THE MORAL LIFE

Second Edition

Steven Luper | Curtis Brown

Trinity University

Australia • Brazil • Japan • Korea • Mexico • Singapore • Spain • United Kingdom • United States

The Moral Life, Second Edition
Steven Luper, Curtis Brown

Executive Editors: Michele Baird, Maureen Staudt, Michael Stranz

Project Development Manager: Linda deStefano

Senior Marketing Coordinators: Sara Mercurio, Lindsay Shapiro

Sr. Production/Manufacturing Manager: Donna M. Brown

PreMedia Services Supervisor: Joel Brennecke

Rights & Permissions Specialist: Kalina Hintz

Cover Image: Getty Image

© 2005 Cengage Learning

ALL RIGHTS RESERVED. No part of this work covered by the copyright herein may be reproduced, transmitted, stored or used in any form or by any means graphic, electronic, or mechanical, including but not limited to photocopying, recording, scanning, digitizing, taping, Web distribution, information networks, or information storage and retrieval systems, except as permitted under Section 107 or 108 of the 1976 United States Copyright Act, without the prior written permission of the publisher.

For product information and technology assistance, contact us at **Cengage Learning Customer & Sales Support, 1-800-354-9706**

For permission to use material from this text or product, submit all requests online at **www.cengage.com/permissions**
Further permissions questions can be emailed to **permissionrequest@cengage.com**

ISBN-13: 978-0-534-61726-4

ISBN-10: 0-534-61726-3

Cengage Learning
5191 Natorp Blvd.
Mason, OH 45040
USA

Cengage Learning is a leading provider of customized learning solutions with office locations around the globe, including Singapore, the United Kingdom, Australia, Mexico, Brazil, and Japan. Locate your local office at **international.cengage.com/region**

Cengage Learning products are represented in Canada by Nelson Education, Ltd.

Visit our corporate website at **www.cengage.com**

Printed in the United States of America
6 7 8 9 10   24 23 22 21 20

PREFACE

Constructing a complete moral view is a daunting task, since we must take a stance on so many issues at so many levels of inquiry. We have designed this volume to help readers undertake this task. We preface each chapter with an introduction to its topic and to the readings that cover it. Our introduction, which has been expanded into an entire chapter for the second edition, describes leading ethical theories that offer solutions to a wide range of ethical issues and now includes three relevant readings. When background factual data are necessary for a proper grasp of the issues at hand, we provide those data. The readings themselves are lively, accessible, thought-provoking, and representative of widely divergent perspectives. At the end of each chapter we ask pointed questions designed to help readers critically assess its selections, and we provide annotated suggestions for further reading.

The feature of our volume in which we take the most pride is its design. We have organized the book so that readers can begin with issues that affect them most directly and then proceed to ones that affect them least. In each part of the book we have collected readings that discuss issues on a single level of inquiry. The first part's focus is most narrow; it deals with the individual and probes issues each of us faces when we design our private lives as best we can. In this section, we encourage readers temporarily to ignore their interaction with other people, focus on their own lives, and deal with such issues as: What is the best way to live my life? What should my attitude be about my own death? New readings in this section include material from Lao Tzu, the Hinayana and Mahayana Scriptures, and Confucius. The scope of subsequent parts broadens gradually. After the individual, our readings discuss interpersonal relationships, then intrasocietal issues, international issues, intergenerational issues, and finally, interspecial issues, ones the human species confronts in its dealings with other species. Thus, when we reach the interpersonal level, our selections consider our relationship to other individuals and ask how they can best be conducted. We want to know how much more importance we should place on our friends and loved ones and what our responsibilities are to these people. Hugh LaFollette's "Morality and Personal Relationships" is an added selection that addresses these concerns. At the next level are intrasocietal issues, which concern how entire societies ought to be designed if they are to be just. At stake here is a plethora of concerns: Does society have the right or responsibility to ban hallucinogenic drugs? (Here, the second edition includes new material from Walter Block and Bonnie Steinbock.) Should society use the death penalty as a punishment for any criminal offenses? What ought to be done with the victims of devastating terminal illnesses: Should we in all cases do everything we can to keep them alive, or should we consider killing those who wish death? Essays in the part on international issues discuss, among other things, the difficult matter of how much help affluent countries are obligated to provide less-developed countries across the globe and the persistent worry that nuclear weapons should be eliminated. New to this second edition is a chapter on terrorism. Our selections for the part on intergenerational issues discuss the divisive abortion issue and several questions raised by the application of genetic engineering to human beings. The readings in the last part of the book deal with such issues as whether and why it is possible to wrong creatures of other species and how we are required to treat them.

We think that readers will find this design most congenial. They may begin with issues that they may find most interesting and that, in any case, must be settled before the issues at other levels can be settled. Then they may move on to less basic concerns, creating as they go an ever clearer and more complete moral view. One demurral: The status of animals, covered in the last part of the book, is not an issue that we are helped to settle by working first through problems individuals confront at increasingly complex levels of interaction. Indeed, an impressive case could be made for considering the status of animals *first*. To identify what is good and bad for human beings, it is helpful to consider what is good and bad for other animals and compare the two.

A good deal of material is gathered in this book. No doubt, instructors (like us) who plan to use it as a text cannot expect to work through the whole of it. However, we believe the range of selections to be a virtue, not a vice. Instructors probably find it taxing to consider the same issues over and over. With this book, they can vary the contents of their courses from term to term, or they may elect to ask their students which issues are of greatest interest and then design their courses accordingly. Groups of students vary greatly, so it is unlikely that any class would opt for precisely the same topics as others.

Several people have helped us edit this book. Conry Davidson not only suggested some of the pieces we included but also handled most of the work of securing permissions to reprint what appears herein. Bernard Rollin provided valuable suggestions about the contents of our chapter on the standing of animals, and David Crocker was very helpful with suggestions about our chapter on the needy. Unfortunately, considerations of length prevented us from incorporating many of the improvements they would like to have seen. Kay Loughrey typed much of the manuscript and handled a good deal of the work of putting together the selections. We would also like to extend our thanks to Karla Barnett for her generous help with many aspects of the preparation of this second edition.

We also found the suggestions of the following "referees" very helpful, and we thank them for their kind assistance: William Aiken, Chatham College; Judith

Brad, Indiana State University; Donna Bestock, Skyline College; Norman Bowie, University of Delaware; William Davie, University of Oregon; Dane Gordon, Rochester Institute of Technology; Tibor Machan, Auburn University; Lawrence McCullough, Baylor College of Medicine; and Louis Pojman, University of Mississippi.

TABLE OF CONTENTS

Preface v

PART ONE: ETHICAL THEORY 1

1. Introduction to Ethical Theory 3
Introduction 3
Readings 17
    Aristotle, *Nicomachean Ethics* 17
    John Stuart Mill, *Utilitarianism* 33
    Immanuel Kant, *Groundwork of the Metaphysic of Morals* 46
Questions for Further Reflection 64
Further Readings 64

PART TWO: THE INDIVIDUAL 67

2. The Individual Life: What Can Make It Worthwhile? 69
Introduction 69
Readings 79
    Religious Faith 79
        Leo Tolstoy, *Confessions* 79
    The Way of Nature 83
        Lao Tzu, *Tao Te Ching* 83
    Contemplation 86
        Aristotle, *Happiness as Contemplation* 86
    Pleasure 89
        Epicurus, *Letter to Menoeceus* 89
        Donatien-Alphonse-François de Sade, *Philosophy in the Bedroom* 92
        J. J. C. Smart, *Hedonism* 94
    Power 99
        Friedrich Nietzsche, *What Is Noble?* 99
    Close Relationships 103
        Carol Gilligan, *Woman's Place in Man's Life Cycle* 103
        Hinayana and Mahayana Scriptures, *Selections* 111
        Confucius, *Analects* 115
    Work 117
        Anthony Storr, *The Significance of Human Relationships* 117
    Self-Creation 121
        Jean-Paul Sartre, *Existentialism and Humanism* 121
    Nothing 124
        Arthur Schopenhauer, *The World as Will and Idea* 124

Questions for Further Reflection   128
Further Readings   128

3. The Individual Death: Is Dying an Evil?   130
Introduction   130
Readings   134

Dying Is Not an Evil   134
  Lucretius, *Death*   134
Dying Is an Evil   136
  Steven Luper, *Annihilation*   136
Not Having Existed Earlier Is an Evil   144
  Derek Parfit, *Why We Should Not Be Biased Towards the Future*   144
Questions for Further Reflection   146
Further Readings   146

4. The Individual Death: Is Suicide Wrong?   148
Introduction   148
Readings   153

Suicide Is a Rational Choice   153
  Thomas S. Szasz, *The Ethics of Suicide*   153
Suicide Is Always Wrong   161
  Immanuel Kant, *Suicide*   161
Suicide Is Almost Always Permissible   163
  David Hume, *Of Suicide*   163
Suicide Is Sometimes Permissible   168
  Jonathan Glover, *Suicide and Gambling with Life*   168
Questions for Further Reflection   174
Further Readings   174

PART THREE: INTERPERSONAL RELATIONSHIPS   175

5. Friendship   177
Introduction   177
Readings   182

Theories of Friendship   182
  Aristotle, *Friendship*   182
  Robert J. Ringer, *The Friendship Hurdle*   187
  Immanuel Kant, *Friendship*   189
The Value of Friendship   192
  Marilyn Friedman, *Friendship and Moral Growth*   192
Friendship and Duty   195
  Hugh LaFollette, *Morality and Personal Relationships*   195
Questions for Further Reflection   202
Further Readings   203

6. Sexual Relationships   205
Introduction   205
Readings   211

Sexual Morality: A Liberal View   211
   Alan H. Goldman, *Plain Sex*   211
Sexual Morality: A Conservative View   220
   Roger Scruton, *Sexual Morality*   220
Prostitution Is Morally Impermissible   229
   Hadley Arkes, *Prostitution*   229
Prostitution Is Morally Permissible   239
   Lars O. Ericsson, *Charges Against Prostitution: An Attempt at a*   239
   Philosophical Assessment
Homosexuality Should Be Discouraged   252
   Michael Levin, *Why Homosexuality Is Abnormal*   252
Homosexuality Should Not Be Discouraged   258
   Timothy F. Murphy, *Homosexuality and Nature: Happiness and*   258
   the Law at Stake
Questions for Further Reflection   264
Further Readings   265

7. Marriage and Family   266

Introduction   266
Readings   272

Marriage: A Traditional View   272
   Roger Scruton, *The Politics of Sex*   272
Marriage: A Marxist View   278
   Frederick Engels, *Marriage*   278
Marriage: A Feminist View   281
   Susan Moller Okin, *Justice, Gender, and the Family*   281
Enforcing the Duties of Parents   290
   Hugh LaFollette, *Licensing Parents*   290
Protecting the Rights of Children   300
   Michael A. Slote, *Obedience and Illusions*   300
Questions for Further Reflection   306
Further Readings   307

PART FOUR: INTRASOCIETAL ISSUES   309

8. Distributive Justice   311

Introduction   311
Readings   317

Classical Liberalism   317
   John Locke, *Property, Labor and the State*   317
Libertarianism   322
   John Hospers, *What Libertarianism Is*   322
The Marxist Critique of Capitalism   330
   Karl Marx, *A Critique of Capitalism*   330
Welfare Liberalism   335
   John Rawls, *Justice as Fairness*   335
Questions for Further Reflection   341
Further Readings   342

9. Euthanasia   343

Introduction   343
Readings   347

   Both Passive and Active Euthanasia Are Permissible   347
      James Rachels, *Active and Passive Euthanasia*   347
   Neither Passive Nor Active Euthanasia Is Permissible   352
      Joseph V. Sullivan, *The Immorality of Euthanasia*   352
   A Rebuttal   357
      James Rachels, *Euthanasia*   357
   Withdrawing Treatment Is Obligatory   362
      Margaret P. Battin, *Age-Rationing and the Just Distribution of Health Care: Is There a Duty to Die?*   362

Questions for Further Reflection   374
Further Readings   374

10. Capital Punishment   376

Introduction   376
Readings   380

   Deserving Death   380
      Stephen Nathanson, *Do Murderers Deserve to Die?*   380
   Execution and Discrimination   390
      Jeffrey Reiman, *The Justice of the Death Penalty in an Unjust World*   390
   Defending the Death Penalty   400
      Ernest van den Haag, *Refuting Reiman and Nathanson*   400

Questions for Further Reflection   403
Further Readings   403

11. Discrimination   405

Introduction   405
Readings   409

   Reverse Discrimination Is Justified   409
      Robert K. Fullinwider, *Reverse Discrimination and Equal Opportunity*   409
   Reverse Discrimination Is Not Justified   418
      Michael Levin, *Affirmative Action*   418

Questions for Further Reflection   429
Further Readings   430

12. Illicit Drugs   431

Introduction   431
Readings   434

   Drugs Should Not Be Legalized   434
      James Q. Wilson, *Against the Legalization of Drugs*   434
   Drugs Should Be Legalized   440
      Walter Block, *Drug Prohibition: A Legal and Economic Analysis*   440
   Drugs and Public Health   450
      Bonnie Steinbock, *Drug Prohibition: A Public-Health Perspective*   450

Questions for Further Reflection   464
Further Readings   464

PART FIVE: INTERNATIONAL ISSUES 465

13. Nuclear Deterrence and Strategic Defense 467

Introduction 467
Readings 471

  Deterrence 471
    David Gauthier, *War and Nuclear Deterrence* 471
  Disarmament 483
    Douglas P. Lackey, *Prisoners and Chickens* 483
  For the Strategic Defense Initiative 495
    Ronald Reagan, *"Star Wars" Speech* 495
    Gen. Daniel O. Graham, *The Non-Nuclear Defense of Cities* 497
  Against the Strategic Defense Initiative 499
    Steven Lee, *The Moral Vision of Strategic Defense* 499
  Questions for Further Reflection 503
  Further Readings 504

14. Terrorism 505

Introduction 505
Readings 509

  Justifications of Terrorism 509
    Carlos Marighella, *Manual of the Urban Guerrilla* 509
    Anonymous, *Freedom Struggle by the Provisional IRA* 512
  Justifications of Terrorism Are Unsuccessful 513
    Michael Walzer, *Terrorism: A Critique of Excuses* 513
    Robert K. Fullinwider, *Understanding Terrorism* 521
  Questions for Further Reflection 531
  Further Readings 531

15. Obligations toward the Needy 532

Introduction 532
Readings 535

  We Are Obligated to Help the Needy 535
    Peter Singer, *Famine, Affluence, and Morality* 535
  We Are Not Obligated to Help the Needy 540
    Garrett Hardin, *Living on a Lifeboat* 540
  Kant and World Hunger 544
    Onora O'Neill, *Kantianism and World Hunger* 544
  Questions for Further Reflection 552
  Further Readings 553

PART SIX: INTERGENERATIONAL ISSUES 555

16. The Genetic Engineering of Human Beings 557

Introduction 557
Readings 562

  Against Germline Therapy 562
    Council for Responsible Genetics of the Human Genetics Committee, 562
    Position Paper on Human Germ Line Manipulation

For Both Positive and Negative Engineering   567
    Jonathan Glover, *Decisions*   567
For Negative but Not Positive Engineering   575
    Michael Ruse, *Genesis Revisited: Can We Do Better Than God?*   575
Questions for Further Reflection   581
Further Readings   581

17. Abortion   582

Introduction   582
Readings   585

A Kantian Critique of Abortion   585
    R. M. Hare, *A Kantian Approach to Abortion*   585
A Rights-based Defense of Abortion   594
    Judith Jarvis Thomson, *A Defense of Abortion*   594
Questions for Further Reflection   606
Further Readings   607

PART SEVEN: INTERSPECIES ISSUES   609

18. The Status of Animals   611

Introduction   611
Readings   614

Rationality Criterion of Standing   614
    Immanuel Kant, *Duties Towards Animals*   614
Pleasure Criterion of Standing   616
    Peter Singer, *Animal Liberation*   616
Interest Criterion of Standing   625
    Ruth Cigman, *Death, Misfortune and Species Inequality*   625
Life Criterion of Standing   630
    Kenneth E. Goodpaster, *On Being Morally Considerable*   630
The Nonsentient Environment   636
    Bernard E. Rollin, *Environmental Ethics and International Justice*   636
Questions for Further Reflection   651
Further Readings   652

THE MORAL LIFE
SECOND EDITION

PART ONE

Ethical Theory

Chapter 1

Introduction to Ethical Theory

Books on particular moral issues are sometimes labeled as books in *applied ethics*. This suggests, misleadingly, that one ought first to develop or choose a theoretical view in ethics and then *apply* it to various particular moral problems. In this view, figuring out what to say about a particular issue is simply a matter of taking a general theory and plugging in the particular facts of this specific issue. This approach makes ethics seem both easier and more hopeless than it really is. The applied ethics approach makes ethics seem *easy* because it is only a matter of more or less mechanically drawing out the consequences of ethical theories. It makes it seem *hopeless*, on the other hand, because the prospects for choosing among competing theoretical views, in this approach, are not good. Kantians will solve moral problems in one way, utilitarians in another, and neither is likely to convince the other of the superiority of his or her own theoretical position.

In fact, ethics is neither this easy nor this hopeless. Possibly, when we have the One True Theory in ethics, we will be able to solve moral problems by "applying" it. But at this stage in the development of ethics, it would be naïve to think that ethicists have identified the One True Theory. Without it, we are forced to continue our struggle to develop defensible opinions about relatively specific cases of right and wrong, good and bad, as well as defensible opinions about more general cases, by adjusting each to cohere with the others. We evaluate our theoretical views by seeing what they imply about particular moral issues and seeing whether we find these implications morally acceptable; at the same time, we develop our views about particular issues in part by seeing which larger theoretical positions are consistent with them and asking whether those positions are plausible or not. This is certainly more difficult than simply "applying" moral theories. But there is room for optimism that, as we compare our theoretical and practical views in the process of adjusting, elaborating, and extending both, we will ultimately arrive at a coherent moral view at all levels of generality. It may even happen that, as we individually sort out our views in these ways, we will also, as a society, find our various views converging more and more.

We all have positions on theoretical as well as practical issues. Our theoretical ideas may be highly elaborate and able to

3

cover a wide range of cases, as Kantianism, for example, is; or they may be somewhat less general—an impression that individual liberties are more important than overall happiness, perhaps, or that everyone has a right to a basic standard of living. No sharp boundary, however, can be drawn between theoretical and practical issues, and our best hope of reaching a satisfactory position is to make use of relatively general principles in thinking through relatively specific issues and then to allow the results to cast light on the acceptability of the general principles. We offer this introduction to some leading ethical theories in the hope that it will provide some concepts and terminology useful in undertaking this task.

Ethical Egoism

A common view about moral obligation is that my only moral duty is to look out for my own happiness, to do the best job I can of getting what I want. This view is known as *ethical egoism*. It should not be confused with *psychological egoism*, which says that as a matter of fact, all people always act so as to maximize their own happiness. If psychological egoism is correct, then ethical egoism, though superficially similar, would seem to have little point: Why enjoin people to look out for their own interests if everyone will of psychological necessity do so anyway? Ethical egoism, the view that we ought to act egoistically, is rare among philosophical writers on ethics, but not uncommon in more popular writings: It seems to be the view advocated in self-help books with titles like *Looking Out for Number One* and also in many writings of Ayn Rand. (Some caution is called for here, though; it may be that these writers justify acting egoistically for utilitarian reasons.)

We need to distinguish between two versions of ethical egoism. All versions of ethical egoism hold that *I* ought to do whatever makes *me* happiest. But what should other people do? One sort of egoistic view might hold that everyone else ought to do whatever makes *me* happiest. This view does not seem inconsistent or self-contradictory. Nevertheless, as a *moral* view it is hopeless. Two problems are worth noticing. First, egoism is not a moral view everyone could agree on. In fact, it is not a *single* moral view at all: Curtis Brown's egoist view will be that everyone ought to do whatever makes Curtis Brown happiest, while Steven Luper's view will be that everyone ought to do whatever makes Steven Luper happiest. Why should we prefer Brown egoism over Luper egoism, or vice versa? If everyone were an egoist, then every egoist would have a moral view in direct contradiction to that of any other egoist (assuming that on at least some occasions, what makes one happy will make others unhappy), and there seems to be no rational ground on which we could decide which view is correct. On the other hand, if Brown succeeded in convincing everyone else that everyone ought to do whatever makes Brown happy, then there would be only one egoist in the world, namely Brown; everyone else would altruistically be working for Brown's happiness. A second, related problem is that this sort of egoism does not satisfy what seems to be a fundamental feature of any moral theory worthy of the name. This feature, often associated with Kant, is *universalizability*. It is the idea that, if an action is wrong for one person in a given situation, it is also wrong for anyone else in the same situation. Any moral claim I make about myself should be one I am prepared to make about anyone in my situation. But if Brown is an egoist of the sort we are now considering, he will hold, for example, that if Luper has an ice-cream cone that Brown wants, Luper should give it to Brown, while if Brown has an ice-cream cone that Luper wants, Brown should keep it. This is unacceptable as a feature of a moral theory.

A second version of ethical egoism, however, is universalizable, namely, the view that each person ought to do whatever will make him or her happiest. Now, if Brown is a universal egoist of this sort, he will hold that Brown ought to do whatever makes Brown happiest *and* that Luper ought to do whatever makes Luper happiest. This is a view everyone in a society could share and one that does not involve regarding oneself as morally different from anyone else. The view has certain attractions; for one thing, it makes being moral a good deal easier and more natural than most moral theories claim.

What, if anything, is wrong with universal ethical egoism? It has sometimes been argued that the view is inconsistent or incoherent. Suppose that Judy and I both want the same ice-cream cone. I then believe that I should try to get it for myself and that Judy should try to get it for herself. Isn't there something fishy about this? Apparently, I think that the best outcome is the one in which I get the cone *and* somehow at the same time think that the best outcome is the one in which Judy gets the cone.

That *would* be a contradiction. However, the egoist does not need to say anything at all about which outcome is best from an agent-neutral point of view, I can hold that the best outcome *for me* is the one in which I get the cone and that the best outcome for Judy is the one in which she gets it, and I may deny that there is an outcome that is best from a neutral point of view.

But doesn't there still remain a tension in my attitudes? I think Judy ought to try to get the cone, but I don't *want* her to succeed. It is not clear, however, that anything is wrong with this sort of tension between how I think she should act and what I want to happen. The very same sort of tension arises in any sort of competition: If I am in a foot-race with Judy, I think I should try to win, but I also think she ought to try to win, even though I do not want her to succeed. If this tension is acceptable in our attitudes about athletic competition, why shouldn't it be acceptable in our moral attitudes generally?

Egoism, in its universalizable version, is not inconsistent. Nevertheless, it suffers, in our view, from a crippling defect: It is a radically *false* view of morality. There might be no way to convince the truly committed egoist of this (you cannot convince the truly committed flat-earther that the earth is round, either). A little thought, however, will reveal to *most* of us that we cannot believe in the correctness of egoism: Its consequences are simply too morally horrifying. Consider: Some people are made happy by killing, torturing, or tormenting others. (A case occurred a few years ago in San Antonio in which an entire family tormented a small child. One of many "games" they played, "The Color Purple Game," consisted of taping the child's nose and mouth shut, watching the child struggle until it turned purple, and then removing the tape.) The egoist is committed to saying that such people are doing what is morally right by killing, torturing, or tormenting. There is no ground on which they can be morally criticized because they are simply doing what makes them happy. Can we really believe a moral theory with such repugnant consequences?

Egoism also presents a more practical difficulty. It provides us with no principled way of setting issues when different people's interests conflict. This is not to say that egoists cannot reach decisions about what to do when they have incompatible desires. If two egoists want the same ice-cream cone, and one is much larger and stronger than the other, then the stronger egoist can simply take it. If the two egoists are equally strong, or if the strong one for some reason does not want to use force (notice that the reason cannot be a *moral* one), then the two can bargain. However, for those of us convinced that a moral decision on such issues cannot be merely a matter of who is stronger or who is in the best bargaining position, egoism provides no satisfactory means of making such decisions.

Deontological versus Teleological Theories

Fortunately, there are many alternatives to egoism. Broadly speaking, there are two primary ways to evaluate possible actions. According to one, our main task is to identify what counts as good. (In philosophical discussions, what counts as good is often simply labeled "the good.") After we have identified the good, we can say that everyone is obligated to participate in a scheme that brings about as much good as possible. Views that identify the good independently from a specification of our obligations and that define our obligations in terms of the good are called *teleological* moral theories. According to hedonistic utilitarianism, for example, only pleasure (and the absence of pain) counts as good, and we are morally obligated to do what we can to maximize the total amount of pleasure.

The primary alternatives to teleological theories are *deontological* theories. Typically, such theories give the concept of right conduct priority over the concept of the good, but a more careful definition of the deontological approach would be this: any approach that is not teleological. Thus, any theory that does not specify the good independently of the right or that does not specify the right in terms of the good is deontological. For example, Kant, the most prominent deontologist, maintained that the only things that are good without qualification are good wills, where one has a good will, roughly, if one always intends to meet one's obligations. Accordingly, he maintained that the complete story about what is good must involve a specification of the right.

All leading ethical theories can be classified as teleological or deontological, but within this classification is a great deal of variety.

Aristotle and Character Ethics

We will discuss two main teleological traditions in ethics: virtue or character ethics, as developed by Aristotle (384–322 B.C.), and utilitarianism, whose most famous proponent is John Stuart Mill (1806–1873). The defining characteristic of teleological views, as we have said, is that they regard the good as fundamental and define right action in terms of it. Teleological views, however, vary widely in the sorts of things they classify as good and in the precise way they relate the good and the right. One key distinction between teleological views concerns the relative priority of *character* and *conduct*. According to utilitarians, someone is a good person or has a good character if he or she tends to act rightly; the most basic thing is the morality of actions, and whether someone is a good or bad person has to do with what sorts of actions he or she performs. (This view about the order of priority of character and conduct is not limited to teleological views; many deontological theorists would agree.) Aristoteleans, on the other hand, hold that character traits are fundamental and that right actions are those that result from a good character. Utilitarians look to the *effects* of our actions to determine the rightness of those actions, while Aristoteleans look to the *causes* of actions: Utilitarians would say that a right action is one that produces or tends to produce good states of affairs, while Aristotelians would claim that a right action is one that is or tends to be produced by a good character.

Let us examine some of the key points in our selection from Aristotle in this chapter. Aristotle opens his *Nicomachean Ethics* by asking what is good in itself. Some things are only *instrumentally* good. A trip to the dentist, for example, is a good thing, but few would claim that it is good in itself; rather, it is good because it has good consequences. If you go to the dentist regularly, you will have healthier teeth, and visits to the dentist are a good thing only because they have this consequence. If some things are good because they lead to other things, it seems, then, that there must also be some things that are *intrinsically* good, good in themselves.

Aristotle suggests that there will be wide agreement that the one and only intrinsic good is *happiness*. (The Greek term that we translate as "happiness" is *eudaimonia*; it has been suggested that a more adequate translation might be "human flourishing" because the Greek notion of happiness is not the notion of having pleasant experiences, which is the idea we tend to associate with the term *happiness*. Indeed, Aristotle explicitly rejects the idea that happiness is essentially the same thing as pleasure.) We want happiness because we find it valuable, not because it leads to something else we value. By contrast, we value each instrumental good not because it is valuable in itself, but because in one way or another it contributes to our happiness.

Aristotle hastens to add, however, that the wide agreement that happiness is good in itself is mainly verbal because people disagree radically over what happiness consists in. We can see the rest of Aristotle's project in the *Ethics* as primarily a matter of explaining and defending a particular conception of what happiness consists in. Aristotle wants to show us what sort of person will flourish or be happy.

The next step in Aristotle's argument is to draw a connection between goodness and function. In a large class of cases, we think that a good _____ is a _____ that performs its function well. For instance, a good knife is one that cuts well, a good chair is one that is comfortable to sit in, a good carpenter is one who builds well, and so on. Aristotle suggests that if there is a specifically *human* function, then a good *person* will be one who performs this function well.

What might such a human function be? In Aristotle's view, it must be something unique to people. The one characteristic of humans that makes us unique, he believes, is our *rationality*. So, a good person will be one whose activities are rational. The best sort of life will be the life governed by reason; such a life will be characterized by certain *virtues*. Aristotle goes on to distinguish two ways in which our lives may be governed by reason, and, correspondingly, two sorts of virtue, two ways of excelling. The distinction between these two sorts of virtue is based on a distinction between different faculties, or "parts of the soul." One capacity we have is that of *reason;* we make use of this whenever we think rationally about things, and especially, for Aristotle, when we engage in philosophical contemplation. When we are disposed to think or philosophize in a rational manner, we have *intellectual* virtue. In addition to reason, though, we have various *appetites*, or desires. These may sometimes accord with reason, as when reason tells me that I need to get some sleep and I find that I also have a strong desire to sleep. However, our appetites or desires may also conflict with reason, as when reason tells me that more ice cream will not be good for me, but I find that I nevertheless strongly crave more ice cream. *Moral* virtue, by Aristotle's account, is a matter of bringing our desires under rational control so that what we want is precisely what reason tells us it is good to want. (According to Aristotle, we also have a third, "nutritive" faculty; this includes such activities as digestion and growth. But because such activities are not under voluntary control, they have nothing to do with rationality, and so no virtues are associated with them.)

Intellectual virtue, Aristotle says, can be taught, but moral virtue cannot. We acquire moral virtue by habituation rather than by education. If we emulate people of good moral character, we will find our own characters improving, but no textbook or series of lectures will make us better people.

Aristotle goes on to provide a general account of the nature of virtue and to discuss in some detail a large number of specific virtues. In Aristotle's account, a virtue aims at a mean between two extremes of emotion or action.

> For instance, both fear and confidence and appetite and anger and pity and in general pleasure and pain may be felt both too much and too little, and in both cases not well; but to feel them at the right times, with reference to the right objects, towards the right people, with the right aim, and in the right way, is what is both intermediate and best, and this is characteristic of excellence [virtue]. Similarly with regard to actions also there is excess, defect, and the intermediate. Now excellence is concerned with passions and actions, in which excess is a form of failure, and so is defect, while the intermediate is praised and is a form of success. . . . Therefore excellence is a kind of mean, since it aims at what is intermediate.

Aristotle's account, unlike many modern accounts, does not even attempt to provide general principles that can be algorithmically applied to particular problems to yield conclusions about what is the morally best thing to do. When Aristotle says that virtue aims at the mean between two extremes, he explicitly does not mean that one can somehow add the extremes together and divide by two in order to find the mean. As a result, Aristotle's view is not as easy to apply to specific social problems as, say, Kant's or Mill's. It is, however, important to us for (at least) three reasons. First, it serves as a reminder that there may simply be no algorithmic way to resolve moral issues. Second, Aristotle's discussion of the human function and the relation between function and goodness provides the historical underpinnings for the influential moral views of St. Thomas Aquinas (1225–1274), according to which actions are impermissible if they conflict with natural purposes. Third, in at least some cases, it can be illuminating to look at a moral problem by asking not which action is right, but rather which traits of character we should strive to endow our children with because those traits will lead to more flourishing lives. (For instance, Roger Scruton applies this Aristotelian strategy to questions of sexual morality in our chapter on sexual relationships.)

Utilitarianism

The most prominent teleological approach is utilitarianism. If we follow Aristotle's strategy of using the word *happiness* to refer to whatever is intrinsically good, without committing ourselves to a particular account of what happiness is, then most utilitarians would accept something like the following claim: An action is morally right if, and only if, it leads to more happiness than any available alternative action. Jeremy Bentham, usually regarded as the inventor of utilitarianism, put it like this: "By the principle of utility is meant that principle which approves or disapproves of every action whatsoever, according to the tendency which it appears to have to augment or diminish the happiness of the party whose interest is in question."[1] Thus, to decide what to do in a given situation, we need to do three main things: determine what our alternatives are; figure out what consequences each would have on overall happiness; and compare these consequences to determine which action would lead to the largest net increase of happiness (or smallest decrease, if all the actions open to us will make people on the whole worse off). Whichever action this is will be the one we morally ought to perform.

The view has an appealing simplicity and directness. The view that we ought to do whatever will make people best off seems natural and plausible, and it also seems to provide a neat and useful means of determining, in any situation, the right thing to do in that situation. However, the formulation of utilitarianism we have just provided leaves many questions unanswered; filling in the answers makes the view more complex and perhaps diminishes its initial appeal.

Here are two of the many questions utilitarians need to answer in filling in the details of their view. (A third will emerge a bit later.) First, what *precisely* is to be maximized? How are we to understand the notion of happiness? Bentham's utilitarianism was *hedonistic;* that is, he held that what utilitarians should maximize was *pleasure:*

> By utility is meant that property in any object, whereby it tends to produce benefit, advantage, pleasure, good, or happiness, (all this in the present case comes to the same thing) or (what comes again to the same thing) to prevent the happening of mischief, pain, evil, or unhappiness to the party whose interest is considered: if that party be the community in general, then the happiness of the community: if a particular individual, then the happiness of that individual.[2]

Contemporary utilitarians typically resist hedonism on several grounds. It is not clear that pleasure can be measured in the way utilitarianism requires, especially when we need to compare the amounts of pleasure different people are feeling. Hedonism also seems to place too much emphasis on *feelings*. Many of the things we care most about may not provide much in the way of pleasant feelings. You may get more pleasure out of watching a soap opera on television than out of reading *War and Peace,* and yet you may value reading *War and Peace* more than you do watching the soap opera. Bentham's student John Stuart Mill tried to meet this problem within a hedonistic framework by claiming that some desires are "higher" than others and that satisfaction of these higher desires is more important than satisfaction of the lower ones. Most contemporary utilitarians have, instead, abandoned hedonism in favor of *preferential* utilitarianism, which holds that we ought to maximize the satisfaction of people's desires, even when thwarting their desires might provide them with more pleasure.

A second question for utilitarians is: Whose happiness counts? The short answer is "everyone's," but it needs to be made clear who "everyone" is. "Everyone" presumably includes all currently existing people. But what about other animals? Dogs and elk and whales can be happy or unhappy; should their happiness count? If so, should it count as much as human

---

[1] Jeremy Bentham, "An Introduction to the Principles of Morals and Legislation," in John Stuart Mill and Jeremy Bentham, *Utilitarianism and Other Essays,* ed. Alan Ryan (Harmondsworth: Penguin, 1987), p. 65, (Bentham's book was first published in 1789; Ryan reprints selections from the 1824 edition.)

[2] Bentham, p. 66.

happiness? Again, should we count only people who are now alive? What about people now dead who had desires for the future? (For instance, is someone's desire to be cremated still important after that person is dead?) What about people who are not yet alive? Should we try to take the desires of future generations into account, for example, in formulating environmental and energy policies?

Utilitarianism also faces a variety of other problems. Many of these involve utilitarianism's failure to give any weight to considerations we ordinarily think of as morally relevant. For instance, utilitarianism gives no special weight to *promises* or *contracts*. If breaking a promise to someone will make her unhappy, then that is a reason not to break it, but if for some reason breaking the promise will not make her unhappy, or if her unhappiness will be outweighed by the happiness of others, then according to the utilitarian, one should break the promise. Suppose someone tells you her most embarrassing secret, and you promise to reveal it to no one. The next evening, you are at a large party, and it occurs to you that the many partygoers would find her embarrassing story hilariously funny. If the enjoyment of the (say) thirty people at the party is enough to outweigh the unhappiness of the unfortunate woman whose story you tell, then according to the utilitarian, you ought to break your promise and tell the story. (If one roomful of happy people is not enough to outweigh one person's unhappiness, you could also tell the story at another party the following night.)

Again, utilitarianism gives no special weight to questions of *justice* or *fairness*. A standard objection is that the principle of utility sometimes requires us to sacrifice a few for the sake of the many. Confronted with the knowledge that the perpetrator of a violent, racially motivated murder cannot be apprehended, a town's mayor may find that the only way to end the public's strident demand that the murderer be brought to justice is to convict an innocent derelict. However, even if the derelict's loss of pleasure really is offset by a great increase of pleasure felt by townspeople who think the murderer has been apprehended, isn't it still obvious that framing an innocent person is wrong?

Utilitarianism also seems to have no room for special moral obligations to one's family and close friends. What matters is simply happiness; it does not matter who gets it. Thus, if you could save only one person from a fire, your spouse or a wealthy philanthropist, most people would usually think you should save your spouse *even if* the philanthropist would do more good. But it seems that the utilitarian must deny this.

Utilitarianism has some further surprising consequences. It seems not to distinguish what would be nice for us to do from what we are morally required to do. For the utilitarian, there can be no such thing as a supererogatory act, one through which we go beyond the requirements of duty, because we are always required to do whatever would maximize the good. But then, most of us are acting in morally impermissible ways most of the time, as there is usually something we could be doing that would do more to maximize happiness than whatever we are now doing.

There are also surprising consequences for our treatment of animals. The utilitarian view is sometimes defended on the grounds that it offers us a basis for dealing with conflicts between the interests of people and the interests of other animals. Bentham himself was one of the earliest proponents of the view that we have obligations with respect to animals. Indeed, utilitarianism does sustain some plausible claims about animals—for example, that it is wrong to subject animals to unnecessary suffering because when we calculate the total amount of happiness, we must weigh in the happiness of all creatures capable of it. But utilitarianism also has far more controversial consequences. Suppose that five caribou would generate slightly more happiness than one human being if kept alive. Suppose also that somehow, because of a food shortage, either five caribou or one human must die. In this case, the utilitarian view has the implausible implication that the human must be sacrificed.

Some of these criticisms may be met by a somewhat different sort of utilitarianism. We have been considering the view that on each occasion of action, you should perform whichever action (of those available to you) would have the best consequences. This version of utilitarianism is now known as *act utilitarianism* and is often abandoned in favor of *rule utilitarianism*, which focuses on kinds of acts, or policies, rather than on individual actions. According to rule utilitarianism, we need to determine which *rules* or policies would, if generally adhered to, maximize overall happiness. Then, on any particular occasion of action, we should simply consult the set of rules we have determined in this way. For instance, it may be that a general policy of keeping promises would lead to greater overall happiness than alternative policies. If so, then I should keep my promise not to tell the embarrassing secret even if, on *this* particular occasion, breaking the promise would lead to more happiness than keeping it. Similarly, a town that adopts a *policy* of framing innocent people will find itself thwarting many desires clustering around the desire not to be subject to arbitrary seizure; because the policy of framing innocent people does not pass the rule utilitarian test, a rule utilitarian will hold that the mayor should not frame the innocent derelict, even if on *this* occasion, doing so would lead to greater happiness.

Kantianism

Utilitarians, we have seen, evaluate acts (act utilitarianism) or policies (rule utilitarianism) by examining certain consequences those acts or policies would actually have. They maintain that if those acts would maximize pleasure (hedonistic utilitarianism) or satisfaction of desire (preferential utilitarianism), then they are morally obligatory. Immanuel Kant's (1724–1804) approach is quite distinct from act utilitarianism, although it is rather closely related to rule utilitarianism.

As he says in the introduction to his *Groundwork of the Metaphysic of Morals*, much of Kant's work in ethics is an attempt "to seek out and establish the supreme principle of morality," which he calls the categorical imperative. Kant offers what he calls three "formulations" of the categorical imperative, all of which he believes to be equivalent. In fact, however, the third formulation is quite different from the first two. Here are the three formulations:

> *Law of nature formulation:* act as if the maxim of your action were to become through your will a universal law of nature.[3]
>
> *End in itself formulation:* act in such a way that you always treat humanity, whether in your own person or in the person of any other, never simply as a means, but always at the same time as an end.[4]
>
> *Autonomy formulation:* act always on the maxim of such a will in us as can at the same time look upon itself as making universal law.[5]

Perhaps the best way to clarify Kant's ethical theory is to focus on the first two

---

[3] Immanuel Kant, *Groundwork of the Metaphysic of Morals*, trans. H.J. Paton (New York: Harper & Row, 1964), p. 89.

[4] Kant, p. 96.

[5] Kant, p. 100.

formulations of the categorical imperative. These formulations state that we are to act as we wish only if the intention behind our act can be universalized in a certain sense. Exactly what sort of universalizability Kant had in mind is extremely controversial, but a fruitful interpretation can be offered by drawing on the writings of John Rawls.[6]

We may explain Kant's procedure for determining whether a maxim is universalizable in terms of a series of steps. Suppose I am trying to decide whether to perform a certain action. (Let us call the action A for now; we will consider specific examples later.)

The *first step* is to determine the *maxim* on which I would be acting if I were to do A. If an action is the result of a considered decision, then it will typically reflect a more general policy. If I am thirsty and drink a glass of water, this is not simply an isolated action with no connection to my other actions; rather, it reflects a general policy of drinking when I am thirsty and have easy access to a drinkable liquid. A maxim, then, is a sort of general policy; it says what I will do in any of a class of relevantly similar situations. A maxim will take a form something like the following:

I will do A whenever I am in circumstances C.

Notice, however, that maxims may be indefinitely complex. For example, if we put the maxim just considered into this form, we get: "I will drink a liquid whenever I am in a situation in which I am thirsty and have easy access to a drinkable liquid." This is not really complex enough to capture my actual policy. I would not drink such a liquid if: I believed someone would shoot me if I did; I were in a contest to see who could refrain from drinking the longest; the only liquid available were a diet soft drink (which I detest), but I knew that in an hour I could get a glass of iced tea; and so on. A maxim that accurately reflected my actual policy would need to be complex enough to account for my behavior in these situations.

The *second step* is to perform a sort of "thought experiment," that is, to try to imagine what things would be like if our world were different in certain respects. Although Kant does not use quite this language, it is useful to think of this step as working out what a certain hypothetical world would be like; we might call this "the world our maxim yields." (Rawls calls this the "perturbed social world paired to our maxim."[7]) The world our maxim yields is the world as it would be if two conditions held. First, *everyone* acts according to the same policy we are considering, that is, everyone acts on our maxim. (In Kant's natural law formulation of the categorical imperative, we are to imagine that everyone acts this way because of "a universal law of nature," that is, a natural, presumably psychological, law that applies to everyone.) The second condition to which the world yielded by our maxim must conform is that it is public knowledge that everyone acts on the maxim in question. The world yielded by our maxim will be a world as similar to the actual world as it can be, given that these two conditions hold. So, for instance, we will imagine that the laws of nature are the same in the world our maxim yields as in the actual world, except for the addition of the psychological law that everyone follows our maxim; we will imagine that the world's population is the same, unless the

---

[6] See John Rawls, *A Theory of Justice* (Cambridge, MA: Harvard University Press, 1971), Section 40, and his essay "Themes in Kant's Moral Philosophy," in Eckart Förster, ed., *Kant's Transcendental Deductions* (Stanford, CA: Stanford University Press, 1989).

[7] Rawls, p. 84.

maxim would involve changing it by, say, dropping bombs or having fewer children; and so on.

The *third* and final *step* is to determine whether the world our maxim yields involves either of two contradictions. Our maxim is universalizable, and so the action we are contemplating is permissible, if and only if neither of these contradictions exists; if there *is* a contradiction of either sort, then it is our moral duty not to perform the contemplated action. Let us consider each sort of contradiction in turn.

First, there must be no contradiction in conception. This means that the world our maxim yields must be a *possible* world; such a world must contain no contradictions or inconsistencies. For example, Kant thinks that there is a contradiction in conception in the thought that all people could have a policy of breaking their promises whenever it was convenient to do so. In a world in which everyone followed this policy and in which this fact was public knowledge, it would quickly become clear that promises had no weight whatsoever, and the practice of making promises would die out. In trying to imagine a world in which everyone breaks promises when it is convenient, then, we have been led to a contradiction: The world is supposed to be one in which promises are made and then broken, but we have concluded that no promises would be made in such a world. There cannot be a world in which promises are broken but also in which there are no promises.

This first test faces two objections. One is that many immoral actions will pass the test. For instance, it is easy to imagine a world in which everyone follows the maxim "I will under no circumstances help others in need," or "I will punch the first person I see every day," although Kant would not say that these are morally acceptable maxims. This objection, however, is not serious at this stage because immoral maxims that yield no contradiction in conception may still yield the second sort of contradiction, which we will soon discuss.

More serious is the objection that some morally acceptable maxims may *not* pass the test. Consider a man who adopts the maxim that he will apply for conscientious objector status in order to avoid military combat. If everyone acted on this maxim, there would be no military combat, and soon there would be no conscientious objector status because there would be no need for it. If there were no conscientious objector status, no one could act on the maxim in question. So it looks as though if everyone acted on the maxim, then no one could. The conscientious objector's maxim appears to lead to a contradiction in conception in the same way that the liar's maxim does. Yet, there is arguably nothing morally wrong with the conscientious objector's maxim.

The second sort of contradiction Kant says we must avoid is a contradiction in will. Very roughly, a contradiction in will occurs if, although there could be a world in which everyone followed the maxim we are considering, we could not will that our world be like that. Let us see in more detail what this means by considering an example. Consider what Kant says about the maxim of someone who wants never to harm anyone but who also resolves never to contribute to anyone's well-being. In the *Groundwork* he says that no contradiction in conception arises in the world this maxim yields, but a contradiction in will does arise:

[A]lthough it is possible that a universal law of nature could subsist in harmony with this maxim, yet it is impossible to *will* that such a principle should hold everywhere as a law of nature. For [the will of a person who] decided in this way would be in conflict with itself, since many a situation might arise in which the [person] needed love and sympathy from others.[8]

What precisely Kant means by a contradiction in will is one of the most puzzling questions about his ethics, as this example reveals. There is a contradiction in will in this case because the agent could not will that the world yielded by the maxim be actual. In the example, the idea seems to be that we could not will the world yielded by the maxim because we sometimes want others to help us, and in the world yielded by our maxim, we never would receive such help.

A serious difficulty arises with Kant's view on this interpretation. *I* sometimes want others to help me, so *I* cannot will the world in question, so if I vowed never to help others in need, my will would contradict itself in Kant's sense. It is not at all clear, though, that absolutely anyone must sometimes want others to help him or her. Can't we imagine someone so independent that he or she never wants to receive assistance from anyone? If this is possible, then the requirements of morality differ from one person to the next, depending on the desires a person happens to have: I am obligated at least sometimes to help those in need, while our hypothesized lover of independence is not. This is a conclusion that Kant himself would have found intolerable.

The interpretation of contradictions in will as involving a conflict between the world my maxim yields and my actual desires involves further difficulties. It has the consequence that *any* action that thwarts my own desires will involve a contradiction in will. This is an unwelcome consequence for two reasons. First, it means that many actions to which morality seems irrelevant will, in fact, be morally required. I am deciding whether to buy chocolate or vanilla ice cream; I prefer chocolate. I consider selecting which flavor to buy by flipping a coin. The contemplated maxim would be, let us say, when buying ice cream, to determine which flavor to buy by flipping a coin. Now I consider a world in which everyone follows this maxim. In that world I will sometimes fail to get what I want: On some occasions, as in fact on the present actual occasion, I will flip a coin, and the flavor thereby determined will not be the flavor I would prefer to eat. This seems to have the consequence that I am morally required not to decide which flavor to buy by flipping a coin. But is this really believable? The coin-flipping method may be a silly one to employ in cases in which I have a clear preference, but surely there is nothing *morally* wrong with it. The second undesirable feature of the view that any action that thwarts my own desires involves a contradiction in my will is that I may, on occasion, have morally despicable desires. Perhaps I want to kill someone once a week, but I am nevertheless considering a policy of not killing anyone. If everyone, including me, follows this policy, then once a week my desires will be thwarted. Surely it ought not to follow that it is morally impermissible for me to follow the policy of not killing anyone.

It looks as though we had better not interpret Kant's requirement that we be able to *will* the world yielded by our maxim as meaning that we must be able to *want* that world to be actual. We cannot interpret it to mean that the world yielded by our maxim must be consistent with *all* our desires. But then, what *does* the requirement mean?

One way to interpret Kant is to say that the world yielded by our maxim must be consistent with *some* of our desires. Which ones? We need to rule out morally

---

[8]Kant, p. 91.

irrelevant and morally reprehensible desires. We also need to be sure that the desires in question are desires that *all* rational agents have, since otherwise, the requirements of morality will differ, depending on the desires we happen to have. Are there such things as desires that all rational agents have?

Evidence suggests that Kant thinks all rational beings want to be happy and rational. This is suggested by two passages, one that makes it clear that all rational beings want to be happy, and another that suggests that all rational beings have their rationality as a goal:

> There is . . . *one* end that can be presupposed as actual in all rational beings . . . and thus there is one purpose which . . . they all *do* have by a natural necessity—the purpose, namely, of *happiness*.[9]
>
> Rational nature exists as an end in itself. This is the way in which [every rational being] necessarily conceives his own existence.[10]

However, in saying that rational beings want to be happy, Kant does not mean to imply that there is a particular conception of happiness that all rational beings share. Happiness could consist of a wide range of things, depending on the nature and circumstances of the various rational agents at hand. Thus, Kant comments that "the concept of happiness is so indeterminate . . . that although every man wants to attain happiness, he can never say definitely . . . what it really is that he wants and wills."[11]

Apparently we are to take it that the goal of rational beings is to achieve some conception of happiness or another. Consequently, Kant is not saying that we are to use a particular conception of happiness when we ask of a maxim whether it generates a contradiction in will. Instead, we are to ask whether we could achieve happiness of one sort or another (as well as become and remain rational) in the world our maxim yields. If we cannot, then our maxim generates a contradiction in will, and the categorical imperative forbids our acting from the maxim.

This interpretation of the notion of a contradiction in will avoids some of the problems of the interpretation with which we began. According to this interpretation, it will not be immoral to choose ice cream by flipping a coin, or for those who enjoy murder to refrain from killing people. On the other hand, it is not clear that the categorical imperative, under this interpretation, will have as many substantive consequences as Kant credits it with. In particular, the problem of the extremely independent individual remains a problem in this interpretation: If such an independent person could be happy and rational in a world in which no one ever helped him or her, then it seems that he or she is not required to give aid to others.

A final twist, motivated on other grounds as well, may alleviate this problem. Consider first another frequently noted problem with Kant's view as presented so far. Some maxims are so specific to our own case that they seem to involve a kind of cheating. One primary motivation behind the categorical imperative is to prevent people from treating themselves as special, from exempting themselves from moral requirements to which they hold others. Kant warns against taking "the liberty of making an exception to [a universal law] for ourselves (or even just for this once). . . ."[12]

---

[9] Kant, p. 83.

[10] Kant, p. 96.

[11] Kant, p. 85.

[12] Kant, p. 91.

But some universalizable maxims nevertheless do involve treating at least small groups of people as special. For example, consider a maxim of selective benevolence. If I am a plumber, I could approve a maxim that makes exceptions of plumbers: I am to help plumbers who are in need, but not anyone else. The world yielded would be one in which all plumbers receive help when they need it, but no one else does. As a plumber, I would have no trouble being happy in a world in which only plumbers receive needed aid, but people in other professions might.

One way to avoid such special treatment of oneself or one's group is to add the following feature to our description of contradictions in will. Let us understand Kant's notion of a contradiction in will to involve some restrictions on knowledge. Let us stipulate that in asking ourselves whether we could become and remain rational and happy in the world a given maxim yields, we do not know which particular conception of happiness we will have in that world, nor where in that world we will find ourselves. A maxim fails to generate a contradiction in will only if we would be willing to be part of the world it yields even though we do not know the particulars about our place in that world nor our individual idea of happiness. Presumably, a maxim has this feature only if people with a wide range of conceptions of happiness could be happy and rational in the world yielded by the maxim, regardless of their social position.

In effect, Kant's categorical imperative asks us to evaluate the way we want to act by considering the consequences if our proposed way of acting were to become a general policy. Looking at it in this way brings out the sense in which the consequences of our acts are relevant to the permissibility of our acts. Often, deontological approaches such as Kant's are contrasted with other approaches called *consequentialist* theories, which are defined as accounts according to which the consequences of our acts are relevant to the moral status of our acts. Kant's view is said to be nonconsequentialist, while utilitarianism is said to be consequentialist. This contrast is misleading, however, since it is the consequences of converting the maxim behind our act into a general policy that determine whether our act is permissible, in Kant's view. True, in Kant's view it is the intention behind our act that is evaluated, while in the act utilitarian approach, a particular act is evaluated regardless of how we motivate it to ourselves. However, in spite of this difference in focus, consequences matter in both views. The difference is that for Kant, it matters what *would* happen if others followed the maxim we propose to act on, while for the act utilitarian, so long as others will not act in the way we propose to act, what would happen if they did is irrelevant to the permissibility of our acting as we propose. Rule utilitarians come even closer to agreeing with Kant because they share his view that the consequences of the general policy of acting as we propose are what determine the moral status of our act.

A more substantial point of disagreement between Kant and utilitarians concerns the way in which the two view nonhuman animals. Kant's view attributes no intrinsic value to nonrational beings and hence, does not take nonhuman animals seriously. His position is that nonrational beings are the property of rational beings and so may be dealt with in any way whatever, as long as those property rights are honored. Utilitarians, we have seen, take animals very seriously, perhaps too seriously.

Nicomachean Ethics

Aristotle

Book I

1. The good as the aim of action

Every art or applied science and every systematic investigation, and similarly every action and choice, seem to aim at some good; the good, therefore, has been well defined as that at which all things aim. But it is clear that there is a difference in the ends at which they aim: in some cases the activity is the end, in others the end is some product beyond the activity. In cases where the end lies beyond the action the product is naturally superior to the activity.

Since there are many activities, arts, and sciences, the number of ends is correspondingly large: of medicine the end is health, of shipbuilding a vessel, of strategy, victory, and of household management, wealth. In many instances several such pursuits are grouped together under a single capacity: the art of bridle-making, for example, and everything else pertaining to the equipment of a horse are grouped together under horsemanship; horsemanship in turn, along with every other military action, is grouped together under strategy; and other pursuits are grouped together under other capacities. In all these cases the ends of the master sciences are preferable to the ends of the subordinate sciences, since the latter are pursued for the sake of the former. This is true whether the ends of the actions lie in the activities themselves or, as is the case in the disciplines just mentioned, in something beyond the activities.

2. Politics as the master science of the good

Now, if there exists an end in the realm of action which we desire for its own sake, an end which determines all our other desires; if, in other words, we do not make all our choices for the sake of something else—for in this way the process will go on infinitely so that our desire would be futile and pointless—then obviously this end will be the good, that is, the highest good. Will not the knowledge of this good, consequently, be very important to our lives? Would it not better equip us, like archers who have a target to aim at, to hit the proper mark? If so, we must try to comprehend in outline at least what this good is and to which branch of knowledge or to which capacity it belongs.

This good, one should think, belongs to the most sovereign and most comprehensive master science, and politics clearly fits this description. For it determines which sciences ought to exist in states, what kind of sciences each group of citizens must learn, and what degree of proficiency each must attain. We observe further that the most honored capacities, such as strategy, household management, and oratory, are contained in politics. Since this science uses the rest of the sciences, and since, moreover, it legislates what people are to do and what they are not to do, its end seems to embrace the ends of the other sciences. Thus it follows that the end of politics is the good for man. For even if the good is the same for the individual and the state, the good of the state clearly is the greater and more perfect thing to attain and to safeguard. The attainment of the good for one man alone is, to be sure, a source of satisfaction; yet to secure it for a nation and for states is nobler and more divine. In short, these are the aims of our investigation, which is in a sense an investigation of social and political matters.

3. The limitations of ethics and politics

Our discussion will be adequate if it achieves clarity within the limits of the subject matter. For precision cannot be expected in the treatment of all subjects alike, any more than it can be expected in all manufactured articles. Problems of what is noble and just, which politics examines, present so much variety and irregularity that some people believe that they exist only by convention and not by nature. The problem of the good, too, presents a similar kind of irregularity, because in many cases good things bring harmful results. There are instances of men ruined by wealth, and others by courage. Therefore, in a discussion of such subjects, which has to start from a basis of this kind, we must be satisfied to indicate the truth with a rough and general sketch: when the subject and the basis of a discussion consist of matters that hold good only as a general rule, but not always, the conclusions reached must be of the same order. The various points that are made must be received in the same spirit. For a well-schooled man is one who searches for that degree of precision in each kind of study which the nature of the subject at hand admits: it is obviously just as foolish to accept arguments of probability from a mathematician as to demand strict demonstrations from an orator.

Each man can judge competently the things he knows, and of these he is a good judge. Accordingly, a good judge in each particular field is one who has been trained in it, and a good judge in general, a man who has received an all-round schooling. For that reason, a young man is not equipped to be a student of politics; for he has no experience in the actions which life demands of him, and these actions form the basis and subject matter of the discussion. Moreover, since he follows his emotions, his study will be pointless and unprofitable, for the end of this kind of study is not knowledge but action. Whether he is young in years or immature in character makes no difference; for his deficiency is not a matter of time but of living and of pursuing all his interests under the influence of his emotions. Knowledge brings no benefit to this kind of person, just as it brings none to the morally weak. But those who regulate their desires and actions by a rational principle will greatly benefit from a knowledge of this subject. So much by way of a preface about the student, the limitations which have to be accepted, and the objective before us.

4. Happiness is the good, but many views are held about it

To resume the discussion: since all knowledge and every choice is directed toward some good, let us discuss what is in our view the aim of politics, i.e., the highest good attainable by action. As far as its name is concerned, most people would probably agree: for both the common run of people and cultivated men call it happiness, and understand by "being happy" the same as "living well" and "doing well." But when it comes to defining what happiness is, they disagree, and the account given by the common run differs from that of the philosophers. The former say it is some clear and obvious good, such as pleasure, wealth, or honor; some say it is one thing and others another, and often the very same person identifies it with different things at different times: when he is sick he thinks it is health, and when he is poor he says it is wealth; and when people are conscious of their own ignorance, they admire those who talk above their heads in accents of greatness. Some thinkers used to believe that there exists over and above these many goods another good, good in itself and by itself, which also is the cause of good in all these things. An examination of all the different opinions would perhaps be a little pointless, and it is sufficient to concentrate on those which are most in evidence or which seem to make some sort of sense.

Nor must we overlook the fact that arguments which proceed from fundamental principles are different from arguments that lead up to them. Plato, too, rightly recognized this as a problem and used to ask whether the discussion was proceeding from or leading up to fundamental principles, just as in a race course there is a difference between running from the judges to the far end of the track and running back again. Now, we must start with the known. But this term has two connotations: "what is known to us" and "what is known" pure and simple. Therefore, we should start perhaps from what is known to us. For that reason, to be a competent student of what is right and just, and of politics generally, one must first have received a proper upbringing in moral conduct. The acceptance of a fact as a fact is the starting point, and if this is sufficiently clear, there will be no further need to ask why it is so. A man with this kind of background has or can easily acquire the foundations from which he must start. But if he neither has nor can acquire them, let him lend an ear to Hesiod's words:

> That man is all-best who himself works out every problem. . . .
> That man, too, is admirable who follows one who speaks well.

> He who cannot see the truth for himself, nor, hearing it from others,
> store it away in his mind, that man is utterly useless.

5. Various views on the highest good

But to return to the point from which we digressed. It is not unreasonable that men should derive their concept of the good and of happiness from the lives which they lead. The common run of people and the most vulgar identify it with pleasure, and for that reason are satisfied with a life of enjoyment. For the most notable kinds of life are three: the life just mentioned, the political life, and the contemplative life.

The common run of people, as we saw, betray their utter slavishness in their preference for a life suitable to cattle; but their views seem plausible because many people in high places share the feelings of Sardanapallus. Cultivated and active men, on the other hand, believe the good to be honor, for honor, one might say, is the end of the political life. But this is clearly too superficial an answer: for honor seems to depend on those who confer it rather than on him who receives it, whereas our guess is that the good is a man's own possession which cannot easily be taken away from him. Furthermore, men seem to pursue honor to assure themselves of their own worth; at any rate, they seek to be honored by sensible men and by those who know them, and they want to be honored on the basis of their virtue or excellence. Obviously, then, excellence, as far as they are concerned, is better than honor. One might perhaps even go so far as to consider excellence rather than honor as the end of political life. However, even excellence proves to be imperfect as an end: for a man might possibly possess it while asleep or while being inactive all his life, and while, in addition, undergoing the greatest suffering and misfortune. Nobody would call the life of such a man happy, except for the sake of maintaining an argument. But enough of this: the subject has been sufficiently treated in our publications addressed to a wider audience. In the third place there is the contemplative life, which we shall examine later on. As for the money-maker, his life is led under some kind of constraint: clearly, wealth is not the good which we are trying to find, for it is only useful, i.e., it is a means to something else. Hence one might rather regard the aforementioned objects as ends, since they are valued for their own sake. But even they prove not to be the good, though many words have been wasted to show that they are. Accordingly, we may dismiss them. . . .

7. The good is final and self-sufficient; happiness is defined

Let us return again to our investigation into the nature of the good which we are seeking. It is evidently something different in different actions and in each art: it is one thing in medicine, another in strategy, and another again in each of the other arts. What, then, is the good of each? Is it not that for the sake of which everything else is done? That means it is health in the case of medicine, victory in the case of strategy, a house in the case of building, a different thing in the case of different arts, and in all actions and choices it is the end. For it is for the sake of the end that all else is done. Thus, if there is some one end for all that we do, this would be the good attainable by action; if there are several ends, they will be the goods attainable by action.

Our argument has gradually progressed to the same point at which we were before, and we must try to clarify it still further. Since there are evidently several ends, and since we choose some of these—e.g., wealth, flutes, and instruments generally—as a means to something else, it is obvious that not all ends are final. The highest good, on the other hand, must be something final. Thus, if there is only one final end, this will be the good we are seeking; if there are several, it will be the most final and perfect of them. We call that which is pursued as an end in itself more final than an end which is pursued for the sake of something else; and what is never chosen as a means to something else we call more final than that which is chosen both as an end in itself and as a means to something else. What is always chosen as an end in itself and never as a means to something else is called final in an unqualified sense. This description seems to apply to happiness above all else: for we always choose happiness as an end in itself and never for the sake of something else. Honor, pleasure, intelligence, and all virtue we choose partly for themselves—for we would choose each of them even if no further advantage would accrue from them—but we also choose them partly for the sake of happiness, because we assume that it is through them that we will be happy. On the other hand, no one chooses happiness for the sake of honor, pleasure, and the like, nor as a means to anything at all.

We arrive at the same conclusion if we approach the question from the standpoint of self-sufficiency. For the final and perfect good seems to be self-sufficient. However, we define something as self-sufficient not by reference to the "self" alone. We do not mean a man who lives his life in isolation, but a man who also lives with parents, children, a wife, and friends and fellow citizens generally, since man is by nature a social and political being. But some limit must be set to these relationships; for if they are extended to include ancestors, descendants, and friends of friends, they will go on to infinity. However, this point must be reserved for investigation later. For the present we define as "self-sufficient" that which taken by itself makes life something desirable and deficient in nothing. It is happiness, in our opinion, which fits this description. Moreover, happiness is of all things the one most desirable, and it is not counted as one good thing among many others. But if it were counted as one among many others, it is obvious that the addition of even the least of the goods would make it more desirable; for the addition would produce an extra amount of good, and the greater amount of good is always more desirable than the lesser. We see then that happiness is something final and self-sufficient and the end of our actions.

To call happiness the highest good is perhaps a little trite, and a clearer account of what it is, is still required. Perhaps this is best done by first ascertaining the proper function of man. For just as the goodness and performance of a flute player, a sculptor, or any kind of expert, and generally of anyone who fulfills some function or performs some action, are thought to reside in his proper function, so the goodness and performance of man would seem to reside in whatever is his proper function. Is it then possible that while a carpenter and a shoemaker have their own proper functions and spheres of action, man as man has none, but was left by nature a good-for-nothing without a function? Should we not assume that just as the eye, the hand, the foot, and in general each part of the body clearly has its own proper function, so man too has some function over and above the functions of his parts? What can this function possibly be? Simply living? He shares that even with plants, but we are now looking for something peculiar to man. Accordingly, the life of nutrition and growth must be excluded. Next in line there is a life of sense perception. But this, too, man has in common with the horse, the ox, and every animal. There remains then an active life of the rational element.

The rational element has two parts: one is rational in that it obeys the rule of reason, the other in that it possesses and conceives rational rules. Since the expression "life of the rational element" also can be used in two senses, we must make it clear that we mean a life determined by the activity, as opposed to the mere possession, of the rational element. For the activity, it seems, has a greater claim to be the function of man.

The proper function of man, then, consists in an activity of the soul in conformity with a rational principle or, at least, not without it. In speaking of the proper function of a given individual we mean that it is the same in kind as the function of an individual who sets high standards for himself: the proper function of a harpist, for example, is the same as the function of a harpist who has set high standards for himself. The same applies to any and every group of individuals: the full attainment of excellence must be added to the mere function. In other words, the function of the harpist is to play the harp; the function of the harpist who has high standards is to play it well. On these assumptions, if we take the proper function of man to be a certain kind of life, and if this kind of life is an activity of the soul and consists in actions performed in conjunction with the rational element, and if a man of high standards is he who performs these actions well and properly, and if a function is well performed when it is performed in accordance with the excellence appropriate to it; we reach the conclusion that the good of man is an activity of the soul in conformity with excellence or virtue, and if there are several virtues, in conformity with the best and most complete.

But we must add "in a complete life." For one swallow does not make a spring, nor does one sunny day; similarly, one day or a short time does not make a man blessed and happy.

This will suffice as an outline of the good: for perhaps one ought to make a general sketch first and fill in the details afterwards. Once a good outline has been made, anyone, it seems, is capable of developing and completing it in detail, and time is a good inventor or collaborator in such an effort. Advances in the arts, too, have come about in this way, for anyone can fill in gaps. We must also bear in mind what has been said above, namely that one should not require precision in all pursuits alike, but in each field precision varies with the matter under discussion and should be required only to the extent to which it is appropriate to the investigation. A carpenter and a geometrician both want to find a right angle, but they do not want to find it in the same sense: the former wants to find it to the extent to which it is useful for his work, the latter, wanting to see truth, [tries to ascertain] what it is and what sort of thing it is. We must, likewise, approach other subjects in the same spirit, in order to prevent minor points from assuming a greater importance than the major tasks. Nor should we demand to know a causal explanation in all matters alike; in some instances, e.g., when dealing with fundamental principles, it is sufficient to point out convincingly that such-and-such is in fact the case. The fact here is the primary thing and the fundamental principle. Some fundamental principles can be apprehended by induction, others by sense perception, others again by some sort of habituation, and others by still other means. We must try to get at each of them in a way naturally appropriate to it, and must be scrupulous in defining it correctly, because it is of great importance for the subsequent course of the discussion. Surely, a good beginning is more than half the whole, and as it comes to light, it sheds light on many problems. . . .

13. The psychological foundations of the virtues

Since happiness is a certain activity of the soul in conformity with perfect virtue, we must now examine what virtue or excellence is. For such an inquiry will perhaps better enable us to discover the nature of happiness. Moreover, the man who is truly concerned about politics seems to devote special attention to excellence, since it is his aim to make the citizens good and law-abiding. We have an example of this in the lawgivers of Crete and Sparta and in other great legislators. If an examination of virtue is part of politics, this question clearly fits into the pattern of our original plan.

There can be no doubt that the virtue which we have to study is human virtue. For the good which we have been seeking is a human good and the happiness a human happiness. By human virtue we do not mean the excellence of the body, but that of the soul, and we define happiness as an activity of the soul. If this is true, the student of politics must obviously have some knowledge of the workings of the soul, just as the man who is to heal eyes must know something about the whole body. In fact, knowledge is all the more important for the former, inasmuch as politics is better and more valuable than medicine, and cultivated physicians devote much time and trouble to gain knowledge about the body. Thus, the student of politics must study the soul, but he must do so with his own aim in view, and only to the extent that the objects of his inquiry demand: to go into it in greater detail would perhaps be more laborious than his purposes require.

Some things that are said about the soul in our less technical discussions are adequate enough to be used here, for instance, that the soul consists of two elements, one irrational and one rational. Whether these two elements are separate, like the parts of the body or any other divisible thing, or whether they are only logically separable though in reality indivisible, as convex and concave are in the circumference of a circle, is irrelevant for our present purposes.

Of the irrational element, again, one part seems to be common to all living things and vegetative in nature: I mean that part which is responsible for nurture and growth. We must assume that some such capacity of the soul exists in everything that takes nourishment, in the embryonic stage as well as when the organism is fully developed; for this makes more sense than to assume the existence of some different capacity at the latter stage. The excellence of this part of the soul is, therefore, shown to be common to all living things and is not exclusively human. This very part and this capacity seem to be most active in sleep. For in sleep the difference between a good man and a bad is least apparent—whence the saying that for half their lives the happy are no better off than the wretched. This is just what we would expect, for sleep is an inactivity of the soul in that it ceases to do things which cause it to be called good or bad. However, to a small extent some bodily movements do penetrate to the soul in sleep, and in this sense the dreams of honest men are better than those of average people. But enough of this subject: we may pass by the nutritive part, since it has no natural share in human excellence or virtue.

In addition to this, there seems to be another integral element of the soul which, though irrational, still does partake of reason in some way. In morally strong and morally weak men we praise the reason that guides them and the rational element of the soul, because it exhorts them to follow the right path and to do what is best. Yet we see in them also another natural strain different from the rational, which fights and resists the guidance of reason. The soul behaves in precisely the same manner as do the paralyzed limbs of the body. When we intend to move the limbs to the right, they turn to the left, and similarly, the impulses of morally weak persons turn in the direction opposite to that in which reason leads them. However, while the aberration of the body is visible, that of the soul is not. But perhaps we must accept it as a fact, nevertheless, that there is something in the soul besides the rational element, which opposes and reacts against it. In what way the two are distinct need not concern us here. But, as we have stated, it too seems to partake of reason; at any rate, in a morally strong man it accepts the leadership of reason, and is perhaps more obedient still in a self-controlled and courageous man, since in him everything is in harmony with the voice of reason.

Thus we see that the irrational element of the soul has two parts: the one is vegetative and has no share in reason at all, the other is the seat of the appetites and of desire in general and partakes of reason insofar as it complies with reason and accepts its leadership; it possesses reason in the sense that we say it is "reasonable" to accept the advice of a father and of friends, not in the sense that we have a "rational" understanding of mathematical propositions. That the irrational element can be persuaded by the rational is shown by the fact that admonition and all manner of rebuke and exhortation are possible. If it is correct to say that the appetitive part, too, has reason, it follows that the rational element of the soul has two subdivisions: the one possesses reason in the strict sense, contained within itself, and the other possesses reason in the sense that it listens to reason as one would listen to a father.

Virtue, too, is differentiated in line with this division of the soul. We call some virtues "intellectual" and others "moral": theoretical wisdom, understanding, and practical wisdom are intellectual virtues, generosity and self-control moral virtues. In speaking of a man's character, we do not describe him as wise or understanding, but as gentle or self-controlled; but we praise the wise man, too, for his characteristic, and praiseworthy characteristics are what we call virtues.

Book II

1. Moral virtue as the result of habits

Virtue, as we have seen, consists of two kinds, intellectual virtue and moral virtue. Intellectual virtue or excellence owes its origin and development chiefly to teaching, and for that reason requires experience and time. Moral virtue, on the other hand, is formed by habit, *ethos*, and its name, *ēthikē*, is therefore derived, by a slight variation, from *ethos*. This shows, too, that none of the moral virtues is implanted in us by nature, for nothing which exists by nature can be changed by habit. For example, it is impossible for a stone, which has a natural downward movement, to become habituated to moving upward, even if one should try ten thousand times to inculcate the habit by throwing it in the air; nor can fire be made to move downward, nor can the direction of any nature-given tendency be changed by habituation. Thus, the virtues are implanted in us neither by nature nor contrary to nature: we are by nature equipped with the ability to receive them, and habit brings this ability to completion and fulfillment.

Furthermore, of all the qualities with which we are endowed by nature, we are provided with the capacity first, and display the activity afterward. That this is true is shown by the senses: it is not by frequent seeing or frequent hearing that we acquired our senses, but on the contrary we first possess and then use them; we do not acquire them by use. The virtues, on the other hand, we acquire by first having put them into action, and the same is also true of the arts. For the things which we have to learn before we can do them we learn by doing: men become builders by building houses, and harpists by playing the harp. Similarly, we become just by the practice of just actions, self-controlled by exercising self-control, and courageous by performing acts of courage.

This is corroborated by what happens in states. Lawgivers make the citizens good by inculcating (good) habits in them, and this is the aim of every lawgiver; if he does not succeed in doing that, his legislation is a failure. It is in this that a good constitution differs from a bad one.

Moreover, the same causes and the same means that produce any excellence or virtue can also destroy it, and this is also true of every art. It is by playing the harp that men become both good and bad harpists, and correspondingly with builders and all the other craftsmen: a man who builds well will be a good builder, one who builds badly a bad one. For if this were not so, there would be no need for an instructor, but everybody would be born as a good or a bad craftsman. The same holds true of the virtues: in our transactions with other men it is by action that some become just and others unjust, and it is by acting in the face of danger and by developing the habit of feeling fear or confidence that some become brave men and others cowards. The same applies to the appetites and feelings of anger: by reacting in one way or in another to given circumstances some people become self-controlled and gentle, and others self-indulgent and short-tempered. In a word, characteristics develop from corresponding activities. For that reason, we must see to it that our activities are of a certain kind, since any variations in them will be reflected in our characteristics. Hence it is no small matter whether one habit or another is inculcated in us from early childhood; on the contrary, it makes a considerable difference, or, rather, all the difference.

2. Method in the practical sciences

The purpose of the present study is not, as it is in other inquiries, the attainment of theoretical knowledge: we are not conducting this inquiry in order to know what virtue is, but in order to become good, else there would be no advantage in studying it. For that reason, it becomes necessary to examine the problem of actions, and to ask how they are to be performed. For, as we have said, the actions determine what kind of characteristics are developed.

That we must act according to right reason is generally conceded and may be assumed as the basis of our discussion. We shall speak about it later and discuss what right reason is and examine its relation to the other virtues. But let us first agree that any discussion on matters of action cannot be more than an outline and is bound to lack precision; for as we stated at the outset, one can demand of a discussion only what the subject matter permits, and there are no fixed data in matters concerning action and questions of what is beneficial, any more than there are in matters of health. And if this is true of our general discussion, our treatment of particular problems will be even less precise, since these do not come under the head of any art which can be transmitted by precept, but the agent must consider on each different occasion what the situation demands, just as in medicine and in navigation. But although such is the kind of discussion in which we are engaged, we must do our best.

First of all, it must be observed that the nature of moral qualities is such that they are destroyed by defect and by excess. We see the same thing happen in the case of strength and of health, to illustrate, as we must, the invisible by means of visible examples: excess as well as deficiency of physical exercise destroys our strength, and similarly, too much and too little food and drink destroys our health; the proportionate amount, however, produces, increases, and preserves it. The same applies to self-control, courage, and the other virtues: the man who shuns and fears everything and never stands his ground becomes a coward, whereas a man who knows no fear at all and goes to meet every danger becomes reckless. Similarly, a man who revels in every pleasure and abstains from none becomes self-indulgent, while he who avoids every pleasure like a boor becomes what might be called insensitive. Thus we see that self-control and courage are destroyed by excess and by deficiency and are preserved by the mean.

Not only are the same actions which are responsible for and instrumental in the origin and development of the virtues also the causes and means of their destruction, but they will also be manifested in the active exercise of the virtues. We can see the truth of this in the case of other more visible qualities, e.g., strength. Strength is produced by consuming plenty of food and by enduring much hard work, and it is the strong man who is best able to do these things. The same is also true of the virtues: by abstaining from pleasures we become self-controlled, and once we are self-controlled we are best able to abstain from pleasures. So also with courage: by becoming habituated to despise and to endure terrors we become courageous, and once we have become courageous we will best be able to endure terror.

3. Pleasure and pain as the test of virtue

An index to our characteristics is provided by the pleasure or pain which follows upon the tasks we have achieved. A man who abstains from bodily pleasures and enjoys doing so is self-controlled; if he finds abstinence troublesome, he is self-indulgent; a man who endures danger with joy, or at least without pain, is courageous; if he endures it with pain, he is a coward. For moral excellence is concerned with pleasure and pain; it is pleasure that makes us do base actions and pain that prevents us from doing noble actions. For that reason, as Plato says, men must be brought up from childhood to feel pleasure and pain at the proper things; for this is correct education.

Furthermore, since the virtues have to do with actions and emotions, and since pleasure and pain are a consequence of every emotion and of every action, it follows from this point of view, too, that virtue has to do with pleasure and pain. This is further indicated by the fact that punishment is inflicted by means of pain. For punishment is a kind of medical treatment and it is the nature of medical treatments to take effect through the introduction of the opposite of the disease. Again, as we said just now, every characteristic of the soul shows its true nature in its relation to and its concern with those factors which naturally make it better or worse. But it is through pleasures and pains that men are corrupted, i.e., through pursuing and avoiding pleasures and pains either of the wrong kind or at the wrong time or in the wrong manner, or by going wrong in some other definable respect. For that reason some people define the virtues as states of freedom from emotion and of quietude. However, they make the mistake of using these terms absolutely and without adding such qualifications as "in the right manner," "at the right or wrong time," and so forth.

We may, therefore, assume as the basis of our discussion that virtue, being concerned with pleasure and pain in the way we have described, makes us act in the best way in matters involving pleasure and pain, and that vice does the opposite.

The following considerations may further illustrate that virtue is concerned with pleasure and pain. There are three factors that determine choice and three that determine avoidance: the noble, the beneficial, and the pleasurable, on the one hand, and on the other their opposites: the base, the harmful, and the painful. Now a good man will go right and a bad man will go wrong when any of these, and especially when pleasure is involved. For pleasure is not only common to man and the animals, but also accompanies all objects of choice: in fact, the noble and the beneficial seem pleasant to us. Moreover, a love of pleasure has grown up with all of us from infancy. Therefore, this emotion has come to be ingrained in our lives and is difficult to erase. Even in our actions we use, to a greater or smaller extent, pleasure and pain as a criterion. For this reason, this entire study is necessarily concerned with pleasure and pain; for it is not unimportant for our actions whether we feel joy and pain in the right or the wrong way. Again, it is harder to fight against pleasure than against anger, as Heraclitus says; and both virtue and art are always concerned with what is harder, for success is better when it is hard to achieve. Thus, for this reason also, every study both of virtue and of politics must deal with pleasures and pains, for if a man has the right attitude to them, he will be good; if the wrong attitude, he will be bad.

We have now established that virtue or excellence is concerned with pleasures and pains; that the actions which produce it also develop it and, if differently performed, destroy it; and that it actualizes itself fully in those activities to which it owes its origin.

4. Virtuous action and virtue

However, the question may be raised what we mean by saying that men become just by performing just actions and self-controlled by practicing self-control. For if they perform just actions and exercise self-control, they are already just and self-controlled, in the same way as they are literate and musical if they write correctly and practice music.

But is this objection really valid, even as regards the arts? No, for it is possible for a man to write a piece correctly by chance or at the prompting of another: but he will be literate only if he produces a piece of writing in a literate way, and that means doing it in accordance with the skill of literate composition which he has in himself.

Moreover, the factors involved in the arts and in the virtues are not the same. In the arts, excellence lies in the result itself, so that it is sufficient if it is of a certain kind. But in the case of the virtues an act is not performed justly or with self-control if the act itself is of a certain kind, but only if in addition the agent has certain characteristics as he performs it: first of all, he must know what he is doing; secondly, he must choose to act the way he does, and he must choose it for its own sake; and in the third place, the act must spring from a firm and unchangeable character. With the exception of knowing what one is about, these considerations do not enter into the mastery of the arts; for the mastery of the virtues, however, knowledge is of little or no importance, whereas the other two conditions count not for a little but are all-decisive, since repeated acts of justice and self-control result in the possession of these virtues. In other words, acts are called just and self-controlled when they are the kind of acts which a just or self-controlled man would perform; but the just and self-controlled man is not he who performs these acts, but he who also performs them in the way just and self-controlled men do.

Thus our assertion that a man becomes just by performing just acts and self-controlled by performing acts of self-control is correct; without performing them, nobody could even be on the way to becoming good. Yet most men do not perform such acts, but by taking refuge in argument they think that they are engaged in philosophy and that they will become good in this way. In so doing, they act like sick men who listen attentively to what the doctor says, but fail to do any of the things he prescribes. That kind of philosophical activity will not bring health to the soul any more than this sort of treatment will produce a healthy body.

5. Virtue defined: the genus

The next point to consider is the definition of virtue or excellence. As there are three kinds of things found in the soul: (1) emotions, (2) capacities, and (3) characteristics, virtue must be one of these. By "emotions" I mean appetite, anger, fear, confidence, envy, joy, affection, hatred, longing, emulation, pity, and in general anything that is followed by pleasure or pain; by "capacities" I mean that by virtue of which we are said to be affected by these emotions, for example, the capacity which enables us to feel anger, pain, or pity; and by "characteristics" I mean the condition, either good or bad, in which we are, in relation to the emotions: for example, our condition in relation to anger is bad, if our anger is too violent or not violent enough, but if it is moderate, our condition is good; and similarly with our condition in relation to the other emotions.

Now the virtues and vices cannot be emotions, because we are not called good or bad on the basis of our emotions, but on the basis of our virtues and vices. Also, we are neither praised nor blamed for our emotions: a man does not receive praise for being frightened or angry, nor blame for being angry pure and simple, but for being angry in a certain way. Yet we are praised or blamed for our virtues and vices. Furthermore, no choice is involved when we experience anger or fear, while the virtues are some kind of choice or at least involve choice. Moreover, with regard to our emotions we are said to be "moved," but with regard to our virtues and vices we are not said to be "moved" but to be "disposed" in a certain way.

For the same reason, the virtues cannot be capacities, either, for we are neither called good or bad nor praised or blamed simply because we are capable of being affected. Further, our capacities have been given to us by nature, but we do not by nature develop into good or bad men. We have discussed this subject before. Thus, if the virtues are neither emotions nor capacities, the only remaining alternative is that they are characteristics. So much for the genus of virtue.

6. Virtue defined: the differentia

It is not sufficient, however, merely to define virtue in general terms as a characteristic: we must also specify what kind of characteristic it is. It must, then, be remarked that every virtue or excellence (1) renders good the thing itself of which it is the excellence, and (2) causes it to perform its function well. For example, the excellence of the eye makes both the eye and its function good, for good sight is due to the excellence of the eye. Likewise, the excellence of a horse makes it both good as a horse and good at running, at carrying its rider, and at facing the enemy. Now, if this is true of all things, the virtue or excellence of man, too, will be a characteristic which makes him a good man, and which causes him to perform his own function well. To some extent we have already stated how this will be true; the rest will become clear if we study what the nature of virtue is.

Of every continuous entity that is divisible into parts it is possible to take the larger, the smaller, or an equal part, and these parts may be larger, smaller, or equal either in relation to the entity itself, or in relation to us. The "equal" part is something median between excess and deficiency. By the median of an entity I understand a point equidistant from both extremes, and this point is one and the same for everybody. By the median relative to us I understand an amount neither too large nor too small, and this is neither one nor the same for everybody. To take an example: if ten is many and two is few, six is taken as the median in relation to the entity, for it exceeds and is exceeded by the same amount, and is thus the median in terms of arithmetical proportion. But the median relative to us cannot be determined in this manner: if ten pounds of food is much for a man to eat and two pounds little, it does not follow that the trainer will prescribe six pounds, for this may in turn be much or little for him to eat; it may be little for Milo and much for someone who has just begun to take up athletics. The same applies to running and wrestling. Thus we see that an expert in any field avoids excess and deficiency, but seeks the median and chooses it—not the median of the object but the median relative to us.

If this, then, is the way in which every science perfects its work, by looking to the median and by bringing its work up to that point—and this is the reason why it is usually said of a successful piece of work that it is impossible to detract from it or to add to it, the implication being that excess and deficiency destroy success while the mean safeguards it (good craftsmen, we say, look toward this standard in the performance of their work)—and if virtue, like nature, is more precise and better than any art, we must conclude that virtue aims at the median. I am referring to moral virtue: for it is moral virtue that is concerned with emotions and actions, and it is in emotions and actions that excess, deficiency, and the median are found. Thus we can experience fear, confidence, desire, anger, pity, and generally any kind of pleasure and pain either too much or too little, and in either case not properly. But to experience all this at the right time, toward the right objects, toward the right people, for the right reason, and in the right manner—that is the median and the best course, the course that is a mark of virtue.

Similarly, excess, deficiency, and the median can also be found in actions. Now virtue is concerned with emotions and actions; and in emotions and actions excess and deficiency miss the mark, whereas the median is praised and constitutes success. But both praise and success are signs of virtue or excellence. Consequently, virtue is a mean in the sense that it aims at the median. This is corroborated by the fact that there are many ways of going wrong, but only one way which is right—for evil belongs to the indeterminate, as the Pythagoreans imagined, but good to the determinate. This, by the way, is also the reason why the one is easy and the other hard: It is easy to miss the target but hard to hit it. Here, then, is an additional proof that excess and deficiency characterize vice, while the mean characterizes virtue: for "bad men have many ways, good men but one."

We may thus conclude that virtue or excellence is a characteristic involving choice, and that it consists in observing the mean relative to us, a mean which is defined by a rational principle, such as a man of practical wisdom would use to determine it. It is the mean by reference to two vices: the one of excess and the other of deficiency. It is, moreover, a mean because some vices exceed and others fall short of what is required in emotion and in action, whereas virtue finds and chooses the median. Hence, in respect of its essence and the definition of its essential nature virtue is a mean, but in regard to goodness and excellence it is an extreme.

Not every action nor every emotion admits of a mean. There are some actions and emotions whose very names connote baseness, e.g., spite, shamelessness, envy; and among actions, adultery, theft, and murder. These and similar emotions and actions imply by their very names that they are bad; it is not their excess nor their deficiency which is called bad. It is, therefore, impossible ever to do right in performing them: To perform them is always to do wrong. In cases of this sort, let us say adultery, rightness and wrongness do not depend on committing it with the right woman at the right time and in the right manner, but the mere fact of committing such action at all is to do wrong. It would be just as absurd to suppose that there is a mean, an excess, and a deficiency in an unjust or a cowardly or a self-indulgent act. For if there were, we would have a mean of excess and a mean of deficiency, and an excess of excess and a deficiency of deficiency. Just as there cannot be an excess and a deficiency of self-control and courage—because the intermediate is, in a sense, an extreme—so there cannot be a mean, excess, and deficiency in their respective opposites: Their opposites are wrong regardless of how they are performed; for, in general, there is no such thing as the mean of an excess or a deficiency, or the excess and deficiency of a mean.

7. Examples of the mean in particular virtues

However, this general statement is not enough; we must also show that it fits particular instances. For in a discussion of moral actions, although general statements have a wider range of application, statements on particular points have more truth in them: actions are concerned with particulars and our statements must harmonize with them. Let us now take particular virtues and vices from the following table.

In feelings of fear and confidence courage is the mean. As for the excesses, there is no name that describes a man who exceeds in fearlessness—many virtues and vices have no name; but a man who exceeds in confidence is reckless, and a man who exceeds in fear and is deficient in confidence is cowardly.

In regard to pleasures and pains—not all of them and to a lesser degree in the case of pains—the mean is self-control and the excess self-indulgence. Men deficient in regard to pleasure are not often found, and there is therefore no name for them, but let us call them "insensitive."

In giving and taking money, the mean is generosity, the excess and deficiency are extravagance and stinginess. In these vices excess and deficiency work in opposite ways: an extravagant man exceeds in spending and is deficient in taking, while a stingy man exceeds in taking and is deficient in spending. For our present purposes, we may rest content with an outline and a summary, but we shall later define these qualities more precisely.

There are also some other dispositions in regard to money: magnificence is a mean (for there is a difference between a magnificent and a generous man in that the former operates on a large scale, the latter on a small); gaudiness and vulgarity are excesses, and niggardliness a deficiency. These vices differ from the vices opposed to generosity. But we shall postpone until later a discussion of the way in which they differ.

As regards honor and dishonor, the mean is high-mindedness, the excess is what we might call vanity, and the deficiency small-mindedness. The same relation which, as we said, exists between magnificence and generosity, the one being distinguished from the other in that it operates on a small scale, exists also between high-mindedness and another virtue: as the former deals with great, so the latter deals with small honors. For it is possible to desire honor as one should or more than one should or less than one should: a man who exceeds in his desires is called ambitious, a man who is deficient unambitious, but there is no name to describe the man in the middle. There are likewise no names for the corresponding dispositions except for the disposition of an ambitious man which is called ambition. As a result, the men who occupy the extremes lay claim to the middle position. We ourselves, in fact, sometimes call the middle person ambitious and sometimes unambitious; sometimes we praise an ambitious and at other times an unambitious man. The reason why we do that will be discussed in the sequel; for the present, let us discuss the rest of the virtues and vices along the lines we have indicated.

In regard to anger also there exists an excess, a deficiency, and a mean. Although there really are no names for them, we might call the mean gentleness, since we call a man who occupies the middle position gentle. Of the extremes, let the man who exceeds be called short-tempered and his vice a short temper, and the deficient man apathetic and his vice apathy.

There are, further, three other means which have a certain similarity with one another, but differ nonetheless one from the other. They are all concerned with human relations in speech and action, but they differ in that one of them is concerned with truth in speech and action and the other two with pleasantness: (a) pleasantness in amusement and (b) pleasantness in all our daily life. We must include these, too, in our discussion, in order to see more clearly that the mean is to be praised in all things and that the extremes are neither praiseworthy nor right, but worthy of blame. Here, too, most of the virtues and vices have no name, but for the sake of clarity and easier comprehension we must try to coin names for them, as we did in earlier instances.

To come to the point; in regard to truth, let us call the man in the middle position truthful and the mean truthfulness. Pretense in the form of exaggeration is boastfulness and its possessor boastful, while pretense in the form of understatement is self-depreciation and its possesor a self-depreciator.

Concerning pleasantness in amusement, the man in the middle position is witty and his disposition wittiness; the excess is called buffoonery and its possessor a buffoon; and the deficient man a kind of boor and the corresponding characteristic boorishness.

As far as the other kind of pleasantness is concerned, pleasantness in our daily life, a man who is as pleasant as he should be is friendly and the mean is friendliness. A man who exceeds is called obsequious if he has no particular purpose in being pleasant, but if he is acting for his own material advantage, he is a flatterer. And a man who is deficient and unpleasant in every respect is a quarrelsome and grouchy kind of person.

A mean can also be found in our emotional experiences and in our emotions. Thus, while a sense of shame is not a virtue, a bashful or modest man is praised. For even in these matters we speak of one kind of person as intermediate and of another as exceeding if he is terror-stricken and abashed at everything. On the other hand, a man who is deficient in shame or has none at all is called shameless, whereas the intermediate man is bashful or modest.

Righteous indignation is the mean between envy and spite, all of these being concerned with the pain and pleasure which we feel in regard to the fortunes of our neighbors. The righteously indignant man feels pain when someone prospers undeservedly; an envious man exceeds him in that he is pained when he sees anyone prosper; and a spiteful man is so deficient in feeling pain that he even rejoices [when someone suffers undeservedly].

But we shall have an opportunity to deal with these matters again elsewhere. After that, we shall discuss justice; since it has more than one meaning, we shall distinguish the two kinds of justice and show in what way each is a mean.

8. The relation between the mean and its extremes

There are, then, three kinds of disposition: two are vices (one marked by excess and one by deficiency), and one, virtue, the mean. Now, each of these dispositions is, in a sense, opposed to both the others: the extremes are opposites to the middle as well as to one another, and the middle is opposed to the extremes. Just as an equal amount is larger in relation to a smaller and smaller in relation to a larger amount, so, in the case both of emotions and of actions, the middle characteristics exceed in relation to the deficiencies and are deficient in relation to the excesses. For example, a brave man seems reckless in relation to a coward, but in relation to a reckless man he seems cowardly. Similarly, a self-controlled man seems self-indulgent in relation to an insensitive man and insensitive in relation to a self-indulgent man, and a generous man extravagant in relation to a stingy man and stingy in relation to an extravagant man. This is the reason why people at the extremes each push the man in the middle over to the other extreme: a coward calls a brave man reckless and a reckless man calls a brave man a coward, and similarly with the other qualities.

However, while these three dispositions are thus opposed to one another, the extremes are more opposed to one another than each is to the median; for they are further apart from one another than each is from the median, just as the large is further removed from the small and the small from the large than either one is from the equal. Moreover, there appears to be a certain similarity between some extremes and their median, e.g., recklessness resembles courage and extravagance generosity; but there is a very great dissimilarity between the extremes. But things that are furthest removed from one another are defined as opposites, and that means that the further things are removed from one another the more opposite they are.

In some cases it is the deficiency and in others the excess that is more opposed to the median. For example, it is not the excess, recklessness, which is more opposed to courage, but the deficiency, cowardice; while in the case of self-control it is not the defect, insensitivity, but the excess, self-indulgence which is more opposite. There are two causes for this. One arises from the nature of the thing itself: when one of the extremes is closer and more similar to the median, we do not treat it but rather the other extreme as the opposite of the median. For instance, since recklessness is believed to be more similar and closer to courage, and cowardice less similar, it is cowardice rather than recklessness which we treat as the opposite of courage. For what is further removed from the middle is regarded as being more opposite. So much for the first cause which arises from the thing itself. The second reason is found in ourselves: the more we are naturally attracted to anything, the more opposed to the median does this thing appear to be. For example, since we are naturally more attracted to pleasure we incline more easily to self-indulgence than to a disciplined kind of life. We describe as more opposed to the mean those things toward which our tendency is stronger; and for that reason the excess, self-indulgence, is more opposed to self-control than is its corresponding deficiency.

9. How to attain the mean

Our discussion has sufficiently established (1) that moral virtue is a mean and in what sense it is a mean; (2) that it is a mean between two vices, one of which is marked by excess and the other by deficiency; and (3) that it is a mean in the sense that it aims at the median in the emotions and in actions. That is why it is a hard task to be good; in every case it is a task to find the median: for instance, not everyone can find the middle of a circle, but only a man who has the proper knowledge. Similarly, anyone can get angry—that is easy—or can give away money or spend it; but to do all this to the right person, to the right extent, at the right time, for the right reason, and in the right way is no longer something easy that anyone can do. It is for this reason that good conduct is rare, praiseworthy, and noble.

The first concern of a man who aims at the median should, therefore, be to avoid the extreme which is more opposed to it, as Calypso advises: "Keep clear your ship of yonder spray and surf." For one of the two extremes is more in error than the other, and since it is extremely difficult to hit the mean, we must, as the saying has it, sail in the second best way and take the lesser evil; and we can best do that in the manner we have described.

Moreover, we must watch the errors which have the greatest attraction for us personally. For the natural inclination of one man differs from that of another, and we each come to recognize our own by observing the pleasure and pain produced in us [by the different extremes]. We must then draw ourselves away in the opposite direction, for by pulling away from error we shall reach the middle, as men do when they straighten warped timber. In every case we must be especially on our guard against pleasure and what is pleasant, for when it comes to pleasure we cannot act as unbiased judges. Our attitude toward pleasure should be the same as that of the Trojan elders was toward Helen, and we should repeat on every occasion the words they addressed to her. For if we dismiss pleasure as they dismissed her, we shall make fewer mistakes.

In summary, then, it is by acting in this way that we shall best be able to hit the median. But this is no doubt difficult; especially when particular cases are concerned. For it is not easy to determine in what manner, with what person, on what occasion, and for how long a time one ought to be angry. There are times when we praise those who are deficient in anger and call them gentle, and other times when we praise violently angry persons and call them manly. However, we do not blame a man for slightly deviating from the course of goodness, whether he strays toward excess or toward deficiency, but we do blame him if his deviation is great and cannot pass unnoticed. It is not easy to determine by a formula at what point and for how great a divergence a man deserves blame; but this difficulty is, after all, true of all objects of sense perception: determinations of this kind depend upon particular circumstances, and the decision rests with our [moral] sense.

This much, at any rate, is clear: that the median characteristic is in all fields the one that deserves praise, and that it is sometimes necessary to incline toward the excess and sometimes toward the deficiency. For it is in this way that we will most easily hit upon the median, which is the point of excellence.

Utilitarianism

John Stuart Mill

Chapter 1

General Remarks

There are few circumstances among those which make up the present condition of human knowledge, more unlike what might have been expected, or more significant of the backward state in which speculation on the most important subjects still lingers, than the little progress which has been made in the decision of the controversy respecting the criterion of right and wrong. From the dawn of philosophy, the question concerning the *summum bonum,* or, what is the same thing, concerning the foundation of morality, has been accounted the main problem in speculative thought, has occupied the most gifted intellects, and divided them into sects and schools, carrying on a vigorous warfare against one another. And after more than two thousand years the same discussions continue, philosophers are still ranged under the same contending banners, and neither thinkers nor mankind

---

Thirteenth edition, London, 1897. First published in 1861.

at large seem nearer to being unanimous on the subject, than when the youth Socrates listened to the old Protagoras, and asserted (if Plato's dialogue be grounded on a real conversation) the theory of utilitarianism against the popular morality of the so-called sophist.

It is true that similar confusion and uncertainty, and in some cases similar discordance, exist respecting the first principles of all the sciences, not excepting that which is deemed the most certain of them, mathematics; without much impairing, generally indeed without impairing at all, the trustworthiness of the conclusions of those sciences. An apparent anomaly, the explanation of which is, that the detailed doctrines of a science are not usually deduced from, nor depend for their evidence upon, what are called its first principles. Were it not so, there would be no science more precarious, or whose conclusions were more insufficiently made out, than algebra; which derives none of its certainty from what are commonly taught to learners as its elements, since these, as laid down by some of its most eminent teachers, are as full of fictions as English law, and of mysteries as theology. The truths which are ultimately accepted as the first principles of a science, are really the last results of metaphysical analysis, practised on the elementary notions with which the science is conversant; and their relation to the science is not that of foundations to an edifice, but of roots to a tree, which may perform their office equally well though they never be dug down to and exposed to light. But though in science the particular truths precede the general theory, the contrary might be expected to be the case with a practical art, such as morals or legislation. All action is for the sake of some end, and rules of action, it seems natural to suppose, must take their whole character and colour from the end to which they are subservient. When we engage in a pursuit, a clear and precise conception of what we are pursuing would seem to be the first thing we need, instead of the last we are to look forward to. A test of right and wrong must be the means, one would think, of ascertaining what is right or wrong, and not a consequence of having already ascertained it.

The difficulty is not avoided by having recourse to the popular theory of a natural faculty, a sense or instinct, informing us of right and wrong. For—besides that the existence of such a moral instinct is itself one of the matters in dispute—those believers in it who have any pretensions to philosophy, have been obliged to abandon the idea that it discerns what is right or wrong in the particular case in hand, as our other senses discern the sight or sound actually present. Our moral faculty, according to all those of its interpreters who are entitled to the name of thinkers, supplies us only with the general principles of moral judgments; it is a branch of our reason, not of our sensitive faculty; and must be looked to for the abstract doctrines of morality, not for perception of it in the concrete. The intuitive, no less than what may be termed the inductive, school of ethics, insists on the necessity of general laws. They both agree that the morality of an individual action is not a question of direct perception, but of the application of a law to an individual case. They recognise also, to a great extent, the same moral laws; but differ as to their evidence, and the source from which they derive their authority. According to the one opinion, the principles of morals are evident *a priori*, requiring nothing to command assent, except that the meaning of the terms be understood. According to the other doctrine, right and wrong, as well as truth and falsehood, are questions of observation and experience. But both hold equally that morality must be deduced from principles; and the intuitive school affirm as strongly as the inductive, that there is a science of morals. Yet they seldom attempt to make out a list of the *a priori* principles which are to serve as the premises of the science; still more rarely do they make any effort to reduce those various principles to one first principle, or common ground of obligation. They either assume the ordinary precepts of morals as of *a priori* authority, or they lay down as the common groundwork of those maxims, some generality much less obviously authoritative than the maxims themselves, and which has never succeeded in gaining popular acceptance. Yet to support their pretensions there ought either to be some one fundamental principle or law, at the root of all morality, or if there be several, there should be a determinate order of precedence among them; and the one principle, or the rule for deciding between the various principles when they conflict, ought to be self evident.

To inquire how far the bad effects of this deficiency have been mitigated in practise, or to what extent the moral beliefs of mankind have been vitiated or made uncertain by the absence of any distinct recognition of an ultimate standard, would imply a complete survey and criticism of past and present ethical doctrine. It would, however, be easy to show that whatever steadiness or consistency these moral beliefs have attained, has been mainly due to the tacit influence of a standard not recognised. Although the non-existence of an acknowledged first principle has made ethics not so much a guide as a consecration of men's actual sentiments, still, as men's sentiments, both of favour and of aversion, are greatly influenced by what they suppose to be the effects of things upon their happiness, the principle of utility, or as Bentham latterly called it, the greatest happiness principle, has had a large share in forming the moral doctrines even of those who most scornfully reject its authority. Nor is there any school of thought which refuses to admit that the influence of actions on happiness is a most material and even predominant consideration in many of the details of morals, however unwilling to acknowledge it as the fundamental principle of morality, and the source of moral obligation. I might go much further, and say to all those *a priori* moralists who deem it necessary to argue at all, utilitarian arguments are indispensable. It is not my present purpose to criticise these thinkers; but I cannot help referring, for illustration, to a systematic treatise by one of the most illustrious of them, the *Metaphysics of Ethics,* by Kant. This remarkable man, whose system of thought will long remain one of the landmarks in the history of philosophical speculation, does, in the treatise in question, lay down an universal first principle as the origin and ground of moral obligation; it is this: — "So act, that the rule on which thou attest would admit of being adopted as a law by all rational beings." But when he begins to deduce from this precept any of the actual duties of morality, he fails, almost grotesquely, to show that there would be any contradiction, any logical (not to say physical) impossibility, in the adoption by all rational beings of the most outrageously immoral rules of conduct. All he shows is that the *consequences* of their universal adoption would be such as no one would choose to incur.

On the present occasion, I shall, without further discussion of the other theories, attempt to contribute something towards the understanding and appreciation of the Utilitarian or Happiness theory, and towards such proof as it is susceptible of. It is evident that this cannot be proof in the ordinary and popular meaning of the term. Questions of ultimate ends are not amenable to direct proof. Whatever can be proved to be good, must be so by being shown to be a means to something admitted to be good without proof. The medical art is proved to be good, by its conducing to health; but how is it possible to prove that health is good? The art of music is good, for the reason, among others, that it produces pleasure; but what proof is it possible to give that pleasure is good? If, then, it is asserted that there is a comprehensive formula, including all things which are in themselves good, and that whatever else is good, is not so as an end, but as a means, the formula may be accepted or rejected, but is not a subject of what is commonly understood by proof. We are not, however, to infer that its acceptance or rejection must depend on blind impulse, or arbitrary choice. There is a larger meaning of the word proof, in which this question is as amenable to it as any other of the disputed questions of philosophy. The subject is within the cognizance of the rational faculty; and neither does that faculty deal with it solely in the way of intuition. Considerations may be presented capable of determining the intellect either to give or withhold its assent to the doctrine; and this is equivalent to proof.

We shall examine presently of what nature are these considerations; in what manner they apply to the case, and what rational grounds, therefore, can be given for accepting or rejecting the utilitarian formula. But it is a preliminary condition of rational acceptance or rejection, that the formula should be correctly understood. I believe that the very imperfect notion ordinarily formed of its meaning, is the chief obstacle which impedes its reception; and that could it be cleared, even from only the grosser misconceptions, the question would be greatly simplified, and a large proportion of its difficulties removed. Before, therefore, I attempt to enter into the philosophical grounds which can be given for assenting to the utilitarian standard, I shall offer some illustrations of the doctrine itself, with the view of showing more clearly what it is, distinguishing it from what it is not, and disposing of such of the practical objections to it as either originate in, or are closely connected with, mistaken interpretations of its meaning. Having thus prepared the ground, I shall afterwards endeavour to throw such light as I can upon the question, considered as one of philosophical theory.

Chapter II
What Utilitarianism Is

A passing remark is all that needs be given to the original blunder of supposing that those who stand up for utility as the test of right and wrong, use the term in that restricted and merely colloquial sense in which utility is opposed to pleasure. An apology is due to the philosophical opponents of utilitarianism, for even the momentary appearance of confronting them with any one capable of so absurd a misconception; which is the more extraordinary, inasmuch as the contrary accusation, of referring everything to pleasure, and that too in its grossest form, is another of the common charges against utilitarianism: and, as has been pointedly remarked by an able writer, the same sort of persons, and often the very same persons, denounce the theory "as impracticably dry when the word utility precedes the word pleasure, and as too practicably voluptuous when the word pleasure precedes the word utility." Those who know anything about the matter are aware that every writer, from Epicurus to Bentham, who maintained the theory of utility, meant by it, not something to be contradistinguished from pleasure, but pleasure itself, together with exemption from pain; and instead of opposing the useful to the agreeable or the ornamental, have always declared that the useful means these, among other things. Yet the common herd, including the herd of writers, not only in newspapers and periodicals, but in books of weight and pretension, are perpetually falling into this shallow mistake. Having caught up the word utilitarian, while knowing nothing whatever about it but its sound, they habitually express by it the rejection, or the neglect, of pleasure in some of its forms; of beauty, of ornament, or of amusement. Nor is the term thus ignorantly misapplied solely in disparagement, but occasionally in compliment; as though it implied superiority to frivolity and the mere pleasures of the moment. And this perverted use is the only one in which the word is popularly known, and the one from which the new generation are acquiring their sole notion of its meaning. Those who introduced the word, but who had for many years discontinued it as a distinctive appellation, may well feel themselves called upon to resume it, if by doing so they can hope to contribute anything towards rescuing it from this utter degradation.*

The creed which accepts as the foundation of morals, Utility, or the Greatest Happiness Principle, holds that actions are right in proportion as they tend to promote happiness, wrong as they tend to produce the reverse of happiness. By happiness is intended pleasure, and the absence of pain; by unhappiness, pain and the privation of pleasure. To give a clear view of the moral standard set up by the theory, much more requires to be said; in particular, what things it includes in the ideas of pain and pleasure; and to what extent this is left an open question. But these supplementary explanations do not affect the theory of life on which this theory of morality is grounded—namely, that pleasure, and freedom from pain, are the only things desirable as ends; and that all desirable things (which are as numerous in the utilitarian as in any other scheme) are desirable either for the pleasure inherent in themselves, or as means of the promotion of pleasure and the prevention of pain.

Now, such a theory of life excites in many minds, and among them in some of the most estimable in feeling and purpose, inveterate dislike. To suppose that life has (as they express it) no higher end than pleasure—no better and nobler object of desire and pursuit—they designate as utterly mean and grovelling; as a doctrine worthy only of swine, to whom the followers of Epicurus were, at a very early period, contemptuously likened; and modern holders of the doctrine are occasionally made the subject of equally polite comparisons by its German, French, and English assailants.

When thus attacked, the Epicureans have always answered, that it is not they, but their accusers, who represent human nature in a degrading light; since the accusation supposes human beings to be capable of no pleasures except those of which swine are capable. If this supposition were true, the charge could not be gainsaid, but would then be no longer an imputation: for if the sources of pleasure were precisely the same to human beings and to swine, the rule of life which is good enough for the one would be good enough for the other. The comparison of the Epicurean life to that of beasts is felt as degrading, precisely because a beast's pleasures do not

---

*The author of this essay has reason for believing himself to be the first person who brought the word utilitarian into use. He did not invent it, but adopted it from a passing expression in Mr. Galt's *Annals of the Parish*. After using it as a designation for several years, he and others abandoned it from a growing dislike to anything resembling a badge or watchword of sectarian distinction. But as a name for one single opinion, not a set of opinions—to denote the recognition of utility as a standard, not any particular way of applying it—the term supplies a want in the language, and offers, in many cases, a convenient mode of avoiding tiresome circumlocution.

satisfy a human being's conceptions of happiness. Human beings have faculties more elevated than the animal appetites, and when once made conscious of them, do not regard anything as happiness which does not include their gratification. I do not, indeed, consider the Epicureans to have been by any means faultless in drawing out their scheme of consequences from the utilitarian principle. To do this in any sufficient manner, many Stoic, as well as Christian elements require to be included. But there is no known Epicurean theory of life which does not assign to the pleasures of the intellect, of the feelings and imagination, and of the moral sentiments, a much higher value as pleasures than to those of mere sensation. It must be admitted, however, that utilitarian writers in general have placed the superiority of mental over bodily pleasures chiefly in the greater permanency, safety, uncostliness, &c., of the former—that is, in their circumstantial advantages rather than in their intrinsic nature. And on all these points utilitarians have fully proved their case; but they might have taken the other, and, as it may be called, higher ground, with entire consistency. It is quite compatible with the principle of utility to recognize the fact, that some *kinds* of pleasure are more desirable and more valuable than others. It would be absurd that while, in estimating all other things, quality is considered as well as quantity, the estimation of pleasures should be supposed to depend on quantity alone.

If I am asked, what I mean by difference of quality in pleasures, or what makes one pleasure more valuable than another, merely as a pleasure, except its being greater in amount, there is but one possible answer. Of two pleasures, if there be one to which all or almost all who have experience of both give a decided preference, irrespective of any feeling of moral obligation to prefer it, that is the more desirable pleasure. If one of the two is, by those who are competently acquainted with both, placed so far above the other that they prefer it, even though knowing it to be attended with a greater amount of discontent, and would not resign it for any quantity of the pleasure which their nature is capable of, we are justified in ascribing to the preferred enjoyment a superiority in quality, so far outweighing quantity as to render it, in comparison, of small account.

Now it is an unquestionable fact that those who are equally acquainted with, and equally capable of appreciating and enjoying, both, do give a most marked preference to the manner of existence which employs their higher faculties. Few human creatures would consent to be changed into any of the lower animals, for a promise of the fullest allowance of a beast's pleasures; no intelligent human being would consent to be a fool, no instructed person would be an ignoramus, no person of feeling and conscience would be selfish and base, even though they should be persuaded that the fool, the dunce, or the rascal is better satisfied with his lot than they are with theirs. They would not resign what they possess more than he, for the most complete satisfaction of all the desires which they have in common with him. If they ever fancy they would, it is only in cases of unhappiness so extreme, that to escape from it they would exchange their lot for almost any other, however undesirable in their own eyes. A being of higher faculties requires more to make him happy, is capable probably of more acute suffering, and is certainly accessible to it at more points, than one of an inferior type; but in spite of these liabilities, he can never really wish to sink into what he feels to be a lower grade of existence. We may give what explanation we please of this unwillingness; we may attribute it to pride, a name which is given indiscriminately to some of the most and to some of the least estimable feelings of which mankind are capable; we may refer it to the love of liberty and personal independence, an appeal to which was with the Stoics one of the most effective means for the inculcation of it; to the love of power, or to the love of excitement, both of which do really enter into and contribute to it: but its most appropriate appellation is a sense of dignity, which all human beings possess in one form or another, and in some, though by no means in exact, proportion to their higher faculties, and which is so essential a part of the happiness of those in whom it is strong, that nothing which conflicts with it could be, otherwise than momentarily, an object of desire to them. Whoever supposes that this preference takes place at a sacrifice of happiness—that the superior being, in anything like equal circumstances, is not happier than the inferior—confounds the two very different ideas, of happiness, and content. It is indisputable that the being whose capacities of enjoyment are low, has the greatest chance of having them fully satisfied; and a highly-endowed being will always feel that any happiness which he can look for, as the world is constituted, is imperfect. But he can learn to bear its imperfections, if they are at all bearable; and they will not make him envy the being who is indeed unconscious of the imperfections, but only because he feels not at all the good which those imperfections qualify. It is better to be a human being dissatisfied than a pig satisfied; better to be Socrates dissatisfied than a fool satisfied. And if the fool, or the pig, is of a different opinion, it is because they only know their own side of the question. The other party to the comparison knows both sides.

It may be objected, that many who are capable of the higher pleasures, occasionally, under the influence of temptation, postpone them to the lower. But this is quite compatible with a full appreciation of the intrinsic superiority of the higher. Men often, from infirmity of character, make their election for the nearer good, though they know it to be less valuable; and this no less when the choice is between two bodily pleasures, than when it is between bodily and mental. They pursue sensual indulgences to the injury of health, though perfectly aware that health is the greater good. It may be further objected, that many who begin with youthful enthusiasm for everything noble, as they advance in years sink into indolence and selfishness. But I do not believe that those who undergo this very common change, voluntarily choose the lower description of pleasures in preference to the higher. I believe that before they devote themselves exclusively to the one, they have already become incapable of the other. Capacity for the nobler feelings is in most natures a very tender plant, easily killed, not only by hostile influences, but by mere want of sustenance; and in the majority of young persons it speedily dies away if the occupations to which their position in life has devoted them, and the society into which it has thrown them, are not favourable to keeping that higher capacity in exercise. Men lose their high aspirations as they lose their intellectual tastes, because they have not time or opportunity for indulging them; and they addict themselves to inferior pleasures, not because they deliberately prefer them, but because they are either the only ones to which they have access, or the only ones which they are any longer capable of enjoying. It may be questioned whether any one who has remained equally susceptible to both classes of pleasures, ever knowingly and calmly preferred the lower; though many, in all ages, have broken down in an ineffectual attempt to combine both.

From this verdict of the only competent judges, I apprehend there can be no appeal. On a question which is the best worth having of two pleasures, or which of two modes of existence is the most grateful to the feelings, apart from its moral attributes and from its consequences, the judgment of those who are qualified by knowledge of both, or, if they differ, that of the majority among them, must be admitted as final. And there needs be the less hesitation to accept this judgment respecting the quality of pleasures, since there is no other tribunal to be referred to even on the question of quantity. What means are there of determining which is the acutest of two pains, or the intensest of two pleasurable sensations, except the general suffrage of those who are familiar with both? Neither pains nor pleasures are homogeneous, and pain is always heterogeneous with pleasure. What is there to decide whether a particular pleasure is worth purchasing at the cost of a particular pain, except the feelings and judgment of the experienced? When, therefore, those feelings and judgment declare the pleasures derived from the higher faculties to be preferable *in kind*, apart from the question of intensity, to those of which the animal nature, disjoined from the higher faculties, is susceptible, they are entitled on this subject to the same regard.

I have dwelt on this point, as being a necessary part of a perfectly just conception of Utility or Happiness, considered as the directive rule of human conduct. But it is by no means an indispensable condition to the acceptance of the utilitarian standard; for that standard is not the agent's own greatest happiness, but the greatest amount of happiness altogether; and if it may possibly be doubted whether a noble character is always the happier for its nobleness, there can be no doubt that it makes other people happier, and that the world in general is immensely a gainer by it. Utilitarianism, therefore, could only attain its end by the general cultivation of nobleness of character, even if each individual were only benefited by the nobleness of others, and his own, so far as happiness is concerned, were a sheer deduction from the benefit. But the bare enunciation of such an absurdity as this last, renders refutation superfluous.

According to the Greatest Happiness Principle, as above explained, the ultimate end, with reference to and for the sake of which all other things are desirable (whether we are considering our own good or that of other people), is an existence exempt as far as possible from pain, and as rich as possible in enjoyments, both in point of quantity and quality; the test of quality, and the rule for measuring it against quantity, being the preference felt by those who, in their opportunities of experience, to which must be added their habits of self-consciousness and self-observation, are best furnished with the means of comparison. This, being, according to the utilitarian opinion, the end of human action, is necessarily also the standard of morality; which may accordingly be defined, the rules and precepts for human conduct, by the observance of which an existence such as has been described might be, to the greatest extent possible, secured to all mankind; and not to them only, but, so far as the nature of things admits, to the whole sentient creation. . . .

I must again repeat, what the assailants of utilitarianism seldom have the justice to acknowledge, that the happiness which forms the utilitarian standard of what is right in conduct, is not the agent's own happiness, but that of all concerned. As between his own happiness and that of others, utilitarianism requires him to be as strictly impartial as a disinterested and benevolent spectator. In the golden rule of Jesus of Nazareth, we read the complete spirit of the ethics of utility. To do as one would be done by, and to love one's neighbour as oneself constitute the ideal perfection of utilitarian morality. As the means of making the nearest approach to this ideal, utility would enjoin, first, that laws and social arrangements should place the happiness, or (as speaking practically it may be called) the interest, of every individual, as nearly as possible in harmony with the interest of the whole; and secondly, that education and opinion, which have so vast a power over human character, should so use that power as to establish in the mind of every individual an indissoluble association between his own happiness and the good of the whole; especially between his own happiness and the practice of such modes of conduct, negative and positive, as regard for the universal happiness prescribes: so that not only he may be unable to conceive the possibility of happiness to himself, consistently with conduct opposed to the general good, but also that a direct impulse to promote the general good may be in every individual one of the habitual motives of action, and the sentiments connected therewith may fill a large and prominent place in every human being's sentient existence. If the impugners of the utilitarian morality represented it to their own minds in this its true character, I know not what recommendation possessed by any other morality they could possibly affirm to be wanting to it: what more beautiful or more exalted developments of human nature any other ethical system can be supposed to foster, or what springs of action, not accessible to the utilitarian, such systems rely on for giving effect to their mandates.

The objectors to utilitarianism cannot always be charged with representing it in a discreditable light. On the contrary, those among them who entertain anything like a just idea of its disinterested character, sometimes find fault with its standard as being too high for humanity. They say it is exacting too much to require that people shall always act from the inducement of promoting the general interests of society. But this is to mistake the very meaning of a standard of morals, and to confound the rule of action with the motive of it. It is the business of ethics to tell us what are our duties, or by what test we may know them; but no system of ethics requires that the sole motive of all we do shall be a feeling of duty; on the contrary, ninety-nine hundredths of all our actions are done from other motives, and rightly so done, if the rule of duty does not condemn them. It is the more unjust to utilitarianism that this particular misapprehension should be made a ground of objection to it, inasmuch as utilitarian moralists have gone beyond almost all others in affirming that the motive has nothing to do with the morality of the action, though much with the worth of the agent. He who saves a fellow creature from drowning does what is morally right, whether his motive be duty, or the hope of being paid for his trouble: he who betrays the friend that trusts him, is guilty of a crime, even if his object be to serve another friend to whom he is under greater obligations. But to speak only of actions done from the motive of duty, and in direct obedience to principle: it is a misapprehension of the utilitarian mode of thought, to conceive it as implying that people should fix their minds upon so wide a generality as the world, or society at large. The great majority of good actions are intended, not for the benefit of the world, but for that of individuals, of which the good of the world is made up; and the thoughts of the most virtuous man need not on these occasions travel beyond the particular persons concerned, except so far as is necessary to assure himself that in benefiting them he is not violating the rights—that is, the legitimate and authorized expectations—of any one else. The multiplication of happiness is, according to the utilitarian ethics, the object of virtue: the occasions on which any person (except one in a thousand) has it in his power to do this on an extended scale, in other words, to be a public benefactor, are but exceptional; and on these occasions alone is he called on to consider public utility; in every other case, private utility, the interest or happiness of some few persons, is all he has to attend to. Those alone the influence of whose actions extends to society in general, need concern themselves habitually about so large an object. In the case of abstinences indeed—of things which people forbear to do, from moral considerations, though the consequences in the particular case might be beneficial—it would be unworthy of an intelligent agent not to be consciously aware that the action is of a class which, if practised generally, would be generally injurious, and that this is the ground of the obligation to abstain from it. The amount of regard for the public interest implied in this recognition, is no greater than is demanded by every system of morals; for they all enjoin to abstain from whatever is manifestly pernicious to society. . . .

Again, defenders of utility often find themselves called upon to reply to such objections as this—that there is not time, previous to action, for calculating and weighing the effects of any line of conduct on the general happiness. This is exactly as if any one were to say that it is impossible to guide our conduct by Christianity, because there is not time, on every occasion on which anything has to be done, to read through the Old and New Testaments. The answer to the objection is, that there has been ample time, namely, the whole past duration of the human species. During all that time mankind have been learning by experience the tendencies of actions; on which experience all the prudence, as well as all the morality of life, is dependent. People talk as if the commencement of this course of experience had hitherto been put off, and as if, at the moment when some man feels tempted to meddle with the property or life of another, he had to begin considering for the first time whether murder and theft are injurious to human happiness. Even then I do not think that he would find the question very puzzling; but, at all events, the matter is now done to his hand. It is truly a whimsical supposition, that if mankind were agreed in considering utility to be the test of morality, they would remain without any agreement as to what *is* useful, and would take no measures for having their notions on the subject taught to the young, and enforced by law and opinion. There is no difficulty in proving any ethical standard whatever to work ill, if we suppose universal idiocy to be conjoined with it, but on any hypothesis short of that, mankind must by this time have acquired positive beliefs as to the effects of some actions on their happiness; and the beliefs which have thus come down are the rules of morality for the multitude, and for the philosopher until he has succeeded in finding better. That philosophers might easily do this, even now, on many subjects; that the received code of ethics is by no means of divine right; and that mankind have still much to learn as to the effects of actions on the general happiness, I admit, or rather, earnestly maintain. The corollaries from the principle of utility, like the precepts of every practical art, admit of indefinite improvement, and, in a progressive state of the human mind, their improvement is perpetually going on. But to consider the rules of morality as improvable, is one thing; to pass over the intermediate generalisations entirely, and endeavour to test each individual action directly by the first principle, is another. It is a strange notion that the acknowledgment of a first principle is inconsistent with the admission of secondary ones. To inform a traveller respecting the place of his ultimate destination, is not to forbid the use of landmarks and direction-posts on the way. The proposition that happiness is the end and aim of morality, does not mean that no road ought to be laid down to that goal, or that persons going thither should not be advised to take one direction rather than another. Men really ought to leave off talking a kind of nonsense on this subject, which they would neither talk nor listen to on other matters of practical concernment. Nobody argues that the art of navigation is not founded on astronomy, because sailors cannot wait to calculate the Nautical Almanack. Being rational creatures, they go to sea with it ready calculated; and all rational creatures go out upon the sea of life with their minds made up on the common questions of right and wrong, as well as on many of the far more difficult questions of wise and foolish. And this, as long as foresight is a human quality, it is to be presumed they will continue to do. Whatever we adopt as the fundamental principle of morality, we require subordinate principles to apply it by: the impossibility of doing without them, being common to all systems, can afford no argument against any one in particular: but gravely to argue as if no such secondary principles could be had, and as if mankind had remained till now, and always must remain, without drawing any general conclusions from the experience of human life, is as high a pitch, I think, as absurdity has ever reached in philosophical controversy. . . .

Chapter IV

Of What Sort of Proof the Principle of Utility Is Susceptible

It has already been remarked, that questions of ultimate ends do not admit of proof, in the ordinary acceptation of the term. To be incapable of proof by reasoning is common to all first principles; to the first premises of our knowledge, as well as to those of our conduct. But the former, being matters of fact, may be the subject of a direct appeal to the faculties which judge of fact—namely, our senses, and our internal consciousness. Can an appeal be made to the same faculties on questions of practical ends? Or by what other faculty is cognizance taken of them?

Questions about ends are, in other words, questions what things are desirable. The utilitarian doctrine is, that happiness is desirable, and the only thing desirable, as an end; all other things being only desirable as means to that end. What ought to be required of this doctrine—what conditions is it requisite that the doctrine should fulfill—to make good its claim to be believed?

The only proof capable of being given that an object is visible, is that people actually see it. The only proof that a sound is audible, is that people hear it; and so of the other sources of our experience. In like manner, I apprehend, the sole evidence it is possible to produce that anything is desirable, is that people do actually desire it. If the end which the utilitarian doctrine proposes to itself were not, in theory and in practice, acknowledged to be an end, nothing could ever convince any person that it was so. No reason can be given why the general happiness is desirable, except that each person, so far as he believes it to be attainable, desires his own happiness. This, however, being a fact, we have not only all the proof which the case admits of, but all which it is possible to require, that happiness is a good: that each person's happiness is a good to that person, and the general happiness, therefore, a good to the aggregate of all persons. Happiness has made out its title as *one* of the ends of conduct, and consequently one of the criteria of morality.

But it has not, by this alone, proved itself to be the sole criterion. To do that, it would seem, by the same rule, necessary to show, not only that people desire happiness, but that they never desire anything else. Now it is palpable that they do desire things which, in common language, are decidedly distinguished from happiness. They desire, for example, virtue, and the absence of vice, no less really than pleasure and the absence of pain. The desire of virtue, is not as universal, but it is as authentic a fact, as the desire of happiness. And hence the opponents of the utilitarian standard deem that they have a right to infer that there are other ends of human action besides happiness, and that happiness is not the standard of approbation and disapprobation.

But does the utilitarian doctrine deny that people desire virtue, or maintain that virtue is not a thing to be desired? The very reverse. It maintains not only that virtue is to be desired, but that it is to be desired disinterestedly, for itself. Whatever may be the opinion of utilitarian moralists as to the original conditions by which virtue is made virtue; however they may believe (as they do) that actions and dispositions are only virtuous because they promote another end than virtue; yet this being granted, and it having been decided, from considerations of this description, what *is* virtuous, they not only place virtue at the very head of the things which are good as means to the ultimate end, but they also recognise as a psychological fact the possibility of its being, to the individual, a good in itself, without looking to any end beyond it; and hold, that the mind is not in a right state, not in a state conformable to Utility, not in the state most conducive to the general happiness, unless it does love virtue in this manner— as a thing desirable in itself, even although, in the individual instance, it should not produce those other desirable consequences which it tends to produce, and on account of which it is held to be virtue. This opinion is not, in the smallest degree, a departure from the Happiness principle.

The ingredients of happiness are very various, and each of them is desirable in itself, and not merely when considered as swelling an aggregate. The principle of utility does not mean that any given pleasure, as music, for instance, or any given exemption from pain, as for example, health, is to be looked upon as means to a collective something termed happiness, and to be desired on that account. They are desired and desirable in and for themselves; besides being means, they are a part of the end. Virtue, according to the utilitarian doctrine, is not naturally and originally part of the end, but it is capable of becoming so; and in those who love it disinterestedly it has become so, and is desired and cherished not as a means to happiness, but as a part of their happiness.

To illustrate this further, we may remember that virtue is not the only thing, originally a means, and which if it were not a means to anything else, would be and remain indifferent, but which by association with what it is a means to comes to be desired for itself, and that too with the utmost intensity. What, for example, shall we say of the love of money? There is nothing originally more desirable about money than about any heap of glittering pebbles. Its worth is solely that of the things which it will buy; the desires for other things than itself, which it is a means of gratifying. Yet the love of money is not only one of the strongest moving forces of human life, but money is, in many cases, desired in and for itself; the desire to possess it is often stronger than the desire to use it, and goes on increasing when all the desires which point to ends beyond it, to be compassed by it, are falling off. It may then be said truly, that money is desired not for the sake of an end, but as part of the end. From being a means to happiness, it has come to be itself a principal ingredient of the individual's conception of happiness. The same may be said of the majority of the great objects of human life—power, for example, or fame; except that to each of these there is a certain amount of immediate pleasure annexed, which has at least the semblance of being naturally inherent in them; a thing which cannot be said of money. Still, however, the strongest natural attraction, both of power and of fame, is the immense aid they give to the attainment of our other wishes; and it is the strong association thus generated between them and all our objects of desire, which gives to the direct desire of them the intensity it often assumes, so as in some characters to surpass in strength all other desires. In these cases the means have become a part of the end, and a more important part of it than any of the things which they are means to. What was once desired as an instrument for the attainment of happiness, has come to be desired for its own sake. In being desired for its own sake it is, however, desired as *part* of happiness. The person is made, or thinks he would be made, happy by its mere possession; and is made unhappy by failure to obtain it. The desire of it is not a different thing from the desire of happiness, any more than the love of music, or the desire of health. They are included in happiness. They are some of the elements of which the desire of happiness is made up. Happiness is not an abstract idea, but a concrete whole; and these are some of its parts. And the utilitarian standard sanctions and approves their being so. Life would be a poor thing, very ill provided with sources of happiness, if there were not this provision of nature, by which things originally indifferent, but conducive to, or otherwise associated with, the satisfaction of our primitive desires, become in themselves sources of pleasure more valuable than the primitive pleasures, both in permanency, in the space of human existence that they are capable of covering, and even in intensity.

Virtue, according to the utilitarian conception, is a good of this description. There was no original desire of it, or motive to it, save its conduciveness to pleasure, and especially to protection from pain. But through the association thus formed, it may be felt a good in itself, and desired as such with as great intensity as any other good; and with this difference between it and the love of money, of power, or of fame, that all of these may, and often do, render the individual noxious to the other members of the society to which he belongs, whereas there is nothing which makes him so much a blessing to them as the cultivation of the disinterested love of virtue. And consequently, the utilitarian standard, while it tolerates and approves those other acquired desires, up to the point beyond which they would be more injurious to the general happiness than promotive of it, enjoins and requires the cultivation of the love of virtue up to the greatest strength possible, as being above all things important to the general happiness.

It results from the preceding considerations, that there is in reality nothing desired except happiness. Whatever is desired otherwise than as a means to some end beyond itself, and ultimately to happiness, is desired as itself a part of happiness, and is not desired for itself until it has become so. Those who desire virtue for its own sake, desire it either because the consciousness of it is a pleasure, or because the consciousness of being without it is a pain, or for both reasons united; as in truth the pleasure and pain seldom exist separately, but almost always together, the same person feeling pleasure in the degree of virtue attained, and pain in not having attained more. If one of these gave him no pleasure, and the other no pain, he would not love or desire virtue, or would desire it only for the other benefits which it might produce to himself or to persons whom he cared for.

We have now, then, an answer to the question, of what sort of proof the principle of utility is susceptible. If the opinion which I have now stated is psychologically true—if human nature is so constituted as to desire nothing which is not either a part of happiness or a means of happiness, we can have no other proof, and we require no other, that these are the only things desirable. If so, happiness is the sole end of human action, and the promotion of it the test by which to judge of all human conduct; from whence it necessarily follows that it must be the criterion of morality, since a part is included in the whole.

Groundwork of the Metaphysic of Morals

Immanuel Kant

Chapter I

Passage from Ordinary Rational Knowledge of Morality to Philosophical

IT is impossible to conceive anything at all in the world, or even out of it, which can be taken as good without qualification, except a *good will*. Intelligence, wit, judgement, and any other *talents* of the mind we may care to name, or courage, resolution, and constancy of purpose, as qualities of *temperament*, are without doubt good and desirable in many respects; but they can also be extremely bad and hurtful when the will is not good which has to make use of these gifts of nature, and which for this reason has the term *'character'* applied to its peculiar quality. It is exactly the same with *gifts of fortune*. Power, wealth, honour, even health and that complete well-being and contentment with one's state which goes by the name of *'happiness'*, produce boldness, and as a consequence often over-boldness as well, unless a good will is present by which their influence on the mind—and so too the whole principle of action—may be corrected and adjusted to universal ends; not to mention that a rational and impartial spectator can never feel approval in contemplating the uninterrupted prosperity of a being graced by no touch of a pure and good will, and that consequently a good will seems to constitute the indispensable condition of our very worthiness to be happy.[1]

Some qualities are even helpful to this good will itself and can make its task very much easier. They have none the less no inner unconditioned worth, but rather presuppose a good will which sets a limit to the esteem in which they are rightly held and does not permit us to regard them as absolutely good. Moderation in affections and passions, self-control, and sober reflexion are not only good in many respects: they may even seem to constitute part of the *inner* worth of a person. Yet they are far from being properly described as good without qualification (however unconditionally they have been commended by the ancients).

---

[1] Translator's references have been omitted—Eds.

For without the principles of a good will they may become exceedingly bad; and the very coolness of a scoundrel makes him, not merely more dangerous, but also immediately more abominable in our eyes than we should have taken him to be without it.

A good will is not good because of what it effects or accomplishes—because of its fitness for attaining some proposed end: it is good through its willing alone—that is, good in itself. Considered in itself it is to be esteemed beyond comparison as far higher than anything it could ever bring about merely in order to favour some inclination or, if you like, the sum total of inclinations. Even if, by some special disfavour of destiny or by the niggardly endowment of step-motherly nature, this will is entirely lacking in power to carry out its intentions; if by its utmost effort it still accomplishes nothing, and only good will is left (not, admittedly, as a mere wish, but as the straining of every means so far as they are in our control); even then it would still shine like a jewel for its own sake as something which has its full value in itself. Its usefulness or fruitlessness can neither add to, nor subtract from, this value. Its usefulness would be merely, as it were, the setting which enables us to handle it better in our ordinary dealings or to attract the attention of those not yet sufficiently expert, but not to commend it to experts or to determine its value.

Yet in this Idea of the absolute value of a mere will, all useful results being left out of account in its assessment, there is something so strange that, in spite of all the agreement it receives even from ordinary reason, there must arise the suspicion that perhaps its secret basis is merely some high-flown fantasticality, and that we may have misunderstood the purpose of nature in attaching reason to our will as its governor. We will therefore submit our Idea to an examination from this point of view.

In the natural constitution of an organic being—that is, of one contrived for the purpose of life—let us take it as a principle that in it no organ is to be found for any end unless it is also the most appropriate to that end and the best fitted for it. Suppose now that for a being possessed of reason and a will the real purpose of nature were his *preservation*, his *welfare*, or in a word his *happiness*. In that case nature would have hit on a very bad arrangement by choosing reason in the creature to carry out this purpose. For all the actions he has to perform with this end in view, and the whole rule of his behaviour, would have been mapped out for him far more accurately by instinct; and the end in question could have been maintained far more surely by instinct than it ever can be by reason. . . .

Since reason is not sufficiently serviceable for guiding the will safely as regards its objects and the satisfaction of all our needs (which it in part even multiplies)—a purpose for which an implanted natural instinct would have led us much more surely; and since none the less reason has been imparted to us as a practical power—that is, as one which is to have influence on the *will*; its true function must be to produce a *will* which is *good*, not as a *means* to some further end, but *in itself*; and for this function reason was absolutely necessary in a world where nature, in distributing her aptitudes, has everywhere else gone to work in a purposive manner. Such a will need not on this account be the sole and complete good, but it must be the highest good and the condition of all the rest, even of all our demands for happiness. In that case we can easily reconcile with the wisdom of nature our observation that the cultivation of reason which is required for the first and unconditioned purpose may in many ways, at least in this life, restrict the attainment of the second purpose—namely, happiness—which is always conditioned; and indeed that it can even reduce happiness to less than zero without nature proceeding contrary to its purpose; for reason, which recognizes as its highest practical function the establishment of a good will, in attaining this end is capable only of its own peculiar kind of contentment—contentment in fulfilling a purpose which in turn is determined by reason alone, even if this fulfilment should often involve interference with the purposes of inclination.

We have now to elucidate the concept of a will estimable in itself and good apart from any further end. This concept, which is already present in a sound natural understanding and requires not so much to be taught as merely to be clarified, always holds the highest place in estimating the total worth of our actions and constitutes the condition of all the rest. We will therefore take up the concept of *duty*, which includes that of a good will, exposed, however, to certain subjective limitations and obstacles. These, so far from hiding a good will or disguising it, rather bring it out by contrast and make it shine forth more brightly.

I will here pass over all actions already recognized as contrary to duty, however useful they may be with a view to this or that end; for about these the question does not even arise whether they could have been done *for the sake of duty* inasmuch as they are directly opposed to it. I will also set aside actions which in fact accord with duty, yet for which men have *no immediate inclination*, but perform them because impelled to do so by some other inclination. For there it is easy to decide whether the action which accords with duty has been done *from duty* or from some purpose of self-interest. This distinction is far more difficult to perceive when the action accords with duty and the subject has in addition an *immediate* inclination to the action. For example, it certainly accords with duty that a grocer should not overcharge his inexperienced customer; and where there is much competition a sensible shopkeeper refrains from so doing and keeps to a fixed and general price for everybody so that a child can buy from him just as well as anyone else. Thus people are served *honestly*; but this is not nearly enough to justify us in believing that the shopkeeper has acted in this way from duty or from principles of fair dealing; his interests required him to do so. We cannot assume him to have in addition an immediate inclination towards his customers, leading him, as it were out of love, to give no man preference over another in the matter of price. Thus the action was done neither from duty nor from immediate inclination, but solely from purposes of self-interest.

On the other hand, to preserve one's life is a duty, and besides this every one has also an immediate inclination to do so. But on account of this the often anxious precautions taken by the greater part of mankind for this purpose have no inner worth, and the maxim of their action is without moral content. They do protect their lives *in conformity with duty*, but not *from the motive of duty*. When on the contrary, disappointments and hopeless misery have quite taken away the taste for life; when a wretched man, strong in soul and more angered at his fate than faint-hearted or cast down, longs for death and still preserves his life without loving it—not from inclination or fear but from duty; then indeed his maxim has a moral content.

To help others where one can is a duty, and besides this there are many spirits of so sympathetic a temper that, without any further motive of vanity or self-interest, they find an inner pleasure in spreading happiness around them and can take delight in the contentment of others as their own work. Yet I maintain that in such a case an action of this kind, however right and however amiable it may be, has still no genuinely moral worth. . . .

Our second proposition is this: An action done from duty has its moral worth, *not in the purpose* to be attained by it, but in the maxim in accordance with which it is decided upon; it depends therefore, not on the realization of the object of the action, but solely on the *principle of volition* in accordance with which, irrespective of all objects of the faculty of desire, the action has been performed. That the purposes we may have in our actions, and also their effects considered as ends and motives of the will, can give to actions no unconditioned and moral worth is clear from what has gone before. Where then can this worth be found if we are not to find it in the will's relation to the effect hoped for from the action? It can be found nowhere but *in the principle of the will*, irrespective of the ends which can be brought about by such an action; for between its *a priori* principle, which is formal, and its *a posteriori* motive, which is material, the will stands, so to speak, at a parting of the ways; and since it must be determined by some principle, it will have to be determined by the formal principle of volition when an action is done from duty, where, as we have seen, every material principle is taken away from it.

Our third proposition, as an inference from the two preceding, I would express thus: *Duty is the necessity to act out of reverence for the law.* For an object as the effect of my proposed action I can have an *inclination*, but *never reverence*, precisely because it is merely the effect, and not the activity, of a will. Similarly for inclination as such, whether my own or that of another, I cannot have reverence: I can at most in the first case approve, and in the second case sometimes even love—that is, regard it as favourable to my own advantage. Only something which is conjoined with my will solely as a ground and never as an effect—something which does not serve my inclination, but outweighs it or at least leaves it entirely out of account in my choice—and therefore only bare law for its own sake, can be an object of reverence and therewith a command. Now an action done from duty has to set aside altogether the influence of inclination, and along with inclination every object of the will; so there is nothing left able to determine the will except objectively the *law* and subjectively *pure reverence* for this practical law, and therefore the maxim* of obeying this law even to the detriment of all my inclinations.

Thus the moral worth of an action does not depend on the result expected from it, and so too does not depend on any principle of action that needs to borrow its motive from this expected result. For all these results (agreeable states and even the promotion of happiness in others) could have been brought about by other causes as well, and consequently their production did not require the will of a rational being, in which, however, the highest and unconditioned good can alone be found. Therefore nothing but the *idea of the law* in itself, *which admittedly is present only in a rational being*—so far as it, and not an expected result, is the ground determining the will—can constitute that pre-eminent good which

---

*A *maxim* is the subjective principle of a volition: an objective principle (that is, one which would also serve subjectively as a practical principle for all rational beings if reason had full control over the faculty of desire) is a practical *law*.

we call moral, a good which is already present in the person acting on this idea and has not to be awaited merely from the result.*

But what kind of law can this be the thought of which, even without regard to the results expected from it, has to determine the will if this is to be called good absolutely and without qualification? Since I have robbed the will of every inducement that might arise for it as a consequence of obeying any particular law, nothing is left but the conformity of actions to universal law as such, and this alone must serve the will as its principle. That is to say, I ought never to act except in such a way *that I can also will that my maxim should become a universal law*. Here bare conformity to universal law as such (without having as its base any law prescribing particular actions) is what serves the will as its principle, and must so serve it if duty is not to be everywhere an empty delusion and a chimerical concept. The ordinary reason of mankind also agrees with this completely in its practical judgements and always has the aforesaid principle before its eyes.

Take this question, for example. May I not, when I am hard pressed, make a promise with the intention of not keeping it? Here I readily distinguish the two senses which the question can have—Is it prudent, or is it right, to make a false promise? The first no doubt can often be the case. I do indeed see that it is not enough for me to extricate myself from present embarrassment by this subterfuge: I have to consider whether from this lie there may not subsequently accrue to me much greater inconvenience than that from which I now escape, and also—since, with all my supposed *astuteness*, to foresee the consequences is not so easy that I can be sure there is no chance, once confidence in me is lost, of this proving far more disadvantageous than all the ills I now think to avoid—whether it may not be a *more prudent* action to proceed here on a general maxim and make it my habit not to give a promise except with the intention of keeping it. Yet it becomes clear to me at once that such a maxim is always founded solely on fear of consequences. To tell the truth for the sake of duty is something entirely different from doing so out of concern for inconvenient results; for in the first case the concept of the action already contains in itself a law for me, while in the second

---

*It might be urged against me that I have merely tried, under cover of the word *"reverence"*, to take refuge in an obscure feeling instead of giving a clearly articulated answer to the question by means of a concept of reason. Yet although reverence is a feeling, it is not a feeling *received* through outside influence, but one *self-produced* by a rational concept, and therefore specifically distinct from feelings of the first kind, all of which can be reduced to inclination or fear. What I recognize immediately as law for me, I recognize with reverence, which means merely consciousness of the *subordination* of my will to a law without the mediation of external influences on my senses. Immediate determination of the will by the law and consciousness of this determination is called *"reverence"*, so that reverence is regarded as the *effect* of the law on the subject and not as the *cause* of the law. Reverence is properly awareness of a value which demolishes my self-love. Hence there is something which is regarded neither as an object of inclination nor as an object of fear, though it has at the same time some analogy with both. The *object* of reverence is the *law* alone—that law which we impose *on ourselves* but yet as necessary in itself. Considered as a law, we are subject to it without any consultation of self-love; considered as self-imposed it is a consequence of our will. In the first respect it is analogous to fear, in the second to inclination. All reverence for a person is properly only reverence for the law (of honesty and so on) of which that person gives us an example. Because we regard the development of our talents as a duty, we see too in a man of talent a sort of *example of the law* (the law of becoming like him by practice), and this is what constitutes our reverence for him. All moral *interest*, so-called, consists solely in *reverence* for the law.

case I have first of all to look around elsewhere in order to see what effects may be bound up with it for me. When I deviate from the principle of duty, this is quite certainly bad; but if I desert my prudential maxim, this can often be greatly to my advantage, though it is admittedly safer to stick to it. Suppose I seek, however, to learn in the quickest way and yet unerringly how to solve the problem "Does a lying promise accord with duty?" I have then to ask myself "Should I really be content that my maxim (the maxim of getting out of a difficulty by a false promise) should hold as a universal law (one valid both for myself and others)? And could I really say to myself that every one may make a false promise if he finds himself in a difficulty from which he can extricate himself in no other way?" I then become aware at once that I can indeed will to lie, but I can by no means will a universal law of lying; for by such a law there could properly be no promises at all, since it would be futile to profess a will for future action to others who would not believe my profession or who, if they did so over-hastily, would pay me back in like coin; and consequently my maxim, as soon as it was made a universal law, would be bound to annul itself.

Thus I need no far-reaching ingenuity to find out what I have to do in order to possess a good will. Inexperienced in the course of world affairs and incapable of being prepared for all the chances that happen in it, I ask myself only "Can you also will that your maxim should become a universal law?" Where you cannot, it is to be rejected, and that not because of a prospective loss to you or even to others, but because it cannot fit as a principle into a possible enactment of universal law. For such an enactment reason compels my immediate reverence, into whose grounds (which the philosopher may investigate) I have as yet no *insight*, although I do at least understand this much: reverence is the assessment of a worth which far outweighs all the worth of what is commended by inclination, and the necessity for me to act out of *pure* reverence for the practical law is what constitutes duty, to which every other motive must give way because it is the condition of a will good *in itself*, whose value is above all else. . . .

Chapter II

Passage from Popular Moral Philosophy to a Metaphysic of Morals

If so far we have drawn our concept of duty from the ordinary use of our practical reason, it must by no means be inferred that we have treated it as a concept of experience. On the contrary, when we pay attention to our experience of human conduct, we meet frequent and—as we ourselves admit—justified complaints that we can adduce no certain examples of the spirit which acts out of pure duty, and that, although much may be done *in accordance with* the commands of *duty*, it remains doubtful whether it really is done *for the sake of duty* and so has a moral value. . . .

In actual fact it is absolutely impossible for experience to establish with complete certainty a single case in which the maxim of an action in other respects right has rested solely on moral grounds and on the thought of one's duty. It is indeed at times the case that after the keenest self-examination we find nothing that without the moral motive of duty could have been strong enough to move us to this or that good action and to so great a sacrifice; but we cannot infer from this with certainty that it is not some secret impulse of self-love which has actually, under the mere show of the Idea of duty, been the cause genuinely determining our will. We are pleased to flatter ourselves with the false claim to a nobler motive, but in fact we can never, even by the most strenuous self-examination, get to the bottom of our secret impulses; for when moral value is in question, we are concerned, not with the actions which we see, but with their inner principles, which we cannot see. . . .

It may be added that unless we wish to deny to the concept of morality all truth and all relation to a possible object, we cannot dispute that its law is of such widespread significance as to hold, not merely for men, but for all *rational beings as such*—not merely subject to contingent conditions and exceptions, but *with absolute necessity*. It is therefore clear that no experience can give us occasion to infer even the possibility of such apodeictic laws. For by what right can we make what is perhaps valid only under the contingent conditions of humanity into an object of unlimited reverence as a universal precept for every rational nature? And how could laws for determining *our* will be taken as laws for determining the will of a rational being as such—and only because of this for determining ours—if these laws were merely empirical and did not have their source completely *a priori* in pure, but practical, reason? . . .

From these considerations the following conclusions emerge. All moral concepts have their seat and origin in reason completely *a priori*, and indeed in the most ordinary human reason just as much as in the most highly speculative: they cannot be abstracted from any empirical, and therefore merely contingent, knowledge. In this purity of their origin is to be found their very worthiness to serve as supreme practical principles, and everything empirical added to them is just so much taken away from their genuine influence and from the absolute value of the corresponding actions. It is not only a requirement of the utmost necessity in respect of theory, where our concern is solely with speculation, but is also of the utmost practical importance, to draw these concepts and laws from pure reason, to set them forth pure and unmixed, and indeed to determine the extent of this whole practical, but pure, rational knowledge—that is, to determine the whole power of pure practical reason. We ought never—as speculative philosophy does allow and even at times finds necessary—to make principles depend on the special nature of human reason. Since moral laws have to hold for every rational being as such, we ought rather to derive our principles from the general concept of a rational being as such, and on this basis to expound the whole of ethics—which requires anthropology for its *application* to man—at first independently as pure philosophy, that is, entirely as metaphysics (which we can very well do in this wholly abstract kind of knowledge). We know well that without possessing such a metaphysics it is a futile endeavour, I will not say to determine accurately for speculative judgement the moral element of duty in all that accords with duty—but that it is impossible, even in ordinary and practical usage, particularly in that of moral instruction, to base morals on their genuine principles and so to bring about pure moral dispositions and engraft them on men's minds for the highest good of the world.

In this task of ours we have to progress by natural stages, not merely from ordinary moral judgement (which is here worthy of great respect) to philosophical judgement, as we have already done, but from popular philosophy, which goes no further than it can get by fumbling about with the aid of examples, to metaphysics. (This no longer lets itself be held back by anything empirical, and indeed—since it must survey the complete totality of this kind of knowledge—goes right to Ideas, where examples themselves fail.) For this purpose we must follow—and must portray in detail—the power of practical reason from the general rules determining it right up to the point where there springs from it the concept of duty.

Everything in nature works in accordance with laws. Only a rational being has the power to act *in accordance with his idea* of laws—that is, in accordance with principles—and only so has he a *will*. Since *reason* is required in order to derive actions from laws, the will is nothing but practical reason. If reason infallibly determines the will, then in a being of this kind the actions which are recognized to be objectively necessary are also subjectively necessary—that is to say, the will is then a power to choose *only that* which reason independently of inclination recognizes to be practically necessary, that is, to be good. But if reason solely by itself is not sufficient to determine the will; if the will is exposed also to subjective conditions (certain impulsions) which do not always harmonize with the objective ones; if, in a word, the will is not *in itself* completely in accord with reason (as actually happens in the case of men); then actions which are recognized to be objectively necessary are subjectively contingent, and the determining of such a will in accordance with objective laws is *necessitation*. That is to say, the relation of objective laws to a will not good through and through is conceived as one in which the will of a rational being, although it is determined by principles of reason, does not necessarily follow these principles in virtue of its own nature.

The conception of an objective principle so far as this principle is necessitating for a will is called a command (of reason), and the formula of this command is called an *Imperative.*

All imperatives are expressed by an 'ought' (*Sollen*). By this they mark the relation of an objective law of reason to a will which is not necessarily determined by this law in virtue of its subjective constitution (the relation of necessitation). They say that something would be good to do or to leave undone; only they say it to a will which does not always do a thing because it has been informed that this is a good thing to do. The practically *good* is that which determines the will by concepts of reason, and therefore not by subjective causes, but objectively—that is, on grounds valid for every rational being as such. It is distinguished from the *pleasant* as that which influences the will, not as a principle of reason valid for every one, but solely through the medium of sensation by purely subjective causes valid only for the senses of this person or that.*

---

*The dependence of the power of appetition on sensations is called an inclination, and thus an inclination always indicates a *need*. The dependence of a contingently determinable will on principles of reason is called an *interest*. Hence an interest is found *only* where there is a dependent will which in itself is not always in accord with reason: to a divine will we cannot ascribe any interest. But even the human will can *take an interest in* something without therefore *acting from interest*. The first expression signifies *practical* interest in the action; the second *pathological* interest in the object of the action. The first indicates only dependence of the will on principles of reason by itself; the second its dependence on principles of reason at the service of inclination—that is to say, where reason merely supplies a practical rule for meeting the need of inclination. In the first case what interests me is the action; in the second case what interests me is the object of the action (so far as this object is pleasant to me). We have seen in Chapter 1 that in an action done for the sake of duty we must have regard, not to interest in the object, but to interest in the action itself and in its rational principle (namely, the law).

A perfectly good will would thus stand quite as much under objective laws (laws of the good), but it could not on this account be conceived as *necessitated* to act in conformity with law, since of itself, in accordance with its subjective constitution, it can be determined only by the concept of the good. Hence for the *divine* will, and in general for a *holy* will, there are no imperatives: '*I ought*' is here out of place, because '*I will*' is already of itself necessarily in harmony with the law. Imperatives are in consequence only formulae for expressing the relation of objective laws of willing to the subjective imperfection of the will of this or that rational being—for example, of the human will.

All *imperatives* command either *hypothetically* or *categorically*. Hypothetical imperatives declare a possible action to be practically necessary as a means to the attainment of something else that one wills (or that one may will). A categorical imperative would be one which represented an action as objectively necessary in itself apart from its relation to a further end.

Every practical law represents a possible action as good and therefore as necessary for a subject whose actions are determined by reason. Hence all imperatives are formulae for determining an action which is necessary in accordance with the principle of a will in some sense good. If the action would be good solely as a means *to something else*, the imperative is *hypothetical;* if the action is represented as good *in itself* and therefore as necessary, in virtue of its principle, for a will which of itself accords with reason, then the imperative is *categorical*.

An imperative therefore tells me which of my possible actions would be good; and it formulates a practical rule for a will that does not perform an action straight away because the action is good—whether because the subject does not always know that it is good or because, even if he did know this, he might still act on maxims contrary to the objective principles of practical reason.

A hypothetical imperative thus says only that an action is good for some purpose or other, either *possible* or *actual*. In the first case it is a *problematic* practical principle; in the second case an *assertoric* practical principle. A categorical imperative, which declares an action to be objectively necessary in itself without reference to some purpose—that is, even without any further end—ranks as an *apodeictic* practical principle.

Everything that is possible only through the efforts of some rational being can be conceived as a possible purpose of some will; and consequently there are in fact innumerable principles of action so far as action is thought necessary in order to achieve some possible purpose which can be effected by it. All sciences have a practical part consisting of problems which suppose that some end is possible for us and of imperatives which tell us how it is to be attained. Hence the latter can in general be called imperatives of *skill*. Here there is absolutely no question about the rationality or goodness of the end, but only about what must be done to attain it. . . .

There is, however, *one* end that can be presupposed as actual in all rational beings (so far as they are dependent beings to whom imperatives apply); and thus there is one purpose which they not only *can* have, but which we can assume with certainty that they all *do* have by a natural necessity—the purpose, namely, of *happiness*. A hypothetical imperative which affirms the practical necessity of an action as a means to the furtherance of happiness is *assertoric*. We may represent it, not simply as necessary to an uncertain, merely possible purpose, but as necessary to a purpose which we can presuppose *a priori* and with certainty to be present in every man because it belongs to his very being. Now skill in the choice of means to one's own greatest well-being can be called *prudence*[2] in the narrowest sense. Thus an imperative concerned with the choice of means to one's own happiness—that is, a precept of prudence—still remains *hypothetical*: an action is commanded, not absolutely, but only as a means to a further purpose.

Finally, there is an imperative which, without being based on, and conditioned by, any further purpose to be attained by a certain line of conduct, enjoins this conduct immediately. This imperative is *categorical*. It is concerned, not with the matter of the action and its presumed results, but with its form and with the principle from which it follows; and what is essentially good in the action consists in the mental disposition, let the consequences be what they may. This imperative may be called the imperative of *morality*. . . .

The question now arises 'How are all these imperatives possible?' This question does not ask how we can conceive the execution of an action commanded by the imperative, but merely how we can conceive the necessitation of the will expressed by the imperative in setting us a task. How an imperative of skill is possible requires no special discussion. Who wills the end, wills (so far as reason has decisive influence on his actions) also the means which are indispensably necessary and in his power. . . .

If it were only as easy to find a determinate concept of happiness, the imperatives of prudence would agree entirely with those of skill . . . . For here as there it could alike be said 'Who wills the end, wills also (necessarily, if he accords with reason) the sole means which are in his power'. Unfortunately, however, the concept of happiness is so indeterminate a concept that although every man wants to attain happiness, he can never say definitely and in unison with himself what it really is that he wants and wills. The reason for this is that all the elements which belong to the concept of happiness are without exception empirical—that is, they must be borrowed from experience; but that none the less there is required for the Idea of happiness an absolute whole, a maximum of well-being in my present, and in every future, state. . . . Thus we cannot act on determinate principles in order to be happy, but only on empirical counsels, for example, of diet, frugality, politeness, reserve, and so on—things which experience shows contribute most to well-being on the average. From this it follows that imperatives of prudence, speaking strictly, do not command at all—that is, cannot exhibit actions objectively as practically *necessary*. . . . Nevertheless, if we assume that the means to happiness could be discovered with certainty, this imperative of prudence would be an analytic practical proposition; for it differs from the imperative of skill only in this—that in the latter the end is merely possible, while in the former the end is given. In spite of this difference, since both command solely the means to something assumed to be willed as an end, the imperative which commands him who wills the end to will the means is in both cases analytic. Thus there is likewise no difficulty in regard to the possibility of an imperative of prudence.

Beyond all doubt, the question 'How is the imperative of *morality* possible?' is the only one in need of a solution; for it is in no way hypothetical, and consequently we cannot base the objective necessity which it affirms on any presupposition, as we can with hypothetical imperatives. . . .

We shall thus have to investigate the possibility of a *categorical* imperative entirely *a priori*, since here we do not enjoy

---

[2]Footnote omitted—Eds.

the advantage of having its reality given in experience and so of being obliged merely to explain, and not to establish, its possibility. . . .

In this task we wish first to enquire whether perhaps the mere concept of a categorical imperative may not also provide us with the formula containing the only proposition that can be a categorical imperative; for even when we know the purport of such an absolute command, the question of its possibility will still require a special and troublesome effort, which we postpone to the final chapter.

When I conceive a *hypothetical* imperative in general, I do not know beforehand what it will contain—until its condition is given. But if I conceive a *categorical* imperative, I know at once what it contains. For since besides the law this imperative contains only the necessity that our maxim* should conform to this law, while the law, as we have seen, contains no condition to limit it, there remains nothing over to which the maxim has to conform except the universality of a law as such; and it is this conformity alone that the imperative properly asserts to be necessary.

There is therefore only a single categorical imperative and it is this: '*Act only on that maxim through which you can at the same time will that it should become a universal law.*'

Now if all imperatives of duty can be derived from this one imperative as their principle, then even although we leave it unsettled whether what we call duty may not be an empty concept, we shall still be able to show at least what we understand by it and what the concept means.

Since the universality of the law governing the production of effects constitutes what is properly called *nature* in its most general sense (nature as regards its form)—that is, the existence of things so far as determined by universal laws—the universal imperative of duty may also run as follows: '*Act as if the maxim of your action were to become through your will a universal law of nature.*'

We will now enumerate a few duties, following their customary division into duties towards self and duties towards others and into perfect and imperfect duties.*

1. A man feels sick of life as the result of a series of misfortunes that has mounted to the point of despair, but he is still so far in possession of his reason as to ask himself whether taking his own life may not be contrary to his duty to himself. He now applies the test 'Can the maxim of my action really become a universal law of nature?' His maxim is 'From self-love I make it my principle to shorten my life if its continuance threatens more evil than it promises pleasure'. The only further question to ask is whether this principle of self-love can become a universal law of nature. It is then seen at once that a system of nature by whose law the very same feeling whose function (*Bestimmung*) is to stimulate the furtherance of life should actually destroy

---

*A *maxim* is a subjective principle of action and must be distinguished from an *objective principle*—namely, a practical law. The former contains a practical rule determined by reason in accordance with the conditions of the subject (often his ignorance or again his inclinations): it is thus a principle on which the subject *acts*. A law, on the other hand, is an objective principle valid for every rational being; and it is a principle on which he *ought to act*—that is, an imperative.

*It should be noted that I reserve my division of duties entirely for a future *Metaphysic of Morals* and that my present division is therefore put forward as arbitrary (merely for the purpose of arranging my examples). Further, I understand here by a perfect duty one which allows no exception in the interests of inclination, and so I recognize among *perfect duties*, not only outer ones, but also inner. This is contrary to the accepted usage of the schools, but I do not intend to justify it here, since for my purpose it is all one whether this point is conceded or not.

life would contradict itself and consequently could not subsist as a system of nature. Hence this maxim cannot possibly hold as a universal law of nature and is therefore entirely opposed to the supreme principle of all duty.

2. Another finds himself driven to borrowing money because of need. He well knows that he will not be able to pay it back; but he sees too that he will get no loan unless he gives a firm promise to pay it back within a fixed time. He is inclined to make such a promise; but he has still enough conscience to ask 'Is it not unlawful and contrary to duty to get out of difficulties in this way?' Supposing, however, he did resolve to do so, the maxim of his action would run thus: 'Whenever I believe myself short of money, I will borrow money and promise to pay it back, though I know that this will never be done'. Now this principle of self-love or personal advantage is perhaps quite compatible with my own entire future welfare; only there remains the question 'Is it right?' I therefore transform the demand of self-love into a universal law and frame my question thus: 'How would things stand if my maxim became a universal law. I then see straight away that this maxim can never rank as a universal law of nature and be self-consistent, but must necessarily contradict itself. For the universality of a law that every one believing himself to be in need can make any promise he pleases with the intention not to keep it would make promising, and the very purpose of promising, itself impossible, since no one would believe he was being promised anything, but would laugh at utterances of this kind as empty shams.

3. A third finds in himself a talent whose cultivation would make him a useful man for all sorts of purposes. But he sees himself in comfortable circumstances, and he prefers to give himself up to pleasure rather than to bother about increasing and improving his fortunate natural aptitudes. Yet he asks himself further 'Does my maxim of neglecting my natural gifts, besides agreeing in itself with my tendency to indulgence, agree also with what is called duty?' He then sees that a system of nature could indeed always subsist under such a universal law, although (like the South Sea Islanders) every man should let his talents rust and should be bent on devoting his life solely to idleness, indulgence, procreation, and, in a word, to enjoyment. Only he cannot possibly *will* that this should become a universal law of nature or should be implanted in us as such a law by a natural instinct. For as a rational being he necessarily wills that all his powers should be developed, since they serve him, and are given him, for all sorts of possible ends.

4. Yet a *fourth* is himself flourishing, but he sees others who have to struggle with great hardships (and whom he could easily help); and he thinks 'What does it matter to me? Let every one be as happy as Heaven wills or as he can make himself; I won't deprive him of anything; I won't even envy him; only I have no wish to contribute anything to his well-being or to his support in distress!' Now admittedly if such an attitude were a universal law of nature, mankind could get on perfectly well—better no doubt than if everybody prates about sympathy and goodwill, and even takes pains, on occasion, to practise them, but on the other hand cheats where he can, traffics in human rights, or violates them in other ways. But although it is possible that a universal law of nature could subsist in harmony with this maxim, yet it is impossible to *will* that such a principle should hold everywhere as a law of nature. For a will which decided in this way would be in conflict with itself, since many a situation might arise in which the man needed love and sympathy from others, and in which, by such a law of nature sprung from his own

will, he would rob himself of all hope of the help he wants for himself.

These are some of the many actual duties—or at least of what we take to be such—whose derivation from the single principle cited above leaps to the eye. We must *be able to will* that a maxim of our action should become a universal law—this is the general canon for all moral judgement of action. Some actions are so constituted that their maxim cannot even be *conceived* as a universal law of nature without contradiction, let alone be *willed* as what *ought* to become one. In the case of others we do not find this inner impossibility, but it is still impossible to *will* that their maxim should be raised to the universality of a law of nature, because such a will would contradict itself. It is easily seen that the first kind of action is opposed to strict or narrow (rigorous) duty, the second only to wider (meritorious) duty; and thus that by these examples all duties—so far as the type of obligation is concerned (not the object of dutiful action)—are fully set out in their dependence on our single principle.

If we now attend to ourselves whenever we transgress a duty, we find that we in fact do not will that our maxim should become a universal law—since this is impossible for us—but rather that its opposite should remain a law universally: we only take the liberty of making an *exception* to it for ourselves (or even just for this once) to the advantage of our inclination. Consequently if we weighed it all up from one and the same point of view—that of reason—we should find a contradiction in our own will, the contradiction that a certain principle should be objectively necessary as a universal law and yet subjectively should not hold universally but should admit of exceptions. Since, however, we first consider our action from the point of view of a will wholly in accord with reason, and then consider precisely the same action from the point of view of a will affected by inclination, there is here actually no contradiction, but rather an opposition of inclination to the precept of reason (*antagonismus*), whereby the universality of the principle (*universalitas*) is turned into a mere generality (*generalitas*) so that the practical principle of reason may meet our maxim half-way. This procedure, though in our own impartial judgement it cannot be justified, proves none the less that we in fact recognize the validity of the categorical imperative and (with all respect for it) merely permit ourselves a few exceptions which are, as we pretend, inconsiderable and apparently forced upon us.

We have thus at least shown this much—that if duty is a concept which is to have meaning and real legislative authority for our actions, this can be expressed only in categorical imperatives and by no means in hypothetical ones. At the same time—and this is already a great deal—we have set forth distinctly, and determinately for every type of application, the content of the categorical imperative, which must contain the principle of all duty (if there is to be such a thing at all). But we are still not so far advanced as to prove *a priori* that there actually is an imperative of this kind—that there is a practical law which by itself commands absolutely and without any further motives, and that the following of this law is duty.

For the purpose of achieving this proof it is of the utmost importance to take warning that we should not dream for a moment of trying to derive the reality of this principle from *the special characteristics of human nature*. For duty has to be a practical, unconditioned necessity of action; it must therefore hold for all rational beings (to whom alone an imperative can apply at all), and *only because of this* can it also be a law for all human wills. . . .

Our question therefore is this: 'Is it a necessary law *for all rational beings* always to judge their actions by reference to those maxims of which they can themselves will that they should serve as universal laws?' If there is such a law, it must already be connected (entirely *a priori*) with the concept of the will of a rational being as such.

The will is conceived as a power of determining oneself to action *in accordance with the idea of certain laws.* And such a power can be found only in rational beings. Now what serves the will as a subjective ground of its self-determination is an *end;* and this, if it is given by reason alone, must be equally valid for all rational beings. What, on the other hand, contains merely the ground of the possibility of an action whose effect is an end is called a *means.* The subjective ground of a desire is an *impulsion (Triebfeder)*; the objective ground of a volition is a *motive (Bewegungsgrund)*. Hence the difference between subjective ends, which are based on impulsions, and objective ends, which depend on motives valid for every rational being. Practical principles are *formal* if they abstract from all subjective ends; they are *material*, on the other hand, if they are based on such ends and consequently on certain impulsions. Ends that a rational being adopts arbitrarily as *effects* of his action (material ends) are in every case only relative; for it is solely their relation to special characteristics in the subject's power of appetition which gives them their value. Hence this value can provide no universal principles, no principles valid and necessary for all rational beings and also for every volition—that is, no practical laws. Consequently all these relative ends can be the ground only of hypothetical imperatives.

Suppose, however, there were something *whose existence* has *in itself* an absolute value, something which as *an end in itself* could be a ground of determinate laws; then in it, and in it alone, would there be the ground of a possible categorical imperative—that is, of a practical law.

Now I say that man, and in general every rational being, *exists* as an end in himself, *not merely as a means* for arbitrary use by this or that will: he must in all his actions, whether they are directed to himself or to other rational beings, always be viewed *at the same time as an end*. All the objects of inclination have only a conditioned value; for if there were not these inclinations and the needs grounded on them, their object would be valueless. Inclinations themselves, as sources of needs, are so far from having an absolute value to make them desirable for their own sake that it must rather be the universal wish of every rational being to be wholly free from them. Thus the value of all objects that can *be produced* by our action is always conditioned. Beings whose existence depends, not on our will, but on nature, have none the less, if they are non-rational beings, only a relative value as means and are consequently called *things*. Rational beings, on the other hand, are called *persons* because their nature already marks them out as ends in themselves—that is, as something which ought not to be used merely as a means—and consequently imposes to that extent a limit on all arbitrary treatment of them (and is an object of reverence). Persons, therefore, are not merely subjective ends whose existence as an object of our actions has a value *for us:* they are *objective ends*—that is, things whose existence is in itself an end, and indeed an end such that in its place we can put no other end to which they should serve *simply* as means; for unless this is so, nothing at all of *absolute* value would be found anywhere. But if all value were conditioned—that is, contingent—then no supreme principle could be found for reason at all.

If then there is to be a supreme practical principle and—so far as the human will is concerned—a categorical imperative, it must be such that from the idea of something which is necessarily an end for every one because it is an *end in itself* it forms an *objective* principle of the will and consequently can serve as a practical law. The ground of this principle is: *Rational nature exists as an end in itself.* This is the way in which a man necessarily conceives his own existence: it is therefore so far a *subjective* principle of human actions. But it is also the way in which every other rational being conceives his existence on the same rational ground which is valid also for me;³ hence it is at the same time an *objective* principle, from which, as a supreme practical ground, it must be possible to derive all laws for the will. The practical imperative will therefore be as follows: *Act in such a way that you always treat humanity, whether in your own person or in the person of any other, never simply as a means, but always at the same time as an end.* We will now consider whether this can be carried out in practice.

Let us keep to our previous examples.

First, as regards the concept of necessary duty to oneself, the man who contemplates suicide will ask 'Can my action be compatible with the Idea of humanity *as an end in itself?*' If he does away with himself in order to escape from a painful situation, he is making use of a person merely as *a means* to maintain a tolerable state of affairs till the end of his life. But man is not a thing—not something to be used *merely* as a means: he must always in all his actions be regarded as an end in himself. Hence I cannot dispose of man in my person by maiming, spoiling, or killing. (A more precise determination of this principle in order to avoid all misunderstanding—for example, about having limbs amputated to save myself or about exposing my life to danger in order to preserve it, and so on—I must here forego: this question belongs to morals proper.)

Secondly, so far as necessary or strict duty to others is concerned, the man who has a mind to make a false promise to others will see at once that he is intending to make use of another man *merely as a means* to an end he does not share. For the man whom I seek to use for my own purposes by such a promise cannot possibly agree with my way of behaving to him, and so cannot himself share the end of the action. This incompatibility with the principle of duty to others leaps to the eye more obviously when we bring in examples of attempts on the freedom and property of others. For then it is manifest that a violator of the rights of man intends to use the person of others merely as a means without taking into consideration that, as rational beings, they ought always at the same time to be rated as ends—that is, only as beings who must themselves be able to share in the end of the very same action.*

Thirdly, in regard to contingent (meritorious) duty to oneself, it is not enough that an action should refrain from conflicting with humanity in our own person as an end in itself: it must also *harmonize with this end.* Now there are in humanity capacities for greater perfection which form part of nature's purpose for humanity in our person. To neglect these can admittedly be

---

*Let no one think that here the trivial "*quod tibi non vis fieri, etc.*" can serve as a standard or principle. For it is merely derivative from our principle, although subject to various qualifications: it cannot be a universal law since it contains the ground neither of duties to oneself nor of duties of kindness to others (for many a man would readily agree that others should not help him if only he could be dispensed from affording help to them), nor finally of strict duties towards others; for on this basis the criminal would be able to dispute with the judges who punish him, and so on.

---

³Footnote omitted—Eds.

compatible with the *maintenance* of humanity as an end in itself, but not with the *promotion* of this end.

Fourthly, as regards meritorious duties to others, the natural end which all men seek is their own happiness. Now humanity could no doubt subsist if everybody contributed nothing to the happiness of others but at the same time refrained from deliberately impairing their happiness. This is, however, merely to agree negatively and not positively with *humanity as an end in itself* unless every one endeavours also, so far as in him lies, to further the ends of others. For the ends of a subject who is an end in himself must, if this conception is to have its *full* effect in me, be also, as far as possible, *my* ends.

This principle of humanity, and in general of every rational agent, *as an end in itself* (a principle which is the supreme limiting condition of every man's freedom of action) is not borrowed from experience; firstly, because it is universal, applying as it does to all rational beings as such, and no experience is adequate to determine universality; secondly, because in it humanity is conceived, not as an end of man (subjectively)—that is, as an object which, as a matter of fact, happens to be made an end—but as an objective end—one which, be our ends what they may, must, as a law, constitute the supreme limiting condition of all subjective ends and so must spring from pure reason. That is to say, the ground for every enactment of practical law lies *objectively in the rule* and in the form of universality which (according to our first principle) makes the rule capable of being a law (and indeed a law of nature); *subjectively*, however, it lies in the *end;* but (according to our second principle) the subject of all ends is to be found in every rational being as an end in himself. From this there now follows our third practical principle for the will—as the supreme condition of the will's conformity with universal practical reason—namely, the Idea *of the will of every rational being as a will which makes universal law.*

By this principle all maxims are repudiated which cannot accord with the will's own enactment of universal law. The will is therefore not merely subject to the law, but is so subject that it must be considered as also *making the law* for itself and precisely on this account as first of all subject to the law (of which it can regard itself as the author).

Imperatives as formulated above—namely, the imperative enjoining conformity of actions to universal law on the analogy of a *natural order* and that enjoining the universal *supremacy* of rational beings in themselves *as ends*—did, by the mere fact that they were represented as categorical, exclude from their sovereign authority every admixture of interest as a motive. They were, however, merely *assumed* to be categorical because we were bound to make this assumption if we wished to explain the concept of duty. That there were practical propositions which commanded categorically could not itself be proved, any more than it can be proved in this chapter generally; but one thing could have been done—namely, to show that in willing for the sake of duty renunciation of all interest, as the specific mark distinguishing a categorical from a hypothetical imperative, was expressed in the very imperative itself by means of some determination inherent in it. This is what is done in the present third formulation of the principle—namely, in the Idea of the will of every rational being as *a will which makes universal law.*

Once we conceive a will of this kind, it becomes clear that while a will *which is subject to law* may be bound to this law by some interest, nevertheless a will which is itself a supreme lawgiver cannot possibly as such depend on any interest; for a will which is dependent in this way would itself require yet a further law in order to restrict the interest of self-love to the condition that this interest should itself be valid as a universal law.

Thus the *principle* that every human will is *a will which by all its maxims enacts universal law**—provided only that it were right in other ways—would be *well suited* to be a categorical imperative in this respect: that precisely because of the Idea of making universal law it is *based on no interest* and consequently can alone among all possible imperatives be *unconditioned*. Or better still—to convert the proposition—if there is a categorical imperative (that is, a law for the will of every rational being), it can command us only to act always on the maxim of such a will in us as can at the same time look upon itself as making universal law; for only then is the practical principle and the imperative which we obey unconditioned, since it is wholly impossible for it to be based on any interest.

We need not now wonder, when we look back upon all the previous efforts that have been made to discover the principle of morality, why they have one and all been bound to fail. Their authors saw man as tied to laws by his duty, but it never occurred to them that he is subject only to *laws which are made by himself* and yet are *universal*, and that he is bound only to act in conformity with a will which is his own but has as nature's purpose for it the function of making universal law. For when they thought of man merely as subject to a law (whatever it might be), the law had to carry with it some interest in order to attract or compel, because it did not spring as a law from *his own* will: in order to conform with the law his will had to be necessitated by *something else* to act in a certain way. This absolutely inevitable conclusion meant that all the labour spent in trying to find a supreme principle of duty was lost beyond recall; for what they discovered was never duty, but only the necessity of acting from a certain interest. This interest might be one's own or another's; but on such a view the imperative was bound to be always a conditioned one and could not possibly serve as a moral law. I will therefore call my principle the principle of the *Autonomy* of the will in contrast with all others, which I consequently class under *Heteronomy*.

The concept of every rational being as one who must regard himself as making universal law by all the maxims of his will, and must seek to judge himself and his actions from this point of view, leads to a closely connected and very fruitful concept—namely, that of *a kingdom of ends*.

I understand by a *'kingdom'* a systematic union of different rational beings under common laws. Now since laws determine ends as regards their universal validity, we shall be able—if we abstract from the personal differences between rational beings, and also from all the content of their private ends—to conceive a whole of all ends in systematic conjunction (a whole both of rational beings as ends in themselves and also of the personal ends which each may set before himself); that is, we shall be able to conceive a kingdom of ends which is possible in accordance with the above principles.

For rational beings all stand under the *law* that each of them should treat himself and all others, *never merely as a means*, but always *at the same time as an end in himself*. But by so doing there arises a systematic union of rational beings under common objective laws—that is, a kingdom. Since these laws are directed precisely to the relation of such beings to one another as ends and means, this kingdom can be

---

*I may be excused from bringing forward examples to illustrate this principle, since those which were first used as illustrations of the categorical imperative and its formula can all serve this purpose here.

called a kingdom of ends (which is admittedly only an Ideal).

A rational being belongs to the kingdom of ends as a *member*, when, although he makes its universal laws, he is also himself subject to these laws. He belongs to it as its *head*, when as the maker of laws he is himself subject to the will of no other.

A rational being must always regard himself as making laws in a kingdom of ends which is possible through freedom of the will—whether it be as member or as head. The position of the latter he can maintain, not in virtue of the maxim of his will alone, but only if he is a completely independent being, without needs and with an unlimited power adequate to his will.

Thus morality consists in the relation of all action to the making of laws whereby alone a kingdom of ends is possible. This making of laws must be found in every rational being himself and must be able to spring from his will. The principle of his will is therefore never to perform an action except on a maxim such as can also be a universal law, and consequently such *that the will can regard itself as at the same time making universal law by means of its maxim*. Where maxims are not already by their very nature in harmony with this objective principle of rational beings as makers of universal law, the necessity of acting on this principle is practical necessitation—that is, *duty*. Duty does not apply to the head in a kingdom of ends, but it does apply to every member and to all members in equal measure.

The practical necessity of acting on this principle—that is, duty—is in no way based on feelings, impulses, and inclinations, but only on the relation of rational beings to one another, a relation in which the will of a rational being must always be regarded as *making universal law*, because otherwise he could not be conceived as *an end in himself*. Reason thus relates every maxim of the will, considered as making universal law, to every other will and also to every action towards oneself: it does so, not because of any further motive or future advantage, but from the Idea of the *dignity* of a rational being who obeys no law other than that which he at the same time enacts himself.

In the kingdom of ends everything has either a *price* or a *dignity*. If it has a price, something else can be put in its place as an *equivalent;* if it is exalted above all price and so admits of no equivalent, then it has a dignity.

What is relative to universal human inclinations and needs has a *market price;* what, even without presupposing a need, accords with a certain taste—that is, with satisfaction in the mere purposeless play of our mental powers—has a *fancy price (Affektionspreis)*; but that which constitutes the sole condition under which anything can be an end in itself has not merely a relative value—that is, a price—but has an intrinsic value—that is, *dignity*.

Now morality is the only condition under which a rational being can be an end in himself; for only through this is it possible to be a law-making member in a kingdom of ends. Therefore morality, and humanity so far as it is capable of morality, is the only thing which has dignity. Skill and diligence in work have a market price; wit, lively imagination, and humour have a fancy price; but fidelity to promises and kindness based on principle (not on instinct) have an intrinsic worth. In default of these, nature and art alike contain nothing to put in their place; for their worth consists, not in the effects which result from them, not in the advantage or profit they produce, but in the attitudes of mind— that is, in the maxims of the will—which are ready in this way to manifest themselves in action even if they are not favoured by success. Such actions too need no recommendation from any subjective disposition or taste in order to meet with immediate favour and approval;

they need no immediate propensity or feeling for themselves; they exhibit the will which performs them as an object of immediate reverence; nor is anything other than reason required to *impose* them upon the will, not to *coax* them from the will—which last would anyhow be a contradiction in the case of duties. This assessment reveals as dignity the value of such a mental attitude and puts it infinitely above all price, with which it cannot be brought into reckoning or comparison without, as it were, a profanation of its sanctity.

What is it then that entitles a morally good attitude of mind—or virtue—to make claims so high? It is nothing less than the *share* which it affords to a rational being *in the making of universal law,* and which therefore fits him to be a member in a possible kingdom of ends. For this he was already marked out in virtue of his own proper nature as an end in himself and consequently as a maker of laws in the kingdom of ends—as free in respect of all laws of nature, obeying only those laws which he makes himself and in virtue of which his maxims can have their part in the making of universal law (to which he at the same time subjects himself). For nothing can have a value other than that determined for it by the law. But the law-making which determines all value must for this reason have a dignity—that is, an unconditioned and incomparable worth—for the appreciation of which, as necessarily given by a rational being, the word '*reverence*' is the only becoming expression. *Autonomy* is therefore ground of the dignity of human nature and of every rational nature.

Questions for Further Reflection

1. According to Aristotle, virtues are character traits that enable us to fulfill the human function. Do you believe there is a human function? If not, why not? If so, do you agree with Aristotle about what it is? Why or why not?

2. Kant writes, of the virtues praised by Aristotle, that, although they are "good in many respects," nevertheless "they are far from being properly described as good without qualifications. . . . For without the principles of a good will they may become exceedingly bad; and the very coolness of a scoundrel makes him, not merely more dangerous, but also immediately more abominable in our eyes than we would have taken him to be without it." How might Aristotle respond?

3. Suppose that you could save the world, but only by sacrificing the life of one completely innocent person. Ought you to sacrifice that person and thus save the world? What would Mill say? What would Kant say? Would either of them be correct?

4. Suppose that you could save the world, but only by sacrificing your own life. Would it be morally permissible for you to do it? Do you have a duty to do it? What would Mill say? What would Kant say? Would either of them be correct?

5. According to Mill, when Kant tries to derive actual duties of morality from his categorical imperative, "he fails, almost grotesquely, to show that there would be any contradiction, any logical (not to say physical) impossibility, in the adoption by all rational beings of the most outrageously immoral rules of conduct. All he shows is that the consequences of their universal adoption would be such as not one would choose to incur." How would Kant respond to Mill?

Further Readings

Paton, H. J. *The Categorical Imperative.* London: Oxford Press, 1947. A commentary on the *Groundwork.*

Smart, J. J. C., and Bernard Williams. *Utilitarianism: For and Against.* Cambridge: Cambridge University Press, 1973. Explication and defense of utilitarianism by Smart; criticism by Williams.

Sparshott, Francis. *Taking Life Seriously: A Study of the Argument of the Nicomachean Ethics.* Toronto: University of Toronto Press, 1994. An accessible study of Aristotle's ethics.

PART TWO

The Individual

Chapter 2

THE INDIVIDUAL LIFE: WHAT CAN MAKE IT WORTHWHILE?

Earlier we distinguished between the concepts of the good and the right. Each of us has a view concerning what is valuable or worthwhile; this view, as we said, is our conception of the good. Unfortunately, these views sometimes lead us to seek ways of life that clash with those sought by others: We cannot attain what we value if they get what *they* value. Such clashes can occur not only when we want different things (one of the last two people on earth wants solitude, the other wants company), but also when we want the same thing (I want all the bananas, and so do you). The main role served by the concept of the right is to establish how such potential conflicts *ought* to be settled. That concept specifies our obligations, what we must do regardless of whether our conception of the good leads us to value doing it or not.

Because we almost always apply the concept of the right in deciding how to avoid potential conflict with others, rather than in deciding how to arrange our affairs when their impact on others is negligible, the role it plays in planning our *private* affairs is not as prominent as the role played by the concept of the good. This is not to say that the concept of the right plays no role in our private affairs; there are prominent accounts of the right that support the idea that individuals have obligations to themselves.

For example, the utilitarian view clearly implies that one has duties to oneself. It stipulates that we are obligated to do everything we can to maximize the net happiness; since our happiness is part of that formula, then in situations in which we can influence no one's life other than our own, we are obligated to maximize our own happiness. Kant also thought that we have obligations to ourselves, but he did not think them to be based on "advantages we reap from doing our duty towards ourselves, but in the worth of manhood. . . . We must reverence humanity in our own person, because apart from this man becomes an object of contempt."[1] We are required never to treat anyone as a mere means; we must always respect humanity by treating no one as a mere means, and we violate this duty when we treat ourselves as a means as fully as when we treat others as a mere means. Accordingly,

---

[1] *Lectures on Ethics*, Louis Infield, trans. (Indianapolis, IN: Hackett, 1930), 121.

The supreme rule is that in all the actions which affect himself a man should so conduct himself that every exercise of his powers is compatible with the fullest employment of them. . . . If I have drunk too much I am incapable of using my freedom and my powers.[2]

Thus, even if I would be happiest were I to slowly drink myself to death, I may not do it. I may not use anyone as a mere means toward my happiness, including myself.

The essays in this chapter rarely raise issues of right, however. Instead, they focus primarily on what it takes to make our lives good or worthwhile. Our lives can be led in a variety of ways, some better than others. If we are to decide how best to plan our affairs, we need to identify features that make lives good, worth living.

Objectivism versus Subjectivism

In some views, we play a substantial role in determining what constitutes a life that is worth living, while in others, the task is taken almost completely out of our hands. Views according to which we play no role whatsoever maintain that objective values determine *all* the ingredients of a worthwhile life, so that regardless of anyone's desires or beliefs to the contrary, a given set of features must be present in a life if it is to be worthwhile. There is an objectively correct account of the good life, and our task is to see to it that our lives have the correct features. Perhaps there will be many different means toward achieving a worthwhile life, but that sort of flexibility does not entail that we have any say in the matter of determining what would *constitute* a worthwhile life.

By contrast, the view that we play a substantial role in determining the requirements of a good life can result from more than one position. We might say that all values are completely subjective, entirely a human invention, so that there are no objective standards to conform to in designing a worthwhile life. However, those who are subjectivists in this sense are not the only people who may think that people have the primary responsibility for deciding what will constitute a worthwhile life. Instead of saying that all values are objective *or* that all values are subjective, we could adopt the view that some values are objective while others are subjective (arguably, most people who identify themselves as objectivists concerning value actually think that only some values are objective). According to this mixed view, we can maintain that only *some* of the features of worthwhile lives are laid out by objective values, but that most are not. The bulk of the features is to be assessed using values that people create. That is, people who are objectivists concerning some values (for example, killing innocent people is bad) can acknowledge that other values, such as those that guide our choice of occupation, are subjective.

Many versions of subjectivism are possible. We can arrive at several by combining the following claims with the subjectivist thesis that all values are entirely an invention: (1) It is up to individuals to invent the standard they will use for assessing their own lives, and it makes no sense to assess anyone else's; (2) individuals invent the standard they will use to assess everyone's life, although this standard may conflict with that of other people; (3) each society invents values for assessing the lives of its members alone; and (4) each society invents values for assessing everyone's life. Moreover, choosing among the possible versions of subjectivism (and among the

---
[2]*Lectures*, 123.

possible standards we might adopt in each version) can be problematic. If I am a subjectivist, what am I doing when, for example, I choose to evaluate lives using the standard I have myself invented rather than the one my society invented? If I take myself to be employing the standard that is *correct* or *best*, what I am saying is incoherent, namely, that although there is no such thing as the objective truth about what constitutes a worthwhile life, my standard, not society's, is objectively correct or best. On the other hand, if I abandon any attempt to appeal to objective considerations and commit myself to the view that any choice among standards is ultimately arbitrary, on what basis can I choose my standard rather than society's or any other standard whatever?

Subjectivism in its many forms appears to have become extremely widespread, even among people who hold other views that are flatly inconsistent with subjectivism. Thus, many of the people who hold the religious belief that it is good to conform to God's will and sinful or bad not to are also subjectivists; they say that their religion-inspired value scheme is merely one alternative among many others people may choose, and no value scheme can claim to be objectively correct. They seem unaware that their religious belief about goodness and sin is incompatible with the idea that values are merely a matter of choice: Can it be that God would punish people for making the wrong (admittedly arbitrary) choice?

Transcendentalism

The most radically objectivist views result from the position (which might be called *transcendentalism*) that an extrahuman order determines what makes lives worthwhile. Theists, or those who believe that a god or gods exist, are the main proponents of this transcendentalist view. According to theists, God's plan gives things any purpose and value they have: They are good in virtue of playing a role in the plan. That the good is determined in this fashion does not entail that our lives are worthwhile no matter what we do, however. It is true that some theists would say that whatever free choices we make (if any) were taken into account by God and worked into God's plan, so that everything that happens is good. In this view, our lives are inevitably worthwhile. However, other theists would say that God's plan *can* be thwarted temporarily by people. Those who opt to honor the plan thereby make their lives worthwhile by ensuring that their lives have the feature (playing a role in the plan) that is definitive of objective value. Those who choose to oppose or ignore it thereby ensure that their lives are not worthwhile. Both versions of theism prompt questions about life's point or purpose and its goodness: Mightn't my life be bad even if it has a point or contributes to God's plan? (Imagine an atheist who is slated for eternal damnation whose life contributes to the plan by serving as an example to others of what not to do.) And mightn't my life be good even if it does not contribute to God's plan? (Imagine an atheist who is happy serving others.)

Count Leo Nikolaevitch Tolstoy (1828–1910) expresses a theistic point of view in his *Confessions* (written in 1879), an excerpt from which is reprinted here. He thought that life could be worthwhile only if we participate in God's plan, for participating in God's plan struck Tolstoy as the only hope for our attaining two essential ingredients in a worthwhile life: immortality and an eternal significance for individual lives. Unfortunately, the more he studied the attempts by people to understand the world, the more convinced he became of the overwhelming likelihood that his existence would end and all trace of his life would eventually vanish. Everything human investigators turned up was water on the fire of Tolstoy's hopes. Because he wanted no part of life under such conditions, however, his search became desperate. Eventually, after many years of agonizing, he came to a conclusion that renewed his hope. He decided that the very *nature* of human investigation made it unable to provide the sort of answers he wanted. For that, he needed something that would link our finite world to an infinite God. Faith provided just the right link. His new faith suggested that he would be immortal and attain "unity with the infinite, God, heaven."

Several aspects of Tolstoy's view are puzzling. Two worries that come immediately to mind are: Is it really true that *only* an eternal life is worth having? And can it really be that life is good *only* if it has eternal significance?

Other puzzling features of Tolstoy's view will stand out if we contrast theism, which is Tolstoy's version of transcendentalism, with a form of transcendentalism that is not theistic: An ancient Chinese philosophy called Taoism, primarily based on the *Tao Te Ching*. The *Tao Te Ching* may have been written by Lao Tzu in the sixth century B.C.E., but the authorship of the *Tao Te Ching* is a disputed matter. In any case, the *Tao Te Ching* maintains that nature is the beginning of all things and that an objectively worthwhile life consists in conforming to the natural order, letting nature go its own way. No assumption is made that God or any other agent is behind the way nature develops; hence, Taoists are not theists. So one question we should ask when reading Tolstoy is, "Even if we adopt the transcendentalist assumption that life is made worthwhile only by being embedded in an extrahuman order that gives it the value it has, why say that this transcendent order must be implemented by (any) God?" (If you are tempted to say that a transcendental order could not exist unless God created it, then ask how God came into existence.) We should also ask, since Taoists do not believe in an afterlife, why assume that a transcendent order guarantees eternal life or eternal significance?

The natural order to which Taoist ethics conforms is exceedingly mysterious, so much so that the *Tao Te Ching* begins with the warning, "the way that can be spoken of is not the constant way." At one point the Tao, or way of nature, is described as "turning back." In various places those who follow the way of nature are said to have freed themselves from having desires and consequently to be inactive. They are like babies or uncarved blocks in that they are not committed to shaping their lives in any particular way. They are self-effacing. Moreover, they do not value "learning," an anti-intellectualist tendency they share with Tolstoy.

Contemplation

Unlike Tolstoy and Lao Tzu, the ancient Greek philosopher Aristotle develops a thoroughgoing objectivist view that attributes the highest value to reason. In his *Nicomachean Ethics,* Aristotle focuses on *eudaimonia,* which is sometimes translated as "happiness" but which is best rendered as "flourishing." The best life, according to him, is one in which people perform their function "according to virtue." By *virtue* Aristotle means "excellence," so "performing our function according to virtue" means performing our function *well.* Because of their structure, members of the human species are able to act in certain ways better than they can in others, and it is their function to do what they do better than other creatures in the world. Engaging in the life of reason, as it turns out, is what we do best, so that is our function, and the best life consists in using reason well. However, there are two sorts of reason, practical and theoretical, and what constitutes the excellent use of one differs from what constitutes the excellent use of the other. We are morally virtuous to the extent that we conduct our affairs as dictated by the excellent use of practical reason; we are intellectually virtuous to the extent that our use of theoretical reason is excellent. In most of the *Ethics*, Aristotle emphasizes the practical use of reason, reason insofar as it is used to bring about some state of affairs. Practically, we reason well when we strike a balance between excess and deficiency of emotion or action, taking into account the particulars of the concrete situation we are in. However, in the selection in this chapter, he suggests that the people who have the best lives are ones who devote their lives as much as possible to theoretical reasoning, which is the contemplation and discovery of fact, for theoretical reasoning is the most pleasant, continuous, self-sufficient, and divine activity of which people are capable.

It is interesting to note that in *Mysticism and Logic* Bertrand Russell joins Aristotle in opposing Tolstoy's denigration of reason. An important mathematical logician in his own right, Russell praises the "art of living in the contemplation of great things"[3] and singles out the study of mathematics as one of the purest instances of such a life. Nonetheless, Russell and Aristotle praise the contemplative life largely in otherworldly terms that would have been congenial to theists such as Tolstoy. This is particularly incongruous in the case of Russell, who was an outspoken atheist and a complete subjectivist concerning values.[4] Thus, Aristotle praised the contemplative life partly on the grounds that it calls on the most divine (godlike) part of our nature, while Russell lauded it on the grounds that it allows us to escape the vicissitudes and hostile passions of the actual world and to focus on a beautiful, orderly, changeless, noble realm; to the extent that we have devoted ourselves to the discovery and appreciation of mathematical truths, "our best hopes are not thwarted."[5]

Hedonism

Hedonists tend to hold the sort of objectivist view according to which individuals have a great deal of autonomy in deciding what constitutes a worthwhile life. It is an objective truth that pleasure is in itself good and that pain is in itself bad, according to hedonism; there is nothing we can do about that. Hedonists tend to equate "happy" with "pleasant," saying that we are happy and our lives worthwhile when we enjoy a preponderance of pleasure over pain. Each of us, though, may find it possible to choose from a considerable range of pleasurable ways of life, and hedonists would say that equally pleasant lifestyles are equally good. Moreover, hedonism is consistent with our having a further sort of autonomy in deciding what is worthwhile. We may be able to train ourselves to find various things pleasurable, using something

---

[3]*Mysticism and Logic* (Totowa, NJ: Barnes & Noble Books, 1981), p. 48.

[4]As he said in *Religion and Science*, pp. 237–238, "if two men differ about values, there is not a disagreement as to any kind of truth."

[5]*Mysticism*, p. 55.

like the conditioning B. F. Skinner championed, for example. If so, then we can determine whether a way of life will have the feature it must have if it is to be objectively valuable.

The view that only pleasure (and the absence of pain) is intrinsically good and that only pain is intrinsically bad is definitive of the term *hedonist*. It is sometimes called *ethical hedonism* to distinguish it from a separate thesis that tends to be (but need not be) adopted by hedonists, namely *psychological hedonism*, which is a theory of motivation: the theory that as a matter of psychological fact, people always act in ways they think will be pleasurable and not painful.

One of the most rigid forms of hedonism was advocated by one of its earliest proponents, Epicurus (341–270 B.C.E.). Epicurus' hedonist position was that the good is happiness, while happiness, in turn, is pleasure and the absence of pain. Upon closer examination, however, we encounter some surprises. At one point, he says that we feel the need of pleasure only when it is painful to be without it and concludes that happiness consists in the absence of painful states. At another, he reinforces the conclusion that freedom from pain is the only requisite for happiness by saying that pleasure *is* the absence of painful states of awareness. No wonder, then, that Epicurus rejected what we now call the life of the Epicure, which involves indulging the senses. He had noted that the chief source of pain was unfulfilled desires, and so he recommended that we transform our desire scheme quite profoundly, abandoning any desire whose fulfillment is difficult. In particular, we should get rid of desires when leaving them ungratified would lead to no pain. We are left with nothing but desires we can surely fulfill (and ones that are necessary if we are to avoid pain); accordingly, we will ask very little of life and rest content with a simple, austere, passive lifestyle.

The view that happiness consists in the absense of pain and suffering existed at least two centuries before Epicurus articulated it. Gautama, or the Buddha (563–483 B.C.E.), maintained that the path to nirvana (literally "extinguishment," as when a flame is snuffed) is the elimination of suffering through the elimination of craving or desires. The Buddha also claimed that the most important craving to abandon is the craving for existence, a craving that is fueled by the false idea that we are selves. His followers are traditionally grouped into two main schools: the Theravada, whose main goal is the individual's extinguishing of craving through one's own efforts, and the Mahayana, who is also concerned to help others eliminate their suffering.

Of course, the negative approach to pleasure is not the only possible one. Taken to its extreme, the view that happiness consists in the absence of pain implies that we would be better off if we did not exist, since only then would we be completely free of pain. The version of hedonism that equates the good with pleasure and the absence of pain does not have this consequence, since we must exist if we are to experience pleasure. However, the latter version has its own share of difficulties. One is that I might take pleasure in activities others consider immoral, offensive, or ignoble—indeed, *I* might find them offensive and immoral even though I enjoy them.

Infamous for his libertine lifestyle, Donatien-Alphonse-François de Sade (1740–1814), better known as the Marquis de Sade, wrote many works designed to shock his readers with the sorts of pleasures he valued. In *Philosophy in the Bedroom*, a set of dialogues published posthumously, he discusses the three preferences of his brand of libertinage: sodomy, sacrilegious fancies, and penchants to cruelty. Since hedonists take all forms of pleasure as good, they must consider even the pleasures sadists experience upon torturing victims as good in themselves. Only the consequences of sadism are bad.

To criticize sadistic pleasures only because of their bad consequences may not seem to go far enough. However, toward the end of his discussion of hedonism, J. J. C. Smart defends the hedonist claim that even sadistic pleasures are intrinsically good. He also picks up a famous discussion between J. S. Mill and Jeremy Bentham in which Mill tried to rebut Bentham's hedonistic claim that pushpin, a trivial game, is as good as poetry, assuming that people get equal amounts of pleasure from each. According to Mill, some pleasures (such as the pleasures of poetry or scientific discovery) are higher than others (such as the pleasures of bowling or sex), and the former weigh more heavily in determining whether someone is happy:

> To suppose that life has (as [many people] express it) no higher end than pleasure—no better and nobler object of desire and pursuit—they designate as utterly mean and groveling, as a doctrine worthy only of swine. . . .
> When thus attacked, the Epicureans have always answered that it is not they, but their accusers, who represent human nature in a degrading light, since the accusation supposes human beings to be capable of no pleasures except those of which swine are capable. . . . The comparison of the Epicurean life to that of beasts is felt as degrading, precisely because a beast's pleasures do not satisfy a human being's conceptions of happiness. . . . Some kinds of pleasure are more desirable and more valuable than others.[6]

Smart notes that in most cases, the higher pleasures can be defended as better than the lower ones on purely hedonistic grounds because the former are more productive of further pleasure in the long run. However, Smart admits (as did Mill) that if Bentham's hedonistic view were correct, then "strictly in itself and at a particular moment, a contented sheep is as good as a contented philosopher."

Power

The German philosopher Friedrich Nietzsche (1844–1900) condemned all religions and philosophical positions that advocated passivity and withdrawal from life. Consequently, Epicurus' hedonism was anathema to Nietzsche, who saw that the way of life advocated by Epicurus was passive and passionless insofar as Epicurus counseled people to aim no higher than the absence of pain and to abandon desires whose satisfaction required effort. Although Nietzsche singled out Epicurus' brand of hedonism for special criticism, he rejected all forms of hedonism because he had contempt for the attitude that our aspirations in designing our lives should not extend beyond pleasure.

Rather than adopt a passive way of life, Nietzsche urged people to fill their lives with active, ambitious pursuits. Those with high aspirations will not focus on mere pleasure. Indeed, a truly worthwhile life might be so difficult to achieve that it would involve a good deal of suffering. As he said in section 225 of *Beyond Good and Evil*, "The discipline of suffering, of *great* suffering—do you not know that only *this* discipline has created all enhancements of man so far?"[7] Moreover, against

---

[6] J. S. Mill, *Utilitarianism* (Indianapolis, IN: Hackett, 1861), 7–8.

[7] Trans. Walter Kaufmann (New York: Vintage Books, 1966).

psychological hedonism he set his own theory of human motivation, which held that healthy people always strive to increase their power, not their pleasure. He replaced ethical hedonism with the view that only power is good. Happiness, he maintained, consists in efficiently augmenting one's power. The drive to increase our power—our "will to power"—is so basic to human nature that Nietzsche is willing to say that anything that weakens people is antilife. Since life is lived in the physical world, and since religions counsel us to value a transcendent realm rather than the physical world, Nietzsche criticizes all religions on the grounds that they are antilife.

Even if the best life is one consisting in ambitious, power-enhancing pursuits, individuals have a great deal of leeway in deciding what will constitute a worthwhile life, for there are many forms of power. Nietzsche appears to have admired power in all its forms, including improving our position at the expense of others. As he says in *The Antichrist*, section 2:

> What is good? Everything that heightens the feeling of power in man, the will to power, power itself.
> What is bad? Everything that is born of weakness.
> What is happiness? The feeling that power is *growing*, that resistance is overcome.
> Not contentedness but more power; not peace but war; not virtue but fitness.[8]

Yet Nietzsche reserved his strongest praise for creativity and individuality, which themselves enhance our power, according to him.

Close Relationships

That interpersonal relationships are a key part of a worthwhile life is an ancient view. Nowhere is it emphasized more emphatically than in the Confucian tradition. Confucius (551–479 B.C.E.) maintained that the highest moral quality is *jen*, translated as benevolence or humaneness, and that *jen* is attained by participating in a particular community, which itself requires respectful conformity to *li*, the traditions or rites of that community. The chief element of the community is the family. Indeed, as Confucius said (*Analects* Book 8, Chapter 2), "when the gentleman feels profound affection for his parents, the common people will be stirred to benevolence."[9] Because forming a community with others is a reciprocal relationship, Confucius emphasized (*Analects* Book 6, Chapter 30) that "a benevolent man helps others to take their stand in so far as he himself wishes to take his stand, and gets others there in so far as he himself wishes to get there."

The emphasis on close interpersonal relationships can also be found in modern psychoanalytic literature, where it is a common theme that the personal relationships we form with others are the central and essential ingredients in a meaningful life. One of the most important ways we make sense of our lives is by adopting a scheme of goals or purposes that help determine what it is important for us to be, and we begin to form this scheme during childhood under the influence of the predisposition to attach ourselves to others, which leads us to center our lives around the people to whom we attach ourselves.

---

[8]*The Portable Nietzsche*, trans. Walter Kaufmann (New York: Viking Press, 1954).

[9]*The Analects*, trans. D. C. Lau (London: Penguin Books, 1979).

Yet many psychologists seem to downplay the importance of relationships to others in the lives of normal, mature people. In "Woman's Place in Man's Life Cycle," Chapter 1 of her book *In a Different Voice*, Carol Gilligan suggests that males tend to develop different values from females, that psychologists such as Freud, Piaget, Erickson, Lever, Kohlberg, and (to a lesser degree) Horner have accepted the values usually associated with males as definitive of a healthy, mature human being because their studies focused on males, and that these pyschologists have therefore concluded that in view of the values they hold, females normally do not mature properly. Males tend to be competitive and individualistic; they tend to attribute great importance to the rules of fair play that govern their competition. Their view of morality is one centered around adjudicating conflicts fairly. Females tend to be cooperative, caring, and deeply attached to others. These values tend to make them shy away from competition and to attribute less importance to rules associated with competition, but one ought not conclude that females are developmentally defective. Instead, Gilligan says, one should conclude that female development is different from male. As a consequence of the values they develop, females tend to view moral issues differently. Their conception of morality "centers moral development around the understanding of responsibility and relationships, just as the conception of morality as fairness ties moral development to the understanding of rights and rules."

Is Gilligan offering a prescription for how to live life well? The answer is complicated by the descriptive style she adopts. She never says that forming attachments is good or that competing is bad. Instead, she says that in contemporary Western culture, females tend to value attachments, that males tend to value competition, and that it is a mistake to say that biology or psychic health dictates developing one set of values rather than the other. One might be tempted to find a prescription in Gilligan's work anyway, for one might say that Gilligan has shown that proper development of women will differ from that of men; it will center around close relationships, and, accordingly, women should emphasize the role of relationships in their lives, while men should not. This conclusion is problematic for more than one reason.

One difficulty is a gulf between the claim that because of their biology, people will normally develop a certain set of values and the conclusion that they ought, therefore, live the life that best accords with those values. However, perhaps this gap can be overcome. It does seem reasonable to assume that if, in the course of normal development, people will come to develop certain values, then the things they come to regard as good through the influence of these values *are* good, other things being equal (but what if Sade is correct in saying that cruelty is natural?). This claim would be consistent with the view of Aristotle, Epicurus, and Nietzsche that there is a tight relationship between the way we are structured to act and the way it would be good to act. But even if we bridge the gap, we still cannot conclude that the good life for women differs from that for men. Gilligan merely claims to establish a contingent tendency for the values of females and males to differ in the ways she describes. The tendency

> is not absolute, and the constrasts between male and female voices are presented . . . to highlight a distinction between two modes of thought and to focus a problem of interpretation rather than to represent a generalization about either sex. . . . No claims are

made about the origins of the differences described or their distribution in a wider population, across cultures, or through time."[10]

In view of the limited scope of Gilligan's thesis, male readers should not assume that she recommends their allegiance to what she classifies as "male values." Nor should female readers suppose that Gilligan recommends their allegiance to "female values." Her main message is that both sorts of values are consistent with being a healthy human being. Still, Gilligan invites her readers to reconsider "female values"; perhaps relationships and cooperativeness should play a more central role in the lives of people than is suggested by the biased psychological studies Gilligan criticizes.

Work

Anthony Storr shares with Aristotle, Epicurus, and Nietzsche the assumption that we are built in such a fashion that in the normal course of events, we will have certain preferences rather than others. Like Gilligan, Storr does not overtly prescribe a way of life, but we can convert his position into a prescription. If Gilligan invites us to give more importance to close relationships, Storr invites us to give them less. Storr argues that close interpersonal relationships need not be the hub of a worthwhile life. Instead, work and other activities that allow people to express themselves can be the main source of meaning in the lives of some people. Everyone needs acquaintances, he admits, but for some, these ties are far less important an ingredient in a worthwhile life than their work, and relationships that are not intimate can often sustain people's sense of belonging to an order in which they are valued. Lives centered around work can be fulfilling, yet comparatively solitary and self-contained, resembling those of the intellectual idealized by Aristotle.

Self-Creation

Jean-Paul Sartre (1905–1980) comes closer than anyone else we have discussed to adopting the thesis that all values are subjective. He called his position *existentialism* and defined it as the doctrine that "existence precedes essence." This vague slogan signifies at least four theses. First, no creator designed us with a purpose in mind, so we have a purpose only if we assign one to ourselves. Second, each one of us invents our self in the sense that one constructs a picture of what one is, what one's projects are, and how one is engaged in the world. Third, nothing about our nature or circumstances determines that we will pursue one set of goals rather than another or that we will synthesize one set of engagements into ourselves rather than another—as Sartre sometimes puts the point, there is no such thing as human nature. Fourth, nothing determines that one set of activities rather than another is good or right. We must *decide* what sorts of thing are good and bad, he concluded, since "God does not exist," and "all possibility of finding values in a heaven of ideas disappears along with him."

Sartre draws two particularly important conclusions from his existentialist doctrine. The first is a version of subjectivism: We are radically free in the sense that we must invent our own values (so that perhaps Sartre overstated matters a bit when he denied the existence of a human nature; our inescapable freedom seems to constitute our nature). Second, "Man is responsible for what he is," and not only in the sense that

---

[10] *In a Different Voice* (Cambridge, MA: Harvard University Press, 1982), 2.

each of us chooses what we are. Instead, Sartre adds a thesis that sits badly with his value subjectivism: "When we say that man is responsible for himself, we . . . mean . . . that he is responsible for all men."

Nothing

In the final selection of the chapter, the philosopher Arthur Schopenhauer, (1788–1860) gives two powerful arguments for the thesis that it is impossible to have a worthwhile life. First, life is pointless, and what we do is completely arbitrary. We think otherwise because we declare living, and various other things that we desire, to be good, and, hence, we think our lives devoted to the pursuit of good things. However, the only reason we have for thinking that what we ultimately desire is good is *that we desire it;* if we are honest, we have to admit that we do not actually have *any* reason whatever for desiring what we do. Second, given inevitable features of the human situation, a fulfilling life is impossible. Schopenhauer supports this forlorn claim with a negative analysis of happiness that is somewhat reminiscent of that of Epicurus. Happiness would consist in our being satisfied, but we are incapable of final satisfaction because we always want something else; moreover, satisfaction consists in nothing more than the momentary ending of a period of unpleasant dissatisfaction, so that our best moments consist merely in long stretches of suffering brought briefly to an end.

RELIGIOUS FAITH

Confessions

Leo Tolstoy

Five years ago something very strange started happening to me. At first I began experiencing moments of bewilderment; my life would come to a standstill, as if I did not know how to live or what to do, and I felt lost and fell into despair. But they passed and I continued to live as before. Then these moments of bewilderment started to recur more frequently, always taking the same form. On these occasions, when life came to a standstill, the same questions always arose: 'Why? What comes next?' . . .

All this was happening to me at a time when I was surrounded on all sides by what is considered complete happiness: I was not yet fifty, I had a kind, loving and beloved wife, lovely children, and a large estate that was growing and expanding with no effort on my part. I was respected by relatives and friends far more than ever before. I was praised by strangers and could consider myself a celebrity without deceiving myself. Moreover I was not unhealthy in mind or body, but on the contrary enjoyed a strength of mind and body such as I had rarely witnessed in my contemporaries. Physically I could keep up with the peasants tilling the fields; mentally I could work for eight or ten hours at a stretch without suffering any ill effects from the effort. And in these circumstances I found myself at the point where I could no longer go on living and, since I feared death, I had to deceive myself in order to refrain from suicide.

I could not attribute any rational meaning to a single act, let alone to my whole life. I simply felt astonished that I had failed to realize this from the beginning. It had all been common knowledge for such a long time. Today or tomorrow sickness and death will come (and they had already arrived) to those dear to me, and to myself, and nothing will remain other than the stench and the worms. Sooner or later my deeds, whatever they may have been, will be forgotten and will no longer exist. What is all the fuss about then? How can a person carry on living and fail to perceive this? That is what is so astonishing! It is only possible to go on living while you are intoxicated with life; once sober it is impossible not to see that it is all a mere trick, and a stupid trick! That is exactly what it is: there is nothing either witty or amusing, it is only cruel and stupid.

There is an old Eastern fable about a traveller who is taken unawares on the steppes by a ferocious wild animal. In order to escape the beast the traveller hides in an empty well, but at the bottom of the well he sees a dragon with its jaws open, ready to devour him. The poor fellow does not dare to climb out because he is afraid of being eaten by the rapacious beast, neither does he dare drop to the bottom of the well for fear of being eaten by the dragon. So he seizes hold of a branch of a bush that is growing in the crevices of the well and clings on to it. His arms grow weak and he knows that he will soon have to resign himself to the death that awaits him on either side. Yet he still clings on, and while he is holding on to the branch he looks around and sees that two mice, one black and one white, are steadily working their way round the bush he is hanging from, gnawing away at it. Sooner or later they will eat through it and the branch will snap, and he will fall into the jaws of the dragon. The traveller sees this and knows that he will inevitably perish. But while he is still hanging there he sees some drops of honey on the leaves of the bush, stretches out his tongue and licks them. In the same way I am clinging to the tree of life, knowing full well that the dragon of death inevitably awaits me, ready to tear me to pieces, and I cannot understand how I have fallen into this torment. And I try licking the honey that once consoled me, but it no longer gives me pleasure.

In my search for answers to the question of life I felt just like a man who is lost in a wood.

I came to a clearing, climbed a tree and saw clearly into the never-ending distance. But there was no house there, nor could there be. I walked into the thicket, into the gloom and saw the darkness, but there was no house there either.

In the same way I wandered in the forest of human knowledge, both amidst the bright rays of mathematical knowledge and experimental knowledge, where wide horizons were opened up to me, but in a direction where I could find no house, and amidst the darkness of speculative knowledge where I was immersed in ever deeper gloom the further I progressed. And I became quite convinced that there was not, and could not be, a way out.

When I inclined to the bright side of knowledge I realized that I was only avoiding facing the question. However bright and attractive those horizons spreading out before me were, and however tempting it was to immerse myself in the infinity of all this knowledge, I already knew that the clearer the knowledge was, the less I needed it, and the less it answered my question. 'Well,' I said to myself, 'I know everything that science so urgently wants to know and along that path there is no answer to the question of the meaning of my life.' In the speculative realm I knew that despite the fact, or rather precisely because of the fact, that the primary purpose of this knowledge is to answer my question, the answer given was none other than the one I had already given myself: what is the meaning of my life? It has none. Or: what will come of my Life? Nothing. Or: why does everything there is exist, and why do I exist? Because it does.

When I put my questions to one branch of human knowledge I received a countless number of precise answers to things I had not asked: the chemical composition of the stars, the movement of the sun towards the constellation Hercules, the origin of the species and of man, the forms of infinitely tiny atoms, the fluctuations of infinitely small and imponderable particles of ether. But the only answer this branch of knowledge provided to my question concerning the meaning of life was this: you are that which you call your life; you are a temporary, incidental accumulation of particles. The mutual interaction and alteration of these particles produces in you something you refer to as your life. This accumulation can only survive for a limited length of time; when the interaction of these particles ceases, that which you call life will cease, bringing an end to all your questions. You are a randomly united lump of something. This lump decomposes and the fermentation is called your life. The lump will disintegrate and the fermentation will end, together with all your questions. This is the answer given by the exact side of knowledge, and if it adheres strictly to its principles, it cannot answer otherwise.

However, the truth is that this answer does not reply to the question. I need to know the meaning of my life, and the fact that it is a particle of infinity not only fails to give it any meaning, but eliminates any possible meaning.

The experimental side of knowledge vaguely compromises with the speculative side in saying that the meaning of life lies in development and in the encouragement of this development. But owing to the inaccuracies and obscurities these cannot be regarded as answers.

Whenever the other side of knowledge, the speculative realm, sticks firmly to its principles and gives direct answers to the question, it has always, throughout the ages, given the same answer: the universe is something infinite and incomprehensible. Man's life is an inscrutable part of this inscrutable 'whole'. . . .

Whether it was thanks to my somewhat strange and instinctive love of the true working people that I was forced to understand them and to realize that they are not as stupid as we thought; or whether it was thanks to the sincerity of my conviction that I knew of nothing better to do than hang myself, I sensed anyway that if I wanted to live and to understand the meaning of life I must not seek it among those who have lost it and wish to kill themselves, but among the millions of people living and dead who have created life, and who carry the weight of our lives together with their own. And I looked around at the enormous masses of simple, uneducated people without wealth, who have lived and who still live, and I saw something quite different. I saw that with a few exceptions all those millions do not fit into my divisions, and that I could not categorize them as people who did not understand the question because they themselves posed, and answered, the question with unusual clarity. Neither could I categorize them as epicureans, since their lives rest more on deprivation and suffering than on pleasure. I could still less regard them as living out their meaningless lives irrationally, since they could explain every act of their lives, including death. They considered suicide the greatest evil. It appeared that mankind as a whole had some kind of comprehension of the meaning of life that I did not acknowledge and derided. It followed that rational knowledge does not provide the meaning of life, but excludes it; while the meaning given to life by the millions of people, by humanity as a whole, is founded on some sort of knowledge that is despised and considered false. . . .

A contradiction arose from which there were only two ways out: either that which I called reasonable was not as reasonable as I thought, or that which I felt to be irrational was not as irrational as I thought. And I started to check the line of argument that stemmed from my rational knowledge.

As I checked this line of argument I found it to be entirely correct. The conclusion that life is nothing was inevitable, but I spotted a mistake. The mistake was that my thinking did not correspond to the question I had posed. The question was: why do I live? Or: is there anything that will remain and not be annihilated of my illusory and transitory life? Or: what meaning has my finite existence in an infinite universe? In order to answer this question I studied life.

Clearly the solution to all the possible questions of life could not satisfy me because my question, however simple it may seem at first, involves a demand for an explanation of the finite by means of the infinite and vice versa.

I had asked: what meaning has life beyond time, beyond space and beyond cause? And I was answering the question: 'What is the meaning of my life within time, space and cause?' The result was that after long and laboured thought I could only answer: none.

In my deliberations I was continually drawing comparisons between the finite and the finite, and the infinite and the infinite, and I could not have done otherwise. Thus I reached the only conclusion I could reach: force is force, matter is matter, will is will, the infinite is the infinite, nothing is nothing; and I could go no further than that.

It was somewhat similar to what happens in mathematics when, trying to resolve an equation, we get an identity. The method of deduction is correct, but the only answer obtained is that a equals a, and x equals x, or o equals o. Precisely the same thing was happening with my reasoning concerning the meaning of life. The only answers the sciences give to this question are identities.

And really, strictly rational knowledge, such as that of Descartes, begins with complete doubt in everything and throws aside any knowledge founded on faith, reconstructing everything along laws of reason and experiment. And it can provide no answer other than the one I reached: an indefinite one. It was only at first that I thought knowledge had given an affirmative answer, Schopenhauer's answer that life has no meaning and is evil. But when I went into the matter I realized that this answer is not affirmative and that it was only my senses that had taken it to be so. Strictly expressed, as it is by the Brahmins, Solomon, and Schopenhauer, the answer is but a vague one, an identity: o equals o, life presented to me as nothing is nothing. Thus, philosophical knowledge denies nothing but simply replies that it cannot solve the question, and that as far as it is concerned any resolution remains infinite.

Having understood this, I realized that it was impossible to search for an answer to my questions in rational knowledge; that the answer given by rational knowledge simply suggests that the answer can only be obtained by stating the question in another way, by introducing the question of the relation of the finite to the infinite. I realized that no matter how irrational and distorted the answers given by faith might be, they had the advantage of introducing to every answer a relationship between the finite and the infinite, without which there can be no solution. Whichever way I put the question: how am I to live? the answer is always: according to God's law. Or to the question: is there anything real that will come of my life? the answer is: eternal torment or eternal bliss. Or, to the question: what meaning is there that is not destroyed by death? the answer is: unity with the infinite, God, heaven.

Thus in addition to rational knowledge, which I had hitherto thought to be the only knowledge, I was inevitably led to acknowledge that there does exist another kind of knowledge—an irrational one—possessed by humanity as a whole: faith, which affords the possibility of living. Faith remained as irrational to me as before, but I could not fail to recognize that it alone provides mankind with the answers to the question of life, and consequently with the possibility of life.

Rational knowledge had led me to recognize that life is meaningless. My life came to a halt and I wanted to kill myself. As I looked around at people, at humanity as a whole, I saw that they lived and affirmed that they knew the meaning of life. I looked at myself, I had lived as long as I knew the meaning of life. For me, as for others, faith provided the meaning of life and the possibility of living.

Having looked around further at people in other countries and at my contemporaries and predecessors, I saw the same thing. Where there is life there is faith. Since the day of creation faith has made it possible for mankind to live, and the essential aspects of that faith are always and everywhere the same.

THE WAY OF NATURE

Tao Te Ching

Lao Tzu

I

The way that can be spoken of
Is not the constant way;
The name that can be named
Is not the constant name.
The nameless was the beginning of heaven and earth;
The named was the mother of the myriad creatures.
Hence always rid yourself of desires in order to observe its secrets;
But always allow yourself to have desires in order to observe its manifestations.
These two are the same
But diverge in name as they issue forth.

Being the same they are called mysteries,
Mystery upon mystery—
The gateway of the manifold secrets.[1]

II

The whole world recognizes the beautiful as the beautiful, yet this is only the ugly; the whole world recognizes the good as the good, yet this is only the bad.
Thus Something and Nothing produce each other;
The difficult and the easy complement each other;
The long and the short off-set each other;
The high and the low incline towards each other;
Note and sound harmonize with each other;
Before and after follow each other.
Therefore the sage keeps to the deed that consists in taking no action and practises the teaching that uses no words.
The myriad creatures rise from it yet it claims no authority;
It gives them life yet claims no possession;
It benefits them yet exacts no gratitude;
It accomplishes its task yet lays claim to no merit.
It is because it lays claim to no merit
That its merit never deserts it.

. . .

XXV

There is a thing confusedly formed,
Born before heaven and earth.
Silent and void
It stands alone and does not change,
Goes round and does not weary.
It is capable of being the mother of the world.

---

[1] Lau's notes have been omitted—Eds.

I know not its name
So I style it 'the way'.
I give it the makeshift name of 'the great'.
Being great, it is further described as receding,
Receding, it is described as far away,
Being far away, it is described as turning back.
Hence the way is great; heaven is great; earth is great; and the king is also great. Within the realm there are four things that are great, and the king counts as one.
Man models himself on earth,
Earth on heaven,
Heaven on the way,
And the way on that which is naturally so.

. . .

XXXVII

The way never acts yet nothing is left undone.
Should lords and princes be able to hold fast to it,
The myriad creatures will be transformed of their own accord.
After they are transformed, should desire raise its head,
I shall press it down with the weight of the nameless uncarved block.
The nameless uncarved block
Is but freedom from desire,
And if I cease to desire and remain still,
The empire will be at peace of its own accord.

. . .

XXXVIII

A man of the highest virtue does not keep to virtue and that is why he has virtue. A man of the lowest virtue never strays from virtue and that is why he is without virtue. The former never acts yet leaves

nothing undone. The latter acts but there are things left undone. A man of the highest benevolence acts, but from no ulterior motive. A man of the highest rectitude acts, but from ulterior motive. A man most conversant in the rites acts, but when no one responds rolls up his sleeves and resorts to persuasion by force. Hence when the way was lost there was virtue; when virtue was lost there was benevolence; when benevolence was lost there was rectitude; when rectitude was lost there were the rites.
The rites are the wearing thin of loyalty and good faith
And the beginning of disorder;
Foreknowledge is the flowery embellishment of the way
And the beginning of folly.
Hence the man of large mind abides in the thick not in the thin, in the fruit not in the flower.
Therefore he discards the one and takes the other.

. . .

LXIII

Do that which consists in taking no action; pursue that which is not meddlesome; savour that which has no flavour.
Make the small big and the few many; do good to him who has done you an injury.
Lay plans for the accomplishment of the difficult before it becomes difficult; make something big by starting with it when small.
Difficult things in the world must needs have their beginnings in the easy; big things must needs have their beginnings in the small.

Therefore it is because the sage never attempts to be great that he succeeds in becoming great.
One who makes promises rashly rarely keeps good faith; one who is in the habit of considering things easy meets with frequent difficulties.
Therefore even the sage treats some things as difficult.
That is why in the end no difficulties can get the better of him.

. . .

LXXX

Reduce the size and population of the state. Ensure that even though the people have tools of war for a troop or a battalion they will not use them; and also that they will be reluctant to move to distant places because they look on death as no light matter.
Even when they have ships and carts, they will have no use for them; and even when they have armour and weapons, they will have no occasion to make a show of them.
Bring it about that the people will return to the use of the knotted rope,
Will find relish in their food
And beauty in their clothes,
Will be content in their abode
And happy in the way they live.
Though adjoining states are within sight of one another, and the sound of dogs barking and cocks crowing in one state can be heard in another, yet the people of one state will grow old and die without having had any dealings with those of another.

CONTEMPLATION

Happiness as Contemplation

Aristotle

What remains is to discuss in outline the nature of happiness, since this is what we state the end of human nature to be. Our discussion will be the more concise if we first sum up what we have said already. We said, then, that it is not a state; for if it were it might belong to some one who was asleep throughout his life, living the life of a plant, or, again, to some one who was suffering the greatest misfortunes. If these implications are unacceptable, and we must rather class happiness as an *activity,* as we have said before, and if some activities are necessary and desirable for the sake of something else, while others are so in themselves, evidently happiness must be placed among those desirable in themselves, not among those desirable for the sake of something else; for happiness does not lack anything, but is self-sufficient. Now those activities are desirable in themselves from which nothing is sought beyond the activity. And of this nature excellent actions are thought to be; for to do noble and good deeds is a thing desirable for its own sake.

Pleasant amusements also are thought to be of this nature; we choose them not for the sake of other things; for we are injured rather than benefited by them, since we are led to neglect our bodies and our property. But most of the people who are deemed happy take refuge in such pastimes, which is the reason why those who are ready-witted at them are highly esteemed at the courts of tyrants; they make themselves pleasant companions in the tyrant's favourite pursuits, and that is the sort of man they want. Now these things are thought to be of the nature of happiness because people in despotic positions spend their leisure in them, but perhaps such people prove nothing; for excellence and thought, from which good activities flow, do not depend on despotic position; nor, if these people, who have never tasted pure and generous pleasure, take refuge in the bodily pleasures, should these for that reason be thought more desirable; for boys, too, think the things that are valued among themselves are the best. It is to be expected, then, that, as different things seem valuable to boys and to men, so they should to bad men and to good. Now, as we have often maintained, those things are both valuable and pleasant which are such to the *good man;* and to each man the activity in accordance with his own state is most desirable, and, therefore, to the good man that which is in accordance with excellence. Happiness, therefore, does not lie in amusement; it would, indeed, be strange if the end were amusement, and one were to take trouble and suffer hardship all one's life in order to amuse oneself. For, in a word, everything that we choose we choose for the sake of something else—except happiness, which is an end. Now to exert oneself and work for the sake of amusement seems silly and utterly childish. But to amuse oneself in order that one may exert oneself, as Anacharsis puts it, seems right; for amusement is a sort of relaxation, and we need relaxation because we cannot work continuously. Relaxation, then, is not an end; for it is taken for the sake of activity.

The happy life is thought to be one of excellence; now an excellent life requires exertion, and does not consist in amusement. And we say that serious things are better than laughable things and those connected with amusement, and that the activity of the better of any two things—whether it be two parts or two men—is the better; but the activity of the better is *ipso facto* superior and more of the nature of happiness. And any chance person—even a slave—can enjoy the bodily pleasures no less than the best man; but no one assigns to a slave a share in happiness—unless he assigns to him also a share in human life. For happiness does not lie in such occupations, but, as we have said before, in excellent activities.

If happiness is activity in accordance with excellence, it is reasonable that it should be in accordance with the highest excellence; and this will be that of the best thing in us. Whether it be intellect or something else that is this element which is thought to be our natural ruler and guide and to take thought of things noble and divine, whether it be itself also divine or only the most divine element in us, the activity of this in accordance with its proper excellence will be complete happiness. That this activity is contemplative we have already said.

Now this would seem to be in agreement both with what we said before and with the truth. For this activity is the best (since not only is intellect the best thing in us, but the objects of intellect are the best of knowable objects); and secondly, it is the most continuous, since we can contemplate truth more continuously than we can *do* anything. And we think happiness has pleasure mingled with it, but the activity of wisdom is admittedly the pleasantest of excellent activities; at all events philosophy is thought to offer pleasures marvellous for their purity and their enduringness, and it is to be expected that those who know will pass their time more pleasantly than those who inquire. And the self-sufficiency that is spoken of must belong most to the contemplative activity. For while a wise man, as well as a just man and the rest, needs the necessaries of life, when they are sufficiently equipped with things of that sort the just man needs people towards whom and with whom he shall act justly, and the temperate man, the brave man, and each of the others is in the same case, but the wise man, even when by himself, can contemplate truth, and the better the wiser he is; he can perhaps do so better if he has fellow-workers, but still he is the most self-sufficient. And this activity alone would seem to be loved for its own sake; for nothing arises from it apart from the contemplating, while from practical activities we gain more or less apart from the action. And happiness is thought to depend on leisure; for we are busy that we may have leisure, and make war that we may live in peace. Now the activity of the practical excellences is exhibited in political or military affairs, but the actions concerned with these seem to be unleisurely. Warlike actions are completely so (for no one chooses to be at war, or provokes war, for the sake of being at war; any one would seem absolutely murderous if he were to make enemies of his friends in order to bring about battle and slaughter); but the action of the statesman is also unleisurely, and—apart from the political action itself—aims at despotic power and honours, or at all events happiness, for him and his fellow citizens—a happiness different from political action, and evidently sought as being different. So if among excellent actions political and military actions are distinguished by nobility and greatness, and these are unleisurely and aim at an end and are not desirable for their own sake, but the activity of intellect, which is contemplative, seems both to be superior in worth and to aim at no end beyond itself, and to have its pleasure proper to itself (and this augments the activity), and the self-sufficiency, leisureliness, unweariedness (so far as this is possible for man), and all the other attributes ascribed to the blessed man are evidently those connected with this activity, it follows that this will be the complete happiness of man, if it be allowed a complete term of life (for none of the attributes of happiness is *in*complete).

But such a life would be too high for man; for it is not in so far as he is man that he will live so, but in so far as something divine is present in him; and by so much as this is superior to our composite nature is its activity superior to that which is the exercise of the other kind of excellence. If intellect is divine, then, in comparison with man, the life according to it is divine in comparison with human life. But we must not follow those who advise us, being men, to think of human things, and, being mortal, of mortal things, but must, so far as we can, make ourselves immortal, and strain every nerve to live in accordance with the best thing in us; for even if it be small in bulk, much more does it in power and worth surpass everything. This would seem, too, to be each man himself, since it is the authoritative and better part of him. It would be strange, then, if he were to choose not the life of himself but that of something else. And what we said before will apply now; that which is proper to each thing is by nature best and most pleasant for each thing; for man, therefore, the life according to intellect is best and pleasantest, since intellect more than anything else *is* man. This life therefore is also the happiest.

But in a secondary degree the life in accordance with the other kind of excellence is happy; for the activities in accordance with this befit our human estate. Just and brave acts, and other excellent acts, we do in relation to each other, observing what is proper to each with regard to contracts and services and all manner of actions and with regard to passions; and all of these seem to be human. Some of them seem even to arise from the body, and excellence of character to be in many ways bound up with the passions. Practical wisdom, too, is linked to excellence of character, and this to practical wisdom, since the principles of practical wisdom are in accordance with the moral excellences and rightness in the moral excellences is in accordance with practical wisdom. Being connected with the passions also, the moral excellences must belong to our composite nature; and the excellences of our composite nature are human; so, therefore, are the life and the happiness which correspond to these. The excellence of the intellect is a thing apart; we must be content to say this much about it, for to describe it precisely is a task greater than our purpose requires. It would seem, however, also to need external equipment but little, or less than moral excellence does. Grant that both need the necessaries, and do so equally, even if the statesman's work is the more concerned with the body and things of that sort; for there will be little difference there; but in what they need for the exercise of their activities there will be much difference. The liberal man will need money for the doing of his liberal deeds, and the just man too will need it for the returning of services (for wishes are hard to discern, and even people who are not just pretend to wish to act justly); and the brave man will need power if he is to accomplish any of the acts that correspond to his excellence, and the temperate man will need opportunity; for how else is either he or any of the others to be recognized? It is debated, too, whether the choice or the deed is more essential to excellence, which is assumed to involve both; it is surely clear that its completion involves both; but for deeds many things are needed, and more, the greater and nobler the deeds are. But the man who is contemplating the truth needs no such thing, at least with a view to the exercise of his activity; indeed they are, one may say, even hindrances, at all events to his contemplation; but in so far as he is a man and lives with a number of people, he chooses to do excellent acts; he will therefore need such aids to living a human life.

But that complete happiness is a contemplative activity will appear from the following consideration as well. We assume the gods to be above all other beings blessed and happy; but what sort of actions must we assign to them? Acts of justice? Will not the gods seem absurd if they make contracts and return deposits, and so on? Acts of a brave man, then, confronting dangers and running risks because it is noble to do so? Or liberal acts? To whom will they give? It will be strange if they are really to have money or anything of the kind. And what would their temperate acts be? Is not such praise tasteless, since they have no bad appetites? If we were to run through them all, the circumstances of action would be found trivial and unworthy of gods. Still, every one supposes that they *live* and therefore that they are active; we cannot suppose them to sleep like Endymion. Now if you take away from a living being action, and still more production, what is left but contemplation? Therefore the activity of God, which surpasses all others in blessedness, must be contemplative; and of human activities, therefore, that which is most akin to this must be most of the nature of happiness.

This is indicated, too, by the fact that the other animals have no share in happiness, being completely deprived of such activity. For while the whole life of the gods is blessed, and that of men too in so far as some likeness of such activity belongs to them, none of the other animals is happy, since they in no way share in contemplation. Happiness extends, then, just so far as contemplation does, and those to whom contemplation more fully belongs are more truly happy, not accidentally, but in virtue of the contemplation; for this is in itself precious. Happiness, therefore, must be some form of contemplation.

PLEASURE

Letter to Menoeceus

Epicurus

Epicurus to Menoeceus, greeting.

Let no young man delay the study of philosophy, and let no old man become weary of it: for it is never too early nor too late to care for the well-being of the soul. The man who says that the season for this study has not yet come or is already past is like the man who says it is too early or too late for happiness. Therefore, both the young and the old should study philosophy, the former so that as he grows old he may still retain the happiness of youth in his pleasant memories of the past, the latter so that although he is old he may at the same time be young by virtue of his fearlessness of the future. We must therefore study the means of securing happiness, since if we have it we have everything, but if we lack it we do everything in order to gain it.

Practice and study without ceasing that which I was always teaching you, being assured that these are the first principles of the good life. After accepting god as the immortal and blessed being depicted by popular opinion, do not ascribe to him anything in addition that is alien to immortality or foreign to blessedness, but rather believe about him whatever can uphold his blessed immortality. The gods do indeed exist, for our perception of them is clear; but they are not such as the crowd imagines them to be, for most men do not retain the picture of the gods that they first receive. It is not the man who destroys the gods of popular belief who is impious, but he who describes the gods in the terms accepted by the many. For the opinions of the many about the gods are not perceptions but false suppositions. According to these popular suppositions, the gods send great evils to the wicked, great blessings [to the righteous], for they, being always well disposed to their own virtues, approve those who are like themselves, regarding as foreign all that is different.

Accustom yourself to the belief that death is of no concern to us, since all good and evil lie in sensation and sensation ends with death. Therefore the true belief that death is nothing to us makes a mortal life happy, not by adding to it an infinite time, but by taking away the desire for immortality. For there is no reason why the man who is thoroughly assured that there is nothing to fear in death should find anything to fear in life. So, too, he is foolish who says that he fears death, not because it will be painful when it comes, but because the anticipation of it is painful; for that which is no burden when it is present gives pain to no purpose when it is anticipated. Death, the most dreaded of evils, is therefore of no concern to us; for while we exist death is not present, and when death is present we no longer exist. It is therefore nothing either to the living or to the dead since it is not present to the living, and the dead no longer are.

But men in general sometimes flee death as the greatest of evils, sometimes [long for it] as a relief from [the evils] of life. [The wise man neither renounces life] nor fears its end; for living does not offend him, nor does he suppose that not to live is in any way evil. As he does not choose the food that is most in quantity but that which is most pleasant, so he does not seek the enjoyment of the longest life but of the happiest.

He who advises the young man to live well, the old man to die well, is foolish, not only because life is desirable, but also because the art of living well and the art of dying well are one. Yet much worse is he who says that it is well not to have been born, but once born, be swift to pass through Hades' gates. If a man says this and really believes it, why does he not depart from life? Certainly the means are at hand for doing so if this really be his firm conviction. If he says it in mockery, he is regarded as a fool among those who do not accept his teaching.

Remember that the future is neither ours nor wholly not ours, so that we may neither count on it as sure to come nor abandon hope of it as certain not to be.

You must consider that of the desires some are natural, some are vain, and of those that are natural, some are necessary, others only natural. Of the necessary desires, some are necessary for happiness, some for the ease of the body, some for life itself. The man who has a perfect knowledge of this will know how to make his every choice or rejection tend toward gaining health of body and peace [of mind], since this is the final end of the blessed life. For to gain this end, namely freedom from pain and fear, we do everything. When once this condition is reached, all the storm of the soul is stilled, since the creature need make no move in search of anything that is lacking, nor seek after anything else to make complete the welfare of the soul and the body. For we only feel the lack of pleasure when from its absence we suffer pain: [but when we do not suffer pain] we no longer are in need of pleasure. For this reason we say that pleasure is the beginning and the end of the blessed life. We recognize pleasure as the first and natural good; starting from pleasure we accept or reject: and we return to this as we judge every good thing, trusting this feeling of pleasure as our guide.

For the very reason that pleasure is the chief and the natural good, we do not choose every pleasure, but there are times when we pass by pleasures if they are outweighed by the hardships that follow; and many pains we think better than pleasures when a greater pleasure will come to us once we have undergone the long-continued pains. Every pleasure is a good since it has a nature akin to ours; nevertheless, not every pleasure is to be chosen. Just so, every pain is an evil, yet not every pain is of a nature to be avoided on all occasions. By measuring and by looking at advantages and disadvantages, it is proper to decide all these things; for under certain circumstances we treat the good as evil, and again, the evil as good.

We regard self-sufficiency as a great good, not so that we may enjoy only a few things, but so that, if we do not have many, we may be satisfied with the few, being firmly persuaded that they take the greatest pleasure in luxury who regard it as least needed, and that everything that is natural is easily provided, while vain pleasures are hard to obtain. Indeed, simple sauces bring a pleasure equal to that of lavish banquets if once the pain due to need is removed; and bread and water give the greatest pleasure when one who is in need consumes them. To be accustomed to simple and plain living is conducive to health and makes a man ready for the necessary tasks of life. It also makes us more ready for the enjoyment of luxury if at intervals we chance to meet with it, and it renders us fearless against fortune.

When we say that pleasure is the end, we do not mean the pleasure of the profligate or that which depends on physical enjoyment—as some think who do not understand our teachings, disagree with them, or give them an evil interpretation—but by pleasure we mean the state wherein the body is free from pain and the mind from anxiety. Neither continual drinking and dancing, nor sexual love, nor the enjoyment of fish and whatever else the luxurious table offers brings about the pleasant life; rather, it is produced by the reason which is sober, which examines the motive for every choice and rejection, and which drives away all those opinions through which the greatest tumult lays hold of the mind.

Of all this the beginning and the chief good is prudence. For this reason prudence is more precious than philosophy itself. All the other virtues spring from it. It teaches that it is not possible to live pleasantly without at the same time living prudently, nobly, and justly, [nor to live prudently, nobly, and justly] without living pleasantly; for the virtues have grown up in close union with the pleasant life, and the pleasant life cannot be separated from the virtues.

Whom then do you believe to be superior to the prudent man: he who has reverent opinions about the gods, who is wholly without fear of death, who has discovered what is the highest good in life and understands that the highest point in what is good is easy to reach and hold and that the extreme of evil is limited either in time or in suffering and who laughs at that which some have set up as the ruler of all things, [Necessity? He thinks that the chief power of decision lies within us, although some things come about by necessity,] some by chance, and some by our own wills; for he sees that necessity is irresponsible and chance uncertain, but that our actions are subject to no power. It is for this reason that our actions merit praise or blame. It would be better to accept the myth about the gods than to be a slave to the determinism of the physicists; for the myth hints at a hope for grace through honors paid to the gods, but the necessity of determinism is inescapable. Since the prudent man does not, as do many, regard chance as a god (for the gods do nothing in disorderly fashion) or as an unstable cause [of all things], he believes that chance does [not] give man good and evil to make his life happy or miserable, but that it does provide opportunities for great good or evil. Finally, he thinks it better to meet misfortune while acting with reason than to happen upon good fortune while acting senselessly; for it is better that what has been well-planned in our actions [should fail than that what has been ill-planned] should gain success by chance.

Meditate on these and like precepts, by day and by night, alone or with a likeminded friend. Then never, either awake or asleep, will you be dismayed; but you will live like a god among men; for life amid immortal blessings is in no way like the life of a mere mortal.

Philosophy in the Bedroom

The Marquis de Sade

I suppose Eugénie is sufficiently disabused on the score of religious errors to be intimately persuaded that sporting with the objects of fools' piety can have no sort of consequence. Sacrilegious fancies have so little substance to them that indeed they cannot heat any but those very youthful minds gladdened by any rupture of restraint; 'tis here a kind of petty vindictiveness which fires the imagination and which, very probably, can provoke a moment or two of enjoyment; but these delights, it would seem to me, must become insipid and cold when one is of an age to understand and to be convinced of the nullity, of the objects of which the idols we jeer at are but meager likenesses. The profanation of relics, the images of saints, the host, the crucifix, all that, in the philosopher's view can amount to no more than the degradation of a pagan statue. Once your scorn has condemned those execrable baubles, you must leave them to contempt, and forget them; 'tis not wise to preserve anything for all that but blasphemy, not that blasphemy has much meaning, for as of the moment

God does not exist, what's the use of insulting his name? but it is essential to pronounce hard and foul words during pleasure's intoxication, and the language of blasphemy very well serves the imagination. Be utterly unsparing; be lavish in your expressions; they must scandalize to the last degree; for 'tis sweet to scandalize: causing scandal flatters one's pride, and though this be a minor triumph, 'tis not to be disdained; I say it openly, Mesdames, such is one of my secret delights: few are the moral pleasures which more actively affect my imagination. . . .

The libertine details of masculine passions, Madame, have little therein to provide suitable stuff for the instruction of a girl who, like Eugénie, is not destined for the whoring profession; she will marry and, such being the hypothesis, one may stake ten to one on it, her husband will have none of those inclinations; however, were he to have them, her wiser conduct is readily to be described: much gentleness, a readiness ever to comply, good humor; on the other hand, much deceit and ample but covert compensation: those few words contain it all. However, were you, Eugénie, to desire some analysis of men's preferences when they resort to libertinage, we might, in order most lucidly to examine the question, generally reduce those tastes to three: *sodomy, sacrilegious fancies,* and *penchants to cruelty.* The first of these passions is universal today; to what we have already said upon it, we shall join a few choice reflections. It divides into two classes, active and passive: the man who embuggers, be it a boy, be it a woman, acquits himself of an active sodomization; he is a passive sodomite when he has himself buggered. . . .

Cruel pleasures comprise the third sort we promised to analyze. This variety is today exceedingly common amongst men, and here is the argument they employ to justify them: we wish to be roused, stirred, they say, 'tis the aim of every man who pursues pleasure, and we would be moved by the most active means. Taking our departure from this point, it is not a question of knowing whether our proceedings please or displease the object that serves us, it is purely a question of exposing our nervous system to the most violent possible shock; now, there is no doubt that we are much more keenly affected by pain than by pleasure: the reverberations that result in us when the sensation of pain is produced in others will essentially be of a more vigorous character, more incisive, will more energetically resound in us, will put the animal spirits more violently into circulation and these, directing themselves toward the nether regions by the retrograde motion essential to them, instantly will ignite the organs of voluptuousness and dispose them to pleasure. Pleasure's effects, in women, are always uncertain; often disappointing; it is, furthermore, very difficult for an old or an ugly man to produce them. When it does happen that they are produced, they are feeble, and the nervous concussions fainter; hence, pain must be preferred, for pain's telling effects cannot deceive, and its vibrations are more powerful. But, one may object to men infatuated by this mania, this pain is afflictive to one's fellow; is it charitable to do others ill for the sake of delighting oneself? In answer thereto, the rascals reply that, accustomed in the pleasure-taking act to thinking exclusively of themselves and accounting others as nothing, they are persuaded that it is entirely reasonable, in accordance with natural impulses, to prefer what they feel to what they do not feel. What, they dare ask, what do these pains occasioned in others do to us? Hurt us? No; on the contrary, we have just demonstrated that from their production there results a sensation delightful to us. For what reason then ought we go softly with an individual who feels one thing while we feel another? Why should we spare him a torment that will cost us never a tear, when it is certain that from this suffering a very great pleasure for us will be born? Have we ever felt a single natural impulse advising us to prefer others to ourselves, and is each of us not alone, and for himself in this world? 'Tis a very false tone you use when you speak to us of this Nature which you interpret as telling us not to do to others what we would not have done to us; such stuff never came but from the lips of men, and weak men. Never does a strong man take it into his head to speak that language. They were the first Christians who, daily persecuted on account of their ridiculous doctrine, used to cry at whosoever chose to hear: "Don't burn us, don't flay us! *Nature says one must not do unto others that which unto oneself one would not have done!*" Fools! How could Nature, who always urges us to delight in ourselves, who never implants in us other instincts, other notions, other inspirations, how could Nature, the next moment, assure us that we must not, however, decide to love ourselves if that might cause others pain? Ah! believe me, Eugénie, believe me, Nature, mother to us all, never speaks to us save of ourselves; nothing has more of the egoistic than her message, and what we recognize most clearly therein is the immutable and sacred counsel: prefer thyself, love thyself, no matter at whose expense. But the others, they say to you, may avenge themselves. . . . Let them! the mightier will vanquish; he will be right. Very well, there it is, the primitive state of perpetual strife and destruction for which Nature's hand created us, and within which alone it is of advantage to her that we remain.

Thus, my dear Eugénie, is the manner of these persons' arguing, and from my experience and studies I may add thereunto that cruelty, very far from being a vice, is the first sentiment Nature injects in us all. The infant breaks his toy, bites his nurse's breast, strangles his canary long before he is able to reason; cruelty is stamped in animals, in whom, as I think I have said, Nature's laws are more emphatically to be read than in ourselves; cruelty exists amongst savages, so much nearer to Nature than civilized men are; absurd then to maintain cruelty is a consequence of depravity. I repeat, the doctrine is false. Cruelty is natural.

Hedonism

J. J. C. Smart

Let us consider Mill's contention that it is better to be Socrates dissatisfied than a fool satisfied.[1] Mill holds that pleasure is not to be our sole criterion for evaluating consequences: the state of mind of Socrates might be less pleasurable than that of the fool, but, according to Mill, Socrates would be happier than the fool. . . .

A man who enjoys pushpin is likely eventually to become bored with it, whereas the man who enjoys poetry is likely to retain this interest throughout his life. Moreover

---

[1] *Utilitarianism*, p. 9. The problem of the unhappy sage and the happy fool is cleverly stated in Voltaire's 'Histoire d'un bon Bramin', *Choix de Contes*, edited with an introduction and notes by F. C. Green (Cambridge University Press, London, 1951), pp. 245–7.

the reading of poetry may develop imagination and sensitivity, and so as a result of his interest in poetry a man may be able to do more for the happiness of others than if he had played pushpin and let his brain deteriorate. In short, both for the man immediately concerned and for others, the pleasures of poetry, are, to use Bentham's word, more *fecund* than those of pushpin.

Perhaps, then, our preference for poetry, over pushpin is not one of intrinsic value, but is merely one of extrinsic value. Perhaps strictly in itself and at a particular moment, a contented sheep is as good as a contented philosopher. However it is hard to agree to this. If we did we should have to agree that the human population ought ideally to be reduced by contraceptive methods and the sheep population more than correspondingly increased. Perhaps just so many humans should be left as could keep innumerable millions of placid sheep in contented idleness and immunity from depredations by ferocious animals. Indeed if a contented idiot is as good as a contented philosopher, and if a contented sheep is as good as a contented idiot, then a contented fish is as good as a contented sheep, and a contented beetle is as good as a contented fish. Where shall we stop?

Maybe we have gone wrong in talking of pleasure as though it were no more than contentment. Contentment consists roughly in relative absence of unsatisfied desires; pleasure is perhaps something more positive and consists in a balance between absence of unsatisfied desires and presence of satisfied desires. We might put the difference in this way: pure unconsciousness would be a limiting case of contentment, but not of pleasure. A stone has no unsatisfied desires, but then it just has no desires. Nevertheless, this consideration will not resolve the disagreement between Bentham and Mill. No doubt a dog has as intense a desire to discover rats as the philosopher has to discover the mysteries of the universe. Mill would wish to say that the pleasures of the philosopher were more valuable intrinsically than those of the dog, however intense these last might be.

It appears, then, that many of us may well have a preference not only for enjoyment as such but for certain sorts of enjoyment. And this goes for many of the humane and beneficent readers whom I am addressing. I suspect that they too have an intrinsic preference for the more complex and intellectual pleasures. . . . Even the most avid television addict probably enjoys solving practical problems connected with his car, his furniture, or his garden. However unintellectual he might be, he would certainly resent the suggestion that he should, if it were possible, change places with a contented sheep, or even a lively and happy dog. Nevertheless, when all is said and done, we must not disguise the fact that disagreements in ultimate attitude are possible between those who like Mill have, and those who like Bentham have not, an intrinsic preference for the 'higher' pleasures. However, it is possible for two people to disagree about ultimate ends and yet agree in practice about what ought to be done. . . .

This [agreement in practice] need not always be so. Some years ago two psychologists, Olds and Milner, carried out some experiments with rats.[2] Through the skull of each rat they inserted an electrode. These electrodes penetrated to various regions of

---

[2] James Olds and Peter Milner, 'Positive reinforcement produced by electrical stimulation of the septal area and other regions of the rat brain', *Journal of Comparative and Physiological Psychology* 47 (1954) 419–27. James Olds, 'A preliminary mapping of electrical reinforcing effect in the rat brain', *ibid.* 49 (1956) 281–5. I. J. Good has also used these results of Olds and Milner in order to discuss ethical hedonism. See his 'A problem for the hedonist', in I. J. Good (ed.). *The Scientist Speculates* (Heinemann, London, 1962). Good takes the possibility of this sort of thing to provide a *reductio ad absurdum* of hedonism.

the brain. In the case of some of these regions the rat showed behaviour characteristics of pleasure when a current was passed from the electrode, in others they seemed to show pain, and in others the stimulus seemed neutral. That a stimulus was pleasure-giving was shown by the fact that the rat would learn to pass the current himself by pressing a lever. He would neglect food and make straight for this lever and start stimulating himself. In some cases he would sit there pressing the lever every few seconds for hours on end. This calls up a pleasant picture of the voluptuary of the future, a bald-headed man with a number of electrodes protruding from his skull, one to give the physical pleasure of sex, one for that of eating, one for that of drinking, and so on. Now is this the sort of life that all our ethical planning should culminate in? A few hours' work a week, automatic factories, comfort and security from disease, and hours spent at a switch, continually electrifying various regions of one's brain? Surely not. Men were made for higher things, one can't help wanting to say, even though one knows that men weren't made for anything, but are the product of evolution by natural selection.

It might be said that the objection to continual sensual stimulation of the above sort is that though it would be pleasant in itself it would be infecund of future pleasures. This is often so with the ordinary sensual pleasures. . . . Maybe if everyone became an electrode operator people would lose interest in everything else and the human race would die out.

Suppose, however, that the facts turned out otherwise: that a man could (and would) do his full share of work in the office or the factory and come back in the evening to a few hours' contented electrode work, without bad aftereffects. This would be his greatest pleasure, and the pleasure would be so great intrinsically and so easily repeatable that its lack of fecundity would not matter. Indeed perhaps by this time human arts, such as medicine, engineering, agriculture and architecture will have been brought to a pitch of perfection sufficient to enable most of the human race to spend most of its time electrode operating, without compensating pains of starvation, disease and squalor. Would this be a satisfactory state of society? Would this be the millennium towards which we have been striving? Surely the pure hedonist would have to say that it was.

It is time, therefore, that we had another look at the concept of happiness. Should we say that the electrode operator was really happy? This is a difficult question to be clear about, because the concept of happiness is a tricky one. But whether we should call the electrode operator 'happy' or not, there is no doubt (a) that he would be *contented* and (b) that he would be *enjoying himself.*

Perhaps a possible reluctance to call the electrode operator 'happy' might come from the following circumstance. The electrode operator might be perfectly contented, might perfectly enjoy his electrode operating, and might not be willing to exchange his lot for any other. And we ourselves, perhaps, once we became electrode operators too, could become perfectly contented and satisfied. But nevertheless, as we are now, we just do not want to become electrode operators. We want other things, perhaps to write a book or get into a cricket team. If someone said 'from tomorrow onwards you are going to be forced to be an electrode operator' we should not be pleased. Maybe from tomorrow onwards, once the electrode work had started, we should be perfectly contented, but we are not contented now at the prospect. We are not satisfied at being told that we would be in a certain state from tomorrow onwards, even though we may know that from tomorrow onwards we should be perfectly satisfied. . . .

This, I think, explains part of our hesitancy about whether to call the electrode operator 'happy'. The notion of happiness ties up with that of contentment: to be fairly happy at least involves being fairly contented, though it involves something more as well. Though we should be contented when we became electrode operators we are not contented now with the prospect that we should become electrode operators. Similarly if Socrates had become a fool he might thereafter have been perfectly contented. Nevertheless if beforehand he had been told that he would in the future become a fool he would have been even more dissatisfied than in fact he was. This is part of the trouble about the dispute between Bentham and Mill. The case involves the possibility of (a) our being contented if we are in a certain state, and (b) our being contented at the prospect of being so contented. Normally situations in which we should be contented go along with our being contented at the prospect of our getting into such situations. In the case of the electrode operator and in that of Socrates and the fool we are pulled two ways at once.

Now to call a person 'happy' is to say more than that he is contented for most of the time, or even that he frequently enjoys himself and is rarely discontented or in pain. It is, I think, in part to express a favourable attitude to the idea of such a form of contentment and enjoyment. That is, for A to call B 'happy', A must be contented at the prospect of B being in his present state of mind and at the prospect of A himself, should the opportunity arise, enjoying that sort of state of mind. That is, 'happy' is a word which is mainly descriptive (tied to the concepts of contentment and enjoyment) but which is also partly evaluative. It is because Mill approves of the 'higher' pleasures, e.g., intellectual pleasures, so much more than he approves of the more simple and brutish pleasures, that, quite apart from consequences and side effects, he can pronounce the man who enjoys the pleasures of philosophical discourse as 'more happy' than the man who gets enjoyment from pushpin or beer drinking.

The word 'happy' is not wholly evaluative, for there would be something absurd, as opposed to merely unusual, in calling a man who was in pain, or who was not enjoying himself, or who hardly ever enjoyed himself, or who was in a more or less permanent state of intense dissatisfaction, a 'happy' man. For a man to be happy he must, as a minimal condition, be fairly contented and moderately enjoying himself for much of the time. Once this minimal condition is satisfied we can go on to evaluate various types of contentment and enjoyment and to grade them in terms of happiness. Happiness is, of course, a long-term concept in a way that enjoyment is not. We can talk of a man enjoying himself at a quarter past two precisely, but hardly of a man being happy at a quarter past two precisely. Similarly we can talk of it raining at a quarter past two precisely, but hardly about it being a wet climate at a quarter past two precisely. But happiness involves enjoyment at various times, just as a wet climate involves rain at various times.

To be enjoying oneself, Ryle once suggested, is to be doing what you want to be doing and not to be wanting to do anything else,[3] or, more accurately, we might say that one enjoys oneself the more one wants to be doing what one is in fact doing and the less one wants to be doing anything else. A man will not enjoy a round of golf if

---

[3]Gilbert Ryle, *The Concept of Mind* (Hutchison, London, 1949), p. 108.

(a) he does not particularly want to play golf, or (b) though he wants to play golf there is something else he wishes he were doing at the same time, such as buying the vegetables for his wife, filling in his income tax forms, or listening to a lecture on philosophy.

The hedonistic ideal would then appear to reduce to a state of affairs in which each person is enjoying himself. Since, as we noted, a dog may, as far as we can tell, enjoy chasing a rat as much as a philosopher or a mathematician may enjoy solving a problem, we must, if we adopt the purely hedonistic position, defend the higher pleasures on account of their fecundity. And that might not turn out to be a workable defence in a world made safe for electrode operators. . . .

So much for the issue between Bentham and Mill. What about that between Mill and Moore? Could a pleasurable state of mind have no intrinsic value at all, or perhaps even a *negative* intrinsic value.[4] Are there pleasurable states of mind towards which we have an unfavourable attitude, even though we disregard their consequences. In order to decide this question let us imagine a universe consisting of one sentient being only, who falsely believes that there are other sentient beings and that they are undergoing exquisite torment. So far from being distressed by the thought, he takes a great delight in these imagined sufferings. Is this better or worse than a universe containing no sentient being at all? Is it worse, again, than a universe containing only one sentient being with the same beliefs as before but who sorrows at the imagined tortures of his fellow creatures? I suggest, as against Moore, that the universe containing the deluded sadist is the preferable one. After all he is happy, and since there is no other sentient being, what harm can he do? Moore would nevertheless agree that the sadist was happy, and this shows how happiness, though partly an evaluative concept, is also partly not an evaluative concept.

It is difficult, I admit, not to feel an immediate repugnance at the thought of the deluded sadist. If throughout our childhood we have been given an electric shock whenever we had tasted cheese, then cheese would have become immediately distasteful to us. Our repugnance to the sadist arises, naturally enough, because in our universe sadists invariably do harm. If we lived in a universe in which by some extraordinary laws of psychology a sadist was always confounded by his own knavish tricks and invariably did a great deal of good, then we should feel better disposed towards the sadistic mentality. Even if we could de-condition ourselves from feeling an immediate repugnance to a sadist (as we could de-condition ourselves from a repugnance to cheese by going through a course in which the taste of cheese was invariably associated with a pleasurable stimulus) language might make it difficult for us to distinguish an extrinsic distaste for sadism, founded on our distaste for the consequences of sadism, from an immediate distaste for sadism as such. Normally when we call a thing 'bad' we mean indifferently to express a dislike for it in itself or to express a dislike for what it leads to. When a state of mind is sometimes extrinsically good and sometimes extrinsically bad, we find it easy to distinguish between our intrinsic and extrinsic preferences for instances of it, but when a state of mind is always, or almost always, extrinsically bad, it is easy for us to confuse an extrinsic distaste for it with an intrinsic one. If we allow for this, it does not seem so absurd to hold that there are no pleasures which are intrinsically bad.

[4]Cf. G. E. Moore, *Principia Ethica*, pp. 209–10.

POWER

What Is Noble?

Friedrich Nietzsche

257. Every elevation of the type "man," has hitherto been the work of an aristocratic society—and so will it always be—a society believing in a long scale of gradations of rank and differences of worth among human beings, and requiring slavery in some form or other. Without the *pathos of distance,* such as grows out of the incarnated difference of classes, out of the constant out-looking and down-looking of the ruling caste on subordinates and instruments, and out of their equally constant practice of obeying and commanding, of keeping down and keeping at a distance—that other more mysterious pathos could never have arisen, the longing for an ever new widening of distance within the soul itself, the formation of ever higher, rarer, further, more extended, more comprehensive states, in short, just the elevation of the type "man," the continued "self-surmounting of man," to use a moral formula in a supermoral sense. To be sure, one must not resign oneself to any humanitarian illusions about the history of the origin of an aristocratic society (that is to say, of the preliminary condition for the elevation of the type "man"): the truth is hard. Let us acknowledge unprejudicedly how every higher civilisation hitherto has *originated!* Men with a still natural nature, barbarians in every terrible sense of the word, men of prey, still in possession of unbroken strength of will and desire for power, threw themselves upon weaker, more moral, more peaceful races (perhaps trading or cattle-rearing communities), or upon old mellow civilisations in which the final vital force was flickering out in brilliant fireworks of wit and depravity. At the commencement, the noble caste was always the barbarian caste: their superiority did not consist first of all in their physical, but in their psychical power—they were more *complete* men (which at every point also implies the same as "more complete beasts").

258. Corruption—as the indication that anarchy threatens to break out among the instincts, and that the foundation of the emotions, called "life," is convulsed—is something radically different according to the organisation in which it manifests itself. When, for instance, an aristocracy like that of France at the beginning of the Revolution, flung away its privileges with sublime disgust and sacrificed itself to an excess of its moral sentiments, it was corruption:—it was really only the closing act of the corruption which had existed for centuries, by virtue of which that aristocracy had abdicated step by step its lordly prerogatives and lowered itself to a *function* of royalty (in the end even to its decoration and parade-dress). The essential thing, however, in a good and healthy aristocracy is that it should *not* regard itself as a function either of the kingship or the commonwealth, but as the *significance* and highest justification thereof—that it should therefore accept with a good conscience the sacrifice of a

legion of individuals, who, *for its sake,* must be suppressed and reduced to imperfect men, to slaves and instruments. Its fundamental belief must be precisely that society is *not* allowed to exist for its own sake, but only as a foundation and scaffolding, by means of which a select class of beings may be able to elevate themselves to their higher duties, and in general to a higher *existence:* like those sun-seeking climbing plants in Java—they are called *Sipo Matador,*—which encircle an oak so long and so often with their arms, until at last, high above it, but supported by it, they can unfold their tops in the open light, and exhibit their happiness.

259. To refrain mutually from injury, from violence, from exploitation, and put one's will on a par with that of others: this may result in a certain rough sense in good conduct among individuals when the necessary conditions are given (namely, the actual similarity of the individuals in amount of force and degree of worth, and their co-relation within one organisation). As soon, however, as one wished to take this principle more generally, and if possible even as *the fundamental principle of society,* it would immediately disclose what it really is—namely, a Will to the *denial* of life, a principle of dissolution and decay. Here one must think profoundly to the very basis and resist all sentimental weakness: life itself is *essentially* appropriation, injury, conquest of the strange and weak, suppression, severity, obtrusion of peculiar forms, incorporation, and at the least, putting it mildest, exploitation;—but why should one for ever use precisely these words on which for ages a disparaging purpose has been stamped? Even the organisation within which, as was previously supposed, the individuals treat each other as equal—it takes place in every healthy aristocracy—must itself, if it be a living and not a dying organisation, do all that towards other bodies, which the individuals within it refrain from doing to each other; it will have to be the incarnated Will to Power, it will endeavour to grow, to gain ground, attract to itself and acquire ascendency—not owing to any morality or immorality, but because it *lives,* and because life *is* precisely Will to Power. On no point, however, is the ordinary consciousness of Europeans more unwilling to be corrected than on this matter; people now rave everywhere, even under the guise of science, about coming conditions of society in which "the exploiting character" is to be absent:—that sounds to my ears as if they promised to invent a mode of life which should refrain from all organic functions. "Exploitation" does not belong to a depraved, or imperfect and primitive society: it belongs to the *nature* of the living being as a primary organic function; it is a consequence of the intrinsic Will to Power, which is precisely the Will to Life.—Granting that as a theory this is a novelty—as a reality it is the *fundamental fact* of all history: let us be so far honest towards ourselves!

260. In a tour through the many finer and coarser moralities which have hitherto prevailed or still prevail on the earth, I found certain traits recurring regularly together, and connected with one another, until finally two primary types revealed themselves to me, and a radical distinction was brought to light. There is *master-morality* and *slave-morality;*—I would at once add, however, that in all higher and mixed civilisations, there are also attempts at the reconciliation of the two moralities; but one finds still oftener the confusion and mutual misunderstanding of them, indeed, sometimes their close juxtaposition—even in the same man, within one soul. The distinctions of moral values have either originated in a ruling caste, pleasantly conscious

of being different from the ruled—or among the ruled class, the slaves and dependents of all sorts. In the first case, when it is the rulers who determine the conception "good," it is the exalted, proud disposition which is regarded as the distinguishing feature, and that which determines the order of rank. The noble type of man separates from himself the beings in whom the opposite of this exalted, proud disposition displays itself: he despises them. Let it at once be noted that in this first kind of morality the antithesis "good" and "bad" means practically the same as "noble" and "despicable";—the antithesis "good" and "*evil*" is of a different origin. The cowardly, the timid, the insignificant, and those thinking merely of narrow utility are despised; moreover, also, the distrustful, with their constrained glances, the self-abasing, the dog-like kind of men who let themselves be abused, the mendicant flatterers, and above all the liars:—it is a fundamental belief of all aristocrats that the common people are untruthful. "We truthful ones"—the nobility in ancient Greece called themselves. It is obvious that everywhere the designations of moral value were at first applied to *men*, and were only derivatively and at a later period applied to *actions*; it is a gross mistake, therefore, when historians of morals start with questions like, "Why have sympathetic actions been praised?" The noble type of man regards *himself* as a determiner of values; he does not require to be approved of; he passes the judgment: "What is injurious to me is injurious in itself"; he knows that it is he himself only who confers honour on things; he is a *creator of values*. He honours whatever he recognises in himself: such morality is self-glorification. In the foreground there is the feeling of plentitude, of power, which seeks to overflow, the happiness of high tension, the consciousness of a wealth which would fain give and bestow:—the noble man also helps the unfortunate, but not—or scarcely—out of pity, but rather from an impulse generated by the superabundance of power. The noble man honours in himself the powerful one, him also who has power over himself, who knows how to speak and how to keep silence, who takes pleasure in subjecting himself to severity and hardness, and has reverence for all that is severe and hard. "Wotan placed a hard heart in my breast," says an old Scandinavian Saga: it is thus rightly expressed from the soul of a proud Viking. Such a type of man is even proud of *not* being made for sympathy; the hero of the Saga therefore adds warningly: "He who has not a hard heart when young, will never have one." The noble and brave who think thus are the furthest removed from the morality which sees precisely in sympathy, or in acting for the good of others, or in *désintéressement*, the characteristic of the moral; faith in oneself, radical enmity and irony toward "selflessness," belong as definitely to noble morality, as do a careless scorn and precaution in presence of sympathy and the "warm heart."—It is the powerful who *know* how to honour, it is their art, their domain for invention. The profound reverence for age and for tradition—all law rests on this double reverence,—the belief and prejudice in favour of ancestors and unfavourable to newcomers, is typical in the morality of the powerful; and if, reversely, men of "modern ideas" believe almost instinctively in "progress" and the "future," and are more and more lacking in respect for old age, the ignoble origin of these "ideas" has complacently betrayed itself thereby. A morality of the ruling class, however, is more especially foreign and irritating to present-day taste in the sternness of its principle that one has duties only to one's equals; that one may act towards beings of a lower rank, towards all that is foreign, just as seems good to one, or "as the heart desires," and in any case "beyond good and evil": it is here that sympathy and similar sentiments can have a place. The ability and obligation to exercise prolonged gratitude and prolonged revenge—both only within the circle of equals,—artfulness in retaliation, *raffinement* of the idea in friendship, a certain necessity to have enemies (as outlets for the emotions of envy, quarrelsomeness, arrogance—in fact, in order to be a good *friend*): all these are typical characteristics of the noble morality, which, as has been pointed out, is not the morality of "modern ideas," and is therefore at present difficult to realise, and also to unearth and disclose.—It is otherwise with the second type of morality, *slave-morality*. Supposing that the abused, the oppressed, the suffering, the unemancipated, the weary, and those uncertain of themselves, should moralise, what will be the common element in their moral estimates? Probably a pessimistic suspicion with regard to the entire situation of man will find expression, perhaps a condemnation of man, together with his situation. The slave has an unfavourable eye for the virtues of the powerful; he has a scepticism and distrust, a *refinement* of distrust of everything "good" that is there honoured—he would fain persuade himself that the very happiness there is not genuine. On the other hand, *those* qualities which serve to alleviate the existence of sufferers are brought into prominence and flooded with light; it is here that sympathy, the kind, helping hand, the warm heart, patience, diligence, humility, and friendliness attain to honour, for here these are the most useful qualities, and almost the only means of supporting the burden of existence. Slave-morality is essentially the morality of utility. Here is the seat of the origin of the famous antithesis "good" and "*evil*":—power and dangerousness are assumed to reside in the evil, a certain dreadfulness, subtlety, and strength, which do not admit of being despised. According to slave-morality, therefore, the "evil" man arouses fear; according to master-morality, it is precisely the "good" man who arouses fear and seeks to arouse it, while the bad man is regarded as the despicable being. The contrast attains its maximum when, in accordance with the logical consequences of slave-morality, a shade of depreciation—it may be slight and well-intentioned—at last attaches itself even to the "good" man of this morality; because, according to the servile mode of thought, the good man must in any case be the *safe* man: he is good-natured, easily deceived, perhaps a little stupid, *un bonhomme*. Everywhere that slave-morality gains the ascendency, language shows a tendency to approximate the significations of the words "good" and "stupid."—A last fundamental difference: the desire for *freedom*, the instinct for happiness and the refinements of the feeling of liberty belong as necessarily to slave-morals and morality, as artifice and enthusiasm in reverence and devotion are the regular symptoms of an aristocratic mode of thinking and estimating.—Hence we can understand without further detail why love *as a passion*—it is our European specialty—must absolutely be of noble origin; as is well known, its invention is due to the Provençal poet-cavaliers, those brilliant ingenious men of the "*gai saber*," to whom Europe owes so much, and almost owes itself.

CLOSE RELATIONSHIPS

Woman's Place in Man's Life Cycle

Carol Gilligan

At a time when efforts are being made to eradicate discrimination between the sexes in the search for social equality and justice, the differences between the sexes are being rediscovered in the social sciences. This discovery occurs when theories formerly considered to be sexually neutral in their scientific objectivity are found instead to reflect a consistent observational and evaluative bias. . . .

The penchant of developmental theorists to project a masculine image, and one that appears frightening to women, goes back at least to Freud (1905), who built his theory of psycho-sexual development around the experiences of the male child that culminate in the Oedipus complex. In the 1920s, Freud struggled to resolve the contradictions posed for his theory by the differences in female anatomy and the different configuration of the young girl's early family relationships. After trying to fit women into his masculine conception, seeing them as envying that which they missed, he came instead to acknowledge, in the strength and persistence of women's pre-Oedipal attachments to their mothers, a developmental difference. He considered this difference in women's development to be responsible for what he saw as women's developmental failure.

Having tied the formation of the superego or conscience to castration anxiety, Freud considered women to be deprived by nature of the impetus for a clear-cut Oedipal resolution. Consequently, women's superego—the heir to the Oedipus complex—was compromised: it was never "so inexorable, so impersonal, so independent of its emotional origins as we require it to be in men." From this observation of difference, that "for women the level of what is ethically normal is different from what it is in men," Freud concluded that women "show less sense of justice than men, that they are less ready to submit to the great exigencies of life, that they are more often influenced in their judgements by feelings of affection or hostility" (1925, pp. 257–258).

Thus a problem in theory became cast as a problem in women's development, and the problem in women's development was located in their experience of relationships. Nancy Chodorow (1974), attempting to account for "the reproduction within each generation of certain general and nearly universal differences that characterize masculine and feminine personality and roles," attributes these differences between the sexes not to anatomy but rather to "the fact that women, universally, are largely responsible for early child care." Because this early social environment differs for and is experienced differently by male and female children, basic sex differences recur in personality development. As a result, "in any given society, feminine personality comes to define itself in relation and connection to other people more than masculine personality does" (pp. 43–44).

In her analysis, Chodorow relies primarily on Robert Stoller's studies which indicate that gender identity, the unchanging core of personality formation, is "with rare exception firmly and irreversibly established for both sexes by the time a child is around three." Given that for both sexes the primary caretaker in the first three years of life is typically female, the interpersonal dynamics of gender identity formation are different for boys and girls. Female identity formation takes place in a context of ongoing relationship since "mothers tend to experience their daughters as more like, and continuous with, themselves." Correspondingly, girls, in identifying themselves as female, experience themselves as like their mothers, thus fusing the experience of attachment with the process of identity formation. In contrast, "mothers experience their sons as a male opposite." and boys, in defining themselves as masculine, separate their mothers from themselves, thus curtailing "their primary love and sense of empathic tie." Consequently, male development entails a "more emphatic individuation and a more defensive firming of experienced ego boundaries." For boys, but not girls, "issues of differentiation have become intertwined with sexual issues" (1978, pp. 150, 166–167).

Writing against the masculine bias of psychoanalytic theory, Chodorow argues that the existence of sex differences in the early experiences of individuation and relationship "does not mean that women have 'weaker' ego boundaries than men or are more prone to psychosis." It means instead that "girls emerge from this period with a basis for 'empathy' built into their primary definition of self in a way that boys do not. . . ."

Consequently, relationships, and particularly issues of dependency, are experienced differently by women and men. For boys and men, separation and individuation are critically tied to gender identity since separation from the mother is essential for the development of masculinity. For girls and women, issues of femininity or feminine identity do not depend on the achievement of separation from the mother or on the progress of individuation. Since masculinity is defined through separation while femininity is defined through attachment, male gender identity is threatened by intimacy while female gender identity is threatened by separation. Thus males tend to have difficulty with relationships, while females tend to have problems with individuation. The quality of embeddedness in social interaction and personal relationships that characterizes women's lives in contrast to men's, however, becomes not only a descriptive difference but also a developmental liability when the milestones of childhood and adolescent development in the psychological literature are markers of increasing separation. Women's failure to separate then becomes by definition a failure to develop.

The sex differences in personality formation that Chodorow describes in early childhood appear during the middle childhood years in studies of children's games. Children's games are considered by George Herbert Mead (1934) and Jean Piaget (1932) as the crucible of social development during the school years. In games, children learn to take the role of the other and come to see themselves through another's eyes. In games, they learn respect for rules and come to understand the ways rules can be made and changed.

Janet Lever (1976) . . . extends and corroborates the observations of Piaget in his study of the rules of the game, where he finds boys becoming through childhood increasingly fascinated with the legal elaboration of rules and the development of fair procedures for adjudicating conflicts, a fascination that, he notes, does not hold for girls. Girls, Piaget observes, have a more "pragmatic" attitude toward rules, "regarding a rule as good as long as the game repaid it" (p. 83). Girls are more tolerant in their attitudes toward rules, more willing to make exceptions, and more easily reconciled to innovations. As a result, the legal sense, which Piaget considers essential to moral development, "is far less developed in little girls than in boys" (p. 77).

The bias that leads Piaget to equate male development with child development also colors Lever's work. The assumption that shapes her discussion of results is that the male model is the better one since it fits the requirements for modern corporate success. In contrast, the sensitivity and care for the feelings of others that girls develop through their play have little market value and can even impede professional success. Lever implies that, given the realities of adult life, if a girl does not want to be left dependent on men, she will have to learn to play like a boy. . . .

Lever concludes that from the games they play, boys learn both the independence and the organizational skills necessary for coordinating the activities of large and diverse groups of people. By participating in controlled and socially approved competitive situations, they learn to deal with competition in a relatively forthright manner—to play with their enemies and to compete with their friends—all in accordance with the rules of the game. In contrast, girls' play tends to occur in smaller, more intimate groups, often the best-friend dyad, and in private places. This play replicates the social pattern of primary human relationships in that its organization is more cooperative. Thus, it points less, in Mead's terms, toward learning to take the role of "the generalized other," less toward the abstraction of human relationships. But it fosters the development of the empathy and sensitivity necessary for taking the role of "the particular other" and points more toward knowing the other as different from the self.

The sex differences in personality formation in early childhood that Chodorow derives from her analysis of the mother-child relationship are thus extended by Lever's observations of sex differences in the play activities of middle childhood. Together these accounts suggest that boys and girls arrive at puberty with a different interpersonal orientation and a different range of social experiences. Yet, since adolescence is considered a crucial time for separation, the period of "the second individuation process" (Blos, 1967), female development has appeared most divergent and thus most problematic at this time. . . .

The problem that female adolescence presents for theorists of human development is apparent in Erikson's scheme. Erikson (1950) charts eight stages of psychosocial development, of which adolescence is the fifth. The task at this stage is to forge a coherent sense of self, to verify an identity that can span the discontinuity of puberty and make possible the adult capacity to love and work. The preparation for the successful resolution of the adolescent identity crisis is delineated in Erikson's description of the crises that characterize the preceding four stages. Although the initial crisis in infancy of "trust versus mistrust" anchors development in the experience of relationship, the task then clearly becomes one of individuation. Erikson's second stage centers on the crisis of "autonomy versus shame and doubt," which marks the walking child's emerging sense of separateness and agency. From there, development goes on through the crisis of "initiative versus guilt," successful resolution of which represents a further move in the direction of autonomy. Next, following the inevitable disappointment of the magical wishes of the Oedipal period, children realize that to compete with their parents, they must first join them and learn to do what they do so well. Thus in the middle childhood years, development turns on the crisis of "industry versus inferiority," as the demonstration of competence becomes critical to the child's developing self-esteem. This is the time when children strive to learn and master the technology of their culture, in order to recognize themselves and to be recognized by others as capable of becoming adults. Next comes adolescence, the celebration of the autonomous, initiating, industrious self through the forging of an identity based on an ideology that can support and justify adult commitments. But about whom is Erikson talking?

Once again it turns out to be the male child. For the female, Erikson (1968) says, the sequence is a bit different. She holds her identity in abeyance as she prepares to attract the man by whose name she will be known, by whose status she will be defined, the man who will rescue her from emptiness and loneliness by filling "the inner space." While for men, identity precedes intimacy and generativity in the optimal cycle of human separation and attachment, for women these tasks seem instead to be fused. Intimacy goes along with identity, as the female comes to know herself as she is known, through her relationships with others.

Yet despite Erikson's observation of sex differences, his chart of life-cycle stages remains unchanged: identity continues to precede intimacy as male experience continues to define his life-cycle conception. But in this male life cycle there is little preparation for the intimacy of the first adult stage. Only the initial stage of trust versus mistrust suggests the type of mutuality that Erickson means by intimacy and generativity and Freud means by genitality. The rest is separateness, with the result that development itself comes to be identified with separation, and attachments appear to be developmental impediments, as is repeatedly the case in the assessment of women. . . .

These observations about sex difference support the conclusion reached by David McClelland (1975) that "sex role turns out to be one of the most important determinants of human behavior; psychologists have found sex differences in their studies from the moment they started doing empirical research." But since it is difficult to say "different" without saying "better" or "worse," since there is a tendency to construct a single scale of measurement, and since that scale has generally been derived from and standardized on the basis of men's interpretations of research data drawn predominantly or exclusively from studies of males, psychologists "have tended to regard male behavior as the 'norm' and female behavior as some kind of deviation from that norm" (p. 81). Thus, when women do not conform to the standards of psychological expectation, the conclusion has generally been that something is wrong with the women.

What Matina Horner (1972) found to be wrong with women was the anxiety they showed about competitive achievement. From the beginning, research on human motivation using the Thematic Apperception Test (TAT) was plagued by evidence of sex differences which appeared to confuse and complicate data analysis. The TAT presents for interpretation an ambiguous cue—a picture about which a story is to be written or a segment of a story that is to be completed. Such stories, in reflecting projective imagination, are considered by psychologists to reveal the ways in which people construe what they perceive, that is, the concepts and interpretations they bring to their experience and thus presumably the kind of sense that they make of their lives. Prior to Horner's work it was clear that women made a different kind or sense than men of situations of competitive achievement, that in some way they saw the situations differently or the situations aroused in them some different response.

On the basis of his studies of men, McClelland divided the concept of achievement motivation into what appeared to be its two logical components, a motive to approach success ("hope success") and a motive to avoid failure ("fear failure"). From her studies of women, Horner identified as a third category the unlikely motivation to avoid success ("fear success"). Women appeared to have a problem with competitive achievement, and that problem seemed to emanate from a perceived conflict between femininity and success, the dilemma of the female adolescent who struggles to integrate her feminine aspirations and the identifications of her early childhood with the more masculine competence she has acquired at school. . . .

Such conflicts about success, however, may be viewed in a different light. Georgia Sassen (1980) suggests that the conflicts expressed by the women might instead indicate "a heightened perception of the 'other side' of competitive success, that is, the great emotional costs at which success achieved through competition is often gained—an understanding which, though confused, indicates some underlying sense that something is rotten in the state in which success is defined as having better grades than everyone else" (p. 15). Sassen points out that Horner found success anxiety to be present in women only when achievement was directly competitive, that is, when one person's success was at the expense of another's failure. . . .

We might on these grounds begin to ask, not why women have conflicts about competitive success, but why men show such readiness to adopt and celebrate a rather narrow vision of success. Remembering Piaget's observation, corroborated by Lever, that boys in their games are more concerned with rules while girls are more concerned with relationships, often at the expense of the game itself—and given Chodorow's conclusion that men's social orientation is positional while women's is personal—we begin to understand why, when "Anne" becomes "John" in Horner's tale of competitive success and the story is completed by men, fear of success tends to disappear. John is considered to have played by the rules and won. He has the *right* to feel good about his success. Confirmed in the sense of his own identity as separate from those who, compared to him, are less competent, his positional sense of self is affirmed. For Anne, it is possible that the position she could obtain by being at the top of her medical school class may not, in fact, be what she wants.

"It is obvious." Virginia Woolf says, "that the values of women differ very often from the values which have been made by the other sex" (1929, p. 76). Yet, she adds. "it is the masculine values that prevail." As a result, women come to question the normality of their feelings and to alter their judgments in deference to the opinion of others. In the nineteenth-century novels written by women, Woolf sees at work "a mind which was slightly pulled from the straight and made to alter its clear vision in deference to external authority." The same deference to the values and opinions of others can be seen in the judgments of twentieth-century women. The difficulty women experience in finding or speaking publicly in their own voices emerges repeatedly in the form of qualification and self-doubt, but also in intimations of a divided judgment, a public assessment and private assessment which are fundamentally at odds.

Yet the deference and confusion that Woolf criticizes in women derive from the values she sees as their strength. Women's deference is rooted not only in their social subordination but also in the substance of their moral concern. Sensitivity to the needs of others and the assumption of responsibility for taking care lead women to attend to voices other than their own and to include in their judgment other points of view. Women's moral weakness, manifest in an apparent diffusion and confusion of judgment, is thus inseparable from women's moral strength, an overriding concern with relationships and responsibilities. The reluctance to judge may itself be indicative of the care and concern for others that infuse the psychology of women's development and are responsible for what is generally seen as problematic in its nature.

Thus women not only define themselves in a context of human relationship but also judge themselves in terms of their ability to care. Women's place in man's life cycle has been that of nurturer, caretaker, and helpmate, the weaver of those networks of relationships on which she in turn relies. But while women have thus taken care of men, men have, in their theories of psychological development, as in their economic arrangements, tended to assume or devalue that care. When the focus on individuation and individual achievement extends into adulthood and maturity is equated with personal autonomy, concern with relationships appears as a weakness of women rather than as a human strength (Miller, 1976).

The discrepancy between womanhood and adulthood is nowhere more evident than in the studies on sex-role stereotypes reported by Broverman, Vogel, Broverman, Clarkson, and Rosenkrantz (1972). The repeated finding of these studies is that the qualities deemed necessary for adulthood—the capacity for autonomous thinking, clear decision-making, and responsible action—are those associated with masculinity and considered undesirable as attributes of the feminine self. The stereotypes suggest a splitting of love and work that relegates expressive capacities to women while placing instrumental abilities in the masculine domain. Yet looked at from a different perspective, these stereotypes reflect a conception of adulthood that is itself out of balance, favoring the separateness of the individual self over connection to others, and leaning more toward an autonomous life of work than toward the interdependence of love and care.

The discovery now being celebrated by men in mid-life of the importance of intimacy, relationships, and care is something that women have known from the beginning. However, because that knowledge in women has been considered "intuitive" or "instinctive," a function of anatomy coupled with destiny, psychologists have neglected to describe its development. In my research, I have found that women's moral development centers on the elaboration of that knowledge and thus delineates a critical line of psychological development in the lives of both of the sexes. The subject of moral development not only provides the final illustration of the reiterative pattern in the observation and assessment of sex differences in the literature on human development, but also indicates more particularly why the nature and significance of women's development has been for so long obscured and shrouded in mystery.

The criticism that Freud makes of women's sense of justice, seeing it as compromised in its refusal of blind impartiality, reappears not only in the work of Piaget but also in that of Kohlberg. While in Piaget's account (1932) of the moral judgment of the child, girls are an aside, a curiosity to whom he devotes four brief entries in an index that omits "boys" altogether because "the child" is assumed to be male, in the research from which Kohlberg derives his theory, females simply do not exist. Kohlberg's (1958, 1981) six stages that describe the development of moral judgment from childhood to adulthood are based empirically on a study of eighty-four boys whose development Kohlberg has followed for a period of over twenty years. Although Kohlberg claims universality for his stage sequence, those groups not included in his original sample rarely reach his higher stages (Edwards, 1975; Holstein, 1976; Simpson, 1974). Prominent among those who thus appear to be deficient in moral development when measured by Kohlberg's scale are women, whose judgments seem to exemplify the third stage of his six-stage sequence. At this stage morality is conceived in interpersonal terms and goodness is equated with helping and pleasing others. This conception of goodness is considered by Kohlberg and Kramer (1969) to be functional in the lives of mature women insofar as their lives take place in the home. Kohlberg and Kramer imply that only if women enter the traditional arena of male activity will they recognize the inadequacy of this moral perspective and progress like men toward higher stages where relationships are subordinated to rules (stage four) and rules to universal principles of justice (stages five and six).

Yet herein lies a paradox, for the very traits that traditionally have defined the "goodness" of women, their care for and sensitivity to the needs of others, are those that mark them as deficient in moral development. In this version of moral development, however, the conception of maturity is derived from the study of men's lives and reflects the importance of individuation in their development. Piaget (1970), challenging the common impression that a developmental theory is built like a pyramid from its base in infancy, points out that a conception of development instead hangs from its vertex of maturity, the point toward which progress is traced. Thus, a change in the definition of maturity does not simply alter the description of the highest stage but recasts the understanding of development, changing the entire account.

When one begins with the study of women and derives developmental constructs from their lives, the outline of a moral conception different from that described by Freud, Piaget, or Kohlberg begins to emerge and informs a different description of development. In this conception, the moral problem arises from conflicting responsibilities rather than from competing rights and requires for its resolution a mode of thinking that is contextual and narrative rather than formal and abstract. This conception of morality as concerned with the activity of care centers moral development around the understanding of responsibility and relationships, just as the conception of morality as fairness ties moral development to the understanding of rights and rules. . . .

Thus it becomes clear why a morality of rights and noninterference may appear frightening to women in its potential justification of indifference and unconcern. At the same time, it becomes clear why, from a male perspective, a morality of responsibility appears inconclusive and diffuse, given its insistent contextual relativism. Women's moral judgments thus elucidate the pattern observed in the description of the developmental differences between the sexes, but they also provide an alternative conception of maturity by which these differences can be assessed and their implications traced. The psychology of women that has consistently been described as distinctive in its greater orientation toward relationships and interdependence implies a more contextual mode of judgment and a different moral understanding. Given the differences in women's conceptions of self and morality, women bring to the life cycle a different point of view and order human experience in terms of different priorities.

The myth of Demeter and Persephone, which McClelland (1975) cites as exemplifying the feminine attitude toward power, was associated with the Eleusinian Mysteries celebrated in ancient Greece for over two thousand years. . . .

Persephone, the daughter of Demeter, while playing in a meadow with her girlfriends, sees a beautiful narcissus which she runs to pick. As she does so, the earth opens and she is snatched away by Hades, who takes her to his underworld kingdom. Demeter, goddess of the earth, so mourns the loss of her daughter that she refuses to allow anything to grow. The crops that sustain life on earth shrivel up, killing men and animals alike, until Zeus takes pity on man's suffering and persuades his brother to return Persephone to her mother. But before she leaves, Persephone eats some pomegranate seeds, which ensures that she will spend part of every year with Hades in the underworld.

The elusive mystery of women's development lies in its recognition of the continuing importance of attachment in the human life cycle. Woman's place in man's life cycle is to protect this recognition while the developmental litany intones the celebration of separation, autonomy, individuation, and natural rights. The myth of Persephone speaks directly to the distortion in this view by reminding us that narcissism leads to death, that the fertility of the earth is in some mysterious way tied to the continuation of the mother-daughter relationship, and that the life cycle itself arises from an alternation between the world of women and that of men. Only when life-cycle theorists divide their attention and begin to live with women as they have lived with men will their vision encompass the experience of both sexes and their theories become correspondingly more fertile

References

Blos, Peter. "The Second Individuation Process of Adolescence." In A. Freud, ed., *The Psychoanalytic Study of the Child*, vol. 22. New York: International Universities Press, 1967.

Broverman, I., Vogel, S., Broverman, D., Clarkson, F., and Rosenkrantz, P. "Sex-role Stereotypes: A Current Appraisal." *Journal of Social Issues* 28 (1972): 59–78.

Chodorow, Nancy. "Family Structure and Feminine Personality." In M. Z. Rosaldo and L. Lamphere, eds., *Woman, Culture and Society* Stanford: Stanford University Press, 1974.

———. *The Reproduction of Mothering*. Berkeley: University of California Press, 1978.

Edwards, Carolyn P. "Societal Complexity and Moral Development: A Kenyan Study." *Ethos* 3 (1975): 505–527.

Erickson, Erik H. *Childhood and Society*. New York: W. W. Norton, 1950.

———. *Identity: Youth and Crisis*. New York: W. W. Norton, 1968.

Freud, Sigmund. *Three Essays on the Theory of Sexuality* (1905). Vol. VII.

———. "Some Psychical Consequences of the Anatomical Distinction Between the Sexes" (1925). Vol. XIX.

Holstein, Constance. "Development of Moral Judgment: A Longitudinal Study of Males and Females." *Child Development* 47 (1976): 51–61.

Horner, Matina S. "Toward an Understanding of Achievement-related Conflicts in Women." *Journal of Social Issues* 28 (1972): 157–175.

Kohlberg, Lawrence. "The Development of Modes of Thinking and Choices in Years 10 to 16." Ph.D. Diss., University of Chicago, 1958.

———. *The Philosophy of Moral Development*. San Francisco: Harper & Row, 1981.

Kohlberg, L., and Kramer, R. "Continuities and Discontinuities in Child and Adult Moral Development." *Human Development* 12 (1969): 93–120.

Lever, Janet. "Sex Differences in the Games Children Play." *Social Problems* 23 (1976): 478–487.

McClelland, David C. *Power: The Inner Experience*. New York: Irvington, 1975.
Mead, George Herbert. *Mind, Self and Society*. Chicago: University of Chicago Press, 1934.
Miller, Jean Baker. *Toward a New Psychology of Women*. Boston: Beacon Press, 1976.
Piaget, Jean. *The Moral Judgment of the Child* (1932). New York: The Free Press, 1965.
―――. *Structuralism*. New York: Basic Books, 1970.

Sassen, Georgia. "Success Anxiety in Women: A Constructivist Interpretation of Its Sources and Its Significance." *Harvard Educational Review* 50 (1980): 13–25.
Simpson, Elizabeth L. "Moral Development Research: A Case Study of Scientific Cultural Bias." *Human Development* 17 (1974): 81–106.
Woolf, Virginia. *A Room of One's Own*. New York: Harcourt, Brace and World, 1929.

Hinayana and Mahayana Scriptures

Hinayāna

The Synopsis of Truth [1]

Thus have I heard. Once when the Lord was staying at Benares in the Isipatana deerpark, he addressed the almsmen as follows: It was here in this very deerpark at Benares that the Truth-finder, *Arahat* [arhat] all-enlightened, set a-rolling the supreme Wheel of the Doctrine—which shall not be turned back from its onward course by recluse or *brāhmin*, god or Māra or Brahmā or by anyone in the universe,— the announcement of the Four Noble Truths, the teaching, declaration, and establishment of those Four Truths, with their unfolding, exposition, and manifestation.

What are these four?—The announcement, teaching . . . and manifestation of the Noble Truth of suffering—of the origin of suffering—of the cessation of suffering—of the path that leads to the cessation of suffering.

Follow, almsmen, Sāriputta and Moggallāna and be guided by them; they are wise helpers unto their fellows in the higher life. . . . Sāriputta is able to announce, teach . . . and manifest the Four Noble Truths in all their details.

Having thus spoken, the Blessed One arose and went into his own cell.

The Lord had not been gone long when the reverent Sāriputta proceeded to the exposition of the Truth-finder's Four Noble Truths, as follows:

What, reverend sirs, is the Noble Truth of suffering?—Birth is a suffering; decay is a suffering; death is a suffering; grief and lamentation, pain, misery and tribulation are sufferings; it is a suffering not to get what is desired;—in brief all the factors of the fivefold grip on existence are suffering.

Birth is, for living creatures of each several class, the being born or produced, the issue, the arising or the re-arising, the appearance of the impressions, the growth of faculties.

Decay, for living creatures of each several class, is the decay and decaying, loss of

---

[1] References have been omitted—Eds.

teeth, grey hair, wrinkles, a dwindling term of life, sere faculties.

Death, for living creatures of each several class, is the passage and passing hence, the dissolution, disappearance, dying, death, decease, the dissolution of the impressions, the discarding of the dead body.

Grief is the grief, grieving, and grievousness, the inward grief and inward anguish of anyone who suffers under some misfortune or is in the grip of some type of suffering.

Lamentation is the lament and lamentation, the wailing and the lamenting of anyone who suffers under some misfortune or is in the grip of some type of suffering.

Pain is any bodily suffering or bodily evil, and suffering bred of bodily contact, any evil feeling.

Misery is mental suffering and evil, any evil feeling of the mind.

Tribulation is the tribulation of heart and mind, the state to which tribulation brings them, in anyone who suffers under some misfortune or is in the grip of some type of suffering.

There remains not to get what is desired. In creatures subject to birth—or decay—or death—or grief and lamentation, pain, misery, and tribulation—the desire arises not to be subject thereto but to escape them. But escape is not to be won merely by desiring it; and failure to win it is another suffering.

What are in brief all the factors of the fivefold grip on existence which are sufferings?—They are: the factors of form, feeling, perception, impressions, and consciousness.

The foregoing, sirs, constitutes the Noble Truth of suffering.

What now is the Noble Truth of the origin of suffering? It is any craving that makes for re-birth and is tied up with passion's delights and culls satisfaction now here now there—such as the craving for sensual pleasure, the craving for continuing existence, and the craving for annihilation.

Next, what is the Noble Truth of the cessation of suffering?—It is the utter and passionless cessation of this same craving,—the abandonment and rejection of craving, deliverance from craving, and aversion from craving.

Lastly, what is the Noble Truth of the Path that leads to the cessation of suffering?—It is just the Noble Eightfold Path, consisting of right outlook, right resolves, right speech, right acts, right livelihood, right endeavour, right mindfulness and right rapture of concentration.

Right outlook is to know suffering, the origin of suffering, the cessation of suffering, and the path that leads to the cessation of suffering.

Right resolves are the resolve to renounce the world and to do no hurt or harm.

Right speech is to abstain from lies and slander, from reviling, and from tattle.

Right acts are to abstain from taking life, from stealing, and from lechery.

Right livelihood is that by which the disciple of the Noble One supports himself, to the exclusion of wrong modes of livelihood.

Right endeavour is when an almsman brings his will to bear, puts forth endeavour and energy, struggles and strives with all his heart, to stop bad and wrong qualities which have not yet arisen from ever arising, to renounce those which have already arisen, to foster good qualities which have not yet arisen, and, finally, to establish, clarify, multiply, enlarge, develop, and perfect those good qualities which are there already.

Right mindfulness is when realizing what the body is—what feelings are—what the heart is—and what the mental states are—an almsman dwells ardent, alert, and mindful, in freedom from the wants and discontents attendant on any of these things.

Right rapture of concentration is when, divested of lusts and divested of wrong dispositions, an almsman develops, and dwells in, the first ecstasy with all its zest and satisfaction, a state bred of aloofness and not divorced from observation and reflection. By laying to rest observation and reflection, he develops and dwells in inward serenity, in [the] focussing of heart, in the zest and satisfaction of the second ecstasy, which is divorced from observation and reflection and is bred of concentration—passing thence to the third and fourth ecstasies.

This, sirs, constitutes the Noble Truth of the Path that leads to the cessation of suffering. . . .

The Theory of No-Soul [or Self]

The body, monks, is soulless. If the body, monks, were the soul, this body would not be subject to sickness, and it would be possible in the case of the body to say, "Let my body be thus, let my body not be thus." Now, because the body is soulless, monks, therefore the body is subject to sickness, and it is not possible in the case of the body to say, "Let my body be thus, let my body not be thus."

Feeling is soulless . . . perception is soulless . . . the aggregates are soulless. . . .

Consciousness is soulless. For if consciousness were the soul, this consciousness would not be subject to sickness, and it would be possible in the case of consciousness to say, "Let my consciousness be thus, let my consciousness not be thus."

Now, because consciousness is soulless, therefore consciousness is subject to sickness, and it is not possible in the case of consciousness to say, "Let my consciousness be thus, let my consciousness not be thus."

What think you, monks, is the body permanent or impermanent?

Impermanent, Lord.

But is the impermanent painful or pleasant?

Painful, Lord.

But is it fitting to consider what is impermanent, painful, and subject to change as, "this is mine, this am I, this is my soul"?

No indeed, Lord.

[And so of feeling, perception, the aggregates, and consciousness.] Therefore in truth, monks, whatever body, past, future, or present, internal or external, gross or subtle, low or eminent, near or far, is to be looked on by him who duly and rightly understands, as, "all this body is not mine, not this am I, not mine is the soul." [And so of feeling, etc.]

Thus perceiving, monks, the learned noble disciple feels *loathing* for the body, for feeling, for perception, for the aggregates, for consciousness. Feeling disgust he becomes free from passion, through freedom from passion he is emancipated, and in the emancipated one arises the knowledge of his emancipation. He understands that destroyed is rebirth, the religious life has been led, done is what was to be done, there is nought [for him] beyond this world.

Mahāyāna

The Twenty Verses on the Great Vehicle

Adoration to Mañjuśrī-kumāra-bhūtā.

Adoration to the Three Treasures.

I. The Buddha who is undefiled and enlightened, elucidates well, being full of mercy, that which is not a word nor is to be expressed in words: therefore I adore the Buddha's power which is beyond thought.

II. From the absolute point of view there is no birth, here again is there no annihilation; the Buddha is like sky, so are beings; they are of one nature.

III. There is no birth on the other side, nor on this side; *nirvāṇa* too in its self-nature exists not. Thus, when surveyed by a knowledge which knows all things, empty are the created.

IV. The self-nature of all things is regarded as like shadows; they are in substance pure, serene, non-dualistic, and same as suchness.

V. [To think of] self or of no-self is not the truth; they are discriminated by the confused; pleasure and pain are relative; so are passions and emancipation from them.

VI. Transmigration in the six paths of existence, the excellence and enjoyability of the heavenly world, or the great painfulness of the purgatories—all these come from apprehending the external world as reality.

VII. One suffers very much when there is nothing pleasurable; even when there are things to enjoy, they pass away because they are impermanent; but it is so settled that goods indeed come from good deeds.

VIII. Things are produced by false discrimination where there is no origination, so, when the purgatories, etc., are manifested, the erroneous are burned like a forest fire.

IX. Like unto things magic-created, so are the deeds of sentient beings who take the external world for reality. The six paths of existence are in substance magic-creations, and they exist conditionally.

X. As the painter painting a terrible monster is himself frightened thereby, so is the fool frightened with transmigration.

XI. As a stupid child making a muddy pool is himself drowned in it, so are sentient beings drowned in the mire of false discrimination and unable to get out of it.

XII. As they regard non-existence as existence they suffer the feeling of pain. In the external world as well as in thought they are bound by the poison of false discrimination.

XIII. Seeing that beings are weak, one with a heart of love and wisdom is to discipline oneself for perfect enlightenment in order to benefit them.

XIV. Again, if one with such a heart accumulates [spiritual] provisions, one attains, from the relative point of view, supreme enlightenment and is delivered from the bondage of false discrimination. Such an enlightened one is a friend of the world.

XV. When a man perceives the true meaning of reality as it becomes, he understands that the paths of existence are empty, and cuts asunder [the chain of] the first, middle, and last.

XVI. Thus regarded, *saṁsāra* and *nirvāṇa* have no real substance. Passions have not any substance. Such notions as the first, middle, and last are done away with when their self-nature is understood.

XVII. As perception takes place in a dream which when awakened disappears, so it is with sleeping in the darkness of ignorance: when awakened, transmigrations no more obtain.

XVIII. When things created by magic are seen as such, they have no existence; such is the nature of all things.

XIX. They are all nothing but mind, they are established as phantoms; therefore a blissful or an evil existence is matured according to deeds good or evil.

XX. When the mind-wheel ceases to exist all things indeed cease to exist; thus there is no ego in the nature of all things and therefore their nature is pure indeed.

XXI. When the ignorant wrapped in the darkness of ignorance conceive eternity or bliss in objects as they appear or as they are in themselves, they drift in the ocean of transmigration.

XXII. Where the great ocean of birth and death is filled with waters of false discrimination, who could ever reach the other shore unless carried by the raft of the Mahāyāna?

XXIII. When it is rightly understood that the world arises conditioned by ignorance, where could false discrimination obtain?

Analects
Confucius

Book I

2. Yu Tzu said, 'It is rare for a man whose character is such that he is good as a son and obedient as a young man to have the inclination to transgress against his superiors; it is unheard of for one who has no such inclination to be inclined to start a rebellion. The gentleman devotes his efforts to the roots, for once the roots are established, the Way will grow therefrom. Being good as a son and obedient as a young man is, perhaps, the root of a man's character.'[1]

. . .

12. Yu Tzu said, 'Of the things brought about by the rites, harmony is the most valuable. Of the ways of the Former Kings, this is the most beautiful, and is followed alike in matters great and small, yet this will not always work: to aim always at harmony without regulating it by the rites simply because one knows only about harmony will not, in fact, work.'

. . .

Book II

3. The Master said, 'Guide them by edicts, keep them in line with punishments, and the common people will stay out of trouble but will have no sense of shame. Guide them by virtue, keep them in line with the rites, and they will, besides having a sense of shame, reform themselves.'

. . .

5. Meng Yi Tzu asked about being filial. The Master answered, 'Never fail to comply.'

Fan Ch'ih was driving. The Master told him about the interview, saying, 'Meng-sun asked me about being filial. I answered, "Never fail to comply."'

Fan Ch'ih asked, 'What does that mean?'

The Master said, 'When your parents are alive, comply with the rites in serving them; when they die, comply with the rites in burying them; comply with the rites in sacrificing to them.'

6. Meng Wu Po asked about being filial. The Master said, 'Give your father and mother no other cause for anxiety than illness.'

7. Tzu-yu asked about being filial. The Master said, 'Nowadays for a man to be filial means no more than that he is able to provide his parents with food. Even hounds and horses are, in some way, provided with food. If a man shows no reverence, where is the difference?'

. . .

19. Duke Ai asked, 'What must I do before the common people will look up to me?'

Confucius answered, 'Raise the straight and set them over the crooked and the common people will look up to you. Raise the crooked and set them over the straight and the common people will not look up to you.'

. . .

Book VI

. . .

30. Tzu-kung said, 'If there were a man who gave extensively to the common people and brought help to the multitude,

---
[1] Lau's notes have been omitted—Eds.

what would you think of him? Could he be called benevolent?

The Master said, 'It is no longer a matter of benevolence with such a man. If you must describe him, "sage" is, perhaps, the right word. Even Yao and Shun would have found it difficult to accomplish as much. Now, on the other hand, a benevolent man helps others to take their stand in so far as he himself wishes to take his stand, and gets others there in so far as he himself wishes to get there. The ability to take as analogy what is near at hand can be called the method of benevolence.'

. . .

BOOK XI

. . .

12. Chi-lu asked how the spirits of the dead and the gods should be served. The Master said, 'You are not able even to serve man. How can you serve the spirits?'

'May I ask about death?'

'You do not understand even life. How can you understand death.?'

. . .

BOOK XII

1. Yen Yüan asked about benevolence. The Master said, 'To return to the observance of the rites through overcoming the self constitutes benevolence. If for a single day a man could return to the observance of the rites through overcoming himself, then the whole Empire would consider benevolence to be his. However, the practice of benevolence depends on oneself alone, and not on others.'

Yen Yüan said, 'I should like you to list the items.' The Master said, 'Do not look unless it is in accordance with the rites; do not listen unless it is in accordance with the rites; do not speak unless it is in accordance with the rites; do not move unless it is in accordance with the rites.'

Yen Yüan said, 'Though I am not quick, I shall direct my efforts towards what you have said.'

2. Chung-kung asked about benevolence. The Master said, 'When abroad behave as though you were receiving an important guest. When employing the services of the common people behave as though you were officiating at an important sacrifice. Do not impose on others what you yourself do not desire. In this way you will be free from ill will whether in a state or in a noble family.'

Chung-kung said, 'Though I am not quick, I shall direct my efforts towards what you have said.'

. . .

19. Chi K'ang Tzu asked Confucius about government, saying, 'What would you think if, in order to move closer to those who possess the Way, I were to kill those who do not follow the Way?'

Confucius answered, 'In administering your government, what need is there for you to kill? Just desire the good yourself and the common people will be good. The virtue of the gentleman is like wind; the virtue of the small man is like grass. Let the wind blow over the grass and it is sure to bend.'

. . .

Book XIV

. . .

34. Someone said,

'Repay an injury with a good turn.

What do you think of this saying?'

The Master said, 'What, then, do you repay a good turn with? You repay an injury with straightness, but you repay a good turn with a good turn.'

. . .

Book XV

. . .

9. The Master said, 'For Gentlemen of purpose and men of benevolence while it is inconceivable that they should seek to stay alive at the expense of benevolence, it may happen that they have to accept death in order to have benevolence accomplished.'

. . .

24. Tzu-kung asked, 'Is there a single word which can be a guide to conduct throughout one's life?' The Master said, 'It is perhaps the word *"shu"*. Do not impose on others what you yourself do not desire.'

Book XVII

. . .

21. Tsai Wo asked about the three-year mourning period, saying, 'Even a full year is too long. If the gentleman gives up the practice of the rites for three years, the rites are sure to be in ruins; if he gives up the practice of music for three years, music is sure to collapse. A full year's mourning is quite enough. After all, in the course of a year, the old grain having been used up, the new grain ripens, and fire is renewed by fresh drilling.'

The Master said, 'Would you, then, be able to enjoy eating your rice and wearing your finery?'

'Yes. I would.'

'If you are able to enjoy them, do so by all means. The gentleman in mourning finds no relish in good food, no pleasure in music, and no comforts in his own home. That is why he does not eat his rice and wear his finery. Since it appears that you enjoy them, then do so by all means.'

After Tsai Wo had left, the Master said, 'How unfeeling Yü is. A child ceases to be nursed by his parents only when he is three years old. Three years' mourning is observed throughout the Empire. Was Yü not given three years' love by his parents?'

WORK

The Significance of Human Relationships

Anthony Storr

Concentration upon interpersonal relationships and upon transference is not characteristic of all forms of analytical practice; but it does link together a number of psychoanalysts and psycho-therapists who may originally have been trained in different schools, but who share two fundamental convictions. The first is that neurotic problems are something to do with early failures in the relation between the child and its parents: the second, that health and happiness entirely depend upon the maintenance of intimate personal relationships.

No two children are exactly alike, and it must be recognized that genetic differences may contribute powerfully to problems in childhood development. The same parent may be perceived quite differently by different children. Nevertheless, I share the conviction that many neurotic difficulties in later life can be related to the individual's early emotional experience within the family.

I am less convinced that intimate personal relationships are the only source of health and happiness. In the present climate, there is a danger that love is being idealized as the only path to salvation. When Freud was asked what constituted psychological health, he gave as his answer the ability to love and work. We have overemphasized the former, and paid too little attention to the latter. In many varieties of analysis, exclusive concentration upon interpersonal relationships has led to failure to consider other ways of finding personal fulfilment, and also to neglecting the study of shifting dynamics within the psyche of the isolated individual.

A number of psycho-analysts contributed to the rise of 'object-relations theory' as opposed to Freud's 'instinct theory'. Amongst these analysts were Melanie Klein, Donald Winnicott, and Ronald Fairbairn. But the most important work in this field has been that of John Bowlby, whose three volumes *Attachment and Loss* are deservedly influential, have inspired a great deal of research, and are widely regarded as having made a major contribution to our understanding of human nature.

Bowlby assumes that the primary need of human beings, from infancy onward, is for supportive and rewarding relationships with other human beings, and that this need for *attachment* extends far beyond the need for sexual fulfilment. . . .

Bowlby's *Attachment and Loss* originated in his work for the World Health Organization on the mental health of homeless children. This led to subsequent study of the effects upon young children of the temporary loss of the mother and to a far greater appreciation of the distress suffered by young children when, for example, they or their mothers have to be admitted to hospital.

Human infants begin to develop specific attachments to particular people around the third quarter of their first year of life. This is the time at which the infant begins to protest if handed to a stranger and tends to cling to the mother or other adults with whom he is familiar. The mother usually provides a secure base to which the infant can return, and, when she is present, the infant is bolder in both exploration and play than when she is absent. If the attachment figure removes herself, even briefly, the infant usually protests. Longer separations, as when children have been admitted to hospital, cause a regular sequence of responses first described by Bowlby. Angry protest is succeeded by a period of despair in which the infant is quietly miserable and apathetic. After a further period, the infant becomes detached and appears no longer to care about the absent attachment figure. This sequence of *protest, despair,* and *detachment* seems to be the standard response of the small child whose mother is removed.

The evidence is sufficiently strong for Bowlby to consider that an adult's capacity for making good relationships with other adults depends upon the individual's experience of attachment figures when a child. A child who from its earliest years is certain that his attachment figures will be available when he needs them, will develop a sense of security and inner confidence. In adult life, this confidence will make it possible for him to trust and love other human beings. In relationships between the sexes in which love and trust has been established, sexual fulfilment follows as a natural consequence. . . .

Anthropologists, sociologists, and psychologists all concur in regarding man as a social being who requires the support and companionship of others throughout his life. In addition to learning, social co-operation has played an essential part in man's survival as a species, just as it has in the survival of sub-human primates, like baboons and chimpanzees. As Konrad Lorenz pointed out, man is neither fleet of foot nor equipped by nature with a tough hide, powerful tusks, claws, or other natural weapons. In order to protect themselves from more powerful species and in order to succeed in hunting large animals, primitive men had to learn co-operation. Their survival depended upon it. Modern man has moved a long way from the social condition of the hunter-gatherer, but his need for social interaction and for positive ties with others has persisted.

There are, therefore, many reasons for giving a high place to attachment in any hierarchy of human needs. Indeed, some sociologists would doubt whether the individual possesses any significance when considered apart from the family and social groups of which he is a member. Most members of Western society assume that close family ties will constitute an important part of their lives; that these ties will be supplemented by other loves and friendships; and that it is these relationships which will give their own lives significance. As Peter Marris has put it:

> The relationships that matter most to us are characteristically to particular people whom we love—husband or wife, parents, children, dearest friend—and sometimes to particular places—a home or personal territory that we invest with the same loving qualities. These specific relationships, which we experience as unique and irreplaceable, seem to embody most crucially the meaning of our lives.[1]

In Marris's view, these unique and irreplaceable relationships act as points of reference which help us to make sense of our experience. We are, as it were, embedded in a structure of which unique relationships are the supporting pillars. We take this so much for granted that we seldom define it, and may hardly be conscious of it until some important relationship comes to an end. As Marris points out, recently bereaved persons often feel, at any rate for a time, that the world has become *meaningless*. When we lose the person who is nearest and dearest to us, we may discover that the meaning of life was bound up with that person to a greater extent than we had supposed. This is the usual pattern; but we must also remember that some people, even after losing a spouse who was dear to them, feel a new sense of freedom and take on a new lease of life.

When Robert S. Weiss studied a number of people whose marriages had recently ended, and who had joined a group for single parents, he found, as might be expected, that, although they gained support from the group, they still complained of loneliness. No amount of friendship was enough to compensate for the loss of close attachment and emotional intimacy which they had experienced in marriage.

But, however crucial such relationships are for most people, it is not only *intimate* personal relationships which provide life with meaning. Weiss also studied married couples who, for one reason or another, had moved a considerable distance from the neighbourhood in which they had been living. Although their intimate attachments to their spouses were unimpaired, they were distressed at no longer feeling part of a group.

In other words, whether or not they are enjoying intimate relationships, human beings need a sense of being part of a larger community than that constituted by the family. The modern assumption that intimate relationships are essential to personal

---

[1] Peter Marris, 'Attachment and Society', in *The Place of Attachment in Human Behavior*, edited by C. Murray Parkes and J. Stevenson-Hinde (London, 1982), p. 185.

fulfilment tends to make us neglect the significance of relationships which are not so intimate. Schizophrenics, and other individuals who are more or less totally isolated, are rightly regarded as pathological; but many human beings make do with relationships which cannot be regarded as especially close, and not all such human beings are ill or even particularly unhappy.

Social structures of the kind found in the army or in a business may not give individuals the same kind of satisfactions which they might obtain from intimate relationships, but they do provide a setting in which the individual feels he has a function and a place. Gellner's contention . . . that modern society is so mobile and fluid that it has made many people feel disorientated and insecure, is to some extent countered by the fact that many workers are reluctant to abandon a familiar setting even if offered more rewarding opportunities. The fact that a man is part of a hierarchy, and that he has a particular job to carry out, gives his life significance. It also provides a frame of reference through which he perceives his relation with others. In the course of daily life, we habitually encounter many people with whom we are not intimate, but who nevertheless contribute to our sense of self. Neighbours, postmen, bank clerks, shop assistants, and many others may all be familiar figures with whom we daily exchange friendly greetings, but are generally persons about whose lives we know very little. Yet, if such a person disappears and is replaced by another, we feel some sense of loss, however transient. We say that we have become 'used to' so-and-so; but what we miss is mutual recognition, acknowledgement of each other's existence, and thus some affirmation, however slight, that each reciprocally contributes something to life's pattern.

Relationships of this kind play a more important role in the lives of most of us than is generally recognized. When people retire from work in offices or institutions, they miss the familiar figures who used to provide recognition and affirmation. It is generally accepted that most human beings want to be loved. The wish to be recognized and acknowledged is at least as important.

In Western societies today, a large number of people live lives in which intimate relationships play little part, however much they recognize the lack, or attempt to compensate for it in phantasy. Instead of being centred on spouse and children, their lives are based upon the office where, although they may not be loved, they are at least recognized and valued. People who have a special need to be recognized, perhaps because their parents accorded them little recognition in childhood, are attracted to office life for this reason. Although some types of work may require short periods of solitary concentration, most office workers spend relatively little time alone, without human interaction, and for the majority, this seems to be an attractive feature of office life.

The importance which less intimate, comparatively superficial relationships play in the lives of most of us is also attested by the kind of conversations we have with acquaintances. When neighbours meet in the street, they may, especially in England, use the weather as an opening gambit. But if the exchange is at all prolonged, the conversation is likely to turn to talk of other neighbours. Even the most intellectual persons are seldom averse to gossip, although they may affect to despise it. It would be interesting to know what proportion of conversation consists of talking about the lives of other people, as compared with talking about books, music, painting, ideas or money. Even amongst the highly educated, the proportion cannot be small.

Failure to make, or to sustain, the kind of intimate attachments which the object-relations theorists maintain are the main source of life's meaning and satisfaction does not imply that a person is necessarily cut off from other, less intimate human relationships. Whilst it is certainly more difficult for most people to find meaning in life if they do not have close attachments, many people can and do lead equable and satisfying lives by basing them upon a mixture of work and more superficial relationships. . . .

SELF-CREATION

Existentialism and Humanism

Jean-Paul Sartre

There are two kinds of existentialists. There are, on the one hand, the Christians, amongst whom I shall name Jaspers and Gabriel Marcel, both professed Catholics; and on the other the existential atheists, amongst whom we must place Heidegger as well as the French existentialists and myself. What they have in common is simply the fact that they believe that *existence* comes before *essence*—or, if you will, that we must begin from the subjective. What exactly do we mean by that?

If one considers an article of manufacture—as, for example, a book or a paper-knife—one sees that it has been made by an artisan who had a conception of it; and he has paid attention, equally, to the conception of a paper-knife and to the pre-existent technique of production which is a part of that conception and is, at bottom, a formula. Thus the paper-knife is at the same time an article producible in a certain manner and one which, on the other hand, serves a definite purpose, for one cannot suppose that a man would produce a paper-knife without knowing what it was for. Let us say, then, of the paper-knife that its essence—that is to say the sum of the formulae and the qualities which made its production and its definition possible—precedes its existence. The presence of such-and-such a paper-knife or book is thus determined before my eyes. Here, then, we are viewing the world from a technical standpoint, and we can say that production precedes existence.

When we think of God as the creator, we are thinking of him, most of the time, as a supernal artisan. Whatever doctrine we may be considering, whether it be a doctrine like that of Descartes, or of Leibnitz himself, we always imply that the will follows, more or less, from the understanding or at least accompanies it, so that when God creates he knows precisely what he is creating. Thus, the conception of man in the mind of God is comparable to that of the paper-knife in the mind of the artisan: God makes man according to a procedure and a conception, exactly as the artisan manufactures a paper-knife, following a definition and a formula. Thus each individual man is the realisation of a certain conception which dwells in the divine understanding. In the philosophic atheism of the eighteenth century, the notion of God is suppressed, but not, for all that, the idea that essence is prior to existence; something of that idea we still find everywhere, in Diderot, in Voltaire and even in Kant. Man possesses a human nature; that "human nature," which is the conception of human being, is found in every man; which means that each man is a particular example of an universal conception, the conception of Man. In Kant, this universality goes so far that the wild man of the woods, man in the state of nature and the bourgeois are all contained in the same definition and have the same fundamental qualities. Here again, the essence of man precedes that historic existence which we confront in experience.

Atheistic existentialism, of which I am a representative, declares with greater consistency that if God does not exist there is at least one being whose existence comes before its essence, a being which exists before it can be defined by any conception of it. That being is man or, as Heidegger has it, the human reality. What do we mean by saying that existence precedes essence? We mean that man first of all exists, encounters himself, surges up in the world—and defines himself afterwards. If man as the existentialist sees him is not definable, it is because to begin with he is nothing. He will not be anything until later, and then he will be what he makes of himself. Thus, there is no human nature, because there is no God to have a conception of it. Man simply is. Not that he is simply what he conceives himself to be, but he is what he wills, and as he conceives himself after already existing—as he wills to be after that leap towards existence. Man is nothing else but that which he makes of himself. That is the first principle of existentialism. And this is what people call its "subjectivity," using the word as a reproach against us. But what do we mean to say by this, but that man is of a greater dignity than a stone or a table? For we mean to say that man primarily exists—that man is, before all else, something which propels itself towards a future and is aware that it is doing so. Man is, indeed, a project which possesses a subjective life, instead of being a kind of moss, or a fungus or a cauliflower. Before that projection of the self nothing exists; not even in the heaven of intelligence; man will only attain existence when he is what he purposes to be. Not, however, what he may wish to be. For what we usually understand by wishing or willing is a conscious decision taken—much more often than not—after we have made ourselves what we are. I may wish to join a party, to write a book or to marry—but in such a case what is usually called my will is probably a manifestation of a prior and more spontaneous decision. If, however, it is true that existence is prior to essence, man is responsible for what he is. Thus, the first effect of existentialism is that it puts every man in possession of himself as he is, and places the entire responsibility for his existence squarely upon his own shoulders. And, when we say that man is responsible for himself, we do not mean that he is responsible only for his own individuality, but that he is responsible for all men. The word "subjectivism" is to be understood in two senses, and our adversaries play upon only one of them. Subjectivism means, on the one hand, the freedom of the individual subject and, on the other, that man cannot pass beyond human subjectivity. It is the latter which is the deeper meaning of existentialism. When we say that man chooses himself, we do mean that every one of us must choose himself; but by that we also mean that in choosing for himself he chooses for all men. For in effect, of all the actions a man may take in order to create himself as he wills to be, there is not one which is not creative, at the same time, of an image of man such as he believes he ought to be. To choose between this or that is at the same time to affirm the value of that which is chosen; for we are unable ever to choose the worse. What we choose is always the better; and nothing can be better for us unless it is better for all. If, moreover, existence precedes essence and we will to exist at the same time as we fashion our image, that image is valid for all and for the entire epoch in which we find ourselves. Our responsibility is thus much greater than we had supposed, for it concerns mankind as a whole. If I am a worker, for instance, I may choose to join a Christian rather than a Communist trade union. And if, by the membership, I choose to signify that resignation is, after all, the attitude that best becomes a man, that man's kingdom is not upon this earth, I do not commit myself alone to that view. Resignation is my will for everyone, and my action is, in consequence, a commitment on behalf of all mankind. Or if, to take a more personal case, I decide to marry and to have children, even though this decision proceeds simply from my situation, from my passion or my desire, I am thereby committing not only myself, but humanity as a whole, to the practice of monogamy. I am thus responsible for myself and for all men, and I am creating a certain image of man as I would have him to be. In fashioning myself I fashion man.

This may enable us to understand what is meant by such terms—perhaps a little grandiloquent—as anguish, abandonment and despair. As you will soon see, it is very simple. First, what do we mean by anguish? The existentialist frankly states that man is in anguish. His meaning is as follows— When a man commits himself to anything, fully realising that he is not only choosing what he will be, but is thereby at the same time a legislator deciding for the whole of mankind—in such a moment a man cannot escape from the sense of complete and profound responsibility. There are many, indeed, who show no such anxiety. But we affirm that they are merely disguising their anguish or are in flight from it. Certainly, many people think that in what they are doing they commit no one but themselves to anything: and if you ask them, "What would happen if everyone did so?" they shrug their shoulders and reply, "Everyone does not do so." But in truth, one ought always to ask oneself what would happen if everyone did as one is doing; nor can one escape from that disturbing thought except by a kind of self-deception. The man who lies in self-excuse, by saying "Everyone will not do it" must be ill at ease in his conscience, for the act of lying implies the universal value which it denies. . . .

And when we speak of "abandonment"—a favourite word of Heidegger—we only mean to say that God does not exist, and that it is necessary to draw the consequences of his absence right to the end. The existentialist is strongly opposed to a certain type of secular moralism which seeks to suppress God at the least possible expense. Towards 1880, when the French professors endeavoured to formulate a secular morality, they said something like this:—God is a useless and costly hypothesis, so we will do without it. However, if we are to have morality, a society and a law-abiding world, it is essential that certain values should be taken seriously; they must have an *à priori* existence ascribed to them. It must be considered obligatory *à priori* to be honest, not to lie, not to beat one's wife, to bring up children and so forth; so we are going to do a little work on this subject, which will enable us to show that these values exist all the same, inscribed in an intelligible heaven although, of course, there is no God. In other words—and this is, I believe, the purport of all that we in France call radicalism—nothing will be changed if

God does not exist; we shall re-discover the same norms of honesty, progress and humanity, and we shall have disposed of God as an out-of-date hypothesis which will die away quietly of itself. The existentialist, on the contrary, finds it extremely embarrassing that God does not exist, for there disappears with Him all possibility of finding values in an intelligible heaven. There can no longer be any good *à priori*, since there is no infinite and perfect consciousness to think it. It is nowhere written that "the good" exists, that one must be honest or must not lie, since we are now upon the plane where there are only men. Dostoievsky once wrote "If God did not exist, everything would be permitted"; and that, for existentialism, is the starting point. Everything is indeed permitted if God does not exist, and man is in consequence forlorn, for he cannot find anything to depend upon either within or outside himself. He discovers forthwith, that he is without excuse. For if indeed existence precedes essence, one will never be able to explain one's action by reference to a given and specific human nature; in other words, there is no determinism—man is free, man *is* freedom. Nor, on the other hand, if God does not exist, are we provided with any values or commands that could legitimise our behaviour. Thus we have neither behind us, nor before us in a luminous realm of values, any means of justification or excuse. We are left alone, without excuse. That is what I mean when I say that man is condemned to be free. Condemned, because he did not create himself, yet is nevertheless at liberty, and from the moment that he is thrown into this world he is responsible for everything he does. The existentialist does not believe in the power of passion. He will never regard a grand passion as a destructive torrent upon which a man is swept into certain actions as by fate, and which, therefore, is an excuse for them. He thinks that man is responsible for his passion. Neither will an existentialist think that a man can find help through some sign being vouchsafed upon earth for his orientation: for he thinks that the man himself interprets the sign as he chooses. He thinks that every man, without any support or help whatever, is condemned at every instant to invent man. . . .

NOTHING

The World as Will and Idea

Arthur Schopenhauer

What Happiness Is

All satisfaction, or what is commonly called happiness, is always really and essentially only *negative*, and never positive. It is not an original gratification coming to us of itself, but must always be the satisfaction of a wish. The wish, *i.e.*, some want, is the condition which precedes every pleasure. But with the satisfaction the wish and therefore the pleasure cease. Thus the satisfaction or the pleasing can never be more than the deliverance from a pain, from a want; for such is not only every actual, open sorrow, but every desire, the importunity of which disturbs our peace, and, indeed, the deadening ennui also that makes life a burden to us. It is, however, so hard to attain or achieve anything; difficulties and troubles without end are opposed to every purpose, and at every step hindrances accumulate. But when finally everthing is overcome and attained, nothing can ever be gained but deliverance from some sorrow or desire, so that we find ourselves just in the same position as we occupied before this sorrow or desire appeared. All that is ever directly given us is merely the want, *i.e.,* the pain. The satisfaction and the pleasure we can only know indirectly through the remembrance of the preceding suffering and want, which ceases with its appearance. Hence it arises that we are not properly conscious of the blessings and advantages we actually possess, nor do we prize them, but think of them merely as a matter of course, for they gratify us only negatively by restraining suffering. Only when we have lost them do we become sensible of their value; for the want, the privation, the sorrow, is the positive, communicating itself directly to us. Thus also we are pleased by the remembrance of past need, sickness, want, and such like, because this is the only means of enjoying the present blessings. . . .

It is really incredible how meaningless and void of significance when looked at from without, how dull and unenlightened by intellect when felt from within, is the course of the life of the great majority of men. It is a weary longing and complaining, a dream-like staggering through the four ages of life to death, accompanied by a series of trivial thoughts. Such men are like clockwork, which is wound up, and goes it knows not why; and every time a man is begotten and born, the clock of human life is wound up anew, to repeat the same old piece it has played innumerable times before, passage after passage, measure after measure, with insignificant variations. Every individual, every human being and his course of life, is but another short dream of the endless spirit of nature, of the persistent will to live; is only another fleeting form, which it carelessly sketches on its infinite page, space and time; allows to remain for a time so short that it vanishes into nothing in comparison with these, and obliterates to make new room. And yet, and here lies the serious side of life, every one of these fleeting forms, these empty fancies, must be paid for by the whole will to live, in all its activity, with many and deep sufferings, and finally with a bitter death, long feared and coming at last. This is why the sight of a corpse makes us suddenly so serious.

The life of every individual, if we survey it as a whole and in general, and only lay stress upon its most significant features, is really always a tragedy, but gone through in detail, it has the character of a comedy. For the deeds and vexations of the day, the restless irritation of the moment, the desires and fears of the week, the mishaps of every hour, are all through chance, which is ever bent upon some jest, scenes of a comedy. But the never-satisfied wishes, the frustrated efforts, the hopes unmercifully crushed by fate, the unfortunate errors of the whole life, with increasing suffering and death at the end, are always a tragedy. Thus, as if fate would add derision to the misery of our existence, our life must contain all the woes of tragedy, and yet we cannot even assert the dignity of tragic characters, but in the broad detail of life must inevitably be the foolish characters of a comedy.

But however much great and small trials may fill human life, they are not able to conceal its insufficiency to satisfy the spirit; they cannot hide the emptiness and superficiality of existence, nor exclude ennui, which is always ready to fill up every pause that care may allow. Hence it arises that the human mind, not content with the cares, anxieties, and occupations which the actual world lays upon it, creates for itself an imaginary world also in the form of a thousand different superstitions, then finds all manner of employment with this, and wastes time and strength upon it, as soon as the real world is willing to grant it the rest which it is quite incapable of enjoying. This is accordingly most markedly the case with nations for which life is made easy by the congenial nature of the climate and the soil, most of all with the Hindus, then with the Greeks, the Romans, and later with the Italians, the Spaniards, &c. Demons, gods, and saints man creates in his own image, and to them he must then unceasingly bring offerings, prayers, temple decorations, vows and their fulfillment, pilgrimages, salutations, ornaments for their images, &c. Their service mingles everywhere with the real, and, indeed, obscures it. Every event of life is regarded as the work of these beings; the intercourse with them occupies half the time of life, constantly sustains hope, and by the charm of illusion often becomes more interesting than intercourse with real beings.

Good, Bad, and Wicked

In all the preceding investigations of human action, we have been leading up to the final investigation, and have to a considerable extent lightened the task of raising to abstract and philosophical clearness, and exhibiting as a branch of our central thought that special ethical significance of action which in life is with perfect understanding denoted by the words *good* and *bad*. . . .

We now wish to discover the significance of the concept *good*, which can be done with very little trouble. This concept is essentially relative, and signifies *the conformity of an object to any definite effort of the will.* Accordingly everything that corresponds to the will in any of its expressions and fulfills its end is thought through the concept *good*, however different such things may be in other respects. Thus we speak of good eating, good roads, good weather, good weapons, good omens, and so on; in short, we call everything good that is just as we wish it to be; and therefore that may be good in the eyes of one man which is just the reverse in those of another. The conception of the good divides itself into two sub-species—that of the direct present satisfaction of any volition, and that of its indirect satisfaction which has reference to the future, *i.e.*, the agreeable and the useful. The conception of the opposite, so long as we are speaking of unconscious existence, is expressed by the word *bad*, more rarely and abstractly by the word *evil*, which thus denotes everything that does not correspond to any effort of the will. . . .

It follows from what has been said above, that the *good* . . . is essentially relative, for its being consists in its relation to a desiring will. *Absolute good* is, therefore, a contradiction in terms; highest good, *summum bonum*, really signifies the same thing—a final satisfaction of the will after which no new desire could arise—a last motive, the attainment of which would afford enduring satisfaction of the will. But, according to the investigations which have already been conducted in this Fourth Book, such a consummation is not even thinkable. The will can just as little cease from willing altogether on account of some particular satisfaction, as time can end or begin; for it there is no such thing as a permanent fulfillment which shall completely and for ever satisfy its craving. It is the vessel of the Danaides; for it there is no highest good, no absolute good, but always a merely temporary good. If, however, we wish to give an honorary position, as it were emeritus, to an old expression, which from custom we do not like to discard altogether, we may, metaphorically and figuratively, call the complete self-effacement and denial of the will, the true absence of will, which alone for ever stills and silences its struggle, alone gives that contentment which can never again be disturbed, alone redeems the world, and which we shall now soon consider at the close of our whole investigation—the absolute good, the *summum bonum*—and regard it as the only radical cure of the disease of which all other means are only palliations or anodynes. In this sense the Greek *telos* and also *finis bonorum* correspond to the thing still better. So much for the words *good* and *bad;* now for the thing itself.

If a man is always disposed to do *wrong* whenever the opportunity presents itself, and there is no external power to restrain him, we call him *bad.* According to our doctrine of wrong, this means that such a man does not merely assert the will to live as it appears in his own body, but in this assertion goes so far that he denies the will which appears in other individuals. This is shown by the fact that he desires their powers for the service of his own will, and seeks to destroy their existence when they stand in the way of its efforts. The ultimate source of this is a high degree of egoism, the nature of which has been already explained. Two things are here apparent. In the first place, that in such a man an excessively vehement will to live expresses itself, extending far beyond the assertion of his own body; and, in the second place, that his knowledge, entirely given up to the principle of sufficient reason and involved in the principle of individuation, cannot get beyond the difference which this latter principle establishes between his own person and every one else. Therefore he seeks his own well-being alone, completely indifferent to that of all others, whose existence is to him altogether foreign and divided from his own by a wide gulf, and who are indeed regarded by him as mere masks with no reality behind them. And these two qualities are the constituent elements of the bad character. . . .

Since man is a manifestation of will illuminated by the clearest knowledge, he is always contrasting the actual and felt satisfaction of his will with the merely possible satisfaction of it which knowledge presents to him. Hence arises envy: every privation is infinitely increased by the enjoyment of others, and relieved by the knowledge that others also suffer the same privation. Those ills which are common to all and inseparable from human life trouble us little, just as those which belong to the climate, to the whole country. The recollection of greater sufferings than our own stills our pain; the sight of the sufferings of others soothes our own. If, now, a man is filled with an exceptionally intense pressure of will,—if with burning eagerness he seeks to accumulate everything to slake the thirst of his egoism, and thus experiences, as he inevitably must, that all satisfaction is merely apparent, that the attained end never fulfills the promise of the desired object, the final appearing of the fierce pressure of will, but that when fulfilled the wish only changes its form and now torments him in a new one; and indeed that if at last all wishes are exhausted, the pressure of will itself remains without any conscious motive, and makes itself known to him with fearful pain as a feeling of terrible desolation and emptiness; if from all this, which in the case of the ordinary degrees of volition is only felt in small measure, and only produces the ordinary degree of melancholy, in the case of him who is a manifestation of will reaching the point of extraordinary wickedness, there necessarily springs an excessive inward misery, an eternal unrest, an incurable pain; he seeks indirectly the alleviation which directly is denied him,—seeks to mitigate his own suffering by the sight of the suffering of others, which at the same time he recognises as an expression of his power. The suffering of others now becomes for him an end in itself, and is a spectacle in which he delights; and thus arises the phenomenon of pure cruelty, blood-thirstiness, which history exhibits so often in the Neros and Domitians, in the African Deis, in Robespierre, and the like. . . .

Questions for Further Reflection

1. Might my life be unworthwhile even though it has a point or purpose? Might it be worthwhile even though it lacks a point or purpose? How exactly are the notions of purpose, point, and value related?
2. Imagine that long ago, aliens visited the earth precisely for the purpose of setting into motion processes that would lead eventually to the existence of human beings. What would the implications be for someone who subscribed to the transcendentalist view that whatever agency guided the development of human beings determines what is worthwhile for us by making plans for us? Would we consider it worthwhile to serve as the aliens' slaves or food if that is what they had intended all along?
3. Suppose that human beings had been built so that what they did best was fight with one another. How would this affect Aristotle's conception of the best life? Does the possibility that we might have been built this way affect the conclusions we can reach about the good life from the work of Storr and Gilligan?
4. Are hedonists correct in saying that pleasure is intrinsically good, no matter what its source? Assuming that a homicidal maniac is going to kill a given group of victims no matter what, is it better that he enjoy the slaughter rather than be indifferent to it or suffer from it?
5. Would a life spent attached to electrodes that stimulate the pleasure centers of the brain be a worthwhile one? Is the stance Smart takes on this issue correct?
6. Is there a tension between Sartre's subjectivism concerning values and his claim that we are responsible for everyone?
7. What role ought the values Gilligan associates with females to play in the lives of men? What role ought the values Gilligan associates with males to play in the lives of women?
8. Suppose that I live in a community, whose traditions I consider to be unacceptable. What should I do according to Confucius?
9. Critically compare the views of Lao Tzu, Confucius, and Gautama on selflessness.
10. What role does pleasure play in Schopenhauer's conception of happiness?
11. Suppose we grant Schopenhauer that our desires are ultimately arbitrary. Would it follow that life cannot be worthwhile? What would Sartre say about this matter?

Further Readings

Blake, Ralph. "Why Not Hedonism?" *Ethics* (1926). *Readings in Ethical Theory*, second edition, edited by W. Sellars and J. Hospers. Englewood Cliffs, NJ: Prentice-Hall, 1970: 392–401. An excellent defense of hedonism.

Chan, Wing-tsit, ed. *A Source Book in Chinese Philosophy.* Princeton, NJ: Princeton University Press, 1963. A good collection of Chinese philosophy for those who wish to examine religions outside the Western tradition, such as Confucianism and Taoism.

Edwards, Rem B. *Pleasures and Pains*. Ithaca, NY: Cornell University Press, 1979. A defense of Mill-style qualitative hedonism.

Glover, Jonathan. "Projects of Self-Creation." In *I: The Philosophy and Psychology of Personal Identity*. London, England: Allen Lane, The Penguin Press, 1988. In this chapter Glover discusses ways we can transform ourselves for the better.

Klemke, E. D., ed. *The Meaning of Life*. Oxford, England: Oxford University Press, 1981. A good collection of essays dealing with the meaning of life.

Luper, Steven. *Invulnerability: On Securing Happiness*. Chicago: Open Court, 1996. Critically discusses several strategies for achieving a worthwhile life.

Mill, John Stuart. *Utilitarianism*. Indianapolis: Hackett, 1861. Discusses and defends a version of hedonism and clarifies the relationship between hedonism and utilitarianism.

Nagel, Thomas. *The View from Nowhere*. Oxford, England: Oxford University Press, 1986. An excellent discussion of the meaning and value of life and of the objectivity of value.

Nietzsche, Friedrich. "On the Preachers of Death." In Walter Kaufmann, ed., *The Portable Nietzsche*. New York: Viking Press, 1968. A sharp critique of otherworldliness.

Noddings, Nell. *Caring: A Feminist Approach to Ethics and Moral Education*. Berkeley: University of California Press, 1984. Noddings argues that the main motivation for ethical behavior is concern for others and that we ought to avoid ethical views that rely heavily on principles. She characterizes her view as "feminist" because she believes her ethics of caring is typical of women, while the ethics of principle is typical of men.

Parkes, C. Murray, et al., eds. *The Place of Attachment in Human Behavior*. London: 1982. A good collection of discussions of the central role that close interpersonal relationships play in life according to psychotherapists.

Pascal, Blaise. *Pensées*. New York: Dutton, 1958. A classic discussion of the Christian perspective on the meaning and value of life.

Radhakrishnan, Sarvepalli, and Charles Moore, eds. *A Source Book in Indian Philosophy*. Princeton, NJ: Princeton University Press, 1957. A good collection of Buddhist and Hindu writings for those who wish to delve into religions outside the Western tradition.

Russell, Bertrand. "The Study of Mathematics." In *Mysticism and Logic*. Totowa, NJ: Barnes and Noble, 1981. In this essay Russell echoes Aristotle's praise of the life of reason and singles out the study of mathematics as one of the purest instances of such a life.

Sidgwick, Henry. *The Methods of Ethics*. Indianapolis: Hackett, 1981. A classic defense of hedonism.

Sumner, William Graham. *Folkways*. 1907. Here Sumner, an anthropologist (1840–1910), gives an influential defense of cultural relativism, the view that our values are determined by the folkways of our society.

Williams, Bernard. "Goodness and Roles." In *Morality: An Introduction to Ethics*. New York: Harper Torchbooks, 1972. Discusses how the roles we play in society affect our identity and worth. A useful companion to Sartre's *Existentialism and Humanism*.

Chapter 3

THE INDIVIDUAL DEATH: IS DYING AN EVIL?

Almost all religions suggest that when we die, our lives are not over. Instead, we begin an afterlife of some sort. (The exceptions include Taoism, Confucianism, and versions of Buddhism.) Most religions suggest that the afterlife is incomparably better than this life and that it lasts forever. If so, then dying would appear to be a good thing (other things being equal) inasmuch as it makes entry into paradise possible. Moreover, those whose religion leads them to regard death as a transition to eternal life are likely to be happy that their lives will never end. It means that they will never have to face the prospect of being utterly annihilated, a fate that those who are not religious think awaits them when they die.

But *would* annihilation be a bad thing? It is natural to think that if life is good, then ending it would be bad, other things being equal, and that how bad ending life would be is directly proportional to how good one's life would have been. So if living a worthwhile life *forever* were a genuine possibility, as some religious people (including Tolstoy) think, then being annihilated would be especially awful. And even if an eternity of worthwhile living were not possible, as atheists think, annihilation would still be bad when it cuts short a worthwhile life.

Yet some philosophers have argued compellingly that being annihilated is a matter of complete indifference, no matter how good the life it interrupts. In fact, Epicurus defended such indifference in his *Letter to Menoeceus,* reprinted in the previous chapter. In this chapter, Epicurus' position will be discussed further. The general topic is what our attitude about our own death should be and how that attitude should affect our attitude about life.

Epicurus and the Triviality of Annihilation

In his *Letter to Menoeceus,* Epicurus argues that the actual event of dying (as opposed to the illness leading up to dying) is a matter of indifference, no matter when it occurs during the course of our lives and no matter how good those lives are when interrupted. He reaches this conclusion on the strength of his brand of ethical hedonism: Only pleasure and the absence of pain (and, indirectly, what causes pleasure) is good, and only pain (and its causes) is bad, so anything that causes neither pleasure nor pain is a matter of indifference. Dying, which Epicurus construes as our complete annihilation, causes neither pleasure nor pain; indeed, it ends our capacity to experience anything at all. So, we should be indifferent about the prospect of dying, no matter when it occurs. It is true that the *anticipation* of dying could cause us pain and hence be a bad thing. But the fact that anticipating death is bad does not entail that dying itself is bad. Moreover, Epicurus would say, it is *irrational* to let the anticipation of death cause us turmoil precisely because dying itself is of no concern.

In evaluating Epicurus' argument, it is important to note that a version of ethical hedonism is possible other than the sort Epicurus himself embraced, a version which can be used as grounds for concern about annihilation. Epicurus granted that pleasure is not the only good; another good is the absence of pain. Why not grant, then, that pain is not the only bad thing? Why not admit that the absence of pleasure is a bad thing? If we adopt *that* sort of hedonism, we must admit that being annihilated is a bad thing when it deprives us of pleasure we would have derived from living.

Epicurus cannot say that the deprivation of pleasure is a bad thing if he is to maintain that annihilation is *always* a matter of indifference. At most, he could say that people who would not experience a net amount of pleasure were they to live on will be indifferent to ending their lives (since their demise deprives them of no pleasure), and that a possible strategy for making ourselves indifferent to the prospect of annihilation is to arrange our lives so that no pleasure is in store for us. However, such a strategy is a bitter pill to swallow; in effect, it is to render death a matter of indifference by eliminating everything that is desirable about living. Wouldn't we be better off regarding death as a bad thing?

Luper and the Evil of Annihilation

One response Epicurus might make is that the extended hedonistic criterion according to which the absence of pleasure is a bad thing is problematic. After all, we do not normally regard the absence of pleasure as a bad thing. At worst, the many times we endure without experiencing any pleasure are matters of indifference, as the example of periods of sleep makes obvious. However, in "Annihilation," Steven Luper finds somewhat different grounds for saying that Epicurus can completely disarm annihilation only by converting life into something that is not good. Luper claims that Epicurus ought to admit that whatever thwarts our desires, or rather those of our desires whose fulfillment we would find gratifying, is a bad thing for us. Having made this admission, Epicurus could insist that annihilation is trivial only to those who have abandoned all desires that their demise would thwart. However, to abandon all such desires is to deprive ourselves of any reason for thinking that living is a good thing. Better, Luper says, to keep our reasons for thinking life good and pay the price of regarding our demise as bad.

Lucretius and the Triviality of Annihilation

Titus Lucretius Carus (c. 99–55 B.C.), a Roman poet who was greatly influenced by Epicurus, introduces other arguments designed to persuade us that our annihilation is unimportant. Two of these are very much in the spirit of Epicurus. First, we have cause to fear something only if it would make us wretched, yet our ceasing to exist cannot cause us to be wretched. Second, many people who persist in regarding their deaths as evil are involved in a certain sort of confusion: In imagining the situation in which they have ceased to exist, they pretend that they are around to witness what happens after their demise (for example, their corpses being mangled), which, of course, could not happen if dying is annihilation.

Two further arguments are not borrowed from Epicurus. One of these reminds us that if we cease to be, we escape the pain and the endless, pointless Sisyphus-like toil of life. (Notice that death's being our ticket out of a wretched condition is not a reason to regard death as a matter of indifference, but rather a reason to say that death is a good thing.) Lucretius' second argument is as follows:

> Look back at time . . . before our birth. In this way Nature holds before our eyes the mirror of our future after death. Is this so grim, so gloomy?

On one reading of this argument, Lucretius is drawing our attention to the fact that no one is unhappy about the fact that there is no way for us to extend our lives into the past. We are content with being born when we were, so why should we want to extend our lives into the future?

Parfit and Our Bias Toward the Future

Epicurus could have joined Lucretius in arguing that our attitude about extending life into the past should be the same as our attitude about extending life into the future, for our not having been born earlier than we were cannot cause us pain or pleasure. Derek Parfit thinks that Epicurus did make something like Lucretius' argument, though the editors can find no such argument. In "Why We Should Not Be Biased Towards the Future," Parfit discusses the following version of Lucretius' argument:

We do not regret our past nonexistence, so we ought not to regret our future nonexistence. Parfit claims that this argument does not work because, as a matter of fact, everyone is biased toward the future, meaning that we care a great deal about events in our futures but little about ones in our past, so that we would rather have a period of agony behind us than before us, a period of enjoyment before us rather than behind us. Given this bias, it makes sense to regret the fact that we will one day cease to exist, even though we do not lament the fact that prior to a certain time, we did not exist. It is reasonable to wish we could extend our lives into the future, even though we do not wish we could extend them into the past.

Parfit also suggests that we would be better off without our bias. We would be happier if we could emulate a person he calls Timeless, described as follows:

> When such a person is reminded that he once had a month of agony, he is as much distressed as when he learns that he will later have such a month. He is similarly neutral with respect to enjoyable events. When he is told that he will later have some period of great enjoyment, he is pleased to learn this. He greatly looks forward to this period. When he is reminded that he once had just such a period, he is equally pleased.[1]

Such people would regret dying considerably less than those of us who are biased toward the future. When they neared death, they could look back over their lives and savor the experiences they had accumulated. The situation of being nearly dead would strike them as exactly like the situation of being newly born (or rather, it would if we imagined that the newly born sprang immediately from oblivion into full

---

[1] *Reasons and Persons* (Oxford, England: Clarendon Press, 1984), 174.

adulthood in a way that mirrors the fashion in which the nearly dead spring immediately from full adulthood into the void). The latter is cause for reduced regret, even though the newly born have nothing to look back on because they have their whole lives to look forward to. And the former is cause for less alarm, even though the nearly dead have nothing to look forward to because they have their whole lives to look back on.

Parfit does not think we can entirely eliminate our bias toward the future, so he thinks that ultimately, Lucretius' argument fails. However, just as Luper suggests that we would do well to adopt a version of the Epicurean strategy for approaching death, so Parfit seems to recommend a version of Lucretius' approach to death. Parfit's recommendation is that we *minimize* our bias toward the future.

Would Immortality Be Evil?

Luper suggests that a death that prevents us from satisfying desires we would find fulfilling is a bad thing. Parfit adds that not being born earlier is a bad thing when it keeps us from things we would regard as good. These suggestions do not entail that living forever (and *having* lived forever) would be a good thing, but they come close. Only if we could continue to satisfy fulfilling desires forever would Luper say that immortality is a good thing (other things being equal), and only if we could always have had good things in our life would Parfit say that having always lived is a good thing (other things being equal). In an essay not included here called "The Makropulous Case: Reflections on the Tedium of Immortality," Bernard Williams argues against the possibility that we could always be in the way of satisfying fulfilling desires. Thereby, he concludes that immortality would be an evil, so that people (such as Tolstoy) who wish to live forever are misled. If he is right, a similar sort of argument can be used to show that having always lived would be an evil.

Williams's key point is that anything we might do over the course of a long enough period will begin to fall into recognizable patterns. At that time, people who want to live out of the impetus of categorical desires (instead of achieving a complete indifference about whether we live or die by emulating the zombie-like Epicureans described by Luper; not only do these Epicureans not mind dying, they do not mind living forever) will find that life has become unbearably tedious. By *categorical desire,* Williams means the same thing as Luper means by *unconditional desire* (having borrowed the notion from Williams). Such a desire is one that is not contingent on our being alive. Instead, it can provide a person with a motivation to remain alive. People who want themselves to be thrust forever into the future by categorical desires must pick ones that involve them in projects that will never fall into patterns whose repetition would only bore them so much that after a time, life would become unbearable. But no such projects are available.

According to Williams, the strategy that comes closest to helping us put together desires that thrust us forever into the future is that of taking up an endless series of lives, so that over time, our character and concerns change completely. The problem with this strategy is that it prevents *us* from living forever. My surviving into the future requires that my character and concerns remain to some (admittedly unclear) degree recognizably the same. Thus, planning that all or most of the features of my personality should periodically be replaced with wholly new features is planning that my body should be occupied by a series of completely distinct persons. The plan is not one by which I survive forever, happy or otherwise. It is one by which an endless series of distinct people live and die.

If immortality really were undesirable, we would have yet another reason to regard our demise as less of a disaster, for we might have thought that living forever (and having always lived) would be a good. The comfort here is only slightly beyond cold, however, for those of us who could make use of a good deal *more* time than is allotted to us. We might even wonder whether Williams has underestimated the possibilities eternity could offer us.

DYING IS NOT AN EVIL

Death

Lucretius

Death
Is nothing to us, has no relevance
To our condition, seeing that the mind
Is mortal. . . .
If there lies ahead
Tough luck for any man, he must be there,
Himself, to feel its evil, but since death
Removes this chance, and by injunction stops
All rioting of woes against our state,
We may be reassured that in our death
We have no cause for fear, we cannot be
Wretched in nonexistence. Death alone
Has immortality, and takes away
Our mortal life. It does not matter a bit
If we once lived before. . . .
So, seeing a man
Feel sorry for himself, that after death
He'll be a rotting corpse, laid in a tomb,
Succumb to fire, or predatory beasts,
You'll know he's insincere, just making noise,
With rancor in his heart, though he believes,
Or tries to make us think so, that death ends all.
And yet, I'd guess, he contradicts himself,
He does not really see himself as gone,
As utter nothingness, but does his best—
Not really understanding what he's doing—
To have himself survive, for, in his life,
He will project a future, a dark day
When beast or bird will lacerate his corpse.
So he feels sorry for himself; he fails
To make the real distinction that exists
Between his castoff body, and the man
Who stands beside it grieving, and imputes
Some of his sentimental feelings to it.
Resenting mortal fate, he cannot see
That in true death he'll not survive himself
To stand there a mourner, stunned by grief
That he is burned or mangled. If in death
It's certainly no pleasure to be mauled
By beak of bird or fang of beast, I'd guess
It's no voluptuous revel to be laid
Over the flames, or packed in honey and ice,
Stiff on the surface of a marble slab,
Or buried under a great mound of earth.

And men behave the same way at a banquet,
Holding the cups or garlanding the brows,

And sighing from the heart, "Ah, life is short
For puny little men, and when it goes
We cannot call it back," as if they thought
The main thing wrong, after their death, will be
That they are very thirsty, or may have
A passionate appetite for who knows what.
"No longer will you happily come home
To a devoted wife, or children dear
Running for your first kisses, while your heart
Is filled with sweet unspoken gratitude.
You will no longer dwell in happy state,
Their sword and shield. Poor wretch," men tell themselves,
"One fatal day has stolen all your gains."
But they don't add, "And all your covetings."
If they could see this clearly, follow it
With proper reasoning, their minds would be
Free of great agony and fear, "As now
You lie asleep in death, forevermore
You will be quit of any sickening pain,
While we, who stood beside your funeral pyre,
Have, with no consolation, mourned your death
In sorrow time will never heal." Well, then,
Ask of your dead what bitterness he finds
In sleep and quiet; why should anyone
Wear himself out in everlasting grief?
No man, when body and soul are lost in sleep,
Finds himself missing, or conducts a search
For his identity; for all we know,
For all we care, that sleep might last forever
And we would never list ourselves as missing.
Yet, all this while, our motes, our atoms, wander
Not far from sense-producing shift and stir,
And suddenly we come to wakefulness.
So we must think of death as being nothing,
As less than sleep, or less than nothing, even,
Since our array of matter never stirs
To reassemble, once the chill of death
Has taken over.
Look back at time—
How meaningless, how unreal!— before our birth.
In this way Nature holds before our eyes
The mirror of our future after death.
Is this so grim, so gloomy? Is it not
A rest more free from care than any sleep?

Now all those things which people say exist
In Hell, are really present in our lives.
The story says that Tantalus, the wretch,
Frozen in terror, fears the massive rock
Balanced in air above him. It's not true.
What happens is that in our lives the fear,
The silly, vain, ridiculous fear of gods,
Causes our panic dread of accident.
No vultures feed on Tityos, who lies
Sprawled out for them in Hell; they could not find
In infinite eternities of time
What they are searching for in that great bulk,
Nine acres wide, or ninety, or the spread
Of all the globe. No man can ever bear
Eternal pain, nor can his body give
Food to the birds forever. We do have
A Tityos in ourselves, and lie, in love,
Torn and consumed by our anxieties,
Our fickle passions. Sisyphus, too, is here
In our own lives; we see him as the man
Bent upon power and office, who comes back
Gloomy and beaten after every vote.
To suffering and punishment, and fears
These will be more than doubled after death.
Hell does exist on earth—in the life of fools.

To seek for power, such an empty thing,
And never gain it, suffering all the while,
This is to shove uphill the stubborn rock
Which over and over comes bouncing down again

To the flat levels where it started from.
Or take another instance: when we feed
A mind whose nature seems unsatisfied,
Never content, with all the blessings given
Through season after season, with all the charms
And graces of life's harvest, this, I'd say,
Is to be like those young and lovely girls,
The Danaids, trying in vain to fill
Their leaky jars with water. Cerberus,
The Furies, and the dark, and the grim jaws
Of Tartarus, belching blasts of heat—all these
Do not exist at all, and never could.
But here on earth we do fear punishment
For wickedness, and in proportion dread
Our dreadful deeds, imagining all too well
Being cast down from the Tarpeian Rock,
Jail, flogging, hangmen, brands, the rack, the knout;
And even though these never touch us, still
The guilty mind is its own torturer
With lash and rowel, can see no end at all.

Finally, what's this wanton lust for life
To make us tremble in dangers and in doubt?
All men must die, and no man can escape.
We turn and turn in the same atmosphere
In which no new delight is ever shaped
To grace our living; what we do not have
Seems better than everything else in all the world,
But should we get it, we want something else.
Our gaping thirst for life is never quenched.
We have to know what luck next year will bring,
What accident, what end. But life, prolonged,
Subtracts not even one second from the term
Of death's continuance. We lack the strength
To abbreviate that eternity. Suppose
You could contrive to live for centuries,
As many as you will. Death, even so,
Will still be waiting for you; he who died
Early this morning has as many years
Interminably before him, as the man,
His predecessor, has, who perished months
Or years, or, even centuries ago.

. . .

Dying Is an Evil

Annihilation

Steven Luper

I do not want to die—no; I neither want to die nor do I want to want to die; I want to live for ever and ever and ever.

Miguel de Unamuno,
The Tragic Sense of Life

Those of us who are bitter about dying are appalled by the cheerful indifference of people who are capable of agreeing with Epicurus' absurd claim that "death is nothing to us." Our first thought is that dying is about the worst thing that could possibly happen to us. Perhaps we would modify this extreme view upon further reflection, but we will still think that dying would almost always be a misfortune for us. What would people have to be *like* to really think that their deaths are nothing to them? The answer, as we shall see, is that to the extent that such people are understandable at all, they are rather coldhearted and passionless. Having said that, I nonetheless want to claim that they are worth careful study. By emulating a certain sort of "Epicurean", as I shall call an individual who is indifferent to dying, it may be possible for others to acquire a measure of equanimity in the face of death without adopting the less desirable characteristics of Epicureans. But before I describe the kind of Epicurean it would behoove us to become, I shall describe others whose ways we should shun.

Dying does not dismay the unflappable Epicureans because they insulate themselves with an overly narrow criterion of evil. On their brand of hedonism, something can be bad only if it causes us pain, and good only if it causes us pleasure; whatever causes us neither pain nor pleasure is a matter of indifference.[1] On the strength of this criterion for good and evil, Epicureans claim that dying is nothing to us since it causes us neither pain nor pleasure. They admit that the disease or aging process which causes us to die may be a bad thing; these causes of death may bring us experiences whose unpleasantness is formidable. But dying causes no sensations at all, they point out. In fact, it brings about an end to all sensing. Once dead, we lack even the opportunity to regret the ending of sensation.

As stated, the hedonistic criterion for good and bad is overly narrow. (Isn't it a tragedy that death deprives us even of the opportunity to experience, to delight, and to regret.) Consider the trouble it gets Epicureans into when they confront situations in which dying would be an *attractive* option for most people. For instance, the prospect of spending eternity in unmitigated agony is about as horrifying as can be; virtually the only thing worse would be spending eternity in *even more intense* agony. It is obvious that dying would be better than either fate. But Epicureans could agree only if they were not completely indifferent to dying. To agree, they must be willing to admit that under some circumstances dying can be the best of all available alternatives because of the escape it provides. Yet they cannot agree. Their criterion for good and bad precludes their doing so. The fact that the Epicureans are completely indifferent to dying means that they never under any circumstances either want to die or want not to die, and that is possible only if under no circumstances do they prefer dying to anything nor anything to dying.

This result makes Epicureans considered as completely indifferent to dying extremely foreign. Hence let us try to describe Epicureans whose indifference is somewhat more limited. Epicurus himself judged an item good for him only to the extent that the item caused him pleasure. Consequently he was unable to judge a death good when it prevented him from suffering. But he could do just that if he modified his hedonistic criterion as follows: something is good only if it causes us pleasure *or it eliminates pain*, bad only if it causes us pain, and a matter of indifference otherwise. A death that spares us from protracted suffering is a good thing on this more expansive criterion.

---

[1] According to Epicurus,

> All good and evil consists in sensation, but death is deprivation of sensation. . . . For we recognize pleasure as the first good innate in us, and from pleasure we begin every act of choice and avoidance, and to pleasure we return again, using the feeling as the standard by which we judge every good. (*Letter to Menoeceus*)

But wait: if the Epicureans say that the absence of pain can be a good thing, why shouldn't they add that the absence of pleasure can be a *bad* thing? The addition has considerable plausibility, but of course it is one that Epicureans would be loath to accept inasmuch as doing so would force them to deplore death. For almost in every case dying does deprive us of pleasure.

In any case, it is not important to decide whether Epicureans who acknowledge that the absence of pain can be good should also say that the absence of pleasure can be bad. For the hedonistic criterion for good and bad is too narrow *even if* it says that something is bad only if it causes pain or eliminates pleasure. To see why, consider some of the consequences of the hedonist criterion. On that criterion, an event which *would* cause me great pain or deprive me of a considerable amount of pleasure if I were to find out about it is a matter of indifference so long as I in fact never do. The fact that my spouse and children have fallen for the lies of my enemy and now hate me but are pretending not to is of no concern to me, according to hedonists, if my ignorance prevents that event from affecting the amount of pleasure and pain I feel. Moreover, hedonists would cheerfully consent to being used in any way we like so long as we promise to precede their treatment with a drug that makes them enjoy what we do to them, or at least a drug which suppresses any unpleasant experiences that might otherwise result from the abuses we have planned for them. They could even be made to welcome our drugging away their free will so that they want to be our slaves.

In view of cases like these, we need a better understanding of misfortune than hedonists have provided. I suggest that whatever prevents us from fulfilling our desires, or at least those of our desires whose fulfillment we would find gratifying, is a misfortune for us.[2] If I am right, it is clear why losing love or being converted into a slave would constitute a misfortune. My desire that my spouse and children continue to love me is thwarted when they fall for the lies of my enemies. My ambition to shape the course of my own life comes to naught if I am converted into a contented slave. However, on this alternative notion of a misfortune, dying is usually a bad thing. For in most circumstances dying *would* thwart our desires. Let 'premature death' refer to a death that thwarts desires whose fulfillment we would find gratifying. Then surely a premature death is a misfortune for its victim.[3]

Surprisingly, however, Epicureans could adopt our understanding of misfortune and

---

[2] Even this criterion is subject to criticism, but it will suffice for our purposes.

[3] I might note that there is another reason, often attributed to Epicurus, for denying that dying can be a bad thing for us. The objection is that 'having died' can never correctly be *attributed* to anyone, since before people die, 'having died' is not true of them, and after they die they have ceased to exist, so that nothing remains for 'having died' to be a property of. Hence 'having died' does not refer to a property anyone can have, and so it cannot be a misfortune for us to have that property. (Arguably, this is what Wittgenstein had in mind when he remarked in *Tractatus*, 6.4311 that "death is not an event in life.")

But this is a mere sophism. Just as I can have properties by virtue of what goes on outside my *spatial* boundaries (for example, being attacked by a cat), so I can have properties by virtue of what is going on outside my temporal boundaries. Thus it is partly due to events that occurred before I came into existence that 'having been conceived' and 'born after Aristotle' are both true of me. And it is partly due to events that will take place after I die that 'will have his will read' and 'will die' are true of me. Death is not an event in a life, but it *is* the event by which a life ends.

still never regard dying as a bad thing. True, they would have to deplore a death that thwarted desires whose satisfaction would be fulfilling. But suppose Epicureans simply avoided having any such desires! Suppose that they so constitute the scheme of their desires that any time death comes it is mature rather than premature. Assuming that Epicureans allow themselves goals, then either they would have to be unfulfilling ones, or else they would have to be ones that could not be thwarted by death. If Epicureans had any other sort of goal, they could not be unconcerned about premature death.

But what would a desire that cannot be thwarted by death be like? One desire that obviously is impervious to death is the desire to die. Desires that set out conditions under which life is so bad that death is preferable would also fit the bill. Call desires of this sort *escape desires*. In effect, they are qualified desires for death: they say that if certain conditions are met, we wish to be dead. But they do not imply that there are any conditions under which we do not want to be dead. Hence death presents no obstacle to our satisfying them.

Nor does the list of relevant desires end there. Some of our aims are such that our chances of successfully accomplishing them are not really affected by what we do in the course of our lives or even by whether or not we *are* alive. Being alive does not help us achieve these ends; hence they cannot be thwarted by our deaths. Since the likelihood that such goals will be achieved does not depend on what we do with our lives, let us call these *independent* goals. Ones whose chances of being achieved do depend on our activities we can call *dependent* goals. My desire that the moon continue to orbit Earth, for example, is an independent goal; it cannot provide me any grounds for deploring death since the behaviour of Earth and its satellite is unaffected by what I do in the course of my life.

There is another, more interesting, type of desire that is invulnerable to our deaths. Suppose that we care about the situation at some future time, but only on the assumption that we shall be alive at that time; if we think that we shall be dead, we are indifferent about the situation. Suicidal depressants, for example, might take this view. They may strongly wish to be dead, and they may be totally indifferent to anything that may or may not happen once they *are* dead; yet they still may have the attitude that if they *are* to be alive, they should be well fed. They desire something—in this case being well fed—only on the assumption or condition that they will continue to be alive. Desires that are *not* in this way contingent on our being alive we can call *unconditional*.

As far as I can tell, the catalogue of desires which cannot be thwarted by death is limited to escape desires, independent desires, and conditional desires. Since limiting their desires to the catalogued sorts is the only way Epicureans could ensure that death is no evil for them, however, we shall want to consider what kind of person they have had to become as a result of that limitation.

Consider their motivation to take up the activities in which we normally engage. Since Epicureans never have any reason to avoid dying, it may appear that they have no reason to do *anything* (with the possible exception of committing suicide). But this is an important mistake. It is true that their independent desires cannot provide Epicureans grounds for any activities, since by definition these are desires about whose fulfillment Epicureans can do nothing of importance. However, conditional desires do provide strong reason for action. Such desires can enable Epicureans to take an interest in things for which life is a precondition. While indifferent to the prospect of dying in their sleep, Epicureans may take the attitude that if they *do* wake, their wakeful days should be spent in vigorous pursuit of an exciting career, in raising a family, etc. And for this to be possible, they will need to seek an education and work long hours in pursuit of a career.

Suppose that someone went around injecting Epicureans with painless but deadly poison. Wouldn't an Epicurean society have to be indifferent about that practice, since it would not interfere with any Epicurean's desires? No, precisely because it *would* interfere. It is true that an Epicurean cannot abhor these murders on the grounds that they are bad for their *victims*. But the murders could be abhorred (unless they involve the massacre of entire societies or the entire human race) because they deprive people of their loved ones. The murders are bad for the survivors, who wanted to share their lives (if lives they will lead) with the victims. Still Epicureans could condemn the murder of pariahs who play no positive role in society only on the grounds that if that sort of thing were permitted it might lead people to kill those who *do* have a role to play. Anyone who is inclined to condemn Epicureans on the grounds that they do not appreciate how bad murder is should, however, recall that the victims *themselves* are to their very cores genuinely indifferent to dying.

So far, adopting the Epicurean approach may not seem terribly unattractive. If something which is a bad thing for us, given our present desires, turns out to be inevitable, then why not alter our desires so that we no longer must regard the inevitable as an evil?[4] Dying is inevitable, so why not disarm it by limiting ourselves to the desires of Epicureans? Unfortunately, the indifference to dying which the Epicurean approach would secure us comes at a price most of us will not be willing to pay. Epicureans think that death is nothing to them only because they think that *life* is nothing to them. For in avoiding all aspirations that can be thwarted by death, Epicureans have had to avoid all desires which are capable of giving Epicureans a reason for living.

The extent to which Epicureans have sabotaged their motivation for living can be brought out by examining the desires to which they are limited, desires that are invulnerable to death. Independent goals (unlike dependent ones) are incapable of giving us reason to remain alive and to avoid dying, since our lives and the things we do with our lives play no role toward the achievement of such goals. Conditional de-

---

[4]This view has been advocated in one form or another by a great number of people for a good while. It is the third "Noble Truth" of Gautama Siddhartha (563–483 B.C.), and is echoed in the following melancholy advice by the tenth century Buddhist lama Milarepa:

> All worldly pursuits have but the one unavoidable and inevitable end, which is sorrow: acquisitions end in dispersion; buildings, in destructions; meetings, in separation; births, in death. Knowing this, one should from the very first renounce acquisition and heaping-up, and building and meeting. . . . Life is short, and the time of death is uncertain. (From W. Evans-Wentz, *Tibet's Great Yogi: Milarepa* (New York, 1969).)

The Roman Stoic Epictetus (ca. A.D. 50–130), who lived about three centuries after Epicurus, also suggests that we alter our desires so that we need not regard the inevitable as a bad thing:

> Ask not that events should happen as you will, but let your will be that events should happen as they do, and you shall have peace. If . . . you try to avoid only what is unnatural in the region within your control, you will escape from all that you avoid; but if you try to avoid disease or death or poverty you will be miserable. (From *The Manual of Epictetus*, in *The Stoic and Epicurean Philosophers*, edited by W. Oates (New York, 1940), pp. 468–84.)

sires are similarly impotent; because they apply only on the assumption that we are alive, they cannot provide grounds for being alive. Like the other desires Epicureans possess, escape desires (as well as the death wish itself) are incapable of providing any reason to remain alive; on the contrary, escape desires provide reason to *die*. Beyond conditional, independent, and escape desires, the only other desires Epicureans can have are unfulfilling ones, and these are obviously as impotent as the others with respect to motivating Epicureans to live. Out of the desires possessed by Epicureans, then, a case for remaining alive cannot be built. Since they limit their desires to those listed above, and so consider dying at least as good as any other option, it is useful to characterize the Epicurean personality as *death-tolerant*.[5] By contrast, the personality of people who have unconditional desires that make living desirable can be called *life-affirming*.

Since Epicureans cannot allow themselves any motivation to live, they must ensure that they never think that it would be *good* to live. For to say that living is good certainly implies that it is preferable to dying, which is a view Epicureans must eschew. On their view, living no sort of life would be better than dying.

Nothing said here supports the claims, occasionally made, that life's being meaningful or worthwhile is due to the fact that we die, or that life is *meaningless* because we die.[6] Both claims imply that it is due to death that life has the value it does, which is not true. A life can be made neither good nor bad by the fact that it will eventually end, any more than a car can be made good or bad by the fact that it will eventually be scrapped. A life has the value it does quite independently of the fact that it will end. In fact, *death* has the value it does due to the value of the life it ends. Speaking roughly, dying is a bad thing when living on would be good, and when living on would be bad, dying is good.

Because Epicureans are not interested in anything that could lead them to regard living as a good thing, they do not care about *anything* that they believe will happen after they die, ignoring what they care about through their independent desires, which (as we have seen) have no motivational power in the Epicureans' lives anyway. Those with a death-tolerant personality live out of inertia most of the time, acting only under the influence of their conditional desires unless life becomes unpleasant enough to opt out of. But the interest which they take in things through the agency of their conditional desires does not extend beyond what they believe to be the

---

[5]Indeed, we might just as well call the Epicurean personality death-*wishing* in view of the facts that conditional desires are much like escape desires and the latter are qualified death wishes. What is plausible about Freud's theory is captured by the view that many people are quite death-tolerant.

[6]In *My Confessions*, trans. Leo Weiner (London, 1905), Tolstoy seems to suggest that life would be meaningless if we died:

> But the answer in this sphere of knowledge to my question what the meaning of my life was, was always: "you are what you call your life; you are a temporal, accidental conglomeration of particles. The inter-relation, the change of these particles, produces in you that which you call life. This congeries will last for some time; then the interaction of these particles will cease, and that which you call life and all your questions will come to an end."

With such an answer it appears that the answer is not a reply to the question. I want to know the meaning of my life, but the fact that it is a particle of the infinite not only gives it no meaning, but even destroys every possible meaning.

temporal boundaries of their lives. For given that their entire attitude about whether or not a given state of affairs X holds at some time *t* is conditional, then if they believed that they would be dead at *t*, then they would be indifferent about whether or not X would hold at *t*. This makes Epicureans peculiar people indeed. Out of her conditional desire for their well-being, an Epicurean mother may well be concerned about whether her children will survive an imminent catastrophe, but *only* if she assumes that she too will survive. Her conditional desires leave her completely indifferent to their welfare if she assumes that she will die. Nor does the peculiar pattern of her concern for her offspring end here. She may well place herself between a crazed beast and her children since she does not think that her life will be bearable to her if they die, and so is willing to risk her life in their defense. Her life means nothing to her in any case. But she is incapable of writing a will or taking out life insurance out of concern for her children's well-being after she dies, even if she knows that they will lead a horrible existence if she fails to act. Whether their lives go well or poorly after she dies is a matter of utter indifference to her.

Still less could Epicureans desire the welfare of future generations. Because their concern for others is conditional, Epicureans cannot believe that the welfare of future generations matters at all, though the welfare of their contemporaries may be important to them.

Nonetheless, it *is* conceivable that Epicureans have a conditional desire to spend their days working for the benefit of future generations. They could take the attitude that so long as they are to go on, they will work for the benefit of posterity. And an Epicurean mother could decide that, so long as she is alive tomorrow, she will spend it working to ensure that her children flourish after she dies. However, these attitudes are not to be mistaken for concern about what occurs after the Epicureans die. Epicureans just do not care what happens then. They are capable only of indifference about the well-being of posterity, and an Epicurean mother could not care less about the welfare of her children after she believes she will die. Therefore, even if Epicureans take an interest in *working for* the welfare of posterity, they remain indifferent to the welfare of posterity. It takes peculiar people to desire to spend time ensuring that some state of affairs holds in the future even though they are indifferent about whether that state of affairs comes to be.

Even the conditionalized form of a purely self-centered desire can be enormously peculiar. Our self-centered projects play an important role in our lives, and most of them can succeed only if we survive, either because we are an essential ingredient in them, as I am in my plan to become President of Money Bank, or my plan to lead a long life of adventure, or else because we play a key role in them. Hence we must conditionalize our concern for these projects if we are to emulate the Epicureans. But is a deep concern about such projects really consistent with the attitude that their failure is a matter of indifference so long as we do not live through their demise? How serious can I be about wanting to discover the cure for cancer if I am just as happy to fail so long as I do not live through my failure? The fact is that a conditionalized passion is not a passion, for we can conditionalize our passions in life only if we no longer take them seriously enough to want to live another day. Once conditionalized, they can no longer play any significant role in what might have been a worthwhile life.

Although we should not emulate the Epicureans we have described, it does seem to me that there *is* a type of Epicurean which we should strive to become. Unlike the ones we have discussed before, the Epicureans I have in mind are anxious to squeeze as much as possible out of life. But these neo-Epicureans (as I will call them) realize that one can squeeze out of a lifetime only as much as a lifetime can hold. Neo-Epicureans have impressed upon themselves the fact that unless further advances in life extension techniques can be expected, they cannot possibly expect much more than a normal lifetime, *and so they cannot allow their happiness to require more*. Neo-Epicureans are not unconcerned about everything that happens after they die. But because they are not indifferent, they try to ensure that those of their concerns that their deaths might leave vulnerable are rendered invulnerable. For example, if they plan to have children, neo-Epicurean parents will see to it that the youngsters grow into relatively self-sufficient adults, or at least that the children's well-being does not depend on the survival of their parents beyond a normal lifetime. Neo-Epicureans know that they cannot expect to survive beyond a normal lifetime, and so make sure that well before then they have fully equipped their children for life.

Neo-Epicureans have a similar approach to all of their other concerns which might be left vulnerable to what occurs after their deaths. They are not indifferent to these matters; instead, and because of their concern, they see to it that the goals they are concerned about are as invulnerable to their deaths as can be. All such goals neo-Epicureans convert to independent goals, so that the success of these projects is not made less likely by their deaths. In short, as their final years approach, neo-Epicureans make themselves completely dispensable to everything they care about. Not worried that the concerns of their lifetimes will come to a bad end with their deaths, they do not regret passing away. They have, we might say, *epicureanized* their desires. Death which comes before they have done what they have set out to do they hate with all their hearts, since it comes between them and what they consider dear. But death which comes after they have accomplished their goals or rendered their goals independent they do not grudge. It will catch the neo-Epicureans only with independent or conditional desires.

Being dispensable, however, is something that neo-Epicureans carefully postpone to the very end. Early on in life, they begin taking steps that will ensure that they will *be* dispensable, but—like a coffin—dispensability is something they want only when they die. For having our lives deeply intertwined with those of others is part of what makes life worthwhile. What neo-Epicureans want is not that their lives should have made no difference to anybody or anything. What they want is that their *deaths* should make no difference. To the extent that our being alive plays no important role in any of the matters we care about (and to the extent that we care about *nothing*), to that extent we have no reason to value our lives. It is the fact that we are indispensable to people and projects we care about that motivates us to live another day; we should undermine this motivation, therefore, only when we are prepared to die.

NOT HAVING EXISTED EARLIER IS AN EVIL

Why We Should Not Be Biased Towards the Future

Derek Parfit

Our bias towards the future is bad for us. It would be better for us if we were like Timeless. [When such a person is reminded that he once had a month of agony, he is as much distressed as when he learns that he will later have such a month. He is similarly neutral with respect to enjoyable events. When he is told that he will later have some period of great enjoyment, he is pleased to learn this. He greatly looks forward to this period. When he is reminded that he once had just such a period, he is equally pleased. I shall call this imagined man *Timeless*.] We would lose in certain ways. Thus we should not be relieved when bad things were in the past. But we should also gain. We should not be sad when good things were in the past.

The gains would outweigh the losses. One reason would be this. When we look backward, we could afford to be selective. We ought to remember some of the bad events in our lives, when this would help us to avoid repetitions. But we could allow ourselves to forget most of the bad things that have happened, while preserving by rehearsing all of our memories of the good things. It would be bad for us if we were so selective when we are looking forward. Unless we think of all the bad things that are at all likely to happen, we lose our chance of preventing them. Since we ought not to be selective when looking forward, but could afford to be when looking backward, the latter would be, on the whole, more enjoyable.

There would be other, greater gains. One would be in our attitude to ageing and to death. Let us first consider the argument with which Epicurus claimed that our future non-existence cannot be something to regret. We do not regret our past non-existence. Since this is so, why should we regret our future non-existence? If we regard one with equanimity, should we not extend this attitude to the other?

Some claim that this argument fails because, while we might live longer, we could not have been born earlier. This is not a good objection. When they learnt that the square root of two was not a rational number, the Pythagoreans regretted this. We can regret truths even when it is logically impossible that these truths be false.

Epicurus's argument fails for a different reason: we are biased towards the future. Because we have this bias, the bare knowledge that we once suffered may not now disturb us. But our equanimity does not show that our past suffering was not bad. The same could be true of our past non-existence. Epicurus's argument therefore has force only for those people who both lack the bias towards the future, and do not regret their past non-existence. Since there are no such people, the argument has force for no one.

Though the argument fails, it may provide some consolation. If we are afraid of death, the argument shows that the object of our dread is not *our non-existence*. It is only our *future* non-existence. That we can think serenely of our past non-existence does not show that it is not something to regret. But since we do not in fact view with dread our past non-existence, we may be able to use this fact to reduce our dread, or depression, when we think about our inevitable deaths. If we often think about, and view serenely, the blackness behind us, some of this serenity may be transferred to our view of the blackness before us.

Let us now suppose that we lack the bias towards the future. We are like Timeless. We should then greatly gain in our attitude to ageing and to death. As our life passes, we should have less and less to look forward to, but more and more to look backward to. This effect will be clearer if we imagine another difference. Suppose that our lives began, not with birth and childhood, but as Adam's did. Suppose that, though we are adults, and have adult knowledge and abilities, we have only just started to exist. We lack the bias towards the future. Should we be greatly troubled by the thought that yesterday we did not exist?

This depends on what is wrong with non-existence. Some think it in itself bad. But the more plausible view is that its only fault is what it causes us to lose. Suppose we take this view. We may then think it a ground for regret that our life is finite, bounded at both ends by non-existence. But, if we had just started to exist, we would not think that something bad was just behind us. Our ground for regret would merely be that we had missed much that would have been good. Suppose that I could now be much as I actually am, even though I had been born as one of the privileged few around 1700. I would then greatly regret that I was in fact born in 1942. I would far prefer to have lived through the previous two and a half centuries, having had among my friends Hume, Byron, Chekhov, Nietzsche, and Sidgwick.

In my imagined case, we are not biased towards the future, and we have just started to exist. Though we would regret the fact that we had not existed earlier, we would not be greatly troubled by the thought that only yesterday we did not exist. We would not regard this fact with the kind of dread or grief with which most actual people would regard the sudden prospect of death tomorrow. We would not have such dread or grief because, though we would have nothing good to look backward to, we would have our whole lives to look forward to.

Now suppose that our lives have nearly passed. We shall die tomorrow. If we were not biased towards the future, our reaction should mirror the one that I have just described. We should not be greatly troubled by the thought that we shall soon cease to exist, for though we now have nothing to look forward to, we have our whole lives to look backward to.

It may be objected: 'You can look backward now. But once you are dead you won't be able to look backward. And you will be dead tomorrow. So you ought to be greatly troubled.' We could answer: 'Why? It is true that after we cease to exist we shall never be able to enjoy looking backward to our lives. We now have nothing at all to look forward to, not even the pleasures of looking backward. But it was equally true that, before we began to exist, we could not enjoy looking forward to our lives. Just after we began to exist, we had nothing at all to look backward to, not even the pleasures of looking forward. But that was then no reason to be greatly troubled, since we could then look forward to our whole lives. Since we can now look backward to our whole lives, why should the parallel fact—that we have nothing to look forward to—give us reason to be greatly troubled?'

This reasoning ignores those emotions which are essentially future-directed. It would not apply to those people for whom the joy in looking forward comes from making plans, or savouring alternatives. But the reasoning seems to be correct when applied to more passive types, those who take life's pleasures as they come. And, since this is partly true of us, this reasoning shows that we would be happier if we lacked the bias towards the future. We would be much less depressed by ageing and the approach of death. If we were like Timeless, being at the end of our lives would be more like being at the beginning. At any point within our lives we could enjoy looking either backward or forward to our whole lives.

I have claimed that, if we lacked the bias towards the future, this would be better for us. This matches the plausible claim that it would be better for us if we lacked the bias towards the near. There is no ground here for criticizing only the latter bias. Both these attitudes to time are, on the whole, bad for us.

Since I believe that this attitude is bad for us, I believe that we ought not to be biased towards the future. This belief does not beg the question about the rationality of this bias. On any plausible moral view, it would be better if we were all happier. This is the sense in which, if we could, we ought not to be biased towards the future. In giving us this bias, Evolution denies us the best attitude to death.

Questions for Further Reflection

1. Some people say that it is not bad to cease to exist because dying is inevitable, natural, and universal to all individuals. Are these good reasons to say that dying is not an evil?
2. Some people, such as Bernard Williams (in "The Makropulous Case: Reflections on the Tedium of Immortality," in his *Problems of the Self* [Cambridge, England: Cambridge University Press, 1973]), argue that immortality would be undesirable since living forever would become insufferably boring. If this claim is correct, mustn't God be miserable? (After all, God is supposed to exist eternally.)
3. If the features of our personality changed gradually over time until they were completely different from our present features, would we be better off than if, instead, we were suddenly to cease to exist? If so, does this show that it would be a good thing were the process of gradual personality change to last forever, and that it is a bad thing that it does not?
4. How should Parfit respond to the following defense of our bias toward the future? We cannot do anything about what is in the past; we can affect only what is in our futures, so we ought to care more about the future than the past.
5. Parfit seems to think that we cannot overcome our bias toward the future. Is he correct?
6. How would Parfit's argument be affected if, in fact, we were irresistibly biased toward the past?

Further Readings

Becker, Ernest. *The Denial of Death.* New York: Free Press, 1973. Pulitzer Prize–winning study of the fear of death.

Donnelly, John, ed. *Language, Metaphysics, and Death.* New York: Fordham University Press, 1978. Contains several interesting discussions of death and some discussions about whether death is a bad thing (including the essay by

Williams referred to in this volume). Thomas Nagel's influential "Death," Richard Taylor's "De Anima," and Slote's "Existentialism and the Fear of Dying" are especially good.

Freud, Sigmund. *Beyond the Pleasure Principle.* J. Strachey, trans. New York: W. W. Norton, 1961. This is where Freud introduces the idea of a death wish. He returns to the idea in his *New Introductory Lectures on Psychoanalysis* (New York: W. W. Norton, 1964).

Kramer, Scott, and Kuang-ming Wu, eds. *Thinking Through Death.* Vols. 1 and 2. Malabar, FL: Krieger, 1988. An exhaustive collection of literature on death, including a good sample from Oriental literature.

Montaigne, Michel de. "That to Philosophize Is to Learn How to Die." In Kramer and Wu, *Thinking Through Death.* A useful collection of common (and bad) arguments against fearing death.

Nagel, Thomas. *The View from Nowhere,* Chapter XI. New York: Oxford University Press, 1986. Expands upon his earlier piece, "Death."

Nietzsche, Friedrich. "On Free Death." In Walter Kaufmann, ed., *The Portable Nietzsche.* New York: Viking Press, 1968. Here Nietzsche suggests that we plan to make our deaths the glorious consummation of our lives.

Nozick, Robert. *Philosophical Explanations,* Section 6. Cambridge, MA: Harvard University Press, 1981. A useful discussion that places death into the larger context of the meaning of life.

Plato. *Phaedo.* In the main, this dialogue is designed to demonstrate the immortality of the soul, but it makes many important points about whether dying is a bad thing.

Schopenhauer, Arthur. *The World as Will and Representation.* Vols. I and II. E. F. J. Payne, trans. New York: Dover, 1956. A difficult discussion that requires weeks to penetrate, but a fascinating attempt to show that it would be better for us not to exist. Those who are interested in Buddhism and Hinduism will find Schopenhauer one of the best interpreters of those doctrines.

Spinoza, Baruch. *Ethics.* Samuel Shirley, trans., Seymour Feldman, ed. Indianapolis: Hackett, 1982. A difficult discussion but an important one.

Unamuno, Miguel de. *The Tragic Sense of Life.* J. E. Crawford Flitch, trans. New York: Dover, 1954. A forceful statement of the view that remaining alive forever is incomparably valuable. See especially Chapter III, "The Hunger of Immortality."

Chapter 4

THE INDIVIDUAL DEATH: IS SUICIDE WRONG?

Deliberately taking one's own life is suicide. In France, it has been legal since the eighteenth century, and it is legal in many other European countries as well. In the United States, many states forbid helping or encouraging anyone to commit suicide, but attempting suicide is a crime only in Texas, Washington, and Oklahoma, while suicide is a crime only in South Carolina and Alabama. Nonetheless, neither attempted suicide nor suicide is punished (although those who attempt suicide are subject to such discriminatory practices as insurance policies that pay no benefits in case of suicide),[1] in view of the fact that punishment would only add to the burdens of people who already find life not to be worth living. Instead, people who attempt suicide are often committed to mental institutions for treatment.

Suicide as a Symptom of Disease

In many cases, committal is based on the assumption that suicide is the product of a mental disorder. However, according to psychologist E. S. Shneidman,

> Nothing like a complete correspondence between suicide and accepted forms of mental disorder has ever been demonstrated. The most profitable approach would seem to be to recognize that the cause of suicide and the causes of mental disorder partly overlap. . . . Thus, virtually the only important theoretical approach to suicide in psychology . . . links the causes of suicide closely with the causes of depression.[2]

In "The Ethics of Suicide," the well-known psychiatrist Thomas Szasz resists the idea that suicide is the product of mental deficiency and argues that suicide is a choice by autonomous agents that must be respected by others who think to intervene.

When mental disorders lead people to take their lives, it makes no sense to ask whether their act is morally blameworthy. If an act is beyond our control, we cannot be morally responsible for it. Suppose, however, that sometimes suicide is not the product of mental disorder. Let us consider

---

[1]David Meyers, *Medico-Legal Implications of Death and Dying* (The Lawyers' Co-operative Publishing Co., 1981), p. 133.

[2]E. S. Shneidman, "Suicide," *Encyclopedia Britannica* (1972), Vol. 21.

people who are of sound mind and ask whether it would be permissible for them to commit suicide.

Arguments for and against the claim that it is morally wrong to commit suicide can be classified according to whether they include the assumption that dying entails annihilation, that is, the assumption that death is not followed by an afterlife. Let us examine the two types of argument, beginning with the one given by people who think that dying is a transition to an afterlife.

Entering the Afterlife

Many theists believe that eternal bliss is available in the afterlife. Such people can find it difficult to explain what is wrong with suicide, supposing that it is a way to achieve bliss straightaway. Indeed, what is to stop utilitarian theists who believe in a blissful afterlife from arguing that it is not only permissible to kill ourselves as quickly as possible, it is our duty, for that is the way to maximize our pleasure?

Some theists simply respond that we may not kill ourselves in order to achieve bliss now because God forbids suicide. Thus, Augustine (354–430) says that killing ourselves and killing others is wrong for the same reason: The Sixth Commandment specifically forbids killing.

> It is not without significance, that in no passage of the holy canonical books there can be found either divine precept or permission to take away our own life, whether for the sake of entering on the enjoyment of immortality, or of shunning, or ridding our selves of anything whatever. Nay, the law, rightly interpreted, even prohibits suicide, where it says, "Thou shalt not kill."[3]

If the Sixth Commandment were a blanket condemnation of all forms of killing, it would be difficult for contemporary Christians to square it with their view that killing in self-defense or in the course of a war is permissible. The main problem with Augustine's response, however, is that it leaves mysterious the reason that God forbade killing in all its forms, and suicide in particular. Even if it is true that God forbids suicide, we will not have an explanation of what is wrong with suicide unless we are told why God forbids it. Presumably, there is a reason why God forbids suicide; otherwise, God's disapproval of suicide would be completely arbitrary.

The Catholic theologian Thomas Aquinas (1225–1274) gives several reasons for saying that suicide is wrong (and hence, several reasons why God might forbid it). One of the points Aquinas makes is that we have to consider the happiness of others who depend on us: If we abandon them in pursuit of a better life beyond, we will deprive them of our help, and, hence, reduce their happiness. However, is this utilitarian retort convincing? If there really is bliss in the life to follow, then wouldn't it be better (and, if we are utilitarians, our duty) to kill everyone we can as quickly as possible, thus securing for them the bliss we ourselves seek, and then take our own lives?

Fortunately, Aquinas gives several more criticisms of suicide, and most of them do not rest on an appeal to the well-being of others:

> It is altogether unlawful to kill oneself, for three reasons. First, because everything naturally loves itself, the result being that everything naturally keeps itself in being, and resists corruptions so far as it can. Wherefore, suicide is contrary to the inclination of nature, and to charity whereby every man should love himself. . . .

---

[3]*The City of God*, trans. Marcus Dods (New York: Random House, 1950), 26 (Book I, Sect. 20).

Secondly, because every part, as such, belongs to the whole. Now every man is part of the community, and so, as such, he belongs to the community. Hence by killing himself he injures the community. . . .

Thirdly, because life is God's gift to man, and is subject to His power, Who kills and makes to live. Hence whoever takes his own life, sins against God, even as he who kills another's slave, sins against that slave's master, and as he who usurps to himself judgment of a matter not entrusted to him. For it belongs to God alone to pronounce sentence of death and life, according to Deut. xxxii. 39, *I will kill and I will make to live*.[4]

It is debatable how cogent these points are. First, suicide might well be the *charitable* (and "self-loving") way to treat ourselves. Given that the afterlife is blissful, even reasonably happy people would seem to do themselves a favor by entering into it without delay. And it is more obvious still that people who are suffering relentlessly would be treating themselves charitably by taking their lives. Now consider Aquinas's complaint that suicide is unnatural. It is far from clear what constitutes an unnatural act and far from obvious that we are morally obligated to refrain from acting in unnatural ways. Depriving oneself of sex is acting contrary to the inclination of nature if anything is, but is abstinence wrong? As for the other concerns, the responses Hume offers in his essay are worth considering, as we shall see.

Augustine's and Aquinas's points were not intended to show that suicide is never permissible. Both were aware of accounts of suicide and certain other sorts of killings in the New Testament, and they tried to find a way to square these with the Sixth Commandment. According to Augustine,

> There are some exceptions made by the divine authority to its own law, that men may not be put to death. . . . They who have waged war in obedience to the divine command, . . . have by no means violated the commandment. "Thou shalt not kill." Abraham indeed was not merely deemed guiltless of cruelty, but was even applauded for his piety, because he was ready to slay his son in obedience to God, not to his own passion. . . . Samson, too, who drew down the house on himself and his foes together, is justified only on this ground, that the Spirit who wrought wonders by him had given him secret instructions to do this.[5]

The claim here is that killing on God's orders is always all right, even when God specifically commands us to take our lives. But again: Is God's decision to require certain suicides completely arbitrary? Or would God have based his decision on the discovery that those suicides were morally right? If the latter, then we still need some way to tell when suicide is right or wrong.

It is worth noting that Arthur Schopenhauer (1788–1860) is one of the few who think that even though death is a transition to an afterlife, suicide is always permissible. He begins his essay "On Suicide" with the following comment:

> As far as I know, none but the votaries of monotheistic, that is to say, Jewish religions, look upon suicide as a crime. This is all the more striking, inasmuch as neither in the Old nor in the New Testament is there to be found any prohibition or positive disapproval of it; so that religious teachers are forced to base their condemnation of suicide on philosophical grounds of their own invention. These are so very bad that writers of this kind endeavor to make up for the weakness of their arguments by the strong terms in

---

[4] *Summa Theologica*, Vol. 2, trans. Fathers of the English Dominican Province (New York: Benziger Brothers, 1947), p. 1469 (Second Part of the Second Part, Question 64).

[5] *The City of God*, p. 27 (Book I, Sect. 21).

which they express their abhorrence of the practice. . . . They tell us that suicide is the greatest piece of cowardice; that only a madman could be guilty of it; and other insipidities of the same kind; or else they make the nonsensical remark that suicide is wrong; when it is quite obvious that there is nothing in the world to which every man has a more unassailable title than to his own life and person. Think of the impression that would be made upon you by the news that some one you know had committed the crime, say, of murder or theft . . . ; and compare it with your feelings when you hear that he has met a voluntary death. While in the one case a lively sense of indignation and extreme resentment will be aroused, and you will call loudly for punishment or revenge, in the other you will be moved to grief and sympathy; and mingled with your thoughts will be admiration for his courage, rather than the moral disapproval which follows upon a wicked action.[6]

Suicide as Annihilation

In "Of Suicide," David Hume (1711–1776) rebuts the theistic arguments of Augustine and Aquinas and goes on to argue that annihilating ourselves is morally permissible in virtually every set of circumstances. He begins with the assumption that if suicide is always wrong, it must always violate either our duty to "God, our neighbour, or ourselves" and then rejects each possibility in turn.

As for the first, he notes (among other things) that we do not normally regard altering the natural course of events as objectionable ("it would be no crime in me to divert the Nile or Danube from its course"), so why say that altering it by committing suicide is wrong? As for the claim that suicide is an encroachment on God's prerogative over life and death, Hume notes that the same reasoning would show that "it would be equally criminal to act for the preservation of life as for its destruction." And Hume adds that if putting our lives in danger were wrong, then no one "could deserve the appellation of Hero, whom glory or friendship transports into the greatest dangers."

If suicide is not a violation of our duty to God, perhaps it is a violation of our duty to other people. But Hume argues otherwise. Only in a trivial sense do we *harm* society if we kill ourselves. Leaning heavily on the distinction between an act and an omission, Hume says that we simply *cease to do good.* Moreover, we are obligated to do good for others only when others bestow good upon us. If we opt out of the situation in which they may do us good, then we may stop doing them good.

Hume does not argue that suicide is never a violation of our duty to ourselves, but he does argue that it often is not. For "age, sickness, or misfortune may render life a burthen, and make it worse even than annihilation."

In arguing that suicide is not a violation of our duty to others, Hume adopted an assumption that libertarians expand upon, namely, that so long as we do not harm others, we are not obligated to help them, except perhaps in exchange for good they do us. Szasz, too, seems inclined toward a libertarian stance. Like Schopenhauer, Szasz says that our lives belong to us, meaning that we should be free to act in any way we wish so long as we do not harm others. Utilitarians would disagree. Even if we have met our duties to others, we still have a duty to ourselves to maximize our happiness. Jonathan Glover defends a (qualified) utilitarian approach in his selection. He draws our attention to the range of acts that

---

[6]*Essays of Arthur Schopenhauer,* trans. T. Bailey Saunders (New York: A. L. Burt, Publisher), 398.

might be called suicidal, including gambling with our lives, and argues that it is not often permissible to commit suicide. Whether it is permissible in a certain set of circumstances depends on how we would affect the lives of others if we were to die and on what our lives would be like if we lived on. Glover goes on to claim that if others believe our lives to be worth living, they may forcibly prevent us from committing suicide, even if we who are contemplating suicide have arrived at our decision in a calm and rational way. Intervening will "give [us] a chance to think again." Ultimately, however, they must stop interfering and respect our autonomy by letting us take our lives. If our decision really was rational, though, why do we need a chance to think again? Won't we simply come to the same conclusion?

Immanuel Kant rejects both the libertarian and the utilitarian position. His objection to suicide, as spelled out in the selection from his *Lectures on Ethics*, seems to presuppose that suicide comes to annihilating ourselves, even though Kant himself thought that in some sense we survive our deaths. Kant makes two main objections to suicide. First, he claims that we are always obligated to respect humanity, whether in ourselves or in others, and, for reasons that are not altogether clear, Kant thinks that killing ourselves is never consistent with respecting ourselves. No doubt, his judgment is based at least in part on his conviction that we may use no one, including ourselves, as a mere means to our happiness, and sometimes that is what people do who annihilate themselves. Their goal might be to maximize their happiness by escaping suffering. But isn't there an important difference between treating ourselves as a mere means to our happiness and treating others as a mere means to our happiness? (How do we explain the fact that we may not do to others what we wish: Doesn't the explanation have something to do with the fact that *they* are the ones who get to decide what to do with their lives?) And must all suicides act with their own happiness in mind? I *might* take my life out of a concern for the happiness of others (wouldn't that still be suicide?), and using ourselves as a means to the happiness of others, interestingly enough, is not a violation of Kant's injunction that we never use anyone as a mere means to our *own* happiness.

Kant's second complaint is that suicide is incompatible with our duty to perfect ourselves. The "supreme rule" for our conduct toward ourselves

> is that in all the actions which affect himself a man should so conduct himself that every exercise of his powers is compatible with the fullest employment of them.

But why are we required to perfect our powers unless we are required to use them to make ourselves (1) able to act morally and (2) happy in a morally permissible manner? If this were the rationale for our duty to perfect ourselves, then to forbid people who are capable of acting morally from maximizing their happiness by killing themselves on the grounds that suicide is wrong would beg the question. It would presuppose that suicide is wrong without explaining why.

SUICIDE IS A RATIONAL CHOICE

The Ethics of Suicide

Thomas S. Szasz

In 1967, an editorial in *The Journal of the American Medical Association* declared that "The contemporary, physician sees suicide as a manifestation of emotional illness. Rarely does he view it in a context other than that of psychiatry."[1] It was thus implied, the emphasis being the stronger for not being articulated, that to view suicide in this way is at once scientifically accurate and morally uplifting. I submit that it is neither; that, instead, this perspective on suicide is both erroneous and evil: erroneous because it treats an act as if it were a happening; and evil, because it serves to legitimize psychiatric force and fraud by justifying it as medical care and treatment.

Before going further, I should like to distinguish three fundamentally different concepts and categories that are combined and confused in most discussions of suicide. They are: 1. Suicide proper, or so-called successful suicide; 2. Attempted, threatened, or so-called unsuccessful suicide; and 3. The attribution by someone (typically a psychiatrist) to someone else (now called a "patient") of serious (that is, probably successful) suicidal intent. The first two concepts refer to acts by an actually or ostensibly suicidal person; the third refers to the claim of an ostensibly normal person about someone else's suicide-proneness.

I believe that, generally speaking, the person who commits suicide intends to die; whereas the one who threatens suicide or makes an unsuccessful attempt at it intends to improve his life, not to terminate it. (The person who makes claims about someone else's suicidal intent does so usually in order to justify his efforts to control that person.)

Put differently, successful suicide is generally an expression of an individual's desire for greater autonomy—in particular, for self-control over his own death; whereas unsuccessful suicide is generally an expression of an individual's desire for more control over others—in particular, for compelling persons close to him to comply with his wishes. Although in some cases there may be legitimate doubt about which of these conditions obtains, in the majority of instances where people speak of "suicide" or "attempted suicide," the act falls clearly into one or the other group.

In short, I believe that successful and unsuccessful suicide constitute radically different acts and categories, and hence cannot be discussed together. Accordingly, I have limited the scope of this essay to suicide proper, with occasional references to attributions of suicidal intent. (The ascription of suicidal intent is, of course, a very different sort of thing from either successful or unsuccessful suicide. Since psychiatrists use it as if it designated a potentially or probably fatal "condition," it is sometimes necessary to consider this concept

---

[1] "Changing Concepts of Suicide," *Journal of the American Medical Association*, Vol. 199, No. 10 (March 6, 1967), p. 162.

together with the phenomenon of suicide proper.) . . .

It is difficult to find "responsible" medical or psychiatric authority today that does not regard suicide as a medical, and specifically as a mental health, problem.

For example, Ilza Veith, the noted medical historian, writing in *Modern Medicine*[2], asserts that ". . . the act [of suicide] clearly represents an illness. . . ."

Bernard R. Shochet, a psychiatrist at the University of Maryland, offers a precise description of the kind of illness it is. "Depression," he writes, "is a serious systemic disease, with both physiological and psychological concomitants, and suicide is a part of this syndrome." And he articulates the intervention he feels is implicit in this view: "If the patient's safety is in doubt, psychiatric hospitalization should be insisted on."[3]

Harvey M. Schein and Alan A. Stone, both psychiatrists at the Harvard Medical School, are even more explicit about the psychiatric coercion justified, in their judgment, by the threat of suicide. "Once the patient's suicidal thoughts are shared," they write, "the therapist must take pains to make clear to the patient that he, the therapist, considers suicide to be a maladaptive action, irreversibly counter to the patient's sane interests and goals; that he, the therapist, will do *everything* [emphasis mine, T.S.] he can to prevent it; and that the potential for such an action arises from the patient's illness. It is equally essential that the therapist believe in the professional stance; if he does not he should not be treating the patient within the delicate human framework of psychotherapy."[4]

Schein and Stone do not explain why the patient's confiding in his therapist to the extent of communicating his suicidal thoughts to him should *ipso facto* deprive the patient from being the arbiter of his own best interests. The thrust of their argument is prescriptive rather than logical. They seek to justify depriving the patient of a basic human freedom—the freedom to grant or withhold consent for treatment: "The therapist must insist that patient and physician—*together* [italics in the original]—communicate the suicidal potential to important figures in the environment, both professional and family. . . . Suicidal intent must not be part of therapeutic confidentiality." And further on they write: "Obviously this kind of patient must be hospitalized. . . . The therapist must be prepared to step in with hospitalization, with security measures, and with medication. . . ."

Schein and Stone thus suggest that the "suicidal" patient should have the right to choose his therapist; and that he should have the right to agree with his therapist and follow the latter's therapeutic recommendation (say, for hospitalization). At the same time, they insist that if "suicidal" patient and therapist disagree on therapy, then the patient should *not* have the right to disengage himself from the first therapist and choose a second—say, one who would consider suicidal intent a part of therapeutic confidentiality.

Many other psychiatric authorities could be cited to illustrate the current unanimity on this view of suicide.

---

[2] "Reflections on the Medical History of Suicide," *Modern Medicine*, August 11, 1969, p. 116.

[3] "Recognizing the Suicidal Patient," *Modern Medicine*, May 18, 1970.

[4] "Psychotherapy Designed to Detect and Treat Suicidal Potential," *American Journal of Psychiatry*, Vol. 125 (March 1969), pp. 1247–51.

Lawyers and jurists have eagerly accepted the psychiatric perspective on suicide, as they have on nearly everything else. An article in the *American Bar Association Journal*[5] by R.E. Schulman, who is both a lawyer and a psychologist, is illustrative.

Schulman begins with the premise that "No one in contemporary Western society would suggest that people be allowed to commit suicide as they please without some attempt to intervene or prevent such suicides. Even if a person does not value his own life, Western society does value everyone's life."

But I should like to suggest, as others have suggested before me, precisely what Schulman claims no one would suggest. Furthermore, if Schulman chooses to believe that Western society—which includes the United States with its history of slavery, Germany with its history of National Socialism, and Russia with its history of Communism—really "values everyone's life," so be it. But to accept this assertion as true is to fly in the face of the most obvious and brutal facts of history.

When a person decides to take his life, and when a physician decides to frustrate him in this action, the question arises: Why should the physician do so?

Conventional psychiatric wisdom answers: Because the suicidal person (now called "patient" for proper emphasis) suffers from a mental illness whose symptom is his desire to kill himself; it is the physician's duty to diagnose and treat illness: *ergo*, he must prevent the "patient" from killing himself and, at the same time, must "treat" the underlying "disease" that "causes" the "patient" to wish doing away with himself. This looks like an ordinary medical diagnosis and intervention. But it is not. What is missing? Everything. This hypothetical, suicidal "patient" is not ill; he has no demonstrable bodily disorder (or if he does, it does not "cause" his suicide); he does not assume the sick role; he does not seek medical help. In short, the physician uses the rhetoric of illness and treatment to justify his forcible intervention in the life of a fellow human being—often in the face of explicit opposition from his so-called "patient."

I do not doubt that attempted or successful suicide may be exceedingly *disturbing* for persons related to, acquainted with, or caring for the ostensible "patient." But I reject the conclusion that the suicidal person is, *ipso facto*, disturbed, that being disturbed equals being *mentally ill*, and that being mentally ill *justifies* psychiatric hospitalization or treatment. I have developed my reasons for this elsewhere, and need not repeat them here.[6] For the sake of emphasis, however, let me state that I consider counseling, persuasion, psychotherapy, or any other *voluntary measure*, especially for persons troubled by their own suicidal inclinations and seeking such help, unobjectionable, and indeed generally desirable, interventions. However, physicians and psychiatrists are usually not satisfied with limiting their help to such measures—and with good reason: from such assistance the individual may gain not only the desire to live, but also the strength to die.

But we still have not answered the question: Why should a physician frustrate an

---

[5]"Suicide and Suicide Prevention: A Legal Analysis," *American Bar Association Journal*, Vol. 54 (September 1968), pp. 855–62.

[6]T. S. Szasz, *Law, Liberty and Psychiatry* (New York: Macmillan, 1963), T. S. Szasz, *Ideology and Insanity* (Garden City, N.Y.: Anchor Books, 1970), especially chapters 9 and 12.

individual from killing himself? As we saw, some psychiatrists answer: Because the physician values the patient's life, at least when the patient is suicidal, more highly than does the patient himself. Let us examine this claim. Why should the physician, often a complete stranger to the suicidal patient, value the patient's life more highly than does the patient himself? He does not do so in medical practice. Why then should he do so in psychiatric practice, which he himself insists is a form of medical practice? Let us assume that a physician is confronted with an individual suffering from diabetes or heart failure who fails to take the drugs prescribed for his illness. We know that this often happens, and that when it does the patient may become disabled and die prematurely. Yet it would be absurd for a physician to consider, much less to attempt, taking over the conduct of such a patient's life, confining him in a hospital against his will in order to treat his disease. Indeed, any attempt to do so would bring the physician into conflict with both the civil and the criminal law. For, significantly, the law recognizes the medical patient's autonomy despite the fact that, unlike the suicidal individual, he suffers from a real disease; and despite the fact that, unlike the nonexistent disease of the suicidal individual, his illness is often easily controlled by simple and safe therapeutic procedures.

Nevertheless, the threat of alleged or real suicide, or so-called dangerousness to oneself, is everywhere considered a proper ground and justification for involuntary mental hospitalization and treatment. Why should this be so?

Let me suggest what I believe is likely to be the most important reason for the profound antisuicidal bias of the medical profession. Physicians are committed to saving lives. How, then, should they react to people who are committed to throwing away their lives? It is natural for people to dislike, indeed to hate, those who challenge their basic values. The physician thus reacts, perhaps "unconsciously" (in the sense that he does not articulate the problem in these terms), to the suicidal patient as if the patient had affronted, insulted, or attacked him: The physician strives valiantly, often at the cost of his own well-being, to save lives; and here comes a person who not only does not let the physician save him, but, *horrible dictu*, makes the physician an unwilling witness to that person's deliberate self-destruction. This is more than most physicians can take. Feeling assaulted in the very center of their spiritual identity, some take to flight, while others fight back.

Some non-psychiatric physicians will thus have nothing to do with suicidal patients. This explains why many people who end up killing themselves have a record of having consulted a physician, often on the very day of their suicide. I surmise that these persons go in search of help, only to discover that the physician wants nothing to do with them. And, in a sense, it is right that it should be so. I do not blame the doctors. Nor do I advocate teaching them suicide prevention—whatever that might be. I contend that because physicians have a relatively blind faith in their life-saving ideology—which, moreover, they often need to carry them through their daily work—they are the wrong people for listening and talking to individuals, intelligently and calmly, about suicide. So much for those physicians who, in the face of the existential attack which they feel the suicidal patient launches on them, run for *their* lives. Let us now look at those who stand and fight back.

Some physicians (and other mental health professionals) declare themselves not only ready and willing to help suicidal patients who seek assistance, but all persons who are or are alleged to be, suicidal.

Since they, too, seem to perceive suicide as a threat, not just to the suicidal person's physical survival but to their own value system, they strike back and strike back hard. This explains why psychiatrists and suicidologists resort, apparently with a perfectly clear conscience, to the vilest methods: they must believe that their lofty ends justify the basest means. Hence the prevalent use of force and fraud in suicide prevention. The consequence of this kind of interaction between physician and "patient" is a struggle for power. The patient is at least honest about what he wants: to gain control over his life *and* death—by being the agent of his own demise. But the (suicide preventing) pyschiatrist is completely dishonest about what he wants: he claims that he only wants to help his patient, while actually he wants to gain control over the patient's life in order to save himself from having to confront his doubts about the value of his own life. Suicide is medical heresy. Commitment and electro-shock are the appropriate psychiatric-inquisitorial remedies for it.

In the West, opposition to suicide, like opposition to contraception and abortion, rests on religious grounds. According to both the Jewish and Christian religions, God created man, and man can use himself only in the ways permitted by God. Preventing conception, aborting a pregnancy, or killing oneself are, in this imagery, all sins: each is a violation of the laws laid down by God, or by theological authorities claiming to speak in His name.

But modern man is a revolutionary. Like all revolutionaries, he likes to take away from those who have and to give to those who have not, especially himself. He has thus taken Man from God and given him to the State (with which he often identifies more than he knows). This is why the State gives and takes away so many of our rights, and why we consider this arrangement so "natural." (Hence the linguistic abomination of referring to the abolition of prohibitions, say against abortion or off-track betting, as the "legalizing" of these acts.)

But this arrangement leaves suicide in a peculiar moral and philosophical limbo. For if a man's life belongs to the State (as it formerly belonged to God), then surely suicide is the taking of a life that belongs not to the taker but to everyone else.

The dilemma of this simplistic transfer of body-ownership from God to State derives from the fundamental difference between a religious and secular world view, especially when the former entails a vivid conception of a life after death, whereas the latter does not (or even emphatically repudiates it). More particularly, the dilemma derives from the problem of how to punish successful suicide? Traditionally, the Roman Catholic Church punished it by depriving the suicide of burial in consecrated ground. As far as I know, this practice is now so rare in the United States as to be practically nonexistent. Suicides are given a Catholic burial, as they are routinely considered having taken their lives while insane.

The modern State, with psychiatry as its secular-religious ally, has no comparable sanction to offer. Could this be one of the reasons why it punishes so severely—so very much more severely than did the Church—the *unsuccessful* suicide? For I consider the psychiatric stigmatization of people as "suicidal risks" and their incarceration in psychiatric institutions a form of punishment, and a very severe one at that. Indeed, although I cannot support this claim with statistics, I believe that accepted psychiatric methods of suicide prevention often aggravate rather than ameliorate the suicidal person's problems. As one reads of the tragic encounters with psychiatry of people like James Forrestal, Marilyn Monroe, or Ernest Hemingway, one gains the impression that they felt demeaned and deeply hurt by the psychiatric indignities inflicted on them, and that, as a result of these experiences, they were even more desperately driven to suicide. In short, I am suggesting that coerced psychiatric interventions may increase, rather than diminish, the suicidal person's desire for self-destruction.

But there is another aspect of the moral and philosophical dimensions of suicide that must be mentioned here. I refer to the growing influence of the resurgent idea of self-determination, especially the conviction that men have certain inalienable rights. Some men have thus come to believe (or perhaps only to believe that they believe) that they have a right to life, liberty, and property. This makes for some interesting complications for the modern legal and psychiatric stand on suicide.

This individualistic position on suicide might be put thus: A man's life belongs to himself. Hence, he has a right to take his own life, that is, to commit suicide. To be sure, this view recognizes that a man may also have a moral responsibility to his family and others, and that, by killing himself, he reneges on these responsibilities. But these are moral wrongs that society, in its corporate capacity as the State, cannot properly punish. Hence the State must eschew attempts to regulate such behavior by means of formal sanctions, such as criminal or mental hygiene laws.

The analogy between life and other types of property means that a person can dispose of it even if in so doing he injures himself and his family. A man may give away, or gamble away, his money. But, significantly, he cannot—our linguistic conventions do not allow it—be said to *steal from himself*. The concept of theft requires at least two parties: one who steals and another from whom is stolen. There is no such thing as "self-theft." The term "suicide" blurs this very distinction. The etymology of this term implies that suicide is a type of homicide, one in which criminal and victim are one and the same person. Indeed, when a person wants to condemn suicide he calls it "self-murder." Schulman, for example, writes: "Surely, self-murder falls within the province of the law."

History does repeat itself. Until recently, psychiatrists castigated as sick and persecuted those who engaged in self-abuse (that is, masturbation);[7] now they castigate as sick and persecute those who engage in self-murder (that is, suicide).

The suicidologist has a literally schizophrenic view of the suicidal person: He sees him as two persons in one, each at war with the other. One-half of the patient wants to die; the other half wants to live. The former, says the suicidologist, is wrong; the latter is right. And he proceeds to protect the latter by restraining the former. However, since these two people are, like Siamese twins, one, he can restrain the suicidal half only by restraining the whole person.

The absurdity of this medical-psychiatric position on suicide does not end here. It ends in extolling mental health and physical survival over every other value, particularly individual liberty.

In regarding the desire to live as a legitimate human aspiration, but not the desire to die, the suicidologist stands Patrick Henry's famous exclamation, "Give me liberty, or give me death!" on its head. In effect, he says: "*Give him* commitment, *give him* electroshock, *give him* lobotomy, *give him* life-long slavery, but *do not let him choose* death!" By so radically invalidating another person's (not his own!) wish to die, the suicide-preventer redefines the aspiration of the Other as not an aspiration at all:

---

[7]T. S. Szasz, *The Manufacture of Madness* (1970), chapter 11.

The wish to die thus becomes something an irrational, mentally diseased being displays, or something that happens to a lower form of life. The result is a far-reaching infantilization and dehumanization of the suicidal person.

For example, Phillip Solomon writes in the *Journal of the American Medical Association*[8], that "We [physicians] must protect the patient from his own [suicidal] wishes." While to Edwin Schneidman, "Suicide prevention is like fire prevention. . . ."[9] Solomon thus reduces the would-be suicide to the level of an unruly child, while Schneidman reduces him to the level of a tree! In short, the suicidologist uses his professional stance to illegitimize and punish the wish to die.

There is, of course, nothing new about any of this. Do-gooders have always opposed personal autonomy or self-determination. In "Amok," written in 1931, Stefan Zweig put these words into the mouth of his protagonist: "Ah, yes, 'It's one's duty to help.' That's your favorite maxim, isn't it? . . . Thank you for your good intentions, but I'd rather be left to myself. . . . So I won't trouble you to call, if you don't mind. Among the 'rights of man' there is a right which no one can take away, the right to croak when and where and how one pleases, without a 'helping hand'."[10]

But this is not the way the scientific psychiatrist and suicidologist sees the problem. He might agree (I suppose) that, in the abstract, man has the right Zweig claimed for him. But, in practice, suicide (so he says) is the result of insanity, madness, mental illness. Furthermore, it makes no sense to say that one has a right to be mentally ill, especially if the illness is one that, like typhoid fever, threatens the health of other people as well. In short, the suicidologist's job is to try to convince people that wanting to die is a disease.

This is how Ari Kiev, director of the Cornell Program in Social Psychiatry and its suicide prevention clinic, does it: "We say [to the patient], look, you have a disease, just like the Hong Kong flu. Maybe you've got the Hong Kong depression. First, you've got to realize you are emotionally ill. . . . Most of the patients have never admitted to themselves that they are sick. . . ."[11]

This pseudo-medical perspective is then used to justify psychiatric deception and coercion of the crudest sort.

Here is how, according to the *Wall Street Journal*, the Los Angeles Suicide Prevention Center operates. A man calls and says he is about to shoot himself. The worker asks for his address. The man refuses to give it. "'If I pull it [the trigger] now I'll be dead,' he [the caller] said in a muffled voice. 'And that's what I want.' Silently but urgently, Mrs. Whitbook [the worker] has signalled a co-worker to begin tracing the call. And now she worked to keep the man talking. . . . An agonizing 40 minutes passed. Then she heard the voice of a policeman come on the phone to say the man was safe."[12]

But surely, if this man was able to call the Suicide Prevention Center, he could have, had he wanted to, called for a policeman himself. But he did not. He was thus deceived by the Center in the "service" he got.

---

[8]"The Burden of Responsibility in Suicide and Homicide," *Journal of the American Medical Association*, Vol. 199, No. 5 (Jan. 30, 1967), pp. 321–4.

[9]"Preventing Suicide," *American Journal of Nursing*, Vol. 65, No. 5 (May 1965), p. 112.

[10]"Amok," in *The Royal Game* (New York: Viking, 1944), p. 137.

[11]*The New York Times*, February 9, 1969, p. 96.

[12]March 6, 1969, p. 1.

I understand that this kind of deception is standard practice in suicide prevention centers, though it is often denied that it is. A report about the Nassau County Suicide Prevention Service corroborates the impression that when the would-be suicide does not cooperate with the suicide-prevention authorities, he is confined involuntarily. "When a caller is obviously suicidal," we are told, "a Meadowbrook ambulance is sent out immediately to pick him up."[13]

One more example of the sort of thing that goes on in the name of suicide prevention should suffice. It is a routine story from a Syracuse newspaper. The gist of it is all in one sentence: "A 28-year-old Minoa [a Syracuse suburb] man was arrested last night on a charge of violation of the Mental Hygiene Law, after police authorities said they spent two hours looking for him in the Minoa woods."[14] But this man has harmed no one; his only "offense" was that someone claimed he might harm himself. Why, then, should the police look for, much less arrest, him? Why not wait until he returns? Or why not look, offer help, but avoid arrest and coerced psychiatry?

These are rhetorical questions. For our answers to them depend on and reflect our concepts of what it means to be a human being.

I submit, then, that the crucial contradiction about suicide viewed as an illness whose treatment is a medical responsibility is that suicide is an action but is treated as if it were a happening. As I showed elsewhere, this contradiction lies at the heart of all so-called mental illnesses or psychiatric problems.[15] However, it poses a particularly acute dilemma for suicide, because suicide is the only fatal "mental illness."

Before concluding, I should like to restate briefly my views on the differences between diseases and desires, and show that by persisting in treating desires as diseases, we only end up treating man as a slave.

Let us take, as our paradigm case of illness, a skier who takes a bad spill and fractures an ankle. This fracture is something that has happened to him. He has not intended it to happen. (To be sure, he may have intended it; but that is another case.) Once it has happened, he will seek medical help and will cooperate with medical efforts to mend his broken bones. In short, the person and his fractured ankle are, as it were, two separate entities, the former acting on the latter.

Let us now consider the case of the suicidal person. Such a person may also look upon his own suicidal inclinations as an undesired, almost alien impulse and seek help to combat it. If so, the ensuing arrangement between him and his psychiatrist is readily assimilated to the standard medical model of treatment: the patient actively seeks and cooperates with professional efforts to remedy his "condition."

But as we have seen this is not the only way, nor perhaps the most important way, that the game of suicide prevention is played. It is accepted medical and psychiatric practice to treat persons for their suicidal desires against their will. And what exactly does this mean? Something quite different from that to which it is often analogized, namely the involuntary (or non-voluntary) treatment of a bodily illness. For a fractured ankle can be set whether or not a patient consents to its being set. That is because setting a fracture is *a mechanical act on the body*. But a threatened suicide cannot be prevented whether or not the "patient" consents to its being prevented. That is because, suicide being

---

[13]*Medical World News*, July 28, 1967, p. 17.

[14]Syracuse *Post Standard*, September 29, 1969, p. 10.

[15]T. S. Szasz, *The Myth of Mental Illness* (New York: Harper & Row, 1961).

the result of human desire and action, suicide prevention is a *political act on the person*. In other words, since suicide is an exercise and expression of human freedom, it can be prevented only by curtailing human freedom. This is why deprivation of liberty becomes, in institutional psychiatry, a form of treatment.

In the final analysis, the would-be suicide is like the would-be emigrant: both want to leave where they are and move elsewhere. The suicide wants to leave life and embrace death. The emigrant wants to leave his homeland and settle in another country.

Let us take this analogy seriously. It is much more faithful to the facts than is the analogy between suicide and illness. A crucial characteristic that distinguishes open from closed societies is that people are free to leave the former but not the latter. The medical profession's stance toward suicide is thus like the Communists' toward emigration: the doctors insist that the would-be suicide survive, just as the Russians insist that the would-be emigrant stay home.

Whether those who so curtail other people's liberties act with complete sincerity, or with utter cynicism, hardly matters. What matters is what happens: the abridgment of individual liberty, justified, in the case of suicide prevention, by psychiatric rhetoric; and, in the case of emigration prevention, by political rhetoric.

In language and logic we are the prisoners of our premises, just as in politics and law we are the prisoners of our rulers. Hence we had better pick them well. For if suicide is an illness because it terminates in death, and if the prevention of death by any means necessary is the physician's therapeutic mandate, then the proper remedy for suicide is indeed liberticide.

SUICIDE IS ALWAYS WRONG

Suicide

Immanuel Kant

The most serious offence against the duty one owes to oneself is suicide. But why should suicide be so abominable? It is no answer to say 'because God forbids it'. Suicide is not an abomination because God has forbidden it; it is forbidden by God because it is abominable. If it were the other way about, suicide would not be abominable if it were not forbidden; and I should not know why God had forbidden it, if it were not abominable in itself. The ground, therefore, for regarding suicide and other transgressions as abominable and punishable must not be found in the divine will, but in their inherent heinousness. Suicide is an abomination because it implies the abuse of man's freedom of action: he uses his freedom to destroy himself. His freedom should be employed to enable him to live as a man. . . .

Man is free to dispose of his condition but not of his person; he himself is an end and not a means; all else in the world is of value only as a means, but man is a person and not a thing and therefore not a means. It is absurd that a reasonable being, an end for the sake of which all else is means, should use himself as a means. It is true that a person can serve as a means for others (e.g. by his work), but only in a way whereby he does not cease to be a person and an end. Whoever acts in such a way that he cannot be an end, uses himself as a means and treats his person as a thing. Man is not free to dispose of his person as a means; and in what follows we shall have more to say on this score.

The duties we owe to ourselves do not depend on the relation of the action to the ends of happiness. If they did, they would depend on our inclinations and so be governed by rules of prudence. Such rules are not moral, since they indicate only the necessity of the means for the satisfaction of inclinations, and cannot therefore bind us. The basis of such obligation is not to be found in the advantages we reap from doing our duty towards ourselves, but in the worth of manhood. This principle does not allow us an unlimited freedom in respect of our own persons. It insists that we must reverence humanity in our own person, because apart from this man becomes an object of contempt, worthless in the eyes of his fellows and worthless in himself. . . .

In all nature there is nothing to injure man in the satisfaction of his desires; all injurious things are his own invention, the outcome of his freedom. We need only instance strong drink and the many dishes concocted to tickle his palate. In the unregulated pursuit of an inclination of his own devising, man becomes an object of utter contempt, because his freedom makes it possible for him to turn nature inside out in order to satisfy himself. Let him devise what he pleases for satisfying his desires, so long as he regulates the use of his devices; if he does not, his freedom is his greatest misfortune. It must therefore be restricted, though not by other properties or faculties, but by itself. The supreme rule is that in all the actions which affect himself a man should so conduct himself that every exercise of his powers is compatible with the fullest employment of them. Let us illustrate our meaning by examples. If I have drunk too much I am incapable of using my freedom and my powers. Again, if I kill myself, I use my powers to deprive myself of the faculty of using them. That freedom, the principle of the highest order of life, should annul itself and abrogate the use of itself conflicts with the fullest use of freedom. But freedom can only be in harmony with itself under certain conditions; otherwise it comes into collision with itself. If there were no established order in Nature, everything would come to an end, and so is it with unbridled freedom. Evils are to be found, no doubt, in Nature, but the true moral evil, vice, only in freedom. We pity the unfortunate, but we hate the vicious and rejoice at their punishment. The conditions under which alone the fullest use of freedom is possible, and can be in harmony with itself, are the essential ends of humanity. It must conform with these. The principle of all duties is that the use of freedom must be in keeping with the essential ends of humanity. Thus, for instance, a human being is not entitled to sell his limbs for money, even if he were offered ten thousand thalers for a single finger. If he were so entitled, he could sell all his limbs. We can dispose of things which have no freedom but not of a being which has free will. A man who sells himself makes himself a thing and, as he has jettisoned his person it is open to anyone to deal with him as he pleases. Another instance of this kind is where a human being makes himself a thing by making himself an object of enjoyment for some one's sexual desire. It degrades humanity, and that is why those guilty of it feel ashamed. . . .

We see, therefore, that just as freedom is the source of virtue which ennobles mankind, so is it also the root of the most dreadful vices—such as, for instance, a *crimen carnis contra naturam,* since it can devise all manner of means to satisfy its inclinations. Some crimes and vices, the result of freedom (e.g. suicide), make us shudder, others are nauseating; the mere mention of them is loathsome; we are ashamed of them because they degrade us below the level of beasts; they are grosser even than suicide, for the mention of suicide makes us shudder, but those other crimes and vices cannot be mentioned without producing nausea. Suicide is the most abominable of the vices which inspire dread and hate, but nausea and contempt indicate a lower level still. . . .

SUICIDE IS ALMOST ALWAYS PERMISSIBLE

Of Suicide

David Hume

If Suicide be criminal, it must be a transgression of our duty, either to God, our neighbour, or ourselves.

To prove, that Suicide is no transgression of our duty to God, the following considerations may perhaps suffice. In order to govern the material world, the almighty creator has established general and immutable laws, by which all bodies, from the greatest planet to the smallest particle of matter, are maintained in their proper sphere and function. To govern the animal world, he has endowed all living creatures with bodily and mental powers; with senses, passions, appetites, memory, and judgment; by which they are impelled or regulated in that course of life, to which they are destined. These two distinct principles of the material and animal world continually encroach upon each other, and mutually retard or forward each other's operation. The powers of men and of all other animals are restrained and directed by the nature and qualities of the surrounding bodies; and the modifications and actions of these bodies are incessantly altered by the operation of all animals. Man is stopped by rivers in his passage over the surface of the earth; and rivers, when properly directed, lend their force to the motion of machines, which serve to the use of man. But tho' the provinces of the material and animal powers are not kept entirely separate, there result from thence no discord or disorder in the creation: On the contrary, from the mixture, union, and contrast of all the various powers of inanimate bodies and living creatures, arises that surprizing harmony and proportion, which affords the surest argument of supreme wisdom.

The providence of the deity appears not immediately in any operation, but governs every thing by those general and immutable laws, which have been established from the beginning of time. All events, in one sense, may be pronounced the action of the almighty: They all proceed from those powers with which he has endowed his creatures. A house, which falls by its own weight, is not brought to ruin by his providence more than one destroyed by the hands of men; nor are the human faculties less his workmanship than the laws of motion and gravitation. When the passions play, when the judgment dictates, when the limbs obey; this is all the operation of God; and upon these animate principles, as well as upon the inanimate, has he established the government of the universe.

Every event is alike important in the eyes of that infinite being, who takes in, at one glance, the most distant regions of space and remotest periods of time. There is no one event, however important to us, which he has exempted from the general laws that govern the universe, or which he has peculiarily reserved for his own immediate action and operation. The revolutions of states and empires depend upon the smallest caprice or passion of single men; and the lives of men are shortened or extended by the smallest accident of air or diet, sunshine or tempest. Nature still continues her progress and operation; and if general laws be ever broke by particular volitions of the deity, 'tis after a manner which entirely escapes human observation. As on the one hand, the elements and other inanimate parts of the creation carry on their action without regard to the particular interest and situation of men; so men are entrusted to their own judgment and discretion in the various shocks of matter, and may employ every faculty, with which they are endowed, in order to provide for their ease, happiness, or preservation.

What is the meaning, then, of that principle, that a man, who, tired of life, and hunted by pain and misery, bravely overcomes all the natural terrors of death, and makes his escape from this cruel scene; that such a man, I say, has incurred the indignation of his creator, by encroaching on the office of divine providence, and disturbing the order of the universe? Shall we assert, that the Almighty has reserved to himself, in any peculiar manner, the disposal of the lives of men, and has not submitted that event, in common with others, to the general laws, by which the universe is governed? This is plainly false. The lives of men depend upon the same laws as the lives of all other animals; and these are subjected to the general laws of matter and motion. The fall of a tower or the infusion of a poison will destroy a man equally with the meanest creature: An inundation sweeps away every thing, without distinction, that comes within the reach of its fury. Since therefore the lives of men are for ever dependent on the general laws of matter and motion; is a man's disposing of his life criminal, because, in every case, it is criminal to encroach upon these laws, or disturb their operation? But this seems absurd. All animals are entrusted to their own prudence and skill for their conduct in the world, and have full authority, as far as their power extends, to alter all the operations of nature. Without the exercise of this authority, they could not subsist a moment. Every action, every motion of a man innovates in the order of some parts of matter, and diverts, from their ordinary course, the general laws of motion. Putting together, therefore, these conclusions, we find, *that* human life depends upon the general laws of matter and motion, and *that* 'tis no encroachment on the office of providence to disturb or alter these general laws. Has not every one, of consequence, the free disposal of his own life? And may he not lawfully employ that power with which nature has endowed him?

In order to destroy the evidence of this conclusion, we must shew a reason, why this particular case is excepted. Is it because human life is of so great importance, that it is a presumption for human prudence to dispose of it? But the life of man is of no greater importance to the universe than that of an oyster. And were it of ever so great importance, the order of nature has actually submitted it to human prudence, and reduced us to a necessity, in every incident, of determining concerning it.

Were the disposal of human life so much reserved as the peculiar province of the almighty that it were an encroachment on his right for men to dispose of their own lives; it would be equally criminal to act for the preservation of life as for its destruction. If I turn aside a stone, which is falling upon my head, I disturb the course of nature, and I invade the peculiar province of the almighty, by lengthening out my life, beyond the period, which, by the general laws of matter and motion, he had assigned to it.

A hair, a fly, an insect is able to destroy this mighty being, whose life is of such importance. Is it an absurdity to suppose, that human prudence may lawfully dispose of what depends on such insignificant causes?

It would be no crime in me to divert the *Nile* or *Danube* from its course, were I able to effect such purposes. Where then is the crime of turning a few ounces of blood from their natural chanels!

Do you imagine that I repine at providence or curse my creation, because I go out of life, and put a period to a being, which, were it to continue, would render me miserable? Far be such sentiments from me. I am only convinced of a matter of fact, which you yourself acknowledge possible, that human life may be unhappy, and that my existence, if farther prolonged, would become uneligible. But I thank providence, both for the good, which I have already enjoyed, and for the power, with which I am endowed, of escaping the ill that threatens me. To you it belongs to repine at providence, who foolishly imagine that you have no such power, and who must still prolong a hated being, tho' loaded with pain and sickness, with shame and poverty.

Do you not teach, that when any ill befalls me, tho' by the malice of my enemies, I ought to be resigned to providence; and that the actions of men are the operations of the almighty as much as the actions of inanimate beings? When I fall upon my own sword, therefore, I receive my death equally from the hands of the deity, as if it had proceeded from a lion, a precipice, or a fever.

The submission, which you require to providence, in every calamity, that befalls me, excludes not human skill and industry; if possibly, by their means, I can avoid or escape the calamity. And why may I not employ one remedy as well as another?

If my life be not my own, it were criminal for me to put it in danger, as well as to dispose of it: Nor could one man deserve the appellation of *Hero*, whom glory or friendship transports into the greatest dangers, and another merit the reproach of *Wretch* or *Miscreant*, who puts a period to his life, from the same or like motives.

There is no being, which possesses any power or faculty, that it receives not from its creator; nor is there any one, which, by ever so irregular an action, can encroach upon the plan of his providence, or disorder the universe. Its operations are his work equally with that chain of events, which it invades; and which ever principle prevails, we may, for that very reason, conclude it to be most favoured by him. Be it animate or inanimate, rational or irrational, 'tis all a case: Its power is still derived from the supreme creator, and is alike comprehended in the order of his providence. When the horror of pain prevails over the love of life: When a voluntary action anticipates the effect of blind causes; it is only in consequence of those powers and principles, which he has implanted in his creatures. Divine providence is still inviolate, and placed far beyond the reach of human injuries.

It is impious, says the old *Roman* superstition, to divert rivers from their course, or invade the prerogatives of nature. 'Tis impious, says the *French* superstition, to inoculate for the small-pox, or usurp the business of providence, by voluntarily producing distempers and maladies. 'Tis impious, says the modern *European* superstition, to put a period to our own life, and thereby rebel against our creator. And why not impious, say I, to build houses, cultivate the ground, and sail upon the ocean? In all these actions, we employ our powers of mind and body to produce some innovation in the course of nature; and in none of them do we any more. They are all of them, therefore, equally innocent or equally criminal.

But you are placed by providence, like a sentinel, in a particular station; and when you desert it, without being recalled, you are guilty of rebellion against your almighty sovereign, and have incurred his displeasure. I ask, why do you conclude, that Providence has placed me in this station? For my part, I find, that I owe my birth to a long chain of causes, of which many and even the principal, depended upon voluntary actions of men. *But Providence guided all these causes, and nothing happens in the universe without its consent and co-operation.* If so, then neither does my death, however voluntary, happen without its consent; and whenever pain and sorrow so far overcome my patience as to make me tired of life, I may conclude, that I am recalled from my station, in the clearest and most express terms.

It is providence, surely, that has placed me at present in this chamber: But may I not leave it, when I think proper, without being liable to the imputation of having deserted my post or station? When I shall be dead, the principles, of which I am composed, will still perform their part in the universe, and will be equally useful in the grand fabric, as when they composed this individual creature. The difference to the whole will be no greater than between my being in a chamber and in the open air. The one change is of more importance to me than the other; but not more so to the universe.

It is a kind of blasphemy to imagine, that any created being can disturb the order of the world, or invade the business of providence. It supposes, that that being possesses powers and faculties, which it received not from its creator, and which are not subordinate to his government and authority. A man may disturb society, no doubt; and thereby incur the displeasure of the almighty: But the government of the world is placed far beyond his reach and violence. And how does it appear, that the almighty is displeased with those actions, that disturb society? By the principles which he has implanted in human nature, and which inspire us with a sentiment of remorse, if we ourselves have been guilty of such actions, and with that of blame and disapprobation, if we ever observe them in others. Let us now examine, according to the method proposed, whether Suicide be of this kind of actions, and be a breach of our duty to our *neighbour* and to society.

A man, who retires from life, does no harm to society. He only ceases to do good; which, if it be an injury, is of the lowest kind.

All our obligations to do good to society seem to imply something reciprocal. I receive the benefits of society, and therefore ought to promote its interest. But when I withdraw myself altogether from society, can I be bound any longer?

But allowing, that our obligations to do good were perpetual, they have certainly some bounds. I am not obliged to do a small good to society, at the expense of a great harm to myself. Why then should I prolong a miserable existence, because of some frivolous advantage, which the public may, perhaps, receive from me? If upon account of age and infirmities, I may lawfully resign any office, and employ my time altogether in fencing against these calamities, and as much as possible, the miseries of my future life: Why may I not cut short these miseries at once by an action, which is no more prejudicial to society?

But suppose, that it is no longer in my power to promote the interest of the public: Suppose, that I am a burthen to it: Suppose, that my life hinders some person from being much more useful to the public. In such cases my resignation of life must not only be innocent but laudable. And most people, who lie under any temptation to abandon existence, are in some such situation. Those, who have health, or power, or authority, have commonly better reason to be in humour with the world.

A man is engaged in a conspiracy for the public interest; is seized upon suspicion; is threatened with the rack; and knows, from his own weakness, that the secret will be extorted from him: Could such a one consult the public interest better than by putting a quick period to a miserable life? This was the case of the famous and brave *Strozzi* of *Florence*.

Again, suppose a malefactor justly condemned to a shameful death; can any reason be imagined, why he may not anticipate his punishment, and save himself all the anguish of thinking on its dreadful approaches? He invades the business of providence no more than the magistrate did, who ordered his execution; and his voluntary death is equally advantageous to society, by ridding it of a pernicious member.

That Suicide may often be consistent with interest and with our duty to *ourselves*, no one can question, who allows, that age, sickness, or misfortune may render life a burthen, and make it worse even than annihilation. I believe that no man ever threw away life, while it was worth keeping. For such is our natural horror of death, that small motives will never be able to reconcile us to it. And tho' perhaps the situation of a man's health or fortune did not seem to require this remedy, we may at least be assured, that any one, who, without apparent reason, has had recourse to it, was curst with such an incurable depravity or gloominess of temper, as must poison all enjoyment, and render him equally miserable as if he had been loaded with the most grievous misfortunes.

If Suicide be supposed a crime, 'tis only cowardice can impel us to it. If it be no crime, both prudence and courage should engage us to rid ourselves at once of existence, when it becomes a burthen. 'Tis the only way, that we can then be useful to society, by setting an example, which, if imitated, would preserve to every one his chance for happiness in life, and would effectually free him from all danger of misery.*

---

*It would be easy to prove, that Suicide is as lawful under the *christian* dispensation as it was to the heathens. There is not a single text of scripture, which prohibits it. That great and infallible rule of faith and practice, which must controul all philosophy and human reasoning, has left us, in this particular, to our natural liberty. Resignation to providence is, indeed, recommended in scripture; but that implies only submission to ills, which are unavoidable, not to such as may be remedied by prudence or courage. *Thou shalt not kill* is evidently meant to exclude only the killing of others, over whose life we have no authority. That this precept like most of the scripture precepts, must be modified by reason and common sense, is plain from the practice of magistrates, who punish criminals capitally, notwithstanding the letter of this law. But were this commandment ever so express against Suicide, it could now have no authority. For all the law of *Moses* is abolished, except so far as it is established by the law of nature; and we have already endeavoured to prove, that Suicide is not prohibited by that law. In all cases, *Christians* and *Heathens* are precisely upon the same footing; and if *Cato* and *Brutus, Arria* and *Portia* acted heroically, those who now imitate their example ought to receive the same praises from posterity. The power of committing Suicide is regarded by *Pliny* as an advantage which men possess even above the deity himself. *Deus non sibi potest mortem consciscere, si velit, quod homini dedit optimum in tantis vitæ pænis.* Lib. ii. Cap. 7. [Pliny, *Natural History* 2.5.27 in the Loeb edition: "(God cannot) even if he wishes, commit suicide, the supreme boon that he has bestowed on man among all the penalties of life" (Loeb translation by H. Rackham).]

Suicide Is Sometimes Permissible

Suicide and Gambling with Life

Jonathan Glover

The view that suicide is morally wrong has been held so strongly that some have treated it as one of the purest cases of an obviously wrong kind of act. Wittgenstein said,

> If suicide is allowed then everything is allowed. If anything is not allowed then suicide is not allowed. This throws a light on the nature of ethics, for suicide is, so to speak, the elementary sin. And when one investigates it it is like investigating mercury vapour in order to comprehend the nature of vapours. Or is even suicide in itself neither good nor evil?[1] . . .

But in the sixty years since these remarks were made, it has come to seem less obvious that suicide is wrong at all, even to people who are far from holding that everything is allowed.

The reaction against responding to suicide with horror and condemnation has made widespread the view that the question is not in any way a moral one. Suicide is sometimes thought of as an irrational symptom of mental disturbance and so as a 'medical' problem. On a different view, it is a matter for each person's free choice: other people should have nothing to say about it, and the question for someone contemplating it is simply one of whether his future life will be worth living. Against these views, it will be argued here that consideration of a possible act of suicide raises moral questions, for the person himself and for other people, of the same complexity as other acts of killing. (It does not, of course, follow from this that it would in some cases be a good thing to revert to traditional attitudes of disapproval towards those who have attempted suicide.) It will also be argued here that the moral case which justifies some acts of intervention to prevent a suicide has implications for social policy on a wider range of issues than is at first apparent.

1 The Variety of Suicidal and Near-Suicidal Acts

There are many different kinds of suicidal act. The act of someone whose life is fundamentally a happy one but who tries to kill himself in a state of severe but temporary depression differs from the act of someone who, after prolonged deliberation, decides to kill himself rather than face any more of his incurable illness. And the case is different again when people kill themselves for reasons that we, even if not Durkheim, can call 'altruistic', perhaps because they do not want to be a burden to others, or as a protest against some political or social evil, or as a gesture in support of some cause. Here distinguishable but related acts vary from voluntary acceptance of a martyr's

---

[1] Ludwig Wittgenstein: *Notebooks*, 1914–16, concluding paragraphs.

death at the hands of others, to slow suicide by hunger strike, and public and dramatic suicide (such as that of Jan Palach in Czechoslovakia or some of the Buddhist suicides in Vietnam).

Apart from these, there is a whole range of acts on the border of suicide. Some of the most interesting work on the explanation of suicide is that of Professor Stengel and others suggesting that many apparent attempts at suicide may not have been intended to succeed.[2] Comparison of those 'attempts' which end in death and those which do not shows some significant differences. More men than women make attempts ending in death, while more women than men make 'attempts' which they survive. The peak age for fatal attempts is between fifty-five and sixty-four, while the peak age for non-fatal ones is between twenty-four and forty-four. Such discrepancies make it plausible to suggest that not all 'attempts' are the result of an equally firm decision to die. Some may be a cry for help without any real intention to die. Others may be made in a state of mind where a gamble is taken with some risk of death and some chance of survival followed by help.

As well as the dramatic case of a suicide 'attempt', there are other instances where people gamble with their lives. People in wars volunteer for high-risk missions, sometimes out of altruism or duty, but sometimes because they do not value their lives much, or even half want to die. The same may be true of some who take on dangerous jobs, such as soldier or war correspondent, or some of those who like dangerous sports. Then there are those who drink or smoke heavily, or who eat too much and exercise too little, all in the knowledge of the earlier death that will probably result.

In the cases mentioned, we would not count a course of action as even near-suicidal unless the risk of death was welcomed, or at least accepted with indifference. A member of a bomb-disposal squad may very much want to live, and do his work out of public spirit: it would be quite inappropriate to call him suicidal. And the same is true of heavy smokers who want a long life but who cannot escape their addiction.

But in all cases where people opt for the risk or certainty of their own death, whether or not with suicidal intent, it is possible to raise two moral questions. Ought they to risk their lives? Should other people intervene to prevent them? One reason for thinking that to raise the question of the morality of an act of suicide is inappropriate is the belief that an act of suicide must be done in such a state of disturbance that moral considerations stand no chance of influencing the decision. But thinking about the variety of suicidal and near-suicidal acts should cast doubt on this belief.

2 Questions for the Person Thinking of Suicide

Where someone contemplating suicide is sufficiently in control of himself to deliberate about his course of action, two factors are relevant to the decision. What would his own future life be like, and would it be worth living? What effect would his decision (either way) have on other people?

The difficulties in answering the question about one's own future life are obvious. If life is at present sufficiently bad to make a person think suicide may be in his own interest, he will need to have some idea of how likely or unlikely is any improvement in his state. This is often hard to predict (except in cases where the blight on his life is an absolutely incurable illness). Most of us are bad at giving enough weight to the

---

[2]Erwin Stengel: *Suicide and Attempted Suicide*, Harmondsworth, 1964.

chances of our lives changing for better or worse. And people sometimes contemplate suicide without exploring the possibility of less radical steps to deal with their problems. Someone who would normally not even consider such upheavals as leaving his family, changing his job, emigrating, or seeking psychiatric help, should not absolutely rule out any of them once he enters the region where killing himself is not ruled out either. And, since many of us are bad at predicting our own futures, it is worth talking to other people who may see the thing differently, whether friends or the Samaritans.

The other difficulty is deciding what sort of life is worth living. One test has to do with the amount of life for which you would rather be unconscious. Most of us prefer to be anaesthetized for a painful operation. If most of my life were to be on that level, I might opt for permanent anaesthesia, or death. But complications arise. It may be that we prefer to be anaesthetized for an operation only because we have plenty of other times to experience life without pain. It may be worth putting up with a greater degree of pain where the alternative is no life at all. And, even if we can decide about when we would rather be unconscious, the question whether a life is worth living cannot be decided simply by totting up periods of time to see if more than half our waking life is below zero in this way. Some brief periods of happiness may be of such intensity as to justify much longer periods of misery. (Equally, some brief periods of agony or despair may outweigh longer periods of mild cheerfulness.)

Our estimates of the quality of our lives are especially vulnerable to temporary changes of mood, so that the only reasonable way to reach a serious evaluation is to consider the question over a fairly long stretch of time. Even this has limitations, because of the difficulty of giving the right weight to estimates made at different times and in different moods, but anything less is hopelessly inadequate.

The other question to be answered is about the effects on other people of a decision for or against the suicide. No doubt there are some people whose lives are so desperately bad that their own interests should come before any loss to other people. But sometimes an act of suicide can shatter the lives of others (perhaps parents) to a degree the person might never have suspected. Suicide cannot be seen to be the right thing to do without the most careful thought about the effects on all those emotionally involved. There is also the question of the loss of any general contribution the person might make to society.

To kill oneself can sometimes be the right thing to do, but much less often than may at first sight appear. (Evidence of a reasonably respectable kind could come from studies of the later lives of those whose 'attempts' fail and of the lives of families after one member kills himself.) To suggest that some acts of suicide may be morally wrong is not to advocate that those who make failed 'attempts' ought to be responded to with condemnation or reproach: it is obvious that the last thing that is helpful is any pressure of this kind.

It is interesting that the case against suicide is also a case against gambling with one's life. There are familiar stories of the wives of racing-car drivers pleading with their husbands to retire. This kind of thing is not just a marginal feature of dangerous jobs or sports, but something which ought to be considered very seriously before starting on them.

3 Intervention: The Problems

The moral question for the person contemplating suicide is simply whether his being dead would be a better state of affairs for himself and others or a worse one. ('Simply' does not imply that this question is easy.) But for other people contemplating intervention to prevent a suicide, the matter is more complicated. They have to ask the same question about whether the death would on the whole be a good or a bad thing. But, if they decide it would be a bad thing, they also must ask the further question, whether it would be right for them to intervene. This will seem not to be a separate question only to someone who thinks that we are always entitled to interfere in other people's lives where they would otherwise do something wrong.

The question of intervention can take various forms. Are we entitled to use our powers of persuasion in an attempt to stop someone killing himself? If our persuasion fails, or we have no opportunity to use it, may we then use coercion? If we can use some coercion, how far may we go? (This problem is clearly illustrated by the use of forcible feeding on people killing themselves by hunger strike.) If someone arrives in hospital after a suicide attempt, should doctors make efforts to revive him?

These questions are related to others not involving suicide: to what extent ought there to be persuasion, social pressure or legislation of a paternalist kind, to try to stop people risking their lives? These questions arise about matters such as seat belts in cars, drugs, smoking, obesity, dangerous sports or safety standards in houses.

4 Intervention: A Policy

Apart from consideration of side-effects, the guiding principles to be applied are two. It is desirable where possible to save a worth-while life. It is desirable where possible to respect a person's autonomy. The prevention of suicide is obviously a place where these two principles will sometimes conflict, and I have no general formula for deciding priorities. The policy to be suggested here is that there should be an attempt to save the maximum number of worth-while lives compatible with using paternalist restrictions of autonomy only temporarily in the case of sane adults. Some people may accept the same general principles, but strike a different balance between them where they conflict.

Where we think someone bent on suicide has a life worth living, it is always legitimate to reason with him and to try to persuade him to stand back and think again. There is no case against reasoning, as it in no way encroaches on the person's autonomy. There is a strong case in its favour, as where it succeeds it will prevent the loss of a worth-while life. (If the person's life turns out not to be worth-while, he can always change his mind again.) And if persuasion fails, the outcome is no worse than it would otherwise have been.

Where someone has decided that his life is not worth living and is not deflected from his decision for suicide by persuasion, it is legitimate to restrain him by force from his first attempt, or even several attempts. (I do not attempt to draw any precise boundary here.) This legitimacy depends on our belief that his life will be worth living: those of us who do not believe in the sanctity of life will not agree to overriding someone's autonomy in order to make him endure a life not worth living. And we ought to limit severely the number of times we use force to frustrate a person's decision to kill himself, because a persistent policy of forcible prevention is a total denial of his autonomy in the matter. If we prevent him once or a few times this gives him a chance to reconsider, and the decision later is still his own. Even those who do not set any independent value on autonomy may feel in the case of a rational person that his persistent suicide attempts cast doubt on their own judgement that his life is worth living.

The endorsement of limited coercion given here does not extend to the forcible feeding of those on hunger strike. Someone set on a slow death of this kind has plenty of time to reconsider the decision, and so the justification of temporary intervention does not apply. In addition, much stronger justification would be needed for imposing the pain and humiliation that normally accompany forcible feeding than for the relatively harmless methods of frustrating a normal suicide attempt.

The question of forcible prevention is easier to answer in the case of a rational person calmly deciding that his life is not worth living than it is in the case of someone prone to bouts of suicidal depression. In the case of the rational person we intervene to give him a chance to think again, but should ultimately respect his decision. But should we equally respect the decision for suicide taken in a temporary but recurring mood of despair?

There is no difficulty in justifying intervention in the case of someone in a suicidal mood for the only time in his life. He is given time to think again, and he never again decides to kill himself. His life has been saved at minimal cost to this autonomy. But what are we to say of someone whose emotional life is a constant series of ups and downs, who alternates between very much wanting to go on living and moods of suicidal depression? If we treat him on a par with the person who calmly and rationally contemplates suicide, we will, after frustrating a few attempts, allow him to go ahead. But the rightness of this seems much more doubtful where moods of temporary depression are involved.

This is partly because a sustained and reflective preference for suicide seems much better evidence that a person's life is not worth living than are frequent changes of mind about it. And it is also because overriding a decision that is the product of a passing mood is less disrespectful of autonomy than overriding a preference that plays a stable role in a person's outlook. Where someone fluctuates between optimism and pessimism about his life, there may be no neutral vantage point from which he can take a 'rational' decision. In such a case, he does not fully possess the desire either to live or to die, in the dispositional sense of 'possess' that is relevant to the autonomy principle. It is hard to see in such a case that we can decide about intervention on any basis other than our views about the likely quality of his future life, together with any side effects we think relevant. (If we are unable to judge whether his future life is likely on balance to be worth living, we may allow the scale to be tipped by the effects of his suicide on his family.)

Some decisions about intervention have to be taken largely in ignorance of the state of mind and reasons behind the person's decision to kill himself. A mere passer-by may be in a position to intervene, or, more often, a doctor in a hospital may be in a position to revive someone after an attempt. In all such cases, the intervention is justified. This is for the same reason that intervention is justified in any first attempt. There is the chance of saving a worth-while life at the cost of only a temporary interference with autonomy: there is a very strong chance that someone calmly determined to kill himself will have other opportunities.

5 Paternalism and Gambling with Life

To what extent is intervention justified when someone places his own life at risk? When ought we to try to persuade people not to run risks or even compel them by law not to do so? These questions again do not have simple answers. We need to take into account the benefits that may result from running the risks, the degree of risk involved and the drawbacks of the different kinds of intervention. Whether or not persuasion should be used may also vary in individual cases according to the likely side-effects of a death. If someone volunteers for a highly useful but dangerous job, such as bomb-disposal, it may not be right to try to argue him out of this. But the position changes if he has a large family and there are plenty of bachelor volunteers. (The arguments for intervention are not all paternalist ones.)

As the benefits from a risky course of action decrease and the risk increases, so the case for trying to persuade someone to change his mind increases. And there comes a point where the risks are so disproportionate to the benefits that, if persuasion is unsuccessful, there is justification for stronger pressure, and perhaps legislation. So much injury and loss of life results from the failure to wear seat belts in cars that it is right for the law to make wearing them compulsory. Those who resist this proposed legislation use arguments appealing to people's freedom from paternalist interference and say that persuasion is better than compulsion. So it is, but freedom from such a trivial piece of compulsion is purchased at too great a cost in lives and happiness.

We rightly value having a large area of our lives free from fussy state interference. And for the state to intervene to prevent us taking any risk to life, however small, would involve an officious paternalism which nearly everyone would find not worthwhile. But when the risks increase, the objections should diminish. Against this, we have to set the benefits for which the risks are run. Having to spend a moment putting on a seat belt is an extremely trivial disadvantage to weigh against avoiding a high risk. But having to give up an activity like mountaineering might be a large sacrifice for those who like it, and so a much larger degree of risk would be necessary to justify banning it.

I do not know where the boundaries of legislation should be. A great deal of investigation and argument is needed. But it is at least fairly clear that our intuitive responses to this question probably need to be revised. Social traditions grow up in which some things are thought of as outside the scope of legislation simply because they have never been legally controlled. We are used to paternalist laws making motorcyclists wear crash helmets, but the idea of laws forbidding people to smoke cigarettes shocks us as an infringement of traditional liberties. Yet our location of smoking within the realm of individual free decisions is a tradition that grew up before we knew the facts about its effects. A rational social policy would be concerned with striking a balance between minimizing risks and minimizing the kinds of restrictions that frustrate people in things that really matter to them. It is not at all clear that our traditional frontiers of legislation achieve this.

The argument here is that reasons for preventing suicides are also reasons for social policies of risk reduction, if necessary by legislation. To some it may appear odd that I have argued in favour of legislation to prevent people taking certain risks with their lives, but have not argued for the reintroduction of legislation against suicide. The reason for this is that suicide is a special case. Legislation seems, hardly surprisingly, to be of little use in reducing the suicide rate, and its main effect was to impose an additional ordeal on those who survived their suicide attempts. There is also the thought that some suicide decisions are quite rational, being taken by people with a very clear assessment of their future lives, so that interference is unjustified. And the appeal to autonomy has much more force where the person's decision is of such importance to him than it has when it concerns a person's decision not to bother to put on his seat belt. There is nothing to be said for a substantial erosion of autonomy that is also ineffective. There is a lot to be said for saving many people who want to live, but who, for trivial advantages, thoughtlessly gamble with their lives.

Questions for Further Reflection

1. If committing suicide is morally permissible in certain circumstances, it ought to be legal in those circumstances, and in such cases people should be legally prohibited from interfering with our attempt to take our lives. However, if it is *wrong*, should it be illegal? If not, should it be legal for people to prevent suicides?
2. Does Hume justify the claim that suicide is *never* a violation of our duties to ourselves?
3. Should Glover say that people whose grounds for committing suicide are irrational should eventually be allowed to do so if repeated intervention does not result in a change of their view? What form should intervention take: Is it enough to prevent suicide attempts for a time, or must we have some plan to make the person stop desiring death?
4. What should Kant say about a case in which I throw myself over a grenade in order to save the lives of several comrades? Here I knowingly sacrifice myself, but my goal is to preserve the lives of my comrades.
5. The previous chapter considered whether dying is a bad thing. How is the issue of whether suicide is permissible affected by death's being a bad thing? If death were a matter of indifference, would suicide be a matter of indifference from the moral point of view?
6. If it is all right to intervene so as to prevent someone from committing suicide, is it also all right to intervene so as to stop someone from engaging in dangerous activities such as racing or sky diving?
7. How might Kant have defended his claim that we have a duty to perfect our powers?

Further Readings

Battin, M. Pabst, and Mayo, David J., eds. *Suicide: The Philosophical Issues.* New York: St. Martin's Press, 1980. A good collection of articles on many aspects of the suicide issue.

Camus, Albert. *The Myth of Sisyphus.* J. O'Brien, trans. New York: Vintage Books, 1955. Argues that we should not commit suicide even if there is no such thing as objective value.

Donne, John. *Biathanatos.* 1644: An interesting defense of the prerogative of suicide.

Durkheim, E. *Suicide.* Glencoe: The Free Press, 1951. Classic sociological study of suicide. Durkheim says that two sorts of suicide are typical in modern society: egoistic, which occurs when an individual is not fully integrated into society, and anomic (from *anomie*, normlessness), which occurs when society's norms are not appropriate to an individual's life.

Leenaars, Antoon. *Suicide Notes: Predictive Clues and Patterns.* New York: Human Sciences Press, 1988. Offers a survey of the views of people who regard suicide as "a human malaise."

Moore, Charles. *A Full Inquiry Into the Subject of Suicide.* London, 1790. A survey of opinion and an attempt to refute Hume.

Seneca. "On Suicide." *Epistles.* E. Barker, trans. Oxford, England: Clarendon Press, 1932. An important classical discussion of suicide.

Shneidman, Edwin. *Death: Current Perspectives.* Palo Alto, CA: Mayfield, 1984. A useful collection of essays about death.

Voltaire. "Of Suicide." In *Works*, Vol. XVII. T. Smollett, trans. Dublin, 1772. Defends the permissibility of suicide.

Williams, Glanville. *The Sanctity of Life and the Criminal Law.* New York, 1957. Discusses whether suicide should be legal.

PART THREE

Interpersonal Relationships

Chapter 5

FRIENDSHIP

Friendships are a vital part of most of our lives, but, if a cursory survey of the self-help books in a bookstore is any indication, we do not think about friendship nearly as frequently as we think about romantic relationships, or for that matter making money, cooking, or car repair. It seems odd that such an important part of our lives should receive so little attention. This chapter provides some material for discussion of the nature of friendship, its values and dangers, and its effect on our moral duties.

What Does It Take to Be a Friend?

What does it take to be friends with someone? One of the earliest accounts, namely that of Aristotle, is still one of the most persuasive. In his *Rhetoric*, Aristotle writes:

> We may describe friendly feeling towards anyone as wishing for him what you believe to be good things, not for your own sake but for his, and being inclined, so far as you can, to bring these things about. A friend is one who feels thus and excites these feelings in return. This being assumed, it follows that your friend is the sort of man who shares your pleasure in what is good and your pain in what is unpleasant, for your sake and for no other reason. This pleasure and pain of his will be the token of his good wishes for you, since we all feel glad at getting what we wish for, and pained at getting what we do not.[1]

As he usually does, Aristotle here packs a number of important points into a few words. Let us identify the chief components of friendship to which he is calling attention. According to Aristotle, you are not friends with someone unless you meet these criteria:

1. You wish the other well; that is, you want things to go well for the other person.
2. This attitude is reciprocated on the part of the other; that is, the other person also wishes you well. (Notice how odd it would be to say "I am her friend but she is not mine.")
3. It is not enough to simply prefer that, other things being equal, things go well for your friend. Your desire for your friend's welfare must actually make a difference to your behavior: As Aristotle says, you must not only wish good things for your friend but also be "inclined, so far as you can, to bring these things about."

---

[1] Aristotle, *Rhetoric*, in Jonathan Barnes, ed., *The Complete Works of Aristotle*, Volume Two (Princeton, NJ: Princeton University Press, 1984), p. 2200, 1380b36–1381a8.

4. Finally, Aristotle stresses that you must wish your friend well "not for your own sake but for his." In Aristotle's view, you are not a genuine friend if you want things to go well for someone else only because, for one reason or another, this is to your own advantage. You are someone's friend only if you regard it as a good thing if things go well for her, regardless of whether or not this benefits you. As Aristotle points out, a good indication that you genuinely want things to go well for someone for her own sake is that you take pleasure in her successes and are pained when things go badly for her.

In our selection from Aristotle in this chapter, he goes a bit further in providing an account of what friendship is. He first provides an account similar to the one we have been considering, writing that: "When people wish for our good in this way [i.e., for our own sake], we attribute good will to them. . . . If the good will is on a reciprocal basis, it is friendship." But he now goes a bit further: "Perhaps we should add: 'provided that we are aware of the good will.'" Aristotle thinks we might have good will toward people we have not even met. For instance, suppose that a close friend of yours has another close friend whom you have not met. Your friend regularly tells you about her other friend, bringing back weekly accounts of her successes and failures. You come to know a good deal about this other friend and may well come to want her to be happy. Of course, it could be that at the same time, your friend tells her other friend about *you* and that the other friend comes to have the same sort of good will toward you that you have toward her. Although the two of you have never met, each of you has what Aristotle calls "good will" toward the other. Perhaps each of you is even willing to contribute toward the other's welfare. Aristotle's point is that this is still not a friendship. He suggests that in addition to the four conditions we have already discussed, we should perhaps add a fifth: Friends "must each be aware of one another's good will."

We have so far identified five features that Aristotle thinks any friendship must have. Is it also true that these five features *define* friendship? Is possessing all five features enough to make a relationship a friendship? Aristotle appears to think he has provided a definition, but in fact, these five features do not seem to be sufficient. Suppose, in the example just discussed, your friend informs both you and her other friend that each of you wants things to go well for the other. This seems to satisfy our fifth condition for friendship, and yet your relationship to your friend's friend *still* does not appear to be one of friendship. What else is needed? Many features might be suggested, but surely one feature of crucial importance is that you must *share* part of your lives with each other. Reciprocated good will is not yet friendship; friends also interact with each other. In fact, in his later discussion, Aristotle seems to presuppose that friends will engage in shared activities; near the end of his discussion, Aristotle even goes so far as to suggest that friends will want to live together (that is, in the same community).

Three Kinds of Friendship

Aristotle goes on to distinguish three kinds of friendship. He claims that we feel affection for people either because they are pleasant, or because they are useful to us, or because they are good. Depending on the basis of our affection for someone, then, our friendship will be of three sorts, sometimes called pleasure-friendships, use-friendships, and character-friendships. You might have a pleasure-friendship, for instance, with someone who has a terrific sense of humor: He entertains you and makes you laugh with a seemingly endless repertoire of amusing stories and jokes. You might form a sort of friendship with such a person even if you thought that behind the façade of his humor, he was really rather unpleasant. You might have a use-friendship with a business contact or, perhaps, with someone with whom you study. Here the basis of the friendship is that your friend is useful to you in your pursuit of money or understanding.

In both these cases, there is a sense in which it is not really the *person* you like, but some more-or-less incidental characteristic of the person. You like the fact that he gives you pleasure or that he can help you understand Aristotle, but you don't necessarily like *him*. In a character-friendship, by contrast, you like your friend, not for some peripheral attribute or quality, but for her good personality or character. Aristotle thinks that as a consequence, character-friendships are more lasting than the other kinds: What you find pleasant may change fairly quickly, and it will be advantageous to be friendly with different people at different times, but people's characters or personalities change only slowly and gradually.

Aristotle's discussion has a peculiar feature. He says that someone wishes his friend well for the friend's own sake, but at the same time, Aristotle seems to imply that the use-friend wishes *his* friend well, not for the friend's sake, but for his own. The use-friend does not want what is best for his "friend" come what may, but only to the extent that helping his friend is also to his own advantage. It is important to see here that Aristotle regards character-friendships as the paradigmatic case of friendship; use-friendships and pleasure-friendships are not really friendships in the full sense, but merely resemble full-blooded friendships in some respects. So Aristotle may think that, while pleasure-friendship and use-friendship have *some* of the defining features of friendship, they do not have them all, and in particular, they do not have the feature that one wishes his friend well for the friend's sake.[2]

Egoism and Friendship

While Aristotle regards use-friendships as practically no friendships at all, Robert J. Ringer seems to defend the view that all friendships are, or ought to be, use-friendships. Ringer is refreshingly blunt about this ("Can you buy friendship? You not only can, you must. It's the *only* way to obtain friends.") Although he does not use this vocabulary, his piece is a defense of an egoistic view of friendship: the view that friendship is always a matter of two individuals each looking out for his or her own interest and discovering that certain exchanges between them are to the advantage of both. Friendship is thus seen on the model of an economic transaction.

Although the kind of friendship Ringer advocates appears to be a sort of use-friendship, it is interesting to note that it has something in common with character-friendship: Ringer argues that friends must admire and respect each other. But this is explained along egoistic lines: "If you don't admire and respect the other fellow, what does he have to trade with you?" But how much force does this rhetorical question really have? Someone you do not admire or respect might have many things to "trade"—business or personal connections,

---

[2]But contrast the article by John Cooper listed in the "Further Readings" for this chapter.

money, knowledge, or a winter home in Hawaii, to mention only a few.

In evaluating Ringer's article, it is useful to keep in mind the distinction between psychological and ethical egoism. We may ask, first, whether all friendships really are based on nothing more than rational self-interest, and, second, whether it *ought* to be the case that all friendships are so based. Ringer seems to think both that friendships will, as a matter of psychological fact, always be based on self-interest and also that it is a good thing that they are so based. It is intriguing to compare his view with that of Schopenhauer, who thinks that usually, though not always, friendships will be based solely on self-interest but who also regards this as a sad and unfortunate truth rather than as something to be pleased about.

Values and Dangers of Friendships

We turn now to issues about what makes friendship a good (or bad) thing. In the case of friendship, as elsewhere, considerations about the good and the right are connected, though distinct. For instance, one of the things that makes friendship good is the contribution it can make to our moral growth, to making us better people; and being a better person involves being more apt to act rightly. Nevertheless, there remains a distinction in principle between the good and the right; in this section we consider the goods and ills of friendship, and in the following section we take up the issue of the relation between friendship and right action, in particular, the extent to which friendship imposes some moral duties and provides exceptions to others.

On the issue of the value of friendship, as on so many others, Aristotle has important things to say. One particularly interesting point Aristotle makes is that we can often see our faults more clearly when they are mirrored in a friend than when we exhibit them ourselves. In the *Magna Moralia,* Aristotle puts the point as follows:

> We are not able to see what we are from ourselves (and that we cannot do so is plain from the way in which we blame others without being aware that we do the same things ourselves; and this is the effect of favour or passion, and there are many of us who are blinded by these things so that we judge not aright); as then when we wish to see our own face, we do so by looking into the mirror, in the same way when we wish to know ourselves we can obtain that knowledge by looking at our friend.[3]

Kant provides another virtue of friendship. Our lives are often extremely compartmentalized; we reveal one side of ourselves to one acquaintance, another side to another acquaintance; one side at work, another at play; and so on. But a relationship with a friend provides the opportunity to reveal all of oneself, to bring all of oneself to bear in a way that few other relationships do. Nor do we need to regard this, as Kant himself seems to, as a matter of revealing a determinately pre-existing self: To some extent, we surely *become* the people we are through our relations with other people. If this is correct, then to some extent friendships help us to *become,* rather than simply to reveal, ourselves as entire, rounded beings rather than as collections of fragments.

Marilyn Friedman calls attention to the role of friendship in moral growth, arguing that in friendships we are often forced for the first time to understand and take seriously systems of values that may be quite different from our own. It is easy to scoff at or dismiss views with which we disagree when they are held by people we do not

---

[3]Aristotle, *Magna, Moralia,* in *Complete Works,* Barnes, ed., p. 1920, 1213a15–23.

much admire or care for; but when a respected friend expresses or reveals values quite different from our own, we are inclined to regard them more carefully.

Most writers on friendship sing its praises. However, it should be kept in mind that friendship carries with it dangers as well as rewards. As Aristotle writes: "The friendship of base people becomes wicked, because, unsteady as they are, they share in base pursuits, and by becoming like one another they become wicked." When we are with friends who do not share our intellectual interests, we do not express or reveal that side of our personalities; similarly, if our friends are less thoughtful, less caring, or less concerned about fairness than we, we will tend in their presence to be less thoughtful, caring, or fair. Friendship also can cement or reinforce unpleasant or immoral attitudes. We are friends with only a few people, and we tend to feel confident of the attitudes we share with our friends and dismissive of the attitudes of those outside our circle. In this way, the exclusiveness that seems to be an essential characteristic of friendship can become dangerous.

It is interesting at this point to look again at Kant. Kant, despite his vivid description of the value of friendship, seems to think that its exclusiveness is inherently a bad thing: It is necessary only because of our human limitations; and the better we are, the less exclusive our friendships will be. In the ideal case, Kant apparently believes, we would not have *special* relationships with anyone but would be friends to everyone:

> Friendship is not of heaven but of the earth; the complete moral perfection of heaven must be universal; but friendship is not universal; it is a peculiar association of specific persons . . . civilized man seeks universal pleasures and a universal friendship, unrestricted by special ties; the savage picks and chooses according to his taste and disposition, for the more primitive the social culture the more necessary such associations are.

Friendship and Duty

We turn now from issues about the good to issues about the right: from the benefits of friendship to its bearing on moral obligations. The relation between friendship and morality is problematic because we often think of morality as involving a requirement of *impartiality*, a requirement that we not give anyone special treatment but that we treat everyone equally, without regard to our special personal feelings or attachments. On the other hand, while morality is often thought to involve impartiality, friendship seems to require its opposite. Friendship seems to involve treating one's friend differently from the way one treats others. At least on the surface, there appears to be a conflict between morality and friendship. It seems that there may be cases where morality requires us to treat our friend no differently from anyone else, while friendship requires us to give him special treatment.

Hugh LaFollette notes that there appears to be a conflict between the view that morality requires impartiality, and the view that personal relationships, such as friendship, which are necessarily partial, are morally permissible (or even morally important). But he argues that, properly understood, morality and personal relationships are in fact mutually reinforcing. LaFollette argues that morality is better understood as a system of habits than as a system of rules. Once we adopt this view of morality as a set of good habits (or virtues, to use the Aristotelian terminology), we can see close personal relationships as a necessary factor in the development of moral habits, including habits of impartiality. We typically learn to care about the needs and interests of others by caring first of all about the needs and interests of those close to us; a world without close relationships would be very unlikely to be a world of universal concern for others! As LaFollette writes, "if we are not motivated to promote the needs of our families or friends, how can we be motivated to promote the needs of strangers?"

Close relationships, then, play an important role in the development of impartial concern for others. Conversely, LaFollette argues, following Aristotle, that moral people are more likely to be capable of strong and lasting friendships.

This chapter on friendship is in some ways a transitional chapter. It is the last chapter concerned mainly with issues about the good. This chapter discusses not only the good of friendship but also the obligations associated with it; in the remainder of the book, as in the previous chapter, we will be primarily concerned with issues about the right thing to do and only to a lesser extent with issues about what sorts of things are good.

THEORIES OF FRIENDSHIP

Friendship

Aristotle

Book VIII

2

The kinds of friendship may perhaps be cleared up if we first come to know the object of love. For not everything seems to be loved but only the lovable, and this is good, pleasant, or useful; but it would seem to be that by which some good or pleasure is produced that is useful, so that it is the good and the pleasant that are lovable as ends. Do men love, then, *the* good, or what is good for *them*? These sometimes clash. So too with regard to the pleasant. Now it is thought that each loves what is good for himself, and that the good is without qualification lovable, and what is good for each man is lovable for him; but each man loves not what is good for him but what seems good. This however will make no difference; we shall just have to say that this is that which seems lovable. Now there are three grounds on which people love; of the love of lifeless objects we do not use the word 'friendship'; for it is not mutual love, nor is there a wishing of good to the other (for it would surely be ridiculous to wish wine well; if one wishes anything for it, it is that it may keep, so that one may have it oneself); but to a friend we say we ought to wish what is good for his sake. But to those who thus wish good we ascribe only goodwill, if the wish is not reciprocated; goodwill when it *is* reciprocal being friendship. Or must we add 'when it is recognized'? For many people have goodwill to those whom they have not seen but judge to be good or useful; and one of these might return this feeling. These people seem to bear goodwill to each other; but how could one call them friends when they do not know their mutual feelings? To be friends, then, they must be mutually recognized as bearing goodwill and wishing well to each other for one of the aforesaid reasons.

3

Now these reasons differ from each other in kind; so therefore, do the corresponding forms of love and friendship. There are therefore three kinds of friendship, equal in number to the things that are lovable; for with respect to each there is a mutual and recognized love, and those who love each other wish well to each other in that respect in which they love one another. Now those who love each other for their utility do not love each other for themselves but in virtue of some good which they get from each other. So too with those who love for the sake of pleasure; it is not for their character that men love ready-witted people, but because they find them pleasant. Therefore those who love for the sake of utility love for the sake of what is good for *themselves,* and those who love for the sake of pleasure do so for the sake of what is pleasant to *themselves,* and not in so far as the other is the person loved but in so far as he is useful or pleasant. And thus these friendships are only incidental; for it is not as being the man he is that the loved person is loved, but as providing some good or pleasure. Such friendships, then, are easily dissolved, if the parties do not remain like themselves; for if the one party is no longer pleasant or useful the other ceases to love him.

Now the useful is not permanent but is always changing. Thus when the motive of the friendship is done away, the friendship is dissolved, inasmuch as it existed only for the ends in question. This kind of friendship seems to exist chiefly between old people (for at that age people pursue not the pleasant but the useful) and, of those who are in their prime or young, between those who pursue utility. And such people do not live much with each other either; for sometimes they do not even find each other pleasant; therefore they do not need such companionship unless they are useful to each other; for they are pleasant to each other only in so far as they rouse in each other hopes of something good to come. Among such friendships people also class the friendship of host and guest. On the other hand the friendship of young people seems to aim at pleasure; for they live under the guidance of emotion, and pursue above all what is pleasant to themselves and what is immediately before them; but with increasing age their pleasures become different. This is why they quickly become friends and quickly cease to be so; their friendship changes with the object that is found pleasant, and such pleasure alters quickly. Young people are amorous too; for the greater part of the friendship of love depends on emotion and aims at pleasure; this is why they fall in love and quickly fall out of love, changing often within a single day. But these people do wish to spend their days and lives together; for it is thus that they attain the purpose of their friendship.

Perfect friendship is the friendship of men who are good, and alike in excellence; for these wish well alike to each other *qua* good, and they are good in themselves. Now those who wish well to their friends for their sake are most truly friends; for they do this by reason of their own nature and not incidentally; therefore their friendship lasts as long as they are good—and excellence is an enduring thing. And each is good without qualification and to his friend, for the good are both good without qualification and useful to each other. So too they are pleasant; for the good are pleasant both without qualification and to each other, since to each his own activities and others like them are pleasurable, and the actions of the good *are* the same or like. And such a friendship is as might be expected lasting since there meet in it all the qualities that friends should have. For all friendship is for the sake of good or of pleasure—good or pleasure either in the abstract or such as will be enjoyed by him who has the friendly feeling—and is based on a certain resemblance; and to a friendship of good men all the qualities we have named belong in virtue of the nature of the friends themselves; for in the case of this kind of friendship the other qualities also are alike in both friends, and that which is good without qualification is also without qualification pleasant, and these are the most lovable qualities. Love and friendship therefore are found most and in their best form between such men.

But it is natural that such friendships should be infrequent; for such men are rare. Further, such friendship requires time and familiarity; as the proverb says, men cannot know each other till they have 'eaten salt together'; nor can they admit each other to friendship or be friends till each has been found lovable and been trusted by each. Those who quickly show the marks of friendship to each other wish to be friends, but are not friends unless they both are lovable and know the fact; for a wish for friendship may arise quickly, but friendship does not. . . .

4

For the sake of pleasure or utility, then, even bad men may be friends of each other, or good men of bad, or one who is neither good nor bad may be a friend to any sort of person, but for their own sake clearly only good men can be friends; for bad men do not delight in each other unless some advantage come of the relation.

The friendship of the good too alone is proof against slander; for it is not easy to trust any one's talk about a man who has long been tested by oneself; and it is among good men that trust and the feeling that he would never wrong me and all the other things that are demanded in true friendship are found. In the other kinds of friendship, however, there is nothing to prevent these evils arising.

For men apply the name of friends even to those whose motive is utility, in which sense states are said to be friendly (for the alliances of states seem to aim at advantage), and to those who love each other for the sake of pleasure, in which sense children are called friends. Therefore we too ought perhaps to call such people friends, and say that there are several kinds of friendship—firstly and in the proper sense that of good men *qua* good, and by similarity the other kinds; for it is in virtue of something good and something similar that they are friends, since even the pleasant is good for the lovers of pleasure. . . .

6

One cannot be a friend to many people in the sense of having friendship of the complete type with them, just as one cannot be in love with many people at once (for love is a sort of excess, and it is the nature of such only to be felt towards one person): and it is not easy for many people at the same time to please the same person very greatly, or perhaps even to be good for him. One must, too, acquire some experience of the other person and become familiar with him, and that is very hard. But with a view to utility or pleasure it is possible that many people should please one; for many people are useful or pleasant, and these services take little time. . . .

9

Friendship and justice seem, as we have said at the outset of our discussion, to be concerned with the same objects and exhibited between the same persons. For in every community there is thought to be some form of justice, and friendship too; at least men address as friends their fellow voyagers and fellow-soldiers, and so too those associated with them in any other kind of community. And the extent of their association is the extent of their friendship, as it is the extent to which justice exists between them. And the proverb 'what friends have is common property' expresses the truth; for friendship depends on community. Now brothers and comrades have all things in common, but the others have definite things in common—some more things, others fewer; for of friendships, too, some are more and others less truly friendships. And the claims of justice differ too; the duties of parents to children and those of brothers to each other are not the same, nor those of comrades and those of fellow-citizens, and so, too, with the other kinds of friendship. There is a difference, therefore, also between the acts that are unjust towards each of these classes of associates, and the injustice increases by being exhibited towards those who are friends in a fuller sense; e.g., it is a more terrible thing to defraud a comrade than a fellow citizen, more terrible not to help a brother than a stranger, and more terrible to wound a father than any one else. And the demands of justice also naturally increase with the friendship, which implies that friendship and justice exist between the same persons and have an equal extension. . . .

13

Those who are friends on the ground of excellence are anxious to do well by each other (since that is a mark of excellence and of friendship), and between men who are emulating each other in this there cannot be complaints or quarrels; no one is offended by a man who loves him and does well by him—if he is a person of nice feeling he takes his revenge by doing well by the other. And the man who excels will not complain of his friend, since he gets what he aims at; for each man desires what is good. Nor do complaints arise much even in friendships of pleasure; for both get at the same time what they desire, if they enjoy spending their time together; and even a man who complained of another for *not* affording him pleasure would seem ridiculous, since it is in his power not to spend his days with him.

But the friendship of utility is full of complaints; for as they use each other for their own interests they always want to get the better of the bargain, and think they have got less than they should, and blame their partners because they do not get all they want and deserve; and those who do well by others cannot help them as much as those whom they benefit want. . . .

Book IX

9

It is also disputed whether the happy man will need friends or not. It is said that those who are blessed and self-sufficient have no need of friends; for they have the things that are good, and therefore being self-sufficient they need nothing further while a friend, being another self, furnishes what a man cannot provide by his own effort; whence the saying 'when fortune is kind, what need of friends?' But it seems strange, when one assigns all good things to the happy man, not to assign friends, who are thought the greatest of external goods. And if it is more characteristic of a friend to do well by another than to be well done by, and to confer benefits is characteristic of the good man and of excellence, and it is nobler to do well by friends than by strangers, the good man will need people to do well by. This is why the question is asked whether we need friends more in prosperity or in adversity, on the assumption that not only does a man in adversity need people to confer benefits on him, but also those who are prospering need people to do well by. Surely it is strange, too, to make the blessed man a solitary; for no one would choose to possess all good things on condition of being alone, since man is a political creature and one whose nature is to live with others. Therefore even the happy man lives with others; for he has the things that are by nature good. And plainly it is better to spend his days with friends and good men than with strangers or any chance persons. Therefore the happy man needs friends.

What then is it that the first party means, and in what respect is it right? Is it that most men identify friends with useful people? Of such friends indeed the blessed man will have no need, since he already has the things that are good; nor will he need those whom one makes one's friends because of their pleasantness, or he will need them only to a small extent (for his life, being pleasant, has no need of adventitious pleasure); and because he does not need *such* friends he is thought not to need friends.

But that is surely not true. For we have said at the outset that happiness is an activity; and activity plainly comes into being and is not present at the start like a piece of property. If happiness lies in living and being active, and the good man's activity is virtuous and pleasant in itself, as we have said at the outset, and if a thing's being one's own is one of the attributes that make it pleasant, and if we can contemplate our neighbours better than ourselves and their actions better than our own, and if the actions of virtuous men who are their friends are pleasant to good men (since these have both the attributes that are naturally pleasant)—if this be so, the blessed man will need friends of this sort, since he chooses to contemplate worthy actions and actions that are his own, and the actions of a good man who is his friend have both these qualities.

Further, men think that the happy man ought to live pleasantly. Now if he were a solitary, life would be hard for him; for by oneself it is not easy to be continuously active; but with others and towards others it is easier. With others therefore his activity will be more continuous, being in itself pleasant, as it ought to be for the man who is blessed; for a good man *qua* good delights in excellent actions and is vexed at vicious ones, as a musical man enjoys beautiful tunes but is pained at bad ones. A certain training in excellence arises also from the company of the good, as Theognis remarks. . . .

12

Does it not follow, then, that, as for lovers the sight of the beloved is the thing they love most, and they prefer this sense to the others because on it love depends most for its being and for its origin, so for friends the most desirable thing is living together? For friendship is a partnership, and as a man is to himself, so is he to his friend; now in his own case the perception of his existence is desirable, and so therefore is that of his friend's, and the activity of this perception is produced when they live together, so that it is natural that they aim at this. And whatever existence means for each class of men, whatever it is for whose sake they value life, in *that* they wish to occupy themselves with their friends; and so some drink together, others dice together, others join in athletic exercises and hunting, or in the study of philosophy, each class spending their days together in whatever they love most in life; for since they wish to live with their friends, they do and share in those things as far as they can. Thus the friendship of bad men turns out an evil thing (for because of their instability they unite in bad pursuits, and besides they become evil by becoming like each other), while the friendship of good men is good, being augmented by their companionship; and they are thought to become better too by their activities and by improving each other; for from each other they take the mould of the characteristics they approve—whence the saying 'noble deeds from noble men. . . .'

The Friendship Hurdle

Robert J. Ringer

Regardless of the degree or variety, what it all boils down to is that a friend is a person who fills a need for you. And from his standpoint, your function is to fill a need for him. It's losing sight of the latter that causes so many friendship problems. When both sides understand the entire equation and perform accordingly, the basis for a solid, value-for-value relationship exists—the only kind of relationship which can be both honest and lasting. . . .

There are two essential elements in the foundation of any worthwhile friendship. The first is the admiration/respect factor. If someone doesn't admire and respect you, how can you possibly fill any of his needs, assuming he's rational and bases his actions on long-term consequences? Likewise, if you don't admire and respect the other fellow, what does he have to trade with you?

On the basis of short-term patching, I guess it's possible to develop a foundationless relationship with someone you don't respect and try to masquerade it as a friendship. . . . Although such a relationship may bring you or him something you desire today (such as companionship), it probably will result in frustration and bad feelings for both parties. If admiration and respect aren't there from the outset, then it's not a friendship; it's an unhealthy relationship.

The other building block of a successful friendship is rational selfishness, which provides the basis for the essential component of value for value. Those who have difficulty making friends are usually afflicted with the negative results of the World-Owes-Me-a-Living Theory. No one owes you, or anyone else, anything—certainly not friendship, love or respect. Don't seek an unearned friendship. Deal with people on an honest, value-for-value basis and you'll be amazed at how willingly they in turn will fill your needs (assuming they, too, are value-for-value oriented).

The modern context in which *friend* is usually used has no doubt been partly responsible for the failure of many people to understand that friendship is something which must be earned. To many, the word somehow implies an individual who will do anything for you, regardless of the circumstances—who can be counted on when a favor, as it were, is needed. And *favor* has likewise evolved—to imply one's receiving something for nothing. The whole syndrome is dangerous. In truth, a friend should be someone you admire and respect and to whom you are attached by affection; a favor should be something you do for a friend because your Weight-and-Balance Happiness Scale tells you that it's in your best interest to do so, long-term.

Therefore, when you "sacrifice" for a friend, it is, hopefully, a conscious, rationally selfish action on your part. It's a goodwill gesture toward another person whose friendship gives you pleasure. It's not a complicated proposition at all, except that you do have to be careful that you're feeding your Scale correct information.

Because a friend is someone who brings you pleasure, it's essential that you understand that he, too, has a Weight-and-Balance Happiness Scale. When you realize that, you're in the correct mental frame of mind to appeal to him intelligently through acts which make him feel good. Because of custom and tradition, many people have trouble accepting the reality that the most meaningful relationships are based on selfishness. But when both of you are operating in this honest and realistic manner, you have a solid foundation for a beautiful, long-lasting, value-for-value relationship.

That's not to say that both parties must derive the same kinds of pleasure from a friendship. One person could be gaining good advice and intellectual stimulation from it, while the other enjoys the interesting conversations and companionship. . . .

Can you buy friendship? You not only can, you must. It's the *only* way to obtain friends. Everyone buys all his friends—in the Free-Enterprise Friendship Market. The prices vary in size and form, but there is always a payment involved. Same rule: everything worthwhile has a price. The payment might require your investing a given number of hours per week in conversation, it might mean that you're counted on for inspiration, or that you have to forgo some facet of your life which you presently enjoy.

Every person in the Free-Enterprise Friendship Market has needs. When you fill one or more of those needs, you're paying for someone's friendship. It's when you aren't willing to pay for a friendship—when you aren't prepared to fill some need of his on a value-for-value basis—that you begin having problems with the Friendship Hurdle. We all have the something-for-nothing urge within us, so don't feel guilty about it; just concentrate on suppressing it, because it produces bad long-term consequences. To the degree you're successful in keeping it under control, your chances of making and keeping friends are greatly increased.

Whenever I become acquainted with someone I think I might enjoy as a friend, I try to determine two things. One is what the price for his friendship is likely to be; the other is whether I'm willing and able to pay it. For example, an interesting conversationalist may require more of my time than I'm willing to give in exchange for such conversation. Don't delude yourself about the total, long-term price. . . .

The easiest way of all to destroy a friendship is to wake up one morning and realize that your accounts payable to someone have far outgrown your receivables. If a person is a good friend, it's easy to be presumptuous and take liberties you wouldn't think of attempting with your worst enemy. Does it make any sense to treat friends worse than enemies? Remember that your friends have Weight-and-Balance Happiness Scales, too. They can't afford to carry overdue receivables on their books forever, any more than you can. When you allow a friendship to become too one-sided, your friend being the creditor and you the debtor, it moves out of the realm of friendship and becomes an obligatory relationship. Your friendship debts become so great that you lose the freedom necessary to look out for Number One. . . .

How do the things I've said in this chapter affect my friendships? Is it wise to let my friendship philosophy be made public? Yes, that's the whole point. I want my friends—and everyone else who might cross my path—to understand exactly what my thoughts are regarding this important subject. By being honest—by advertising the real me—I increase the chances of drawing to myself those people with whom I have the most in common. It also brings me closer to existing friends who see friendship in the same value-for-value light that I do.

On the other side of the coin, it operates as a self-policing device. It eliminates from my life those people who don't understand the necessity of paying for friends. Rather, it would be more correct to say that they eliminate themselves. This in turn spares me the unpleasant ramifications of becoming involved with the wrong kind of people, as well as the discomfort of having to break off any existing friendships which are, or could later become, unhealthy.

Friendship

Immanuel Kant

Friendship is the hobby-horse of all rhetorical moralists; it is nectar and ambrosia to them.

There are two motives to action in man. The one—self-love—is derived from himself, and the other—the love of humanity—is derived from others and is the moral motive. In man these two motives are in conflict. If the purposes of self-love did not demand our attention, we would love others and promote their happiness. On the other hand, we recognize that acts of self-love have no moral merit, but have at most the sanction of the moral law, while acts prompted by our love of mankind and by our desire to promote the happiness of the human race, are most meritorious. Yet we attach particular importance to whatever promotes the worth of our own person. Here friendship comes in; but how are we to proceed? Are we first, from our self-love, to secure our own happiness, and having done that, look to the happiness of our fellows; or should the happiness of others be our first concern? In the first case we subordinate the happiness of others to our own, the inclination towards our own happiness becomes stronger and stronger, the pursuit of our own happiness has no term, and so care for the happiness of others is altogether suppressed; in the second case, we think of others and our own happiness loses ground in the race. If men, however, were so minded that each one looked to the happiness of others, then the welfare of each would be secured by the efforts of his fellows. If we felt that others would care for our happiness as we for theirs, there would be no reason to fear that we should be left behind. The happiness I gave to another would be returned to me. There would be an exchange of welfare and no one would suffer, for another would look after my happiness as well as I looked after his. It might seem as if I should be the loser by caring for the happiness of others, but if this care were reciprocated, there would be no loss; and the happiness of each would be promoted by the generosity of the others. This is the Idea of friendship, in which self-love is superseded by a generous reciprocity of love.

Let us now examine the other side of the picture. Let us see what would happen if every man concerned himself only with his own happiness and was indifferent to the happiness of others. Everyone is then entitled to care for his own happiness. There is no merit in this, though it has the sanction of the moral rule. Provided that, in furthering my own, I do not hinder my neighbour in his pursuit of happiness, I commit no moral fault, although I achieve no moral merit.

But if I had to choose between friendship and self-love, which should I choose? On moral grounds I should choose friendship, but on practical grounds self-love, for no one could see to my happiness so well as I could myself. In either case, however, my choice would be bad. If I chose only friendship, my happiness would suffer; if I chose only self-love, there would be no moral merit or worth in my choice.

Friendship is an Idea, because it is not derived from experience. Empirical examples of friendship are extremely defective. It has its seat in the understanding. In ethics, however, it is a very necessary Idea. Let us take this opportunity to define the significance of the terms 'an Idea' and 'an Ideal'. We require a standard for measuring degree. The standard may be either natural or arbitrary, according as the quantity is or is not determined by means of concepts a priori. What then is the determinate standard by means of which we measure quantities which are determined a priori? The standard in such cases is the upper limit, the maximum possible. Where this standard is employed as a measure of lesser quantities, it is an Idea; when it is used as a pattern, it is an Ideal. Now if we compare the affectionate inclinations of men, we find that the degrees and proportions in which men distribute their love as between themselves and their fellows vary greatly. The maximum reciprocity of love is friendship, and friendship is an Idea because it is the measure by which we can determine reciprocal love. The greatest love I can have for another is to love him as myself. I cannot love another more than I love myself. But if I am to love him as I love myself I must be sure that he will love me as he loves himself, in which case he restores to me that with which I part and I come back to myself again. This Idea of friendship enables us to measure friendship and to see the extent to which it is defective. When, therefore, Socrates remarks, 'My dear friends, there are no friends', he implies thereby that there is no friendship which fully conforms to the Idea of friendship. And he is right; for any such absolute conformity is impossible; but the Idea is true. Assume that I choose only friendship, and that I care only for my friend's happiness in the hope that he cares only for mine. Our love is mutual; there is complete restoration. I, from generosity, look after his happiness and he similarly looks after mine; I do not throw away my happiness, but surrender it to his keeping, and he in turn surrenders his into my hands; but this Idea is valuable only for reflection; in practical life such things do not occur.

But if every one cared only for himself and never troubled about any one else, there would be no friendship. The two things must, therefore, be combined. Man cares for his own happiness and for that of others also. But as in this matter no limits are fixed and the degrees and proportions cannot be defined, the measure of friendship in the mixture cannot be determined by any law or formula. I am bound to look to my wants and to my satisfaction. If I cannot secure the happiness of my neighbour otherwise than by refraining from satisfying the needs of life, no one can place upon me the obligation of looking to his happiness and showing friendship towards him. But as each of us has his own measure of need and can raise the standard at will, the point at which the satisfaction of needs should give place to friendship is indeterminate. There is no question, however, that many of our needs, or things we have made our needs, are of such a nature that we can well sacrifice them for friendship. . . .

In ordinary social intercourse and association we do not enter completely into the social relation. The greater part of our disposition is withheld; there is no immediate outpouring of all our feelings, dispositions and judgments. We voice only the judgments that seem advisable in the circumstances. A constraint, a mistrust of others, rests upon all of us, so that we withhold something, concealing our weaknesses to escape contempt, or even withholding our opinions. But if we can free ourselves of this constraint, if we can unburden our heart to another, we achieve complete communion. That this release may be achieved, each of us needs a friend, one in whom we can confide unreservedly, to whom we can disclose completely all our dispositions and judgments, from whom we can and need hide nothing, to whom we can communicate our whole self. On this rests the friendship of dispositions and fellowship. It can exist only between two or three friends. We all have a strong impulse to disclose ourselves, and enter wholly into fellowship; and such self-revelation is further a human necessity for the correction of our judgments. To have a friend whom we know to be frank and loving, neither false nor spiteful, is to have one who will help us to correct our judgment when it is mistaken. This is the whole end of man, through which he can enjoy his existence. But even between the closest and most intimate of friends there are still some things which call for reserve, for the other's sake more than for one's own. There can be perfect and complete intimacy only in matters of disposition and sentiment, but we have certain natural frailties which ought to be concealed for the sake of decency, lest humanity be outraged. Even to our best friend we must not reveal ourselves, in our natural state as we know it ourselves. To do so would be loathsome.

To what extent do we make things better for ourselves by making friends? It is not man's way to embrace the whole world in his good-will; he prefers to restrict it to a small circle. He is inclined to form sects, parties, societies. The most primitive societies are those based on family connexion, and there are men who move only in the family circle. Then there are religious sects. These also are societies, associations formed by men for the cultivation of their common religious views and sentiments. This is on the face of it a laudable purpose, but it tends to harden the heart against and to ostracize those who stand outside the pale of the particular sect; and any tendency to close the heart to all but a selected few is detrimental to true spiritual goodness, which reaches out after a good-will of universal scope. Friendship, likewise, is an aid in overcoming the constraint and the distrust man feels in his intercourse with others, by revealing himself to them without reserve. In this form of association also we must guard against shutting out from our heart all who are not within the charmed circle. Friendship is not of heaven but of the earth; the complete moral perfection of heaven must be universal; but friendship is not universal; it is a peculiar association of specific persons; it is man's refuge in this world from his distrust of his fellows, in which he can reveal his disposition to another and enter into communion with him. . . .

The more civilized man becomes, the broader his outlook and the less room there is for special friendships; civilized man seeks universal pleasures and a universal friendship, unrestricted by special ties; the savage picks and chooses according to his taste and disposition, for the more primitive the social culture the more necessary such associations are. . . .

What then is that adaptation of man to man that constitutes the bond of friendship? Not an identity of thought; on the contrary, difference in thought is a stronger foundation for friendship, for then the one makes up the deficiencies of the other. Yet on one point they must agree. Their intellectual and moral principles must be the same, if there is to be complete understanding between them. Otherwise, there will always be discrepancy in their decisions and they will never agree.

THE VALUE OF FRIENDSHIP

Friendship and Moral Growth

Marilyn Friedman

The Moral Possibilities Presented by Special Relationships

Various philosophers have explored many of the values provided by friendship.[1] I wish to call attention to one important good made possible by friendship which seems to have been neglected in other contemporary discussions. This good is moral growth—of a certain particular sort. Clearly, one's first values and moral rules are learned in the course of the moral socialization which most people receive from their early caretakers, usually parents or family. Against the background of these earliest learned moral abstractions, many of us find ourselves undergoing remarkable changes of commitment in later life. I wish to draw attention to one way in which friendship can be a source of such moral transformation.

The sort of moral growth which I have in mind is that which occurs when we learn to grasp our experiences in a new light, or in different terms. Abstract moral guidelines are "tested" by concrete human lives. The more we know about real lives lived according to, or under the influence of, various abstract moral guidelines, the more we gain insight into the living realities of those guidelines. Our everyday experiences can seem to confirm or to disconfirm our abstract moral guidelines, or they can seem inconclusive or irrelevant. Widening the experiential base against which we make our

---

[1]Footnote deleted—Eds.

assessments promotes our more adequate evaluation of those guidelines. Because we might comprehend our own personal experience in limited terms, or because our own experience might be narrow in virtue of the restricted opportunities of our own lives, we do not always have the experiential or conceptual resources *on our own* to gain new moral insights or to surpass our prior moral outlook.

The needs, wants, fears, experiences, projects, and dreams of our friends can frame for us new standpoints from which we can explore the significance and worth of moral values and standards. In friendship, our commitments to our friends, as such, afford us access to whole ranges of experience beyond our own. Friendship offers such access in virtue of the shared trust which underlies friendship. This trust manifests itself in a variety of forms. There is the obvious trust in the friend's good will and good intentions with respect to one's own well-being. But a rather different sort of trust is even more important for the moral growth which I am considering.

In friendship, there is a substantial measure of trust in the ability of our friends to bear what I call reliable "moral witness" to their own experiences. Among friends, there is generally a mutual sharing of stories about past and present experiences. Friendship enables us to come to know the experiences and perspectives of our friends from their own points of view. So long as our friends confide their experiences authentically, sensitively, and insightfully, we can gain knowledge of lives lived in accord with moral rules and values which differ from our own. Based on this "empirical" grasp of the morally relevant features of the experiences of our friends, we broaden and enrich our own "empirical" base for evaluating both the abstract moral guidelines which we already hold and alternatives which we might consider.

What is the distinctive experiential contribution of *friendship?* Friendship is a close relationship in which trust, intimacy, and disclosure open for us whole standpoints other than our own. Through seeing what my friend counts as a harm done to her, for example, and seeing how she suffers from it, and what she does in response, I can "try on," as it were, her interpretive claim and its implications for moral practice, that is, its call for resistance or redress.

Because we come to know, in minute and intimate detail, so much of what is happening to a good friend, those experiences live for us with narrative specificity and richness. However, a friend inevitably differs from oneself, in regard to the ways in which she conceptualizes experience and comprehends its significance. Due to those differences, the narratives and assessments which she shares will implicitly reveal a moral perspective unlike one's own. The stories which she tells will be informed by her conceptualizations, values, and standards; these stories will, thus, live for us in the terms which reflect our friend's perspective and not our own.

Obviously, moral induction is not limited to relationships of friendship. A dependent child whom I nurture, for example, becomes a touchstone for assessing my own behavior in its success in meeting the child's needs, and also for determining the appropriate societal arrangements for enabling those needs to be met. My principles about social justice, no less than my principles about how I should nurture, are brought into question when I confront the hunger of a child whom I cannot adequately feed. Other relationships, as well, inform us of experiences which "test" various moral guidelines. But friendship, that is, a relationship of some degree of mutual intimacy, benevolence, interest, and concern, constitutes a context of trust and shared perspectives which fosters *vicarious participation in the very experience of moral alternatives.*

What does my friend consider important in the situations which she faces? What harms her? What offends her? What gives her hope and courage? How does she respond? How does she feel about what happens to her? When does she take the initiative? When does she let go? How does she explain, in her reflective moments, what she has done? As she narrates her stories, she reveals her own moral conceptions and principles *in practice:* her conceptions for discerning what happens to her and her principles for determining her own behavior. In virtue of understanding the experiences of our friends in *their own terms,* we not only widen our inductive basis for moral assessment, but, as well, we enrich the range of *conceptual* resources which we can use for interpreting and evaluating all the morally significant experience which we can comprehend.

There are, at least, two different kinds of "inductive" moral knowledge which one can gain from one's friends. First, one can see how a friend is affected by the various social arrangements in which she lives and by the behavior of others toward her. These effects reveal something about the adequacy of the standards which shape the social arrangements and the human actions which impinge upon her.

Second, one can observe how the course of her life "tests" the moral guidelines according to which she herself lives. One can reflect on that which motivates, guides, or affects her. One will be inspired to take it seriously because one takes *her* seriously. It becomes a living option for oneself. Through intimate knowledge of one's friend, one participates vicariously in the living which *embodies and realizes* her divergent values. One learns what life is like for someone who is motivated by springs of action different from one's own, and one sees how the moral abstractions which inform and affect her life fare in practice.

Because of these opportunities for growth in our moral knowledge, friendship permits us to orient ourselves in times when we doubt our own moral rules, values, or principles. When we don't know *what* to believe, we can try to determine *whom* to believe. Trusted friends offer us one important sort of guide through our uncertainties. Even if we have not yet doubted our own moral standards, commitments to particular persons may still surprise us with the inspiration to consider new values and principles. Thus, when we least expect it, our friendships may stimulate our moral transformation. . . .

Moral change obviously offers the possibility of enabling us to improve the moral quality of our lives. As well, it may facilitate our moral autonomy. Autonomy is promoted when one acquires a plurality of standpoints from which to assess one's choices, one's values and principles, one's very character.[2] The greater the diversity of perspectives which one can adopt for assessing rules, values, principles, and character, the greater will be the degree of one's autonomy in making moral choices. People to whom we are affiliated, especially our friends, afford us standpoints from which to comprehend, in their experiential significance, alternative perspectives on our own abstract moral guidelines. Through fostering our moral growth, our friends may, thus, occasion our moral autonomy. . . .

---

[2] For a discussion of the way in which autonomy is fostered by access to a plurality of perspectives, cf. Marilyn Friedman, "Autonomy in Social Contex," in *Proceedings of the Second International Conference of the North American Society for Social Philosophy,* eds. James Sterba and Creighton Peden (Edwin Mellen Press, forthcoming 1987).

FRIENDSHIP AND DUTY

Morality and Personal Relationships

Hugh LaFollette

Throughout this book, I have made frequent reference to a wide range of moral issues: honesty, jealousy, sexual fidelity, commitment, paternalism, caring, etc. This suggests there is an intricate connection between morality and personal relationships. There is. Of course personal relationships do not always promote moral values, nor do people find all relationships salutary. Some friendships, marriages, and kin relationships are anything but healthy or valuable. We all know (and perhaps are in) some relationships which hinder personal growth, undermine moral values, and diminish both parties' happiness—in short, relationships which systematically undermine the values they should promote.

Arguably such relationships are not close in any robust sense of the term. Nonetheless, I think many of them are personal. They are personal inasmuch as each person loves the other as a specific, unique individual. However, they are not close inasmuch as the parties cannot or will not take the interests of the others as their own. I suspect many of these marginal relationships fail because they are founded on a rigid love. Rigid love, if you may recall, is tied to a particular organism, not to that particular person with specific, embodied characteristics. Since this form of love is indifferent to the beloved's particular characteristics, the lover is likely less sensitive to the beloved's interests, needs, and desires.

The presence of detrimental relationships, however, does not undermine the claim that personal relationships are intricately connected with morality. Throughout the book I have offered numerous examples which indicate the pervasiveness and breadth of this connection. Here I want to bring these disparate suggestions together to defend an Aristotelian-type two-pronged thesis: that (1) close personal relationships are likely to be formed and persist only among morally good people, and that (2) close personal relationships are prerequisites for the development of morally good people.

Many people, I suspect, will think these claims are mistaken. Some will object to them on empirical grounds: they will claim that some corrupt people have close personal relationships, while some good people do not. Although I think this occurs far less often than the objectors might think, neither Aristotle's nor my account asserts that it is *impossible* for immoral people to be close friends—especially if the term "immoral" is construed weakly enough. Nor need either account claim it is impossible for those without close relationships to be morally good. What both accounts do suggest is that people who are moral are considerably more likely to have close personal relationships, and that the personal relationships of immoral people are in jeopardy.

Some philosophers reject my thesis on purely theoretical grounds. In their view, not only are morality and personal relationships not intricately connected, they are often diametrically opposed. It is not difficult to see why. Morality, as typically conceived, requires impartiality. The principle of impartiality (or the equal consideration of interests) specifies that we must treat all humans (creatures?) alike unless there is some general and morally relevant difference between them which justifies a difference in treatment. This principle is central to traditional ethical theory. According to J. L. Mackie, it is "in some sense beyond dispute" (1977: 83). The principle of impartiality does permit treating different people differently, but any difference in treatment must be justified by general features of the circumstances, so that others in like circumstances should act similarly (Singer 1971; Frankena 1973; Hare 1963). Specifically, impartiality forbids any deviation in one's moral duties because of one's "variable inclinations" (Gewirth 1978: 24) or "generic differences between persons" (Mackie 1977: 97). Put differently, "the class of persons alleged to be an exception to the rule cannot be a unit class" (Singer 1971: 87). Thus, a teacher should give equal grades to students who perform equally; unequal grades are justified only if there is some general and relevant reason which justifies that difference. For example, it is legitimate to give a better grade to a student who does superior work; it is illegitimate to give her a better grade because she is pretty, wears pink, or is named "Molly."

On the other hand, personal relationships are partial to the core: the subject of attention is *always* "a unit class" — ". . . its particular focus [is] the unique concatenation of wants, desires, identity, history, and so on, of a particular person" (Friedman 1993: 190–1). That is why personal relationships (which have partiality at their core) clash with morality, typically conceived (which has impartiality at its core). How, if at all, can this conflict be resolved? . . .

Why an accommodation is difficult

But an accommodation will not be easy. For there are elements of traditional morality which make it more likely to conflict with personal relationships. Specifically, widely held views of morality: (1) construe moral rules legalistically and, therefore, (2) give limited scope to moral judgement. Moreover, they (3) have a narrow understanding of moral motivation and are, therefore, (4) unconcerned about how people can develop the appropriate moral motivation.

Immanuel Kant, as traditionally interpreted, embodies just such a view of morality. Kant apparently embraces a legalistic view of morality according to which moral rules uniquely determine what we ought to do — at least they uniquely determine what Kant deems our "perfect duties" (1981: 30–3). Legalistic views naturally leave little room for moral judgement: moral agents need judge only how to apply the exceptionless moral rules. Moreover, those who embrace such views are relatively unconcerned about how to make people behave morally. Kant claims, for instance, that an act is devoid of moral worth if we are motivated by self-interest or inclination (1981: 7–12). Put differently, an action has moral worth only if we are motivated exclusively by the desire to do our duty. He has no suggestions about how to inculcate the desire to do our duty. Indeed, he couldn't. It is not hard to see why: any suggestion would inevitably make reference to other motives (self-interest, inclination, love, etc.) and, on his view, it would be morally inappropriate to develop moral motives for non-moral reasons or by non-moral means.

In a series of influential articles (1993; 1985; 1983), Barbara Herman challenges this standard interpretation of Kant. However, even if Herman is correct, many people do interpret Kant in these ways; moreover, whether Kantian or not, it is a view many people do hold. Even William Frankena, who more than 20 years ago recognized the potential appeal of "virtue ethics," nonetheless describes the first job of morality as determining our "moral obligations"—where his examples of obligations are described in terms of specific actions we should perform (1973: 10–11).

However, this Kantian view of morality fails to give specific guidance about how we should behave in real-life situations. Moreover, this account makes it nigh impossible to understand or inculcate moral dispositions. To help understand these defects of a legalistic morality, I will borrow an example from an earlier paper. Suppose I have a friend who, some months ago, experienced a profound personal tragedy. How should I relate to her? Should I be a non-judgemental listener, sensitive to her continuing pain? Should I offer advice, even if it is not requested? Or should I simply ignore, or at least play down, the trauma to help her "get on with her life"?

Clearly it is desirable—though doubtless annoying—to have friends play these (and other) diverse roles. If everyone were a sensitive listener, she could get mired in her trauma. If everyone offered her unsolicited advice, she could lose her self-respect. If everyone refused to discuss the trauma, she might never be able to satisfactorily resolve it. A mixture of reactions is not simply permissible, it may well be crucial for her recovery. One response will not help her (LaFollette 1991: 148–9).

Hence no general rule will tell me what I should do. I must judge what I, with my particular temperament and abilities, can best do to respond to her sensitively, given her needs and the character of our relationship. If I have inculcated sensitivity and kindness, I may act appropriately. Yet there is no precise description of what "acting appropriately" would be.

But on a traditional Kantian account of morality, abstract rules—not concrete moral judgement—should direct my action. In this view, the only role for judgement is to apply exceptionless moral principles—much like a referee. The rules of the football game may be variously interpreted and, even if the rule is unambiguous, its application in a particular case may be uncertain. Therefore, someone must apply those rules: that is the referee's task. Likewise for ethics in the traditional view. Ethical rules are exceptionless; but agents must apply them to individual circumstances. That is the (only) proper role of moral judgement.

However, this analogy gives inadequate scope to judgement. In football there are clearly delineated rules all referees must follow. Moral agents, however, do not merely apply rules, certainly not in the case under discussion. It *might* be tempting to say that all her friends are following a rule, perhaps one like: "Be loving to your intimates." However, this is not a rule, at least not one comparable to the rules of football. It is vague. (A comparably vague, and thus totally useless, rule in football might be: "Play fairly.") This rule has no content. Any attempt to give it precise content will either fail, yield an unacceptable rule, or reduce to some more precise rule. Consequently, since this case describes moral choices people frequently do face, then this Kantian account of moral judgement will be inadequate to the task.

Relatedly, this standard view is relatively indifferent about what motivates people to be moral and how they can become moral. Admittedly some traditional theorists are quite concerned about moral education and morality. For instance, J. S. Mill, who is often portrayed as endorsing a rule conception of morality, recognizes the importance of judgement and the need for moral education:

> As the means of making the nearest approach to this ideal, utility would enjoin, first, that laws and social arrangements should place the happiness . . . of every individual, as nearly as possible in harmony with the interest of the whole; and secondly, that education and opinion, which have so vast a power over human character, should so use that power as to establish in the mind of every individual an indissoluble association between his own happiness and the good of the whole; . . . so that not only he may be unable to conceive the possibility of happiness to himself, consistently with conduct opposed to the general good, but also that a direct impulse to promote the general good may be in every individual one of the habitual motives of action (1979: 17).

In fact, a growing number of philosophers are concerned about moral development (Flanagan 1991; Thomas 1991). Embedded in a richer understanding of moral development and moral psychology we will find an account of morality that both supports and is informed by personal relationships.

Moral habits

The key to understanding the interplay of morality and personal relationships is understanding that morality is, at its core, not a continuous series of choices, but a network of habits. By "habits" I do not mean some mere behavioral repetition, like biting one's nails. I follow Dewey in seeing habits as working adaptations of the organism with its environment. Habits are "that kind of human activity which is influenced by prior activity, which contains within itself a certain order of systemization of minor elements of action; which is projective, dynamic in quality, ready for overt manifestation; and which is operative in some subdued subordinate form even when not obviously dominating activity" (Dewey 1988: 39).

Most human activity is habitual. It couldn't be otherwise. We couldn't walk or write or drive or think if we had to consciously determine to take the next step, write the next word, apply the brakes, or add two numbers. Morality joins thinking, emotions, and work as habits. "Habit means special sensitiveness of accessibility to certain classes of stimuli, standing predilections and aversions, rather than bare recurrence of specific acts. It means will" (41).

For instance, thinking is generally thought to be the paradigm of a conscious, self-directed activity. Dewey and I would beg to differ: thinking is also a habit, albeit a complex one. A thoughtful person does not *decide* to think about an important issue, nor does she typically have to decide *how* to think about it. Her education and training make her sensitive to certain types of problems; they instill a disposition to think about those problems in a certain way. Emotions are also habits. Certain kinds of situations (or people) typically incite anger or desire or fear. I do not have to decide to become angry if someone attacks my child. I do so, and I do so habitually.

However, I wish to emphasize again: habits are not mere repetitions of behavior. Habits—at least those of interest here—are very fine-grained: they prompt different responses to different situations. For instance, the habit of thinking does not require that we think about all problems in exactly the same way. The habit can be sufficiently complex and supple so that we make suitable adjustments in the *way* we think about a problem, depending on the nature of that problem.

Morality—like thinking—is not some mysterious and inexplicable practice of abstract rational contemplation, but a complex habit. To treat morality as primarily the conscious adherence to a set of rules inevitably spells its failure. If in each and every case we had to consciously decide to be moral, we would be even less moral than we are. Moral education (whether by others or by ourselves) is successful if we become habitually sensitive to the needs and interests of others. That is, if we are moral we do not have to decide to consider the interests of others, we just will consider their interests. And, since moral habits, like habits of thought, can be very complex, very fine-grained, they empower us to respond sensitively to others in a variety of circumstances.

Once we appreciate the habitual nature of morality, the weakness of Kant's views (as traditionally understood) becomes apparent. We are not—nor could we be—moral if, on each and every occasion, we had to (1) decide what was morally relevant, (2) decide to fully consider all that is morally relevant, and (3) decide to act upon the results of our deliberations. Rather, if we are moral we do habitually what we should do (Aristotle 1985: 34). A truly moral person is not forced to act morally; rather it is something she does by inclination—it is part of her, that is, it is one of her habits, one of her deeper-disposing traits.

Of course to acknowledge that morality is a habit does not mean we need never deliberate, nor does it imply that we need never act against our current habits (although the ability to abandon or modify a current habit is, itself, a different type of habit, a meta-habit if you will). As Kant rightly points out, morality sometimes demands that we act against our inclinations. Modifying our habits so that we are inclined to do what we ought is a crucial element of morality. Unfortunately, many of us do not have the strength—or the sufficiently ingrained meta-habits—to do that. My point here is simply that *most* behavior—including moral behavior—is habitual. Thus, if we do not have deeply ingrained and finely textured moral habits, then we will behave immorally.

Inculcating moral habits

Once we see that morality is a habit, we are better equipped to understand two ways in which morality and personal relationships are supportive: (1) close personal relationships give us the knowledge and the motivation to develop impartial moral habits; and (2) intimacy flourishes in an environment which impartially recognizes the needs and interests of all. Understanding these connections will not dissolve the tensions between impartial moral demands and close personal relationships, but it will certainly make them more amenable to resolution.

For instance, close personal relationships can empower us to act morally, they are grist for the moral mill. Ethical theorists disagree about the extent of our concern for others, but all agree we should morally consider, even promote, the interests of others. But how do we learn how to promote others' interests? How do we become motivated to promote those interests? These are questions Kant does not ask; indeed, he couldn't. But they are questions we should ask.

Suppose, for example, you are standing next to someone who has an epileptic seizure, but you have never heard of epilepsy, let alone witnessed a seizure. Or suppose you are stranded on an elevator with someone having a heart attack, but you don't know people have hearts, let alone that they can malfunction. In short, try to imagine that you were in one of these circumstances when you were seven years old. You would do nothing. Or if you tried, it would likely do more harm than good; any success would surely be serendipitous.

It is difficult to imagine how we could develop the knowledge necessary to act morally had we not been in personal relationships. No one knows how to do mathematics or to play football without acquaintance with the discipline or the game. So why should we think we could know how to promote the interests of others if we had no close acquaintance with others? Someone reared by uncaring parents, who never established close personal ties with her peers, will be unlikely to know how to look after or promote the interests of intimates or strangers. We cannot promote interests we cannot identify, and the way we learn to identify the interests of others is by interacting with them. Most of us learned from our parents how to recognize the needs of others. Our parents comforted us when we were hurt; they laughed with us when we were happy. Eventually, we learned to identify their and our siblings' interests.

Equally importantly, that is likely how we learned to be concerned about the interests of others. Indeed, unless we had personal relationships, it is difficult to know how we would be motivated to care for others. Though I expect we may have *some* biologically inherited sympathetic tendencies, these wither unless others care for us, and we for them. If we are not motivated to promote the needs of our families or friends, how can we be motivated to promote the needs of strangers?

On the other hand, if we develop empathy toward our friends, we will have some inclination to generalize it to others. In close relationships we become so vividly aware of our intimates' needs that we are willing to help them, even when it is difficult to do so. Since empathy tends to be non-specific, by learning to respond to the interests of friends we learn to respond to the interests of acquaintances and even strangers.

My point is not simply that a person must have some exposure to loving, personal relationships in order to know how to care and to be motivated to care. There is also a strong correlation between the *extent* of our involvement in close relationships and the extent of our ability and motivation to care for strangers. That is, if we have had numerous close relationships, our moral horizons will be wider than if we had only one. We will learn how to respond to different intimates' needs, in a variety of circumstances. We will learn what causes them pain. And we will learn how to ease their pain. Generally, we will learn the myriad ways we can promote the interests of others.

That is not to say that those who develop close relationships always come to care for strangers. My point is simply that a person needs some exposure to personal relationships to acquire the knowledge and motivation to be moral. Put differently, a person cannot be just or moral in a vacuum; she can become just only within an environment which countenances personal relationships.

On the other hand, an environment which recognizes the needs of strangers (i.e., an impartialist's morality) will be one in which intimacy is more likely to flourish. A society concerned about the needs and interests of everyone, including strangers, is one in which empathy, caring, and honesty, etc. are prized. And a society which prizes these behaviors will be one which thereby equips its citizens for close personal relationships.

We can see this clearly if we try to think about attempted personal relationships between non-moral people. Their relationships will be at risk. Morally wicked people cannot be close friends. I recognize this claim is rather controversial; many people would consider it patently false. I think, though, that is because they do not fully appreciate what it means to have a close relationship. Let me rehearse a number of arguments from throughout the book to support this claim.

First, in a close personal relationship each party must have, as one of her interests, an interest in the other. Thus, if Al and Frank are close personal friends, then one of Al's interests must be to promote Frank's interests, and one of Frank's interests is to promote Al's. Put differently, neither Frank nor Al can be entirely egoistic. Each must be concerned with something besides himself, i.e., his friend. But can a morally wicked person have such concerns? I don't see how. Moral wickedness is paradigmatically a complete disregard for the interests of others. (Of course not all evil in the world stems from morally wicked people. Arguably most evil stems from the ignorance and inattention of morally decent people. My point here, though, is not about the primary sources of evil, but about the troubles wicked people will have in establishing and maintaining close relationships.)

All this seems too easy. Surely even crooks and gangsters— whom we typically consider morally wicked—can have close friends. We do think this, but perhaps we shouldn't. If (and this is a big if) these people do have close relationships—if they really do care for other people—then, although they are doubtless immoral in some respects (as are we all) we should conclude that they are not completely wicked. They are good inasmuch as they really care about others. In fact, I suspect this is the right way to think about most criminals; the world is not neatly divided into "the good guys" and "the bad guys." We all have flaws and foibles. Even the worst person has good features and the most saintly person is riddled with faults.

However, let us think, for a moment, about two people who are paradigmatically evil, yet appear to be friends. Do these people have genuine friendships? My answer is a guarded "No." There are other plausible explanations for their seeming friendly behavior. Suppose Al and Frank are kingpins in organized crime. By all outward appearances they are the best of friends. They say they care for each other; they are friends. I would suggest, however, that they are friendly merely because they are afraid not to be. What makes them act amicably toward each other is not that each wishes the other well (one of the criteria of friendship). Rather, it is that each thinks he can best promote his own interests by maintaining an air of friendship with the other.

But that air can be polluted suddenly if either thinks the other is in some way jeopardizing "the family business." Chronicles of gangland days in the United States are replete with cases where one boss would kill his best friend or even members of his family because they had violated some code. In these cases Frank and Al do not have a friendship; rather they have a role relationship supported by an unwritten code of conduct. What keeps the "relationship" together is not mutual well-wishing, but a fear of what will happen if either breaks that code. And that, most surely, is not at the center of close personal relationships.

We can understand the failure of these relationships in general terms by citing each person's exclusive attention to his own interests. There are, however, more fine-grained explanations. Close relationships, as I have argued throughout the book, are possible only inasmuch as each party trusts the other. . . . Each must trust the other will not hurt or abuse her, each must trust the other to care for her. But trust cannot survive, let alone flourish, in an environment of distrust and hate.

Intimates must also be honest with one another; dishonesty will chip away at the foundations of the relationship. . . . Yet people cannot be honest in the ways they need to be if they are immersed in a subculture built on dishonesty and deceit. Dishonesty, like all traits, is not something we can turn on and off. If we are dishonest with large numbers of people at work, we will be similarly inclined at home. Assuming Frank and Al are not stupid, they know that. That is why each will be cautious of the other; each will always be suspicious that the other is lying. And, to connect concerns about honesty with the previously mentioned concern about trust, we cannot really be honest with others unless we trust them. Mistrust constrains honesty.

In short, the possibility of genuine personal relationships is limited, if not eliminated, in an unjust environment. More especially, a person is unlikely to have close relationships unless she is moral. Anyone unconcerned with the welfare of other people, that is anyone who is amoral or immoral, will enter a relationship for her own benefit. Thus the relationship will not be personal in the relevant sense.

Consequently, personal relationships and morality are not at odds in the ways many philosophers have supposed. Rather, they are mutually supportive. Experience and involvement in close relationships will enhance our interest in and sympathy for the plight of others. Conversely, concern about the plight of the stranger will help us develop the traits necessary for close personal relationships.

Of course not everyone who has friends is concerned for strangers and not everyone who is concerned about strangers will be a good friend—though I suspect each will at least be capable of doing so. Nonetheless, these concerns could not exist in isolation. They are mutually supportive; they are not in constant conflict. Conflicts do arise. They arise in the same way that any moral conflicts arise; for instance, duties to two friends may conflict as may duties to two strangers. But such conflicts do not show that morality is impossible; they only show that it is sometimes difficult to achieve. But then, we already knew that.

References

Dewey, J. 1988: *Human Nature and Conduct*. Carbondale, IL: Southern Illinois University Press.
Flanagan, O. 1991: *Varieties of Moral Personality*. Cambridge, MA: Harvard University Press.
Frankena, W. 1973: *Ethics*. Englewood Cliffs, NJ: Prentice-Hall.
Gewirth, A. 1978: *Reason and Morality*. Chicago: University of Chicago Press.
Hare, R. M. 1963: *Freedom and Reason*. Oxford: Oxford University Press.
Herman, B. 1993: *The Practice of Moral Judgement*. Cambridge, MA: Harvard University Press.
——— 1985: *The Practice of Moral Judgement*. Journal of Philosophy, **82**, 414–36.
——— 1983: *Impartiality and Integrity*. The Monist, **66**, 233–50.
Kant, I. 1981: *Grounding for the Metaphysics of Morals*, J. W. Ellington (tr.). Indianapolis, IN: Hackett Publishing.
LaFollette, H. 1991: *The Truth in Ethical Relativism. Social Philosophy*.
Mackie, J. L. 1977: *Ethics: Inventing Right and Wrong*. New York: Penguin.
Mill, J. S. 1979: *Utilitarianism*, G. Sher (ed.). Indianapolis, IN: Hackett Publishing.
Wasserstrom, R. 1977: *Racism, Sexism, and Preferential Treatment*. UCLA Law Review, **24**, 581–622.
Wolf, S. 1982: *Moral Saints*. Journal of Philosophy, **79**, 419–39.

Questions for Further Reflection

1. Aristotle says that the character-friend wishes his friend well because the friend is a good person. It seems to follow from Aristotle's view that evil people cannot

have character-friendships. But could an evil person like someone and wish him well because that someone was an evil person—if, for instance, he liked and respected evil? If not, why not? If so, would such a relationship count as a friendship?

2. Aristotle says that if you are someone's friend, you wish her well for her own sake. He also says that it would be absurd to wish wine well for *its* own sake. What can have a "sake"? Can we wish dogs well for their own sakes? What about plants?

3. Ringer suggests that the only reason one would wish one's friend well is for one's own sake. Is this really true? Suppose that right now, as far as you know, your friend is fine. Still, he has been rather quiet tonight, and it occurs to you that he may be secretly unhappy about something. Suppose you will never know for certain whether this is so. Don't you hope, however, that your friend is not unhappy? This won't make *you* any happier, since you will never know whether he is unhappy or not. So, if you do hope that your friend is not unhappy, doesn't this show that the egoistic account of friendship is false?

4. Kant seems to think that the only reason we have only a few friends is that we do not trust other people with our secrets—if people were trustworthy, we would not need special friends. What would Aristotle say about this? (Think about his discussion of the reasons we can have only a few friends.) What do you think?

5. Kant says that although friends do not need to think exactly alike, still "on one point they must agree. Their intellectual and moral principles must be the same, if there is to be complete understanding between them." Do you agree with this? How does this affect Marilyn Friedman's claim that friendship can lead to moral growth?

6. LaFollette argues that close relationships help us learn to extend our sympathies more broadly and impartially. This might suggest a picture according to which we should grow out of our need for special relationships. Compare: We learn to count by taking groups of particular objects and combining them, but we soon become able to add two numbers without worrying about which particular objects we are counting. Perhaps we could similarly learn concern for others by being concerned about particular people, then learn to care about the interests of others in general, without worrying about whose interests are concerned. How might LaFollette defend the *continuing* need for close relationships?

Further Readings

Annis, David B. "The Meaning, Value, and Duties of Friendship." *American Philosophical Quarterly* 24 (1987). Argues that we have moral duties to our friends that we do not have to others, so that in some situations we not only may but should give our friends special treatment.

Brain, Robert. *Friends and Lovers.* New York: Pocket Books, 1977. Intriguing anthropological study; explains the surprising rituals associated with friendship in a number of societies and draws parallels with our own.

Cooper, John. "Aristotle on Friendship." In Amelie O. Rorty, ed., *Essays on Aristotle's Ethics.* Berkeley: University of California Press, 1980. Discusses both the types of friendship and its benefits. Argues (among other things) that use-friends and pleasure-friends *can* to some extent want another's good for the other's own sake.

Emerson, Ralph Waldo. "Friendship." In Michael Pakaluk, ed., *Other Selves: Philosophers on Friendship.* Rather obscurely written, but intriguing. Argues, among other things, that it is best not to see one's friends too often—an interesting contrast with Aristotle's view that friends should live together.

LaFollette, Hugh. *Personal Relationships: Love, Identity, and Morality.* Oxford: Blackwell, 1996. The book from which the selection by LaFollette in the present chapter is excerpted.

Pakaluk, Michael, ed. *Other Selves: Philosophers on Friendship.* Indianapolis: Hackett, 1991. A good collection of historical discussions of friendship by Plato, Aristotle, Cicero, Emerson, and others.

Thomas, Laurence. *Living Morally: A Psychology of Moral Character.* Philadelphia: Temple University Press, 1989. Chapters 4 and 5 offer a sensitive discussion of the nature of friendship.

Chapter 6

Sexual Relationships

This chapter addresses three interrelated issues about sexual morality. The first and most general issue concerns the relation between sex and love; the second and third concern the moral status of prostitution and homosexuality.

What ought the relation between sex and love to be? Let us begin by considering relationships in which sex is motivated by love and then consider various kinds of relationships in which sex and love are divorced. Finally, we will consider homosexual relationships, which, like heterosexual ones, may or may not involve love or affection.

Loving Sexual Relationships

Few people seem to see anything morally problematic about sexual relationships motivated by love. There are, of course, ascetic views, according to which *any* sort of sexual relationship is morally suspect; St. Paul, for instance, seems to think that marriage is desirable only for those too weak to resist the temptations of the flesh. And many who find nothing objectionable about sex *per se* nevertheless think there ought to be restrictions on loving sexual relationships, in particular, that there should be no sex outside marriage. Disagreements also exist about whether loving sexual relationships ought to be monogamous, whether within or without marriage. Some think extramarital sex is morally unobjectionable, but only with one partner at a time; some think polygamous marriage is morally permissible. Aside from such disputes over the conditions under which loving sex is permissible, however, opposition to sex motivated by love is rare. Much of the debate over sexual morality concerns the moral status of sex *without* love.

Sex without Love

Many sexual relationships involve affection but no deep or lasting love: Sexual relationships that last only a short time, from one night to a few weeks, are fairly common, and while these may be very affectionate and friendly, it seems unlikely that many of them are genuinely loving. Even longer relationships, including some marriages, may involve affection without love.

Alan Goldman, in "Plain Sex," argues against the traditional view that sex is undesirable unless coupled with love. Goldman argues that there is no reason to suppose that sex is a good thing only when engaged in for some larger purpose, such as procreation or the expression of love. He argues that there is nothing wrong with "plain sex," sex engaged in simply for its own sake rather than as a means of reproduction or as a way of expressing love. Roger Scruton, by contrast, defends the traditional view that sex ought to involve love: "Love is the fulfillment of desire, and therefore love is its *telos* [goal or purpose]." Scruton defends traditional sexual morality by arguing that erotic love is desirable and rewarding, and urging that erotic love is more likely to be available to those who embody the values of traditional sexual morality. The various sorts of activity prohibited by traditional morality in different ways inhibit the possibility of erotic love: Infidelity leads to jealousy, for example, while masturbation and prostitution lead to a separation of the personal from the sexual.

Sex with Mutual Agreement

Sexual relationships are sometimes the result of a noncoercive mutual agreement and yet involve neither love nor even affection. Prostitutes agree to engage in sex for a price, without being motivated by attraction or affection; their customers, too, typically pay them for sex not because of any affection for a particular prostitute, but simply in order to have sex with *someone*; it matters little with whom. Something similar may be true of various sorts of anonymous sexual encounters, in a park or restroom, perhaps, where two or more people engage in sex with little communication and no expectation of ever meeting again. In this chapter, we focus on prostitution as an example of sex by agreement but without affection.

Hadley Arkes argues that prostitution is immoral, and he insists that the immorality of prostitution is not because of any sort of unpleasant consequence; rather, prostitution is *intrinsically* wrong. Arkes believes that prostitution is morally on a par with other extramarital sex; indeed, he seems to approve of the purported fact that "women are labeled freely as 'prostitutes' when they are promiscuous, and when they engage often in sexual intercourse outside the relation of marriage." His argument that we are morally obligated not to engage in extramarital sex seems to involve several steps. First is the claim that we ought to engage in sex only with those we love. (Actually, Arkes explicitly says only that the sort of intimate fusion involved in sex "would be unthinkable unless one were motivated by the deepest personal love." Obviously this is *not*, in fact, "unthinkable," since many people not only think of but engage in sex without love. Presumably, then, what Arkes means to say is that sex without love is morally impermissible rather than literally unthinkable.) Second is the claim that we ought not to love someone deeply without committing ourselves to that person. (Again, Arkes does not quite say this: He says only that when love is present, "it becomes a proper ground for commitment." To complete his argument for the conclusion that prostitution is immoral, he must assume that love morally *requires* commitment, not that love is simply one ground for commitment.) Third and finally is the claim that if we are committed to someone we love, we ought to marry him or her. (Arkes says only that marriage is "the most appropriate symbol of a moral connection between lovers," but again, his argument seems to require the stronger claim.) If these three claims are true, then it follows that sex outside marriage is morally impermissible.

Each of these three claims provides an objection to prostitution, since sex with a prostitute is sex outside marriage, without commitment, and without love. The most important of the three is the claim that we should have sex only with those we love, since commitment and marriage acquire their role in the argument by virtue of the fact that, in Arkes' view, love requires them. Goldman, as we have already mentioned, attacks the view that there is anything wrong with sex without love, or, more generally, with "plain sex." Sex, like many other activities, *may* be engaged in out of love, but as with those other activities, there is nothing morally suspect about sex which is not engaged in for that purpose.

Arkes mentions Goldman's argument and makes two points relevant to it. These two points are not so much counterarguments as they are attempts to show that, in fact, we do not regard sex, and prostitution in particular, as morally on a par with other activities and pursuits. Arkes points out, first, that we regard rape as a more serious crime than simple assault. A beating, even if it causes as much pain and distress as a rape, does not seem to us to be as heinous an offense. However, the only apparent difference is that rape involves sex, so we apparently do not regard sex as morally on a par with other activities. Arkes' second point is that even those who claim to find nothing wrong with prostitution *per se* still do not want children to engage in it. We do not object to children acting or modeling for retail catalogs; why do we object to their being prostitutes? It must be, Arkes suggests, because we think that there is something intrinsically wrong with prostitution.

Lars O. Ericsson comes to the defense of prostitution and responds to a number of arguments against it. Of the many he considers and rejects, perhaps the "charge from conventional morality" and the "sentimentalist" charge come closest to capturing Arkes' view. Ericsson agrees with Arkes that the fundamental issue concerns the intrinsic acceptability or unacceptability of prostitution; utilitarian arguments about the bad consequences of prostitution are much less important. Unlike Arkes, however, Ericsson argues that there is nothing intrinsically wrong with prostitution; the negative features of prostitution are "the avoidable result of values and attitudes of the society wherein prostitution occurs," and the right response to these negative features is not to condemn prostitution but to change society's values and attitudes.

Sex without Mutual Agreement

Although none of the readings in this chapter focuses primarily on rape, there are certainly important philosophical issues involving the notion. There seems to be universal agreement that rape is morally despicable, one of the clearest imaginable violations of the Kantian injunction that we should never treat another as a mere means. However, there is less consensus than one might hope concerning which acts count as rapes. One study reported that, of a sample of about 7,000 college students, "most men (88%) who reported an assault that met legal definitions of rape were adamant that their behavior was definitely not rape,"[1] while "only 27% of the women whose experience met legal definitions of rape labeled themselves as rape victims."[2] Clearly there are some serious disagreements over which acts count as rapes, due mainly to disagreement over where free consent ends and

---

[1] Mary Koss, "Hidden Rape: Sexual Aggression and Victimization in a National Sample of Students in Higher Education," in Ann Wolbert Burgess, ed., *Rape and Sexual Assault II* (New York: Garland, 1988), p. 19.

[2] Koss, p. 16.

coercion begins. (There has been some controversy over the interpretation of the survey results just mentioned,[3] but this controversy is itself an indication of how dramatically views differ about the proper understanding of rape.)

Is Homosexuality an Evil?

So far, we have been classifying sexual relationships on the basis of the motives out of which we engage in sex. For some purposes, though, it is also useful to classify such relationships according to the type of partner with whom one engages in sex. There are issues about the moral propriety of engaging in sex with partners significantly older or younger than oneself; of sex with members of other races; of sex with people related in various ways to oneself (e.g., parents or children, siblings, students or teachers); of sex with members of other species; and so on. Perhaps the liveliest issue of this sort concerns the moral propriety of sex with members of one's own gender. Homosexuality does not fit neatly into our classification so far, since homosexual relationships may fall into any of the categories we have discussed: loving, affectionate but not loving, and so on.

Homosexuality has been criticized on two main grounds. The first is *utilitarian* and holds that homosexuality is a bad thing because it leads to bad consequences. An extreme version of this view was held by the emperor Justinian, who held that homosexuality caused "famines, earthquakes, and plagues."[4] A more common argument is that homosexuality is bad because it leads to unhappiness. Supposing that this is true, one must still ask *why* it leads to unhappiness; if the main cause is social attitudes toward homosexuality, then it may be the attitudes themselves that ought to be changed (compare Ericsson's similar argument in the case of prostitution).

The other main argument against homosexuality is that it is *unnatural*. The Roman Catholic view of sexuality, as codified by Saint Thomas Aquinas, holds that every human activity has its own natural end or purpose. We have an obligation to act in such a way that these natural purposes may be fulfilled. The purpose of sex, in Aquinas' view, is the production and raising of children; every act of sex, then, should both allow the possibility of biological reproduction and also be engaged in within a relationship that will allow for a stable environment in which to bring up and educate the resulting children, if any. The requirement that sex allow the possibility of biological reproduction rules out masturbation, contraception, and homosexuality; the requirement that it be engaged in only within a stable relationship rules out most extramarital sex.

For many contemporary readers, Aquinas' argument is not terribly persuasive. Two main objections to it are first, that the notion of natural ends or purposes no longer seems as clear as it did to Aquinas, and second, even supposing that reproduction is in some sense what sex is *for*, it is not clear what normative consequences follow from this. It may be that feet are, in some sense, for standing and walking on. Houdini also used his feet to untie knots, thus

---

[3]See Chapter 10, "Rape Research," in Christina Hoff Sommers, *Who Stole Feminism: How Women Have Betrayed Women* (New York: Simon and Schuster, 1994).

[4]Quoted in Sir Patrick Devlin, *The Enforcement of Morals* (New York: Oxford University Press, 1965), p. 15.

using them to accomplish a purpose for which they were not designed, but it is difficult to see why this should be morally questionable. Similarly, many people find it difficult to believe that there is anything necessarily wrong about using our sex organs to accomplish purposes for which they were not designed (if indeed they were designed for a purpose at all).

Michael Levin's article can be seen as an attempt to combine the utilitarian argument against homosexuality with the argument that it is unnatural, and to meet the difficulties with both. Levin attempts to explain the notion of the *purpose* of an organ in sociobiological terms, thus responding to the first worry with Aquinas' argument. He also attempts to meet the worry that no normative consequences follow from facts about an organ's purpose by adding a utilitarian dimension to his argument. Using our organs in ways for which they were not designed, in Levin's view, leads to unhappiness; for this reason we should discourage people from using their organs in such ways.

Because Levin argues that homosexual *behavior* is a misuse of sexual organs, it is worth pointing out that homosexuality is usually thought of not as an activity in which one might or might not engage, but as a disposition or state of character, so that one might be a homosexual without ever engaging in a homosexual act. However, it is difficult to construe homosexuality understood in this way as a misuse of organs. As Timothy Murphy points out, "If one accepts the condition that homosexuality is primarily a psychic phenomenon, and if one wanted to argue its abnormality along the lines Levin has suggested, it would seem that one would have to argue that homoeroticism is somehow a misuse of the brain!" Murphy also argues that it is likely that, to the extent that homosexuals are unhappy, this is because of adverse social circumstances rather than because of biological reasons, in which case the best way to alleviate this unhappiness would be for society to become more, rather than less, tolerant of homosexuality.

Is Heterosexuality an Evil?

In striking contrast to Levin's view that heterosexual sex is better because it uses the sex organs in accordance with their natural functions, Andrea Dworkin has suggested that heterosexual intercourse is undesirable because it is oppressive to women. She writes, in her provocative but fascinating book, *Intercourse*, that "intercourse remains a means or the means of physiologically making a woman inferior. . . . In the experience of intercourse, she loses her capacity for integrity because her body— the basis of privacy and freedom in the material world for all human beings—is entered and occupied; the boundaries of her physical body are—neutrally speaking—violated."[5] In the current social and political climate, sexual intercourse is one among many arenas in which men are dominant, and intercourse serves Dworkin as a kind of metaphor for all sorts of male oppression of women. But she also suggests that it is more than just a metaphor. Dworkin strongly hints that the purported oppressiveness of intercourse is not merely socially caused, but is actually biologically based. Intercourse may be not just a metaphor for various sorts of oppression, but a chief *cause* of women's oppression.

---

[5]Andrea Dworkin, *Intercourse* (New York: The Free Press, A Division of Macmillan, Inc., 1987), p. 137.

On this view, intercourse may be a bad thing even though our bodies are "designed" for it. Moreover, we *could* now do without it if we became convinced it was an evil. Dworkin mentions that, as a result of new reproductive technologies, intercourse is no longer necessary for biological survival. Just because we are biologically suited for an activity does not mean that we must or even should engage in it, and Dworkin strongly implies that a world in which children were produced by *in vitro* fertilization and our sexual needs were met in lesbian or gay relationships might be a much better world than the one we actually live in.

Still, what of the fact that most women *want* sexual relationships with men? How can intercourse be oppressive when it is freely engaged in by women who want it? Dworkin describes women who want intercourse as "collaborators" in their own oppression: Under present unequal conditions, intercourse "destroys in women the will to political freedom. . . . We become female: occupied; collaborators against each other, especially against those among us who resist male domination."[6] On this view women who acquiesce in heterosexual arrangements are analogous to citizens of a country who willingly assist an occupying force.

Types of Ethical Issues

Our discussion so far has concealed a good deal of complexity. It is natural to discuss various sorts of sexual practice as though they raised a single moral issue, roughly, whether they are morally acceptable or unacceptable. In fact, a number of moral issues about such practices need to be disentangled. We need to distinguish at least the following issues:

1. Is a certain sort of sex good sex? This is an ethical issue in a broad sense because it concerns the components of a good life, but it is not a moral issue in the usual sense. It has to do with what sorts of sex are most rewarding or worthwhile, but an answer to this question has no immediate consequences for the issue of whether we are obligated not to engage in certain sorts of sex. It may be that sex with a prostitute is usually inferior, *per se*, to sex with a lover; it does not follow that we ought not to have sex with prostitutes. Goldman's "Plain Sex" is primarily concerned with the issue of whether plain sex is necessarily bad sex and only secondarily with issues about our duties or obligations in matters of sex.

2. Is a given sort of sex morally permissible? (Do we have a duty not to engage in sex of certain sorts?) In general, utilitarianism takes a permissive attitude toward many sexual practices. As long as both partners enjoy a practice and it does not cause too much pain to others, there will be no utilitarian objection to it. (It may be that utilitarianism is more permissive about sexual practices than most of us will be able to accept. Imagine a husband who derives great pleasure from forcing his unwilling wife to engage in sex. On some occasions, she may find this only mildly unpleasant and frustrating; on such occasions, the husband's action produces a net increase of pleasure and so is apparently acceptable on utilitarian grounds. To most of us, however, his action nevertheless seems plainly to be morally unacceptable.) It is less clear what sort of advice Kantianism offers on matters of sexual morality. The notion of using someone as a mere means seems potentially useful in this

---
[6]Dworkin, *Intercourse*, p. 143.

regard, but it is puzzling how this notion is to be applied. It is clear that loving sex does not involve using one's partner as a mere means, and it is clear that rape does. It is less clear what to say about intermediate cases, such as prostitution. This may depend on the extent to which one thinks prostitutes are exploited or coerced.

3. Is one sort of sex morally preferable to other sorts? (Sex without love, for example, might be permissible but less morally desirable than sex with love, as, for example, failing to help a starving stranger may be permissible but less morally desirable than helping him.) Scruton's article argues that Aristotelianism supports a very conventional and conservative view of sexual morality. Like utilitarianism, Scruton's Aristotelianism is teleological: He recommends instilling in people, especially one's children, the sort of character that will, on the whole, lead them to have happier lives. If Scruton is correct, then we have an obligation to encourage our children to act according to the dictates of traditional sexual morality, but it does not follow that they have a moral obligation to follow these dictates: If they fail to live up to traditional standards, they will very likely, in Scruton's view, be less happy or fulfilled than otherwise, but they will not necessarily have done anything morally wrong.

4. Finally, there is the issue of how the law ought to treat various sorts of sexual practice. One may think that a particular sexual practice is unrewarding, less morally desirable than another practice, or even morally impermissible, without necessarily holding that it ought to be made illegal. A tradition of liberal political thought, famously expressed in John Stuart Mill's *On Liberty*, holds that private morality should not be legally enforced. According to this view, the law should not come into play unless a practice harms people who do not knowingly and without coercion engage in it.

SEXUAL MORALITY: A LIBERAL VIEW

Plain Sex

Alan H. Goldman

I

Before we can get a sensible view of the relation of sex to morality, perversion, social regulation, and marriage, we require a sensible analysis of the concept itself; one which neither understates its animal pleasure nor overstates its importance within a theory or system of value. I say "before," but the order is not quite so clear, for questions in this area, as elsewhere in moral philosophy, are both conceptual and normative at the same time. Our concept of sex will partially determine our moral view of it, but as philosophers we should formulate a concept that will accord with its proper moral status. What we require here, as elsewhere, is "reflective equilibrium," a goal not achieved by traditional and recent analyses together with their moral implications. Because sexual activity, like other natural functions such as eating or exercising, has become imbedded in layers of cultural, moral, and superstitious superstructure, it is hard to conceive it in its simplest terms. But partially for this reason, it is only by thinking about plain sex that we can begin to achieve this conceptual equilibrium.

I shall suggest here that sex continues to be misrepresented in recent writings, at least in philosophical writings, and I shall criticize the predominant form of analysis which I term "means-end analysis." Such conceptions attribute a necessary external goal or purpose to sexual activity, whether it be reproduction, the expression of love, simple communication, or interpersonal awareness. They analyze sexual activity as a means to one of these ends, implying that sexual desire is a desire to reproduce, to love or be loved, or to communicate with others. All definitions of this type suggest false views of the relation of sex to perversion and morality by implying that sex which does not fit one of these models or fulfill one of these functions is in some way deviant or incomplete.

The alternative, simpler analysis with which I will begin is that sexual desire is desire for contact with another person's body and for the pleasure which such contact produces; sexual activity is activity which tends to fulfill such desire of the agent. Whereas Aristotle and Butler were correct in holding that pleasure is normally a byproduct rather than a goal of purposeful action, in the case of sex this is not so clear. The desire for another's body is, principally among other things, the desire for the pleasure that physical contact brings. On the other hand, it is not a desire for a particular sensation detachable from its causal context, a sensation which can be derived in other ways. This definition in terms of the general goal of sexual desire appears preferable to an attempt to more explicitly list or define specific sexual activities, for many activities such as kissing, embracing, massaging, or holding hands may or may not be sexual, depending upon the context and more specifically upon the purposes, needs, or desires into which such activities fit. The generality of the definition also represents a refusal (common in recent psychological texts) to overemphasize orgasm as the goal of sexual desire or genital sex as the only norm of sexual activity. . . .

Central to the definition is the fact that the goal of sexual desire and activity is the physical contact itself, rather than something else which this contact might express. By contrast, what I term "means-end analyses" posit ends which I take to be extraneous to plain sex, and they view sex as a means to these ends. Their fault lies not in defining sex in terms of its general goal, but in seeing plain sex as merely a means to other separable ends. I term these "means-end analyses" for convenience, although "means-separable-end analyses," while too cumbersome, might be more fully explanatory. The desire for physical contact with another person is a minimal criterion for (normal) sexual desire, but is both necessary and sufficient to qualify normal desire as sexual. Of course, we may want to express other feelings through sexual acts in various contexts; but without the desire for the physical contact in and for itself, or when it is sought for other reasons, activities in which contact is involved are not predominantly sexual. Furthermore, the desire for physical contact in itself, without the wish to express affection or other feelings through it, is sufficient to render sexual the activity of the agent which fulfills it. Various activities with this goal alone, such as kissing and caressing in certain contexts, qualify as sexual even without the presence of genital symptoms of sexual excitement. The latter are not therefore necessary criteria for sexual activity.

This initial analysis may seem to some either over- or underinclusive. It might seem too broad in leading us to interpret physical contact as sexual desire in activities such as football and other contact sports. In these cases, however, the desire is not for contact with another body per se, it is not directed toward a particular person for that purpose, and it is not the goal of the activity—the goal is winning or exercising or knocking someone down or displaying one's prowess. If the desire is purely for contact with another specific person's body, then to interpret it as sexual does not seem an exaggeration. A slightly more difficult case is that of a baby's desire to be cuddled and our natural response in wanting to cuddle it. In the case of the baby, the desire may be simply for the physical contact, for the pleasure of the caresses. If so, we may characterize this desire, especially in keeping with Freudian theory, as sexual or protosexual. It will differ nevertheless from full-fledged sexual desire in being more amorphous, not directed outward toward another specific person's body. It may also be that what the infant unconsciously desires is not physical contact per se but signs of affection, tenderness, or security, in which case we have further reason for hesitating to characterize its wants as clearly sexual. The intent of our response to the baby is often the showing of affection, not the pure physical contact, so that our definition in terms of action which fulfills sexual desire *on the part of the agent* does not capture such actions, whatever we say of the baby. (If it is intuitive to characterize our response as sexual as well, there is clearly no problem here for my analysis.) The same can be said of signs of affection (or in some cultures polite greeting) among men or women: these certainly need not be homosexual when the intent is only to show friendship, something extrinsic to plain sex although valuable when added to it.

Our definition of sex in terms of the desire for physical contact may appear too narrow in that a person's personality, not merely her or his body, may be sexually attractive to another, and in that looking or conversing in a certain way can be sexual in a given context without bodily contact. Nevertheless, it is not the contents of one's thoughts per se that are sexually appealing, but one's personality as embodied in certain manners of behavior. Furthermore, if a person is sexually attracted by another's personality, he or she will desire not just further conversation, but actual sexual contact. While looking at or conversing with someone can be interpreted as sexual in given contexts it is so when intended as preliminary to, and hence parasitic upon, elemental sexual interest. Voyeurism or viewing a pornographic movie qualifies as a sexual activity, but only as an imaginative substitute for the real thing (otherwise a deviation from the norm as expressed in our definition). The same is true of masturbation as a sexual activity without a partner.

That the initial definition indicates at least an ingredient of sexual desire and activity is too obvious to argue. We all know what sex is, at least in obvious cases, and do not need philosophers to tell us. My preliminary analysis is meant to serve as a contrast to what sex is not, at least, not necessarily. I concentrate upon the physically manifested desire for another's body, and I take as central the immersion in the physical aspect of one's own existence and attention to the physical embodiment of the other. One may derive pleasure in a sex act from expressing certain feelings to one's partner or from awareness of the attitude of one's partner, but sexual desire is essentially desire for physical contact itself: it is a bodily desire for the body of another that dominates our mental life for more or less brief periods. Traditional writings were correct to emphasize the purely physical or animal aspect of sex; they were wrong only in condemning it. This characterization of sex as an intensely pleasurable physical activity and acute physical desire may seem to some to capture only its barest level. But it is worth distinguishing and focusing upon this least common denominator in order to avoid the false views of sexual morality and perversion which emerge from thinking that sex is essentially something else.

II

We may turn then to what sex is not, to the arguments regarding supposed conceptual connections between sex and other activities which it is necessary to conceptually distinguish. The most comprehensible attempt to build an extraneous purpose into the sex act identifies that purpose as reproduction, its primary biological function. While this may be "nature's" purpose, it certainly need not be ours (the analogy with eating, while sometimes overworked, is pertinent here). While this identification may once have had a rational basis which also grounded the identification of the value and morality of sex with that applicable to reproduction and childrearing, the development of contraception rendered the connection weak. Methods of contraception are by now so familiar and so widely used that it is not necessary to dwell upon the changes wrought by these developments in the concept of sex itself and in a rational sexual ethic dependent upon that concept. In the past, the ever present possibility of children rendered the concepts of sex and sexual morality different from those required at present. There may be good reasons, if the presence and care of both mother and father are beneficial to children, for restricting reproduction to marriage. Insofar as society has a legitimate role in protecting children's interests, it may be justified in giving marriage a legal status, although this question is complicated by the fact (among others) that children born to single mothers deserve no penalties. In any case, the point here is simply that these questions are irrelevant at the present time to those regarding the morality of sex and its potential social regulation. (Further connections with marriage will be discussed later.)

It is obvious that the desire for sex is not necessarily a desire to reproduce, that the psychological manifestation has become, if it were not always, distinct from its biological roots. There are many parallels, as previously mentioned, with other natural functions. The pleasures of eating and exercising are to a large extent independent of their roles in nourishment or health (as the junk-food industry discovered with a vengeance). Despite the obvious parallel with sex, there is still a tendency for many to think that sex acts which can be reproductive are, if not more moral or less immoral, at least more natural. These categories of morality and "naturalness," or normality, are not to be identified with each other, as will be argued later, and neither is applicable to sex by virtue of its connection to reproduction. The tendency to identify reproduction as the conceptually connected end of sex is most prevalent now in the pronouncements of the Catholic church. There the assumed analysis is clearly tied to a restrictive sexual morality according to which acts become immoral and unnatural when they are not oriented towards reproduction, a morality which has independent roots in the Christian sexual ethic as it derives from Paul. However, the means-end analysis fails to generate a consistent sexual ethic: homosexual and oral-genital sex is condemned while kissing or caressing, acts equally unlikely to lead in themselves to fertilization, even when properly characterized as sexual according to our definition, are not.

III

Before discussing further relations of means-end analyses to false or inconsistent sexual ethics and concepts of perversion, I turn to other examples of these analyses. One common position views sex as essentially an expression of love or affection between the partners. It is generally recognized that there are other types of love besides sexual, but sex itself is taken as an expression of one type, sometimes termed "romantic" love.[1] Various factors again ought to weaken this identification. First, there are other types of love besides that which it is appropriate to express sexually, and "romantic" love itself can be expressed in many other ways. I am not denying that sex can take on heightened value and meaning when it becomes a vehicle for the expression of feelings of love or tenderness, but so can many other usually mundane activities such as getting up early to make breakfast on Sunday, cleaning the house, and so on. Second, sex itself can be used to communicate many other emotions besides love, and, as I will argue later, can communicate nothing in particular and still be good sex.

On a deeper level, an internal tension is bound to result from an identification of sex, which I have described as a physical-psychological desire, with love as a long-term, deep emotional relationship between two individuals. As this type of relationship, love is permanent, at least in intent, and more or less exclusive. A normal person cannot deeply love more than a few individuals even in a lifetime. We may be suspicious that those who attempt or claim to love many love them weakly if at all. Yet, fleeting sexual desire can arise in relation to a variety of other individuals one finds sexually attractive. It may even be, as some have claimed, that sexual desire in humans naturally seeks variety, while this is obviously false of love. For this reason, monogamous sex, even if justified, almost always represents a sacrifice or the exercise of self-control on the part of the spouses, while monogamous love generally does not. There is no such thing as casual love in the sense in which I intend the term "love." It may occasionally happen that a spouse falls deeply in love with someone else (especially when sex is conceived in terms of love), but this is relatively rare in comparison to passing sexual desire for others; and while the former often indicates a weakness or fault in the marriage relation, the latter does not.

If love is indeed more exclusive in its objects than is sexual desire, this explains why those who view sex as essentially an expression of love would again tend to hold a repressive or restrictive sexual ethic. As in the case of reproduction, there may be good reasons for reserving the total commitment of deep love to the context of marriage and family—the normal personality may not withstand additional divisions of ultimate commitment and allegiance. There is no question that marriage itself is best sustained by a deep relation of love and affection; and even if love is not

---

[1] Even Bertrand Russell, whose writing in this area was a model of rationality, at least for its period, tends to make this identification and to condemn plain sex in the absence of love: "sex intercourse apart from love has little value, and is to be regarded primarily as experimentation with a view to love." *Marriage and Morals* (New York: Bantam, 1959), p. 87.

naturally monogamous, the benefits of family units to children provide additional reason to avoid serious commitments elsewhere which weaken family ties. It can be argued similarly that monogamous sex strengthens families by restricting and at the same time guaranteeing an outlet for sexual desire in marriage. But there is more force to the argument that recognition of a clear distinction between sex and love in society would help avoid disastrous marriages which result from adolescent confusion of the two when sexual desire is mistaken for permanent love, and would weaken damaging jealousies which arise in marriages in relation to passing sexual desires. The love and affection of a sound marriage certainly differs from the adolescent romantic variety, which is often a mere substitute for sex in the context of a repressive sexual ethic.

In fact, the restrictive sexual ethic tied to the means-end analysis in terms of love again has failed to be consistent. At least, it has not been applied consistently, but forms part of the double standard which has curtailed the freedom of women. It is predictable in light of this history that some women would now advocate using sex as another kind of means, as a political weapon or as a way to increase unjustly denied power and freedom. The inconsistency in the sexual ethic typically attached to the sex-love analysis, according to which it has generally been taken with a grain of salt when applied to men, is simply another example of the impossibility of tailoring a plausible moral theory in this area to a conception of sex which builds in conceptually extraneous factors.

I am not suggesting here that sex ought never to be connected with love or that it is not a more significant and valuable activity when it is. Nor am I denying that individuals need love as much as sex and perhaps emotionally need at least one complete relationship which encompasses both. Just as sex can express love and take on heightened significance when it does, so love is often naturally accompanied by an intermittent desire for sex. But again love is accompanied appropriately by desires for other shared activities as well. What makes the desire for sex seem more intimately connected with love is the intimacy which is seen to be a natural feature of mutual sex acts. Like love, sex is held to lay one bare psychologically as well as physically. Sex is unquestionably intimate, but beyond that the psychological toll often attached may be a function of the restrictive sexual ethic itself, rather than a legitimate apology for it. The intimacy involved in love is psychologically consuming in a generally healthy way, while the psychological tolls of sexual relations, often including embarrassment as a correlate of intimacy, are too often the result of artificial sexual ethics and taboos. The intimacy involved in both love and sex is insufficient in any case in light of previous points to render a means-end analysis in these terms appropriate. . . .

I have now criticized various types of analysis sharing or suggesting a common means-end form. I have suggested that analyses of this form relate to attempts to limit moral or natural sex to that which fulfills some purpose or function extraneous to basic sexual desire. The attempts to brand forms of sex outside the idealized models as immoral or perverted fail to achieve consistency with intuitions that they themselves do not directly question. The reproductive model brands oral-genital sex a deviation, but cannot account for kissing or holding hands. . . .

The sex-love model makes most sexual desire seem degrading or base. These views condemn extramarital sex on the sound but irrelevant grounds that reproduction and deep commitment are best confined to family contexts. The romanticization of sex and the confusion of sexual desire with love operate in both directions: sex outside the context of romantic love is repressed; once it is repressed, partners become more difficult to find and sex becomes romanticized further, out of proportion to its real value for the individual.

What all these analyses share in addition to a common form is accordance with and perhaps derivation from the Platonic-Christian moral tradition, according to which the animal or purely physical element of humans is the source of immorality, and plain sex in the sense I defined it is an expression of this element, hence in itself to be condemned. All the analyses examined seem to seek a distance from sexual desire itself in attempting to extend it conceptually beyond the physical. The love and communication analyses seek refinement or intellectualization of the desire; plain physical sex becomes vulgar, and too straightforward sexual encounters without an aura of respectable cerebral communicative content are to be avoided. Solomon explicitly argues that sex cannot be a "mere" appetite, his argument being that if it were, subway exhibitionism and other vulgar forms would be pleasing.[2] This fails to recognize that sexual desire can be focused or selective at the same time as being physical. Lower animals are not attracted by every other member of their species, either. Rancid food forced down one's throat is not pleasing, but that certainly fails to show that hunger is not a physical appetite. Sexual desire lets us know that we are physical beings and, indeed, animals; this is why traditional Platonic morality is so thorough in its condemnation. Means-end analyses continue to reflect this tradition, sometimes unwittingly. They show that in conceptualizing sex it is still difficult, despite years of so-called revolution in this area, to free ourselves from the lingering suspicion that plain sex as physical desire is an expression of our "lower selves," that yielding to our animal natures is subhuman or vulgar.

VI

Having criticized these analyses for the sexual ethics . . . they imply, it remains to contrast my account along these lines. To the question of what morality might be implied by my analysis, the answer is that there are no moral implications whatever. Any analysis of sex which imputes a moral character to sex acts in themselves is wrong for that reason. There is no morality intrinsic to sex, although general moral rules apply to the treatment of others in sex acts as they apply to all human relations. We can speak of a sexual ethic as we can speak of a business ethic, without implying that business in itself is either moral or immoral or that special rules are required to judge business practices which are not derived from rules that apply elsewhere as well. Sex is not in itself a moral category, although like business it invariably places us into relations with others in which moral rules apply. It gives us opportunity to do what is otherwise recognized as wrong, to harm others, deceive them or manipulate them against their wills. Just as the fact that an act is sexual in itself never renders it wrong or adds to its wrongness if it is wrong on other grounds (sexual acts towards minors are wrong on other grounds as will be argued below), so no wrong act is to be excused because done from a sexual motive. If a "crime of passion" is to be excused, it would have to be on grounds of temporary insanity rather than sexual context (whether insanity does constitute a legitimate excuse for certain actions is too big a topic to argue

---

[2]Robert Solomon. "Sex and Perversion," *Philosophy and Sex*, ed. R. Baker and F. Elliston (Buffalo: Prometheus, 1975), p. 285.

here). Sexual motives are among others which may become deranged, and the fact that they are sexual has no bearing in itself on the moral character, whether negative or exculpatory, of the actions deriving from them. Whatever might be true of war, it is certainly not the case that all's fair in love or sex.

Our first conclusion regarding morality and sex is therefore that no conduct otherwise immoral should be excused because it is sexual conduct, and nothing in sex is immoral unless condemned by rules which apply elsewhere as well. The last clause requires further clarification. Sexual conduct can be governed by particular rules relating only to sex itself. But these precepts must be implied by general moral rules when these are applied to specific sexual relations or types of conduct. The same is true of rules of fair business, ethical medicine, or courtesy in driving a car. In the latter case, particular acts on the road may be reprehensible, such as tailgating or passing on the right, which seem to bear no resemblance as actions to any outside the context of highway safety. Nevertheless their immorality derives from the fact that they place others in danger, a circumstance which, when avoidable, is to be condemned in any context. This structure of general and specifically applicable rules describes a reasonable sexual ethic as well. To take an extreme case, rape is always a sexual act and it is always immoral. A rule against rape can therefore be considered an obvious part of sexual morality which has no bearing on nonsexual conduct. But the immorality of rape derives from its being an extreme violation of a person's body, of the right not to be humiliated, and of the general moral prohibition against using other persons against their wills, not from the fact that it is a sexual act.

The application elsewhere of general moral rules to sexual conduct is further complicated by the fact that it will be relative to the particular desires and preferences of one's partner (these may be influenced by and hence in some sense include misguided beliefs about sexual morality itself). This means that there will be fewer specific rules in the area of sexual ethics than in other areas of conduct, such as driving cars, where the relativity of preference is irrelevant to the prohibition of objectively dangerous conduct. More reliance will have to be placed upon the general moral rule, which in this area holds simply that the preferences, desires, and interests of one's partner or potential partner ought to be taken into account. This rule is certainly not specifically formulated to govern sexual relations; it is a form of the central principle of morality itself. But when applied to sex, it prohibits certain actions, such as molestation of children, which cannot be categorized as violations of the rule without at the same time being classified as sexual. I believe this last case is the closest we can come to an action which is wrong *because* it is sexual, but even here its wrongness is better characterized as deriving from the detrimental effects such behavior can have on the future emotional and sexual life of the naive victims, and from the fact that such behavior therefore involves manipulation of innocent persons without regard for their interests. Hence, this case also involves violation of a general moral rule which applies elsewhere as well.

Aside from faulty conceptual analyses of sex and the influence of the Platonic moral tradition, there are two more plausible reasons for thinking that there are moral dimensions intrinsic to sex acts per se. The first is that such acts are normally intensely pleasurable. According to a hedonistic, utilitarian moral theory, they therefore should be at least prima facie morally right, rather than morally neutral in themselves. To me this seems incorrect and reflects unfavorably on the ethical theory in question. The pleasure intrinsic to sex acts is a good, but not, it seems to me, a good with much positive moral significance. Certainly I can have no duty to pursue such pleasure myself, and while it may be nice to give pleasure of any form to others, there is no ethical requirement to do so, given my right over my own body. The exception relates to the context of sex acts themselves, when one partner derives pleasure from the other and ought to return the favor. This duty to reciprocate takes us out of the domain of hedonistic utilitarianism, however, and into a Kantian moral framework, the central principles of which call for just such reciprocity in human relations. Since independent moral judgments regarding sexual activities constitute one area in which ethical theories are to be tested, these observations indicate here, as I believe others indicate elsewhere, the fertility of the Kantian, as opposed to the utilitarian, principle in reconstructing reasoned moral consciousness.

It may appear from this alternative Kantian viewpoint that sexual acts must be at least prima facie wrong in themselves. This is because they invariably involve at different stages the manipulation of one's partner for one's own pleasure, which might appear to be prohibited on the formulation of Kant's principle which holds that one ought not to treat another as a means to such private ends. A more realistic rendering of this formulation, however, one which recognizes its intended equivalence to the first universalizability principle, admits no such absolute prohibition. Many human relations, most economic transactions for example, involve using other individuals for personal benefit. These relations are immoral only when they are one-sided, when the benefits are not mutual, or when the transactions are not freely and rationally endorsed by all parties. The same holds true of sexual acts. The central principle governing them is the Kantian demand for reciprocity in sexual relations. In order to comply with the second formulation of the categorical imperative, one must recognize the subjectivity of one's partner (not merely by being aroused by her or his desire, as Nagel describes). Even in an act which by its nature "objectifies" the other, one recognizes a partner as a subject with demands and desires by yielding to those desires, by allowing oneself to be a sexual object as well, by giving pleasure or ensuring that the pleasures of the acts are mutual. It is this kind of reciprocity which forms the basis for morality in sex, which distinguishes right acts from wrong in this area as in others. (Of course, prior to sex acts one must gauge their effects upon potential partners and take these longer range interests into account.)

VII

I suggested earlier that in addition to generating confusion regarding the rightness or wrongness of sex acts, false conceptual analyses of the means-end form cause confusion about the value of sex to the individual. My account recognizes the satisfaction of desire and the pleasure this brings as the central psychological function of the sex act for the individual. Sex affords us a paradigm of pleasure, but not a cornerstone of value. For most of us it is not only a needed outlet for desire but also the most enjoyable form of recreation we know. Its value is nevertheless easily mistaken by being confused with that of love, when it is taken as essentially an expression of that emotion. Although intense, the pleasures of sex are brief and repetitive rather than cumulative. They give value to the specific acts which generate them, but not the lasting kind of value which enhances one's whole life. The briefness of these pleasures contributes to their intensity (or perhaps their intensity makes them necessary brief), but it also relegates them to the periphery of most rational plans for the good life.

By contrast, love typically develops over a long-term relation; while its pleasures may be less intense and physical, they are of more cumulative value. The importance of love to the individual may well be central in a rational system of value. And it has perhaps an even deeper moral significance relating to the identification with the interests of another person, which broadens one's possible relationships with others as well. Marriage is again important in preserving this relation between adults and children, which seems as important to the adults as it is to the children in broadening concerns which have a tendency to become selfish. Sexual desire, by contrast, is desire for another which is nevertheless essentially self-regarding. Sexual pleasure is certainly a good for the individual, and for many it may be necessary in order for them to function in a reasonably cheerful way. But it bears little relation to those other values just discussed, to which some analyses falsely suggest a conceptual connection.

SEXUAL MORALITY: A CONSERVATIVE VIEW

Sexual Morality

Roger Scruton

We must now . . . ask whether there is such a thing as sexual virtue, and, if so, what is it, and how is it acquired? Clearly, sexual desire, which is an interpersonal attitude with the most far-reaching consequences for those who are joined by it, cannot be morally neutral. On the contrary, it is in the experience of sexual desire that we are most vividly conscious of the distinction between virtuous and vicious impulses, and most vividly aware that, in the choice between them, our happiness is at stake.

The Aristotelian strategy enjoins us to ignore the actual conditions of any particular person's life, and to look only at the permanent features of human nature. We know that people feel sexual desire; that they feel erotic love, which may grow from desire; that they may avoid both these feelings, by dissipation or self-restraint. Is there anything to be said about desire, other than that it falls within the general scope of the virtue of temperance, which enjoins us to desire only what reason approves?

The first, and most important, observation to be made is that the capacity for love in general, and for erotic love in particular, is a virtue. . . . Erotic love involves an element of mutual self-enhancement; it generates a sense of the irreplaceable value, both of the other and of the self, and of the activities which bind them. To receive and to give this love is to achieve something of incomparable value in the process of self-fulfilment. It is to gain the most powerful of all interpersonal *guarantees;* in erotic love the subject becomes conscious of the full reality of his personal existence, not only in his own eyes, but in the eyes of another. Everything that he is and values gains sustenance from his love, and every project receives a meaning beyond the moment. All that exists for us as mere hope and hypothesis—the attachment to life and the body—achieves under the rule of *erōs* the aspect of a radiant certainty. Unlike the cold glances of approval, admiration and pride, the glance of love sees value precisely in that which is the source of anxiety and doubt: in the merely contingent, merely 'empirical', existence of the flesh, the existence which we did not choose, but to which we are condemned. It is the answer to man's fallen condition—to his *Geworfenheit*.[1]

To receive erotic love, however, a person must be able to give it: or if he cannot, the love of others will be a torment to him, seeking from him that which he cannot provide, and directing against him the fury of a disappointed right. It is therefore unquestionable that we have reason to acquire the capacity for erotic love, and, if this means bending our sexual impulses in a certain direction, that will be the direction of sexual virtue. Indeed, the argument of the last two chapters has implied that the development of the sexual impulse towards love may be impeded: there are sexual habits which are vicious, precisely in neutralising the capacity for love. The first thing that can be said, therefore, is that we all have reason to avoid those habits and to educate our children not to possess them.

Here it may be objected that not every love is happy, that there are many—Anna Karenina, for example, or Phaedra—whose capacity for love was the cause of their downfall. But we must remind ourselves of the Aristotelian strategy. In establishing that courage or wisdom is a virtue, the Aristotelian does not argue that the possession of these virtues is in every particular circumstance bound to be advantageous. A parable of Derek Parfit's, adapted from T. C. Schelling,[2] adequately shows what is at stake: Suppose a man breaks into my house and commands me to open the safe for him, saying that, if I do not comply, he will begin to shoot my children. He has heard me telephone the police, and knows that, if he leaves any of us alive, we will be able to give information sufficient to arrest him if he takes what the safe contains. Clearly it is irrational in these circumstances to open the safe—since that will not protect any of us—and also not to open it, since that would cause the robber to kill my children one by one in order to persuade me of his sincerity. Suppose, however, I possess a drug that causes me to become completely irrational. I swallow the pill, and cry out: 'I love my children, therefore kill them'; the man tortures me and I beg him to continue; and so on. In these changed circumstances, my assailant is powerless to obtain what he wants and can only flee before the police arrive. In other words, in such a case, it is actually in the interests of the subject to be irrational: he has overwhelming circumstantial *reason* to be irrational, just as Anna Karenina had an overwhelming circumstantial *reason* to be without the

---

[1]Thrown-ness—Heidegger's term for the condition in which the agent first confronts the objective world (*Being and Time*, tr. J. Macquarrie and E. S. Robinson, New York, 1962). The term describes the agent's situation as *perceived:* before I have taken responsibility for my existence, my being has a quality of arbitrariness which afflicts me with anxiety.

[2]Parfit, *Reasons and Persons*, pp. 12–13, drawing on T. C. Schelling's *Strategy of Conflict*, Cambridge, Mass., 1960.

capacity for love. Clearly, however, it would be absurd, on these grounds, to inculcate a habit of irrationality in our children; indeed no *reason* could be given, in the absence of detailed knowledge of a person's future, for acquiring such a habit. In so far as reasons can be given now, for the cultivation of this or that state of character, they must justify the cultivation of rationality before all else—for how can I flourish according to my nature as a rational agent if I am not at least rational?

In like manner, it is not the particular personal tragedy but the generality of the human condition that determines the basis of sexual morality. Tragedy and loss are the rare but necessary outcomes of a process which we all have reason to undergo. (Indeed, it is part of the point of tragedy that it divorces in our imagination the right and the good from the merely prudential: that it sets the value of life against the value of mere survival.) We wish to know, in advance of any particular experience, which dispositions a person must have if he is successfully to express himself in sexual desire and to be fulfilled in his sexual endeavours. Love is the fulfilment of desire, and therefore love is its *telos*. A life of celibacy may also be fulfilled; but, assuming the general truth that most of us have a powerful, and perhaps overwhelming, urge to make love, it is in our interests to ensure that love—and not some other thing—is made.

Love, I have argued, is prone to jealousy, and the object of jealousy is defined by the thought of the beloved's desire. Because jealousy is one of the greatest of psychical catastrophes, involving the possible ruin of both partners, a morality based in the need for erotic love must forestall and eliminate jealousy. It is in the deepest human interest, therefore, that we form the habit of fidelity. This habit is natural and normal; but it is also easily broken, and the temptation to break it is contained in desire itself—in the element of generality which tempts us always to experiment, to verify, to detach ourselves from that which is too familiar in the interest of excitement and risk. Virtuous desire is faithful; but virtuous desire is also an artefact, made possible by a process of moral education which we do not, in truth, understand in its complexity.

If that observation is correct, a whole section of traditional sexual morality must be upheld. The fulfillment of sexual desire defines the nature of desire: *to telos phuseis estin*. And the nature of desire gives us our standard of normality. There are enormous varieties of human sexual conduct, and of 'common-sense' morality: some societies permit or encourage polygamy, others look with indifference upon premarital intercourse, or regard marriage itself as no more than an episode in a relation that pre-exists and perhaps survives it. But no society, and no 'common-sense' morality—not even, it seems, the morality of Samoa[3]—looks with favour upon promiscuity or infidelity, unless influenced by a doctrine of 'emancipation' or 'liberation' which is dependent for its sense upon the very conventions which it defies. Whatever the institutional forms of human sexual union, and whatever the range of permitted partners, sexual desire is itself inherently 'nuptial': it involves concentration upon the embodied existence of the other, leading through tenderness to the 'vow' of erotic love. It is a telling observation that the civilisation which has most tolerated the institution of polygamy—the Islamic—has also, in its erotic literature, produced what are perhaps the intensest

---

[3]See again the criticisms offered to Margaret Mead by Derek Freeman, *Margaret Mead and Samoa*, Cambridge, Mass., 1983.

and most poignant celebrations of monogamous love, precisely through the attempt to capture, not the institution of marriage, but the human datum of desire.[4]

The nuptiality of desire suggests, in its turn, a natural history of desire: a principle of development which defines the 'normal course' of sexual education. 'Sexual maturity' involves incorporating the sexual impulse into the personality, and so making sexual desire into an expression of the subject himself, even though it is, in the heat of action, a force which also overcomes him. If the Aristotelian approach to these things is as plausible as I think it is, the virtuous habit will also have the character of a 'mean': it will involve the disposition to desire what is desirable, despite the competing impulses of animal lust (in which the intentionality of desire may be demolished) and timorous frigidity (in which the sexual impulse is impeded altogether). Education is directed towards the special kind of temperance which shows itself, sometimes as chastity, sometimes as fidelity, sometimes as passionate desire, according to the 'right judgement' of the subject. In wanting what is judged to be desirable, the virtuous person wants what may also be loved, and what may therefore be obtained without hurt or humiliation.

Virtue is a matter of degree, rarely attained in its completion, but always admired. Because traditional sexual education has pursued sexual virtue, it is worthwhile summarising its most important features, in order to see the power of the idea that underlies and justifies it.

The most important feature of traditional sexual education is summarised in anthropological language as the 'ethic of pollution and taboo'.[5] The child was taught to regard his body as sacred, and as subject to pollution by misperception or misuse. The sense of pollution is by no means a trivial side-effect of the 'bad sexual encounter': it may involve a penetrating disgust, at oneself, one's body and one's situation, such as is experienced by the victim of rape. Those sentiments—which arise from our 'fear of the obscene'—express the tension contained within the experience of embodiment. At any moment we can become 'mere body', the self driven from its incarnation, and its habitation ransacked. The most important root idea of personal morality is that I am *in* my body, not (to borrow Descartes' image) as a pilot in a ship, but as an incarnate self. My body is identical with me, and sexual purity is the precious guarantee of this.

Sexual purity does not forbid desire: it simply ensures the status of desire as an interpersonal feeling. The child who learns 'dirty habits' detaches his sex from himself, sets it outside himself as something curious and alien. His fascinated enslavement to the body is also a withering of desire, a scattering of erotic energy and a loss of union with the other. Sexual purity sustains the *subject* of desire, making him present as a self in the very act which overcomes him.

The extraordinary, spiritual significance accorded to sexual 'purity' has, of course, its sociobiological and its psychoanalytical explanations. But what, exactly, is its *meaning*, and have people been right to value it? In Wagner's *Parsifal*, the 'pure fool' is uniquely credited with the power to heal the terrible wound which is the physical

---

[4]Cf. the love poetry of Hafiz, of Omar Khayyam, and of the Divan poets; and also the tales of faithful love in the *Thousand and One Nights*.

[5]See Mary Douglas, *Implicit Meanings*, London, 1975, and *Purity and Danger*, London, 1966, for a study of the phenomena of disgust and pollution among African tribes.

sign of Amfortas's sexual 'pollution'. He alone can redeem Kundry, the 'fallen' woman, whose sexual licence is so resistant to her penitent personality, that it must be confined to another world, of which she retains only a dim and horrified consciousness. That other world is a world of pleasure and opportunity, a world of the 'permitted'. It is governed, however, by the impure eunuch Klingsor, whose rule is a kind of slavery. Wagner finds the meaning of Christian redemption in the fool's chastity, which leads him to renounce the rewards of an impure desire for the sake of another's salvation. Parsifal releases Amfortas from the hold of 'magic' from the 'charm' which tempts Szymanowski's King Roger towards a vain apotheosis.[6] Parsifal is the harbinger of peace and freedom, in a world that has been enslaved by the magic of desire.

The haunting symbols of this opera owe their power to feelings that are too deep to be lightly dismissed as aesthetic artefacts. But what is their meaning for people who live unsheltered by religion? The answer is to be found, not in religious, but in sexual, feeling. The purely human redemption which is offered to us in love is dependent, in the last analysis, upon public recognition of the value of chastity, and of the sacrilege involved in a sexual impulse that wanders free from the controlling impulse of respect. The 'pollution' of the prostitute is not that she gives herself for money, but that she gives herself to those whom she hates or despises. This is the 'wound' of unchastity, which cannot be healed in solitude by the one who suffers it, but only by his acceptance into a social order which confines the sexual impulse to the realm of intimate relations. The chaste person sustains the ideal of sexual innocence, by giving honourable form to chastity as a way of life. Through his example, it becomes not foolish but admirable to ignore the promptings of a desire that brings no intimacy or fulfilment. Chastity is not a private policy, followed by one individual alone for the sake of his peace of mind. It has a wider and more generous significance: it attempts to draw others into complicity, and to sustain a social order that confines the sexual impulse to the personal sphere. . . .

The child was traditionally brought up to achieve sexual fulfilment only *through* chastity, which is the condition which surrounds him on his first entering the adult world—the world of commitments and obligations. At the same time, he was encouraged to ponder certain 'ideal objects' of desire. These, presented to him under the aspect of an idealised physical beauty, were never *merely* beautiful, but also endowed with the moral attributes that fitted them for love. This dual inculcation of 'pure' habits and 'ideal' love might seem, on the face of it, to be unworthy of the name of education. Is it not, rather, like the mere *training* of a horse or a dog, which arbitrarily forbids some things and fosters others, without offering the first hint of a reason why? And is it not the distinguishing mark of education that it engages with the rational nature of its recipient, and does not merely mould him indifferently to his own understanding of the process? Why, in short, is this moral education, rather than a transference into the sexual sphere—as Freud would have it—of those same processes of interdiction that train us to defecate, not in our nappies, but in a porcelain pot?

---

[6] *King Roger* is, I believe, an important expression of a certain vision of the erotic, which is seen as essentially *outside* society, chthonic, unintelligible and subversive of established things. I have discussed the opera and its meaning in 'Between Decadence and Barbarism: the Music of Szymanowski', in M. Bristiger, R. Scruton and P. Weber-Bockholdt (eds), *Karol Szymanowski in seiner Zeit*, Munich, 1984, pp. 159–78.

The answer is clear. The cult of innocence is an attempt to *generate* rational conduct, by incorporating the sexual impulse into the self-activity of the subject. It is an attempt to impede the impulse, until such a time as it may attach itself to the interpersonal project that leads to its fulfilment: the project of union with another person, who is wanted not merely for his body, but for the person who *is* this body. Innocence is the disposition to avoid sexual encounter, except with the person whom one may fully desire. Children who have lost their innocence have acquired the habit of gratification through the body alone, in a state of partial or truncated desire. Their gratification is detached from the conditions of personal fulfilment and wanders from object to object with no settled tendency to attach itself to any, pursued all the while by a sense of the body's obscene dominion. 'Debauching of the innocent' was traditionally regarded as a most serious offence, and one that offered genuine *harm* to the victim. The harm in question was not physical, but moral: the undermining of the process which prepares the child to enter the world of *erōs*. (Thus Nabokov's Lolita, who passes with such rapidity from childish provocativeness to a knowing interest in the sexual act, finds, in the end, a marriage devoid of passion, and dies without knowledge of desire.)

The personal and the sexual can become divorced in many ways. The task of sexual morality is to unite them, to sustain thereby the intentionality of desire, and to prepare the individual for erotic love. Sexual morality is the morality of embodiment: the posture which strives to unite us with our bodies, precisely in those situations when our bodies are foremost in our thoughts. Without such a morality the human world is subject to a dangerous divide, a gulf between self and body, at the verge of which all our attempts at personal union falter and withdraw. Hence the prime focus of sexual morality is not the attitude to others, but the attitude to one's own body and its uses. Its aim is to safeguard the integrity of our embodiment. Only on that condition, it is thought, can we inculcate either innocence in the young or fidelity in the adult. Such habits are, however, only one part of sexual virtue. Traditional morality has combined its praise of them with a condemnation of other things—in particular of the habits of lust and perversion. And it is not hard to find the reason for these condemnations.

Perversion consists precisely in a diverting of the sexual impulse from its interpersonal goal, or towards some act that is intrinsically destructive of personal relations and of the values that we find in them. The 'dissolution' of the flesh, which the Marquis de Sade regarded as so important an element in the sexual aim, is in fact the dissolution of the soul; the perversions described by de Sade are not so much attempts to destroy the flesh of the victim as to rid his flesh of its personal meaning, to wring out, with the blood, the rival perspective. That is true in one way or another of all perversion, which can be simply described as the habit of finding a sexual release that avoids or abolishes the *other*, obliterating his embodiment with the obscene perception of his body. Perversion is narcissistic, often solipsistic, involving strategies of replacement which are intrinsically destructive of personal feeling. Perversion therefore prepares us for a life without personal fulfilment, in which no human relation achieves foundation in the acceptance of the other, as this acceptance is provided by desire.

Lust may be defined as a genuine sexual desire, from which the goal of erotic love has been excluded, and in which whatever tends towards that goal—tenderness, intimacy, fidelity, dependence—is curtailed or obstructed. There need be nothing perverted in this. Indeed the special case of lust which I have discussed under the title of Don Juanism, in which the project of intimacy is constantly abbreviated by the flight towards another sexual object, provides one of our paradigms of desire. Nevertheless, the traditional condemnation of lust is far from arbitrary, and the associated contrast between lust and love far from a matter of convention. Lust is also a habit, involving the disposition to give way to desire, without regard to any personal relation with the object. (Thus perversions are all forms of lust even though lust is not in itself a perversion.) Naturally, we all feel the promptings of lust, but the rapidity with which sexual acts become sexual habits, and the catastrophic effect of a sexual act which cannot be remembered without shame or humiliation, give us strong reasons to resist them, reasons that Shakespeare captured in these words:

> Th'expence of Spirit in a waste of shame
> Is lust in action, and till action, lust
> Is perjur'd, murdrous, blouddy, full of blame,
> Savage, extreame, rude, cruell, not to trust,
> Injoyd no sooner but dispised straight,
> Past reason hunted, and no sooner had,
> Past reason hated as a swollowed bayt,
> On purpose layd to make the taker mad:
> Mad in pursuit and in possession so,
> Had, having, and in quest to have, extreame,
> A blisse in proofe, and prov'd, a very woe,
> Before a joy proposd, behind, a dreame,
> > All this the world well knowes, yet none knowes well
> > To shun the heaven that leads men to this hell.

In addition to the condemnation of lust and perversion, however, some part of traditional sexual education can be seen as a kind of sustained war against fantasy. It is undeniable that fantasy can play an important part in all our sexual doings, and even the most passionate and faithful lover may, in the act of love, rehearse to himself other scenes of sexual abandon than the one in which he is engaged. Nevertheless, there is truth in the contrast (familiar, in one version, from the writings of Freud)[7] between fantasy and reality, and in the sense that the first is in some way destructive of the second. Fantasy replaces the real, resistant, objective world with a pliant substitute—and that, indeed, is its purpose. Life in the actual world is difficult and embarrassing. Most of all it is difficult and embarrassing in our confrontation with other people, who, by their very existence, make demands that we may be unable or unwilling to meet. It requires a great force, such as the force of sexual desire, to overcome the embarrassment and self-protection that shield us from the most intimate encounters. It is tempting to take refuge in substitutes, which neither embarrass us nor resist the impulse of our spontaneous cravings. The habit grows, in masturbation, of creating a compliant world of desire, in which unreal objects become the focus of real emotions, and the emotions themselves are rendered incompetent to participate in the building of personal relations. The fantasy blocks the passage to reality, which becomes inaccessible to the will.

Even if the fantasy can be overcome so far as to engage in the act of love with another, a peculiar danger remains. The other becomes veiled in substitutes; he is never fully himself in the act of love; it is never clearly *him* that I desire, or *him* that I possess, but always rather a composite object, a universal body, of which he is but one among a potential infinity of instances. Fantasy fills our thoughts with a sense of the obscene, and the orgasm becomes, not the possession of another, but

---

[7] 'Formulations Regarding the Two Principles in Mental Functioning' (1911), in *Collected Papers*, tr. J. Riviere, New York, 1924–50, vol. IV.

the expenditure of energy on his depersonalised body. Fantasies are private property, which I can dispose according to my will, with no answerability to the other whom I abuse through them. He, indeed, is of no intrinsic interest to me, and serves merely as my opportunity for self-regarding pleasure. For the fantasist, the ideal partner is indeed the prostitute, who, because she can be purchased, solves at once the moral problem presented by the presence of another at the scene of sexual release.

The connection between fantasy and prostitution is deep and important. The effect of fantasy is to 'commodify' the object of desire, and to replace the law of sexual relationship between people with the law of the market. Sex itself can then be seen as a commodity:[8] something that we pursue and obtain in quantifiable form, and which comes in a variety of packages: in the form of a woman or a man; in the form of a film or a dream; in the form of a fetish or an animal. In so far as the sexual act is seen in this way, it seems morally neutral—or, at best, impersonal. Such criticism as may be offered will concern merely the dangers for the individual and his partner of this or that sexual package: for some bring diseases and discomforts of which others are free. The most harmless and hygienic act of all, on this view, is the act of masturbation, stimulated by whatever works of pornography are necessary to prompt the desire for it in the unimaginative. This justification for pornography has, indeed, recently been offered.

As I have already argued, however, fantasy does not exist comfortably with reality. It has a natural tendency to realise itself: to remake the world in its own image. The harmless wanker with the video-machine can at any moment turn into the desperate rapist with a gun. The 'reality principle' by which the normal sexual act is regulated is a principle of personal encounter, which enjoins us to respect the other person, and to respect, also, the sanctity of his body, as the tangible expression of another self. The world of fantasy obeys no such rule, and is governed by monstrous myths and illusions which are at war with the human world—the illusions, for example, that women wish to be raped, that children have only to be awakened in order to give and receive the intensest sexual pleasure, that violence is not an affront but an affirmation of a natural right. All such myths, nurtured in fantasy, threaten not merely the consciousness of the man who lives by them, but also the moral structure of his surrounding world. They render the world unsafe for self and other, and cause the subject to look on everyone, not as an end in himself, but as a possible means to his private pleasure. In his world, the sexual encounter has been 'fetishised', to use the apt Marxian term,[9] and every other human reality has been poisoned by the sense of the expendability and replaceability of the other.

It is a small step from the preoccupation with sexual virtue, to a condemnation of obscenity and pornography (which is its published form). Obscenity is a direct assault on the sentiment of desire, and therefore on the social order that is based in desire and which has personal love as its goal and fulfilment. There is no doubt that the normal conscience cannot remain neutral towards obscenity, any more than it can remain neutral towards paedophilia and rape (which is not to say that obscenity

---

[8] An eccentric and politicised, but frequently perceptive, critique of this 'commodification' of sex is contained in Stephen Heath, *The Sexual Fix*, London, 1982.

[9] Karl Marx, *Capital*, tr. S. Moore and E. Aveling, ed. F. Engels, London, 1887, vol I, part I, ch. I, section 4.

must also be treated as a *crime*). It is therefore unsurprising that traditional moral education has involved censorship of obscene material, and a severe emphasis on 'purity in thought, word and deed'—an emphasis which is now greeted with irony or ridicule.

Traditional sexual education was, despite its exaggerations and imbecilities, truer to human nature than the libertarian culture which has succeeded it. Through considering its wisdom and its shortcomings, we may understand how to resuscitate an idea of sexual virtue, in accordance with the broad requirements of the Aristotelian argument that I have, in this chapter, been presenting. The ideal of virtue remains one of 'sexual integrity': of a sexuality that is entirely integrated into the life of personal affection, and in which the self and its responsibility are centrally involved and indissolubly linked to the pleasures and passions of the body.

Traditional sexual morality has therefore been the morality of the body. Libertarian morality, by contrast, has relied almost entirely on a Kantian view of the human subject, as related to his body by no coherent moral tie. Focussing as he does on an ideal of purely personal respect, and assigning no distinctive place to the body in our moral endeavour, the Kantian inevitably tends towards permissive morality. No sexual act can be wrong merely by virtue of its physical character, and the ideas of obscenity, pollution and perversion have no obvious application. His attitude to homosexuality is conveniently summarised in this passage from a Quaker pamphlet:

> We see no reason why the physical nature of the sexual act should be the criterion by which the question whether it is moral should be decided. An act which (for example) expresses true affection between two individuals and gives pleasure to them both, does not seem to us to be sinful by reason *alone* of the fact that it is homosexual. The same criteria seem to apply whether a relationship is heterosexual or homosexual.[10]

Such sentiments are the standard offering of the liberal and utilitarian moralities of our time. However much we may sympathise with their conclusions, it is not possible to accept the shallow reasoning that leads up to them, and which bypasses the great metaphysical conundrum to which all sexual morality is addressed: the conundrum of embodiment. Lawrence asserts that 'sex is *you*', and offers some bad but revealing lines on the subject:

> And don't, with the nasty, prying mind, drag it out from its deeps
> And finger it and force it, and shatter the rhythm it keeps
> When it is left alone, as it stirs and rouses and sleeps.

If anything justifies Lawrence's condemnation of the 'nasty, prying mind', it is the opposite of what he supposes. Sex 'sleeps' in the soul precisely because, and to the extent that, it is buried there by education. If sex is you, it is because you are the product of that education, and not just its victim. It has endowed you with what I have called 'sexual integrity': the ability to be *in* your body, in the very moment of desire.

The reader may be reluctant to follow me in believing that traditional morality is largely justified by the ideal of sexual integrity. But if he accepts the main tenor of my argument, he must surely realise that the ethic of 'liberation', far from promising the release of the self from hostile bondage, in fact heralds the dissipation of the self in loveless fantasy: th'expence of Spirit, in a waste of shame.

---

[10] A. Heron (ed.), *Towards a Quaker View of Sex*, London, 1963, quoted in Ronald Atkinson, *Sexual Morality*, London, 1965, p. 148.

PROSTITUTION IS MORALLY IMPERMISSIBLE

Prostitution

Hadley Arkes

Prostitution: Framing the Problem

Whatever defines, in principle, the wrong of prostitution would probably have to apply to the fashionable courtesans, as well as to the common prostitute on the street. The courtesan may not seem to present the same difficulty because she may be hidden from public display, and because the prostitute on the street may branch out more easily into muggings and thefts, which will present other problems that the police will be compelled to deal with. But if a law on prostitution were established on its proper ground of principle, the courtesan would not stand so clearly out of reach as she appears to stand today. For the heart of the matter, I think, has to do with the acceptance of sexual intercourse outside the special context of law and intimacy that is defined by marriage and the family. From the free employment of the epithet "whore," it is evident that common usage takes its guide from these very gross, and very clear, markers: women are labeled freely as "prostitutes" when they are promiscuous, and when they engage often in sexual intercourse outside the relation of marriage. That engagement may be extended; it may be offered impersonally, to a larger section of the public, without discrimination, and for the payment of a fee. But no threshold is crossed here; all of these steps merely confirm the criteria that underlay the original judgment: that the movement to prostitution was a movement away from relations of personal commitment and love concentrated in a marriage, and it involved a shift (at the extreme) toward sexual intercourse on an impersonal basis; with members of the public, without commitment and without love.

There is little doubt that it would be far easier for the law to define prostitution if it could use as the core of its definition the unambiguous test of whether sexual intercourse takes place in the context of a legal marriage. But apart from the clarity it would furnish to the law, this standard probably points rather precisely, also, to the moral grounds on which the condemnation of prostitution would ultimately rest. In that event one would arrive at a recognition that one might almost prefer these days to leave undiscovered—namely, that the law which condemns prostitution stood on a much firmer ground in an earlier period, a period characterized by a more stringent regulation of public morals, when the law was willing to condemn as "fornication" all sexual intercourse outside marriage. It seems hardly imaginable, of course, that we could return in our own time to that state of the laws. And yet if the moral rejection of prostitution depends at its foundation on the special significance of *human* love and the unique commitments of family, it is sobering to consider the possibility that the law which restrains prostitution stood on a much firmer ground of principle in an earlier day than it does now, in our own.

The law today must be far less clear about the moral ground on which it would condemn prostitution, and the result is that when the law seeks to address the problem, the tendency has been to deal mainly with the peripheral aspects or the most outward manifestations of prostitution. The inclination has often been to ban "public solicitation" or restrict the zone of solicitation—to treat the problem, in other words, as a matter of "aesthetic regulation" or the abatement of nuisances. Now it is true, of course, that solicitation may be a "nuisance" or a form of harassment on independent grounds, quite apart from whether it would beckon people to activities that are illegitimate. The courts have upheld the rights of communities to ban sound trucks or neon signs, regardless of whether the activities that were being advertised were legitimate. Yet it is virtually inconceivable that the law could ban all forms of advertisement for products and services that are recognized as legitimate.

In the case of prostitution, however, a ban on all public advertising and solicitation has not been considered beyond question. It should be apparent that a measure as sweeping as that could not be separated from a judgment in principle about the legitimacy of prostitution itself, but still there has been no disposition in the law to come to terms with that fact. A case in point has been offered by New York City in its recent efforts to counter the bogus "massage parlors," which have really been brothels in disguise. As the City initially prepared legislation on the subject, its approach was characteristic of the line of attack that would be pursued by most lawyers: in the spirit of Holmes, they would try to banish every word of moral significance from the law altogether, which is to say that they would try to deal with a moral problem while using descriptions and regulations that were notably free of moral import. The result was, and persistently has been, a minor burlesque in the law. The City would require, for example, that "real" massage parlors establish their authenticity by appearing either in hotels with more than two hundred rooms, or in centers that contain facilities for sports, such as swimming pools (with a minimum of 1500 square feet), squash courts (which must be 25 feet wide, 45 feet long, and 20 feet high), or other kinds of courts whose dimensions may be specified with equal precision.[1] The extraordinary precision, of course, reflects the ritual of empty exactitude that the law is forced to undertake in defining the surface features of a problem when the authorities are either unable or unwilling to define the moral essence of the offense itself.

In point of principle, it is not at all clear as to why a real massage parlor must be annexed to all of these additional facilities if it has a claim to be what it says it is, and therefore a right to stay in business. In the meantime, the return on the bogus massage parlors might be high enough that the owners could afford to build larger establishments, containing hotel rooms and swimming pools and squash courts. After that, the law would presumably have to begin specifying the number of patrons who must make use of these facilities, or perhaps even the proportion of hotel rooms that must be occupied in order to have a legitimate hotel. In this respect the exercise is as ultimately meaningless as the measures that require these "massage parlors" and pornography shops to be at least 1,000 feet apart and no closer than 500 feet to

---

[1] City Planning Commission, December 10, 1975/ Calendar = 22. CP-23116, pp. 1 and 10.

churches and schools. If the businesses in question were law firms, few people are likely to suggest that it would be salutary for the community to keep these businesses 1,000 feet apart—and 500 feet away from churches and schools. The measure becomes plausible only when it is assumed that there is something in the nature of the enterprises themselves that is unwholesome and illegitimate. But if one could explain the grounds of principle on which they are found to be obnoxious in the first place, then these establishments could be banned or restricted without the need for these charades in legal draftsmanship.[2]

The charade becomes ever more functional, however, when the people who are most earnest in resisting the "legislation of morals" become quite insistent, nevertheless, that the culture of prostitution and pornography be removed from their immediate vicinity. In this manner, *The New York Times* has been quite firm in defending the legality of pornography under the First Amendment, but it has also been willing to countenance the use of legal ploys to harass the purveyors of pornography and prostitution and "clean up" Times Square.[3]

Similarly, many liberals on the West Side of New York who were inclined to consider prostitution as a "victimless crime" became rather concerned when prostitutes began soliciting in large numbers in the more fashionable precincts of the West 70's and 80's.[4] Doorbells would be rung; neighbors would be awakened in the middle of the night by men looking for prostitutes. As the prostitutes settled into the neighborhood, along with "topless" and "bottomless" bars, they would attract a clientele that had a taste for these services, and the clientele, in turn, would attract muggers and pickpockets. For their own part, the liberal residents of the West Side would have been content to see the police deal with the problem under the cover of "nuisances" without bothering to spell out the grounds on which the law may properly restrict prostitution itself.

Some have argued, of course, that prostitution becomes open to legal restraint precisely because of these ancillary harms that it generates—the increase of street crime, the propositioning of other women in the neighborhood, and the blight that affects the community with this culture of commercial sex. But once again the weight of the argument is placed on empirical effects or material injuries without any account of what would be wrong in principle with prostitution itself. In the absence of that principled argument, the mustering of evidence on the "effects" of prostitution simply yields, once again, a mere collection of correlations that entail no conclusions. It is certainly true, for example, that the presence of prostitutes seems to bring an increase in thefts and muggings. But similar effects may be generated by many legitimate entertainments that happen to bring out large crowds. The incidence of pickpocketing is likely to rise in and around

---

[2] The same observation would have to be made, for example, in response to the contention of the authorities in New York that "if a land use is so incompatible with the predominant uses of a district's zoning as to change the character of the area, it is appropriate to remove that use." See ibid., p. 3. If one entertains the possibility that the "new" use of a building may be for a law firm or a good restaurant in a district that formerly contained no law firms or good restaurants, the statement would reveal its own vacuity. Once again, the policy of the city would make sense only if it were underlain by a substantive argument as to why brothels are illegitimate businesses. In the absence of that kind of argument, the legal measures of the city become reduced to so many legal formulas, without substance or justification on their own terms.

[3] See Walter Berns, "Absurdity at *The New York Times*," *Harper's* (May 1973), pp. 34ff.

[4] See *The New York Times*, April 4, 1976, p. 47.

Yankee Stadium when the Yankees are playing an important series, or in Grand Central Station on Friday afternoons; and yet it would be inadmissible to suggest that these legitimate activities ought to be suppressed because of the opportunities they afford for crime. In all strictness, it would be as invalid in principle to ban these activities as it would have been wrong, in the case mentioned earlier, to ban the ice cream wagon because its presence on the town common induced people to tread on the grass. . . .

The argument over prostitution cannot be settled, then, by charting material injuries and pointing to harmful, ancillary effects. None of these items of evidence can have a decisive weight in the absence of a showing that there is something in principle wrong with prostitution itself; and it is on that point, ultimately, that all other judgments must turn.

Prostitution and "Plain Sex": The Search for a Principled Argument

Whether prostitution has been legalized in any place or not, "prostitute" and "whore" have always functioned as terms of contempt. And if we sought to account for the source of this aversion, it would probably be found in the disparity that exists, in prostitution, between the special intimacy of the sexual act and a context that is radically unsuited to that intimacy. There are many tiers of closeness, we know, but there is nothing precisely equal to the intimacy of the sexual act and the moral portents that envelop it. The sense of "penetrating" and enclosing, of coupling embraces and fusing bodies, marks a relation quite apart from anything that is accorded even to close friends and confidants. It suggests the image of two bodies seeking to become one, and it draws to itself all of the symbolic import of a "union" or a "wedding." To admit a fusion in that way with another person would be unthinkable unless one were motivated by the deepest personal love. But to say that two people are bound together in love is to say that they are connected by more than a casual attraction. And that connection finds its proper ground when it proceeds from an understanding of those things which make one's partner truly worthy of being loved.

When that deeper source of attachment is present it becomes a proper ground for commitment. And few things express the sense of that commitment as literally as a tie made solemn and binding with the public imprint of law. Nothing could signify more precisely the nature of that commitment than the willingness of lovers to forgo their own freedom to quit this relation when it no longer suits their convenience. It might be said that the union consecrated by law stands as the most appropriate symbol of a moral connection between lovers. For as we have seen, law arises in the most proper sense only from imperatives of moral standing; moral propositions entail the existence of law because the logic of morals is a logic of commitment. The binding of a marriage with law may draw to itself then the same sense of solemnity and moral import that invests the notion of "law."

In addition, of course, two people in a marriage will often produce children, who embody in their physical presence, in their mingling of features from both parents, the spiritual union of the two lovers. If the marriage does produce children, then it is all the more important that these children are brought into the world and nurtured in a setting that is already defined by the legal commitment of a marriage. I venture no commentary here on the question of whether "broken" homes are more destructive for children than families in which both parents are present. A single parent with goodness and sense would clearly be better than two indifferent and irresponsible parents. I simply take account of the fact that the first agency of moral tutelage for the child is inevitably the family, and in point of principle it matters profoundly that the child is introduced to the moral world through a structure that embodies visibly, concretely, the meaning of a moral commitment.

Perhaps it has been part of the odd appeal of prostitution over the years that it stands as a reproach to the conventions that reflect these moral understandings; but that is precisely the source also of the wrong that prostitution represents in principle. Prostitution inescapably implies that the intimacy of sexual intercourse need not be connected to any authentic sentiment of love and that it need not take place in a setting marked by the presence of commitment. In that sense it might be said that prostitution patronizes the corruption of physical love: it reduces physical love to the kind of hydraulic action that animals may share, and as it does that it detaches the act of intercourse from the kind of love that is distinctly human. The love that may arise between human beings is not simply a matter, after all, of successful orgasm; it may also involve, at its highest level, a respect for that character or principle of which one's partner is an example.

To the extent that prostitution disparages the notion of a love that is distinctly human, the argument has been made that prostitution strikes at those institutions, like the family, which depend most importantly on the ties of love. But care must be taken here to avoid the form and properties of an "empirical" argument. Principles clearly have consequences, and we ought to be aware that the erosion of certain moral understandings may have serious, adverse results for the family. And yet, the case against prostitution cannot depend on predictions of this kind. It cannot rest on any proposition to the effect that a higher incidence of prostitution will cause an increase in the breakup of families. Even if that notion found some statistical support, it would still represent nothing more than a *contingent* proposition, rather than a proposition that must hold true as a matter of necessity. At the same time, the argument would become vulnerable to any showing that certain people are in fact capable of preserving their families, along with a special love for their spouses, even while they seek other satisfactions in prostitution. The matter of the family becomes pertinent only as it stands as the instance of a larger principle that is engaged in the question of prostitution.

From that perspective, the importance of the family is that it is the most immediate school of moral instruction, and this moral import of the family is in fact central to its definition. A. I. Melden once pointed out that the obligations which children are thought to have to their parents cannot be entailed simply by a biological connection. A man who sires a child and then deserts his family cannot claim later the duties owed to a father. Those obligations are predicated on moral terms, on the understanding that the father has discharged the responsibilities of a parent in the care of his child.[5] Parental rights, then, cannot flow to a father simply by virtue of his biological definition; they can be claimed only by the man who has fulfilled the *moral* definition of a father. We might say here more strictly what any child would understand: that a father who does not satisfy the moral definition of a father is not really a father; or, as the saying goes, he is a father in name only.

---

[5] A. I. Melden, *Rights and Right Conduct* (Oxford: Basil Blackwell, 1959), Secs. III–VI, pp. 9–20.

In the same way it could be said that a family is a family only in its moral definition. A natural biological group cannot be considered a family if it is not constituted in the first place on terms that recognize the binding force of principle. A man and woman "living together" informally with their child may furnish, for all we know, a sense of affection and care which exceeds that of many legal families. But quite apart from their performance, there is an independent ground of concern for the terms on which this "living arrangement" is constituted. There is something fearful in a family life whose founding doctrine is that no one may be bound ultimately when he chooses not to be bound. This doctrine is at war with the very notion of morals, and it is not hard to consider what its consequences may be if it comes to pervade the life of the family. (And if it is not meant to define the character of the family, we would be left to wonder why the partners would make this understanding the cornerstone of their "relationship.") It may be liberating to know that responsibilities are accepted out of affection rather than compulsion; and yet that sense may be fostered in many legal families as well, while the informal "living arrangements" are incapable of teaching what is manifest in the very constitution of a legal family. The child of an authoritarian father may find his parent disagreeable, but he may come to understand in a number of ways that his father is committed to certain responsibilities for his care by a law outside the family. He may know that the commitments of his parents cannot be discarded at will, and that his claim to their care will not end when he ceases to please them. In that way even some of the least appealing legal families may nevertheless impart to their children the meaning of lawfulness; and children who have absorbed that lesson have cultivated also an awareness of the rudiments of morals.

It does not strictly matter, then, what the evidence may tell us about the "health" of children raised in legal families or informal "living units." As a matter of principle—as an emanation from the very notion of principle itself—a family in its moral definition must be constituted by commitments made manifest in law; it must represent in its very structure an awareness of a moral universe; and if it does not have these features, it is not really a family.

Some critics may intervene at this point and grant all of this to be true, but they may raise the question of why all sex must be confined to the family, and why all sex must be "serious" sex. They may concede, as Alan Goldman does, that sex may be affected with a much larger significance when it is enveloped by love and commitment, but he would suggest, quite aptly, that many other prosaic activities may also be transformed when they are animated by deep personal love. (One thinks of a mother in middle years, anticipating a visit from her married son, and concentrating all her loving care in the preparation of his favorite tuna casserole.) And yet sex may also be, as Goldman says, "plain sex": it may involve simply "a desire for contact with another person's body and for the pleasure which such contact produces."[6] What is central here is "the immersion in the physical aspect of one's own existence and attention to the physical embodiment of the other."

The serious mistake, says Goldman, comes in confusing love and sex: there can be no such thing as "casual love" as there may be "casual sex." Love, he suggests, is properly monogamous; it involves "a long-term, deep emotional relationship between

---

[6]Alan H. Goldman, "Plain Sex," *Philosophy and Public Affairs*, Vol. 6, no. 3 (Spring 1977), pp. 267–87, at 268. [Reprinted in this volume—Eds.]

two individuals." For that reason it is possible, as he argues, that men and women may be attracted erotically to a number of people; they may be drawn by the beauty of others, they may even extend their love and admiration to people who genuinely merit love; but none of this may disrupt the unique love and the special relation that they have with one other person.

Still, what if that "other person" has a different reaction? What if a wife happens to feel less "unique,"and somehow diminished, if the intimacies she regarded as special and exclusive were now shared easily with many others? But if the issue really turned on the injured feelings of spouses, then the problem would essentially dissolve in those instances when the spouses do not object (and where they may in fact claim the same franchise for themselves). When the spouses do feel injured, the pursuit of sexual pleasure may take on the additional purpose of inflicting injury on another, and the sexual act, *in that aspect*, would be subject to condemnation. That kind of case would not be different from a class of other cases in which people pursue their sexual pleasure in ways that are designed to shock or assault others—for example, the men who expose themselves in public, or the couples who have intercourse in the streets—and these people would no doubt be subject to reproach and restraint.

But when sexual intercourse is not used to harm another without justification, then it is Goldman's argument that it must be treated just like any other innocent activity that is pursued for its own pleasure. It has been a necessary part of my own argument in these pages that people have a claim to the exercise of their personal freedom in all of its expressions unless they do something that is in principle wrong, and it is only on the basis of a principle that the law may restrain that freedom. Goldman's argument probably ought to be understood in this light when he seeks to argue that "there are no moral implications whatever [in sex]. Any analysis of sex which imputes a moral character to sex acts in themselves is wrong for that reason. There is no morality intrinsic to sex, although general moral rules apply to the treatment of others in sex acts as they apply to all human relations."[7] That is, there is no morality intrinsic to sex any more than there is a morality intrinsic to driving a car or hitting a golf ball. But the man who drives recklessly, or the sportsman who finds his satisfaction in stroking his golf balls through other people's windows, may suffer the restraint of his freedom. And yet, until they misuse their freedom in this way, they have a right to their freedom to drive or play golf, and Goldman would make essentially the same claim for "plain sex" pursued, with an innocent mind, for the special pleasure that sex may afford.

If we have reservations about an argument of this kind, they would no doubt begin with the conviction, nourished by generations and consecrated by song, that there is, after all, something different about sex. Of course any activity may be innocent until it is directed toward wrongful ends, and on that point there would indeed be no difference between sex and parachute-jumping (though one should be fearful, I suppose, of marrying someone who did not know the difference). But sex may be different in ways that are morally significant, and the recognition that it is different is often borne out indirectly by people who are inclined to take an "advanced" position on matters of sex. A few years ago a group of undergraduate women at Yale demanded that rape should be recognized, in the code of student conduct, as a crime quite apart from others. Presumably assault was already a crime according to the statutes of

---

[7]Ibid., p. 280.

Yale, and if rape were nothing more than another assault—an unwarranted setting upon the body of another person—then it would have been no more necessary to make any further specifications for rape than it would have been to distinguish assaults directed at the head, say, from assaults directed at the legs. Why then should rape have been different?

There was an awareness, I think, of rape as not merely a striking of the body, but an act of larger arrogance and violation. There *is* something different, after all, about the penetration, the forceful access to an intimacy that is reserved only for people with whom the woman has a special connection. It may be hard to put the matter artfully, but it must be said also that this is an assault in which the assailant presumes to engage the reproductive capacity of the woman. That is, altogether, quite different from the average mugging or the lifting of a wallet: this assault, unlike other assaults, may actually generate new life, and one does not typically engage in anything as grave as that with anyone who just happens along on the street. And in the passions that have ever been aroused over this crime, the child that is conceived as the innocent issue of the crime has often been marked as a fit candidate for abortion, as though he were, in himself, a memorial to the trauma, or as though he somehow shared responsibility for the original crime. In that way there seems to be immanent in the agony of this violation an impulse to efface the original injustice with another one more lethal.

It is hard to account, I think, for the revulsion that marks rape as a crime apart from others without recognizing what is different about the intimacy of sex and the portentousness of reproduction. At the same time it should be apparent that the revulsion would not be diminished in any way by the news that the assailant or the victim was sterile. Our understanding of the crime is formed by our awareness of the special significance and the moral import that invests the act of sex. That is why the moral outrage which the crime elicits is virtually indifferent to any showing that the probability of conception in rape is very slight (which it is) or that the participants were incapable of generating children. The same reason may also inform the traditional objections to casual sexual encounters by people who may not seem impressed with the unique significance of sex, or who are conspicuously less than awed by an inventory of consequences that truly merits their awe.

But the outrage that has arisen traditionally in response to rape has held a tendency also to moderate with the showing that the woman involved was notoriously unselective in admitting people to her intimacies; that her consent, in effect, to enter was usually bestowed with no more hesitation than is shown by the average ticket-taker; and that she was willing to risk the engagement of her reproductive capacities—perhaps even with strangers in the dark—for a price that was not overly demanding. In short, the awareness of a wrong diminishes as the putative victim comes closer to that pattern of conduct which fits, more or less strictly, the sense of prostitution.

Again, the popular understanding here is probably a more accurate guide to the nature of the problem than the more ingenious offerings of social scientists. The wrong of prostitution cannot be found in any contingent reckonings about venereal disease, the stimulation of crime, or the breakup of families. It must be found rather in principle—in a principle, we might say, that begins with the awareness of principle itself and of beings that alone have access to the understanding of principles. The aversion to prostitution finds its proper ground in the recognition that there is something of inescapable moral significance about sex in creatures who may have moral reasons for extending or withdrawing their love; whose purposes in conceiving children may be enveloped with a far more complicated understanding than the motives that inspire procreation in animals; and who treat as profoundly serious the terms of principle on which sexual franchises are tendered.

What is finally unacceptable, in principle, about prostitution is that it must deny implicitly this kind of significance in sex. It must reject this understanding because it is compelled to deny the ultimate and insistent sovereignty that is entailed in our lives, in all aspects of our lives, by the capacity of human beings for moral judgment. In that sense I think it may be said that the wrong of prostitution would be drawn, in Kantian fashion, from the idea of morals itself and from the nature of that creature which has the capacity for morals. It would arise, that is, as a matter of necessity if one is compelled to acknowledge the special significance of sex in creatures that have access to moral understanding.

Child Prostitution, Pornography, and "Legal Paternalism"

A friend recalled for me once, with lingering admiration, the brothels he came to know in China and Japan after the Second World War. The services in those establishments were rendered with all the delicacy and exquisiteness that comes with the cultivation of a fine art. My friend began to make the case for legalized prostitution along the familiar lines of argument, and he contended, in addition, that the existence of legalized prostitution in China and Japan did not seem to threaten the institution of the family there (although he thought it might have a corrosive effect on that institution in the United States). But could prostitution be regarded, then, as a "business" just like other businesses? Would he have been willing to see his daughter work in a brothel during her vacations from school—as willing as he would be, say, to see her work in a restaurant or an office? The answer, unequivocally, was no.

If the argument I have been offering here is correct, this ultimate aversion to prostitution is grounded in something more substantial than convention, and it is not likely to disappear in future generations. We would expect that, twenty years from now, even parents holding the most advanced views are not likely to offer a standing ovation when their son announces that he is about to withdraw from medical school in order to become a male prostitute.[8] But the opinion of parents cannot be unaffected by the things that society teaches through the law about the kinds of occupations that are respectable; and if the laws become equivocal in regard to matters like prostitution and pornography, we should not be surprised to find even parents taking a more relaxed view of these enterprises, especially if they themselves can turn a small profit. The most bizarre example, which has burst upon us just in the past few years, is the growth of child prostitution and what has been called "kiddie porn" (or child pornography). Parents were found hiring out children as young as three and four years old to perform sexual acts for pornographic magazines and films. In January 1977 a couple in Colorado were

---

[8]Of course if prostitution should ever become a legitimate profession, we should expect that it will show the same banal urges of other professions to adorn itself with a vocabulary that will support its pretensions to professionalism. Its practitioners will probably carry attaché cases, and state universities will probably offer both preprofessional and M.A. programs in Sexual Therapy, perhaps as part of an overall School of Therapeutic Sciences.

arrested for "selling" their twelve-year-old son for sexual purposes for $3,000. In Rockford, Illinois, a social worker was convicted for permitting his three adopted sons to perform sexual acts before a camera for $150 each.[9] In some cases the parents performed with their own children, and according to Judianne Densen-Gerber, this new vogue in incest managed to produce, in two grotesque cases, gonorrhea of the throat in infants as young as 9 and 18 months old.[10]

These outrages produced one of the rare moments of unity these days in the political class of the country. Political figures and commentators, on the Left as well as the Right, joined the call for legislation. (The only reservations came from sections of the American Civil Liberties Union, which feared that the government might not merely prohibit the use of children in pornography, but that it might actually go on to prevent adults from viewing these productions!)[11] The result of this rising national sentiment was the Act for the "Protection of Children Against Sexual Exploitation," which forbade the employment of children in pornographic enterprises. The act also carried penalties for parents and guardians who knowingly permitted their children to be used for these purposes.[12]

But the consensus achieved on this issue temporarily masked the differences among the supporters and the serious difficulties that some of them would have in working out a rationale for the legislation. It was no particular problem to support laws that restricted the use of children in prostitution and pornography if one was generally in favor of restricting both prostitution and pornography. And yet if one happened to believe that prostitution should be legalized or that pornography should generally be available without restriction to mature adults, then it was far harder to produce an argument that came anywhere near the expression of a principle. . . .

The easiest rationale, for the Left as well as the Right, was that the legislation, after all, was about minors. With a few notable exceptions, it was still common to assume that young people do not have the maturity to manage the most consequential decisions in their lives, and restrictions have been accepted on minors that would not be established for adults. It was thought, in this respect, that the engagement in sexual acts for public display was one such grave matter that minors might not have the maturity to determine for themselves. (This judgment was freely offered, it must be said, even by people who were also quite convinced that minors had the maturity to decide for themselves whether to have abortions, without the knowledge or consent of their parents.) Beyond that, it was argued that the employment of children in pornography could be treated without strain as another incident in the restriction of child labor more generally.

And yet that explanation did not entirely satisfy. The restrictions on child labor carried many exemptions, and some of the most notable were the exemptions granted to children to act in legitimate movies or to model clothes in catalogues. There was reason to believe that children who were thrust, at young ages, into the role of celebrities could suffer alterations in

---

[9]*Congressional Record*, March 31, 1977, p. H2853.

[10]Notes on Press Conference, Washington, D.C. (February 14, 1977).

[11]See the statement of Ira Glasser reported in the *Congressional Record*, March 31, 1977, p. H2853.

[12]18 U.S.C.A. 2252 (1978). The problem of prostitution was covered under the old "White Slave Act," but Congress amended the section on the "Coercion or enticement of minor female" and changed it to the "Transportation of minors." In that way the act was broadened to take in male children as well. 18 U.S.C.A. 2423.

personality and character that were not always wholesome. It was apparent, also, that the parents who sought to propel their children to stardom were often moved by impulses that were no less self-serving than the motivations of those parents who traded off the careers of their children in pornography. But the legislation on child pornography was supported, as I have said, by many people who professed to regard the production of pornography as a legitimate business, as legitimate as making movies for Disney and catalogues for Sears. It goes without saying that there was no move to restrict children from participating in movies for Disney or modeling in catalogues for Sears, and the obvious question must be put: Why this discrimination? Would it not be apparent that the difference between the cases must turn, not on the labor of children, but on the things that separate Disney movies and Sears catalogues from pornography and prostitution? And how could the legislation be defended then unless we were finally able to explain what it is that makes prostitution and pornography *in principle* offensive in a way that Disney movies and Sears catalogues are not? . . .

PROSTITUTION IS MORALLY PERMISSIBLE

Charges Against Prostitution: An Attempt at a Philosophical Assessment*

Lars O. Ericsson

I. A Neglected Philosophical Task

The debate over prostitution is probably as old as prostitution itself. And the discussion of the oldest profession is as alive today as it ever was. New books and articles are constantly being published, new scientific reports and theories presented, and new committees and commissions formed.[1] Yet while the scientific and literary discussion is very much alive, the philosophical discussion of it seems never even to have come to life. How is this to be explained? And is there any justification for it? . . .

The alleged Archimedean point from which practically all discussion of harlotry takes off is the view that *prostitution is*

---

*I wish to acknowledge my indebtedness to Harry Benjamin and R. E. L. Masters. Their well-argued plea for a rational reevaluation of prostitution and for an assessment of it freed from emotional prejudice has been a great source of inspiration. Their empirical studies have also provided me with a large share of my factual insights concerning mercenary sex. I also wish to thank Harald Ofstad for his valuable criticism of an earlier version of this essay.

[1] For a comprehensive bibliography, see Vern Bullough et al., eds. *A Bibliography of Prostitution* (New York and London: Garland Publishers, 1977).

undesirable. And on *this* presupposition, the crucial issues become scientific and political, not philosophical. Science is called in to explain the undesirable phenomenon and to invent a cure to be put in the hands of the politicians. And moralists of all shades and colors act as their cheerleaders. The philosophical contributions have mainly consisted of the discussion of such derivative issues, as, Does society have the right to pass judgment at all on matters of sexual morals? and, If so, does it also have the right to use the weapon of the law to enforce what it considers to be sexual immorality?[2]

It is the purpose of this paper to undertake a critical assessment of the view that prostitution is an undesirable social phenomenon that ought to be eradicated. I shall do this by examining what seem to me (and to others) the most important and serious charges against prostitution. I shall try to show that mercenary love per se must, upon closer inspection, be acquitted of most of these charges. Instead, I shall argue, the major culprit is the hostile and punitive attitudes which the surrounding hypocritical society adopts toward promiscuous sexual relations in general and prostitution in particular.

II. The Charge from Conventional Morality

By far the most common ground for holding that prostitution is undesirable is that it constitutes a case of sexual immorality. Society and conventional morality condemn it. The law at best barely tolerates it; sometimes, as in most states in the United States, it downright prohibits it. In order to improve prostitution, we must first and foremost improve our attitudes toward it. Contrary to what is usually contended, I shall conclude that prostitution, although not in any way *ultimately* desirable, is still conditionally desirable because of certain ubiquitous and permanent imperfections of actual human societies.

The prostitute, according to the moralist, is a sinful creature who ought to be banned from civilized society. Whoredom is "the great social evil" representing a flagrant defiance of common decency. The harlot is a threat to the family, and she corrupts the young. To engage in prostitution signifies a total loss of character. To choose "the life" is to choose a style of living unworthy of any decent human being. And so on.

There is also a less crude form of moralism, which mixes moral disapproval with a more "compassionate" and "concerned" attitude. The fate of a whore is "a fate worse than death." The hustler is a poor creature who has to debase herself in order to gratify the lusts of immoral men. Prostitution is degrading for all parties involved, but especially for the woman. . . .

How are the hostile and punitive attitudes of society toward prostitution to be explained? It seems to be an anthropological fact that sexual institutions are ranked on the basis of their relation to reproduction. Hence, in virtue of its intimate relation to reproduction, the monogamous marriage constitutes the sexual institution in society which is ranked the highest and which receives the strongest support from law and mores. On the other hand, the less a sexual practice has to do with the bearing and rearing of children, the less sanctioned it is. Therefore, when coitus is practiced for pecuniary reasons (the hooker), with pleasure

---

[2]I am thinking here of the debate between Devlin and Hart which followed upon the publication of the *Wolfenden Report* on homosexual offenses and prostitution in 1957 (see Lord Devlin, *The Enforcement of Morals* [London: Oxford University Press, 1965], and H. L. A. Hart, *Law, Liberty, and Morality* [Stanford, Calif.: Stanford University Press, 1963]).

and not procreation in mind (the client), we have a sexual practice that, far from being sanctioned, finds itself at the opposite extreme on the scale of social approval. . . . [3]

An explanation of our antiprostitution attitudes and their probably prehistoric roots must not, however, be confused with a *rationale* for their continuation in our own time. That we understand why the average moralist, who is a predominantly unreflecting upholder of prevailing rules and values, regards prostitution and prostitutes as immoral gives us no good reason to shield those rules and values from criticism, especially if we find, upon reflection, that they are no longer adequate to our present social conditions.

That prostitution neither is nor ever was a threat to reproduction within the nuclear family is too obvious to be worth arguing for. Nor has it ever been a threat to the family itself. People marry and visit whores for quite different reasons. In point of fact, the greatest threat to the family is also the greatest threat to prostitution, namely, complete sexual liberty for both sexes. The conclusion we must draw from this is that neither the value of future generations nor the importance of the family (if it is important) warrants the view that prostitution is bad and undesirable.

It is hardly likely, however, that the moralist would be particularly perturbed by this, for the kernel of his view is rather that to engage in prostitution is *intrinsically* wrong. Both whore and customer (or at least the former) act immorally, according to the moralist, even if neither of them nor anyone else gets hurt. Mercenary love per se is regarded as immoral.

---

[3]Here I am indebted to Kingsley Davis (see his "The Sociology of Prostitution," reprinted in *Deviance, Studies in the Process of Stigmatization and Social Reaction*, ed. A. C. Clarke, S. Dinitz, and R. R. Dynes (New York: Oxford University Press, 1975).

Personally, I must confess that I, upon reflection, am no more able to see that coition for a fee is intrinsically wrong than I am able to see that drunkenness is. There is something fanatic about both of these views which I find utterly repelling. If two adults voluntarily consent to an economic arrangement concerning sexual activity and this activity takes place in private, it seems plainly absurd to maintain that there is something intrinsically wrong with it. In fact, I very much doubt that it is wrong at all. To say that prostitution is intrinsically immoral is in a way to refuse to give any arguments. The moralist simply "senses" or "sees" its immorality. And this terminates rational discussion at the point where it should begin.

III. The Sentimentalist Charge

There is also a common contention that harlotry is undesirable because the relation between whore and customer must by the nature of things be a very poor relation to nonmercenary sex. Poor, not in a moral, but in a nonmoral, sense. Since the majority of the objections under this heading have to do with the quality or the feelings and sentiments involved or with the lack of them, I shall refer to this critique as "the sentimentalist charge."

Sex between two persons who love and care for one another can of course be, and often is, a very good thing. The affection and tenderness which exist between the parties tend to create an atmosphere in which the sexual activities can take place in such a way as to be a source of mutual pleasure and satisfaction. Sexual intercourse is here a way of becoming even more intimate in a relation which is already filled with other kinds of intimacies.

Now, according to the sentimentalist, mercenary sex lacks just about all of these qualities. Coitus between prostitute and client is held to be impoverished, cold, and impersonal. The association is regarded as characterized by detachment and emotional noninvolvement. And the whole thing is considered to be a rather sordid and drab affair.

In order to answer this charge, there is no need to romanticize prostitution. Mercenary sex usually *is* of poorer quality compared with sentimental sex between lovers. To deny this would be simply foolish. But does it follow from this that hustling is undesirable? Of course not! That would be like contending that because 1955 Ch. Mouton-Rothschild is a much better wine than ordinary claret, we should condemn the act of drinking the latter.

The sentimentalist's mistake lies in the comparison on which he relies. He contrasts a virtual sexual ideal with prostitutional sex, which necessarily represents an entirely different kind of erotic association and which therefore fulfills quite different social and individual functions. Only a minute share of all sex that takes place deserves to be described as romantic sex love. And if, in defending mercenary sex, we should beware of romanticizing *it*, the same caution holds for the sentimentalist when he is describing nonprostitutional sex. The sex lives of ordinary people often fall miles short of the sentimentalist's ideal. On the other hand, the sexual services performed by harlots are by no means always of such poor quality as we are conditioned to think. And we would most likely think better of them were we able to rid ourselves of the feelings of guilt and remorse that puritanism and conventional morality create in us. . . .

The sentimentalistic critique of the prostitute-customer relationship, however, has also another side to it. This consists in the notion that sex without love or affection—sex "pure and simple"—is "no good." I have already admitted the obvious here—namely, that sex love is a beautiful thing. But this seems to me no reason for embracing the romantic notion that sex without love or mutual affection must be valueless. On the contrary, satisfaction of sexual desires is, qua satisfaction of a basic need, *intrinsically good,* love or no love.

The argument fails to show that prostitution is undesirable. If it shows anything at all it shows lack of contact with reality. As I pointed out earlier, sex between lovers hardly dominates the scene of human sex quantitatively. Consequently, the argument entails that a major part of the sex that takes place between humans is worthless. And how interesting is this? Even if correct, it does not show that there is something *particularly* or *distinctively* bad about prostitution.

In conclusion, I would like to counter the charge that the prostitute-customer relationship is bad on the ground that it involves the selling of something that is too basic and too elementary in human life to be sold. This is perhaps not a sentimentalist charge proper, but since it seems to be related to it I shall deal with it here.

Common parlance notwithstanding, what the hustler sells is of course not her body or vagina, but sexual *services*. If she actually did sell herself, she would no longer be a prostitute but a sexual slave. I wish to emphasize this simple fact, because the popular misnomer certainly contributes to and maintains our distorted views about prostitution.

But is it not bad enough to sell sexual services? To go to bed with someone just for the sake of money? To perform fellatio on a guy you neither love nor care for? In view of the fact that sex is a fundamental need, is it not wrong that anyone should have to pay to have it satisfied and that anyone should profit from its satisfaction? Is it not a deplorable fact that in the prostitute-customer relationship sexuality is completely alienated from the rest of the personality and reduced to a piece of merchandise?

In reply to these serious charges I would, first, like to confess that I have the greatest sympathy for the idea that the means necessary for the satisfaction of our most basic needs should be free, or at least not beyond the economic means of anyone. We all need food, so food should be available to us. We all need clothes and a roof over our heads, so these things should also be available to us. And since our sexual desires are just as basic, natural, and compelling as our appetite for food, this also holds for them. But I try not to forget that this is, and probably for a long time will remain, an *ideal* state of affairs.

Although we live in a society in which we have to pay (often dearly) for the satisfaction of our appetites, including the most basic and natural ones, I still do not regard food vendors and the like with contempt. They fulfill an important function in the imperfect world in which we are destined to live. That we have to pay for the satisfaction of our most basic appetites is no reason for socially stigmatizing those individuals whose profession it is to cater to those appetites. With this, I take it, at least the nonfanatical sentimentalist agrees. But if so, it seems to me inconsistent to hold that prostitution is undesirable on the ground that it involves the selling of something that, ideally, should not be sold but freely given away. Emotional prejudice aside, there is on *this* ground no more reason to despise the sex market and those engaged in it than there is to despise the food market and those engaged in it. . . .

As for the charge that in the prostitute-customer relationship sexuality is completely alienated from the rest of the personality—this is no doubt largely true. I fail to see, however, that it constitutes a very serious charge. My reason for this is, once again, that the all-embracing sex act represents an ideal with which it is unfair to compare the prostitute-customer relationship, especially if, as is often the case, such an all-embracing sex act does not constitute a realizable alternative. Moreover, there is no empirical evidence showing that sex between two complete strangers must be of poor quality.

IV. The Paternalistic Charge

It is a well-established fact that the occupational hazards connected with prostitution constitute a serious problem. The prostitute runs the risk of being hurt, physically as well as mentally. On the physical side there is always the risk of getting infected by some venereal disease. Certain forms of urosis are known to be more common among harlots than among women in general. And then there is the risk of assault and battery from customers with sadistic tendencies. On the mental side we encounter such phenomena as depression and neurosis, compulsive behavior, self-degrading and self-destructive impulses, etc.

It is therefore not uncommon to find it argued that prostitution is undesirable because it is not in the best interest of the prostitute to be what she is. It is held that society should, for the prostitutes' own good, try to prevent people from becoming prostitutes and to try to "rehabilitate" those who already are. This type of criticism I shall refer to as "the paternalistic charge."

I shall not consider the question—discussed by Mill, Devlin, Hart, and others—of whether society has the *right* to interfere with a person's liberty for his own good. I shall limit my discussion to the question of whether the fact that the hustler runs the risks that she runs is a good reason for holding that prostitution is undesirable.

A comparison with other fields clearly shows that the fact that a certain job is very hazardous is not regarded as a good reason for the view that the type of job in question is undesirable. Take, for instance, a miner: he runs considerable risks in his job, but we hardly think that this warrants the conclusion that mining should be prohibited. What we do think (or at least ought to think) is that, since the miner is doing a socially valuable job, everything possible should be done to minimize those risks by improving his working conditions by installing various safety devices, introducing shorter working hours, etc. It seems to me, therefore, that in cases like this—and there are many of them—paternalistic considerations carry no weight. The individual is not to be protected from himself (for wanting to take risks) but from certain factors in the environment. It is not the individual who should be changed but the milieu in which he has to place himself in order to be able to follow his occupational inclinations.

Unless the paternalist simply assumes what remains to be proven, namely, that what the prostitute does is of no value to society, a similar argument also applies in the case of prostitution. The individual whore does not need to be protected from herself if her hustling is voluntary in the same sense of "voluntary" as someone's choice of profession may be voluntary. What she does need protection from are detrimental factors in the social environment, especially the hostile, punitive, or condescending attitudes of so-called respectable citizens. It is not the hooker who should be changed, reformed, or rehabilitated but the social milieu in which she works.

The paternalistic charge is not an independent argument against prostitution. It only seems to work because it has already given in to conventional morality. To oppose prostitution by referring to the welfare, good, happiness, needs, or interest of the prostitute may seem very noble and humanitarian; but in reality it serves the status quo by leaving the norms and values of the surrounding society intact, viewing prostitution through the unreflected spectacles of a conservative public opinion, and placing the "blame" exclusively on the individual. . . .

VI. The Feminist Charge

In this essay I have deliberately desisted from trying to *define* "prostitution." I have simply relied upon the fact that we seem to know pretty well what we mean by this term. My reason for resisting the well-known predilection of philosophers for definitional questions is that ordinary usage seems to me sufficiently precise for my present purposes.[4] In consequence, I have up till now referred to the prostitute as "she" and to the customer as "he." For in ordinary parlance the whore is a woman and her customer a man. I do not think, however, that ordinary usage is such that this is true by definition. I rather suspect that our habit of thinking of the hustler as a *she* and her customer as a *he* simply reflects the empirical fact that most prostitutes are women and most customers men.

I shall in this section discuss a group of arguments in support of the thesis that prostitution is undesirable, whose common feature is this fact. Prostitution is held to be undesirable on the ground that it constitutes an extreme instance of the inequality between the sexes. Whoredom is regarded

---

[4]I should perhaps stress, however, that I use the term "prostitution" in a neutral, descriptive sense, disregarding the ordinary negative value association of the term. In a later section (X) a normative concept 'sound prostitution' will be developed.

as displaying the male oppression of the female in its most naked form. It is contended that the relation between hooker and "John" is one of object to subject—the prostitute being reified into a mere object, a thing for the male's pleasure, lust, and contempt. The customer-man pays to use the whore-woman and consequently has the upper hand. He is the dominating figure, the master. It is the whore's task to oblige, to satisfy his most "perverse" and secret desires, desires that the male is unable to reveal to his wife or girl friend. Prostitution, it is argued, reduces the woman to a piece of merchandise that anyone who can pay the price may buy. The unequal nature of prostitution is also contended to consist in the fact that it represents a way out of *misère sexuel* only for men. Instead of trying to solve the sexual problems together with his wife, the married man can resort to the services of the hustler; but the married woman lacks the same advantage, since there are not so many male heterosexual prostitutes around. I shall refer to this group of arguments as "the feminist charge."

Like the moralist and the Marxist, the feminist is of the opinion that prostitution can and ought to be eradicated.[5] Some feminists, like the moralist, even want to criminalize prostitution. But unlike the moralist they want to criminalize both whore and customer.

The core of the feminist charge—that prostitution is unequal and disfavors the female sex—deserves to be taken seriously. For social inequality is a serious matter both morally and politically. And inequalities based on differences with regard to race, color of skin, religious belief, sex, and the like are particularly serious. Thus, if valid, the feminist critique would constitute powerful support for the view that prostitution is undesirable.

Before I proceed to an attempt to counter the feminist charge, I would like to add a few nuancing facts to the prostitute-customer picture outlined at the beginning of this section.[6] No one denies that a majority of prostitutes are women, and no one denies that a majority of customers are men. But it is clear from the evidence that a large portion of the prostitutes, especially in metropolitan areas, are male homosexuals.[7] There is also lesbian prostitution, though this is not (at least not yet) sufficiently widespread to be of any great social importance. And finally, there is male heterosexual prostitution, the prevalence of which is also rather limited. We may sum up by saying that, rather than constituting a dichotomy between the sexes, prostitution has the characteristic that a considerable portion of the prostitutes are men, and a small minority of the customers are women. I mention this because I think that a rational assessment should not be based on an incomplete picture of the phenomenon under assessment and I consider these data to have some relevance with respect to the feminist charge against prostitution.

There are at least two types of inequalities. In the one, the inequality consists in the fact that some *benefit* is withheld from

---

[5]The empirical part of this opinion will be examined critically in the next section.

[6]My major source of information has here as elsewhere been Benjamin and Masters (n. 4) Harry Benjamin and R. E. L. Masters, *Prostitution and Morality* (New York: Julian Press, 1964)., esp. chaps. 5, 6, and,10. I have also consulted the reports of Jersild (Jens Jersild, *Boy Prostitution* [Copenhagen: G.E.C. Gad, 1956]) and Butts (W. B. Butts "Boy Prostitutes of the Metropolis," *Journal of Clinical Psychopathology* [1947], pp. 673–81).

[7]A ratio of 60/40 has been mentioned for big city areas like New York and Los Angeles. I do not regard this (or any other) figure as completely reliable, however. The empirical material available does not seem to allow any exact conclusions.

some group or individual. A typical example: only white members of a society are allowed to vote. In the other, the inequality consists in the fact that some *burden* is placed only on some group or individual. A typical example: a feudal society in which peasants and artisans are the only ones who have to pay taxes. We may also distinguish between unequal practices, which, like racial discrimination, are best dealt with through a complete *abolition* of them, and unequal practices which, like male franchise, are best dealt with by *modifying* them (in the case of male franchise, by granting the franchise to women). The one type of unequal practice is always and under all conditions undesirable: there is no remedy to the inequality of apartheid but abolition. The other type of unequal practice is also undesirable, but it had the seed of something defensible or valuable in it: the franchise is something good, although the franchise restricted to males is not. Obviously, these two pairs of categories are not mutually exclusive. On the contrary, all combinations of them are possible.

After these preliminaries, we come to the question of how prostitution is to be classified. Is harlotry an unequal practice? And if so, in what precisely does its inequality consist?

If it is conceded that in exchange for his money the customer receives a service—something that at least the sentimentalist seems most reluctant to concede—it could be argued that harlotry is unequal in the sense that some benefit is withheld from or denied women that is not withheld from or denied men. This is perhaps how the argument that hustling represents a way out only for men should be understood. However, if this is what the feminist charge amounts to, two things appear to be eminently clear. The first is that prostitution is unequal in a less serious way than, for instance, male franchise. For in the latter the benefit (opportunity to vote) which is withheld from women is withheld from them in the strong sense that it is not legally possible for the women to vote, while in the former no such legal or formal obstacle stands in their way. In fact, instead of saying that the sex services of prostitutes are withheld or denied women, it would be more appropriate to say that centuries of cultural and social conditioning makes them desist from asking for them. It is after all only recently that women have begun to define their sexuality and require that their sexual needs and desires be recognized. Rowbotham reminds us that "'Nymphomania' was actually used in the 1840s to describe any woman who felt sexual desire, and such women were seen as necessarily abandoned, women of the streets, women of the lower classes."[8] The second point is that if, through prostitution, a benefit is "withheld" the female sex, the best way to deal with this inequality would not be an attempt to stamp out the institution but an attempt to modify it, by making the benefit in question available to both sexes.

Could it be then that the inequality of whoredom consists in the fact that some burden is unequally placed on the two sexes and in disfavor of the female sex? This allegation can be interpreted in several different ways. And I shall in what follows consider those that seem to me the most important.

To begin with, this allegation can be understood in accordance with the view that it is women, and not men, who are in peril of becoming prostitutes. But first of all, this is largely untrue since, as I have argued earlier, a great many prostitutes are men. Moreover, the perils of being a prostitute, although existent today (due to factors discussed in Sec. IV), do not constitute a good

---

[8]Rowbotham [*Women, Resistance, and Revolution* (London: Penguin Press, 1972)], p. 66.

reason for abolishing harlotry; rather they constitute a good reason for a social reform that will reduce the perils to a minimum tomorrow.[9]

Another way of intepreting this allegation is to say that prostitution constitutes exploitation of the female sex, since harlots are being exploited by, inter alia, sex capitalists and customers, and a majority of harlots are women. This interpretation of the allegation merits careful study, and I shall therefore in the first instance limit my discussion to the capitalist exploitation of prostitutes.

It is of course true that not all prostitutes can be described as workers in the sex industry. Some are in point of fact more adequately described as small-scale private entrepreneurs. Others are being exploited without being exploited by sex capitalists. Those who can be regarded as workers in the sex industry—the growing number of girls working in sex clubs and similar establishments for instance—are, of course, according to Marxist theory, being exploited in the same sense as any wage worker is exploited. But exploitation in this Marxist sense, although perhaps effective as an argument against wage labor in general, is hardly effective as an argument against prostitution.

There is no doubt, however, that practically all harlots—irrespective of whether they are high-class call girls, cheap streetwalkers, or sex-club performers—are being exploited, economically, in a much more crude sense than that in which an automobile worker at General Motors is being exploited. I am thinking here of the fact that all of them—there are very few exceptions to this—have to pay usury rents in order to be able to operate. Many are literally being plundered by their landlords—sex capitalists who often specialize in letting out rooms, flats, or apartments to people in the racket. Not a few prostitutes also have to pay for "protection" to mafiosi with close connections to organized crime.

What makes all this possible? And what are the implications of the existence of conditions such as these for the question of the alleged undesirability of prostitution? With respect to the first of these questions the answer, it seems to me, is that the major culprit is society's hypocritical attitude toward harlotry and harlots. It is this hypocrisy which creates the prerequisites for the sex-capitalist exploitation of the prostitutes. Let me exemplify what I mean by society's hypocritical—and, I might add, totally inconsistent—attitude here. On the one hand, most societies, at least in the West (one deplorable exception is the United States), have followed the UN declaration which recommends that prostitution in itself should not be made illegal.[10] One would therefore expect that someone who pursues a legal activity would have the right to rent the necessary premises, to advertise her services, and so on. But not so! The penal code persecutes those who rent out rooms, apartments, and other premises to prostitutes. And an editor of a Swedish newspaper was recently convicted for having accepted ads from "models" and "masseuses." In what other legal field or branch would contradictions such as these be considered tolerable? None of course! One of the first to point out this double morality of society was Alexandra Kollontai, who as early as 1909 wrote: "But if the state tolerates the prostitutes and thereby supports their profession, then it must also accept housing for them and even—in the interest of social health and order—institute houses where they could pursue their

---

[9] To those who find this statement a bit too categorical I suggest a quick glance back to Sec. IV.

[10] United Nations, *Study on Traffic in Persons and Prostitution* (New York, 1959).

occupation."[11] And the most incredible of all is that the official motivation for outlawing persons prepared to provide harlots with the premises necessary for their legal activity is a paternalistic one: so doing is in the best interest of the hustlers themselves, who would otherwise be at the mercy of unscrupulous landlords! In practice, the risk of being thrown in jail of course scares away all but the unscrupulous individuals, who can charge sky-high rents (after all, they take a certain risk) and who often are associated with the criminal world. How can anyone, therefore, be surprised at the fact that not so few hustlers display "antisocial tendencies"?

The conclusion I draw from this is that the crude economic exploitation of the prostitutes is not an argument against prostitution. It rather constitutes an accusation against the laws, regulations, and attitudes which create the preconditions for that exploitation. Society cannot both allow harlotry and deprive harlots of reasonable working conditions (as a concession to "common decency") and still expect that all will be well.

A third way of interpreting the charge that prostitution is unequal in the sense that it places a burden on women that it does not place on men is to say that whores are being oppressed, reified, and reduced to a piece of merchandise by their male customers. To begin with the last version of this charge first, I have already pointed out the obvious, namely, that whores do not sell themselves. The individual hooker is not for sale, but her sexual services are. One could therefore with equal lack of propriety say of any person whose job it is to sell a certain service that he, as a result thereof, is reduced to a piece of merchandise. I cannot help suspecting that behind this talk of reduction to a piece of merchandise lies a good portion of contempt for prostitutes and the kind of services they offer for sale.

As for the version according to which the whore is reified—turned into an object, a thing—it can be understood in a similar way as the one just dealt with. But it can also be understood as the view that the customer does not look upon the prostitute as a human being but as "a piece of ass." He is not interested in her as a person. He is exclusively interested in her sexual performance. As far as I can see, this version of the charge collapses into the kind of sentimentalistic critique that I discussed in Section III. Let me just add this: Since when does the fact that we, when visiting a professional, are not interested in him or her as a person, but only in his or her professional performance, constitute a ground for saying that the professional is dehumanized, turned into an object?

The "reification charge" may, however, be understood in still another way. It may be interpreted as saying that the whore is nothing but a means, a mere instrument, for the male customer's ends. This also comes rather close to the sentimentalist charge. Its Kantian character does perhaps deserve a few words of comment, however. First of all, that the customer treats the harlot as a means to his ends is only partly true. The other part of the truth is that the prostitute treats her customer as a means to *her* ends. Thus, the complete truth (if it deserves to be called that) is that prostitute and customer treat *one another* as means rather than as ends.

I have to say, however, that I do not find much substance in this Kantian-inspired talk about means and ends. The kind of relationship that exists between prostitute and customer is one that we find in most service professions. It is simply cultural

---

[11] A. Kollontai, *Brak i semeinaja problema* [Marriage and the family problem] (1909).

blindness and sexual taboos that prevent so many of us from seeing this. Moreover, in virtue of the prevalence of this type of relationship—a contractual relation in which services are traded—I suspect that those who talk about the badness of it in the case of prostitute-customer relationship have in fact long before decided that the relationship is bad on some *other*—not declared—ground. The means-ends talk is just a way of rationalizing a preconceived opinion.

I shall conclude this section by considering the charge that harlotry constitutes oppression of the female sex. Prostitution is here regarded as displaying male oppression of the female in its most overt and extreme form. The seriousness of this charge calls, to begin with, for a clarification of the meaning of the word "oppression." If A oppresses B, I take it that B's freedom of choice and action is severely reduced, against his will, as a result of actions undertaken by A against B. In the case of a political oppression, for example, A thwarts B's desire to form unions and political parties, prevents B from expressing his political opinions, throws B in jail if he refuses to comply, and so on.

It can hardly be disputed that prostitutes are oppressed in this sense. They would not have chosen to become hustlers if some better alternative had been open to them. They are very much aware of the fact that to be a prostitute is to be socially devalued; to be at the bottom of society. To become a hooker is to make just the reverse of a career. It should be observed, however, that none of this warrants the charge that prostitution means the oppression of the female by the male sex. The oppression just described is not an oppression on the basis of sex, as male franchise would be. The "oppressor" is rather those social conditions—present in practically all known social systems—which offer some individuals (both men and women) no better alternative than hustling.

But perhaps what the charge amounts to is that the male sex's oppression of the female sex consists in the oppression of the whore by her male customer. It certainly happens that customers treat prostitutes in ways which could motivate use of the term "oppression." But this does not mean that this term typically applies to the prostitute-customer relationship. Moreover, harlots usually develop a keen eye for judging people, and that helps them to avoid many of the (latently) dangerous customers. For it is just a myth that their freedom of choice and action is reduced to a point where they have to accept customers indiscriminately. This is not even true of prostitutes in the lowest bracket, and it certainly is not true of girls in the higher ones.

It is not seldom argued from feminist quarters that the liberation of women must start with the liberation of women from exploitation of their sex. Hence the crusade against prostitution, pornography, and the use of beautiful women in commercial advertising, etc. It is argued that women's lib must have as its primary goal the abolition of the (ab)use of the female sex as a commodity. As long as the female sex is up for sale, just like any other commercial object, there can be no true liberation from oppression.

To the reader who has read this far it should be obvious that, at least in part, this type of reasoning rests on or is misguided by such misnomers as "the whore sells her body," "to live by selling oneself," "to buy oneself a piece of ass," etc. So I need not say any more about that. Instead I wish to make a comparison between a typical middle-class housewife in suburbia and her prostitute counterpart, the moderately successful call girl. And I ask, emotional prejudice aside, which of them needs to be "liberated" the most? Both are doing fairly well economically, but while the housewife is totally dependent on her husband, at least economically, the call girl in that respect stands on her own two feet. If she has a pimp, it is she, not he, who is the breadwinner in the family. Is she a traitor to her own sex? If she is (which I doubt), she is no more a traitor to her own sex than her bourgeois counterpart. For, after all, Engels was basically right when he said that the major difference between the two is that the one hires out her body on piecework while the other hires it out once and for all.

All this does not mean that I am unsympathetic toward the aspirations of the feminist movement. It rather means that I disagree with its order of priorities.

Both men and women need to be liberated from the harness of their respective sex roles. But in order to be able to do this, we must liberate ourselves from those mental fossils which prevent us from looking upon sex and sexuality with the same naturalness as upon our cravings for food and drink. And, contrary to popular belief, we may have something to learn from prostitution in this respect, namely, that coition resembles nourishment in that if it can not be obtained in any other way it can always be bought. And bought meals are not always the worst. . . .

X. Some Policy Suggestions

In several of the previous sections of this essay I have had occasion to discuss the negative features of prostitution as it functions today (and has long functioned) in most societies: the great professional hazards; the economic exploitation; the antisocial tendencies of people in the racket, their frequent association with the criminal world and organized crime, and the stigma attached to their profession; etc. But in distinction to all those who hold these negative features against prostitution (as if they were intrinsic to it), I regard them as the avoidable result of values and attitudes of the society wherein prostitution occurs. And these values and attitudes are not only detrimental to prostitution, *they are also detrimental to the relations between the sexes generally.* But more of this presently. . . .

It seems to me impossible to come to grips with the negative aspects of harlotry without a change of our values and attitudes. Which values and attitudes? And why should they be changed? It would take an essay of its own to deal with these questions exhaustively, so I shall have to confine myself to a few examples and the outlines of a justification.

In my view, contempt for whores and contempt for women are closely related. The devaluation of the female sex is a permanent part of the Western tradition of ideas, reinforced by the Christian so-called culture. As an early example, according to Aristotle we should "look upon the female state as being as it were a deformity though one which occurs in the ordinary course of nature."[12] And according to Freud, who in many respects echoes Aristotle, woman is pictured as partial man: "She [the female child] acknowledges the fact of her castration, and with it too, the superiority of the male."[13] The influence of these and numerous other similar ideas has, with the passage of the years and often in vulgarized form, been sedimented in public opinion.

---

[12] Aristotle. *The Generation of Animals*, quoted in Caroline Whitbeck. "Theories of Sex Difference." *Philosophical Forum* 5, nos. 1 and 2 (1973–74): 54–80, quote from p. 56.

[13] Sigmund Freud, *Female Sexuality*, quoted in Whitbeck, p. 69.

In order to see the relationship between contempt for women and contempt for harlots, another important part of the Western tradition of ideas must be added, namely, the devaluation of sexuality. Both contempt for the female sex and the devaluation of sexuality have their roots in the ancient notion that man consists of two distinct parts, body and soul, of which the second is immensely more valuable than the first. As is well known, the soul, according to Plato, does not really belong here in our material world, the world of the senses. It belongs to the spiritual world, although it temporarily takes its seat (or is imprisoned) in the body. These ideas were later developed by Aristotle and the purveyor of philosophy to the Catholic church, Thomas Aquinas. The originally Orphic distinction between body and soul was soon transformed, especially under the influence of Christian thinkers such as Saint Augustine, to a general devaluation of the body, bodily functions, and sexuality. Saint Augustine, for instance, seems to have been greatly disappointed in the Creator for not having made human reproduction possible in a less crudely bodily and pleasurable way. In the Christian tradition generally the body and its functions, especially when associated with pleasure, have typically been regarded as sinful.

In a culture where both the female sex and sexuality are devaluated it is only "logical" to place the prostitute—an individual who is not only a female but who also earns her living by means of her female sex by selling sexual services—at the bottom of the scale of social approval. . . .

Our attitudes toward sexual expression in general, and mercenary sex in particular, ought to be modified or abandoned partly because of the damage that they do, partly because they represent prejudices in the sense that they are rooted in false beliefs. Women are not partial men nor is the female sex a deformity. And the distinction between body and soul, with all its metaphysical and religious ramifications, apart from being philosophically highly dubious, is the source of more human misery than almost any other.

A sound prostitution is, first of all, a prostitution that is allowed to function in a social climate freed from emotional prejudice of the kind described above. Prostitution can never be rid of its most serious negative aspects (primarily the suffering the prostitutes have to endure) in a society where females are regarded as inferior to males and where man's physical nature is regarded as inferior to his spiritual nature.

A sound prostitution is, furthermore, a prostitution such that those who become prostitutes are adults who are not compelled to prostitute themselves but who freely choose to do so in the same sense of "freely" as anyone's trade or occupation may be said to be freely chosen. A sound prostitution is, in other words, a prostitution of voluntary, not compulsive, hustlers.

A sound prostitution is, third, a prostitution that is legal, and where the prostitutes are not persecuted but attributed the same rights as ordinary citizens as a recognition of the fact that they fulfill a socially valuable function by, inter alia, decreasing the amount of sexual misery in society.

A sound prostitution is, fourth, a prostitution such that the prostitutes are no more economically exploited than wage workers in general.

A sound prostitution is, finally, a prostitution that is equally available to both sexes.

Of these conditions I regard the first as the most fundamental. Without it being at least partially satisfied, the satisfaction of the others seems most difficult. Thus, if I were to sum up the principal view put forward in this concluding section, it would be formulated as follows: *in order to improve prostitution, we must first and foremost improve our attitudes toward it.*

I admit that a sound prostitution in this sense is far from easy to realize, but this does not mean that I think that it is unrealistic. As far as I can see, we have at least begun to liberate ourselves from some of the archaic strands of Western thought. But we surely still have a long way ahead of us.

In conclusion, I wish to emphasize once again that I do not regard prostitution, not even a sound prostitution, as in any way *ultimately* desirable. Its desirability is conditional upon certain ubiquitous and permanent imperfections of actual human societies. In a perfectly good society, however, it would be superfluous.

HOMOSEXUALITY SHOULD BE DISCOURAGED

Why Homosexuality Is Abnormal*

Michael Levin

1. Introduction

This paper defends the view that homosexuality is abnormal and hence undesirable—not because it is immoral or sinful, or because it weakens society or hampers evolutionary development, but for a purely mechanical reason. It is a misuse of bodily parts. Clear empirical sense attaches to the idea of *the use* of such bodily parts as genitals, the idea that they are *for* something, and consequently to the idea of their misuse. I argue on grounds involving natural selection that misuse of bodily parts can with high probability be connected to unhappiness. I regard these matters as prolegomena to such policy issues as the rights of homosexuals, the rights of those desiring not to associate with homosexuals, and legislation concerning homosexuality, issues which I shall not discuss systematically here. However, I do in the last section draw a seemingly evident corollary, from my view that homosexuality is abnormal and likely to lead to unhappiness.

I have confined myself to male homosexuality for brevity's sake, but I believe that much of what I say applies *mutatis mutandis* to lesbianism. There may well be significant differences between the two: the data of [2], for example, support the popular idea that sex *per se* is less important to women and in particular lesbians than it is to men. On the other hand, lesbians are generally denied motherhood, which seems more important to women

---

*Arthur Caplan, R. M. Hare, Michael Slote, Ed Erwin, Steven Goldberg, Ed Sagarin. Charles Winnick, Robert Gary, Thomas Nagel, David Benfield, Michael Green and my wife Margarita all commented helpfully on earlier drafts of this paper, one of which was read to the New York chapter of the Society for Philosophy and Public Policy. My definition of naturalness agrees to some extent with Gary's in [5], and I have benefited from seeing an unpublished paper by Michael Ruse.

than is fatherhood—normally denied homosexual males—to men. On this matter, [2] offers no data. Overall, it is reasonable to expect general innate gender differences to explain the major differences between male homosexuals and lesbians.

Despite the publicity currently enjoyed by the claim that one's "sexual preference" is nobody's business but one's own, the intuition that there is something unnatural about homosexuality remains vital. The erect penis fits the vagina, and fits it better than any other natural orifice; penis and vagina seem made for each other. This intuition ultimately derives from, or is another way of capturing, the idea that the penis is not *for* inserting into the anus of another man—that so using the penis is not the way it is *supposed,* even *intended,* to be used. Such intuitions may appear to rest on an outmoded teleological view of nature, but recent work in the logic of functional ascription shows how they may be explicated, and justified, in suitably naturalistic terms. Such is the burden of Section 2, the particular application to homosexuality coming in Section 3. Furthermore, when we understand the sense in which homosexual acts involve a misuse of genitalia, we will see why such misuse is bad and not to be encouraged. (The case for this constitutes the balance of Section 3.) . . .

But before turning to these issues, I want to make four preliminary remarks. The first concerns the explicitness of my language in the foregoing paragraph and the rest of this paper. Explicit mention of bodily parts and the frank description of sexual acts are necessary to keep the phenomenon under discussion in clear focus. Euphemistic vagary about "sexual orientation" or "the gay lifestyle" encourage one to slide over homosexuality without having to face or even acknowledge what it really is. Such talk encourages one to treat "sexual preference" as if it were akin to preference among flavors of ice-cream. Since unusual taste in ice-cream is neither right nor wrong, this usage suggests, why should unusual taste in sex be regarded as objectionable? Opposed to this usage is the unblinkable fact that the sexual preferences in question are such acts as mutual fellation. Is one man's taste for pistachio ice-cream really just like another man's taste for fellation? Unwillingness to call this particular spade a spade allows delicacy to award the field by default to the view that homosexuality is normal. Anyway, such delicacy is misplaced in a day when "the love that dare not speak its name" is shouting its name from the rooftops.[1]

My second, related, point concerns the length of the present paper. . . . [We have shortened Levin's paper considerably.—Eds.]

The third point is this. The chain of intuitions I discussed earlier has other links, links connected to the conclusion that homosexuality is bad. They go something like this: Homosexual acts involve the use of the genitals for what they aren't for, and it is a *bad* or at least *unwise* thing to use a part or your body for what it isn't for. Calling homosexual acts "unnatural" is intended to sum up this entire line of reasoning.

---

[1]"Sexual preference" typifies the obfuscatory language in which the homosexuality debate is often couched. "Preference" suggests that sexual tastes are voluntarily chosen, whereas it is a commonplace that one cannot decide what to find sexually stimulating. True, we talk of "preferences" among flavors of ice-cream even though one cannot choose what flavor of ice-cream to like: such talk is probably a carryover from the voluntariness of *ordering* ice-cream. "Sexual preference" does not even sustain this analogy, however, since sex is a forced choice for everyone except avowed celibates, and especially for the relatively large number of homosexuals who cruise regularly (see Appendix [deleted from this abridged version of Levin's essay—Eds.]).

"Unnatural" carries disapprobative connotations, and any explication of it should capture this.... To have anything to do with our intuitions—even if designed to demonstrate them groundless—an explication of "abnormal" must capture the analytic truth that the abnormality of a practice is a reason for avoiding it. If our ordinary concept of normality turns out to be ill-formed, so that various acts are at worst "abnormal" in some nonevaluative sense, this will simply mean that, as we ordinarily use the expression, *nothing is abnormal*. (Not that anyone really believes this—people who deny that cacophagia or necrophilia are abnormal do so only to maintain the appearance of consistency.)

Fourth, I should mention Steven Goldberg's defense of a position similar to mine ([3])....

2. On "Function" and Its Cognates

To bring into relief the point of the idea that homosexuality involves a misuse of bodily parts, I will begin with an uncontroversial case of misuse, a case in which the clarity of our intuitions is not obscured by the conviction that they are untrustworthy. Mr. Jones pulls all his teeth and strings them around his neck because he thinks his teeth look nice as a necklace. He takes puréed liquids supplemented by intravenous solutions for nourishment. It is surely natural to say that Jones is misusing his teeth, that he is not using them for what they are for, that indeed the way he is using them is incompatible with what they are for. Pedants might argue that Jones's teeth are no longer part of him and hence that he is not misusing any bodily parts. To them I offer Mr. Smith, who likes to play "Old MacDonald" on his teeth. So devoted is he to this amusement, in fact, that he never uses his teeth for chewing—like Jones, he takes nourishment intravenously. Now, not only do we find it perfectly plain that Smith and Jones are misusing their teeth, we predict a dim future for them on purely physiological grounds, we expect the muscles of Jones's jaw that are used for—that *are* for—chewing to lose their tone, and we expect this to affect Jones's gums. Those parts of Jones's digestive tract that are for processing solids will also suffer from disuse. The net result will be deteriorating health and perhaps a shortened life. Nor is this all. Human beings enjoy chewing. Not only has natural selection selected in muscles for chewing and favored creatures with such muscles, it has selected a tendency to find the use of those muscles reinforcing. Creatures who do not enjoy using such parts of their bodies as deteriorate with disuse, will tend to be selected out. Jones, product of natural selection that he is, descended from creatures who at least tended to enjoy the use of such parts. Competitors who didn't simply had fewer descendants. So we expect Jones sooner or later to experience vague yearnings to chew something, just as we find people who take no exercise to experience a general listlessness. Even waiving for now my apparent reification of the evolutionary process, let me emphasize how little anyone is tempted to say "each to his own" about Jones or to regard Jones's disposition of his teeth as simply a deviation from a statistical norm. This sort of case is my paradigm when discussing homosexuality.

The main obstacle to talk of what a process or organic structure is for is that, literally understood, such talk presupposes an agent who intends that structure or process to be used in a certain way. Talk of function derives its primitive meaning from the human use of artifacts, artifacts being for what purposive agents intend them for. Indeed, there is in this primitive context a natural reason for using something for what it is for: to use it otherwise would frustrate the intention of some purposeful agent. Since it now seems clear that our bodily parts were not emplaced by purposeful agency, it is easy to dismiss talk of what they are for as "theologically" based on a faulty theory of how we came to be built as we are:

> The idea that sex was designed for propagation is a theological argument, but not a scientific one. . . . To speak of the "fit" of penis and vagina as proof of nature's intention for their exclusive union is pure theological reasoning—imposing a meaning or purpose upon a simple, natural phenomenon ([4]. 63).

Barash—who elsewhere uses its cognates freely—dismisses "unnatural" as a mere term of abuse: "people with a social or political axe to grind will call what they don't like 'unnatural' and what they do, 'natural'" ([I], 237). Hume long ago put the philosopher's case against the term 'natural' with characteristic succinctness: "'Tis founded on final Causes; which is a consideration, that appears to me pretty uncertain & unphilosophical. For pray, what is the End of Man? Is he created for Happiness or for Virtue? For this Life or the next? For himself or for his Maker?" ([5], 134). . . .

An organ is for a given activity if the organ's performing that activity helps its host or organisms suitably related to its host, *and* if this contribution is how the organ got and stays where it is. . . . This definition . . . distinguishes what something is for from what it may be *used* for on some occasion. Teeth are for chewing—we have teeth because their use in chewing favored the survival of organisms with teeth— whereas Jones is using his teeth for ornamentation.

[This account of what it is for an organ to be *for* a certain activity] explains our intuition that, since their efficacy in chewing got them selected in, teeth are for masticating and Jones is preventing his teeth from doing their proper job. . . . Nature is interested in making its creatures like what is (inclusively) good for them. A creature that does not enjoy using its teeth for chewing uses them less than does a toothed competitor who enjoys chewing. Since the use of teeth for chewing favors the survival of an individual with teeth, and, other things being equal, traits favorable to the survival of individuals favor survival of the relevant cohort, toothed creatures who do not enjoy chewing tend to get selected out. We today are the filtrate of this process, descendants of creatures who liked to chew. . . .

Jones's behavior is ill-advised not only because of the avertible objective consequences of his defanging himself, but because he will feel that something is missing. Similarly, this is why you should exercise. It is not just that muscles are for running. We have already heard the sceptic's reply to that: "So what? Suppose I don't mind being flabby? Suppose I don't give a hang about what will propagate my genetic cohort?" Rather, running is good because nature made sure people like to run. This is, of course, the prudential "good," not the moral "good"—but I disavowed at the outset the doctrine that misuse of bodily parts is *morally* bad, at least in any narrow sense. You ought to run because running was once necessary for catching food: creatures who did not enjoy running, if there ever were any, caught less food and reproduced less frequently than competitors who enjoyed running. These competitors passed on their appetites along with their muscles *to you*. This is not to say that those who suffer the affective consequences of laziness must recognize them as such, or even be able to identify them against their general background feeling-tone. They may not realize they would feel better if they exercised. They may even doubt it. They may have allowed their muscles to deteriorate beyond the point at which satisfying exercise is possible. For all that, evolution has decreed that a life involving regular exercise is on the whole more enjoyable than a life without. The same holds for every activity that is the purpose of an organ.

3. Applications to Homosexuality

The application of this general picture to homosexuality should be obvious. There can be no reasonable doubt that one of the functions of the penis is to introduce semen into the vagina. It does this, and it has been selected in because it does this. . . . Nature has consequently made this use of the penis rewarding. It is clear enough that any proto-human males who found unrewarding the insertion of penis into vagina have left no descendants. In particular, proto-human males who enjoyed inserting their penises into each other's anuses have left no descendants. This is why homosexuality is abnormal, and why its abnormality counts prudentially against it. Homosexuality is likely to cause unhappiness because it leaves unfulfilled an innate and innately rewarding desire. And should the reader's environmentalism threaten to get the upper hand, let me remind him again of an unproblematic case. Lack of exercise is bad and even abnormal not only because it is unhealthy but also because one feels poorly without regular exercise. Nature made exercise rewarding because, until recently, we had to exercise to survive. Creatures who found running after game unrewarding were eliminated. Laziness leaves unreaped the rewards nature has planted in exercise, even if the lazy man cannot tell this introspectively. If this is a correct description of the place of exercise in human life, it is by the same token a correct description of the place of heterosexuality.

It hardly needs saying, but perhaps I should say it anyway, that this argument concerns tendencies and probabilities. Generalizations about human affairs being notoriously "true by and large and for the most part" only, saying that homosexuals are bound to be less happy than heterosexuals must be understood as short for "Not coincidentally, a larger proportion of homosexuals will be unhappy than a corresponding selection of the heterosexual population." There are, after all, genuinely jolly fat men. To say that laziness leads to adverse affective consequences means that, because of our evolutionary history, the odds are relatively good that a man who takes no exercise will suffer adverse affective consequences. Obviously, some people will get away with misusing their bodily parts. Thus, when evaluating the empirical evidence that bears on this account, it will be pointless to cite cases of well-adjusted homosexuals. I do not say they are non-existent; my claim is that, of biological necessity, they are rare. . . .

Talk of what is "in the genes" inevitably provokes the observation that we should not blame homosexuals for their homosexuality if it is "in their genes." True enough. Indeed, since nobody decides what he is going to find sexually arousing, the moral appraisal of sexual object "choice" is entirely absurd. However, so saying is quite consistent with regarding homosexuality as a misfortune, and taking steps—this being within the realm of the will—to minimize its incidence, especially among children. Calling homosexuality involuntary does not place it outside the scope of evaluation. Victims of sickle-cell anemia are not blameworthy, but it is absurd to pretend that there is nothing wrong with them. Homosexual activists are partial to genetic explanations and hostile to Freudian environmentalism in part because they see a genetic cause as exempting homosexuals from blame. But surely people are equally blameless for indelible traits acquired in early childhood. And anyway, a blameless condition may still be worth trying to prevent. . . .

Utilitarians must take the present evolutionary scenario seriously. The utilitarian attitude toward homosexuality usually runs something like this: even if homosexuality is in some sense unnatural, as a matter of brute fact homosexuals take pleasure in sexual contact with members of the same sex. As long as they don't hurt anyone else, homosexuality is as great a good as heterosexuality. But the matter cannot end here. Not even a utilitarian doctor would have words of praise for a degenerative disease that happened to foster a certain kind of pleasure (as sore muscles uniquely conduce to the pleasure of stretching them). A utilitarian doctor would presumably try just as zealously to cure diseases that feel good as less pleasant degenerative diseases. A pleasure causally connected with great distress cannot be treated as just another pleasure to be toted up on the felicific scoreboard. Utilitarians have to reckon with the inevitable consequences of pain-causing pleasure. . . .

6. On Policy Issues

Homosexuality is intrinsically bad only in a prudential sense. It makes for unhappiness. However, this does not exempt homosexuality from the larger categories of ethics—rights, duties, liability. Deontic categories apply to acts which increase or decrease happiness or expose the helpless to the risk of unhappiness.

If homosexuality is unnatural, legislation which raises the odds that a given child will become homosexual raises the odds that he will be unhappy. The only gap in the syllogism is whether legislation which legitimates, endorses or protects homosexuality does increase the chances that a child will become homosexual. If so, such legislation is *prima facie* objectionable. The question is not whether homosexual elementary school teachers will molest their charges. Pro-homosexual legislation might increase the incidence of homosexuality in subtler ways. If it does, and if the protection of children is a fundamental obligation of society, legislation which legitimates homosexuality is a dereliction of duty. I am reluctant to deploy the language of "children's rights," which usually serves as one more excuse to interfere with the prerogatives of parents. But we do have obligations to our children, and one of them is to protect them from harm. If, as some have suggested, children have a right to protection from a religious education, they surely have a right to protection from homosexuality. So protecting them limits somebody else's freedom, but we are often willing to protect quite obscure children's rights at the expense of the freedom of others. There is a movement to ban TV commercials for sugar-coated cereals, to protect children from the relatively trivial harm of tooth decay. Such a ban would restrict the freedom of advertisers, and restrict it even though the last clear chance of avoiding the harm, and thus the responsibility, lies with the parents who control the TV set. I cannot see how one can consistently support such legislation and also urge homosexual rights, which risk much graver danger to children in exchange for increased freedom for homosexuals. (If homosexual behavior is largely compulsive, it is falsifying the issue to present it as balancing risks to children against the freedom of homosexuals.) The right of a homosexual to work for the Fire Department is not a negligible good. Neither is fostering a legal atmosphere in which as many people as possible grow up heterosexual.

It is commonly asserted that legislation granting homosexuals the privilege or right to be firemen endorses not homosexuality, but an expanded conception of human liberation. It is conjectural how sincerely this can be said in a legal order that forbids employers to hire whom they please and demands hours of paperwork for an interstate shipment of hamburger. But in any case legislation "legalizing homosexuality" cannot be neutral because passing it would have an inexpungeable speech-act dimension. Society cannot grant unaccustomed rights and privileges to homosexuals while remaining neutral about the value of homosexuality. Working from the assumption that society rests on the family and its consequences, the Judaeo-Christian tradition has deemed homosexuality a sin and withheld many privileges from homosexuals. Whether or not such denial was right, for our society to grant these privileges to homosexuals *now* would amount to declaring that it has rethought the matter and decided that homosexuality is not as bad as it had previously supposed. . . .

Up to now, society has deemed homosexuality so harmful that restricting it outweighs putative homosexual rights. If society reverses itself, it will in effect be deciding that homosexuality is not as bad as it once thought.

References

[1] Barash, D. *The Whispering Within.* New York: Harper & Row, 1979.
[2] Bell, A. and M. Weinberg. *Homosexualities.* New York: Simon and Schuster, 1978.
[3] Goldberg, S. "What is 'Normal'? Logical Aspects of the Question of Homosexual Behavior." *Psychiatry* (1975).
[4] Gould, R. "What We Don't Know about Homosexuality." *New York Times Magazine,* Feb. 24, 1974.
[5] Gary, R. "Sex and Sexual Perversion." *Journal of Philosophy* 74 (1978): 189–99.
[6] Mossner, E. *The Life of David Hume,* 1st. ed. New York: Nelson & Sons, 1954.

HOMOSEXUALITY SHOULD NOT BE DISCOURAGED

Homosexuality and Nature: Happiness and the Law at Stake

Timothy F. Murphy

The nature and legitimacy of homosexual behaviour continue to generate considerable controversy. Since 1973, the American Psychiatric Association has formally professed that homosexuality per se is no disease entity,[1] but one may still seek and find

---
[1]RONALD BAYER (1981) *Homosexuality and American Psychiatry* (New York, Basic Books).

practitioners of sexual conversion therapy.[2] While some religious thinkers have become more tolerant of it,[3] others continue to conceptualize homosexuality as a sin of the first order, a sin said to be formally condemned in strong Old and New Testament language. While at present 26 states of the Union do *not* have criminal statutes for private consensual homosexual behaviour, the US Supreme Court recently held that states may criminalize such behaviour if they so choose.

There are many ways used to argue against the moral legitimacy of homosexual behaviour, whether such behaviour is transient or exclusive. Some seek recourse to concepts of sinfulness, disease or crime in order to flesh out objections. Others appeal to the argument that homosexuality, its religious, medical, and criminal implications apart, is a kind of unnatural aberration which undermines its practitioners' prospects for happiness. I will consider this kind of argument here and contend that such an argument fails to establish that homosexuality is any significant abnormality and that neither its purported abnormality nor the unhappiness said to be associated with such behaviour can constitute a basis for criminalizing consensual homosexual behaviour or for failing to provide equal protections under the law for homosexuals in the area of public housing, service, jobs, and so on. I consider Michael Levin's 'Why homosexuality is abnormal' as paradigmatic of the kind of argument I wish to investigate. Although I confine myself to his specific argument and frequently use its language, my position is applicable *a fortiori* to all similar kinds of position.

The Argument from Nature

. . .

Despite the effort which Levin takes to show that homosexual behaviour falls outside the behaviour upon which human adaptive success depended, I cannot say that I think this argument is even remotely convincing. Indeed, I believe it to be subject to a damning criticism. Even if it were certainly established that homosexuality was not part of originally adaptive behaviour, I do not see how that conclusion alone could establish the abnormality of homosexuality because there is neither a premise that natural selection has any kind of ultimate normative force nor a premise that human beings are bound to continue to be the kind of things that cosmic accident brought them to be. There is nothing in Levin's argument to sustain a claim that departures from a blind, accidental force of nature, or whatever metaphor of randomness is chosen, must be resisted. Without a logically prior and controlling premise that patterns of adaptive success possess ultimate, normative force, then it seems that human beings are completely at liberty to dispose of their world, their behaviour, and even such things as their anatomy and physiology as they see fit. H Tristram Engelhardt has made an argument along similar lines: that we human beings may choose our futures and are in no metaphysically binding sense bound to continue being the kind of persons blind determinants of nature have brought us to be.[4] Violations of a random order of nature carry no inherent

---

[2]Mark Schwartz & William H. Masters (1984) The Masters and Johnson Program for Dissatisfied Homosexual Men, *American Journal of Psychiatry*, 141, pp. 173–181.

[3]See some of the selections in Edward Batchelor, Jr. (Ed.) (1980) *Homosexuality and Ethics* (New York, Pilgrim Press).

[4]See H. Tristram Engelhardt, Jr. (1986) *The Foundation of Bioethics*, pp. 375–387 (New York, OUP).

penalty for there is no ultimate enforcer, or at least none is specified by this argument. Levin believes that he can show the abnormality of homosexuality without having to show that it violates some cosmic principle, by showing its inherent obstacles to adaptive success. But I think it is because no cosmic principle is invoked that we can judge that adaptive success itself is no binding force. The only guide available for human beings in respect of their lives, sexuality, and future is their will and imagination. Should the entire population of the planet choose to become exclusive homosexuals, for example, leaving the business of reproduction to ectogenesis, I cannot think of a reason *derived from nature* why they should not do so.

Levin's argument, and others like it, ignore the prospects of beneficial departures from the naturally adaptive order. His argument assumes that each departure from our adaptive heritage will be unhappy in result. The argument, too, assumes that *all* behaviour of *all* persons must serve the purpose of adaption. Clearly, it is possible that some departures from the adaptive order are possible which do not threaten a species' survival as a whole. If a species can survive if only a majority of its members use their organs in a particular fashion, then it may enjoy a surplus of adaptive protection even for those who act in wholly non-procreative fashion. Homosexuality, then, might have served some beneficial advantage (as sociobiology asserts) or it may have been (and this is more important for my argument) no impediment to selective adaptation. If this is so, it is hard to see in what sense homosexuality would have to be reckoned as a natural aberration.

Even if one were to accept Levin's suggestions regarding the abnormality of homosexuality with respect to natural selection, it seems to me that his definition of homosexuality is highly problematic. He defines homosexuality behaviourally, i.e., as something one does with one's body, specifically with one's organs. It is *behaviour* which is said to be unnatural. Since there are, after all, self-identified gay men and lesbians who have never had sexual relations with a member of the same (or opposite) sex, this definition seems ill-advised. By their own lights, adolescents and closeted adults see themselves as homosexual, their sexual continence notwithstanding. How is one to understand the nature of their sexual dispositions if there is no overt behaviour? Is their homoerotic desire itself abnormal? Or is only behaviour abnormal? I believe that homosexuality is better defined as primarily a psychic phenomenon and that specific homosexual behaviour is virtually epiphenomenal, merely a matter of what biology makes possible (this claim would also apply to heterosexuality). Most psychiatric texts follow this approach.[5] If one accepts the condition that homosexuality is primarily a psychic phenomenon, and if one wanted to argue its abnormality along the lines Levin has suggested, it would seem that one would have to argue that homoeroticism is somehow a misuse of the brain! There are arguments, of course, that attempt to show homosexuality as a result of some psychic disrepair, but even though these arguments are themselves the matter of much debate, that debate is only about physical development, not about uses of the brain. It is hard to imagine that one could show homoeroticism as a misuse of the brain. . . .

---

[5]MICHAEL GELDER, DENNIS GATH & RICHARD MAYOU (1983) *Oxford Textbook of Psychiatry*, p. 468 (Oxford, OUP).

Prospects for Happiness

Levin makes a great deal of the supposed link between homosexuality and unhappiness. One may assume that he would reply to my foregoing remarks by admitting that even if it were true that humans are not bound by any ultimate metaphysical sexual directive, then it would still remain true that prudential cautions obtain against homosexuality and that these cautions are sufficient to ground legal measures designed to minimize the occurrence of homosexuality. "Homosexuality," Levin says, "is likely to cause unhappiness because it leaves unfulfilled an innate and innately rewarding desire,"[6] a desire supposedly ingrained through millennia of evolutionary selection. One might find some happy homosexuals, but Levin believes that such exceptions are inconsequential and do not disable his argument. He does not say that happy homosexuals are non-existent, only that they are rare and that their lives will be inherently less rewarding than those of heterosexuals. . . .

To put specific quarrels about evidence aside, it seems to me that Levin fails almost culpably to imagine what a society would have to be like in order to be free of the oppressive elements which contribute to the putative unhappiness of homosexuals. In order to see the extent to which homosexual unhappiness is caused by social repressions and to what extent it is intrinsic, society would have to be completely free at every significant level of bias against homosexuals. To begin with—let's call this Phase I of the agenda: there should be no gratuitous assumption of heterosexuality in education, politics, advertising, and so on, just as a gender-neutral society would not presume the priority, real and symbolic, of males. For example, in education, texts and films ought to incorporate the experiences of gay men and lesbians. Educational measures should attempt to reduce anti-homosexuality in the same ways and to the same extent they educate against racism. In a society reconstructed along these lines, moreover, there would also have to be no right of access or entitlement possessed by a heterosexual that could be denied to a homosexual. *Only* in such a radically restructured society would one be able to see if homosexual unhappiness were immune to social deconstruction. Even if it weren't, one could still argue that homosexuals are not necessarily unhappy but that their happiness requires social protections or accommodations unrequired by heterosexuals. That is, homosexuals might need, as Phase II of the agenda, entitlements which heterosexuals do not—in the way, for example, that legally mandated minority hiring quotas serve other specific populations. Of course, one might want to argue that such entitlements would be anti-democratic and therefore objectionable. This protestation however would not by itself diminish the point being made: that homosexual unhappiness is perhaps adventitious and that the only way of discovering this is to protect homosexuals in their lives, jobs, and interests in ways that are not presently served. . . .

Issues at Law

Levin believes that the abnormality of homosexuality, and its attendant unhappiness are warrant enough to ground legal enactments against homosexuality and this is a matter of protecting citizens from lives impoverished by the loss of heterosexual rewards. Any legislation therefore that raises the odds that a child will become homosexual ought to be rejected as prima facie

---

[6]Levin, p. 261.

objectionable, as a dereliction of the duty of protecting children from the unhappy homosexual selves they might become.[7] The US Supreme Court recently ruled in Bowers v. Hardwick that states may enact, if they choose, statutes proscribing private consensual homosexual behaviour since, according to the opinion, there is nothing in the Constitution making such behaviour a fundamental right.[8] Levin's argument would presumably extend further since private consensual homosexual behaviour is socially invisible and unlikely as such to influence persons to become homosexual. Although he does not specifically mention what kinds of laws ought to be called for, or what kinds of laws ought to be rejected, presumably he means denying homosexuals protections in jobs, housing, foster-parenting, and so on. In short, the law would presumably have to serve the function of rendering homosexuality entirely invisible else there would continue to exist subtle promptings to homosexuality by virtue of degree of acceptance extended to it. Levin says he does not believe that this legal scenario would put any undue burden on any actual homosexual since, unlike members of racial minorities, he or she can always stay in the closet while applying for jobs, housing and the like. Therefore to give homosexuals protections they don't really need would have to be interpreted as a de facto social legitimation of homosexuality. This implied approval might be causally involved in the production of more homosexuals and therefore ought to be rejected.

I do not believe that this argument is convincing. First of all, the 'cause' or 'causes' of homosexuality are a matter of continuing controversy. There are metaphysical arguments that homosexuality is the result of some cosmic principle of world ordering: Plato's *Symposium* depicts homosexuals (and heterosexuals) as the result of an angry god's punishment. Biological theories hold homosexuality to be the result of some developmental variance or organismal dysfunction. Genetic theories try to locate the origins of homosexuality at the lowest level of biological causality, the gene. The most numerous kinds of theories are psychosocial theories which see homoeroticism as the result of either original psychical constitution or some developmental influences. Even the briefest perusal of the literature of the 'cause' of homosexuality leaves one with the conclusion that the 'cause' is an essentially disputed concept. There is not even agreement that homosexuality is a reifiable trait (any more than, say, courage) that can be explained by reference to a universally pre-existing set of conditions.[9] This dispute is important to consider since Levin seems to hold, without justification (at least without explanation), a developmental theory of homosexuality, a theory that homosexuals are made not born. This may or may not be true, but it seems wrong-headed to establish legal policy on the basis of one particular speculative theory of the origins of homosexual behaviour. If homosexuality is primarily a function of biological variance, for example, such laws and forbearances that Levin would see as desirable would have no effect whatever on the production of more homosexuals. Even if the law diligently erased all evidence of homosexual behaviour and persons from public view, one could not automatically assume a reduced number of homosexuals or a decrease in homosexual behaviour. I suspect

---

[7]Levin, p, 274.

[8]Bowers v. Hardwick, No. 85–140 (30 June, 1986).

[9]DOUGLAS FUTUYMA & STEPHEN J. RISCH (1984) Sexual orientation, sociobiology and evolution, in: J. P. DECECCO & M. G. SHIVELEY (Eds) *Bisexual and Homosexual Identities: critical theoretical issues*, pp. 157–168 (New York, Haworth Press).

that most persons are homosexual and become homosexual in ways completely immune to the written or enforced statutes of the various states. Children who never hear a word about homosexuality in their youth nevertheless become homosexuals. Children who walk past homosexual clubs and persons in the streets of certain American cities do not thereby automatically become homosexuals. Would it really be the case that there are more homosexuals spawned in West Virginia because there are no laws against private, consensual homosexual behaviour there than in Virginia where there are such laws?[10] The net result of efforts to criminalize and reduce the visibility of homosexuality then would be to impose burdens on those who are perhaps involuntarily homosexual. At the very least, Levin's theory gratuitously supposes a developmental theory of homosexuality, a theory which has its insistent critics. One should also point out that even if some developmental theory of homosexuality were true, it is not necessarily the case that changing statutes would halt the flow of homosexuals since there may be other pathways to homosexuality. It is also the suspicion of many psychologists that homosexual tendencies are established very early on in childhood, in which case one presumes fairly that statutes criminalizing sodomy and lacks of protection in housing on the basis of sexual orientation have little to do with either ingraining or stifling homosexual dispositions.

If the reason that Levin suggests anti-homosexual measures is to contain human unhappiness, then his argument may be turned on its head. If the reason, or part of the reason that homosexuals are unhappy is because of the existence of certain legally permissible discriminations (or what comes to the same thing: fear of such), then it can certainly be suggested that laws ought to be changed in order to protect and enlarge the happiness of homosexuals, whether their homosexuality is elective or involuntary. In the name of their happiness, they ought to be afforded protections under the law, freedom from fear of prosecution for their private consensual behaviour and freedom to occupy jobs as the persons they are, not as the persons others would have them be. The law could further protect them by saving them from blackmailers who would expose their homosexuality to employers, landlords, and so on. It is eminently clear that the law could at least enlarge the happiness of gay men and lesbians in these respects even if it cannot vouchsafe them absolute satisfaction in their lives.

Interestingly enough, even if all the unhappiness said to be associated with being homosexual were not eliminated by a dogged social reconstruction that achieved full parity between homosexuality and heterosexuality, it would still not follow that the law ought to be put to the purpose of eliminating homosexuality (assuming it could). Life, sad to say, is in some of its aspects inherently tragic. For example, in some important ways, law or society could never fully compensate the atheist for the lost rewards of religion. Atheism can discover in the world no incentives to conduct, no promise of the eventual recompense for injustices borne, and no guarantee that the heart's desires will be met.[11] Society might provide such consolations as it can, but it is certainly the case that a certain tragedy antagonistic to human happiness is an irreducible element of atheistic thought. That atheism leads to this measure of unhappiness would certainly not be a reason for instituting social and legal barriers to atheism

---

[10]Sodomy laws in US (illus.), *New York Times*, 1 July 1986, p. A19.

[11]ERNEST NAGEL (1965) A defense of atheism, in: P. EDWARDS & A. PAP *A Modern Introduction to Philosophy*, pp. 460–472, rev edn (New York, Free Press).

on the theory that children ought to be glowingly happy (if self-deceived) theists rather than unhappy atheists. Human dignity is not automatically overthrown by a position of atheism; the atheist accepts and honours those satisfactions that are within his or her power. That homosexuality too might lead to a certain amount of unhappiness does not thereby overthrow the dignity of homosexual persons. One realizes merely that the law is no unfailing conduit to human happiness.

Levin's conclusions that legal measures ought to be taken to minimize the possibility that children become themselves the sad new recruits of homosexuality therefore cannot stand. I believe, on the contrary, that the law ought to do what it can to protect homosexuals from socially inflicted unhappiness. Levin's point that to decriminalize homosexual behaviour and to provide legal protections for homosexual persons would be seen as social legitimization of homosexuality (and not just tolerance) is correct. But this is no point over which to despair, for this inference is precisely compatible with the underlying metaphysics of gay activism, that homosexuality is no degrading impoverishment of human life. On the contrary, it has an integrity of its own apart from invidious comparison with heterosexuality. Therefore, lest society be a political enforcer of sexual ideology, homosexuals ought to be afforded equal standing and protections under the law, and this in the name of serving human happiness. . . .

Questions for Further Reflection

1. Goldman writes that "the desire for physical contact with another person . . . is both necessary and sufficient to qualify normal desire as sexual." Goldman discusses and responds to some purported counterexamples to this analysis. How successful are his responses? Is it really the case that caressing a baby's skin is a sexual act? That masturbation is not (unless it is "an imaginative substitute for the real thing")? And what about fetishism?

2. Goldman argues that a clear distinction between sex and love would "help avoid disastrous marriages" and "weaken damaging jealousies." Evaluate these claims.

3. In keeping with his view that "there is no morality intrinsic to sex," Goldman argues that "the immorality of rape derives from its being an extreme violation of a person's body, of the right not to be humiliated, and of the general moral prohibition against using other persons against their wills, not from the fact that it is a sexual act." Is this account capable of explaining why we regard rape as more horrible than mere assault? (Compare Arkes' discussion of this issue.)

4. Scruton writes that: "Love is the fulfillment of desire, and therefore love is its *telos* [goal or purpose]." According to Goldman, on the other hand, the only necessary goal of sexual desire is physical contact. Defend one or the other of these views.

5. Goldman and Scruton agree that infidelity can lead to jealousy. But they recommend opposite remedies: Goldman recommends separating love from sex so that sexual infidelity no longer seems like a betrayal of love; Scruton recommends forming "the habit of fidelity." Who is right?

6. Scruton intriguingly suggests that the goal of sexual morality is to integrate "the personal and the sexual," to ensure that in sex we relate to ourselves and our lovers as persons rather than just as bodies. How important is this? What would Goldman think of this view?

7. Arkes suggests that moral condemnation of prostitution stands or falls with moral condemnation of promiscuity. Is he right? If so, what conclusion should we draw?
8. Evaluate Arkes' response to Goldman. Include a discussion of Arkes' point that our objection to child prostitution suggests that there is something intrinsically wrong with prostitution.
9. Arkes holds that prostitution is intrinsically wrong, not wrong merely because of its consequences. Ericsson, in his discussion of "the charge from conventional morality," suggests that to make this claim "is in a way to refuse to give any arguments." Is this fair as a response to Arkes?
10. Ericsson argues that prostitution is morally acceptable even though it would not exist in a perfectly good society. Explain and evaluate his attempted reconciliation of these two views.
11. Levin regards homosexuality as analogous to lack of exercise and suggests that just as lack of exercise makes you feel bad, so the "misuse" of sex organs involved in homosexuality leads to unhappiness. Evaluate the analogy. (Incidentally, which part of the body does lack of exercise misuse?)
12. Levin suggests that homosexuality is bad for the people who engage in it because it makes them unhappy. Suppose that he is right. Evaluate his claim that this justifies opposing gay rights. (Eating too much fat and sugar is bad for you, but no one objects to equal rights for fat- and sugar-eaters.)

Further Readings

Murphy, Timothy F., ed. *Gay Ethics: Controversies in Outing, Civil Rights, and Sexual Science.* New York: Haworth Press, 1994. An excellent collection of essays on a variety of issues regarding homosexuality.

Pateman, Carole. "Defending Prostitution: Charges against Ericsson." *Ethics* 93 (1983): 561–565. Argues that Ericsson misunderstands and so fails to respond to feminist objections to prostitution.

Richards, David A. J. *Sex, Drugs, Death, and the Law: An Essay on Human Rights and Overcriminalization.* Totowa, NJ: Rowman & Littlefield, 1982. Chapter 3 is an informative discussion of the empirical, moral, and legal issues surrounding prostitution.

Solomon, Robert C., and Kathleen M. Higgins, eds. *The Philosophy of (Erotic) Love.* Lawrence, KS: University Press of Kansas, 1991. Interesting collection of essays, both historical and contemporary.

Taylor, Richard. *Having Love Affairs.* Buffalo, NY: Prometheus, 1982. A defense of adultery.

Tong, Rosemarie. *Women, Sex, and the Law.* Totowa, NJ: Rowman & Allanheld, 1984. Chapter 2 is a good overview of various feminist responses to prostitution.

Vannoy, Russell. *Sex without Love: A Philosophical Exploration.* Buffalo, NY: Prometheus, 1980. Defends the superiority of sex without love over sex with love.

Chapter 7

Marriage and Family

In this chapter, we are concerned with two collections of issues: issues about the relations between married couples, and issues about the relations between parents and children. The first set of issues focuses on *marriage*, and the second on the *family*. With respect to marriage, there are two particularly interesting moral issues. The first has to do with the value of marriage as an institution, and the second has to do with the notion that sex ought to be limited to marriage.

Marriage as an Institution

It is useful to distinguish four different views about marriage, which we will label the romantic, contractual, traditional, and radical attitudes, respectively.

The Romantic View

The romantic attitude is not discussed in the readings in this chapter but provides a useful background for them. It is criticized in the nineteenth-century Danish philosopher Søren Kierkegaard's intriguing piece "The Aesthetic Validity of Marriage."[1] Kierkegaard describes the character of much romantic literature as follows:

> For through many centuries have not knights and adventurers undergone incredible pains and trouble in order to come to harbor in the quiet peace of a happy marriage? Have not novelists and novel readers worked their way through one volume after another in order to stop with a happy marriage? And has not one generation after another endured the troubles and complications of four acts if only there was some likelihood of a happy marriage in the fifth? . . . For this precisely is the pernicious, the unwholesome feature of such works, that they end where they ought to begin. After the many fates they have overcome the lovers finally sink into one another's arms. The curtain falls, the book ends; but the reader is none the wiser. [80]

Kierkegaard's point is that the curtain falls after the lovers have finally come together, but before they have had to *live* together; the whole story concerns their courtship rather than the marriage that follows it. (This is also true of most contemporary "romance" novels.)

---

[1]Søren Kierkegaard, "The Aesthetic Validity of Marriage," in Kierkegaard, *Either/Or*, Volume II, trans. Walter Lowrie (Princeton, NJ: Princeton University Press, 1971).

Kierkegaard also notes that the distinguishing feature of romantic love is "that it is *immediate:* to see her was to love her; or, though she saw him only once through a slit in the shuttered window of her chamber, nevertheless from this instant she loved him, him alone in the whole world" [82]. This immediacy has two features. First, it is "based upon the sensuous." If one immediately falls in love, then this love cannot be based on any very deep facts of personality or character, but rather only on the loved one's appearance and manner. Second, when one falls in love in this way, it at least *feels* to those involved as though it is permanent, as though the relationship will last forever.

This combination of immediacy and permanence is unstable. In the romantic conception, love is a matter of the powerful feelings that overcome one when one sees or contemplates the loved one, and these feelings lead one to think that the relationship will last forever. However, there is no guarantee that the powerful feelings will not fade or change or that one will not later feel at least as powerfully about someone else; so there is no guarantee of permanence in the relationship.

The romantic lover is therefore likely to reject marriage as undesirable and dangerous. Since love has to do with feeling, formal commitments are alien to it and, in fact, may even be dangerous, because they lock one into a relationship regardless of whether the powerful feelings on which it is based continue.

Arguments against the Romantic View

The romantic critique of marriage has its attractions, perhaps especially in a period like ours, in which an estimated half of all marriages end in divorce. We can, however, offer at least two considerations that favor marriage, or at least some sort of formalized commitment to remaining together. The first consideration is a *utilitarian* one: It suggests that the benefits of commitment outweigh the disadvantages. When one makes a long-term commitment, one shuts off a number of possibilities, many of which might be quite pleasant. If you find several people attractive, then the thought of committing yourself exclusively to one may be disturbing because it rules out intimacy with the others. And of course, even if you find a single person overwhelmingly attractive, the strong possibility remains that you will later find someone else equally attractive. On the other hand, a long-term relationship with a single person may be richer and deeper than any short-term relationship can be. Even if there is no *one* person with whom you could be happiest, because you could be happy in different ways with many different people, nevertheless a long-term relationship with (any) one of them still may be more rewarding than a mere succession of short-term relationships.

In this respect, finding a partner may be a bit like choosing a musical instrument or a profession. It is difficult to devote yourself to the oboe, since this may mean paying less attention than you would like to the charms of the French horn or the electric guitar; but refusing to commit yourself to any of these instruments because you cannot give up the others may mean that you will not become truly expert at any of them, and this may well be less rewarding than devoting yourself to any one of them would have been. The same thing is perhaps even more clearly true in your choice of a profession.

A second consideration in support of long-term commitment is *metaphysical.* It seems, in fact, to be Kierkegaard's own principal reason for favoring a committed relationship. He suggests that there is a legitimate sense in which, without commitment, one is not genuinely a *person*. A person is someone with a more-or-less stable personality, someone with a character that remains largely constant despite changes in pursuits and interests. To the extent that one simply gives in to whatever passions strike at the moment, drifting from one impulse to the next, one does not have the sort of stability which, he suggests, is necessary to genuinely be a person rather than a succession of momentary person-stages which are not linked together by anything coherent [103].

Of course, even supposing that this picture of the acquisition of personhood is correct, it does not follow that everyone ought to get married, but rather only that if one is genuinely to be a person, one must make *some* lasting commitments. However, a commitment to marriage is at least an example of the sort of commitment that can make one a person.

The Contractual View

Both remaining views of marriage take seriously the idea that commitment is valuable and important, but they understand the notion of commitment differently. The second is what we call the contractual view; it is the view criticized by Roger Scruton in "The Politics of Sex." This attitude holds that the obligations one incurs in marriage are acquired only by virtue of an explicit contract or agreement between the marriage partners. Going through a marriage ceremony does not somehow magically result in the acquisition of a whole raft of moral obligations one did not have before; to the extent that one acquires new obligations in marriage, this is only because both partners have agreed to act in certain ways toward each other.

This attitude leads to three consequences of interest. First, if the moral obligations of marriage are acquired only because of an agreement, then it seems useful to make the agreement as explicit as possible; thus, we see various sorts of prenuptial agreements and explicit marriage contracts that attempt to spell out in detail the rights and duties to be associated with a particular marriage. Second, if marriage is essentially a contract between two people, then the contract ought to be dissolvable whenever the two partners agree to dissolve it. There would seem to be no basis for insisting on *grounds* for a divorce if both partners want one; if they both agree to separate, that ought to conclusively settle the issue. Third, there would seem to be no reason why the contract should be the same for all married couples. If marriage is to be thought of as a contract, then it may as well be a *different* contract in each case.

The Traditional View

Roger Scruton, in "The Politics of Sex," argues vigorously against this contractual conception and in favor of what we might call the traditional conception of marriage. According to the traditional conception, marrying someone involves a variety of commitments, like the contractual conception; however, the two views differ over the nature and grounds of these commitments. Where the contractual view says that the only source of marital obligations lies in the free agreement of the partners, the traditional view holds that one acquires commitments by entering into a marriage whether or not the two married partners ever explicitly agree to these commitments. The source of the commitments lies in the partners' participation in the institution of marriage as it has developed over a long period. As a result, the nature of the obligations acquired in marriage also differs in the two views. According to the contractual view, the only marital obligations partners have are those to which they explicitly agree. If the explicit agreement between the partners does not cover various sorts of unforeseen consequences, then those circumstances cannot give rise to new specific obligations. For example, suppose two married partners have agreed that each will pursue a career and their explicit agreement presupposes throughout that they will live on two incomes. If an accident then renders one unable to work, neither partner has any particular obligations to the other with respect to income.

The contractual view of marriage is a kind of Enlightenment view: It involves a rejection of the notion that tradition deserves respect, holding instead that rather than submit themselves to the traditional conception of marriage, partners ought to begin from scratch and build their own agreement, define their own possibly unique version of marriage. It is illuminating to contrast Scruton's reverence for tradition with a more iconoclastic view. Scruton writes that the tradition of marriage is "a smooth handle on experience, which has been passed from generation to generation, and, in the passing, slowly worn itself into the shape required by human nature." Compare this with, for example, Bertrand Russell: "Sex . . . can dispense with an ethic based solely upon ancient prohibitions propounded by uneducated people in a society wholly unlike our own."[2]

Arguments against the Contractual View

What sorts of arguments can be offered against the contractual conception and in favor of the traditional conception? Scruton offers two.

First, Scruton suggests that an explicit agreement will not be able to foresee all the relevant future circumstances; as a result, to limit obligations to those explicitly agreed to will inevitably leave out many of what we would ordinarily regard as moral duties. "Who, when faced with his wife's fatal illness, can justify divorce on the ground that this was not an eventuality that he had foreseen, or a duty that he had willingly undertaken? . . . 'taking responsibility' is not to be summarized in a promise. For its terms cannot be stated, nor can its duties be foretold."

Second, Scruton suggests that the survival of marriage requires a *shared* conception of marriage; marriage needs to be a public institution in a way it cannot be if each couple designs its own. "If marriage survives it is because people seek public recognition for their intimacies. Only an institution which imposes a single, invariable obligation on all who elect to join it can create this public recognition."

The Radical View

The contractual conception of marriage has also been attacked from the opposite direction. While traditionalists attack the contractual conception for ignoring the value of marriage as it has evolved over time, Marxist and feminist thinkers have attacked it for allowing historical inequities between women and men to have too much influence over marital arrangements. The terms of any contract are the result of a bargaining process, and feminists have argued that present inequalities mean that women are seriously disadvantaged in any such process. Thus, making the terms of a marriage a matter of contract has the effect of preserving inequitable family arrangements that unfairly benefit men.

---

[2]Bertrand Russell, "Marriage and Morals," in Al Seckel, ed., *Bertrand Russell on Ethics, Sex and Marriage* (Buffalo, NY: Prometheus, 1987), p. 264.

Feminists and others disagree over solutions to this problem. Frederick Engels argues that the view of marriage as a contract freely entered into is an acceptable ideal which, however, can only be realized once all private property is abolished. Others have argued that the family is inevitably oppressive to women and should itself be abolished. (See the article by Sheila Cronan in Jaggar and Rothenberg, *Feminist Frameworks*, listed in the "Further Readings" for this chapter.) Susan Moller Okin, in her selection in this chapter, takes a somewhat less radical approach. She argues that ideally, marriages and families would not be differentiated at all along gender-related lines, but she acknowledges that most people at present prefer marriages and families that make gender-related distinctions. In such marriages, she argues, the partner who is responsible for child care — normally the woman — should be protected in various ways, notably by receiving half of what we now think of as the money earned by the working partner.

A deeper and more problematic criticism of the contractual conception may be suggested by Okin's claim that traditional marriage is unjust even when preferred by the women involved. This suggests that a marital contract may be unjust not only because women are in a weaker bargaining position, but also because even with equal power, they may not act in their own best interest: They may be so thoroughly co-opted by the oppressive system of male domination that their very desires and beliefs are tainted by it. According to this view, many women need to be protected not only from men but also from themselves.

Marriage and Sex

In many cultures, marriage does not involve a requirement of sexual exclusivity.

For instance, marriage among the ancient Greeks did not preclude homosexual love affairs; moreover, in Japan it has until recently been widely accepted for married men to have mistresses (a few years ago, a Japanese prime minister resigned after Western news media made an issue of his unconcealed arrangement with a mistress[3]). The Judaeo-Christian tradition, however, places heavy weight on a prohibition of extramarital sex (including premarital sex; see Deuteronomy 22:13ff, which commands that a wife found not to be a virgin at the time of marriage be stoned to death).

The traditional view of marriage holds that extramarital sex is wrong precisely *because* there is a long tradition prohibiting it, perhaps supplementing this point with a defense of tradition as the inherited wisdom of previous generations. Unsurprisingly, Scruton, who defends the traditional view of marriage, also opposes extramarital sex. A contractual approach to marriage, on the other hand, has to maintain that whether extramarital sex is permissible depends on the specific contract into which a particular married couple has entered. If both partners have agreed not to engage in sex outside the marriage, then having an affair would amount to breaking a promise and could be criticized on that ground. However, if the particular marriage involves no such agreement, then there are no grounds on which to object to extramarital sex.

Parents and Children

The other main issue this chapter addresses concerns the relations between parents and

---

[3]Then-Prime Minister Sousuke Uno's affair with a geisha is discussed, for example, in "The End of the Affair?" *Newsweek* 114 (July 10, 1989): 22–23. Uno resigned shortly thereafter.

children. In particular, what do parents owe their children, and what do children owe their parents?

Rather than discuss these issues in the abstract, we have chosen two readings that address specific issues that fall into these two categories. Hugh LaFollette, in "Licensing Parents," suggests that whatever obligations parents have toward their children, they certainly have an obligation not to abuse them. His article is primarily concerned with a suggestion about how to enforce this obligation—the suggestion, namely, that we require prospective parents to obtain a license and that we deny such licenses to people who seem likely to be abusive parents. LaFollette argues that licensing an activity is appropriate where the activity is potentially harmful to others, where its safe performance requires competence, and where we have a reasonably reliable procedure by means of which to determine whether someone is competent at the activity. All these criteria are met, he argues, in the case of being a parent.

At the end of his article, LaFollette makes an interesting suggestion about why his proposal is likely to be met with horror. The reason we find the thought of licensing parents so unappealing, he argues, is that we hold the view that children are property of their parents: We believe that "parents own, or at least have natural sovereignty over, their children." LaFollette claims that "this belief is abhorrent and needs to be supplanted," but he devotes little space to arguing against it.

Michael Slote's article, "Obedience and Illusions," can be seen as an attempt to fill this gap. The article is devoted to arguing that parents do not have anything like "natural sovereignty" over their children. Slote addresses the question whether children have a moral duty to obey their parents. His answer, perhaps surprisingly, is that they do not have such a duty. The idea that there is a duty to obey one's parents, Slote argues, is simply an illusion.

Actually, Slote claims to identify two illusions involved in the notion of parental authority. The first is the illusion that we are mere things, without will or choice, that we *must* do what our parents say. One reason for succumbing to this illusion is the feeling of safety it engenders. Making choices is difficult and often frightening, and the illusion that one cannot make choices can free one from this disturbing prospect.

The second illusion arises, Slote argues, out of an attempt to protect the first illusion. In order to continue avoiding choices, we develop rationalizations for the authority of our parents, coming to the conclusion that they have a moral right to command us and that we have a moral duty to obey.

Regardless of how persuasive we find Slote's account of the illusions involved in parental authority, he raises the difficult question of just how parental authority is to be justified, if at all. There are, surely, limits to parental authority. A parent cannot legitimately command a child to do *anything* (e.g., work for twelve hours a day, or hold her hands in boiling water). If a parent, though, commands her ten-year-old son to take out the garbage, doesn't the son have an obligation to do so? Would it really be legitimate for him to reply, "I don't owe you obedience, Mom; you don't have a moral right to order me around. I'm not going to touch that smelly garbage." If Mom really does have a moral right to command her son to take out the garbage, where does this right come from? What grounds it? Slote is surely right that the mere fact that your parents brought you into existence does not automatically give them the right to order you around.

It may be worth returning briefly to three of the views of marriage we distinguished earlier, applying them now to parenthood. The *romantic* view of parenthood would hold that in a good family, the notion of obligation is simply irrelevant. Parents will care for their children out of love and affection; children will do what their parents wish because they love them and want to please them; and the notion of obligation need never rear its ugly head. Unfortunately, families often do not work this way, and when they do not, questions of moral obligation become pressing.

The *contractual* view holds that obligations arise only out of explicit agreements. In this view, the only obligations of the child to her parents will be those which result from explicit agreements she makes (when she is old enough to make agreements at all). Slote seems to be drawn to this view; the closest thing to a duty of obedience he recognizes is an obligation that a farm child, for example, might have to cooperate with her parents in order to share in the benefits of the farm. But in such a case, a child who did not care to share in the benefits would also have no obligation to help out.

Finally, there is a *traditional* conception of the family, according to which parents do have authority over their children. Can we say that parental authority simply arises from tradition? This seems problematic. Even those who find the traditional view of the obligations of marriage attractive may be reluctant to apply a similarly traditional view of parenthood. Someone who does not want the obligations of a traditional marriage can always simply choose not to marry, but a child cannot choose not to be a child (though it has been suggested that children *ought* to be able to choose people other than their natural parents to supervise their upbringing[4]).

---

[4]John Holt, *Escape from Childhood* (New York: Ballantine, 1974), p. 157; quoted in Jeffrey Blustein, *Parents and Children: The Ethics of the Family* (New York: Oxford University Press, 1982), p. 209. Some feminists have advocated a similarly radical view: See, for example, Shulamith Firestone, *The Dialectic of Sex: The Case for Feminist Revolution* (New York: Bantam, 1970).

MARRIAGE: A TRADITIONAL VIEW

The Politics of Sex

Roger Scruton

The state protects and ratifies the institutions of civil society, by endowing them with legal and moral personality. By casting over all social arrangements the protective mantle of sovereignty and law, it removes the arbitrariness from custom and agreement. Associations, such as the family, the club, the firm, the government and the state itself, cease to be mere contracts between private people for purposes of their own and become instead recognisable entities—artificial persons, with rights, duties and liabilities, which present an intelligible face to the world and can be understood in personal terms. By associating himself with such collectives the individual expands his own capacity for action, and acquires also an expanded image of himself, as a bearer of functions and roles. No civil society can persist in stable form, unless these collective entities become institutions, with personality, agency and the capacity to survive their present membership, and to acquire a history and an identity of their own. One of the principal functions of the state is to provide the legal and political framework within which that transaction can occur. And in doing so, the state is inevitably selective, providing protection for some institutions (for example, for the family), and removing it from others (for example, from the private army).

Liberalism is the natural philosophy of the 'desacralised' world. For the liberal conscience, obligations do not surround us in the *Lebenswelt*, but are created by our individual choices. 'There is', said Hobbes, 'no obligation on any man which ariseth not from some act of his own'.[1] Hence there can be no obligation between you and me without an agreement which binds us. With a little strain, many social arrangements can be seen in those terms, as 'voluntary associations', arising out of the common consent, and common expectations, of their members. At the same time, however, there is something extremely artificial about the liberal way of seeing things, even when formulated in the sophisticated manner of Rawls, who sees the obligations of civil society as founded, not in an actual, but in a hypothetical contract.[2] Men join an association not as a rule because they seek agreement with existing members, but either because they have no choice, or because they seek to be part of the association itself, as an entity which is something more than a mutual promise. People are expanded and set free by association, precisely because associations transcend their capacities to 'agree on terms'. And the two most important of all human associations—the family which nurtures us, and the state which governs us from birth to death—are not, and could not be, founded in a social contract'.[3]

One should not be surprised, therefore, if at every important juncture in civil association—every point at which a decision of *membership* has to be made—we find, not just associations, but also institutions. People worship and pray together, but through the institution of church or mosque; they compete and play, but through clubs and local societies; they learn and teach, but through educational institutions which exert the widest possible influence over those who attend them. And their sexual union too seems to crave for its institutional realisation—for the publicly recognisable form whereby it is enlarged into something other than a mutual agreement.

Such a form is marriage, which imposes on the bond of erotic love the noncontractual and pious arrangement of the home. Marriage is a public endorsement of the passion which separates lovers from their surroundings. It is the public acceptance of their exclusive privacy. In entering a marriage they do not merely exchange promises: they pass together into a condition that is

---

[1] Thomas Hobbes, *Leviathan*, II.

[2] John Rawls. *A Theory of Justice*, Oxford, 1971. Pertinent criticism of this idea is offered by Ronald Dworkin, in 'The Original Position', in Norman Daniels (ed.), *Reading Rawls*, Oxford, 1975, reprinted as ch. 6 of *Taking Rights Seriously*, London, 1977.

[3] See Hegel, *The Philosophy of Right*. The essential contrast, in terms of which the Hegelian view of political order is to be expressed, is that between piety and justice. The first, which consists in the ability to accept and be bound by obligations that were never chosen, is denounced by the liberal conscience as mere superstition. I have defended piety in my *Meaning of Conservatism*.

not of their own devising, and which contains the deposits of countless previous experiences of intimacy. Marriage, like every worthwhile institution, is also a tradition—a smooth handle on experience, which has been passed from generation to generation, and, in the passing, slowly worn itself into the shape required by human nature. It has a story attached to it: its comic and tragic aspects are a familiar part of popular culture; its hardships and joys can be anticipated and also shared; it has the respect and the understanding of others. Moreover, it translates itself into legal forms, and endeavours to reconstitute as legal rights the many and mysterious obligations which arise from domestic proximity. In many societies a marriage is a 'legal person' in itself, with agency and answerability that are not those of the partners. If there is an 'ethical idea of marriage',[4] it lies at least partly in this subsumption of the 'merely private' bond of love under laws that are open, disputable and a matter of moral and legal right.

The marriage ceremony is therefore one of the most important of human ceremonies, and one which marks a transition from one state of existence to another. At such moments, man is confronted with his fragility and dependence. As at the moments of death and birth, he is beset by awe. This feeling is a recognition of the sacred: of the intrusion into the human world of obligations that cannot be created by an act of choice, and which therefore demand a transcendental meaning. The sacred is 'the subjectivity of objects'—the presentation, in the contours of day-to-day things, of a meaning that sees 'from I to I'. Out of the mute objectivity of the surrounding world, a voice suddenly calls to me, with a clear and intelligible command. It tells me who I am, and enjoins me to enter the place that has been kept for me. In marriage I 'undertake' an obligation that precedes my choice, and which resides in the scheme of things. Not surprisingly, therefore, marriage is a religious 'sacrament', comparable to the sacraments of baptism and extreme unction. The universal participation of religions in the marriages of believers is testimony to the shared perception of this sacred quality. And like all sacred matters, marriage presents different aspects to the participant and to the observer. The sacred is a personal concept, one that features in the intentional understanding of the person who *participates* in a certain social practice. From the scientific point of view, however, there is no such reality as that of the sacred. At best there is, in anthropological language, an 'initiation rite', in which the transition of a person from one state of social existence to another is confirmed by the mass participation of the tribe.[5]

In order to understand the marriage obligation in its full political meaning, it is necessary to distinguish the ceremony of marriage from the institution which is created by it. The first is an attempt to embody, in publicly intelligible form, the experience of a sacred obligation. It represents marriage as a point of *transition*, which, like death, permits of no return, but which, unlike death, establishes a new life in this world for those who undergo it. 'To apprehend / The point of intersection of the timeless / With time, is an occupation for the saint,' wrote Eliot. His sentiment was, however, heretical. This point of intersection is apprehended in every experience of the sacred. Matrimony, as Eliot reminds us,

---

[4]The phrase is Kierkegaard's: see *Either/Or*, tr. W. Lowrie, New York, 1959, vol. II.

[5]Telling anthropological studies of 'initiation rites' include M. Fortes and G. Evans-Pritchard. *African Political Systems*, Oxford, 1940; and J. Beattie, *Other Cultures*, London, 1964.

is a 'dignified and commodious sacrament', and if every true marriage yearns for ceremony, it is in order to record this fact, and to confirm the apprehension of sacred things by making them matters of public knowledge and public concern.

The institution of marriage is, however, something more than the ceremony with which it begins. And it is as necessary for the state to join in the institution as it is for the church to join in its beginning. For marriage is a moral and legal reality, which takes its meaning from the two most fundamental forms of human love: erotic love, and love between parent and child. Both loves have their natural history; both vary from the intensity of passion to the serenity of day-to-day assurance. But both demand recognition, not only from those who are bound by them, but also from the surrounding world, which might otherwise threaten their exclusiveness, or rebel against the unfair privilege which every love contains. If marriage survives it is because people seek public recognition for their intimacies. Only an institution which imposes a single, invariable obligation on all who elect to join it can create this public recognition, by making clear that the meaning of the individual action is to be found, not in the private desire which prompted it, but in the public custom which gives it form. Hence the bond of marriage, even in the secular state, has a 'transcendental' meaning—one that cannot be summarised in terms of contract or consent. The obligations of marriage are not contracted between the partners, but imposed by the institution, which endeavours to translate into articulate form the constant upsurge of new responsibilities between those who have entered it together. The greatest threat to marriage—as indeed to all institutions which permit the enlargement of the human spirit—is the 'ideology of contract': the view that no man can be bound except by terms to which he has consented. Who, when faced with his wife's fatal illness, can justify divorce on the ground that this was not an eventuality that he had foreseen, or a duty that he had willingly undertaken? It is of course true that a man 'takes responsibility' for another's life in marriage. But this 'taking responsibility' is not to be summarised in a promise. For its terms cannot be stated, nor can its duties be foretold. Thus it is that the transition from private passion to public institution gives substance to the 'vow' of erotic love. To remake marriage as a personal contract, with conditions and terms, is in fact to abolish it, and thereby to threaten both the obligations which it protects and the state of mind which dares to confront them. (Hence sentences of the ecclesiastical courts, which release the parties *a vinculo matrimonii* are not releases from a 'marriage contract', but declarations that a marriage never existed.) The world of the 'consenting adult', the world remade in accordance with the 'social contract' of the enlightened liberal conscience, is, in the last analysis, a world too timid for love.

It might be argued that, if the obligations of love are private, they need no public institution to protect them. But to argue thus is, I believe, to make a serious mistake about the character of civil society. It is to suppose that social relations can simply sustain themselves, without the complicity of the social world. On the contrary, however, social existence is 'existence under observation'. It involves activities which place us continually before the curious, envious or condoning eyes of ethers. The moral sense itself arises from the habit of turning upon ourselves the eyes which we turn on other persons. Their eyes on us direct our eyes also. And if we develop the capacity for the vow of love, it is because we see ourselves reflected in this public observation, as objects of judgement that can make no exceptions in their own favour, and who must take life as it is offered. This public pressure on the individual is made bearable by marriage, which instructs others to avert their eyes and to create the legitimacy of a life lived privately. The division between the public and the private *creates* the private, by creating the space from which others are excluded. In doing so, it brings to a resolution that dialectical anxiety of lovers, who wish constantly to be assured of love, but who cannot demand it. . . . Marriage brings inquisition to a close, and fills the resulting silence with an unspoken answer.

It is perhaps unnecessary to contrast the unhappy condition of the adulterer, who must be secret in all his works and for whom the privacy demanded by love is a rare achievement, no sooner enjoyed than threatened with discovery. However, it is not only the adulterer who is in this predicament. The element of generality in our sexual feelings—the element which leads us to look on people as 'fair game'—leads to a curiosity about the sexual lives of others, and a nascent jealousy, that can be extinguished only by the closing of doors. Marriage, which is legitimate exclusion, creates a peculiar safety and inwardness between lovers. One philosopher has even written of 'the domestic' as a separate 'phenomenological category'.[6]

Stani, a character in Hofmannsthal's *Der Schwierige*, utters the outrageous opinion that women are of two kinds: those you marry and those you love. There are many reasons for marriage apart from love; why, therefore, does marriage not pollute love with considerations that are unworthy of it? Marriage has an economic and also a philoprogenitive meaning. Marriage may be a means to something else, and valued for no intrinsic reason. Love, however, is never a means, and contains its virtue intrinsically. In comparison with marriage—*le ron-ron monotone du pot-au-feu conjugale*, as Sardou described it—adultery seems more exciting, and often more pure: as indeed it was for the medieval expositors of the ethic of courtly love.[7] It may even seem as though *only* adultery is worthy of the higher transports of erotic love, since only adultery can show that it is love alone which creates its obligations, and not the external morality of a public institution polluted by others' purposes and others' needs.

That Tristanian justification of adultery is also, however, a plea for the public acceptance of marriage, as the necessary background for these forbidden pleasures. The adulterer trades security for excitement, and intimacy for a precarious exposure to jealousy and pain. The desire of the adulterer is greater, just as the desire for food is greater in the hungry man. The value of marriage lies, however, not in the heightening of desire, but in the fulfilling of it. Marriage creates thereby the objective conditions for the genesis of desire, and if desire sometimes strays towards the forbidden and the fruitless, this is made possible only because it also has a normal course which sustains its wayward intensities.

It is a small step from the institution of marriage to that of private property. The exclusive erotic relation fights also for its exclusive territory; for the right to close a door. Within that territory everything is 'shared', and since only what is privately owned can be privately shared, the sphere of marriage and of the family is one of private ownership. Moreover, ownership of the home (in the wide sense of 'tenure' as

---

[6] E. Husserl, *Die Krisis der europäischen Wissenschaften und die transzendentale Phänomenologie*, ed. W. Biemel, The Hague, 1976.

[7] Cf. Demosthenes, *Against Naicea:* 'mistresses we keep for the sake of pleasure, concubines for the daily care of our person, but wives to bear us legitimate offspring, and to be faithful guardians of the hearth.'

this concept has been developed in English law) is ownership of a stake in the means of production. The home is not merely the 'means of consumption', as the Marxists would have us believe. It is a place of collective labour, where things are not only consumed but also *made* for consumption. Agricultural produce may be grown and sold; carpets and clothes may be sewn and embroidered; the home itself may be improved and passed on. In short, the home has a natural tendency to realise itself as capital, and will do so upon the death of parents, unless some political system exists which prevents the transition from residence to sale. Hence, as Hegel wrote:

> The family, as person, has its real external existence in property; and it is only when this property takes the form of capital that it becomes the embodiment of the substantial personality of the family.[8]

That passage serves to remind us of a deep and important truth. The institutions of the world into which we were born have the appearance of political contrivances; they may seem, under the impact of this or that revolutionary theory, to be no more than passing phases of man's historical condition. But those appearances may also be mistaken. It may be that human nature, which enjoins us to love, imposes upon us the religious, civil and legal institutions that abounded everywhere in the world, until exultant intellectuals decided that the time had come to dispense with them. No account of erotic love will be either politically innocent or politically neutral. And it will be the greatest error of a political system that it overlooks the demands of love. This error was made, I believe, by the nineteenth-century communists, in their demand for a society without exclusive relations either between people or between people and things: a kind of dance of death, performed by indistinguishable noumenal selves.

This book ends, however, with the defence of marriage. All that I have said about other institutions is no more than a hint, and must await wider argument. In place of that argument, I here give only a gesture. Many social and political changes have swept the world clean of the apprehension of sacred things: the rejection of custom and ceremony; the conversion of marriage into a defeasible contract; the relaxing of the laws governing sexual conduct and obscenity; the decline of faith and saintliness. As those changes take their effect, the experience of erotic love becomes dangerous and uncertain in its outcome. Our responsibility retreats further from the confused terrain of sexual experience, and threatens even to void it of desire.

Hence, it might be said, my ability to reflect, in so neutral and philosophical a fashion, on the nature of this phenomenon is perhaps already an index of its decline: of the fact that desire does not, now, have the importance for us that formerly caused men to conceal it in poetry or overcome it through prayer. What we understand of our condition may also pass from us in the act of understanding. For we were never meant to have knowledge of this thing; we were meant only to be subject to its command. No phenomenon, perhaps, illustrates more profoundly the great poetical utterance of Hegel; that

> When philosophy paints its grey in grey, then has a shape of life grown old. By philosophy's grey in grey it cannot be rejuvenated but only understood. The owl of Minerva spreads its wings only with the gathering of the dusk.

On the other hand, it is a century and a half since Hegel wrote those words, and life goes on.

---

[8]See Chapter 8, and especially the work by Capellanus there referred to.

Marriage: A Marxist View

Marriage

Frederick Engels

Our jurists . . . hold that the progress of legislation to an increasing degree removes all cause for complaint on the part of the woman. Modern civilised systems of law are recognising more and more, first, that, in order to be effective, marriage must be an agreement voluntarily entered into by both parties; and secondly, that during marriage, too, both parties must be on an equal footing in respect to rights and obligations. If, however, these two demands were consistently carried into effect, women would have all that they could ask for.

This typical lawyer's reasoning is exactly the same as that with which the radical republican bourgeois dismisses the proletarian. The labour contract is supposed to be voluntarily entered into by both parties. But it is taken to be voluntarily entered into as soon as the law has put both parties on an equal footing *on paper*. The power given to one party by its different class position, the pressure it exercises on the other—the real economic position of both—all this is no concern of the law. And both parties, again, are supposed to have equal rights for the duration of the labour contract, unless one or the other of the parties expressly waived them. That the concrete economic situation compels the worker to forego even the slightest semblance of equal rights—this again is something the law cannot help.

As far as marriage is concerned, even the most progressive law is fully satisfied as soon as the parties formally register their voluntary desire to get married. What happens behind the legal curtains, where real life is enacted, how this voluntary agreement is arrived at—is no concern of the law and the jurist. And yet the simplest comparison of laws should serve to show the jurist what this voluntary agreement really amounts to. In countries where the children are legally assured of an obligatory share of their parents' property and thus cannot be disinherited—in Germany, in the countries under French law, etc.—the children must obtain their parents' consent in the question of marriage. In countries under English law, where parental consent to marriage is not legally requisite, the parents have full testatory freedom over their property and can, if they so desire, cut their children off with a shilling. It is clear, therefore, that despite this, or rather just because of this, among those classes which have something to inherit, freedom to marry is not one whit greater in England and America than in France or Germany.

The position is no better with regard to the juridical equality of man and woman in marriage. The inequality of the two before the law, which is a legacy of previous social conditions, is not the cause but the effect of the economic oppression of women. In the old communistic household, which embraced numerous couples and their children, the administration of the household, entrusted to the women, was just as much a public, a socially necessary industry as the providing of food by the men. This situation changed with the patriarchal family, and even more with the monogamian individual family. The administration of the household lost its public character. It was no longer the concern of society. It became a *private service*. The wife became the first domestic servant, pushed out of participation in social production. Only modern large-scale industry again threw open to her—and only to the proletarian woman at that—the avenue to social production; but in such a way that, when she fulfils her duties in the private service of her family, she remains excluded from public production and cannot earn anything; and when she wishes to take part in public industry and earn her living independently, she is not in a position to fulfil her family duties. What applies to the woman in the factory applies to her in all the professions, right up to medicine and law. The modern individual family is based on the open or disguised domestic enslavement of the woman; and modern society is a mass composed solely of individual families as its molecules. Today, in the great majority of cases, the man has to be the earner, the bread-winner of the family, at least among the propertied classes, and this gives him a dominating position which requires no special legal privileges. In the family, he is the bourgeois; the wife represents the proletariat. In the industrial world, however, the specific character of the economic oppression that weighs down the proletariat stands out in all its sharpness only after all the special legal privileges of the capitalist class have been set aside and the complete juridical equality of both classes is established. The democratic republic does not abolish the antagonism between the two classes; on the contrary, it provides the field on which it is fought out. And, similarly, the peculiar character of man's domination over woman in the modern family, and the necessity, as well as the manner, of establishing real social equality between the two, will be brought out into full relief only when both are completely equal before the law. It will then become evident that the first premise for the emancipation of women is the reintroduction of the entire female sex into public industry; and that this again demands that the quality possessed by the individual family of being the economic unit of society be abolished. . . .

But the closing of contracts presupposes people who can freely dispose of their persons, actions and possessions, and who meet each other on equal terms. To create such "free" and "equal" people was precisely one of the chief tasks of capitalist production. Although in the beginning this took place only in a semiconscious manner, and in religious guise to boot, nevertheless, from the time of the Lutheran and Calvinistic Reformation it became a firm principle that a person was completely responsible for his actions only if he possessed full freedom of the will when performing them, and that it was an ethical duty to resist all compulsion to commit unethical acts. But how does this fit in with the previous practice of matrimony? According to bourgeois conceptions, matrimony was a contract, a legal affair, indeed the most important of all, since it disposed of the body and mind of two persons for life. True enough, formally the bargain was struck voluntarily; it was not done without the consent of the parties; but how this consent was obtained, and who really arranged the marriage was known only too well. But if real freedom to decide was demanded for all other contracts, why not for this one? Had not the two young people about to be paired the right freely to dispose of themselves, their bodies and organs? Did not sex love become the fashion as a consequence of chivalry, and was not the love of husband and wife its correct bourgeois form, as against the adulterous love of the knights? But if it was the duty of married people to love each other, was it not just as much the duty of lovers to marry each other and nobody else? And did not the right of these lovers stand higher than that of parents, relatives and other traditional marriage brokers and matchmakers? If the right of free personal investigation unceremoniously forced its way into church and religion, how could it halt at the intolerable claim of the older generation to dispose of body and soul, the property, the happiness and unhappiness of the younger generation?

These questions were bound to arise in a period which loosened all the old social ties and which shook the foundations of all traditional conceptions. At one stroke the size of the world had increased nearly tenfold. Instead of only a quadrant of a hemisphere the whole globe was now open to the gaze of the West Europeans who hastened to take possession of the other seven quadrants. And the thousand-year-old barriers set up by the mediaeval prescribed mode of thought vanished in the same way as did the old, narrow barriers of the homeland. An infinitely wider horizon opened up both to man's outer and inner eye. Of what avail were the good intentions of respectability, the honoured guild privileges handed down through the generations, to the young man who was allured by India's riches, by the gold and silver mines of Mexico and Potosi? It was the knight-errant period of the bourgeoisie; it had its romance also, and its love dreams, but on a bourgeois basis and, in the last analysis, with bourgeois ends in view.

Thus it happened that the rising bourgeoisie, particularly in the Protestant countries, where the existing order was shaken up most of all, increasingly recognised freedom of contract for marriage also and carried it through in the manner described above. Marriage remained class marriage, but, within the confines of the class, the parties were accorded a certain degree of freedom of choice. And on paper, in moral theory as in poetic description, nothing was more unshakably established than that every marriage not based on mutual sex love and on the really free agreement of man and wife was immoral. In short, love marriage was proclaimed a human right; not only as man's right (*droit de l'homme*) but also, by way of exception, as woman's right (*droit de la femme*).

But in one respect this human right differed from all other so-called human rights. While, in practice, the latter remained limited to the ruling class, the bourgeoisie—the oppressed class, the proletariat, being directly or indirectly deprived of them—the irony of history asserts itself here once again. The ruling class continues to be dominated by the familiar economic influences and, therefore, only in exceptional cases can it show really voluntary marriages; whereas, as we have seen, these are the rule among the dominated class.

Thus, full freedom in marriage can become generally operative only when the abolition of capitalist production, and of the property relations created by it, has removed all those secondary economic considerations which still exert so powerful an influence on the choice of a partner. Then, no other motive remains than mutual affection.

Since sex love is by its very nature exclusive—although this exclusiveness is fully realised today only in the woman—then marriage based on sex love is by its very nature monogamy. We have seen how right Bachofen was when he regarded the advance from group marriage to individual marriage chiefly as the work of the women; only the advance from pairing marriage to monogamy can be placed to the men's account, and, historically, this consisted essentially in a worsening of the position of women and in facilitating infidelity on the part of the men. With the disappearance of the economic considerations which compelled women to tolerate the customary infidelity of the men—the anxiety about their own livelihood and even more about the future of their children—the equality of woman thus achieved will, judging from all previous experience, result far more effectively in the men becoming really monogamous than in the women becoming polyandrous.

What will most definitely disappear from monogamy, however, is all the characteristics stamped on it in consequence of its having arisen out of property relationships. These are, first, the dominance of the man, and secondly, the indissolubility of marriage. The predominance of the man in marriage is simply a consequence of his economic predominance and will vanish with it automatically. The indissolubility of marriage is partly the result of the economic conditions under which monogamy arose, and partly a tradition from the time when the connection between these economic conditions and monogamy was not yet correctly understood and was exaggerated by religion. Today it has been breached a thousandfold. If only marriages that are based on love are moral, then, also, only those are moral in which love continues. The duration of the urge of individual sex love differs very much according to the individual, particularly among men; and a definite cessation of affection, or its displacement by a new passionate love, makes separation a blessing for both parties as well as for society. People will only be spared the experience of wading through the useless mire of divorce proceedings.

Thus, what we can conjecture at present about the regulation of sex relationships after the impending effacement of capitalist production is, in the main, of a negative character, limited mostly to what will vanish. But what will be added? That will be settled after a new generation has grown up: a generation of men who never in all their lives have had occasion to purchase a woman's surrender either with money or with any other means of social power, and of women who have never been obliged to surrender to any man out of any consideration other than that of real love, or to refrain from giving themselves to their beloved for fear of the economic consequences. Once such people appear, they will not care a rap about what we today think they should do. They will establish their own practice and their own public opinion, comfortable therewith, on the practice of each individual—and that's the end of it.

MARRIAGE: A FEMINIST VIEW

Justice, Gender, and the Family

Susan Moller Okin

Some who are critical of the present structure and practices of marriage have suggested that men and women simply be made free to make their own agreements about family life, contracting with each other, much as business contracts are made.[1] But this takes insufficient account of the history of gender in our culture and our own psychologies, of the present substantive inequalities between the sexes, and, most important, of the well-being of the children who result from the relationship. As has long been recognized in the realm of labor relations, justice is by no means always enhanced by the maximization of freedom of contract, if the individuals involved are in unequal positions to start with. Some have even suggested that it is consistent with justice to leave spouses to work out their own divorce settlement.[2] By this time, however, the two people ending a marriage are likely to be far *more* unequal. Such a practice would be even more catastrophic for most women and children than is the present system. Wives in any but the rare cases in which they as individuals have remained their husbands' socioeconomic equals could hardly be expected to reach a just solution if left "free" to "bargain" the terms of financial support or child custody. What would they have to bargain *with?*

There are many directions that public policy can and should take in order to make relations between men and women more just.... Let us begin by asking what kind of arrangements persons in a Rawlsian original position would agree to regarding marriage, parental and other domestic responsibilities, and divorce. What kinds of policies would they agree to for other aspects of social life, such as the workplace and schools, that affect men, women, and children and relations among them? And let us consider whether these arrangements would satisfy Walzer's separate spheres test—that inequalities in one sphere of life not be allowed to overflow into another. Will they foster equality within the sphere of family life? For the protection of the privacy of a domestic sphere in which inequality exists is the protection of the right of the strong to exploit and abuse the weak.

Let us first try to imagine ourselves, as far as possible, in the original position, knowing neither what our sex nor any other of our personal characteristics will be once the veil of ignorance is lifted.[3] Neither do we know our place in society or our particular conception of the good life. Particularly relevant in this context, of course, is our lack of knowledge of our beliefs about the characteristics of men and women and our related convictions about the appropriate division of labor between the sexes. Thus the positions we represent must include a wide variety of beliefs on these matters. We may, once the veil of ignorance is lifted, find ourselves feminist men or feminist women whose conception of the good life includes the minimization of social differentiation between the sexes. Or we may find ourselves traditionalist men or women, whose conception of the good life, for religious or other reasons, is bound up in an adherence to the

---

[1] See, for example, Marjorie Maguire Schultz, "Contractual Ordering of Marriage: A New Model for State Policy," *California Law Review* 70, no. 2 (1982); Lenore Weitzman, *The Marriage Contract: Spouses, Lovers, and the Law* (New York: The Free Press, 1981), parts 3–4.

[2] See, for example, David L. Kirp, Mark G. Yudof, and Marlene Strong Franks, *Gender Justice* (Chicago: University of Chicago Press, 1986), pp. 183–85. Robert H. Mnookin takes an only slightly less laissez-faire approach, in "Divorce Bargaining: The Limits on Private Ordering." *University of Michigan Journal of Law Reform* 18, no. 4 (1985).

[3] I say "so far as possible" because of the difficulties already pointed out in chapter 5. Given the deep effects of gender on our psychologies, it is probably more difficult for us, having grown up in a gender-structured society, to imagine not knowing our sex than anything else about ourselves. Nevertheless, this should not prevent us from trying.

conventional division of labor between the sexes. The challenge is to arrive at and apply principles of justice having to do with the family and the division of labor between the sexes that can satisfy these vastly disparate points of view and the many that fall between.

There are some traditionalist positions so extreme that they ought not be admitted for consideration, since they violate such fundamentals as equal basic liberty and self-respect. We need not, and should not, that is to say, admit for consideration views based on the notion that women are inherently inferior beings whose function is to fulfill the needs of men. Such a view is no more admissible in the construction of just institutions for a modern pluralist society than is the view, however deeply held, that some are naturally slaves and others naturally and justifiably their masters. We need not, therefore, consider approaches to marriage that view it as an inherently and desirably hierarchical structure of dominance and subordination. Even if it were conceivable that a person who did not know whether he or she would turn out to be a man or a woman in the society being planned would subscribe to such views, they are not admissible. Even if there were no other reasons to refuse to admit such views, they must be excluded for the sake of children, for everyone in the original position has a high personal stake in the quality of childhood. Marriages of dominance and submission are bad for children as well as for their mothers, and the socioeconomic outcome of divorce after such a marriage is very likely to damage their lives and seriously restrict their opportunities.

With this proviso, what social structures and public policies regarding relations between the sexes, and the family in particular, could we agree on in the original position? I think we would arrive at a basic model that would absolutely minimize gender. I shall first give an account of some of what this would consist in. We would also, however, build in carefully protective institutions for those who wished to follow gender-structured modes of life. These too I shall try to spell out in some detail.

Moving Away from Gender

First, public policies and laws should generally assume no social differentiation of the sexes. Shared parental responsibility for child care would be both assumed and facilitated. Few people outside of feminist circles seem willing to acknowledge that society does not have to choose between a system of female parenting that renders women and children seriously vulnerable and a system of total reliance on day care provided outside the home. While high-quality day care, subsidized so as to be equally available to all children, certainly constitutes an important part of the response that society should make in order to provide justice for women and children, it is only one part.[4] If we start out with the reasonable assumption that women and men are equally parents of their children, and have equal responsibility for both the unpaid effort that goes into caring for them and their economic support, then we must rethink the demands of work life throughout the period in which a worker of either sex is a parent of a small child. We can no longer cling to the by now largely mythical assumption that every worker has "someone else" at home to raise "his" children.

The facilitation and encouragement of equally shared parenting would require

---

[4]It seems reasonable to conclude that the effects of day care on children are probably just as variable as the effects of parenting—that is to say, very widely variable depending on the quality of the day care and of the parenting. . . .

substantial changes.[5] It would mean major changes in the workplace, all of which could be provided on an entirely (and not falsely) gender-neutral basis. Employers must be required by law not only completely to eradicate sex discrimination, including sexual harassment. They should also be required to make positive provision for the fact that most workers, for differing lengths of time in their working lives, are also parents, and are sometimes required to nurture other family members, such as their own aging parents. Because children are borne by women but can (and, I contend, should) be raised by both parents equally, policies relating to pregnancy and birth should be quite distinct from those relating to parenting. Pregnancy and childbirth, to whatever varying extent they require leave from work, should be regarded as temporarily disabling conditions like any others, and employers should be mandated to provide leave for all such conditions.[6] Of course, pregnancy and childbirth are far *more* than simply "disabling conditions," but they should be treated as such for leave purposes, in part because their disabling effects vary from one woman to another. It seems unfair to mandate, say, eight or more weeks of leave for a condition that disables many women for less time and some for much longer, while *not* mandating leave for illnesses or other disabling conditions. Surely a society as rich as ours can afford to do both.

Parental leave during the post-birth months must be available to mothers and fathers on the same terms, to facilitate shared parenting; they might take sequential leaves or each might take half-time leave. All workers should have the right, without prejudice to their jobs, seniority, benefits, and so on, to work less than full-time during the first year of a child's life, and to work flexible or somewhat reduced hours at least until the child reaches the age of seven. Correspondingly greater flexibility of hours must be provided for the parents of a child with any health problem or disabling condition. The professions whose greatest demands (such as tenure in academia or the partnership hurdle in law) coincide with the peak period of child rearing must restructure their demands or provide considerable flexibility for those of their workers who are also participating parents. Large-scale employers should also be required to provide high-quality on-site day care for children from infancy up to school age. And to ensure equal quality of day care for all young children, *direct government subsidies* (not tax credits, which benefit the better-off) should make up the difference between the cost of high-quality day care and what less well-paid parents could reasonably be expected to pay.

There are a number of things that schools, too, must do to promote the minimization of gender. As Amy Gutmann has

---

[5]Much of what I suggest here is not new; it has formed part of the feminist agenda for several decades, and I first made some of the suggestions I develop here in the concluding chapter of *Women in Western Political Thought* (Princeton: Princeton University Press, 1979). Three recent books that address some of the policies discussed here are Fuchs, *Women's Quest*, chap. 7; Philip Green, *Retrieving Democracy: In Search of Civic Equality* (Totowa, NJ: Rowman and Allanheld, 1985), pp. 96–108; and Anita Shreve, *Remaking Motherhood: How Working Mothers Are Shaping Our Children's Future* (New York: Fawcet Columbine, 1987), pp. 173–78. . . .

[6]The dilemma faced by feminists in the recent California case *Guerra v. California Federal Savings and Loan Association*, 107 S. Ct. 683 (1987) was due to the fact that state law mandated leave for pregnancy and birth that it did *not* mandate for other disabling conditions. Thus to defend the law seemed to open up the dangers of discrimination that the earlier protection of women in the workplace had resulted in. (For a discussion of this general issue of equality versus difference, see, for example, Wendy W. Williams, "The Equality Crisis: Some Reflections on Culture, Courts, and Feminism." *Women's Rights Law Reporter* 7, no. 3 [1982].) The Supreme Court upheld the California law on the grounds that it treated workers equally in terms of their rights to become parents.

recently noted, in their present authority structures (84 percent of elementary school teachers are female, while 99 percent of school superintendents are male), "schools do not simply reflect, they perpetuate the social reality of gender preferences when they educate children in a system in which men rule women and women rule children." She argues that, since such sex stereotyping is "a formidable obstacle" to children's rational deliberation about the lives they wish to lead, sex should be regarded as a relevant qualification in the hiring of both teachers and administrators, until these proportions have become much more equal.[7]

An equally important role of our schools must be to ensure in the course of children's education that they become fully aware of the politics of gender. This does not only mean ensuring that women's experience and women's writing are included in the curriculum, although this in itself is undoubtedly important.[8] Its political significance has become obvious from the amount of protest that it has provoked. Children need also to be taught about the present inequalities, ambiguities, and uncertainties of marriage, the facts of workplace discrimination and segregation, and the likely consequences of making life choices based on assumptions about gender. They should be discouraged from thinking about their futures as *determined* by the sex to which they happen to belong. For many children, of course, personal experience has already "brought home"
the devastating effects of the traditional division of labor between the sexes. But they do not necessarily come away from this experience with positive ideas about how to structure their own future family lives differently. As Anita Shreve has recently suggested, "the old home-economics courses that used to teach girls how to cook and sew might give way to the new home economics: teaching girls *and boys* how to combine working and parenting."[9] Finally, schools should be required to provide high-quality after-school programs, where children can play safely, do their homework, or participate in creative activities.

The implementation of all these policies would significantly help parents to share the earning and the domestic responsibilities of their families, and children to grow up prepared for a future in which the significance of sex difference is greatly diminished. Men could participate equally in the nurturance of their children, from infancy and throughout childhood, with predictably great effects on themselves, their wives or partners, and their children. And women need not become vulnerable through economic dependence. In addition, such arrangements would alleviate the qualms many people have about the long hours that some children spend in day care. If one parent of a preschooler worked, for example, from eight to four o'clock and the other from ten to six o'clock, a preschool child would be at day care for only six hours (including nap time), and with each one or both of her or his parents the rest of the day. If each parent were able to work a six-hour day, or a four-day week, still less day care would be needed. Moreover, on-site provision of day care would enable mothers to continue to

---

[7] Amy Gutmann, *Democratic Education* (Princeton: Princeton University Press, 1987), pp. 112–15; quotation from pp. 113–14. See also Elisabeth Hansot and David Tyack, "Gender in American Public Schools: Thinking Institutionally," *Signs* 13, no. 4 (1988).

[8] A classic text on this subject is Dale Spender, ed., *Men's Studies Modified: The Impact of Feminism on the Academic Disciplines* (Oxford: Pergamon Press, 1981).

[9] Shreve, *Remaking Motherhood*, p. 237.

nurse, if they chose, beyond the time of their parental leave. . . . [10]

[M]arital separation and divorce . . . would be significantly altered in a society not structured along the lines of gender. Even if rates of divorce were to remain unchanged (which is impossible to predict), it seems inconceivable that separated and divorced fathers who had shared equally in the nurturance of their children from the outset would be as likely to neglect them, by not seeing them or not contributing to their support, as many do today. It seems reasonable to expect that children after divorce would still have two actively involved parents, and two working adults economically responsible for them. Because these parents had shared equally the paid work and the family work, their incomes would be much more equal than those of most divorcing parents today. Even if they were quite equal, however, the parent without physical custody should be required to contribute to the child's support, *to the point where the standards of living of the two households were the same.* This would be very different from the situation of many children of divorced parents today, dependent for both their nurturance and their economic support solely on mothers whose wage work has been interrupted by primary parenting.

It is impossible to predict all the effects of moving toward a society without gender. Major current injustices to women and children would end. Men would experience both the joys and the responsibilities of far closer and more sustained contact with their children than many have today. Many immensely influential spheres of life—notably politics and the professional occupations—would for the first time be populated more or less equally by men and women, most of whom were also actively participating parents. This would be in great contrast to today, when most of those who rise to influential positions are either men who, if fathers, have minimal contact with their children, or women who have either forgone motherhood altogether or hired others as full-time caretakers for their children because of the demands of their careers. These are the people who make policy at the highest levels—policies not only *about* families and their welfare and about the education of children, but about the foreign policies, the wars and the weapons that will determine the future or the lack of future for all these families and children. Yet they are almost all people who gain the influence they do in part by never having had the day-to-day experience of nurturing a child. This is probably the most significant aspect of our gendered division of labor, though the least possible to grasp. The effects of changing it could be momentous.

Protecting the Vulnerable

The pluralism of beliefs and modes of life is fundamental to our society, and the genderless society I have just outlined would certainly not be agreed upon by all as desirable. Thus when we think about constructing relations between the sexes that could be agreed upon in the original position, and are therefore just from all points of view, we must also design institutions and practices acceptable to those with more traditional beliefs about the characteristics of men and women, and the appropriate division of labor between them. It is essential, if men and women are to be allowed to so divide their labor, as they must

---

[10]Although 51 percent of infants are breast-fed at birth, only 14 percent are entirely breast-fed at six weeks of age. Cited from P. Leach, *Babyhood* (New York: Alfred A. Knopf, 1983), by Sylvia Ann Hewlett, in *A Lesser Life: The Myth of Women's Liberation in America* (New York: Morrow, 1986), p. 409n34.

be if we are to respect the current pluralism of beliefs, that society protect the vulnerable. Without such protection, the marriage contract seriously exacerbates the initial inequalities of those who entered into it, and too many women and children live perilously close to economic disaster and serious social dislocation; too many also live with violence or the continual threat of it. . . . There is no need for the division of labor between the sexes to involve the economic dependence, either complete or partial, of one partner on the other. Such dependence can be avoided if both partners have *equal legal entitlement* to all earnings coming into the household. The clearest and simplest way of doing this would be to have employers make out wage checks equally divided between the earner and the partner who provides all or most of his or her unpaid domestic services. . . .

What I am suggesting is *not* that the wage-working partner pay the homemaking partner for services rendered. I do not mean to introduce the cash nexus into a personal relationship where it is inappropriate. I have simply suggested that since both partners in a traditional or quasi-traditional marriage work, there is no reason why only one of them should get paid, or why one should be paid far more than the other. The equal splitting of wages would constitute public recognition of the fact that the currently unpaid labor of families is just as important as the paid labor. If we do *not* believe this, then we should insist on the complete and equal sharing of both paid and unpaid labor, as occurs in the genderless model of marriage and parenting described earlier. It is only if we *do* believe it that society can justly allow couples to distribute the two types of labor so unevenly. But in such cases, given the enormous significance our society attaches to money and earnings, we should insist that the earnings be recognized as equally earned by the two persons. To call on Walzer's language, we should do this in order to help prevent the inequality of family members in the sphere of wage work to invade their domestic sphere. . . .

The same fundamental principle should apply to separation and divorce, to the extent that the division of labor has been practiced within a marriage. Under current divorce laws, as we have seen, the terms of exit from marriage are disadvantageous for almost all women in traditional or quasi-traditional marriages. Regardless of the consensus that existed about the division of the family labor, these women lose most of the income that has supported them *and* the social status that attached to them because of their husband's income and employment, often at the same time as suddenly becoming single parents, and prospective wage workers for the first time in many years. This combination of prospects would seem to be enough to put most traditional wives off the idea of divorcing even if they had good cause to do so. In addition, since divorce in the great majority of states no longer requires the consent of both spouses, it seems likely that wives for whom divorce would spell economic and social catastrophe would be inhibited in voicing their dissatisfactions or needs within marriage. The terms of exit are very likely to affect the use and the power of voice in the ongoing relationship. At worst, these women may be rendered virtually defenseless in the face of physical or psychological abuse. This is not a system of marriage and divorce that could possibly be agreed to by persons in an original position in which they did not know whether they were to be male or female, traditionalist or not. It is a fraudulent contract, presented as beneficial to all but in fact to the benefit only of the more powerful.

For all these reasons, it seems essential that the terms of divorce be redrawn so as to reflect the gendered or nongendered character of the marriage that is ending, to a far greater extent than they do now.[11] The legal system of a society that allows couples to divide the labor of families in a traditional or quasi-traditional manner *must* take responsibility for the vulnerable position in which marital breakdown places the partner who has completely or partially lost the capacity to be economically self-supporting. When such a marriage ends, it seems wholly reasonable to expect a person whose career has been largely unencumbered by domestic responsibilities to support financially the partner who undertook these responsibilities. This support, in the form of combined alimony and child support, should be far more substantial than the token levels often ordered by the courts now. *Both postdivorce households should enjoy the same standard of living.* Alimony should not end after a few years, as the (patronizingly named) "rehabilitative alimony" of today does; it should continue for at least as long as the traditional division of labor in the marriage did and, in the case of short-term marriages that produced children, until the youngest child enters first grade and the custodial parent has a real chance of making his or her own living. After that point, child support should continue at a level that enables the children to enjoy a standard of living equal to that of the noncustodial parent. There can be no reason consistent with principles of justice that some should suffer economically vastly more than others from the breakup of a relationship whose asymmetric division of labor was mutually agreed on.

I have suggested two basic models of family rights and responsibilities, both of which are currently needed because this is a time of great transition for men and women and great disagreement about gender. Families in which roles and responsibilities are equally shared regardless of sex are far more in accord with principles of justice than are typical families today. So are families in which those who undertake more traditional domestic roles are protected from the risks they presently incur. In either case, justice as a whole will benefit from the changes. Of the two, however, I claim that the genderless family is more just, in the three important respects that I spelled out at the beginning of this book: it is more just to women; it is more conducive to equal opportunity both for women and for children of both sexes; and it creates a more favorable environment for the rearing of citizens of a just society. Thus, while protecting those whom gender now makes vulnerable, we must also put our best efforts into promoting the elimination of gender.

The increased justice to women that would result from moving away from gender is readily apparent. Standards for just social institutions could no longer take for granted and exclude front considerations of justice much of what women now do, since men would share in it equally. Such central components of justice as what counts as productive labor, and what count as needs and deserts, would be greatly affected by this change. Standards of justice would become *humanist,* as they have never been before. One of the most important effects of this would be to change radically the situation of women as citizens. With

---

[11]My suggestions for protecting traditional and quasi-traditional wives in the event of divorce are similar to those of Lenore Weitzman in *The Divorce Revolution: The Unexpected Social and Economic Consequences for Women and Children in America* (New York: The Free Press, 1985), chap. 11, and chap. 2. Although they would usually in practice protect traditional wives, the laws should be gender-neutral so that they would equally protect divorcing men who had undertaken the primary functions of parenting and homemaking. Mary Ann Glendon, *Abortion and Divorce in Western Law* (Cambridge, Mass.: Harvard University Press, 1987).

egalitarian families, and with institutions such as workplaces and schools designed to accommodate the needs of parents and children, rather than being based as they now are on the traditional assumption that "someone else" is at home, mothers would not be virtually excluded from positions of influence in politics and the workplace. They would be represented at every level in approximately equal numbers with men.

In a genderless society, children too would benefit. They would not suffer in the ways that they do now because of the injustices done to women. It is undeniable that the family in which each of us grows up has a deeply formative influence on us—on the kind of persons we want to be as well as the kind of persons we are.[12] This is one of the reasons why one *cannot* reasonably leave the family out of "the basic structure of society," to which the principles of justice are to apply. Equality of opportunity to become what we want to be would be enhanced in two important ways by the development of families without gender and by the public policies necessary to support their development. First, the growing gap between the economic well-being of children in single-parent and those in two-parent families would be reduced. Children in single-parent families would benefit significantly if fathers were held equally responsible for supporting their children, whether married to their mothers or not; if more mothers had sustained labor force attachment; if high-quality day care were subsidized; and if the workplace were designed to accommodate parenting. These children would be far less likely to spend their formative years in conditions of poverty, with one parent struggling to fulfill the functions of two.

Their life chances would be significantly enhanced.

Second, children of both sexes in gender-free families would have (as some already have) much more opportunity for self-development free from sex-role expectations and sex-typed personalities than most do now. Girls and boys who grow up in highly traditional families, in which sex difference is regarded as a determinant of everything from roles, responsibilities, and privileges to acceptable dress, speech, and modes of behavior, clearly have far less freedom to develop into whatever kind of person they want to be than do those who are raised without such constraints. . . .

Finally, it seems undeniable that the enhancement of justice that accompanies the disappearance of gender will make the family a much better place for children to develop a sense of justice. We can no longer deny the importance of the fact that families are where we first learn, by example and by how we are treated, not only how people do relate to each other but also how they *should*. How would families not built on gender be better schools of moral development? First, the example of co-equal parents with shared roles, combining love with justice, would provide a far better example of human relations for children than the domination and dependence that often occur in traditional marriage. The fairness of the distribution of labor, the equal respect, and the *inter*dependence of his or her parents would surely be a powerful first example to a child in a family with equally shared roles. Second, as I have argued, having a sense of justice requires that we be able to empathize, to abstract from our own situation and to think about moral and political issues from the points of view of others. We cannot come to either just principles or just specific decisions by thinking, as it were, as if we were nobody, or thinking from nowhere; we

---

[12]Here I paraphrase Rawls's wording in explaining why the basic structure of society is basic. "The Basic Structure as Subject," *American Philosophical Quarterly* 14, no. 2 (1977): 160.

must, therefore, learn to think from the point of view of others, including others who are different from ourselves.

To the extent that gender is deemphasized in our nurturing practices, this capacity would seem to be enhanced, for two reasons. First, if female primary parenting leads, as it seems to, to less distinct ego boundaries and greater capacity for empathy in female children, and to a greater tendency to self-definition and abstraction in males, then might we not expect to find the two capacities better combined in children of both sexes who are reared by parents of both sexes? Second, the experience of *being* nurturers, throughout a significant portion of our lives, also seems likely to result in an increase in empathy, and in the combination of personal moral capacities, fusing feelings with reason, that just citizens need.[13]

---

[13]See, for example, Sara Ruddick, "Maternal Thinking," *Feminist Studies* 6, no. 2 (1980); Diane Ehrensaft, "When Women and Men Mother," in *Mothering: Essays in Feminist Theory*, ed. Joyce Trebilcot (Totowa, NJ: Rowman and Allanheld, 1984); Judith Kegan Gardiner, "Self Psychology as Feminist Theory," *Signs* 12 no. 4 (1987), esp. 778–80.

ENFORCING THE DUTIES OF PARENTS

Licensing Parents

Hugh LaFollette

In this essay I shall argue that the state should require all parents to be licensed. My main goal is to demonstrate that the licensing of parents is theoretically desirable, though I shall also argue that a workable and just licensing program actually could be established.

My strategy is simple. After developing the basic rationale for the licensing of parents, I shall consider several objections to the proposal and argue that these objections fail to undermine it. I shall then isolate some striking similarities between this licensing program and our present policies on the adoption of children. If we retain these adoption policies—as we surely should—then, I argue, a general licensing program should also be established.

Finally, I shall briefly suggest that the reason many people object to licensing is that they think parents, particularly biological parents, own or have natural sovereignty over their children.

Regulating Potentially Harmful Activities

Our society normally regulates a certain range of activities; it is illegal to perform these activities unless one has received prior permission to do so. We require automobile operators to have licenses. We forbid people from practicing medicine, law, pharmacy, or psychiatry unless they have satisfied certain licensing requirements.

Society's decision to regulate just these activities is not ad hoc. The decision to restrict admission to certain vocations and to forbid some people from driving is based on an eminently plausible, though not often explicitly formulated, rationale. We require drivers to be licensed because driving an auto is an activity which is potentially harmful to others, safe performance of the activity requires a certain competence, and we have a moderately reliable procedure for determining that competence. The potential harm is obvious: incompetent drivers can and do maim and kill people. The best way we have of limiting this harm without sacrificing the benefits of automobile travel is to require that all drivers demonstrate at least minimal competence. We likewise license doctors, lawyers, and psychologists because they perform activities which can harm others. Obviously they must be proficient if they are to perform these activities properly, and we have moderately reliable procedures for determining proficiency.[1] Imagine a world in which everyone could legally drive a car, in which everyone could legally perform surgery, prescribe medications, dispense drugs, or offer legal advice. Such a world would hardly be desirable.

Consequently, any activity that is potentially harmful to others and requires certain demonstrated competence for its safe performance, is subject to regulation—that is, it is theoretically desirable that we regulate it. If we also have a reliable procedure for determining whether someone has the requisite competence, then the action is not only subject to regulation but ought, all things considered, to be regulated.

It is particularly significant that we license these hazardous activities, even though denying a license to someone can severely inconvenience and even harm that person. Furthermore, available competency tests are not 100 percent accurate. Denying someone a driver's license in our society, for example, would inconvenience that person acutely. In effect that person would be prohibited from working, shopping, or visiting in places reachable only by car. Similarly, people denied vocational licenses are inconvenienced, even devastated. We have all heard of individuals who had the "life-long dream" of becoming physicians or lawyers, yet were denied that dream. However, the realization that some people are disappointed or inconvenienced does not diminish our conviction that we must regulate occupations or activities that are potentially dangerous to others. Innocent people must be protected even if it means that others cannot pursue activities they deem highly desirable.

Furthermore, we maintain licensing procedures even though our competency tests are sometimes inaccurate. Some people competent to perform the licensed activity (for example, driving a car) will be unable to demonstrate competence (they freeze up on the driver's test). Others may be incompetent, yet pass the test (they are lucky or certain aspects of competence—for example, the sense of responsibility—are not tested). We recognize clearly—or should recognize clearly—that no test will pick out all and only competent drivers, physicians, lawyers, and so on. Mistakes are inevitable. This does not mean we should forget that innocent people may be harmed by faulty regulatory procedures. In fact, if

---

[1] "When practice of a profession or calling requires special knowledge or skill and intimately affects public health, morals, order or safety, or general welfare, legislature may prescribe reasonable qualifications for persons desiring to pursue such professions or calling and require them to demonstrate possession of such qualifications by examination on subjects with which such profession or calling has to deal as a condition precedent to right to follow that profession or calling." 50 SE 2nd 735 (1949). Also see 199 US 306, 318 (1905) and 123 US 623, 661 (1887).

the procedures are sufficiently faulty, we should cease regulating that activity entirely until more reliable tests are available. I only want to emphasize here that tests need not be perfect. Where moderately reliable tests are available, licensing procedures should be used to protect innocent people from incompetents.[2]

These general criteria for regulatory licensing can certainly be applied to parents. First, parenting is an activity potentially very harmful to children. The potential for harm is apparent: each year more than half a million children are physically abused or neglected by their parents.[3] Many millions more are psychologically abused or neglected—not given love, respect, or a sense of self-worth. The results of this maltreatment are obvious. Abused children bear the physical and psychological scars of maltreatment throughout their lives. Far too often they turn to crime.[4] They are far more likely than others to abuse their own children.[5] Even if these maltreated children never harm anyone, they will probably never be well-adjusted, happy adults. Therefore, parenting clearly satisfies the first criterion of activities subject to regulation.

The second criterion is also incontestably satisfied. A parent must be competent if he is to avoid harming his children; even greater competence is required if he is to do the "job" well. But not everyone has this minimal competence. Many people lack the knowledge needed to rear children adequately. Many others lack the requisite energy, temperament, or stability. Therefore, child-rearing manifestly satisfies both criteria of activities subject to regulation. In fact, I dare say that parenting is a paradigm of such activities since the potential for harm is so great (both in the extent of harm any one person can suffer and in the number of people potentially harmed) and the need for competence is so evident. Consequently, there is good reason to believe that all parents should be licensed. The only ways to avoid this conclusion are to deny the need for licensing *any* potentially harmful activity; to deny that I have identified the standard criteria of activities which should be regulated; to deny that parenting satisfies the standard criteria; to show that even though parenting satisfies the standard criteria there are special reasons why licensing parents is not theoretically desirable; or to show that there is no reliable and just procedure for implementing this program.

---

[2] What counts as a moderately reliable test for these purposes will vary from circumstance to circumstance. For example, if the activity could cause a relatively small amount of harm, yet regulating that activity would place extensive constraints on people regulated, then any tests should be extremely accurate. On the other hand, if the activity could be exceedingly harmful but the constraints on the regulated person are minor, then the test can be considerably less reliable.

[3] The statistics on the incidence of child abuse vary. Probably the most recent detailed study (Saad Nagi, *Child Maltreatment in the United States*, Columbia University Press, 1977) suggests that between 400,000 and 1,000,000 children are abused or neglected each year. Other experts claim the incidence is considerably higher.

[4] According to the National Committee for the Prevention of Child Abuse, more than 80 percent of incarcerated criminals were, as children, abused by their parents. In addition, a study in the *Journal of the American Medical Association* 168, no. 3: 1755–1758, reported that first-degree murderers from middle-class homes and who have "no history of addiction to drugs, alcoholism, organic disease of the brain, or epilepsy" were frequently found to have been subject to "remorseless physical brutality at the hands of the parents."

[5] "A review of the literature points out that abusive parents were raised in the same style that they have recreated in the pattern of rearing children. . . . An individual who was raised by parents who used physical force to train their children and who grew up in a violent household has had as a role model the use of force and violence as a means of family problem solving." R. J. Gelles, "Child Abuse as Psychopathology—a Sociological Critique and Reformulation," *American Journal of Orthopsychiatry* 43, no. 4 (1973): 618–19.

While developing my argument for licensing I have already identified the standard criteria for activities that should be regulated, and I have shown that they can properly be applied to parenting. One could deny the legitimacy of regulation by licensing, but in doing so one would condemn not only the regulation of parenting, but also the regulation of drivers, physicians, druggists, and doctors. Furthermore, regulation of hazardous activities appears to be a fundamental task of any stable society.

Thus only two objections remain. In the next section I shall see if there are any special reasons why licensing parents is not theoretically desirable. Then, in the following section, I shall examine several practical objections designed to demonstrate that even if licensing were theoretically desirable, it could not be justly implemented.

Theoretical Objections to Licensing

Licensing is unacceptable, someone might say, since people have a right to have children, just as they have rights to free speech and free religious expression. They do not need a license to speak freely or to worship as they wish. Why? Because they have a right to engage in these activities. Similarly, since people have a right to have children, any attempt to license parents would be unjust.

This is an important objection since many people find it plausible, if not self-evident. However, it is not as convincing as it appears. The specific rights appealed to in this analogy are not without limitations. Both slander and human sacrifice are prohibited by law; both could result from the unrestricted exercise of freedom of speech and freedom of religion. Thus, even if people have these rights, they may sometimes be limited in order to protect innocent people. Consequently, even if people had a right to have children, that right might also be limited in order to protect innocent people, in this case children. Secondly, the phrase "right to have children" is ambiguous; hence, it is important to isolate its most plausible meaning in this context. Two possible interpretations are not credible and can be dismissed summarily. It is implausible to claim either that infertile people have rights to be *given* children or that people have rights to intentionally create children biologically without incurring any subsequent responsibility to them.

A third interpretation, however, is more plausible, particularly when coupled with observations about the degree of intrusion into one's life that the licensing scheme represents. On this interpretation people have a right to rear children if they make good-faith efforts to rear procreated children the best way they see fit. One might defend this claim on the ground that licensing would require too much intrusion into the lives of sincere applicants.

Undoubtedly one should be wary of unnecessary governmental intervention into individuals' lives. In this case, though, the intrusion would not often be substantial, and when it is, it would be warranted. Those granted licenses would face merely minor intervention; only those denied licenses would encounter marked intrusion. This encroachment, however, is a necessary side-effect of licensing parents—just as it is for automobile and vocational licensing. In addition, as I shall argue in more detail later, the degree of intrusion arising from a general licensing program would be no more than, and probably less than, the present (and presumably justifiable) encroachment into the lives of people who apply to adopt children. Furthermore, since some people hold unacceptable views about what is best for children (they think children should be abused regularly), people do not automatically have rights to rear children just because they will rear them in a way they deem appropriate.[6]

Consequently, we come to a somewhat weaker interpretation of this right claim: a person has a right to rear children if he meets certain minimal standards of child rearing. Parents must not abuse or neglect their children and must also provide for the basic needs of the children. This claim of right is certainly more credible than the previously canvassed alternatives, though some people might still reject this claim in situations where exercise of the right would lead to negative consequences, for example, to overpopulation. More to the point, though, this conditional right is compatible with licensing. On this interpretation one has a right to have children only if one is not going to abuse or neglect them. Of course the very purpose of licensing is just to determine whether people *are* going to abuse or neglect their children. If the determination is made that someone will maltreat children, then that person is subject to the limitations of the right to have children and can legitimately be denied a parenting license.

In fact, this conditional way of formulating the right to have children provides a model for formulating all alleged rights to engage in hazardous activities. Consider, for example, the right to drive a car. People do not have an unconditional right to drive, although they do have a right to drive if they are competent. Similarly, people do not have an unconditional right to practice medicine; they have a right only if they are demonstrably competent. Hence, denying a driver's or physician's license to someone who has not demonstrated the requisite competence does not deny that person's rights. Likewise, on this model, denying a parenting license to someone who is not competent does not violate that person's rights.

Of course someone might object that the right is conditional on actually being a person who will abuse or neglect children, whereas my proposal only picks out those we can reasonably predict will abuse children. Hence, this conditional right *would* be incompatible with licensing.

There are two ways to interpret this objection and it is important to distinguish these divergent formulations. First, the objection could be a way of questioning our ability to predict reasonably and accurately whether people would maltreat their own children. This is an important practical objection, but I will defer discussion of it until the next section. Second, this objection could be a way of expressing doubt about the moral propriety of the prior restraint licensing requires. A parental licensing program would deny licenses to applicants judged to be incompetent even though they had never maltreated any children. This practice would be in tension with our normal skepticism about the propriety of prior restraint.

Despite this healthy skepticism, we do sometimes use prior restraint. In extreme circumstances we may hospitalize or imprison people judged insane, even though they are not legally guilty of any crime, simply because we predict they are likely to harm others. More typically, though, prior restraint is used only if the restriction is not terribly onerous and the restricted activity is one which could lead easily to serious harm. Most types of licensing (for example, those for doctors, drivers, and druggists) fall into this latter category. They require prior restraint to prevent serious harm, and generally the

---

[6]Some people might question if any parents actually believe they should beat their children. However, that does appear to be the sincere view of many abusing parents. See, for example, case descriptions in *A Silent Tragedy* by Peter and Judith DeCourcy (Sherman Oaks, CA.: Alfred Publishing Co., 1973).

restraint is minor—though it is important to remember that some individuals will find it oppressive. The same is true of parental licensing. The purpose of licensing is to prevent serious harm to children. Moreover, the prior restraint required by licensing would not be terribly onerous for many people. Certainly the restraint would be far less extensive than the presumably justifiable prior restraint of, say, insane criminals. Criminals preventively detained and mentally ill people forcibly hospitalized are denied most basic liberties, while those denied parental licenses would be denied only that one specific opportunity. They could still vote, work for political candidates, speak on controversial topics, and so on. Doubtless some individuals would find the restraint onerous. But when compared to other types of restraint currently practiced, and when judged in light of the severity of harm maltreated children suffer, the restraint appears *relatively* minor.

Furthermore, we could make certain, as we do with most licensing programs, that individuals denied licenses are given the opportunity to reapply easily and repeatedly for a license. Thus, many people correctly denied licenses (because they are incompetent) would choose (perhaps it would be provided) to take counseling or therapy to improve their chances of passing the next test. On the other hand, most of those mistakenly denied licenses would probably be able to demonstrate in a later test that they would be competent parents.

Consequently, even though one needs to be wary of prior restraint, if the potential for harm is great and the restraint is minor relative to the harm we are trying to prevent—as it would be with parental licensing—then such restraint is justified. This objection, like all the theoretical objections reviewed, has failed.

Practical Objections to Licensing

I shall now consider five practical objections to licensing. Each objection focuses on the problems or difficulties of implementing this proposal. According to these objections, licensing is (or may be) theoretically desirable; nevertheless, it cannot be efficiently and justly implemented.

The first objection is that there may not be, or we may not be able to discover, adequate criteria of "a good parent." We simply do not have the knowledge, and it is unlikely that we could ever obtain the knowledge, that would enable us to distinguish adequate from inadequate parents.

Clearly there is some force to this objection. It is highly improbable that we can formulate criteria that would distinguish precisely between good and less than good parents. There is too much we do not know about child development and adult psychology. My proposal, however, does not demand that we make these fine distinctions. It does not demand that we license only the best parents; rather it is designed to exclude only the very bad ones.[7] This is not just a semantic difference, but a substantive one. Although we do not have infallible criteria for picking out good parents, we undoubtedly can identify bad ones—those who will abuse or neglect their children. Even though we could have a lively debate about the range of freedom a child should be given or the appropriateness of corporal punishment, we do not wonder if a parent who severely beats or neglects a child is

---

[7] I suppose I might be for licensing only good parents if I knew there were reasonable criteria and some plausible way of deciding if a potential parent satisfied these criteria. However, since I don't think we have those criteria or that method, nor can I seriously envision that we will discover those criteria and that method, I haven't seriously entertained the stronger proposal.

adequate. We know that person isn't. Consequently, we do have reliable and usable criteria for determining who is a bad parent; we have the criteria necessary to make a licensing program work.

The second practical objection to licensing is that there is no reliable way to predict who will maltreat their children. Without an accurate predictive test, licensing would be not only unjust, but also a waste of time. Now I recognize that as a philosopher (and not a psychologist, sociologist, or social worker), I am on shaky ground if I make sweeping claims about the present or future abilities of professionals to produce such predictive tests. Nevertheless, there are some relevant observations I can offer.

Initially, we need to be certain that the demands on predictive tests are not unreasonable. For example, it would be improper to require that tests be 100 percent accurate. Procedures for licensing drivers, physicians, lawyers, druggists, etc., plainly are not 100 percent (or anywhere near 100 percent) accurate. Presumably we recognize these deficiencies yet embrace the procedures anyway. Consequently, it would be imprudent to demand considerably more exacting standards for the tests used in licensing parents.

In addition, from what I can piece together, the practical possibilities for constructing a reliable predictive test are not all that gloomy. Since my proposal does not require that we make fine line distinctions between good and less than good parents, but rather that we weed out those who are potentially very bad, we can use existing tests that claim to isolate relevant predictive characteristics—whether a person is violence-prone, easily frustrated, or unduly self-centered. In fact, researchers at Nashville General Hospital have developed a brief interview questionnaire which seems to have significant predictive value.

Based on their data, the researchers identified 20 percent of the interviewees as a "risk group"—those having great potential for serious problems. After one year they found "the incidence of major breakdown in parent-child interaction in the risk group was approximately four to five times as great as in the low risk group."[8] We also know that parents who maltreat children often have certain identifiable experiences, for example, most of them were themselves maltreated as children. Consequently, if we combined our information about these parents with certain psychological test results, we would probably be able to predict with reasonable accuracy which people will maltreat their children.

However, my point is not to argue about the precise reliability of present tests. I cannot say emphatically that we now have accurate predictive tests. Nevertheless, even if such tests are not available, we could undoubtedly develop them. For example, we could begin a longitudinal study in which all potential parents would be required to take a specified battery of tests. Then these parents could be "followed" to discover which ones abused or neglected their children. By correlating test scores with information on maltreatment, a usable, accurate test could be fashioned. Therefore, I do not think that the present unavailability of such tests (if they are unavailable) would count against the legitimacy of licensing parents.

The third practical objection is that even if a reliable test for ascertaining who would

---

[8]The research gathered by Altemeir was reported by Ray Helfer in "Review of the Concepts and a Sampling of the Research Relating to Screening for the Potential to Abuse and/or Neglect One's Child." Helfer's paper was presented at a workshop sponsored by the National Committee for the Prevention of Child Abuse, 3–6 December 1978.

be an acceptable parent were available, administrators would unintentionally misuse that test. These unintentional mistakes would clearly harm innocent individuals. Therefore, so the argument goes, this proposal ought to be scrapped. This objection can be dispensed with fairly easily unless one assumes there is some special reason to believe that more mistakes will be made in administering parenting licenses than in other regulatory activities. No matter how reliable our proceedings are, there will always be mistakes. We may license a physician who, through incompetence, would cause the death of a patient; or we may mistakenly deny a physician's license to someone who would be competent. But the fact that mistakes are made does not and should not lead us to abandon attempts to determine competence. The harm done in these cases could be far worse than the harm of mistakenly denying a person a parenting license. As far as I can tell, there is no reason to believe that more mistakes will be made here than elsewhere.

The fourth proposed practical objection claims that any testing procedure will be intentionally abused. People administering the process will disqualify people they dislike, or people who espouse views they dislike, from rearing children.

The response to this objection is parallel to the response to the previous objection, namely, that there is no reason to believe that the licensing of parents is more likely to be abused than driver's license tests or other regulatory procedures. In addition, individuals can be protected from prejudicial treatment by pursuing appeals available to them. Since the licensing test can be taken on numerous occasions, the likelihood of the applicant's working with different administrative personnel increases and therefore the likelihood decreases that intentional abuse could ultimately stop a qualified person from rearing children. Consequently, since the probability of such abuse is not more than, and may even be less than, the intentional abuse of judicial and other regulatory authority, this objection does not give us any reason to reject the licensing of parents.

The fifth objection is that we could never adequately, reasonably, and fairly enforce such a program. That is, even if we could establish a reasonable and fair way of determining which people would be inadequate parents, it would be difficult, if not impossible, to enforce the program. How would one deal with violators and what could we do with babies so conceived? There are difficult problems here, no doubt, but they are not insurmountable. We might not punish parents at all—we might just remove the children and put them up for adoption. However, even if we are presently uncertain about the precise way to establish a just and effective form of enforcement, I do not see why this should undermine my licensing proposal. If it is important enough to protect children from being maltreated by parents, then surely a reasonable enforcement procedure can be secured. At least we should assume one can be unless someone shows that it cannot.

An Analogy with Adoption

So far I have argued that parents should be licensed. Undoubtedly many readers find this claim extremely radical. It is revealing to notice, however, that this program is not as radical as it seems. Our moral and legal systems already recognize that not everyone is capable of rearing children well. In fact, well-entrenched laws require adoptive parents to be investigated—in much the same ways and for much the same reasons as in the general licensing program advocated here. For example, we do not allow just anyone to adopt a child; nor do we let someone adopt without first estimating the likelihood of the person's being a good parent. In fact, the adoptive process is far more rigorous than the general licensing procedures I envision. Prior to adoption the candidates must first formally apply to adopt a child. The applicants are then subjected to an exacting home study to determine whether they really want to have children and whether they are capable of caring for and rearing them adequately. No one is allowed to adopt a child until the administrators can reasonably predict that the person will be an adequate parent. The results of these procedures are impressive. Despite the trauma children often face before they are finally adopted, they are five times less likely to be abused than children reared by their biological parents.[9]

Nevertheless we recognize, or should recognize, that these demanding procedures exclude some people who would be adequate parents. The selection criteria may be inadequate; the testing procedures may be somewhat unreliable. We may make mistakes. Probably there is some intentional abuse of the system. Adoption procedures intrude directly in the applicants' lives. Yet we continue the present adoption policies because we think it better to mistakenly deny some people the opportunity to adopt than to let just anyone adopt.

Once these features of our adoption policies are clearly identified, it becomes quite apparent that there are striking parallels between the general licensing program I have advocated and our present adoption system. Both programs have the same aim—protecting children. Both have the same drawbacks and are subject to the same abuses. The only obvious dissimilarity is that the adoption requirements are *more* rigorous than those proposed for the general licensing program. Consequently, if we think it is so important to protect adopted children, even though people who want to adopt are less likely than biological parents to maltreat their children, then we should likewise afford the same protection to children reared by their biological parents.

I suspect, though, that many people will think the cases are not analogous. The cases are relevantly different, someone might retort, because biological parents have a natural affection for their children and the strength of this affection makes it unlikely that parents would maltreat their biologically produced children.

Even if it were generally true that parents have special natural affections for their biological offspring, that does not mean that all parents have enough affection to keep them from maltreating their children. This should be apparent given the number of children abused each year by their biological parents. Therefore, even if there is generally such a bond, that does not explain why we should not have licensing procedures to protect children of parents who do not have a sufficiently strong bond. Consequently, if we continue our practice of

---

[9]According to a study published by the Child Welfare League of America, at least 51 percent of the adopted children had suffered, prior to adoption, more than minimal emotional deprivation. See *A Follow-up Study of Adoptions: Post Placement Functioning of Adoption Families*, Elizabeth A. Lawder et al., New York 1969.

According to a study by David Gil (*Violence Against Children*, Cambridge: Harvard University Press, 1970) only .4 percent of abused children were abused by adoptive parents. Since at least 2 percent of the children in the United States are adopted (*Encyclopedia of Social Work*, National Association of Social Workers, New York, 1977), that means the rate of abuse by biological parents is five times that of adoptive parents.

regulating the adoption of children, and certainly we should, we are rationally compelled to establish a licensing program for all parents.

However, I am not wedded to a strict form of licensing. It may well be that there are alternative ways of regulating parents which would achieve the desired results—the protection of children—without strictly prohibiting nonlicensed people from rearing children. For example, a system of tax incentives for licensed parents, and protective services scrutiny of nonlicensed parents, might adequately protect children. If it would, I would endorse the less drastic measure. My principal concern is to protect children from maltreatment by parents. I begin by advocating the more strict form of licensing since that is the standard method of regulating hazardous activities.

I have argued that all parents should be licensed by the state. This licensing program is attractive, not because state intrusion is inherently judicious and efficacious, but simply because it seems to be the best way to prevent children from being reared by incompetent parents. Nonetheless, even after considering the previous arguments, many people will find the proposal a useless academic exercise, probably silly, and possibly even morally perverse. But why? Why do most of us find this proposal unpalatable, particularly when the arguments supporting it are good and the objections to it are philosophically flimsy?

I suspect the answer is found in a long-held, deeply ingrained attitude toward children, repeatedly reaffirmed in recent court decisions, and present, at least to some degree, in almost all of us. The belief is that parents own, or at least have natural sovereignty over, their children.[10] It does not matter precisely how this belief is described, since on both views parents legitimately exercise extensive and virtually unlimited control over their children. Others can properly interfere with or criticize parental decisions only in unusual and tightly prescribed circumstances—for example, when parents severely and repeatedly abuse their children. In all other cases, the parents reign supreme.

This belief is abhorrent and needs to be supplanted with a more child-centered view. Why? Briefly put, this attitude has adverse effects on children and on the adults these children will become. Parents who hold this view may well maltreat their children. If these parents happen to treat their children well, it is only because they want to, not because they think their children deserve or have a right to good treatment. Moreover, this belief is manifestly at odds with the conviction that parents should prepare children for life as adults. Children subject to parents who perceive children in this way are [un]likely to be adequately

---

[10]We can see this belief in a court case chronicled by DeCourcy and DeCourcy in *A Silent Tragedy*. The judge ruled that three children, severely and regularly beaten, burned, and cut by their father, should be placed back with their father since he was only "trying to do what is right." If the court did not adopt this belief would it even be tempted to so excuse such abusive behavior? This attitude also emerges in the all-too-frequent court rulings (see S. Katz, *When Parents Fail*, Boston: Beacon Press, 1971) giving custody of children back to their biological parents even though the parents had abandoned them for years, and even though the children expressed a strong desire to stay with foster parents.

In "The Child, the Law, and the State" (*Children's Rights: Toward the Liberation of the Child*, Leila Berg et al., New York: Praeger Publishers, 1971), Nan Berger persuasively argues that our adoption and foster care laws are comprehensible only if children are regarded as the property of their parents.

prepared for adulthood. Hence, to prepare children for life as adults and to protect them from maltreatment, this attitude toward children must be dislodged. As I have argued, licensing is a viable way to protect children. Furthermore, it would increase the likelihood that more children will be adequately prepared for life as adults than is now the case.

For helpful comments and criticisms, I am indebted to Jeffrey Gold, Chris Hackler, James Rachels, and especially to William Aiken, George Graham, and the Editors of the journal. A somewhat different version of this essay will appear in the Proceeding of the Loyola University (Chicago) Symposium, *Justice for the Child within the Family Context*.

Thanks are due to the directors of the symposium for kind permission to publish the essay in *Philosophy & Public Affairs*.

PROTECTING THE RIGHTS OF CHILDREN

Obedience and Illusions

Michael A. Slote

1. Obligations to Obey

Not long ago, the following reasoning would to many people have seemed compelling, if not inescapable:

> We are all God's children. He has done for us what parents do for their children: created us and given us all we have. We owe Him a debt of gratitude of the kind children owe to (good) parents, and therefore owe Him the kind of obedience children owe to parents.

Today, most of us live in a world where reasoning like this has lost its power to persuade. Has the widespread loss of belief in God made the difference? In some measure, perhaps. But I think the change is also largely the result of the way our thoughts about childhood have matured. I shall spend much of this paper explaining the implications and significance of this last remark. I shall talk about authority and childhood, about divine authority and the important ways it resembles parental authority. Although I shall in no way be attacking religion or theism per se, I shall argue that both divine authority and parental authority are underlaid by illusions that must be shed in order to complete the process of growing up, and that the very knowledge that this is so is part of the ongoing maturation of our culture and ourselves.

The argument given at the beginning of the paper can be "stood on its head" in two different ways. First, it can be used to prove the very opposite of what it purports to prove. To many of us, it seems obvious that children have no *obligation* to obey their parents, any more than they have duties of *filial piety*. So any force there is to the analogy between God's creation and parental begetting can, for modern ways of seeing, tend to show that we have no duty to obey God, if He exists.

Moreover, one can reach this conclusion without necessarily holding that children have *no* obligations, owe *nothing*, to their parents. It may well be that good parents are owed a debt of gratitude—though the notion of "debt" here is probably somewhat loose and metaphorical, since it is difficult to believe that one has any moral *duty* to show gratitude for benefits one has not requested. Perhaps children also have a moral obligation to care for their parents when they become sick or infirm. But in neither case does anything seem to follow about debts or duties of obedience. If a stranger, unasked, gives me the money for a college education, I at most owe him a debt of gratitude, not of obedience. And why should it be any different with parents?

Furthermore, it seems entirely gratuitous to suppose that *very young children* have any moral obligations at all, even to their parents. Such obligations, it would seem, exist, if at all, only when moral concepts are firmly implanted. But, on the other hand, if we think of older children—say, adolescents—duties of obedience seem to vanish in another direction. Young children seem to be too young to have any *obligations* or *duties* of obedience or anything else. But older children, precisely because they are more mature, seem to possess a right to determine for themselves how they should live, and this seems to undermine any duty of *obedience* to parents. After reaching a certain age, children, e.g., on a family farm may have duties of cooperation; at least, they have no right to a share of the farm produce unless they cooperate. And such cooperation may entail doing what their more knowledgeable parents tell them to do. But it is unlikely that this constitutes any duty of obedience. Even if the child has a duty to cooperate, and cooperation, in a particular instance, requires doing what a more knowledgeable parent says to do, it does not follow that the child has any general obligation to follow parental instructions or any duty to *obey* his parents in the particular instance.

In addition, I have emphasized that the obligation to cooperate exists, if at all, only to the degree that the older child wants or demands some share in the goods produced by the family. There is, I think, no duty of fair play that requires him to stay with the family and share in its life and benefits because of his parents' past beneficence. The duty of fair play presumably exists only where benefits are voluntarily accepted within a cooperative scheme, and we can hardly suppose that a child has voluntarily accepted his role in (the cooperative scheme of) family life. The (older) child, then, may always opt out of his whole family situation, and we have, in all, found no reason to believe that any child has a duty to obey his parents.

The reasoning at the beginning of this paper needs to be stood on its head in another sense, because it implies an inverted picture of the nature and causality of parental and divine authority. It implies that our acknowledgement of or submission to parental (or divine) authority is (often) powered by our sense of the moral validity of such authority, and just the reverse seems to me to be the case. I believe that moral arguments for duties of obedience to authority are typically epiphenomena: secondary rationalizations of deeper feelings, habits, and (illusory) ideas connected with authority. People do not submit to authority because they recognize a duty to do so on the basis of abstract moral reasoning. Rather, they are, first, under the yoke or such authority—in certain matters feeling, for example, that they have no choice but to do what God or their parents tell them—and only then, or on that basis, make an intellectual accommodation with that authority.

I shall now argue that we are faced with (at least) two levels of illusion when we consider the nature of authority. Submission to authority, by its very nature, involves certain illusions about matters other than the nature of authority itself. However, such submission also typically gives rise to ideological support and reinforcement for the first illusions in the form of illusions *about what authority is,* and the illusion that parental authority (causally) derives from a moral sense of its legitimacy is a good example of such derivative "ideology of authority." We need to understand both these levels of illusion and their modes of interaction.

2. Illusions of Authority

Most parents have some legal authority over their children, but they almost always also have that "aura" of authority that makes their children accept most of their dictates unquestioningly. It is this sort of submission to parental authority that I mean to refer to when I speak hereafter of parental authority, and I believe that parental authority, in this sense, is closely related to the acceptance of divine authority by the devoutly religious.

When people submit to divine authority, they seem to think that they have no choice but to obey God. And I believe that when a devout person, confronted by what he takes to be God's will, thinks, "I have no choice in the matter," he represents himself as a mere object that lacks choice and will altogether—a mere instrument of divine purposes. No doubt, it will immediately be replied that in thinking this way, a devout person may simply be using a harmless metaphor and thus be under no illusion about what he is. But the devout person who thinks or says this sort of thing is typically not, at that moment, clear in his own mind about the merely metaphorical nature of his utterance. If my wife wants me to stay in bed in the morning, and I tell her, "I have no choice in the matter; I have to get to work," I speak in all *seriousness* and in order to *justify* my departure. I need to be *reminded* that what I am saying is not literally true, and am not, therefore, like someone who says that his wife has a heart of gold and never suffers any initial unclarity or confusion about the literal falsity of what he says. Similarly, I think someone who believes he has no choice once God has spoken is not, at least initially, as clear in his own mind about the literal falsity of what he says as is the person who says his wife has a heart of gold. And this gives us at least some reason to claim that religious people, at some point and at some level, actually imagine they lack choice and are mere instruments or things. I think, moreover, that having such illusory thoughts is part of what it is fully to accept God's authority. To see clearly that one has a choice—perhaps a coerced and threatened choice, but a choice, nonetheless—about whether to do as God asks is precisely *not* to submit to divine authority in the manner of the devout.

Important additional evidence for the existence of these illusions comes from the fact that someone who submits to divine authority invariably feels that the presence of God in the universe makes an automatic and total difference to his life and its meaning. The difference he supposes God to make does not seem to consist *merely* in the fact that if God exists, there is a totally wise and good being in the world from whom one can learn; nor can it simply involve God's ability to get us to do what He wants or to impose dire punishments if we do not. And it is very difficult to explain why so many religious people think God makes a total difference to life and its meaning. But we *can* explain this belief if we say that those who hold it are under the illusions we have discussed. For if we are choiceless things because of God's presence in the universe, then that presence clearly does make a total difference to one's life, since it in effect destroys human life and replaces it with the existence of a mere thing. If, by virtue of the divine presence, we are mere instruments of God's purposes, then our lives have no meaning (of their own), and surely it makes a total difference to the meaning of a human life whether that life has or lacks meaning (of its own).[1]

What we have just said about submission to divine authority carries over, in great part, to the authority of parents. I think that children, like the devout, feel their submission to their parents as a loss of will. The child under effective parental authority feels that he has no choice or will of his own in certain matters where his parents have prescribed. And there is every reason to believe that if devout people are under illusions about whether they have choice and wills (or purposes) of their own, children who accept parental authority are under similar illusions. I shall now attempt to explain why children come to have such illusions of choicelessness and willlessness.

Many things can stand in the way of a child's development of autonomy. To learn to think and act for himself, he must also, along the way, rely heavily on his parents or parental substitutes: he must take some things for granted. The child is thus subject to a number of conflicting pressures. He seeks autonomy and is constantly tugging against parental bonds, and yet he needs his parents and has to depend on them for many things. And even as far as the drive for autonomy itself is concerned, parents represent both opportunity and threat. They themselves subject the child to conflicting pressures, wanting the child to grow up and mature, but almost always also seeking to impose more intellectual, moral and emotional baggage on the child than he needs to make his own way in the world.

But parents are not the only threat to a child's developing autonomy. Autonomy has its own risks, anxieties, and frustrations, and these can frighten a child and cause him to regress into dependency. Such a child may then desire to be taken care of again like an infant, to have others make his choices, to lose autonomy. Alternatively, if the parents themselves seek to block the child's autonomy with prohibitions, threats, or hostile accusations of ingratitude, the child may become panicky about the impending loss of his autonomy. And rather than fight his parents, who may seem practically omnipotent in his eyes, he may acquiesce in their domination. Faced with a losing battle, the child may try, defensively, to convince himself that he really didn't want to be autonomous in the first place. Or he may reason that he really has nothing to lose from his parents' domination because he has, in fact, no will of his own to

---

[1] Of course, in using this explanation, we assume that the belief that God can or does make an automatic total difference to our lives is as illusory as the beliefs that explain it. But I think it is impossible to specify a way in which God actually could make an automatic total difference to human life and its meaning; let the reader try for himself, if he will. So, I think the religious assumption that God can make such a difference is as illusory as the assumptions about choicelessness, etc., that are needed to explain it.

Perhaps the first philosopher to hold that submission to authority involves illusions was Sartre in *Being and Nothingness* and in his play "The Flies." But Sartre's conception of the content of those illusions differs considerably from what I have been saying here and is open to serious criticism. (On this, see my "Existentialism and the Fear of Dying," *American Philosophical Quarterly* 12 (1975) p. 27.) Most significantly of all, perhaps, Sartre does not see that the illusory religious belief that God can make a total difference provides some of the best evidence for the illusory character of submission to divine, or parental, authority. (In fact, in his essay "Existentialism is a Humanism," Sartre comes close to *endorsing* the idea that God makes a total difference to human life.)

be thwarted. He may welcome the loss of autonomy or imagine he never had any autonomy that could be taken away, in order to console himself for, or reconcile himself to, the loss he so greatly fears. That fear is not so much destroyed by these devices as kept out of direct awareness.

Such phenomena are not psychologically, atypical or rare. It is, for example, a truism of psychiatry and a fact ordinary people are commonly aware of that an overwhelming anxiety in the face of impending death may give rise to the defensive thought-feeling that one doesn't really care if one dies, or even that one welcomes death. Similarly, when things take a dramatic turn *for the better,* people often say: I must be dreaming all this. And the explanation is fairly obvious. One tries to convince oneself that it is all a dream, and thus, that one has nothing to lose, in order to counteract and submerge one's fears of losing what one has suddenly gained and to soften the blow if one *does* lose it. And this is very close to what happens when a child who faces a loss of autonomy imagines he has no will of his own.

I think, then, that when children accept parental authority without question, even after they have arrived at a stage where they desire considerable autonomy for themselves, a kind of regression has occurred as a means of alleviating anxiety—anxiety at the frustrations of autonomy itself, anxiety over parental attempts to thwart the child's desires for autonomy, and perhaps other forms of anxiety as well. This regression involves an attempt to retreat to the stage of infancy where decisions were made for one and life was a blissful ease of dependency.[2] And to do this, one erects psychic structures of indifference to the loss of autonomy, either welcoming the loss one thinks will occur or denying that there is anything to lose. The acceptance of parental authority in such circumstances, then, is an easy retreat from threats and frustration, but it involves the illusion that one has no choice or will of one's own, a repudiation of one's real and persisting desires to be autonomous, and a certain amount of internal conflict as a result.

What I have just said, moreover, indicates that the threat power of parents lies behind, even if it is not the same as, their authority. It is their power to circumvent or coerce the child's will, their power to deprive it of the autonomy it seeks, that sends some children scurrying into the defenses and illusions that constitute submission to parental authority.[3] So, we must contrast living in fear of parental attempts to limit one's autonomy, which may involve no illusions at all, with submitting to those attempts, or to parental authority, which does. Since, in addition, the illusions involved in acquiescing in parental authority are part of the way children cope with and allay powerful anxieties, we should expect that they would resist exposure. To see that they were illusions would be to become

---

[2] It is conventional psychiatric wisdom that if one's infancy was *not* very happy or tranquil, one will seek to regress to infancy when life is frustrating, in order to *make up for,* or *overcome,* that earlier lack of satisfaction.

[3] Submission to authority need not, I think, imply that there *is* an authority to whom one submits. However, it is not clear whether we should want to say that parents *lack* the authority that children attribute to them because they cannot take away their children's choice in the way children imagine: or whether we should not, instead, say that parents *have* authority over submissive children because to have authority is just to be in a position where others have certain habits and illusions. But whatever we decide to say about this question, we needn't conclude that there is any *validity* to parental authority of the kind we are focusing on. Authority cannot, I think, be valid when it *has to be* based on false beliefs or illusions. Cf. my "Morality and Ignorance," *Journal of Philosophy,* LXXIV (1977), pp. 745–767, for a lengthy elaboration of this and related themes.

partly free of them and thus no longer able to "use" them as part of one's psychological defenses. To protect the illusions involved in submission to authority, people often develop complicated and clever secondary rationalizations of such authority. This is the derivative "ideology of authority" I mentioned earlier. The illusions of authority can be defended from discovery and preserved by means of a distorted intellectual picture of what submission to authority actually is. One will, for example, moralize about authority using the reasoning at the beginning of this paper. One will somehow be convinced that it is morality, and the rational acknowledgment of moral requirements, that powers one's submission to parental authority. So, the illusions intrinsic to authority naturally give rise to illusions *about* (submission to) authority—illusions that, in effect, deny the illusory character that submission to authority actually has. And these illusions about illusions serve to perpetuate the illusions they are about.[4]

3. Being Adult

What can we conclude from the fact that people so often seek an authority that involves illusions? To begin with, it may well be true that children in some measure *need* to submit to parental authority during childhood if they are later to have successful or satisfying adult lives. Perhaps the illusions of authority are "noble lies" of childhood, and it is good for children to believe such lies the way it is good for them to believe the fairy tales they hear.

But even if we need to have illusions about parental authority as children, it hardly seems likely that we are better off having such illusions when we become older. I have said that the child who submits to parental authority out of fear of parental threats to his autonomy is in a state of conflict. He retreats into dependence on his parents, yet never really loses his desire for autonomy; so, he both needs and resents his parents. He will not show that resentment for fear of retaliation, and if his parents continue to impose upon him well into adulthood, he may never get over his fearful submission to them. He will then frequently become the kind of parent his parents were to him—displaying to his children an aggression he could never vent against his parents. The "authoritarian personality" that often develops with submission to parental authority tends to perpetuate itself, generation after generation, and what is most clear about such continuing cycles of submission and domination is that *no one* has grown up completely. The dominating authoritarian parent acts as he does as a result of his own illusory and childish submissiveness to his parents. To become fully an adult, one has to cease submitting to the authority of one's parents—to become one's own parent, as it is said—and gain that autonomy that parents who seek to impose authority on a child may *seem to have* and that children themselves seek, but often permanently give away, before fully attaining it. If what I have been saying here is correct, the person who gains such autonomy will have to free himself from

---
[4] In many ways, my account of the desire for autonomy and of the ways we regress into dependency when it is threatened derives from Erich Fromm's *Escape from Freedom* (New York: Holt, 1941). But, more in the manner of Sartre, I have emphasized the illusions of authority. And Fromm not only ignores this aspect of authority but sometimes seems *himself* to fall under some of the illusions of authority I have described. He often says that when we submit to authority, we give up our freedom and individuality. And he speaks of both the annihilation and the loss of the self, in this connection. (See *Escape from Freedom*, pp. 140f., 154f., 185f., 206.) At the very least, he does not distinguish clearly enough between the *illusion* that we have no self or will of our own, an illusion involved in submitting to authority, and the (impossible) state of affairs that that illusion is *about*.

various illusions of authority, and from the inordinate fear of his parents that results in defensive submission to their authority and in internal conflicts between a desire for autonomy and a desire for dependence. That person will unequivocally accept his autonomy despite its risks and frustrations, and he fulfills (a great part of) my idea of what it is to be, morally speaking, an adult.[5]

Finally, I think that our culture has itself grown up to the degree that it has freed itself from various illusions of authority. There is evidence of this maturation, for example, in the present powerlessness of the argument with which we began. That we no longer see any need to believe in the child's moral obligation to obey his parents shows, it seems to me, that our culture no longer encourages as much submission to parental authority as it used to. Some of the illusions of parental authority are now harder to foster and maintain. Perhaps the development and spread of political democracy has aided the discovery of the illusions of parental and divine authority. When the authority of kings came into question, it perhaps became easier to recognize the illusions, rationalizations, and conflicts inherent in other kinds of submission to authority. I hope, however, that I am under no illusions about the "progress" that has been made in discarding the illusions connected with authority. I do not doubt that the insights that have been developed are very frail reeds, pawns to future history and to the very needs and fears that so often give rise to submission to authority. I do not, then, believe that further progress in this area is inevitable, and sadly enough, it seems quite possible that our insight into the illusions of authority and our greater present freedom from submission to authority should someday, somehow, be lost.[6]

Questions for Further Reflection

1. Scruton suggests that the contractual account of marital obligations is inadequate because we cannot foresee, and make provision for, all the various things that will happen to us. Is this a good argument? Could one make the same sort of argument against other sorts of contracts, for example, a contract to buy a house? If not, why not?

2. Another argument Scruton offers against the contractual account is that the survival of marriage requires public recognition of the institution, and this in turn requires that the institution be the same for all. Is he right about this?

3. Okin recommends that employers of members of gendered marriages pay both marriage partners equally. On the other hand, in gender-neutral marriages, each partner would be paid by his or her employer in the normal way. What practical problems might face such a proposal, and how might they be addressed? (For instance, what about marriages in which one partner provides most of the domestic services but also works full- or part-time?)

4. On the proposal to split earnings, it seems that a working person with a nonworking spouse will make half as much money for the same job as either an unmarried person or one married to a working spouse. Is this fair?

---

[5]To the degree, moreover, that submission to divine authority—as opposed to simple belief in or fear of God—involves similar illusions, resentments, and conflicts, adulthood may be incompatible with religious submissiveness of the sort I have been describing.

[6]I am indebted to Arthur Fine, the editors of [*Having Children: Philosophical and Legal Reflections on Parenthood*], and especially, Hans Kleinschmidt and David Levin, for helpful criticisms and suggestions.

5. Evaluate Okin's proposal that, in gendered marriages, alimony and child-support levels should guarantee that "both postdivorce households should enjoy the same standard of living."
6. LaFollette proposes denying a parenting license to people who, according to a test of some sort, seem likely to be abusive parents. The test need not be, he suggests, perfectly reliable, since we do not require perfect reliability of tests in comparable cases, for example, driving tests or bar exams. But are these cases really analogous? Parenthood is more important to many people than driving a car or being a physician. Does this mean that the need for reliability is more crucial?
7. LaFollette does not discuss a number of issues about the implementation of his proposal. It may be worth considering, for example, what happens if one member of a married couple passes the licensing test for parenthood but the other fails. How often would the test be given? Suppose parents pass the test and are licensed, then have children, and at a later date take the test again and fail it. Should their children be removed?
8. Just as some people are abusive parents, some are abusive dates. Dating is potentially harmful to others (e.g., in cases of date rape); its safe performance requires competence (e.g., someone who thinks forcing sex on one's date is appropriate behavior is not a competent dater); and it seems as plausible that a reliable test could be found for abusive dates as for abusive parents. Should we license dating?
9. Slote suggests that the illusion involved in the idea that children are obligated to be obedient is the illusion that one is a thing without free choice. Think of the young children you know. Do they really regard obeying their parents in this light? ("Eat your cereal, Johnny." "But I don't *want* raisin bran.")
10. Slote seems to regard our view that children are obligated to be obedient as a mere rationalization, the purpose of which is to protect the illusion that we are choiceless things. Is this coherent? If I obey because I believe that I am morally obligated to obey, then it seems that I think of myself as making a moral choice, and so, as *not* a mere thing.
11. Consider the following suggestion about the source of parental authority. Parents have a duty to care for their children; children have a correlative right to parental care. This is a right which young children, at least, cannot give up (since they are not yet fully rational agents). Because children cannot give up their right to child care, they have a duty to facilitate their parents' carrying out of *their* duties of child care. The duty to obey your parents is a result of this duty to help your parents care for you, since it facilitates the parents' task considerably. (Roughly this suggestion is made by Jeffrey Blustein, *Parents and Children*, p. 171.)

Further Readings

Blustein, Jeffrey. *Parents and Children: The Ethics of the Family*. New York: Oxford University Press, 1982. The first half of this book is an extremely helpful history of Western philosophical thought about the family; the second half takes up issues about the duties of parents and children.

Houlgate, Laurence D. *Family and State: The Philosophy of Family Law*. Totowa, NJ: Rowman and Littlefield, 1988. Chapters 3 ("The Justification of the Family"), 5 ("The Justification of Legal Marriage"), and 6 ("Privileges and Liabilities of the Marital Status") are especially relevant. A useful discussion of both philosophical and legal aspects of marriage and the family. Chapter 5 includes discussion of the traditional conception of marriage and of contractual alternatives to marriage.

Hunter, Nan D. "Marriage, Law, and Gender: A Feminist Inquiry." In David S. Caudill and Steven Jay Gold, eds., *Radical Philosophy of Law: Contemporary Challenges to Mainstream Legal Theory and Practice.* Atlantic Highlands, NJ: Humanities Press, 1995. Discusses arguments for and against same-sex marriage.

Jaggar, Alison M., and Paula S. Rothenberg. *Feminist Frameworks,* second edition. New York: McGraw-Hill, 1984, Part 3. This book contains an excellent collection of feminist pieces on marriage, including pieces by liberal, radical, and socialist feminists, among others. Includes a sample marriage contract proposed by Alix Kates Shulman and an argument for the abolition of marriage by Sheila Cronan.

Midgley, Mary, and Judith Hughes. "Trouble with Families?" In Brenda Almond, ed., *Introducing Applied Ethics.* Oxford: Blackwell, 1995. Discusses a number of issues related to the "breakdown of the family."

Sommers, Christina. "Philosophers Against the Family." In Christina Sommers and Fred Sommers, eds., *Vice and Virtue in Everyday Life,* second edition. San Diego: Harcourt Brace Jovanovich, 1989. A critique of feminist attacks on the family and also of the contractual conception of moral obligation.

Weitzman, Lenore J. *The Marriage Contract: Spouses, Lovers, and the Law.* New York: Macmillan, The Free Press, 1981. An exhaustive analysis of the nature and consequences of the traditional conception of marriage, and an argument in favor of the contractual approach.

PART FOUR

Intrasocietal Issues

Chapter 8

DISTRIBUTIVE JUSTICE

In this chapter we offer brief statements of some of the major views about how the rights, duties, benefits, and burdens associated with society must be distributed if society is to be just. The conceptions of justice we survey are classical liberalism, libertarianism, and welfare liberalism. We also glance at the Marxist critique of classical liberalism.

John Locke and Classical Liberalism

An excerpt from John Locke's *Second Treatise of Government* represents the classical liberal view. Writing in seventeenth-century England, Locke (1632–1704) defended a consentual and contractarian form of government against royal absolutism. In Locke's view, governments do not create moral rights or responsibilities. Even in the absence of political authority, in the state of nature, we have rights and responsibilities. They are literally God-given. These rights and duties are dictated by natural law, which Locke thought of as the component of the law proclaimed by God that is made evident to us on the basis of facts we can observe about the natural world. Moreover, the natural law limits the powers of legitimate political regimes. To see how these limits work, we must begin with a sketch of Locke's derivation of rights and duties from the natural law.

Perhaps our most important natural *right* is the right to political jurisdiction over ourselves. Locke justifies the claim that we have this right on the grounds that because God has legitimate authority over us as our creator, only God has the right to set some people in authority over others. We know, however, that God did not place any person in authority over others, since God gave each of us the same natural faculties and the same advantages of nature. Because God has given no one else jurisdiction over us, we have jurisdiction over ourselves.

Perhaps our most important natural *duties* are the duty to preserve ourselves and, when our own lives are not at stake, to preserve others as well. We have these duties because we are God's property, and we are obligated to preserve and protect God's property.

Other natural rights and duties are derived by Locke from the right to equal political jurisdiction and our duty to preserve ourselves and others. For example, Locke derives property rights and the right to punish from the preservation duties: If we did not have the right to property, we could not stay alive, and we can protect people's lives against violations of the laws of nature only if we can punish transgressors. Locke also assumes a right to compensation from violators of the laws of nature, since we may need reparations to preserve ourselves.

So Locke's view is that because we are bound by the natural law, we are subject to an extensive catalog of rights and responsibilities, and these are in no way dependent on the existence of any political regime. In fact, our rights and responsibilities help determine what it takes for a political regime to be just. Most importantly, it is Locke's view that a regime cannot legitimately exercise any powers that individuals could not voluntarily have transferred to it. And they cannot transfer a power not given them in the first place by natural law. We do not, for example, have the right to make ourselves slaves (since it would interfere with our responsibility to preserve ourselves), and so we cannot transfer any such right to a regime.

Theoretically, people could have remained in a state of nature. They could have decided not to bind themselves to any regime. However, it was in the interest of people to leave the state of nature. In the state of nature, people would violate our rights, since people acting individually lack the power to enforce their rights effectively. Another inconvenience of the state of nature would be the absence of a judge with the authority to punish violators of our rights. Primarily, therefore, people left the state of nature because it was in their interest to set up a regime that would protect their rights. In initiating the new political order, they voluntarily entered into a certain sort of *contract* between themselves and a political authority: They agreed to transfer some of their rights to an authority, who in turn agreed to secure the rights and meet the moral obligations that had been transferred.

As we said earlier, the fact that we can transfer only rights and duties that we would have in the state of nature greatly limits the powers of a legitimate regime. However, there is another limitation on those powers, namely, the fact that as rational people, we would not be willing to transfer some of our rights. Rather than doing so, we would be better off remaining in the state of nature. For example, it would be irrational for us to transfer the right to do with our property whatever we see fit. Protecting the right to keep property, after all, would be one of the main reasons to set up a regime in the first place.

So royal absolutism is illegitimate. Not only would it be irrational for people to give unlimited powers to any single individual, it would also be impossible, since no individuals have such powers in the first place. As Locke says, an absolute monarch is someone who "retains all the liberty of the state of nature, increased with power and made licentious by impunity." By contrast, the only legitimate regime in Locke's view is a minimal state.

It is possible to criticize many of the features of Locke's view. Locke's theistic defense of natural law is subject to a familiar criticism of such defenses: If the rights and duties God endorses are not arbitrary, then even God must uphold them because God sees that they are morally defensible, and that defense is precisely what Locke should provide. A far more worrisome criticism, however, is that Locke's criterion for a legitimate form of political regime is extremely weak. This is partly explained by the fact that Locke's primary goal was to defeat the legitimacy of royal absolutism, and it does not require a strong criterion of legitimacy to rule out so grossly unjust a type of regime. However, it is worth noting that Locke ends up tolerating substantial inequalities, including political inequalities. By his criterion, a just type of regime must be one that people voluntarily could have contracted into consistently with the rights and responsibilities given them by the natural law. Yet inequalities in the state of nature will affect the sort of agreements people will be able to arrive at when it comes time to enter into the social compact. In positioning for an agreement about what form of regime to adopt, people who owned property in the state of nature would have an edge over those who did not. In particular, landowners would hold out for concessions from those who needed access to land. The upshot might be many sorts of inequality, such as a social contract favoring a weighted voting system that gave preference to the propertied.

John Hospers and Libertarianism

Libertarianism is closely allied with the classical liberal view advocated by Locke and elaborated upon by the eighteenth-century economist Adam Smith (1723–1790). Locke argues that the introduction of the institution of money and the inequalities in possessions it helped create are to everyone's advantage. Smith argues that people are best off in a state in which the market is allowed to operate without interference. He suggests that people are best off if each pursues his or her own individual interests in competition with others and describes an "invisible hand" that directs selfishly motivated people to do what is to the greatest advantage of society as a whole, primarily because agents in this capitalist (free-market) system will supply what people demand at prices they are willing to pay.

Like Locke and Smith, contemporary libertarians all emphasize the importance of liberty and the absence of state interference in the lives of individuals. They disagree, however, on how extensive individual autonomy must be in a just society. Some libertarians such as Robert Paul Wolff are anarchists; they think that individual liberty must be so extensive that no sort of state whatever may exist. Others think that a minimal state roughly along the lines advocated by Locke would be desirable and legitimate. John Hospers, a contemporary philosopher, is such a libertarian. The powers of a just state are limited to enforcing contracts and protecting the liberties of its citizens. States may not, for example, use taxation to force people to support others.

One problem with the libertarian view is that it does not clearly identify which specific liberties we are to have. Many liberties are incompatible with others: My freedom to live where I wish interferes with your freedom to live in solitude. How will the libertarian go about choosing a particular mix of freedoms?

Because libertarians suggest that states may not forcibly redistribute wealth, they are often accused of callousness toward the needy. Libertarians argue that taxation schemes that take away a portion of someone's income and transfer it elsewhere, even to people who admittedly are badly off, are simply a means of stealing property. But some critics of libertarians believe that in just societies, everyone's needs must be met. Other critics believe that justice requires an equal distribution of goods within society, and to meet everyone's needs or to distribute goods equally, a society must be prepared to transfer the fruits of some people's labor to others.

Karl Marx and the Critique of Capitalism

The German philosopher Karl Marx (1818–1883) was a critic of the classical liberal view in general and of the free-market system in particular. However, Marx himself did little by way of assessing the justice of capitalism or of any other economic system. To do so, he would have had to assume the truth of a conception of justice. Yet he considered views about justice to be the product of a society's means of production. A society's economic system also generates its class structure and even the religions and conceptions of the good of individuals, according to Marx. Each economic system favors a distinctive class structure; in turn, the dominant class reinforces social ideals and views of justice that maintain its power and support the economic system on which it relies.

Although Marx does not criticize capitalism as unjust, he does believe that through irresistible forces, it will be displaced by economic arrangements that are more conducive to creative activity, which is something human beings need by their very nature. Marx thinks that capitalism is one stage in an inexorable process whereby social conditions are becoming more suited to meeting human needs. What generates the changes are shifts in economic arrangements. As means of production change, so do class structures, according to Marx. New technology and novel reorganizations of the labor force tend to favor social groups other than ones favored by the old means of production. As a result, the older classes (and the social ideals they favor) come to be forcibly displaced by newer ones. Inevitably, by such a violent transition, capitalist societies will come to be ruled by socialist dictatorships, which will transform them into fully communist societies, according to Marx. Capitalist societies are divided into two classes: the bourgeoisie, or controllers of the means of production, and the proletariat, or workers. When the transition is made to fully communist societies, class divisions will be eliminated.

Consequently, the state, insofar as it is the instrument through which the dominant class maintains its power over others, will cease to exist. What will remain is not the minimalist state envisioned by classical liberals and libertarians, however. Rather, the state, now identified with society as a collectivity, will retain control over production. Marx's protégé Frederick Engels (1820–1895) describes the role of the state as follows: "State interference in social relations becomes . . . superfluous, and then dies out of itself; the government of persons is replaced by the administration of things, and by the conduct of processes of production."[1]

Marx says little about the features of a fully communist society. In the following passage from *Critique of the Gotha Programme*, he is as explicit as he is anywhere in telling us about a fully communist society:

> In a higher phase of communist society, after the enslaving subordination of the individual to the division of labour, and therewith also the antithesis between mental and physical labour, has vanished; after labour has become not only a means of life but life's prime want; after the productive forces have also increased with the all-round development of the individual, and all the springs of co-operative wealth flow more abundantly—only then can the narrow horizon of bourgeois right be crossed in its entirety and society inscribe on its banners: from each according to his ability, to each according to his needs.[2]

Clearly, Marx's vision of communist society is a utopian one in which machinery is so efficient and resources so abundant that no

---

[1] *Anti-Dühring: Herr Eugen Dühring's Revolution in Science* (Moscow: Progress Publishers, 1978), p. 341.

[2] In David McLellan, *Karl Marx: Selected Writings* (Oxford: Oxford University Press, 1977), p. 569.

one need toil at the repetitive, dull, overspecialized work that typically is available in capitalist society. A main reason that Marx thinks communist society will generate such abundance is that he believes that cooperative activity is much more productive than the competitive activity found in capitalist society. More can be accomplished if people cooperate to produce the goods everyone needs to flourish. In a productive communist society, everyone will find it possible to undertake the sorts of tasks that, since they draw on a wide range of his or her talents and abilities, he or she will find intrinsically good. Through making creative contributions, each will develop into a well-rounded individual.

However, a fully communist society can emerge only after capitalism has played its historical role of creating an efficient means of production. Meanwhile, workers in a capitalist state must endure various indignities that Marx describes in his many works. We cannot cover all of these, so we instead focus on Marx's account of the exploitation of workers in capitalist societies.

Workers in free markets are exploited primarily in that they supply surplus value, or unpaid labor. In our excerpt, Marx explains how this is possible in spite of the fact that workers *appear* to be providing their labor through their own free choice. Marx thinks that the extraction of surplus value has been hidden from the participants in free-market systems and that its being hidden has helped allow it to occur. However, he also thinks that laborers who remain in a free-market society have no real choice but to allow themselves to be exploited, for owners will supply workers with the natural resources that are the necessities of life only if the latter provide surplus value. Workers who refuse to meet owners' demands will simply starve.

Here is Marx's explanation of the hidden mechanism through which surplus value is extracted: Capitalists offer laborers a subsistence wage, which is just enough to keep a worker alive and working. If the amount of working time required to produce enough to keep a worker alive for a day is six hours, then a day's labor is valued at six hours. So, if a dollar is the equivalent of an hour's work—if a dollar buys the worker one-sixth of the means to stay alive for a day—then a worker will receive $6.00 for a day's work. However, there would be no point to a capitalist's asking a worker to labor for six hours and then paying him $6.00. Under such an arrangement, the capitalist would simply be turning over to the worker a paycheck that is the exact equivalent of what the worker produced. Instead, capitalists require that workers labor for eight, or twelve, or more hours, yet continue to pay them only $6.00. Surplus value is the value of the labor that workers expend over and above the labor for which they are paid. It is the source of the capitalist's profit.

Marx's critique brings out many features of capitalism that need correction. Arguably, no countries on earth are fully capitalist, and this may be in some measure because of the influence of Marx. On the other hand, several aspects of his view are dubious. His thesis that inexorable forces lead inevitably to a violent revolution in which the proletariat brings about a communist society has been disproven by the course of history: The closest candidates for violent communist revolutions occurred in countries such as Russia that were hardly capitalist at all. None occurred in societies such as Great Britain and the United States, the countries with the most nearly capitalist economies. Moreover, the states in the former Soviet Union appear to be moving in exactly the opposite direction from that predicted by Marx. Such states are incorporating aspects of capitalism, not withering away into fully communist societies in which everyone can achieve a worthwhile life through work.

John Rawls and Welfare Liberalism

Like Locke, contemporary philosopher John Rawls offers a contractarian justification for his principles of justice. In order to help us decide on the best conception of justice, he suggests that we imagine a hypothetical assembly of people, each of whom represents a member of society, and such that everyone in society is represented. These hypothetical representatives will collectively agree on a conception of justice on behalf of us, their wards. Rawls' idea is that if we constrain the circumstances (the "initial situation") under which the representatives rank alternative conceptions of justice in such a fashion that they represent their wards fairly, then the conception of justice they favor will itself be fair. Hence his term *justice as fairness*.

Rawls represents citizens fairly by stipulating that the representatives be granted the same powers in ranking alternatives. He ensures that only relevant features of citizens' moral personality affect the chosen conception of justice by imposing restrictions on the information available to the representatives. As Rawls says, the representatives are situated behind a "veil of ignorance." He calls his interpretation of the initial situation that meets all these demands the *original position* and describes it as one in which rational representatives rank alternatives solely according to how well they further the interests of the representatives' wards. Yet the representatives are largely ignorant of their wards' situations in society. Consider an arbitrarily chosen representative called Nel, whose ward is Len. Nel knows that Len lives in a society in which cooperation is advantageous, that Len wants to exercise his moral power to understand, apply, and act from the conception of justice that eventually will be adopted, and also that Len wants to advance his goals in life and to pursue his values. However, Nel knows nothing else about her ward; for example, she does not know her ward's class position, sex, race, natural assets, or the particulars of Len's society. Hence such factors cannot affect the choice of a conception of justice. In fact, no representative knows anything that would allow her to single out Len so as to show him special favor when it comes to choosing a conception of justice. The representatives have no choice but to make their decision based on the possibility that their ward might be anyone in society at all. Hence they must treat everyone fairly, or so Rawls suggests.

Using the apparatus of the original position, Rawls argues that the minimal state advocated by Locke and other classical liberals is not extensive enough. Like many utilitarians, he defends a kind of welfare liberalism, which emphasizes that a just society must redistribute goods so as to meet the needs of those who are less well off than others. More precisely, Rawls' position is that the institutions of a just society must conform to the following two principles:

1. Each person is to have an equal right to the most extensive total system of liberty for all (the *liberty principle*).
2. Social and economic inequalities are to be arranged so that they are (a) to the greatest benefit of the least advantaged (the *difference principle*) and (b) are attached to offices and positions open to all under conditions of fair equality of opportunity.*

---

*I here ignore the fact that the difference principle is constrained by the just-savings principle; see Section 44 of *A Theory of Justice*.

Like classical liberals, Rawls emphasizes the importance of liberty in a just state. His emphasis on liberty is embodied in the liberty principle, which directs us to offer people as many liberties as is possible while offering the same liberties to everyone, as well as in the fact that his first principle takes priority over his second: We are to fully implement the liberty principle before applying the second principle. However, he departs from classical liberals in suggesting that a just society should have a substantial redistributive component. His difference principle requires that goods such as income, wealth, and the advantages of office be distributed in such a fashion that the least well off in a just society are as well off as they could possibly be.

It is worth noting that Rawls has revised his liberty principle and that the new version no longer requires that we institute as many liberties as possible. The version of his principle quoted above is the one he defends in *A Theory of Justice*. In "The Basic Liberties and Their Priority,"[3]

---

[3]*Liberty, Equality, and Law: Selected Tanner Lectures on Moral Philosophy*, Sterling McMurrin, ed. (Salt Lake City: University of Utah Press, 1987).

Rawls reformulates the liberty principle as follows:

> Each person has an equal right to a fully adequate scheme of equal basic liberties which is compatible with a similar scheme of liberties for all. (p. 5)

Instead of requiring that we institute as many liberties as possible, Rawls wants to identify certain liberties that play a crucial role in our developing and exercising two fundamental moral capacities. The first of these moral capacities is the ability to have and act from a conception of the good, which sets out our view of a good life. The second is the ability to have and act from a conception of justice. Liberties that are crucial toward the development of these moral powers Rawls calls "basic," and it is the basic liberties that the first principle is designed to guarantee. The basic liberties are

> freedom of thought and liberty of conscience; the political liberties and freedom of association, as well as the freedoms specified by the liberty and integrity of the person; and finally, the rights and liberties covered by the rule of law. (p. 5)

CLASSICAL LIBERALISM

Property, Labor and the State

John Locke

To understand political power right, and derive it from its original, we must consider, what state all men are naturally in, and that is, a *state of perfect freedom* to order their actions, and dispose of their possessions and persons, as they think fit, within the bounds of the law of nature, without asking leave, or depending upon the will of any other man.

A *state* also *of equality*, wherein all the power and jurisdiction is reciprocal, no one having more than another; there being nothing more evident, than that creatures of the same species and rank, promiscuously born to all the same advantages of nature, and the use of the same faculties, should also be equal one amongst another without subordination or subjection, unless the lord and master of them all should, by any manifest declaration of his will, set one above another, and confer on him, by an evident and clear appointment, an undoubted right to dominion and sovereignty. . . .

But though this be a *state of liberty*, yet *it is not a state of licence:* though man in that state have an uncontroulable liberty to dispose of his person or possessions, yet he has not liberty to destroy himself, or so much as any creature in his possession, but where some nobler use than its bare preservation calls for it. The *state of nature* has a law of nature to govern it, which obliges every one: and reason, which is that law, teaches all mankind, who will but consult it, that being all *equal and independent*, no one ought to harm another in his life, health, liberty, or possessions: for men being all the workmanship of one omnipotent, and infinitely wise maker; all the servants of one sovereign master, sent into the world by his order, and about his business; they are his property, whose workmanship they are, made to last during his, not one another's pleasure: and being furnished with like faculties, sharing all in one community of nature, there cannot be supposed any such *subordination* among us, that may authorize us to destroy one another, as if we were made for one another's uses, as the inferior ranks of creatures are for our's. Every one, as he is *bound to preserve himself,* and not to quit his station wilfully, so by the like reason, when his own preservation comes not in competition, ought he, as much as he can, to *preserve the rest of mankind,* and may not, unless it be to do justice on an offender, take away, or impair the life, or what tends to the preservation of the life, the liberty, health, limb, or goods of another.

And that all men may be restrained from invading others' rights, and from doing hurt to one another, and the law of nature be observed, which willeth the peace and *preservation of all mankind,* the *execution* of the law of nature is, in that state, put into every, man's hands, whereby every one has a right to punish the transgressors of that law to such a degree, as may hinder its violation: for the *law of nature* would, as all other laws that concern men in this world, be in vain, if there were no body that in the state of nature had a *power to execute* that law, and thereby preserve the innocent and restrain offenders. And if any one in the state of nature may punish another for any evil he has done, every one may do so: for in that *state of perfect equality,* where naturally there is no superiority or jurisdiction of one over another, what any may do in prosecution of that law, every one must needs have a right to do.

And thus, in the state of nature, *one man comes by a power over another;* but yet no absolute or arbitrary power, to use a criminal, when he has got him in his hands, according to the passionate heats, or boundless extravagancy of his own will; but only to retribute to him, so far as calm reason and conscience dictate, what is proportionate to his transgression, which is so much as may serve for *reparation* and *restraint:* for these two are the only reasons, why one man may lawfully do harm to another, which is that we call *punishment.* In transgressing the law of nature, the offender declares himself to live by another rule than that of reason and common equity, which is that measure God has set to the actions of men, for their mutual security. . . .

Besides the crime which consists in violating the law, and varying from the right rule of reason, whereby a man so far becomes degenerate, and declares himself to quit the principles of human nature, and to be a noxious creature, there is commonly *injury* done to some person or other, and some other man receives damage by his transgression: in which case he who hath received any damage, has, besides the right of punishment common to him with other men, a particular right to seek *reparation* from him that has done it: and any other person, who finds it just, may also join with him that is injured, and assist him in recovering from the offender so much as may make satisfaction for the harm he has suffered.

From these *two distinct rights,* the one of *punishing* the crime *for restraint,* and preventing the like offence, which right of punishing is in every body; the other of taking *reparation,* which belongs only to the injured party, comes it to pass that the magistrate, who by being magistrate hath the common right of punishing put into his hands, can often, where the public good demands not the execution of the law, *remit* the punishment of criminal offences by his own authority, but yet cannot *remit* the satisfaction due to any private man for the damage he has received....

By the same reason may a man in the state of nature *punish the lesser breaches* of that law. It will perhaps be demanded, with death? I answer, each transgression may be *punished* to that *degree,* and with so much *severity,* as will suffice to make it an ill bargain to the offender, give him cause to repent, and terrify others from doing the like....

To those that say, there were never any men in the state of nature, I will not only oppose the authority of the judicious Hooker, *Eccl. Pol. lib.* i. *sect.* 10. where he says, *The laws which have been hitherto mentioned,* i.e. the laws of nature, *do bind men absolutely, even as they are men, although they have never any settled fellowship, never any solemn agreement amongst themselves what to do, or not to do: but for asmuch as we are not by ourselves sufficient to furnish ourselves with competent store of things, needful for such a life as our nature doth desire, a life fit for the dignity of man; therefore to supply those defects and imperfections which are in us, as living single and solely by ourselves, we are naturally induced to seek communion and fellowship with others: this was the cause of men's uniting themselves at first in politic societies.* But I moreover affirm, that all men are naturally in that state, and remain so, till by their own consents they make themselves members of some politic society; and I doubt not in the sequel of this discourse, to make it very clear....

Of Property

Though the earth, and all inferior creatures, be common to all men, yet every man has a *property* in his own *person:* this no body has any right to but himself. The *labour* of his body, and the *work* of his hands, we may say, are properly his. Whatsoever then he removes out of the state that nature hath provided, and left it in, he hath mixed his *labour* with, and joined to it something that is his own, and thereby makes it his *property.* It being by him removed from the common state nature hath placed it in, it hath by this *labour* something annexed to it, that excludes the common right of other men: for this *labour* being the unquestionable property of the labourer, no man but he can have a right to what that is once joined to, at least where there is enough, and as good, left in common for others....

It will perhaps be objected to this, that if gathering the acorns, or other fruits of the earth, etc. makes a right to them, then any one may *ingross* as much as he will. To which I answer, Not so. The same law of nature, that does by this means give us property, does also *bound* that *property* too. *God has given us all things richly*, I Tim. vi. 12. is the voice of reason confirmed by inspiration. But how far has he given it us? *To enjoy.* As much as any one can make use of any advantage of life before it spoils, so much he may by his labour fix a property in: whatever is beyond this, is more than his share, and belongs to others. Nothing was made by God for man to spoil or destroy. And thus, considering the plenty of natural provisions there was a long time in the world, and the few spenders; and to how small a part of the provision the industry of one man could extend itself, and ingross it to the prejudice of others; especially keeping within the *bounds*, set by reason, of what might serve for his *use*; there could be then little room for quarrels or contentions about property so established.

But the *chief matter of property* being now not the fruits of the earth, and the beasts that subsist on it, but *the earth itself*; as that which takes in and carries with it all the rest; I think it is plain, that *property* in that too is acquired as the former. *As much land* as a man tills, plants, improves, cultivates, and can use the product of, so much is his *property.* . . .

Nor was this *appropriation* of any parcel of *land*, by improving it, any prejudice to any other man, since there was still enough, and as good left; and more than the yet unprovided could use. So that, in effect, there was never the less left for others because of his inclosure for himself: for he that leaves as much as another can make use of, does as good as take nothing at all. No body could think himself injured by the drinking of another man, though he took a good draught, who had a whole river of the same water left him to quench his thirst: and the case of land and water, where there is enough of both, is perfectly the same. . . .

And thus, without supposing any private dominion, and property in *Adam*, over all the world, exclusive of all other men, which can no way be proved, nor any one's property be made out from it; but supposing the *world* given, as it was, to the children of men *in common*, we see how *labour* could make men distinct titles to several parcels of it, for their private uses; wherein there could be no doubt of right, no room for quarrel.

Nor is it so strange, as perhaps before consideration it may appear, that the *property of labour* should be able to overbalance the community of land: for it is *labour* indeed that *puts the difference of value* on every thing; and let any one consider what the difference is between an acre of land planted with tobacco or sugar, sown with wheat or barley, and an acre of the same land lying in common, without any husbandry upon it, and he will find, that the improvement of *labour makes* the far greater part of the value. . . .

The greatest part of *things really useful* to the life of man, and such as the necessity of subsisting made the first commoners of the world look after, as it doth the *Americans* now, *are* generally things of *short duration;* such as, if they are not consumed by use, will decay and perish of themselves: gold, silver and diamonds, are things that fancy or agreement hath put the value on, more than real use, and the necessary support of life. Now of those good things which nature hath provided in common, every one had a right (as hath been said) to as much as he could use, and *property* in all that he could effect with his labour; all that his *industry* could extend to, to alter from the state nature had put it in, was his. He that *gathered* a hundred bushels of acorns or apples, had thereby a *property* in them, they were his goods as soon as gathered. He was only to look, that he used them before they spoiled, else he took more than his share, and robbed others. And indeed it was a foolish thing, as well as dishonest, to hoard up more than he could make use of. If he gave away a part to any body else, so that it perished not uselessly in his possession, these he also made use of. And if he also bartered away plums, that would have rotted in a week, for nuts that would last good for his eating a whole year, he did no injury; he wasted not the common stock; destroyed no part of the portion of goods that belonged to others, so long as nothing perished uselessly in his hands. Again, if he would give his nuts for a piece of metal, pleased with its colour: or exchange his sheep for shells, or wool for a sparkling pebble or a diamond, and keep those by him all his life, he invaded not the right of others, he might heap up as much of these durable things as he pleased; the *exceeding of the bounds of his just property* not lying in the largeness of his possession, but the perishing of any thing uselessly in it. . . .

But since gold and silver, being little useful to the life of man in proportion to food, raiment, and carriage, has its *value* only from the consent of men, whereof *labour* yet *makes*, in great part, *the measure*, it is plain, that men have agreed to a disproportionate and unequal *possession of the earth*, they having by a tacit and voluntary consent, found out a way how a man may fairly possess more land than he himself can use the product of, by receiving in exchange for the overplus gold and silver, which may be hoarded up without injury to any one; these metals not spoiling or decaying in the hands of the possessor. This partage of things in an inequality of private possessions, men have made practicable out of the bounds of society, and without compact, only by putting a value on gold and silver, and tacitly agreeing in the use of money: for in governments, the laws regulate the right of property, and the possession of land is determined by positive constitutions. . . .

Of the Ends of Political Society and Government

If man in the state of nature be so free, as has been said; if he be absolute lord of his own person and possessions, equal to the greatest, and subject to no body, why will he part with his freedom? why will he give up this empire, and subject himself to the dominion and control of any other power? To which it is obvious to answer, that though in the state of nature he hath such a right, yet the enjoyment of it is very uncertain, and constantly exposed to the invasion of others: for all being kings as much as he, every man his equal, and the greater part no strict observers of equity and justice, the enjoyment of the property he has in this state is very unsafe, very unsecure. This makes him willing to quit a condition, which, however free, is full of fears and continual dangers: and it is not without reason, that he seeks out, and is willing to join in society with others, who are already united, or have a mind to unite, for the mutual *preservation* of their lives, liberties and estates, which I call by the general name, *property*.

The great and *chief end*, therefore, of men's uniting into common-wealths, and putting themselves under government, *is the preservation of their property*. To which in the state of nature there are many things wanting.

First, There wants an *established*, settled, known *law*, received and allowed by common consent to be the standard of right and wrong, and the common measure to decide all controversies between them: for though the law of nature be plain and intelligible to all rational creatures; yet men being biased by their interest, as well as ignorant for want of study of it, are not apt to allow of it as a law binding to them in the application of it to their particular cases.

Secondly, In the state of nature there wants *a known and indifferent judge,* with authority to determine all differences according to the established law: for every one in that state being both judge and executioner of the law of nature, men being partial to themselves, passion and revenge is very apt to carry them too far, and with too much heat, in their own cases; as well as negligence, and unconcernedness, to make them too remiss in other men's.

Thirdly, In the state of nature there often wants *power* to back and support the sentence when right, and to *give* it due *execution.* They who by any injustice offended, will seldom fail, where they are able, by force to make good their injustice; such resistance many times makes the punishment dangerous, and frequently destructive, to those who attempt it.

Thus mankind, notwithstanding all the privileges of the state of nature, being but in an ill condition, while they remain in it, are quickly driven into society. Hence it comes to pass, that we seldom find any number of men live any time together in this state. The inconveniences that they are therein exposed to, by the irregular and uncertain exercise of the power every man has of punishing the transgressions of others, make them take sanctuary under the established laws of government, and therein seek *the preservation of their property.* It is this makes them so willingly give up every one his single power of punishing, to be exercised by such alone, as shall be appointed to it amongst them; and by such rules as the community, or those authorized by them to that purpose, shall agree on. And in this we have the original *right and rise of both the legislative and executive power,* as well as of the governments and societies themselves.

LIBERTARIANISM

What Libertarianism Is

John Hospers

The political philosophy that is called libertarianism (from the Latin *libertas,* liberty) is the doctrine that every person is the owner of his own life, and that no one is the owner of anyone else's life; and that consequently every human being has the right to act in accordance with his own choices, unless those actions infringe on the equal liberty of other human beings to act in accordance with *their* choices.

There are several other ways of stating the same libertarian thesis:

1. *No one is anyone else's master, and no one is anyone else's slave.* Since I am the one to decide how my life is to be conducted, just as you decide about yours, I

have no right (even if I had the power) to make you my slave and he your master, nor have you the right to become the master by enslaving me. Slavery is *forced* servitude, and since no one owns the life of anyone else, no one has the right to enslave another. Political theories past and present have traditionally been concerned with who should be the master (usually the king, the dictator, or government bureaucracy) and who should be the slaves, and what the extent of the slavery should be. Libertarianism holds that no one has the right to use force to enslave the life of another, or any portion or aspect of that life.

2. *Other men's lives are not yours to dispose of.* I enjoy seeing operas; but operas are expensive to produce. Opera-lovers often say, "The state (or the city, etc.) should subsidize opera, so that we can all see it. Also it would be for people's betterment, cultural benefit, etc." But what they are advocating is nothing more or less than legalized plunder. They can't pay for the productions themselves, and yet they want to see opera, which involves a large number of people and their labor; so what they are saying in effect is, "Get the money through legalized force. Take a little bit more out of every worker's paycheck every week to pay for the operas we want to see." But I have no right to take by force from the workers' pockets to pay for what I want.

Perhaps it would be better if he *did* go to see opera—then I should try to convince him to go voluntarily. But to take the money from him forcibly, because in my opinion it would be good for *him*, is still seizure of his earnings, which is plunder.

Besides, if I have the right to force him to help pay for my pet projects, hasn't he equally the right to force me to help pay for his? Perhaps he in turn wants the government to subsidize rock-and-roll, or his new car or a house in the country? If I have the right to milk him, why hasn't he the right to milk me? If I can be a moral cannibal, why can't he too? . . .

3. *No human being should be a nonvoluntary mortgage on the life of another.* I cannot claim your life, your work, or the products of your effort as mine. The fruit of one man's labor should not be fair game for every freeloader who comes along and demands it as his own. The orchard that has been carefully grown, nurtured, and harvested by its owner should not be ripe for the plucking for any bypasser who has a yen for the ripe fruit. The wealth that some men have produced should not be fair game for looting by government, to be used for whatever purposes its representatives determine, no matter what their motives in so doing may be. The theft of your money by a robber is not justified by the fact that he used it to help his injured mother.

It will already be evident that libertarian doctrine is embedded in a view of the rights of man. Each human being has the right to live his life as he chooses, compatibly with the equal right of all other human beings to live their lives as they choose.

All man's rights are implicit in the above statement. Each man has the right to life: any attempt by others to take it away from him, or even to injure him, violates this right, through the use of coercion against him. Each man has the right to liberty: to conduct his life in accordance with the alternatives open to him without coercive action by others. And every man has the right to property: to work to sustain his life (and the lives of whichever others he chooses to sustain, such as his family) and to retain the fruits of his labor.

People often defend the rights of life and liberty but denigrate property rights, and yet the right to property is as basic as the other two; indeed, without property rights no other rights are possible. Depriving you of property is depriving you of the means by which you live.

> . . . All that which an individual possesses by right (including his life and property) are morally his to use, dispose of and even destroy, as he sees fit. If I own my life, then it follows that I am free to associate with whom I please and not to associate with whom I please. If I own my knowledge and services it follows that I may ask any compensation I wish for providing them for another, or I may abstain from providing them at all, if I so choose. If I own my house, it follows that I may decorate it as I please and live in it with whom I please. If I control my own business, it follows that I may charge what I please for my products or services, hire whom I please and not hire whom I please. All that which I own in fact, I may dispose of as I choose to in reality. For anyone to attempt to limit my freedom to do so is to violate my rights.
>
> Where do my rights end? Where yours begin. I may do anything I wish with my own life, liberty and property without your consent; but I may do nothing with your life, liberty and property without your consent. If we recognize the principle of man's rights, it follows that the individual is sovereign of the domain of his own life and property, and is sovereign of no other domain. To attempt to interfere forcibly with another's use, disposal or destruction of his own property is to initiate force against him and to violate his rights.

I have no right to decide how *you* should spend your time or your money. I can make that decision for myself, but not for you, my neighbor. I may deplore your choice of life-style, and I may talk with you about it provided you are willing to listen to me. But I have no right to use force to change it. Nor have I the right to decide how you should spend the money you have earned. I may appeal to you to give it to the Red Cross, and you may prefer to go to prize-fights. But that is your decision, and however much I may chafe about it I do not have the right to interfere forcibly with it, for example by robbing you in order to use the money in accordance with *my* choices. (If I have the right to rob you, have you also the right to rob me?)

When I claim a right, I carve out a niche, as it were, in my life, saying in effect, "This activity I must be able to perform without interference from others. For you and everyone else, this is off limits." And so I put up a "no trespassing" sign, which marks off the area of my right. Each individual's right is his "no trespassing" sign in relation to me and others. I may not encroach upon his domain any more than he upon mine, without my consent. Every right entails a duty, true—but the duty is only that of *forbearance*— that is, of *refraining* from violating the other person's right. If you have a right to life, I have no right to take your life; if you have a right to the products of your labor (property), I have no right to take it from you without your consent. The non-violation of these rights will not guarantee you protection against natural catastrophes such as floods and earthquakes, but it will protect you against the aggressive activities *of other men*. And rights, after all, have to do with one's relations to other human beings, not with one's relations to physical nature.

Nor were these rights created by government; governments—some governments, obviously not all—*recognize* and *protect* the rights that individuals already have. Governments regularly forbid homicide and theft; and, at a more advanced stage, protect individuals against such things as libel and breach of contract. . . .

The *right to property* is the most misunderstood and unappreciated of human rights, and it is one most constantly violated by governments. "Property" of course does not mean only real estate; it includes anything you can call your own—your clothing, your car, your jewelry, your books and papers.

The right of property is not the right to just *take* it from others, for this would interfere with *their* property rights. It is rather the right to work for it, to obtain non-coercively, the money or services which you can present in voluntary exchange.

The right to property is consistently underplayed by intellectuals today, sometimes even frowned upon, as if we should feel guilty for upholding such a right in view of all the poverty in the world. But the right to property is absolutely basic. It is your hedge against the future. It is your assurance that what you have worked to earn will still be there, and be yours, when you wish or need to use it, especially when you are too old to work any longer.

Government has always been the chief enemy of the right to property. The officials of government, wishing to increase their power, and finding an increase of wealth an effective way to bring this about, seize some or all of what a person has earned—and since government has a monopoly of physical force within the geographical area of the nation, it has the power (but not the right) to do this. When this happens, of course, every citizen of that country is insecure: he knows that no matter how hard he works the government can swoop down on him at any time and confiscate his earnings and possessions. A person sees his life savings wiped out in a moment when the tax-collectors descend to deprive him of the fruits of his work; or, an industry which has been fifty years in the making and cost millions of dollars and millions of hours of time and planning, is nationalized overnight. Or the government, via inflation, cheapens the currency, so that hard-won dollars aren't worth anything any more. The effect of such actions, of course, is that people lose hope and incentive: if no matter how hard they work the government agents can take it all away, why bother to work at all, for more than today's needs? Depriving people of property is *depriving them of the means by which they live*—the freedom of the individual citizen to do what he wishes with his own life and to plan for the future. Indeed, only if property rights are respected is there any point to planning for the future and working to achieve one's goals. *Property rights are what makes long-range planning possible*—the kind of planning which is a distinctively human endeavor, as opposed to the day-by-day activity of the lion who hunts, who depends on the supply of game tomorrow but has no real insurance against starvation in a day or a week. Without the right to property, the right to life itself amounts to little: how can you sustain your life if you cannot plan ahead? and how can you plan ahead if the fruits of your labor can at any moment be confiscated by government? . . .

How can any of man's rights be violated? Ultimately, only by the use of force. I can make suggestions to you, I can reason with you, entreat you (if you are willing to listen), but I cannot *force* you without violating your rights; only by forcing you do I cut the cord between your free decisions and your actions. Voluntary relations between individuals involve no deprivation of rights, but murder, assault, and rape do, because in doing these things I make you the unwilling victim of my actions. A man who is beating his wife involves no violation of rights if she *wanted* to be beaten. *Force is behavior that requires the unwilling involvement of other persons.*

Thus the use of force need not involve the use of physical violence. If I trespass on your property or dump garbage on it, I am violating your property rights, as indeed I am when I steal your watch; although this is not force in the sense of violence, it *is* a case of your being an unwilling victim of my action. Similarly, if you shout at me so that I cannot be heard when I try to speak, or blow a siren in my ear, or start a factory next door which pollutes my land, you are again violating my rights (to free speech, to property); I am, again, an unwilling victim of your actions. Similarly, if you steal a manuscript of mine and publish it as your own, you are confiscating a piece of my property and thus violating my right to keep what is the product of my labor. Of course, if I give you the manuscript with permission to sign your name to it and keep the proceeds, no violation of rights is involved—any more than if I give you permission to dump garbage on my yard.

According to libertarianism, the role of government should be limited to the retaliatory use of force against those who have initiated its use. It should not enter into any other areas, such as religion, social organization, and economics.

Government is the most dangerous institution known to man. Throughout history it has violated the rights of men more than any individual or group of individuals could do: it has killed people, enslaved them, sent them to forced labor or concentration camps, and regularly robbed and pillaged them of the fruits of their expended labor. Unlike individual criminals, government has the power to arrest and try; unlike individual criminals, it can surround and encompass a person totally, dominating every aspect of one's life, so that one has no recourse from it but to leave the country (and in totalitarian nations even that is prohibited). Government throughout history has a much sorrier record than any individual, even that of a ruthless mass murderer. The signs we see on bumper stickers are chillingly accurate: "Beware: the Government is Armed and Dangerous."

The only proper role of government, according to libertarians, is that of the protector of the citizen against aggression by other individuals. The government, of course, should never initiate aggression; its proper role is as the embodiment of the *retaliatory* use of force against anyone who initiates its use. . . .

What then should be the function of government? In a word, the *protection of human rights*.

1. *The right to life:* libertarians support all such legislation as will protect human beings against the use of force by others, for example, laws against killing, attempted killing, maiming, beating, and all kinds of physical violence.

2. *The right to liberty:* there should be no laws compromising in any way freedom of speech, of the press, and of peaceable assembly. There should be no censorship of ideas, books, films, or of anything else by government.

3. *The right to property:* libertarians support legislation that protects the property rights of individuals against confiscation, nationalization, eminent domain, robbery, trespass, fraud and misrepresentation, patent and copyright, libel and slander.

Someone has violently assaulted you. Should he be legally liable? Of course. He has violated one of your rights. He has knowingly injured you, and since he has initiated aggression against you he should be made to expiate.

Someone has negligently left his bicycle on the sidewalk where you trip over it in the dark and injure yourself. He didn't do it intentionally; he didn't mean you any harm. Should he be legally liable? Of course; he has, however unwittingly, injured you, and since the injury is caused by him and you are the victim, he should pay.

Someone across the street is unemployed. Should you be taxed extra to pay for his expenses? Not at all. You have not injured him, you are not responsible for the fact that he is unemployed (unless you are a senator or bureaucrat who agitated for further curtailing of business, which legislation passed, with the result that your neighbor was laid off by the curtailed business). You may voluntarily wish to help him out, or better still, try to get him a job to put him on his feet again; but since you have initiated no aggressive act against him, and neither purposely nor accidentally injured him in any way, you should not be legally penalized for the fact of his unemployment. (Actually, it is just such penalties that increase unemployment.)

One man, A, works hard for years and finally earns a high salary as a professional man. A second man, B, prefers not to work at all, and to spend wastefully what money he has (through inheritance), so that after a year or two he has nothing left. At the end of this time he has a long siege of illness and lots of medical bills to pay. He demands that the bills be paid by the government—that is, by the taxpayers of the land, including Mr. A.

But of course B has no such right. He chose to lead his life in a certain way—that was his voluntary decision. One consequence of that choice is that he must depend on charity in case of later need. Mr. A chose not to live that way. (And if everyone lived like Mr. B, on whom would he depend in case of later need?) Each has a right to live in the way he pleases, but each must live with the consequences of his own decision (which, as always, fall primarily on himself). He cannot, in time of need, claim A's beneficence as his right. . . .

Property rights can be violated by physical trespass, of course, or by anyone entering on your property for any reason without your consent. (If you *do* consent to having your neighbor dump garbage on your yard, there is no violation of your rights.) But the physical trespass of a person is only a special case of violation of property rights. Property rights can be violated by soundwaves, in the form of a loud noise, or the sounds of your neighbor's hi-fi set while you are trying to sleep. Such violations of property rights are of course the subject of action in the courts.

But there is another violation of property rights that has not thus far been honored by the courts; this has to do with the effects of *pollution* of the atmosphere.

> From the beginnings of modern air pollution, the courts made a conscious decision not to protect, for example, the orchards of farmers from the smoke of nearby factories or locomotives. They said, in effect, to the farmers: yes, your private property is being invaded by this smoke, but we hold that "public policy" is more important than private property, and public policy holds factories and locomotives to be good things. These goods were allowed to override the defense of property rights—with our consequent headlong rush into pollution disaster. The remedy is both "radical" and crystal clear, and it has nothing to do with multibillion dollar palliative programs at the expense of the taxpayers which do not even meet the real issue. The remedy is simply to enjoin anyone from injecting pollutants into the air, and thereby invading the rights of persons and property. Period. The argument that such an injunction prohibition would add to the costs of industrial production is as reprehensible as the pre-Civil War argument that the abolition of slavery would add to the costs of growing cotton, and therefore should not take place. For this means that the polluters are able to impose the high costs of pollution upon those whose property rights they are allowed to invade with impunity. . . . [1]

What about property which you do not work to earn, but which you *inherit* from someone else? Do you have a right to that? You have no right to it until someone decides to give it to you. Consider the man

---

[1] Murray Rothbard, "The Great Ecology Issue," *The Individualist*, 2, no. 2 (Feb. 1970), p. 5.

who willed it to you: it was his, he had the right to use and dispose of it as *he* saw fit; and if he decided to give it to you, this is a windfall for you, but it was only the exercise of *his* right. Had the property been seized by the government at the man's death, or distributed among numerous other people designated by the government, it *would* have been a violation of his rights: for he, who worked to earn and sustain it, would not have been able to dispose of it according to his own judgment. If he doesn't have the right to determine who shall have it, who does? . . .

Laws may be classified into three types: (1) laws protecting individuals against themselves, such as laws against fornication and other sexual behavior, alcohol, and drugs; (2) laws protecting individuals against aggressions by other individuals, such as laws against murder, robbery, and fraud; (3) laws requiring people to help one another; for example, all laws which rob Peter to pay Paul, such as welfare.

Libertarians reject the first class of laws totally. Behavior which harms no one else is strictly the individual's own affair. Thus, there should be no laws against becoming intoxicated, since whether or not to become intoxicated is the individual's own decision; but there should be laws against driving while intoxicated, since the drunken driver is a threat to every other motorist on the highway (drunken driving falls into type 2). Similarly, there should be no laws against drugs (except the prohibition of sale of drugs to minors) as long as the taking of these drugs poses no threat to anyone else. Drug addiction is a psychological problem to which no present solution exists. Most of the social harm caused by addicts, other than to themselves, is the result of thefts which they perform in order to continue their habit—and then the *legal* crime is the theft, not the addiction. The actual cost of heroin is about ten cents a shot; if it were legalized, the enormous traffic in illegal sale and purchase of it would stop, as well as the accompanying proselytization to get new addicts (to make more money for the pusher) and the thefts performed by addicts who often require eighty dollars a day just to keep up the habit. Addiction would not stop, but the crimes would: it is estimated that 75 percent of the burglaries in New York City today are performed by addicts, and all these crimes could be wiped out at one stroke through the legalization of drugs. (Only when the taking of drugs could be shown to constitute a threat to *others,* should it be prohibited by law. It is only laws protecting people against *themselves* that libertarians oppose.)

Laws should be limited to the second class only: aggression by individuals against other individuals. These are laws whose function is to protect human beings against encroachment by others; and this, as we have seen, is (according to libertarianism) the sole function of government.

Libertarians also reject the third class of laws totally: no one should be forced by law to help others, not even to tell them the time of day if requested, and certainly not to give them a portion of one's weekly paycheck. Governments, in the guise of humanitarianism, have given to some by taking from others (charging a "handling fee" in the process, which, because of the government's waste and inefficiency, sometimes is several hundred percent). And in so doing they have decreased incentive, violated the rights of individuals, and lowered the standard of living of almost everyone.

All such laws constitute what libertarians call *moral cannibalism.* A cannibal in the physical sense is a person who lives off the flesh of other human beings. A *moral* cannibal is one who believes he has a right to live off the "spirit" of other human beings—who believes that he has a moral claim on the productive capacity, time, and effort expended by others.

It has become fashionable to claim virtually everything that one needs or desires as one's *right*. Thus, many people claim that they have a right to a job, the right to free medical care, to free food and clothing, to a decent home, and so on. Now if one asks, apart from any specific context, whether it would be desirable if everyone had these things, one might well say yes. But there is a gimmick attached to each of them: *At whose expense?* Jobs, medical care, education, and so on, don't grow on trees. These are goods and services *produced only by men*. Who, then, is to provide them, and under what conditions?

If you have a right to a job, who is to supply it? Must an employer supply it even if he doesn't want to hire you? What if you are unemployable, or incurably lazy? (If you say "the government must supply it," does that mean that a job must be created for you which no employer needs done, and that you must be kept in it regardless of how much or little you work?) If the employer is forced to supply it at his expense even if he doesn't need you, then isn't *he* being enslaved to that extent? What ever happened to *his* right to conduct his life and his affairs in accordance with his choices?

If you have a right to free medical care, then, since medical care doesn't exist in nature as wild apples do, some people will have to supply it to you for free: that is, they will have to spend their time and money and energy taking care of you whether they want to or not. What ever happened to *their* right to conduct their lives as they see fit? Or do you have a right to violate theirs? Can there be a right to violate rights?

All those who demand this or that as a "free service" are consciously or unconsciously evading the fact that there is in reality no such thing as free services. All man-made goods and services are the result of human expenditure of time and effort. There is no such thing as "something for nothing" in this world. If you demand something free, you are demanding that other men give their time and effort to you without compensation. If they voluntarily choose to do this, there is no problem; but if you demand that they be *forced* to do it, you are interfering with their right not to do it if they so choose. "Swimming in this pool ought to be free!" says the indignant passerby. What he means is that others should build a pool, others should provide the materials, and still others should run it and keep it in functioning order, so that *he* can use it without fee. But what right has he to the expenditure of *their* time and effort? To expect something "for free" is to expect it *to be paid for by others* whether they choose to or not.

Many questions, particularly about economic matters, will be generated by the libertarian account of human rights and the role of government. Should government have no role in assisting the needy, in providing social security, in legislating minimum wages, in fixing prices and putting a ceiling on rents, in curbing monopolies, in erecting tariffs, in guaranteeing jobs, in managing the money supply? To these and all similar questions the libertarian answers with an unequivocal no.

"But then you'd let people go hungry." comes the rejoinder. This, the libertarian insists, is precisely what would not happen; with the restrictions removed, the economy would flourish as never before. With the controls taken off business, existing enterprises would expand and new ones would spring into existence satisfying more and more consumer needs; millions more people would be gainfully employed instead of subsisting on welfare, and all kinds of research and production, released from the stranglehold of government, would proliferate, fulfilling man's needs and desires as never before. It has always been so whenever government has permitted men to be free traders on a free market. But *why* this is so, and how the free market is the best solution to all problems relating to the material aspect of man's life, is another and far longer story. It is told in detail in chapters 3 to 9 of my book, *Libertarianism*.

The Marxist Critique of Capitalism

A Critique of Capitalism

Karl Marx

Let us now examine production as a creation of value.

We know that the value of each commodity is determined by the quantity of labour expended on and materialised in it, by the working-time necessary, under given social conditions, for its production. This rule also holds good in the case of the product that accrued to our capitalist, as the result of the labour-process carried on for him. Assuming this product to be 10 lbs. of yarn, our first step is to calculate the quantity of labour realised in it.

For spinning the yarn, raw material is required; suppose in this case 10 lbs. of cotton. We have no need at present to investigate the value of this cotton, for our capitalist has, we will assume, bought it at its full value, say of ten shillings. In this price the labour required for the production of the cotton is already expressed in terms of the average labour of society. We will further assume that the wear and tear of the spindle, which, for our present purpose, may represent all other instruments of labour employed, amounts to the value of 2s. If, then, twenty-four hours' labour, or two working days, are required to produce the quantity of gold represented by twelve shillings, we have here, to begin with, two days' labour already incorporated in the yarn.

We must not let ourselves be misled by the circumstance that the cotton has taken a new shape while the substance of the spindle has to a certain extent been used up. By the general law of value, if the value of 40 lbs. of yarn = the value of 40 lbs. of cotton + the value of a whole spindle, *i.e.*, if the same working time is required to produce the commodities on either side of this equation, then 10 lbs. of yarn are an equivalent for 10 lbs. of cotton, together with one-fourth of a spindle. In the case we are considering the same working time is materialised in the 10 lbs. of yarn on the one hand, and in the 10 lbs. of cotton and the fraction of a spindle on the other. Therefore, whether value appears in cotton, in a spindle, or in yarn, makes no difference in the amount of that value. The spindle and cotton, instead of resting quietly side by side, join together in the process, their forms are altered, and they are turned into yarn; but their value is no more affected by this fact than it would be if they had been simply exhanged for their equivalent in yarn. . . .

The values of the means of production, *i.e.*, the cotton and the spindle, which values are expressed in the price of twelve shillings, are therefore constituent parts of the value of the yarn, or, in other words, of the value of the product.

Two conditions must nevertheless be fulfilled. First, the cotton and spindle must concur in the production of a use-value; they must in the present case become yarn. Value is independent of the particular use-value by which it is borne, but it must be embodied in a use-value of some kind. Secondly, the time occupied in the labour of production must not exceed the time really necessary under the given social conditions of the case. . . .

We now know what portion of the value of the yarn is owing to the cotton and the spindle. It amounts to twelve shillings or the value of two days' work. The next point for our consideration is, what portion of the value of the yarn is added to the cotton by the labour of the spinner.

We have now to consider this labour under a very different aspect from that which it had during the labour-process; there, we viewed it solely as that particular kind of human activity which changes cotton into yarn; there, the more the labour was suited to the work, the better the yarn, other circumstances remaining the same. The labour of the spinner was then viewed as specifically different from other kinds of productive labour, different on the one hand in its special aim, viz., spinning, different, on the other hand, in the special character of its operations, in the special nature of its means of production and in the special use-value of its product. For the operation of spinning, cotton and spindles are a necessity, but for making rifled cannon they would be of no use whatever. Here, on the contrary, where we consider the labour of the spinner only so far as it is value-creating, *i.e.*, a source of value, his labour differs in no respect from the labour of the man who bores cannon, or (what here more nearly concerns us), from the labour of the cotton-planter and spindle-maker incorporated in the means of production. It is solely by reason of this identity, that cotton planting, spindle making and spinning, are capable of forming the component parts, differing only quantitatively from each other, of one whole, namely, the value of the yarn. Here, we have nothing more to do with the quality, the nature and the specific character of the labour, but merely with its quantity. And this simply requires to be calculated. We proceed upon the assumption that spinning is simple, unskilled labour, the average labour of a given state of society. Hereafter we shall see that the contrary assumption would make no difference.

While the labourer is at work, his labour constantly undergoes a transformation: from being motion, it becomes an object without motion; from being the labourer working, it becomes the thing produced. At the end of one hour's spinning, that act is represented by a definite quantity of yarn; in other words, a definite quantity of labour, namely that of one hour, has become embodied in the cotton. We say labour, *i.e.*, the expenditure of his vital force by the spinner, and not spinning labour, because the special work of spinning counts here, only so far as it is the expenditure of labour-power in general, and not in so far as it is the specific work of the spinner.

In the process we are now considering it is of extreme importance, that no more time be consumed in the work of transforming the cotton into yarn than is necessary under the given social conditions. . . .

If in one hour 1²/₃ lbs. of cotton can be spun into 1²/₃ lbs. of yarn, then 10 lbs. of yarn indicate the absorption of 6 hours' labour. Definite quantities of product, these quantities being determined by experience, now represent nothing but definite quantities of labour, definite masses of crystallized labour-time. They are nothing more than the materialisation of so many hours or so many days of social labor. . . .

We assumed, on the occasion of its sale, that the value of a day's labour-power is three shillings, and that six hours' labour are incorporated in that sum; and consequently that this amount of labour is requisite to produce the necessaries of life daily required on an average by the labourer. If now our spinner by working for one hour, can convert 1²/₃ lbs. of cotton into 1²/₃ lbs. of yarn,[1] it follows that in six hours he will convert 10 lbs. of cotton into 10 lbs. of yarn. Hence, during the spinning process, the cotton absorbs six hours' labour. The same quantity of labour is also embodied in a piece of gold of the value of three shillings. Consequently by the mere labour of spinning, a value of three shillings is added to the cotton.

Let us now consider the total value of the product, the 10 lbs. of yarn. Two and a half days' labour have been embodied in it, of which two days were contained in the cotton and in the substance of the spindle worn away, and half a day was absorbed during the process of spinning. This two and a half days' labour is also represented by a piece of gold of the value of fifteen shillings. Hence, fifteen shillings is an adequate price for the 10 lbs. of yarn, or the price of one pound is eighteenpence.

Our capitalist stares in astonishment. The value of the product is exactly equal to the value of the capital advanced. The value so advanced has not expanded, no surplus-value has been created, and consequently money has not been converted into capital. The price of the yarn is fifteen shillings, and fifteen shillings were spent in the open market upon the constituent elements of the product, or, what amounts to the same thing, upon the factors of the labour-process; ten shillings were paid for the cotton, two shillings for the substance of the spindle worn away, and three shillings for the labour-power. . . .

Let us examine the matter more closely. The value of a day's labour-power amounts to 3 shillings, because on our assumption half a day's labour is embodied in that quantity of labour-power, *i.e.*, because the means of subsistence that are daily required for the production of labour-power, cost half a day's labour. But the past labour that is embodied in the labour-power, and the living labour that it can call into action; the daily cost of maintaining it, and its daily expenditure in work, are two totally different things. The former determines the exchange-value of the labour-power, the latter is its use-value. The fact that half a day's labour is necessary to keep the labourer alive during 24 hours, does not in any way prevent him from working a whole day. Therefore, the value of labour-power, and the value which that labour-power creates in the labour process, are two entirely different magnitudes; and this difference of the two values was what the capitalist had in view, when he was purchasing the labour-power. The useful qualities that labour-power possesses, and by virtue of which it makes yarn or boots, were to him nothing more than a *conditio sine qua non;* for in order to create value, labour must be expended in a useful manner. What really influenced him was the specific use-value

---

[1] These figures are quite arbitrary.

which this commodity possesses of being *a source not only of value, but of more value than it has itself*. This is the special service that the capitalist expects from labour-power, and in this transaction he acts in accordance with the "eternal laws" of the exchange of commodities. The seller of labour-power, like the seller of any other commodity, realises its exchange-value, and parts with its use-value. He cannot take the one without giving the other. The use-value of labour-power, or in other words, labour, belongs just as little to its seller, as the use-value of oil after it has been sold belongs to the dealer who has sold it. The owner of the money has paid the value of a day's labour-power; his, therefore, is the use of it for a day; a day's labour belongs to him. The circumstance, that on the one hand the daily sustenance of labour-power costs only half a day's labour, while on the other hand the very same labour-power can work during a whole day, that consequently the value which its use during one day creates, is double what he pays for that use, this circumstance is, without doubt, a piece of good luck for the buyer, but by no means an injury to the seller.

Our capitalist foresaw this state of things, and that was the cause of his laughter. The labourer therefore finds, in the workshop, the means of production necessary for working, not only during six, but during twelve hours. Just as during the six hours' process our 10 lbs. of cotton absorbed six hours' labour, and became 10 lbs. of yarn, so now, 20 lbs. of cotton will absorb 12 hours' labour and be changed into 20 lbs. of yarn. Let us now examine the product of this prolonged process. There is now materialised in this 20 lbs. of yarn the labour of five days, of which four days are due to the cotton and the lost steel of the spindle, the remaining day having been absorbed by the cotton during the spinning process. Expressed in gold, the labour of five days is thirty shillings. This is therefore the price of the 20 lbs. of yarn, giving, as before, eighteenpence as the price of a pound. But the sum of the values of the commodities that entered into the process amounts to 27 shillings. The value of the yarn is 30 shillings. Therefore the value of the product is $1/9$ greater than the value advanced for its production; 27 shillings have been transformed into 30 shillings; a surplus-value of 3 shillings has been created. The trick has at last succeeded; money has been converted into capital. . . .

If we now compare the two processes of producing value and of creating surplus-value, we see that the latter is nothing but the continuation of the former beyond a definite point. If on the one hand the process be not carried beyond the point, where the value paid by the capitalist for the labour-power is replaced by an exact equivalent, it is simply a process of producing value; if, on the other hand, it be continued beyond that point, it becomes a process of creating surplus-value. . . .

In considering the labour-process, we began . . . by treating it in the abstract, apart from its historical forms, as a process between man and nature. We . . . stated . . . "If we examine the whole labour-process from the point of view of its result, it is plain that both the instruments and the subject of labour are means of production, and that the labour itself is productive labour." And . . . we further added: "This method of determining, from the standpoint of the labour-process alone, what is productive labour, is by no means directly applicable to the case of the capitalist process of production." We now proceed to the further development of this subject.

So far as the labour-process is purely individual, one and the same labourer unites in himself all the functions, that later on become separated. When an individual appropriates natural objects for his livelihood, no one controls him but himself. Afterwards he is controlled by others. A single man cannot operate upon nature without calling his own muscles into play under the control of his own brain. As in the natural body head and hand wait upon each other, so the labour-process unites the labour of the hand with that of the head. Later on they part company and even become deadly foes. The product ceases to be the direct product of the individual, and becomes a social product, produced in common by a collective labourer, *i.e.*, by a combination of workmen, each of whom takes only a part, greater or less, in the manipulation of the subject of their labour. As the co-operative character of the labour-process becomes more and more marked, so, as a necessary consequence, does our notion of productive labour, and of its agent the productive labourer, become extended. In order to labour productively, it is no longer necessary for you to do manual work yourself; enough, if you are an organ of the collective labourer, and perform one of its subordinate functions. The first definition given above of productive labour, a definition deduced from the very nature of the production of material objects, still remains correct for the collective labourer, considered as a whole. But it no longer holds good for each member taken individually.

On the other hand, however, our notion of productive labour becomes narrowed. Capitalist production is not merely the production of commodities, it is essentially the production of surplus-value. The labourer produces, not for himself, but for capital. It no longer suffices, therefore, that he should simply produce. He must produce surplus-value. That labourer alone is productive, who produces surplus-value for the capitalist, and thus works for the self-expansion of capital. If we may take an example from outside the sphere of production of material objects, a schoolmaster is a productive labourer, when, in addition to belabouring the heads of his scholars, he works like a horse to enrich the school proprietor. That the latter has laid out his capital in a teaching factory, instead of in a sausage factory, does not alter the relation. Hence the notion of a productive labourer implies not merely a relation between work and useful effect, between labourer and product of labour, but also a specific, social relation of production, a relation that has sprung up historically and stamps the labourer as the direct means of creating surplus-value. To be a productive labourer is, therefore, not a piece of luck, but a misfortune. . . .

The prolongation of the working day beyond the point at which the labourer would have produced just an equivalent for the value of his labour-power, and the appropriation of that surplus-labour by capital, this is production of absolute surplus-value. It forms the general groundwork of the capitalist system, and the starting point for the production of relative surplus-value. The latter presupposes that the working day is already divided into two parts, necesssary labour, and surplus-labour. In order to prolong the surplus-labour, the necessary labour is shortened by methods whereby the equivalent for the wages is produced in less time. The production of absolute surplus-value turns exclusively upon the length of the working day; the production of relative surplus-value, revolutionises out and out the technical processes of labour, and the composition of society. It therefore presupposes a specific mode, the capitalist mode of production, a mode which, along with its methods, means, and conditions, arises and develops itself spontaneously on the foundation afforded by the formal subjection of labour to capital. In the course of this development, the formal subjection is replaced by the real subjection of labour to capital. . . .

WELFARE LIBERALISM

Justice as Fairness

John Rawls

I. The Notion of a Well-Ordered Society

The aim of a theory of justice is to clarify and to organize our considered judgments about the justice and injustice of social forms. Thus, any account of these judgments, when fully presented, expresses an underlying conception of human society, that is, a conception of the person, of the relations between persons, and of the general structure and ends of social cooperation. Now there are, I believe, rather few such conceptions; and these are sharply distinct so that the choice between them is a choice between disparate things: one cannot continuously vary their basic features so as to pass gradually from one to another. Thus, to formulate a theory of justice, we must specify its underlying conception in a particular though still abstract way. Justice as fairness does this by bringing together certain general features of any society that it seems one would, on due reflection, wish to live in and want to shape our interests and character. The notion of a well-ordered society is the result: it embodies these features in a definite way and indicates how to describe the original position, which is introduced in the next section. I begin by enumerating the features of such a society.[1]

First of all, a well-ordered society is defined as one that is effectively regulated by a public conception of justice. That is, it is a society in which:

1. Everyone accepts, and knows that others accept, the same principles (the same conception) of justice.
2. Basic social institutions and their arrangement into one scheme (the basic structure of society) satisfy, and are with reason believed by everyone to satisfy, these principles.
3. The public conception of justice is founded on reasonable beliefs that have been established by generally accepted methods of inquiry.

It is assumed second that the members of a well-ordered society are, and view themselves as, free and equal moral persons. More specifically, they may be described as follows:

4. They each have, and view themselves as having, a sense of justice (the content of which is defined by the principles of the public conception) that is normally effective (the desire to act on this conception determines their conduct for the most part).
5. They each have, and view themselves as having, fundamental aims and interests (a conception of their good) in the name of which it is legitimate to make claims on one another in the design of their institutions.
6. They each have, and view themselves as having, a right to equal respect and

---

[1] The advantage of beginning the exposition with the notion of a well-ordered society was suggested to me by Ronald Dworkin's discussion in "The Original Position," *Chicago Law Review*, XL (1973), esp. 519–23.

consideration in determining the principles by which the basic structure of their society is to be regulated.

In addition, a well-ordered society is said to be stable with respect to its conception of justice. This means that, viewing the society as a going concern, its members acquire as they grow up a sufficiently strong and effective sense of justice, one that usually overcomes the temptations and stresses of social life. Thus:

7. Basic social institutions generate an effective supporting sense of justice.

Since we are interested in a theory of justice, we shall restrict our attention to well-ordered societies that exist under circumstances that require some conception of justice and give point to its peculiar role. Although natural resources and the state of technology are assumed to be such so as to make social cooperation both possible and necessary, and mutually advantageous arrangements are indeed feasible; nevertheless, the benefits they yield fall short of the demands that people make. Therefore:

8. Conditions of moderate scarcity exist.

But also, we assume that persons and groups have conceptions of the good that incline them in contrary directions and make claims and counterclaims on one another (see (5) above). Furthermore, people have opposing basic beliefs (religious, philosophical, and moral) and different ways of assessing evidence and arguments in many essential cases, and so:

9. There is a divergence of fundamental interests and ends, and a variety of opposing and incompatible basic beliefs.

As for the usefulness of social institutions, we assume that the arrangements of a well-ordered society are productive; they are not, so to speak, a zero-sum game in which one person's (or group's) gain is another's loss. Thus:

10. The scheme of basic institutions is a more or less self-sufficient and productive scheme of social cooperation for mutual good.

Given these circumstances of justice ((8)–(10)), we can delineate the role and subject of justice. Since many of their fundamental aims and beliefs stand in opposition, the members of a well-ordered society are not indifferent as to how the greater benefits produced by their cooperation are distributed. Hence a set of principles is required for adjudicating between social arrangements that shape this division of advantages. We express this by:

11. The role of the principles of justice (the public conception) is to assign rights and duties in the basic structure of society and to specify the manner in which it is appropriate for institutions to influence the overall distribution of benefits and burdens.

To which we add finally:

12. The members of a well-ordered society take the basic structure of society (that is, basic social institutions and their arrangement into one scheme) as the primary subject of justice (as that to which the principles of justice are in the first instance to apply).

Thus the principles of social justice are macro and not necessarily micro principles.

This enumeration of conditions shows that the notion of a well-ordered society under circumstances of justice is extremely complicated. It may help to observe that the various conditions go together. Thus, (1)–(7) specify the notion of a well-ordered society: (1), (2), and (3) characterize publicity; (4), (5), and (6) fill in the idea of free and equal moral persons; and (7), stability, concludes this part of the list. Conditions (8), (9), and (10) characterize the circumstances of justice, which restrict the class of relevant cases in the way appropriate for a theory of justice; and (11) and (12) describe the role and subject of justice. . . .

Clearly the value of the notion of a well-ordered society, and the force of the reasoning based upon it, depends on the assumption that those who appear to hold incompatible conceptions of justice will nevertheless find conditions (1) to (7) congenial to their moral convictions, or at least would do so after consideration. Otherwise, there would be no point in appealing to these conditions in deciding between different principles of justice. But we should recognize that they are not morally neutral (whatever that would be) and certainly they are not trivial. Those who feel no affinity for the notion of a well-ordered society, and who wish to specify the underlying conception in a different form, will be unmoved by justice as fairness (even granting the validity of its argument), except of course as it may prove a better way to systematize their judgments of justice.

II. The Role of the Original Position

The idea of the original position arises in the following way. Consider the question: Which conception of justice is most appropriate for a well-ordered society, that is, which conception best accords with the above conditions? Of course, this is a vague question. One can sharpen it by asking which of a few representative conceptions, drawn from the tradition of moral philosophy, is the closest fit. Assume, then, that we have to decide between but a few conceptions (e.g., a variant of intuitionism and of utilitarianism, and certain principles of justice). Justice as fairness holds that the particular conception that is most suitable for a well-ordered society is the one that would be unanimously agreed to in a hypothetical situation that is fair between individuals conceived as free and equal moral persons, that is, as members of such a society. Alternatively, the conception that is most appropriate for a society is the one that persons characteristic of the society would adopt when fairly situated with respect to one another. This hypothetical situation is the original position. Fairness of the circumstances under which agreement is reached transfers to the fairness of the principles agreed to; and since these principles serve as principles of justice, the name "justice as fairness" seems natural.

We assume that in the original position the parties have the general information provided by natural science and social theory. This meets condition I (3). But in order to define the original position as fair between the individuals conceived as free and equal moral persons, we imagine that the parties are deprived of certain morally irrelevant information. For example, they do not know their place in society, their class position or social status, their fortune in the distribution of natural talents and abilities, their deeper aims and interests, or finally, their particular psychological makeup. And to insure fairness between generations, we must add that they do not know to which generation they belong and thus information about natural resources, the level of productive techniques, and the like, is also forbidden to them. Excluding this knowledge is necessary if no one is to be advantaged or disadvantaged by natural contingencies and social chance in the adoption of principles. Since all are similarly situated, and the parties do not know how to frame principles to favor their peculiar condition, each will reason in the same way. There is no need to have a binding vote, and any agreement reached is unanimous. (Thus, being in the original position is always to be contrasted with being in society.)

The description of the original position must satisfy two conditions: first, it is to be a fair situation, and second, the parties are to be conceived as members of a well-ordered society. Thus, this description contains elements drawn from the notion of fairness, for example, that the parties are symmetrically situated and subject to the veil of ignorance. It also includes features drawn from the nature and relations of persons in a well-ordered society: the parties view themselves as having final aims and interests in the name of which they think it legitimate to make claims on one another; and that they are adopting what is to serve as a public conception of justice and must, therefore, assess principles in part by their publicity effects. They must also check for stability. So long as each part of the description of the original position has a legitimate pedigree, or we are prepared to accept certain conditions in view of their implications, everything is in order.

The aim of the description of the original position is to put together in one conception the idea of fairness with the formal conditions expressed by the notion of a well-ordered society, and then to use this conception to help us select between alternative principles of justice. A striking feature of the preceding account is that we have not said anything very specific about the content of the principles of justice in a well-ordered society. We have simply combined certain rather formal and abstract conditions. One possibility is that these conditions determine unambiguously a unique conception of justice. More likely the constraints of the original position only narrow down the class of admissible conceptions; but this is still significant if it turns out that some ostensibly plausible moral conceptions are ruled out.

Finally, that the original position is hypothetical poses no difficulty. We can simulate being in that situation simply by reasoning in accordance with the stipulated constraints. If we accept the values expressed by these constraints, and therefore the formal values embodied in the notion of a well-ordered society, the idea of fairness, and the rest, we must accept the resulting limitations on conceptions of justice and reject those principles that are excluded. The attempt to unify the more formal and abstract elements of moral thought so as to bring them to bear on questions of lesser generality is characteristic of Kantian theory.

III. The First Pair-Wise Comparison: Two Principles of Justice vs. the Principle of Utility

What alternative conceptions are available in the original position? We must avoid the general case where the parties are to decide between all possible conceptions of justice, since one cannot specify this class in a useful way. We need to simplify greatly if we are to gain an intuitive understanding of the combined force of the conditions that characterize the original position. Thus we imagine that the parties are to choose from a short list of conceptions drawn from the tradition of moral philosophy. Actually, I shall at this point discuss only one pair-wise comparison. Doing this serves to fix ideas and enables me to note a few points that will be required as we proceed.

Now one aim of contract theory has been to give an account of justice that is both superior to utilitarianism and a more adequate basis for a democratic society. Therefore, let us imagine a choice between (α), a conception defined by the principle that average utility (interpreted in the classical sense) is to be maximized, and (β), a conception defined by two principles that express on their face, as it were, a democratic idea of justice. These principles read as follows:

1. Each person has an equal right to the most extensive scheme of equal basic liberties compatible with a similar scheme of liberties for all.
2. Social and economic inequalities are to meet two conditions: they must be (a) to the greatest expected benefit of the least advantaged (the maximin criterion); and (b) attached to offices and positions open to all under conditions of fair equality of opportunity.

The first of these principles is to take priority over the second; and the measure of benefit to the least advantaged is in terms of an index of social primary goods. These I define roughly as rights, liberties, and opportunities, income and wealth, and the social bases of self-respect; they are things that individuals are presumed to want whatever else they want, or whatever their final ends. And the parties are to reach their agreement on this supposition. (I shall come back to primary goods below.) I assume also that everyone has normal physical needs so that the problem of special health care does not arise.

Which of these two conceptions (α) or (β) would be agreed to depends, of course, on how the persons in the original position are conceived. Since they represent free moral persons, as earlier defined, they regard themselves as having fundamental aims and interests, the claims of which they must protect, if this is possible. It is partly in the name of these interests that they have a right to equal consideration and respect in the design of society. The religious interest is a familiar historical example; the interest in the integrity of the person is another (freedom from psychological oppression and physical assault belong here). In the original position the parties do not know what particular form these interests take. But they do assume that they have such interests; and also that the basic liberties necessary for their protection are guaranteed by the first principle. Here it is essential to note that basic liberties are defined by a certain list of liberties; prominent among them are freedom of thought and liberty of conscience, freedom of the person and political liberty. These liberties have a central range of application within which they can be limited and adjusted only because they clash with other basic liberties. None of these liberties, therefore, is absolute, since they may conflict with one another; but, however they are adjusted to form one's system, this system is to be the same for all. Liberties not on the list, for example, the right to own property and freedom of contract as understood in the doctrine of laissez-faire are not basic: they are not protected by the priority of the first principle.

To consider the above pair-wise comparison, we must first say how one is to understand the principle of average utility. It is to be taken in the classical sense, which permits (by definition) interpersonal comparisons of utility that can at least be assessed at the margin; and utility is to be measured from the standpoint of individuals in society (and not from the standpoint of the original position) and means the degree of satisfaction of their interests. If accepted, this is how the principle will be understood and applied in society. But then it might sometimes lead, when consistently applied over time, to a basic structure securing the basic liberties; but there is no reason why it should do so in general. And even if this criterion often ensures the necessary freedoms, it would be pointless to run the risk of encountering circumstances when it does not. The two principles of justice, however, will protect these liberties; and since in the original position the parties give a special priority to their fundamental interests (which they assume to be of certain general kinds), each would far rather adopt these principles (at least when they are the only alternative).

One must also take into account other special features of a well-ordered society. For example, the principles adopted are to serve as a public conception, and this means that the effects of publicity must be assessed. Particularly important are the effects on the social bases of self-respect; for when self-respect is lacking, we feel our ends not worth pursuing, and nothing has much value. Now it would seem that people who regard themselves as free and equal moral persons are much more likely to find their self-esteem supported and confirmed by social institutions satisfying the two principles of justice than by those answering to the standard of average utility. For such institutions announce by the principles they are publicly known to satisfy the collective intent that all should have equal basic liberty and that social and economic inequalities are to be regulated by the maximum criterion. Obviously this reasoning is highly speculative; but it illustrates the kind of considerations introduced by the publicity conditions of a well-ordered society.

The reasoning that favors the two principles can be strengthened by spelling out in more detail the notion of a free person. Very roughly, the parties regard themselves as having a highest-order interest in how all their other interests, including even their fundamental ones, are shaped and regulated by social institutions. They do not think of themselves as inevitably bound to, or as identical with, the pursuit of any particular complex of fundamental interests that they may have at any given time, although they want the right to advance such interests (provided they are admissible). Rather, free persons conceive of themselves as beings who can revise and alter their final ends and who give first priority to preserving their liberty in these matters. Hence, they not only have final ends that they are in principle free to pursue or to reject, but their original allegiance and continued devotion to these ends are to be formed and affirmed under conditions that are free. Since the two principles secure a social form that maintains these conditions, they would be agreed to. Only by this agreement can the parties be sure that their highest-order interest as free persons is guaranteed.

I shall conclude this section with a few remarks about primary goods. As noted earlier these are things that, from the standpoint of the original position, it is reasonable for the parties to assume that they want, whatever their final ends. For the description of the original position to be plausible, this motivation assumption must be plausible; and the (thin) theory of the good is intended to support it. In any case, an essential part of a conception of justice is the rules governing its application by members of a well-ordered society. When the parties adopt a conception, the understanding about these rules must be made explicit. Thus while the motivation of the persons in the original position is different from the motivation of individuals in society, the interpretation of the principles agreed to must be the same.

Now an important feature of the two principles is that they assess the basic structure in terms of certain primary goods: rights, liberties, and opportunities, income and wealth, and the social bases of self-respect. The latter are features of the basic structure that may reasonably be expected to affect people's self-esteem in important ways. In the maximin criterion (part (a) of the second principle) the measure of benefits is an index of these goods. Certainly there are difficulties in defining a satisfactory index,² but the points to stress here are (a) that primary goods are certain objective characteristics of social institutions and people's situation with respect to them, and therefore the index is not a measure of overall satisfaction or dissatisfaction; and (b) that the same index of these goods is used to compare everyone's social circumstances. Interpersonal comparisons are based on this index. . . . In agreeing to the two principles, the parties agree that in making judgments of justice, they are to use such an index. Of course, the precise weights can hardly be determined in the original position; these may be determined later, for example, at the legislative stage.³ What can be settled initially is certain constraints on these weights, as illustrated by the priority of the first principle.

Implicit in the use of primary goods is the following conception. We view persons as able to control and to adjust their wants and desires in the light of circumstances and who are to be given the responsibility for doing so (assuming that the principles of justice are fulfilled). Society on its part assumes the responsibility for maintaining certain basic liberties and opportunities and for providing a fair share of primary goods within this framework, leaving it to individuals and groups to form and to revise their aims and preferences accordingly. Thus there is an understanding among members of a well-ordered society that as citizens they will press claims only for certain kinds of things and as allowed for by the principles of justice. Strong feelings and zealous aspirations for certain goals do not, as such, give people a claim upon social resources or the design of public institutions. It is not implied that those with the same index have equal well-being, all things considered; for their ends are generally different and many other factors are relevant. But for purposes of social justice this is the appropriate basis of comparison. The theory of primary goods is a generalization of the notion of needs, which are distinct from aspirations and desires. So we could say: as citizens the members of a well-ordered society collectively take responsibility for dealing justly with one another on the basis of a public measure of (generalized) needs, while as individuals and members of associations they take responsibility for their preferences and devotions. . . .

Questions for Further Reflection

1. How convincing is the Marxist critique of capitalism? Is Rawls' welfare liberalism subject to the same critique?
2. Consider Hospers' claim that "every human being has the right to act in accordance with his own choices, unless those actions infringe on the equal liberty of other human beings to act in accordance with *their* choices." Given this formulation, how can we determine whether we have a specific liberty or not? For example, suppose you and I both want to take a given parcel of land. How can we decide who may take it?
3. Hospers claims that it would be unjust to tax you to pay for the expenses of someone who is unemployed. Would Rawls disagree? If so, who would be correct, and why?

---

²K. J. Arrow ("Some Ordinalist-Utilitarian Notes on Rawls' Theory of Justice," *Journal of philosophy*, LXX (1973). p. 254) has noted that special health needs, which I assume here not to arise, will be a particularly difficult problem. This question requires a separate discussion.

³See *A Theory of Justice* (Cambridge: Harvard University Press, 1971), p. 198f. At this stage we have much more information and within the constraints can adjust the index to existing social conditions.

4. Contrast the libertarian, utilitarian, and welfare liberal views on the issue of whether there should be laws restricting sexual behavior and drug usage.

Further Readings

Daniels, Norman, ed. *Reading Rawls.* New York: Basic Books, Inc., 1976. Contains an excellent collection of critical discussions of Rawls' view.

Machan, Tibor. *The Libertarian Alternative: Essays in Social and Political Philosophy.* Chicago: Nelson-Hall Company, 1974. A useful collection of libertarian essays on a number of topics.

Nozick, Robert. *Anarchy, State and Utopia.* New York: Basic Books, Inc., 1974. One of the best developments of the libertarian view, which contains engaging critical discussions of welfare liberalism.

Rawls, John. *A Theory of Justice.* Cambridge, MA: Harvard University Press, 1971. The full statement of Rawls' theory of justice. "The Basic Liberties and Their Priority," *Tanner Lectures on Human Values III* (Salt Lake City: University of Utah Press, 1982), "Justice as Fairness: Political Not Metaphysical," *Philosophy and Public Affairs* (1985): 223–251, and "The Idea of an Overlapping Consensus," *Oxford Journal of Legal Studies* 7 (1987): 1–24 record more recent developments of Rawls' position.

Tucker, Robert, ed. *The Marx-Engels Reader,* second edition. New York: W. W. Norton & Company, 1972. An excellent collection of Marx's writings.

Wolff, Robert Paul. *In Defense of Anarchism.* New York: Harper Torchbooks. 1976. An excellent defense of anarchist libertarianism.

Chapter 9

EUTHANASIA

Tragically, many people are struck with afflictions, such as cancer or extensive burns, that fill their lives with extreme suffering and that threaten to persist until they die. Many of them implore us to kill them or let them die. Other people are the victims of accidents that destroy their very personalities and deprive them even of the ability to ask us to end their lives. Moreover, all too often, infants are born with defects, such as the lack of a brain, that rule out the possibility of their leading a worthwhile life. Ought we do everything possible to keep such people alive? Or should we not sometimes end their lives, or at least let them die, so as to relieve them of the burden of living an unworthwhile existence? In a word: Is euthanasia, or "mercy killing," ever acceptable, or even obligatory?

Some Terminology

It will help if we ask what *constitutes* mercy killing, for many different sorts of things have been called *euthanasia*. Some argue that standing by and allowing people to die is not the same thing as killing them, and so ought not to be construed as mercy killing, as euthanasia. Others extend the meaning of the term *euthanasia* to cover some cases of both killing and letting die. Either way a difficulty arises: It is sometimes clear when we are killing and when we are letting someone die, but in other cases, it is very hard to say. Am I killing you if I disconnect you from some apparatus that is helping to keep you alive? Or am I letting you die?

Construing the term *euthanasia* as neutral between killing and letting die allows us to provide a classification that will be useful in the framing of the issues that euthanasia provokes. *Active* euthanasia is the act of killing someone in order to relieve that person's suffering. *Passive* euthanasia is also aimed at relieving someone's suffering, but it is the act of refraining from doing something that would keep that person alive. In either case, we can draw further distinctions depending on whether or not the individual at hand wants to die. A case of euthanasia (whether active or passive) is *voluntary* if, in view of the circumstances, the person at hand wants to die. It would be *involuntary* if the individual wished not to die, and *nonvoluntary* if the person were incapable of having a preference (due to severe physical damage, for example). Often the term *nonvoluntary euthanasia* is also applied to the killing of the bodies of people who arguably are already dead, as when damage to their brains is so extensive that their personalities are completely destroyed but their bodies live on under the aid of artificial support. Unlike the other cases of euthanasia, these situations can seem to raise the issue of whether a body is to die, not the issue of whether a *person* is to die.

Close connections exist between the topic of euthanasia and the topic of suicide, covered in Chapter 4. First, if suicide is sometimes permissible, then clearly, some forms of euthanasia are, too; for if suicide is all right in certain circumstances, then it is permissible to allow people to commit suicide in those circumstances. Yet not interrupting a suicide attempt *is* refraining from doing something that would keep that person alive, so if refraining from interrupting someone's attempt to commit suicide is permissible, then at least some cases of passive voluntary euthanasia are permissible. Second, if suicide were always wrong, so would active and passive euthanasia be (although euthanasia cannot be criticized on some of the grounds on which Kant condemned suicide: Perhaps I would be treating myself as a mere means to my own happiness or to the happiness of others if I killed myself, but if I killed *other* people for *their* own sake, I would not be using them as a mere means to my happiness). If I cannot justifiably take my own life, even if it would be in my interest to do so, no one else can either, and if they allow me to do so, they are permitting a wrong to occur.

In view of the second point, therefore, readers of Chapter 4 who conclude that suicide is always impermissible will no doubt dismiss all forms of euthanasia out of hand. However, if we assume that suicide and voluntary passive euthanasia are both permissible in at least some circumstances, many issues remain, among them: Should only certain forms of passive euthanasia be considered permissible, or are there forms of active euthanasia that are allowable (or even required) as well? Another issue: Given that certain forms of active and/or passive euthanasia are morally permissible, which forms of euthanasia ought to be legalized, if any?

Only Passive Euthanasia Is Permissible

Among people who countenance euthanasia at all, the most conservative are those who maintain that only passive euthanasia is permissible. Some conservatives emphasize an important moral difference between killing someone and standing by while someone dies. In the former case, one may be guilty of murder, while in the latter, one is at worst guilty of a far less serious wrong. Moreover, some terminal patients have nothing to look forward to except great misery, so to save them would cause them great misfortune. On balance, therefore, it is acceptable to stand by while such unfortunate people die; passive euthanasia in some such cases is permissible, although active euthanasia—actively killing someone—is unacceptable.

According to James Rachels, this is the position of the American Medical Association. In Rachels's interpretation, the AMA forbids active euthanasia but maintains that passive euthanasia is allowable, both in its voluntary and its nonvoluntary forms (although not in its involuntary form).

Both Passive and Active Euthanasia Are Permissible

Rachels himself argues that from the moral point of view, active and passive euthanasia are on a par, because killing someone and letting someone die are morally on a par; that is, killing someone is no worse (nor better) than letting someone die. Thus, contrast two situations: In one, I stand by while a child I had intended to kill accidentally drowns; in the other, I drown the child. According to Rachels, what I have done in the first situation is equally as bad as what I have done in the second. Hence, he objects to the American Medical Association's policy of forbidding active euthanasia while allowing passive euthanasia. Of course, the mere fact that passive and active euthanasia are on a par does not show that either is permissible; one might argue that neither is permissible and that the AMA ought to condemn both. Rachels argues that both are defensible, for both are aimed at relieving the intense suffering of terminally ill patients.

Neither Passive nor Active Euthanasia Is Permissible

In his article "The Immorality of Euthanasia," Joseph Sullivan argues that all forms of euthanasia are wrong and ought to be illegal. In Sullivan's view, my act is one of euthanasia only if I intend to kill someone or to let someone die through acting as I have. So understood, *euthanasia* is always wrong, according to Sullivan, because we ought never to act from the intention of letting someone die or of killing someone; doing so is "direct killing." Nevertheless, it *is* sometimes permissible to do what we *foresee* will be fatal, as long as we do not *intend* to allow or to bring about the fatality. Thus, it can be permissible for a physician to abort a fetus to save the life of a mother, and it is possible for physicians to act in a way that *looks* like passive euthanasia. What would the physician's motivation be? In a different essay, Sullivan describes it as follows:

> [T]he unwillingness of the physician to use extra-ordinary means for preserving life may be prompted not by a determination to bring about death, but by other motives. For example, he may realize that further treatment may offer little hope of reversing the dying process and/or be excruciating, as in the case when a massively necrotic bowel condition in a neonate is out of control. The doctor who does what he can to comfort the infant but does not submit it to further treatment or surgery may foresee that the decision will hasten death, but it certainly doesn't follow from that fact that he intends to bring about its death.[1]

Sullivan's arguments against euthanasia include a version of one we have seen before: We may not "play God." God owns us, Sullivan claims, and no one (except God) may destroy God's property, even if that property wants to be killed. David Hume rejected the argument that we may not play God by noting that saving lives is playing God fully as much as is killing, but it is not clear that Hume's criticism applies to Sullivan's version of the "playing God" argument. As Sullivan says, it is reasonable to say that caretakers of God's property may save it from destruction but unreasonable to say that caretakers of God's property may destroy it. (But doesn't it matter that the "property" here under discussion is human beings? If it really is in my interest to die now rather than suffer unnecessary pain, why assume that God's claim to own me would lead God not to want you to accept my request to kill me?)

Withdrawing Treatment Is Morally Obligatory

Margaret Battin would agree with Rachels's claim that active and passive voluntary and nonvoluntary euthanasia are permissible,

---

[1] "Active and Passive Euthanasia: An Impertinent Distinction?" *Human Life Review* III (1977), pp. 40–46.

but she defends a much stronger thesis as well. When medical resources cannot be provided for everyone who needs them, these life-saving resources must be withheld from certain individuals, even though they themselves want to be kept alive. Letting people die on the grounds that it is just is not the same thing as mercy killing. But while Battin recommends withholding medical treatment in certain conditions on the grounds that doing so is a requirement of justice, nonetheless, one of the reasons she thinks her policy is just is that it would benefit everyone (except the generation of people who first adopt her suggestion).

Battin defends her view on Rawlsian grounds: If parties in Rawls's original position were to work out how they would distribute medical resources that were so expensive and scarce as to be unavailable to everyone who could benefit from them, the parties would turn resources that might have gone to the elderly over to the young. In doing so, they would be more likely to ensure that more people live a long life relative to the norm for the human species, for a unit of health care is more effective when applied to the young than to the old. In practice, this policy of "age rationing by denial of treatment" amounts to saying to some of the elderly people who want costly resources, "You cannot have the resources because it would be unjust to allow you to have them." If the elderly are tempted to respond that they are being treated unfairly, the response would be that they themselves have benefited from the policy by having had greater access to health care when they were younger than they would have had in the absence of an age-rationing policy.

Of course, many of the people who are denied costly treatment will face great suffering (particularly if the withheld treatment is itself a costly procedure for minimizing their pain). Consequently, the parties in the original position would institute active euthanasia, or the killing of people who otherwise would suffer. However, Battin claims, the parties would opt only for voluntary, not involuntary, active euthanasia. People denied further treatment would be killed on request, but otherwise, they would be allowed to suffer on, for involuntary active euthanasia is so easily abused that the parties would avoid it.

Should Euthanasia Be Legal?

As we have seen, Battin would argue that a just society, in which health-care resources are scarce, would require withholding resources from some people. If scarcity were unavoidable, she would hope to see her suggestion built into the legal institutions of society. Sullivan takes a diametrically opposed stance. He argues that all forms of euthanasia ought to be illegal. One reason is that euthanasia is wrong in his view. But he also bases his conclusion on what he calls "the argument from the wedge principle" (which is more often called the "slippery slope argument"): If voluntary euthanasia were legalized, so would involuntary euthanasia be, closely followed by the killing of "all incurable charity patients, the aged who are a public care, wounded soldiers, captured enemy soldiers, all deformed children, the mentally afflicted, and so on. Before long the danger would be at the door of every citizen."

In his response to Sullivan's wedge argument, Rachels defends a position that is less conservative than Sullivan's but less liberal than Battin's. He notes that we certainly are not *rationally committed* to moving from accepting voluntary euthanasia to accepting the other practices that Sullivan worries we will. He goes on to give some reasons that, as a matter of psychological fact, we are unlikely to make the move that worries Sullivan. Rachels ends with a proposal for how to legalize euthanasia: Pleas of mercy killing ought to be accepted as legitimate defenses against the charge of murder.

How likely is it that Rachels's suggestion will be implemented? It is very difficult to say, but the Supreme Court shows little sign of countenancing *active* killings even if motivated by mercy. However, the Court has now made it clear that in certain circumstances, it will countenance the withdrawal of medical treatment so as to allow people to die. In these cases, no plea of mercy killing would be necessary.

The key decision came on June 25, 1990, when the Supreme Court issued its decision in *Cruzan v. Director, Missouri Department of Health*. The Court decided that "for purposes of this case, we assume that the United States Constitution would grant a competent person a constitutionally protected right to refuse lifesaving hydration and nutrition."[2] However, the Court allowed States to set their own standards for evidence that a patient desires water and nutrition withheld.

---

[2]Quoted in McDermott, Will, and Emery, *Health Law Update* 7 (June 1990).

BOTH PASSIVE AND ACTIVE EUTHANASIA ARE PERMISSIBLE

Active and Passive Euthanasia

James Rachels

The distinction between active and passive euthanasia is thought to be crucial for medical ethics. The idea is that it is permissible, at least in some cases, to withhold treatment and allow a patient to die, but it is never permissible to take any direct action designed to kill the patient. This doctrine seems to be accepted by most doctors, and it is endorsed in a statement adopted by the House of Delegates of the American Medical Association on December 4, 1973:

> The intentional termination of the life of one human being by another—mercy killing—is contrary to that for which the medical profession stands and is contrary to the policy of the American Medical Association.

The cessation of the employment of extraordinary means to prolong the life of the body when there is irrefutable evidence that biological death is imminent is the decision of the patient and/or his immediate family. The advice and judgment of the physician should be freely available to the patient and/or his immediate family.

However, a strong case can be made against this doctrine. In what follows I will set out some of the relevant arguments, and urge doctors to reconsider their views on this matter.

To begin with a familiar type of situation, a patient who is dying of incurable cancer of the throat is in terrible pain, which can no longer be satisfactorily alleviated. He is certain to die within a few days, even if present treatment is continued, but he does not want to go on living for those days since the pain is unbearable. So he asks the doctor for an end to it, and his family joins in the request.

Suppose the doctor agrees to withhold treatment, as the conventional doctrine says he may. The justification for his doing so is that the patient is in terrible agony, and since he is going to die anyway, it would be wrong to prolong his suffering needlessly. But now notice this. If one simply withholds treatment, it may take the patient longer to die, and so he may suffer more than he would if more direct action were taken and a lethal injection given. This fact provides strong reason for thinking that, once the initial decision not to prolong his agony has been made, active euthanasia is actually preferable to passive euthanasia, rather than the reverse. To say otherwise is to endorse the option that leads to more suffering rather than less, and is contrary to the humanitarian impulse that prompts the decision not to prolong his life in the first place.

Part of my point is that the process of being "allowed to die" can be relatively slow and painful, whereas being given a lethal injection is relatively quick and painless. Let me give a different sort of example. In the United States about one in 600 babies is born with Down's syndrome. Most of these babies are otherwise healthy—that is, with only the usual pediatric care, they will proceed to an otherwise normal infancy. Some, however, are born with congenital defects such as intestinal obstructions that require operations if they are to live. Sometimes, the parents and the doctor will decide not to operate, and let the infant die. Anthony Shaw describes what happens then:

When surgery is denied [the doctor] must try to keep the infant from suffering while natural forces sap the baby's life away. As a surgeon whose natural inclination is to use the scalpel to fight off death, standing by and watching a salvageable baby die is the most emotionally exhausting experience I know. It is easy at a conference, in a theoretical discussion to decide that such infants should be allowed to die. It is altogether different to stand by in the nursery and watch as dehydration and infection wither a tiny being over hours and days. This is a terrible ordeal for me and the hospital staff—much more so than for the parents who never set foot in the nursery.*

I can understand why some people are opposed to all euthanasia, and insist that such infants must be allowed to live. I think I can also understand why other people favor destroying these babies quickly and painlessly. But why should anyone favor letting "dehydration and infection wither a tiny being over hours and days"? The doctrine that says that a baby may be allowed to dehydrate and wither, but may not be given an injection that would end its life without suffering, seems so patently cruel as to require no further refutation. The strong language is not intended to offend, but only to put the point in the clearest possible way.

My second argument is that the conventional doctrine leads to decisions concerning life and death made on irrelevant grounds.

Consider again the case of the infants with Down's syndrome who need operations for congenital defects unrelated to the syndrome to live. Sometimes, there is no operation, and the baby dies, but when there is no such defect, the baby lives on. Now, an operation such as that to remove

---

*Shaw, Anthony, "Doctor, Do We Have a Choice?" *The New York Times Magazine*, January 30, 1972, p. 54.

any intestinal obstruction is not prohibitively difficult. The reason why such operations are not performed in these cases is, clearly, that the child has Down's syndrome and the parents and the doctor judge that because of that fact it is better for the child to die.

But notice that this situation is absurd, no matter what view one takes of the lives and potentials of such babies. If the life of such an infant is worth preserving, what does it matter if it needs a simple operation? Or, if one thinks it better that such a baby should not live on, what difference does it make that it happens to have an unobstructed intestinal tract? In either case, the matter of life and death is being decided on irrelevant grounds. It is the Down's syndrome, and not the intestines, that is the issue. The matter should be decided, if at all, on that basis, and not be allowed to depend on the essentially irrelevant question of whether the intestinal tract is blocked.

What makes this situation possible, of course, is the idea that when there is an intestinal blockage, one can "let the baby die," but when there is no such defect there is nothing that can be done, for one must not "kill" it. The fact that this idea leads to such results as deciding life or death on irrelevant grounds is another good reason why the doctrine would be rejected.

One reason why so many people think that there is an important moral difference between active and passive euthanasia is that they think killing someone is morally worse than letting someone die. But is it? Is killing, in itself, worse than letting die? To investigate this issue, two cases may be considered that are exactly alike except that one involves killing whereas the other involves letting someone die. Then, it can be asked whether this difference makes any difference to the moral assessments. It is important that the cases be exactly alike, except for this one difference, since otherwise one cannot be confident that it is this difference and not some other that accounts for any variation in the assessments of the two cases. So, let us consider this pair of cases:

In the first, Smith stands to gain a large inheritance if anything should happen to his six-year-old cousin. One evening while the child is taking his bath, Smith sneaks into the bathroom and drowns the child, and then arranges things so that it will look like an accident.

In the second, Jones also stands to gain if anything should happen to his six-year-old cousin. Like Smith, Jones sneaks in planning to drown the child in his bath. However, just as he enters the bathroom Jones sees the child slip and hit his head, and fall face down in the water. Jones is delighted; he stands by, ready to push the child's head back under if it is necessary, but it is not necessary. With only a little thrashing about, the child drowns all by himself, "accidentally," as Jones watches and does nothing.

Now Smith killed the child, whereas Jones "merely" let the child die. That is the only difference between them. Did either man behave better, from a moral point of view? If the difference between killing and letting die were in itself a morally important matter, one should say that Jones's behavior was less reprehensible than Smith's. But does one really want to say that? I think not. In the first place, both men acted from the same motive, personal gain, and both had exactly the same end in view when they acted. It maybe inferred from Smith's conduct that he is a bad man, although the judgment may be withdrawn or modified if certain further facts are learned about him—for example, that he is mentally deranged. But would not the very same thing be inferred about Jones from his conduct? And would not the same further considerations also be relevant to any modification of this judgment? Moreover, suppose Jones pleaded, in his own defense, "After all, I didn't do anything except just stand there and watch the child drown. I didn't kill him; I only let him die." Again, if letting die were in itself less bad than killing, this defense should have at least some weight. But it does not. Such a "defense" can only be regarded as a grotesque perversion of moral reasoning. Morally speaking, it is no defense at all.

Now, it may be pointed out, quite properly, that the cases of euthanasia with which doctors are concerned are not like this at all. They do not involve personal gain or the destruction of normal healthy children. Doctors are concerned only with cases in which the patient's life is of no further use to him, or in which the patient's life has become or will soon become a terrible burden. However, the point is the same in these cases: the bare difference between killing and letting die does not, in itself, make a moral difference. If a doctor lets a patient die, for humane reasons, he is in the same moral position as if he had given the patient a lethal injection for humane reasons. If his decision was wrong—if, for example, the patient's illness was in fact curable—the decision would be equally regrettable no matter which method was used to carry it out. And if the doctor's decision was the right one, the method used is not in itself important.

The AMA policy statement isolates the crucial issue very well; the crucial issue is "the intentional termination of the life of one human being by another." But after identifying this issue, and forbidding "mercy, killing," the statement goes on to deny that the cessation of treatment is the intentional termination of a life. This is where the mistake comes in, for what is the cessation of treatment, in these circumstances, if it is not "the intentional termination of the life of one human being by another"? Of course it is exactly that, and if it were not, there would be no point to it.

Many people will find this judgment hard to accept. One reason, I think, is that it is very easy to conflate the question of whether killing is, in itself, worse than letting die, with the very different question of whether most actual cases of killing are more reprehensible than most actual cases of letting die. Most actual cases of killing are clearly terrible (think, for example, of all the murders reported in the newspapers), and one hears of such cases every day. On the other hand, one hardly ever hears of a case of letting die, except for the actions of doctors who are motivated by humanitarian reasons. So one learns to think of killing in a much worse light than of letting die. But this does not mean that there is something about killing that makes it in itself worse than letting die, for it is not the bare difference between killing and letting die that makes the difference in these cases. Rather, the other factors—the murderer's motive of personal gain, for example, contrasted with the doctor's humanitarian motivation—account for different reactions to the different cases.

I have argued that killing is not in itself any worse than letting die; if my contention is right, it follows that active euthanasia is not any worse than passive euthanasia. What arguments can be given on the other side? The most common, I believe, is the following:

> The important difference between active and passive euthanasia is that, in passive euthanasia, the doctor does not do anything to bring about the patient's death. The doctor does nothing, and the patient dies of whatever ills already afflict him. In active euthanasia, however, the doctor does something to bring about the patient's death: he

kills him. The doctor who gives the patient with cancer a lethal injection has himself caused his patient's death; whereas if he merely ceases treatment, the cancer is the cause of the death.

A number of points need to be made here. The first is that it is not exactly correct to say that in passive euthanasia the doctor does nothing, for he does do one thing that is very important: he lets the patient die. "Letting someone die" is certainly different, in some respects, from other types of action—mainly in that it is a kind of action that one may perform by way of not performing certain other actions. For example, one may let a patient die by way of not giving medication, just as one may insult someone by way of not shaking his hand. But for any purpose of moral assessment, it is a type of action nonetheless. The decision to let a patient die is subject to moral appraisal in the same way that a decision to kill him would be subject to moral appraisal: it may be assessed as wise or unwise, compassionate or sadistic, right or wrong. If a doctor deliberately let a patient die who was suffering from a routinely curable illness, the doctor would certainly be to blame for what he had done, just as he would be to blame if he had needlessly killed the patient. Charges against him would then be appropriate. If so, it would be no defense at all for him to insist that he didn't "do anything." He would have done something very serious indeed, for he let his patient die.

Fixing the cause of death may be very important from a legal point of view, for it may determine whether criminal charges are brought against the doctor. But I do not think that this notion can be used to show a moral difference between active and passive euthanasia. The reason why it is considered bad to be the cause of someone's death is that death is regarded as a great evil—and so it is. However, if it has been decided that euthanasia—even passive euthanasia—is desirable in a given case, it has also been decided that in this instance death is no greater an evil than the patient's continued existence. And if this is true, the usual reason for not wanting to be the cause of someone's death simply does not apply.

Finally, doctors may think that all of this is only of academic interest—the sort of thing that philosophers may worry about but that has no practical bearing on their own work. After all, doctors must be concerned about the legal consequences of what they do, and active euthanasia is clearly forbidden by the law. But even so, doctors should also be concerned with the fact that the law is forcing upon them a moral doctrine that may be indefensible, and has a considerable effect on their practices. Of course, most doctors are not now in the position of being coerced in this matter, for they do not regard themselves as merely going along with what the law requires. Rather, in statements such as the AMA policy statement that I have quoted, they are endorsing this doctrine as a central point of medical ethics. In that statement, active euthanasia is condemned not merely as illegal but as "contrary to that for which the medical profession stands," whereas passive euthanasia is approved. However, the preceding considerations suggest that there is really no moral difference between the two, considered in themselves (there may be important moral differences in some cases in their *consequences*, but, as I pointed out, these differences may make active euthanasia, and not passive euthanasia, the morally preferable option). So, whereas doctors may have to discriminate between active and passive euthanasia to satisfy the law, they should not do any more than that. In particular, they should not give the distinction any added authority and weight by writing it into official statements of medical ethics.

NEITHER PASSIVE NOR ACTIVE EUTHANASIA IS PERMISSIBLE

The Immorality of Euthanasia

Joseph V. Sullivan

In this essay I will discuss the moral aspects of mercy killing, whether voluntary or compulsory. The thesis that I will attempt to prove is that it is never lawful for man on his own authority to kill the innocent directly. If the thesis is morally sound, it follows that mercy killing is never permissible.

Under certain conditions one may kill a person who without authorization attacks him or another party. It is the more common opinion that the killing of an unjust aggressor may be only indirect, in the manner that will be explained below.[1] No private individual has authority over the life of another person, and therefore to place by his own authority an act that has as its only immediate end the death of an unjust aggressor, is a grave crime. It must be remembered that even though a man makes an attack upon another, he does not forfeit his life to that other person. Accordingly, if a criminal attacks a man, the man may not aim at the criminal's death, but he may place whatever acts are necessary for protecting his own life, even if in doing this the criminal's death would follow as a concomitant effect. It would appear that in self-defense the aim is always and first of all the stopping of the attack. . . .

Lastly the thesis is concerned with *direct* killing. Direct killing means an action or omission that has no other immediate end than the death of a person. The death is intended as an end in itself or as a means to an end.[2] If a man is killed out of revenge, then the death is inflicted as an end desirable in itself and hence is direct killing. If a man is killed in order that a secret be maintained or that an end be put to his sufferings, then the death is inflicted as a means to an end, but this is also direct killing. In either of these cases the death inflicted is the only immediate effect. Direct killing must be understood in contradistinction to indirect killing, which may be defined as an action or omission having some other immediate effect in addition to the death of a person. Such a death, even when foreseen to follow an act, need not be intended in itself, but can be merely permitted.[3] Thus, if the brakes of an automobile fail and the machine begins to dash downhill into a

---

[1] M. Cronin, *The Science of Ethics*, II, p. 97; J. Aertnys-C. Damen, *Theologia moralis*, I, nr. 571; H. Noldin-A. Schmitt, *Summa theologiae moralis*, II, nr. 333; B. Merkelbach, *Summa theologiae moralis*, II, nr. 361-sub. 4; H. Jone-U. Adelman, *Moral Theology*, nr. 215.3; A. Koch-A. Preuss, *Handbook of Moral Theology*, V, p. 125; St. Thomas, *Summa theologica*, II, II, Q. 64, Art 7.

[2] B. Merkelbach. *Summa theologiae moralis*, II, nr. 349; H. Noldin-A. Schmitt, *Summa theologiae moralis*, II, nr. 326; J. Aertnys-C. Damen, *Theologia moralis*, nr. 566; H. Davis, *Moral and Pastoral Theology*, II, p. 152.

[3] B. Merkelbach, *Summa theologiae moralis*, II, nr. 349; J. Aertnys-C. Damen, *Theologia moralis*, I, nr. 566.

large crowd, the driver may steer it aside even at the risk of running over one person. In this event there are two immediate effects—the avoidance of a great number of (at least probable) deaths and the (at least probable) death of one individual. Again, a lawful military objective may be bombarded in time of war even though as another immediate effect some civilians will lose their lives. These two examples illustrate indirect killing.[4]

Argument from Reason

. . .

Supreme dominion over life belongs to God alone. God has sovereign dominion over all things, even over the essences of things. According to His providence He has given man a natural dominion over things of the earth inferior to himself to the extent that man may make use of them for his own utility.[5] Man has not full dominion over his life. He has only the use of it; and the natural law obliges man while using a thing that is under the dominion of another not to destroy it. The life of man is solely under the dominion of God. Wherefore, as man may not take his life, neither may another man take it (apart from exceptions given above), since another man would have even less dominion over it.[6] . . . In a word, it is the belief of Catholics that according to the natural law man does not have direct dominion over human life—either his own life or the life of another man. Yet euthanasia, whether it is voluntary euthanasia or compulsory euthanasia, is the destruction of human life. Destruction is an act proper to the master alone. Hence euthanasia violates God's absolute dominion over human life. The fact that the victim wills to die is an irrelevant consideration. The patient is innocent and hence apart from a divine command and may not be killed directly whether he wills it or not.

An objection might be presented that the common good may sometimes require the killing of an innocent person. If, for example, a diseased man became a grave danger to a community so that unless he were put out of the way many others would die, the state could kill the diseased patient for the common good. It might seem that the state would have the right to cut off a member of its body for the health and safety of the whole body, as a man may cut off a member of his body when it is necessary for the health of the whole body. This is confirmed by the fact that although the state does not have dominion over the life of the citizen, it is permitted to kill a citizen in punishment for a crime, because the punishment is useful and vital to the common good of the whole state. Therefore, when it is equally or even more necessary to kill an innocent member for the common good, it seems that it should be permissible.

Some might answer that for the health of the whole body a sick or evil member may be cut off, not a healthy one; thus in like manner a malefactor may be cut off from the state, but not an innocent member.[7] The diseased man is an innocent member of the community and therefore to kill him, to administer compulsory euthanasia to him, is a violation of God's absolute dominion over life.

To such a defense it could be answered—and justly, I believe—that even a healthy member of the natural body of a

---

[4]H. Jone-U. Adelman, *Moral Theology*, p. 146.

[5]J. De Lugo, *De Justitia et Jure* (Lyons: 1670), I, Sect. 4. nr. 102f.

[6]*Ibid.*, p. 259, nr. 102 f.

[7]J. De Lugo, *De Justitia et Jure*, Vol. I, Sect. IV, p. 259, nr. 103.

man may be cut off if it is necessary to save the life of the whole person, as for example when an arm is amputated in order that a person may escape a death trap. It might seem therefore that even a healthy member of society, an innocent member of the community, may be cut off for the sake of the whole. If such is permissible then the original thesis is unsound.

The true response to this objection, therefore, is to be found in the great difference between the members of the natural body of man and the members of the political body. A member of the natural body has no independent existence and no individual rights. The person itself has the right to use the members for they exist for the utility of the person. Wherefore properly they may be cut off when it is necessary for the conservation of the person, for the sake of which they exist.[8] It is a very different relation that exists between the individual human being and the state. The citizens do not exist for the sake of the state, but for their own sake, and to attain their own destiny.[9] A citizen does not serve the utility of the state in the sense that the state has full dominion over him. It is the state that exists for the utility of the citizen.[10]

Hence the state may not cut off or kill an innocent citizen merely for its utility, because this is an encroachment of a fundamental personal right, at least when there is a question of compulsory euthanasia. Even if a sick person were to agree to his own death for the common good and undergo voluntary euthanasia, there would still be committed a grave violation of God's absolute dominion over life. Since man does not have full dominion over his own life, he obviously cannot give up a dominion he does not have.

There is another objection that may be advanced, especially as regards voluntary, euthanasia. It might be maintained that life is a gift and as such may be renounced. The answer, however, is that life is not merely a gift. It is indeed a gift, but it has grave obligations, both to God and to one's fellow man, inseparably affixed thereto. Life is given man not only for himself but also for the service of his fellow man and God.

It may further be objected that even though God does have absolute dominion over man's life, yet man does presume the right to mutilate a member of that body when necessary for the good of the whole. And furthermore, it seems, man may even mutilate a part of his body, within certain limits, out of charity for his neighbor.[11] If these two presumptions are permissible it might seem likely that God would allow a man a merciful death out of charity to himself and to those who must care for him. Once a presumption of a minor or a major mutilation is allowed it would appear at least doubtful as to where to draw the line.

This objection is not valid. One can presume reasonably that when he has the administration of a thing belonging to another, a part may be sacrificed when it is necessary to save the whole. Hence it is a reasonable presumption that man may mutilate a part of his body when it is necessary to save the whole body. There is quite a difference between saying this and saying that man may destroy outright what belongs to his master because to retain it causes pain and inconvenience. If a ship is carrying a precious cargo to its owner in a distant port, and it becomes evident to the ship's captain that a part of the cargo must be thrown overboard lest the whole cargo be lost, the captain may presume reasonably

---

[8]*Ibid.*, nr. 104.

[9]*Ibid.*

[10]*Ibid.*

[11]B. Cunningham, *The Morality of Organic Transplantation* (Washington: Catholic University Press. 1944), p. 100.

that the owner of the cargo would allow him to sacrifice a part of it in order that the whole cargo not be lost. But it would be unreasonable to conclude from this that therefore the captain could destroy the owner's whole cargo because some inconvenience is involved in taking care of it. The line of demarcation seems very evident. It must be remembered that in the two presumptions presented in the objection, it was actually for the prolongation of life that the mutilation was allowed.

Surely, it is illogical to argue that since man is permitted to take certain measures to prolong his life, he may therefore sometimes take measures to destroy it. Man has only the use of his life, and when man uses what belongs to another he has the obligation of taking ordinary care of it. When dealing with a human life, this ordinary care may involve some necessary mutilation for the preservation of that life. Hence man's right to presume a reasonable mutilation of his body not only does not argue against God's supreme dominion over life but rather confirms it. It is because God has the absolute dominion over life that man may even be required to mutilate his body, when this is a part of the ordinary care due what belongs to another.

Another objection that is often advanced by advocates of euthanasia is that to maintain that God would object to killing an incurable sufferer, a useless member of society, one who is a burden to all, is unreasonable. There is no point in forcing certain physically and mentally defective persons to live a miserable existence. To hold the contrary is to manifest a heartless attitude toward the sufferers themselves and to place an unbearable physical, emotional, and financial burden upon the families of many of these unfortunate persons.

The Christian has the only answer to this objection. He knows that no human being is a useless member either to himself or to society or at least need not be, no matter what his physical status may be. If the suffering patient is of sound mind and capable of making an act of divine resignation, then his sufferings become a great means of merit whereby he can gain reward for himself and also win great favors for the souls in Purgatory, perhaps even release them from their suffering.[12] Likewise the sufferer may give good example to his family and friends and teach them how to bear a heavy cross in a Christlike manner.

As regard those that must live in the same house with the incurable sufferer, they have a great opportunity to practice Christian charity. They can learn to see Christ in the sufferer and win the reward promised in the Beatitudes.[13] This opportunity for charity would hold true even when the sufferer is deprived of the use of reason. It may well be that the incurable sufferer in a particular case may be of greater value to society than when he was of some material value to himself and his community. . . .

Argument from the "Wedge Principle"

The "wedge principle" means that an act that would injure humanity if raised to a general line of conduct is wrong even in an individual case. Ordinarily the act even individually is evil, but it can happen in exceptional instances that the act causes no harm but nevertheless on account of the common danger there is a general prohibition. By this principle one may conclude that any course of conduct that works destruction when practiced generally may not be permitted in an individual case. Thus divorce and remarriage might be harmless in some individual case. It may be that the

---

[12] A. Tanquerey, *Synopsis theologiae dogmaticae* (Paris: Desclée et Socii, 1938), p. 797, nr. 1125; *Decretum de purgatorio* (DBU, 983, p. 342); II Machab., 12:43.

[13] St. Matthew, 5:7.

innocent party and her children would be greatly benefited by her second marriage. Perhaps in this particular case there may be many good reasons why a second marriage would be helpful to all concerned, especially the children. Nevertheless, if one exception is allowed to the rule of no marriage after a divorce, other exceptions will soon follow and society will suffer much. (We are concerned with the natural law—not with any exceptions that God Himself may have introduced.)

This principle of the wedge may be applied to euthanasia, both voluntary euthanasia and compulsory euthanasia. Here for the sake of argument it will be presumed that the suffering patient wishes euthanasia and that no evil effects will result to his friends or the common good from the single act of administering the euthanasia to him. Nevertheless, euthanasia must not be administered, for to permit in a single instance the direct killing of an innocent person would be to admit a most dangerous wedge that might eventually put all life in a precarious condition. Once a man is permitted on his own authority to kill an innocent person directly, there is no way of stopping the advancement of that wedge. There exists no longer any rational grounds for saying that the wedge can advance so far and no further. Once the exception has been admitted it is too late; hence the grave reason why no exception may be allowed. That is why euthanasia under any circumstances must be condemned. We are making use of this as a secondary argument; for the primary argument is found in the intrinsic malice of the direct killing of an innocent person. But even one who would not admit this should acknowledge the value of the present argument.

If voluntary euthanasia were legalized, there is good reason to believe that at a later date another bill for compulsory euthanasia would be legalized,[14] Once the respect for human life is so low that an innocent person may be killed directly even at his own request, compulsory euthanasia will necessarily be very near. This could lead easily to killing all incurable charity patients, the aged who are a public care, wounded soldiers, captured enemy soldiers, all deformed children, the mentally afflicted, and so on. Before long the danger would be at the door of every citizen.

Politics also would enter and perhaps political parties would use the law to destroy personae non gratae. This might be done by getting a court order stating that the person in question is an incurable mental case. The possibilities of abusing euthanasia are many. Dishonesty and graft have found their way into nearly every field. There would be many opportunities for these evils to operate under legalized euthanasia to a great danger of society. It is common knowledge that not infrequently a person goes into court to seek the administration of property by having the real owner declared insane. A more effective way of securing property would be open to unscrupulous relatives if euthanasia were legalized.

The most outstanding examples of the extremes to which legalized euthanasia can go are found in the mass eugenic murders within Germany and her conquered territories during the war. Those considered by the state as physically unfit or mentally unfit could be put to death as they were regarded as a grave burden to the common good. Likewise any undesirable citizen could be exterminated, whether man, woman, or child. As a rule the death was an easy death in a gas chamber.[15] Many

---

[14] J. Brown. "Taking Life Legally." *Magazine Digest* (March 1937), p. 43.

[15] A. Kinkel, *Put to Death Legally* (London: Davis Co., 1946), p. 37.

present-day advocates of euthanasia might accept this procedure as within reason since the unfit and the undesirable are no benefit to society. The point is, however, that all persons unfriendly to the Nazi government were considered by those in power as undesirable citizens. Those who held a philosophy contrary to that of the government might well be considered as mental cases. Hence many thousands were put to death without mercy.[16] It is estimated that thousands of Jews in Austria alone were sent to their death by the government for no reason save that they were non-Aryan and undesirable to the state. Reports indicate that these murders were considered legal by reason of existing compulsory euthanasia legislation.[17] At the time these laws were enacted it was thought that only the incurable mental cases, monstrosities, and the incurables that were a burden to the state would be put to death. However, once the state held this power of life and death over even the innocent members of society, the lives of all the citizens were in danger.

This example of the Nazi government in Germany with regard to euthanasia might be followed by any other government once that government possessed such a power. One might say that the mentality of the American people would never accept such abuse of human life. The point is, however, that once the American people depart so far from Christian tradition as to allow an innocent person to be put to death legally because he is a monstrosity or wills euthanasia, it is difficult to predict how much further this abuse of the power over human life would go.

It is obvious, therefore, that if euthanasia is legalized, even with strict limitation, it would lead to many downright murders and hence by reason of the "wedge principle" may not be allowed in any individual case.

[16]*Ibid.*, p. 39.
[17]*Ibid.*, p. 40.

A REBUTTAL

Euthanasia

James Rachels

An Argument against Legalizing Active Euthanasia: The Slippery Slope

Now we shall examine the most widely used argument *against* legalizing active euthanasia, the slippery-slope argument.

Statement of the Argument

The basic idea of the argument is that if euthanasia were legally permitted, it would lead to a general decline in respect for human life. In the beginning, we might kill people only to put them out of extreme agony. Our motives would be honorable, and the results might be good. However, once we had started cold-bloodedly killing people, where would it stop? Where would we draw the line? The point is that once we accept killing in some cases, we have stepped onto a "slippery slope," which we will inevitably slide down, and in the end life will be held cheap. Sometimes a different analogy—called the "wedge" argument—is used; then it is said that once we admit the thin edge of the wedge, we are on the way to abandoning our traditional view of the importance of human life.

Bishop Sullivan puts the argument this way:

> . . . to permit in a single instance the direct killing of an innocent person would be to admit a most dangerous wedge that might eventually put all life in a precarious condition. Once a man is permitted on his own authority to kill an innocent person directly, there is no way of stopping the advancement of that wedge. There exists no longer any rational grounds for saying that the wedge can advance so far and no further. Once the exception has been made it is too late; hence the grave reason why no exception may be allowed. That is why euthanasia under any circumstances must be condemned. . . .

Although Sullivan writes from a Catholic point of view, it is clear that this argument is not a religious one. It requires no religious assumptions of any kind. And, in fact, non-Catholics have used this argument, too. Philippa Foot is a leading British moral philosopher. Unlike Sullivan, she thinks that in some individual cases, active euthanasia is *morally* all right. However, she thinks it should not be legalized, because of "the really serious problem of abuse":

> Many people want, and want very badly, to be rid of their elderly relatives and even of their ailing husbands or wives. Would any safeguards ever be able to stop them describing as euthanasia what was really for their own benefit? And would it be possible to prevent the occurrence of acts which were genuinely acts of euthanasia but morally impermissible because infringing the rights of a patient who wished to live? . . . The possibility of active voluntary euthanasia might change the social scene in ways that would be very bad. As things are, people do, by and large, expect to be looked after if they are old or ill. This is one of the good things that we have, but we might lose it, and be much worse off without it. It might come to be expected that someone likely to need a lot of looking after should call for the doctor and demand his own death. Something comparable could be good in an extremely poverty-stricken community where the children genuinely suffered from lack of food; but in rich societies such as ours it would surely be a spiritual disaster.[1]

The conclusion of the argument is that no matter what view you take of individual instances of mercy killing, as a matter of social policy we ought to enforce a rigorous rule against it. Otherwise, we are courting disaster.

To assess this argument, we need to distinguish between two very different forms it might take. We may call these the *logical* version of the argument and the *psychological* version.

The Logical Interpretation of the Slippery Slope

The logical form of the argument goes like this. Once a certain practice is accepted, from a logical point of view we are committed to accepting certain other practices as well, since there are no good reasons for not going on to accept the additional practices once we have taken the all-important first step. But, the argument continues, the

---

[1] "Euthanasia," *Philosophy and Public Affairs*. 6:2 (Winter 1977), 111–112.

additional practices are plainly unacceptable; therefore, the first step had better not be taken.

Interpreted in this way, the slippery-slope argument makes a point about *what you are logically committed to* once certain practices are accepted. It says that once you allow euthanasia for the patient in terrible agony, *you are logically committed* to approving of euthanasia in other cases as well. Bishop Sullivan, in the passage previously quoted, apparently intends this, for he says that "Once a man is permitted on his own authority to kill an innocent person directly . . . *there exists no longer any rational grounds* for saying that the wedge can advance so far and no further." But this is clearly false. There *are* rational grounds for distinguishing between the man in agony who wants to die and other cases, such as that of an old infirm person who does not want to die. It is easy to say what the rational ground is. It is simply that in the first case the person requests death, whereas in the second case the person does not request it. Moreover, in the first case, the person is suffering terribly, and in the second case the person is not. These are morally relevant differences to which we can appeal in order to distinguish the cases; therefore, we are *not* logically committed to accepting "euthanasia" in the second case merely because we approve it in the first. Thus, the logical form of the slippery-slope argument does not work in the case of euthanasia. It does not prove that active euthanasia ought to be legally prohibited in every case.

The Psychological Interpretation of the Slippery Slope

This form of the argument is very different. It claims that once certain practices are accepted, *people shall in fact* go on to accept other, more questionable practices. This is simply a claim about what people will do and not a claim about what they are logically committed to. Thus, this form of the argument says that if we start off by killing people to put them out of extreme agony, we shall *in fact* end up killing them for other reasons, regardless of logic and nice distinctions. Therefore, if we want to avoid the latter, we had better avoid the former. This is the point that Mrs. Foot is making, and it is a much stronger argument than what I have called the "logical" version of the slippery slope.

How strong is the psychological version of the argument? Does it show that active euthanasia ought to be illegal? The crucial question is whether legalizing active euthanasia would in fact lead to terrible consequences. This is an empirical question—a question of fact—about which philosophers have no special inside information. But then, neither does anyone else; there is no definitive "scientific" answer to this question. Each of us is left to form his or her own best estimate concerning what would happen in our society if active euthanasia came to be accepted. For myself, I do *not* believe that it would lead to any sort of general breakdown in respect for life, for several reasons.

First, we have a good bit of historical and anthropological evidence that approval of killing in one context does not necessarily lead to killing in different circumstances. As has been previously mentioned, in ancient Greece, people killed defective infants without any feeling of shame or guilt—but this did *not* lead to the easy approval of other types of killing. Many instances of this kind could be cited. In Eskimo societies, the killing of infants and feeble old people was widely accepted as a measure to avoid starvation; but among the Eskimos murder was virtually unheard of. Such evidence suggests that people are able to distinguish between various types of cases, and keep them separated fairly well.

Second, in our own society killing has been, and still is, accepted in many circumstances. For example, we allow killing in self-defense. But what if it were argued that we should not allow this, on the grounds that acceptance of killing in self-defense would inevitably lead to a breakdown in respect for life? Of course, we know that this is not true, because we know that acceptance of killing in self-defense *has not* led to any such consequences. But why hasn't it? Because, first, it is rather unusual for anyone to have to kill in self-defense—most of us never face such a situation—and second, we are not so stupid that we are unable to distinguish this case, in which killing is justified, from other cases in which it is not justified. Exactly the same seems to be true of killing people who ask to be killed to put them out of misery. Such cases would be fairly rare—most of us know of such cases only by reading of them—and we can distinguish them from other, very different cases fairly easily.

Third, Mrs. Foot fears that "It might come to be expected that someone likely to need a lot of looking after should call for the doctor and demand his own death." But this situation would become possible *only if* it were legal for doctors to kill *anyone* who requests it. It would not be possible under a legal arrangement that authorized doctors administer euthanasia only to terminal patients of special kinds.

Finally, it must be admitted that if active euthanasia were legalized, there would inequitably be *some* abuses, just as there are abuses of virtually every social practice. No one can deny that. The crucial issue is whether the abuses, or the bad consequences generally, would be *so* numerous as to outweigh the advantages of legalized euthanasia. We must remember that the choice is not between a present policy that is benign and an alternative that is potentially dangerous. The present policy has its evils too. . . . We must not forget that these evils have to be weighed against any feared disadvantages of the alternative. For these reasons, my own conclusion is that the psychological version of the slippery-slope argument does *not* provide a decisive reason why active euthanasia should be kept illegal. The possibility of bad consequences should perhaps make us proceed cautiously in this area; but it should not stop us from proceeding at all.

How to Legalize Active Euthanasia: A Modest Proposal

Opposition to the legalization of active euthanasia comes from those who believe it is immoral, from those who fear the consequences of legalization, and from those who believe that, although it may be a fine idea in theory, in practice it is impossible to devise any workable laws to accommodate active euthanasia. This last point is important. If we wanted to legalize active euthanasia, exactly how could we go about doing it? Who should be granted the awesome power to decide when a person may be put to death? Should patients or doctors or the patient's family be allowed to decide on their own? Or should some sort of hospital committee be authorized to make the decision? And if so, exactly who should sit on such a committee? What if those who are given the power abuse it? Shall they then be liable to charges of murder? If so, then it would seem that they do not really have the power to decide; but if not, their power is unchecked and they have a license to do as they please. It is easy to think of objections to almost any proposed scheme, so it is no wonder that even those who approve active euthanasia in theory are often wary of actually legalizing it.

I want to make a modest proposal concerning how active euthanasia might be legalized so as to avoid all these problems. Before outlining this proposal, I need to make some elementary points about American law.

Individuals charged with a crime have no obligations to prove their innocence. The burden of proof is on the prosecution, and the defense may consist entirely in pointing out that the prosecution has not decisively proven guilt. If the prosecution has not discharged its obligation to prove guilt, the jury's duty is to acquit the defendant.

However, if the prosecution does establish a strong case against the defendant, a more active defense is required. Then there are two options available. The defendant may deny having done the criminal act in question. Or, while admitting to the act, the defendant may nevertheless argue that he or she should not be punished for it.

There are two legally accepted ways of arguing that a person should not be punished for an act even while admitting that the act is prohibited by law and that the person did it. First, an *excuse* may be offered, such as insanity, coercion, ignorance of fact, unavoidable accident, and so on. If it can be shown that the defendant was insane when the crime was committed or that he was coerced into doing it or that it was an unavoidable accident, then the defendant may be acquitted. Second, a *justification* may be offered. A plea of self-defense against a charge of murder is an example of a justification. The technical difference between excuses and justifications need not concern us here.

Here is an example to illustrate these points. Suppose you are charged with murdering a man, and the prosecution can make a strong case that you did in fact kill the victim. You might respond by trying to show that you did *not* kill him. Or you might admit that you killed him, and then have your lawyers argue that you were insane or that the killing was a tragic accident for which you are blameless or that you had to kill him in self-defense. If any of these defenses can be made out, then you will be acquitted of the crime even though you admittedly did kill the victim.

When such a defense is offered, the burden of proof is on the defense, and not the prosecution, to show that the facts alleged are true. The prosecution does not have to show that the defendant was sane; rather, the defendant (or the defendant's lawyers) must prove that he or she was insane. The prosecution does not have to prove that the killing was not done in self-defense; instead the defense must prove that it was. Thus it is not quite accurate to say that under American law the burden of proof is always on the prosecution. If the defendant concedes to having performed the act in question but claims an excuse or justification for the act, the burden of proof may shift so that the defense is required to show that the excuse or justification should be accepted.

Now, my proposal for legalizing active euthanasia is that a plea of mercy killing be acceptable as a defense against a charge of murder in much the same way that a plea of self-defense is acceptable as a defense. When people plead self-defense, it is up to them to show that their own lives were threatened and that the only way of fending off the threat was by killing the attacker first. Under my proposal, someone charged with murder could also plead mercy killing; and then, if it could be proven that the victim while competent requested death, and that the victim was suffering from a painful terminal illness, the person pleading mercy killing would also be acquitted.

Under this proposal no one would be "authorized" to decide when a patient should be killed any more than people are "authorized" to decide when someone may be killed in self-defense. There are no committees to be established within which people may cast private votes for which they are not really accountable; people who choose to mercy kill bear full legal responsibility, as individuals, for their actions. In practice, this would mean that anyone contemplating mercy killing would have to be very sure that there are independent witnesses to testify concerning the patient's condition and desire to die; for otherwise, one might not be able to make out a defense in a court of law—if it would come to that—and would be legally liable for murder. However, if this proposal were adopted, it would *not* mean that every time active euthanasia was performed a court trial would follow. In clear cases of self-defense, prosecutors simply do not bring charges, since it would be a pointless waste of time. Similarly, in clear cases of mercy killing, where there is no doubt about the patient's hopeless condition or desire to die, charges would not be brought for the same reason.

Thus, under this proposal, the need to write difficult legislation permitting euthanasia is bypassed. The problems of formulating a statute, which were mentioned at the beginning of this section, do not arise. We would rely on the good sense of judges and juries to separate the cases of justifiable euthanasia from the cases of unjustifiable murder, just as we already rely on them to separate the cases of self-defense and insanity and coercion. Some juries are already functioning in this way but without legal sanction: when faced with genuine mercy killers, they refuse to convict. The main consequence of my proposal would be to sanction officially what these juries already do. . . .

WITHDRAWING TREATMENT IS OBLIGATORY

Age-Rationing and the Just Distribution of Health Care: Is There a Duty to Die?

Margaret P. Battin

Do elderly persons who are irreversibly ill, whose lives can be continued only with substantial medical support, have—as one contemporary political figure is said to have put it—a "duty to die?" A number of conspicuous voices in the historical tradition have advanced such a view (among them Plato, Thomas More, and Nietzsche), variously recommending denial of treatment, euthanasia, or socially assisted "rational" suicide. Various primitive and historical societies (including the Eskimo, the early Japanese, certain migratory American Indian tribes, and the Greeks on the island of Ceos) give evidence of senicide practices, including abandonment, direct killing, and socially enforced suicide. Such societies communicate to their members that when they reach advanced old age or become irreversibly ill, it is time to die, and an old, ill person should acquiesce or cooperate in bringing death about. The question to be explored here, in the light of current issues concerning distributive justice in health care, is whether there is any moral warrant at all to such views. . . .[1]

Justice and Age Rationing

If societal resources are insufficient to provide all the health care all persons in all medical conditions need, some sort of limiting distributive practice will of necessity emerge. Several recent writers have argued that rather than let the market control the distribution of health care, a rationally defended rationing policy can be developed under accepted principles of justice, and that this policy will justify rationing by age: old people should be the first to be excluded from medical care. However, assuming the underlying formal principle of justice to require that like cases and groups be treated alike, it is by no means initially clear that plausible material principles of justice will differentiate the elderly from other claimants for care. For instance, if an individual's claim to care were taken to be a function of the contributions society may expect as a return on its investment in him, this might seem to support age rationing, disfavoring those no longer capable of making contributions; but of course the elderly have already made contributions, contributions which are in fact more secure than the still potential contributions of the young. Alternatively, it might be argued that the elderly have greater claims to care in virtue of their greater vulnerability, in virtue of the respect owed elders, or in virtue of the intrinsic value of old age. This sort of discussion, characteristic of many analyses of distributive justice, involves identifying the possible desert bases of claims to health care and then considering whether the elderly can satisfy these conditions as well as other age groups. If they can (which I think likely), policies which restrict the access of the elderly to health care must be seen as the product of simple age bias.

But an influential conceptual observation has been made by Norman Daniels.[2] Most analyses of distributive justice, Daniels observes, assume that the elderly constitute one among a variety of age groups, including infants, adolescents, and the middle-aged, all of which compete for scarce resources in health care. But this, in Daniels's view, is misleading; the elderly should be viewed as the same persons at a later stage of their lives. The mistake lies in considering distributive problems as problems in allocating resources among competing groups and among competing individuals, when they are more correctly understood as problems of allocating resources throughout the duration of lives. Given this conceptual shift, Daniels then employs Rawlsian strategies to determine just allocations of care. He considers what distributive policies prudential savers—the rational, self-interest-maximizing parties of the Rawlsian original position—would adopt if, unable to know their own medical conditions, genetic predispositions, physical susceptibilities, environmental situations, health maintenance habits, or ages, they must decide in advance on a spending plan, budgeting a fixed amount of medical care across their whole lives. He quite plausibly

---

[1]This is a condensation of the original first paragraphs of this article. References to thinkers and societies mentioned are available in the original.—Eds.

[2]Daniels, "Justice between Age Groups: Am I My Parents' Keeper?" *Milbank Memorial Fund Quarterly* 61, (1983), pp. 489–522.

conjectures that prudential savers behind the veil of ignorance in this original position would choose, where scarcity obtains, to allocate a greater amount of resources to care and treatment required for conditions that occur earlier in life, from infancy through middle age, but not to underwrite treatment which would prolong life beyond its normal span. By freeing resources which might otherwise have been devoted to prolonging the lives of the elderly for use instead in the treatment of diseases which cause death or opportunity-restricting disability earlier in life, such a policy would maximize one's chances of getting a reasonable amount of life within the normal species-typical, age-relative opportunity range. . . .

If the Rawls/Daniels strategy is employed, then, possible practices and policies for effecting age rationing, including denial or refusal of treatment, senicide, euthanasia, and socially mandated "rational" suicide, are to be assessed in terms of whether rational self-interest maximizers behind the veil of ignorance would agree to accept such policies or not. Consequently, it is necessary to consider—as far as possible independently of cultural constraints—what policies for putting age rationing into practice the hypothetical rational, self-interest-maximizing persons in the original position would accept, given that they have antecedently consented to policies assigning enhanced care to the early and middle years but reducing care to the aged. Parties to the original position have disenfranchised themselves, so to speak; but it remains to be seen what form they would agree this disenfranchisement should take.

Age Rationing by Denial of Treatment

Although parties to the original position will have already agreed to ration health care to the elderly (in order to enhance health care available to younger and middle-aged people and, thus, maximize the possibility of each person's reaching a normal life span at all); they must be assumed to have enough general information to see what the consequences of this antecedent agreement will be. First, under an appropriately thin veil of ignorance of this sort, they will know that a given measure of health care is not equally effective at all age ranges, but much more effective in younger years, much less effective in old age. Because old persons typically have more complex medical problems, compounded by a decline in the function of many organs and by reduced capacities for healing and homeostasis, trade-offs between earlier and later years cannot be made on a one-to-one basis: by and large, a unit of medical care consumed late in life will have much less effect in preserving life and maintaining normal species-typical function than a unit of medical care consumed at a younger age. It is this that will have in part induced the rational self-interest maximizers of the original position to consent to an age-rationing policy in the first place; but it will also influence how they choose to put an age-rationing policy into effect. Once the multiple infirmities of old age begin to erode an individual's functioning, comparatively larger amounts of health care are likely to be required to raise it again. Therapy which can successfully maintain comfort, or restore functioning, or preserve life may be very much more expensive in older patients, if indeed success is possible at all.

Parties to the original position will also know that under a rationing scheme it will be necessary, given their antecedent distributive decision, to restrict or eliminate most of the comparatively elaborate kinds of care. Presumably, if care is to be denied, it will be the highest-cost, least-gain varieties of care, including care which does not directly serve to maintain life. Of course, "cheap treatment" such as common antibiotics could be retained for elderly patients, since these are low cost and, given their potential for saving life, high gain; but expensive diagnostic procedures and therapies like CAT scans or nuclear magnetic resonance imaging, renal dialysis, organ transplants, hip replacements, hydrotherapy, respiratory support, total parenteral nutrition, individualized physical therapy, vascular grafting, major surgery, and high tech procedures generally would be ruled out.[3] Hospitalization, and the nearly equally expensive inpatient hospice care, might not be permitted, except perhaps briefly; sustained nursing home care (at twenty thousand dollars a year) would no doubt also be excluded. When the elderly person over an appropriate age ceiling or exceeding a predetermined level of deterioration begins to show symptoms of a condition more serious than a transitory, easily cured illness, he would simply be counted ineligible for treatment. "I'm sorry, Mr. Smith," we can expect the physician to say, "there is nothing more we can do."

Knowing these things, parties to the original position can then assess the impact of age rationing by denial of treatment. While they will know that age rationing of some of the more expensive, elaborate treatment modalities, like renal dialysis and organ transplantation, is now prevalent in Britain[4] and is to an uneven extent also evident in the United States,[5] they will also understand that under the general age-rationing policy they have agreed to, the frequency and finality of such denials of treatment would be much more severe. Though allocations to the elderly would of course be a fluctuating function of scarcity in health care resources as a whole, it is probably fair to estimate that were the degree of scarcity approximately equivalent to what it is now, a just distribution of health care would demand that a very large proportion of all health care expenses now devoted to the elderly be reassigned to younger age groups. The elderly now use nearly a third of all health care.[6] Were these resources reassigned to the younger and middle-aged groups, the probability would be dramatically increased that all or virtually all these persons (except the worst-off newborns and those catastrophically injured or killed outright in accidents, homicide, or suicide) would not only reach a normal life span but reach it in reasonably good health. Although the temporary life expectancy (or average

---

[3]Parties to the original position are not only hypothetical but ahistorical, having no knowledge of what historical period they live in. The parties described here, however, seem to have an extraordinary amount of information about health care costs in the 1980s. But this is simply part of the general information such parties are assumed to have (ibid., sec. 24, p. 142); it can be assumed that they also have similarly detailed information about health care costs in other historical periods, both before and after the 1980s. Regardless of the degree of technological development of medicine in these historical periods, however, in all of them providing extensive care in end-of-life illness is more costly than denying care or directly terminating life; hence in all of them the age-rationing problem will look very much like it does now.

[4]See H. J. Aaron and W. B. Schwartz, *The Painful Prescription: Rationing Hospital Care* (Washington, D.C.: Brookings Institution, 1984) for an account of age rationing in Britain.

[5]I have in mind non-medically-indicated age ceilings for heart transplants at Stanford, waiting lists in the Veterans Administration system for hip replacements, Medicaid's reduction of physical therapy for nursing home patients from twice daily to once daily, and the like.

[6]Health care expenditures for the elderly were estimated to reach 3.3 percent of the GNP in 1984, or nearly a third of the 10.5 percent of the GNP which represents all health care. See Daniel R. Waldo and Helen C. Lazenby, "Demographic Characteristics and Health Care Use and Expenditures by the Aged in the United States: 1977–1984," *Health Care Financing Review* 6 (1984): 1–29, p. 8.

number of years a group of persons at the beginning of an age interval will live during that age interval) is already very high, especially for the intervals zero to twenty and twenty to forty-five,[7] it is still the case that a sizable number of people do not reach a normal life span or reach it only in poor health.[8] Reallocation of substantial health care resources would do a great deal to change this, particularly if the transfers were used for preventive medicine and support programs, such as prenatal nutrition and life-style change, as well as direct assaults on specific diseases. But, to achieve this effect, if the degree of overall scarcity of medical resources could not be altered, a substantial portion of the care now given the elderly would have to be withdrawn. At most, perhaps, minimal home hospice care and inexpensive pain relief could be routinely granted, together with some superficial care in transient acute illness not related to chronic conditions or interdependent diseases, But treatment for the elderly could not be escalated very much beyond this point if, within a fixed degree of scarcity, a just distribution of resources were still to be achieved: if only a significantly lesser portion of the care now devoted to the elderly were reassigned to younger age groups, there would be no substantial redistributive achievement and no significant increase in the propects for persons generally for reaching a normal life span. Minimal and erratic age rationing of the sort now practiced in the United States would accomplish virtually no redistributive goal at all.

In some cases, to deny the elderly treatment beyond minimal home hospice care and inexpensive pain relief would simply result in earlier deaths. This would, presumably, be the case in many sorts of acute conditions—heart attacks or sudden-onset renal failure, for instance—where emergency medical intervention is clearly lifesaving. But, especially in old age, such starkly life versus death episodes are less likely to occur in isolation; it is much more likely that an elderly person will already suffer from a number of related or unrelated chronic conditions, each of which could be relieved at least to some degree by treatment but which together make a fairly substantial and expensive list of complaints. . . .

Clearly, even hypothetical parties to the original position, under an appropriately thin veil of ignorance, will be dismayed by the consequences of the initial distributive decision they have made. Total hip replacements, for instance, could no longer be offered the elderly; but it will be evident that there is a substantial difference in the character of life for an elderly person who remains ambulatory and one no longer able to walk. It will be evident, too, that the person who needs, but does not get, a pacemaker or a coronary bypass may lead a quite restricted life, seriously limited in his activities, and that life with renal failure or cardiac arrhythmias or pulmonary insufficiency can be restrictive, painful, or frightening. Indeed, what may be most dismaying to those peering through this thin veil of ignorance is that elderly persons who are not allocated treatment do not simply die; rather, they suffer their illness and disabilities without adequate aid. Even symptom control in conditions like cancer, if not simply obliterative of consciousness, can be quite expensive, since effective relief may require

---

[7]Olshansky and Ault. pp. 4–5.

[8]The "normal life span" is not to be confused with the "average life span," the latter of which 50 percent of the people do not reach and 50 percent exceed. The conception of "normal life span" employed by Daniels and others is not defined as a statistical notion but appears to have to do with the rough boundary between middle and old age or between early old age and late old age.

constant titration and monitoring; if so, it too would presumably be ruled out. Worse still, common antibiotics and the few other kinds of cheap treatment that would still be available may simply serve to prolong this period of decline, not to reduce its discomfort, while labor-intensive care that might make it tolerable—like physical therapy or psychiatric support and counseling—would also be ruled out. To deny treatment does not always simply bring about earlier deaths that maximal care would postpone; denial of treatment also means denial of expensive palliative measures, both physical and psychological, which maximal care would permit at whatever age death occurs.

Nor can it be supposed that to deny care to the elderly is to simply allow them to die as their fathers and forefathers did; to deny care now is to subject persons to a medically new situation. Not only has it been comparatively unlikely until quite recently that a person would reach old age at all (in the United States, life expectancy at birth in 1900 was only 47.3 years, compared to 74.5 in 1982),[9] but in the past most deaths were caused by parasitic and infectious diseases, many of which were rather rapidly fatal. Modern sanitation, inoculation, and antibiotic therapy have changed that, and for the first time the specter of old age as a constellation of various sublethal but severely limiting and discomforting conditions has become the norm. Hence, any notion that denial of treatment to the elderly will simply allow a return to the more "natural" modes of death enjoyed by earlier, simpler generations is a dangerously romanticized misconception. To ration health care by denial of treatment is not simply to abandon the patient to death but, often, to abandon him to a prolonged period of morbidity, only later followed by death.

But, of course, this is a prospect which the rational self-interest maximizer, behind the veil of ignorance about whether he himself will succumb quickly in an acute crisis or be consigned without substantial medical assistance to a long-term decline, will be concerned to protect against. Parties to the original position will thus find many reasons to reject policies which ration health care by denying treatment to the aged; the question for them will be whether they can devise better alternative methods.

Squaring the Curve

Since the publication in 1980 of James Fries's provocative article on the compression of morbidity,[10] there has been a good deal of discussion of the prospects for the reduction of senescence, or the end-of-life morbidity characteristic of old age. Although the average life span in the United States has increased by more than twenty-seven years between 1900 and the present, as Fries points out, the maximum life span has not increased; there is no greater percentage of centenarians, for instance, and there are no documented cases of survival, he claims, beyond 114 years. The result is an increasingly "rectangularized" mortality curve, as more and more people reach old age but the maximum old age is not extended. Furthermore, since this rectangularization results from postponement of the onset of chronic illness, it means an increasingly rectangularized morbidity curve as well. On this basis, Fries optimistically predicts that the number of extremely old persons will not increase, that the average period of diminished physical vigor or senescence will decrease, that chronic

---

[9]See Waldo and Lazenby, p. 2.

[10]James F. Fries, "Aging, Natural Death, and the Compression of Morbidity," *New England Journal of Medicine* 303 (July 17, 1980): 130–35.

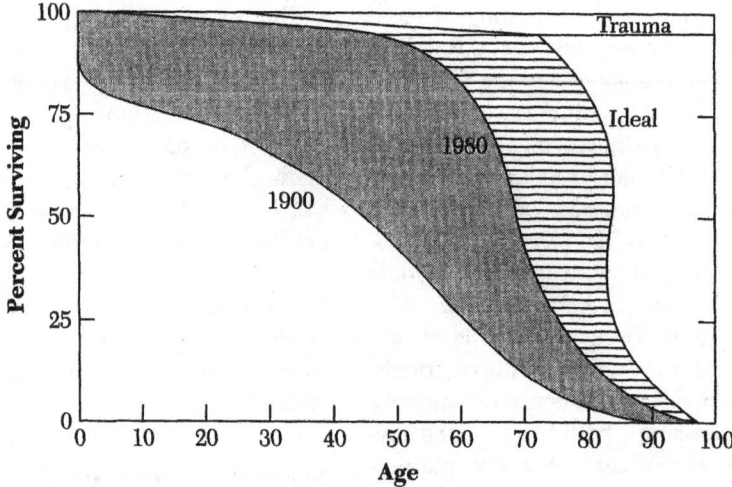

FIGURE 1
Fries's increasingly rectangular survival curve. About 80 percent (stippled area) of the difference between the 1900 curve and the ideal curve had been eliminated by 1980. Trauma is now the dominant cause of death in early life. (From James F. Fries, "Aging, Natural Death, and the Compression of Morbidity," *New England Journal of Medicine* 303 [July 17, 1980]: 131. fig. 2.)

disease will occupy a smaller proportion of the typical life span, and that the need for medical care in late life will decrease. Good health, in short, will extend closer and closer to the ideal average life span of about eighty-five, but life will not be extended much beyond this point (see Fig. 1).

Fries's conclusions about "squaring the curve," as it is often called, have been vigorously disputed by Schneider and Brody,[11] among others. They see no evidence of declining morbidity and disability in any age group, particularly those just prior to old age, but they do observe that increasing numbers of people are reaching advanced ages and point out that this fast-growing segment of the population is the one most vulnerable to chronic disease. While some writers set the biologic limit to the human life span at about one hundred, much higher than Fries's original estimate of eighty-five, others believe that there is no such limit. In either case, most of these comparatively pessimistic writers fear that a large increase in the number of individuals who reach old age will mean a large increase in the number of persons who spend long proportions of their lives afflicted with chronic disease. Advances in medicine will, they believe, prolong old age rather than delay its onset.

Clearly this issue is one with enormous consequences for health care planning. But it has been debated as an empirical issue only; nowhere has it been recognized that the empirical question cloaks a central moral issue as well. What is crucial to note

---

[11]Edward L. Schneider and Jacob A. Brody, "Aging, Natural Death, and the Compression of Morbidity: Another View," *New England Journal of Medicine* 309 (October 6, 1983): 854–55.

is that both the optimistic and pessimistic panics to this dispute agree, or tacitly agree, on one thing: that a squared morbidity curve is a desirable thing. This is by no means surprising: the squared curve represents a situation in which life is, as Fries puts it, "physically, emotionally, and intellectually vigorous until just before its close."[12] Death without illness, or without sustained, long-term illness, rational self-interest maximizers would surely agree, is a desirable thing. But if this is so, the empirical disagreement between the optimists and the pessimists grows irrelevant. For regardless of whether or not changes in lifestyle or improvements in medical care would naturally flatten or square the mortality and morbidity curves, these curves can also be deliberately altered by other distributive and policy-based interventions as well—including those which implement age-rationing schemes. . . .

For the most part, the age-rationing practices now followed in Britain and the United States as well as elsewhere involve denial of treatment, for instance, in the form of age ceilings for organ transplants, renal dialysis, or joint replacement. But I wish to argue that rational self-interest maximizers in the original position would prefer the direct-killing practices which are the contemporary analogues of the historical and primitive practices of senicide, early euthanasia, and culturally encouraged suicide to those which involve allowing to die. Parties to the original position, after all, are fully informed about the possible societal consequences of their choices (except about the impact on themselves) and are not hesitant—as rational persons—to look the circumstances of death squarely in the face. There are, I think, two principal reasons why they would agree on direct-termination policies involving the causing of death, that is, on "squaring the curve."

Avoidance of Suffering

Except for persons who believe, on religious or other grounds, that suffering is of intrinsic merit or is of extrinsic value in attaining salvation or some other valued goal, rational persons eager to maximize their self-interests seek to avoid discomfort, disability, and pain. Of course, a good deal of suffering may willingly be endured by those who hope to survive a critical episode and return to a more normal condition of life; but terminal suffering known to be terminal is not prized. In medical situations where the prognosis is uncertain and sophisticated techniques are employed to support survival, the risk of suffering is one the rational person may well wish to take, since the odds of survival may be either unknown or large enough to make it worth the risk. But under an age-rationing system which proceeds by denial of treatment, medical support will be minimal and, hence, comparatively ineffective in supporting survival; the chance of survival of an episode of illness is thereby drastically reduced. Thus, the possible gains to be achieved by enduring suffering disappear. Willingness to endure suffering may be a prudent, self-interest-favoring posture in a medical climate in which support is provided—even if that support is erratic or the chance of success is unknown—but it is not a prudent posture where age rationing precludes nearly all such support across the board.

Maximization of Life

Parties to the original position will also give preference to a policy which involves an overall distributive gain, benefiting all but giving the greatest benefit to the least advantaged. Since the allocation of resources

---

[12]Fries, p. 135.

may affect the overall total of resources available, they will prefer policies which maximize resources in a just distribution, and it is this that "squaring the curve" would accomplish. Of course, individuals surveying the possibility of policies which permit or require the direct termination of the existence of human beings may believe that their lives are to be sacrificed in the interests of other, younger people, and were this the case they would rightly resist this sort of utilitarian trade-off. But individuals who view these prospective policies in this way make a fundamental error: they view the effects of these policies from their own immediate perspective only and fail to see the larger impact these policies have. Quite the contrary, the overall effect of direct-termination policies is to *maximize* the preservation of life, not reduce it. This is a function of the fact, as pointed out earlier, that medical care is less efficient in old age, more efficient at younger ages, and that a unit of medical care consumed late in life will have much less effect in preserving life and maintaining normal species-typical function than a unit of medical care consumed at a younger age. The effect of rationing policies which allocate care away from elderly persons to younger ones is to increase the effectiveness of these resources, and thus greatly increase the chances for younger persons to reach a normal life span. Of course, since mortality in the zero to twenty and twenty to forty-five age ranges is already quite low, the increase in temporary life expectancy will be greatest for those forty-five to sixty-five; but, it must be remembered, the veil of ignorance for those in the original position excludes all but the vaguest knowledge of likelihoods of their own positions,[13] and *any* possibly preventable mortality or morbidity in these younger age ranges will constitute a situation rational self-interest maximizers will work to avoid.

Furthermore, and for the same reasons of efficiency, the reallocation decreases by a much smaller amount the chances for older persons to live beyond a normal life span, since, after all, those chances were never very great. For example, ten units of medical care given to a ninety-two-year-old man with multiple chronic conditions might make it possible for him to live an additional two years, but ten units of care given to an eight-year-old girl in an acute episode might make it possible for her to live a normal life span, or about sixty-four additional years. The mistake the disgruntled elderly individual facing a rationing-mandated death makes is in failing to calculate not only the immediate loss he faces but also the benefit he has already gained from policies which have enhanced his chances of reaching his current age: his temporary life expectancy in the ranges zero to twenty, twenty to forty-five, and forty-five to sixty-five will have been much elevated, even though his total life expectancy may decline. The less care provided at the end of life and, hence, the greater the amount of transfer to earlier ages, the greater his gain in life prospects will have been. (Of course, this effect could not be achieved in the first generation of the implementation of such policies.) Furthermore, direct-termination policies are more effective in maximizing overall gains in life saved than denial-of-treatment policies. Since denial of treatment still always involves some costs as persons with multiple conditions in interrelated degenerative diseases are granted even minimal hospice and palliative care during their downhill courses, the proportion of savings is smaller, and less is transferred to earlier age groups.

Consequently, the disgruntled individual also makes a second mistake: he fails to see

---

[13] John Rawls, *A Theory of Justice* (Cambridge: Harvard University Press, 1971), sec. 26, p. 155.

that because direct termination rather than denial of treatment maximizes the amount of transfer to younger age groups, such a policy will have maximized his own chances (except in the first generation) not just of reaching old age but also of entering it with fewer chronic, preexisting conditions. Furthermore, this policy will have done the same for all other persons as well. But as the number of persons entering old age with chronic conditions decreases, the normal life span will tend to increase (at least to any natural limit there may be) and, with it, the chances of any individual's reaching this mark. The long-term effect of such policies—despite the fact that they involve deliberately causing death in people who might continue to live—is to gradually increase the normal life span by delaying the onset of seriously debilitating and eventually fatal disease.

The rational person in the original position, then, who counts among his self-interests both the avoidance of suffering and the preservation of his life, will correctly see that social policies providing for the direct termination of his life at the onset of substantial morbidity in old age will more greatly enhance his prospects in satisfying these self-interests than any alternative open in a scarcity situation. After all, as a party to the original position, he has no knowledge of his own medical condition or age at any given time. Of course, if there were no benefits to older as well as to younger persons from this reallocation but, rather, merely the sacrifice of the interests of some people for those of others, parties to the original position could not agree to such policies; but this is not the case. Since such policies do provide benefits for all, and indeed the greatest benefits for the least advantaged (i.e., those who would otherwise die young), they will receive the agreement of all rational persons in the original position. This agreement, then, provides the basis for counting such policies just. . . .

The Issue of Abuse

. . . Direct-termination age-rationing policies would need to incorporate at least three features as protections against abuse. Without these features, rational self-interest maximizers in the original position could not consent to them.

Preservation of Choice

First, compliance with direct-termination policies would need to be experienced as essentially voluntary at the level of individual choice. This does not mean that individual choice would not be shaped by more general social expectations, but the individual could not be coerced, either legally or socially, into ending his life. Any individual who chose to resist the social expectation that it is time to die, and hence to endure the disenfranchisement from treatment that would be his lot, would have to be guaranteed the freedom to do so. Hence, in such a world, it could not be said that the ill, elderly individual has a "duty to die"; what he has is a duty to refrain from further use of medical resources. . . . Preservation of choice is crucial because state or social coercion not only causes harms but also invites rebellion; it is inherently unstable. But the justice of age rationing in the first place depends on stable enough functioning of the scheme so that the distributive gains in overall life prospects are actually realized, and a scheme which is clearly unstable enough to make such redistributive effects impossible cannot be said to be just.

Rejection of a Fixed Age of Death

Second, the timing of direct-termination rationing policies must be based on expected time left until death, not on a fixed cutoff age such as sixty-five (as on the Greek island of Ceos), seventy-two (the approximate average life expectancy), eighty-five (Fries's conjecture)—or, for that matter, any other fixed age. This is because the underlying purpose of rationing is to enhance the length of life span for *all* members of society; though it will most greatly benefit those who now die earliest, it must also benefit the elderly as well. The central mechanism of redistributive age rationing is reallocation of treatment from older years to younger ones, where treatment is more efficacious and where the prospects of a longer life span are enhanced for all, especially for those whose life spans would otherwise be quite short. But if a fixed age cutoff point for the elderly were selected, whereby persons below the cutoff receive full treatment and persons above it were expected to end their lives, the fundamental purpose of rationing would be undermined. The use of a fixed-age cutoff point would be extraordinarily inefficient, since it would allocate some resources to persons on a clearly terminal course, where the possibility of extension of life is small, and it would also exterminate life where there was no medical treatment required to sustain it. It is not old age itself which is medically expensive; it is the last month, six months, or year or two of life. Variations in costs and efficacy of treatment are not so much a function of time since birth as time to death.[14] Many octogenerians are vigorously healthy; so are some people in their nineties and beyond. On the other hand, dying can be expensive and medical efforts futile even for those whose ages are not advanced. Still more important, avoidance of a fixed-age cutoff point protects the health care system from political encroachments, particularly those which seek cost containment or other political objectives by adjusting the cutoff age downward.

Consequently, parties to the original position would not favor a fixed-age rationing policy but, rather, one which, depending on the degree of scarcity, encouraged direct termination via senicide, early euthanasia, or rational suicide only during the last month, half-year, or year of life. Of course, the precise antemortem period can be identified with certainty only retrospectively. However, even this does not constitute a fully effective counterargument, since it is usually possible for the experienced physician to recognize with at least a fair degree of accuracy the onset of what is likely to be a downhill course ending in death—especially in an elderly patient. Nevertheless, even if such predictions are sometimes inaccurate, the rational self-interest maximizer will still prefer reliance on them in order to maximize his opportunities for continuing life and normal functioning, something which would be jeopardized much more severely by a rigid age cutoff.

Furthermore, since some declines are comparatively rapid, even if not instantaneous, and some prolonged, parties to the original position will seek to maximize their overall opportunities not by agreeing to a policy in which a fixed amount of time at the end of life is held ineligible for care and in which direct termination may be practiced but by supporting a policy in which disenfranchisement begins only at the onset of profound illness or irremediable chronic disease. After all, the precise duration of a downhill course can rarely be predicted with accuracy, although it can typically be accurately predicted that the course will indeed be downhill. Consequently, parties to the original position will consent to policies which impose disenfranchisement not long after the diagnosis and

---

[14]Victor Fuchs, "'Though Much Is Taken': Reflections on Aging, Health, and Medical Care," *Milbank Memorial Fund Quarterly/Health and Society* 62 (1984): 143–66, pp. 151–52.

onset of symptoms of an eventually terminal disease, or at least long enough after the onset to confirm the diagnosis and for the need for medical care to have become pronounced. Hence, the curve would in fact never be perfectly squared, and individuals would not have their lives discontinued while they remained in full health, but the timing of disenfranchisement from care and the expectation that it is "time to die" would fall just after the onset of a characteristic downhill course. Just how far down this slope the cutoff point might come would be a function, of course, of the scarcity situation itself and also of individual, voluntary choices mentioned above.

Public Awareness

Third, it is crucial that not only parties to the original position but also actual persons affected by such policies both know the policies and understand the rationale for them; secretive or propagandistic policies cannot be rationally chosen, nor can ill-founded ones. It is crucial for the stability and, hence, justice of "time to die" policies that persons affected by them understand their own distributive gain; without this understanding, they will remain in the posture of the disgruntled individual mentioned earlier, who sees only his own loss. But individuals who see only their own losses under a policy constitute a force for change. This in turn renders the policy itself in practice unstable, and an unstable policy cannot operate in a way to produce a just distribution. It is crucial that the man in the street who reaches old age understands that the very fact that he has been able to do so is in part the product of his cooperation with policies which have him accept the claim that it is time to die when serious morbidity sets in. As said earlier, the rational person will choose policies which promise both freedom from pain and as long a life as possible; it is only if the man in the street understands the theory and the operations of the policy that he too will be able to see that it accomplishes both.

Conclusion: A Warning

This argument, that in an age-rationing system direct termination of the lives of the elderly more nearly achieves justice than denying them treatment, may seem to be a reductio, but it is not. In a society characterized by substantial scarcity of resources, this contemporary analogue of ancient practices is the only fair response. However, this view does not—*repeat, NOT*—entail that contemporary society should impose age rationing or exterminate those among its elderly who are in poor health. For one thing, it is by no means clear that rationing either by denial of treatment or direct termination is better than providing full medical care for all the elderly who wish it, even at the expense of other social goods. Age rationing is a rationally defensible policy only if the alleged scarcity is real and cannot be relieved without introducing still greater injustices. . . .

Second, a redistributive policy cannot be just without adequate guarantees that resources will in fact be redistributed as required. To deprive the elderly of health care without reassigning the savings in the form of health care for younger age groups is not just and ought not to be advertised in this way. Inasmuch as the erratic age rationing practiced in the United States (perhaps unlike that in the closed system, such as within the British National Health Service)[15] is not tied directly to redistribution of this care to others, it can hardly be described as just but, rather, as the product of

---

[15] See Norman Daniels, "Why Saying No to Patients in the United States Is So Hard: Cost Containment, Justice, and Provider Autonomy." *New England Journal of Medicine* 314 (May 22, 1986): 1380–83.

ordinary, socially entrenched age bias. Furthermore, a just rationing system requires a background of just institutions to ensure its operation, and neither the United States nor Britain can boast a full set of these—nor, for that matter, can any of the primitive or historical societies mentioned at the outset. Consequently, although I believe there is a cogent argument for the moral preferability of a quite startling form of age rationing in a scarcity situation—voluntary but socially encouraged killing or self-killing of the elderly as their infirmities overcome them, in preference to the medical abandonment they would otherwise face—this is in no way a recommendation for the introduction of such practices in our present world. As Daniels remarks, if the basic institutions of a given society do not comply with acceptable principles of distributive justice, then rationing by age may make things worse[16]—and surely age rationing by direct-termination practices could make things very much worse indeed. Thus, while this paper argues that direct-termination practices would be just in a scarcity-characterized ideal world, it casts a quite skeptical eye on the sorts of arbitrary, unthinking age rationing we are toying with now.

Questions for Further Reflection

1. If, as Battin suggests, authorities in a just society withhold expensive treatment from an aged, ill patient, knowing that she will die as a consequence, are they guilty of murder? Would they escape the charge of murder if they did not intend to bring about death (consider Sullivan's view in this context)?
2. Rachels claims that killing and letting die are morally on a par. Is this claim compatible with Battin's position that in a just society, physicians would withhold expensive treatment from aged, ill patients but would not kill them unless they agreed to be killed?
3. Battin rejects the possibility of killing aged, terminally ill patients on the grounds that people would rebel. Can the same complaint be made against her recommended policy of withholding expensive treatment?
4. Some elderly, seriously ill patients cannot afford to pay for their health care, which is then provided by public funds. Others are wealthy enough to pay for their own treatment. Should the same health-care allocation policies apply to both? How would denying resources (other than scarce organs) to the elderly who are able to pay for them make any more resources available to younger or less seriously ill patients?
5. Sullivan seems to want to allow for the possibility that physicians would sometimes stop treating patients who could be kept alive longer if they were treated further. Describe the circumstances under which Sullivan would allow this.
6. Rachels seems to want to limit the plea of mercy killing to people who kill those who are terminally ill. Should the plea be extended further, say, to people who kill individuals who request death and who are suffering horrible afflictions that are not likely to kill them but will make their lives miserable? Should the plea be extended to people who kill *anyone* who requests death? (If so, should we worry that some version of Sullivan's "wedge" argument applies?)

Further Readings

Daniels, Norman. "Justice between Age Groups: Am I My Parents' Keeper?" *Milbank Memorial Fund Quarterly* 61 (1983), pp. 489–522. Important for further investigation of Battin's position.

---

[16]Daniels, "Justice between Age Groups," p. 519.

Kohl, Marvin, ed. *Beneficent Euthanasia.* Buffalo, NY: Prometheus Books, 1975. See also the annotated bibliography provided.

Ladd, J., ed. *Ethical Issues Relating to Life and Death.* Oxford: Oxford University Press, 1979. Several of these essays are helpful.

Regan, Tom, ed. *Matters of Life and Death: New Introductory Essays in Moral Philosophy.* New York: Random House, 1980. Chapter 2 of this book is a useful discussion by James Rachels ("Euthanasia" is an excerpt from this essay). Rachels includes suggestions for further reading.

Weir, Robert, ed. *Ethical Issues in Death and Dying.* New York: Columbia University Press, 1986. Part 5 of this collection includes useful discussions of euthanasia.

Chapter 10

CAPITAL PUNISHMENT

The debate over whether execution is an acceptable form of punishment involves a complicated collection of legal, empirical, and moral issues. The Eighth Amendment to the United States Constitution prohibits "cruel and unusual punishment," and so the legal debate has tended to center around whether capital punishment is cruel or unusual. In many states, the death penalty was legal and fairly widely used until 1972. (The largest number of executions, an average of 167 per year, took place in the 1930s; there were fewer than 200 in the entire decade of the 1960s, and only a little more than 100 in the 1980s.) In 1972, the Supreme Court, in *Furman v. Georgia,* ruled that all the death-penalty statutes in existence at the time were unconstitutional. This was not on the ground that execution was inherently cruel and unusual: The problem was held to be not with the death penalty itself, but with its administration. The Court held that there was too much arbitrariness in determining which convicts would receive the death penalty.[1] In response to this Supreme Court decision, many states began drawing up revised statutes that would make sentencing less arbitrary. In 1976, in *Gregg v. Georgia,* the Supreme Court ruled that several of these new statutes were constitutional. For several years afterward there were few executions, but by the mid-1980s, the average was about 20 per year. In 1995, 56 people were executed—25 more than the previous year. An additional 3,054 people were in prison under sentence of death.

According to the Supreme Court, then, the death penalty as currently administered is constitutional. But is it just? Is it a penalty we morally ought to apply?

Theories of Punishment

To think clearly about whether we ought to carry out executions at all, it is helpful to begin with an overview of different views about the justification of punishment. We can divide justifications of punishment into two broad categories: deontological and utilitarian. The principal deontological account of punishment is *retributivism,* which holds that if someone commits a crime, he or she *deserves* punishment. In this view, the goal of punishment is to serve justice, to do what is fair. There are two main varieties of retributivism. The first is *lex talionis,* or the law of retaliation, which

---

[1]Actually, it is difficult to make generalizations about the ruling. The decision was five to four, with no majority opinion: Each of the five justices in the majority wrote a separate opinion, and their reasons varied.

holds that the criminal deserves as punishment the same thing he or she did to the victim, or at least a punishment as similar to the crime as is practically feasible. Proportional retributivism, on the other hand, holds that the punishment should be proportional to the crime but that it may be less extreme: What matters is that the penalty for murder be more severe than the penalty for punching someone in the jaw, not that the puncher be punched and the murderer murdered.

Utilitarian views of punishment are rather different. For the utilitarian, punishment is to be evaluated in terms of its consequences; a punishment is justified if the consequences are better than those of alternative possible punishments. The relevant consequences may be of various kinds, including at least the following: *prevention* of crime while the criminal is being punished; *rehabilitation* of the criminal so that the criminal will not commit further crimes after his or her release; and *deterrence,* or making other people less likely to commit the same crime.

Deterrence

Utilitarian discussions of capital punishment commonly focus on deterrence. Both imprisonment and execution can prevent a criminal from repeating a crime. Execution obviously makes rehabilitation impossible, but imprisonment has not proven to be effective in rehabilitating people either. A key question from the utilitarian point of view is whether the execution of some murderers makes others less likely to commit murder. If the death penalty *did* deter murderers more than alternative penalties, that would clearly be a point in its favor—although not a conclusive point, since some possible punishments, such as torture, are so horrible that most people would not think them morally justified even if they were far more effective deterrents than alternative punishments.

How effective a deterrent is the death penalty? Common sense offers conflicting indications. It seems likely that many people would prefer life imprisonment to death, and one might suppose that the prospect of being executed would make such people somewhat less likely to commit murder. On the other hand, many murders are carried out in the heat of the moment, often while the killer is intoxicated, without any weighing of the consequences. Anyway, as things currently stand, the *likelihood* that one will be executed for murder is vanishingly small.[2] So what is the net deterrent effect? Common sense is of little use here; what is needed is empirical research. In light of the research conducted to date, the clear consensus among scholars is that there is no good evidence for any deterrent effect.[3]

Ernest van den Haag has suggested that if there is a *chance* that the death penalty deters, that chance is enough grounds for using it: The possible saving of a few innocent lives is worth the certain death of a murderer. "It seems morally indefensible to

---

[2]For a very rough idea of *how* small the chances are, consider that in 1988, about 16,000 people were arrested for murder or nonnegligent manslaughter, while eleven people were executed. If these figures are reasonably typical, they suggest that *if* one is arrested for murder, one's chance of being executed is on the order of .07 percent, or about one in 1,450. (In 1987, there were about 17,000 murder arrests and 25 executions, or about one in 680.)

[3]For references and a quick survey of relevant research, see, for example, Phoebe C. Ellsworth, "Unpleasant Facts: The Supreme Court's Response to Empirical Research on Capital Punishment," in Kenneth C. Haas and James A. Inciardi, eds., *Challenging Capital Punishment: Legal and Social Science Approaches* (Newbury Park, CA.: SAGE Publications, 1988), 178–82.

let convicted murderers survive at the probable—even at the merely possible—expense of the lives of innocent victims who might have been spared had the murderers been executed."[4] This judgment, however, is not as straightforward as it may seem. The only study to suggest a deterrent effect of execution, a study now widely discredited, suggested an effect of only seven or eight lives saved for each execution: In 1988, this would have amounted to fewer than 100 lives overall. Given our unwillingness to adopt less expensive and less uncertain ways of saving this many innocent lives, such as further reducing the speed limit on our highways, it seems unclear that a merely possible deterrent effect justifies capital punishment. Moreover, the matter is further complicated by the possibility that innocent people will be executed by mistake. Hugo Adam Bedau and Michael L. Radelet have gathered evidence that, since 1900, there have been at least "23 cases of what we believe were erroneous executions, and 21 other cases in which a defendant, later exonerated, came to within 72 hours of execution."[5]

Retribution

Partly because the evidence about deterrence is so inconclusive, recent discussions of capital punishment have centered on the notion of retributive justice. The selections in this chapter address two primary questions: whether murderers deserve to die, and if they do, whether we ought to execute them.

Do murderers deserve to die? Immanuel Kant argued that they did; in a famous passage he presents an extreme version of this view:

> Even if a civil society were to dissolve itself by common agreement of all its members (for example, if the people inhabiting an island decided to separate and disperse themselves around the world), the last murderer remaining in prison must be executed, so that everyone will duly receive what his actions are worth and so that the bloodguilt thereof will not be fixed on the people because they failed to insist on carrying out the punishment; for if they fail to do so, they may be regarded as accomplices in the public violation of legal justice.[6]

Stephen Nathanson, in this chapter, argues that what a criminal morally deserves depends on more factors than the courts can reasonably be expected to determine. What punishment one morally deserves for performing an illegal act, he argues, depends not only on the action performed, but also on the intention with which it was performed and the amount of effort that would have been required to refrain from performing it. And, while the courts can determine what action was performed and perhaps make a reasonable determination as to motive, the degree of effort involved is simply too complex a matter to be reliably determined by the courts.

Jeffrey Reiman makes a slightly different version of Nathanson's point about the importance of effort. Nathanson thinks that someone is not to blame if it would have cost him or her unreasonable effort not to

---

[4]Ernest van den Haag, "The Collapse of the Case Against Capital Punishment," *The National Review*, March 31, 1978, 395–407.

[5]Michael L. Radelet and Hugo Adam Bedau, "Fallibility and Finality: Type II Errors and Capital Punishment," in Haas and Inciardi, eds., *Challenging Capital Punishment*, 101.

[6]Immanuel Kant, *The Metaphysical Elements of Justice*, trans. John Ladd (Indianapolis: Bobbs-Merrill, 1965), 102, quoted in Jeffrie G. Murphy, *Kant: The Philosophy of Right* (London: Macmillan, 1970), 141.

perform a certain action: "If a person faces such powerful obstacles to moral behavior that it would require extraordinary amounts of effort to act well, then, though he acts badly, he is not morally to blame." Reiman speaks of responsibility rather than blameworthiness but makes the similar point that "if social factors; especially poverty, are in some way a cause of crime, then it is no longer reasonable to characterize criminals, especially poor ones, as *wholly* responsible for their crimes." Reiman suggests that "poverty mitigates culpability" in something like the way entrapment does.

Van den Haag responds to such claims by arguing that "predictability does not reduce responsibility." If one genuinely *could not* have done otherwise—if one was forced to do something, or perhaps was seriously mentally ill—then one is not responsible for one's action, but provided that the individual had a genuine choice, he or she is morally responsible. (By the way, we should clarify something that could be confusing. Although van den Haag's piece is titled "Refuting Reiman and Nathanson," and although he responds to some of the points made in the selections from Reiman and Nathanson, it is not a direct response to their pieces reprinted here, but rather to articles they published in *Philosophy and Public Affairs* in 1985.)

It is striking that when Nathanson is developing the point that a criminal is less blameworthy if it would have required great effort to do otherwise, he does not use any examples involving murder. However, murder is the only crime currently punishable by execution. It might require great psychological effort for someone in impoverished circumstances to, say, return a dropped $100 bill, but how much effort can it take to refrain from murdering someone? Is it really plausible that in many cases of murder, the effort required *not* to kill someone is so great that the murderer is not blameworthy?

At any rate, Nathanson holds that, since whether someone deserves to die depends on factors we cannot expect the courts to determine, we ought not to permit the death penalty. Nathanson's argument takes a twist at the end of our selection from his book, however. If the courts cannot determine what someone morally deserves, that would seem to be an argument against assessing *any* penalties. However, Nathanson suggests that the purpose of the law is not to ensure that people get what they morally deserve: "Even if we cannot guarantee that people are genuinely morally deserving of punishments, we can set up fair institutions that protect people and that are justified by their protective role rather than by the conception of the law as the enforcement arm of morality." If the justification of the criminal justice system is that it protects the innocent, not that it gives the guilty the punishments they deserve, and if capital punishment does not deter potential murderers more than imprisonment does, and so provides no more protection than imprisonment, then there would seem to be no justification for the penalty.

Nathanson, then, holds that murderers do *not* deserve to die, or at least that we cannot reliably determine that they do deserve this. Reiman's view, by contrast, is that many murderers *do* deserve to die but that, nevertheless, we ought not to execute them. Reiman holds that, *in principle*, the death penalty is just, since retribution is a way of reaffirming "society's commitment to the equality of the victim with the offender." However, this shows only that it is morally permissible to execute murderers, not that it is morally required; and although society has a right to execute murderers, Reiman believes that, *in practice*, there are good reasons not to exercise this right.

In particular, Reiman holds that, in practice, the administration of the death penalty is deeply discriminatory; in Reiman's view, not having a death penalty at all is preferable to having a discriminatorily administered death penalty.

Reiman identifies several sorts of discrimination. Probably the most important is discrimination "in the application of the death penalty among convicted murderers." This discrimination is of two sorts. First, among convicted murderers, blacks are more likely to be executed than whites. (Reiman does not mention that studies that control for aggravating factors have *not* shown that, among murderers in equally aggravated crimes, blacks are any more likely to be executed.[7]) Second, it is quite clear that killers of whites are more likely to be executed than killers of blacks.

Does any of this matter? Van den Haag suggests that, since murderers deserve to die, any discrimination in who gets the death penalty results only in guilty persons avoiding the punishment they deserve, not in anyone getting a punishment he or she does *not* deserve. As a result, he argues, while discrimination is unjust and should be eliminated, it is not unjust to those sentenced to death, but only to those who escape the death penalty, so that the discriminatory application of the penalty gives no reason for abolishing it. Van den Haag also points out that the sort of discrimination for which there is the best evidence—discrimination against killers of whites and in favor of killers of blacks—is *not* a form of discrimination against blacks because most black murder victims are killed by blacks.

---

[7]Ellsworth mentions this in "Unpleasant Facts." See also Samuel R. Gross and Robert Mauro, *Death and Discrimination: Racial Disparities in Capital Sentencing* (Boston: Northeastern University Press, 1989).

DESERVING DEATH

Do Murderers Deserve to Die?

Stephen Nathanson

An Eye for an Eye?

Suppose we . . . try to determine what people deserve from a strictly moral point of view. How shall we proceed?

The most usual suggestion is that we look at a person's actions because what someone deserves would appear to depend on what he or she does. A person's actions, it seems, provide not only a basis for a moral appraisal of the person but also a guide to how he should be treated. According to the *lex talionis* or principle of "an eye for an eye," we ought to treat people as they have treated others. What people deserve as recipients of rewards or punishments is determined by what they do as agents.

This is a powerful and attractive view, one that appears to be backed not only by moral common sense but also by tradition and philosophical thought. The most famous statement of philosophical support for this view comes from Immanuel Kant, who linked it directly with an argument for the death penalty. Discussing the problem of punishment, Kant writes,

> What kind and what degree of punishment does legal justice adopt as its principle and standard? None other than the principle of equality . . . the principle of not treating one side more favorably than the other. Accordingly, any undeserved evil that you inflict on someone else among the people is one that you do to yourself. If you vilify, you vilify yourself; if you steal from him, you steal from yourself; if you kill him, you kill yourself. Only the law of retribution (*jus talionis*) can determine exactly the kind and degree of punishment.[1]

Kant's view is attractive for a number of reasons. First, it accords with our belief that what a person deserves is related to what he does. Second, it appeals to a moral standard and does not seem to rely on any particular legal or political institutions. Third, it seems to provide a measure of appropriate punishment that can be used as a guide to creating laws and instituting punishments. It tells us that the punishment is to be identical with the crime. Whatever the criminal did to the victim is to be done in turn to the criminal.

In spite of the attractions of Kant's view, it is deeply flawed. When we see why, it will be clear that the whole "eye for an eye" perspective must be rejected.

Problems with the Equal Punishment Principle

There are two main problems with this view. First, appearances to the contrary, it does not actually provide a measure of moral desert. Second, it does not provide an adequate criterion for determining appropriate levels of punishment.

Let us begin with the second criticism, the claim that Kant's view fails to tell us how much punishment is appropriate for particular crimes. We can see this, first, by noting that for certain crimes, Kant's view recommends punishments that are not morally acceptable. Applied strictly, it would require that we rape rapists, torture torturers, and burn arsonists whose acts have led to deaths. In general, where a particular crime involves barbaric and inhuman treatment, Kant's principle tells us to act barbarically and inhumanly in return. So, in some cases, the principle generates unacceptable answers to the question of what constitutes appropriate punishment.

This is not its only defect. In many other cases, the principle tells us nothing at all about how to punish. While Kant thought it obvious how to apply his principle in the case of murder, his principle cannot serve as a general rule because it does not tell us how to punish many crimes. Using the Kantian version or the more common "eye for an eye" standard, what would we decide to do to embezzlers, spies, drunken drivers, airline hijackers, drug users, prostitutes, air polluters, or persons who practice medicine without a license? If one reflects on this question, it becomes clear that there is simply no answer to it. We could not in fact design a system of punishment simply on the basis of the "eye for an eye" principle.

In order to justify using the "eye for an eye" principle to answer our question about murder and the death penalty, we would first have to show that it worked for a whole range of cases, giving acceptable answers to questions about amounts of punishment. Then, having established it as a satisfactory general principle, we could apply it to the case of murder. It turns out, however, that when we try to apply the principle generally, we find that it either gives wrong answers or no answers at all. Indeed, I suspect that the principle of "an eye for an

---

[1] Kant, *Metaphysical Elements of Justice*, translated by John Ladd (Indianapolis: Bobbs-Merrill, 1965), 101.

eye" is no longer even a principle. Instead, it is simply a metaphorical disguise for expressing belief in the death penalty. People who cite it do not take it seriously. They do not believe in a kidnapping for a kidnapping, a theft for a theft, and so on. Perhaps "an eye for an eye" once was a genuine principle, but now it is merely a slogan. Therefore, it gives us no guidance in deciding whether murderers deserve to die. . . .

Proportional Retributivism

The view we have been considering can be called "equality retributivism," since it proposes that we repay criminals with punishments equal to their crimes. In the light of problems like those I have cited, some people have proposed a variation on this view, calling not for equal punishments but rather for punishments which are *proportional* to the crime. In defending such a view as a guide for setting criminal punishments, Andrew von Hirsch writes:

> If one asks how severely a wrongdoer deserves to be punished, a familiar principle comes to mind: Severity of punishment should be commensurate with the seriousness of the wrong. Only grave wrongs merit severe penalties; minor misdeeds deserve lenient punishments. Disproportionate penalties are undeserved—severe sanctions for minor wrongs or vice versa. This principle has variously been called a principle of "proportionality" or "just deserts"; we prefer to call it commensurate deserts.[2]

Like Kant, von Hirsch makes the punishment which a person deserves depend on that person's actions, but he departs from Kant in substituting proportionality for equality as the criterion for setting the amount of punishment.

In implementing a punishment system based on the proportionality view, one would first make a list of crimes, ranking them in order of seriousness. At one end would be quite trivial offenses like parking meter violations, while very serious crimes such as murder would occupy the other. In between, other crimes would be ranked according to their relative gravity. Then a corresponding scale of punishments would be constructed, and the two would be correlated. Punishments would be proportionate to crimes so long as we could say that the more serious the crime was, the higher on the punishment scale was the punishment administered.

This system does not have the defects of equality retributivism. It does not require that we treat those guilty of barbaric crimes barbarically. This is because we can set the upper limit of the punishment scale so as to exclude truly barbaric punishments. Second, unlike the equality principle, the proportionality view is genuinely general, providing a way of handling all crimes. Finally, it does justice to our ordinary belief that certain punishments are unjust because they are too severe or too lenient for the crime committed.

The proportionality principle does, I think, play a legitimate role in our thinking about punishments. Nonetheless, it is no help to death penalty advocates, because it does not require that murderers be executed. All that it requires is that if murder is the most serious crime, then murder should be punished by the most severe punishment on the scale. The principle does not tell us what this punishment should be, however, and it is quite compatible with the view that the most severe punishment should be a long prison term. . . .

---

[2]*Doing Justice* (New York: Hill & Wang, 1976), 66; reprinted in *Sentencing*, edited by H. Gross and A. von Hirsch (Oxford University Press, 1981), 243. For a more recent discussion and further defense by von Hirsch, see his *Past or Future Crimes* (New Brunswick, NJ: Rutgers University Press, 1985).

Neither of these retributive views, then, provides support for the death penalty. The equality principle fails because it is not in general true that the appropriate punishment for a crime is to do to the criminal what he has done to others. In some cases this is immoral, while in others it is impossible. The proportionality principle may be correct, but by itself it cannot determine specific punishments for specific crimes. Because of its flexibility and open-endedness, it is compatible with a great range of different punishments for murder.[3]

A More Serious Objection

So far, in looking at these versions of retributivism, I have tried to show that they do not help us to determine the appropriate punishment for specific crimes. That is, they do not really tell us what sort of treatment is deserved by people who have acted in certain ways.

There is a more serious defect of both versions of the theory, however. Neither one succeeds in basing punishment on what a person morally deserves. Why is this? Because both theories focus solely on the action that a person has performed, and this action is not the proper basis for determining moral desert. We cannot tell what a person deserves simply by examining what he has done.

While it may sound odd to say that a person's degree of moral desert is not determined by his actions, the point is actually a matter of common sense morality. We can see this by considering the following examples, all of which are cases of rescuing a drowning person.

1. A and B have robbed a bank, but B has hidden the money from A. A finds B at the beach and sees that he is drowning. A drags B from the water, revives him, finds out the location of the money, and then shoots him, leaving him for dead. The shot, however, is not fatal. A has saved B's life.
2. C recognizes D, a wealthy businessman, at the beach. Later, she sees D struggling in the water and, hoping to get a reward, she saves him. C would not have saved D if she had not thought that a reward was likely.
3. E is drowning at the beach and is spotted by F, a poor swimmer. F leaps into the water and, at great risk to her own life, manages to save E.
4. G is drowning at the beach but is spotted by Superman, who rescues him effortlessly.

In each of these cases, the very same act occurs. One person saves another from drowning. Yet, if we attempt to assess what each rescuer morally deserves, we will arrive at very different answers for each case. This is because judgments of desert are moral judgments about people and not just about their actions or how they should be treated. Our moral judgments about A, C, F, and Superman in the examples above are quite different, in spite of the similarity of their actions. From a moral point of view, we would not rate A as being praiseworthy at all because he had no concern for B's well-being and in fact wished him dead, C, the rescuer motivated by the prospect of a reward, wished D no harm but is also less praiseworthy because her act was not motivated by genuine concern for D's well-being. Finally, while F, the poor swimmer, and Superman both acted from benevolent

---

[3]For more positive assessments of these theories, see Jeffrey Reiman, "Justice, Civilization, and the Death Penalty," *Philosophy and Public Affairs* 14 (1985): 115–48; and Michael Davis, "How to Make the Punishment Fit the Crime," *Ethics* 93 (1983).

motives. F is more deserving of praise because of the greater risk which she took and the greater difficulties she faced in accomplishing the rescue.

What these cases make clear is that there is no direct connection between what a person does and his or her degree of moral desert. To make judgments of moral desert, we need to know about a person's intentions, motivations, and circumstances, not just about the action and its result. Since both Kant and von Hirsch base their judgments concerning appropriate punishments simply on the act that has been committed, they do not succeed in basing their recommended punishments on what a person morally deserves, for what a person deserves depends on factors which they do not consider.

It is quite ironic that Kant overlooks this and provides an exclusively act-oriented account of assessing people in his discussion of punishment. In other writings, Kant insists that the fact that an action is harmful or helpful does not by itself tell us how to assess the moral value of the agent's performing it.[4] He lays great stress on the significance of motivation, claiming that the moral value of actions depends *entirely* on whether they are done from a moral motive. . . .

A More Complex View of Moral Desert

One might think that by delaying the discussion of criteria of desert, which include motivation, intention, and other relevant factors, I have been unfair to proponents of the death penalty. No one would deny that these factors are relevant, and the law explicitly includes them in the definition of murder and other crimes. The legal doctrine of *mens rea* makes the presence of certain intentions necessary even for a crime to have occurred. These factors enter into the definitions of murder, manslaughter, and other criminal acts. In addition, variations in motive and intention are frequently used to determine the severity of the punishment. Most death penalty supporters probably believe that death is the appropriate punishment only for those who kill intentionally and whose acts display an especially high degree of callousness, indifference, or brutality.

These judgments suggest a kind of retributive theory that is more enlightened and attractive than the one expressed by the "eye for an eye" principle. It will be worth seeing how we might develop such a view of moral desert in a systematic way. Then we can examine its implications for the death penalty.

A plausible version of this view can be sketched along the following lines.[5] If a person is correctly judged to be negatively deserving or morally blameworthy, then he must have violated some moral rule. The violation must have been done knowingly and voluntarily, for in most cases, we do not

---

[4] Consider the following more representative statement by Kant: "To be beneficent when we can is a duty; and besides this, there are many minds so sympathetically constituted that . . . they find a pleasure in spreading joy around them, and can take delight in the satisfaction of others so far as it is their own work. But I maintain that in such a case an action of this kind, however proper, however amiable it may be, has nevertheless no true moral worth. . . . For the maxim lacks the moral import, namely, that such actions be done *from duty*, not from inclination." See *Fundamental Principles of the Metaphysic of Morals*, translated by T. Abbott (New York: Liberal Arts Press, 1949), 15–16.

[5] In presenting this account, I am indebted to Elizabeth Lane Beardsley's illuminating paper "Moral Worth and Moral Credit." *Philosophical Review* 66 (1957), especially 306–7; reprinted in *Moral Philosophy*, edited by J. Feinberg and H. West (Belmont, Calif.: Dickenson, 1977).

consider someone morally blameworthy if his behavior was accidental or involuntary (unless he was reckless or negligent in some way). Moreover, he must have acted from a motive that we regard as bad, for even if someone causes harm, we may not think him morally blameworthy if he "meant well."

In addition to guiding our judgments about when a person is morally blameworthy, this approach will also guide us in deciding the degree of personal blameworthiness. Because moral rules vary in importance, violating some moral rules will make one more blameworthy than violating others. It is worse to kill someone than to tell a lie, and therefore murderers are more blameworthy than liars. Likewise, some breaches of a moral rule are more serious than others. It is worse for me to steal your life savings than your weekly paycheck, although both actions violate the same rule. In addition, there are degrees of voluntariness, and we recognize that duress or provocation may make people less blameworthy for their deeds. Finally, there are degrees of badness in motives and intentions. We would usually rank an act done from sadistic cruelty as worse than one done in anger or from jealousy.

These kinds of criteria could presumably be worked out in much greater detail. Even with this short sketch, however, we can see why not all killings are murders, why murder is so grave a crime, and why some murders are worse than others. First, not all killings are done "knowingly and voluntarily," and in many cases, when these factors are missing, we totally absolve a person of moral responsibility. (Where negligence is a factor, of course, a person may still be blameworthy to some degree.) Murder does always involve a breach of a moral rule—the rule against unjustified killing. The gravity of murder is a function of the fact that the rule against killing is an extremely serious moral rule, more important than prohibitions against lying or breaking promises. Finally, the person's motive or desire must be bad if he is to be fully blameworthy. Whatever one thinks about the morality of euthanasia, it is clear that the "mercy killer" is less reprehensible than the killer for hire because the mercy killer is motivated by a benevolent desire. Moreover, the worse the motive, the more blameworthy is the murderer.

There is much more that needs to be said and done in order to work out a complete scheme that orders types of killings according to their degrees of gravity. Much of the law of homicide has been a continuing attempt to do this, and the intent often (though not always) seems to be a desire to make the law conform to our moral sense of how wrong certain sorts of acts are. Let us assume that this enterprise could be completed and that we would have a full list of categories of killings, one that is sensitive to differences in motive and intention and that ranks types of killings according to their moral gravity. Presumably, defenders of the "murderers deserve to die" thesis would then settle on those acts which appear to be among the worst murders and would claim that people who commit these acts are morally blameworthy to an extremely high degree. Finally, they would conclude that people who are morally blameworthy to this degree deserve to die and ought to be executed.

The Failure of the More Complex View of Desert

This view, though far superior to the simpler theories of desert with which we started, is still unsatisfactory and does not provide real support for the death penalty. There are a number of reasons for this.

First, even if we could construct an adequate scale of personal moral desert, it would not follow from the fact that a person received the maximum negative rating that he deserved to be killed. The view we have been discussing assumes that some form of proportionality retributivism is true and therefore that punishments should be proprortional to crimes. Yet, as we saw in discussing von Hirsch's "commensurate deserts" idea, a proportionality system does not require any specific form of punishment for any type of crime. Even after we have ranked crimes according to gravity, there is no necessity in fixing the minimum or maximum levels of punishment at any particular point. The worst murderers (as judged by our complex moral desert scale) would deserve the worst punishments, but the worst punishment in the system need not be death. It could be a "fate worse than death," such as prolonged torture, followed by eventual execution. Or, it could be a less severe punishment, such as life in prison, exile, ten years of hard labor, or a $500 fine. All of these are consistent with the proportionality view, since it does not specify the degree of punishment for crimes. Someone could accept the proportionality view, agree that a particular murderer is extreme in his moral depravity, and still not know what specific punishment is appropriate to this person. . . .

Efforts and Obstacles

We have seen that even if an approach which considers intentions and motives provides an adequate measure of personal moral desert, it still does not justify particular punishments for particular crimes. That is not its only weakness, however. In spite of its superiority over the crude views discussed earlier, this conception of moral desert is itself badly flawed. Like the earlier view, it leaves out factors that are relevant to judgments of moral desert and therefore does not really give us adequate criteria for making personal moral appraisals.

We can see this most easily by considering the actions of the insane, who may intentionally perform wrong actions with malicious motives and still not be morally blameworthy. The same is true of young children. In both cases, we do not regard the people involved as full-fledged moral agents. For this reason, we do not make negative moral judgments of them, in spite of their wrong actions and their bad intentions. This shows that the "actions plus intentions" view is not a complete account of the criteria of moral desert.

We need not focus on children or the insane, however, in order to see the insufficiency of the view we are discussing. We can see it by continuing to think generally about how we appraise people and their degrees of desert. When we judge moral desert, we do not look solely at people's actions, motives, and intentions. We often look at other factors. In particular, we are frequently concerned with the amount of effort required for someone to act or refrain from acting in a certain way. The importance of this factor is emphasized by Elizabeth Beardsley in her study of moral desert. She writes,

> As agents, we are often convinced that acts eliciting a considerable amount of praise from outsiders were somehow for us unusually "easy," and in these cases we do not seem to ourselves to deserve high praise. Correspondingly (and doubtless far more often) we are convinced as agents that certain acts eliciting considerable blame from outsiders were for us such that acts alternative to them would have been somehow unusually "difficult," and here we feel that we do not deserve much blame.[6]

---

[6]"Moral Worth and Moral Credit," 313.

Beardsley's remarks remind us of the importance which effort often has in our judgments, and they suggest the insufficiency of desert judgments based only on information about actions and motives. Even if someone acted badly with bad motives, there may be other factors that made it especially difficult for that person to act in any other manner. If we discover this, we may retract or modify our judgment about the degree to which the person is negatively deserving.[7]

While Beardsley appeals to judgments about ourselves, we often have similar feelings about the erroneousness of moral appraisals of others. Herman Schwartz, commenting on von Hirsch's "commensurate deserts" principle, raises the issue in quite concrete form. Registering his dissent from the principle, he asks rhetorically,

> Can one really say that someone *deserves* to be punished for breaking the law, when that person may have been hooked on heroin by the time he was a teenager, was confronted with racism or other prejudice, grew up in a broken home amid violence, filth, and brutality, was forced to go to substandard schools, and had no honest way to make a decent living.[8]

Schwartz expresses a familiar and plausible view here. His question suggests that a person brought up in extremely unfortunate circumstances may not be fully deserving of blame if he fails to act in a morally appropriate manner. His acts may be wrong, but he himself is not morally blameworthy or at least not as blameworthy as he would have been had he benefited from more fortunate surroundings. This is because his conditions made it especially difficult or perhaps impossible for him to act otherwise.[9]

The central point here is that a person's degree of moral desert is determined primarily by considerations of what could reasonably be expected of him. If a person faces such powerful obstacles to moral behavior that it would require extraordinary amounts of effort to act well, then, though he acts badly, he is not morally to blame. Almost anyone in that situation would have acted similarly, and different behavior could not reasonably be expected. The causes of difficulty need not be environmental. They could be physical, psychological, or of any sort, but if they make alternative actions extremely difficult or impossible, a person is not fully blameworthy for his deeds, even if they were wrong acts triggered by bad motives.

The importance of effort as a central factor in determining genuine moral desert will be recognized by many people. The effort-oriented criterion of moral desert is a part of moral common sense and is reflected in many of our ordinary beliefs. We tend to think that people who have worked hard are more deserving of their wealth than people who have inherited money or won lotteries. We think that one who trains hard deserves to win a race more than one who just naturally can run very fast. Likewise, in the rescue examples, the poor swimmer deserves more credit for rescuing the drowning person than does Superman. She had to overcome both her fears and the objective difficulties of the rescue, while Superman could perform the rescue

---

[7] Beardsley herself does not reach this conclusion. She believes that there are different types of desert judgments which are independent of one another and rejects the view that one type is basic. On this, see both the paper "Moral Worth and Moral Credit," which I have already cited, as well as her "Determinism and Moral Perspectives," *Philosophy and Phenomenological Research* 21 (1960).

[8] A. von Hirsch, *Doing Justice* (New York: Hill & Wang, 1976), 177.

[9] On these issues, see John Hospers, "What Means This Freedom?" in *Determinism and Freedom in the Age of Science*, edited by S. Hook (New York: Collier Books, 1971).

effortlessly. We give people the most moral credit when their good deeds require them to exert a great deal of effort, and we think that people are not fully deserving of blame when we judge that the effort required for acting rightly is greater than what could reasonably be expected of them.

The importance of effort is likewise reflected in the familiar maxim that we ought not to judge another person unless we know what it would be like to be "in his shoes." The idea here seems to be that we cannot legitimately blame someone unless we know that it was possible for that person to act otherwise than he did and that we could only know whether this was possible by being in the other person's shoes, that is, by seeing and feeling things from his perspective. One need not agree with this view to recognize that it is a common one and that it reflects an awareness in moral common sense that many of our immediate judgments of people fail to take the difficulties of their situation seriously enough.

What Follows?

What is the upshot of these reflections? What are the implications of the "effort criterion" of moral desert?

The first thing that follows is that making adequate judgments of moral desert is not easy. Matters are difficult enough when we are trying to discern a person's motives and intentions. They become more difficult still when we try to grasp whether someone was in a position to behave in ways other than he did. . . .

Second, if this "effort" view of desert is true, then there is no automatic connection between having performed a certain action with certain motives and being praiseworthy or blameworthy to some degree. The same act could be performed by two people with the same intentions, yet one would be morally blameworthy and the other not. Why? Because one's background or psychological makeup made it especially difficult or impossible for him not to act this way, while the other's background made it relatively easy.

The extreme difficulty of making these judgments of moral desert suggests that we should adopt a somewhat skeptical attitude toward them. This skepticism might take several forms. We might conclude that it is impossible for us ever to know just how morally blameworthy a person is. There are simply too many factors and too much information required for a full and reliable assessment. . . .

This extreme skepticism is not the only possibility. A more moderate view would be that although such judgments are very difficult to make, they are not impossible. With sufficient care, effort, and attention, one could take into account enough of the relevant factors and make reasonable moral appraisals of people. Like all judgments, these could be wrong, but there is no insuperable barrier to making them. Nonetheless. according to this second view, it is not reasonable to expect that our legal institutions will produce such subtle and complex judgments in a rational and unbiased way. Judges, prosecutors, jurors, and other officials who act within the legal system are under many practical constraints and are influenced by many factors that have nothing to do with the moral desert of an accused person. We have already seen the influence of racial prejudice and other arbitrary factors on legal decisions about degrees of guilt. Because of these influences, we cannot count on our legal institutions to make judgments of moral desert in a fair, informed, and rational way. Therefore, even if knowledge about what people morally deserve is theoretically possible, we ought not to expect it to be obtained in the legal context.

There is a third conclusion that is less radical than the extreme skepticism of the first view and that would help explain the arbitrariness of institutional judgments emphasized by the second view. According to this third view, there are no precise amounts of moral desert, and it is therefore impossible to develop a precise scale for measuring desert. . . .

Doesn't Anyone Deserve Anything?

I want to be careful not to be misunderstood, especially since my view is open to a particularly unattractive misinterpretation.

Someone might think that I am arguing that no one is responsible for what he does at all and that we can never say of someone that he deserves good or ill. Neither of these things follows from my view. . . . The basic justification for holding people responsible is that this practice provides support for important human and social values.[10] This pragmatic, utilitarian justification for holding people responsible is especially appropriate to our discussion, because it is the primary justification for the criminal law and the institution of punishment. As I have argued earlier, the primary purpose of the law is protective. So, even if we cannot guarantee that people are genuinely morally deserving of punishments, we can set up fair institutions that protect people and that are justified by their protective role rather than by the conception of the law as the enforcement arm of morality.

Indeed, the focus on effort and desert brings out an additional aspect of social standards of responsibility. One of the factors that influences the degree to which people can maintain control and act in the face of difficulties is the extent to which others expect them to do so. In a society in which no one was held responsible and all immoral actions were thought to be the product of unavoidable causes, people would accept the fact that they could not maintain self-control and would be more likely to act badly. Where people are expected to act decently, even in the face of provocation, temptation, and other obstacles, they are more likely to retain control of themselves. So there is good reason to maintain standards of responsibility, even if we are skeptical that we can know in particular cases that people are fully responsible.

From this perspective, we do not have to be capable of making pure judgments of moral desert because these do not provide the basis of our system of moral and legal responsibility. We punish and blame not because we are certain that our moral appraisals are true but rather because punishment and blame, like reward and praise, provide important support for human values. The defense of these practices is both moral and pragmatic. The pragmatic aspect stresses the usefulness of holding people responsible, while the moral side stresses the fact that the standards are being used on behalf of important human values. . . .

What my arguments do require is that we reject the view that there is a precise moral desert scale which can be used to show that those who murder with certain motives or in certain circumstances deserve to die. Likewise, it is a mistake to think of the criminal law as an institution for giving people what they morally deserve. The law and the system of punishments may be justified even when we are uncertain what people morally deserve, and given the difficulties of determining degrees of moral desert, this is quite fortunate.

---

[10] My argument here is indebted to Richard Brandt, "Determinism and the Justifiability of Moral Blame," in S. Hook, ed., *Determinism and Freedom in the Age of Modern Science*.

EXECUTION AND DISCRIMINATION

The Justice of the Death Penalty in an Unjust World

Jeffrey Reiman

Justice in Principle and in Practice

When it is pointed out to Ernest van den Haag, perhaps America's best known intellectual defender of capital punishment, that the death penalty has been and is still likely to be administered in a discriminatory fashion, he replies that the question of the justice of the death penalty and that of its administration are two separate questions. In his book, *Punishing Criminals*, van den Haag (1975: 221) writes:

> [O]bjections to unwarranted discrimination are relevant to the discriminatory distribution of penalties, not to the penalties distributed. Penalties themselves are not inherently discriminatory; distribution, the process which selects the persons who suffer the penalty, can be. Unjust distribution—either through unjust convictions or through unjust (unequal and biased) penalization of equally guilty convicts—can occur with respect to any penalty. The vice must be corrected by correcting the distributive process that produces it.

Having said this, van den Haag believes that he has disposed of the objection concerning discrimination, since he has shown that discriminatory application, though admittedly wrong, is not something wrong with the death penalty itself. And thus he returns to the business at hand, namely, justifying the death penalty as the appropriate response to crimes like murder.

Van den Haag is correct in believing that these two questions are distinct and that distinguishing them shields the death penalty from the force of the objection. It does so, however, at a considerable price. He is correct because the justice of a penalty and the justice of a penalty's distribution are theoretically separate matters: We can consistently believe that hanging is, in principle, an excessive and thus unjust penalty for double-parking while believing that it is administered evenhandedly, and we can consistently believe that fining double-parkers in a discriminatory fashion is unjust while believing that fines are in principle a fitting and thus just penalty for double-parking. It is possible to admit that the discriminatory application of a penalty is unjust and still maintain that the penalty itself is in principle a just one. Thus van den Haag can agree with his critics that the discriminatory application of the death penalty is unjust, and still maintain that the penalty itself is in principle a just response to murder.

But this way of disposing of the objection carries a high price tag because the very separation of the questions by means of which van den Haag evades the objection dramatically limits the scope of the conclusions he can reach from that point on. *The reason for this is that the moral question of whether the death penalty is a just punishment for murder is not the same as the moral question of whether it would be just for us to adopt the policy of executing murderers.* Consequently, an affirmative answer to the former question does not imply an affirmative answer to the latter question.

Let's call the question of whether the death penalty is a just punishment for murder "the question of the justice of the death penalty *in principle*," and call the question of whether it would be just for us—here and now in the United States, under foreseeable conditions—to adopt the policy of executing murderers "the question of the justice of the death penalty *in practice*." The reason that the two questions are different is that when we choose to adopt a policy, we are not simply affirming it in a vacuum. We are choosing to initiate a course of events that includes the actual way the policy will be carried out. We normally hold people responsible for the foreseeable consequences of their choices, even those consequences that they would rather not have happen. The foreseeable consequences of adopting a policy include the foreseeable ways that the policy will actually be administered. If we have reason to expect that a just policy will be administered unjustly, then choosing to adopt the policy is choosing to do something unjust—even though the policy itself is just in principle. . . .

Moral assessment of the way a penalty is actually going to be carried out is a necessary ingredient in any determination of the justice of adopting that penalty as our policy. By separating the question of the justice of the death penalty itself from that of the justice of the way it is likely to be carried out, van den Haag separates as well his answer to the question of the justice of the death penalty itself from any answer to the question whether the death penalty is just as an actual policy. As a result, van den Haag may prove that the death penalty is in principle a just response to murder—but at the cost of losing the right to assert that it is just for us to adopt it in practice here and now in America.

Further, if there is reason to believe that a policy will be administered unjustly, then that is reason for believing that it is *unjust* to adopt that policy here and now in America, even though the policy is just in principle. This is not to say that injustice in the administration of a policy automatically makes it wrong to adopt the policy. It might still be that all the available alternatives are worse, such that on balance we do better by adopting this policy than by adopting any of the other possible candidates. However, in the absence of a showing that all alternatives are worse, I take it that it is wrong to adopt an unjust policy, and thus that the likelihood of substantially unjust administration of a policy has the effect of making it wrong to adopt that policy. I say "substantially" here in order to make clear that I do not claim that every, even the slightest, injustice has this effect. Given the inevitability of human error, some miscarriages of justice are inevitable in implementing any policy. Unless we are to be paralyzed by the specter of human fallibility, we have to allow that a policy may be administered justly "on the whole" even though there is some small measure of unavoidable error. But, it is not the *unavoidability* of the error that allows us to call the policy justly administered "on the whole," it is the *smallness* of the error that allows this. If we knew that some policy had a likelihood of many grave though unavoidable errors, we would have to consider these as morally relevant costs of adopting the policy though they are unavoidable—for the simple reason that *we* can prevent these errors by not adopting the policy. Thus, I shall say that in situations in which we have reason to expect that a policy will be administered with *substantial* injustice, then that policy will likely be unjust *in practice,* and in situations in which there is not reason to believe that all alternative policies will be worse, it would be wrong to adopt a policy that is likely to be unjust *in practice* even if it was just *in principle*. . . .

I shall first sketch an argument for the justice of the death penalty in principle as a response to murder. I believe that this argument accounts for the appeal that the death penalty continues to have for large numbers of people in civilized nations. I shall then consider a number of features of the actual conditions under which the death penalty is likely to be carried out in America that, notwithstanding the justice of the penalty in principle, imply that the penalty is not just in America now and in the foreseeable future. I believe that this second argument accounts for the resistance to the death penalty felt by large numbers of Americans, and thus that the two arguments together go some way toward explaining the seesawing, schizophrenic attitude toward capital punishment that has characterized the American body politic in recent decades. . . .

The Justice of the Death Penalty . . .

Justifications of the death penalty as the appropriate punishment for murder normally come under one of two heads, namely, deterrence and retribution. Both sorts of justification have characteristic strengths and difficulties.

Consider first, deterrence. If it could be shown that capital punishment was the most effective way to deter potential murderers, then capital punishment would be justified as an extention to society of the individual's right of self-defense—surely one of the least controversial of moral rights. The greatest difficulty facing this justification is establishment of the fact that capital punishment is more effective as a deterrent to murder than less harsh penalties, such as life in prison without chance of parole, or penalties even less harsh. It is crucial that capital punishment be shown to be more effective in deterring murder than less harsh penalties, since if punishment is justified by its deterrent impact, then only so much punishment as is needed for deterrence is justified. Punishment beyond this is strictly speaking pointless suffering, and pointless suffering is cruel if not unusual, and surely unjustified.

Although I take the deterrence justification to rest on the right of self-defense, its more usual foundation is utilitarianism. But either way, only the least harsh means of achieving deterrence is justified. . . .

[However,] research done on the effects of the death penalty by no means indicates that it is a superior deterrent than less harsh penalties, and indeed the weight of empirical research on this issue tends to the opposite conclusion, namely, that jurisdictions without the death penalty experience no greater number of homicides than comparable jurisdictions with it.

In 1970, based on a review of the findings of empirical research on the impact of the death penalty on homicide rates (including the classic study by Thorsten Sellin), Hugo Bedau (1970) concluded that the claim that the death penalty is superior to life imprisonment as a deterrent to crimes generally, and to the crime of murder particularly, "has been disconfirmed," because the evidence shows uniformly the nonoccurrence of the results that one would expect were the death penalty a superior deterrent. In 1975, Isaac Ehrlich, a University of Chicago econometrician, published the results of a statistical study purporting to prove that in the period from 1933 to 1969, each execution may have deterred as many as eight murders. This, however, did not deter the authors of a National Academy of Sciences' study of the impact of punishment from writing in 1978: "In summary, the flaws in the earlier analyses (i.e., Sellin's and others) and the sensitivity of the more recent analyses to minor variations in model specification and the serious temporal instability of the results lead the panel to conclude that the available studies provide no useful evidence on the deterrent effect of capital punishment" (Blumstein, Cohen, and Nagin, 1978: 9). Though there is much that can be said in criticism of the death penalty/deterrence research, it remains that it is all we've got. And a society that thinks the taking of life is so grave an act that it should be done only to prevent other killing should not execute anyone in the absence of reliable evidence that other killing will be prevented as a result. For this reason, I shall set aside the deterrence justification of capital punishment for the moment as unsupported in the present state of our knowledge. I shall have more to say about it at the close.

Unlike deterrence justifications, retributivist justifications of capital punishment are not hostage to empirical research. On retributivist grounds, the death of the murderer is justified not by its effects on other potential murderers, but by the murderer's own moral guilt. By choosing to end his victim's life the murderer *earns* the loss of his own as his *just deserts*. The characteristic difficulty with such a justification is to show that it is not simply a rationalization for satisfying the desire for revenge, a desire that many find unworthy of social affirmation since it seems to be a desire for nothing else but the pointless suffering of the guilty. This difficulty can be met, however, if a better face can be put on revenge by showing that the suffering it desires is not pointless. This is complicated by the fact that there is a feature of the desire for revenge that is truly unworthy of social affirmation. This is the fact that the desire for revenge, powered as it is by the anger and suffering of the victim or his kin, is or can be literally bottomless. To give in to a bottomless desire to see wrongdoers suffer is surely barbaric. In this respect, the ancient Code of Hammurabi, often blamed for legitimating revenge in affirming the maxim of "an eye for an eye," was actually an attempt to limit the desire for revenge to the measure of suffering caused by the wrongdoer.

So limited, the desire for revenge is the desire that the wrongdoer experience suffering in the amount that he has imposed it on another. And though the point of such suffering is not to prevent other suffering, neither is it pointless. Its point is very much the same point as that of the golden rule, namely, to establish a kind of equilibrium or symmetry between persons such that each treats the other as of equal worth to himself. Doing unto others what one would want others to do unto one treats others as of equal worth to oneself because testing the acceptability of one's own actions by whether one would accept being on the receiving end of them limits one to doing only those things that a being equal to oneself in worth (namely, oneself in the other's shoes) could accept. The acts that prompt the desire for revenge are acts that the doer would not accept being on the receiving end of, acts that he does because he can avoid being on the receiving end. By doing to the other what one would not accept done to oneself, a person treats himself as, in effect, of greater worth than his victim. The desire to do back to him what he does in this case is the desire to demonstrate to him that he is not of greater worth than his victim, that since he is of equal worth with others, whatever he does to others may rightly be done to him.

The desire that the wrongdoer experience suffering in the amount he has imposed it on another is simply the desire to have the golden rule executed by force on those who refuse to comply with it voluntarily. And as long as the desire for revenge is limited to the desire to impose suffering equal to the amount that has been imposed, there is nothing shady or barbaric about this desire. If the point of the golden rule is to establish a kind of equilibrium among persons as equal in worth to one another, the point of retribution is to reestablish this equilibrium when it has been upset. This should not be taken as a metaphor. Retribution truly does reestablish equilibrium in at least two ways. First of all, by imposing suffering on the offender equal to that which he imposed on his victim, the offender is literally forced to recognize his likeness to his victim as a person vulnerable to suffering and desiring to avoid it. Second, retribution announces to the whole society that the suffering of each person is equally a calamity, and thus reaffirms the society's commitment to the equality of the victim with the offender that the offender has violated.

That retributive punishment can be thought of as having the same point as the golden rule shows, I believe, that doing to a person what he has intentionally done to another cannot be unjust. And this suffices to show that the death penalty is just on retributive grounds. But, in my view, what this argument establishes is the *right* to execute murderers, not the *duty* to do so. Thus it does not imply that it is unjust to impose a less harsh penalty than death on murderers. It may well be that other considerations, such as a desire not to ape the cruelty of the cruelest criminals, may justify our toning our punishments down. Thus, although I shall treat the argument as justifying the *lex talionis,* an eye for an eye, and thus a life for a life, it is also compatible with the view called "proportional retributivism," in which the severity of punishment is proportioned to the severity of crime (the worst crime gets the worst punishment, the next-to-worst crime gets the next-to-worst punishment, and so on) with no attempt to match the suffering of the punishment to that caused by the crime.

There is, to be sure, much else that would have to be added to this brief sketch in order to complete the argument for the retributive justification of the death penalty for murderers.[1] However, since my purpose is to offer a plausible case for the justice of the death penalty in principle in order to see how it fares in light of the actual conditions under which the penalty is likely to be applied in America, this incomplete argument should suffice. Before proceeding, two features of this argument should be noted since they will figure in what follows. First, the retributive justification of the death penalty that I have defended depends on its capacity to affirm or act out the equal worth of persons. Second, the death penalty affirms the equal worth of persons only on the assumption that the murderer is wholly responsible for his or her crime. This is a necessary condition of the legitimacy of asking him or her to pay the whole price of the harm he or she has caused, namely, a life for a life. I shall consider four conditions under which the death penalty is likely to be applied in America. Three of them are forms of discrimination (though only in the first of these is the form referred to in the quotation from van den Haag), and the fourth is the notion that life on death row awaiting execution is torture. Though I believe that

---

[1] For a more extensive presentation and defense of this argument for the justice of the death penalty as well as the reasons for not instituting it despite its justice, see Reiman, 1985: 115–148. A reply by Ernest van den Haag appears in the same issue of the journal.

all four of these conditions are not only actual but likely to be with us for the foreseeable future. I shall not present extensive evidence to this effect in this short space. Thus, the argument that follows may be taken as evaluating the justice of the death penalty in practice *if* any or all of the four conditions obtain.

. . . In an Unjust World

(1) *Discrimination in the application of the death penalty among convicted murderers.* A long line of researchers has found that among equally guilty murderers, the death penalty is more likely to be given to blacks than to whites, and to poor defendants than to well-off ones. Though racial discrimination was the main ground upon which death penalty statutes were ruled unconstitutional in *Furman v. Georgia* in 1972, there is strong evidence (though not uncontested) that it remains in the sentencing procedures ruled constitutional after *Furman:* "Among killers of whites [in Florida], blacks are five times more likely than whites to be sentenced to death." This pattern of discrimination was also evidenced, though in less pronounced form, in Texas, Ohio, and Georgia (the other three states surveyed). These four states "accounted for approximately 70 percent of the nation's death sentences" between 1972 and 1977 (Bowers and Pierce, 1982: 210, 211). More recently, studies have presented evidence for discrimination among convicted murderers on the basis of the race of their victims, with killers of whites standing a considerably larger chance of being sentenced to death than killers of blacks (see *McCleskey v. Kemp*, 753 F.2d 877, 1985).

It should be clear that a society that adopts the death penalty when it is likely to be applied in this way chooses to bring injustice into existence. At the very least, any society that punishes in such a discriminatory fashion loses the right to appeal to the retributive justification of the death penalty defended earlier. This is because that justification depends on the penalty's affirmation of the equal worth of persons, and a society that reserves the death penalty for murderers coming from certain racial and socioeconomic groups clearly treats these people as of less worth than others. Likewise, a society that reserves the death penalty for the killers of whites but not of blacks, treats blacks as of less worth than whites. Since its punishing behavior is incompatible with respect for the equal worth of persons, such a society loses the right to appeal to the equal worth of persons to justify its punishments. Moreover, insofar as actions speak louder than words, such a society loses the right to justify its executions as appropriate responses to the crime of murder, since its actions indicate that it is executing people not because they are murderers but because they are black or poor, or because their victims are white, or all of the above.

(2) *Discrimination in the definition of murder.* Those acts that the law calls "murder"—and whose perpetrators are treated by the criminal justice system as "murderers"—are by no means the only ways that people kill their fellow citizens in America. There is, for example, considerable evidence that many more Americans die as a result of diseases caused by preventable conditions in the workplace (toxic chemicals, coal and textile dust, and so on) than die at the hands of the murderers who show up in arrest and conviction records or on death row (see Reiman, 1984: 45–76). In 1985, three corporate executives were found guilty of murder and sentenced to 25 years in prison for the death of an employee that was caused by exposure to hydrogen cyanide in a film reprocessing plant (Facts on File, 1985: 495). The executives,

it was held, knew fully the dangerousness of the situation and failed to warn their employees. Most interesting for our purposes is that this was recognized as *the first case of its kind*. The uniqueness of this case and its outcome testify that general practice is to ignore or treat lightly the subjection of workers to lethal hazards on the job.

It might be thought unfair to class such things as the failure to remove deadly occupational hazards as murder because this failure is not an act intentionally aimed at ending life. This objection misconceives the nature of intentions as they function in the attribution of criminal responsibility. If I shoot someone in the head and kill him although I really intended only to scare him by grazing his hair as a prank, the law holds me responsible for (at least) reckless homicide even though I intended only to have some fun and not to kill anyone. As long as his victims have not freely and knowingly consented to put themselves at risk, the law treats the individual as intending—and thus responsible for—all the foreseeable likely consequences of his acts, *regardless of the particular outcome he hopes for when he acts*. Thus, if loss of life is among the foreseeable likely consequences of failure to remove occupational hazards, as long as the victims have not freely and knowingly consented to put themselves at risk, the individual responsible for this failure ought to be held to have intended the loss of life and thus be treated as responsible for (at least) reckless homicide, regardless of the particular outcome he hoped for when he acted. It is reasonable to assume that there is some ordinary level of risk that is accepted by all members of society as an implicit condition of enjoying the benefits of progress, and of course there are some cases in which workers can be said to have freely and knowingly consented to risk the special occupational hazards that accompany their jobs—but there are as well a large number of cases in which individuals taking hazardous jobs had no realistic alternative and a large number of cases in which extraordinary hazards were known only to management, and concealed. In these cases, employees can hardly be held to have freely put themselves at risk.

There is also evidence that the number of people who die from other practices not normally treated as murder, such as performance of unnecessary surgery and prescription of unneeded drugs, is higher than the number of reported murder victims. And these examples can be multiplied. Moreover, it is arguable that the difference between the kinds of killings that are treated as murder and the kinds that are not is not an arbitrary or haphazard difference; it is a quite systematic identification of the ways that poor people kill as "murder" and the ways that well-off people kill as something else: "disasters," "social costs of progress," or "regulatory violations" at worst (Reiman, 1984: 34–45).

If it is the case that in our society murder is not the intentional taking of life but the intentional taking of life *by poor people*, this has quite the same moral effect as the first sort of discrimination. It has the effect of treating well-off killers as of greater worth than poor killers, and supports the presumption that in our society murderers are not punished because they are murderers, but because they are poor. Then, adoption of the death penalty in practice amounts to instituting this unjust discriminatory treatment of the poor. And this disqualifies the society from claiming that it is executing murderers to pay them in kind for their crimes and to affirm the equal worth of human beings.

(3) *Discrimination in the recruitment of murderers.* The first two sorts of discrimination just considered are built into the

criminal justice system; the sort that I shall now take up is arguably built into the structure of the society that that criminal justice system is supposed to protect. That the death rows of our nation are populated primarily with poor people is not only the result of discriminatory sentencing. In large measure, it is the result of the fact that murder, or at least what we call murder, is done primarily by such people. For example, most defendants in capital cases cannot afford to hire their own lawyers and thus must have attorneys appointed by the state (Johnson, 1981: 138). Accordingly, if discrimination in the handing down of death sentences was completely eliminated, it is still likely that the overwhelming majority of death row inmates would come from the bottom of society. Now, unless we assume that poor people are inherently more evil than better-off people, we must recognize that there is something about poverty (and its accompanying conditions: lack of education, transient communities, and so on) that substantially increases the likelihood of a person committing murder. And this implies that, although the media as well as law-and-order politicians like to picture violent crime as the result of individual moral defect, there is considerable evidence to suggest that violent crime has social causes.

That virtually every wave of immigrant laborers to come to the United States passed through a stage of poverty and crime, and then passed out of crime as they ascended the economic ladder, strongly suggests that much crime results from conditions associated with poverty, as opposed to such things as genetic endowment, cultural traditions, and so on, which are relatively stable during the transition from poverty to a higher standard of living. Similarly, cross-national studies in crime rates show that virtually every country that undergoes the transition from an agrarian to an industrial society endures the same pattern of changes in the composition and magnitude of its criminality. All go from low crime rates, in which violent crime predominates over property crime, to high crime rates, in which property crime predominates over violent crime: "The changes in crime patterns observed first in England, Germany, and France as a result of the industrial revolution have accompanied modernization elsewhere.... In terms of crime the hallmark of modernization is the transition from a society dominated by violent crime to one characterized by increasing property crime" (Shelley, 1981: 138–139). The persistence of this pattern across countries different in so many other respects is strong evidence that features of the structure of society importantly affect the incidence and nature of the society's crime.

If social factors, especially poverty, are in some way a cause of crime, then it is no longer reasonable to characterize criminals, especially poor ones, as *wholly* responsible for their crimes. This is particularly the case with a factor like poverty that is not only correctable, but from which the rest of society derives certain benefits, such as the availability of cheap labor to do the jobs others find either too hard or distasteful. A society that not only allows correctable crime-producing conditions to exist, but derives benefits from those conditions, can hardly turn around and hold the criminals thereby produced *wholly* responsible for their crimes. Rather the society must share some of the blame, and that means that it cannot exact from the murderer the "full price" for his or her act, his or her life for the life taken. When such a society takes the murderer's life as the price of his or her crime, it effectively takes more than it is entitled to from the murderer, and commits an injustice. . . .

My argument does not claim that criminals, murderers in particular, cannot control their actions, and thus I do not claim that they are not responsible for their actions. I do, however, argue that under current foreseeable conditions, many criminals cannot be held *wholly* responsible for their actions. But this, in my view, arises because the society shares some of that responsibility, not because the criminals can't help doing what they do.

I think we do better to understand the way poverty mitigates culpability by (rough) analogy with the *entrapment* defense, rather than by analogy with the *insanity* defense. In entrapment, without doubting that the offender could have controlled his actions, we excuse him from criminal responsibility because the state has played a role in making a criminal act a temptingly reasonable option for him when it would not have been otherwise. . . .

Insofar as we as a society tolerate the existence of remediable conditions that make crime a more reasonable alternative for a specific segment of society than for other segments, we are accomplices in the crimes that quite predictably result. As such, we lose the right to extract the full price from the criminal, and this means we lose the right to take the murderer's life in return for the life he has taken. Consequently, since the vast majority of murderers will come from the bottom of society, adopting the death penalty as their punishment imposes more harm on them than they have earned—and that means that adopting the death penalty in practice amounts to bringing about injustice.

(4) *Life on death row as torture.* The argument that the person condemned to be executed lives a life of torture stems from Albert Camus . . . (Camus, 1961: 205). . . . [It] has been fleshed out in fuller psychological detail by Robert Johnson (1981: 129 ff.) who, in his book *Condemned to Die,* recounts the painful psychological deterioration suffered by a substantial majority of the death row prisoners he studied. Since the death row inmate faces execution, he is viewed as having nothing to lose, and thus treated as the most dangerous of criminals. As a result, his confinement and isolation are nearly total. Since he has no future to be rehabilitated for, he receives the least and the worst of the prison's facilities. Since his guards know they are essentially warehousing him until his death, they treat him as something less than human—and so he is brutalized, taunted, powerless, and constantly reminded of it. The result of this confinement, as Johnson reports it, is quite literally the breaking down of the structures of the ego—a process not unlike that caused by brainwashing. Since we do not reserve the term *torture* only for processes resulting in physical pain, but recognize processes that result in psychological pain as torture as well (consider the so-called Chinese water torture), Johnson's application of this term to the conditions of death row confinement seems reasonable. . . .

Although it is possible that the worst features of death row might be ameliorated, it is not at all clear that its torturous nature is ever likely to be eliminated, or even that it is possible to eliminate it. In order to protect themselves against natural, painful, and ambivalent feelings of sympathy for a person awaiting a humanly inflicted death, it may be psychologically necessary for the guards who oversee a condemned person to think of him as less than human and treat him as such. Johnson (personal communication) writes: "I think it can also be argued . . . that humane death rows will *not* be achieved in practice because the purpose of death row confinement is to facilitate executions by dehumanizing both the prisoners and (to a lesser degree) their executioners and thus make it easier for both to conform to the etiquette of ritual killing."

Suppose that conditions on death row are, and are likely to continue to be, a real form of psychological torture, what are the implications for the justice of the death penalty in practice? At the very least, one must admit that it is no longer merely a penalty of death—it is now a penalty of torture-until-death. And if this is so, then it can no longer be thought of as an amount of suffering equal to that imposed by the murderer—leaving aside those murderers who have tortured their victims. Thus, at least for ordinary murderers, the death penalty would exceed the suffering they had caused, and could not be justified on the retributivist basis defended above. As to whether it would be justified retribution for murderers who had tortured their victims, perhaps it would, but I suspect not. The reason is that as we move away from common instrumental murders to the pointlessly cruel ones, we move at the same time toward offenders who are more likely to be sociopaths and less likely to be fully in control of their actions in the way that legitimates retributive punishment. There may of course be torturers of whom this is not true, but its general likelihood counts against reserving the death penalty as a special punishment for torture-murderers. In any event, since current death penalty laws do not reserve the penalty only for such murderers, this argument tells against those laws and their kin, even if not against a law that would reserve the penalty for torturers.

I think it will be granted that the four conditions I have been discussing constitute substantial injustices. If, as I think is the case, any or all of the four conditions are likely to characterize the imposition of the death penalty in the United States in the foreseeable future, it follows that adopting the death penalty under current and foreseeable conditions is willfully initiating a course of events characterized by substantial injustice. Though injustices will result from imposing lesser penalties on murderers, these are likely to be lesser in the same degree as penalties are lesser. In any event, there is no reason to assume that the injustices connected with not executing murderers will be worse than those that accompany executing them. Consequently, I conclude that it would be wrong to adopt the death penalty *in practice* in the United States as punishment for murder—although the penalty itself is *in principle* a just punishment for murder. . . .

References

ALTMAN, A. and LEE, S. (1983) "Legal entrapment." *Philosophy & Public Affairs* 12, 1 (Winter): 51–69.

BEDAU, H. A. (1970) "Deterrence and the death penalty: A reconsideration." *Journal of Criminal Law, Criminology and Police Science* 61, 4:539–548.

BLUMSTEIN, A., COHEN, J., and NAGIN, D. [eds.] (1978) *Deterrence and Incapacitation: Estimating the Effects of Criminal Sanctions on Crime Rates*. Washington, DC: National Academy of Sciences.

BOWERS, W. J. and PIERCE, G. L. (1982) "Racial discrimination and criminal homicide under post-*Furman* capital statutes," pp. 206–224 in H. A. Bedau (ed.) *The Death Penalty in America* (3rd ed.). New York: Oxford University Press.

CAMUS, A. (1961) "Reflections on the guillotine," pp. 173–234 in A. Camus, *Resistance, Rebellion and Death*. New York: Knopf.

EHRLICH, I. (1975) "The deterrent effect of capital punishment: A question of life and death." *American Economic Review* 65 (June): 397–417.

Facts on File (1985). New York: Facts on File.

JOHNSON, R. (1981) *Condemned to Die: Life Under Sentence of Death*. New York: Elsevier.

MURPHY, J. G. (1979) "Marxism and retribution," pp. 491–512 in R. Wasserstrom (ed.) *Today's Moral Problems* (2nd ed.). New York: Macmillan.

REIMAN, J. H. (1984) *The Rich Get Richer and the Poor Get Prison: Ideology, Class and Criminal Justice* (2nd ed.). New York: John Wiley.

REIMAN, J. H. (1985) "Justice, civilization, and the death penalty: Answering van den Haag." *Philosophy & Public Affairs* 14, 2 (Spring): 115–148.

SHELLEY, L. I. (1981) *Crime and Modernization*. Carbondale, IL: Southern Illinois University Press.

TOCH, H. (1980) *Violent Men*. New York: Schenkman.

VAILLANT, G. (1977) *Adaptation to Life*. Boston: Little, Brown.

VAN DEN HAAG, E. (1975) *Punishing Criminals*. New York: Basic Books.

Defending the Death Penalty

Refuting Reiman and Nathanson

Ernest van den Haag

. . .

Poverty and Culpability

Reiman believes "that the vast majority of murders in America are a predictable response to the frustrations and disabilities of impoverished social circumstances" which could be, but are not remedied because "others in America benefit," wherefore we have "no right to exact the full cost . . . from our murderers until we have done everything possible to rectify the conditions that produce their crimes."[1] Murder here seems to become the punishment for the sins of the wealthy. According to Reiman, "the vast majority" of current murderers are not fully culpable, since part of the blame for their crimes must be placed on those who fail to "rectify the conditions that produce their crimes."

I grant that certain social conditions predictably produce crime more readily than others. Does it follow that those who commit crimes in criminogenic conditions are less responsible, or blameworthy, than they would be if they did not live in these conditions? Certainly not. Predictability does not reduce responsibility. Reiman remains responsible for his predictable argument. Culpability is reduced only when the criminal's ability to control his actions, or to realize that they are wrong, is abnormally impaired. If not, the social conditions in which the criminal lives have no bearing on his responsibility for his acts. Conditions, such as poverty, just or unjust, may increase the temptation to commit crimes. But poverty is neither a necessary nor a sufficient condition for crime, and thus certainly not a

---

[1] Reiman does not say here that murder deserves less than the death penalty, but only that "the vast majority of murderers" deserve less because impoverished. However, wealthy murderers can be fully culpable, so that we may "exact the full cost" from them.

coercive one. If there is no compulsion, temptation is no excuse. The law is meant to restrain, and to hold responsible, those tempted to break it. It need not restrain those not tempted, and it cannot restrain those who are unable to control their actions.

Reiman's claim, that even "though criminals can control their actions, when crimes are predictable responses to unjust circumstances, then those who benefit from and do not remedy those conditions bear some responsibility for the crimes and thus the criminals cannot be held *wholly* responsible for them . . ." seems quite unjustified. Those responsible for unjust conditions must be blamed for them,[2] but not for crimes that are "predictable responses to unjust circumstances," if the respondents could have avoided these crimes, as most people living in unjust conditions do.

If crimes are political, that is, address not otherwise remediable "unjust circumstances," they may be held to be morally, if not legally, excusable, on some occasions.[3] But the criminal's moral, let alone legal, responsibility for a crime which he committed for personal gain and could have avoided, is not diminished merely because he lives in unjust circumstances, and his crime was a predictable response to them. Suppose the predictable response to unjust wealth were drunken driving, or rape. Would his wealth excuse the driver or the rapist? Why should poverty, if wealth would not.[4]

Crime is produced by many circumstances, "just" and "unjust." The most just society may have no less crime than the least just (unless "just" is defined circularly as the absence of crime). Tracing crime to causal circumstances is useful and may help us to control it. Suggesting that they *eo ipso* are excuses confuses causality with nonresponsibility. *Tout comprendre ce n'est pas tout pardonner,* Mme. de Staël's followers to the contrary notwithstanding. Excuses require specific circumstances that diminish the actor's control over his actions.

Since "unjust circumstances" do not reduce the responsibility of criminals for their acts, I shall refrain from discussing whether Reiman's circumstances really are unjust, or merely unequal, and whether they do exist because someone benefits from them and could be eliminated if the alleged beneficiaries wished to eliminate them. I am not sure that unjust circumstances always can be remedied, without causing worse injustices. Nor do I share Reiman's confidence that we know what social justice is, or how to produce it. . . .

Discrimination

Disagreeing with the Supreme Court, Stephen Nathanson believes that the death penalty still is distributed in an excessively capricious and discriminatory manner. He thinks capital punishment is "unjust" because poor blacks are more likely to be sentenced to death than wealthy whites. Further, blacks who murdered whites are more likely to be executed than those who

---

[2]Who are they? They are not necessarily the beneficiaries, as Reiman appears to believe. I benefit from rent control, which I think unjust to my landlord, but I'm not responsible for it. I may benefit from low prices for services or goods, without being responsible for them, or for predictable criminal responses to them. Criminals benefit from the unjust exclusionary rules of our courts. Are they to blame for these rules?

[3]See my *Political Violence & Civil Disobedience,* passim (New York: Harper & Row, 1972) for a more detailed argument.

[4]Suppose unjust wealth tends to corrupt, and unjust poverty does not. Would the wealthy be less to blame for their crimes?

murdered blacks.[5] This last discrimination has been thrown into relief recently by authors who seem to be under the impression that they have revealed a new form of discrimination against black murderers. They have not. The practice invidiously discriminates against black victims of murder, who are not as fully, or as often, vindicated as white victims are. However, discrimination against a class of victims, although invidious enough, does not amount to discrimination against their victimizers. The discrimination against black victims, the lesser punishment given their murderers, actually favors black murderers, since most black victims are killed by black murderers. Stephen Nathanson and Jeffrey Reiman appear to think that they have captured additional discrimination against black defendants. They are wrong.

Neither the argument from discrimination against black victims, nor the argument from discrimination against black murderers, has any bearing on the guilt of black murderers, or on the punishment they deserve.

Invidious discrimination is never defensible. Yet I do not see wherein it, in Reiman's words, "would constitute a separate and powerful argument for abolition," or does make the death penalty "unjust" for those discriminatorily selected to suffer it, as Stephen Nathanson believes.[6] If we grant that some (even all) murderers of blacks, or, some (even all) white and rich murderers, escape the death penalty, how does that reduce the guilt of murderers of whites, or of black and poor murderers, so that they should be spared execution too? Guilt is personal. No murderer becomes less guilty, or less deserving of punishment, because another murderer was punished leniently, or escaped punishment altogether. We should try our best to bring every murderer to justice. But if one got away with murder wherein is that a reason to let anyone else get away? A group of murderers does not become less deserving of punishment because another equally guilty group is not punished, or punished less. We can punish only a very small proportion of all criminals. Unavoidably they are selected accidentally. We should reduce this accidentality as much as possible but we cannot eliminate it.[7]

Equal Injustice and Unequal Justice

Reiman and Nathanson appear to prefer equal injustice—letting all get away with murder if some do—to unequal justice: punishing some guilty offenders according to desert, even if others get away. Equal justice is best, but unattainable. Unequal justice is our lot in this world. It is the only justice we can ever have, for not all murderers can be apprehended or convicted, or sentenced equally in different courts. We should constantly try to bring every offender to justice. But meanwhile unequal justice is the only justice we have, and certainly better than equal injustice—giving no murderer the punishment his crime deserves. . . .

---

[5]Despite some doubts, I am here granting the truth of both hypotheses.

[6]Stephen Nathanson, "Does It Matter if the Death Penalty Is Arbitrarily Administered?" *Philosophy & Public Affairs* 14, no. 2.

[7]Discrimination or capriciousness is (when thought to be avoidable and excessive) sometimes allowed by the courts as a defense. Apparently this legal device is meant to reduce discrimination and capriciousness. But those spared because selected discriminatorily for punishment do not become any less deserving of it as both Reiman and Nathanson think, although not punishing them is used as a means to foster the desired equality in the distributions of punishments.

Questions for Further Reflection

1. Nathanson suggests that what one deserves depends on the amount of effort that would have been required for one to do otherwise. He apparently means this to include not only just physical effort (as in the Superman example) but also psychological effort (for example, perhaps you deserve more credit for visiting your sick grandmother if you would prefer to go to the movies than you deserve if visiting her is what you most want to do anyway). The result, however, seems to be that the worse someone's moral character is, the less blame one deserves for one's criminal actions. Is this plausible? Do we perhaps need a distinction between how blameworthy someone is and what punishment it would be just to impose on that person? We might well blame a thoroughly degraded habitual thief less for shoplifting than we would a wealthy teenager who does it for fun. But does it follow that it would be unjust to apply the same punishment to both?

2. How relevant to capital punishment is Nathanson's point about effort? He claims that if there are factors which "make alternative actions extremely difficult or impossible, a person is not fully blameworthy for his deeds." But how difficult can one's environment or psyche make it *not* to murder someone? Can we seriously imagine someone saying, "I tried as hard as I could not to pull the trigger, but not pulling it was just more than I could manage"?

3. Although Nathanson argues that the courts cannot be expected to determine what one morally deserves, he also claims that punishment need not be based on what one morally deserves. If so, why couldn't capital punishment be justified on grounds *other than* moral desert?

4. Suppose that it is true both that murderers deserve to die and that in our present circumstances, it is inevitable that the administration of a death penalty will be discriminatory. Is it better to have a death penalty, even though some people will escape it for discriminatory reasons (as van den Haag holds), or would it be better to have no death penalty at all (as Reiman argues)? It may be interesting to compare the following case (presented by Nathanson in a different article). Suppose that a professor announces that anyone who fails to turn in a paper will fail the course. Three people do not turn in the paper. But the professor fails only one, selected in a discriminatory way (the only black, or the only woman, or the only one the professor does not like). Presumably, it would have been better to fail all three. But given that the professor does not do that, is it better to fail one or to fail none? (Nathanson thinks it better to fail none; van den Haag thinks it better to fail one, since in that way, at least one receives what justice demands.)

5. Reiman holds that the definition of murder is discriminatory, since it includes ways of killing people employed mainly by the poor (e.g., shooting and stabbing) but does not include ways of killing employed mainly by the rich (e.g., not cleaning up hazardous materials from a work site). Is there any moral justification for counting the former ways of killing, but not the latter, as murder? If so, what?

Further Readings

Amnesty International. *United States of America: The Death Penalty*. London: Amnesty International Publications, 1987. Contains a wealth of clearly presented factual information, together with some (less helpful) discussion of the moral issues involved. Amnesty International also publishes an annual update; the most recent as of this writing is *United States of America: Developments in the Death Penalty 1995* (New York: Amnesty International USA, 1996).

Bedau, Hugo Adam, ed. *The Death Penalty in America: Current Controversies*. New York: Oxford University Press, 1997. A substantial collection of essays.

Gross, Samuel R., and Robert Mauro. *Death and Discrimination: Racial Disparities in Capital Sentencing*. Boston: Northeastern University Press, 1989. A useful presentation of the authors' research on racial factors in death sentencing, together with an overview of other related research.

Haas, Kenneth C., and James A. Inciardi, eds. *Challenging Capital Punishment: Legal and Social Science Approaches*. Newbury Park, CA: SAGE Publications, 1988. A good collection of essays by opponents of the death penalty.

Murphy, Jeffrie G., ed. *Punishment and Rehabilitation*, third edition. Belmont, CA: Wadsworth, 1995. A collection of historical and contemporary writing on punishment, including but not limited to the death penalty.

Nathanson, Stephen. *An Eye for an Eye? The Morality of Punishing by Death*. Totowa, NJ: Rowman & Littlefield, 1987. The book from which this chapter's selection by Nathanson is taken.

Reiman, Jeffrey H. "Justice, Civilization, and the Death Penalty: Answering van den Haag." *Philosophy and Public Affairs* 14 (1985): 115–148. A more detailed and sophisticated presentation of the position presented in Reiman's essay in this chapter. The same issue contains a useful piece by Stephen Nathanson and the full version of Ernest van den Haag's response to Reiman and Nathanson, excerpted in this chapter.

Sorrell, Tom. *Moral Theory and Capital Punishment*. Oxford: Basil Blackwell, 1987. A clearly written, theoretically oriented discussion of various philosophical arguments about capital punishment; concludes with a retributivistic defense of the death penalty.

Van den Haag, Ernest, and John P. Conrad. *The Death Penalty: A Debate*. New York: Plenum, 1983. Surveys many of the relevant arguments.

Chapter 11

Discrimination

In its most basic meaning, to *discriminate* is simply to *distinguish*. A color-blind person, for instance, is unable to discriminate red from green. This, of course, is *not* the sense of discrimination most relevant to moral philosophy, but it is related to the relevant sense. To discriminate, in the sense with which we are concerned here, is to treat or favor someone on the basis of irrelevant considerations: hiring a white rather than a more qualified black, for instance, simply *because* the person is white, even though race is irrelevant to how well one will perform the job. Someone who made hiring decisions in a nondiscriminatory fashion would act, for the purpose of making the hiring decision, as though he or she were blind to racial or other irrelevant considerations: He or she would act as though unable to distinguish black from white just as the color-blind person cannot distinguish red from green.

In focusing on discrimination in job hiring, we avoid some delicate issues. For one thing, there seems to be a large difference between what is permissible in the public sphere, for example, in job hiring and university or professional school admissions, and what is permissible in the private sphere: I am presumably violating no moral duty if I refuse to marry members of certain races, or if I am friendlier toward men than women, or if I seek out white male salespeople when I visit a used-car lot. Such actions may be morally unpleasant, but many would argue that they fall within the legitimate exercise of my rights. Some cases, of course, seem poised uneasily between the public and private spheres. For example, may I refuse to admit blacks or women to my private club? Another delicate issue concerns which characteristics are irrelevant. It is fairly clear which qualities are irrelevant to job performance, but in other cases, things may be muddier. In college admissions, for example, selection committees typically attempt to admit an entering class that is balanced by race, sex, and geographic region; is this discriminatory, or are these properties relevant in the appropriate sense to one's suitability for a particular school?

Discrimination in the pejorative sense comes in many varieties, some more puzzling than others. For example, Christopher Jencks has helpfully distinguished four sorts of discrimination.[1] There is, first, *malicious* discrimination, in which one treats poorly members of some group, such as blacks or women, simply out of hostility

---

[1] Christopher Jencks, "Discrimination and Thomas Sowell," *New York Review of Books* 30 no. 3 (March 3, 1983), pp. 33–38.

toward that group. As Jencks writes, "If an employer refuses to promote a black worker he knows is better qualified than any available white, on the grounds that putting blacks in positions of power over whites will undermine white supremacy in society as a whole, that is malicious discrimination."[2] In the case of someone making hiring decisions, malicious discrimination seems undeniably unjust; but pure cases of malicious discrimination are probably also rare.

A second form of discrimination is *myopic* discrimination. This is discrimination based on a false belief about members of a certain group. If I am hiring someone to fill a management-level position and will not consider women for the job because I am convinced that no woman really wants to work, then I am guilty of myopic discrimination. If my belief were *true*, it might constitute good grounds for my behavior, but the belief is not true. This sort of discrimination is no doubt less blameworthy than malicious discrimination: I didn't *intend* to consider anything but relevant characteristics. But, blameworthy or not, it seems clearly unjust.

A third form is what we might call *correlational* discrimination.[3] This involves treating members of a certain group differently because there is a correlation between belonging to the group and some property that would be a genuine liability. For instance, if statistics showed that members of one ethnic group were more likely than members of another to steal from their employers, someone who refused to hire members of that group for that reason would be engaged in correlational discrimination.

A final category of discrimination is perhaps the most troubling of all. This is *consumer-directed* discrimination. Suppose you are hiring a car salesperson, and your customers are all racist bigots. (Perhaps they are all members of the Ku Klux Klan.) No matter how knowledgeable, persuasive, and dedicated he is, a black salesman will have little luck selling cars to these customers. If, recognizing this fact, you hire an otherwise less-qualified white, Jencks will say that you have engaged in consumer-directed discrimination. There seems to be at best a fine line between this sort of case and other cases in which race or sex are perfectly legitimate qualifications. Presumably, no one would object to a casting director who considered being black a qualification for playing the part of Malcolm X in a film biography or who considered being white a qualification for playing John F. Kennedy.

Remedies

It is clear that discrimination on the basis of race and sex have played a large role in our history and, to some extent, continue today. What should be done about it? It is useful to distinguish between several possible responses. One response to discrimination is *passive nondiscrimination*, which seeks to evaluate job applicants solely on the basis of their qualifications, with no attention to race or sex. *Affirmative action* takes things a step further; it involves actively encouraging minorities to join the applicant pool for a position but is consistent with leaving the selection criteria unchanged. *Preferential hiring* takes matters a step further still and involves giving preference to members of groups that historically

---

[2] Jencks, p. 37.

[3] Jencks, following Lester Thurow, uses the term "statistical discrimination," but this could be confusing, as that term also might suggest holding that some group has been discriminated against on the basis of the fact that members are statistically underrepresented in some field.

have been discriminated against. When this practice involves actually picking a less-qualified minority over a better-qualified white male (as opposed to considering race or gender only when other qualifications are equal), it is often called *reverse discrimination*. (Actually, there is no single standard usage of the latter three terms; sometimes they are used interchangeably, and sometimes they are differently distinguished. But the usage outlined here is fairly common and marks some useful distinctions.)

In many ways, the most attractive course is simply passive nondiscrimination. Discrimination is unjust because it involves making hiring decisions based on factors irrelevant to qualifications. So why not simply ignore such factors?

One might think that passive nondiscrimination is insufficient by itself for several reasons. For one thing, in some cases the criteria for a certain position may be irrelevant to the qualifications really necessary for performing the job and may simply have the effect of disqualifying minorities—for instance, requiring that partners in a certain law firm must be taller than 5 feet 7 inches would exclude most women, and would do so for reasons that have nothing to do with how well they would perform. (Somewhat more complicated are cases where criteria that exclude blacks or women are relevant as things stand, but need not be: being rather tall might be necessary in operating certain sorts of equipment—commercial aircraft, say—and yet it might also be the case that the equipment could be differently designed so as not to require tall operators.)

A second point is that there may be cases in which prejudice is so ingrained that trying to apply criteria fairly and impartially simply will not work: The personnel officer might sincerely believe that each and every black he saw was unqualified for a legitimate reason, not recognizing that the real reason for his conviction did not concern qualifications.

The first point makes us realize that discrimination may be embedded in the criteria for a certain job and not only in the application of those criteria; the solution is presumably to change the criteria as well as their application. It is not clear what to do about the second point. Hire a different personnel officer? Or ask the officer to hire less-qualified blacks on the theory that only then will he hire blacks who in fact are better qualified anyway? Neither point justifies *genuine,* as opposed to apparent, reverse discrimination. However, two further sorts of complaint against passive nondiscrimination do purport to show that reverse discrimination is necessary.

Reverse Discrimination: Backward-looking Defenses

The first argument for reverse discrimination is that we owe it to victims of past discrimination to *compensate* them. This is what Fullinwider terms a *backward-looking* defense of reverse discrimination. The trouble with passive nondiscrimination, in this view, is that while it prevents future harm from discrimination, it does not do anything to set past harms right. Similarly, if Joe has been stealing from Fred for years, making sure he no longer steals from Fred does not seem like solution enough: Fred deserves to be repaid the money he lost during those years of theft.

But, as Fullinwider cogently explains, this line of defense has serious problems. For one thing, the people helped by policies of reverse discrimination are not necessarily those most harmed by past discrimination; reverse discrimination policies still seek to hire the most able minorities, and those most able are likely also to be those most advantaged. As a result, it seems that reverse discrimination will aid minorities roughly in *inverse* proportion to the amount of harm they have suffered from discrimination.

Another difficulty is that people harmed by reverse discrimination—those passed over in favor of less-qualified minorities—are not necessarily the perpetrators of the original discrimination. No matter how convinced we are that Fred should be paid back for the money he lost to Joe, we would hardly think it fair to arbitrarily take the money from Jane, who has never stolen in her life. This is true even if Jane is Joe's landlord and Joe's monthly rent has been paid in part by the money stolen from Fred; similarly, it does not seem fair to harm those who have not discriminated, even if they have benefited from the discrimination. (Levin offers these criticisms and more against the compensation argument; he is specifically objecting to the argument as a defense of quotas in the hiring of women, but his considerations could be applied to racial quotas and even to reverse discrimination without quotas.)

Reverse Discrimination: Forward-looking Defenses

A different sort of justification of reverse discrimination, as Fullinwider explains, appeals not to the need to set past harms right, but rather to the need to create a more desirable future. The *goal* of a discrimination-free society, one might argue, simply cannot be met by pursuing only passive discrimination. We simply cannot get there from here without taking stronger measures. This is a broadly utilitarian style of argument, because it justifies reverse discrimination in terms of its consequences, although consequences such as equal opportunity are not the sort to which the utilitarian typically appeals.

The forward-looking defense, then, argues that reverse discrimination is necessary as a temporary measure that alone will make possible the ultimate acquisition of some much-desired goal. But what precisely *is* the goal of reverse discrimination? Fullinwider mentions several possibilities. The one he stresses most is "equality of employment opportunity, understood as selection without bias." He offers a specific example involving AT&T in which, he argues, genuinely equal opportunity simply could not have been achieved without the "shock treatment" of reverse discrimination.

A second possible goal might be achieving a significant number of women and minorities in jobs they have typically not had. Fullinwider indeed suggests that a significant change in the number of women and minorities in a field may be necessary in order to attain genuine equality of opportunity. Still another possible goal, also mentioned by Fullinwider (and criticized by Levin), is to provide role models for women and minorities so that they will see that a certain field is genuinely an option for them. Evaluating the extent to which goals such as these justify reverse discrimination is a complex and difficult task.

REVERSE DISCRIMINATION IS JUSTIFIED

Reverse Discrimination and Equal Opportunity

Robert K. Fullinwider

The United States began, in the mid-1960s, an extensive assault on racial and sexual discrimination. The omnibus Civil Rights Act of 1964 (as amended in 1972) and Executive Order 11246 (as amended in 1968) were major legislative and regulatory initiatives. Some of the programs and policies that evolved from these initiatives generated enormous controversy even among those opposed in principle to racial and sexual discrimination. These programs and policies appear to, or actually do, permit or require businesses, professional schools, municipal agencies, and other institutions to give special favorable weight to the race or sex of minorities and females. Such favorable treatment, on the view of its critics, transgresses the very principle of nondiscrimination established in the 1960s.

Can race and sex properly be used as factors in hirings, promotions, layoffs, school admissions, and similar choices? Do programs of preferential treatment have, or lack, moral, legal, and constitutional foundations? . . .

Initially, defenses of preferential treatment rooted in appeals to compensation seemed attractive.[1] They promised to tie preferences to a very deep and widely shared moral conviction: that justice requires past wrongs to be righted; that where wrongful injury has been done, a duty exists to make restitution. When conjoined with our society's history of flagrant denial of basic rights and opportunities to blacks and women, this deep conviction suggests a powerful claim for the legitimacy of giving preferences to blacks and women. Preferential programs yield to blacks and women what they are owed.[2] However, philosophical writings offered no sophisticated account of compensation. They were content to exploit our intuitions through

---

[1] A word of caution is necessary about the word 'compensation.' It is used in different senses in the literature being discussed here. Thomson uses it more or less synonymously with 'restitution' or 'reparation,' to mean making good on damage or harm caused by wrongful action. Sometimes, however, the term is used by writers in its generic sense, which means simply to make up for some lack or deficiency. Bernard Boxill, in "The Morality of Reparations, *Social Theory and Practice* 2 (Spring 1972), contrasts compensation with reparation, calling the former a 'forward-looking' device for alleviating disabilities however they came about (p. 117). However, in his recent book, *Blacks and Social Justice* (Totowa, NJ: Rowman & Allanheld, 1984), he uses 'compensation' to refer to the same backward-looking practice encompassed by 'reparation.' The reader is advised to take care when encountering 'compensation' and 'compensatory' in a work. I use the term throughout this essay as Thomson used it, to refer to a practice that looks back to a wrongful action or deed producing harm.

[2] In addition to the works of Thomson and Boxill, see Anne C. Minas, 'How Reverse Discrimination Compensates Women,' *Ethics* 88 (October 1977), pp. 74–79, and Howard McGary, Jr., 'Justice and Reparations,' *Philosophical Forum* 9 (Winter-Spring 1977–78), pp. 250–63.

reliance on simple examples or simple principles. Bernard Boxill introduced the reader to the concept of compensation with a story of a stolen bicycle that must be returned.[3] Judith Thomson relied on the principle that he who wrongs another owes him compensation.[4] These simple examples or principles generally command our agreement, but they do not quite apply to the programs they are supposed to justify. They need to be augmented and elaborated. As the elaborations are made, the compensation defense becomes more applicable to the programs in need of justification, but at the same time loses the direct intuitive appeal from which it begins.

The *simple model* of compensation, around which our common intuitions focus, contains four elements related thus: (1) an agent, (2) acting wrongfully, (3) causes injury or harm (4) to a victim. In any case of compensation there are three crucial questions: *Who* owes *what* to *whom?* The formula of the simple model tells us how to construct an answer: the wrongful actor owes, the victim is owed, and what he is owed is restoration to his pre-injury condition (or to some approximation of this). So, to look at a concrete example, in Boxill's story the individual who wrongfully took the bicycle is duty-bound to return it (undamaged) to its original possessor.

This simple model does not directly match the circumstances in which preferential treatment is being practiced. Consider the complications that arise in trying to answer in regard to preferential programs the three questions implied by any compensation claim.

1 *Who owes?* Those who bear the cost of current preferential programs are generally those white, male applicants or workers denied positions, awards, or promotions they otherwise would have received; yet the wrongs for which compensation is owed were not the personal wrongs of these individuals but were corporate wrongs, namely, legislatively enacted and judicially enforced discrimination supported by social custom. How is the community (the debtor according to the simple model) warranted in transferring the costs of its debt to nondebtors? One strategy is to argue that white males are not wholly 'innocent' parties; thus, just as persons complicit in an agent's wrongdoing may have to share responsibility, so too white male applicants or job-holders can properly be assessed the costs of the community's programs of preferential treatment. Thomson, for example, argues that it is 'not inappropriate' that the costs of the programs fall on white males since they have profited from the wrongful discrimination imposed by the community.[5]

Now, the shift from 'he who wrongfully harms another must pay' to 'he who benefits from someone else's wrongs must pay' is a major variation from the simple model, and it is far from clear that there is any consensus at the level of intuition supporting the latter principle. We are apt to judge one thing where benefits were received knowingly and willingly and another thing where benefits were unavoidable and unwanted. We are apt to feel more disposed toward a required return of a benefit where it is easily transferable from the recipient back to its original possessor, and less disposed where it has become intermixed with other things and can't simply be transferred back to where it once lay. Bernard Boxill has insisted that *merely* receiving benefits

---

[3]Boxill, 'The Morality of Reparations,' p. 119.

[4]Thomson, 'Preferential Hiring,' *Philosophy & Public Affairs* 2 (Summer 1973), p. 380.

[5]Ibid., 383. Similar contentions are made by Boxill and McGary.

produced by injustice is enough to make one personally liable to compensate the victim of injustice, but this claim doesn't have much intuitive plausibility and the example he uses to support it carries little force. Suppose, he says, that a surgeon transplants a heart into Harry from Dick's corpse without getting permission from Dick's next-of-kin. When Harry recovers, he is bound, according to Boxill, to make 'suitable reparation' to Dick's family.[6] But I doubt readers will have the same intuitions about this.

The proposition that all white males have benefited from racial and sexual discrimination is offered fairly casually in the literature. It seems, perhaps, too obviously true to need arguing. However, it is not enough that all white males have benefited from discrimination. If they are liable to make compensation, then they must have received *net* benefits. Now, this observation forces us to a prior question: how are we to understand gain and loss when it comes to matters of compensation? As a first approximation, it seems reasonable to impute gain from discrimination to an individual who is better off than he would have been had discrimination never occurred, and to impute loss to an individual who is worse off than he would have been had discrimination never occurred. Given this account, it will not be obviously clear that all white males are or were net gainers from either racial or sexual discrimination. . . .

2 *Who is owed?* Programs of preferential treatment confer their benefits on those minority and female individuals who happen to apply for affected positions and who are qualified above some threshold. Do such programs actually compensate victims of discrimination? That is to say, do we have reason to feel confident that qualified minority and female applicants who happen to apply for affected positions are themselves victims of past discrimination? Judith Thomson in her 1973 article declared it 'absurd to suppose that young blacks and women now of age to apply for jobs have not been wronged.'[7] Likewise, Bernard Boxill in his 1984 book insists: 'We *know* that all blacks, lower class, middle class, and upper class, have been wronged by racial injustice.'[8]

As these two claims are framed, they raise yet another question about the nature of compensation: do we compensate a person for being *wronged* or being *harmed?* This is an important question because it is possible to be wronged without being harmed. Suppose an enemy spreads vicious lies about my behavior. He clearly wrongs me in doing so. But suppose no one believes the charges (they are too transparently lies), I do not fear they will be believed, no damage is done to my business, and I suffer no anxiety about my future. It is hard to see any way I have been *harmed* by the lying attack. This is not to say the lies had no effect on me. They made me angry, and indignant. The lies *hurt* even if they did not *harm.*

Now, leaving aside the issue of punitive damages, which has to do with retribution rather than restitution, it does not appear I have a claim against my attacker for compensation, although I surely have a claim for public retraction and apology.

Boxill's recent attempt to rehabilitate the compensation defense of preferential treatment exhibits how inattention to these questions—Are hurts harms? Do we compensate wrongs or harms?—can result in elusive arguments. Blacks 'deserve compensation for the wrongful *harms* of

---

[6]Boxill, 'The Morality of Reparations,' p. 121.

[7]Thomson, 'Preferential Hiring,' p. 381.

[8]Boxill, *Blacks and Social Justice*, p. 164.

discrimination,' declares Boxill.⁹ Do *all* blacks then deserve compensation? All have been *wronged* by discrimination, he argues. Discrimination materially damages the life prospects of many blacks; in addition, those blacks who 'escape discrimination,' who are 'spared' discrimination, nevertheless 'feel threatened and insulted' at the discrimination against other blacks.¹⁰ All blacks are 'wronged and *liable to be wrongfully harmed*,'¹¹ 'wronged and, *probably harmed*,'¹² 'wronged and *possibly harmed*'¹³ by racial discrimination. These claims do not amount to the proposition that all blacks have been harmed, which is the ground Boxill himself establishes for compensation.

Are insult and threat to be construed as harms? Discrimination attacks the 'self-confidence and self-respect' of blacks,¹⁴ but attack can toughen as well as weaken. We want to be careful about implying that discrimination has turned all blacks into psychological cripples. (Likewise we want to be wary of similar generalizations about women.) *Hurt, harm,* and *wrong* need to be clarified and given appropriate places in a compensation argument.¹⁵

3 *What is owed?* Finally, even if we concede that every black or woman has been harmed by discrimination, it is still not clear we can adequately defend preferential treatment programs in the name of compensation. The simple model tells us to make good the victim's loss. Consequently, we would expect compensation practices to exhibit *proportionality*, matching benefit to loss. Those most harmed would receive more compensation than those least harmed. Many critics of preferential treatment view it as virtually reversing the expected proportionality. Preferential programs benefit those qualified blacks and women who happen to be making job searches, requests for transfer or promotion, or applications to school. These will be disproportionately younger individuals. If we suppose that younger, qualified blacks and women have been least victimized by discrimination, then 'a policy of preferential treatment directed toward groups as a whole will invert the ratio of past harm to present benefit, picking out just those individuals for present preference who least deserve compensation relative to other members.'¹⁶ Preferential programs seem *perverse* as compensation schemes. . . .

One reason we may remain skeptical of getting any broadly compensatory defense to 'fit' the policies of preferences that actually exist is that such a defense is at variance with the justifications these policies offer for themselves. Let us turn to an actual use of preferential treatment.

II

In 1973, American Telephone and Telegraph Company (AT&T) and the Federal

---

⁹Ibid., p. 153; emphasis added.

¹⁰Ibid., pp. 151, 152.

¹¹Ibid., p. 152; emphasis added.

¹²Ibid., p. 150, emphasis added.

¹³Ibid., p. 151: emphasis added.

¹⁴Ibid., p. 152.

¹⁵Apology rather than compensation is the appropriate response to insult. Some may value preferential programs less for what they actually accomplish than for what they symbolize; public acknowledgment and expatiation of past wrong. As to the question about wrong, harm, and hurt; it isn't as if there are no resources at hand for working out answers about their places in compensation. Several hundred years of Anglo-American legal practice have grappled with the kinds of harm and injury the law ought to cognize, the responsibility and liabilities or various parties involved, the appropriateness of various kinds of restitution, and so on. Philosophers, however, had not made much use of this resource.

¹⁶Alan Goldman, *Justice and Reverse Discrimination* (Princeton, NJ: Princeton University Press, 1979). pp. 90–1.

government entered into a consent decree that required extensive changes in the company's employment practices.[17] Among other things the decree called for extensive use of preferences, primarily gender preferences.[18] It is instructive to look at the conditions that gave rise to the consent decree and at the government's specific aims in imposing it.

In 1970, AT&T employed over 800,000 persons (excluding Bell Labs and Western Electric), more than half of whom were women.[19] This ratio between men and women in overall employment was not reflected, however, through the various job classifications in the company. Eighty per cent of the women were in three classifications: operator, clerical, secretarial. This was no accident. Explicit sex segregation was the practice at AT&T. Men and women applicants were given different entrance exams and channeled into different career paths. 'Men's' jobs in outside crafts, inside crafts, and management paid more, of course, than 'women's' jobs as clerk, operator, secretary, or inside sales representative, and carried greater advancement opportunities.

Even when men and women happened to do the same job, women were paid less. At Michigan Bell, the inside craft job of switchroom helper was performed by women, but at the other Bell companies the job was 'frameman' and was performed by men. When AT&T entered into the consent decree in 1973, it had to raise switchroom helper salaries substantially to bring them into line with those for framemen.

Women made up 1 per cent of career management positions. The company recruited management personnel from two sources. It promoted workers from craft jobs—male jobs—into management ranks, and it also recruited college students into management training programs—recruitment that excluded women.

In deliberations before the Federal Communications Commission and the Equal Employment Opportunities Commission in 1971 and 1972, AT&T defended its failure to put women in craft and management jobs. Women 'weren't qualified' for craft jobs, the company averred. Women couldn't be given management positions because they 'weren't mobile,' because they 'think differently from men,' because there would be 'suspicions of favoritism' in male superiors promoting women subordinates. Women were 'not interested' in craft and management jobs.

AT&T's defense of its maldistribution of men and women revealed deep-seated conceptions about the nature of women and men and the work they were fit for. Relations between men and women were viewed as primarily sexual or matrimonial, thus the natural suspicion of favoritism should a male superior promote a female subordinate. Women were viewed as having limited career aspirations and as being incompetent at craft work.

A vivid illustration of how 'women's work' was perceived as a less serious matter than 'men's work' was provided by the different responses Bell companies made to the same kind of complaints made by men and women. A company study of male workers' complaints—that their pay was too low, their skills underutilized, and the prospects of advancement too few—recommended speeding up promotions,

---

[17] A consent decree is an agreement, supervised by a court, in which the government refrains from pressing legal charges to a full decision if the company complies with the terms agreed to.

[18] Although the decree also affected minority hiring and promotions, its main effect was on women. I confine my discussion of the AT&T case to this main effect.

[19] The details in the next several paragraphs are drawn from Robert Fullinwider, *The AT&T Case and Affirmative Action* (Dover, MA: Case Publishing Company, 1981).

increasing pay, and tailoring jobs to skills. Another study of similar complaints by operators recommended that the company in question stop hiring women who complain and seek women who were 'more realistic about their goals' and 'not looking for a glamorous career.'[20]

The ambitions of men to get ahead and earn more were taken seriously by AT&T; the similar ambitions of women were not. Women were expected to be 'realistic' because their primary vocation was to be homemakers and not breadwinners. It was a fault in women to 'look for glamorous careers.'

The consent decree entered into by AT&T, under the threat of extensive litigation, was designed to change the company's employment practices. Among other things, it required the company to set broad hiring and promotion 'targets' for fifteen job classifications. Fulfillment of the targets meant the company would on many occasions have to give sexual preferences. Provision was made for this in the consent decree. The prevailing union-management agreement called for promotion of the 'most senior' from among the 'best qualified.' When strict adherence to this agreement failed to produce enough of the right sex, the consent decree provided for an 'affirmative action override,' in which a person of the right sex could be selected from among 'basically qualified' workers. Hiring goals required similar deviation from standard selection criteria.

The operations of the consent decree produced a considerable amount of preferential selection of women.[21] This resulted in a lot of disgruntlement among male workers.[22] One worker expressed his feelings this way:

> One thing that really bothers me is moving up in the company. I am white, male, 25. I am not a brain, but average. I have a lot of drive and want to go ahead. I have just been notified there is some kind of freeze which will last 3 or 4 months. (Note: frequently, when a target couldn't be met, all promotions would be frozen until a person of the right sex could be found.) In that time, if I am passed over, the company will go to the street. This is not fair. I work for the company, but my chances are less than someone on the street.[23]

However, the operations of the consent decree did not uniformly work against men. The decree included male 'targets' in clerical and operator jobs. This meant that some women were denied positions because of their sex. One such woman, Bertha Biel, unsuccessfully sued in Federal court when she was denied a promotion. In the words of the Court:

> In October 1973 the Company had one job class II opening to be filled for the remainder of the year. It had not met its intermediate goals for that year since no males had sought the opening. Accordingly, it filled its last opening for the year by hiring a male not previously employed by the Company.[24]

Like her male colleague (let's call him 'Bert'), the company passed Bertha over and went 'to the street' in order to fill a sexual quota. She could with justice echo Bert's own lament: 'It's not fair!'

---

[20]Judith Long Laws, 'The Bell System,' in Phyllis A. Wallace, ed., *Equal Employment Opportunity and the AT&T Case* (Cambridge, Mass: MIT Press, 1976). p. 159.

[21]I estimate in excess of 45,000 instances between 1973–9. See *The AT&T Case and Affirmative Action*, p. 5, for the grounds of this estimate.

[22]The company's affirmative action efforts under the decree resulted in thousands of grievances and two dozen lawsuits.

[23]Herbert R. Nothrup and John A. Larson, *The Impact of the AT&T-EEO Consent Decree* (Philadelphia: The Wharton School, University of Pennsylvania, 1979), p. 78.

[24]*Telephone Workers Union v. N.J. Bell Tel.*, 584 F. 2d 31 (1978), at 32.

What was accomplished at the cost of this unfairness? By 1979, the gender profiles of job classifications at the company had changed significantly. For example, between 1973 and 1979 there was a 38 per cent increase in the number of women employed in the top three job classifications (officials and managers), while there was only a 5.3 per cent increase in the number of men. Women made significant strides in sales positions, increasing in numbers by 53 per cent (a growth rate seven times faster than that of white males), and in inside crafts, increasing by 68 per cent (white males were decreasing by 10 per cent). In the outside crafts, the number of women grew by 5,300 while the number of men declined by 6,700.

On the other hand, AT&T increased the proportion of men in clerical and operator positions. It did this by meeting male hiring and promotion targets, and by making clerical positions entry jobs for men. In 1973, 17 per cent of men hired in Bell companies entered through clerical positions, while 83 per cent entered through craft positions. In 1979, 43.7 per cent of men hired entered through clerical positions, while only 56.3 per cent entered through crafts. Overall, the percentage of men in clerical roles grew from 5.9 to 11.1 per cent.

At the end of 1972, AT&T employed 415,725 women (52.4 per cent of all employees); at the beginning of 1979, it employed 408,671 women (50.8 per cent of all employees). This overall decline was not inconsistent with the principal aim of the consent decree, which was to break down and destroy the 'culture of sex segregation' at AT&T. One signal fact at the company dominated management attitudes, job organization, physical layout, equipment design, work-rules, and employee expectations: that there were 'men's' jobs and 'women's' jobs. The purpose of the consent decree, with its targets and affirmative action overrides, was to destroy this fact and the institutional inertia surrounding it. Women would be force-fed in significant numbers into positions from which they had previously been excluded; men would be assigned to 'women's' jobs.

Through this shock treatment enough women would become lodged in nontraditional jobs to effect lasting changes in the work environment, creating a more hospitable climate for women, and making unbiased employment practices truly possible.

If the government had simply required AT&T to eliminate its formal job segregation and to change its employment practices to make them facially unbiased, it is likely that in 1979 the gender profiles of job classifications at the company would have looked remarkably similar to those in 1970. Two reasons suggest this conclusion. First, everything about the company was stacked against women's success in nontraditional jobs even if non-biased procedures were nominally adopted. The introduction of token women into alien and non-supportive work environments would have produced a high rate of failure and attrition, simply confirming the already prevailing belief among management that women would not succeed in 'men's' jobs and were out of place in them. Second, the period 1973–9 was not a period of growth but a period of employment decline for the company. Consequently, women would have been competing for very few positions, and getting but few of those. In 1979, AT&T would still have been a thoroughly segregated place to work, although giving lip service to equality of opportunity and bemoaning its inability to find 'qualified women.'

Even with the best of will, nominally unbiased procedures would not have produced a truly unbiased workplace. The *aspiration* to treat women fairly would have foundered against institutional *habits* reflecting a very different and long-standing *reality:* sex segregation. The strategy of the consent decree was not to change the reality by changing the habits but to change the habits by changing the reality.

Now, the underlying justification for preferential treatment that we can extract from the principal aim and the operations of the consent decree is forward-looking. The aim of law and policy is to achieve equality of employment opportunity, understood as selection without bias.[25] The use of preferences is a tool to this aim. The apparently paradoxical nature of using deliberate biases to undermine bias is dissipated by offering a credible account of an institution and its habits that reveals deep blockages to achieving truly unbiased selections, blockages not dislodgeable without resort to the drastic measure of preferential treatment.

This forward-looking justification, made in terms of promoting equality of opportunity, has a number of virtues apart from its mirroring the avowed aims of the laws and regulations under which the AT&T consent decree was formulated. First, if we view preferential programs as essentially compensatory or restitutive, then that portion of the consent decree requiring male quotas appears indefensible and out of line with the remaining aspects of the decree. On the forward-looking defense, this particular feature of the consent decree makes sense; it works to undermine the existence of 'men's' jobs and 'women's' jobs. Second, the fact that preferential programs benefit the best qualified blacks or women instead of the most injured constitutes an embarrassment for the compensatory defense, but not for the defense in terms of equal opportunity. If the aim is to reform institutional habits, then it is irrelevant that those whose presence can most effectively accomplish this change are themselves relatively advantaged.

The forward-looking defense does not have to find some special deservingness in the beneficiaries of preference, since it does not view them as receiving their benefits by right. They are given preferences because it serves the larger aim. Likewise, the forward-looking defense does not have to search about to find reasons why those who lose out under preferential programs deserve their fate. At AT&T, both Bertha and Bert lost out, and for the very same *impersonal* reason: being in the wrong place at the wrong time.

Now, no individual will be particularly happy at losing out on a job or promotion as a result of a program of preferences; Bert lamented his circumstances and Bertha went to court. Nevertheless, the equal opportunity defense of such a program allows us to justify it to losers in terms of values they cannot easily disavow. If an individual declares he just wants the promotion coming to him, he's not interested in equal opportunity, then he is in no position to complain that denying him the promotion violates his right to equal opportunity. On the other hand, if the loser bases his complaint on the value of equality of opportunity, he must concede that if a preferential program is truly necessary to create conditions for equal opportunity *for all*, adopting the program is not arbitrary and does not simply sacrifice his interests for some gain unrelated to his own values.

The equal opportunities defense has merit from a more abstract point of view as well. In many political theories equality of opportunity ranks as a primary value. Its pursuit has high priority. Alan Goldman, a vigorous critic of preferential treatment by race or sex, nevertheless offers a theoretical defense of such treatment in terms of equality of opportunity:

> The rule for hiring the most competent (he says) . . . (is) justified as part of a right to equal opportunity . . . (which would be

---

[25]Title VII, Civil Rights Act of 1984, 42 U.S.C. 2000e-2; Executive Order 11246 (as amended), 42 U.S.C. 2000e; Revised Order No. 4, 41 C.F.R. 60) 2ff.

rationally willed by all actual members of society). Since it is justified in relation to a right to equal opportunity, and since application of the rule may simply compound injustices when opportunities are unequal elsewhere in the system, the creation of more equal opportunities takes precedence when in conflict with the rule for awarding positions. Thus short-run violations of the rule are justified to create a more just distribution of benefits by applying the rule itself in future years.[26]

In short, if preferences would create a situation that would 'result in fewer violations of rights in the future,' they would be justified.[27] Goldman himself does *not* support giving preferences on the basis of race or sex, but this is because he believes that *as a matter of fact* 'strict enforcement' of antibias regulations short of preferential treatment will succeed in creating genuine nondiscrimination. Given his principles, Goldman could repudiate the use of preferences at AT&T only by holding that the institutional habits of the company were not so recalcitrant as to require the drastic measures imposed by the consent decree.

Finally, the forward-looking defense being considered here has two further features. First, it suggests that preferential programs will not have an unlimited duration. The program need persist only until *enough* minorities or women are lodged in place to create appropriate changes in attitudes and habits. Proportional representation has no independent value: at best it is a proxy for the level of women and minorities sufficient to effect the desired changes. The consent decree at AT&T ended after six years. Although the company was far from having proportional representation of women in its assorted job classifications, nevertheless enough women had been moved into nontraditional positions to *institutionalize* the expectations and the reality of women's presence in management, crafts, sales, and so on.

Moreover, the forward-looking justification does not imply that preferential programs are appropriate at every institution. Where institutional habits are *not* so frozen that facially unbiased procedures would be ineffective, there is no reason provided by the equal opportunity defense for giving anyone a preference because of race or sex. The possibilities of creating equality of opportunity without resort to preferences will vary according to the type of institution, its location, its history or lack of history of segregation, its prospects for growth or decline, and so on. The circumstances we actually encounter may suggest the need for preferential treatment of women but not minorities, of minorities but not women, of both, or of neither.

The equal opportunity defense of preferences is not the only possible forward-looking justification. Preferences might be defended as serving other goals. A frequent defense of preferentially admitting blacks to medical and law schools is the anticipation that this will eventually improve the delivery of medical and legal services to the black community.[28] Richard Wasserstrom has argued that including substantial numbers of blacks in otherwise white educational programs enriches the educational

---

[26] Goldman, *Justice and Reverse Discrimination*, p. 165. The interpolated section comes from p. 29. See pp. 23ff.

[27] Ibid., p. 193. A similar argument is found in Thomas Nagel. 'Equal Treatment and Compensatory Discrimination,' *Philosophy & Public Affairs* 2 (Summer 1973), in the footnote at the bottom of p. 362. Nagel reports a suggestion by Adam Morton that the defense of preferences lies in their ability to contribute to a more just situation in the future. Another writer who anticipates the form if not the details of the equal opportunity argument is Marlene Gerber Fried. 'In Defense of Preferential Hiring,' *Philosophical Forum* 5 (Fall-Winter 1973-74). pp. 308-19.

[28] See Nagel, 'Equal Treatment and Compensatory Discrimination,' p. 361.

climate by adding new perspectives on social issues, and that preferential admissions can serve this end.[29] Many have argued for the need to create female and black role models in the professions, the university, and the corporation as inspirations for other women and blacks to aspire to careers they otherwise would have feared to enter.[30]

These and other forward-looking defenses may or may not individually offer as much justification for preferential programs as the equal opportunity defense of the AT&T consent decree; but they can all probably be assimilated one way or another into a broader equal opportunity aim: to break down the barriers that impede the free access of blacks and women into all aspects of economic, political, and social life.[31]

---

[29]Richard Wasserstrom, 'The University and the Case for Preferential Treatment,' *American Philosophical Quarterly* 13 (April 1976), pp. 165–70.

[30]See, e.g., Michael Martin, 'Pedagogical Arguments for Preferential Hiring and Tenuring of Women Teachers in the University,' *Philosophical Forum* 5 (Fall-Winter 1973–74), pp. 325–33.

[31]This essay was written during a period of support from the National Endowment for the Humanities for work on equal opportunity in American social policy.

REVERSE DISCRIMINATION IS NOT JUSTIFIED

Affirmative Action

Michael Levin

The Free Market and Feminism

Judged historically, the free market is the most successful economic arrangement. Permitting people to trade and associate freely for productive purposes has created unparalleled prosperity, along with support for the democratic institutions on which other forms of individual liberty have been found to depend. It is inevitable that feminists reject the free market, however, because they must interpret the expressions of sex differences facilitated by the freedom of the market as products of adverse socialization and discrimination.

Certainly, the observed differences between male and female labor market behavior are not in dispute; men and women do different sorts of work, and women earn lower average wages. It is also widely agreed that the immediate cause of these differences are differences in the motives which lead men and women into the labor market. Most married working women work to supplement their husbands' incomes, which is regarded as the mainstay of the family budget.[1] Working mothers are

---

[1]Donna Shalala estimates that 80 percent of full-time working women work out of perceived economic

expected to care for their children as well, or at any rate to supervise the arrangements for their care, an expectation that does not fall nearly so heavily upon fathers. Unmarried women often see work as an interregnum between school and marriage. For these reasons, women gravitate to jobs permitting easy entry, exit and re-entry to and from the workforce. Nor, finally, is it seriously questioned that men tend to seek (although of course not always find) more prestigious jobs and to try to "get ahead" more than women do. In short, men and women invest their human capital differently.[2]

As always, the question is why these things are so. Feminist theory takes them to be consequences of oppression. In the words of the Committee on Women's Employment and Related Social Issues of the National Research Council of the National Science Foundation:

> to the extent that sex segregation in the workplace connotes the inferiority of women or contributes to maintaining women as men's inferiors, it has great symbolic significance. To this extent, we believe it is fundamentally at odds with the established goals of equal opportunity and equality under the law in American society.[3]

This theory is contradicted by the close match between many of the major differences in skills brought by men and women to the workplace and a number of the innate differences . . . . Together with the greater innate dominance-aggression of men, which manifests itself economically as greater competitiveness, this match strongly suggests that differences in workplace behavior are not best explained as products of the denial of equal opportunity. . . .

In 1980, the National Opinion Research Center administered the Armed Services Vocational Aptitude Battery of ten tests to 12,000 randomly selected males and females between the ages of eighteen and twenty-three.[4] The ASVAB was then factored into four composite tests for "mechanical," "electronic," "administrative," and "general" aptitudes.[5] It was found that

---

necessity (presentation to the National Convention of the Council on Foundations, Detroit, April 29, 1982). According to a survey conducted by *Newsweek*, 56 percent of working women say they work "for money" ("A Mother's Choice." *Newsweek* [March 31, 1986]: 51). Presumably, the figure is much higher for working mothers. For the economist, no one (except perhaps those facing imminent starvation) "has" to work; work is preferred to not working. Let us say that a woman has to work if she would not work were her husband's salary increased by an amount equal to her own (or, if she is unmarried, she suddenly acquired a suitably salaried husband).

[2] On male and female commitment to employment, see June O'Neill and Rachel Braun, *Women and the Labor Market: A Survey of Issues and Policies in the United States* (Washington, D.C.: Urban Institute, 1981).

[3] Barbara F. Reskin and Heidi I. Hartmann, eds., *Women's Work, Men's Work: Sex Segregation on the Job* (Washington, D.C.: National Academy Press, 1985). Cited in *The Women's Rights Issues of the 1980s*, undated pamphlet distributed by National Academy Press.

[4] *Profile of American Youth: 1980 National Administration of Armed Service Vocational Aptitude Battery* (Department of Defense, Office of the Assistant Secretary of Defense for Manpower, March 1982). The ten ASVAB subtests are: Arithmetic Reasoning, Numerical Operations, Paragraph Comprehension, Work Knowledge, Coding Speed, General Science, Mathematics Knowledge, Electronics Information, Mechanical Comprehension, and Automotive-Shop Information.

[5] Mechanical includes: Mechanical Comprehension, Automotive-Shop Information, and General Science, Administrative includes: Coding Speed, Numerical Operations, Paragraph Comprehension, and Word Knowledge. General includes: Arithmetical Reasoning, Paragraph Comprehension, and Word Knowledge. Electronics includes: Arithmetic Reasoning, Electronics Information, General Science, and Mathematics Knowledge (Ibid., p. 27, table 13).

men scored considerably higher than women in mechanical and electronic aptitude, and slightly higher in general aptitude, while women exhibited greater administrative aptitude.[6] (On the individual tests, men for instance did considerably better on mechanical comprehension and women did considerably better on coding speed.[7]) These differences in aptitude were constant at all educational levels. Since the average female has 11.9 years of schooling to the average male's 11.8, these differences do not represent an educational deficit.[8] One might still wish to explain these aptitude differences in terms of socialization, but however they are explained they show that occupational segregation is not wholly the result of employer discrimination working on a homogeneous population of men and women.

Some innate sex differences correlate closely with aptitude for specific occupations, many of them prestigious, remunerative, and important in industrial society. Spatial ability is requisite for pipe fitting, technical drawing, and wood working,[9] and is the most important component of mechanical ability.[10] Only about 20 percent of girls in the elementary grades reach the average level of male performance on tests of spatial ability, and, according to the U.S. Employment Service, all classes of engineering and drafting as well as a high proportion of scientific and technical occupations require spatial ability in the top 10 percent of the U.S. population.[11] While one should normally be chary of explaining any social phenomenon *directly* in terms of some innate gender dimorphism, male domination of the technical and engineering professions is almost certainly due to the male's innate cognitive advantage rather than to a culturally induced female disadvantage.[12] Proportionally fewer women enter the technical fields than there are women in the population with the requisite raw skills, to be sure, but this is most plausibly attributed to the Goldberg feedback effect which selectively discourages women with marginal levels of skill—an injustice, perhaps, but one also borne by men with atypical skills. In any case, the sex segregation of the workforce is essentially the result of innate sex differences and unmanipulated expectations.

However, if one assumes that women would, given the opportunity, be as interested in and as suited for virtually the same work as men, one is compelled to interpret the continuing statistical segregation of the workforce as evidencing discrimination. And, as the 1964 Civil Rights Act outlawed sex discrimination in all phases of employment, the claim that discrimination not only persists but is so pervasive as to demand extraordinary remedies must involve an unusual construction of "discrimination." One

---

[6] Expressed in mean percentiles (so that a score of *n* for a group means that the average member of the group scored as well as *n* percent of the population): Mechanical-Male, 51; Mechanical-Female, 26; Administrative-M, 44; Administrative-F, 51; General-M, 52; General-F, 48; Electronics-M, 53; Electronics-F, 41 (ibid, p. 32).

[7] Ibid., p. 90, table C-14.

[8] Ibid., tables C-10–C-13, pp. 86–89.

[9] See I. Smith, *Spatial Ability* (San Diego: R. R. Knopp, 1964), pp. 135–55.

[10] See L. M. Terman and Leona Tyler, "Psychological Sex Differences," in *Manual of Child Psychology*, 2nd ed., ed. L. Charmichael (New York: Wiley, 1954), pp. 1064–1114.

[11] *Estimates of Worker Trait Requirements for 4000 Jobs* (Washington, D.C.: U.S. Government Printing Office, 1957).

[12] For a survey of occupationally relevant sex differences, see F. L. Schmidt, "Sex Differences in Some Occupationally Relevant Traits: The Viewpoint of an Applied Differential Psychologist," manuscript (Washington, D.C.: Office of Personnel Management, 1972).

such construction prominent in government research on the question, . . . is that women's own preferences obstruct equality of opportunity. A study by the Labor Department, *Women in Traditionally Male Jobs*, cites "the lack of female interest in many blue-collar jobs" as a "ubiquitous problem" in achieving "equal opportunity goals."[13] The Congressional Office of Technology Assessment cites "sex discrimination and sex stereotyping" as the barriers to women entering science and engineering:

> As long as women expect to assume the major role in housekeeping and child-rearing, and to sacrifice their professional interests to those of their husbands, they will be less likely than men to select occupations like science and engineering that require major educational and labor force commitment.[14] . . .

The Case for Quotas

There are three basic arguments for quotas, yielding as corollaries the three basic arguments for gender quotas. I cannot demonstrate that every argument that anyone might offer for quotas falls under one of these three, but if these three fail, it seems extremely unlikely that any entirely new argument is going to be successful.

Quotas Create Role Models

"Role models" are needed in unusual jobs to let women know that their options are wider than prevalent sex stereo-types now permit them to realize. A self-sustaining influx of women into nontraditional jobs will be triggered once enough women—a number never specified—are in place. The VERA Institute of justice argues that the lower felony arrest rate for female officers shows the need for more female officers to create an atmosphere in which females feel comfortable enough to do a better job.[15] Janet Richards puts the argument clearly:

> What we want to achieve is . . . *an improvement of the position of women until society is fair to them,* and as a matter of fact probably the best way to achieve this is to appoint to positions of importance women who are rather less good at the work than the men who are in competition with them. As long as they are not such hopeless failures as to confirm everyone's ideas that women are not capable of any serious work, their holding those positions will be enough to make others set their sights higher, and make people in general more used to seeing women in former male preserves and expecting more of them.[16]

A variant of this argument in the NOW amicus brief in *Rostker v. Goldberg*[17] claimed that registering and conscripting women would improve their image and decrease the incidence of rape.

Advocates of gender quotas have not pressed this argument with great enthusiasm. It rather conspicuously ignores the possible consequences of inserting less-than-the-best candidates into positions on which lives depend (like surgery or piloting commercial airliners). It seems to assume that the differences between incompetence, competence, and excellence are for the most part trivial, and that most people could do most things pretty well if given the chance.

---

[13]*Women in Traditionally Male Jobs: The Experience of Ten Public Utility Companies*, Department of Labor Research and Development Monograph 65 (Washington, D.C.: U.S. Government Printing Office, 1978), p. 117.

[14]"Panel Report Sex Disparity in Engineering," *New York Times* (December 16, 1985); A15.

[15]*Women on Patrol: A Pilot Study of Police Performance in New York City* (New York: VERA Institute, 1978).

[16]*The Sceptical Feminist*, p. 111.

[17]*Rostker v. Goldberg* 101 SCE 2646, 453 US 57 (1981).

Properly understood, furthermore this argument has nothing to do with equality of opportunity. The creation of role models is not intended to guarantee women freedom equal to men's to pursue the occupations they wish, which is how equality of opportunity is usually understood, but to induce women to want to pursue occupations they do not want (and whose pursuit would allegedly make them happier than they are now). Not that there is any evidence for a role model effect of the appropriate sort; psychologists coined "role model" to refer to the function performed by parents in influencing the ego ideals of very young children, and ego ideals are formed before the age of five.

But the most serious difficulty with the role model argument is this: Even if there were a demonstrable role model effect, and women would be happier (if not freer) attempting nontraditional pursuits, *and* the damage done by placing incompetent women in important jobs was tolerable, the question would remain whether quotas were fair to the individual males bypassed in the process, males not themselves responsible for women's currently constricted aspirations. If quotas do men an injustice, the role model defense is unpersuasive.

Quotas as Preventive Measures

This argument maintains that discrimination is, while illegal, so subtle, pervasive, and vicious that it must be stopped in advance:

> Another depressing topic at [the Congressional Black Caucus] was the Administration's late-August announcement that it would sharply decrease the enforcement of federal affirmative-action regulations designed to prevent discrimination against women and against blacks and other minorities—a curtailment Representative Charles Rangel . . . charged would be a signal to those in the private sector that they "need no longer worry about the government looking over their shoulders" and would in most cases be free to go back to indulging in the prejudices and biases that come naturally to many Americans.[18]

It is frequently added that discrimination is too difficult to prove to be attacked on an individual, case-wise basis.

This argument, too, founders on the question of justice. Preventive coercion is justified only in emergencies. It is generally agreed that the government may prevent grave wrongs clearly about to be done (it can disrupt conspiracies) and more remote but potentially catastrophic possibilities, but must otherwise act after the fact. It would be regarded as impermissibly unfair to reduce the felony rate by incarcerating all eighteen-year-old males, since males who were never going to attack anyone would inevitably be swept along. To be sure, sex discrimination is sometimes described as an evil of sufficient magnitude to warrant preventive measures too extreme to be deployed elsewhere, but this supplementary argument must also await consideration of the issue of justice.

The argument from preemption is also empirically vulnerable. To stop discrimination before it occurs by enforcing the outcome that would obtain without discrimination presupposes knowledge of what the nondiscriminatory outcome would be, and if that outcome is taken to be statistical proportionality, it is being assumed that the only possible causes of aggregate differences in outcomes are malign forces. This is the complete environmentalism which we have seen to be wholly untenable.

There is a close connection between quotas conceived as preventive detention and the concept of institutional discrimination. Quotas are necessary, it is argued,

---

[18]"Around City Hall," *New York* (September 18, 1981): 161.

because the very structure of institutions and the unconcious assumptions that accompany them result in minorities and women being excluded from certain activities. Still, in order for quotas to be an appropriate response, it must be demonstrated that the *particular blacks and women* who gain admission to otherwise structurally discriminatory institutions would have been excluded but for quotas. After all, it cannot be assumed that structural discrimination discriminates against absolutely every member of every unprotected class. Similarly, it must be somehow demonstrated that the particular white males penalized by preventive quotas are just those who would have benefited from institutional discrimination—we cannot just assume that *every* white male so benefits. Even if there is such a phenomenon as institutional discrimination, it does not follow that quotas are consistent with justice.

Quotas as Indemnification

We come to the *nervus probandi:* quotas are not only not unjust, they are demanded by justice, for they give today's Blacks and women the jobs they would have gotten had there been no sexual or racial discrimination in the past. Judging today's Blacks and women by sex-blind and race-blind merit standards unfairly disadvantages them by allowing past discrimination to perpetuate itself. Quotas make whole today's Blacks and women by "neutralizing the *present* competitive disadvantages caused by those past privations",[19] quotas compensate Blacks and women for the competitive abilities they would have had had their ancestors been treated properly. Reserving jobs for less qualified women and Blacks is fair to the bypassed, better-qualified White males, who would not have been better qualified in a nondiscriminatory world. To let better-qualified White males claim those jobs is to let them profit from wrong-doing, even if not their own. As for which White males have profited from the mistreatment of which Blacks and females, it must be assumed that every male enjoys an unfair advantage over every Black and female:

> Surely every white person, however free of direct implication in victimizing non-whites, is still a daily beneficiary of white dominance—past and present. . . . Though, of course, there are obvious and important differences, women too have been victimized as a group.[20]

This final phase of the argument may seem gratuitous paranoia, but it is actually crucial. To use any other indicator of victimhood which merely correlates with race or sex as a basis for preference—poverty, let us say—will entitle a poor White male, although a relatively rarer specimen, to the same preference as an equally poor Black woman. (And to call for affirmative action for Blacks or women to attack poverty, without claiming the support of justice, is still to call for the equally special treatment of equally poor Whites, Blacks, men, and women.) Unless race and sex are in themselves the stigmata of victimhood racial and gender quotas are inappropriate instruments of compensation. . . .

Compensatory Quotas for Women

A compensation claim is a thought experiment in which we return the world to the

---

[19]George Sher, "Justifying Reverse Discrimination in Employment," *Philosophy and Public Affairs* 4 (Winter 1975): 163.

[20]Haywood Burns, "The Bakke Case and Affirmative Action: Some Implications for the Future," *Freedomways* (First Quarter 1978); 6.

moment when a wrong was done and imagine how the world would have evolved had the wrong not been done. What the injured party would have possessed in this ideal world is what he *should* possess in the real world; the difference between his two positions in the two worlds is what the wrong cost the injured party and what the tortfeasor owes him. Despite the obvious uncertainties that beset such reasoning, the courts are able to carry it out in limited contexts—but not merely by observing the truism that people deserve what they wrongfully lost. Five specific conditions must be met to establish a compensation claim: (1) Injury must be shown; (2) the injured party must be identified; (3) the cost to the injured party must be established; (4) those who inflicted or profited from the injury must be identified. The complainant's loss cannot be restored at the expense of the innocent. Moreover, while those who do not inflict a wrong may be compensatorily liable if they profit from it, they must profit from it *directly*. If a terrorist bomb detonated a half-mile away loosens a treasure hidden in someone's ceiling, he does not owe the treasure to the terrorist's victim. (5) Restitution must be feasible, and feasibility constraints may dictate the replacement of what has been lost by an equivalent. Since the dancer cannot get back his mangled toe, the jury awards him compensatory damages in the amount he would have earned in performance fees had the moving man not clumsily dropped the piano on his foot. Indemnificatory quotas fail all five conditions; gender quotas far more completely than racial quotas.

Was injury done? The beginnings of a case for compensating contemporary Blacks can be based on the injuries done to their ancestors by slavery, segregation, and the lynch mob. No remotely comparable injuries have been done to women. Rape is occasionally cited as such an injury, but there is no evidence that rape adversely affects female acquisition of job skills. Because no palpable, physical injuries have been done to women, advocates of gender quotas are forced back on psychological injury supposedly done by sex role stereotyping. The most able defender of the compensation argument known to me is able to marshal only the following evidence of injury to women: "The feminist movement has convincingly documented the ways in which sexual bias is built into the information received by the young."[21]

It scarcely needs repeating that, if the arguments of chapters 3 and 4 are correct, sex stereotypes are no more than reports of the inevitable manifestations of innate sex differences. Stereotypes are true, and possess little independent power. But even supposing sex stereotypes baseless, it is moral lunacy to equate them with racial animosity. Within living memory, a Black man risked a beating or far worse for drinking from a Whites-only fountain. The feelings of an employer uncomfortable about putting a woman on the assembly line bears no resemblance to the hatred that led to what newspapers of the last century shamelessly called "negro barbecues." No matter how frequently it is repeated, the comparison of the sufferings of women to those of Blacks remains offensive to reason.

Who was injured? Who inflicted the injury? Who benefited? That Blacks were actually injured in the past does not justify racial quotas today. The perpetrators of those wrongs have died, and it is impossible to trace in detail the effects of those wrongs. It is therefore impossible to determine which particular Blacks are worse off than they should have been, or by how much, or which Whites are better off. Slavery cannot be said, by the standards of law, science, or

---

[21]Sher, n.6.

common sense, to have benefited today's second-generation Greek-American. It is if anything more speculative to claim that a particular White man has benefited from the wrongs which have disadvantaged a particular Black man. It simply cannot be determined whether every Black promoted over Brian Weber would have been his senior had there been no discrimination.

That the basic showing of injury cannot be sustained for women makes it superfluous to ask how the women injured by sexist discrimination, and the men who have benefited from this injury, are to be identified. Janet Richards writes: "The only men excluded [from jobs] on this principle would be the ones who, as far as we could tell, would not have succeeded anyway if the situation had been fair."[22] This merely restates the problem without some account of how one *is* to tell which men these are and what net advantage they enjoy over particular women.

Current Black disadvantages at least *appear* traceable to past wrongs because Blacks form a coherent subgroup within the general population. It is clear that parents may transmit handicaps to their children within coherent subpopulations (although this effect is attenuated by the social mobility characteristic of industrial democracies). Whatever slight support this transmission of handicaps may lend to the case for racial quotas, it is entirely inappropriate for women. Women do not form an autonomous subpopulation within which norms and traditions are transmitted. Women's ancestors are *everybody*. To the extent that a person's competitive position reflects that of his parents, the average woman must be assumed to have gained as much from her father's ill-gotten advantages as she has lost from her mother's undeserved handicaps. What is particularly ludicrous about the comparison of Blacks and females in the workforce is that *women marry men* whereas Blacks do not typically marry Whites. For most practical purposes a wife has full use of her husband's assets. If the average man is better off than he should have been because the average woman is worse off, they pool their resources and split the difference when they marry. Since virtually all men and women marry, gender quotas harm virtually all women. If compensatory quotas harmed a Black for every Black they helped, they would defeat their own purpose. But whenever a man loses a job, promotion or training to a woman, just because he is a man, another woman, namely the man's wife, is deprived of precisely what the quota beneficiary gained. Gender quotas self-defeatingly compensate some members of the allegedly victimized group by depriving others.

So far as I know, this self-evident point has been overlooked in the literature on quotas. This oversight is due in part to the central role played in the case for gender quotas by the young woman seeking a nontraditional career, a woman less likely than average to be married. A more fundamental cause of this oversight is the repeated portrayal of men and women as competing groups. The motif of woman-as-outsider is a staple of feminist rhetoric;[23] as I mentioned, even feminist evolutionary biology treats men and women as competitors.[24] In addition to the ambitious career woman, much attention has been given to the single mother who must support her family alone

---

[22]Janet Richards, *The Sceptical Feminist* (Boston: Routledge & Kegan Paul, 1980), p. 118.

[23]"I am not real to my civilization. I am not real to the culture that has spawned me and made use of me" (Vivian Gornick, "Woman as Outsider," in *Woman in Sexist Society*, ed. Vivian Gornick and Betty Moran (New York: Mentor, 1971), p. 144.)

[24]See Chapter 4, fn. 15.

and would benefit from an affirmative action boost to a high salary job. Quite apart from the irrelevance of her plight to the justification of affirmative action—men also have families to support, and a single mother is not usually single because of the actions of the men against whom she is competing for jobs—the single mother does not make men and women disparate groups.

What was lost? "Lost competitive ability" is too obscure to justify compensation, although again its application to race must be distinguished from its application to sex. Compensation theory emphasizes the need for tangible criteria of loss, some *goods* lost, since the career of a physical object can be relatively easily traced. If you steal my car, it is possible many years later to identify it as what I lost. There are limits even on the use of physical objects and sums of money as guides to compensation, since the identity of a (stolen) physical object can be blurred by the contributions of subsequent recipients and bystanders. The common law will not dispossess the current holders of land that has been transferred in good faith for a number of generations, despite proof from a claimant that the land was stolen from his ancestors; too much honest labor is now part of the land.

Even in the racial case, "inability to compete" fails the test of identifiability. No Black can point to a successful White and claim that he would have had just *that* much competitive ability had the world been fair. Allan Bakke, a White denied admission to the University of California medical school under a racial quota system, had an undergraduate grade point average of 3.8 out of a possible 4, while the Blacks chosen over him had averages no higher than 2.38.[25] If competitive ability is operationalized as college average, defenders of the University of California quota must be prepared to claim that the Blacks selected over Bakke would have had grade averages at least 1.42 points higher had the world been fair. It is not clear how anyone could know this. And if competitive ability is not operationalized in some such way, it is not clear what advocates of compensatory quotas have in mind when they speak of it.

In marked contrast, no detours into the metaphysics of compensation are needed to see how much less substantial is the corresponding claim about women's "lost competitive abilities." Dominance-aggression, the ability most crucial for success in competitive situations, is physiologically determined and could not have been shared more equally by women in any physiologically possible world, however just it might be. Blacks and Whites want to get to the top equally badly, but Blacks lack some of the skills possessed by Whites. There is this much sense to talk of Black/White competitive abilities being discrepant. The difference between men and women is that women do not want to get to the top as badly as men do and men do not want to do the things women prefer intensely to do.

The basic trouble with speculating about the abilities people would have had in a better world is that it ignores the constitutive contribution of competitive abilities to the human personality and indeed to personal identity. Intelligence, persistence, a sense of detachment toward setbacks—all make a person who he is. Failure to recognize this is the profound error of the shackled runner analogy. We understand what real shackles cost a shackled runner because it is easy to imaginatively remove the shackles and speculate about how *he* would perform without them. Competitive traits are not so easily prised off their possessors. One cannot "unshackle" an ordinary person

---

[25]*Bakke v. University of California Regents*, 438 U.S. 265 (1978), in which the Supreme Court approved race-conscious admissions policies.

from his ordinariness by imagining him brilliant, decisive, and unquenchably ambitious; it would not be the same person. You are imagining somebody else who looks to your mind's eye like the man you thought you were imagining. Compensation arguments which posit far more gifted counterparts, for various actually existing people are describing *replacements*, whose hypothetical performances imply nothing about the entitlements of anybody who actually exists.[26]

Is rectification feasible? Quotas require the award of jobs to individuals who by hypothesis are not the best able to perform them and are in some cases absolutely unable to perform them. Quotas thus violate feasibility constraints that normally limit compensation. The dancer crippled by the careless piano mover does not ask the moving company to hire him to perform *Swan Lake*, for the dancer's complaint, after all, is that—thanks to the moving company's negligence—he can no longer dance very well. He asks for the monetary equivalent of his lost skill, not the right to perform actions for which the lost skill is necessary. (There are reidentification problems even in this case, and perhaps an element of convention enters into the jury's determination of what the dancer would have earned over a lifetime had his skill level remained unimpaired by negligence; these difficulties show that estimates of lost higher-order abilities, like the ability to compete, are even less well founded than I suggested above.) It is therefore odd that compensation for Blacks and women, assuming it to be deserved, should take the form of jobs, when the grounds for compensating them is their lack of the skills necessary for those jobs. The normal mode of reparation in such cases is monetary. If, instead of money, Blacks and women deserve the very jobs they should have been but are not able to fill, if no substitutes are acceptable, Black and female students deserve the grades they should have but are not able to earn. If no substitutes are acceptable, why not allow a free felony, one major crime without punishment, to compensate each Black for all the undeserved punishments inflicted on his ancestors by a legal system once unjust to Blacks? In fact, there *are* government-mandated grading quotas. The U.S. State Department awards five extra points to Blacks taking its Foreign Service, and girls in the Australian Capital Territory receive five extra points on their college entrance examinations.

Feasibility constraints are disregarded when the subject is quotas, I suspect, because discrimination is taken to be morally special, not just one wrong among many others all competing for rectification, but the worst wrong imaginable, a sin. The world must be remade just as it would have been had this blot on humanity never happened at all. It is this assumption that elicits defense of preventive discrimination from people who would not think of preventively detaining potential murderers. Sin is a theological doctrine which cannot profitably be judged by an unbeliever, but it might be instructive to ask the actual victims of a variety of wrongs which one they think worse and in more urgent need of remedy. Would the average Black man prefer to lose a job because of his skin color, or be murdered? Would the average woman

---

[26]For further discussion of these points, see Michael Levin. "Reverse Discrimination, Shackled Runners, and Personal Identity," *Philosophical Studies* 37 (1980): 139–49. It is sometimes argued that the biologically determined differential success rates of men and women are unjust since, had women been treated fairly over the millennia, the market would have evolved to reward female talents as much as it now rewards male talents. Trying to substantiate a conditional this counterfactual is like trying to determine whether Julius Caesar would have used atomic weapons had they been available 2,000 years ago.

prefer to be robbed at knifepoint or be told that driving a truck is unladylike? Which does she want back first, her freedom to realize herself, or her pocketbook?

Racial discrimination seems special because people tend to reify races into entities in their own right, and think of the race itself, not merely the particular victims of discriminatory practices, as having suffered. This is a mistake in its own right—only individuals can suffer—and leads to the further mistake of forgetting that particularly grave discriminatory acts, like lynching, are grave precisely because they fall under nonracial headings like intimidation and murder. No doubt the female sex has also been reified into a victim by the ontologically careless, but, again, it remains crazy to compare the "romantic paternalism"[27] with which many nineteenth-century American males may have viewed women to the racial hatred endured by Blacks. . . .

The Trouble with Reverse Discrimination

Quotas deny benefits and impose burdens on individuals not responsible for any wrongs. They cannot be justified as compensation, inspiration, or prevention, and they decrease economic efficiency. So much alone suffices to close the case against them, but it does not clarify why quotas strike most people as *unfair.* Quotas burden innocent, well-qualified White males—but what is wrong with that?

The usual explanations are unsatisfactory. Quotas cannot sin against the right of the best qualified to a job, since, as far as I can see, there is no such right. The rights and correlative obligations that control employment are created by the mutual agreements of employers and employees. If every individual has a right to refuse to enter agreements with anyone he pleases, an employer may refuse to enter an agreement with anyone, including the person best able to perform a job the employer wants done. If the employer has no right to refuse an offer the best-qualified individual makes him, the employer is to that extent his slave, and has no right to associate *or not* with other people as he pleases. The employer may be irrational in refusing to deal with the best-qualified individual, but the employer does not *harm* him. The employer is simply *refusing to help* that individual (and himself).

For similar reasons, I do not see how White males or anyone else can have a right to be "free from discrimination."[28] Private discrimination is not a force that attacks White males (or anyone else) minding their own business. A White male is discriminated against in employment when, after he offers his services to an employer, the employer turns him down for no other reason than his sex and skin color. It was the White male who initiated proceedings. The potential employer who was minding his own business, has simply refused to enter a mutually beneficial arrangement with the White male; the White male has been made no worse off than he was before proceedings began. If the employer has no right not to bargain with White males as such, White males to that extent *own* him.

There is no injustice in discriminating against White males, *just as, in logical consistency, there is no injustice in discriminating against Black males, females, or*

---

[27]U.S. Commission on Civil Rights, 1980, p. 9.

[28]John Bunzel speaks of "the right to be free of discrimination" in "Rescuing Equality," in *Sidney Hook,* ed. Paul Kurtz (Buffalo, N.Y.: Prometheus, 1983), p. 179. "Mr. Celler: The bill seeks simply to protect the right of American citizens to be free from racial and religious discrimination." *Legislative History of Title VII,* p. 3283.

members of any other group. Favoritism, injustice, and moral arbitrariness enter when the government permits and demands preference for one group while forbidding preference toward another. If, as the Supreme Court held in *Weber*, preference for Blacks is a legitimate exercise of an employer's freedom of association, preference for Whites must also, in consistency, be considered a legitimate exercise of the same freedom. The unfairness of the present quota system lies in the government's disadvantaging White males by permitting—and encouraging and requiring—employer discrimination against them while forbidding employer discrimination against non-White males. The government thereby denies to White males a protection it extends to Blacks, Hispanics, females and other populations.

There are two ways to restore symmetry. It might be argued that, since there are utilitarian reasons to forbid private discrimination,[29] the government should impartially forbid preference of any sort. (If the government rejects the "right" not to be discriminated against but forbids discrimination for the general good, it might wish to rethink the equation of Blacks and women when redrawing the limits of permissible favoritism.) On the other hand, it might be argued that the government should leave freedom of association unlimited and impartially permit preference of any sort. In the latter case, employers persuaded by the arguments for quotas would be free to treat Blacks and females preferentially; employers persuaded of the virtues of merit criteria would be free to use pure merit criteria; and employers persuaded that by now White males deserve some reverse reverse discrimination would be free to prefer White males. The government would revert to a neutral, nondiscriminatory stance under either alternative.

As for the government's own hiring policies, it is clearly impermissible for the state to confer benefits like employment on the basis of race alone, and state action could easily be race blind, so long as proportionally was not the test of race blindness. It is not so clear that the state could ever be blind to sex. The state will always have to impose the burden of defense on men, which is a form of discrimination against them (unless it is argued that combat positions open to male volunteers are a public benefit discriminatorily denied woman—an argument which must be withdrawn whenever the shooting starts). It is unthinkable that the state could pursue its functions without taking some account of biological sex differences.

Questions for Further Reflection

1. Fullinwider argues that, at AT&T, women could not be treated without discrimination until the "shock treatment" of reverse discrimination ensured that substantial numbers of women held traditionally male jobs. Do you agree that in this case, mere nondiscrimination could not have worked? If so, how generalizable is this case? Does it give grounds for reverse discrimination in predominantly white male universities, law firms, or banks?

2. One complicating factor in issues about discrimination is that less well qualified minorities may be less qualified precisely because of past discrimination, which may have damaged their educational opportunities, their social environment, and their expectations. What effect should such causes of underqualification have on hiring practices, if any?

---

[29]This position is defended in Kent Greenawalt, *Discrimination and Reverse Discrimination* (New York: Borzoi, 1983).

3. Levin argues that statistical underrepresentation in a field is not a good indication of discrimination, since underrepresentation of a certain group may also occur because members of the group are not interested in the field or because on the whole they are not good at it. Do you agree? If so, what *would* be good evidence of discrimination? Do you agree with Levin that there cannot be unintended discrimination?
4. Levin suggests that the "role models" argument for reverse discrimination is based on the goal of changing people's desires rather than on satisfying the ones they already have. To what extent is changing people's desires a legitimate goal of social policy? Might role models be desirable for reasons other than changing people's desires?
5. Levin claims that it is unfair to permit discrimination against white males while prohibiting discrimination against blacks or women. He suggests that *either* prohibiting all discrimination *or* permitting discrimination against anyone would be preferable. He seems to prefer the latter: "There is no injustice in discriminating against Black males, females, or members of any other group." This raises a basic question: What, if anything, is wrong with discrimination?

Further Readings

Cohen, Marshall, et al., eds. *Equality and Preferential Treatment*. Princeton, NJ: Princeton University Press, 1977. An excellent collection of essays first published between 1973 and 1976 in *Philosophy and Public Affairs*. The introduction by Thomas Nagel is a helpful entry into the issue.

D'Souza, Dinesh. *The End of Racism*. New York: The Free Press, 1995. An all-out attack on affirmative action. More journalistic than philosophical, but contains some interesting material.

Fullinwider, Robert K. *The Reverse Discrimination Controversy: A Moral and Legal Analysis*. Totowa, NJ: Rowman and Littlefield, 1981. An exhaustive and clearly written study. The first two chapters are a good introduction to the issue; remaining chapters explore specific topics.

Goldman, Alan H. "Affirmative Action." *Philosophy and Public Affairs* 5 (1976), reprinted in Cohen et al. A critique of reverse discrimination, unless in favor of individuals who have previously been discriminated against in job hiring.

Greenawalt, Kent. *Discrimination and Reverse Discrimination*. New York: Alfred A. Knopf, 1983. A very clear introduction to both the legal and philosophical issues surrounding reverse discrimination. Includes a good selection of relevant cases and other legal material.

Thomson, Judith Jarvis. "Preferential Hiring." *Philosophy and Public Affairs* 2 (1973), reprinted in Cohen et al. An important defense of reverse discrimination on compensatory grounds.

Wolgast, Elizabeth H. "Is Reverse Discrimination Fair?" In M. A. Steward, ed., *Law, Morality and Rights*. Dordrecht: D. Reidel, 1983, 295–313. An interesting discussion of difficulties with an equal-opportunity defense of reverse discrimination. (The same volume contains several other useful pieces on reverse discrimination.)

Chapter 12

ILLICIT DRUGS

One of the few things about which most members of both major political parties in the United States agree is that our current prohibition of many drugs should be maintained or strengthened. In 1988, when the House Select Committee on Narcotics Abuse and Control held two days of hearings on drug legalization, nearly all members of the committee opposed legalization, and many objected even to holding hearings on the issue. When a few years later, in December 1993, Dr. Joycelin Elders, the Surgeon General, suggested that legalization was worthy of study, a number of members of Congress called for her resignation, and President Clinton's spokeswoman reported that "the President is firmly against legalizing drugs, and he is not inclined in this case to even study the issue."

The "war on drugs" in the United States raises a number of moral questions, for example: Is there something morally suspect about the pleasure obtained by using drugs, or is pleasure valuable no matter how it is obtained? To what extent is government interference in the free choices of individuals permissible? Are there differences between alcohol and nicotine, on one hand, and marijuana, heroin, and cocaine, on the other, which justify their different treatment under the law? Are heroin, marijuana, and cocaine themselves similar enough to justify collecting them into a single moral category? In this chapter we explore some of the issues in the context of the question of whether some or all illicit drugs should be legalized or decriminalized. We do not address many other interesting issues about drugs, such as the permissibility of steroid use by athletes, the justification of the distinction between prescription and non-prescription drugs, and whether drug screening in the workplace should be permitted or required.

Costs and Benefits

The most commonly heard arguments for and against legalizing drugs are broadly utilitarian in character: They involve weighing the consequences of criminalization against those of decriminalization and making a judgment as to which set of consequences is more acceptable. Such cost-benefit analysis is extremely difficult to perform in the case of drugs, in part because it is difficult to obtain unbiased information on the effects of drugs and to sort out the causal relationships between drug use and crime, and in part because we can only speculate about what would happen to drug use if drugs were legalized. However, we can at least note some of the most important issues.

Clearly, there are costs associated with our current drug laws. Enforcing them requires large amounts of money, prison space, and court time.[1] Moreover, the criminalization of drugs makes huge profits possible for drug traffickers; as Ethan Nadelmann has noted, "More than half of all organized crime revenues are believed to derive from the illicit drug business; estimates of the dollar value range between $10 and $50 billion per year."[2] This creation of huge profits for drug traffickers directly leads not only to illegal transportation and sale of drugs, but also to violent crime; Nadelmann claims that "most law enforcement authorities agree that the dramatic increases in urban murder rates during the past few years can be explained almost entirely by the rise in drug dealer killings, mostly of one another."[3]

Legalization of drugs, then, might be expected to free resources for other law enforcement purposes and to reduce the crime associated with illegal drug trafficking. But legalization would have its own costs. It seems likely that if drug use were legal, and if, as a result, the cost of drugs were much lower, the levels of drug use would increase. As a result, we could expect more people to damage their health with drugs, more traffic and work-related accidents caused by drug use to occur, and perhaps crime to increase by people whose inhibitions have been reduced or whose violent tendencies have been exacerbated by drugs. How dramatic would these consequences be? In their selections in this chapter, Walter Block and James Q. Wilson disagree. Block argues that drug use would not increase dramatically if drugs were legalized, while Wilson offers grounds for thinking that it would. Whether legalization would be desirable on utilitarian grounds clearly depends on who is correct. It seems impossible to be certain, though, or even reasonably sure, who is correct about this issue. Wilson claims that, given this uncertainty, it is better to retain our drug laws; he writes: "If I am right, and the legalizers prevail anyway, then we will have consigned millions of people, hundreds of thousands of infants, and hundreds of neighborhoods to a life of oblivion and disease."

Consistency

Are our drug laws consistent? We treat marijuana, heroin, cocaine, and other illicit drugs very differently from alcohol and nicotine. Are they as different as our laws would suggest? Certainly as things now stand, far more harm is done by alcohol and nicotine than by illicit drugs. Nadelmann's figures again are helpful: In the United States, between 50,000 and 200,000 people per year die as a direct or indirect result of alcohol use; approximately 320,000 people each year die earlier than they otherwise would have because of tobacco use; while in 1985, 3,562 people were known to have died from using all illicit drugs combined.[4] Moreover, alcohol is well known to play a role in a great many violent crimes—perhaps more than half of all violent crimes.[5] If we do not think that this much crime and ill health are a sufficient reason to criminalize the use of alcohol or nicotine, why do we think similar considerations reason enough to criminalize other drugs?

---

[1] Ethan A. Nadelmann, "Drug Prohibition in the United States: Costs, Consequences, and Alternatives," *Science* 245 (1 September 1989): 939–947, at 940–941.

[2] Nadelmann, 941.

[3] Nadelmann, 942.

[4] Nadelmann, 943.

[5] Nadelmann, 941.

Walter Block, in his selection in this chapter, implies that there is no good reason for the distinctions we draw here—for what Stephen Jay Gould has called "an absurd dichotomy" and "a false and senseless classification."[6] Wilson, on the other hand, offers justifications for treating alcohol and nicotine differently from illegal drugs. He points out that although the harmful consequences of nicotine and alcohol are, as things now stand, far worse than those of illegal drugs, it is hard to say how much worse the consequences of drug use would be if drugs were legalized. In the case of alcohol, he suggests a purely practical reason for treating it differently from illicit drugs: Given our historical circumstances, there is not the smallest chance that we could contain the harmful consequences of alcohol use by making alcohol illegal, while it is arguable that existing drug laws *can* help contain the harmful consequences of other drugs. (Wilson in fact suggests that if we currently had fewer alcohol abusers, we should very seriously consider criminalization of alcohol.) In the case of nicotine, Wilson suggests an important *moral* difference from the illicit drugs: Nicotine "does not destroy the user's essential humanity. Tobacco shortens one's life, cocaine debases it. Nicotine alters one's habits, cocaine alters one's soul." Wilson's claim here should be contrasted with Block's portrayal of drug use as simply a ration economic choice by means of which an agent attempts to enhance his or her welfare.

Liberty

One of the most basic questions raised by the drug issue concerns the extent of personal autonomy and liberty and the circumstances under which it is appropriate for government to restrict one's choices. Drug use, or at least the regular use of some drugs, is certainly harmful to one's health and may contribute to a lifestyle we would not regard as productive. And, of course, drug use may be involved in clearly harmful behavior; crack-addicted mothers may give birth to crack-addicted babies whom they then abandon, and people using drugs may, as William Bennett writes, "behave in chilling and horrible ways." (Of course, people not addicted to or using drugs also abuse and abandon children and otherwise act in horrible ways, so the causal relationships are difficult to untangle.) What is the appropriate social response to these problems?

One answer, the one defended by Block, is that we should seek to control behavior directly harmful to others by legal means, for example, by having and enforcing laws forbidding abandoning or abusing children, laws forbidding driving or operating machinery while under the influence of drugs, and so on. However, according to Block, we should not use the law to forbid people to risk their health or to require people to be productive members of society. People should be free to choose their own ways of life, even if the ways they choose are ones of which we disapprove.

Another, very different response is defended by Wilson. Rejecting the libertarian picture Block paints, Wilson writes that "society is not and could never be a collection of autonomous individuals. We all have a stake in ensuring that each of us displays a minimal level of dignity, responsibility, and empathy." In this view, the law should be used not only to keep people from actively interfering with or harming one another, but also to ensure that people live up to certain basic moral standards. The use of crack or heroin, Wilson suggests, is incompatible with living up to these standards and so should be prohibited.

---

[6]Stephen Jay Gould, "Taxonomy as Politics: The Harm of False Classification," *Dissent* (Winter 1990), pp. 73–78.

Block's essay defends a drug policy at the opposite extreme from the current policy, endorsed by Wilson, of completely prohibiting "illicit" drugs. It should be noted that various intermediate policies are possible. We could legalize some drugs, but not others; we could legalize drugs, but impose severe restrictions on who can use them and where they can be purchased; we could reduce or eliminate penalties for drug use, while continuing to penalize the sale of drugs.

Bonnie Steinbock, in her essay in this chapter, argues for a kind of middle ground between the extreme positions of Wilson and Block. Steinbock agrees with Block that banning drugs restricts people's freedom to choose how to design their own lives. But she argues that freedom is not the only value that we should protect. We should also promote the health and well-being of people affected by drug use, both drug users and others they interact with, especially children harmed by drug-using caregivers. When liberty and utility conflict, she argues, we need to balance the two rather than simply taking one to have priority over the other; the public-health perspective she advocates involves taking both sorts of values into account.

DRUGS SHOULD NOT BE LEGALIZED

Against the Legalization of Drugs

James Q. Wilson

In 1972, the President appointed me chairman of the National Advisory Council for Drug Abuse Prevention. Created by Congress, the Council was charged with providing guidance on how best to coordinate the national war on drugs. (Yes, we called it a war then, too.) In those days, the drug we were chiefly concerned with was heroin. When I took office, heroin use had been increasing dramatically. Everybody was worried that this increase would continue. Such phrases as "heroin epidemic" were commonplace.

That same year, the eminent economist Milton Friedman published an essay in *Newsweek* in which he called for legalizing heroin. His argument was on two grounds: as a matter of ethics, the government has no right to tell people not to use heroin (or to drink or to commit suicide); as a matter of economics, the prohibition of drug use imposes costs on society that far exceed the benefits. Others, such as the psychoanalyst Thomas Szasz, made the same argument.

We did not take Friedman's advice. (Government commissions rarely do.) I do not recall that we even discussed legalizing heroin, though we did discuss (but did not take action on) legalizing a drug, cocaine, that many people then argued was benign.

Our marching orders were to figure out how to win the war on heroin, not to run up the white flag of surrender.

That was 1972. Today, we have the same number of heroin addicts that we had then—half a million, give or take a few thousand. Having that many heroin addicts is no trivial matter, these people deserve our attention; But not having had an increase in that number for over fifteen years is also something that deserves our attention. What happened to the "heroin epidemic" that many people once thought would overwhelm us?

The facts are clear: a more or less stable pool of heroin addicts has been getting older, with relatively few new recruits. In 1976 the average age of heroin users who appeared in hospital emergency rooms was about twenty-seven; ten years later it was thirty-two. More than two-thirds of all heroin users appearing in emergency rooms are now over the age of thirty. Back in the early 1970's, when heroin got onto the national political agenda, the typical heroin addict was much younger, often a teenager. Household surveys show the same thing—the rate of opiate use (which includes heroin) has been flat for the better part of two decades. More fine-grained studies of inner-city neighborhoods confirm this. John Boyle and Ann Brunswick found that the percentage of young blacks in Harlem who used heroin fell from 8 percent in 1970–71 to about 3 percent in 1975–76.

Why did heroin lose its appeal for young people? When the young blacks in Harlem were asked why they stopped, more than half mentioned "trouble with the law" or "high cost" (and high cost is, of course, directly the result of law enforcement). Two-thirds said that heroin hurt their health; nearly all said they had had a bad experience with it. We need not rely, however, simply on what they said. In New York City in 1973–75, the street price of heroin rose dramatically and its purity sharply declined, probably as a result of the heroin shortage caused by the success of the Turkish government in reducing the supply of opium base and of the French government in closing down heroin-processing laboratories located in and around Marseilles. These were short-lived gains for, just as Friedman predicted, alternative sources of supply—mostly in Mexico—quickly emerged. But the three-year heroin shortage interrupted the easy recruitment of new users.

Health and related problems were no doubt part of the reason for the reduced flow of recruits. Over the preceding years, Harlem youth had watched as more and more heroin users died of overdoses, were poisoned by adulterated doses, or acquired hepatitis from dirty needles. The word got around: heroin can kill you. By 1974 new hepatitis cases and drug-overdose deaths had dropped to a fraction of what they had been in 1970.

Alas, treatment did not seem to explain much of the cessation in drug use. Treatment programs can and do help heroin addicts, but treatment did not explain the drop in the number of *new* users (who by definition had never been in treatment) nor even much of the reduction in the number of experienced users.

No one knows how much of the decline to attribute to personal observation as opposed to high prices or reduced supply. But other evidence suggests strongly that price and supply played a large role. In 1972 the National Advisory Council was especially worried by the prospect that U.S. servicemen returning to this country from Vietnam would bring their heroin habits with them. Fortunately, a brilliant study by Lee Robins of Washington University in St. Louis put that fear to rest. She measured drug use of Vietnam veterans shortly after they had returned home. Though many had used heroin regularly while in Southeast Asia, most gave up the habit when back in the United States. The reason: here, heroin was less available and sanctions on its use were more pronounced. Of course, if a veteran had been willing to pay enough—which might have meant traveling to another city and would certainly have meant making an illegal contact with a disreputable dealer in a threatening neighborhood in order to acquire a (possibly) dangerous dose—he could have sustained his drug habit. Most veterans were unwilling to pay this price, and so their drug use declined or disappeared. . . .

Back to the Future

Now cocaine, especially in its potent form, crack, is the focus of attention. Now as in 1972 the government is trying to reduce its use. Now as then some people are advocating legalization. Is there any more reason to yield to those arguments today than there was almost two decades ago?*

I think not. If we had yielded in 1972 we almost certainly would have had today a permanent population of several million, not several hundred thousand, heroin addicts. If we yield now we will have a far more serious problem with cocaine.

Crack is worse than heroin by almost any measure. Heroin produces a pleasant drowsiness and, if hygienically administered, has only the physical side effects of constipation and sexual impotence. Regular heroin use incapacitates many users, especially poor ones, for any productive work or social responsibility. They will sit nodding on a street corner, helpless but at least harmless. By contrast, regular cocaine use leaves the user neither helpless nor harmless. When smoked (as with crack) or injected, cocaine produces instant, intense, and short-lived euphoria. The experience generates a powerful desire to repeat it. If the drug is readily available, repeat use will occur. Those people who progress to "bingeing" on cocaine become devoted to the drug and its effects to the exclusion of almost all other considerations—job, family, children, sleep, food, even sex. Dr. Frank Gawin at Yale and Dr. Everett Ellinwood at Duke report that a substantial percentage of all high-dose, binge users become uninhibited, impulsive, hypersexual, compulsive, irritable, and hyperactive. Their moods vacillate dramatically, leading at times to violence and homicide.

Women are much more likely to use crack than heroin, and if they are pregnant, the effects on their babies are tragic. Douglas Besharov, who has been following the effects of drugs on infants for twenty years, writes that nothing he learned about heroin prepared him for the devastation of cocaine. Cocaine harms the fetus and can lead to physical deformities or neurological damage. Some crack babies have for all practical purposes suffered a disabling stroke while still in the womb. The long-term consequences of this brain damage are lowered cognitive ability and the onset of mood disorders. Besharov estimates that about 30,000 to 50,000 such babies are born every year, about 7,000 in New York City alone. There may be ways to treat such infants, but from everything we now know the treatment will be long, difficult, and expensive. Worse, the mothers who are most likely to produce crack babies are precisely the ones who, because of poverty or temperament, are least able and willing to obtain such treatment. In fact, anecdotal evidence suggests that crack mothers are likely to abuse their infants.

---
*I do not here take up the question of marijuana. For a variety of reasons—its widespread use and its lesser tendency to addict—it presents a different problem from cocaine or heroin. For a penetrating analysis, see Mark Kleiman. *Marijuana: Costs of Abuse, Costs of Control* (Greenwood Press, 217 pp., $37.95).

The notion that abusing drugs such as cocaine is a "victimless crime" is not only absurd but dangerous. Even ignoring the fetal drug syndrome, crack-dependent people are, like heroin addicts, individuals who regularly victimize their children by neglect, their spouses by improvidence, their employers by lethargy, and their co-workers by carelessness. Society is not and could never be a collection of autonomous individuals. We all have a stake in ensuring that each of us displays a minimal level of dignity, responsibility, and empathy. We cannot, of course, coerce people into goodness, but we can and should insist that some standards must be met if society itself—on which the very existence of the human personality depends—is to persist. Drawing the line that defines those standards is difficult and contentious, but if crack and heroin use do not fall below it, what does? . . .

Have We Lost?

Many people who agree that there are risks in legalizing cocaine or heroin still favor it because, they think, we have lost the war on drugs. "Nothing we have done has worked" and the current federal policy is just "more of the same." Whatever the costs of greater drug use, surely they would be less than the costs of our present, failed efforts.

That is exactly what I was told in 1972—and heroin is not quite as bad a drug as cocaine. We did not surrender and we did not lose. We did not win, either. What the nation accomplished then was what most efforts to save people from themselves accomplish: the problem was contained and the number of victims minimized, all at a considerable cost in law enforcement and increased crime. Was the cost worth it? I think so, but others may disagree. What are the lives of would-be addicts worth? I recall some people saying to me then, "Let them kill themselves." I was appalled. Happily, such views did not prevail. . . .

It took about ten years to contain heroin. We have had experience with crack for only about three or four years. Each year we spend perhaps $11 billion on law enforcement (and some of that goes to deal with marijuana) and perhaps $2 billion on treatment. Large sums, but not sums that should lead anyone to say, "We just can't afford this any more."

The illegality of drugs increases crime, partly because some users turn to crime to pay for their habits, partly because some users are stimulated by certain drugs (such as crack or PCP) to act more violently or ruthlessly than they otherwise would, and partly because criminal organizations seeking to control drug supplies use force to manage their markets. These also are serious costs, but no one knows how much they would be reduced if drugs were legalized. Addicts would no longer steal to pay black-market prices for drugs, a real gain. But some, perhaps a great deal, of that gain would be offset by the great increase in the number of addicts. These people, nodding on heroin or living in the delusion-ridden high of cocaine, would hardly be ideal employees. Many would steal simply to support themselves, since snatch-and-grab, opportunistic crime can be managed even by people unable to hold a regular job or plan an elaborate crime. Those British addicts who get their supplies from government clinics are not models of law-abiding decency. Most are in crime, and though their per-capita rate of criminality may be lower thanks to the cheapness of their drugs, the total volume of crime they produce may be quite large. Of course, society could decide to support all unemployable addicts on welfare, but that would mean that gains from lowered rates of crime would have to be offset by large increases in welfare budgets.

Proponents of legalization claim that the costs of having more addicts around would be largely if not entirely offset by having more money available with which to treat and care for them. The money would come from taxes levied on the sale of heroin and cocaine.

To obtain this fiscal dividend, however, legalization's supporters must first solve an economic dilemma. If they want to raise a lot of money to pay for welfare and treatment, the tax rate on the drugs will have to be quite high. Even if they themselves do not want a high rate, the politicians' love of "sin taxes" would probably guarantee that it would be high anyway. But the higher the tax, the higher the price of the drug, and the higher the price the greater the likelihood that addicts will turn to crime to find the money for it and that criminal organizations will be formed to sell tax-free drugs at below-market rates. If we managed to keep taxes (and thus prices) low, we would get that much less money to pay for welfare and treatment and more people could afford to become addicts. There may be an optimal tax rate for drugs that maximizes revenue while minimizing crime, bootlegging, and the recruitment of new addicts, but our experience with alcohol does not suggest that we know how to find it. . . .

The Benefits of Illegality

. . . We are now investing subtantially in drug-education programs in the schools. Though we do not yet know for certain what will work, there are some promising leads. But I wonder how credible such programs would be if they were aimed at dissuading children from doing something perfectly legal. We could, of course, treat drug education like smoking education: inhaling crack and inhaling tobacco are both legal, but you should not do it because it is bad for you. That tobacco is bad for you is easily shown; the Surgeon General has seen to that. But what do we say about crack? It is pleasurable, but devoting yourself to so much pleasure is not a good idea (though perfectly legal)? Unlike tobacco, cocaine will not give you cancer or emphysema, but it will lead you to neglect your duties to family, job, and neighborhood? Everybody is doing cocaine, but you should not?

Again, it might be possible under a legalized regime to have effective drug-prevention programs, but their effectiveness would depend heavily, I think, on first having decided that cocaine use, like tobacco use, is purely a matter of practical consequences; no fundamental moral significance attaches to either. But if we believe—as I do—that dependency on certain mind-altering drugs *is* a moral issue and that their illegality rests in part on their immorality, then legalizing them undercuts, if it does not eliminate altogether, the moral message.

That message is at the root of the distinction we now make between nicotine and cocaine. Both are highly addictive; both have harmful physical effects. But we treat the two drugs differently, not simply because nicotine is so widely used as to be beyond the reach of effective prohibition, but because its use does not destroy the user's essential humanity. Tobacco shortens one's life, cocaine debases it. Nicotine alters one's habits, cocaine alters one's soul. The heavy use of crack, unlike the heavy use of tobacco, corrodes those natural sentiments of sympathy and duty that constitute our human nature and make possible our social life. To say, as does Nadelmann, that distinguishing morally between tobacco and cocaine is "little more than a transient prejudice" is close to saying that morality itself is but a prejudice.

The Alcohol Problem

Now we have arrived where many arguments about legalizing drugs begin: is there any reason to treat heroin and cocaine differently from the way we treat alcohol?

There is no easy answer to that question because, as with so many human problems, one cannot decide simply on the basis either of moral principles or of individual consequences; one has to temper any policy by a common-sense judgment of what is possible. Alcohol, like heroin, cocaine, PCP, and marijuana, is a drug—that is, a mood-altering substance—and consumed to excess it certainly has harmful consequences: auto accidents, barroom fights, bedroom shootings. It is also, for some people, addictive. We cannot confidently compare the addictive powers of these drugs, but the best evidence suggests that crack and heroin are much more addictive than alcohol.

Many people, Nadelmann included, argue that since the health and financial costs of alcohol abuse are so much higher than those of cocaine or heroin abuse, it is hypocritical folly to devote our efforts to preventing cocaine or drug use. But as Mark Kleiman of Harvard has pointed out, this comparison is quite misleading. What Nadelmann is doing is showing that a *legalized* drug (alcohol) produces greater social harm than *illegal* ones (cocaine and heroin). But of course. Suppose that in the 1920's we had made heroin and cocaine legal and alcohol illegal. Can anyone doubt that Nadelmann would now be writing that it is folly to continue our ban on alcohol because cocaine and heroin are so much more harmful? . . .

If I Am Wrong . . .

No one can know what our society would be like if we changed the law to make access to cocaine, heroin, and PCP easier. I believe, for reasons given, that the result would be a sharp increase in use, a more widespread degradation of the human personality, and a greater rate of accidents and violence.

I may be wrong. If I am, then we will needlessly have incurred heavy costs in law enforcement and some forms of criminality. But if I am right, and the legalizers prevail anyway, then we will have consigned millions of people, hundreds of thousands of infants, and hundreds of neighborhoods to a life of oblivion and disease. To the lives and families destroyed by alcohol we will have added countless more destroyed by cocaine, heroin, PCP, and whatever else a basement scientist can invent.

Human character is formed by society; indeed, human character is inconceivable without society, and good character is less likely in a bad society. Will we, in the name of an abstract doctrine of radical individualism, and with the false comfort of suspect predictions, decide to take the chance that somehow individual decency can survive amid a more general level of degradation?

I think not. The American people are too wise for that, whatever the academic essayists and cocktail-party pundits may say. But if Americans today are less wise than I suppose, then Americans at some future time will look back on us now and wonder, what kind of people were they that they could have done such a thing?

Drugs Should Be Legalized

Drug Prohibition: A Legal and Economic Analysis

Walter Block

Introduction

This paper shall argue the case for the legalization of addictive drugs such as marijuana, cocaine, and heroin. In section two the claim is defended that there are no "market failures" which could justify a banning of these substances. Section three makes this point with regard to the libertarian theory of law. In section four several objections to this thesis are explored and rejected, and section five concludes with an analysis of the benefits of legalization.

Economics

There is nothing in the tenets of value-free economics that would preclude the legalization of drugs. On the contrary, the presumption from this quarter is that a free market in marijuana, cocaine, heroin, and other such substances will enhance economic welfare.

This somewhat startling conclusion emanates from the axiomatic nature of the proposition that there are always gains from trade. Whenever any two persons engage in commercial activity—whether it be barter, or for employment, or the purchase or sale of consumer goods or intermediate products—both must gain in the *ex ante* sense. That is, neither party would agree to take part in the endeavor did he not expect to be made better off as a result of it. If I purchase a newspaper for fifty cents, I do so only because I predict that I will enjoy its perusal more than any other usage of this money; conversely, the vendor prefers the coins I give him more than the paper and ink he must give over to my possession.

The claim being made here, strictly speaking, is *not* that a free market in drugs (or anything else for that matter) will enhance economic welfare *ex post*, but rather only in the *ex ante* sense. When one views a trade *ex ante*, he does so from a time perspective before it actually takes place; he anticipates that he will benefit from it. And that is the reason he agrees to take part in it in the first place. Economic welfare from the *ex post* sense is from the perspective of after the trade occurs. For him to have gained in this regard, the participant must continue to regard himself as better off because of it.

There is indeed a strong presumption that trade benefits both partners in both senses. However it must be acknowledged that every once in a while a consumer regrets making a purchase; perhaps the price has fallen in the interim between the point of sale and the *ex post* evaluation. Or a vendor later regrets selling an item, because he now thinks it was of higher quality than he estimated when he agreed to the sale.

If this insight applies to ordinary trades, it holds no less in the case under consideration. Were I to sell to you an ounce of cocaine for $100, it must be true that at the point of sale, I value the money more than the opiate, and that you rank the two items in the inverse order. Since trade is a positive sum game, we both gain.

It cannot be denied that third parties to this arrangement will often feel themselves aggrieved. There are legions of decent citizens who are sometimes affronted when consenting adults engage in voluntary capitalist acts. Temperance leagues object to alcohol sales, health nuts are enraged at cigarette advertising, and, for all we know, there may be people who are in principle opposed to the publication, sale, and reading of newspapers. None of this, however, vitiates our original economic insight. The market, the concatenation of all voluntary trades, still enhances the welfare of all participants (Rothbard, 1977). These objectors may be participants in other market activities, but as third parties, their misgivings are simply not included in our welfare calculations.

There are several good reasons for disregarding the welfare of third parties.

First, a praxeological reason. According to the old saw, "talk is cheap, action is what counts." Any third party is free, of course, to verbally oppose any given trade. For example, feminists and conservatives oppose the sale of pornography; teetotalers argue against the purchase of intoxicants; Jews and Muslims decry markets for pork. The point is, however, that these opponents are limited in their opposition, to talk; there is no action which necessarily reveals their true assessment. At least they cannot demonstrate their preference in the manner in which the trade of the two parties to the transaction indicates a positive evaluation of the item received compared to that which is given up.

Second, a pragmatic one. In theory, *no* trade can escape this criticism. There can always be found at least one person who will object to each and every trade ever made. Dyed-in-the-wool Marxists fit this bill; they see commercial activity as necessarily exploitative. Additionally, those who favor self-sufficiency and carry this to its logical conclusion, are in principle committed to disputing the propriety of all exchanges. This applies as well to those who think that we ought to be giving each other presents instead of buying and selling to one another. However, it is rather an unfair hurdle to expect a market defense of legalized drugs to satisfy a philosophy, which can even call into question the pedestrian exchange of fifty cents for a newspaper.

Third, a reason that clarifies the claim being made in the present paper. We are not affirming that the market makes everyone on earth better off; on the contrary, it merely enriches those who take part in it. Third parties, by definition, do not, in the specific and limited contexts in which they are third parties, take part in market transactions. Therefore, no benefit accrues to them on those occasions. Our interest is not in maximizing overall welfare; merely that of market participants. Anyone of course, is free to enter the market, and offer goods or services in trade. On such occasions, their economic welfare can or will be enhanced. But the welfare of third parties qua third parties cannot be counted, since we do not contend that they will be enhanced.

Law

There are basically two kinds of law in this context: normative and positive. The latter is confined to actual legislative enactments, and judicial interpretations. Since the bottom line on this literature is that certain drugs are now illegal in the U.S., a discussion of this aspect of law would be uninteresting and unedifying.

Instead, we concentrate on the former. In particular we focus on the libertarian legal code, insofar as this is one philosophy consistent with full legalization, the position we wish to defend. In this John Locke–based perspective, man is the owner of his own body, since he, in effect, "homesteaded" it, and likewise of all parts of the natural world with which he has mixed his labor. Given that he legitimately owns these properties, he can do with them whatever he wishes, provided that he respects the equal human and property rights of all other people. Thus, a man can use his domicile for target practice, provided he keeps the bullets confined to his own premises; if ever they stray onto the property or bodies of other persons, his actions are no longer consonant with the libertarian legal code.

Under such a regime, a man can properly attain new property by any legitimate noncoercive means (Nozick, 1974): inheritance, gambling, work, and, particularly relevant to our concerns, trade. That is to say, if A homesteaded some land, and grew marijuana plants on it, and B earned some money in any other legitimate occupation, then it is entirely legitimate for B to purchase this commodity from A. Even more important, it is then proper (e.g., it *should* be legal for B) to use this item in any manner, shape, or form which does not violate the right of others to use their persons and property in a manner of their own choosing. That is to say, B is allowed under the libertarian legal code to ingest or smoke the marijuana, but not to use it as a projectile to throw at his (unwilling) neighbor.

The implication of an interference with this right of marijuana use is (partial) slavery. The problem with this "curious" institution is that the control of each of us over our own bodies is abrogated. Are we being hysterical in categorizing present drug law as a form of slavery? It is all a matter of degree; there is never total abrogation. For example, in the epoch of U.S. slavery before the close of the Civil War, slaves were denied the right to come and go as they wished, and to work for any willing employer. Rather, they were typically confined to one particular plantation, and owned by other people. However, they did have a certain limited control over their bodies: they were allowed to sleep; they were allowed to eat; they were allowed to engage in their other bodily functions.

It is no different with the prohibition of dope, except in the matter of degree. In both cases our control over our bodies is restricted. In slavery, this occurs almost but not quite totally; in the present case, the limitations concern merely the right of ingestion of illegal substances. But insofar as interference with our control over ourselves is proscribed, we are to that extent enslaved.

Objections

1. Addictive materials are physically harmful to the person who uses them. They should therefore be banned.

Given the purely economic perspective, we are entitled to deduce from the fact that a man buys narcotics the conclusion that he values them more than their cost. And that is all. It cannot be shown, as attempted by Stigler and Becker (1977) that there are "beneficial" and "harmful" addictions, according to whether or not they enhance, or detract from, the earning of income in the future. Why is it necessarily "beneficial" ("harmful") to engage in activity which promotes an upward (downward) sloping lifetime-earnings profile? Whether the individual chooses an example put forth by these authors in the former category (e.g., classical music) or in the latter (alcohol), the value-free economist cannot categorize them as beneficial or harmful. All he can conclude is that, in the view of the economic actor, at the time the decision was made, the choice of consumption, whether alcohol or Amadeus, was made in order to enhance his welfare.

If pure economic theory cannot support this distinction between "good" and "bad" addictions, even less so can it be used in behalf of the case for interdiction. For even if it could somehow be established that heroin is a harmful addictive substance, in the absence of a value judgment it by no means follows that it should be outlawed.

The paternalistic argument (bad addictive materials should be legally prohibited) undoubtedly rings true from a health point of view, in that if there were any such substances, ending their use would be a medical accomplishment. But this is irrelevant to public-policy analysis, at least from the libertarian legal perspective. There are many other things that are deleterious; for example, chocolate, ice cream, hang gliding, ice skating, boxing, fatty foods, automobile racing, fried chicken. Were we to accept this argument in the present case, logic would require that we forbid all such items, and activities. But this would surely be an infringement on self-ownership rights.

Let us now concede for the sake of argument that heroin is harmful. Even so, injury is a relative, not an absolute concept. Harmful, but compared to what? Alcohol? Tobacco? Many more people—even proportional to actual use—die of the latter two than of the former. If foreclosure is indicated, it is thus by no means clear as to which item it should be applied. Further, legal suppression does not improve, but rather exacerbates the health problem. This is because of the potency effect of prohibition: the mere existence of prohibition, and the more severely it is administered, the stronger will be the potency of the ensuing drugs. A smuggler would rather risk transporting a suitcase full of cocaine than marijuana, because of its greater value. The same phenomenon occurred with alcohol in the early part of the twentieth century: beer manufacture declined, while that for hard liquor increased. This, too, is the explanation for the most recent generation of chemical substitutes: crack, ice, PCP, etc.

If anything is harmful for human consumption, rat poison and carbon monoxide fit the bill. And yet our society has not so far legally excluded these items from commerce. There are some people who even go so far as advocate entrenching into law the right of suicide. These individuals, as in the case of the pro-choicers, are logically obligated to support repeal. For at worst addictive drugs are a (slow) form of suicide. If we do not advocate disallowing these other death aids, nor even doing away with oneself, how then can we logically proscribe substances such as heroin?

2. Addictive drugs are financially harmful to the persons other than the one who uses them. They should therefore be forbidden.

This is true, but only under a regime of socialized medicine. There, we are indeed each "our brother's keepers." If you overeat, and contract heart disease, I, along with everyone else, am forced to pay for it. If I smoke cigarettes and fall victim to cancer, you, and all other citizens, must foot the bill. We therefore each have a clear and focused interest in the health habits of everyone else. The individual is a "clear and present" financial danger to the group. In such a situation, there certainly is a case for the injunction of addictive material: the rest of us can save money if we can reduce the incidence of use.

But why accept this context as a fact of nature? Coercive medical insurance schemes have many shortcomings, not the least of which is the problem of moral hazard, which encourages all parties to overuse scarce health services since they are priced at subsidized costs. Given a free market in medicine, this reason for restraint of drug markets all but vanishes.

Further, alcohol and tobacco, as we have seen, are far more harmful than addictive drugs. To the extent that this objection has any merit, we should first enact legislation against the former, and only then prohibit the latter.

In contrast, this Hobbesian war of each of us against the other does not occur under a market regime. There, it is to the financial interest of private medical insurance companies to set prices which reflect the best estimated risk of future healthcare needs. For example, if a person smokes, or drinks, or engages in any number of dangerous activities such as chocolate, ice cream, hang gliding, ice skating, boxing, fatty foods, etc., their insurance premiums will tend to take this into account. In equilibrium, the risk of these dangers will be fully incorporated, no more, no less: the charges cannot be any higher than the levels predicted by these activities due to competition from other firms; they will not be any lower, since bankruptcy will eliminate such practices.

But what of the objection that insurance companies do not currently charge lower rates to non-alcoholics? There are several replies to this. First of all, we do not at present have an insurance industry based fully on free-market principles. There are simply too many barriers to entry—regulations, prohibitions against foreign carriers in the local market, domestic entry restrictions—for that. Were there no barriers to entry, and if it were profitable for companies to discriminate against alcoholics, the presumption is that this is precisely what would occur. Secondly, ill health is now dealt with by the courts as a handicap, and handicap is now in the process of becoming a status against which it is illegal to discriminate. If alcohol is interpreted as more of a protected handicap than tobacco, due, perhaps, to secondary effects, this may explain why insurance companies are loath to apply their cigarette policy to liquor. If there were absolutely no law against discrimination, insurance companies would likely be able to ensure that one person need not subsidize another's indulging in chocolate or fatty-food consumption: they could measure the blood pressure, height and weight, etc., of their clients. They could subject them to other medical tests: heart-beat rate after five minutes on a treadmill. They could ask them to sign a statement attesting to the fact that they do not engage in activities such as skiing or hang gliding: violations would annul insurance coverage. Needless to say, any such market responses (which would tend to make our lives safer) would be severely dealt with by the courts (Epstein, 1992).

3. Addictive drugs promote crime, and should therefore be banished.

This is perhaps the weakest objection of all so far, in that it is the suppression of narcotics that leads to criminal behavior, not these substances themselves.

If left to the market, the prices of heroin, cocaine, marijuana, and all the rest would be exceedingly modest. After all, they are based for the most part on very hardy plants, which cost little to harvest and process. The reason they are so expensive at present is because of their legal status: it is highly risky to bring them to market. The high prices they can fetch, however, create vast profits. These attract people whose adherence to the niceties of the law are less than totally thorough.

Crime comes about in three ways based on this scenario. First, the farmers, refiners, transporters, street vendors, etc., involved in the practice are per se considered criminals, since they break the law. But this is not "real crime," since there are no victims of these commercial interactions; all the way from planting the seed to final consumption there are only willing participants involved.

Second, because of the exorbitant costs of the drugs, addicts must resort to crime (burglaries, auto theft, assault and battery, etc.) in order to obtain the funds necessary to feed their habits. Here, there is at last real crime, since the victims by no stretch of the imagination can be considered to have given their permission to the burglar.

Third, there are those who pay the ultimate penalty as a result of gun battles in the streets between different gangs contending for turf. These "mushrooms" are also entirely innocent, and lose their lives not because of drugs in and of themselves, but rather due to the law. This is because it is not possible for an aggrieved drug gang member to utilize the courts and police; rather, he must "take the law into his own hands." A similar situation occurred during the epoch of alcohol prohibitionism, and the same people then as now are ultimately responsible for the deaths of the innocents: the legislators who enacted the law, and the police and jurists who administer it.

Despite the foregoing, there are claims to the effect that narcotic usage creates crime in a very different way: by turning the addict into a crazed, enraged lunatic, uncontrollable in his lust to lay waste to the countryside, and all who reside in it. This "Godzilla" effect is entirely erroneous when applied to the traditional opiates. There are three bits of evidence which can be adduced in behalf of this claim. One is the British experience with legalization, where doctors in hospitals would not start newcomers out on this path, but would administer the drug to confirmed addicts. The finding from this source (Judson, 1974) is that the recipients of this medication were able to lead normal lives without any extraordinary involvement in criminal activity. Second are the opium dens of Chinese origin.

The denizens of these establishments, too, were not given over to violence; if anything, the very opposite was the case. This substance induced lethargy, if anything. And third is the example of the one segment of U.S. society which now has almost full access to such material at cut-rate prices: physicians. Experience has failed to show enraged, antisocial behavior as a result.

However, let us consider the contrary-to-fact-conditional. That is, let us assume, if only for the sake of argument, that there is indeed an addictive (or even non-addictive) "Godzilla" drug. Should it be prohibited? The answer, at least from the realms of value-free economics and the libertarian legal code, is no. From the former perspective, we must still deduce from the sale of this product that both parties gained economic welfare in the *ex ante* sense. From the latter, it is still unjustified to initiate violence against non-initiators, and the imbiber of "Godzilla" will, by stipulation, not begin his crazed rantings, ravings, and waves of murder until at least a few seconds after ingestion. Thus, there is no case for prior restraint on these grounds. It would not be unreasonable, however, for the forces of law and order to carefully monitor such people. Then, as the early stages of this mania begin to take effect (pounding on the chest, drooling, snapping of teeth, whatever) the police can subject him to the fullest penalties of the "real" criminal law as soon as he makes even a slight aggressive move in the direction of a victim. There might be some slight risk of criminal behavior under these circumstances, but it would be far less than in the present situation, where public policy truly unleashes the whirlwind.

A few words of clarification on this matter.

At what point would it be all right for officers of the law to intervene? They could do so as soon as there were any indication whatsoever that the person taking this drug were about to go on a rampage. In the extreme case, if we knew with absolute certainty that the Godzilla pill leads necessarily to mayhem (we can never know this, since it is an empirical matter) it would be justified for the police to open fire on the person as soon as ingestion took place. Just as the police may fire at a gunman in order to protect innocent victims long before his bullet has left the pistol chamber, so may they act against "Godzilla" before he actually commits violence.

The only difference between the system of legalized drugs advocated in this paper and the present legal regime would be in the motivation of the forces of law and order. They would be executing a murderer, not a drug taker; they would be killing a person not because he took drugs, but because he was about to commit murder, and in order to prevent him from so doing. This might not matter, much, to the user of the Godzilla drug, but this places in stark contrast the difference between prohibition of drugs and prohibition of murder.

We wouldn't hesitate to impose prior constraint to prevent people from swallowing a nuclear bomb. But cannot the Godzilla pill be looked upon akin to a thermonuclear device? No, there is a relevant difference. If a nuclear device blows up, it is beyond the power of the police, or anyone else, to prevent harm to innocent persons. In contrast, if a person swallows the Godzilla pill, the forces of law and order will be able to stop him in his tracks the moment he gives any indication on incipient violence. At most, then, this analysis can support a law calling on purveyors of the Godzilla pill to notify the police of an upcoming sale; it cannot justify prohibition. With the bomb, things are very different; the clear and present danger it constitutes (to say nothing of the fact that it is intrinsically an offensive weapon and should be prohibited on that ground alone) provides reason for its proscription.

Of course, if the Godzilla pill makes the person who takes it all but omnipotent, as well as murderous, then and only then is there a case for prohibition. But in this scenario, Godzilla has left the realm of (addictive?) drugs and entered that of atom bombs.

4. If narcotics are legalized, they will gain an imprimatur from the state. Their present legal status should therefore be preserved.

The problem with this objection is that legalization does not imply sanction. If it did, extant law with regard to tobacco, alcohol, and gambling would suggest that the government favored these goods and services. And yet they are usually subjected to extra taxes, e.g., "sin" taxes. As well, there are many other disreputable activities which are nonetheless legal, at least at present. For example, lying, gossiping, disloyalty to employers, jilting fiancees right at the altar, disrespect to parents, nose picking, cheating at solitaire, not keeping one's lawn trimmed, cutting corners, not taking regular baths, breaking promises to children. If it were true that a failure to legally interdict these activities is reducible to approval of them, then our society, insofar as it does not fine or imprison perpetrators, actually recommends and esteems them. Needless to say, nothing could be further from the truth.

5. The elasticity of demand for narcotics is very high. Small reductions in price will call forth large increases in demand. The gigantic fall in price likely to emerge with legalization would create a stupendously gigantic elevation in use. Were these agents to be legalized, the whole society would become drugged out of its gourd.

Although posed in a rather exaggerated form, this objection is a very powerful one indeed. Even ardent advocates of repeal such as Friedman (1989) would change their position on the issue were this elasticity claim to be proven correct. Fortunately for the position taken in this chapter, however, the evidence suggests that the elasticity is likely to be far lower than that depicted in the doomsday scenario. Why?

First of all, the elasticity for drugs in general is very low. This is because such items are usually seen by their consumers as necessities, not luxuries. While one might severely reduce demand for the latter in the face of an increased price, or even give it up entirely in the extreme, this does not apply to the former. But if such behavior is characteristic of most drugs, it applies even more so in the case of addictive substances. For at least in the mind of the addict, these are the most difficult of all from which to refrain.

Secondly, the effect of legalization—in markedly reducing profits—will be to greatly decrease the incentive for "pushing." No longer will it pay for addicts to go to schoolyards, offering free samples, in an attempt to "hook" children into a life of addiction in order to support their own habits. With a free market, where these products will be exceedingly cheap, there will be no temptation to resort to these extraordinary means of salesmanship.

Third, even if quantity increases, potency will fall, as we have seen above. Given this effect, a greater amount of total drugs may be less harmful to the population than what is presently consumed, as heroin and cocaine begin to take the place of the more deleterious chemical derivatives, and as marijuana begins to replace those two.

Given this wealth of evidence, we must conclude that it is extremely unlikely that elasticity will prove very high at all. A much more reasonable expectation is that when prices fall due to legalization, quantity will not increase much if at all.

We must, however, squarely face the Armageddon scenario. Suppose for argument's sake that evidence to the contrary notwithstanding, what will really happen upon repeal is accurately portrayed by the exaggerated fears of the objection under consideration. Assume, for instance, that 75 percent of the population, just to pick a number out of a hat, were to become addicted. We still maintain that there is again nothing in the realm of positive economics, nor of normative libertarian political theory, that can serve as the basis for prohibition. It will still be true that all parties concerned will gain, in their own subjective estimates, from their participation in the drug market. It will still be true that the industry will be a totally voluntary one, with no one forced to take part. Hence, libertarian theory still proscribes interdiction. To be sure, G.N.P. will not be as high under such a regime, at least at the outset; but this calculation is a very imperfect estimator of economic welfare, which will be maximized by allowing people to freely choose their consumption patterns. In any case, for those inordinately fond of G.N.P. calculations, there is a consolation. If addiction really is the killer feared by some, the likelihood is that in the long term G.N.P. will rise at least on a per-capita basis, as the death by slow suicide of the addicts raises the average productivity of those who remain.

Advantages

1. Decrease in crime

As legalization takes the vast profits out of the drug business, the incentives toward criminality will tend to disappear *pari passu*. And this is no accident, since the one stems from the other. According to some estimates (Trebach, 1978), this factor alone accounts for some 50 percent of crime in urban America. In addition, with fewer criminals, there will be less overcrowding of prisons; expenditures in this direction will fall. Another saving will be in terms of the monies now expended on crime prevention. Less money will have to be wasted on locksmiths, burglar alarms, gated communities, and fewer ulcers will be generated due to fear and worry about crime.

This point highlights the reason for the difficulty of "fighting the War on Drugs." Every time a battle is won in this "war," paradoxically, the enemy is strengthened, not weakened. If one ton of cocaine is seized, the price of this commodity increases; but this subsequent higher value only succeeds in raising the profit incentives attendant upon production. Thus, the more vigorous and successful the activities of the Drug Enforcement Agency, the greater the strength of the illicit drug industry. The way to "win" the war is not by fighting the alligators, but by draining the swamp. As jurists and law enforcement agents in South American and Asian countries have long known, and as their counterparts in the U.S. are in the process of ascertaining for themselves, these alligators, the drug gangs, have very sharp teeth indeed. Better to ruin their business by deflating the profit balloon than by acting in a way (prohibition) which only supports them. The present drug war is so far from being won that the authorities cannot even stop their spread in prisons, where civil liberties niceties do not play any nugatory role, and their control is as total as it will ever be in any sector of society (Thornton, 1991).

2. Better health protection

If even a small part of the money now fruitlessly spent on banning narcotics were instead allocated to the *medical* problem of curing people of the malady of drug addiction, the average level of health in this country would be vastly improved. *This* battle is a winnable one, as shown by the great strides made recently in fighting the depredations of alcohol and tobacco. The lowered use of these commodities, especially in the upper classes, which usually set consumption patterns for the rest of society, is a pattern which can and must be emulated for narcotics.

In addition, there is the problem of AIDS. Drug prohibition plays its part in the tragic spread of this dreaded disease because of shared needles. Like so much else, this is a result of the outlawry, not of the narcotics themselves, as can be seen from the fact that insulin addicts (diabetics, that is) need never resort to shared needles. On the contrary, they can avail themselves of the finest medical care that our society can offer. Were we to reverse matters, that is, legalize narcotics but prohibit insulin, there is no doubt that the results would be reversed as well. Crazed and enraged insulin junkies would then commit crimes and spread AIDS through shared needles, while heroin addicts would lead relatively calm and unthreatened lives.

The health of addicts would moreover improve. Lenny Bruce died not from an overdose of heroin, but from impurities in the sample with which he injected himself. This is the modern equivalent of "bathtub gin." If Squibb, Pfizer, Upjohn, Ciba-Giegy, Glaxo, Merck, and their ilk were in charge of production instead of a bunch of fly-by-night outfits, there is little doubt that the quality-control safeguards would be immeasurably enhanced. Suppose you were about to die and had a child addicted to narcotics. Would you prefer a situation where he had to run around like a half-crazed wretch, doing all sorts of unspeakable things in order to raise the requisite funds for his habit, never knowing where his next fix was coming from, nor what would be in it, or one where he could be given an injection in safe, comfortable, clean hospital surroundings, under the care of a physician?

3. Civil liberties

Because drug sales are a victimless crime, the police labor under a disadvantage compared to auto theft, rape, assault, arson, etc. There is no formal complainant. Therefore, if they want to solve the "crime," they must often resort to tactics and techniques which would otherwise prove unnecessary and repugnant. This is why they ride roughshod over civil liberties in a way that occurs with regard to few if any other crimes. As a result, we have witnessed teen curfews; "zero tolerance," where boats and automobiles have been seized upon the finding of minuscule amounts of marijuana; strip searches; National Guard patrols on our city streets; and legal prosecutions for the parents of teen addicts. Political leaders have gone so far as to advocate flogging, cutting off a finger for each drug conviction, the death penalty, and sending the U.S. military to foreign countries to interdict supplies. The civilized world was properly outraged by the shooting down by the Russians of the Korean Airlines commercial jet which strayed from its flight path; what are we to make in this context of the suggestion of Customs Commissioner William von Raab (Bandow, 1989) that planes suspected of carrying illegal drugs should be shot out of the sky?

As well, drug legalization—of possession, use, sale, transport, "trafficking," merchandising, advertising, etc.—is a litmus test for the philosophy of civil liberties. One can hardly be a civil libertarian and favor prohibitionism. Advocacy of legalization, or at least decriminalization, is a necessary albeit not sufficient condition for a civil libertarian.

NOTES

Nothing in this article should be taken as an indication that the present author favors the use of the drugs discussed herein. Actually, the very opposite is the case. While he opposes prohibition, he advocates all noncoercive methods—arguments, counseling, advertising, etc.—which lead to decreased or zero usage of these pernicious and immoral materials and substances.

References

Gary Anderson and Walter Block, "The Economics and Ethics of Paternalism: A Reply to George Akerloff," mimeo, 1992.

Doug Bandow, "Once Again, a Drug-War Panic," *Chicago Tribune,* March 22, 1989.

Walter Block, *Defending the Undefendable,* New York: Laissez-Faire Books, (1976) 1991.

Walter Block, *The U.S. Bishops and Their Critics: An Economic and Ethical Perspective* (Vancouver: The Fraser Institute, 1986).

David Boaz, ed., *The Crisis in Drug Prohibition* (Washington, DC: The Cato Institute, 1990).

Richard Epstein, *Forbidden Grounds* (Cambridge: Harvard University Press, 1992).

Milton Friedman, "An Open Letter to Bill Bennett," *Wall Street Journal,* September 7, 1989.

Ron Hamowy, ed., *Dealing with Drugs: Consequences of Government Control* (San Francisco: The Pacific Institute, 1987).

Hans Hermann Hoppe, *A Theory of Socialism and Capitalism* (Boston: Kluwer, 1989).

Horace F. Judson, *Heroin Addiction in Britain* (New York: Harcourt Brace Jovanovich, 1974).

Robert Nozick, *Anarchy, State and Utopia* (New York: Basic Books, 1974).

Murray N. Rothbard, *For a New Liberty* (Macmillan: New York, 1973).

Murray N. Rothbard, *The Ethics of Liberty* (Humanities Press: Atlantic Highlands, N.J., 1982).

Murray N. Rothbard, "Toward a Reconstruction of Utility and Welfare Economics" (San Francisco: Center for Libertarian Studies, Occasional Paper #3, 1977).

George Stigler and Gary Becker, "De Gustibus Non Est Disputandum," *American Economic Review* 67 (March), pp. 76–90.

Thomas Szasz, *Ceremonial Chemistry: The Ritual Persecution of Drugs, Addicts and Push-*

ers, rev. ed. (Holmes Beach, FL: Learning Publications, 1985).

Mark Thornton, *The Economics of Prohibition* (Salt Lake City: University of Utah Press, 1991).

Arnold Trebach, "The Potential Impact of 'Legal' Heroin in America," in *Drugs, Crime and Politics,* Arnold Trebach, ed. (New York: Praeger, 1978).

DRUGS AND PUBLIC HEALTH

Drug Prohibition: A Public-Health Perspective

Bonnie Steinbock

The Drug Problem

It is estimated that over six million Americans are heavy drug users.[1] Between 1986 and 1988, the number of cocaine addicts in New York City more than tripled, with an estimated total of 600,000 in 1988, most addicted to crack.[2] Although middle-class cocaine use in the United States as a whole is on the decline — it has dropped 22 percent since 1988 — Federal officials say that 6.4 million Americans used cocaine last year. In the poorest neighborhoods, cocaine smoking and snorting is on the rise, and a flood of potent heroin is creating new addicts.[3] Drug abuse has caused problems for individuals, families, and society as a whole for years, but the introduction of crack cocaine has made things much worse. Let me mention just a few of the effects attributed to crack in New York City.

- Drug-related crime is far worse than it was twenty years ago. From 1987 to 1988, the number of murders in New York rose 10.4 percent. Police say that drugs, in particular, crack, played a role in at least 38 percent of the 1,867 murders in 1988, compared with generally constant rate of 20 percent for years.

- Crack contributed to a tripling of cases in which parents under the influence of drugs abused or neglected their children. In 1987, 73 percent of the deaths in abuse and neglect cases resulted from parents abusing drugs, up from 11 percent in 1985.[4]

- Between 1986 and 1988, the number of newborn children in New York City testing positive for drugs—mostly cocaine—almost quadrupled, going from 1,325 to 5,088. Because of crack, in some inner-city hospitals, the number of babies going directly from the hospital into foster homes has risen from 2 percent to 15 percent.[5] Urban child-welfare workers estimate that 70 percent of children they see are raised by grandmothers or other relatives after parents abandon them for drugs.[6]

The impact of the crack epidemic on children is perhaps the most heartrending aspect of the drug problem. Other effects of crack, such as the tremendous increase in the prison population — up from 9,815 in New York City in 1985 to over 17,500 in 1989 — can be laid to the fact that crack is *illegal*. Legalize addictive drugs, and drug arrests (1.2 million a year in the United

States), which are overwhelming the criminal justice system, causing overcrowding in the prisons, and costing billions of dollars, would disappear. Moreover, according to Ira Glasser, Executive Director of the American Civil Liberties Union (ACLU) and a proponent of legalization, three-quarters of "drug-related" homicides are caused by territorial disputes and other incidents relating to the criminal trafficking system. "Only 7.5 percent of the homicides were related to the effects of the drug itself, and two-thirds of those involved alcohol, not crack."[7]

By contrast, the effects of crack on children, both pre- and postnatally, will not be diminished by legalization. Dr. Linda A. Randolph, director of the State Office of Public Health, says that, because of drug abuse, particularly crack, "we are seeing dramatic increases in infant mortality, in congenital syphilis, and in the number of AIDS-infected women who are giving birth."[8] Intensive hospital care for *each* crack baby costs about $90,000. That translates into $2.5 billion annually for the nation.

Crack can have devastating effects on the nervous systems of newborns. T. Berry Brazelton describes the clinical manifestations this way:

> They are either limp and unresponsive or are hyper-sensitive and behave chaotically. They have difficulty receiving and responding to the stimuli of a soothing voice or face. When they are cuddled or rocked, they react with piercing wails and jerky motions. Few people could love these babies. They are likely to suffer later from learning disabilities and to be either hyperactive or emotionally flat. They also tend to be at the mercy of their impulses. The social programs required to educate them will cost billions of dollars.[9]

It should be noted that, although crack is ingested during pregnancy, the harmful effects are imposed on the newborn, the infant, and even the older child. The pregnant crack addict does not risk harm only to herself, but also to the baby she will bear, if she decides not to abort. The term "fetal abuse," often used to describe the use of drugs during pregnancy, is something of a misnomer, since the damage is not confined to the fetus, but is done also to the born child. However one views the fetus, born children have full legal rights, including the right not to be injured prior to live birth.[10] That is why there is no logical contradiction in supporting the right to abortion and maintaining that women have an obligation not to harm their not-yet-born children through ingestion of drugs during pregnancy.[11]

While there is debate among the experts about how bad and long-lasting the physical damage is to children born to crack users, there is agreement that these babies are especially susceptible to child abuse. They suffer from neglect because, as one article put it, ". . . people who hardly bother with food for themselves can't be expected to give up precious crack to feed a baby, can they?"[12] And they are at risk for child abuse because their screaming and nonresponsiveness make them unattractive and difficult to care for. As Brazelton asks, "What would an addicted parent in an addicted environment do to such a baby? The ingredients for child abuse were all there."[13]

The Libertarian Approach

Even this brief recounting indicates a major social problem, something with which society is entitled—even obligated—to concern itself. Yet the libertarian perspective offered by Professor Block suggests otherwise. He holds that people gain when they are able freely to buy the drugs they want. And if both parties gain, what possible justification can there be for interfering with the liberty of the parties to trade? Block's advocacy for the legalization of addictive drugs follows from "the axiomatic nature of gains from trade":

> Whenever any two persons engage in commercial activity—whether it be barter, or for employment, or the purchase or sale of consumer goods or intermediate products—both must gain in the *ex ante* sense. That is, neither party would agree to take part in the endeavor did he not expect to be made better off as a result of it. . . . If this insight applies to ordinary trades, it holds no less in the case under consideration. Were I to sell to you an ounce of cocaine for $100, it must be true that at the point of sale, I value the money more than the opiate, and that you rank the two items in the inverse order. Since trade is a positive sum game, we both gain. (pp. 199–200; all references to Block are to his essay in this volume.)

Block is aware that "third parties" may feel affronted when consenting adults engage in voluntary capitalist acts, but so what? "The market, the concatenation of all voluntary trades, still enhances the *welfare of all participants*."

Strictly speaking, the claim is merely that a free market (in drugs or anything else) enhances welfare only in the *ex ante*, not in the *ex post*, sense. Block maintains that there is a strong presumption that trade benefits both partners in both senses, although he concedes, somewhat grudgingly, that "every once in a while a consumer regrets making a purchase" and therefore does not benefit in the *ex post* sense. However, it is benefit in the *ex post* sense that is essential for his argument, for the argument in favor of a free market is premised on the notion that, in such a market, everyone actually benefits, and not merely expects to benefit. Since everyone benefits, there is no justification for intervention. However, we cannot assume that people will gain when they expect to gain, without making further assumptions. One

important assumption is that the buyer has adequate and truthful information about the item purchased. Unfortunately, sellers do not always provide such information; sometimes they even make false claims. Trades made under these conditions are neither voluntary nor fair. Intervention in the free market to assure that consumers have the information they need to make rational and voluntary purchases is entirely justified. It is for this reason that we have such agencies as the Better Business Bureau and the Food and Drug Administration (FDA), and laws requiring "truth in advertising." Even libertarians should welcome such laws, as the constraints they place on manufactures ensure that capitalist acts are genuinely voluntary.

The FDA goes beyond laws requiring "truth in advertising." It has the power to prevent drugs that have not been shown to be effective or that are harmful from being put on the market. From a libertarian perspective, this is unjustifiable. So long as people have the information they need to make a voluntary choice, their choices should be unconstrained. However, we may question the plausibility of the libertarian view. Most people acknowledge that they have neither the knowledge to make judgments about the safety or efficacy of medications nor the time to research the issues. Most of us are willing to sacrifice the liberty to buy useless or dangerous medications in return for increased safety.[14]

Absence of knowledge is only one factor that prevents trade from being a positive sum game. Another is coercion. If one is forced to trade ("Your money or your life"), then one does not gain, even in the *ex ante* sense. How does this relate to the sale of narcotics? Some drugs, such as crack cocaine, are highly addictive. The choices of addicts are not fully voluntary, perhaps not voluntary at all. They are constrained, comparable to the "choice" of a person who has a gun to his head. However persuasive the economic analysis may be in the case of voluntary transactions, it is of limited application in the case of addictive drugs. For these reasons, economic axioms about commercial activity do not support non-intervention into the drug market (legalization).

However, the economic analysis is only part of Block's argument. In addition, he espouses a libertarian philosophy that regards the value of individual liberty higher than any other value. The libertarian principle can be traced back to John Stuart Mill, who argued in *On Liberty* that the only purpose for which it was permissible to restrict individual freedom was to prevent harm to others. A person's own good was never sufficient warrant. Mill's principle has been applied in all sorts of ways: from opposition of seatbelt and helmet laws to opposition to closing gay bathhouses in an effort to stop the spread of AIDS.[15]

Mill attempted to defend his absolute prohibition against paternalistic intervention on utilitarian grounds, but this has been notoriously unsuccessful. There is no reason to think that the harm of paternalistic intervention will necessarily outweigh the benefit to be attained. Philosopher Gerald Dworkin persuasively argues that it was not utilitarian calculation that led Mill to his absolute rejection of paternalism, but rather a non-contingent, non-utilitarian argument about what it means to be a person, an autonomous agent. Dworkin says, "It is because coercing a person for his own good denies this status as an independent entity that Mill objects to it so strongly and in such absolute terms."[16] Dworkin goes on to argue that some paternalistic intervention can be justified, even on Millian grounds, namely, restrictions that preserve a wider range of freedom for the individual in question.

The Public-Health Approach

Whereas Dworkin can be seen as attempting to justify very limited paternalistic measures, within a Millian perspective, Dan Beauchamp, a professor of public health, is a more outright critic of Mill. Beauchamp notes that some restrictions on individual liberty result in considerable social gain. Consider the example of seat belts. Each year roughly forty-five thousand people in the United States are killed in car crashes. Laws requiring the wearing of seat belts or making air bags compulsory would save roughly ten thousand lives a year. That's a lot of lives, a considerable social good. Libertarians object to seat-belt laws as being objectionably paternalistic. Why shouldn't I decide for myself whether to buckle up? Refusing to buckle up doesn't cause "harm to others" and so laws forcing people to use seat belts are not warranted on Millian grounds. But Beauchamp argues that, since the infringement on individual freedom is minuscule, and the social good so great, the intrusion is warranted. He supports "reasonable, minimally intrusive restrictions that yield significant gains in the health and safety of the public."[17]

I think that Beauchamp's public-health approach is far more useful in thinking about the legalization of drugs than the libertarian approach.[18] The libertarian insists that there isn't a drug problem, since trade is a positive sum game, and both parties gain. No one who has any experience with drug abuse and the social upheaval it has caused will agree with that conclusion. Instead of insisting, on ideological grounds, that individuals should have the right to buy whatever they want, regardless of the social costs, we should examine carefully the costs of prohibition and the costs of legalization. This means that the argument about legalization is not primarily a philosophical one. Rather, it is an empirical argument about the likely consequences of different strategies for dealing with the drug problem.

While the public-health approach rejects Mill's absolutist antipaternalism, it entirely agrees with Mill on one thing: the rejection of moralism. Mill argued that legal or social prohibitions on behavior could never be justified simply on the ground that the behavior in question was regarded by the majority as wicked or sinful. He insisted that infringements on individual liberty have to be justified by demonstrating that the conduct in question was likely to cause harm to others.

Of course it is not always easy to settle the question of whether an activity will cause harm to others: the example of violent pornography is a case in point. However, the rejection of moralism at least makes it clear what *kind* of argument is necessary to support coercive intervention. Empirical evidence of injury or the risk of injury is essential. Simply referring to moral principles, no matter how widely accepted, or moral feelings, no matter how strongly held, will not do. Someone who takes a public-health perspective may be willing to consider closing gay bathhouses *if* it is reasonable to think that this will slow the spread of a deadly disease, but will not be willing to infringe on individual liberty because the activities in such places are viewed by many as nasty or evil.

Why does the public-health perspective reject moralism? After all, if it is willing to acknowledge collective or communal values, such as health, why not acknowledge that there can be collective or communal *moral* values? Indeed, aren't free speech, equal opportunity, and the democratic process, which are essential to a democratic republic, *moral* values? Of course. The rejection of moralism does not consist in rejection of or neutrality toward all moral values. Rather, the rejection of moralism consists in opposition to coercion (as opposed to education and persuasion) to eradicate sin and vice or to make individuals morally better.

It might be objected that a public-health approach is based on a false distinction between different kinds of values. On a public-health approach, some government coercion is acceptable for the sake of certain values (for example, those connected to public health) but not others (for example, those related to private sexual behavior). A libertarian might argue that if it is permissible to infringe individual liberty for the sake of social goals, there is no principled reason for insisting that the goals to be achieved must be of a certain kind. If the majority in a society thinks that homosexuality is bad for society, then why shouldn't it pass laws against homosexuality? What justifies coercion for some social goals, but not others?[19] The answer has to do with a certain conception of the common good. The common good should not be understood in terms of whatever the majority values or wants. Such a conception would indeed threaten individual liberty through, in Mill's phrase, "the tyranny of the majority." Rather, I suggest that we think of the common good in terms of what Rawls calls "primary goods": "things which it is supposed a rational man wants whatever else he wants."[20] Health is an example of a primary good. By restricting our conception of the common good to primary goods, we avoid imposing goals and values on individuals that they do not happen to share. However, it may be objected that, even if it is true that everyone has reason to value his or her own health, it does not follow that everyone has reason to value the health of the community. (This was the mistake that Mill is supposed to have made in his proof of the principle of utility.) What if I am not interested in saving ten thousand lives a year? What justifies forcing me to buckle up?

I am not sure that it can be demonstrated that not caring about aggregate welfare or the good of society as a whole is *irrational*. However, the communitarian or republican morality of "We're all in this together" seems to me infinitely preferable to the extreme individualism which is concerned only with individuals' interests and rights. Republican morality balances individual virtues like self-reliance and individual responsibility against community virtues like beneficence, cooperation, and justice. As Dan Beauchamp puts it:

> Beneficence means that we wish the good and welfare of others as well as ourselves, while cooperation and justice mean that we as citizens are disposed to see that the common welfare is extended to all alike and do not allow our private interests to frustrate achievement of the common good. While the principles of individuality and community can often pull in opposite directions, both principles are needed to assure the fullest development of the individual and his dignity both as an autonomous person and as a member of the political fellowship.[21]

Recognition that there is a common good, as well as the separate welfares of individuals, does not preclude controversy over its nature. Moreover, even when individuals acknowledge a collective good, such as disease prevention, they may differ as to its importance relative to other collective goods. A public-health approach does not demand that we value life and health above all else. It merely supports minimally intrusive restrictions on individual liberty to promote the common good.

A related objection holds that even if it is possible to differentiate among social goods, so that infringement of individual liberty is restricted to primary collective goods, such as health, there is still a danger of imposing majoritarian moral views on individuals, because there is no morally neutral way to characterize even basic goods.

All people may want to be healthy, but one's conception of health depends on one's particular moral or religious views. Whether one regards drug use, for example, as "unhealthy" depends on one's views about the body, altered consciousness, pleasure, industriousness, and, in general, the right way to live. It is this inability to characterize, in an objective fashion, basic goods that leads the libertarian to maintain that the assessment about what is worth pursuing should be left to individuals.

I think we can agree that there is an overlap between health and morality without conceding that it is impossible to distinguish the two. Individuals from widely divergent religious and moral backgrounds can agree on whether someone is sick, what disease he or she has, and whether something is a health risk. This suggests that there is a difference between health and morals, which makes it possible, in general, to distinguish arguments and reasons based on health considerations from those based on moral and religious values.

It must be admitted that much of American drug policy has been drenched in moralism. This moralistic attitude is revealed both in regarding addiction as a failure of willpower ("Just say no") and in wildly exaggerated descriptions of the effects of addiction. Here is a description of the effects of heroin from a concurring opinion by Justice Douglas in a 1962 United States Supreme Court decision:

> To be a confirmed drug addict is to be one of the walking dead. . . . The teeth have rotted out; the appetite is lost and the stomach and intestines don't function properly. The gall bladder becomes inflamed; eyes and skin turn a bilious yellow. In some cases membranes of the nose turn a flaming red; the partition separating the nostrils is eaten away—breathing is difficult. Oxygen in the blood decreases; bronchitis and tuberculosis develop. Good traits of character disappear

and bad ones emerge. Sex organs become affected. Veins collapse and livid purplish scars remain. Boils and abscesses plague the skin; gnawing pain racks the body. Nerves snap; vicious twitching develops. Imaginary and fantastic fears blight the mind and sometimes complete insanity results. Often times, too, death comes—much too early in life. . . . Such is the torment of being a drug addict; such is the plague of being one of the walking dead.[22]

Similar lies were propagated about LSD in various newspaper stories, and about marijuana in such films as *Reefer Madness*. The effect, ironically enough, was to persuade a generation that any warnings about drug usage were likely to be completely untrustworthy.

Moralism about drugs is often coupled with hypocrisy about legal drugs. Schoolchildren are taught about the evils of illicit drugs, but the dangers of legal drugs are downplayed or ignored. A recent ad on television depicts a father confronting his child with marijuana found in his room, asking, "Who taught you to do this?" only to be told, "You did, Dad!" The announcer solemnly intones, "Parents who use drugs will have children who use drugs." Yet we don't see ads warning, "Parents who smoke and drink will have children who smoke and drink," despite the fact—as Professor Block notes—that far more people die from cigarettes and alcohol than from illegal drugs.

A public-health approach is pragmatic and non-ideological. It rejects moralism, and insists on sound empirical evidence for its claims. It recognizes the values of liberty and privacy, and supports the right of people to make their own choices about how they will live, free from governmental interference. At the same time, it recognizes that private acts can have social consequences.[23] Thus, a public-health approach balances the harm to individuals of coercive laws against the social good to be achieved. It is willing to sacrifice some individual liberty in order to achieve important collective goals, such as the saving of thousands of lives or the eradication of disease.

Implications for Drug Policy

The Failure of the War on Drugs

There is wide consensus on one thing: the penal approach to the drug problem has been a dismal failure. The United States has poured nearly $70 billion into fighting drugs in the last twenty years,[24] with very little to show for it. The reasons for the failure of the War on Drugs are primarily economic. Illicit drugs are big business. Seventy-nine billion dollars are generated every year by the sale of illicit drugs.[25] Only the Exxon Corporation has higher annual revenues.

In many less-developed countries, drug trafficking, which has provided a new way to earn vast sums of hard currency, is transforming whole economies. In poor Third World countries, coca is one of the few cash crops that grows well, much better than coffee or oranges. In Colombia, Bolivia, and Peru, many farmers have turned from growing food crops to growing marijuana and coca, which make them three or four times as much money a year.[26] In Bolivia, cocaine is estimated to generate as much as ten times the amount of Bolivia's leading official export, tin. Drug traffickers are at least as powerful as the government. They have more money than—and weapons and equipment as least as good as—the armed forces or the police. Moreover, drug traffickers are regarded by much of the populace as benefactors, not criminals. Even with the best will in the world, the government can do little to enforce laws that run counter to the vital economic interests of large numbers of its citizens.

And that will is not always present. Mathea Falco, former Assistant Secretary of State for International Narcotics Matters, writes:

> It is very difficult to convince a foreign government to take the serious political and economic risks that are entailed by an all-out campaign against, say, cocaine production when the American public's predilection for cocaine is so well known. And it is virtually impossible to persuade foreign growers of marijuana to stop producing when one American in four has tried the drug—and billions of dollars in profits are being made by marijuana growers in the United States.[27]

Occasionally, the U.S. government has been able to solicit the cooperation of foreign governments to stop production, but often with unexpected results. In 1975, the Mexican government, with American assistance, began a program to eliminate the marijuana crop by spraying it with paraquat. Mexico, then a major supplier to the U.S. market of relatively cheap, low-potency marijuana, effectively destroyed much of the crop. Jamaica and Colombia, previously only minor suppliers of marijuana, quickly stepped up production, producing a plant of much higher potency. In addition, American domestic production of marijuana began to boom. Marijuana is currently the second-largest cash crop in the United States, just after corn and ahead of soybeans.

Throughout the 1980s, the Reagan and Bush administrations acted aggressively in mobilizing the agencies of the federal government in a coordinated attack on the drug supply from abroad and the distribution of drugs within the United States. Total federal spending on the War on Drugs rose from approximately $1 billion to $9 billion during the 1980s.[28] The crackdown yielded record numbers of drug seizures, arrests, and convictions. The Drug Enforcement Administration (DEA), the FBI, and Customs seized nearly half a billion dollars in drug-related assets in 1986. That year, the DEA arrested twice as many drug offenders as in 1982. From the end of 1980 to June 30, 1987, the prison population soared from 329,021 to 570,519. Roughly 40 percent of new prison inmates are incarcerated for drug offenses.

Should we conclude that the War on Drugs was a success? Not at all. None of this activity had any impact on either drug consumption or the drug market. Domestic marijuana cultivation took off and the black market in cocaine grew to record size. As the result of an abundant supply of cocaine, prices plummeted. "In 1980–81, a gram of cocaine cost $100 and averaged 12 percent purity at street level. By 1986, the price had fallen to as low as $80 ($50 in Miami), and the purity had risen to more than 50 percent. It rose to 70 percent purity in 1988. Around the nation, crack was marketed in $5 and $10 vials to reach the youth and low-income markets."[29] In hospitals, cocaine-related emergencies rose from 4,277 in 1982 to more than 46,000 in 1988. That trend began to go down in late 1989, but a new Federal report shows a 13 percent increase in hospital emergencies attributed to cocaine in the third quarter of 1991 and a 10 percent increase in emergency room visits from the use of heroin.[30]

This rapid expansion of supply and decline in price occurred despite President Reagan's increasing the federal anti-drug enforcement budget from $645 million in fiscal year 1981 to over $4 billion in fiscal year 1987. A third of that budget was specifically devoted to interdiction. Commenting in 1987 specifically upon the interdiction budget, the Office of Technology Assessment concluded:

> Despite a doubling of Federal expenditures on interdiction over the past five years, the quantity of drugs smuggled into the United States is greater than ever. . . . There is no clear correlation between the level of

expenditures or effort devoted to interdiction and the long-term availability of illegally imported drugs in the domestic market.[31]

In 1992, the Bush Administration spent nearly $12 billion on drugs, more than double what was spent in Mr. Reagan's last year in office, two-thirds of it going to interdiction. "It reminds me of that cartoon," says Dr. Herbert Kleber, professor of medicine at Columbia University and a former deputy director of the Office of National Drug Control Policy who quit when he couldn't get more money shifted to treatment. "This king is slamming his fist on the table, saying, 'If all my horses and all my men can't put Humpty Dumpty together again, then what I need is *more* horses and *more* men.'"[32]

Why has the government continued to pour money and other resources into a failed policy? For the same reason, I suspect, that we stayed in Vietnam. In *The March of Folly*, Barbara Tuchman suggests that "Woodenheadedness . . . plays a remarkably large role in government. It consists in assessing a situation in terms of preconceived fixed notions while ignoring or rejecting any contrary signs. It is acting according to wish while not allowing oneself to be deflected by the facts."[33]

The War on Drugs has not simply failed. It's made things much worse. Steven Wisotsky writes:

> It has spun a spider's web of black-market pathologies, including roughly 25 percent of all urban homicides, widespread corruption of police and other public officials, street crime by addicts, and subversive "narco-terrorist" alliances between Latin American guerrillas and drug traffickers. In the streets of the nation's major cities, violent gangs of young drug thugs armed with automatic rifles engage in turf wars. Federal agents estimated in 1988 that more than 10,000 members of "posses" or Jamaican drug gangs were responsible for about 1,000 deaths nationwide. Innocent bystanders and police officers are among their victims.[34]

Another negative effect of the War on Drugs has been a reduction in civil liberties.[35] The Supreme Court has upheld searches without probable cause, warrantees searches of automobiles, adopted a "good-faith exception" to the exclusionary rule, and authorized search of "open fields" adjacent to a residence. The power of the police to stop, question, detain, investigate, and search vehicles has expanded significantly. Wisotsky comments, "The net result of the War on Drugs is gradually, but inexorably, to expand enforcement powers at the expense of personal freedom."[36]

The War on Drugs mentality has prevented doctors from making authorized use of many controlled substances having valuable therapeutic applications. In 1984, the House of Representatives killed a bill that would have made injectable heroin available to dying cancer patients suffering severe, intense and intractable pain, when other drugs were ineffective. In California, patients with extremely debilitating cases of rheumatoid arthritis exhibited remarkable pain-free ability when they smoked freebase cocaine. Nevertheless, the government ended the experiment.

Most recently, the fight has centered around the use of marijuana as a medicinal drug. In March 1992, the Drug Enforcement Administration refused to reclassify marijuana as a Schedule II drug so doctors could prescribe it for patients suffering from glaucoma, cancer, muscular sclerosis, and AIDS.[37] A Federal appeals court had ruled the previous April that the government was using illogical criteria in prohibiting the use of marijuana for medical purposes, because the agency had based a conclusion that marijuana had no "currently accepted medical use" on factors like the drug's general availability, its use by a substantial number of doctors, and recognition of its use in medical texts. Since the drug is illegal, the court said, meeting these criteria would be all but impossible.

Robert C. Bonner, chief of the DEA, said that marijuana had not been shown to be as safe and effective as legal alternatives, such as Marinol, a synthetic form of THC, the active ingredient in marijuana. In his response to the appeals court, Bonner said, "Beyond doubt, the claims that marijuana is medicine are false, dangerous and cruel. Sick men, women and children can be fooled by these claims and experiment with the drug. Instead of being helped, they risk serious side effects." Although made in the guise of scientific information, this is pure moralism. As Dr. Lester Grinspoon, an associate professor of psychiatry at Harvard Medical School who is the author of several books on marijuana's medicinal uses, says, "It's absolutely extraordinary that our government is behaving the way it is toward cannibis. They see legalizing it for medical use as a Trojan Horse for recreational use."[38]

There has been a surge in the last year in requests for medical marijuana by AIDS patients, and some advocates argue that this inspired the recent Government actions. "The government is not doing this to protect patients," said Kennington Wall, a spokesman for the Drug Policy Foundation in Washington, which advocates a liberal national drug policy. "They're doing this to protect their political agenda."[39]

Should Drugs Be Legalized?

If the War on Drugs has been a disaster, should drugs be legalized? A simple "yes" or "no" is impossible, partly because different drugs may require different responses, and partly because there are factual issues yet to be resolved. For example, what would be the effect of legalization on access and consumption? Some argue that would have little impact on access, because illegal drugs are already easily available. More than half the high school seniors questioned by University of Michigan researchers in 1991 said that finding cocaine was "fairly easy" or "very easy." Nearly 40 percent said the same for crack and about a third for heroin.[40]

Others are convinced that, even if illegal drugs are already easy to obtain, legalization would make drugs even more accessible. This would lead to higher addiction rates, and thus worsen the already massive problems faced by the inner city. Many advocates for inner-city communities view illegal drugs as one aspect of the dominant society's oppression of their communities. Legalization "is construed as an expression of disdain for and dismissal of the misery that drugs bring to inner cities."[41]

Block thinks that legalization will not increase the number of addicts for three reasons. First, although the price of drugs can be expected to go down, this will have little effect on the behavior of addicts who regard drugs as a necessity, not a luxury. Second, there will be little incentive for addicts to try to "hook" others to support their own habits. Third, even if quantity increases, potency will fall. Prohibition leads to stronger and stronger drugs, which are both more concentrated and have higher value. Therefore, even if greater amounts of drugs are consumed under legalization, they are likely to be less harmful to the population.

Block may be right about the effect of legalization on consumption and addiction. Still, it should be remembered that *three times* as many Americans abuse alcohol as use illegal drugs. Why? Because alcohol is legal, it is easy to buy, it is an accepted part of our culture. If addictive drugs were legal, it seems likely that entrepreneurs would cultivate or manufacture them, package them, and advertise them, just as they do alcohol. And it is reasonable to believe that this would result in higher consumption, greater abuse, and a higher rate of addiction.

If the end result of legalization is higher addiction rates, this is a serious argument against legalization, from a public-health perspective. Astoundingly, it has no bearing at all on a libertarian view. Block says:

> Assume, for instance, that 75 percent of the population, just to pick a number out of a hat, were to become addicted. We still maintain that there is again nothing in the realm of positive economics, nor of normative libertarian political theory, that can serve as the basis for prohibition. It will still be true that all parties concerned will gain, in their own subjective estimates, from their participation in the drug market. It will still be true that the industry will be a totally voluntary one, with no one forced to take part. Hence, libertarian theory still proscribes interdiction. (p. 211)

However, this is less an argument for legalization than an argument against libertarianism. When a theory has absurd results—in this case, a total disregard for the disastrous effects of addiction on society—the adequacy of the theory must be questioned.

Sometimes the argument in favor of legalization is based on claims about what we learned from Prohibition. It is often said that Prohibition "didn't work": that people went right on drinking in speakeasies, which facilitated the rise of organized crime and led ordinary citizens to lose respect for the law. In fact, by public-health standards, narrowly construed, Prohibition was a success. Consumption of alcohol fell by more than two-thirds, and cirrhosis rates fell to half the level that obtained in 1910. Two years after repeal, total consumption of alcohol was only one-third of the 1910 level.[42]

Nevertheless, Prohibition was a failure, because it was unduly moralistic, restrictive, and repressive. Moreover, it was unnecessary. As Beauchamp says, ". . . most of what we could accomplish in health and safety under Prohibition could be achieved through more stringent regulation of alcohol. Prohibition is something like ringing a doorbell with a cannon."[43]

It might be argued that it is equally unnecessary to ban addictive drugs, even if one is concerned about their impact on the nation's health and safety. Perhaps we could legalize or decriminalize the sale of addictive drugs, while keeping their availability severely restricted. However, there is an important difference between alcohol and illicit drugs, and that is simply that alcohol is currently legal. Millions of Americans have grown up regarding alcohol as a normal and socially acceptable part of life. Having wine in a restaurant, champagne at weddings, and beer at picnics are pleasures of which many Americans would resent being deprived. Prohibition of alcohol is politically impossible.

Because narcotic and opiate drugs have been illegal since the beginning of this century, they aren't viewed by most people as something to which they have a right. *Keeping* drugs illegal would not engender widespread anger and resentment, as *making* alcohol illegal would. The question faced by policy-makers and ordinary citizens is whether we should opt for changing the law, and legalizing addictive drugs. The risks and harms posed by addictive drugs provide a powerful argument against changing the status quo. No doubt it is for this reason that Beauchamp supports "a policy that combines legal suppression of supply, both here and abroad, with more humane and compassionate treatment of users and addicts, even offering some form of maintenance as an alternative to obtaining drugs in illegal settings."[44]

Interestingly enough, Block does not seem so far from Beauchamp on this matter. He says, "Suppose you . . . had a child addicted to narcotics. Would you prefer a situation where he had to run around like a half-crazed wretch, doing all sorts of unspeakable things in order to raise the requisite funds for his habit, never knowing where his next fix was coming from, nor what would be in it, or one where he could be given an injection in safe, comfortable, clean hospital surroundings, under the care of a physician?" (pp. 213-214) Here, Block seems to drop his libertarian stance. As he acknowledges in endnote 11, a real libertarian is committed to allowing drugs to be advertised and marketed, like alcohol. In suggesting something along the lines of the British model, where registered addicts receive drugs by prescription, Block is adopting something that resembles a public-health approach. This approach recognizes that an all-out War on Drugs and a completely free market are not the only two possibilities.

A pragmatic approach also requires us to distinguish between drugs. The case for keeping cocaine and heroin illegal is much stronger than the case for keeping marijuana illegal. Marijuana is not addictive, that is, there is no physical dependence or withdrawal. Psychological dependence appears to be minimal or nonexistent.[45] Sixty-two million Americans have tried marijuana at least once, and roughly 18 million use it regularly.[46] While marijuana is not risk-free (especially for adolescents and pregnant women), there is considerable evidence that it is much less harmful than alcohol. Yet there are approximately one-half million arrests per year for marijuana, almost all for simple possession or petty sale offenses.[47] It is hard to see what social goals require that the criminal justice system be overburdened in this way.

A public-health approach toward drugs would require various measures. First and foremost, it requires continuing education about the benefits and dangers of both legal and illegal drugs. But a public-health approach goes beyond mere education. It supports getting tough on the legal drugs by such measures as getting rid of cigarette vending machines so that cigarettes are not so readily available to minors; restricting the hours of sale of liquor; and levying raising taxes on these items, commensurate with their social costs—billions of dollars in property damage, disease, and lost productivity.[48] At the same time, the respect for individual choice and the rejection of moralism that are part of the public-health approach[49] require that we remain open to the possibility that some currently illegal but comparatively harmless drugs, such as marijuana, should be legalized. And even if we decide to keep cocaine and heroin illegal, the emphasis should be on treatment. For most of the Reagan years, only about 20 percent of the budget went to treatment and education. This rose to about 30 percent under Bush. Despite Clinton's campaign rhetoric, it is still woefully inadequate, according to many experts. Studies indicate that present prevention and treatment efforts reach only 10 percent of alcohol and drug abusers.[50] In addition, there is also very limited research on which prevention and treatment programs work. Dr. Herbert D. Kleber, a former deputy director in the Federal Office of National Drug Control Policy and one of the organizers of the recently created Center on Addiction and Substance Abuse in Manhattan, jokes about the "four-two-one" syndrome in medical school, meaning that in four years of medical school, students get two hours of instruction on the nation's No. 1 health problem, drug abuse. Obviously, this lack of attention must be addressed if we are to combat effectively the drug problem.

Conclusion

This paper does not attempt to answer the complex question whether drugs should be legalized. The answer to that question hinges on various empirical issues, such as whether legalization would increase addiction rates. Instead, my aim has been to show that the right approach to the problem of drug addiction is a public-health perspective, as opposed to the libertarian analysis provided by Professor Block. Whereas the libertarian insists on absolute freedom of choice, regardless of social costs, the public-health approach balances the values of liberty and autonomy against the values of health and safety. It rejects the uncompromising stances characteristic of both moralism and libertarian ideology. Above all, a public-health approach insists that policies must be based on an honest appraisal of the problem and accurate empirical evidence about what does and does not work to solve it.[51]

Notes

1. Joseph B. Treaster, "Hospital Visits Show Abuse of Drugs Is Still on the Rise," *New York Times*, May 14, 1992, A16. According to other estimates, 2 million Americans are addicted to cocaine; 1 million use heroin; 18 million have drinking problems or are alcoholics, and 10 million abuse barbiturates or other prescription drugs. (Kathleen Teltsch, "3 Joining to Start Center Against Substance Abuse," *New York Times*, May 18, 1992, B3.)
2. Michel Marriott, "After 3 Years, Crack Plague in New York Only Gets Worse," *New York Times*, February 20, 1989, A1.
3. Joseph B. Treaster, "20 Years of War on Drugs, and No Victory Yet," *New York Times*, Sunday, June 14, 1992, E7.
4. The above facts come from Michel Marriott (see note 2). There are signs that the crack epidemic, which peaked in 1988, is beginning to abate. A decline in the use of cocaine by pregnant women, combined with improved prenatal care, helped significantly reduce infant mortality in New York City in 1990 for the first time in four years. (Celia W. Dugger, "Infant Mortality in New York City Declines for First Time in 4 Years," *New York Times*, April 20, 1991, p. 1.)
5. Anna Quindlen, "Hearing the Cries of Crack," *New York Times*, October 7, 1990, E19.
6. Editorial in *New York Times*, May 28, 1989, E14.
7. Letter to the Editor, *New York Times*, November 20, 1989, A22.
8. Howard W. French, "New York Sees Rise in Babies Hurt by Drugs," *New York Times*, October 18, 1989, B1.
9. T. Berry Brazelton, "Is America Failing Its Children?" *New York Times Magazine*, September 9, 1990, p. 90.
10. The right of a surviving child to recover in a civil suit for prenatally caused injuries has been upheld in the United States since the landmark case of *Bonbrest v. Kotz*, 65 F. Supp. 138 (1946).
11. For a fuller discussion of this point, see my *Life Before Birth: The Moral and Legal Status of Embryos and Fetuses* (Oxford University Press, 1992), especially Chapter 4, "Maternal-Fetal Conflict."
12. "Hour by Hour: Crack," *Newsweek*, November 28, 1988, p. 75.
13. Brazelton (see note 9), p. 90.
14. This argument for limited paternalism works only when there are alternative safe medications. If conventional medicine can do nothing for someone who is going to die, it is rational to want access to new treatments, even if they are unproven and potentially dangerous. This kind of argument is often heard from terminally ill cancer patients and AIDS activists. However, even AIDS activists do not want to abolish the FDA, only relax some of its standards for new drugs to treat AIDS.
15. See Richard D. Mohr, "AIDS, Gays, and State Coercion," *Bioethics* 1:1 (1987), pp. 35–50.
16. Gerald Dworkin, "Paternalism," *The Monist* 56:1. Reprinted in Ronald Munson, ed., *Intervention and Reflection: Basic Issues in*

Medical Ethics, 4th edition (Belmont, CA: Wadsworth, 1992), pp. 276–87, at p. 282.

17. Dan E. Beauchamp, *The Health of the Republic: Epidemics, Medicine, and Moralism as Challenges to Democracy* (Philadelphia: Temple University Press, 1988), p. 89. Actually, Beauchamp objects to characterizing laws requiring the wearing of seat belts as "paternalism." The reason is that, in this case, the individual is not coerced for his *own* good— the chance of any one individual being killed in a car crash is minuscule. Rather, the good to be achieved is a communal or collective good, namely, a reduction in aggregate levels of death and injury.

18. For a detailed application of a public-health approach to the drug problem, see James F. Mosher and Karen I. Yanagisako, "Public Health, Not Social Warfare: A Public Health Approach to Illegal Drug Policy," *Journal of Public Health Policy* (Autumn 1991), pp. 278–321.

19. This objection was suggested to me by Betty Daniel.

20. John Rawls, *A Theory of Justice* (Cambridge, MA: Harvard University Press, 1971), p. 92.

21. Dan Beauchamp, "Life-Style, Public Health and Paternalism," in S. Doxiadis, ed., *Ethical Dilemmas in Health Promotion*, Chapter 7 (John Wiley & Sons Ltd, 1987), p. 71.

22. *Robinson v. California*, 370 U.S. 660, 672 (1962) Douglas, W.O., concurring.

23. *Private Acts, Social Consequences* (The Free Press, 1989) is the title of a book about AIDS by Ronald Bayer, professor of public health at the Columbia University School of Public Health.

24. Treaster, "20 Years of War on Drugs" (see note 3).

25. Mathea Falco, "The Big Business of Illicit Drugs," in Robert Emmet Long, ed., *Drugs and American Society* (New York: The H.W. Wilson Company, 1986), p. 8.

26. Ibid., p. 10.

27. Ibid., pp. 15–16.

28. Steven Wisotsky, *Beyond the War on Drugs: Overcoming a Failed Public Policy* (Buffalo, NY: Prometheus Books, 1990), p. xviii.

29. Ibid., p. xix.

30. Treaster, "Hospital Visits Show Abuse of Drugs Is Still on the Rise" (see note 1).

31. Cited in Wisotsky (see note 28), p. xx.

32. Treaster, "20 Years of War on Drugs" (see note 3).

33. Barbara Tuchman, *The March of Folly: From Troy to Vietnam* (New York: Ballantine Books, 1984), p. 7.

34. Wisotsky (see note 28), p. xx.

35. In light of this, it is ironic that Mill thought that the preventive function of government was more dangerous to liberty than the punitory function. Beauchamp argues that Mill had this exactly backward (see note 21, p. 77).

36. Wisotsky (see note 28), p. 125.

37. Joseph B. Treaster, "Agency Says Marijuana Is Not Proven Medicine," *New York Times*, Thursday, March 19, 1992, B11.

38. Katherine Bishop, "Marijuana Still a Drug, Not a Medicine," *New York Times*, March 22, 1992, E5.

39. Treaster, "Agency Says Marijuana Is Not Proven Medicine" (see note 37).

40. Treaster, "20 Years of War on Drugs" (see note 3).

41. Although they do not accept this analysis, Mosher and Yanagisako acknowledge that it is a widely held view among advocates for inner-city communities. (See note 18), p. 314.

42. Beauchamp (see note 21), p. 179.

43. Ibid., p. 189.

44. Ibid., p. 196.

45. James C. Weissman, *Drug Abuse: The Law and Treatment Alternatives* (Anderson Publishing Company, 1978), p. 89.

46. National Institute on Drug Abuse, "Highlights of the 1985 National Household Survey on Drug Abuse: National Institute on Drug Abuse," *NIDA Capsules* (November 1986).

47. Wisotsky (see note 28), p. xxv.

48. Ibid., p. xxviii.

49. For a detailed defense of the view that respect for privacy and autonomy are not opposed to, but part of, a public-health approach, see Beauchamp, *The Health of the Republic* (note 21).

50. Kathleen Teltsch (see note 1).

51. I would like to thank Professor Dan E. Beauchamp of the School of Public Health

at the University at Albany, Professor Steven Burton of the University of Iowa Law School and Professor Betty Daniel of the Economics Department at the University at Albany for helpful comments on an earlier version of this paper.

Questions for Further Reflection

1. Wilson suggests that the key argument against legalization is that drug use is degrading and immoral. For Block, whether drug use is degrading is simply irrelevant to whether it should be permitted or not. Who is correct, and why?
2. Compare the justification of drug laws with one or more of the following: seatbelt laws, consumer protection laws, laws against prostitution and pornography.
3. William Bennett has written that "a citizen in a drug-induced haze, whether on his back-yard deck or on a mattress in a ghetto crack house, is not what the founding fathers meant by the 'pursuit of happiness'." Is the pleasure of drugs so degrading that people should not be able to pursue it? What would Bennett say about a citizen on his backyard deck in an *alcohol*-induced haze?
4. Wilson suggests that drug education is more likely to be credible if drugs are illegal. If drugs were legal, he suggests, then arguments against their use would sound rather hollow. He writes: "That tobacco is bad for you is easily shown; the Surgeon General has seen to that. But what do we say about crack? It is pleasurable, but devoting yourself to so much pleasure is not a good idea (though perfectly legal)? Unlike tobacco, cocaine will not give you cancer or emphysema, but it will lead you to neglect your duties to family, job, and neighborhood?" If, as Wilson seems to suggest, these arguments would not be credible as reasons not to use drugs, are they more credible as reasons drugs should not be legal?
5. Block argues that "value-free economics" gives reasons to favor legalization. But are the economic principles to which he appeals (for example, the principle that the welfare of "third parties" not directly involved in an economic transaction is irrelevant to the value of the transaction) really "value-free"?
6. Block argues that, on libertarian grounds, legalization should be pursued regardless of how much this might increase drug use. Steinbock responds that "this is less an argument for legalization than an argument against libertarianism." Which view do you favor, and why?

Further Readings

Bennett, William J. "Restoring Authority." *New Perspectives Quarterly* 6 (Summer 1989): 4–7. The first "Drug Czar" discusses the drug problem as a failure of moral authority. Also interesting is Bennett's essay "Should Drugs Be Legalized?" in the March 1990 *Reader's Digest*; the latter essay is the source of the quotation from Bennett in Question 3.

Husak, Douglas. *Drugs and Rights*. Cambridge: Cambridge University Press, 1992. An excellent discussion, philosophically sophisticated and empirically well-informed.

Luper-Foy, Steven, and Curtis Brown, eds. *Drugs, Morality, and the Law*. New York: Garland, 1994. A collection of essays on a variety of issues about drug policy.

Nadelmann, Ethan A. "Drug Prohibition in the United States: Costs, Consequences, and Alternatives." *Science* 245 (1 September 1989): 939–947. A defense of legalization, with an extensive and well-documented discussion of its costs and benefits.

Richards, David A. J. *Sex, Drugs, Death, and the Law: An Essay on Human Rights and Overcriminalization*. Totowa, NJ: Rowman & Littlefield, 1982, Chapter 4. Detailed argument for legalization and response to arguments against it.

PART FIVE

International Issues

Chapter 13

NUCLEAR DETERRENCE AND STRATEGIC DEFENSE

Until recently, the United States has protected itself and the NATO powers against the possibility of nuclear attack by threatening to use nuclear weapons against assailants. This policy of nuclear deterrence has involved deploying offensive nuclear weapons and targeting cities or weapons of potential aggressors. The lessening of tensions between the United States and the former Soviet Union has reduced the threat of aggression, but there is reason to believe that the number of nations that possess nuclear weapons will continue to grow. Hence, the issue of nuclear policy is as pressing as ever, and if the rapprochement between the United States and the nations of the former Soviet Union continues, there may be a real opportunity to implement new solutions.

Is there a need for a new policy? Increasingly, people have objected to nuclear deterrence on moral grounds, insisting that using nuclear weapons to retaliate against aggressors would be morally impermissible. Some critics have urged that deterrence be replaced with a policy of disarmament. More recently, however, there have been critics who suggest that deterrence be replaced with a purely defensive policy, which would obviate the need to retaliate against aggressors who use nuclear weapons. Many have argued that a space-based system would be too vulnerable to serve as a means of defense but that perhaps other, more effective defensive systems could be devised. In this chapter, we examine some of the arguments that have been given for and against the replacement of deterrence with a defensive policy or with disarmament.

Background

The bulk of the world's nuclear weapons is possessed by the nations of the former Soviet Union and the United States, but other nations possess nuclear arms as well. Great Britain, China, France, and (it is widely believed) Israel have them, and Iran, Iraq, and Libya are among the nations with programs for developing nuclear weapons, according to William Webster, a former director of the CIA. Altogether, the collection of nuclear weapons is enormous. About 50,000 nuclear warheads exist today, and each has astonishing power. The atomic bombs the U.S. dropped on Japan in 1945 were about 10,000 times more powerful than the most powerful conventional bombs ("blockbusters") used in World War II, but today's warheads are 1-megaton bombs. Each is 75 times more powerful than the atomic bombs dropped on Japan.[1]

The Soviet Union acquired nuclear-weapons technology shortly after World War II. Initially, the United States strove to maintain military superiority over the U.S.S.R., and, until well into the sixties, the United States did have a clearly superior nuclear force. During the Eisenhower years of the fifties, the United States took advantage of its superiority to maintain a policy of deterring aggression by threatening massive retaliation. The Kennedy administration refined the policy of massive retaliation during the sixties, replacing it with a five-step sequence of ever more serious options so that, as John McNamara explained, the focus of nuclear attack would be military targets.

This unilateral policy of flexible response held sway until pressures began to mount in the United States in favor of developing an effective defensive weapons system in general and antiballistic missile (ABM) systems in particular. After the Soviets deployed an ABM system around Moscow in 1966, McNamara supported the development of an ABM system to defend U.S. cities against accidental Soviet launches or attacks by China. In the ensuing debate over the wisdom of developing an ABM system, McNamara began to defend the need for the United States to retain the capacity for the "assured destruction" of Soviet society should the latter strike first. The ABM proposal itself was eventually defeated; it was criticized on the grounds that it could not be effective (the Soviets could overwhelm it with decoys and a buildup of missiles) and on the grounds that any side that had an effective ABM system would be tempted to strike first because it would have less concern about retaliation.

Although initially the Nixon administration followed that of Kennedy in pressing for an ABM system (now to protect intercontinental ballistic missiles rather than cities), it eventually decided that such systems were "destabilizing" in that they could be construed as the first step toward a first strike. President Nixon decided that a policy of nuclear deterrence was preferable and in 1972 signed a treaty with the Soviets to abandon ABM systems.

Under the Reagan administration, the policy of assured destruction came under renewed attack, and the grounds against developing a defensive weapons system were reexamined. In 1983, Reagan announced the Strategic Defense Initiative (SDI), which at least initially was aimed at developing a space-based nationwide defense system against all missiles. The proposal was immediately criticized on the grounds that a system that would deflect every missile the Soviets might launch could not possibly be developed. However, Reagan apparently was willing to settle for the development of a system that would fall short of complete defense, and debate about this proposal rages on.[2]

Alternatives

The United States has four main choices as far as nuclear policy is concerned. It could maintain the policy it has favored longest,

---

[1] Paul Craig and John Jungerman, *Nuclear Arms Race: Technology and Society* (New York: McGraw-Hill, 1986), p. 4.

[2] The background material was drawn in part from Douglas Lackey, ed., *Ethics and Strategic Defense* (Belmont, CA: Wadsworth Publishing Company, 1986).

which is roughly one of *deterrence* (with offensive weapons), or it could opt for *complete disarmament* (either unilateral, in concert with some other nuclear powers, or in concert with all other nuclear powers), *defense* (with purely defensive weapons), or the *combination of deterrence with defense*.

The readings that follow fall into two main groups. The first group of readings focuses on the issue of how deterrence stacks up against the second choice, disarmament. Here the question will be whether deterrence, which involves using the threat of nuclear retaliation as a deterrent to nuclear aggression, is better than disarmament. The second group of readings considers the relative merits of deterrence vis-à-vis the last two choices. The question will be which is best: deterrence with no defense, defense with no deterrence, or some combination of the two.

Deterrence or Disarmament?

David Gauthier defends deterrence over unilateral disarmament. He thinks that multilateral disarmament would be the best option for all nuclear powers, so that the United States should offer to disarm if all others do, but that it ought not to disarm unilaterally. Instead, it ought to maintain a deterrence posture if others refuse to disarm. Douglas Lackey, by contrast, defends unilateral disarmament. His position is that the United States ought to disarm even if no other nuclear power does.

Gauthier bases his defense of deterrence on both prudential and moral grounds. The moral defense rests on his view that the rules of morality are those that communities would find mutually advantageous to follow. A policy of nuclear deterrence would have no place in a moral community, Gauthier admits, but it is our duty nonetheless, because deterrence is necessary for *bringing about* the sort of community in which people can act morally. Nations with nuclear weapons must give each other the incentive to disarm by (1) threatening to retaliate if attacked, (2) threatening to remain armed if others do, and (3) promising to disarm if others do.

Gauthier spends the bulk of his essay in an attempt to show that multilateral disarmament and deterrence can be rational policies in spite of certain paradoxes. Many philosophers have noticed that in considering the possibility of disarmament, nuclear powers find themselves in a Prisoner's Dilemma. In this situation, each side attempts to do what is best for it, yet the net result is an outcome that is a disaster for all concerned. A puzzle Gauthier terms the *disarmament dilemma* occurs as a result: Suppose that the United States and its nuclear opponents were perfectly rational, completely prudent. If they were, they would appear forced to choose to remain armed. The United States would prefer the situation in which it alone is armed over the situation in which no one is, and it would prefer the situation in which it and its opponents are armed over the situation in which only the opponents are armed. So no matter what its opponents do, the United States would consider itself better off if it remained armed. All, however, would be better off if all disarmed, yet how can prudential rationality prevent the United States and its opponents from choosing an outcome that would be best for all concerned?

The second puzzle Gauthier wrestles with he terms the *deterrence dilemma*. Here the problem is not that nuclear powers are in a Prisoner's Dilemma, but rather that they appear to be in the sort of situation in which juveniles find themselves when playing Chicken. In this game, winning requires appearing less rational than one's opponents, since doing the threatened thing would be irrational. In the case of the two superpowers, each maintains the threat to retaliate if attacked, which is an irrational threat, since actual retaliation would simply cause pointless suffering. Yet how can it be rational to play a game in which one makes irrational threats?

Lackey argues that the United States would not find itself in a Prisoner's Dilemma with its opponents in deciding to disarm and that it is not playing Chicken with its opponents if both retain a deterrence policy. Whether they are in either situation depends on the facts about how the two powers rank several options. Thus Gauthier's charge that they are playing Chicken is based on the assumption that each ranks the alternatives in the following order:

1. Attack without counterattack.
2. Neither side attacks.
3. Be attacked without counterattack.
4. Be attacked and counterattack.

Lackey insists that U.S. presidents think that retaliation would be rational; perhaps it would even help prevent the occupation of the United States. So option 4 beats option 3. Moreover, insists Lackey, neither the United States nor the former Soviet Union appear to prefer striking without any reprisal to not striking at all, since among other reasons, striking would destroy anything in the attacked country that the attackers might covet. So option 2 beats option 1.

Gauthier's concern that the United States and the former Soviet Union are in a prisoner's dilemma vis-à-vis deterrence is based on the assumption that they adopt the following ranking of alternatives:

1. Possess nuclear weapons when the other side does not.
2. Neither side has any nuclear weapons.
3. Both sides have nuclear weapons.
4. Only the other side has nuclear weapons.

But, Lackey says, NATO powers appeared to prefer mutual retention of nuclear weapons to mutual disarmament because it was cheaper to offset Soviet conventional power with nuclear weapons than it would have been to match its conventional forces. So option 3 beat option 2. Moreover, unilateral disarmament was better for the United States than both sides having nuclear weapons, for several reasons. Among them was the fact that being armed made possible an all-out nuclear war that would destroy life on most of the planet.

Lackey also rejects Gauthier's suggestion that morally, the best policy is one of threatening retaliation if attacked and disarming only multilaterally. Even if that policy maximizes utility, it does not follow that it is obligatory, and even if it were morally obligatory to threaten retaliation, it would not follow that executing the threat would be obligatory. Indeed, Lackey believes that "the moral impermissibility of executing the threat spills backwards into the moral impermissibility of making it."

Deterrence or Defense?

In his so-called "star wars" speech of February 1983, reprinted here, President Reagan *seemed* to argue that a purely defensive policy was morally preferable to a deterrence policy, because the former is a matter of "dealing with other nations and human beings by threatening their existence." To keep any offensive arms whatever, even at reduced levels, is to "rely on the specter of retaliation," and "that is a sad commentary on the human condition." "Wouldn't it be better," he went on to ask, "to save lives than to avenge them?" He also called on scientists to provide the means to render "nuclear weapons impotent and obsolete." Whether Reagan should be read as advocating a policy of pure defense, however, is problematic. Among other things, the strategic defense initiative (SDI) he announced called for measures against nuclear bombs carried by intercontinental ballistic missiles only, not ones carried by other means, such as aircraft or boat. Would he advocate retaining a deterrence policy against the use of these delivery systems?

Reagan's speech covers some of the same ground as a book by General Daniel Graham called *The Non-Nuclear Defense of Cities* (Cambridge, MA: Abt Books, 1983), from which we have included an excerpt. Graham was one of the people who helped influence the Reagan administration to reevaluate U.S. policy on defensive systems versus deterrence ones. Like many thinkers who oppose nuclear deterrence, Graham argues that a deterrence policy is immoral and against the military code of ethics because it involves targeting innocent civilians in Soviet cities. A policy of defense would be subject to no such objection. (Having given this justification of defensive measures, however, Graham goes on to make the puzzling suggestion that the United States retain its offensive capability as a deterrent to a first strike.)

In his essay, Steven Lee seizes on the fact that defenders of defense policies are rarely willing to defend *purely* defensive policies and instead prefer combining defense with some measure of deterrence. A policy that combines defense with deterrence cannot be given the kind of justification to which a policy of pure defense is susceptible, for the mixed policy still involves targeting innocent civilians. At best, one might attempt to defend the mixed policy on the grounds that it makes nuclear war less likely, Lee suggests. That is, the combination policy is a more effective deterrent than a pure deterrence policy. But Lee argues that this defense would fail: The combination policy is not more effective than pure deterrence, for adding defensive measures to deterrence increases the chances that the other side will initiate a preemptive attack in times of crisis.

DETERRENCE

War and Nuclear Deterrence

David Gauthier

. . . Thinking about war in the nuclear age is difficult. One source of this difficulty is the complexity of modern weaponry. Another is the unimaginability of full-scale nuclear war. Were there such a war, the survivors, if any, would not find it unimaginable, but for us, now, it falls too far beyond anything we have experienced. Let us hope that it always remains so, but let us not forget how our inability to imagine nuclear war limits our reactions.

A third source of difficulty in thinking about nuclear war involves analyzing the strategic structure of interaction among

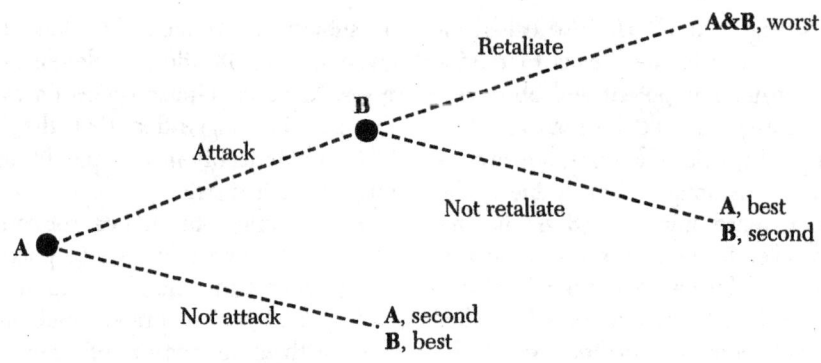

FIGURE 1 THE DETERRENCE DILEMMA

nations with opposed interests but similar nuclear capacities. One feature of this analysis is that it reveals, almost immediately, some quite simple but deeply puzzling features of our conception of practical rationality. This is my primary theme—to examine what I shall call the rational dilemmas of deterrence and disarmament. But there is at least one other source of difficulty in thinking about nuclear war, which is that our ordinary moral ideas and rules have not been shaped as guides for such an apocalyptic possibility. I shall not ignore the morality of deterrence and disarmament, although what I shall say about them will follow from what I shall first try to establish about their rationality.

The Rational Dilemmas of Deterrence and Disarmament

Let us begin with the dilemmas, for it is here that philosophic thinking can make a contribution that requires neither a technical understanding nor an imaginative insight to which I, as a philosopher, could make no special claim. These dilemmas, I must emphasize, need not arise whenever deterrence or disarmament is an issue. Rather, they relate to extreme cases, in which many of the usual characteristics of international interaction get stripped away. But discussion of nuclear war has been un-

able to avoid these extreme cases.[1] The deterrence dilemma threatens the credibility of deterrence policies; the disarmament dilemma threatens the practicability of disarmament policies. What, then, are these dilemmas?

The deterrence dilemma exhibits the seeming irrationality of threat behavior; I exhibit its structure in Figure 1. Party A chooses whether or not to attack Party B, which then chooses whether or not to retaliate. The dilemma arises for B, which seeks a strategy to deter A from attacking. For deterrence to be a concern, B must believe that A prefers, or at least may prefer, an unretaliated attack to no attack. Otherwise, B would have nothing to deter. Furthermore, B must believe that A would prefer no attack to an attack with retaliation. Otherwise, B would have nothing with which to deter. B wants to deter A from attacking by threatening to retaliate against an attack.

In itself, B's concern to deter does not create a dilemma. For B to have such a concern, it must prefer not to be attacked; if B prefers to retaliate if attacked rather than not to retaliate, then its only problem

---

[1] Indeed, even the U.S. secretary of defense focuses on the extreme: "The policy of deterrence is difficult for some to grasp because it is based on a paradox." Caspar Weinberger, letter of August 23, 1982, in *New York Review of Books*, November 4, 1982, p. 27.

	B Disarm	B Not disarm
A Disarm	Mutual second best	A, worst; B, best
A Not disarm	A, best; B, worst	Mutual third best

FIGURE 2 THE DISARMAMENT DILEMMA

would be to get A to recognize B's preferences. But if B prefers not to retaliate if attacked, supposing that retaliation does it no good, or at least insufficient good to outweigh the harm of escalating conflict by retaliating, then B faces a dilemma. To deter A, B must credibly threaten to retaliate if attacked, although B prefers not to retaliate. Thus, a threat would be seemingly irrational. If A believes B to be rational, then A will reason that if attacked, B will not retaliate; thus, B's deterrent threat will lack credibility.

Successful deterrence would protect B from attack; thus, B acts rationally in seeking to deter A. But B can succeed, it seems, only if A believes that B is prepared to act irrationally and retaliate should its deterrent threat fail, and B may have no way of inducing A to believe this, short of actually being willing to retaliate.

The deterrence dilemma arises from a conflict between intention and possible action. It seems rational for B to intend retaliation if attacked because such an intention, communicated to A, minimizes B's risk of being attacked and so yields B its best outcome. But it does not seem rational for B actually to retaliate if attacked because such an action yields B's worst outcome. How can B rationally form an intention believing, even at the time of formation, that it would not be rational to carry the intention out?

The disarmament dilemma is structurally quite different from the deterrence dilemma and takes a form now familiar in the literature of rational choice and also moral philosophy—the form of a Prisoner's Dilemma. I exhibit the structure of the deterrence dilemma in Figure 2. Each party chooses whether or not to disarm and makes its choice independently of the other. Should the choices be fully interdependent, so that both parties must disarm together or not at all, then there is no dilemma; disarmament is straightforwardly best.

Each party has the same preferences for the four possible outcomes relative to its own position. Each party prefers most to be the sole armed power. Each party has mutual disarmament as its second preference and mutual armament as its third. Each party least prefers to be the sole disarmed power. This ordering reflects the desire of each to be dominant and the fears, on the one hand, of war provoked by mutual armament and, on the other hand, of being dominated.[2] Given these preferences each party prefers not to disarm whatever the other does; remaining armed enables the party to avoid being dominated if the other party remains armed, and to be dominant if the other party disarms. So it seems that each party acts rationally in not disarming. But the outcome, both parties agree, is less

---

[2] If we remove the desire to dominate, so that each prefers mutual disarmament to being the sole armed power, then we transform the situation into a form of the Assurance Game. More attention should be paid to this structure in examining the problems of disarmament.

desirable than mutual disarmament. Hence the dilemma—rational behavior leads to a mutually undesirable outcome.

The disarmament dilemma arises from a conflict between action and possible outcome. There is an outcome—mutual disarmament—that both parties prefer to the one that by seemingly rational action they bring into being. More technically, the conflict is between choosing a dominant course of action and attaining an optimal outcome. A course of action is dominant if it is a party's best response whatever the other party chooses. Not disarming is dominant. An outcome is optimal if no alternative is preferred by all parties. The outcome if neither disarms is not optimal; both prefer mutual disarmament. It seems irrational for two parties to end up with an outcome that is not optimal; both are needlessly disadvantaged. But it seems irrational for any party not to choose a dominant course of action; the party is needlessly disadvantaged.

To think about war in the nuclear age we must think about these dilemmas. But when faced with a dilemma, we are not likely to know what to think. However sophisticated our understanding of the technology of nuclear weaponry, and however imaginative our conception of nuclear holocaust, we do not thereby resolve the dilemmas of deterrence and disarmament. We need more thought, more reflection about rationality.

But first, let us ask about the applicability of our discussion. I assume that it is plausible to think of such nations as the United States and the Soviet Union as facing these dilemmas. Now one very reasonable response, if one faces a dilemma, is to endeavor to restructure one's situation so that it disappears. Thus, one seeks a deterrent response that one can plausibly represent, to a potential attacker, as one's preferred choice in the face of attack. One also seeks a disarmament strategy that can be fully mutual—a lock-step procedure in which each party can link its actions with those of the other, so that each can be sure that it disarms if and only if the other does. In this way, the possibilities of being either dominant or dominated are removed.

One may go farther. The dilemmas arise out of certain perceptions that nations have of each other and that lead to the fear that one is in danger of being attacked by a power that seeks forcible dominance. These perceptions may be accurate. But they are dangerous. A nation will want to be sure that it does not mistakenly perceive others, or behave so that others misperceive it, in ways that give rise to fears that invite deterrence and preclude mutual disarmament.[3]

If I thought that by appropriate restructuring and reorientation, the United States and the Soviet Union could move beyond the impasses of the dilemmas, then I should think it unprofitable and even undesirable to continue discussing them. For we should not needlessly complicate thinking about war and the avoidance of war in the nuclear age. But I believe instead that the dilemmas frustrate our thinking about deterrence and disarmament policies. Therefore, as a philosopher I find myself concerned with problems about rationality that, as a citizen, seem to me to have serious practical implications.

Practical Rationality

I return to my concern with rationality. I shall address these questions: Is deterrence rational? Is disarmament rational? In addressing them, I shall assume that deterrence and disarmament involve interactions

---

[3]Misperception characteristically leads one party to perceive the other's preferences as they would be in a Prisoner's Dilemma rather than as in an Assurance Game (see note 2).

that give rise to the dilemmas that I have sketched. However, I shall begin by setting the dilemmas to one side. Let us define a deterrence policy simply as "retaliate if attacked," and let us define a disarmament policy as "disarm if you expect the other party (or parties) to disarm." Now if we set the dilemmas aside, we may suppose that a nation can adopt, and make credible its adoption of, one or both of these policies. We ignore the fact that each seems to commit one to be conditionally prepared to perform a dispreferred action—to retaliate if attacked or to disarm if one expects others to disarm. Or perhaps we bypass this by adopting the fiction that in choosing a policy one ties one's hands, leaving no choice but to carry it out.

In the usual maximizing view of practical rationality, an agent, faced with a choice, explicitly or implicitly determines an expected value or utility for each alternative and selects one with the greatest expected value. Although the dilemmas raise problems for this view, it is, I believe, the only plausible account of practical rationality. This view simply requires fine-tuning to remove the dilemmas. Rationality is instrumental; the rational person is the one who acts to realize what she or he values to the fullest extent possible. Let us apply this view to answer our questions.

Is deterrence a rational policy? Compare it with acquiescence. An acquiescence policy is "do not retaliate if attacked." The benefit of a deterrence policy is that it reduces the probability of being attacked. The cost is that the policy increases the probability of retaliation. To evaluate deterrence in relation to acquiescence, we need to make some estimate of these probabilities. We also need to make some estimate of the relative values, to the would-be deterrer, of the three possible outcomes—not being attacked, being attacked with no retaliation, and being attacked with retaliation.

Different estimates yield different results. Roughly speaking, we balance the expectation of success against the cost of failure. But as a philosopher my business is not to make such estimates, and in any event, sensible estimates will vary for differing circumstances. . . .

Kavka's Case

Deterrence and disarmament may be the best policies. But that one's best policy may commit one to performing a dispreferred act leading to one's worst outcome may seem more than paradoxical. It may seem self-contradictory. . . .

Consider an example, which I owe to Gregory Kavka.[4] An eccentric millionaire offers to deposit $100,000 to your bank account at midnight tonight, provided that at that time he believes that you intend to, and actually will, take a pill tomorrow morning that will make you mildly ill for several hours. You are assured, on the best possible medical advice, that this is the only effect the pill will have; you will be nauseous and run a slight fever—nothing more. Let us suppose that it is worth $100,000 to you to be mildy ill tomorrow. So it is rational for you to form the intention to take the pill.

Tomorrow comes. Either the eccentric millionaire has deposited the money in your account or he has not. You will not find out until the bank opens, and you must take the pill, or refuse it, earlier in the morning. But what you do cannot affect whether or not the money is in your account. Surely you would be downright foolish to take the pill. Why endure a few hours' sickness for nothing? If taking the pill could affect the millionaire's decision, then you would have good reason to take it, but taking it now can

---

[4]See Gregory S. Kavka, "The Toxin Puzzle," *Analysis* 43 (1983): 33–36.

have no such effect. If someone in the same position were to ask you, "Shall I take the pill?" you would surely advise her or him not to do so. Therefore, you have no reason to take it yourself.

But now the same problem arises that I noted in introducing the deterrence dilemma; there is a conflict between intention and action. If you realize, when the millionaire makes the offer, that come tomorrow you will have no reason to take the pill, but instead good reason not to take it, then how can you, today, form the intention to take it? But you must form this intention if the millionaire is to expect you to take the pill and so deposit the money to your account.

It may be urged that frequently we intend to perform some action, or at least to try performing it, knowing that we may be unable or simply unwilling to do it when the time comes. I put off an unpleasant task, forming the intention to do it tomorrow, even though I have some doubt that I will then bring myself to do it. So can't you form the intention to take the pill, even though you doubt that you will carry it out? Such an intention might do you little good; the millionaire, sharing your doubt, might not put any money into your bank account. But this apart, can you form the intention? For it is not that you have some doubt that you will actually bring yourself to carry it out. It seems that you have no doubt at all that, come tomorrow, it would be positively unreasonable for you to take the pill. Surely, you have no doubt that you will not do something that, at the time, you will neither desire to do nor think reasonable to do. You might enlist the services of a professional hypnotist in the hope that you could bring yourself to take the pill as the result of posthypnotic suggestion, but this would not be, in any ordinary sense, to form an intention to take the pill, even if you bring it about that you have the intention.

Suppose then that you cannot form the intention to take the pill even though if you could, it would be advantageous for you to do so. Now apply this conclusion to our dilemmas. It seems that you cannot adopt a policy that may require you to choose a dispreferred action, for the same reason that you cannot form an intention to take the pill. Adopting the policy requires forming the intention to act in accordance with it, and this you cannot do. Granted that it would be beneficial for you to adopt the policy if you could; the fact is, or so it seems, that you cannot.

This may seem regrettable. But many inabilities are regrettable. One could frequently expect to benefit if one could perform actions that are beyond one's powers. But one's powers are limited, and one limitation, although perhaps not one of which we are usually aware, has to do with the capacity to form intentions. One cannot just form the intention to do anything at all. In particular, one cannot form the intention to do what one believes that one would neither desire nor have reason to do.

If we accept this argument, then we have resolved the dilemmas of deterrence and disarmament. Neither is a policy possible whenever its adoption would commit its holder, should certain conditions come about, to do something that he or she cannot do—in the case of deterrence, to retaliate when he or she would prefer to acquiesce; in the case of disarmament, to disarm when the holder would prefer to remain armed.

Rethinking Kavka's Case

But how strange that it is not possible for us to adopt policies that, could we but adopt them, would be in our interest, and that do not call for actions exceeding our physical or mental capacities. Let us reconsider the argument of the preceding section. So let us rethink Kavka's example. Perhaps it is not downright foolish for you to take the pill. Consider how you might respond to someone asking you why you were taking it. You might say that it had been to your advantage to commit yourself to taking the pill, that committing yourself and then carrying out your commitment were clearly better than not committing yourself at all, and now you are simply carrying out your commitment. You could point out that if you did not take the pill, then given that the circumstances are just what you anticipated in making the commitment, you could not really have committed yourself.

Could you say more? Suppose that when the eccentric millionaire offered you the opportunity, you realized that a bondage freak would have no problem arranging to take the pill the following morning. Before midnight, she (or he) would lock herself into her favorite chains, so arranging it that a time-release device would drop the pill into her mouth—wired open—the next morning, and only later would a further device drop the key into a position from which she could reach it to unlock her chains. Now you, unless you are a bondage freak, would no doubt find this unpleasant—but for $100,000? If the millionaire allowed you this method of committing yourself to take the pill, would it not be rational for you to adopt it in lieu of a better one?

But of course there is a better method (for those of us who are not bondage freaks). You can avoid the cost of being chained up all night with your mouth wired open. You can simply make up your mind to take the pill no matter what. If it would be rational for you to undergo some real unpleasantness to ensure your taking the pill, then is it not rational for you to adopt a procedure that leads to your taking the pill without incurring that cost? The least costly procedure is simply to commit yourself.

Resorting to bondage would be a way of denying yourself the choice between taking and not taking the pill. If you believe that, given the choice, you would not take the pill, then you would want to deny yourself the choice. But if you would want to deny yourself the choice rather than choose not to take the pill, then is it not rational for you to choose to take it, rather than either denying yourself the choice at some cost or choosing not to take it? If it is not downright foolish, but rather perfectly sensible, to force the pill on yourself at some cost, then is it not even more sensible, and not foolish at all, simply to choose to take the pill? Is it not an irrational inability to resist temptation that might lead you not to take it, rather than a determination to choose rationally? I think it is.

Keeping Promises

Rational people can commit themselves to perform a dispreferred action and carry out their commitment. This is my claim. It may seem even more plausible if we consider a very different example. Consider one of our fundamental moral practices—promising.

One might treat promising as a device for coordinating the actions of different persons and for communicating intentions. But the obligatory character of a promise bespeaks something more. One is expected to keep one's promise even if doing so is not in one's interest— not one's preferred or utility-maximizing action. Of course, one's promise does not override all concern with one's interest. If I promise to meet you at the ballgame tomorrow, you would not expect me to endanger my life in order to show up, but you would expect me to decline some more attractive prospect should it present itself. One might then think of promising as a practice from which everyone expects to benefit given that one may expect to gain more on balance as promisee than one loses as promisor. But were this all, it would seem to be in one's interest to accept promises but not to make them. Rather, I suggest, promising is a practice whereby one commits oneself, where it is to one's advantage at the time of making the commitment, to be committed. It is then a device for denying oneself the right to act on some subsequent occasion on one's usual basis of choosing one's most preferred act.

Consider this example. Suppose that next week you will help me to harvest my crops, provided you can count on my assistance in harvesting your crops the following week. But at the end of the season I am giving up farming and retiring to Florida; I will have nothing to gain, in terms of future dealings with you or others in our community, by helping you. But it is worth my while to get your help in exchange for helping you. I need a device to commit myself, to give you the assurance that if you help me, I will help you even if, after receiving your assistance, I have nothing further to gain. Promising is just this device. In making a sincere promise, I commit myself to helping you—not, to be sure, no matter what, but despite the usual temptations that may arise. Absent such a device, I have no way of giving you the assurance you need so that I may gain your assistance next week.

Promising, we think, creates a moral obligation, and in this view it does, in the sense that it commits promise-makers to act without regard to their direct preferences. But promising does this because it is advantageous to us to have available a practice of commitment and to be able to put ourselves under obligation. We do not think it downright foolish to carry out our obligations, even if carrying them out runs counter to our interests.

This may seem a low view of promising and its attendant moral obligation. On the contrary, I think this view demystifies promising and its obligatory character. We can see clearly the point of having a practice, adherence to which requires that one be willing to override one's usual concern with fulfilling one's preferences. My analysis does not explain away the obligation, but rather makes it intelligible by placing it within the framework of rationality.

Understanding the existence of and rationale for practices by which we commit ourselves to act in ways that, absent such practices, we should deem irrational— ways that lead us to incur costs that do not themselves bring about greater benefits— enables us to understand the rationality and possibility of deterrence and disarmament policies. We resolve the dilemmas of rationality that seem to plague these policies by recognizing that each requires a commitment on the part of the agent to act, given certain conditions, in an otherwise irrational manner, and that the agent may have sufficient reason to undertake such a commitment. A nation faced with the need to deter, or the desire to disarm, does not want to be free to act in its ordinary way because such freedom would prevent it giving some other party the assurance needed to influence its behavior in the way that maximizes the nation's expectation of benefit.

In defending the rationality of deterrence and disarmament policies, in those contexts in which adopting the policies maximizes one's expectation of benefit, I am implicitly advocating a revision in our usual account of rationality. I am arguing that the rationality of a particular action or choice must be judged, not in isolation, but in an appropriate context. Intentions, plans, commitments, and dispositions are all tied to particular choices in ways that rule out certain combinations—one cannot sincerely commit oneself to do x if one is quite sure that one will actually do y: A person disposed to promise-keeping cannot consistently fail to ignore his or her particular promises. Thus, I suppose that although it is indeed rational to seek the greatest fulfillment of one's preferences, it is rational to do this at the level of one's overall set of dispositions, intentions, and particular choices.[5] Hence, one is not rationally prevented from adopting a policy because it calls for particular actions that in themselves run counter to one's preferences. The apparent dilemmas of deterrence and disarmament arise from an inadequate understanding of rationality. If agents expect to do best by adopting a deterrence or disarmament policy, then it is rational for them to do so, and it is within their capacity to form and to carry out any necessary commitments to particular dispreferred actions.

Integrating Deterrence with Disarmament

Before turning explicitly to the morality of deterrence and disarmament policies, I want to examine some of their effects and the linkages among them. A successful deterrence policy is primarily redistributive, making the deterring party better off and the deterred party worse off than they would otherwise have been. An unsuccessful deterrence policy is mutually costly, leading to the outcome least preferred by both parties. Thus, there need be no possible net gain, but there must be a possible net loss, from a deterrence policy. A disarmament policy is productive and cooperative. If successful, it makes both parties better off than had they remained armed. If unsuccessful, a disarmament policy either preserves the status quo—not expecting the other to disarm, one remains armed oneself—or is redistributive—one party mistakenly disarms unilaterally, making it worse off and the other better off than they would otherwise have been. Therefore, there need be no possible net loss, but there must be a possible net gain, from a disarmament policy.

This difference between deterrence and disarmament policies suggests that we should evaluate the need for each very differently. To resort to deterrence must be unwelcome, whereas to participate in mutual disarmament should be welcome. Both policies may be rational, but the rationality of a policy in given circumstances is one thing; the desirability of the circumstances, and hence the rationality of seeking or continuing them, is quite another. It is obviously rational to avoid, prevent, or terminate the circumstances that would make deterrence rational, whereas it is equally rational to seek or maintain the circumstances in which disarmament is rational. A rational deterrence policy thus looks to its own supercession—to ending the danger of an attack against which the best defense is the threat to retaliate. That it would be costly to carry out the threat makes it an unwelcome mode of defense, even when rational. Thus, to suppose that a situation of mutual deterrence should be considered stable and desirable would be quite mistaken. On the other hand, a rational disarmament policy looks to its own realization—to converting a conditional willingness to disarm if others may be expected to do likewise into an actual willingess because others are equally willing.

The need to resort to a deterrence policy should be a strong spur to the adoption of a disarmament policy. Recognizing that in existing circumstances, one's best defense involves making a threat that one would clearly not want to carry out, one

---

[5]This scratches the surface of very complex and controversial issues about maximizing rationality that I cannot pursue here. For some first words on the issues, see my *Morals by Agreement* (Oxford: Clarendon Press, 1986), pp. 182–187.

sees the need for transforming these circumstances. The surest transformation, if existing weaponry is such as to make deterrence rational, is to do away, multilaterally, with the weaponry. A nation that believes that because it can deter, it does not need to be willing to disarm, is pursuing a deeply irrational policy.

But if the need to resort to deterrence should lead to awareness of the rationality of mutual disarmament, the success of a rational disarmament policy may itself be furthered by the existence of a rational deterrence policy. The prospect of achieving mutual disarmament depends not only on saying, "I will disarm if I expect that you will," but also on reminding, "And I will not disarm if I expect that you will not." The most effective way of emphasizing this reminder may involve a firm policy of deterrence; thus, one says both "I will if you will" and "I will not, and what's more I'll surely retaliate, if you will not, and I will think then that you may attack." The need to deter thus creates an incentive for oneself to be willing to disarm, and the willingness to deter then creates an incentive for the other party to be willing to disarm. Neither of these incentives should be overlooked.

Thus, deterrence and disarmament can and should be viewed as linked policies, in precisely the way advocated four hundred years ago by Thomas Hobbes, when he said that "it is a precept, or generall rule of Reason, That every man, ought to endeavour Peace, as farre as he has hope of obtaining it; and when he cannot obtain it, that he may seek, and use, all helps, and advantages of Warre."[6] To seek peace is to be willing to disarm if others also are willing. To use all advantages of war is to be willing to retaliate if others attack. The costs of having to resort to the advantages of war should prevent one from being remiss in seeking peace. The willingness, nevertheless, to resort to those advantages should encourage others not to be remiss in seeking peace.

The lesson here is hard to learn and one that, in the real world, has yet to be learned sufficiently. There has been little serious attention given to the development of a policy that would integrate deterrence and disarmament. Such a policy would aim at bringing about a stable condition of multilateral disarmament in which the danger of nuclear warfare would be minimized in the long run and in which our present dependence on deterrence would be ended, not by abandoning deterrence unilaterally, but by using the commitment to deter in the absence of any better alternative as a means to motivate the agreement to provide such an alternative through disarming. We should deter in order to be able to disarm and then disarm so that we should no more need to deter.

Morality and Rationality

The link between deterrence and disarmament may help us understand their morality. This is my final theme, and I must be brief and, in one sense, dogmatic. For I shall have to appeal to a conception of morality that, given the scope of this chapter, I cannot defend here, although I do develop and defend it elsewhere.[7] I do not suppose that this conception, or its implications, will sit comfortably with everyone. Persons have radically different views, not only of the requirements and prohibitions of morality, but also of the appropriate way of grounding these requirements and prohibitions. Those who understand morality as based on divine command, or on natural

---

[6]Thomas Hobbes, *Leviathan* (London, 1651), Ch. 14.

[7]See, especially, Gauthier, *Morals by Agreement*.

rights, or on the greatest happiness of the greatest number, may all find my position unconvincing. But I cannot argue with these persons here. All that I can do is to sketch why I believe that a disarmament policy may be morally required and a deterrence policy morally acceptable when and insofar as each is rationally justifiable.

I have shown that there can be circumstances in which it is not only rational to commit oneself to deterrence or to disarmament, but irrational not so to commit oneself because commitment would offer one a better prospect than any alternative. I now want to insist that whatever morality may require or prohibit, it does not contravene rationality. In principle, morality may extend beyond rationality in prohibiting actions that are rationally permissible and requiring actions whose omissions are not rationally forbidden. But morality may not require actions that are rationally forbidden or prohibit those that are rationally required. A morality that would do either of these latter things would be irrational and therefore mistaken.

How precisely does morality relate to rationality? I have shown that in some circumstances it is rational to dispose oneself to act in ways that need not be in one's interest. One such way, relevant to our present concern, is promise-keeping, and this offers us the appropriate clue. Moral requirements override the pursuit of one's interests or the endeavor to fulfill one's preferences. But not all cases in which the pursuit of one's own interest is overridden constitute moral requirements. It would be peculiar to suppose that, in Kavka's example, you would be morally required to take the pill. When the pursuit of one's own interests is overridden for the benefit of others, we speak naturally of moral requirements. Such requirements are endorsed by reason in just the way we have seen in our discussion of promising. Insofar as people may expect to benefit by a practice that requires them not to act directly to further their own particular interests, then where that practice benefits others, it is not only rational but also moral.

This gives us a test for correct moral practices. For we need not and should not suppose that all of the practices, with their sundry requirements and prohibitions, that we have come to accept as part of our everyday morality will in fact receive the necessary seconding of reason. The true morality, in my view, is constituted by the set of mutually advantageous constraints on individual preference-satisfaction.

It is now easy to see that a willingness to disarm, if others are also willing, may well be a requirement of morality. For to refuse is to reject a constraint that if accepted by everyone, benefits each. My willingness to disarm promotes your good, just as your willingness promotes mine. Thus, if I am unwilling, I am giving in to the temptation to be a free-rider, to take advantage of others if they disarm, and to refuse to cooperate with them in bringing about a mutually beneficial state of affairs.

I want to praise the morality of mutual disarmament. But I also want to allay concern about the morality of deterrence, in those circumstances in which a deterrence policy is rationally adopted. This should not be surprising, given the way in which the policies are related. But let me argue the point directly. In the view of the morality I espouse, we may think of a moral community as a group of persons linked to each other by the mutually advantageous constraints needed for cooperation and sociability to be genuinely possible. Within such a community, deterrence would have no place, for it is a form of threat behavior, and one of the constraints that would surely be operative would be a prohibition of threats. To be sure, such a ban would not operate alone. The point of a deterrent threat is to prevent attack; within a moral community each person or party would be constrained from attacking or more generally from seeking to dominate or to control other community members. A moral community embraces free and autonomous individuals who respect and value each other's freedom and autonomy.

It is surely apparent that in the real world of nations, a moral community is in many cases limited or even absent. It would be foolish to suppose that the rules constraining behavior within such a community apply straightforwardly outside it. We must make Hobbes' distinction between validity *in foro interno* and *in foro externo*. Although the rules of a moral community are *in foro interno* valid—they represent the possibility of mutually advantageous and rational cooperation and sociability among both individual persons and nations—yet these rules are not therefore *in foro externo* valid; people who put these rules into direct practice where they are not followed by others would simply worsen their own position[8] and would more likely be victims of those who do not comply.

If we now ask how we might best bring about a moral community, where none initially exists, then it is plausible to suppose that such a community requires not only a willingness to abide by mutually beneficial constraints, but also a clear refusal to do so unilaterally. For if I am willing to constrain myself whether or not you do, then you have no initial incentive to join in a moral community with me. Instead, I simply make it easier for you to dominate me and to survive without putting yourself under any constraints in the pursuit of your own interest.

This suggests a general defense that may be offered for policies that would rightly be condemned within a moral community as admissible and even necessary if one is to bring such a community into being. But there are more particular considerations to note about deterrence. It is tempting to suppose that given the horrific consequences of escalating nuclear war by retaliation, the cost is so great that the risk of deterrence failure can never outweigh the benefit of preventing attack. But although the failure of deterrence, given a commitment to retaliate, does escalate nuclear war, the willingness to acquiesce without retaliation is no guarantee that such war will be avoided.

Let us return, briefly and speculatively, to the real-world situation. Some talk as if, were the United States to renounce its nuclear arsenal, then the threat of nuclear war would vanish because the Soviet Union would not use nuclear weapons against a non-nuclear opponent. But even now, several other nations have the capacity to engage in large-scale nuclear warfare, and their number must be expected to increase. It is surely in the strong interest of the United States to try preventing any outbreak of nuclear conflict as well as to avoid participating in such conflict itself. To that end, it is in the strong interest of the United States to promote multilateral nuclear disarmament. But, I believe, the United States can do this effectively only if it does not unilaterally renounce its own nuclear weapons or commit itself never to use them. I return to the idea that a deterrence policy is an incentive to others to move beyond deterrence and more generally beyond the development of and reliance on a nuclear arsenal. The hard truth here is that only a power willing to use nuclear weapons in some circumstances may expect to play a significant role in moving the world away from those circumstances in which nuclear weapons might be used.

---

[8]Hobbes, *Leviathan*, Ch. 15.

Hence, I have an operational test of both the rationality and the morality of a policy about nuclear weapons. Does it offer the best chance, all things considered, of moving the world away from those circumstances in which nuclear war might become a reality? That such a policy may involve short-run risks of the very war it would avoid, and that it may require us to embrace those risks in a way that, however rational, must be profoundly unwelcome, is one of the somber lessons that must be drawn from an analysis of the structure and relations of deterrence and disarmament policies.

DISARMAMENT

Prisoners and Chickens

Douglas P. Lackey

David Gauthier has a longstanding interest in the theory of games and in decision theory, and it is only natural that he should try to apply the insights of these disciplines to problems of nuclear weapons policy. This he has attempted to do in two recent and interesting analyses, "Deterrence, Maximization, and Rationality," (DMR) *Ethics* (April 1984), and "War and Nuclear Deterrence," first published in *Problems of International Justice* (Boulder: Westview Press, 1988). Roughly speaking, the focus of the earlier analysis is on nuclear deterrence; the later analysis addresses both deterrence and the nuclear arms race. Gauthier's argument implies that in certain conditions, conditions that many responsible parties believe presently to exist, nuclear deterrence is a game of Chicken and the nuclear arms race is a Prisoner's Dilemma. Given what he believes about Chicken and the Prisoner's Dilemma, he concludes that it is rational and moral to continue practicing nuclear deterrence and irrational and immoral to engage in unilateral nuclear disarmament. Any analysis of Gauthier's views, then, must address three issues: Is nuclear deterrence really a game of Chicken, and are the nuclear superpowers really in a Prisoner's Dilemma as regards nuclear weapons possession? Second, if we are playing Chicken and if we are in a Prisoner's Dilemma, are Gauthier's instructions as to how we should behave in these situations rationally justifiable? Third, if we are playing Chicken and if we are in a Prisoner's Dilemma and if Gauthier's instructions as to how we should behave in these situations are rationally justifiable, can we infer that rational conduct in these situations is also morally acceptable conduct?

What Games Are We Playing?

Is This Chicken?

The analysis of nuclear deterrence as Chicken goes back to Bertrand Russell's *Common Sense and Nuclear Warfare* (1959), in which Russell described Chicken as a game played by "elder statesmen and youthful degenerates."[1] Two cars deliberately speed toward each other head on. Each driver thinks that his best outcome is not swerving when the other swerves; his next best, swerving when the other swerves; his third best, swerving when the other does not; and his worst outcome, not swerving when the other does not. Russell noticed that this game was like mutual nuclear deterrence, in which each nation would prefer most to attack without being counterattacked; would prefer next to not attack if the other does not attack; would prefer next to be attacked without counterattacking; and would prefer least to be attacked and then to counterattack. (The reason why not counterattacking after a nuclear first strike is preferred to counterattacking is that such a counterattack is, according to Russell, "useless revenge.")

At the time, Thomas Schelling and others[2] noticed that this situation created a paradox as regards the rationality of threatening to counterattack. If your opponent, studying your own preference schedule, becomes confident that you will not counterattack when attacked, then your opponent, gunning for his or her best outcome, will attack, giving you your third best outcome. On the other hand, if you credibly threaten to counterattack when attacked, this will force your opponent to not attack, giving you your second best outcome. Given that your second best outcome beats your third, it seems ineluctably rational to threaten counterattacking when attacked. But now suppose that your opponent does not believe your threats and chooses to attack. If you stick by your threats, given what your opponent does, the result is your fourth best outcome, which is worse than your third.

If you are rational and free to choose what to do when the opponent attacks, you always will choose not to counterattack. Thus, your threats are never credible, and your opponent is free to attack if you are free to choose. Schelling's celebrated solution to this credibility problem was "the threat that leaves something to chance." If the decision to counterattack when attacked is automated, then the opponent cannot count on your free and rational choice not to respond. Because rationally you do not wish to respond when attacked and because it is not necessary to threaten an absolutely certain response in order to deter the opponent, Schelling's analysis suggests that the best strategy is not only automatic but randomized. One of the more exquisite results of decision-theoretic analysis in the late 1950s is that simple formulas determine the correct randomization ratios for "counterattack" and "do not counterattack" in this automated response, given what the opponent would hope to gain from attacking without being attacked and what the opponent would hope to lose by attacking and then suffering counterattack.[3]

Now what is historically relevant about Schelling's line of thought is that it was never incorporated into mainstream strategic thinking by those U.S. decisionmakers who could have chosen to implement it. Part of the reason for this lack of enthusiasm was that the notion of a threat that leaves something to chance was (perhaps unfairly) associated with the brinkmanship of John Foster Dulles, and, in the

---

[1] For Russell's priority, see Douglas P. Lackey, "Bertrand Russell's Contribution to the Study of Nuclear Weapons Policy," *Russell* 4, no. 2 (Winter 1984–85).

[2] The relevant papers from the late 1950s are collected in Thomas Schelling, *The Strategy of Conflict* (Cambridge, Mass.: Harvard University Press, 1960).

[3] Daniel Ellsberg, "The Crude Analysis of Strategic Choice." *American Economic Review* (May 1961).

light of developing Soviet nuclear capacity, brinkmanship in the late 1950s was falling out of fashion. (It revived in October 1962.) The automated threat idea was also discredited by its Grand Guignol development into the doomsday machine described in Herman Kahn's *On Thermonuclear War* (Princeton, 1960); Kahn hypothesized that the perfect deterrent would be a credible device that would automatically blow up the world in the event of nuclear attack. But easily the strongest motive for not introducing automation and randomization into nuclear choices was the understandable reluctance of key decisionmakers to adopt policies that would put normally controllable actions beyond control at certain points in time. Presidents who precommit the nation to an automated and randomized chance of using nuclear weapons render themselves powerless to control events at the most crucial moment in U.S. history. Presumably persons who seek the presidency enjoy power. They are hardly likely to welcome or comprehend suggestions that in the deterrence game, impotence is bliss. Parallel psychological observations apply to the Soviet leadership.

I am not saying that Schelling's suggestions necessarily require the automation and randomization of Kahn's doomsday machine. On the contrary, it might be possible to develop a posture that gives the president the power to control the decision to use nuclear weapons, but that also acknowledges and publicizes the fact that in the radioactive fog of modern war there is a certain likelihood that U.S. nuclear weapons will be used even in the face of explicit presidential (or National Command Authority) orders to desist. The ineliminable chance of such unauthorized use might be high enough to provide a credible deterrent against Soviet or Warsaw Pact attack. But it does not seem that U.S. leaders around 1960 thought of "the threat that leaves something to chance" along these lines, nor did they design command and control systems to facilitate what came to be known as "the rationality of irrationality."

What John Kennedy, Robert McNamara, William Kaufmann, and Daniel Ellsberg sought to do when they replaced Massive Retaliation with Flexible Response was to design nuclear weapons policies that transcended the game of Chicken altogether. To do this, it was necessary to design nuclear second strikes whose launch would be rational in the event of a Soviet first strike. The single-massive-attack option provided to the president in the first single-integrated operational plan of 1960 was replaced by five attack options in the plan of 1962. In 1974, Secretary of Defense James R. Schlesinger broadened the scope of presidential choice by introducing a variety of limited nuclear options over and above the five big strikes of the 1962 plan.[4] On the European front, a succession of presidents repeatedly refused to endorse a pledge of "no first use" of tactical and intermediate-range nuclear weapons. From all this, we can infer that U.S. leaders have believed since 1962 and continue to believe that in the event of Soviet attacks of various types it would be rational to use nuclear weapons, *at that moment,* independently of all prior considerations of deterrence. Indeed, the situations in which U.S. leaders consider it rational to use nuclear weapons are the very situations in which U.S. leaders threaten to use them. If this is so, the United States is not playing Chicken with its nuclear threats. U.S. leaders believe that it is better to counterattack when attacked than to not counterattack when attacked.

This is not the only reason why Chicken is an inappropriate model for nuclear deterrence as it is currently practiced by

---

[4]Desmond Ball. *Targeting for Strategic Deterrence* (London: Institute for Strategic Studies, 1983).

the superpowers. In Chicken, each player prefers attacking if not counterattacked to not attacking at all. But if the attack in question is a nuclear attack, it is not clear that the Soviets would prefer to launch a nuclear attack, assuming no counterattack, over not launching a nuclear attack at all. Nuclear attacks on land destroy assets that one might seek to exploit, and even in the case of nuclear attacks at sea, it is possible to accomplish everything one might wish to achieve militarily with precision-guided conventional weapons in lieu of nuclear weapons. The Soviets have always presumed the superiority of their conventional forces, which is why they have always been prepared to endorse an agreement for "no first use." Why then would they prefer launching a nuclear attack to launching a conventional attack? Why, indeed, would they prefer any attack on the West at all, given their firsthand knowledge of the horrors of conventional war, and given their need to sell natural gas and maintain trade with freely and thereby eagerly cooperating Western states?

A person who maintains that Chicken correctly models the present superpower confrontation must maintain that, regardless of leadership beliefs, presently planned nuclear responses in fact are not rational, when assessed after a first strike and independently of prior considerations concerning deterrence. But current plans contain a wide variety of nuclear responses to a wide variety of Soviet provocations. What is the argument that *every one* of these responses is irrational? Clearly some of them are irrational, but some might not be. Among the clearly irrational I would include all responses that require a first use of tactical nuclear weapons when the Soviets have used none yet or a first use of strategic weapons when the Soviets have used none yet. But how about using tactical nuclear weapons after the Soviets have already used them and using strategic weapons after the Soviets have already used them? Is it so obvious that all types of these uses are irrational? Will every tit-for-tat response escalate the conflict, or will some tit-for-tat responses persuade the opponent to stop at that level?

Let us consider one of the grisliest first-strike scenarios, in which the USSR launches an all-out counterforce strike against the United States. After the strike, Soviet and Cuban troops, *Red Dawn*-style, prepare to occupy the United States. Assume that, despite everything, one U.S. nuclear submarine remains undestroyed at sea. Would it be irrational for the submarine commander, independently of prior considerations of deterrence, to launch a limited counterforce nuclear attack on the Soviet Union? Perhaps not, if such a strike could forestall the occupation of the United States.

My conclusion is that across a broad spectrum of situations, and independently of prior considerations of deterrence, it would not be irrational to execute nuclear threats. If so, the deterrence game is not a Chicken game. Such executions of nuclear threats in nearly all cases would be immoral, but that is another matter.

Is This a Prisoner's Dilemma?

Gauthier and nearly all authors who write about the nuclear arms race assume that the present situation as regards nuclear weapons acquisition and possession is a Prisoner's Dilemma. In this view, it is better for neither side to possess nuclear weapons than for both sides to possess them, but it is best for each to possess them when the other side does not, and it is worst for each to not possess nuclear weapons when the other side does. This preference pattern forms a Prisoner's Dilemma, and the usual grim results follow, in particular the result that it is better for each to possess nuclear weapons regardless of what the other side does. On the strength of this argument each side chooses to possess. Both sides end up with nuclear weapons, even though each side realizes it would be better off if neither possessed them.

Despite near unanimity on this subject, I do not believe that the Prisoner's Dilemma is the correct model for superpower weapons choices.[5] First, it is not obvious that the NATO countries believe that mutual nonpossession of nuclear weapons is better than mutual possession. When the NATO states decided to introduce tactical and intermediate-range nuclear weapons into NATO forces after the Lisbon meeting in 1953, they did so because they were not prepared, politically or financially, to field enough divisions to offset the strength of Soviet conventional forces. Nuclear weapons were billed as providing more bang for the buck, which made them congenial both to the budget-conscious Eisenhower administration and to Western European leaders, whose sense of the Red Menace was subsiding after the death of Joseph Stalin. It remains true today that NATO states are not prepared to bear the costs of achieving conventional parity in the European theater, even though the gap between NATO conventional strength and Warsaw Pact conventional strength, given recent developments in antitank weaponry, is perhaps smaller now than at any time since the Warsaw Pact was founded in 1955.

Second, although this is much tougher sledding, it is not clear to me that it is preferable for the United States to possess nuclear weapons when the other side possesses them, compared with not possessing them when the other side possesses them.[6] A full test of the rationality of U.S. nuclear possession in the face of Soviet nuclear arms must take into account the full range of costs of nuclear weapons possession for the United States, compared with unilateral nonpossession. These costs include (a) the possibility of involvement in a nuclear war that begins with a first strike or first use by the United States; (b) the possibility of involvement in an all-out, two-sided nuclear war that destroys life on most of the planet; (c) an increased chance of a Soviet first strike intended to preempt a presumed U.S. first strike; (d) the deterioration of U.S. conventional military capability due to a high-tech strategic emphasis focused around nuclear weapons and nuclear delivery systems; (e) the deterioration of the U.S. economy due to a monopoly of top scientific and engineering talent by the strategic weapons fraction of the national research budget; and (f) a decline in civil liberties and in democratic involvement in federal decisionmaking due to the secrecy within which nuclear weapons systems are necessarily enshrouded.

These costs must be carefully weighed against the costs of unilateral nuclear disarmament, of which the most frequently mentioned is a substantially increased chance of nuclear blackmail. A full assessment of the risks of nuclear blackmail cannot be given here,[7] but I must say that I

---

[5]For an attack on the appropriateness of the Prisoner's Dilemma model, see D. Lackey, "Ethics and Nuclear Deterrence." in *Moral Problems*, edited by James Rachels (New York: Harper and Row, 1975).

[6]This argument is presented in my "Missiles and Morals," *Philosophy and Public Affairs* 11 (Summer 1982): 189–232.

[7]The best assessment of nuclear blackmail known to me is Jeffrey McMahan's chapter, "Nuclear Blackmail," in *Dangers of Deterrence*, edited by Nigel Blake and Kay Pole (London: Routledge and Kegan Paul, 1983).

think that these risks have been very much exaggerated. There are few genuine conflicts of interest between the United States and the Soviet Union, conflicts of the sort that would lead to a military confrontation that the Soviet Union would win if it held the nuclear cards. There are, of course, ideological conflicts between the superpowers—we would like to see the Soviet Union out of Afghanistan, off of Poland's back, less repressive toward its own dissidents, and so forth. (I call these "ideological" conflicts because their outcome does not affect U.S. domestic liberty or the U.S. standard of living.) But the current possession of nuclear weapons by the United States does not seem to have intimidated the Soviets into withdrawing from Afghanistan or accepting Solidarity, nor is it likely that there are many new repressive schemes that the Soviets would inflict on their own people in the face of unilateral U.S. nuclear disarmament. On the contrary, the presence of a palpable external nuclear threat only assists the Soviets in the business of domestic repression. Furthermore, one must recognize that what matters in nuclear blackmail is not whether it will be attempted but whether it will succeed, and it will not succeed if we are determined to resist it.

I recognize the heresy in this argument, and I am well aware of the fear that grips Americans at the prospect of unilateral nuclear disarmament. Why then, critics say, the Soviets could destroy the United States in the flicker of an eye. To which comes the obvious reply: They can do that now. If this argument is right, we are not forced into possession by the argument that possession dominates nonpossession, as the noncooperative choice dominates the cooperative choice in a Prisoner's Dilemma. If we acquire and retain nuclear weapons, we do so not on game-theoretic grounds but on the expectations of utility maximization that may well be empirically mistaken.

What Is Rational Play?

Chicken and the Deterrence Paradox

Suppose that the preceding arguments are unsound and that nuclear deterrence is indeed a Chicken game. In this view, it is irrational to carry out a threat to counterattack if attacked, assuming that we evaluate the counterattack independently of all prior considerations concerning deterrence. Then the critical problem for decision theory becomes whether or not it is rational to make such threats.

We can make such threats in four ways: We can threaten insincerely, intending not to counterattack when attacked and retaining full capacity to desist if attacked. We can threaten neutrally, not forming an intention to counterattack and not forming an intention not to counterattack. We can threaten sincerely, committing ourselves to carrying out a counterattack and guaranteeing this commitment by rendering ourselves unable to not counterattack when attacked. Or we can threaten sincerely, forming an intention to counterattack when attacked.

The first sort of threat, essentially a bluff, is recommended by the National Council of Catholic Bishops.[8] Neutral threats were described and recommended by David Fisher in his book *Morality and the Bomb*.[9] The third sort of threat, sincere and helplessly committed, was recommended by Thomas Schelling, and its moral respectability has recently been defended by Daniel Farrell in the first issue

---

[8] The National Council of Catholic Bishops, *The Challenge of Peace: God's Promise and Our Response* (Washington, D.C.: United States Catholic Conference, 1983), p. 17.

[9] David Fisher, *Morality and the Bomb* (New York: St. Martin's Press, 1985), p. 76.

of *Public Affairs Quarterly*.[10] The fourth sort, sincere and freely committed, is defended by David Gauthier. What Gauthier says is that if your threat to counterattack is utility maximizing, then it is rational to execute the threat, even though it is not utility maximizing to execute it and even if it is within your power to not execute it. What this means is that if it is utility maximizing for the United States to threaten a nuclear second strike of type A after experiencing a first strike of type B, then in the event of a first strike of type B it is rationally required to launch a second strike of type A, even though *at that time* it would not be utility maximizing to do so.

Despite the attraction of nuclear bluffs, it is exceedingly unlikely that the United States could maintain a policy in which threats of counterattack are completely insincere. The U.S. right wing would discover this policy and call it treason, and the United States would have a new administration in four years or less. Likewise, the option of neutral threats is a nonstarter if we are really playing Chicken; if we leave open the choice of responding or not responding, we will always, when the attack comes, choose not to respond because we have no reason to respond, not even the reason that we have made a prior commitment to do so. If the neutrality of our posture became known, our threats would fail to deter because the opponent would recognize that we would always decide not to carry them out. All real deterrent threats, in a Chicken game, must be sincere threats.

Among sincere threats, the most convincing sort require relinquishing the ability to not execute the threat. For reasons given previously, policies involving such threats have never been popular in Washington, although some strategies have suggested a semiautomated launch-on-warning system as a remedy for ICBM vulnerability. Given the stories that have leaked out during the years and throughout the 1980s about difficulties in the U.S. attack assessment system,[11] there is a justified fear that an automated system might turn sorcerer's apprentice and set off a nuclear attack in response to a nonexistent first strike. Once the disutility of mistaken and accidental launches is added in, it appears likely that automated deterrent threats do not maximize expected value and therefore should not even be made, much less executed.

What about the rationality of sincere threats that involve a commitment to a freely chosen second strike? Here we can reason in three ways. We could argue that because the execution of the threat is irrational, the making of the threat must be irrational, too. This is the standard view. Or we could argue that because the making of the threat is rational, the execution of the threat must be rational as well. The second view is Gauthier's in DMR. The third view is that the rationality of threat-making is logically independent of threat execution.

Because making a threat and executing a threat are distinct events, it would seem to follow that they must be logically independent of each other and that the third view is correct. But if by "making a threat" we mean making a sincere threat that includes forming the intention to execute the threat if conditions warrant, then threat-making and threat execution are logically related. The reason, explicated by Gregory Kavka,[12] is that it is logically impossible to form an

---

[10]Daniel M. Farrell, "Strategic Planning and Moral Norms: The Case of Deterrent Nuclear Threats," *Public Affairs Quarterly* 1. no. 1 (January 1987): 61–78.

[11]For anecdotes that would make for comedy were they not all too real, see Daniel Ford. *The Button* (New York: Simon and Schuster, 1985).

[12]Gregory Kavka, "The Toxin Puzzle," *Analysis* 43 (June 1983): 33–36.

intention to do X unless one feels that there will be good reasons to do X when the time comes to do it. One cannot form intentions at will, in the absence of reasons, no more than one can form beliefs at will, in the absence of what one takes to be evidence. For this sort of sincere threat, the threat-making and the threat execution must be both rational or both irrational. But which is it?

Why should we say that if executing such a threat is irrational, making the threat must be irrational as well? The main reason is that rational action is simply utility-maximizing action. If it is clear that executing the threat is not utility maximizing at the time of executing it, then it is not rational to execute the threat, and from this it follows that it is not rational to make the threat. Indeed, in Kavka's view, it is not even possible to make the threat because we cannot form an intention to perform an action that we know will be irrational at the time of performance.

The trouble with this argument is that it seems to work equally well in the opposite direction. If making the threat is utility maximizing, then it is rational to make it, and from this it follows that it would be rational to carry the threat out. Because it would be rational to carry the threat out, it is quite possible to form the intention to carry it out. So far, the result is stalemate.

When Kavka says that executing the threat is irrational and Gauthier says that executing the threat is rational, they are not in fact contradicting each other because they are using the word *rational* in different senses. When Kavka says that executing the threat is irrational, he means simply that executing the threat is not utility maximizing at the time of execution, and Gauthier certainly agrees that it is not utility maximizing *then* to execute the threat. Gauthier is arguing that it is rational to execute the threat because execution follows from a utility-maximizing policy, and Kavka certainly would agree that executing the threat proceeds from a utility-maximizing policy adopted at an earlier point in time. Which sense of rationality is true rationality, the sort that a rational person should follow when subjected to attack?

Gauthier believes that his sense of "rational" is clearly superior because "the fully rational actor is not one who assesses her actions from now but who subjects the largest, rather than the smallest, segments of her activity to primary rational scrutiny, proceeding from policies to performances, letting assessment of the latter be ruled by assessment of the former."[13] The background force of Gauthier's argument is Platonic: If we evaluate from the point of execution, we are bound up in time; if we evaluate from the stretch of time that includes both the threat-making and the threat execution, we are comparatively emancipated from time, looking at things sub specie aeternitatis, as philosophers should. If this is his argument, there are three ways in which it might be going wrong.

The first problem is that the argument assumes a continuity of self through the stretch of time that includes the threat-making and the threat execution. If we are Buddhists or Humeans and believe that things in the universe are loosely connected, then such continuity of self cannot be presumed. We have instead many selves at many points in time, each undertaking a rational evaluation from its own point of view. The same conclusion follows if we endorse a solipsism of the present moment, which seems to have led Aristippus to his view that the truly rational person seeks to maximize the pleasures of each present moment.

---

[13]David Gauthier, "Deterrence, Maximization, and Rationality," *Ethics* (April 1984): 488.

The second problem is that Gauthier's view might not be as temporally emancipated as he believes it is. Is it really the case that the person who evaluates the rationality of executing a threat from the time of execution is making the evaluation in a "small" stretch of time, while the person who evaluates the rationality of executing the threat from the standpoint of a policy regarding threat execution is making the evaluation in a "larger" stretch of time? Is it not rather the case that the policy of threat execution is adopted at a certain point in time, the point at which the threat is made, and that this point in time is no "larger" than the point of threat execution? If so, all that Gauthier is arguing is that the evaluation from the earlier point should prevail over the evaluation from the later point. Other things being equal, the preference for the earlier point is odd because at the later point we have more information relevant to the question of what we ought to do, especially the information that an attack has occurred. What, at the point of threat-making, is simply a probability of attack becomes, at the time of threat execution, a certainty of attack. (The wave packet of attack probability collapses at that point!) All that we are doing, at each point in time, is making choices that maximize utility in the future, and to assist us in making these choices we are rationally required to use all the information we can get.

The third and final problem is that it is not self-evident that philosophical wisdom consists in viewing matters sub specie aeternitatis. If time is unreal, then it is indeed wise to adopt this stance, but if time is real, then the stance is unwise.

Consider the following puzzle, suggested by Derek Parfit. You wake up and discover that you are in a hospital, with no memory of what happened the day before. You ask the nurse for information, and she says that her memory is bad but you are one of two persons: Person A, who had a terribly painful operation without anaesthetic the day before and then was hypnotized to forget the whole thing, or Person B, who is due to have a mildly painful operation tomorrow. Which person would you rather be? If you prefer the alternative that maximizes utility in your life, you prefer to be person B. If you prefer the alternative that maximizes utility in the stretch of life that remains before you, you prefer to be person A. Despite his affection, in other contexts, for non-utility-maximizing actions, Gauthier would clearly prefer to be person B. Most people, thinking that what matters are pains and pleasures yet to come, would prefer to be person A. Because such persons prefer lives in which there is more pain over other lives with less pain, ceteris paribus, Gauthier would dismiss the preferences of these persons as irrational.

Nevertheless, it seems to me that it is rational to prefer being person A, the person whose pain is over and done with. The reason is that our standards of rationality judge actions by their effects, and all the effects of an action come after the act. The "choice" in Parfit's example is confusing because it appears that you are given a choice as to what life you are to have, rather than a choice as to what action you will take in that life.

The choice of which person you would rather be instead of which action you would rather undertake is like the choice of a Leibnizian God who is choosing among possible worlds, each with their complete and inalterable histories. But in human life there are no such choices of lives, only choices within lives. If we chose lives before we lived them, who would be making the choice? Even if the philosopher should view things sub specie aeternitatis, the decision theorist should not.

Escaping Prisoner's Dilemmas

Gauthier's advice as regards the arms race is considerably less radical than is his advice regarding deterrence. He counsels that we should disarm if the other side disarms, but we should not disarm if we expect that the other side will not. Multilateral disarmament is wise; unilateral disarmament is very unwise. This is simple advice, but there are problems with it.

To begin, Gauthier does not acknowledge that there is a relationship between deterrence and the arms race. If you feel that it is necessary to play the deterrence game so long as your opponent has any nuclear weapons at all, then you will not be able to go through with a policy of multilateral disarmament. Suppose serendipitously the United States and the Soviet Union adopt a plan under which 10 percent of their nuclear arsenals, matched for strategic importance, will be scrapped each month. At the start, as the arsenals come down, each side will retain the ability to deter the other with threats of a second strike. Unfortunately, given the fact that each nuclear weapon when used can knock several opposing nuclear weapons out of commission, a time will come in the disarmament process when each side, if it attacks first, will be able to destroy enough of the strategic weapons of the other side that it may be utility maximizing to attempt a first strike. Furthermore, as soon as it begins to look possible and profitable for each side to launch a first strike, pressure increases on each side to launch a preemptive first strike, on the fear that the other side might succumb to temptation. If the preferences of nations are as Gauthier describes them (contrary to the account at the beginning of this chapter)—that nations prefer attack without retaliation to no attack—then the mutual disarmament process may well be doomed. To escape the armaments trap we must escape the deterrence trap first.

A second difficulty with Gauthier's "disarm mutually" program is that it provides no incentive for taking unilateral first steps. I may be prepared to disarm if and when my opponent disarms; my opponent may be prepared to disarm if and when I disarm. Even if we both prefer mutual disarmament to mutual armament, there is no way to move from mutual armament to mutual disarmament, unless one side is prepared to act first. If Gauthier's distrust of unilateral disarmament extends to distrust of such unilateral steps, then the mutually advantageous result will never be reached. The fact that Gauthier analyzes the arms race in terms of conditional strategies such as "disarm if the other side does" shows that he is perhaps thinking of the arms race not as a simple Prisoner's Dilemma but as a repeated game in which previous moves are kept in account. Then the strategy he proposes is "disarm if the other side has chosen to disarm in the most recent play of the game." Many authors have suggested such repeated play routes out of the iterated Prisoner's Dilemma, and Robert Axelrod's computer tournaments have shown that if the world is a system in which different players play repeated Prisoner's Dilemmas against each other, round robin, you will probably be best off if you (a) cooperate after the other side does, (b) do not cooperate after the other side does not, and (c) never are first not to cooperate (this strategy is known as Tit For Tat).[14]

The problem for nations in the real world—not Axelrod's computer world—is this: If the superpowers are locked in a Prisoner's Dilemma, as Gauthier thinks they are, will Tit For Tat get them out of it? I think not, for two reasons.

---

[14] Robert Axelrod, *The Evolution of Cooperation* (New York: Basic Books, 1984).

First, many strategists exude confidence about Tit For Tat,[15] but the results of Axelrod's tournaments, fascinating in themselves, have little application to the current superpower confrontation. Tit For Tat "defeated" opposing strategies only in the sense that it scored highest in a round robin tournament. In pairwise confrontations, Tit For Tat never managed better than a tie. In short, Tit For Tat beat no one; the other strategies beat each other. Now, in the present historical situation, the superpowers play each other, while the other powers largely cheer from the sidelines. In such pairwise situations, there is no reason to think that Tit For Tat will do best in the long run.

Second, all repeated play escapes from the Prisoner's Dilemma require both sides to correctly identify the moves of the opponent and to remember those moves in succeeding plays of the game. But on the superpower scene there is little charity extended when interpreting the moves of the other side—does anyone on the U.S. side believe that the Krasnoyark radar might be, as the Soviets say, just a satellite tracking system?—and the ability of both sides to remember past moves seems to be sorely limited. The efforts of a generation toward mutual disarmament can be sabotaged in a week by a president with faulty memory, especially if he has at his side a legal staff prepared to interpret past agreements not in the light of what was agreed to then but in conformity with what is convenient now.

What Is Moral Play?

The Morality of Deterrence

The bulk of Gauthier's arguments intends to show that nuclear retaliation can be rational and that unilateral disarmament is irrational. Confident that these judgments are rational, he claims that they are morally obligatory as well. Certainly, in the moral system developed in his splendid book, *Morals by Agreement* (Oxford: Clarendon Press, 1986), Gauthier repeatedly alleges that there is an intimate connection between the moral and the rational; morality, it turns out, is simply constrained maximization. To dispute Gauthier's conclusions, it seems, is to begin the descent into irrationalism and barbarism.

But of course the contractarian system developed in *Morals by Agreement* is not the only moral system that carries the torch for rationality. Jeremy Bentham considered himself to be establishing morality as an exact science, and Immanuael Kant felt that he had discovered the rules of conduct for all rational beings. Hence, the question we should address is not whether Gauthier is right in claiming a deep connection between rationality and morality but whether he has discovered the right connection.

Let us go back to Gauthier's argument for the rationality of nuclear retaliation. Let us assume that it really is utility maximizing to threaten nuclear second strikes, but that such threats are utility maximizing only if we form intentions to carry them out. Unfortunately, our threats fail and we suffer a first strike. In that event, says Gauthier, we are rationally bound to carry out a second strike. The parallel argument for morality, then, must be that it is morally obligatory to make second strike threats and that if it is morally obligatory to make such threats, it must be morally obligatory to carry them out when conditions warrant. This parallel claim, however, raises a host of problems.

First, where is Gauthier's argument that it is morally obligatory to make the threat? He suggests hesitantly that the threat is utility maximizing, but the fact that an act is utility maximizing for the agent is hardly

---

[15] One such is Bruce Russett, *The Prisoners of Insecurity* (San Francisco: W. H. Freeman, 1983).

sufficient, even in Gauthier's system, for demonstrating the moral obligatoriness of the act. Even if Gauthier believes, as I do not, that the second-strike nuclear threats of the United States are utility maximizing for humankind, I do not think that this constitutes a proof that it is morally obligatory to make these threats.

Second, even if we assume that making the threat is morally obligatory, where is the proof that the moral obligatoriness of making the threat carries over to the moral obligatoriness of executing the threat? Gauthier argues, you will recall, that the rationality of threat-making carried over into the rationality of threat execution because the rationality of threat-making involved a policy that covered a "larger stretch of time" than did the policy involved in threat execution. We found that there was reason to challenge this argument. But even if the argument goes through for the rationality of threat-making, what reason is there to think that it goes through for the morality of threat-making? Isn't making a moral decision a matter that involves the condition of one's soul at the time that the decision is made? Isn't one's character affected by what one imagines oneself doing if one adopts the policy? We are considering here a policy that requires a conditional commitment to killing millions of human beings, and the conditions that provoke such killing are not fully under our control. I cannot believe that people of good character can morally commit themselves to this course of action, even conditionally. If I am right, it follows that the moral impermissibility of executing the threat spills backward into the moral impermissibility of making it.

Morality and Disarmament

Just as we are rationally obliged to forgo maximizing utility when we execute our deterrent threats, we are rationally obliged to forgo maximizing utility and meet moves toward disarmament by our opponents with disarmament moves of our own. But we are not obliged, and for Gauthier not permitted, to make disarmament moves that are not reciprocated. But suppose that unilateral disarmament by one party, although a disadvantage to that party, would be a great advantage to the world as a whole. For example, if one side gave up its nuclear weapons unilaterally, this would eliminate the chance of an all-out, two-sided nuclear war, the kind of nuclear war that at a minimum would throw the human race back to the Stone Age. If so, then utilitarianism would require that the United States make such a move and unilaterally give up its nuclear weapons. (Utilitarianism makes such a demand on the USSR as well, but the two demands are logically independent, and what the USSR does makes no difference as to what the United States should do.)

Now, it is one of the features of Gauthier's concept, not Bentham's, of the rational basis of morality that morality as a whole cannot require individuals to take such losses. Morality may constrain us from maximizing as much as we might, but it cannot constrain us so much that we are worse off, at least in terms of expected value, under the moral regime than we would be if there were no moral regime at all. Thus, Gauthier's system will not require any nation to make sacrifices for the welfare of humankind, unless humankind is prepared to make some sacrifices in return. This idea of confining morality to mutually advantageous sacrifices is appealing, but in such cases where the harm to the individual is relatively small and the gain to the human race is great, I think unilateral sacrifices are in fact moral duties. Rational cooperation, then, is not the ultimate moral standard; rather, insistence on rational cooperation is impermissible if the overall results of cooperation for the human race are markedly inferior to those obtainable by unilateral sacrifice.

The improvements in the human condition brought about by rational cooperation are so extensive and dramatic that one may be swept away into thinking that rational cooperation can do no harm and that every breach of the standards for cooperation can do no good. But now and then situations arise in which the threat to the common interest of humanity is so great and the obstacles to cooperation are so substantial that an insistence on a mutual approach to the difficulty may cause enough delay to ensure disaster. Perhaps the possession of nuclear weapons by antagonistic superpowers is just such a situation. For humanity's sake, then, unilateral sacrifices are morally required. But for those of us who consider nuclear weapons worse than useless for the nations that possess them, this is a sacrifice in name only.

FOR THE STRATEGIC DEFENSE INITIATIVE

"Star Wars" Speech

Ronald Reagan

. . .

My predecessors in the Oval Office have appeared before you on other occasions to describe the threat posed by Soviet power and have proposed steps to address that threat. But since the advent of nuclear weapons, those steps have been increasingly directed toward deterrence of aggression through the promise of retaliation. This approach to stability through offensive threat has worked. We and our allies have succeeded in preventing nuclear war for more than three decades.

In recent months, however, my advisors, including in particular the Joint Chiefs of Staff, have underscored the necessity to break out of a future that relies solely on offensive retaliation for our security. Over the course of these discussions, I have become more and more deeply convinced that the human spirit must be capable of rising above dealing with other nations and human beings by threatening their existence. Feeling this way, I believe we must thoroughly examine every opportunity for reducing tensions, and for introducing greater stability into the strategic calculus on both sides.

One of the most important contributions we can make is, of course, to lower the level of all arms, and particularly nuclear arms. We are engaged right now in several negotiations with the Soviet Union to bring about a mutual reduction of weapons. . . .

I am totally committed to this course. If the Soviet Union will join with us in our effort to achieve major reduction, we will have succeeded in stabilizing the nuclear balance.

Nevertheless, it will still be necessary to rely on the specter of retaliation, on mutual threat. And that is a sad commentary on the human condition. Wouldn't it be better to save lives than to avenge them? Are we not capable of demonstrating our peaceful intentions by applying all our abilities and our ingenuity to achieving a truly lasting stability?

I think we are. Indeed, we must. After careful consultation with my advisors, including the Joint Chiefs of Staff, I believe there is a way. Let me share with you a vision of the future which offers hope. It is that we embark on a program to counter the awesome Soviet missile threat with measures that are defensive. Let us turn to the very strengths in technology that spawned our great industrial base, and that have given us the quality of life we enjoy today.

What if free people could live secure in the knowledge that their security did not rest upon the threat of instant U.S. retaliation to deter a Soviet attack, that we could intercept and destroy strategic ballistic missiles before they reached our own soil or that of our allies?

I know this is a formidable technical task, one that may not be accomplished before the end of this century. Yet current technology has attained a level of sophistication where it is reasonable for us to begin this effort. It will take years, probably decades, of effort on many fronts. There will be failures and setbacks, just as there will be successes and breakthroughs. And as we proceed, we must remain constant in preserving the nuclear deterrent and maintaining a solid capability for flexible response.

But isn't it worth every investment necessary to free the world from the threat of nuclear war? We know it is. In the meantime, we will continue to pursue real reductions in nuclear arms, negotiating from a position of strength that can be assured only by modernizing our strategic forces.

At the same time, we must take steps to reduce the risk of a conventional military conflict escalating to nuclear war by improving our non-nuclear capabilities. America does possess—now—the technologies to attain very significant improvements in the effectiveness of our conventional, non-nuclear forces. Proceeding boldly with these new technologies, we can significantly reduce any incentive that the Soviet Union may have to threaten attack against the United States or its allies.

As we pursue our goal of defensive technologies, we recognize that our allies rely upon our strategic offensive power to deter attacks against them. Their vital interests and ours are inextricably linked. Their safety and ours are one. And no change in technology can or will alter that reality. We must and shall continue to honor our commitments.

I clearly recognize that defensive systems have limitations and raise certain problems and ambiguities. If paired with offensive systems, they can be viewed as fostering an aggressive policy, and no one wants that.

But with these considerations firmly in mind, I call upon the scientific community in our country, those who gave us the nuclear weapons, to turn their great talents now to the cause of mankind and world peace, to give us the means of rendering these nuclear weapons impotent and obsolete.

Tonight, consistent with our obligations of the ABM Treaty and recognizing the need for closer consultation with our allies, I'm taking an important first step. I am directing a comprehensive and intensive effort to define a long-term research and development program to begin to achieve our ultimate goal of eliminating the threat posed by strategic nuclear missiles. This could pave the way for arms control measures to eliminate the weapons themselves. We seek neither military superiority nor political advantage. Our only purpose—one all people share—is to search for ways to reduce the danger of nuclear war.

My fellow Americans, tonight we're launching an effort that holds the promise of changing the course of human history.

There will be risks, and results take time. But I believe we can do it. As we cross this threshold, I ask for your prayers and your support. Thank you. Good night. And God bless you.

The Non-Nuclear Defense of Cities

Gen. Daniel O. Graham

. . .

In April of 1981, the Space Shuttle Columbia made its dramatic maiden voyage into space and back safely to Earth. This event was not merely another admirable feat of American space technology. It marked the advent of a new era of human activity on the High Frontier of space. The Space Shuttle is a development even more momentous for the future of mankind than was the completion of the transcontinental railway, the Suez and Panama Canals, or the first flight of the Wright brothers. It can be viewed as a "railroad into space" over which will move the men and materials necessary to open broad new fields of human endeavor in space and to free us from the brooding menace of nuclear attack.

This is an historic opportunity—history, is driving us to seize it.

A few thousand years ago, man's activities—his work, his commerce, his communications, all of his activities, including armed conflict—were confined to the land.

Eventually man's technology and daring thrust his activities off the land areas of the continents and into the coastal seas. His work, commerce, communications, and military capabilities moved strongly into this new arena of human activity. Those nations that had either the wit or the luck to establish the strongest military and commercial capabilities in the new arena reaped enormous strategic advantages. For example, the Vikings, although never a very numerous people, became such masters of the coastal seas that their power spread from their homes in Scandinavia over all the coasts of Europe and into the Mediterranean Sea, up to the very gates of Byzantium. . . .

In the lifetime of many of us, man's activity moved strongly into yet another arena, the coastal seas of space—the air. And once again the nations which quickly and effectively made use of this new arena for commerce and defense gained great advantages. As Americans we can take pride that the greatest commercial and military successes in aviation have been achieved by our nation.

But today, following the epic voyages of our astronauts to the Moon and our unmanned explorer satellites to the rings of Saturn and beyond, we find man's activities moving strongly into yet another new arena—the high seas of space. Already the United States and other major nations, including the Soviet Union, are making huge investments in space. Much of our communications, intelligence, weather forecasting, and navigation capabilities are now heavily dependent on space satellites. And, as history teaches us well, those nations or groups of nations that become preeminent in space will gain the decisive advantage of this strategic "high ground."

We must be determined that these advantages shall accrue to the peoples of the Free World; not to any totalitarian power. We can improve the Shuttle, our railway into space, placing space stations at its terminals and sharply reducing the cost-per-pound of material put into space. We can thus open the doors of opportunity to develop entire new space based industries, promising new products and new jobs for our people on Earth. We can eventually create the means to bring back to Earth the minerals and the inexhaustible solar energy available in space. By doing so, we can confound the gloomy predictions of diminishing energy and material resources available here on Earth. This will not only enhance the prosperity of the advanced, industrialized nations of our Free World, but will also provide the means to solve many of the hitherto intractable problems of the developing countries.

Further, we can place into space the means to defend these peaceful endeavors from interference or attack by any hostile power. We can deploy in space a purely defensive system of satellites using nonnuclear weapons which will deny any hostile power a rational option for attacking our current and future space vehicles or for delivering a militarily effective first strike with its strategic ballistic missiles on our country or on the territory of our allies. Such a global ballistic missile defense system is well within our present technological capabilities and can be deployed in space in this decade, at less cost than other options that might be available to us to redress the strategic balance.

We need not abrogate current treaties to pursue these defensive options. A United Nations Treaty prohibits the emplacement of weapons of mass destruction in space, but does not prohibit defensive space weapons. The ABM Treaty requires discussion among Soviet and U.S. representatives of any decision to proceed with defensive systems "based on other principles" such as space systems. We should initiate such discussions and propose revisions, if necessary, in the ABM Treaty which is scheduled for review in 1982.

Essentially, this is a decision to provide an effective defense against nuclear attack for our country and our allies. It represents a long overdue concrete rejection by this country of the "Mutual Assured Destruction" theory which held that the only effective deterrent to nuclear war was a permanent threat by the United States and the Soviet Union to heap nuclear devastation on the cities and populations of each other. The inescapable corollary of this theory of MAD (perhaps the most apt acronym every devised in Washington) was that civilian populations should *not* be defended, as they were to be considered hostages in this monstrous balance of terror doctrine. The MAD doctrine, which holds that attempting to defend ourselves would be "destabilizing" and "provocative," has resulted not only in the neglect of our active military and strategic defenses and our civil defense, it has also resulted in the near total dismantlement of such strategic defenses as we once had.

For years, many of our top military men have decried the devastating effect the MAD theory has had on the nation's security. In fact, our military leaders have, over the years, denied its validity and tried within the limits of their prerogatives to offset its ill effects. But those effects are readily evident. The only response permitted under MAD to increased nuclear threats to the United States or to its allies was to match these threats with increased nuclear threats against the Soviet Union.

Further, a U.S. strategy which relied at its core on the capability to annihilate civilians and denied the soldier his traditional role of defending his fellow citizens has had a deleterious effect on the traditional American military ethic, and on the relationship between the soldier and the normally highly supportive public.

This legacy of MAD lies at the heart of many current problems of U.S. and allied security. We should abandon this immoral and militarily bankrupt theory of MAD and move from "Mutual Assured Destruction" to "Assured Survival." Should the Soviet Union wish to join in this endeavor—to make Assured Survival a mutual endeavor—we would, of course, not object. We have an abiding and vital interest in assuring the survival of our nation and our allies. We have no interest in the nuclear devastation of the Soviet Union.

If both East and West can free themselves from the threat of disarming nuclear first strikes, both sides will have little compulsion to amass ever larger arsenals of nuclear weapons. This would almost certainly produce a more peaceful and stable world than the one we now inhabit. And it would allow us to avoid leaving to future generations the horrendous legacy of a perpetual balance of terror.

What we propose is not a panacea which solves all the problems of our national security. Spaceborne defense does not mean that our nuclear retaliatory capabilities can be abandoned or neglected. The United States would still maintain strategic offensive forces capable of retaliation in case of attack. The Soviets, while losing their advantage in first strike capabilities, would still be able to retaliate in case of attack. Nor does our approach to the strategic nuclear balance eliminate the need to build and maintain strong conventional capabilities.

We Americans have always been successful on the frontiers; we will be successful on the new High Frontier of space. We need only be as bold and resourceful as our forefathers.

AGAINST THE STRATEGIC DEFENSE INITIATIVE

The Moral Vision of Strategic Defense

Steven Lee

The proponents of the Strategic Defense Initiative (SDI) have made a move uncommon in the forty-year-old history of the debate over nuclear weapons policy: they have introduced morality as a significant factor in the public discussion. The SDI has, from its inception, been supported by a specific moral vision. One of the most prominent arguments publicly put forth in favor of the SDI, going back to President Reagan's initiation of the public debate in March of 1983, has been that it is morally preferable to achieve military security through defensive capability rather than through deterrent threats to innocent Soviet citizens. Assured defense is morally superior to assured destruction. This moral vision has led some to charge that Reagan has irresponsibly joined the group of naive idealists who reject nuclear deterrence, a group heretofore populated exclusively by those advocating nuclear disarmament. In any case, the opening of the public debate to moral argument gives philosophers their best opportunity in a long time: a chance through discourse in their area of expertise to have a real impact on the public understanding of a crucial policy issue.

The moral vision constitutes what I call the thesis of the moral novelty of the SDI: unlike most technological innovations in strategic systems proposed over the past forty years, the SDI promises to make a fundamental difference in the moral status of strategic policy. The difference is this. Nuclear deterrence has always been based, at least ultimately, on the threat to destroy the opponent's population centers, so-called countervalue targets. However successful this policy has been at achieving deterrence, it has involved the conditional intention to attack noncombatants, an indiscriminate intention and morally unacceptable in terms of just war theory. The resulting moral paradox has been uncomfortable for many. Counterforce targeting, aiming nuclear weapons at military rather than at population targets, has been proposed as one way out of this paradox, and the shift in recent years to a more strongly counterforce policy has been applauded on moral grounds. The SDI, however, promises a much clearer escape from the paradox, a more radical moral break with our nuclear-policy past. The moral novelty of the SDI is its promise to make nuclear weapons obsolete. The technology promises that military security can be achieved without the intention to attack anyone.

Unfortunately, the thesis of the moral novelty of the SDI is false, and is seen as such even by most of the proponents of the program. To make nuclear weapons obsolete, the SDI would have to make nuclear deterrence unnecessary. But nuclear deterrence would be unnecessary only if the opponent's nuclear weapons posed no significant threat to one's nation, and this would be the case only if the opponent lacked the capability to explode any nuclear weapons on one's territory. The great destructive power of nuclear weapons makes utterly unacceptable any attack in which even a few nuclear warheads would get through. In fact, however, the SDI cannot create a "rainbow shield," a perfect leakproof defense against nuclear warheads. Some nuclear warheads would get through even the best defense envisioned. The assumption behind a layered set of defensive systems, central to the SDI concept, is that no one mode of defense will be sufficient to stop all warheads. But perfection cannot be achieved by layering imperfect systems: given the large numbers of Soviet nuclear warheads, some will get through. In addition, the SDI as currently envisioned is directed primarily against ballistic missile warheads, ignoring other existing modes of delivery, such as the cruise missile.

In the absence of a perfect defense, one's opponent must still be dissuaded from attacking, and for this a policy of deterrence would presumably still be required. Most proponents of the SDI now speak of its goal as being that of enhancing deterrence, not replacing it. But this is not just a matter of the goals that have in fact been adopted by those working on the SDI. It is part of the basic logic of the strategic situation: any strategic system deployed in a situation in which an attack cannot be perfectly defended against becomes by its very existence part of the effort to deter an attack.

Where does this leave the moral vision of strategic defense? The falsity of the moral novelty thesis makes the moral vision behind the SDI more mundane, but at the same time more problematic. This makes the moral assessment of the SDI less intrinsically interesting, but of greater practical importance. The moral vision behind the SDI is more mundane because it is now seen to be one of reducing the risk of nuclear war, through enhanced deterrence, rather than eliminating its possibility. The moral vision is more problematic because there are serious doubts about whether the SDI would reduce the risk of nuclear war. The moral vision behind the SDI partially merges with the moral vision behind counterforce policy: each claims to reduce the risk of nuclear war through enhancing deterrence. But the SDI appears to provide a more effective way than does counterforce policy of reducing this risk, because it seems to provide a more effective way of limiting nuclear war. It is this understanding of the moral vision of the SDI that I will examine below.

Because the moral vision of the SDI partially merges with the moral vision of counterforce policy, it will be helpful to begin by considering the moral advantages that are claimed for counterforce policy. Counterforce policy is said to have two main kinds of moral advantage over countervalue (or assured destruction) policy. First, as mentioned just above, counterforce policy is said to lessen the risk of nuclear war by providing a more effective form of deterrence (one involving more credible retaliatory threats) than does countervalue policy. This is a form of utilitarian moral advantage which in fact happens to coincide with what is taken to be the strategic or prudential advantage of counterforce policy. Second, counterforce policy is said to have the more traditional moral advantage of satisfying just war theory's principle of discrimination. Unlike countervalue policy, counterforce policy does not involve the conditional intention to attack noncombatants; by the doctrine of double effect, the deaths of many noncombatants from a nuclear retaliation, though foreseen, are not intended. This is the way in which counterforce policy is said to resolve the moral paradox of nuclear deterrence referred to at the beginning.

The second of the moral advantages claimed for counterforce policy, however, is not relevant to assessing the moral vision behind the SDI. Given the falsity of the moral novelty thesis, the SDI cannot claim by itself to secure any advantage for strategic policy in terms of the principle of discrimination. Since the SDI would not make nuclear weapons obsolete, it would be deployed on top of an existing set of offensive weapons systems already designed to achieve deterrence. The addition of the defensive systems would not alter the status of the offensive systems in terms of the principle of discrimination. Hence, the SDI would make no moral difference in this regard. While I would argue that no system of offensive nuclear weapons, no matter how they are targeted, can satisfy the principle of discrimination, this issue is irrelevant to the moral assessment of the SDI itself.

The first moral advantage claimed for counterforce policy is, however, relevant to the moral assessment of the SDI, because it is claimed that the SDI, like counterforce targeting, would enhance deterrence. What is the argument that counterforce policy enhances deterrence, and so decreases the risk of nuclear war? For a threat to be effective, it must be credible. But the threat of countervalue retaliation is thought not to be credible, especially in the face of Soviet counterforce capability. If the U.S. had only countervalue capability, it is thought unlikely to retaliate for any aggression short of the destruction of its own cities, for countervalue retaliation in such circumstances would certainly bring on the destruction of these very cities by Soviet counterretaliation. If, however, the U.S. had counterforce capability, it is more likely to retaliate, since counterforce retaliation would not destroy Soviet cities, and so would be unlikely to bring about the destruction of U.S. cities in response. The more likely one is to carry out a retaliatory threat, the more credible the threat, and the greater its deterrent value.

Another way to put this argument is to say that counterforce policy is thought to make possible limited nuclear war. The threat to retaliate is the threat to engage in nuclear war, and this threat is credible only if engaging in nuclear war could be a rational act. Given the great destruction potential in nuclear weapons, nuclear war could be rational (i.e., could be an instrument to achieve some political purpose) only if such war were limited. Counterforce capability creates the possibility of limited nuclear war by making possible a nuclear war in which cities would not be destroyed. The actual mechanism by which a nuclear war would be kept limited requires a sufficiently strong counterforce capability to achieve what is called escalation dominance; one must be superior to one's opponent at every potential level of nuclear (and nonnuclear) conflict so that the opponent has a strong incentive not to escalate any conflict that arises.

Thus, the argument that counterforce policy enhances deterrence depends crucially on the possibility (or at least the perceived possibility) of limited nuclear war. Similarly, the SDI is conceived to enhance deterrence, for the SDI would provide another mechanism by which nuclear war could be kept limited. Moreover, the argument that the SDI would enhance deterrence seems to be even stronger than the argument that counterforce policy would do so, since the mechanism of limitation seems to be much more effective. Counterforce policy must rely on an exercise of human restraint to limit nuclear war: escalation dominance provides a kind of intra-war deterrence through which one hopes to encourage escalatory restraint on the part of one's opponent. But the SDI relies on a technological mechanism to limit nuclear war, *viz.*, our ability to destroy a high portion of incoming nuclear warheads. The technological mechanism seems to be a more effective form of limitation than human restraint. So, the SDI promises a greater enhancement of the effectiveness of deterrence: by increasing the likelihood that nuclear war could be kept limited beyond that resulting from counterforce policy, it would make retaliation seem an even more rational act, and hence more greatly increase the credibility of the retaliatory threat.

Does the SDI have the moral advantage of lessening the likelihood of nuclear war? It does not, and for the same reason that counterforce policy does not. The argument, just rehearsed, that the SDI and counterforce policy have this moral advantage rests on too narrow an understanding of how a strategic posture can lead to nuclear war. It is true that, other things being equal, the more credible a nuclear threat, the more likely it is to deter a nuclear attack. But a nuclear attack may occur in circumstances where the credibility of the retaliatory threat is not the most important factor in the attacker's deliberations, and in these circumstances the SDI and counterforce policy could increase the likelihood of nuclear war. To see this, consider two ways in which nuclear war might start: first, by a so-called bolt-from-the-blue; and second, by a pre-emptive attack in a crisis. A bolt-from-the-blue is a nuclear first-strike in a situation in which it is completely unexpected, when there is no crisis between the nuclear powers. The argument based on greater credibility does, presumably, speak to this case: the more certain one's opponent is that one will retaliate, and a defensive capability and a major counterforce capability give some greater certainty here, the less likely the opponent is to launch a surprise attack.

But things are very different regarding the likelihood of a pre-emptive attack in a crisis. A major counterforce capability as well as a strategic defense capability (when coupled with an offensive capability) significantly increase the risk that one's opponent will launch a pre-emptive attack in a crisis. (This is the argument that these strategic postures are crisis destabilizing.) A major counterforce capability makes it more advantageous for one to strike first, for in doing so one can destroy a large portion of the opponent's nuclear weapons. In a crisis, the opponent, recognizing this advantage (and perhaps also able to achieve this advantage itself through its own counterforce capability), and coming to think war inevitable in those circumstances, would be greatly tempted to launch what it would view as a pre-emptive attack. The incentive would be, as is said, to use the weapons or to lose them. The credibility of one's retaliatory threat obviously would play little role in such deliberations. The same strategic posture that gives greater credibility to one's retaliatory threat also makes a first strike to one's advantage. Whatever the gain in a lesser likelihood or a bolt-from-the-blue, a major counterforce capability would increase the overall risk of nuclear war due to a much greater likelihood of crisis pre-emption.

The same argument applies to a strategic defense capability, when this is coupled with a strategic offensive capability, as it would if the defenses were part of a deterrence policy. Since the defenses are not perfect, they do a better job against a smaller attack than against a larger; and the way to reduce the size of the attack is to destroy some of the opponent's weapons in a first strike. This is the first-strike advantage resulting from a strategic defense capability, and again, it gives the opponent a strong incentive to launch a pre-emptive attack in a crisis. Defenses in conjunction with offensive forces are themselves perceived as offensive. Ironically, the more effective the defensive systems, or more precisely, the more effective they are perceived to be, the greater the incentive they provide to the other side to attack pre-emptively. But this is just a consequence of the fact that the situation of least pre-emptive incentive is one where there is no defensive capability at all. The moral vision of strategic defenses is fundamentally flawed.

Finally, something should be said about the damage-limitation function of strategic defenses. It should be counted as a moral advantage of the SDI that it would limit the damage that would occur if deterrence fails. But again, this would decide the moral case in favor of the SDI only other things being equal. Other things are not equal: the nuclear war whose damage the SDI would limit would likely be a result of the very offensive/defensive posture of which the SDI would be a part. The value of the damage the SDI would avoid if there is a nuclear war is outweighed morally by the disvalue of the significantly greater risk of war consequent on such a strategic posture.

Questions for Further Reflection

1. If it is important to minimize or eliminate nuclear weapons, is it also important to minimize or eliminate conventional weapons? How about chemical weapons? (The United States and the former Soviet Union signed a treaty that forbade either side from using chemical weapons first but permitted stockpiling

chemical weapons.) Or is there a good reason to treat the three as incommensurable?
2. Is the policy of nuclear deterrence a form of terrorism?
3. The deterrence policy is sometimes defended against the charge that it involves targeting innocent civilians in cities on the grounds that the real targets are military units; civilian deaths are merely foreseen, not intended. How convincing is this appeal to the doctrine of double effect?
4. Suppose that the world's powers had only defensive systems. Should they then go on to disarm completely? Which is better: a policy of pure defense or one of complete disarmament?

Further Readings

Cohen, Avner, and Steven Lee, eds. *Nuclear Weapons and the Future of Humanity: The Fundamental Questions.* Totowa, NJ: Rowman & Allanheld, Publishers, 1986. A nice collection.

Craig, Paul, and John Jungerman. *Nuclear Arms Race: Technology and Society.* New York: McGraw-Hill, 1986. Gives a great deal of technical information about nuclear weapons in a readable way.

Ford, Dan. *The Button.* New York: Simon & Schuster, 1958. An excellent account of the problems faced by the U.S. system of nuclear deterrence.

Gray, Colin. *American Military Space Policy.* Cambridge, MA: Abt Books, 1982. A useful account of the development of space policy.

Hardin, Russell, ed. *Ethics* 95 (April 1985). The entire issue is devoted to the ethics of nuclear deterrence.

Lackey, Douglas, ed. *Ethics and Strategic Defense.* Belmont, CA: Wadsworth Publishing Company, 1986. An excellent collection of essays that also contains helpful introductory and bibliographical materials.

U.S. Catholic Conference. *The Challenge of Peace: God's Promise and Our Response.* Office of Publishing Services, U.S.C.C. In this pastoral letter, Catholic bishops condemn any use of nuclear weapons on the grounds that it kills innocent civilians.

Chapter 14

TERRORISM

Terrorist acts are a much-publicized aspect of contemporary life. In the summer of 1997, news stories included the following: the militant Islamic group Hamas claimed responsibility for a suicide bombing that killed 13 people in a Jerusalem market; the Irish Republican Army, which had declared a "cease-fire" in late 1994, then resumed detonating bombs in England in February 1996, declared a new cease-fire; Timothy McVeigh was convicted of bombing the Alfred P. Murrah Federal Building in Oklahoma City on April 19, 1995, an attack that killed 168 people; two Palestinians were arrested in New York City and charged with planning suicide bombings of New York City buses and subways; and Ramzi Ahmed Yousef was on trial for allegedly masterminding the 1993 bombing of the World Trade Center. Despite the headlines, however, few of us are aware of the social or political reasons for terrorist acts, and we rarely stop to think about whether such activity could ever be morally justifiable. These issues are addressed in the present chapter.

What Is Terrorism?

Very little agreement exists about terrorism. Not only is there disagreement about whether terrorism is ever justified, about which groups or acts are terroristic, and about the appropriate response to terrorism; there is even considerable disagreement over what terrorism *is*. There are as many definitions of terrorism as there are writers on the subject. Here are just two of the disputes over the definition of terrorism.

First, there is disagreement over whether terrorism is *by nature* unjustified. Michael Walzer, in his selection in this chapter, argues that there can be no justification for terrorism, but only excuses; this suggests that terrorism is by definition without moral justification. Similarly, former President Ronald Reagan has been described as characterizing terrorism as "the deliberate maiming or killing of innocent people," and terrorists as "base criminals."[1] On the other hand, many people have argued that to *define* terrorism as evil or unjustified is to close off debate too early; terrorists themselves often offer justifications for their actions, and we cannot prove them wrong by definition. In this chapter, we will not assume that terrorism is wrong by definition, although of course it may nevertheless be that in fact it is always wrong.

---

[1] Haig Khatchadourian, "Terrorism and Morality," *Journal of Applied Philosophy* 5 (1988): 131–145, at p. 131.

Disagreement also arises over whether there can be state terrorism, in addition to terrorism on the part of nongovernmental groups or individuals. The activities that are usually described in the media as terroristic are typically not performed by states; usually they are performed by resistance or liberation movements. It is interesting, however, that in its original meaning, *terrorism* referred to state activity. Our words *terrorism* and *terrorist* apparently derive from the French words *terrorisme* and *terroriste*, which emerged in revolutionary France and referred to "the systematic employment of violence and the guillotine by the Jacobin and Thermidorian regimes."[2] At least in its original meaning, then, the term *terrorism* referred to state violence, and some have argued that by far the majority of terrorist acts today are carried out by states, including liberal Western democracies. Our readings will focus on nongovernmental terrorism, but it is worth keeping in mind the question whether and to what extent states act in ways that are relevantly similar to nongovernmental terrorism.

Ignoring further disagreements, let us see what features terrorism is generally agreed to have. First, the methods of terrorists are intentionally *violent:* They include bombings, assassinations, hijackings, and the taking of hostages. Second, terrorist acts are performed in the interest of accomplishing some political aim. This might be to overthrow a government, to get prisoners released, or even, as in the Algerian revolution, to provoke a violent governmental response in the hope that this will lead the population as a whole to revolt.

(Often terrorist acts are intended to accomplish a goal by causing terror, as the term itself suggests, but perhaps this is not necessary; whether terrorism *must* involve terror is yet another area of disagreement among writers on the subject.) Mere random violence for no particular purpose is not terrorism as that term is commonly understood. (But perhaps the aim need not be political in any narrow sense; the many bombings and killings carried out by Latin American drug cartels would usually be counted as terrorist, for example, although their principal aim is monetary rather than political.[3]) Third, terrorist acts are usually carried out by organized groups, such as the ones Robert Fullinwider lists: factions of the PLO, the IRA, the Red Brigades, and so on.

Our characterization so far does not account for the horror with which we view terrorism. Violence in support of a political aim on the part of an organized group is in many contexts something we feel able to support: Most of us think that some wars are justified, for instance, and that in some contexts it is necessary for police forces to use violence. What inclines us to regard terrorism as beyond the pale is perhaps the following two further features. Fourth, then, terrorist activity is *criminal*, in violation of the laws of the societies in which it occurs. (This will not be true of at least some state terrorism, but it is true of nongovernmental terrorism.) Violence on the part of police or armies is typically sanctioned by the law and the governing authorities; violence on the part of terrorist organizations is not. Fifth and finally,

---

[2]Michael Stohl, "Demystifying Terrorism," in *The Politics of Terrorism*, third edition, ed. Michael Stohl (New York: Marcel Dekker, 1988), p. 8; compare Jenny Teichman, "How to Define Terrorism," *Philosophy* 64 (1989): 505–517, at p. 507.

[3]Khatchadourian suggests that the aims of terrorists may be monetary, retaliatory, or moral rather than political (p. 133), and Teichman characterizes terrorist actions as "carried out for political or other social purposes, including some large-scale mercenary purposes" (p. 513).

terrorist acts usually target people who *in some sense* are innocent. Hijackings and bombings in public places, for instance, clearly have victims most of us would regard as innocent. However, Fullinwider shows that it may be question-begging to characterize terrorism as involving innocent targets, since in many cases the victims of terrorism are carefully chosen and, by the terrorists' lights, not at all innocent. It may nevertheless be useful to describe the victims of terrorism as *noncombatants*.[4] They are often neither guilty of anything officially recognized as a crime nor directly engaged in violent action against the terrorists or those they purport to represent.

Can Terrorism Be Justified?

The central question about terrorism is whether it can ever be morally justified. Walzer begins his essay by presupposing that terrorism is morally indefensible, and goes on to consider whether several "excuses" might nevertheless have some force. It may be that Walzer describes his own view in a misleading way here. Fullinwider points out that these "excuses" *are* justifications in the ordinary sense of the term. But perhaps the view Walzer means to discuss is the position that, although terrorist acts involve doing something morally wrong, they may nonetheless be the best actions available to the terrorist. The terrorist may view his or her situation as a moral dilemma, in which all the available options are morally unacceptable, and in which the best one can do is therefore to choose the least awful possibility.[5] If a regime is sufficiently oppressive and tyrannical, for example, and if the potential terrorist is convinced that no means short of terrorism will dislodge it, then such a person may well believe that, however horrible terrorist acts may be in themselves, they are the best option available.

Walzer argues that in fact terrorism is never the best available option. It is never the *last* option, because there will always be others to try; it may be that no other option seems likely to succeed, but if so, this must be because the movement considering terrorism lacks popular support, in which case it should not pretend to act on behalf of the populace; it is never the only effective method, because in fact it is never effective.

Whether or not they agree with the way Walzer sets up the issues, most people (or at least most of the people likely to be reading this text) will probably agree with the conclusion that terrorism is not only morally wrong, but also rarely if ever even the best option of a bad lot. So what makes terrorism philosophically interesting? As Fullinwider helps us see, what is especially interesting about terrorism is the difficulty of saying why it is wrong. (Of course, if it turns out to be impossible to satisfactorily explain why it is always and inevitably wrong, we may be led to change our opinion that it *is* always and inevitably wrong.) Fullinwider points out that terrorists could often offer justifications of their actions. It may be difficult to say what is wrong with such justifications without also ruling out as unjustifiable other forms of violence that in fact we do not reject.

---

[4]Compare C. A. J. Coady, "The Morality of Terrorism," *Philosophy* 60 (1985): 47–69, at pp. 52, 54, and especially 58–60.

[5]Whether there are moral dilemmas in this sense is controversial, but many philosophers have argued that there are. See, for example, E. J. Lemmon, "Moral Dilemmas," *Philosophical Review* 71 (1962): 139–158; Ruth Barcan Marcus, "Moral Dilemmas and Consistency," *Journal of Philosophy* 77 (1980): 121–136.

We suggested earlier that the features that make terrorist actions seem morally unacceptable are their criminal nature and the fact that they target people who by ordinary standards are innocent. Consider criminality first. It seems too simple to say that terrorism is immoral *because* it is criminal. For there is a crucial distinction between legality and morality. There certainly are regimes that are unjust through and through, and in which acting morally requires acting illegally. We do not want to say that criminality is automatically immoral; the cost would be insisting that those who helped Jews escape Nazi Germany were acting immorally, that the American revolution was immoral, that the Chinese students who demonstrated against their government in Tiananmin Square were acting immorally. When the law itself is unjust, morality may require acting illegally, and it is important to remember that by the terrorists' lights, the regimes they are defying are thoroughly corrupt. We need to consider indictments of particular societies on their merits, without insisting that whatever a regime dictates is automatically moral.

The second especially troubling feature of terrorism concerns its targets, who often are, by ordinary standards, innocent of wrongdoing. Indeed, this is probably the main reason that we so often find terroristic acts not just wrong but horrifying. Most of us take for granted an absolute prohibition on the intentional killing of the innocent. This is true even in wartime; as Michael Walzer has elsewhere noted, it is an important part of "the war convention"[6] that "non-combatants cannot be attacked at any time."[7] Terrorism seems to violate our view that attacks on innocents cannot be justified.

As Fullinwider points out, however, matters unfortunately are not so simple. The distinction between the innocent and the guilty is a difficult one to make, and it is typical of terrorists that, whatever *our* view of the matter, *they* do not regard their victims as innocent. This may be seen, for instance, in our selection from the IRA. In this selection the authors list a number of bombing targets; these include not only military and police targets, but also "factories, firms, stores . . . owned in whole or part by British financiers or companies, or who in any way are a contributory factor to the well-being of Her Majesty's invading forces." It is clear here that the authors regard those who provide any sort of assistance or contribution to the presence of British forces in Ireland as legitimate targets: The fact that these institutions provide support is enough to make them guilty, even though they are not themselves *directly* engaged in violence. Similarly, Carlos Marighella describes legitimate targets of the Brazilian "urban guerrilla" as including "top government leaders, their subordinates, and the stooges of the North American imperialists." We may suspect that the notion of a "stooge of the North American imperialists" might be interpreted rather broadly.

The terrorist, then, may regard *complicity* with the unjust ruling authority as a kind of guilt, and view anyone guilty in this way as a legitimate target. Killing those who are complicitous is often regarded by terrorists as a kind of execution: Fullinwider discusses the "execution" of Aldo Moro, and Marighella says that any "firing team" may independently decide to "execute an agent of the dictatorship." If we take seriously this notion of terrorist killing as *execution*, a form of punishment, we may perhaps see a line of

---

[6] Walzer defines the "war convention" as "the set of articulated norms, customs, professional codes, legal precepts, religious and philosophical principles, and reciprocal arrangements that shape our judgments of military conduct." Walzer, *Just and Unjust Wars* (New York: Basic Books, 1977), p. 44.

[7] Walzer, p. 151.

response to the position that terrorism is justified because merely participating in, or supporting, or profiting from an unjust regime amounts to a kind of guilt. There is first of all something peculiar in the notion that killing people on individual initiative can be regarded as a kind of punishment. Punishment seems to require a richer institutional background than this. Second and more important, however, we saw in our chapter on capital punishment that those who defend retributive theories of punishment defend either an "eye for an eye" doctrine, according to which one deserves to be paid back in kind for what one has done, or the somewhat milder "proportional retributivism," according to which the punishment should be proportional to the crime but need not be as severe as the crime itself. On either view, the killing of those complicitous with an unjust regime could be justified only if they were not merely guilty, but guilty of *murder*. It seems difficult to see how the guilt of noncombatants could extend this far.

Difficult, but perhaps not impossible. It is interesting to compare the point we have now reached with a view that is sometimes held about world hunger. James Rachels has argued that allowing someone to starve is just as bad as actively killing someone, and that people who do not do what they can to alleviate hunger are allowing people to starve.[8] Although Rachels does not go this far, we may notice that, if execution is an appropriate punishment for murder, and not alleviating hunger is tantamount to murder, than it might be appropriate to execute people for not contributing to charity. Perhaps the attitude of terrorists is something like this. The regimes they regard as unjust may be unjust not only because of assassinations, "disappearances," and the like, but also because of an inequitable distribution of wealth that results in the death by starvation and disease of many members of the underclass. The terrorist may take the attitude that anyone who does nothing to try to remedy this situation is guilty of allowing people to die; if allowing someone to die is as bad as murder, then execution may be an appropriate response. This strikes us, no doubt, as a primitive and unjustifiable view, but it is surprising to see how close it is to views that seem at first to be enlightened and, even if mistaken, at least worthy of respect.

---

[8]James Rachels, "Killing and Starving to Death," *Philosophy* 54 (1979): 159–171.

JUSTIFICATIONS OF TERRORISM

Manual of the Urban Guerrilla

Carlos Marighella

The Nature of the Urban Guerrilla

The upsurge of revolutionary activity in Brazil is a product of its chronic structural crisis and resultant political instability.

The urban guerrilla employs weapons in unconventional warfare in his struggle against the military dictatorship. He is a political revolutionary. An ardent patriot. A freedom fighter. A friend of the masses and a lover of freedom. The urban guerrilla's theatre of war is Brazil's large cities. Do not mistake the urban guerilla for the bandits or outlaws who flourish in the larger cities. Urban guerrillas are often blamed for the acts of these outlaws.

The urban guerrilla, however, is no outlaw. The outlaw benefits personally from his act, robbing equally the exploited and the exploiter. He numbers among his victims the common men and women. In contrast, the urban guerrilla seeks a political goal, targeting only the government, wealthy capitalists, and foreign imperialists, particularly North Americans.

No less dangerous than the outlaw is the right-wing counter-revolutionary who adds to the chaos by robbing banks, hurling bombs, kidnappings, and assassinations. Right-wing counter-revolutionaries commit the worst crimes imaginable against the urban guerrilla, revolutionary priests, students, and all citizens opposing fascism and striving for liberty.

The urban guerrilla is an implacable enemy of the government, systematically inflicting damage on established authority, and those who exercise power to exploit the nation. The urban guerrilla's main task is to confuse, harrass, and demoralize the militarists, the dictatorship, and its repressive forces. It is no less important to destroy the Brazilian rich, the foreign company managers, and the wealth and property of the North Americans.

The urban guerrilla does not fear dismantling and destroying the present Brazilian economic, political, and social system. That is because he joins hands with the social and political order, under the leadership of the armed masses. . . .

. . . As the class struggle inevitably and necessarily sharpens, the armed struggle of the urban guerrilla points towards two essential objectives:

(a) the physical liquidation of the generals and commanders in the armed forces and police; and,
(b) the expropriation of the resources of the government and big businesses, the stooges of foreigners, and the imperialists. Limited expropriation objectives will serve to support the individual urban guerrilla; large expropriations serve the revolution itself.

Clearly the armed struggle of the urban guerrilla has other objectives as well. But these must follow expropriation. Only through expropriation of the enemy's wealth and arms can the urban guerrilla kill policemen and all others dedicated to repression. This is accomplished by taking from the wealthy capitalists, the stooges of the foreigners, and the imperialists themselves. . . .

Urban guerrillas make certain that the tremendous costs of the revolution are paid for by the agents of the dictatorship, the large capitalists, the imperialists, the stooges of the imperialists, and the state and federal government agencies. All are exploiters and oppressors of the masses.

Top government leaders, their subordinates, and the stooges of the North American imperialists must pay with their lives for their crimes against the Brazilian people. . . .

The Fire Team

The urban guerrilla functions best in small teams. A fire team is made up of no more than four or five members. Two or more fire teams, separated and sealed off from other fire teams for security reasons, and directed or coordinated by one or two leaders, is known as a fire group. . . .

Tasks handed down from the urban guerrilla strategic command take precedence over all other operations. Still each fire team is not a team unless it maintains its own initiative. For this reason rigidity in organization must be avoided so that the independent fire team retains a full measure of initiative. The old forms of organization exemplified by traditional left-wing Communist movements do not exist in our organization.

Therefore, any fire team can decide to attack a bank, to kidnap, or to execute an agent of the dictatorship, a person identified with reaction, or a North American spy, or issue propaganda materials, or conduct a war of nerves against the enemy, without prior consultation with the strategic command. The strategic command only sets the priority of objectives for individual fire teams and fire groups. . . .

Executions

The urban guerrilla executes North American spies, agents of the dictatorship, police torturers, and fascist government officials involved in crimes against or persecution of revolutionary patriots. Urban guerrillas also execute stool pigeons, informers, police agents, and police provocateurs. Those who voluntarily denounce or accuse urban guerrillas to the police, or who provide evidence, or who finger suspects, must also be executed.

Executions should be highly secret operations involving a minimum number of urban guerrillas. In many cases, a simple execution may be carried out by one sniper, who waits patiently, alone and unknown. The sniper functions in complete secrecy, and kills in cold blood.

Kidnapping

The urban guerrilla kidnaps and detains in a secret place a police agent, North American spy, a high-ranking political figure, or any other notorious or dangerous enemy of the revolutionary movement.

Kidnapping is used as a means of exchanging or liberating imprisoned revolutionary comrades, or to force the military dictatorship to end the torture of prisoners. Kidnapping of non-political national figures, such as well-known artists, sports personalities, or publicized individuals in other fields, may be useful as a form of revolutionary propaganda. It is important that these forms of kidnapping encourage public sympathy and acceptance.

The kidnapping of North Americans working in Brazil, or visiting Brazil as tourists, constitutes a form of protest against U.S. imperialism, and its penetration and exploitation of our country. . . .

Terrorism

Terrorism is normally accomplished by placing a bomb or incendiary device so that its destructive power causes an irreparable loss of life to the enemy. The terrorist act is no different from any other urban guerrilla tactic, apart from the apparent facility with which it can be carried out. All depend for their success on revolutionary planning and organization. In committing the terrorist act, the urban guerrilla must do his job with extreme cold-bloodedness, remaining calm himself, while acting with bold decisiveness.

Terrorism normally is brought on by explosion. Yet there are cases in which execution or arson is terrorist in nature. An important weapon in revolutionary terrorism is the incendiary bomb or gasoline bomb.

Terrorism is a weapon the revolution can not do without.

Freedom Struggle by the Provisional IRA

Quite frankly it suited IRA strategy to carry out selective bombings in Belfast, Derry, and other towns in Occupied Ulster. They see these actions as a legitimate part of war, the targets chosen being military and police barracks, outposts, customs offices, administrative and government buildings, electricity transformers and pylons, certain cinemas, hotels, clubs, dance halls, pubs, all of which provide relaxation and personal comforts for the British forces; also business targets e.g., factories, firms, stores (sometimes under the guise of CO-OPs) owned in whole or part by British financiers or companies, or who in any way are a contributory factor to the well-being of Her Majesty's invading forces, and in certain instances residences of people known to harbor or be in league with espionage personnel or *agents provocateurs* namely the S.A.S., MRF, and S.I.B. In many ways this campaign is reminiscent of that carried out by the underground Resistance in France during World War II.

In all cases IRA bomb squads give adequate warning though these warnings are sometimes withheld or delayed deliberately by the British army as a counter-tactic, with view to making optimum publicity out of the injured and the dead in their propaganda war on the IRA. In no instance has the "warning rule" been violated by the guerrilla forces in sharp contrast with the "no warning" methods used by the Unionist gangs and British army *agents provocateurs*.

The Abercorn Restaurant, McGurk's Bar, Benny's Bar and more recently McGlades Bar are frightening examples of the latter type of instant bombing. Naturally it presents less risk to the bombers in terms of personal safety and lessens the chances of being apprehended. As well as giving warnings, the IRA always claims full responsibility for all military action taken even should this redound unfavorably on the Republican Movement's popularity; E.B.N.I. and Donegall Street are classic examples of this. Over the years the press has learned to accept the veracity of Irish Republican Publicity Bureau statements, whereas, with the British army's constant propaganda handouts, various versions of incidents and blatant covering-up of tracks have created for them a gross credibility gap.

The effect of the IRA bombing campaign can be gauged in many different ways. Firstly, they have struck at the very root of enemy morale, confining and tying down large numbers of troops and armored vehicles in center city areas, thus relieving much of the pressure on the much-oppressed nationalist areas. In terms of direct financial loss (structural damage, goods, machinery), also in the crippling of industrial output and perhaps worst of all in the scaring-off of foreign capital investments, IRA bombs have hit Britain where she feels it most—in her pocket.

England always found unfortunate soldiers quite dispensable and to a certain extent replaceable, but she always counted in terms of cost to the Treasury. Any peace through the granting of freedom emanating to rebellious colonies from London came by means of calculation—the cost of occupation. Since 1969 a bill of warfare running to at least a conservative £500,000,000 has not gone unnoticed back home in Britain where recent opinion polls showed that over 54 percent of the ordinary people wanted the troops withdrawn forthwith.

Already some 1,500 troops have left Northern Ireland never to return. In many cases death certificates have been issued as for fatal road accident victims to the unsuspecting next-of-kin of soldiers killed in action in a heartless attempt at cooking records and hiding telling manpower losses. Suddenly Northern Ireland has become England's Vietnam. In the knowledge that the will to overcome of a risen people can never be defeated by brute force or even overwhelming odds more enlightened British politicians have seen the light and are themselves thinking along Tone's famous dictum: "Break the connection!"

Great Britain too, of course, has suffered losses other than bomb damage and loss of personnel. Her prestige and credibility in terms of world opinion and world finance have been severely shaken; her duplicity and selective sense of justice have been seriously exposed; her puerile hankering after "holding the last vestige of the Empire" has marked her as a recidivist nation, psychologically vulnerable, unstable, and mentally immature. These considerations have not been lost on the European Common Market countries, especially France and Monsieur Pompidou. Britain's dilemma in Ireland is of her own making and is now seen as a black mark against her in the new capital—Brussels. Time is running out along the Thames.

JUSTIFICATIONS OF TERRORISM ARE UNSUCCESSFUL

Terrorism: A Critique of Excuses

Michael Walzer

No one these days advocates terrorism, not even those who regularly practice it. The practice is indefensible now that it has been recognized, like rape and murder, as an attack upon the innocent. In a sense, indeed, terrorism is worse than rape and murder commonly are, for in the latter cases the victim has been chosen for a purpose; he or she is the direct object of attack, and the attack has some reason, however twisted or ugly it may be. The victims of a terrorist attack are third parties, innocent bystanders; there is no special reason for attacking them; anyone else within a large class of (unrelated) people will do as well. The attack is directed indiscriminately against the entire class. Terrorists are like killers on a rampage, except that their rampage is not just expressive of rage or madness; the rage is purposeful and programmatic. It aims at a general vulnerability: Kill these people in order to terrify those. A relatively small number of dead victims makes for a very large number of living and frightened hostages.

This, then, is the peculiar evil of terrorism—not only the killing of innocent people but also the intrusion of fear into everyday life, the violation of private purposes, the insecurity of public spaces, the endless coerciveness of precaution. A crime wave might, I suppose, produce similar effects, but no one plans a crime wave; it is the work of a thousand individual decision-makers, each one independent of the others, brought together only by the invisible hand. Terrorism is the work of visible hands; it is an organizational project, a strategic choice, a conspiracy to murder and intimidate . . . you and me. No wonder the conspirators have difficulty defending, in public, the strategy they have chosen.

The moral difficulty is the same, obviously, when the conspiracy is directed not against you and me but against *them*—Protestants, say, not Catholics; Israelis, not Italians or Germans; blacks, not whites. These "limits" rarely hold for long; the logic of terrorism steadily expands the range of vulnerability. The more hostages they hold, the stronger the terrorists are. No one is safe once whole populations have been put at risk. Even if the risk were contained, however, the evil would be no different. So far as individual Protestants or Israelis or blacks are concerned, terrorism is random, degrading, and frightening. That is its hallmark, and that, again, is why it cannot be defended.

But when moral justification is ruled out, the way is opened for ideological excuse and apology. We live today in a political culture of excuses. This is far better than a political culture in which terrorism is openly defended and justified, for the excuse at least acknowledges the evil. But the improvement is precarious, hard won, and difficult to sustain. It is not the case, even in this better world, that terrorist organizations are without supporters. The support is indirect but by no means ineffective. It takes the form of apologetic descriptions and explanations, a litany of excuses that steadily undercuts our knowledge of the evil. Today that knowledge is insufficient unless it is supplemented and reinforced by a systematic critique of excuses. That is my purpose in this chapter. I take the principle for granted: that every act of terrorism is a wrongful act. The wrongfulness of the excuses, however, cannot be taken for granted; it has to be argued. The excuses themselves are familiar enough, the stuff of contemporary political debate. I shall state them in stereotypical form. There is no need to attribute them to this or that writer, publicist, or commentator; my readers can make their own attributions.[1]

The Excuses for Terrorism

The most common excuse for terrorism is that it is a last resort, chosen only when all else fails. The image is of people who have literally run out of options. One by one, they have tried every legitimate form of political and military action, exhausted every possibility, failed everywhere, until no alternative remains but the evil of terrorism. They must be terrorists or do nothing at all. The easy response is to insist that, given this description of their case, they should do nothing at all; they have indeed exhausted their possibilities. But this response simply reaffirms the principle, ignores the excuse; this response does not attend to the terrorists' desperation. Whatever the cause to which they are committed, we have to recognize that, given the commitment, the one thing they cannot do is "nothing at all."

But the case is badly described. It is not so easy to reach the "last resort." To get there, one must indeed try everything (which is a lot of things) and not just once, as if a political party might organize a single demonstration, fail to win immediate victory, and claim that it was now justified in moving on to murder. Politics is an art of repetition. Activists and citizens learn from experience, that is, by doing the same thing over and over again. It is by no means clear when they run out of options, but even under conditions of oppression and war, citizens have a good run short of that. The same argument applies to state officials who claim that they have tried "everything" and are now compelled to kill hostages or bomb peasant villages. Imagine such people called before a judicial tribunal and required to answer the question, What exactly did you try? Does anyone believe that they could come up with a plausible list? "Last resort" has only a notional finality; the resort to terror is ideologically last, not last in an actual series of actions, just last for the sake of the excuse. In fact, most state officials and movement militants who recommend a policy of terrorism recommend it as a first resort; they are for it from the beginning, although they may not get their way at the beginning. If they are honest, then, they must make other excuses and give up the pretense of the last resort.

The second excuse is designed for national liberation movements struggling against established and powerful states. Now the claim is that nothing else is possible, that no other strategy is available except terrorism. This is different from the first excuse because it does not require would-be terrorists to run through all the available options. Or, the second excuse requires terrorists to run through all the options in their heads, not in the world, notional finality is enough. Movement strategists consider their options and conclude that they have no alternative to terrorism. They think that they do not have the political strength to try anything else, and thus they do not try anything else. Weakness is their excuse.

But two very different kinds of weakness are commonly confused here: the weakness of the movement vis-à-vis the opposing state and the movement's weakness vis-à-vis its own people. This second kind of weakness, the inability of the movement to mobilize the nation, makes terrorism the "only" option because it effectively rules out all the others: nonviolent resistance, general strikes, mass demonstrations, unconventional warfare, and so on.

These options are only rarely ruled out by the sheer power of the state, by the pervasiveness and intensity of oppression. Totalitarian states may be immune to nonviolent or guerrilla resistance, but all the evidence suggests that they are also immune to terrorism. Or, more exactly, in totalitarian states state terror dominates every other sort. Where terrorism is a possible strategy for the oppositional movement (in liberal and democratic states, most obviously), other strategies are also possible if the movement has some significant degree of popular support. In the absence of popular support, terrorism may indeed be the one available strategy, but it is hard to see how its evils can then be excused. For it is not weakness alone that makes the excuse, but the claim of the terrorists to represent the weak; and the particular form of weakness that makes terrorism the only option calls that claim into question.

One might avoid this difficulty with a stronger insistence on the actual effectiveness of terrorism. The third excuse is simply that terrorism works (and nothing else does); it achieves the ends of the oppressed even without their participation. "When the act accuses, the result excuses."[2] This is a consequentialist argument, and given a strict understanding of consequentialism, this argument amounts to a justification rather than an excuse. In practice, however, the argument is rarely pushed so far. More often, the argument begins with an acknowledgment of the terrorists' wrongdoing. Their hands are dirty, but we must make a kind of peace with them because they have acted effectively for the sake of people who could not act for themselves. But, in fact, have the terrorists' actions been effective? I doubt that terrorism has ever achieved national liberations—no nation that I know of owes its freedom to a campaign of random murder—although terrorism undoubtedly increases the power of the terrorists within the national liberation movement. Perhaps terrorism is also conducive to the survival and notoriety (the two go together) of the movement, which is now dominated by terrorists. But even if we were to grant some means-end relationship between terror and national liberation, the third excuse does not work unless it can meet the further requirements of a consequentialist argument. It must be possible to say that the desired end could not have been achieved through any other, less wrongful, means. The third excuse depends, then, on the success of the first or second, and neither of these look likely to be successful.

The fourth excuse avoids this crippling dependency. This excuse does not require the apologist to defend either of the improbable claims that terrorism is the last resort or that it is the only possible resort. The fourth excuse is simply that terrorism is the universal resort. All politics is (really) terrorism. The appearance of innocence and decency is always a piece of deception, more or less convincing in accordance with the relative power of the deceivers. The terrorist who does not bother with appearances is only doing openly what everyone else does secretly.

This argument has the same form as the maxim "All's fair in love and war." Love is always fraudulent, war is always brutal, and political action is always terrorist in character. Political action works (as Thomas Hobbes long ago argued) only by generating fear in innocent men and women. Terrorism is the politics of state officials and movement militants alike. This argument does not justify either the officials or the militants, but it does excuse them all. We hardly can be harsh with people who act the way everyone else acts. Only saints are likely to act differently, and sainthood in politics is supererogatory, a matter of grace, not obligation.

But this fourth excuse relies too heavily on our cynicism about political life, and cynicism only sometimes answers well to experience. In fact, legitimate states do not need to terrorize their citizens, and strongly based movements do not need to terrorize their opponents. Officials and militants who live, as it were, on the margins of legitimacy and strength sometimes choose terrorism and sometimes do not. Living in terror is not a universal experience. The world the terrorists create has its entrances and exits.

If we want to understand the choice of terror, the choice that forces the rest of us through the door, we have to imagine what in fact always occurs, although we often have no satisfactory record of the occurrence: A group of men and women, officials or militants, sits around a table and argues about whether or not to adopt a terrorist strategy. Later on, the litany of excuses obscures the argument. But at the time, around the table, it would have been no use for defenders of terrorism to say, "Everybody does it," because there they would be face to face with people proposing to do something else. Nor is it historically the case that the members of this last group, the opponents of terrorism, always lose the argument. They can win, however, and still not be able to prevent a terrorist campaign; the would-be terrorists (it does not take very many) can always split the movement and go their own way. Or, they can split the bureaucracy or the police or officer corps and act in the shadow of state power. Indeed, terrorism often has its origin in such splits. The first victims are the terrorists' former comrades or colleagues. What reason can we possibly have, then, for equating the two? If we value the politics of the men and women who oppose terrorism, we must reject the excuses of their murderers. Cynicism at such a time is unfair to the victims.

The fourth excuse can also take, often does take, a more restricted form. Oppression, rather than political rule more generally, is always terroristic in character, and thus, we must always excuse the opponents of oppression. When they choose terrorism, they are only reacting to someone else's previous choice, repaying in kind the treatment they have long received. Of course, their terrorism repeats the evil—innocent people are killed, who were never themselves oppressors—but repetition is not the same as initiation. The oppressors set the terms of the struggle. But if the struggle is fought on the oppressors' terms, then the oppressors are likely to win. Or, at least, oppression is likely to win, even if it takes on a new face. The whole point of a liberation movement or a popular mobilization is to change the terms. We have no reason to excuse the terrorism reactively adopted by opponents of oppression unless we are confident of the sincerity of their opposition, the seriousness of their commitment to a nonoppressive politics. But the choice of terrorism undermines that confidence.

We are often asked to distinguish the terrorism of the oppressed from the terrorism of the oppressors. What is it, however, that makes the difference? The message of the terrorist is the same in both cases: a denial of the peoplehood and humanity of the groups among whom he or she finds victims. Terrorism anticipates, when it does not actually enforce, political domination. Does it matter if one dominated group is replaced by another? Imagine a slave revolt whose protagonists dream only of enslaving in their turn the children of their masters. The dream is understandable, but the fervent desire of the children that the revolt be repressed is equally understandable. In neither case does understanding make for excuse—not, at least, after a politics of universal freedom has become possible. Nor does an understanding of oppression excuse the terrorism of the oppressed, once we have grasped the meaning of "liberation."

These are the four general excuses for terror, and each of them fails. They depend upon statements about the world that are false, historical arguments for which there is no evidence, moral claims that turn out to be hollow or dishonest. This is not to say that there might not be more particular excuses that have greater plausibility, extenuating circumstances in particular cases that we would feel compelled to recognize. As with murder, we can tell a story (like the story, that Richard Wright tells in *Native Son*, for example) that might lead us, not to justify terrorism, but to excuse this or that individual terrorist. We can provide a personal history, a psychological study, of compassion destroyed by fear, moral reason by hatred and rage, social inhibition by unending violence—the product, an individual driven to kill or readily set on a killing course by his or her political leaders.[3] But the force of this story will not depend on any of the four general excuses, all of which grant what the storyteller will have to deny: that terrorism is the deliberate choice of rational men and women. Whether they conceive it to be one option among others or the only one available, they nevertheless argue and choose. Whether they are acting or reacting, they have made a decision. The human instruments they subsequently find to plant the bomb or shoot the gun may act under some psychological compulsion, but the men and women who choose terror as a policy act "freely." They could not act in any other way, or accept any other description of their action, and still pretend to be the leaders of the movement or the state. We ought never to excuse such leaders.

The Response to Terrorism

What follows from the critique of excuses? There is still a great deal of room for argument about the best way of responding to terrorism. Certainly, terrorists should be resisted, and it is not likely that a purely defensive resistance will ever be sufficient. In this sort of struggle, the offense is always ahead. The technology of terror is simple; the weapons are readily produced and easy to deliver. It is virtually impossible to protect people against random and indiscriminate attack. Thus, resistance will have to be supplemented by some combination of repression and retaliation. This is a dangerous business because repression and retaliation so often take terroristic forms and there are a host of apologists ready with excuses that sound remarkably like those of the terrorists themselves. It should be clear by now, however, that counterterrorism cannot be excused merely because it is reactive. Every new actor, terrorist or counterterrorist, claims to be reacting to someone else, standing in a circle and just passing the evil along. But the circle is ideological in character; in fact, every actor is a moral agent and makes an independent decision.

Therefore, repression and retaliation must not repeat the wrongs of terrorism, which is to say that repression and retaliation must be aimed systematically at the terrorists themselves, never at the people for whom the terrorists claim to be acting. That claim is in any case doubtful, even when it is honestly made. The people do not authorize the terrorists to act in their name. Only a tiny number actually participate in terrorist activities; they are far more likely to suffer than to benefit from the terrorist program. Even if they supported the program and hoped to benefit from it, however, they would still be immune from attack—exactly as civilians in time of war who support the war effort but are not themselves part of it are subject to the same immunity. Civilians may be put at risk by attacks on military targets, as by attacks on terrorist targets, but the risk must be kept to a minimum, even at some cost to the attackers. The refusal to make ordinary people into targets, whatever their nationality or even their politics, is the only way to say no to terrorism. Every act of repression and retaliation has to be measured by this standard.

But what if the "only way" to defeat the terrorists is to intimidate their actual or potential supporters? It is important to deny the premise of this question: that terrorism is a politics dependent on mass support. In fact, it is always the politics of an elite, whose members are dedicated and fanatical and more than ready to endure, or to watch others endure, the devastations of a counterterrorist campaign. Indeed, terrorists will welcome counterterrorism; it makes the terrorists' excuses more plausible and is sure to bring them, however many people are killed or wounded, however many are terrorized, the small number of recruits needed to sustain the terrorist activities.

Repression and retaliation are legitimate responses to terrorism only when they are constrained by the same moral principles that rule out terrorism itself. But there is an alternative response that seeks to avoid the violence that these two entail. The alternative is to address directly, ourselves, the oppression the terrorists claim to oppose. Oppression, they say, is the cause of terrorism. But that is merely one more excuse. The real cause of terrorism is the decision to launch a terrorist campaign, a decision made by that group of people sitting around a table whose deliberations I have already described. However, terrorists do exploit oppression, injustice, and human misery generally and look to these at least for their excuses. There can hardly be any doubt that oppression strengthens their hand. Is that a reason for us to come to the defense of the oppressed? It seems to me that we have our own reasons to do that, and do not need this one, or should not, to prod us into action. We might imitate those movement militants who argue against the adoption of a terrorist strategy—although not, as the terrorists say, because these militants are prepared to tolerate oppression. They already are opposed to oppression and now add to that opposition, perhaps for the same reasons, a refusal of terror. So should we have been opposed before, and we should now make the same addition.

But there is an argument, put with some insistence these days, that we should refuse to acknowledge any link at all between terrorism and oppression—as if any defense of oppressed men and women, once a terrorist campaign has been launched, would concede the effectiveness of the campaign. Or, at least, a defense of oppression would give terrorism the appearance of effectiveness and so increase the likelihood of terrorist campaigns in the future. Here we have the reverse side of the litany of excuses; we have turned over the record. First oppression is made into an excuse for terrorism, and then terrorism is made into an excuse for oppression. The first is the excuse of the far left; the second is the excuse of the neoconservative right.[4] I doubt that genuine conservatives would think it a good reason for defending the status quo that it is under terrorist attack; they would have independent reasons and would be prepared to defend the status quo against any attack. Similarly, those of us who think that the status quo urgently requires change have our own reasons for thinking so and need not be intimidated by terrorists or, for that matter, antiterrorists.

If one criticizes the first excuse, one should not neglect the second. But I need to state the second more precisely. It is not so much an excuse for oppression as an excuse for doing nothing (now) about oppression. The claim is that the campaign against terrorism has priority over every other political activity. If the people who take the lead in this campaign are the old oppressors, then we must make a kind of peace with them—temporarily, of course, until the terrorists have been beaten. This is a strategy that denies the possibility of a two-front war. So long as the men and women who pretend to lead the fight against oppression are terrorists, we can concede nothing to their demands. Nor can we oppose their opponents.

But why not? It is not likely in any case that terrorists would claim victory in the face of a serious effort to deal with the oppression of the people they claim to be defending. The effort would merely expose the hollowness of their claim, and the nearer it came to success, the more they would escalate their terrorism. They would still have to be defeated, for what they are after is not a solution to the problem but rather the power to impose their own solution. No decent end to the conflict in Ireland, say, or in Lebanon, or in the Middle East generally, is going to look like a victory for terrorism—if only because the different groups of terrorists are each committed, by the strategy they have adopted, to an indecent end.[5] By working for our own ends, we expose the indecency.

Oppression and Terrorism

It is worth considering at greater length the link between oppression and terror. To pretend that there is no link at all is to ignore the historical record, but the record is more complex than any of the excuses acknowledge. The first thing to be read out of it, however, is simple enough: Oppression is not so much the cause of terrorism as terrorism is one of the primary means of oppression. This was true in ancient times, as Aristotle recognized, and it is still true today. Tyrants rule by terrorizing their subjects; unjust and illegitimate regimes are upheld through a combination of carefully aimed and random violence.[6] If this method works in the state, there is no reason to think that it will not work, or that it does not work, in the liberation movement. Wherever we see terrorism, we should look for tyranny and oppression. Authoritarian states, especially in the moment of their founding, need a terrorist apparatus—secret police with unlimited power, secret prisons into which citizens disappear, death squads in unmarked cars. Even democracies may use terror, not against their own citizens, but at the margins, in their colonies, for example, where colonizers also are likely to rule tyrannically. Oppression is sometimes maintained by a steady and discriminate pressure, sometimes by intermittent and random violence—what we might think of as terrorist melodrama—designed to render the subject population fearful and passive.

This latter policy, especially if it seems successful, invites imitation by opponents of the state. But terrorism does not spread only when it is imitated. If it can be invented by state officials, it can also be invented by movement militants. Neither one need take lessons from the other; the circle has no single or necessary starting point. Wherever it starts, terrorism in the movement is tyrannical and oppressive in exactly the same way as is terrorism in the state. The terrorists aim to rule, and murder is their method. They have their own internal police, death squads, disappearances. They begin by killing or intimidating those comrades who stand in their way, and they proceed to do the same, if they can, among the people they claim to represent. If terrorists are successful, they rule tyrannically, and their people bear, without consent, the costs of the terrorists' rule. (If the terrorists are only partly successful, the costs to the people may be even greater: What they have to bear now is a war between rival terrorist gangs.) But terrorists cannot win the ultimate victory they seek without challenging the established regime or colonial power and the people it claims to represent, and when terrorists do that, they themselves invite imitation. The regime may then respond with its own campaign of aimed and random violence. Terrorist tracks terrorist, each claiming the other as an excuse.

The same violence can also spread to countries where it has not yet been experienced; now terror is reproduced not through temporal succession but through ideological adaptation. State terrorists wage bloody wars against largely imaginary enemies: army colonels, say, hunting down the representatives of "international communism." Or movement terrorists wage bloody wars against enemies with whom, but for the ideology, they could readily negotiate and compromise: nationalist fanatics committed to a permanent irredentism. These wars, even if they are without precedents, are likely enough to become precedents, to start the circle of terror and counterterror, which is endlessly oppressive for the ordinary men and women where the state calls its citizens and the movement its "people."

The only way to break out of the circle is to refuse to play the terrorist game. Terrorists in the state and the movement warn us, with equal vehemence, that any such refusal is a sign of softness and naiveté. The self-portrait of the terrorists is always the same. They are tough-minded and realistic; they know their enemies (or privately invent them for ideological purposes); and they are ready to do what must be done for victory. Why then do terrorists turn around and around in the same circle? It is true: Movement terrorists win support because they pretend to deal energetically and effectively with the brutality of the state. It also is true: State terrorists win support because they pretend to deal energetically and effectively with the brutality of the movement. Both feed on the fears of brutalized and oppressed people. But there is no way of overcoming brutality with terror. At most, the burden is shifted from these people to those; more likely, new burdens are added for everyone. Genuine liberation can come only through a politics that mobilizes the victims of brutality and takes careful aim at its agents, or by a politics that surrenders the hope of victory and domination and deliberately seeks a compromise settlement. In either case, once tyranny is repudiated, terrorism is no longer an option. For what lies behind all the excuses, of officials and militants alike, is the predilection for a tyrannical politics.

Notes

1. I cannot resist a few examples: Edward Said, "The Terrorism Scam," *The Nation*, June 14, 1986; and (more intelligent and circumspect) Richard Falk, "Thinking About Terrorism," *The Nation*, June 28, 1986.
2. Machiavelli, *The Discourses* I:ix. As yet, however, there have been no results that would constitute a Machiavellian excuse.
3. See, for example, Daniel Goleman, "The Roots of Terrorism Are Found in Brutality of Shattered Childhood," *New York Times*, September 2, 1986, pp. C1, 8. Goleman discusses the psychic and social history of particular terrorists, not the roots of terrorism.
4. The neoconservative position is represented, although not as explicitly as I have stated it here, in Benjamin Netanyahu, ed., *Terrorism: How the West Can Win* (New York: Farrar, Straus & Giroux, 1986).
5. The reason the terrorist strategy, however indecent in itself, cannot be instrumental to some decent political purpose is because any decent purpose must somehow accommodate the people against whom the terrorism is aimed, and what terrorism expresses is precisely the refusal of such an accommodation, the radical devaluing of the Other. See my argument in *Just and Unjust Wars* (New York: Basic Books, 1977), pp. 197–206, especially 203.
6. Aristotle, *The Politics* 1313–1314a.

Understanding Terrorism

Robert K. Fullinwider

I hold that a little rebellion now and then is a good thing, & as necessary in the political world as storms in the physical.

What signify a few lives lost in a century or two? The tree of liberty must be refreshed from time to time with the blood of patriots & tyrants. It is its natural manure.

— Thomas Jefferson

It belongs to men to judge the law at the risk of being judged by it.

— Maurice Merleau-Ponty

"No one these days advocates terrorism," writes Michael Walzer, "not even those who regularly practice it." This is because there is no moral defense available to the terrorist, no justification. Terrorism is worse than murder and rape, and no one can justify them. The only thing we can do with terrorists is excuse them. But the standard excuses we might offer are themselves lame and unpersuasive. So Walzer begins his analysis.

It is a puzzling analysis. First, there is no precise characterization of the terrorist. We do not know exactly who it is that is beyond justification, and so we remain unclear as to why. Second, and more puzzling, Walzer does not talk about excuses at all. The arguments he criticizes are all defenses of terrorism.

Consider the second point first. The avowed aim of the chapter is to examine excuses made for terrorism. According to Walzer, there are basically four of them: Terrorism is an act of last resort; terrorism is a tool of the weak; terrorism is the only effective tool the weak have; everybody practices terrorism. But these are not excuses, strictly speaking.

We excuse people by arguing that they acted in ignorance or under compulsion.[1] This is not what the apologists of terrorism say about terrorists. As Walzer himself points out, the four "excuses" he discusses acknowledge that terrorism is the deliberate choice of rational men and women. The apologists for terrorism do not offer an *apology* but an *apologia*. They put forward arguments that say the terrorist, all things considered, did not act wrongly.

So it is puzzling to find half of Walzer's chapter attacking defenses of terrorism when he begins by saying that no defense is available, that he will simply take for granted that every act of terrorism is a wrongful act. To reintroduce the first point: This puzzlement is compounded by the lack of a clear account in the chapter of who the terrorist is. Walzer pictures the terrorist as attacking "innocent bystanders," as killing or harming "indiscriminately." This is not a picture likely to enlist our sympathetic ear to the terrorist's case. We are going to take it for granted, too, that the terrorist is wrong. But some of Walzer's own later observations belie his initial description. Terrorists are often very discriminate in their targets.

I press these points because the outrage we feel for terrorist acts too easily prompts us to make and support blanket condemnations of terrorism by resort to equivocation or word play.[2] Therefore, it is important not to be vague about who the terrorist is and not to blur distinctions or relevant questions.

Who are terrorists? Here is a list: Basque separatists, factions of the PLO, the IRA, the Red Brigades, Croatian nationalists, the Tupamaros, the Puerto Rican National Liberation Front, the Baader-Meinhof Gang, Black September, Shining Path, Posse Comitatus, South Moluccan nationalists, Armenian revanchists, the Symbionese Liberation Army. Why is there no defense for what they do? Why are they beyond justification? It must be because (1) they make no claims and arguments at all or in terms we can understand or (2) they make claims and arguments so flimsy that it is a waste of energy to go through the exercise of answering them.

Benzion Netanyahu takes the first path by diabolizing the terrorist. "The terrorist," he claims, "represents a new breed of man which takes humanity back to prehistoric times, to the times when morality was not yet born. Divested of any moral principle, he has no moral sense, no moral controls, and is therefore capable of committing any crime, like a killing machine, without shame or remorse."[3] If this is the terrorist, then he or she is so alien from our own moral experience that there is no ground for understanding him or her. There are no moral claims and arguments to answer.

Even Walzer's characterization of terrorists as indiscriminate killers of the innocent puts terrorists and their cause beyond the pale. What recognizable moral view could these killers possibly employ? What arguments could there be for us to take seriously? Walzer, in fact, uneasily straddles the line between the first and second paths. There *are* arguments, although Walzer puts them not in the mouths of terrorists—what could indiscriminate killers say?—but in the mouth of the apologist for terrorism. These arguments are "excuses" too incomplete or shallow to be taken very seriously.

The slaughter of Jewish worshippers in the Neve Shalom Synagogue in Istanbul last year exemplifies the mad and indiscriminate terrorism that Walzer obviously has in mind. During services, two terrorists entered the synagogue, barred the doors, and machine-gunned twenty-two people to death before exploding grenades to destroy themselves and all identity of who they were.[4] The worshippers in Istanbul met their deaths because they were Jews and because their attackers were willing to target Jews as such in the former's "war against Zionism." The slaughter was so horrible and revolting that it may strike us as too morally grotesque to understand, from their point of view, the goals and the values that animated the slaughterers.

But the Turkish synagogue episode is less typical of terrorism during the last one hundred years—or even the past twenty years—than is, for example, the kidnapping and murder of Aldo Moro in 1978. The Red Brigades abducted Moro, probably the most respected political leader in Italy, subjected him to a "trial" for his "crimes" (as representative and principal agent of the "rotten" and "repressive" Italian state), and "executed" him. The abduction had been planned over several months and followed a period of kidnappings and kneecappings of industrialists and lesser political figures. There was nothing indiscriminate about the taking of Aldo Moro.

Are the *brigatisti*, too, morally beyond the pale, subhuman throwbacks to a prehistoric time, divided from us by some moral chasm, their aims not worth a charitable understanding? It is, unfortunately, too easy to foreclose questions of justification here by definitional sleights of hand. Benjamin Netanyahu agrees with Walzer that "terrorism is always unjustifiable."[5] This seems to follow from Netanyahu's definition ("Terrorism is the deliberate and systematic murder, maiming, and menacing of the innocent to inspire fear for political ends"[6]) and from the fact that deliberately killing innocents is wrong. But Netanyahu gets the kidnappers of Aldo Moro under his proscription only by sliding over to a characterization of terrorists as attackers of *civilians*, implicitly equating "innocents" and "civilians."[7] According to the Netanyahu definition—and under Walzer's characterization—the Red Brigades' kidnapping of Aldo Moro does not qualify as terrorism unless we characterize Moro as an *innocent* civilian, but that just begs the question against the Red Brigades. They chose Moro because he was *not* innocent (by their lights).

Italy was convulsed by the Aldo Moro kidnapping not because the actions of the Red Brigades were incomprehensible but because the actions were fully comprehensible in moral terms. Everybody understands crime and punishment. The arguments of the Red Brigades were so understandable, in fact, that the Italian establishment feared they might even seduce many Italian citizens.

The political parties of Italy from the onset of the Moro crisis locked themselves into a rigid position: No negotiations for Moro's release. The parties did not take this position because they thought the arguments of the Red Brigades had no credibility. If the Red Brigades had defended their kidnapping of Moro on the grounds that he was guilty of secretly poisoning all the water in Italy with fluorides, or that he had betrayed the planet earth to galactic enemies, the Italian government would not have felt that negotiations for Moro's life risked giving the kidnappers widespread legitimacy among the populace. It was precisely because the Red Brigades' arguments had enough facial credibility to start with that the government saw any concessions as undermining its own legitimacy.[8] Its policy on Moro amounted to an argument-by-deed addressed to the Italian public that there was no truth to the charge that the state was rotten, repressive, and illegitimate.

Thus, not only were the arguments of the Red Brigades comprehensible; they had to be answered. The answers were not, and are not, transparent. They have to be worked at, especially if they are not to beg the central questions. Simply taking for granted that every act of terrorism is wrong may allow us to make short work of the Red Brigades, but not honest work. Pushing aside the question of justification as pointless is more likely to impede rather than advance our understanding of terrorism.

The Appeal to Morality versus the Appeal to Law

Benzion Netanyahu gets the matter exactly backward: Terrorists are not throwbacks to a prehistoric time "when morality was not yet born." If anything, terrorists are throwbacks to a "time" when morality was not yet under control. What is often scary about terrorists is that they appeal to morality without appealing to the law. Let me explain.

Political theorists tell a story about the "state of nature" to explain and defend government. The state of nature proves to be intolerable for its inhabitants, whose lives are "solitary, poore, nasty, brutish, and short."[9] Contrary to common impressions, however, the problem in the state of nature is not that people are so immoral—so selfish and rapacious that they persistently endanger each other. The problem is that people are so moral—so determined to vindicate rights or to uphold honor at any costs that they become a menace to one another.

The distinctive feature of the state of nature, as John Locke points out, is not the absence of morality but the absence of law. It is a circumstance in which "the law of nature"—the moral law—must be enforced by each person. Each is responsible for vindicating his or her own rights and the rights of others. All prosecution of crime and injustice in the state of nature is free-lance. Such a situation is the inevitable spawning ground of the neverending chain of retaliation and counter-retaliation of the blood feud. "For every one in that state being both Judge and Executioner of the Law of Nature, Men being partial to themselves, Passion and Revenge is very apt to carry them too far, and with too much heat, in their own Cases; as well as negligence, and unconcernedness, to make them too remiss, in other Mens."[10]

Even if persons were not biased in their own favor, the problems of enforcing justice in the state of nature would remain deadly. How would crime be defined? How would evidence for its commission be gathered? Who is to be punished, and in what manner? Nothing about the state of nature ensures any common understanding about these questions. The contrary is the case. Private understanding pitted against private understanding produces an escalation of response and counter-response that lets violence erupt and feed on itself.

The solution, of course, is "an establish'd, settled, known *Law*, received and allowed by common consent to be the Standard of Right and Wrong, and the common measure to decide all Controversies" and "a known and indifferent Judge, with Authority to determine all differences according to the established Law."[11] Conventions, established standards, and enforced rulings keep the peace, and when they exist by "common consent," they do justice as well.

"Consent of the governed" is the ideal that underlies democratic regimes, at least in Anglo-American cultures. It is an attractive ideal. When a regime of law is "chosen" by "free and rational persons," the "strains of commitment" will be minimal.[12] That is to say, there will be widespread willingness to obey the law and accept its rulings.

But in the real governments we live under—even the best of them—the strains of commitment often are severe. Impatience with the existing procedures of law can, and does, lead people to resort to "irregular justice," including political violence. Such "irregular justice," even when it is violent and rebellious, need not repudiate the existing rule of law. Irregular justice may be directed only at egregious failures of the law or at illegality tolerated as law.

Ordinary political violence can itself have all the earmarks of terrorism. The Molly Maguires—a secret band of Irish miners in mid-nineteenth century Pennsylvania—carried on a decade-long labor "war" with mine owners and police. Emerging from violent resistance among Pennsylvania Irish to the Civil War draft, the Molly Maguires had their own way of dealing with the labor strife of the time. They resorted to arson, beatings, and murder, directed against mine foremen, superintendents, policemen, and others against whom the Molly Maguires had grievances. The violence was meant to intimidate (targeted foremen, for example, often left the community after receiving threats) for political ends.[13] The Molly Maguires resorted to war because they perceived both the law and its enforcers to be in the pockets of owners and bankers.

A less remote situation is the bombing and burning of scores of abortion facilities in the United States during the last decade. The aim of the attackers is to stop or impede abortions, and these attackers resort to "irregular justice" because the law fails to protect the unborn. They appeal to a "higher law," to morality itself.[14]

Our responses to political violence of this kind are ambivalent. In general we do not want free-lance justice; we do not want people arrogating to themselves decisions the law should make. But in particular cases, our sympathies often are enlisted on the side of the violent, even if we go through pro forma condemnations of their actions. We as often romanticize the Molly Maguires of our history as vilify them.

This is not surprising because it is a part of U.S. political tradition that we may be forced, in Merleau-Ponty's words, "to judge the law at the risk of being judged by it."[15] "I like a little rebellion now and then," wrote Thomas Jefferson to Abigail Adams. "The spirit of resistance to government is so valuable on certain occasions, that I wish it to be always kept alive. It will often be exercised when wrong, but better so than not to be exercised at all."[16] Political violence serves the useful function of shaking government out of its unresponsiveness to the rights and interests of some of its citizens."[17] The violence strains but does not rupture the rule of law because the appeal to morality made by the rebels draws from the same principles embodied in the law.

It is not Jeffersonian rebellions and outbreaks that truly frighten and disturb us, but revolutionary violence directed against a whole existing regime of law, including its underlying principles. The kidnapping and trial of Aldo Moro were an assault against the very idea of capitalist and bourgeois legality. They were acts of war on behalf of a new social order that would emerge from the ruins of "rotten" Italy.

Political violence that strikes against the very regime itself is doubly disturbing. For one thing, such violence is more frightening than ordinary dissidence or rebellion because the underlying common allegiance to the principles of the law that we expect to moderate or contain the violence of the dissident or rebel is absent. It is false to say that the revolutionary terrorist has no moral limits; but it is true that he or she repudiates the conventional boundaries that guide our own actions.

More importantly for our purposes, revolutionary violence is more frustrating because it is hard to answer the challenge of revolutionaries without begging the question against them. We can condemn ordinary political violence, including ordinary terrorism, by appealing to the "constitution," that is, the basic ideas of legality upon which our political, economic, and cultural institutions rest. Revolutionaries repudiate the "constitution." They do so in the name of recognizable moral ideas: creating a just or humane society, ending oppression and misery. But "just," "humane," and so on are abstractions that we typically fill in by reference to the principles and practices of our existing social order. If we cannot resort to this strategy in answering revolutionaries, then how do we convincingly repudiate their claims of justice? How do we show their violence to be condemned rather than supported by morality?

I do not mean we have to answer these questions for the satisfaction of revolutionaries. They have already pulled a gun. It is for our own satisfaction that we would like to give an intellectually honest answer to revolutionaries' rejectionism. We appeal to the law; they reject our law and appeal to morality. We claim morality, too, but then notice we have filled it up with our law.

Attacking the Innocent

The ease with which we beg the question against revolutionaries is illustrated by Walzer's depiction of terrorists as killers of the innocent. How are we to understand "innocence"? Aldo Moro was clearly innocent in one sense: He had never been convicted of any wrong by a duly authorized judge or jury of any state or officially recognized international agency. But this sense of innocence is not terribly helpful for condemning the Red Brigades. Many instances of political violence that any of us would endorse are directed against innocents in this respect. Was Moro innocent in a deeper sense: not causally or morally responsible for the "crimes" of Italy, not an accessory, not complicit?

If we accept that the Italian state is a "criminal" enterprise, a repressive and unjust system, then it was clearly reasonable directly to connect Moro with it and its "crimes." Few other figures in Italy were so centrally involved in maintaining the rule of Christian democratic governments since World War II. Other targets of the Red Brigades were similarly connected in some important way to the political, military, or economic functioning of the state. If we *grant* the premises of the Red Brigades, then the charge that they killed innocent people is not so readily sustainable.

But aren't there some lines to be drawn that are independent of point of view, lines that everyone must acknowledge? Perhaps so, but finding an institutionally contextless conception of innocence will not be easy.[18] Consider the infamous massacre of the Israeli athletes at the 1972 Munich Olympics. Weren't they uncontroversially innocent? Yet a case can be made, from the point of view of their attackers, that these athletes were legitimate targets. They were willing and knowing representatives of their state to an international affair in which their presence and participation would lend yet further international credibility and legitimacy to Israel. Thus, from the point of view of their attackers, the athletes were active and informed accessories in a continuing "crime"—the support of the "criminal" state of Israel.

Of course, by international convention, unarmed athletes participating in the Olympics *are* "innocent." The willingness of terrorists to violate this convention burdens their defense. A great deal can be said in favor of such a convention; even terrorists are unlikely to prefer a world in which every "criminal" is an open target. Nevertheless, the circumstances, as the terrorists saw them, may have justified "irregular justice." Like the Molly Maguires, the terrorists saw themselves as attacking fair targets that current conventions protect. Such terrorists concede that they attack the "conventionally innocent," but not that they attack the "really innocent."

What about the victims of the slaughter at Neve Shalom Synagogue in Istanbul? Surely *they* cannot be connected to "crimes" of any sort. Their only connection to "Zionist imperialism" was that they were Jews; and if that is enough of a connection to make them fair targets, then "immunity of the innocent" is emptied as a moral notion and there will be no one who is "really innocent."

There is, doubtless, some point of view from which the slaughter in Istanbul makes sense, but it is a point of view that comes close to being too alien for us to comprehend or even credit as a moral point of view. Here the claims of Walzer and the rhetoric of Netanyahu seem appropriate. But I say "comes close" because the rationalization of the Istanbul massacre may be less alien than we expect.

Walzer's response to terrorism, or the terrorism I am describing now, flows from a conception of universal human rights.[19] Every human individual has an inviolability and dignity *just as a human being*. Independently of any feature of his or her social environment or historical circumstance, a person has a claim to our moral concern, a claim expressed in the possession of basic human rights. The "immunity thesis"—that innocent persons cannot be made the targets of violent assault—describes one of those rights.

An alternative view denies the moral individualism and universalism underlying the human rights approach. This view claims that the value of a person is wholly exhausted in his or her class or group membership. There is no transgroup or extraclass "humanity" that creates moral pull. Moral universalism is false.

Stated so starkly, perhaps this is a view not subscribed to by anyone. But there clearly are views that show considerable kinship. For example, at least some forms of Marxism imply, in present historical circumstances, that a person's rights and duties are wholly a function of his or her class.[20] Moreover, parochial moralities that see the universe from the point of view of God's, or history's, chosen people are not hard to imagine or even to find in history.

Another alternative conception sees the modern world as so dehumanized, so devoid of value, that it is perverse to agonize over the protection of innocents, to erect conventions, make law, and pass judgments as if current humanity itself had any value. Modern humans are deracinated and deformed, a mockery of what a fully realized humanity could be. That such beings are incidentally slaughtered, maimed, and terrorized in the upheaval of a revolution for a transformed social order is of no importance. What will their deaths signify in a century or two, from the perspective of a new order and a new humanity?[21]

Thus, two basic ideas compete against the idea of universal human rights. One measures the worth of people according to their group membership. The other measures the worth of people against an ideal of humanity. These measures are not alien and incomprehensible to us. In attenuated and confined forms, they are a part of the moral armory of even those of us who, like Walzer, subscribe to universal human rights. We value community and cherish special relations of affinity and kinship. We hold ideals and strive for collective reform and improvement.

We thus can comprehend the role of these ideas for those who acknowledge no limits on their force. Even the maddest terrorism shows a familiar face. Moreover, within our own philosophical culture, we cannot say with confidence that the intellectual foundations of human rights are clear or that they are universally acknowledged. The reigning fashions in the academy today include various attacks on "liberal individualism." In contrast to the "atomistic" individual supposedly subscribed to by liberalism, current critics offer pictures of individuals "essentially connected" to others in community, individuals whose identities are "constituted by community."[22]

The ideas of essence and constitution in these pictures are not made clear; these ideas may turn out to be innocuous enough and hardly at odds with anything except a caricature of individualism. But lurking within them are possible interpretations that would make the grounds of moral universalism obscure. To say that people are *essentially related* to community may mean they have no value outside *some* community or other; or it may mean they have no value outside their own community. "Community" may encompass the loosest human associations and the most casual forms of sociability, or it may mean a highly structured group bound by corporate values. Out of these options there can emerge interpretations that render the view that human beings have a worth and dignity independently of *any* of their relations a proposition too abstract and empty to hold.

Perhaps other grounds of universalism are available; or perhaps a conception of human rights can be erected on nonuniversalist views. But our intellectual house is not in such good order that rationally irrefutable barriers are in place against an extreme extension of the quest for community or the quest for ideals—both of which can lead us to discount rather sharply the value of some humans. Then the rationalization of Neve Shalom is not so far away.

To understand terrorists and to take their self-justification seriously is not to acquiesce in the terrorists' deeds or concede them any measure of right. Rather, the point is to see the full spectrum of political violence realistically, without demonization, for our *own* sake, not the sake of terrorists. Because revolutionary terrorists repudiate so much of what is settled and in place, we struggle to make sense of the meaning they give to the moral notions they deploy. But they invite us to see how rotten the existing system is and to trust that in destroying it a new and morally preferable society will emerge. If terrorists war on us, we can war on them without compunction, but that does not answer their invitation. To do that, we have to say why the existing rule of law deserves allegiance.

Terrorists typically appeal to history for vindication. We can appeal to history, too, in defense of the conventions and practices terrorists revolt against or violate. Some terrorism we can condemn by appeal to those very conventions, some we can condemn by appeal to abstract principle, but most we must condemn because we judge the terrorists grotesquely mistaken in their understanding of historical possibilities. The Red Brigades deluded themselves into thinking the kidnapping of Aldo Moro would bring on the revolution. The Molly Maguires might have thought their violence was an effective—or the only—way to bring justice for the miners. Walzer's discussion of the four "excuses" eloquently shows the burden of proof that terrorism, ordinary or revolutionary, seldom meets. But this failure is contingent, not necessary. We cannot define terrorism into a moral corner where we do not have to worry any more about justification.

NOTES

I am grateful to Steven Luper-Foy and to my colleagues at the Center for Philosophy and Public Policy, especially Claudia Mills, for comments on an earlier draft of this chapter.

1. See J. L. Austin, "A Plea for Excuses," *Philosophical Papers*, 2nd ed. (London: Oxford University Press, 1970), p. 176: "In the one defence [i.e., justifying], briefly, we accept responsibility but deny [of the conduct] that it was bad. In the other [i.e., excusing], we admit [of the conduct] that it was bad but don't accept full, or any, responsibility." In subsequent correspondence, Michael Walzer writes that what he is talking about *are* excuses because they "have this construction: 'of course it is wrong to kill innocent people, but. . . .'" This construction, however, is ambiguous between "of course it is *ordinarily* wrong to kill innocent people, but there are special circumstances in this case to justify it," and "of course it is wrong to kill innocent people and *it was wrong in this case*, but there are special circumstances that excuse it," the special circumstances in this second construction being the presence of responsibility-relieving factors. Because Walzer acknowledges that the apologist for terrorism does not deny the terrorists' responsibility, I take the apologies to have the form of the first rather than the second construction and thus to be justificatory in nature. In any case, I do not want to make too much of the difference between excusing and justifying or of the way I draw the distinction.

2. I have benefited, on this point, from reading Judith Lichtenberg's unpublished essay, "Beneath the Rhetoric of Terrorism."

3. Benzion Netanyahu, "Terrorists and Freedom Fighters," in Benjamin Netanyahu, ed., *Terrorism: How the West Can Win* (New York: Farrar, Straus, Giroux, 1986), pp. 29–30.

4. See the account by Judith Miller, "The Istanbul Synagogue Massacre: An Investigation," *New York Times Magazine*, January 4, 1987, pp. 14–18.

5. "Defining Terrorism," in Netanyahu, *Terrorism*, p. 12.

6. Ibid., p. 9.

7. Ibid., p. 10. Netanyahu explicitly refers to the Red Brigades. Walzer's writings are usually rich with examples and cases but in the present case, we never meet any real examples of terrorism. Part of the initial puzzlement I express at the beginning of this chapter derived from uncertainty about whether Walzer's initial characterization of terrorists as indiscriminate killers was meant as a *description* of those individuals and groups most frequently referred to as terrorists (and this would include the Red Brigades) or was meant as a *stipulative definition*, marking off as terrorists only those who engage in indiscriminate murder. In subsequent correspondence, Walzer writes, "I do not believe that the kidnapping of Aldo Moro was a terrorist act . . . [and] I don't think that it unduly restricts the idea of terrorism to insist on its randomness: the carpet bombing of cities, the bomb in the pub, cafe, bus station, supermarket—all this is common enough, and awful enough, to deserve a name."

8. Nations also resist negotiating with terrorists in order not to encourage future terrorism. This was a secondary consideration in the present case. On the Italian policy of no-negotiations, and on the Moro kidnapping generally, see Robin Erica Wagner-Pacifici, *The Moro Morality Play: Terrorism as Social Drama* (Chicago: University of Chicago Press, 1986), pp. 47–163; and

Robert Katz, *Days of Wrath: The Ordeal of Aldo Moro* (Garden City, N.Y.: Doubleday, 1980), p. 70ff.
9. Thomas Hobbes, *Leviathan* (Baltimore, Md.: Penguin Books, 1968), p. 186.
10. John Locke, *Two Treatises of Government* (New York: New American Library, 1965), pp. 395–396.
11. Ibid., p. 396.
12. John Rawls, *A Theory of Justice* (Cambridge, Mass.: Harvard University Press, 1971), pp. 175–183.
13. The Molly Maguires clearly count as terrorists on some definitions. See, for example, C. A. J. Coady, "The Morality of Terrorism," *Philosophy* 60 (January 1985): 52.
14. "Perhaps it *is* terrorism to use violence to intimidate. But which is the greater terror: the destruction of two dozen buildings without loss of life in 1984, or the destruction of 1.5 million human beings because they were inconvenient to the mothers who carried them?" Patrick Buchanan, *Washington Times*, January 4, 1985, p. C1.
15. Maurice Merleau-Ponty, *Humanism and Terror* (Boston: Beacon Press, 1969), p. xxxix.
16. Thomas Jefferson, *Writings* (New York: Library of America, 1984), pp. 889–890. For the quotations at the beginning of this chapter, see p. 882 (letter to James Madison, January 1787), and p. 911 (letter to William Smith, November 1787).
17. Shay's Rebellion, which was the occasion for Jefferson's comments, is a case in point. To a certain extent we owe our Constitution to this insurrection of desperate farmers in western Massachusetts (but it apparently would have failed Walzer's strictures about last resort). A few lives were lost in the affair. See Marion L. Starkey, *A Little Rebellion* (New York: Knopf, 1955).
18. Less easy, perhaps, than I supposed in R. Fullinwider, "War and Innocence," *Philosophy & Public Affairs* 5 (Fall 1975):90–97.
19. See Michael Walzer, *Just and Unjust Wars* (New York: Basic Books, 1977), pp. 134–135. See also his *Spheres of Justice* (New York: Basic Books, 1983), p. xv.
20. "The correct basis for what is morally good, what one's duty is, what the right thing to do is, what is fair to do . . . is one's place in one's society. The correct basis is not the human person taken in isolation. Rather, the focus is on the groups in society to which a person belongs. . . . The right thing to do is determined by a consideration of what ultimately, in view of the primacy of class, advances the realization of the tendencies of one's class." Milton Fisk, *Ethics and Society. A Marxist Interpretation of Value* (New York: New York University Press, 1980), pp. xiii, xvi.

"Whoever does not care to return to Moses, Christ, or Mohammed; whoever is not satisfied with eclectic *hodge-podges* must acknowledge that morality is a product of social development; that there is nothing immutable about it; that it serves social interests; that these interests are contradictory; that morality more than any other form of ideology has a class character.

"But do not elementary moral precepts exist, worked out in the development of humanity as a whole and indispensable for the existence of every collective body? Undoubtedly such precepts exist but the extent of their action is extremely limited and unstable. Norms 'obligatory upon all' become the less forceful the sharper the character assumed by the class struggle. The highest form of the class struggle is civil war, which explodes into midair all moral ties between the hostile classes." Leon Trotsky, *Their Morals and Ours* (New York: Pathfinder Press, 1973), p. 21.
21. For a discussion of views that find the modern world generally worthless, see Bernard Yack, *The Longing for Total Revolution: Philosophic Sources of Social Discontent from Rousseau to Marx and Nietzsche* (Princeton, N.J.: Princeton University Press, 1986).
22. For a typical recent attack on "liberal individualism," see Suzanna Sherry, "Civic Virtue and the Feminine Voice in Constitutional Adjudication," *Virginia Law Review* 72 (April 1986): 546ff, and her citations of Alasdair MacIntyre, Michael Sandel, Carol Gilligan, and so forth.

Questions for Further Reflection

1. A commonly heard slogan is that "one man's terrorist is another man's freedom fighter." Are there objective means of distinguishing between terrorists and freedom fighters? (Or, perhaps, for deciding which freedom fighters are terrorists and which are not?) If so, what might they be?
2. Is it possible to distinguish between the innocent and the guilty in an oppressive regime? If so, where is the line to be drawn? For instance, are wealthy members of the society, who support the oppressive government and in turn profit from it, innocent or guilty of oppression?
3. Is it ever permissible to attack noncombatants? There are many military cases in which noncombatants are killed; any sort of bombing raid, for example, is likely to kill noncombatants. Are the killings of noncombatants in these cases morally permissible? If so, is there an important difference between these cases and terrorist attacks in which noncombatants are killed?
4. Can you think of any example, actual or imaginary, in which terrorist acts are or would be justified? If so, what are they? If there could be no such examples, why not?

Further Readings

Coady, C. A. J. "The Morality of Terrorism." *Philosophy* 60 (1985): 47–69. Includes a good discussion of the combatant/noncombatant distinction.

Khatchadourian, Haig. "Terrorism and Morality." *Journal of Applied Philosophy* 5 (1988): 131–145. Discusses the definition of terrorism, and argues that "terrorism, in all its types and forms, is always wrong."

Laqueur, Walter. *The Age of Terrorism.* Boston: Little, Brown, 1987. A very readable overview of terrorism, focused mainly on the contemporary scene but including a discussion of the nineteenth-century origins of modern terrorism.

Laqueur, Walter, and Yonah Alexander, eds. *The Terrorism Reader*, revised edition. New York: NAL Penguin, 1987. A helpful collection of writings about terrorism, including a selection of writings by terrorists.

Stohl, Michael, ed. *The Politics of Terrorism*, third edition. New York: Marcel Dekker, 1988. A useful collection of essays, mainly by political scientists. Michael Stohl's introductory chapter, "Demystifying Terrorism," is especially helpful. (It is interesting to contrast the ten "myths" he identifies about terrorism with the ten "erroneous beliefs" discussed in Laqueur's introduction to *The Age of Terrorism.*)

Teichman, Jenny. "How to Define Terrorism." *Philosophy* 64 (1989): 505–517. Distinguishes between wide and narrow senses.

Wallace, Gerry. "War, Terrorism, and Ethical Consistency." In Brenda Almond, ed., *Introducing Applied Ethics.* Oxford: Basil Blackwell, 1995. Considers whether it is consistent to defend some wars while holding all terrorist activity to be impermissible.

Chapter 15

OBLIGATIONS TOWARD THE NEEDY

What sort of obligations do we have to help those less well off than we are? To make matters more concrete, what obligations do we have, if any, to alleviate hunger in countries other than our own?

That world hunger is a large and significant problem is beyond dispute. In the recent past, there have been famines in the Sahara, Bangladesh, Ethiopia, and elsewhere. However, merely counting famines gives a misleading picture of the problem, since a great many people who are not actually starving are nonetheless severely malnourished. As Robert Van Wyk notes, "Estimates of the number of severely malnourished people in the world have ranged from seventy million, to 460 million, to one billion."[1] Hunger is clearly the cause of a great deal of suffering. But what, if anything, is it our moral duty to do about it? It may be useful to divide this question into two: Are we obligated to help the needy? If so, what ought we to do?

Are We Obligated to Help the Needy?

In an article that has become a classic, Peter Singer argues on utilitarian grounds that we should do a great deal to help those in need. Our duty to help others in need, according to Singer, is as important and central as our duty not to harm others. The key premise in Singer's argument is that, "if it is in our power to prevent something bad from happening, without thereby sacrificing something of comparable moral importance, we ought, morally, to do it." It is difficult, of course, to say what is of "comparable moral importance." Is my children's college education of comparable moral importance to food for a starving Biafran child? Presumably, eating is more important than going to college, but also we normally think we have special obligations to our own children, that our duties to our own children are more pressing than our duties to other children. This, however, does little damage to Singer's point, for many of the things on which we expend our resources surely have *no* moral importance, or at best a vanishingly small amount. One's acquisition of a new compact disc player, a

---

[1] Robert N. Van Wyk, "Perpectives on World Hunger and the Extent of Our Positive Duties." *Public Affairs Quarterly* 2 (1988): 75–90, at p. 75.

second or third television set, or an expensive dinner at a fancy restaurant is surely of virtually *no* moral importance. So even what Singer calls the "more moderate" version of his principle—that we should give as much as we can without giving up something of moral significance—has the consequence that nearly all of us ought to be doing far more than we are to help the world's hungry, provided that there are effective ways of spending our money or time so as to help them.

It is useful to contrast Singer's view with one that regards morality not as a matter of maximizing utility but as a matter of not getting in one another's way. A more libertarian account, of the sort defended by John Hospers or Robert Nozick, for example, might hold that all duties are *negative* in the sense that they proscribe interfering with the liberties of others. There are no *positive* duties, no duties to help others meet their needs or accomplish their goals. In this sort of view, we are not *obligated* to do anything to help the hungry, although if we want to, of course, we *may*, since we can do anything we like with our property, including donating it to charity.

Amartya Sen has suggested that it is the wide acceptance of something like this view that, in some cases, has led to famines. He points out that famines have taken place in years when the per capita food supply in the countries in which they occur is average or even above average. The problem is not so much lack of food as the loss by some citizens of the resources by means of which to acquire it.[2]

Robert Van Wyk has suggested that even on libertarian grounds, we have an obligation to help the poor. Van Wyk holds that even on Nozick's grounds, we would have an obligation of compensatory justice toward the world's hungry, as their hunger is arguably due in part to the economic and political treatment of underdeveloped countries by developed ones. By way of example, Van Wyk cites the case of Bengal, which was at one time highly prosperous but which was reduced to poverty by British practices, including taxes and trade restrictions. Van Wyk writes: "Those who benefited from the Industrial Revolution in England, including those alive today, would still have duties to aid Bengal, just as those who inherited a fortune partially based on stolen money have a duty to return what was stolen, with interest, even though they themselves are in no way guilty of theft."[3] (But how plausible is Van Wyk's claim that the inheritor of stolen money should pay it back? If you buy my house with stolen money, do I then have an obligation to give the money to the person from whom you stole it? Doesn't that obligation still rest with you? Is the situation different if you *give* me the money rather than *paying* me with it?)

Garrett Hardin, in this chapter, rejects the idea that we owe aid to the hungry for compensatory reasons, pointing out that similar reasoning would suggest that we ought now to give back all the land in the United States to the Native Americans. Indeed, Hardin rejects not only compensatory arguments but any argument that we ought to provide food to the hungry. It is not clear whether this is because he adopts a libertarian moral view or because he is simply combining utilitarian principles with a different assessment than Singer's of the facts of the case. Hardin argues that provision of food or resources to the hungry in third-world nations will, in the end, be counterproductive: Aid will simply allow

---

[2] See Amartya Sen, "Property and Hunger," *Economics and Philosophy* 4 (1988): 57–68, at pp. 60–62, and other works of Sen's cited there.

[3] Van Wyk, p. 80.

We Are Obligated to Help the Needy

Famine, Affluence, and Morality

Peter Singer

As I write this, in November 1971, people are dying in East Bengal from lack of food, shelter, and medical care. The suffering and death that are occurring there now are not inevitable, not unavoidable in any fatalistic sense of the term. Constant poverty, a cyclone, and a civil war have turned at least nine million people into destitute refugees; nevertheless, it is not beyond the capacity of the richer nations to give enough assistance to reduce any further suffering to very small proportions. The decisions and actions of human beings can prevent this kind of suffering. Unfortunately, human beings have not made the necessary decisions. At the individual level, people have, with very few exceptions, not responded to the situation in any significant way. Generally speaking, people have not given large sums to relief funds; they have not written to their parliamentary representatives demanding increased government assistance; they have not demonstrated in the streets, held symbolic fasts, or done anything else directed toward providing the refugees with the means to satisfy their essential needs. At the government level, no government has given the sort of massive aid that would enable the refugees to survive for more than a few days. . . .

What are the moral implications of a situation like this? In what follows, I shall argue that the way people in relatively affluent countries react to a situation like that in Bengal cannot be justified; indeed, the whole way we look at moral issues—our moral conceptual scheme—needs to be altered, and with it, the way of life that has come to be taken for granted in our society.

In arguing for this conclusion I will not, of course, claim to be morally neutral. I shall, however, try to argue for the moral position that I take, so that anyone who accepts certain assumptions, to be made explicit, will, I hope, accept my conclusion.

I begin with the assumption that suffering and death from lack of food, shelter, and medical care are bad. I think most people will agree about this, although one may reach the same view by different routes. I shall not argue for this view. People can hold all sorts of eccentric positions, and perhaps from some of them it would not follow that death by starvation is in itself bad. It is difficult, perhaps impossible, to refute such positions, and so for brevity I will henceforth take this assumption as accepted. Those who disagree need read no further.

My next point is this: if it is in our power to prevent something bad from happening, without thereby sacrificing anything of comparable moral importance, we ought, morally, to do it. By "without sacrificing anything of comparable moral importance" I mean without causing anything else comparably bad to happen, or doing something that is wrong in itself, or failing to promote some moral good, comparable in significance to the bad thing that we can prevent. This principle seems almost as uncontroversial as the last one. It requires us only to prevent what is bad, and not to promote what is good, and it requires this of us only when we can do it without sacrificing anything that is, from the moral point of view, comparably important. I could even, as far as the application of my argument to the Bengal emergency is concerned, qualify the point so as to make it: if it is in our power to prevent something very bad from happening, without thereby sacrificing anything morally significant, we ought, morally, to do it. An application of this principle would be as follows: if I am walking past a shallow pond and see a child drowning in it, I ought to wade in and pull the child out. This will mean getting my clothes muddy, but this is insignificant, while the death of the child would presumably be a very bad thing.

The uncontroversial appearance of the principle just stated is deceptive. If it were acted upon, even in its qualified form, our lives, our society, and our world would be fundamentally changed. For the principle takes, firstly, no account of proximity or distance. It makes no moral difference whether the person I can help is a neighbor's child ten yards from me or a Bengali whose name I shall never know, ten thousand miles away. Secondly, the principle makes no distinction between cases in which I am the only person who could possibly do anything and cases in which I am just one among millions in the same position.

I do not think I need to say much in defense of the refusal to take proximity and distance into account. The fact that a person is physically near to us, so that we have personal contact with him, may make it more likely that we *shall* assist him, but this does not show that we *ought* to help him rather than another who happens to be further away. If we accept any principle of impartiality, universalizability, equality, or whatever, we cannot discriminate against someone merely because he is far away from us (or we are far away from him). Admittedly, it is possible that we are in a better position to judge what needs to be done to help a person near to us than one far away, and perhaps also to provide the assistance we judge to be necessary. If this were the case, it would be a reason for helping those near to us first. This may once have been a justification for being more concerned with the poor in one's town than with famine victims in India. Unfortunately for those who like to keep their moral responsibilities limited, instant communication and swift transportation have changed the situation. From the moral point of view, the development of the world into a "global village" has made an important, though still unrecognized, difference to our moral situation. Expert observers and supervisors, sent out by famine relief organizations or permanently stationed in famine-prone areas, can direct our aid to a refugee in Bengal almost as effectively as we could get it to someone in our own block. There would seem, therefore, to be no possible justification for discriminating on geographical grounds.

There may be a greater need to defend the second implication of my principle—that the fact that there are millions of other people in the same position, in respect to the Bengali refugees, as I am, does not make the situation significantly different from a situation in which I am the only person who can prevent something very bad from occurring. Again, of course, I admit that there is a psychological difference between the cases; one feels less guilty about doing nothing if one can point to others, similarly placed, who have also done nothing. Yet this can make no real difference to our moral obligations. Should I consider that I am less obliged to pull the drowning child out of the pond if on looking around I see other people, no further away than I am, who have also noticed the child but are doing nothing? One has only to ask this question to see the absurdity of the view that numbers lessen obligation. It is a view that is an ideal excuse for inactivity; unfortunately most of the major evils—poverty, overpopulation, pollution,—are problems in which everyone is almost equally involved.

The view that numbers do make a difference can be made plausible if stated in this way: if everyone in circumstances like mine gave £5 to the Bengal Relief Fund, there would be enough to provide food, shelter, and medical care for the refugees; there is no reason why I should give more than anyone else in the same circumstances as I am; therefore I have no obligation to give more than £5. Each premise in this argument is true, and the argument looks sound. It may convince us, unless we notice that it is based on a hypothetical premise, although the conclusion is not stated hypothetically. The argument would be sound if the conclusion were: if everyone in circumstances like mine were to give £5, I would have no obligation to give more than £5. If the conclusion were so stated, however, it would be obvious that the argument has no bearing on a situation in which it is not the case that everyone else gives £5. This, of course, is the actual situation. It is more or less certain that not everyone in circumstances like mine will give £5. So there will not be enough to provide the needed food, shelter, and medical care. Therefore by giving more than £5 I will prevent more suffering than I would if I gave just £5. . . .

If my argument so far has been sound, neither our distance from a preventable evil nor the number of other people who, in respect to that evil, are in the same situation as we are, lessens our obligation to mitigate or prevent that evil. I shall therefore take as established the principle I asserted earlier. As I have already said, I need to assert it only in its qualified form: if it is in our power to prevent something very bad from happening, without thereby sacrificing anything else morally significant, we ought, morally, to do it.

The outcome of this argument is that our traditional moral categories are upset. The traditional distinction between duty and charity cannot be drawn, or at least, not in the place we normally draw it. Giving money to the Bengal Relief Fund is regarded as an act of charity in our society. The bodies which collect money are known as "charities." These organizations see themselves in this way—if you send them a check, you will be thanked for your "generosity." Because giving money is regarded as an act of charity, it is not thought that there is anything wrong with not giving. The charitable man may be praised, but the man who is not charitable is not condemned. People do not feel in any way ashamed or guilty about spending money on new clothes or a new car instead of giving it to famine relief. (Indeed, the alternative does not occur to them.) This way of looking at the matter cannot be justified. When we buy new clothes not to keep ourselves warm but to look "well-dressed" we are not providing for any important need. We would not be sacrificing anything significant if we were to continue to wear our old clothes, and give the money to famine relief. By doing so, we would be preventing another person from starving. It follows from what I have said earlier that we ought to give money away, rather than spend it on clothes which we do not need to keep us warm. To do so is not charitable, or generous. Nor is it the kind of act which philosophers and theologians have called "supererogatory"—an act which it would be good to do, but not wrong not to do. On the contrary, we ought to give the money away, and it is wrong not to do so.

I am not maintaining that there are no acts which are charitable, or that there are no acts which it would be good to do but not wrong not to do. It may be possible to redraw the distinction between duty and charity in some other place. All I am arguing here is that the present way of drawing the distinction, which makes it an act of charity for a man living at the level of affluence which most people in the "developed nations" enjoy to give money to save someone else from starvation, cannot be supported. It is beyond the scope of my argument to consider whether the distinction should be redrawn or abolished altogether. There would be many other possible ways of drawing the distinction—for instance, one might decide that it is good to make other people as happy as possible, but not wrong not to do so.

Despite the limited nature of the revision in our moral conceptual scheme which I am proposing, the revision would, given the extent of both affluence and famine in the world today, have radical implications. These implications may lead to further objections, distinct from those I have already considered. I shall discuss two of these.

One objection to the position I have taken might be simply that it is too drastic a revision of our moral scheme. People do not ordinarily judge in the way I have suggested they should. Most people reserve their moral condemnation for those who violate some moral norm, such as the norm against taking another person's property. They do not condemn those who indulge in luxury instead of giving to famine relief. But given that I did not set out to present a morally neutral description of the way people make moral judgments, the way people do in fact judge has nothing to do with the validity of my conclusion. My conclusion follows from the principle which I advanced earlier, and unless that principle is rejected, or the arguments shown to be unsound, I think the conclusion must stand, however strange it appears. . . .

The second objection to my attack on the present distinction between duty and charity is one which has from time to time been made against utilitarianism. It follows from some forms of utilitarian theory that we all ought, morally, to be working full time to increase the balance of happiness over misery. The position I have taken here would not lead to this conclusion in all circumstances, for if there were no bad occurrences that we could prevent without sacrificing something of comparable moral importance, my argument would have no application. Given the present conditions in many parts of the world, however, it does follow from my argument that we ought, morally, to be working full time to relieve great suffering of the sort that occurs as a result of famine or other disasters. Of course, mitigating circumstances can be adduced—for instance, that if we wear ourselves out through overwork, we shall be less effective than we would otherwise have been. Nevertheless, when all considerations of this sort have been taken into account, the conclusion remains: we ought to be preventing as much suffering as we can without sacrificing something else of comparable moral importance. This conclusion is one which we may be reluctant to face. I cannot see, though, why it should be regarded as a criticism of the position for which I have argued, rather than a criticism of our ordinary standards of behavior. Since most people are self-interested to some degree, very few of us are likely to do everything that we ought to do. It would, however, hardly be honest to take this as evidence that it is not the case that we ought to do it. . . .

I accept that the earth cannot support indefinitely a population rising at the present rate. This certainly poses a problem for anyone who thinks it important to prevent famine.... However, one could accept the argument without drawing the conclusion that it absolves one from any obligation to do anything to prevent famine. The conclusion that should be drawn is that the best means of preventing famine, in the long run, is population control. It would then follow from the position reached earlier that one ought to be doing all one can to promote population control (unless one held that all forms of population control were wrong in themselves, or would have significantly bad consequences). Since there are organizations working specifically for population control, one would then support them rather than more orthodox methods of preventing famine.

[Another] point raised by the conclusion reached earlier relates to the question of just how much we all ought to be giving away. One possibility, which has already been mentioned, is that we ought to give until we reach the level of marginal utility—that is, the level at which, by giving more, I would cause as much suffering to myself or my dependents as I would relieve by my gift. This would mean, of course, that one would reduce oneself to very near the material circumstances of a Bengali refugee. It will be recalled that earlier I put forward both a strong and a moderate version of the principle of preventing bad occurrences. The strong version, which required us to prevent bad things from happening unless in doing so we would be sacrificing something of comparable moral significance, does seem to require reducing ourselves to the level of marginal utility. I should also say that the strong version seems to me to be the correct one. I proposed the more moderate version—that we should prevent bad occurrences unless, to do so, we had to sacrifice something morally significant—only in order to show that even on this surely undeniable principle a great change in our way of life is required. On the more moderate principle, it may not follow that we ought to reduce ourselves to the level of marginal utility, for one might hold that to reduce oneself and one's family to this level is to cause something significantly bad to happen. Whether this is so I shall not discuss, since, as I have said, I can see no good reason for holding the moderate version of the principle rather than the strong version. Even if we accepted the principle only in its moderate form, however, it should be clear that we would have to give away enough to ensure that the consumer society, dependent as it is on people spending on trivia rather than giving to famine relief, would slow down and perhaps disappear entirely. There are several reasons why this would be desirable in itself. The value and necessity of economic growth are now being questioned not only by conservationists, but by economists as well.[1] There is no doubt, too, that the consumer society has had a distorting effect on the goals and purposes of its members. Yet looking at the matter purely from the point of view of overseas aid, there must be a limit to the extent to which we should deliberately slow down our economy; for it might be the case that if we gave away, say, forty percent of our Gross National Product, we would slow down the economy so much that in absolute terms we would be giving less than if we gave twenty-five percent of the much larger GNP that we would have if we limited our contribution to this smaller percentage.

I mention this only as an indication of the sort of factor that one would have to take into account in working out an ideal. Since Western societies generally consider one percent of the GNP an acceptable level for overseas aid, the matter is entirely academic. Nor does it affect the question of how much an individual should give in a so-

---

[1] See for instance. John Kenneth Galbraith, *The New Industrial State* (Boston, 1967); and E. J. Mishan, *The Costs of Economic Growth* (London, 1967).

ciety in which very few are giving substantial amounts.

It is sometimes said, though less often now than it used to be, that philosophers have no special role to play in public affairs, since most public issues depend primarily on an assessment of facts. On questions of fact, it is said, philosophers as such have no special expertise, and so it has been possible to engage in philosophy without committing oneself to any position on major public issues. No doubt there are some issues of social policy and foreign policy about which it can truly be said that a really expert assessment of the facts is required before taking sides or acting, but the issue of famine is surely not one of these. The facts about the existence of suffering are beyond dispute. Nor, I think, is it disputed that we can do something about it, either through orthodox methods of famine relief or through population control or both. This is therefore an issue on which philosophers are competent to take a position. The issue is one which faces everyone who has more money than he needs to support himself and his dependents, or who is in a position to take some sort of political action. These categories must include practically every teacher and student of philosophy in the universities of the Western world. If philosophy is to deal with matters that are relevant to both teachers and students, this is an issue that philosophers should discuss.

Discussion, though, is not enough. What is the point of relating philosophy to public (and personal) affairs if we do not take our conclusions seriously? In this instance, taking our conclusion seriously means acting upon it. The philosopher will not find it any easier than anyone else to alter his attitudes and way of life to the extent that, if I am right, is involved in doing everything that we ought to be doing. At the very least, though, one can make a start. The philosopher who does so will have to sacrifice some of the benefits of the consumer society, but he can find compensation in the satisfaction of a way of life in which theory and practice, if not yet in harmony, are at least coming together.

WE ARE NOT OBLIGATED TO HELP THE NEEDY

Living on a Lifeboat

Garrett Hardin

Environmentalists have emphasized the image of the earth as a spaceship—Spaceship Earth. Kenneth Boulding (1966) is the principal architect of this metaphor. It is time, he says, that we replace the wasteful "cowboy economy" of the past with the frugal "spaceship economy" required for continued survival in the limited world we now see ours to be. The metaphor is notably useful in justifying pollution control measures.

Unfortunately, the image of a spaceship is also used to promote measures that are suicidal. . . .

For the metaphor of a spaceship to be correct the aggregate of people on board would have to be under unitary sovereign control (Ophuls 1974). A true ship always has a captain. It is conceivable that a ship could be run by a committee. But it could not possibly survive if its course were determined by bickering tribes that claimed rights without responsibilities.

What about Spaceship Earth? It certainly has no captain, and no executive committee. The United Nations is a toothless tiger, because the signatories of its charter wanted it that way. The spaceship metaphor is used only to justify spaceship demands on common resources without acknowledging corresponding spaceship responsibilities. . . .

Before taking up certain substantive issues let us look at an alternative metaphor, that of a lifeboat. In developing some relevant examples the following numerical values are assumed. Approximately two-thirds of the world is desperately poor, and only one-third is comparatively rich. The people in poor countries have an average per capita GNP (Gross National Product) of about $200 per year; the rich, of about $3,000. (For the United States it is nearly $5,000 per year.) Metaphorically, each rich nation amounts to a lifeboat full of comparatively rich people. The poor of the world are in other, much more crowded lifeboats. Continuously, so to speak, the poor fall out of their lifeboats and swim for a while in the water outside, hoping to be admitted to a rich lifeboat, or in some other way to benefit from the "goodies" on board. What should the passengers on a rich lifeboat do? This is the central problem of "the ethics of a lifeboat."

First we must acknowledge that each lifeboat is effectively limited in capacity. The land of every nation has a limited carrying capacity. The exact limit is a matter for argument, but the energy crunch is convincing more people every day that we have already exceeded the carrying capacity of the land. We have been living on "capital"—stored petroleum and coal—and soon we must live on income alone.

Let us look at only one lifeboat—ours. The ethical problem is the same for all, and is as follows. Here we sit, say 50 people in a lifeboat. To be generous, let us assume our boat has a capacity of 10 more, making 60. (This, however, is to violate the engineering principle of the "safety factor." A new plant disease or a bad change in the weather may decimate our population if we don't preserve some excess capacity as a safety factor.)

The 50 of us in the lifeboat see 100 others swimming in the water outside, asking for admission to the boat, or for handouts. How shall we respond to their calls? There are several possibilities.

One. We may be tempted to try to live by the Christian ideal of being "our brother's keeper," or by the Marxian ideal (Marx 1875) of "from each according to his abilities, to each according to his needs." Since the needs of all are the same, we take all the needy into our boat, making a total of 150 in a boat with a capacity of 60. The boat is swamped, and everyone drowns. Complete justice, complete catastrophe.

Two. Since the boat has an unused excess capacity of 10, we admit just 10 more to it. This has the disadvantage of getting rid of the safety factor, for which action we will sooner or later pay dearly. Moreover, *which* 10 do we let in? "First come, first served?" The best 10? The neediest 10? How do we *discriminate?* And what do we say to the 90 who are excluded?

Three. Admit no more to the boat and preserve the small safety factor. Survival of the people in the lifeboat is then possible (though we shall have to be on our guard against boarding parties).

The last solution is abhorrent to many people. It is unjust, they say. Let us grant that it is.

"I feel guilty about my good luck," say some. The reply to this is simple: *Get out and yield your place to others.* Such a selfless action might satisfy the conscience of those who are addicted to guilt but it would not change the ethics of the lifeboat. The needy person to whom a guilt-addict yields his place will not himself feel guilty about his sudden good luck. (If he did he would not climb aboard.) The net result of conscience-stricken people relinquishing their unjustly held positions is the elimination of their kind of conscience from the lifeboat. The lifeboat, as it were, purifies itself of guilt. The ethics of the lifeboat persist, unchanged by such momentary aberrations.

This then is the basic metaphor within which we must work out our solutions. Let us enrich the image step by step with substantive additions from the real world.

Reproduction

The harsh characteristics of lifeboat ethics are heightened by reproduction, particularly by reproductive differences. The people inside the lifeboats of the wealthy nations are doubling in numbers every 87 years; those outside are doubling every 35 years, on the average. And the relative difference in prosperity is becoming greater. . . .

Suppose that all these countries, and the United States, agreed to live by the Marxian ideal, "to each according to his needs," the ideal of most Christians as well. Needs, of course, are determined by population size, which is affected by reproduction. Every nation regards its rate of reproduction as a sovereign right. If our lifeboat were big enough in the beginning it might be possible to live *for a while* by Christian-Marxian ideals. *Might.* . . .

Ruin in the Commons

The fundamental error of the sharing ethics is that it leads to the tragedy of the commons. Under a system of private property the man (or group of men) who own property recognize their responsibility to care for it, for if they don't they will eventually suffer. A farmer, for instance, if he is intelligent, will allow no more cattle in a pasture than its carrying capacity justifies. If he overloads the pasture, weeds take over, erosion sets in, and the owner loses in the long run.

But if a pasture is run as a commons open to all, the right of each to use it is not matched by an operational responsibility to take care of it. It is no use asking independent herdsmen in a commons to act responsibly, for they dare not. The considerate herdsman who refrains from overloading the commons suffers more than a selfish one who says his needs are greater. (As Leo Durocher says, "Nice guys finish last.") Christian-Marxian idealism is counterproductive. That it *sounds* nice is no excuse. With distribution systems, as with individual morality, good intentions are no substitute for good performance.

A social system is stable only if it is insensitive to errors. To the Christian-Marxian idealist a selfish person is a sort of "error." Prosperity in the system of the commons cannot survive errors. If *everyone* would only restrain himself, all would be well; but it takes *only one less than everyone* to ruin a system of voluntary restraint. In a crowded world of less than perfect human beings—and we will never know any other—mutual ruin is inevitable in the commons. This is the core of the tragedy of the commons. . . .

World Food Banks

In the international arena we have recently heard a proposal to create a new commons, namely an international depository of food reserves to which nations will contribute according to their abilities, and from which nations may draw according to their needs. . . .

The search for a rational justification can be short-circuited by interjecting the word "emergency. . . ." What is an "emergency?" It is surely something like an accident, which is correctly defined as *an event that is certain to happen, though with a low frequency* (Hardin 1972). A well-run organization prepares for everything that is certain, including accidents and emergencies. It budgets for them. It saves for them. It expects them—and mature decision-makers do not waste time complaining about accidents when they occur.

What happens if some organizations budget for emergencies and others do not? If each organization is solely responsible for its own well-being, poorly managed ones will suffer. But they should be able to learn from experience. They have a chance to mend their ways and learn to budget for infrequent but certain emergencies. The weather, for instance, always varies and periodic crop failures are certain. A wise and competent government saves out of the production of the good years in anticipation of bad years that are sure to come. This is not a new idea. The Bible tells us that Joseph taught this policy to Pharaoh in Egypt more than 2,000 years ago. Yet it is literally true that the vast majority of the governments of the world today have no such policy. They lack either the wisdom or the competence, or both. Far more difficult than the transfer of wealth from one country to another is the transfer of wisdom between sovereign powers or between generations.

"But it isn't their fault! How can we blame the poor people who are caught in an emergency? Why must we punish them?" The concepts of blame and punishment are irrelevant. The question is, what are the operational consequences of establishing a world food bank? If it is open to every country every time a need develops, slovenly rulers will not be motivated to take Joseph's advice. Why should they? Others will bail them out whenever they are in trouble.

Some countries will make deposits in the world food bank and others will withdraw from it: there will be almost no overlap. Calling such a depository-transfer unit a "bank" is stretching the metaphor of *bank* beyond its elastic limits. The proposers, of course, never call attention to the metaphorical nature of the word they use.

The Ratchet Effect

An "international food bank" is really, then, not a true bank but a disguised one-way transfer device for moving wealth from rich countries to poor. . . .

Only under a strong and farsighted sovereign—which theoretically could be the people themselves, democratically organized—can a population equilibrate at some set point below the carrying capacity, thus avoiding the pains normally caused by periodic and unavoidable disasters. For this happy state to be achieved it is necessary that those in power be able to contemplate with equanimity the "waste" of surplus food in times of bountiful harvests. It is essential that those in power resist the temptation to convert extra food into extra babies. On the public relations level it is necessary that the phrase "surplus food" be replaced by "safety factor."

But wise sovereigns seem not to exist in the poor world today. The most anguishing problems are created by poor countries that are governed by rulers insufficiently wise and powerful. If such countries can draw on a world food bank in times of "emergency," the population *cycle* . . . will be replaced by [a] population *escalator*. . . .

The input of food from a food bank acts as the pawl of a ratchet, preventing the population from retracing its steps to a lower level. Reproduction pushes the population upward, inputs from the world bank prevent its moving downward. Population size escalates, as does the absolute magnitude of "accidents" and "emergencies." The process is brought to an end only by the total collapse of the whole system, producing a catastrophe of scarcely imaginable proportions.

Such are the implications of the well-meant sharing of food in a world of irresponsible reproduction.

References

Boulding, K. 1966. The economics of the coming Spaceship earth. *In* H. Jarrett, ed. Environmental Quality in a Growing Economy, Johns Hopkins Press, Baltimore.

Hardin, G. 1972. Pages 81–82 *in* Exploring New Ethics for Survival: The Voyage of the Spaceship *Beagle*. Viking, N.Y.

Marx, K. 1875. Critique of the Gotha program. Page 388 *in* R. C. Tucker, ed. The Marx-Engels Reader. Norton, NY., 1972.

Ophuls, W. 1974. The scarcity society. *Harpers* 248 (1487): 47–52.

KANT AND WORLD HUNGER

Kantianism and World Hunger

Onora O'Neill

Controversies about Avoiding Famines

When we ask *how* famine and hunger can best be ended and whether it is at all likely that they will be ended, there is great controversy. All agree that the task of ending famine is at best enormous and daunting. But even experts disagree about what is possible. Some awareness of these disagreements is helpful in considering moral problems raised by famine.

Some experts—often spoken of as neo-Malthusians—think that the only secure way to end famine is by limiting population growth. In the long run no increase in available food could match population increase. Other experts—often called developmentalists—think that the first aim must be economic growth, which is a prerequisite of lowering population growth.

Developmentalists themselves disagree whether the most important changes are economic or political. They debate whether economic policies available within current political structures, such as foreign aid and international loans and investments by transnational corporations, provide an adequate framework to develop the now underdeveloped world. Are there—as some political economists believe—features of the present structure of aid and trade that prevent such policies from transforming the economic prospects of underdeveloped regions but which might be changed by political transformations? Is it even possible that the main obstacle to economic growth in the poorest regions lies in the present international economic order, despite its ostensible commitment to the goal of development?

These debates are ethically important because social inquiry itself is no matter of ethically neutral "facts." The debates between different experts often show that their disputes are *already* moral disagreements. There is no way in which those who want to do something about world hunger and poverty can hope that experts will present "the facts," and equally no way in which those who take action can shirk making informed judgments about what is possible.

Malthusian Controversies

Neo-Malthusians take their name from Thomas Malthus (1766–1834), who noted in his *Summary View of the Principle of Population* (1830), "a tendency in mankind to increase, if unchecked, beyond the possibility of an adequate supply of food in a limited territory."[1]

Of course, Malthus knew well enough that such increase always was "checked." The check might be what he called "prudential restraint on marriage and population," or it might be high mortality. If there was much "imprudence," the ultimate check might even be the highly visible mortality of famine.

Recent neo-Malthusians hold that famine is not only the *ultimate* check on population growth but an imminent one. Some characterize population growth as a bomb that economic growth cannot defuse, whose explosion threatens all. Others compare the lives of those who appear well off to the plight of passengers on a lifeboat, who can rescue those who drown around them only at the risk of sinking and drowning everybody. Still others allege that the only responsible approach to the distribution of resources must follow the tough-minded principle of "triage," offering help neither to the better off nor to the destitute but only to the "best risks" for whom alone (they think) help can make a difference. These powerful images suggest that population growth cannot be sustained indefinitely and that, to avoid catastrophe, we must forthwith abandon rather than rescue the neediest.

Various reasons are given for these views. Some neo-Malthusians claim that the rapid growth of population of recent centuries cannot be sustained because readily exploited natural resources have already been used and further exploitation will be harder because of pollution and low yields. The continued evasion of famine would require sustained technological advance, which we cannot guarantee. Other neo-Malthusians stress economic and political rather than natural barriers to sustained economic growth. It is apparent enough that there is nothing automatic about economic growth and that long periods of history have shown nothing more fundamental than succeeding lean and fat years. The risk of famine is greatest in just those places where economic growth will be hardest. Underdeveloped countries may lack investment capital and know-how; there may be resistance to the introduction of technology that will change existing and preferred ways of life, and an often accurate perception that not everybody will share the economic benefits which new

---

[1] Thomas Malthus, *Summary View of the Principle of Population*, reprinted in *On Population: Three Essays*, ed. F. Notestein, New York: Mentor, 1960, p. 55.

technology is said to bring. Nor is it easy to transfer resources from areas of economic surplus to poorer regions. The richer nations are often reluctant to share their surplus, and the very process of transfer can harm the economic system of undeveloped regions.

In the eyes of neo-Malthusians, these obstacles to economic growth are matched by difficulty in controlling population growth. In spite of the "contraceptive revolution," it remains true that the only wholly safe and reliable modes of contraception are forms of sterilization that are not reliably reversible and are therefore unpopular. Reversible techniques (IUDs, rubber devices, chemical contraception) may be neither entirely reliable nor safe nor easy for those living in great poverty to use or to afford. They are also rejected by some on religious grounds. Abortion is even more widely rejected, and it is least available and safe where poverty is harshest.

Even if these difficulties were overcome, some neo-Malthusians argue,[2] the populations that most risk famine might not have the "prudence" to limit their increasing populations. Access to contraceptive technology does not guarantee smaller families; nor does lack of access always prevent reduction in family size. In the now developed countries of Europe and North America, a *demographic transition* has taken place, and these countries now have, despite long-lived populations and little emigration, either low or negative rates of population increase. By contrast, no such demographic transition has yet taken place in many now underdeveloped countries. Death rates have fallen, but fertility levels remains high and population increase is rapid. In other Third World countries (not generally in the poorest ones), fertility is now falling. This is particularly evident in some Southeast Asian countries.

An interesting and vitally important question to ask these neo-Malthusians is why they are so pessimistic about the longer-term prospects for economic development and fertility control in the Third World. Why, for example, do they not think the economic development and controlled population growth of the now developed world evidence that success is possible? After all, it is not so long since the whole world was underdeveloped. What is it that makes the development of the now underdeveloped world appear so hard that it demands abandoning those most at risk? Harsh measures may be necessary in certain emergencies, but we need to be sure that there is an emergency before we take or advocate emergency measures.

Developmentalist Rejoinders

Developmentalist views of prospects for economic growth in the underdeveloped world and for ending the risk of famine are more optimistic. Like neo-Malthusians, these writers hold a great variety of views, and only a selection can be mentioned. The optimism which developmentalist writers often show is only a *relative* optimism. Most of them do not think that economic development and ending the risk of famine can be either easy or rapid; many stress that huge political and social as well as economic changes may have to be made if the enterprise is to succeed.

The optimism is based on an awareness of the many ways in which economic advance takes place. Recent growth rates in the Third World have often been high. However, the picture is one only of *qualified* optimism for several reasons. First, many of the poor do not benefit from growth; second, when population growth remains rapid, improvement in living standards must

---

[2]This line of argument has been pressed by Garrett Hardin.

be slight even if the benefits of economic growth are evenly distributed. Few developmentalist writers today expect economic growth in poor countries to resolve all problems of dire poverty and hunger merely by some automatic "trickle down" of benefits toward the most vulnerable.

However, many of these more optimistic writers do not think that population growth is an insuperable barrier to economic growth. The most optimistic even argue that various countries are held back economically not by excess but by sparse population. More commonly, they think reduction in population growth rates is feasible. They point out that reduced fertility rates have generally succeeded rather than preceded economic growth. The demographic transition of the now developed world was not the prelude to but a result of increasing standards of living. They point out that, for the very poor, large families may appear an asset rather than a liability. Their children have a shorter period of economic dependence than children in more developed areas, and only children can provide for old age or illness or other contingencies which in richer countries may be handled by social or private insurance schemes. Developmentalists think that Third World populations will undergo a demographic transition *only when they begin to be less poor.* Trying to achieve economic growth by limiting population growth is going about the problem the wrong way round. "Prudence" in having children cannot be expected of those who can best secure their future by having many children.[3]

Developmentalists also view the present economic plight of poorer countries less as a natural inevitability, to which these countries must prudently adapt their expectations and their population growth, and more as the result of changeable economic and political structures. Many point out that the poverty of specific Third World countries is in part due to a history of colonialism, under which these economies stagnated because the imperial power either prevented or discouraged certain forms of trade or manufacture, or encouraged the production of goods that did not compete with the industries of the developed world (such as palm oil, coffee, rubber, and other tropical agricultural products that were often grown on the plantation system). While the *political* independence of former colonies is now virtually complete, the trade and economic policies of former imperial powers and other powerful developed nations often hinder development.

Developmentalist writers disagree not only about the detailed interpretation of the sources of economic vulnerability of Third World economies but also about the best strategy for economic progress and the part that redistribution has to play in it. Some stress the unnecessary consumption of developed countries and the grotesque size of their armaments expenditure, and the resulting possibilities for redistribution of resources. But many are unsure how these resources can be redistributed to the benefit of those whose poverty puts them at risk of famine.

One common view has been that policies stressing foreign aid, and in particular food aid, have a major part to play in overcoming the risk of famine. What could seem more sensible than the provision of food from the unsaleable agricultural surpluses of wealthier temperate-zone nations, particularly in North America and western Europe? But while such aid clearly benefits the farmers of the developed world, its impact on the Third World is often ambiguous. Food relieves hunger; in some emergencies, only the rapid delivery of food can prevent famine deaths. But when free or subsidized

---

[3] See, for example, Ester Boserup, *Population and Technology*, Oxford, England: Blackwell, 1981, esp. chap. 14.

grain is standardly available, marginal farmers in poor regions may be unable to sell their crops; they may stop growing grain and even migrate to the shantytowns of Third World cities, where their chance of sharing in food aid is greater but their prospects of economic progress may be slight. Over the last twenty years, more and more countries have become dependent on food imports and food aid, especially in Africa.[4] The transfer of food can harm even when it is intended to benefit.

Many developmentalist writers have therefore focused less on the (far from simple) policy of transferring food to those who are hungry than on the (even more complex) requirements for achieving economic development within Third World countries. The underlying thought is the simple one expressed in the proverb often quoted by famine relief agencies: Give a man a fish and you feed him for a day; teach a man to fish and he will be fed for life. The proverb may have an obvious interpretation in a simple and traditional social world; but its interpretation in an interdependent world is no more obvious than the interpretation of the parable of the good Samaritan. Economic development needs capital investment, technological innovation, and trading opportunities. All three are scarce or difficult to acquire for most Third World countries. Poor countries cannot easily raise large capital sums for developmental projects: their problem is, after all, precisely that they still lack a developed economy in which there is accumulated capital. But they can attract international capital only if they offer comparatively favorable investment opportunities. Investment then has to reflect criteria other than those of need. For example, if irrigation or rural development projects would meet more needs but offer little return on investment, investment will not be in these areas; but if selling luxury goods to the small urban elite who already have more than subsistence incomes is profitable, then such less needed development will attract investment.

Technological innovation, even if successful, may not benefit most those who need most. For example, "miracle" strains of rice or wheat may need fertilizer and irrigation that only wealthier farmers can afford. Agricultural mechanization may reduce opportunities for work and earnings for the landless poor.

Trading opportunities nowadays are internationally regulated, and the developed world can often meet its own needs more cheaply without trading with Third World countries (except for a few tropical products). Even when Third World products are cheaper, developed countries may prevent their import, since competition from "cheap labor" is not acceptable to the high-earning workers of richer countries.

In spite of these difficulties, developmentalist writers argue that there is no more fundamental reason why the Third World should remain poverty-stricken forever than there was in the case of the developed world. Development is *always* difficult. It is true that Third World countries lack both colonies, whose imports they can keep cheap or whose markets they can preserve for their own industry, and a frontier or colonies for their own expanding population, and they do not control the international economic order. However, they have some advantages. Many forms of technology, including contraceptive technology, are already developed; there are interests and groups within the developed world that seek global development and are prepared

---

[4] See in particular Tony Jackson, *Against the Grain: the Dilemma of Project Food Aid*, Oxford, England: Oxfam, 1982.

to argue and agitate for aid, trade, and other policies that may help Third World countries develop. Above all, it is now well established that economic development and a better-than-subsistence standard of life can be reached by whole populations. We can no longer take it as given that "the poor are always with us." . . .

[Editors' note: Having discussed the principal views about the most effective means of eliminating hunger, O'Neill now turns to a discussion of the implications of Kant's ethical theory for our treatment of the needy.]

Using Others as Mere Means

[According to Kant's ethical theory, we] use others as *mere means* if what we do reflects some maxim *to which they could not in principle consent*. . . . If a false promise is given, the party that accepts the promise is not just used but used as a mere means, because it is *impossible* for consent to be given to the fundamental principle or project of deception that must guide every false promise, whatever its surface character. Those who accept false promises *must* be kept ignorant of the underlying principle or maxim on which the "undertaking" is based. . . .

Another standard way of using others as mere means is by coercing them. Coercers, like deceivers, standardly don't give others the possibility of dissenting from what they propose to do. In deception, "consent" is spurious because it is given to a principle that couldn't be the underlying principle of *that* act at all; but the principle governing coercion may be brutally plain. Here any "consent" given is spurious because there was no option *but* to consent. If a rich or powerful landowner or nation threatens a poorer or more vulnerable person, group, or nation with some intolerable difficulty unless a concession is made, the more vulnerable party is denied a genuine choice between consent and dissent. While the boundary that divides coercion from mere bargaining and negotiation varies and is therefore often hard to discern, we have no doubt about the clearer cases. Maxims of coercion may threaten physical force, seizure of possessions, destruction of opportunities, or any other harm that the coerced party is thought to be unable to absorb without grave injury or danger. A money lender in a Third World village who threatens not to make or renew an indispensable loan, without which survival until the next harvest would be impossible, uses the peasant as mere means. The peasant does not have the possibility of genuinely consenting to the "offer he can't refuse." The outward form of some coercive transactions may *look* like ordinary commercial dealings: but we know very well that some action that is superficially of this sort is based on maxims of coercion. To avoid coercion, action must be governed by maxims that the other party can choose to refuse and is not bound to accept. The more vulnerable the other party in any transaction or negotiation, the less their scope for refusal, and the more demanding it is likely to be to ensure that action is noncoercive. . . .

Treating Others as Ends in Themselves

For Kant, as for utilitarians, justice is only one part of duty. We may fail in our duty, even when we don't use anyone as mere means (by deception or coercion), if we fail to treat others as "ends in themselves." To treat others as "Ends in Themselves" we must not only avoid using them as mere means but also treat them as rational and autonomous beings with their own maxims. . . . Human action is limited not only by various sorts of physical barrier and inability but by further sorts of (mutual or asymmetrical) dependence. To treat one another as ends in themselves such beings have to base their action on principles that do not undermine but rather sustain and extend one another's capacities for autonomous action. A central requirement for doing so is to share and support one another's ends and activities at least to some extent. Since finite rational beings cannot generally achieve their aims without some help and support from others, a general refusal of help and support amounts to failure to treat others as rational and autonomous beings, that is as ends in themselves. Hence Kantian principles require us not only to act justly, that is in accordance with maxims that don't coerce or deceive others, but also to avoid manipulation and to lend some support to others' plans and activities. Since famine, great poverty and powerlessness all undercut the possibility of autonomous action, and the requirement of treating others as ends in themselves demands that Kantians standardly act to support the possibility of autonomous action where it is most vulnerable, Kantians are required to do what they can to avert, reduce, and remedy famine. On a Kantian view, beneficence is as indispensable as justice in human lives. . . .

Justice to the Vulnerable in Kantian Thinking

For Kantians, justice requires action that conforms (at least outwardly) to what could be done in a given situation while acting on maxims neither of deception nor of coercion. Since anyone hungry or destitute is more than usually vulnerable to deception and coercion, the possibilities and temptations to injustice are then especially strong.

Examples are easily suggested. I shall begin with some situations that might arise for somebody who happened to be part of a famine-stricken population. Where shortage of food is being dealt with by a reasonably fair rationing scheme, any mode of cheating to get more than one's allocated share involves using some others and is unjust. Equally, taking advantage of others' desperation to profiteer—for example, selling food at colossal prices or making loans on the security of others' future livelihood, when these are "offers they can't refuse"—constitutes coercion and so uses others as mere means and is unjust. Transactions that have the outward form of normal commercial dealing may be coercive when one party is desperate. Equally, forms of corruption that work by deception—such as bribing officials to gain special benefits from development schemes, or deceiving others about their entitlements—use others unjustly. Such requirements are far from trivial and frequently violated in hard times; acting justly in such conditions may involve risking one's own life and livelihood and require the greatest courage.

It is not so immediately obvious what justice, Kantianly conceived, requires of agents and agencies who are remote from destitution. Might it not be sufficient to argue that those of us fortunate enough to live in the developed world are far from famine and destitution, so if we do nothing but go about our usual business will successfully avoid injustice to the destitute? This conclusion has often been reached by those who take an abstract view of rationality and forget the limits of human rationality and autonomy. In such perspectives it can seem that there is nothing more to just action than meeting the formal requirements of nondeception and noncoercion in our dealings with one another. But once we remember the limitations of human rationality and autonomy, and the particular ways in which they are limited for those living close to the margins of subsistence, we can see that mere conformity to ordinary standards of commercial honesty and political bargaining is not enough for justice toward the destitute. If international agreements themselves can constitute "offers that cannot be refused" by the government of a poor country, or if the concessions required for investment by a transnational corporation or a development project reflect the desperation of recipients rather than an appropriate contribution to the project, then (however benevolent the motives of some parties) the weaker party to such agreements is used by the stronger.

In the earlier days of European colonial penetration of the now underdeveloped world it was evident enough that some of the ways in which "agreements" were made with native peoples were in fact deceptive or coercive or both. "Sales" of land by those who had no grasp of market-practices and "cessation of sovereignty" by those whose forms of life were prepolitical constitute only spurious consent to the agreements struck. But it is not only in these original forms of bargaining between powerful and powerless that injustice is frequent. There are many contemporary examples. For example, if capital investment (private or governmental) in a poorer country requires the receiving country to contribute disproportionately to the maintenance of a developed, urban "enclave" economy that offers little local employment but lavish standards of life for a small number of (possibly expatriate) "experts," while guaranteeing long-term exemption from local taxation for the investors, then we may doubt that the agreement could have been struck without the element of coercion provided by the desperation of the weaker party. Or if a trade agreement extracts political advantages (such as military bases) that are incompatible with the fundamental political interests of the country concerned, we may judge that at least some leaders of that country have been "bought" in a sense that is not consonant with ordinary commercial practice.

Even when the actions of those who are party to an agreement don't reflect a fundamental principle of coercion or deception, the agreement may alter the life circumstances and prospects of third parties in ways to which they patently could not have not consented. For example, a system of food aid and imports agreed upon by the government of a Third World country and certain developed countries or international agencies may give the elite of that Third World country access to subsidized grain. If that grain is then used to control the urban population and also produces a destitution among peasants (who used to grow food for that urban population), then those who are newly destitute probably have not been offered any opening or possibility of refusing their new and worsened conditions of life. If a policy is imposed, those affected *cannot* have been given a chance to refuse it: had the chance been there, they would either have assented (and so the policy would not have been *imposed*) or refused (and so proceeding with the policy would have been evidently coercive).

Beneficence to the Vulnerable in Kantian Thinking

In Kantian moral reasoning, the basis for beneficent action is that we cannot, without it, treat others of limited rationality and autonomy as ends in themselves. This is not to say that Kantian beneficence won't make others happier, for it will do so whenever they would be happier if (more) capable of autonomous action, but that happiness secured by purely paternalistic means, or at the cost (for example) of manipulating others' desires, will not count as beneficent in the Kantian picture. Clearly the vulnerable position of those who lack the very means of life, and their severely curtailed possibilities for autonomous action, offer many different ways in which it might be possible for others to act beneficently. Where the means of life are meager, almost any material or organizational advance may help extend possibilities for autonomy. Individual or institutional action that aims to advance economic or social development can proceed on many routes. The provision of clean water, of improved agricultural techniques, of better grain storage systems, or of adequate means of local transport may all help transform material prospects. Equally, help in the development of new forms of social organization—whether peasant self-help groups, urban cooperatives, medical and contraceptive services, or improvements in education or in the position of women—may help to extend possibilities for autonomous action. Kantian thinking does not provide a means by which all possible projects of this sort could be listed and ranked. But where some activity helps secure possibilities for autonomous action for more people, or is likely to achieve a permanent improvement in the position of the most vulnerable, or is one that can be done with more reliable success, this provides reason for furthering that project rather than alternatives.

Clearly the alleviation of need must rank far ahead of the furthering of happiness in the Kantian picture. I might make my friends very happy by throwing extravagant parties: but this would probably not increase anybody's possibility for autonomous action to any great extent. But the sorts of development-oriented changes that have just been mentioned may *transform* the possibilities for action of some. Since famine and the risk of famine are always and evidently highly damaging to human autonomy, any action that helps avoid or reduce famine must have a strong claim on any Kantian who is thinking through what beneficence requires. Depending on circumstances, such action may have to take the form of individual contribution to famine relief and development organizations, of individual or collective effort to influence the trade and aid policies of developed countries, or of attempts to influence the activities of those Third World elites for whom development does not seem to be an urgent priority. Some activities can best be undertaken by private citizens of developed countries; others are best approached by those who work for governments, international agencies, or transnational corporations. Perhaps the most dramatic possibilities to act for a just or an unjust, a beneficent or selfish future belong to those who hold positions of influence within the Third World. But wherever we find ourselves, our duties are not, on the Kantian picture, limited to those close at hand. Duties of justice arise whenever there is some involvement between parties—and in the modern world this is never lacking. Duties of beneficence arise whenever destitution puts the possibility of autonomous action in question for the more vulnerable. When famines were not only far away, but nothing could be done to relieve them, beneficence or charity may well have begun—and stayed—at home. In a global village, the moral significance of distance has shrunk, and we may be able to affect the capacities for autonomous action of those who are far away. . . .

Questions for Further Reflection

1. Singer writes that "if we accept any principle of impartiality, universalizability, equality, or whatever, we cannot discriminate against someone merely because he is far away from us." Do you agree? We often think we have stronger duties to our families, our friends, members of our communities, and citizens of our nation (in that order) than we do to others. Is this really inconsistent with impartiality or universalizability? What if

everyone has a duty (for example) to put his or her family's interests ahead of the interests of others?

2. Singer argues that many actions we normally consider acts of charity are actually our moral duties, and the fact that most people do not live up to their moral duty makes our duties even more stringent than they would be if all people did their share. On Singer's principles, would it be a good idea to tax people and use the proceeds for charitable purposes? Singer aside, do *you* think this is a good idea? If so, would you tax people enough to ensure that they do their duty by Singer's lights? If you do not think it is a good idea, what is your attitude toward charitable purposes on which our government currently spends tax dollars?

3. Garrett Hardin suggests that food aid will lead to a version of the "tragedy of the commons." Just as multiple farmers grazing cattle on a common pasture will build their herds too large and overgraze it, so needy people with access to a common stock of food (such as a world food bank) will produce populations too large for the food supply. How persuasive is this analogy?

4. O'Neill suggests that agreements with underdeveloped countries are often coercive agreements that would not have been made "without the element of coercion provided by the desperation of the weaker party." How can we distinguish coercive from noncoercive agreements in cases in which one party to the agreement is extremely needy? If a needy party is willing to give up a great deal for food, why shouldn't we "drive a hard bargain"?

5. O'Neill is not very specific about how much we should sacrifice in order to help the needy, but she does write that "the alleviation of need must rank far ahead of the furthering of happiness in the Kantian picture." Will this lead to conclusions rather like Singer's? If the importance of alleviating need in Africa ranks far ahead of the pleasure I gain from my compact disc collection, should I sell my discs and contribute the proceeds to aid organizations?

Further Readings

Aiken, William, and Hugh LaFollette, eds. *World Hunger and Morality*. Englewood Cliffs, NJ: Prentice-Hall, 1996. A useful collection of essays. (Revised and updated version of a 1977 book entitled *World Hunger and Moral Obligations*.)

Lucas, George R., Jr. "African Famine: New Economic and Ethical Perspectives." *Journal of Philosophy* 87 (1990): 629–641. Makes use of the work by Sen listed below. See also the reply by William Aiken in the same issue.

Sen, Amartya. "The Right Not to Be Hungry." In G. Floistad, ed., *Contemporary Philosophy: A New Survey*, vol. 2. The Hague: Martinus Nijhof, 1982, 343–360. A highly theoretical but illuminating discussion. See also Jean Dreze and Amartya Sen, *Hunger and Public Action* (Oxford: Oxford University Press, 1989).

Singer, Peter. *Practical Ethics*. Cambridge, England: Cambridge University Press, 1979, Chapter 8 ("Rich and Poor"). A slightly more recent version of the argument of his selection in this chapter; includes some useful responses to objections.

O'Neill, Onora. *Faces of Hunger*. London: George Allen and Unwin, 1985. Develops the views O'Neill advances in her selection in this chapter. See also O'Neill. "Perplexities of Famine and World Hunger," in Tom Regan, ed., *Matters of Life and Death: New Introductory Essays in Moral Philosophy*, second edition (New York: Random House, 1986). This is the longer essay from which our selection is excerpted: It includes discussions of Hardin and Singer and some practical suggestions.

Unger, Peter. *Living High and Letting Die: Our Illusion of Innocence*. Oxford: Oxford University Press, 1996. Argues that moral standards we already accept show that we are morally required to do much more than we actually do.

Part Six

Intergenerational Issues

Chapter 16

THE GENETIC ENGINEERING OF HUMAN BEINGS

Through genetic engineering—the direct alteration of the blueprint genes use to control the development and structure of life forms—scientists have produced types of life that would never have existed naturally. Genetic engineering is being used to correct genetically based human health problems and one day may be used to change human structure in dramatic new ways. As things stand, the morality and legality of many uses of genetic engineering are unclear, especially uses involving human beings. The potential benefits of the new technology are great, and so are the potential dangers. In this chapter, we examine some of the arguments people have given both for and against the application of genetic engineering techniques to human beings.

Background

It is widely known that the development of living things proceeds in accordance with the information encoded by the sequences of nucleotides that make up the DNA present in each cell of every animal. Spontaneous changes in these sequences, called mutations, are a key element in the evolution of new life forms. For centuries, people have been speeding up (or interfering with) this process of evolution; through selective breeding, they have produced types of animals especially suitable for human needs. Genetic engineering technology, developed in the 1970s, has made it possible to introduce new types of living creatures far more efficiently. Enzymes are used by scientists to chop up strands of DNA and then to recombine them. Bits of DNA that are associated with undesirable features can be eliminated. More impressively, the DNA from animals of one species can be combined with bits from the same or different species to create creatures with quite different structures.

The new technology had enough potential for danger that in 1974, a voluntary moratorium was called by researchers in the field. Scientists were worried that life forms could be developed through their new techniques that might conceivably constitute a hazard to existing life, and that such forms could interfere with evolution in unforeseen and unfortunate ways. A group of seven scientists formed a committee chaired by Paul Berg and published a letter expressing their concerns in *Science*. After the Berg letter was published, an international conference was held at

Asilomar, California, in 1975. Here, discussion was sufficiently encouraging that the moratorium was conditionally lifted. Soon after, the National Institutes of Health wrote guidelines for the conduct of research involving the new techniques, and in 1976 created the Recombinant DNA Advisory Committee (RAC) to oversee projects funded by the federal government. The RAC also screens proposals voluntarily submitted by many researchers in the field.

Another important development in the dispute over recombinant DNA research occurred on June 16, 1980. At that time, the U.S. Supreme Court made a decision in the *Diamond, Commissioner of Patents and Trademarks, v. Chakrabarty* case. Ananda Chakrabarty was a molecular biologist who sought to patent a bacterium he had developed through altering an existing strain of bacteria. The new sort was able to break down crude oil. Chakrabarty was denied his patent by the Patent Office, whose officials claimed that life cannot be patented. Upon review, the Court of Customs and Patent Appeals maintained that Chakrabarty should be granted his patent, and the Supreme Court agreed. It held that given the existing patent law (Section 101 of Title 35 of the United States Code), "a live, human-made microorganism is patentable subject matter." Chakrabarty got his patent. More followed. In 1987, for example, a patent was granted to Harvard University for *any nonhuman* type of animal engineered to carry certain genes that cause cancer.[1] So, as things stand, plants and nonhuman animals produced through genetic engineering techniques are patentable, and although human beings are not patentable, human material, such as bone marrow stem cells, have been patented.[2]

The availability of patents on useful living things has provided economic incentives for the development of life forms by granting the right to exclusive control. It also tends to commercialize research; thus in 1987, a company (called "Genome") was begun in Cambridge, Massachusetts, whose aim is to conduct research necessary to create, copyright, and sell an "atlas" giving all the genetic information contained in human DNA. In the same year, however, plans were announced for what is now a 3-billion-dollar NIH project aimed at charting human DNA[3] and Europeans announced plans for an international Human Genome Organization (HUGO), which aims to map the human genome.[4]

Since the Chakrabarty decision, experiments have been conducted cautiously and only after considerable legal battles waged by environmentalists and others. In 1987, however, the first genetically altered organisms were released into the environment: ice-minus bacteria, derived from *Pseudomona* bacteria by eliminating the gene that produces a protein that prompts ice crystals to form on plants. Other striking experiments quickly followed. For example, researchers have inserted the genetic code of the AIDS virus into mice.[5] More significantly, human tissues have been submitted to genetic alteration. For example, lymphocytes, altered so as to be more effective against melanoma, have been introduced into patients.[6]

---

[1] *Science* 240 (May 1988), 1142.
[2] "Staking Claims on the Human Body," *U.S. News & World Report* (November 18, 1991).

[3] *Discover* (January 1988), 85–86 and *Science* 240 (June 1988), 1728.
[4] *Science* 241 (July 1988), 165.
[5] *Science* 239 (January 1988), 341–343.
[6] *Science* 256 (May 1992), 808–813.

Possible Applications

Genetic engineering techniques may be applied to human beings in several ways. The least controversial is using the new techniques to identify the role various genes play in determining human characteristics. On the basis of such information, however, we could do several additional things.

Some of these do not involve any further bioengineering: (1) We can detect diseases and treat them using traditional methods, such as drug therapy; (2) we can screen fetuses and abort those who have undesirable genetic profiles; or (3) we can use *in vitro* fertilization and transfer embryos whose genetic profiles are suitable, thus avoiding the resort to abortion.

Other measures we can take involve further bioengineering. The aim is to directly alter genetic profiles. This alteration might be either germline or somatic. *Germline therapy* involves altering the genetic makeup of germ (reproductive) cells, and such changes would be passed down to future generations. (Thus, the use of germline therapy can be one form of *eugenics*, a blanket term covering any attempt to correct defects or make heritable improvements in human beings.) Such alteration could be performed on adults before they reproduce or on zygotes. *Somatic therapy* involves changes that are not inherited, the alteration of the genetic makeup of cells that have already differentiated, that is, cells that have already been programmed as a subcomponent of an organism (such as bone cells).

Both germline and somatic therapy could take two forms. *Negative engineering* is the use of bioengineering to overcome defects or disease. More than 3,000 diseases are caused by either the presence of genes that normally are absent or the absence of genes that normally are present. *Positive engineering* is the use of bioengineering to make improvements over and above the elimination of defects. Obviously, the distinction between negative and positive engineering will not always be clear: Some people's genetic constitution allows them to run faster than others; would making everyone able to run as fast as the fastest constitute overcoming a defect, or would it be a different sort of improvement? (Indeed, what makes an abnormality of one sort a defect while another is not? One could imagine slow people arguing that abnormal speed is the defect to be eliminated.)

Should Human Beings Be Engineered?

Few argue that genetic engineering should not be applied to human beings in any way whatever. Such a ban would prevent researchers from using the new tools to gather information that could be used to help us detect genetically linked disorders that could be treated using conventional methods, such as surgery or drug therapy. Still, one can imagine arguments in favor of a total ban on genetic engineering, even as used only in an information-gathering capacity.

People who consider the killing of zygotes to be morally objectionable might favor a complete ban on the grounds that information-gathering that exploits bioengineering techniques involves killing zygotes. Whether killing zygotes is wrong is an issue discussed in a later chapter, but even if readers take this view about the status of zygotes, it does not follow that bioengineering should be completely banned, for, of course, there is no reason in principle why bioengineering aimed at gathering information must involve killing zygotes. Instead, information might be gathered by applying bioengineering to somatic cells.

Other critics might defend a ban using a slippery-slope argument: If we permit researchers to use bioengineering in one area, we cannot stop them from using it in more clearly objectionable ways. However, the slippery-slope argument is subject to the response that we can stop bioengineering in one area while using it in another as long as there is a good argument that its use is wrong in the one area but not in the other. Proponents of bioengineering will maintain that we can clearly identify at least some uses that would be extremely beneficial, even if others would be extremely detrimental. Hence, we should not ban bioengineering in principle but should instead adopt a policy of careful review of each proposed innovation and make our choices on a case-by-case basis. This approach is the one that has won out in the United States, where, at present, the reviewing is done by the NIH.

If we continue to permit bioengineering, it is likely that we will permit it in research aimed at discovering the roles genes play in controlling human structure. Should we go beyond such pure research?

Negative Engineering

The next step, presumably, is to allow negative engineering so as to treat genetically linked diseases, such as cystic fibrosis and Tay-Sachs disease. On the "con" side is an argument from ignorance: For all we know, any attempt to eliminate or add genes whose presence or absence is linked to defects might have disastrous consequences. Because consequences might be noticeable only in adulthood, when it is too late to reverse the therapy, we should not permit any negative engineering (or any positive engineering, for that matter). Moreover, eliminating the many genes known to be associated with diseases might result in a people who are not robust enough to adapt to changing future conditions.

One problem with this argument as stated is that it does not acknowledge the distinction between germline therapy and somatic therapy, the latter of which is now a fairly uncontroversial practice. The addition or subtraction of genes in germ cells would have more far-reaching consequences than would the addition or subtraction of genes in somatic cells, for only the former would result in heritable features. So if an application of somatic therapy led to a flaw in a group of people, the therapy could be discontinued, and the victims could still produce normal children without any further intervention (unless, of course, the flaw blocks reproduction). Moreover, somatic therapy might be a welcome option for parents who discover that their fetus has a serious genetic defect but who oppose abortion.

Dealing with flaws using germline therapy would be somewhat more complicated and is opposed by the Council for Responsible Genetics in their essay. If the victims agreed that they were flawed, they could opt to have no children, or they could allow experts to reverse the effects of the unfortunate germ therapy. It may happen, though, that the effects are so subtle that they go unnoticed for a few generations, so that a large number of people are involved. Or perhaps the effects cannot be reversed, either because they are not fully understood or because the means turn out to be too complicated. Moreover, as Jonathan Glover points out, it may be that altered people will not agree that they are flawed; if so, we may have to resign ourselves to their being a permanent part of the population. Thus, suppose we try to eliminate retardation and end up making people more violent instead. We might want to erase our mistake and begin again, hoping to persuade the people of the new generation to sterilize themselves or alter their descendants. However, the newly engineered people we consider defective may not agree (they may consider *us* defective), and, because they *are* people, mustn't our respect for their autonomy lead us to allow them to reproduce?

Positive Engineering

If we allow germ or somatic gene therapy to correct defects, why not allow gene therapy (whether germ or somatic) aimed at improving human nature? The improvements we could make may in time turn out to be substantial. Perhaps we could make people brilliant, long-lived, beautiful, and extremely physically powerful; perhaps, in the more distant future, we could even adjust human structure so that people could survive comfortably in extreme conditions, such as those on other planets or even in the oceans of the earth.

However, some substantial reasons exist for worrying about the application of positive engineering. One source of concern is the argument from ignorance already discussed in conjunction with negative engineering. Another is that even if we had the technology to produce any sort of human being we wished, doubts would remain about the desirability and permissibility of improving people. In his essay, Michael Ruse takes it for granted that we ought to correct defects using negative engineering, but he argues against the implementation of positive engineering. His claim is that even if without any unfortunate side effects we could "improve" human beings in the ways that seem at first desirable, it would be a bad idea to do so. One of the reasons he gives is that "the worth of human accomplishments is comparative:" My accomplishment has worth only insofar as it compares favorably to those of others. So if we were all smarter or more adept, none of us would be any better off.

Another set of concerns about improving people through a fool-proof technology stems from the fact that unless we let anybody create any sort of "child," we must identify some sort of mechanism whereby proposed departures from the norm are permitted. At a minimum, presumably we would be permitted to develop children whose features depart from the norm only in ways that are improvements. Otherwise, we would be gratuitously handicapping these children. However, people differ greatly in their views concerning what constitutes an improvement, and it is difficult to see how an objective criterion could be provided. Perhaps the most obvious criterion would be that the putative improvement must be welcomed by the altered individual once that individual comes to maturity. But what if the improvement at hand is accompanied by an alteration in the values of the improved individual so that she or he is simply engineered to welcome the improvement? In the absence of an overwhelmingly obvious criterion for what constitutes an improvement, how are we to decide on permissible improvements in human beings?

Jonathan Glover suggests a "mixed system" in which we leave the decisions about whether and how to depart from the natural lottery up to parents but empower some governmental body with the authority to veto any parents' proposals. By depriving the government of the authority to initiate projects for improving human beings, Glover hopes to meet worries about Hitler-like schemes for enslaving the population, and by stopping short of allowing parents to fashion their children in any way they choose, he hopes to prevent demented parents from bringing miserable creatures into existence.

AGAINST GERMLINE THERAPY

Position Paper on Human Germ Line Manipulation

Council for Responsible Genetics, Human Genetics Committee (Fall, 1992)

The Position of the Council for Responsible Genetics

The Council for Responsible Genetics (CRG) strongly opposes the use of germ line gene modification in humans. This position is based on scientific, ethical, and social concerns.

Proponents of germ line manipulation assume that once a gene implicated in a particular condition is identified, it might be appropriate and relatively easy to change, supplement or otherwise modify the gene by some form of therapy. However, biological characteristics or traits usually depend on interactions among many genes, and these genes are themselves affected by processes that occur both inside the organism and in its surroundings. This means that scientists cannot predict the full effect that any gene modification will have on the traits of people or other organisms. In purely biological terms, the relationship between genes and traits is not well enough understood to guarantee that by eliminating or changing genes associated with traits one might want to avoid, we may not simultaneously alter or eliminate traits we would like to preserve. Even genes that are associated with diseases that may cause problems in one context can be beneficial in another context.

Two frequently destructive aspects of contemporary culture are linked together in an unprecedented fashion in germ line gene modification. The first is the notion that the value of a human being is dependent on the degree to which he or she approximates some ideal of biological perfection. The second is the ideology that all limitations imposed by nature can and should be overcome by technology. To make intentional changes in the genes that people will pass on to their descendants would require that we, as a society, agree on how to identify 'good' and 'bad' genes. We do not have such criteria, nor are there mechanisms for establishing them. Any formulation of such criteria would necessarily reflect current social biases.

Moreover, the definition of the standards and the technological means for implementing them would largely be determined by the economically and socially privileged. By implementing a program of germ line manipulation these groups would exercise unwarranted influence over the common biological heritage of humanity.

What Is "Germ Line Manipulation"?

The undifferentiated cells of an early embryo develop into either germ cells or somatic cells. *Germ* cells, or reproductive cells, are those that develop into the egg or sperm of a developing organism and transmit all its heritable characteristics. *Somatic* cells, or body cells, refer to all other cells of the body. While both types of cells contain chromosomes, only the chromosomes of germ cells are passed on to future generations.

Techniques are now available to change chromosomes of animal cells by inserting new segments of DNA into them. If this insertion is performed on specialized or *differentiated* body tissues, such as liver, muscle, or blood cells, it is referred to as *somatic cell* gene modification, and the changes do not go beyond the individual organism. If it is performed on sperm or eggs before fertilization, or on the undifferentiated cells of an early embryo, it is called *germ cell* or *germ line* gene modification, and the changes are not limited to the individual organism. For when DNA is incorporated into an embryo's germ cells, or undifferentiated cells that give rise to germ cells, the introduced gene or genes will be passed on to future generations and may become a permanent part of the gene pool.

Deliberate gene alterations in humans are often referred to as 'gene therapy.' The Council for Responsible Genetics (CRG) prefers to use the terms 'gene modification' and 'gene manipulation' because the word 'therapy' promises health benefits, and it is not yet clear that gene manipulations are beneficial.

Why Might Germ Line Modification Be Attempted in Humans?

If one or both partners carry a version of a gene that could predispose their offspring to inherit a condition they want to avoid, genetic manipulation may appear to be a potential way to prevent the undesired outcome. The earlier during embryonic development the targeted gene or genes are replaced, the less likely is the resulting individual to be affected by the unwanted gene. But while the immediate goal of such a modification might be to alter the genetic constitution of a single individual, modifications made at the early embryonic stages would incidentally result in germ line modification, and so all the offspring of this person would have and pass on the modification.

Alternatively, germ line modification may be the intended consequence of the procedure. One goal might be to 'cleanse' the gene pool of 'deleterious' genes. For example, Daniel E. Koshland, Jr., a molecular biologist, and the editor-in-chief of *Science,* has written, "keeping diabetics alive with insulin, which increases the propagation of an inherited disease, seems justified only if one ultimately is willing to do genetic engineering to remove diabetes from the germ line and thus save the anguish and cost to millions of diabetics." (1) Another goal of germ line manipulation may be to avoid multiple treatments of somatic gene modification that would be required under proposed treatment protocols for certain conditions such as cystic fibrosis.

Some people may also look forward to the possibility of introducing genes into the germ line that can 'enhance' certain characteristics desired by parents or other custodians of the resulting offspring. In the article referred to above, Koshland raises the possibility that germ line alterations could be perceived to meet future 'needs' to design individuals "better at computers, better as musicians, better physically."

The attempt to improve the human species biologically is known as *eugenics,* and was the basis of a popular movement in Europe and North America during the first half of this century. Eugenics was advocated by prominent scientists across the entire political spectrum, who represented it as the logical consequence of the most advanced biological thinking of the period. In the U.S., eugenic thinking resulted in social policies that called for forced sterilization of individuals regarded as inferior because they were 'feeble minded or paupers.' In Europe, the Nazis took up these ideas, and their attempts at implementation led to widespread revulsion against the concept of eugenics. Today public discussion in favor of influencing the genetic constitution of future generations has gained new respectability with the increased possibility for intervention presented by in-vitro fertilization and embryo implantation technologies. Although it is once again espoused by individuals with a variety of political perspectives, the doctrine of social advancement through biological perfectibility underlying the new eugenics is almost indistinguishable from the older version so avidly embraced by the Nazis.

It is important to recognize that the dream of eliminating 'harmful' genes (such as those associated with cystic fibrosis or Duchenne muscular dystrophy) from the entire human gene pool could be realized only over time scales of thousands of years, and then only with massive, coercive programs of germ line manipulation. Such a program would be neither feasible nor morally acceptable. As a practical matter then, any presumed beneficial effects of germ line modification would pertain to individual families, not to the human population as a whole. This is in contrast to harmful effects, which would be widely disseminated.

Furthermore, parents who carry a gene which they would not want a child of theirs to inherit could arrange to have unaffected, biologically-related offspring *without* germ line modification. If a gene is well enough characterized to consider gene manipulation, there will always be a diagnostic test available to identify a fetus that carries that gene and parents, if they choose, may then terminate the pregnancy. Given that there are alternatives for avoiding the inheritance of unwanted genes, the main selling point of germ line modification techniques over the long term would appear to be the prospect of enhancement of desired traits.

What Is the Feasibility of Modifying the Germ Line of Humans?

Both somatic and germ line modification are widely performed on laboratory animals for research purposes. Somatic gene modifications have already been performed on humans and additional experimental protocols are being approved by the National Institutes of Health in increasing numbers.

No published reports have yet appeared on germ line modification in humans, but there appear to be no technical obstacles to such experiments, and articles proposing these procedures are becoming more and more common in the literature (2,3,4). Germ line gene modification has actually proved technically easier than somatic modification in mice and other vertebrate animals which have been employed as 'models' for human biology in the past, because the cells of early embryos incorporate foreign DNA and synthesize corresponding functional proteins more readily than most differentiated somatic cells. A widely-reported example of the successful experimental use of the germ line technique was the introduction of an extra gene that specified growth hormone into fertilized mouse eggs. In the presence of the high levels of growth hormone produced, the mice grew to double their normal size. Germ line techniques are also being used in attempts to modify farm animals, with stated goals of increasing yields or enhancing nutritional quality of meat and other animal products.

Given what has been accomplished in animals, the only remaining technical requirements for germ line gene modification in humans are procedures for collecting a woman's eggs, fertilizing them outside her body, and implanting them in the uterus of the same or another woman, where they can be brought to term. These are already well established procedures for humans and are widely used in in-vitro fertilization clinics.

What Are the Technical Pitfalls?

Current methods for germ line gene modification of mammals are inefficient, requiring the microinjection of numerous eggs with foreign DNA before an egg is successfully modified. Moreover, introduction of a foreign gene (even if there is a copy of one already present) into an inappropriate location in an embryo's chromosomes can have unexpected consequences. For example, the offspring of a mouse that received an extra copy of the normally present *myc* gene developed cancer at 40 times the rate of the unmodified strain of mice. (5)

Techniques to introduce foreign DNA into eggs, however, are constantly being improved and eventually will be portrayed as efficient and reliable enough for human applications. It may soon be possible to place a gene into a specified location on a chromosome while simultaneously removing the unwanted gene. This will increase the accuracy of the procedures, but does not eliminate the possibility that gene combinations will be created that will be harmful to the modified embryo, and its descendants in future generations. Such inadvertent damage could be caused by technical error, or more importantly, by biologists' inability to predict how genes or their products interact with one another and with the organism's environment to give rise to biological traits. It would have been impossible to predict, *a priori*, for example, that someone who has even *one* copy of the gene for a blood protein known as hemoglobin-S would be protected against malaria, whereas a person who has *two* copies of this gene would have sickle cell disease.

This unpredictability applies with equal force to genetic modifications introduced to 'correct' presumed disorders and to those introduced to enhance characteristics. Inserting new segments of DNA into the germ line could have major, unpredictable consequences for both the individual and the future of the species that include the introduction of susceptibilities to cancer and other diseases into the human gene pool.

What Are the Social and Ethical Implications of Germ Line Modification?

Clinical trials in humans to treat Adenosine Deaminase Deficiency—a life-threatening immune disorder—and terminal cancer with somatic gene modification are already in progress and experiments to treat diabetes and hypertension are under development. It is important to distinguish the ethical problems raised by these protocols from the additional, and more profound, questions raised by germ line modification. While the biological effects of somatic manipulations reside entirely in the individual in which they are attempted, such treatments are not strictly analogous to other therapies with individual risk. Radiation, chemical or drug treatment can be withdrawn if they prove harmful to the patient, while some forms of somatic modification cannot. Thus, somatic gene modification requires a person to forfeit his/her rights to withdraw from a research study because the intervention cannot be stopped, whether harmful or not. Valid objections have also been raised to the fact that the first somatic gene modification experiments, involving

Adenosine Deaminase Deficiency, were carried out on young children who were not themselves in a position to give informed consent. While it appears that somatic gene modification techniques will be used increasingly in the future, the CRG urges that they be used with greatest caution, and only for clearly life-threatening conditions.

Germ line modification, in contrast, has not yet been attempted in humans. The Council for Responsible Genetics opposes it unconditionally. Ethical arguments against germ line modification include many of those that pertain to somatic cell modification, as well as the following:

- Germ line modification is not needed in order to save the lives or alleviate suffering of existing people. Its target population[s] are 'future people' who have not yet even been conceived.
- The cultural impact of treating humans as biologically perfectible artifacts would be entirely negative. People who fall short of some technically achievable ideal would increasingly be seen as 'damaged goods.' And it is clear that the standards for what is genetically desirable will be those of the society's economically and politically dominant groups. This will only reinforce prejudices and discrimination in a society where they already exist.
- Accountability to individuals of future generations who are harmed or stigmatized by wrongful or unsuccessful germ line modifications of their ancestors is unlikely.

In conclusion, the Council calls for a ban on germ line modification.

References

1. Koshland Jr., Daniel E., "The Future of Biological Research: What Is Possible and What Is Ethical?", *MBL* [Marine Biological Laboratory] *Science*. v. 3, no. 2, pp. 11–15, 1988.
2. Walters, LeRoy, "Human Gene Therapy: Ethics and Public policy," *Human Gene Therapy*, v. 2, pp. 115–122, 1991.
3. Working Group on Genetic Screening and Testing, *Report of Discussions in Genetics, Ethics and Human Values*, XXIVth CIOMS Conference, Tokyo and Inuyama, Japan, 24–26 July 1990.
4. Buster, John E. and Carson, Sandra A., "Genetic Diagnosis of the Preimplantation Embryo," *American Journal of Medical Genetics*, v. 34, pp. 211–216, 1989.
5. Leder, A. et al, "Consequences of Widespread Deregulation of the c-myc Gene in Trangenic Mice: Multiple Neoplasms and Normal Development," *Cell*, v. 45, p. 485, 1986.

Notes

This document was written by the Human Genetics Committee of the Council for Responsible Genetics (CRG). The Council is a Cambridge-based national organization of scientists, public health advocates, trade unionists, women's health activists and others who want to see biotechnology developed safely and in the public interest. The Council believes that an informed public can and should play a leadership role in setting the direction for emerging technologies. A fundamental goal of the CRG is to prevent genetic discrimination.

The Human Genetics Committee has 14 members with backgrounds in the biological sciences, public health, law, disability rights, occupational health and safety, and women's health. Members include: Abby Lippman, Professor of Epidemiology, McGill University, Chairperson; Philip Bereano, Professor of Engineering and Public Policy, University of Washington; Paul Billings, Chief of Genetic Medicine, Pacific Presbyterian Medical Center; Colin Gracey, Head of the Religious Life Office, Northeastern University; Mary Sue Henifin, Deputy Attorney General, State of New Jersey; Ruth Hubbard, Professor Emerita of Biology at Harvard University; Sheldon Krimsky, Associate Professor of Urban and Environmental Policy, Tufts University; Richard Lewontin, Alexander Agassiz Professor of Zoology, Harvard University; Karen Messing, Professor of Biology, University of Quebec in Montreal; Stuart Newman, Professor of Cell Biology and Anatomy, New York Medical College; Judy Norsigian, Co-Director, Boston Women's Healthbook Collective; Marsha Saxton, Director, Project on Women and Disability; Doreen Stabinsky, California Biotechnology Action Council and University of California at Davis; and Nachama L. Wilker, Executive Director, Council for Responsible Genetics.

FOR BOTH POSITIVE AND NEGATIVE ENGINEERING

Decisions

Jonathan Glover

Like everyone else, philosophers measure their personal emotional responses to various alternatives as though consulting a hidden oracle. That oracle resides deep in the emotional centres of the brain, most probably within the limbic system . . .

E. O. Wilson: *On Human Nature*

Some of the strongest objections to positive engineering are not about specialized applications or about risks. They are about the decisions involved. The central line of thought is that we should not start playing God by redesigning the human race. The suggestion is that there is no group (such as scientists, doctors, public officials, or politicians) who can be entrusted with decisions about what sort of people there should be. And it is also doubted whether we could have any adequate grounds for basing such decisions on one set of values rather than another.

This chapter is about the 'playing God' objection: about the question 'Who decides?', and about the values involved. I shall argue that these issues raise real problems, but that, contrary to what is often supposed, they do not add up to an overwhelming case against positive engineering.

1 Not Playing God

Suppose we could use genetic engineering to raise the average IQ by fifteen points. (I mention, only to ignore, the boring objection that the average IQ is always by definition 100.) Should we do this? Objectors to positive engineering say we should not. This is not because the present average is preferable to a higher one. We do not think that, if it were naturally fifteen points higher, we ought to bring it down to the present level. The objection is to our playing God by deciding what the level should be.

On one view of the world, the objection is relatively straightforward. On this view, there really is a God, who has a plan for the world which will be disrupted if we stray outside the boundaries assigned to us. (It is *relatively* straightforward: there would still be the problem of knowing where the boundaries came. If genetic engineering disrupts the programme, how do we know that medicine and education do not?)

The objection to playing God has a much wider appeal than to those who literally believe in a divine plan. But, outside such a context, it is unclear what the objection comes to. If we have a Darwinian view, according to which features of our nature have been selected for their contribution to gene survival, it is not blasphemous, or obviously disastrous, to start to control the process in the light of our own values. We may value other qualities in people, in preference to those which have been most conducive to gene survival.

The prohibition on playing God is obscure. If it tells us not to interfere with natural selection at all, this rules out medicine, and most other environmental and social changes. If it only forbids interference with natural selection by the direct alteration of genes, this rules out negative as well as positive genetic engineering. If these interpretations are too restrictive, the ban on positive engineering seems to need some explanation. If we can make positive changes at the environmental level, and negative changes at the genetic level, why should we not make positive changes at the genetic level? What makes this policy, but not the others, objectionably God-like?

Perhaps the most plausible reply to these questions rests on a general objection to any group of people trying to plan too closely what human life should be like. Even if it is hard to distinguish in principle between the use of genetic and environmental means, genetic changes are likely to differ in degree from most environmental ones. Genetic alterations may be more drastic or less reversible, and so they can be seen as the extreme case of an objectionably God-like policy by which some people set out to plan the lives of others.

This objection can be reinforced by imagining the possible results of a programme of positive engineering, where the decisions about the desired improvements were taken by scientists. Judging by the literature written by scientists on this topic, great prominence would be given to intelligence. But can we be sure that enough weight would be given to other desirable qualities? And do things seem better if for scientists we substitute doctors, politicians or civil servants? Or some committee containing businessmen, trade unionists, academics, lawyers and a clergyman?

What seems worrying here is the circumscribing of potential human development. The present genetic lottery throws up a vast range of characteristics, good and bad, in all sorts of combinations. The group of people controlling a positive engineering policy would inevitably have limited horizons, and we are right to worry that the limitations of their outlook might become the boundaries of human variety. The drawbacks would be like those of town-planning or dog-breeding, but with more important consequences.

When the objection to playing God is separated from the idea that intervening in this aspect of the natural world is a kind of blasphemy, it is a protest against a particular group of people, necessarily fallible and limited, taking decisions so important to our future. This protest may be on grounds of the bad consequences, such as loss of variety of people, that would come from the imaginative limits of those taking the decisions. Or it may be an expression of opposition to such concentration of power, perhaps with the thought: 'What right have *they* to decide what kinds of people there should be?' Can these problems be sidestepped?

2 The Genetic Supermarket

Robert Nozick is critical of the assumption that positive engineering has to involve any centralized decision about desirable qualities: 'Many biologists tend to think the problem is one of *design*, of specifying the best types of persons so that biologists can proceed to produce them. Thus they worry over what sort(s) of person there is to be and who will control this process. They do not tend to think, perhaps because it diminishes the importance of their role, of a system in which they run a "genetic supermarket", meeting the individual specifications (within certain moral limits) of prospective parents. Nor do they think of seeing what limited number of types of persons people's choices would converge upon, if indeed there would be any such convergence. This supermarket system has the great virtue that it involves no centralized decision fixing the future human type(s).'[1]

This idea of letting parents choose their children's characteristics is in many ways an improvement on decisions being taken by some centralized body. It seems less likely to reduce human variety, and could even increase it, if genetic engineering makes new combinations of characteristics available. (But we should be cautious here. Parental choice is not a guarantee of genetic variety, as the influence of fashion or of shared values might make for a small number of types on which choices would converge.)

To those sympathetic to one kind of liberalism, Nozick's proposal will seem more attractive than centralized decisions. On this approach to politics, it is wrong for the authorities to institutionalize any religious or other outlook as the official one of the society. To a liberal of this kind, a good society is one which tolerates and encourages a wide diversity of ideals of the good life. Anyone with these sympathies will be suspicious of centralized decisions about what sort of people should form the next generation. But some parental decisions would be disturbing. If parents chose characteristics likely to make their children unhappy, or likely to reduce their abilities, we might feel that the children should be protected against this. (Imagine parents belonging to some extreme religious sect, who wanted their children to have a religious symbol as a physical mark on their face, and who wanted them to be unable to read, as a protection against their faith being corrupted.) Those of us who support restrictions protecting children from parental harm after birth (laws against cruelty, and compulsion on parents to allow their children to be educated and to have necessary medical treatment) are likely to support protecting children from being harmed by their parents' genetic choices.

No doubt the boundaries here will be difficult to draw. We already find it difficult to strike a satisfactory balance between protection of children and parental freedom to choose the kind of upbringing their children should have. But it is hard to accept that society should set no limits to the genetic choices parents can make for their children. Nozick recognizes this when he says the genetic supermarket should meet the specifications of parents 'within certain moral limits'. So, if the supermarket came into existence, some centralized policy, even if only the restrictive one of ruling out certain choices harmful to the children, should exist. It would be a political decision where the limits should be set.

There may also be a case for other centralized restrictions on parental choice, as well as those aimed at preventing harm to the individual people being designed. The genetic supermarket might have more oblique bad effects. An imbalance in the ratio between the sexes could result. Or parents might think their children would

---

[1] *Anarchy, State and Utopia*, New York, 1974, p. 315.

be more successful if they were more thrusting, competitive and selfish. If enough parents acted on this thought, other parents with different values might feel forced into making similar choices to prevent their own children being too greatly disadvantaged. Unregulated individual decisions could lead to shifts of this kind, with outcomes unwanted by most of those who contribute to them. If a majority favour a roughly equal ratio between the sexes, or a population of relatively uncompetitive people, they may feel justified in supporting restrictions on what parents can choose. (This is an application to the case of genetic engineering of a point familiar in other contexts, that unrestricted individual choices can add up to a total outcome which most people think worse than what would result from some regulation.)

Nozick recognizes that there may be cases of this sort. He considers the case of avoiding a sexual imbalance and says that 'a government could require that genetic manipulation be carried on so as to fit a certain ratio'.[2] He clearly prefers to avoid governmental intervention of this kind, and, while admitting that the desired result would be harder to obtain in a purely libertarian system, suggests possible strategies for doing so. He says: 'Either parents would subscribe to an information service monitoring the recent births and so know which sex was in shorter supply (and hence would be more in demand in later life), thus adjusting their activities, or interested individuals would contribute to a charity that offers bonuses to maintain the ratios, or the ratio would leave 1:1, with new family and social patterns developing.' The proposals for avoiding the sexual imbalance without central regulation are not reassuring. Information about likely prospects for marriage or sexual partnership might not be decisive for parents' choices. And, since those most likely to be 'interested individuals' would be in the age group being genetically engineered, it is not clear that the charity would be given donations adequate for its job.[3]

If the libertarian methods failed, we would have the choice between allowing a sexual imbalance or imposing some system of social regulation. Those who dislike central decisions favouring one sort of person over others might accept regulation here, on the grounds that neither sex is being given preference: the aim is rough equality of numbers.

But what about the other sort of case, where the working of the genetic supermarket leads to a general change unwelcome to those who contribute to it? Can we defend regulation to prevent a shift towards a more selfish and competitive population as merely being the preservation of a certain ratio between characteristics? Or have we crossed the boundary, and allowed a centralized decision favouring some characteristics over others? The location of the boundary is obscure. One view would be that the sex-ratio case is acceptable because the desired ratio is equality of numbers. On another view, the acceptability derives from the fact that the present ratio is to be preserved. (In this second view, preserving altruism would be acceptable, so long as no attempt was made to raise the proportion of altruistic people in the population. But is *this* boundary an easy one to defend?)

If positive genetic engineering does become a reality we may be unable to avoid some of the decisions being taken at a social level. Or rather, we could avoid this, but only at what seems an unacceptable cost, either to the particular people being designed, or to their generation as a whole. And, even if the social decisions are only

---

[2] Op. cit., p. 315.

[3] This kind of unworldly innocence is part of the engaging charm of Nozick's dotty and brilliant book.

restrictive, it is implausible to claim that they are all quite free of any taint of preference for some characteristics over others. But, although this suggests that we should not be doctrinaire in our support of the liberal view, it does not show that the view has to be abandoned altogether. We may still think that social decisions in favour of one type of person rather than another should be few, even if the consequences of excluding them altogether are unacceptable. A genetic supermarket, modified by some central regulation, may still be better than a system of purely central decisions. The liberal value is not obliterated because it may sometimes be compromised for the sake of other things we care about.

3 A Mixed System

The genetic supermarket provides a partial answer to the objection about the limited outlook of those who would take the decisions. The choices need not be concentrated in the hands of a small number of people. The genetic supermarket should not operate in a completely unregulated way, and so some centralized decisions would have to be taken about the restrictions that should be imposed. One system that would answer many of the anxieties about centralized decision-making would be to limit the power of the decision-makers to one of veto. They would then only check departures from the natural genetic lottery, and so the power to bring about changes would not be given to them, but spread through the whole population of potential parents. Let us call this combination of parental initiative and central veto a 'mixed system'. If positive genetic engineering does come about, we can imagine the argument between supporters of a mixed system and supporters of other decision-making systems being central to the political theory of the twenty-first century, parallel to the place occupied in the nineteenth and twentieth centuries by the debate over control of the economy.[4]

My own sympathies are with the view that, if positive genetic engineering is introduced, this mixed system is in general likely to be the best one for taking decisions. I do not want to argue for an absolutely inviolable commitment to this, as it could be that some centralized decision for genetic change was the only way of securing a huge benefit or avoiding a great catastrophe. But, subject to this reservation, the dangers of concentrating the decision-making create a strong presumption in favour of a mixed system rather than one in which initiatives come from the centre. And, if a mixed system was introduced, there would have to be a great deal of political argument over what kinds of restrictions on the supermarket should be imposed. Twenty-first-century elections may be about issues rather deeper than economics.

If this mixed system eliminates the anxiety about genetic changes being introduced by a few powerful people with limited horizons, there is a more general unease which it does not remove. May not the limitations of one generation of parents also prove disastrous? And, underlying this, is the problem of what values parents should appeal to in making their choices. How can we be confident that it is better for one sort of person to be born than another?

4 Values

The dangers of such decisions, even spread through all prospective parents, seem to me very real. We are swayed by fashion. We do not know the limitations of our own

---

[4]Decision-taking by a central committee (perhaps of a dozen elderly men) can be thought of as a 'Russian' model. The genetic supermarket (perhaps with genotypes being sold by TV commercials) can be thought of as an 'American' model. The mixed system may appeal to Western European social democrats.

outlook. There are human qualities whose value we may not appreciate. A generation of parents might opt heavily for their children having physical or intellectual abilities and skills. We might leave out a sense of humour. Or we might not notice how important to us is some other quality, such as emotional warmth. So we might not be disturbed in advance by the possible impact of the genetic changes on such a quality. And, without really wanting to do so, we might stumble into producing people with a deep coldness. This possibility seems one of the worst imaginable. It is just one of the many horrors that could be blundered into by our lack of foresight in operating the mixed system. Because such disasters are a real danger, there is a case against positive genetic engineering, even when the changes do not result from centralized decisions. But this case, resting as it does on the risk of disaster, supports a principle of caution rather than a total ban. We have to ask the question whether there are benefits sufficiently great and sufficiently probable to outweigh the risks.

But perhaps the deepest resistance, even to a mixed system, is not based on risks, but on a more general problem about values. Could the parents ever be justified in choosing, according to some set of values, to create one sort of person rather than another?

Is it sometimes better for us to create one sort of person rather than another? We say 'yes' when it is a question of eliminating genetic defects. And we say 'yes' if we think that encouraging some qualities rather than others should be an aim of the upbringing and education we give our children. Any inclination to say 'no' in the context of positive genetic engineering must lay great stress on the two relevant boundaries. The positive–negative boundary is needed to mark off the supposedly unacceptable positive policies from the acceptable elimination of defects. And the genes–environment boundary is needed to mark off positive engineering from acceptable positive aims of educational policies. But it is not clear that confidence in the importance of these boundaries is justified.

The positive–negative boundary may seem a way of avoiding objectionably God-like decisions, on the basis of our own values, as to what sort of people there should be. Saving someone from spina bifida is a lot less controversial than deciding he shall be a good athlete. But the distinction, clear in some cases, is less sharp in others. With emotional states or intellectual functioning, there is an element of convention in where the boundaries of normality are drawn. And, apart from this, there is the problem of explaining why the positive–negative boundary is so much more important with genetic intervention than with environmental methods. We act environmentally to influence people in ways that go far beyond the elimination of medical defects. Homes and schools would be impoverished by attempting to restrict their influence on children to the mere prevention of physical and mental disorder. And if we are right here to cross the positive–negative boundary, encouraging children to ask questions, or to be generous and imaginative, why should crossing the same boundary for the same reasons be ruled out absolutely when the means are genetic?

It may be said that the genes–environment boundary, is important because environmentally created changes can be reversed in a way that genetically based characteristics can not. But this perhaps underrates the permanence of the effects of upbringing. It may be that the difference is at best a matter of degree. And it is also hard to believe that irreversibility can be our main objection to crossing the genes–environment boundary. In bringing up our children, we try to encourage kindness and generosity. Would we really stop doing this if we were so effective that cruelty and meanness became impossible for them? It is not clear that our concern to develop their autonomy requires keeping open *all* possibilities, at whatever cost to our other values.

Yet there remains an unease about positive policies of moulding people in one direction rather than another, however much they are already incorporated in our child-rearing, and however reluctant we would be to abandon them altogether. And the unease is intensified when the methods are genetic, perhaps because the changes are likely to be less reversible, and perhaps because they may be more extreme. It may be said that we do not see the human race from the God-like perspective that seems to be required for making these decisions. We have our values, but perhaps we ought to be modest about them. E. O. Wilson's speculation that intuitions about values have their basis in the limbic system might be right. If so, perhaps genetic engineering could alter the limbic system, and so alter the values by which people judge these issues. And this raises the question of what basis we have for saying that genetic changes are improvements.

The sceptical case has been strongly stated by Bernard Williams. He talks of a difficulty

> about the basis of values on which these supposed improvements would be introduced. One would have to take the kind of standpoint in which one regarded as self-evident to oneself what the future of the human race should be, presuppose that you knew what the human race was here for, and take all the steps you could to make it reach that ideal goal. But it is not at all clear where one is supposed to get that knowledge or information from.[5]

Talk of 'knowledge' and 'information' sets the standard rather high, requiring the proponents of positive genetic engineering to have solved problems about objectivity in ethics which we do not expect people arguing other cases to have solved. But the point can be freed from this implication by being put as a question: on what basis can we decide between bringing into existence different types of people?

If we take decisions of this sort, we cannot but be guided by our own values (which would perhaps have been different had our limbic systems been different). But this is a feature of any moral or political decision. And it is not obvious that we are the best possible people in terms of our own values. People more generous, braver and less conformist than ourselves may be people *we* can recognize would be better than us. This need not commit us to some utopian blueprint about what the human race is for, but could be a matter of piecemeal genetic engineering. We take a view about what sort of people we prefer when we make decisions about schooling, without claiming to know what the human race is here for. And, as with educational decisions, decentralized choices at the genetic stage could lead to variety rather than uniformity.

There is, of course, a general problem about the basis of the values we bring to any decision. But it is questionable how far this is an argument against intervention to change what people are like, whether the means are genetic or environmental. Why should we assume that opting for the genetic status quo involves less commitment to a world view than opting for a change? And, if we are sure that some genetic changes would be for the worse, and so want to restrict the genetic supermarket, is it really plausible to say we have no basis for thinking some changes would be for the better? The scepticism seems unjustifiably selective.

If positive genetic engineering is to be justified, there must be benefits to

---

[5]'Genetics and Moral Responsibility', in A. Clow (ed.), *Morals and Medicine*. London, 1970.

outweigh the risks. And the benefits have to be even greater if centralized social decisions are taken, not merely to filter out certain parental initiatives, but positively to encourage the development of some characteristics. I have argued that there should be a presumption in favour of decentralized choices, which are more likely to preserve or increase variety than decisions taken from the narrow viewpoint of the members of some central body. But this is a presumption rather than an absolute ban on any central initiative. The chance of securing some great benefit, or of avoiding some great catastrophe, might justify overriding the presumption. It is hard to imagine being persuaded of the rightness of such a policy if adopted undemocratically or if imposed by coercion. But, even with a democratically chosen policy, using only persuasion or incentives, there is still the liberal resistance to government endorsement of some types of people as more desirable than others.

5 Changing Human Nature

Positive genetic engineering raises two issues. Could we be justified in trying to change human nature? And, if so, is genetic change an acceptable method? Most of us feel resistance to genetic engineering, and these two questions are often blurred together in our thinking. One aim of the discussion has been to separate the different sources of our resistance. Another has been to try to isolate the justifiable doubts. These have to do with risks of disasters, or with the drawbacks of imposed, centralized decisions. They need not justify total rejection of positive engineering. The risks are good reasons for extreme caution. The other drawbacks are good reasons for decentralized decisions, and for resisting positive genetic engineering in authoritarian societies. But these good reasons are quite separable from any opposition in principle to changing human nature.

The idea of 'human nature' is a vague one, whose boundaries are not easy to draw. And, given our history, the idea that we must preserve all the characteristics that are natural to us is not obvious without argument. Some deep changes in human nature may only be possible if we do accept positive genetic engineering. It is true that our nature is not determined entirely by our genes, but they do set limits to the sorts of people we can be. And the evolutionary competition to survive has set limits to the sorts of genes we have. Perhaps changes in society will transform our nature. But there is the pessimistic thought that perhaps they will not. Or, if they do, the resulting better people may lose to unreconstructed people in the evolutionary struggle. On either of these pessimistic views, to renounce positive genetic engineering would be to renounce any hope of fundamental improvement in what we are like. And we cannot yet be sure that these pessimistic views are both false.

Given the risks that positive genetic engineering is likely to involve, many people will think that we should reject it, even if that means putting up with human nature as it is. And many others will think that, quite apart from risks and dangers, we ought not to tamper with our nature. I have some sympathy with the first view. The decision involves balancing risks and gains, and perhaps the dangers will outweigh the benefits. We can only tell when the details are clearer than they are now, both about the genetic techniques and about the sort of society that is in existence at the time.

It is less easy to sympathize with opposition to the principle of changing our nature. Preserving the human race as it is will seem an acceptable option to all those who can watch the news on television and feel satisfied with the world. It will appeal to those who can talk to their children about the history of the twentieth century without wishing they could leave some things out.

When, in the rest of this book, the case for and against various changes is considered, the fact that they *are* changes will be treated as no objection at all.

FOR NEGATIVE BUT NOT POSITIVE ENGINEERING

Genesis Revisited: Can We Do Better Than God?

Michael Ruse

... Genetic ailments are bad things; it would be a morally good act to eliminate them; therefore, one should strive so to eliminate them. That is the framework within which discussion must take place. Hammering out details is incredibly difficult. But they are detail, nevertheless.[1]

In this paper, therefore, I want to look at far more hypothetical issues, where the right direction is not at all so obvious. I want to suppose that medical technology is very much more powerful than it is now and that we have virtually unlimited ability to recreate Homo sapiens in any genetic form or shape we desire. The question I want to ask is What can we—what should we—desire for our descendants, or (assuming that technology prefers to start anew rather than to tinker with the old) our replacements? ...

Bigger and Better Sensations?

... What, if anything, would be an improvement? Suppose a genetic fairy godmother did appear, prepared to wave her wand over any human feature and to grant any change requested. What changes could we ask for? What changes would it be sensible to ask for?

You may think this is all a bit silly. After all, what you really want is that everything be bigger and better. If we could raise everybody's IQ by twenty points and could make everyone a little more caring about neighbors, not to mention enemies, then humans would be far improved beings. Add a couple of wings and the potential to live for 10,000 years, and who knows what marvellous things we might be and do!

I am not sure that matters are quite this simple, as I will try to show. But first, we must ask about ... the organs of sensation and their products. *Prima facie,* the prospect of a little improvement here seems like a wonderful thing. We would all like the eyes of a hawk and the ears of a

---

[1] I say this despite the recent manifesto, designed by Jeremy Rifkin and signed by many clergymen, calling for a stop to all genetic interventions on humankind (Briggs 1983). Failure to avoid the agony of severe genetic disease—if one can—is a gross moral lapse.

bat, not to mention the x-ray visual powers of Superman. Or would we?

Consider the options. Minimally, we might hope to perfect the organs we have already. Next, we might hope to add powers that other organisms have but that we do not have. At most, we would desire altogether new powers, like those of Superman, or even powers that we do not even know or think of. I suspect, however, that satisfaction of any of these options would not bring happiness. Indeed, such satisfaction might well make us very uncomfortable.

Take the question of the organs we have already. I am sure that all baseball fans would love to have the power of their eyesight increased significantly, and I suppose there is nothing too much wrong with this—although how easy the game itself would be to play, given that everyone had fantastic eyesight, could be queried. But, super-strong hearing would be quite another thing. Imagine how hard it would be to concentrate if every crackle of paper were to sound like a clap of thunder or the roll of a drum! And a super-strong sense of smell would be downright disgustingly burdensome. Every time you entered a room, you would be greeted with a wave of armpits and feet. Pity the poor nonsmoker forced to sit next to a man with a pipe! No doubt, we would learn to discriminate; but, if the noise were really loud or the smell really strong, a great deal of brain "rewiring" might be needed before we could tolerate it.

Of course, the simple fact of the matter is that we do not need and cannot properly use a strong sense of smell. Contrast us with dogs, who can and do use such a sense. Their faces are close to the ground, and so they are positioned to use their noses efficiently. Furthermore, their territorial-cum-mating proclivities need this sense.

Male dogs have to check out for intruders on their territory, hence, the urinating against lampposts, to mark home ground. Males also have to sniff around the rears of other dogs, looking for rivals and for females in heat. Humans, however, just do not work that way. Males do not have to smell out receptive females. Indeed, it would be disastrous to human society, as we know it, if they did. Can you imagine if women came into heat?! (See Symons 1979, for related thoughts.)

In short, I am far from convinced that we need much-improved organs of sense, and analogous doubts spoil the prospect of developing new trends of organs of sense. . . .

You might argue that it is the new slant that counts, not the added information-gathering power. A rose smells good, quite apart from its visual beauty. Perhaps, then, the rose as chemical entity will be even more stunning. But, rose-lover though I am, I remain unmoved. How can I deny the joys of chemical information about roses, until I have sensed them? However, the new slant will only go so far. It is not as if any new sense is going to unlock mysteries more profound than dreamed of in our philosophies. An insect using pheromones avoids the same objects as a human using sight or touch. Any new sense is a different way of getting at the same world, not a way of getting at a whole new world.

In short, however efficient, a new sense's value is limited. If you doubt this, consider the relationship between the sense of sight and the sense of touch. Seen-circles and touched-circles are not the same, but they do not contradict each other or suggest that the world as revealed by the one sense is not the world as revealed by the other sense (Berkeley 1963; Turbayne 1962).

Finally, what about pretend senses? Unless someone can spell out in some way what they are supposed to do, they can hardly be of much concern, and they are certainly not things to strongly desire. Further, those pretend senses which often are proposed seem of dubious value. X-ray eyes will certainly help you if you cannot remember whether you packed your toothbrush. But do you want everyone in the room to know what color underwear you have on today? Or if indeed you have underwear on at all? Is life to be one long nude-beach party? Even the oft-desired ability to read thoughts would be burdensome. Can you imagine any relationship—even the most loving (especially the most loving)—without some degree of mental privacy?

I conclude that drastic changes in . . . our organs of sense would not at once lead to total happiness, and there are good reasons to think the reverse might be the case.

Analogous arguments apply fairly readily to . . . the feelings, the emotions, and their associated organs. Those of us subject to strong depressions or to desperate pain from cancer will surely cry for relief, and who could deny such cries? But this is far from saying that—all other things being equal—we want some emotions blocked right off or that we want other emotions strongly intensified. Pain certainly serves a vital purpose. I for one am far from eager to replace it with a light bulb in the middle of my forehead—a bulb which flashes on whenever there is something wrong with my body.

Conversely, think how devastating the emotion of love can be when it gets out of hand. Do we really want to spend our days as aging Romeos and Juliets, able to think of nothing but the sweet objects of our affections? I am reminded in this context of Cephalus's reply to Socrates about the joys of old age. "For instance, I remember someone asking Sophocles, the poet, whether he was still capable of enjoying a woman. 'Don't talk in that way,' he answered: 'I am only too glad to be free of all that; it is like escaping from bondage to a raging madman.' I thought that a good answer at the time, and I still think so: for certainly a great peace comes when age sets us free from passions of that sort" (Plato 1941, 5).

I hasten to add that I am not arguing for the deletion of sexual passions *per se*. Apart from the disastrous effects this would have on society, life without sex and love would be very drab. Do you really want to do philosophy all of the time? Nor am I arguing for drastic alteration of the passions. Radical feminists and others sometimes argue for the desirability of such a transformation, where one would take heterosexual passions and turn them into something androgynous, making for indifference as to the sex of one's partner. Frankly, I enjoy being a man and feeling sexual attractions towards women. Others, male and female, likewise enjoy sexual feelings. So why change them? (I am not denying the joys of homosexual attractions for those inclined that way. Nor am I saying that male and female feelings are identical, or that one should accept complacently every last aspect of today's male-female distribution of goods or power.[2])

Changing Regulative Principles

Let us move on now to . . . the ways in which we humans process and interpret the

---

[2] Some of the strongest supporters of my position would be conventional sex researchers, who have neither philosophical nor biological axes to grind. They point out that those who are most unhappy sexually are those with no firm sense of sexual identity. See Green (1974).

data of our senses and our emotions. They speak of what neo-Kantians call "regulative principles" and what sociobiologists have dubbed "epigenetic rules." . . .

I am sure there have been times for all of us when we have wished that we could more clearly appreciate basic principles of thinking about the world and about ourselves and our relations to others, but this is far from wanting wholesale change. In fact, it is hard to see what case could be made for such change.

Take as an example the kind of principle which informs our thinking about causality. When something happens, we look for a cause. "Things do not just happen!" We look for a uniformity between cause and effect. If you strike a match and it ignites on one occasion, then you expect it to ignite on other occasions. If it does not, then you want to know why.

Now, as I have pointed out, there are obvious biological advantages to thinking this way. The child that does not learn to fear the fire—the child that does not think that fire causes burning—simply is not going to survive long enough to reproduce. Hence, to speak quite bluntly: if we start tampering with the way in which we think causally, we can predict wholesale disaster in fairly short order. Hume may be right about there being no objective causality, but this is not to deny the selective advantage of thinking that there is (Quine 1969; Lorenz 1962). In other words, attempts to change the way we suppose causes to operate in the world seem downright foolish!

But, you might complain, we do not have to think causally—at least we are not forced to think in a conventional way. Quantum mechanics proves this (Nagel 1961). Perhaps this is so, but nothing I have said is affected. In everyday life we do have to think in a straightforward, causal fashion.

Just suppose some student claimed that the isomorphism between his answer and that of a friend was due to random, unpredictable factors! In any case, even in such subjects as quantum mechanics one is hardly discarding regulative principle or governed thought. You modify some claims, like causality, in order to save more basic ones, like the principle of noncontradiction (Hanson 1958).

Finally, you may object that my whole line of argument is circular. Trapped as I am within my selectively produced thought patterns, I simply cannot pronounce on it. Perhaps, if I could only know, life without causal thinking would be bliss. There is, I admit, something in this objection. It is true that, literally, I cannot conceive of a noncausal world; hence I can hardly argue for its undesirability! But I would also point out that, because something is inconceivable, this does not mean that it is a possible option—certainly not a possible reasonable option, which I should allow for at this moment (Ruse 1984). So I reaffirm that without causality, my claims about natural selection and everything else simply collapse into a meaningless morass. Life without causality is inconceivable; and that is that. It is certainly not something for which we should strive.

Similar arguments apply to the principles of moral thought. Even if it is conceivable to have a life without any moral perceptions whatsoever, it is hardly desirable. A human who has absolutely no moral feelings for his or her fellow humans is no more going to be able to function than a human who has no sense of causation. My own feeling is that, in an important sense, you cannot really conceive of human life without any morality. I doubt we could have such life, if everyone hated everyone else from the moment of conception.

Although he is no evolutionist and although indeed he thinks morality belongs to a sphere above the animal passions—a sphere of reason—I believe my point is the one Kant was trying to make when he justified the first version of the Categorical Imperative: "Act only according to that maxim by which you can at the same time will that it should become a universal law."[3] Breaking with the imperative leads to what Kant calls "contradictions"—these are not logical contradictions, but they do point to the collapse of society and to personal ill-effects from the break.

Suppose a man refuses to repay a loan and says to himself that he will always refuse.

> He changes the pretension of self-love into a universal law and then puts the question: How would it be if my maxim became a universal law? He immediately sees that it could never hold as a universal law of nature and be consistent with itself; rather it must necessarily contradict itself. For the universality of a law which says that anyone who believes himself to be in need could promise what he pleased with the intention of not fulfilling it would make the promise itself and the end to be accomplished by it impossible; no one would believe what was promised to him but would only laugh at any such assertion as vain pretense (Kant 1959, 40).

I endorse Kant's argument, but I would give it an evolutionary interpretation. If you do not cooperate with your fellows, then you will be less well off than if you do (Trivers 1971). For this reason, I cannot imagine why one would want to change our moral awareness in any significant way. (I have argued in an earlier section that perhaps our moral awareness is not perfect—as is so often the case with the products of evolution—and that sometimes it fails as in the case of the individual/group conflicts. I am certainly not arguing against fine tuning of the products by evolution, here or elsewhere, although I am not quite sure what form the fine tuning would take in this case.)

Changing Abilities

Finally, let us turn to . . . categories which cover humans as beings able to put their thoughts and principles into action, both mentally and physically. Even here, I am doubtful about the benefits of significant changes from the present state. Take the . . . development of systems of pure thought like mathematics and science and then the applications of these systems as technology.

A priori, it is attractive to think of us all being mathematical superstars, but is it not all going to be a bit self-defeating? Consider, analogously, the genius of Wolfgang Mozart. Think of the sheer, undiluted pleasure that that man has brought to so many people. What if each and every one of us were busily churning out forty-one symphonies, an opera of the greatness of *Don Giovanni*, and four exquisite gems of horn concerti? Would the work of each and every one of us have equal value and give equal pleasure, as Mozart achieves? The mind boggles at the thought of the Canadian Opera Company trying to put on twenty-five million different operas—one for each man, woman, and child in the country. Then, if we each follow up our first success with our own equivalent of *The Magic Flute* . . . !!

The sad truth is that the worth of human accomplishments is comparative. It is far from obvious that, if we were all that much brighter and more adept, we would be that

---

[3] Supposedly, this version is equivalent to a second version, making individual rights supreme: "Act so that you treat humanity, whether in your own person or in that of another, always as an end and never as a means only" (Kant 1959, 170).

much better off. This is not a neo-Luddite cry against science and technology. I am all in favor of both. It is to suggest that twice as much of a good thing is not necessarily twice as good a thing—whatever elementary economics texts may say.

Perhaps you accept my position about science and technology . . . but are loath to accept it for the application of morality. . . . After all, if we were all a lot more moral, this would be a much better world. If we felt the same sentiments of love for the Russians (and they for us) as we do for our own family and if we were prepared to take the same amount of effort and to make the same sacrifices for strangers as for friends, then everyone would be better off—those in the West and those in the East.

Heretical though it may sound, I am inclined to think that a world peopled by Mother Teresas would be no better than a world peopled by Mozarts. Morally, the hunger of any one child sets up the same obligations as the hunger of any other child. But could any one of us function if we felt the same pangs and urge to action about every child in Africa as we do about our own children?

I do not want to appear deliberately callous. I am not saying we have no obligations to the starving poor. We do! I am not saying Mother Teresa is not a wonderful model. Of course she is—as was Mozart! I am simply pointing out that, if we all worried equally about every individual, we would have a collective nervous breakdown long before we did any good. It is far better to be able to work on helping a few than to pine after helping all.

In this context, I am reminded how, in the movie *Gandhi*, the Mahatma jokes that his friends say that they cannot afford the expense of keeping him in poverty! This is my point. You can have a saint or two, if the rest of us are "sinners"; but if everyone aspires to sainthood, giving up all to serve the poor, everything falls apart.[4]

So, . . . here you have my conclusion—a conclusion which, I must confess, somewhat surprised me at first—that God did not do such a bad job after all! Before we plunge headlong into massive programs of genetic redesign, perhaps we should consider where we stand today. It may just be that it is not such a bad place to stand.

Berkeley, G. 1963. *Works on Vision*. Indianapolis, Ind.: Library of Liberal Arts.

Hanson, N. R. 1958. *Patterns of Discovery*. Cambridge: Cambridge Univ. Press.

Kant, Immanuel. 1959. *Foundations of the Metaphysics of Morals*. Trans. L. W. Beck. Indianapolis, Ind.: Bobbs-Merrill.

Lorenz, Karl. 1962. "Kant's Doctrine of the A Priori in the Light of Contemporary Biology." *General Systems* 7:23–25.

Nagel, E. 1961. *The Structure of Science*. New York: Harcourt, Brace & World.

Plato. 1941. *The Republic*. Trans. F. M. Cornford. Oxford: Oxford Univ. Press.

Quine, W. V. O. 1969. "Natural Kinds." In *Ontological Relativity and Other Essays*. New York: Columbia Univ. Press.

Ruse, Michael. 1984. "Is Rape Wrong on Andromeda: Philosophical Reflections on Extra-Terrestrial Life." In *The Search for Extra-Terrestrial Intelligence*, ed. E. Regis. New York: Cambridge Univ. Press.

Symons, D. 1979. *The Evolution of Human Sexuality*. New York: Oxford Univ. Press.

Trivers, R. 1971. "The Evolution of Reciprocal Altruism." *Quarterly Review of Biology* 46:35–57.

Turbayne, C. M. 1962. *The Myth of Metaphor*. New Haven: Yale Univ. Press.

---

[4] I certainly do not want to defend priestly celibacy, but it is surely the case that Mother Teresa functions as effectively as she does in part because she has no family obligations. You cannot spend all day helping the poor in Calcutta if you have small children at home—nor should you.

Questions for Further Reflection

1. We have examined various arguments for and against genetically engineering people, but what should we say about engineering nonhuman animals? Combine your reflections about animal rights with your conclusions about engineering people into a coherent view about engineering life in general.
2. Suppose it becomes possible to engineer people's values in such a way as to make them happily accept any task assigned them. What, if any, would be the objections to creating people who would happily perform tasks that no one else in society wanted to perform? (Even parents might conceivably do something like this: Perhaps they want to ensure that their children will happily enter the family business, for example.)
3. Future children cannot now consent to any engineering that affects their genetic makeup. Does it follow that we may not engineer them?
4. Suppose that in the future parents are subject to criminal prosecution if they opt to avoid negative engineering and knowingly produce a child with a glaring defect. *Would* such parents have done something morally objectionable? *Should* they be prosecuted?
5. Recall that in an earlier chapter, LaFollette argued that parents should be licensed. How should genetic policy fit into a licensing proposal?
6. Suppose that a foreign country creates a future generation of aggressive, bright, and violent people. Should this concern prompt our country to respond in kind? In thinking through your answer, consider the arguments people give in connection with nuclear disarmament.

Further Readings

Brooks, D. H. M. "Dogs and Slaves: Genetics, Exploitation and Morality." *Proceedings of the Aristotelian Society* 88 (1987–1988). Gives a lively discussion of difficult moral issues that arise if the values of people are engineered.

Fletcher, John, and W. French Anderson. "Germ-Line Gene Therapy: A New Stage of Debate." *Law, Medicine and Health Care* 20 (1992): 26–39. Anderson is one of the pioneers in gene therapy.

Glover, Jonathan, et al. *Ethics of New Reproductive Technologies: The Glover Report to the European Commission.* DeKalb: Northern Illinois University Press, 1989. Makes recommendations concerning several reproductive technologies, including genetic engineering.

Lamb, David, Teifon Davies, and Marie Roberts, eds. *Explorations in Medicine.* Avebury and Brookfield: 1987. Contains several helpful discussions; for example, George Agich, in "Justice and Genetic Engineering," uses the issue of genetic engineering to explore gaps in Rawls's theory of justice.

Lappe, Marc. *Broken Code: The Exploitation of DNA.* San Francisco: Sierra Club Books, 1984. A helpful, single-author discussion of the issue.

Chapter 17

ABORTION

Few moral issues are as controversial and emotionally argued as that of the permissibility of abortion. Opponents of abortion claim that abortion is murder and that the current widespread practice of abortion is a tragedy on the same scale as that of the Holocaust. Defenders of abortion rights, on the other hand, insist that women have a fundamental right to determine what happens to their bodies and that abortion can be an important tool in controlling one's life.

In a landmark ruling in 1973, the United States Supreme Court in *Roe v. Wade* overturned a Texas anti-abortion statute. Dividing pregnancy into three twelve-week periods, or "trimesters," the Court held that states cannot restrict a woman's right to abortion in the first trimester and, in the second trimester, can restrict abortion only to protect the woman's health; in the third trimester, abortions can be banned except where they are necessary for health reasons. In the years since this decision, abortions have become quite common. According to data from the Centers for Disease Control, there are approximately 1.3 million abortions per year, and approximately 32 abortions for every 100 live births.[1] In 1989, in *William L. Webster v. Reproductive Health Services,* the Supreme Court upheld the constitutionality of a Missouri law prohibiting the use of public facilities or employees to perform abortions. Although this decision did not overturn *Roe v. Wade,* it was widely seen as suggesting that the Court might in the future overturn the earlier decision. However, in a 1992 decision, *Planned Parenthood v. Casey,* the Court again reaffirmed *Roe* in a 5–4 decision, while also upholding a number of Pennsylvania restrictions on the availability of abortions, including a requirement that a minor seeking an abortion obtain the consent of one parent.

The abortion controversy has at its center two separate but related moral issues: when, if ever, it is morally permissible for a pregnant woman to have her fetus aborted, and whether states should be able to prohibit abortions. Presumably, if there is no moral objection to certain abortions, the state should not intervene to prevent them. However, even if abortion is always a moral mistake, it may be that the state should not intervene. Many prominent politicians (such as former Governor Mario Cuomo of New York) have held that, while they personally oppose abortion, they believe that the choice of whether or not to have one should be available to mothers. Although

---

[1] Centers for Disease Control, *Morbidity and Mortality Weekly Report*, vol. 45, nos. 51 & 52 (January 3, 1997). The data are as of 1994.

much of the public uproar over abortion concerns the issue of what the state ought or ought not to do to regulate or prevent abortions, most of the discussion in this chapter concerns the question of the morality of abortion itself.

The Status of the Fetus

The issue that receives the most attention in popular discussions of abortion concerns whether the unborn child is a person or not. In thinking about the issue, it is helpful to keep in mind some of the biological facts about the development of the unborn child. At the earliest stage, the ovum and spermatozoa come together to produce a *single-cell zygote*. The zygote begins developing as it moves through the Fallopian tube to the uterus. After implantation in the uterus, by the end of the second week, the unborn human is called an *embryo*. The embryonic stage lasts until the eighth week, when brain activity becomes detectable. In careful usage, the term *fetus* is reserved for the unborn human from the eighth week until birth,[2] but the term is sometimes used more broadly to refer to any prenatal stage after conception. Because it is useful to have such a term, we use *fetus* in the broader sense in this discussion.

Some striking facts about very early stages of development are worth noting.[3] It is not clearly correct to identify a fertilized egg or its early products as an individual organism until at least after the second week.

In mice, two four-cell embryos can *fuse* to form a single individual. In humans, at the eight-cell stage, cells can be added or deleted, and a single, normal individual will still result. After embedding in the uterus wall, an embryo can still undergo twinning, so even at this stage, it is indefinite *how many* individuals the embryo is.

Those who hold that abortion is never or seldom permissible often do so on the basis of the claim that the fetus is a person and, as such, has the rights a person has. In particular, it is claimed, the fetus has a right to life. On the other hand, those who defend a woman's right to choose abortion sometimes do so on the basis of the claim that the fetus is *not* yet a person.

It is important to distinguish two issues that are often conflated. The important question is sometimes taken to be whether the unborn child is a *human being*. It can then seem that a moral issue can be settled by an empirical fact, because whether the fetus is human seems an empirical matter. It seems obvious that the fetus *is* a human being, a member of the species *Homo sapiens*; after all, it has human genetic material. However, the fact that the fetus is a member of the same species as we are will settle no moral issues. Human corpses are clearly human but do not have the same rights people do. The genuinely important question is not whether the fetus is human but whether it is a *person*; only if the fetus is a person do we have the same sort of obligations toward it as we have toward other people.

It has become conventional to distinguish among three broad views on the issue of whether the fetus is a person. The *conservative* view holds that the fetus is a person from the moment of conception. The *liberal* view is that one is not a person until after birth, so that at no point during the pregnancy is the fetus a person, the *moderate* view is that the fetus gradually becomes

---

[2]This terminology is standard and can be found, for example, in Joel Feinberg, "Introduction," in Feinberg, ed., *The Problem of Abortion*, second edition (Belmont, CA: Wadsworth, 1984), 2–3.

[3]The biological information in this paragraph is from Clifford Grobstein, "Hereditary Constitution and Individual Life." *Society* 19 (1982): 54–58.

a person as it develops, so that while it is not a person at conception, by the time of birth it is.

Each view has its difficulties. Each of the two extreme views, the conservative view and the liberal view, seems to give rise by means of a slippery slope to an implausible conclusion. The conservative must hold that even a one-celled zygote is a person, even though, as Joel Feinberg notes, it has "no face, no limbs, no organs, no brain, no nervous system, no consciousness, no rationality, no concepts—nothing at all that we would recognize as belonging to an actual person, even though it is undeniably a potential person."[4] The liberal must hold that even immediately before birth, the fetus is not a person; given that being born does not change the fetus in any very interesting way, the liberal is in danger of being forced to say that even young babies are not people. The implausibility of these extreme views might make us inclined to favor the moderate view, but it has its difficulties as well; in particular, there seems to be no point in the development of the fetus that has much plausibility as a dividing line between personhood and nonpersonhood.

Other Issues

Although the issue of whether the fetus is a person is often taken to be the key issue in the abortion debate, others may be equally important. R. M. Hare argues that it is useless to appeal to the personhood of the fetus to solve the moral problem of whether abortion is permissible because being a person in the relevant sense is *constituted by* one's possession of certain rights: To try to settle the issue of whether the fetus has a right to life by determining whether it is a person is to argue in a circle. Hare therefore offers an argument against abortion that does not appeal to whether the fetus is a person. He argues on Kantian grounds that, because each of us is glad not to have been aborted, we ought, in order to be consistent, to avoid aborting others.

Judith Thomson circumvents the issue of whether the fetus is a person in another way. She argues that, even if we suppose that the fetus is a person, the impermissibility of abortion does not follow. Even if we suppose that the fetus has a right to life, we must balance that right against other relevant rights. For example, the woman presumably also has a right to life, and so in cases in which her life is threatened by pregnancy, it may be permissible for her to abort the fetus in self-defense. But Thomson does not stop here. Using a series of elaborate and intriguing (if far-fetched) examples, she argues further that a person's right to determine what happens in and to her body may override another person's right to life, so that the fetus's right to life, if there is such a right, does not entail that it has a right to use the woman's body for food and shelter. Although it would be kinder to allow the fetus to continue developing, in at least some cases this would be an act of good Samaritanism rather than something one is morally required to do.

---

[4]Feinberg, p. 4.

A KANTIAN CRITIQUE OF ABORTION

A Kantian Approach to Abortion

R. M. Hare

The position of somebody wondering whether to have an abortion is usually too wretched for it to be decent for a philosopher to try to make her decision depend on the definitions of words that could in principle have several different definitions.[1] So let us start by putting to rest the question "Is the foetus a person?", which has occupied so many pages in discussions of this problem. It leads straight to a dead end, and we would best avoid it. We know what a foetus is, in the sense that if anybody were to ask whether an object before us or even inside us was a human foetus, there would be no difficulty in principle in determining whether it was. For the same sort of reason, we know how to determine some of the properties the foetus has. We know, for example, that it has the *potentiality* of becoming a human adult—that is, that *if* the pregnancy comes to term, it will have turned into a baby, and if the baby survives it will turn into an adult more or less like us.

Copyright 1989 by R. M. Hare
From *Social Theory and Practice* Vol. 15, No. 1 (Spring 1989).

[1] I have tried in this paper to improve the argument in my "Abortion and the Golden Rule", *Philosophy and Public Affairs* 4 (1975): 20–22: German translation in A. Leist, ed., *Um Leben und Tod*, forthcoming. There are, however, some important points in that earlier paper which are not here repeated.

There are some things of the same ordinary sort about which we cannot be so certain, but which do not present great problems. For example, we do not know for certain whether foetuses, at any rate at a late stage of pregnancy, may not have some rudimentary conscious experiences, including experiences of suffering. It is fairly certain that at earlier stages, before their nervous systems have become at all developed, they do not have such experiences. So let us avoid this question by supposing, either that the abortion in question would be at such an early stage of pregnancy, or, if later, that it could be done without causing pain to the foetus (for example, by anaesthesia).

As I said, there seems to be no difficulty in principle in deciding *these* facts about the foetus. They are facts which may be, and I think are, morally relevant when we are deciding what it is all right to do to the foetus. But what about the question whether the foetus is a *person*? How would we answer that? We have to see that it is not the same kind of question at all as the question "Will the foetus, if the pregnancy continues and the child survives, turn into a human adult like us, or into, say, a horse?" The reason is that it is uncertain what we *mean* by "person", whereas it is not uncertain what we mean by "horse", or "human adult". We all know how to tell whether something is a horse or a human adult. But we do not know how to tell whether the foetus is a person. To that extent the term "person" is unclear.

The main trouble is that "person", and other words like "human being" which have been used in this dispute, all have several different meanings. There is a clear sense in which a foetus is *not* a person. It is altogether too different from the things which we instantly recognize as people. If the notice in the elevator says it may not carry more than six persons, a pregnant woman is still allowed to have five adult companions in the elevator.

At the opposite extreme, there is a sense in which it is a necessary condition for something's being called a person that it has the rights which persons have, or that the duties are owed to it which we owe to persons. Obviously, if the foetus were a person in that sense, it would have the rights that other persons have, and to kill it would be murder. But for that very reason, if having the rights is a qualification for being called a person, then we cannot know whether the foetus is a person without *first* deciding whether the foetus has the rights. But that was the question we started with. So it is obviously no use trying to settle that question by asking whether the foetus is a person; we shan't know whether it is, in the required sense, until we have already decided the question about its rights.

There are going to be a lot of senses of "person" besides these, or in between these, and there will not be room even to list them all. It should be clear already that most of the disputes about this allegedly crucial question of whether the foetus is a person are going to be a waste of time and can never get anywhere.

How do people get into this impasse? The cause is this: they have some excellent firm principles about murder and about liberty, and in this difficult case of abortion it looks as if the principles conflict. If one forbids the abortion, one infringes the liberty of the mother; if one allows it, one is allowing murder. So people take sides for one principle or the other, call themselves "pro-life" or "pro-choice", and stop thinking. They even start bombing one another.

We start with these good firm simple principles about life and liberty (though we do not know how to formulate them clearly and explicitly), and then they come into conflict. If we terminate a pregnancy, we are offending against the principle requiring us to preserve life. If we stop women terminating their pregnancies, we are offending against the other principle requiring us to preserve liberty or choice. The right thing to do in this predicament is to think some more and try to formulate the principles exactly and apply them to this case, and see whether we can find forms of them that do *not* conflict with each other. That indeed is what people are trying to do when they argue about whether the foetus is a person. For if there were a sense in which the foetus is *not* a person, the conflict might be resolved; in killing the foetus, one would not be committing a murder, because killing is not murder unless it is the killing of people. And so we could observe the principle about liberty by letting the foetus be killed, without breaking the principle about murder.

As we saw, this manoeuvre does not do any good, because the word "person" is indeterminate; taken one way, we can say that it is all right to kill the foetus because it is not a person (in the sense of occupying one person's place in the elevator); but the side that does not think the foetus ought to be killed was not using the word in that sense. It was using it in the sense in which to be a person is to be a possessor of the rights that ordinary persons have. And we are not in a position to say whether the foetus is a person in *that* sense. This is a moral, not a factual question, and we cannot answer it until we have settled the prior question of whether we have the duties to the foetus that we have to ordinary adults, that is, whether the foetus has the same rights as adults have.

So what ought we to do, instead of disputing endlessly about whether the foetus is a person? My advice is that we forget about the word "person", and ask instead about the properties of the foetus that might be reasons why we ought not to kill it—properties in the ordinary factual sense in which we can *determine* whether or not it has them. It may be that the word "person" stands for some combination of these properties, or ambiguously for more than one possible set of them. In that case, if we can isolate a set of ordinary properties of the foetus which together constitute a reason why we ought not to let it be killed, we might sum up this set of properties by saying that the foetus is a person. But, for the reasons I have given, we should be able to do this only *after* first answering the moral question. The word "person" would not have helped in the argument; it would at most be a convenient way of summarizing its conclusion. The real work would have been done in identifying the ordinary properties of the foetus that made us want to say (if that was what we did want to say) that it ought not to be killed. The hard part of the moral thinking is that involved in this identification of the ordinary properties which are the reasons for or against killing the foetus.

What then are these ordinary properties? One is that, if the foetus suffered while being killed, then that would be *a* reason for not inflicting this suffering on it, though there could be reasons on the other side. But we can ignore this property if we confine ourselves, as I have proposed, to cases where we can be sure it will not suffer.

What other properties of the foetus, besides its capacity for suffering which we have now discounted, could give us reasons for not killing it? I cannot think of any besides the foetus's potentiality, already mentioned, of turning into someone like us. Here is an example that will illustrate why I cannot think of any. Suppose that in the case of a given pregnancy we can be absolutely certain that for reasons beyond anybody's control the foetus will not survive. It has, say, some recognizable disease from which foetuses never recover. Let us suppose additionally that, if we did kill the foetus, we could do so painlessly, say by using an anaesthetic. In such a case is there any reason for not killing the foetus if there are other grounds for killing it (say the health of the mother)? This case illustrates rather well what is wrong with what I shall call the absolutist pro-life position. It also illustrates the difference between foetuses and ordinary human persons. In the case of an ordinary person who you were certain would die in a month, there *would* be reasons for not killing that person. It would disappoint hopes of what he (or she) might have done in the remaining month; the process of killing might cause fear; it might cause sorrow to others; the terminally ill patient might be deprived of the chance of ordering his financial affairs for the benefit of his family, or even reconciling himself and them to his impending death. There could be reasons, all the same, on the other side, such as the suffering he would undergo if his life were prolonged. None of these reasons applies to the foetus. The foetus does not have *now*, at the present moment, properties which are reasons for not killing it, given that it will die in any case before it acquires those properties which ordinary human adults and even children have, and which are our reasons for not killing *them*. A foetus before it has achieved sentience does not *currently* possess any properties that could be morally relevant to its treatment and which are not possessed equally by oysters and earthworms.

If we are to find reasons for not killing the foetus, we must look for some properties which it does not have now, but which it *will* have later if it survives. Philosophers call these *potential* properties, and argue about whether the potentiality that the foetus has of turning into someone like us is morally relevant to what we may or may not do to the foetus now. The case that I have just described shows that defenders of the foetus, if they are going to make good their defence, have nothing else that they can rely on *except* the foetus's potentiality. But I shall be arguing in a moment, against the views of many philosophers like Michael Tooley,[2] that potentiality does provide a powerful weapon with which to defend the foetus *in normal cases*.

In order to set up this argument I shall have to do a little ethical theory, though I will try to make as light work of it as I can. The ethical theory I am going to use is of a more or less Kantian sort.[3] I am also going, for reasons which I hope will become clear in a moment, to make a time-switch into the past. Suppose that it is not this woman now who is deciding whether or not to have an abortion, but some other woman in the past. Suppose, for example, it was my own mother deciding whether or not to terminate the pregnancy which actually resulted in *me*. In that case, am I going to say that it is morally quite all right for her to have an abortion?

Please note that the question is *not* "What *would* I say if I were speaking to her at that time?" Nor is it "What *would* I say now if I did not exist?" I have deliberately formulated the question in such a way as to avoid the difficulties with those other questions. The question is, "What *do* I (a presently existing person) now say about this past situation?"

I will draw attention to an obvious reason why I might not like to say that it was all right for her to have an abortion. It is a reason which might be outweighed by other reasons, but it is at least *a* reason. The reason is that if she had had an abortion, I would not now have existed. Let us suppose that I am able to reach back in time and give instructions to my mother as to what she should do. Suppose, even, that she is able to ask me questions about what she ought to do. In order to get into a position in which I can communicate with her at that time, I shall have to penetrate some noumenal world outside time (this is really getting very Kantian) and have access to her in that past time. This of course raises deep philosophical problems, into which I am not going to go. But just suppose I can do it. What shall I say to her?

I am sure I shall not say "Carry on, have the abortion; it's all the same to me." Because my existence now is valuable to me, I shall not, other things being equal, will (to use another Kantian term) that she should have the abortion, thereby depriving me of the possibility of existence. I value my existence, not for its own sake, but for the sake of the nice things that happen to me, which couldn't happen if I did not exist. There is a sentence in the Anglican Prayer Book in

---

[2]M. Tooley, "Abortion and Infanticide", *Philosophy and Public Affairs* 2 (1972): 37–65, revised in Joel Feinberg, ed., *The Problem of Abortion* (Belmont, Calif.: Wadsworth, 1973).

[3]The theory can also be put into a utilitarian form, and I have often so put it. The idea that Kantianism and utilitarianism are irreconcilable is the result of attempts by modern deontologists to borrow Kant's authority for their own intuitionist positions; but they seldom document their claims about Kant, and it could in fact be shown that a properly formulated utilitarianism and a properly formulated Kantianism need not conflict. For hints, see references to Kant in index to my *Moral Thinking* (Oxford: Oxford University Press, 1981), and my "Punishment and Retributive Justice," *Philosophical Topics* 14 (1986): 219; reprinted in my *Essays on Political Morality* (Oxford University Press, 1989) pp. 211–15.

which we thank God for our creation, preservation, and all the blessings of this life.[4] If there were no blessings but only curses, then we could not thank him for our creation either; but he has been good enough to arrange things otherwise for most of us. That we can thank him for our creation does not show that mere existence in itself is a good; but it does show that it is a good at least as a means to the other good things that those who exist can have. Therefore, faced with the possibility of either existing now or not existing now, the normally happy person will tell his mother not to have the abortion. And therefore, all things being equal (if, for example, *she* is not going to die if the pregnancy is not terminated), he will say that she ought not to have it.

I put the whole dialogue in the past, because of an argument which is sometimes used by philosophers who write about this question. They say that *potential* people or *merely* possible people do not have any rights, and we cannot have any duties to them. But in the case I described we were talking about an actual person, namely myself. I am asking myself, as an actual person, to prescribe what ought to have been done at a time in the past when my mother was contemplating having an abortion. Potential people do not come into this argument.

It is a part of ethical theory that is accepted by almost all moral philosophers, however, that if one makes a moral judgement about any case or situation, one must, to be consistent, make the same moral judgement about any other case which resembles it in all its non-moral particulars. For example, if it is all right for one person to do something (call him A), it must be all right for anybody else to do the same thing in exactly the same situation. By "the same situation", I mean the same in all respects, and these include the properties of the people in it. So I am not saying that if it is all right for A to tickle B when B likes being tickled, it must be all right for B to tickle A who hates being tickled. What I am saying is that if the circumstances and all the properties, including the wishes, of the people are the same, the moral judgement has to be the same.

In applying this theoretical doctrine, which, as I said, is accepted by nearly all moral philosophers, at least all who understand what the doctrine is (some have denied it through *not* understanding it) we have to apply it to hypothetical cases as well as to actual ones. If it *was* wrong for my mother to have an abortion, then it *would be* wrong for any other mother to have an abortion in exactly the same circumstances, and therefore would now be wrong for the woman we started with to have an abortion, if the circumstances were the same. And this, in general, is the prima facie case for being against abortion, as most of us are *in general.* By that I mean that most of us, if asked whether it just does not matter in the least whether people have abortions or not, would say that we think that in most cases it does matter; most pregnancies ought to be allowed to continue; those who want to legalize abortion want to do so because that will leave the decision to the individuals concerned in *special* cases where there are strong grounds for termination. Nobody thinks that *no* abortions matter, except those who do not care whether the human race survives or not, or who even want it not to survive.

The reason why most of us think that *all things being equal* pregnancies should not be terminated, is that we think that on the whole they are likely to result in people being born who will in the course of their lives be glad to have been born. There is of

---

[4]*Book of Common Prayer* (old and new versions), the General Thanksgiving.

course a problem about having too many people: if there were so many people, and the results of over-population made them so unhappy, that they wished they had not been born, that would be different; but I am assuming that this is not the case yet. I shall be returning to this point.

Reverting for a moment, however, to the dialogue between myself in the present and my mother in the past, there is one other thing that I *might* think I could say. We have considered two things I might say, namely "Do not have the abortion" and "You ought to have the abortion." What I said was that I would not say "You ought to have the abortion", because this would be a prescription to her to have the abortion, and I do not want that. So, if those were the only two things I could say, I would choose the first, "Do not have the abortion", and rule out the second "You ought to have the abortion." But a third thing I might say is "I do not say you ought to have an abortion; but I do not claim, either, that you ought not to have it; of course I want you not to have it, because otherwise I shall not exist; so I still go on saying, so far as I am concerned 'Do not have it.' But if you ask me whether it is the case, morally speaking, that you ought not to have it, I would not go so far as that. You will not be doing wrong if you have it, but please do not."

This possibility, though important, raises difficulties which are really too great for me to deal with here. If I am trying to give my mother positive moral guidance, I shall be confined to the two answers, "You ought" and "You ought not"; and, if this is so then, because I prefer to be existing now, I shall not say "You ought", and shall therefore have to say "You ought not."[5]

There is, then, a reason for accepting the *general* principle which forbids abortions in ordinary cases. The question is, then, whether we ought to allow any exceptions to this principle, and whether they ought to extend further than the exceptions that can be made to the principle that we should not kill adults. Let us ask what are the reasons for having the latter principle. We have looked at some of them already. Nearly all of us want not to be killed, and want not to live in fear of being killed. So, when faced with a choice between a universal prohibition on killing people and a universal license to kill them, we would choose the former. But most of us do not want to have to choose between these stark alternatives; we want to make *some* exceptions to the principle forbidding killing people, of which killing in self-defence is an obvious one, and killing in war or as a penalty for murder are more controversial. If we are speaking, as we are, of a general principle to be inculcated in children when we bring them up, and protected by the law, the principle has to be fairly simple and cannot contain too many complicated exceptions. So we allow killing in self-defence and perhaps in these other cases, but try to keep the prohibition as simple as we can. This is in the interests of workability.

It is sometimes said that if one allows exceptions to such simple principles one will be inserting the thin end of a wedge, or starting down a slippery slope. This is indeed sometimes the case: but sometimes it is not. Whether it is will depend on whether there is a clear stopping-place on the slope where we can dig in our heels—and sometimes there is. When it was decided in the United States to allow cars to turn right at a red light after stopping, did anybody say "You are starting down a slippery slope: if you let people turn right on a red light, then you will have breached the absolute ban on crossing a red light, and

---

[5] I deal at length with this problem in my *Moral Thinking*, pp. 182 ff.

people will soon begin crossing it when they want to go straight ahead or turn left."? People realized that it was quite easy to distinguish the cases in which it was now to be legal to cross the red light from those in which it was still to be forbidden. So the slope was not slippery.

Similarly, nobody says that we ought to forbid killing *even* in self-defence because if you allow that, people will start killing for other reasons too. In this case, there is a real difficulty in deciding what counts as self-defence, and no doubt there are volumes of cases in the criminal law in which this has had to be sorted out. But even so (even though, that is, the slope is a little bit slippery) we do allow killing in self-defence, and the slope has not in practice proved *too* slippery.

In principle, we could do the same for abortion. The argument is sometimes used that if we allow the killing of foetuses, people will soon be killing adults *ad lib*. I cannot see much force in this argument. In many countries the killing of foetuses has been legalized under certain conditions, and in others it has never been illegal. I know of no evidence that this has led to a greater incidence of ordinary murder.

Although the slope from killing foetuses to killing adults is not slippery, there *is* a slippery slope from killing foetuses under certain conditions to killing them under other conditions. This is because it is rather difficult to delimit precisely in law the conditions under which abortion is allowable. Expressions like "congenital defect" and "the health of the mother" are capable of being stretched. Whether we think it is dangerous that this slope is slippery, however, will depend on what view we take about the general question of what abortions should be allowed, and who should make the decision. For example, *if* we took the view that abortion should be allowed freely and the mother should decide, we should not mind the law being stretched in this way. I do not myself take so extreme a view; but I do not think it bad that the law has been stretched a bit, as it has been in different ways in different countries.

But at any rate the slope from killing foetuses to killing adults is not slippery. So we can reasonably ask whether it would be all right to allow an exception, in the case of foetuses, to the general ban on killing. How would we decide such a question? The general ban on killing has a point, as we saw earlier, namely that people want not to be killed. But does this point extend to foetuses? *They* do not want to be killed.

I have argued that most people prefer not *to have been* killed when they were foetuses; and that this gives us a general reason for having a principle that we ought not to kill foetuses. But here we have to be rather careful. The general preference for existence over non-existence does not justify the principle that we ought to bring into existence all the people we *could* bring into existence. If we tried to do that, there would obviously be too many people, and perhaps a majority of those people would wish that we had *not* brought them into existence, thus destroying the premiss of our argument. So evidently any principle that we are likely to accept is going to allow some limitation of the population, if only by the use of the methods approved by the Pope.

However we limit the population, it is going to result in some people not being born who *could* have been born. We have to ask next, "Is there any reason for giving precedence to some of these people over others?" Notice that the argument used earlier in defence of the foetus does not provide any such reason. Suppose that if this woman does not have a baby now she will have one in a year's time, but that she will not have that other baby if she has one now. Each of these people, if born, will, we hope, have reason to be thankful that he or she was born; but, other things being equal, neither will have any *more* reasons for being thankful than the other has. So, given that we are going to limit the population, does it make any difference *which* of the possible people is born, and which gets excluded? The argument used so far does not provide any reason for saying that it makes a difference.

There are certainly factors which could make a difference. If, for example, the mother is not at present married but hopes to be soon, this might mean that the present foetus, if born, will not have such a good start in life as the other would. Or, to take a case which points in the opposite direction: if the mother is thirty-five years old, there is a reason for having a child in the next five years. The reason is that if she postpones having it until she is forty, the chance of the child being born with Down's syndrome is greater. So there can be reasons for choosing to have a child later rather than now, or the reverse. But we have so far not been able to discover any general reason for giving precedence to the child that this foetus would turn into over other possible future children, given that one or another of them is going to be born.

Are there any strong reasons for preferring the child that this foetus would turn into? The feeling many people have that it should have precedence may be due to a false analogy between foetuses and adults. Certainly it would be wrong to kill an adult in order to replace him or her with some other person who might be born. This is because the existing adult has desires (above all the desire to live) which will be frustrated if he is killed. That is the reason why we have the general ban on killing adults. And this applies even to young children. Whether it applies to neonates, who do not have the desire to live, is a controversial question which there is no room to discuss here. It certainly applies to children from a very early age. But it clearly does not apply to foetuses; so at any rate *that* reason for saying that foetuses ought not to be killed lacks force.

At this point it will be claimed that the argument so far provides no reason for forbidding abortions that does not apply equally to contraception or even to abstinence. I think that this is right. So far we have no such reason. Perhaps reasons can be found, but they are relatively weak ones. Abortion is a more tricky procedure medically than contraception. But there are contraceptive methods which are really abortifacients, because, when used before or during copulation, they kill the zygote (perhaps by preventing implantation) after it has been formed. There is no clear reason for distinguishing such methods from the kind which prevents the formation of zygotes. Again, the feeling that there is a difference is due to a false analogy.

There is also the consideration that normally the foetus attracts feelings of affection on the part of the mother and perhaps others—feelings which do not yet attach to a possible future child that she might have. To kill the foetus, even if the mother herself desires this all things considered, is bound to wound those feelings. She might feel that it would have been better to have used contraception.

There is also what might be called the "bird in the hand" argument. The foetus is *there*, and will turn into an adult if it survives; future conceptions and births are more problematical. Given, however, that there is likely to be a child that will be born, if not to this family, then to some other family, and so occupy the place in the demography that this child would occupy, that does not seem a very strong argument.

If, as already argued, abortions are in general wrong, but allowable in particular cases, what such exceptions ought the law to allow, and who should have the task of deciding when to perform an abortion? The general principle is that, if there are interests affected by a decision, then, since we have to treat people as ends, those interests should be protected impartially; and this is most likely to happen if those who have the interests have a say in the decision, or, if they are not in a position to have a say, are in some way represented, and if the greater interests have the greater say. This is likely to result in the maximal and impartial protection of the interests. Those who like to speak about rights (and I see no harm in that) can speak equally well of the protection of their rights. But interests will do for the present argument.

Obviously the mother has a very great interest in the outcome. That is the justification for the claim that the mother ought to have the only say; and this would indeed be so if there were no other interests affected. But there *are* other interests, and we must consider them. The father has an interest—certainly a smaller one than the mother, but not negligible. The person into whom the foetus would turn if not aborted has an interest—a very great one. But this interest may be counterbalanced by those of other children who might be born thereafter, if the family is in any case to be limited. Certainly, if it is known that this foetus is seriously defective (the mother, say, had rubella) but she could have a normal child later, the interest of that normal child is much greater than that of the defective child who would be born from this pregnancy.

There is also the interest of doctors, surgeons, and nurses who may be called upon to perform the abortion. If ever we have an abortifacient pill that can be bought at pharmacies and used at any stage in early pregnancy, that would cut out the doctors; but I think it unlikely that such a pill will be developed soon which could safely be sold without prescription, although an abortion pill is now available on prescription in France. So for the moment we have to consider the interest of the doctor who is being asked to act against his conscience—and this *is* an interest, even if the conscience is misguided.

The question of who should decide whether to allow an abortion is the question of how best to be fair to all these interests. The mother's interest is preponderant but not the sole one. What the best procedure is depends on a lot of factors which I am not able to assess with confidence. But I am inclined to think that there are procedures now followed in some countries which have worked well in practice and have done reasonable justice between the interests affected. In any case, that is what we should be aiming at.[6]

---

[6]This is a revised version of a paper presented at a colloquium with R. B. Brandt at Florida State University on March 11, 1988. This paper also appears in *Right Conduct: Theories and Applications*, 2nd ed., ed. by Michael D. Bayles and Kenneth Henley (New York: Random House, 1989).

A Rights-Based Defense of Abortion

A Defense of Abortion[1]

Judith Jarvis Thomson

Most opposition to abortion relies on the premise that the fetus is a human being, a person, from the moment of conception. The premise is argued for, but, as I think, not well. Take, for example, the most common argument. We are asked to notice that the development of a human being from conception through birth into childhood is continuous; then it is said that to draw a line, to choose a point in this development and say "before this point the thing is not a person, after this point it is a person" is to make an arbitrary choice, a choice for which in the nature of things no good reason can be given. It is concluded that the fetus is, or anyway that we had better say it is, a person from the moment of conception. But this conclusion does not follow. Similar things might be said about the development of an acorn into an oak tree, and it does not follow that acorns are oak trees, or that we had better say they are. Arguments of this form are sometimes called "slippery slope arguments"—the phrase is perhaps self-explanatory—and it is dismaying that opponents of abortion rely on them so heavily and uncritically.

I am inclined to agree, however, that the prospects for "drawing a line" in the development of the fetus look dim. I am inclined to think also that we shall probably have to agree that the fetus has already become a human person well before birth. Indeed, it comes as a surprise when one first learns how early in its life it begins to acquire human characteristics. By the tenth week, for example, it already has a face, arms and legs, fingers and toes; it has internal organs, and brain activity is detectable.[2] On the other hand, I think that the premise is false, that the fetus is not a person from the moment of conception. A newly fertilized ovum, a newly implanted clump of cells, is no more a person than an acorn is an oak tree. But I shall not discuss any of this. For it seems to me to be of great interest to ask what happens if, for the sake of argument, we allow the premise. How, precisely, are we supposed to get from there to the conclusion that abortion is morally impermissible? Opponents of abortion commonly

---

From "A Defense of Abortion" by Judith Jarvis Thomson, *Philosophy & Public Affairs*, vol. 1, no. 1 (copyright © 1971 by Princeton University Press), pp. 47–66. Reprinted by permission of Princeton University Press.

[1] I am very much indebted to James Thomson for discussion, criticism, and many helpful suggestions.

[2] Daniel Callahan, *Abortion: Law, Choice and Morality* (New York, 1970), p. 373. This book gives a fascinating survey of the available information on abortion. The Jewish tradition is surveyed in David M. Feldman, *Birth Control in Jewish Law* (New York, 1968), Part 5; the Catholic tradition in John T. Noonan, Jr., "An Almost Absolute Value in History," in *The Morality of Abortion*, ed. John T. Noonan, Jr. (Cambridge, Mass., 1970). Noonan's essay is in this volume, pp. 9–14.

spend most of their time establishing that the fetus is a person, and hardly any time explaining the step from there to the impermissibility of abortion. Perhaps they think the step too simple and obvious to require much comment. Or perhaps instead they are simply being economical in argument. Many of those who defend abortion rely on the premise that the fetus is not a person, but only a bit of tissue that will become a person at birth; and why pay out more arguments than you have to? Whatever the explanation, I suggest that the step they take is neither easy nor obvious, that it calls for closer examination than it is commonly given, and that when we do give it this closer examination we shall feel inclined to reject it.

I propose, then, that we grant that the fetus is a person from the moment of conception. How does the argument go from here? Something like this, I take it. Every person has a right to life. So the fetus has a right to life. No doubt the mother has a right to decide what shall happen in and to her body; everyone would grant that. But surely a person's right to life is stronger and more stringent than the mother's right to decide what happens in and to her body, and so outweighs it. So the fetus may not be killed; an abortion may not be performed.

It sounds plausible. But now let me ask you to imagine this. You wake up in the morning and find yourself back to back in bed with an unconscious violinist. A famous unconscious violinist. He has been found to have a fatal kidney ailment, and the Society of Music Lovers has canvassed all the available medical records and found that you alone have the right blood type to help. They have therefore kidnapped you, and last night the violinist's circulatory system was plugged into yours, so that your kidneys can be used to extract poisons from his blood as well as your own. The director of the hospital now tells you. "Look, we're sorry the Society of Music Lovers did this to you—we would never have permitted it if we had known. But still, they did it, and the violinist now is plugged into you. To unplug you would be to kill him. But never mind, it's only for nine months. By then he will have recovered from his ailment, and can safely be unplugged from you." Is it morally incumbent on you to accede to this situation? No doubt it would be very nice of you if you did, a great kindness. But do you *have* to accede to it? What if it were not nine months, but nine years? Or longer still? What if the director of the hospital says, "Tough luck, I agree, but you've now got to stay in bed, with the violinist plugged into you, for the rest of your life. Because remember this. All persons have a right to life, and violinists are persons. Granted you have a right to decide what happens in and to your body, but a person's right to life outweighs your right to decide what happens in and to your body. So you cannot ever be unplugged from him." I imagine you would regard this as outrageous, which suggests that something really is wrong with that plausible-sounding argument I mentioned a moment ago.

In this case, of course, you were kidnapped; you didn't volunteer for the operation that plugged the violinist into your kidneys. Can those who oppose abortion on the ground I mentioned make an exception for a pregnancy due to rape? Certainly. They can say that persons have a right to life only if they didn't come into existence because of rape; or they can say that all persons have a right to life, but that some have less of a right to life than others, in particular, that those who came into existence because of rape have less. But these statements have a rather unpleasant sound. Surely the question of whether you have a right to life at all, or how much of it you have, shouldn't turn on the question of whether or not you are the product of a rape. And in fact the people who oppose abortion on the ground I mentioned do not make this distinction, and hence do not make an exception in case of rape.

Nor do they make an exception for a case in which the mother has to spend the nine months of her pregnancy in bed. They would agree that would be a great pity, and hard on the mother; but all the same, all persons have a right to life, the fetus is a person, and so on. I suspect, in fact, that they would not make an exception for a case in which, miraculously enough, the pregnancy went on for nine years, or even the rest of the mother's life.

Some won't even make an exception for a case in which continuation of the pregnancy is likely to shorten the mother's life; they regard abortion as impermissible even to save the mother's life. Such cases are nowadays very rare, and many opponents of abortion do not accept this extreme view. All the same, it is a good place to begin: a number of points of interest come out in respect to it.

1. Let us call the view that abortion is impermissible even to save the mother's life "the extreme view." I want to suggest first that it does not issue from the argument I mentioned earlier without the addition of some fairly powerful premises. Suppose a woman has become pregnant, and now learns that she has a cardiac condition such that she will die if she carries the baby to term. What may be done for her? The fetus, being a person, has a right to life, but as the mother is a person too, so has she a right to life. Presumably they have an equal right to life. How is it supposed to come out that an abortion may not be performed? If mother and child have an equal right to life, shouldn't we perhaps flip a coin? Or should we add to the mother's right to life her right to decide what happens in and to her body, which everybody seems to be ready to grant—the sum of her rights now outweighing the fetus' right to life?

The most familiar argument here is the following. We are told that performing the abortion would be directly killing[3] the child, whereas doing nothing would not be killing the mother, but only letting her die. Moreover, in killing the child, one would be killing an innocent person, for the child has committed no crime, and is not aiming at his mother's death. And then there are a variety of ways in which this might be continued. (1) But as directly killing an innocent person is always and absolutely impermissible, an abortion may not be performed. Or, (2) as directly killing an innocent person is murder, and murder is always and absolutely impermissible, an abortion may not be performed.[4] Or, (3) as one's duty to refrain from directly killing an innocent person is more stringent than one's duty to keep a person from dying, an abortion may not be performed. Or, (4) if one's only options are directly killing an innocent person or letting a person die, one must prefer

---

[3]The term "direct" in the arguments I refer to is a technical one. Roughly, what is meant by "direct killing" is either killing as an end in itself, or killing as a means of some end, for example, the end of saving someone else's life. See footnote 6 for an example of its use.

[4]Cf. *Encyclical Letter of Pope Pius XI on Christian Marriage*, St. Paul Editions (Boston, n.d.), p. 32: "however much we may pity the mother whose health and even life is gravely imperiled in the performance of the duty allotted to her by nature, nevertheless what could ever be a sufficient reason for excusing in any way the direct murder of the innocent? This is precisely what we are dealing with here." Noonan (*The Morality of Abortion*, p. 43) reads this as follows: "What cause can ever avail to excuse in any way the direct killing of the innocent? For it is a question of that."

letting the person die, and thus an abortion may not be performed.[5]

Some people seem to have thought that these are not further premises which must be added if the conclusion is to be reached, but that they follow from the very fact that an innocent person has a right to life.[6] But this seems to me to be a mistake, and perhaps the simplest way to show this is to bring out that while we must certainly grant that innocent persons have a right to life, the theses in (1) through (4) are all false. Take (2), for example. If directly killing an innocent person is murder, and thus is impermissible, then the mother's directly killing the innocent person inside her is murder, and thus is impermissible. But it cannot seriously be thought to be murder if the mother performs an abortion on herself to save her life. It cannot seriously be said that she *must* refrain, that she *must* sit passively by and wait for her death. Let us look again at the case of you and the violinist. There you are, in bed with the violinist, and the director of the hospital says to you, "It's all most distressing, and I deeply sympathize, but you see this is putting an additional strain on your kidneys, and you'll be dead within the month. But you *have* to stay where you are all the same. Because unplugging you would be directly killing an innocent violinist, and that's murder, and that's impermissible." If anything in the world is true, it is that you do not commit murder, you do not do what is impermissible, if you reach around to your back and unplug yourself from that violinist to save your life.

The main focus of attention in writings on abortion has been on what a third party may or may not do in answer to a request from a woman for an abortion. This is in a way understandable. Things being as they are, there isn't much a woman can safely do to abort herself. So the question asked is what a third party may do, and what the mother may do, if it is mentioned at all, is deduced, almost as an afterthought, from what it is concluded that third parties may do. But it seems to me that to treat the matter in this way is to refuse to grant to the mother that very status of person which is so firmly insisted on for the fetus. For we cannot simply read off what a person may do from what a third party may do. Suppose you find yourself trapped in a tiny house with a growing child. I mean a very tiny house, and a rapidly growing child—you are already up against the wall of the house and in a few minutes you'll be crushed to death. The child on the other hand won't be crushed to death: if nothing is done to stop him from growing he'll be hurt, but in the end he'll simply burst open the house and walk out a free man. Now I could well understand it if a bystander were to say, "There's nothing we can do for you. We cannot choose between your life and his, we cannot be the ones to decide who is to live, we cannot intervene." But it cannot be concluded that you too can do

---

[5]The thesis in (4) is in an interesting way weaker than those in (1), (2), and (3): they rule out abortion even in cases in which both mother *and* child will die if the abortion is not performed. By contrast, one who held the view expressed in (4) could consistently say that one needn't prefer letting two persons die to killing one.

[6]Cf. the following passage from Pius XII, *Address to the Italian Catholic Society of Midwives:* "The baby in the maternal breast has the right to life immediately from God.—Hence there is no man, no human authority, no science, no medical, eugenic, social, economic or moral 'indication' which can establish or grant a valid juridical ground for a direct deliberate disposition of an innocent human life, that is a disposition which looks to its destruction either as an end or as a means to another end perhaps in itself not illicit.—The baby, still not born, is a man in the same degree and for the same reason as the mother" (quoted in Noonan, *The Morality of Abortion,* p. 45).

nothing, that you cannot attack it to save your life. However innocent the child may be, you do not have to wait passively while it crushes you to death. Perhaps a pregnant woman is vaguely felt to have the status of house, to which we don't allow the right of self-defense. But if the woman houses the child, it should be remembered that she is a person who houses it.

I should perhaps stop to say explicitly that I am not claiming that people have a right to do anything whatever to save their lives. I think, rather, that there are drastic limits to the right of self-defense. If someone threatens you with death unless you torture someone else to death, I think you have not the right, even to save your life, to do so. But the case under consideration here is very different. In our case there are only two people involved, one whose life is threatened, and one who threatens it. Both are innocent: the one who is threatened is not threatened because of any fault, the one who threatens does not threaten because of any fault. For this reason we may feel that we bystanders cannot intervene. But the person threatened can.

In sum, a woman surely can defend her life against the threat to it posed by the unborn child, even if doing so involves its death. And this shows not merely that the theses in (1) through (4) are false; it shows also that the extreme view of abortion is false, and so we need not canvass any other possible ways of arriving at it from the argument I mentioned at the outset.

2. The extreme view could of course be weakened to say that while abortion is permissible to save the mother's life, it may not be performed by a third party, but only by the mother herself. But this cannot be right either. For what we have to keep in mind is that the mother and the unborn child are not like two tenants in a small house which has, by an unfortunate mistake, been rented to both: the mother *owns* the house.

The fact that she does adds to the offensiveness of deducing that the mother can do nothing from the supposition that third parties can do nothing. But it does more than this: it casts a bright light on the supposition that third parties can do nothing. Certainly it lets us see that a third party who says "I cannot choose between you" is fooling himself if he thinks this is impartiality. If Jones has found and fastened on a certain coat, which he needs to keep him from freezing, but which Smith also needs to keep him from freezing, then it is not impartiality that says "I cannot choose between you" when Smith owns the coat. Women have said again and again "This body is *my* body!" and they have reason to feel angry, reason to feel that it has been like shouting into the wind. Smith, after all, is hardly likely to bless us if we say to him, "Of course it's your coat, anybody would grant that it is. But no one may choose between you and Jones who is to have it."

We should really ask what it is that says, "no one may choose" in the face of the fact that the body that houses the child is the mother's body. It may be simply a failure to appreciate this fact. But it may be something more interesting, namely the sense that one has a right to refuse to lay hands on people, even where it would be just and fair to do so, even where justice seems to require that somebody do so. Thus justice might call for somebody to get Smith's coat back from Jones, and yet you have a right to refuse to be the one to lay hands on Jones, a right to refuse to do physical violence to him. This, I think, must be granted. But then what should be said is not "no one may choose," but only "*I* cannot choose," and indeed not even this, but "*I* will not *act*," leaving it open that somebody else can or should, and in particular that anyone in a position of authority, with the job of securing people's rights, both can and should. So this is no difficulty. I have not been arguing that any given third party must accede to the mother's request that he perform an abortion to save her life, but only that he may.

I suppose that in some views of human life the mother's body is only on loan to her, the loan not being one which gives her any prior claim to it. One who held this view might well think it impartiality to say "I cannot choose." But I shall simply ignore this possibility. My own view is that if a human being has any just, prior claim to anything at all, he has a just, prior claim to his own body. And perhaps this needn't be argued for here anyway, since, as I mentioned, the arguments against abortion we are looking at do grant that the woman has a right to decide what happens in and to her body.

But although they do grant it, I have tried to show that they do not take seriously what is done in granting it. I suggest the same thing will reappear even more clearly when we turn away from cases in which the mother's life is at stake, and attend, as I propose we now do, to the vastly more common cases in which a woman wants an abortion for some less weighty reason than preserving her own life.

3. Where the mother's life is not at stake, the argument I mentioned at the outset seems to have a much stronger pull. "Everyone has a right to life, so the unborn person has a right to life." And isn't the child's right to life weightier than anything other than the mother's own right to life, which she might put forward as ground for an abortion?

This argument treats the right to life as if it were unproblematic. It is not, and this seems to me to be precisely the source of the mistake.

For we should now, at long last, ask what it comes to, to have a right to life. In some views having a right to life includes having a right to be given at least the bare minimum one needs for continued life. But suppose that what in fact *is* the bare minimum a man needs for continued life is something he has no right at all to be given? If I am sick unto death, and the only thing that will save my life is the touch of Henry Fonda's cool hand on my fevered brow, then all the same, I have no right to be given the touch of Henry Fonda's cool hand on my fevered brow. It would be frightfully nice of him to fly in from the West Coast to provide it. It would be less nice, though no doubt well meant, if my friends flew out to the West Coast and carried Henry Fonda back with them. But I have no right at all against anybody that he should do this for me. Or again, to return to the story I told earlier, the fact that for continued life that violinist needs the continued use of your kidneys does not establish that he has a right to be given the continued use of your kidneys. He certainly has no right against you that *you* should give him continued use of your kidneys. For nobody has any right to use your kidneys unless you give him such a right; and nobody has the right against you that you shall give him this right—if you do allow him to go on using your kidneys, this is a kindness on your part, and not something he can claim from you as his due. Nor has he any right against anybody else that *they* should give him continued use of your kidneys. Certainly he had no right against the Society of Music Lovers that they should plug him into you in the first place. And if you now start to unplug yourself, having learned that you will otherwise have to spend nine years in bed with him, there is nobody in the world who must try to prevent you, in order to see to it that he is given something he has a right to be given.

Some people are rather stricter about the right to life. In their view, it does not include the right to be given anything, but amounts to, and only to, the right not to be killed by anybody. But here a related difficulty arises. If everybody is to refrain from killing that violinist, then everybody must refrain from doing a great many different sorts of things. Everybody must refrain from slitting his throat, everybody must refrain from shooting him—and everybody must refrain from unplugging you from him. But does he have a right against everybody that they shall refrain from unplugging you from him? To refrain from doing this is to allow him to continue to use your kidneys. It could be argued that he has a right against us that *we* should allow him to continue to use your kidneys. That is, while he had no right against us that we should give him the use of your kidneys, it might be argued that he anyway has a right against us that we shall not now intervene and deprive him of the use of your kidneys. I shall come back to third-party interventions later. But certainly the violinist has no right against you that *you* shall allow him to continue to use your kidneys. As I said, if you do allow him to use them, it is a kindness on your part, and not something you owe him.

The difficulty I point to here is not peculiar to the right to life. It reappears in connection with all the other natural rights; and it is something which an adequate account of rights must deal with. For present purposes it is enough just to draw attention to it. But I would stress that I am not arguing that people do not have a right to life— quite to the contrary, it seems to me that the primary control we must place on the acceptability of an account of rights is that it should turn out in that account to be a truth that all persons have a right to life. I am arguing only that having a right to life does not guarantee having either a right to be given the use of or a right to be allowed continued use of another person's body— even if one needs it for life itself. So the right to life will not serve the opponents of abortion in the very simple and clear way in which they seem to have thought it would.

4. There is another way to bring out the difficulty. In the most ordinary sort of case, to deprive someone of what he has a right to is to treat him unjustly. Suppose a boy and his small brother are jointly given a box of chocolates for Christmas. If the older boy takes the box and refuses to give his brother any of the chocolates, he is unjust to him, for the brother has been given a right to half of them. But suppose that, having learned that otherwise it means nine years in bed with that violinist, you unplug yourself from him. You surely are not being unjust to him, for you gave him no right to use your kidneys, and no one else can have given him any such right. But we have to notice that in unplugging yourself, you are killing him; and violinists, like everybody else, have a right to life, and thus in the view we were considering just now, the right not to be killed. So here you do what he supposedly has a right you shall not do, but you do not act unjustly to him in doing it.

The emendation which may be made at this point is this: the right to life consists not in the right not to be killed, but rather in the right not to be killed unjustly. This runs a risk of circularity, but never mind: it would enable us to square the fact that the violinist has a right to life with the fact that you do not act unjustly toward him in unplugging yourself, thereby killing him. For if you do not kill him unjustly, you do not violate his right to life, and so it is no wonder you do him no injustice.

But if this emendation is accepted, the gap in the argument against abortion stares us plainly in the face: it is by no means enough to show that the fetus is a person, and to remind us that all persons have a right to life—we need to be shown also that killing the fetus violates its right to life, i.e., that abortion is unjust killing. And is it?

I suppose we may take it as a datum that in a case of pregnancy due to rape the mother has not given the unborn person a right to the use of her body for food and shelter. Indeed, in what pregnancy could it be supposed that the mother has given the unborn person such a right? It is not as if there were unborn persons drifting about the world, to whom a woman who wants a child says "I invite you in."

But it might be argued that there are other ways one can have acquired a right to the use of another person's body than by having been invited to use it by that person. Suppose a woman voluntarily indulges in intercourse, knowing of the chance it will issue in pregnancy, and then she does become pregnant; is she not in part responsible for the presence, in fact the very existence, of the unborn person inside her? No doubt she did not invite it in. But doesn't her partial responsibility for its being there itself give it a right to the use of her body?[7] If so, then her aborting it would be more like the boy's taking away the chocolates, and less like your unplugging yourself from the violinist—doing so would be depriving it of what it does have a right to, and thus would be doing it an injustice.

And then, too, it might be asked whether or not she can kill it even to save her own life: If she voluntarily called it into existence, how can she now kill it, even in self-defense?

The first thing to be said about this is that it is something new. Opponents of abortion have been so concerned to make out the independence of the fetus, in order to establish that it has a right to life, just as its mother does, that they have tended to overlook the possible support they might gain from making out that the fetus is *dependent* on the mother, in order to establish that she has a special kind of responsibility for it, a responsibility that gives it rights against her which are not possessed by any independent person—such as an ailing violinist who is a stranger to her.

On the other hand, this argument would give the unborn person a right to its mother's body only if her pregnancy resulted from a voluntary act, undertaken in full knowledge of the chance a pregnancy might result from it. It would leave out entirely the unborn person whose existence is due to rape. Pending the availability of some further argument, then, we would be left with the conclusion that unborn persons whose existence is due to rape have no right to the use of their mothers' bodies, and thus that aborting them is not depriving them of anything they have a right to and hence is not unjust killing.

And we should also notice that it is not at all plain that this argument really does go even as far as it purports to. For there are cases and cases, and the details make a difference. If the room is stuffy, and I therefore open a window to air it, and a burglar climbs in, it would be absurd to say, "Ah, now he can stay, she's given him a right to the use of her house—for she is partially responsible for his presence there, having voluntarily done what enabled him to get in, in full knowledge that there are such things as burglars, and that burglars burgle." It would be still more absurd to say this if I had had bars installed outside my windows, precisely to prevent burglars from getting in, and a burglar got in only because of a defect in the bars. It remains equally absurd if we imagine it is not a burglar who climbs in, but an innocent person who blunders or falls in. Again, suppose it were like this: people-seeds drift about in the air like pollen, and if you open your windows, one may drift in and take root in

---

[7]The need for a discussion of this argument was brought home to me by members of the Society for Ethical and Legal Philosophy, to whom this paper was originally presented.

your carpets or upholstery. You don't want children, so you fix up your windows with fine mesh screens, the very best you can buy. As can happen, however, and on very, very rare occasions does happen, one of the screens is defective; and a seed drifts in and takes root. Does the person-plant who now develops have a right to the use of your house? Surely not—despite the fact that you voluntarily opened your windows, you knowingly kept carpets and upholstered furniture, and you knew that screens were sometimes defective. Someone may argue that you are responsible for its rooting, that it does have a right to your house, because after all you *could* have lived out your life with bare floors and furniture, or with sealed windows and doors. But this won't do—for by the same token anyone can avoid a pregnancy due to rape by having a hysterectomy, or anyway by never leaving home without a (reliable!) army.

It seems to me that the argument we are looking at can establish at most that there are *some* cases in which the unborn person has a right to the use of its mother's body, and therefore *some* cases in which abortion is unjust killing. There is room for much discussion and argument as to precisely which, if any. But I think we should sidestep this issue and leave it open, for at any rate the argument certainly does not establish that all abortion is unjust killing.

5. There is room for yet another argument here, however. We surely must all grant that there may be cases in which it would be morally indecent to detach a person from your body at the cost of his life. Suppose you learn that what the violinist needs is not nine years of your life, but only one hour: all you need do to save his life is to spend one hour in that bed with him. Suppose also that letting him use your kidneys for that one hour would not affect your health in the slightest. Admittedly you were kidnapped. Admittedly you did not give anyone persmission to plug him into you. Nevertheless it seems to me plain you *ought* to allow him to use your kidneys for that hour—it would be indecent to refuse.

Again, suppose pregnancy lasted only an hour, and constituted no threat to life or health. And suppose that a woman becomes pregnant as a result of rape. Admittedly she did not voluntarily do anything to bring about the existence of a child. Admittedly she did nothing at all which would give the unborn person a right to the use of her body. All the same it might well be said, as in the newly emended violinist story, that she *ought* to allow it to remain for that hour—that it would be indecent of her to refuse.

Now some people are inclined to use the term "right" in such a way that it follows from the fact that you ought to allow a person to use your body for the hour he needs, that he has a right to use your body for the hour he needs, even though he has not been given that right by any person or act. They may say that it follows also that if you refuse, you act unjustly toward him. This use of the term is perhaps so common that it cannot be called wrong; nevertheless it seems to me to be an unfortunate loosening of what we would do better to keep a tight rein on. Suppose that box of chocolates I mentioned earlier has not been given to both boys jointly, but was given only to the older boy. There he sits, stolidly eating his way through the box, his small brother watching enviously. Here we are likely to say "You ought not to be so mean. You ought to give your brother some of those chocolates." My own view is that it just does not follow from the truth of this that the brother has any right to any of the chocolates. If the boy refuses to give his brother any, he is greedy, stingy, callous—but not unjust. I suppose that the people I have in mind will say it does follow that the brother has a right to some of the chocolates, and thus that the boy does act unjustly if he refuses to give his brother any. But the effect of saying this is to obscure what we should keep distinct, namely the difference between the boy's refusal in this case and the boy's refusal in the earlier case, in which the box was given to both boys jointly, and in which the small brother thus had what was from any point of view clear title to half.

A further objection to so using the term "right" that from the fact that A ought to do a thing for B, it follows that B has a right against A that A do it for him, is that it is going to make the question of whether or not a man has a right to a thing turn on how easy it is to provide him with it; and this seems not merely unfortunate, but morally unacceptable. Take the case of Henry Fonda again. I said earlier that I had no right to the touch of his cool hand on my fevered brow, even though I needed it to save my life. I said it would be frightfully nice of him to fly in from the West Coast to provide me with it, but that I had no right against him that he should do so. But suppose he isn't on the West Coast. Suppose he has only to walk across the room, place a hand briefly on my brow—and lo, my life is saved. Then surely he ought to do it, it would be indecent to refuse. Is it to be said "Ah, well, it follows that in this case she has a right to the touch of his hand on her brow, and so it would be an injustice in him to refuse"? So that I have a right to it when it is easy for him to provide it, though no right when it's hard? It's rather a shocking idea that anyone's rights should fade away and disappear as it gets harder and harder to accord them to him.

So my own view is that even though you ought to let the violinist use your kidneys for the one hour he needs, we should not conclude that he has a right to do so—we should say that if you refuse, you are, like the boy who owns all the chocolates and will give none away, self-centered and callous, indecent in fact, but not unjust. And similarly, that even supposing a case in which a woman pregnant due to rape ought to allow the unborn person to use her body for the hour he needs, we should not conclude that he has a right to do so; we should conclude that she is self-centered, callous, indecent, but not unjust, if she refuses. The complaints are no less grave; they are just different. However, there is no need to insist on this point. If anyone does wish to deduce "he has a right" from "you ought," then all the same he must surely grant that there are cases in which it is not morally required of you that you allow that violinist to use your kidneys, and in which he does not have a right to use them, and in which you do not do him an injustice if you refuse. And so also for mother and unborn child. Except in such cases as the unborn person has a right to demand it—and we were leaving open the possibility that there may be such cases—nobody is morally *required* to make large sacrifices, of health, of all other interests and concerns, of all other duties and commitments, for nine years, or even for nine months, in order to keep another person alive.

6. We have in fact to distinguish between two kinds of Samaritan: the Good Samaritan and what we might call the Minimally Decent Samaritan. The story of the Good Samaritan, you will remember, goes like this:

> A certain man went down from Jerusalem to Jericho, and fell among thieves, which stripped him of his raiment, and wounded him, and departed, leaving him half dead.
>
> And by chance there came down a certain priest that way; and when he saw him, he passed by on the other side.
>
> And likewise a Levite, when he was at the place, came and looked on him, and passed by on the other side.

> But a certain Samaritan, as he journeyed, came where he was; and when he saw him he had compassion on him.
>
> And went to him, and bound up his wounds, pouring in oil and wine, and set him on his own beast, and brought him to an inn, and took care of him.
>
> And on the morrow, when he departed, he took out two pence, and gave them to the host, and said unto him, "Take care of him; and whatsoever thou spendest more, when I come again. I will repay thee."
>
> (Luke 10:30–35)

The Good Samaritan went out of his way, at some cost to himself, to help one in need of it. We are not told what the options were, that is, whether or not the priest and the Levite could have helped by doing less than the Good Samaritan did, but assuming they could have, then the fact they did nothing at all shows they were not even Minimally Decent Samaritans, not because they were not Samaritans, but because they were not even minimally decent.

These things are a matter of degree, of course, but there is a difference, and it comes out perhaps most clearly in the story of Kitty Genovese, who, as you will remember, was murdered while thirty-eight people watched or listened, and did nothing at all to help her. A Good Samaritan would have rushed out to give direct assistance against the murderer. Or perhaps we had better allow that it would have been a Splendid Samaritan who did this, on the ground that it would have involved a risk of death for himself. But the thirty-eight not only did not do this, they did not even trouble to pick up a phone to call the police. Minimally Decent Samaritanism would call for doing at least that, and their not having done it was monstrous.

After telling the story of the Good Samaritan, Jesus said "Go, and do thou likewise." Perhaps he meant that we are morally required to act as the Good Samaritan did. Perhaps he was urging people to do more than is morally required of them. At all events it seems plain that it was not morally required of any of the thirty-eight that he rush out to give direct assistance at the risk of his own life, and that it is not morally required of anyone that he give long stretches of his life—nine years or nine months—to sustaining the life of a person who has no special right (we were leaving open the possibility of this) to demand it.

Indeed, with one rather striking class of exceptions, no one in any country in the world is *legally* required to do anywhere near as much as this for anyone else. The class of exceptions is obvious. My main concern here is not the state of the law in respect to abortion, but it is worth drawing attention to the fact that in no state in this country is any man compelled by law to be even a Minimally Decent Samaritan to any person; there is no law under which charges could be brought against the thirty-eight who stood by while Kitty Genovese died. By contrast, in most states in this country women are compelled by law to be not merely Minimally Decent Samaritans, but Good Samaritans to unborn persons inside them. This doesn't by itself settle anything one way or the other, because it may well be argued that there should be laws in this country—as there are in many European countries—compelling at least Minimally Decent Samaritanism.[8] But it does show that there is a gross injustice in the existing state of the law. And it shows also that the groups currently working against liberalization of abortion laws, in fact working toward having it declared

---

[8] For a discussion of the difficulties involved, and a survey of the European experience with such laws, see *The Good Samaritan and the Law*, ed. James M. Ratcliffe (New York, 1966).

unconstitutional for a state to permit abortion, had better start working for the adoption of Good Samaritan laws generally, or earn the charge that they are acting in bad faith.

I should think, myself, that Minimally Decent Samaritan laws would be one thing, Good Samaritan laws quite another, and in fact highly improper. But we are not here concerned with the law. What we should ask is not whether anybody should be compelled by law to be a Good Samaritan, but whether we must accede to a situation in which somebody is being compelled—by nature, perhaps—to be a Good Samaritan. We have, in other words, to look now at third-party interventions. I have been arguing that no person is morally required to make large sacrifices to sustain the life of another who has no right to demand them, and this even where the sacrifices do not include life itself; we are not morally required to be Good Samaritans or anyway Very Good Samaritans to one another. But what if a man cannot extricate himself from such a situation? What if he appeals to us to extricate him? It seems to me plain that there are cases in which we can, cases in which a Good Samaritan would extricate him. There you are, you were kidnapped, and nine years in bed with that violinist lie ahead of you. You have your own life to lead. You are sorry, but you simply cannot see giving up so much of your life to the sustaining of his. You cannot extricate yourself, and ask us to do so. I should have thought that—in light of his having no right to the use of your body—it was obvious that we do not have to accede to your being forced to give up so much. We can do what you ask. There is no injustice to the violinist in our doing so.

7. Following the lead of the opponents of abortion, I have throughout been speaking of the fetus merely as a person, and what I have been asking is whether or not the argument we began with, which proceeds only from the fetus' being a person, really does establish its conclusion. I have argued that it does not.

But of course there are arguments and arguments, and it may be said that I have simply fastened on the wrong one. It may be said that what is important is not merely the fact that the fetus is a person, but that it is a person for whom the woman has a special kind of responsibility issuing from the fact that she is its mother. And it might be argued that all my analogies are therefore irrelevant—for you do not have that special kind of responsibility for that violinist, Henry Fonda does not have that special kind of responsibility for me. And our attention might be drawn to the fact that men and women both *are* compelled by law to provide support for their children.

I have in effect dealt (briefly) with this argument in section 4 above; but a (still briefer) recapitulation now may be in order. Surely we do not have any such "special responsibility" for a person unless we have assumed it, explicitly or implicitly. If a set of parents do not try to prevent pregnancy, do not obtain an abortion, and then at the time of birth of the child do not put it out for adoption, but rather take it home with them, then they have assumed responsibility for it, they have given it rights, and they cannot *now* withdraw support from it at the cost of its life because they now find it difficult to go on providing for it. But if they have taken all reasonable precautions against having a child, they do not simply by virtue of their biological relationship to the child who comes into existence have a special responsibility for it. They may wish to assume responsibility for it, or they may not wish to. And I am suggesting that if assuming responsibility for it would require large sacrifices, then they may refuse. A Good Samaritan would not refuse—or anyway, a Splendid Samaritan, if the sacrifices that had to be made were enormous. But then so would a Good Samaritan assume responsibility for that violinist; so would Henry Fonda, if he is a Good Samaritan, fly in from the West Coast and assume responsibility for me.

8. My argument will be found unsatisfactory on two counts by many of those who want to regard abortion as morally permissible. First, while I do argue that abortion is not impermissible, I do not argue that it is always permissible. There may well be cases in which carrying the child to term requires only Minimally Decent Samaritanism of the mother, and this is a standard we must not fall below. I am inclined to think it a merit of my account precisely that it does *not* give a general yes or a general no. It allows for and supports our sense that, for example, a sick and desperately frightened fourteen-year-old schoolgirl, pregnant due to rape, may *of course* choose abortion, and that any law which rules this out is an insane law. And it also allows for and supports our sense that in other cases resort to abortion is even positively indecent. It would be indecent in the woman to request an abortion, and indecent in a doctor to perform it, if she is in her seventh month, and wants the abortion just to avoid the nuisance of postponing a trip abroad. The very fact that the arguments I have been drawing attention to treat all cases of abortion, or even all cases or abortion in which the mother's life is not at stake, as morally on a par ought to have made them suspect at the outset.

Secondly, while I am arguing for the permissibility of abortion in some cases, I am not arguing for the right to secure the death of the unborn child. It is easy to confuse these two things in that up to a certain point in the life of the fetus it is not able to survive outside the mother's body; hence removing it from her body guarantees its death. But they are importantly different. I have argued that you are not morally required to spend nine months in bed, sustaining the life of that violinist; but to say this is by no means to say that if, when you unplug yourself, there is a miracle and he survives, you then have a right to turn round and slit his throat. You may detach yourself even if this costs him his life; you have no right to be guaranteed his death, by some other means, if unplugging yourself does not kill him. There are some people who will feel dissatisfied by this feature of my argument. A woman may be utterly devastated by the thought of a child, a bit of herself, put out for adoption and never seen or heard of again. She may therefore want not merely that the child be detached from her, but more, that it die. Some opponents of abortion are inclined to regard this as beneath contempt—thereby showing insensitivity to what is surely a powerful source of despair. All the same, I agree that the desire for the child's death is not one which anybody may gratify, should it turn out to be possible to detach the child alive.

At this place, however, it should be remembered that we have only been pretending throughout that the fetus is a human being from the moment of conception. A very early abortion is surely not the killing of a person, and so is not dealt with by anything I have said here.

Questions for Further Reflection

1. A moderate about the moral status of the fetus must hold either that there is some very important stage in fetal development at which the fetus becomes a person (for example, the development of a nervous system or the point at which the fetus could live outside the womb) or that the change from a nonperson to a person is gradual, with no sharp dividing line. Is either of these views plausible? Why or why not?

2. Hare argues that, if I could give my mother advice about whether to abort me, the fact that I am glad to be alive would prevent me from telling her she ought to have an abortion, and therefore if I were to give her moral advice I would have to tell her she ought not to have an abortion. How does Hare argue against the thought that I might simply say that I would prefer that she not have the abortion without saying either that she should or that she should not? How persuasive is Hare's response to this possibility?

3. No doubt there are many people who either would not now be alive, or who would have less happy lives, if their mothers had not aborted one or more other unborn children. How, if at all, does this affect Hare's argument?

4. Thomson claims that even if being disconnected will result in his death, the famous violinist has no right to the use of her kidneys. Do you agree? Why or why not?

5. Is the analogy between the violinist and the fetus strong enough that, if the violinist has no right to the use of Thomson's kidneys, the fetus has no right to the use of her body? If not, why not?

6. Thomson considers the argument that in pregnancies resulting from voluntary intercourse, the mother has implicitly granted the unborn child a right to the use of her body. Thomson denies this, using the example of the people-seeds to make her point. How is the people-seeds analogy supposed to work? How good is the analogy?

Further Readings

Bermudez, Jose Luis. "The Moral Significance of a Birth." *Ethics* 106 (1996): 378–403. Argues that there are morally significant differences between newborns and fetuses just about to be born—contrary to what most philosophers have supposed.

English, Jane. "Abortion and the Concept of a Person." *Canadian Journal of Philosophy* 5 (1975): 233–243. Argues that whether the fetus is a person is not as important as is often assumed: "If a fetus is a person, abortion is still justifiable in many cases; and if a fetus is not a person, killing it is still wrong in many cases."

Feinberg, Joel. "Abortion." In Tom Regan, ed., *Matters of Life and Death*, third edition. New York: Random House, 1993. A very clear and helpful synoptic discussion of the issues.

Feinberg, Joel, ed. *The Problem of Abortion*, second edition. Belmont, CA: Wadsworth, 1984. An excellent collection of critical essays on abortion.

Gallagher, Janet. "Prenatal Invasions and Interventions: What's Wrong with Fetal Rights." *Harvard Women's Law Journal* 10 (1987): 9–58. A critique of the view that fetuses have or ought to have legal rights.

Harris, George W. "Fathers and Fetuses." *Ethics* 96 (1986): 594–603. Argues that "in some cases it would be morally impermissible for a woman to have an abortion because it would be a wrongful harm to the father and a violation of his autonomy."

Thomson, Judith Jarvis. "Abortion." *The Boston Review* 20, no. 3 (January 1994/December 1995). Interesting new contribution by Thomson. Available online at http://www-polisci.mit.edu/BostonReview/BR20.3/thomson.html. There are replies and a rejoinder in the following issue of the same journal, also available online.

Part Seven

Interspecies Issues

Chapter 18

The Status of Animals

From the fact that a creature is not capable of acting morally, it does not follow that we may treat it in any way we wish. Very young children are not yet capable of appreciating the difference between right and wrong. For that reason, they are not *moral agents:* They are not the sort of agents capable of restricting themselves to what they see to be morally permissible behavior. But those of us who *are* moral agents nevertheless have many obligations toward children. While children are not moral agents, they are moral *patients:* They are among the creatures who may be wronged by moral agents and to whom agents may have obligations. In this sense, they have moral *standing*.

However, to say that a creature has moral standing is not to say that it is due the same treatment as a normal adult human being. In fact, if we know of a creature only that it has standing, we do not yet know how we must treat it. We cannot simply treat it in any way we wish; but it may be that our obligations toward it are extremely limited. So granting that animals have moral standing may be granting very little. For example, it is possible that while we may not torture animals, we may kill and consume them.

Do creatures other than human beings have standing? What is necessary for a creature to have standing? In this chapter we consider a range of suggestions about the conditions under which creatures have standing and examine some issues about how they legitimately may be treated, given their standing.

The Rationality Criterion

The traditional Western understanding of the status of animals is the *anthropocentric* view (contrast the status assigned animals in the Hindu tradition). It is the view advocated in the Christian tradition, for example, and the one inherited from that tradition by John Locke. In this traditional picture, God gave the whole of the earth to human beings to exploit at will. In *Summa Contra Gentiles,* Aquinas goes out of his way to say that not only land and plants, but animals as well, are there for us to use in any way we wish. He cites *Genesis* 9:3 to justify his claim that "animals are ordered to man's use in the natural course of things, according to divine providence. Consequently, man uses them without any injustice, either by killing them or by employing them in any other way."

This is not to say that anyone may do to an animal, plant, or tract of land anything he or she wishes, but it is to say that animals cannot themselves be wronged and, hence, that they do not have standing. According to the anthropocentric criterion, a creature must be a human being to have standing. So the only important issue to be resolved before we can know how we may treat an animal is which *human* rights will be affected by that treatment. Once it as established that a particular kitten (say) is yours, then *I* may not pour gasoline over it and set it on fire. But you may.

One of the primary difficulties facing the anthropocentric view as defended on theistic grounds (a problem we have pressed against theistic approaches in other chapters as well) is that it does not tell us *why* it is permissible to treat anything aside from people in any way we wish. To say that God elected to turn everything over to people to use as they wish is not to say why it is permissible for us to deal with the nonhuman world as we wish, and unless theists adopted the implausible view that God's decision was arbitrary, they would presumably admit that God would not have done what he did unless he saw that it is morally acceptable for us to use the nonhuman world as we wish.

Of course, it is possible to defend the anthropocentric criterion of standing on nontheistic grounds. Descartes is notorious for suggesting that nonhuman animals and plants are merely soulless machines. As machines, they would have the status of clocks and other gadgets and could be used by their owners as they chose. As the selection by Kant makes clear, he thinks animals capable of feeling (he says that they care for their young and that it is possible to be cruel to animals), and hence, he does not classify them as mere machines, but he defends a version of the anthropocentric view, anyway. The only sense in which we have duties toward animals, in Kant's view, is that certain ways of treating animals are psychologically impossible for people who are motivated to treat human beings morally. Thus, we cannot avoid cruelty to human beings without avoiding cruelty to animals. (But doesn't this suggest that a feature common to both human and nonhuman animals makes cruelty wrong?) His version of anthropocenticism is the *rationality criterion:* nonhuman animals are not rational, self-conscious beings and hence cannot be ends in themselves, which are the only things to which (by the *rationality criterion*) we must show moral consideration. In effect, he simply assumes without argument that the only moral patients are moral agents, for while it is clear that lack of rationality blocks a creature from appreciating the distinction between right and wrong, it is by no means clear why the lack of rationality prevents a creature from having standing.

The Hedonistic Criterion

The earliest opposition to the rationality criterion came from utilitarians such as Bentham, who paved the way for later animal-rights advocates such as Peter Singer. As Singer notes, Bentham's retort to Kant was:

> A full-grown horse or dog is beyond comparison a more rational, as well as a more conversable animal, than an infant of a day, or a week, or even a month, old. But suppose the case were otherwise, what would it avail? the question is not, Can they *reason?* nor, Can they *talk?* but, Can they *suffer?*

In this passage, Bentham gives two separate responses to Kant. One is that some animals are rational, and the other is that animals have standing for the same reason human beings and other rational creatures do: Both generate pleasure and pain. In that sense, they meet what may be called the *hedonistic criterion* for standing.

Like Bentham, Singer adopts the hedonistic criterion. He then moves quickly to the view that every animal that meets that criterion should be treated with the respect due a human being. Following Richard Ryder, he condemns "the belief that we are entitled to treat members of other species in a way in which it would be wrong to treat members of our own species." He labels this practice "speciesism" so as to bring out the parallel with racism and sexism. Given that we must avoid speciesism, we may not exploit animals in the many ways in which we are accustomed to doing. Eating them is out of the question, and experimenting on them is as bad as experimenting on orphan children would be.

The Interest Criterion

Advocates of the *interest criterion* would criticize Kant's defense of the rationality criterion and Singer's defense of the hedonistic criterion by noting the existence of features aside from rationality and the ability to experience pleasure or pain that we take to be relevant to the issue of how we may treat a creature. According to those who subscribe to the interest criterion, what gives a creature standing is its having *interests*, and rationality and the ability to generate pleasure and pain are simply two of the things in which a creature may take an interest.

Ruth Cigman accepts a version of the interest criterion. All and only creatures with interests have standing, she would say, and she would add that we have an interest in something only if it would be a misfortune for us to be deprived of that thing. However, she criticizes Singer's attempt to compare speciesism with racism and sexism. On Cigman's reading, Singer's view is that members of other species are morally our equals in the sense that they have "equality over a range of fundamental rights." Cigman rejects this view and (elaborating on an argument by Michael Tooley) suggests instead that animals do not have even the right to life. She begins with the assumption that a creature can have a right to something only if depriving the creature of that thing would be a misfortune for the creature. Then she argues that dying cannot be a misfortune for an animal. To be a misfortune, what happens to an animal would have to thwart one of its desires, or at least a desire that it could have, she asserts. So dying could be a misfortune for an animal only if it could have an unconditional or categorical desire for something, as opposed to a conditional one. Conditional desires are contingent on their bearer's being alive; unconditional, or categorical, desires are not. Only unconditional desires can be thwarted by death (though some would not be), but animals cannot have such desires, Cigman says.

This reasoning is a bit quick, for it is not clear why animals cannot have unconditional desires. One might have thought that *conditional* desires would be the ones animals could not manage, for, unlike unconditional desires, conditional desires are contingent on their bearer's life, so conditional desires can be possessed only by creatures who can conceive of their own temporally extended lives. (Perhaps Cigman means to argue that a creature could have an unconditional desire only if it could grasp the distinction between conditional and unconditional desires, which is not possible. But doesn't a creature's inability to make that distinction show at worst that it cannot *categorize* its desires into conditional or unconditional, not that it cannot *have* unconditional desires?)

The Life Criterion

Kenneth Goodpaster defends yet another criterion of standing. His suggestion is that any living thing has standing, including plants. Sentience, the ability to feel pleasure and pain, is merely one of the mechanisms by which certain creatures avoid damage, and we can imagine intelligent life forms that do not rely on pain as a way to help stay alive. Some of these creatures would clearly have standing, so the capacity to experience pain and pleasure must not be necessary for standing, Goodpaster concludes.

Of course, the fact that creatures other than ones that feel pain can have standing does not show that plants have standing. It is possible that all and only creatures that feel pain *and creatures that are conscious and intelligent* have standing. But if this possibility is defended on the grounds that all and only creatures with interests have standing, then Goodpaster thinks the defense is misguided. In his view, the interest criterion for standing is a good one, but it does not deny plants standing, for plants have interests in the sense that they have needs or conditions without which their lives would end. They do not have desires, Goodpaster acknowledges, but he adds that "psychological or hedonic capacities seem unnecessarily sophisticated when it comes to locating the minimal conditions for something's deserving to be valued for its own sake."

The Nonsentient Environment

It is sometimes argued that parts of the environment, such as mountains and streams, should have moral standing even though they are not alive. In the final essay of this chapter, Bernard Rollin considers some of the reasons for saying this and rejects them. Rollin also points out that a powerful defense of the environment can be built without assuming that the nonliving world has standing. Indeed, a powerful case can be built even without assuming that plants have standing. Essentially the idea would be that sentient beings, such as people and other animals, have moral standing, and, because destroying their environments is against their interests, it is wrong.

Unfortunately, it is not possible for single nations to devise adequate environmental policies on their own. Rollin notes, for example, that if one nation bans practices that deplete the ozone in the atmosphere and other nations do not, all sentient beings will still suffer. The environment is global, and hence a suitable environmental policy would have to be global.

RATIONALITY CRITERION OF STANDING

Duties Towards Animals

Immanuel Kant

Baumgarten speaks of duties towards beings which are beneath us and beings which are above us. But so far as animals are concerned, we have no direct duties. Animals are not self-concious and are there merely as a means to an end. That end is man. We can ask, 'Why do animals exist?' But to ask, 'Why does man exist?' is a meaningless question. Our duties towards animals are merely indirect duties towards humanity. Animal nature has analogies to human nature, and by doing our duties to animals in respect of manifestations which correspond to manifestations of human nature, we indirectly do our duty towards humanity. Thus, if a dog has served his master long and faithfully, his service, on the analogy of human service, deserves reward, and when the dog has grown too old to serve, his master ought to keep him until he dies. Such action helps to support us in our duties towards human beings, where they are bounden duties. If then any acts of animals are analogous to human acts and spring from the same principles, we have duties towards the animals because thus we cultivate the corresponding duties towards human beings. If a man shoots his dog because the animal is no longer capable of service, he does not fail in his duty to the dog, for the dog cannot judge, but his act is inhuman and damages in himself that humanity which it is his duty to show towards mankind. If he is not to stifle his human feelings, he must practise kindness towards animals, for he who is cruel to animals becomes hard also in his dealings with men. We can judge the heart of a man by his treatment of animals. Hogarth[1] depicts this in his engravings. He shows how cruelty grows and develops. He shows the child's cruelty to animals, pinching the tail of a dog or a cat; he then depicts the grown man in his cart running over a child; and lastly, the culmination of cruelty in murder. He thus brings home to us in a terrible fashion the rewards of cruelty, and this should be an impressive lesson to children. The more we come in contact with animals and observe their behaviour, the more we love them, for we see how great is their care for their young. It is then difficult for us to be cruel in thought even to a wolf. Leibnitz used a tiny worm for purposes of observation, and then carefully replaced it with its leaf on the tree so that it should not come to harm through any act of his. He would have been sorry—a natural feeling for a humane man—to destroy such a creature for no reason. Tender feelings towards dumb animals develop humane feelings towards mankind. In England butchers and doctors do not sit on a jury because they are accustomed to the sight of death and hardened. Vivisectionists, who use living animals for their experiments, certainly act cruelly, although their aim is praiseworthy, and they can justify their cruelty, since animals must be regarded as man's instruments; but any such cruelty for sport cannot be justified. A master who turns out his ass or his dog because the animal can no longer earn its keep manifests a small mind. The Greeks' ideas in this respect were high-minded, as can be seen from the fable of the ass and the bell of ingratitude. Our duties towards animals, then, are indirect duties towards mankind.

---

[1] Hogarth's four engravings. 'The Stages of Cruelty', 1751.

Pleasure Criterion of Standing

Animal Liberation

Peter Singer

I

We are familiar with Black Liberation, Gay Liberation, and a variety of other movements. With Women's Liberation some thought we had come to the end of the road. Discrimination on the basis of sex, it has been said, is the last form of discrimination that is universally accepted and practiced without pretense, even in those liberal circles which have long prided themselves on their freedom from racial discrimination. But one should always be wary of talking of "the last remaining form of discrimination." If we have learned anything from the liberation movements, we should have learned how difficult it is to be aware of the ways in which we discriminate until they are forcefully pointed out to us. A liberation movement demands an expansion of our moral horizons, so that practices that were previously regarded as natural and inevitable are now seen as intolerable.

Animals, Men and Morals is a manifesto for an Animal Liberation movement. . . . It is a demand for a complete change in our attitudes to nonhumans. It is a demand that we cease to regard the exploitation of other species as natural and inevitable, and that, instead, we see it as a continuing moral outrage. Patrick Corbett, Professor of Philosophy at Sussex University, captures the spirit of the book in his closing words:

> . . . We require now to extend the great principles of liberty, equality and fraternity over the lives of animals. Let animal slavery join human slavery in the graveyard of the past.

The reader is likely to be skeptical. "Animal Liberation" sounds more like a parody of liberation movements than a serious objective. The reader may think: We support the claims of blacks and women for equality because blacks and women really are equal to whites and males—equal in intelligence and in abilities, capacity for leadership, rationality, and so on. Humans and nonhumans obviously are not equal in these respects. Since justice demands only that we treat equals equally, unequal treatment of humans and nonhumans cannot be an injustice.

This is a tempting reply, but a dangerous one. It commits the non-racist and non-sexist to a dogmatic belief that blacks and women really are just as intelligent, able, etc., as whites and males—and no more. Quite possibly this happens to be the case. Certainly attempts to prove that racial or sexual differences in these respects have a genetic origin have not been conclusive. But do we really want to stake our demand for equality on the assumption that there are no genetic differences of this kind between the different races or sexes? Surely the appropriate response to those who claim to have found evidence for sure genetic differences is not to stick to the belief that there are no differences, whatever the evidence to the contrary; rather one should be clear that the claim to equality does not depend on IQ. Moral equality is distinct from factual equality. Otherwise it would be nonsense to talk of the equality of human beings, since humans, as individuals, obviously differ in intelligence and almost any ability one cares to name. If possessing greater intelligence does not entitle one human to exploit another, why should it entitle humans to exploit nonhumans?

Jeremy Bentham expressed the essential basis of equality in his famous formula: "Each to count for one and none for more than one." In other words, the interests of every being that has interests are to be taken into account and treated equally with the like interests of any other being. Other moral philosophers, before and after Bentham, have made the same point in different ways. Our concern for others must not depend on whether they possess certain characteristics, though just what that concern involves may, of course, vary according to such characteristics.

Bentham, incidentally, was well aware that the logic of the demand for racial equality did not stop at the equality of humans. He wrote:

> The day *may* come when the rest of the animal creation may acquire those rights which never could have been withholden from them but by the hand of tyranny. The French have already discovered that the blackness of the skin is no reason why a human being should be abandoned without redress to the caprice of a tormentor. It may one day come to be recognized that the number of the legs, the villosity of the skin, or the termination of the *os sacrum*, are reasons equally insufficient for abandoning a sensitive being to the same rate. What else is it that should trace the insuperable line? Is it the faculty of reason, or perhaps the faculty of discourse? But a full-grown horse or dog is beyond comparison a more rational, as well as a more conversable animal, than an infant of a day, or a week, or even a month, old. But suppose they were otherwise, what would it avail? The question is not, Can they *reason?* nor Can they *talk?* but, Can they *suffer?*[1]

Surely Bentham was right. If a being suffers, there can be no moral justification for refusing to take that suffering into consideration, and, indeed, to count it equally with the like suffering (if rough comparisons can be made) of any other being.

So the only question is: Do animals other than man suffer? Most people agree unhesitatingly that animals like cats and dogs can and do suffer, and this seems also to be assumed by those laws that prohibit wanton cruelty to such animals. Personally, I have no doubt at all about this and find it hard to take seriously the doubts that a few people apparently do have. The editors and contributors of *Animals, Men and Morals* seem to feel the same way, for although the question is raised more than once, doubts are quickly dismissed each time. Nevertheless, because this is such a fundamental point, it is worth asking what grounds we have for attributing suffering to other animals.

It is best to begin by asking what grounds any individual human has for supposing that other humans feel pain. Since pain is a state of consciousness, a "mental event," it can never be directly observed. No observations, whether behavioral signs such as writhing or screaming or physiological or neurological recordings, are observations of pain itself. Pain is something one feels, and one can only infer that others are feeling it from various external indications. The fact that only philosophers are ever skeptical about whether other humans feel pain shows that we regard such inference as justifiable in the case of humans.

Is there any reason why the same inference should be unjustifiable for other

---

[1] *The Principles of Morals and Legislation*, ch. XVII, sec. 1, footnote to paragraph 4. (Italics in original.)

animals? Nearly all the external signs which lead us to infer pain in other humans can be seen in other species, especially "higher" animals such as mammals and birds. Behavioral signs—writhing, yelping, or other forms of calling, attempts to avoid the source of pain, and many others—are present. We know, too, that these animals are biologically similar in the relevant respects, having nervous systems like ours which can be observed to function as ours do.

So the grounds for inferring that these animals can feel pain are nearly as good as the grounds for inferring other humans do. Only nearly, for there is one behavioral sign that humans have but nonhumans, with the exception of one or two specially raised chimpanzees, do not have. This, of course, is a developed language. As the quotation from Bentham indicates, this has long been regarded as an important distinction between man and other animals. Other animals may communicate with each other, but not in the way we do. Following Chomsky, many people now mark this distinction by saying that only humans communicate in a form that is governed by rules of syntax. (For the purposes of this argument, linguists allow those chimpanzees who have learned a syntactic sign language to rank as honorary humans.) Nevertheless, as Bentham pointed out, this distinction is not relevant to the question of how animals ought to be treated, unless it can be linked to the issue of whether animals suffer.

This link may be attempted in two ways. First, there is a hazy line of philosophical thought, stemming perhaps from some doctrines associated with Wittgenstein, which maintains that we cannot meaningfully attribute states of consciousness to beings without language. I have not seen this argument made explicit in print, though I have come across it in conversation. This position seems to me very implausible, and I doubt that it would be held at all if it were not thought to be a consequence of a broader view of the significance of language. It may be that the use of a public, rule-governed language is a precondition of conceptual thought. It may even be, although personally I doubt it, that we cannot meaningfully speak of a creature having an intention unless that creature can use a language. But states like pain, surely, are more primitive than either of these, and seem to have nothing to do with language.

Indeed, as Jane Goodall points out in her study of chimpanzees, when it comes to the expression of feelings and emotions, humans tend to fall back on non-linguistic modes of communication which are often found among apes, such as a cheering pat on the back, an exuberant embrace, a clasp of hands, and so on.[2] Michael Peters makes a similar point in his contribution to *Animals, Men and Morals* when he notes that the basic signals we use to convey pain, fear, sexual arousal, and so on are not specific to our species. So there seems to be no reason at all to believe that a creature without language cannot suffer.

The second, and more easily appreciated way of linking language and the existence of pain is to say that the best evidence that we can have that another creature is in pain is when he tells us that he is. This is a distinct line of argument, for it is not being denied that a non-language-user conceivably could suffer, but only that we could know that he is suffering. Still, this line of argument seems to me to fail, and for reasons similar to those just given. "I am in pain" is not the best possible evidence that the speaker is in pain (he might be lying) and it is certainly not the only possible evidence. Behavioral signs and knowledge of the animal's biological

---

[2] Jane van Lawick-Goodall, *In the Shadow of Man* (Houghton Mifflin, 1971), p. 225.

similarity to ourselves together provide adequate evidence that animals do suffer. After all, we would not accept linguistic evidence if it contradicted the rest of the evidence. If a man was severely burned, and behaved as if he were in pain, writhing, groaning, being very careful not to let his burned skin touch anything, and so on, but later said he had not been in pain at all, we would be more likely to conclude that he was lying or suffering from amnesia than that he had not been in pain.

Even if there were stronger grounds for refusing to attribute pain to those who do not have a language, the consequences of this refusal might lead us to examine these grounds unusually critically. Human infants, as well as some adults, are unable to use language. Are we to deny that a year-old infant can suffer? If not, how can language be crucial? Of course, most parents can understand the responses of even very young infants better than they understand the responses of other animals, and sometimes infant responses can be understood in the light of later development. . . .

The grounds we have for believing that other mammals and birds suffer are, then, closely analogous to the grounds we have for believing that other humans suffer. It remains to consider how far down the evolutionary scale this analogy holds. Obviously it becomes poorer when we get further away from man. To be more precise would require a detailed examination of all that we know about other forms of life. With fish, reptiles, and other vertebrates the analogy still seems strong, with molluscs like oysters it is much weaker. Insects are more difficult, and it may be that in our present state of knowledge we must be agnostic about whether they are capable of suffering.

If there is no moral justification for ignoring suffering when it occurs, and it does occur in other species, what are we to say of our attitudes toward these other species? Richard Ryder, one of the contributors to *Animals, Men and Morals*, uses the term "speciesism" to describe the belief that we are entitled to treat members of other species in a way in which it would be wrong to treat members of our own species. The term is not euphonious, but it neatly makes the analogy with racism. The nonracist would do well to bear the analogy in mind when he is inclined to defend human behavior toward nonhumans. "Shouldn't we worry about improving the lot of our own species before we concern ourselves with other species?" he may ask. If we substitute "race" for "species" we shall see that the question is better not asked. "Is a vegetarian diet nutritionally adequate?" resembles the slaveowner's claim that he and the whole economy of the South would be ruined without slave labor. There is even a parallel with skeptical doubts about whether animals suffer, for some defenders of slavery professed to doubt whether blacks really suffer in the way that whites do.

I do not want to give the impression, however, that the case for Animal Liberation is based on the analogy with racism and no more. On the contrary, *Animals, Men and Morals* describes the various ways in which humans exploit nonhumans, and several contributors consider the defenses that have been offered, including the defense of meat-eating mentioned in the last paragraph. Sometimes the rebuttals are scornfully dismissive, rather than carefully designed to convince the detached critic. This may be a fault, but it is a fault that is inevitable, given the kind of book this is. The issue is not one on which one can remain detached. . . .

II

The logic of speciesism is most apparent in the practice of experimenting on nonhumans in order to benefit humans. This is because the issue is rarely obscured by allegations that nonhumans are so different from humans that we cannot know anything about whether they suffer. The defender of vivisection cannot use this argument because he needs to stress the similarities between man and other animals in order to justify the usefulness to the former of experiments on the latter. The researcher who makes rats choose between starvation and electric shocks to see if they develop ulcers (they do) does so because he knows that the rat has a nervous system very similar to man's, and presumably feels an electric shock in a similar way.

Richard Ryder's restrained account of experiments on animals made me angrier with my fellow men than anything else in this book. Ryder, a clinical psychologist by profession, himself experimented on animals before he came to hold the view he puts forward in his essay. Experimenting on animals is now a large industry, both academic and commercial. In 1969, more than 5 million experiments were performed in Britain, the vast majority without anesthetic (though how many of these involved pain is not known). There are no accurate U.S. figures, since there is no federal law on the subject, and in many cases no state law either. Estimates vary from 20 million to 200 million. Ryder suggests that 80 million may be the best guess. We tend to think that this is all for vital medical research, but of course it is not. Huge numbers of animals are used in university departments from Forestry to Psychology, and even more are used for commercial purposes, to test whether cosmetics can cause skin damage, or shampoos eye damage, or to test food additives or laxatives or sleeping pills or anything else.

A standard test for foodstuffs is the "LD50." The object of this test is to find the dosage level at which 50 percent of the test animals will die. This means that nearly all of them will become very sick before finally succumbing or surviving. When the substance is a harmless one, it may be necessary to force huge doses down the animals, until in some cases sheer volume or concentration causes death.

Ryder gives a selection of experiments, taken from recent scientific journals. I will quote two, not for the sake of indulging in gory details, but in order to give an idea of what normal researchers think they may legitimately do to other species. The point is not that the individual researchers are cruel men, but that they are behaving in a way that is allowed by our speciesist attitudes. As Ryder points out, even if only 1 percent of the experiments involve severe pain, that is 50,000 experiments in Britain each year, or nearly 150 every day (and about fifteen times as many in the United States, if Ryder's guess is right). Here then are two experiments:

> O. S. Ray and R. J. Barrett of Pittsburg gave electric shocks to the feet of 1,042 mice. They then caused convulsions by giving more intense shocks through cup-shaped electrodes applied to the animal's eyes or through pressure spring clips attached to their ears. Unfortunately some of the mice who "successfully completed Day One training were found sick or dead prior to testing on Day Two." [*Journal of Comparative and Physiological Psychology*, 1969, vol. 67, pp. 110–116]

> At the National Institute for Medical Research, Mill Hill, London, W. Feldberg and S. L. Sherwood injected chemicals into the brains of cats— "with a number of widely different substances, recurrent patterns of reaction were obtained. Retching, vomiting, defaecation, increased salivation and greatly accelerated respiration leading to panting were common features." . . .

> The injection into the brain of a large dose of Tubocuraine caused the cat to jump "from the table to the floor and then straight into

its cage, where it started calling more and more noisily whilst moving about restlessly and jerkily . . . finally the cat fell with legs and neck flexed, jerking in rapid clonic movements, the condition being that of a major [epileptic] convulsion . . . within a few seconds the cat got up, ran for a few yards at high speed and fell in another fit. The whole process was repeated several times within the next ten minutes, during which the cat lost faeces and foamed at the mouth."

This animal finally died thirty-five minutes after the brain injection. [*Journal of Physiology*, 1954, vol. 123, pp. 148–167]

There is nothing secret about these experiments. One has only to open any recent volume of a learned journal, such as the *Journal of Comparative and Physiological Psychology*, to find full descriptions of experiments of this sort, together with the results obtained—results that are frequently trivial and obvious. The experiments are often supported by public funds.

It is a significant indication of the level of acceptability of these practices that, although these experiments are taking place at this moment on university campuses throughout the country, there has, so far as I know, not been the slightest protest from the student movement. Students have been rightly concerned that their universities should not discriminate on grounds of race or sex, and that they should not serve the purposes of the military or big business. Speciesism continues undisturbed, and many students participate in it. There may be a few qualms at first, but since everyone regards it as normal, and it may even be a required part of a course, the student soon becomes hardened and, dismissing his earlier feelings as "mere sentiment," comes to regard animals as statistics rather than sentient beings with interests that warrant consideration.

Argument about vivisection has often missed the point because it has been put in absolutist terms: Would the abolitionist be prepared to let thousands die if they could be saved by experimenting on a single animal? The way to reply to this purely hypothetical question is to pose another: Would the experimenter be prepared to experiment on a human orphan under six months old, if it were the only way to save many lives? (I say "orphan" to avoid the complication of parental feelings, although in doing so I am being overfair to the experimenter, since the nonhuman subjects of experiments are not orphans.) A negative answer to this question indicates that the experimenter's readiness to use nonhumans is simple discrimination, for adult apes, cats, mice, and other mammals are more conscious of what is happening to them, more self-directing, and, so far as we can tell, just as sensitive to pain as a human infant. There is no characteristic that human infants possess that adult mammals do not have to the same or a higher degree.

(It might be possible to hold that what makes it wrong to experiment on a human infant is that the infant will in time develop into more than the nonhuman, but one would then, to be consistent, have to oppose abortion, and perhaps contraception, too, for the fetus and the egg and sperm have the same potential as the infant. Moreover, one would still have no reason for experimenting on a nonhuman rather than a human with brain damage severe enough to make it impossible for him to rise above infant level.)

The experimenter, then, shows a bias for his own species whenever he carries out an experiment on a nonhuman for a purpose that he would not think justified him in using a human being at an equal or lower level of sentience, awareness, ability to be self-directing, etc. No one familiar with the kind of results yielded by these experiments can have the slightest doubt that if this bias were eliminated the number of experiments performed would be zero or very close to it.

III

If it is vivisection that shows the logic of speciesism most clearly, it is the use of other species for food that is at the heart of our attitudes toward them. Most of *Animals, Men and Morals* is an attack on meat-eating—an attack which is based solely on concern for nonhumans, without reference to arguments derived from considerations of ecology, macrobiotics, health, or religion.

The idea that nonhumans are utilities, means to our ends, pervades our thought. Even conservationists who are concerned about the slaughter of wild fowl but not about the vastly greater slaughter of chickens for our tables are thinking in this way—they are worried about what we would lose if there were less wildlife. Stanley Godlovitch, pursuing the Marxist idea that our thinking is formed by the activities we undertake in satisfying our needs, suggests that man's first classification of his environment was into Edibles and Inedibles. Most animals came into the first category, and there they have remained.

Man may always have killed other species for food, but he has never exploited them so ruthlessly as he does today. Farming has succumbed to business methods, the objective being to get the highest possible ratio of output (meat, eggs, milk) to input (fodder, labor costs, etc.). Ruth Harrison's essay "On Factory Farming" gives an account of some aspects of modern methods, and of the unsuccessful British campaign for effective controls, a campaign which was sparked off by her *Animal Machines* (Stuart: London, 1964).

Her article is in no way a substitute for her earlier book. This is a pity since, as she says, "Farm produce is still associated with mental pictures of animals browsing in the fields, . . . of hens having a last forage before going to roost. . . ." Yet neither in her article nor elsewhere in *Animals, Men and Morals* is this false image replaced by a clear idea of the nature and extent of factory farming. We learn of this only indirectly, when we hear of the code of reform proposed by an advisory committee set up by the British government.

Among the proposals, which the government refused to implement on the grounds that they were too idealistic, were: "*Any animal should at least have room to turn around freely.*"

Factory farm animals need liberation in the most literal sense. Veal calves are kept in stalls five feet by two feet. They are usually slaughtered when about four months old, and have been too big to turn in their stalls for at least a month. Intensive beef herds, kept in stalls only proportionately larger for much longer periods, account for a growing percentage of beef production. Sows are often similarly confined when pregnant, which, because of artificial methods of increasing fertility, can be most of the time. Animals confined in this way do not waste food by exercising, nor do they develop unpalatable muscle.

"*A dry bedded area should be provided for all stock.*" Intensively kept animals usually have to stand and sleep on slatted floors without straw, because this makes cleaning easier.

"*Palatable roughage must be readily available to all calves after one week of age.*" In order to produce the pale veal housewives are said to prefer, calves are fed on an all-liquid diet until slaughter, even though they are long past the age at which they would normally eat grass. They develop a craving for roughage, evidenced by attempts to gnaw wood from their stalls. (For the same reason, their diet is deficient in iron.)

"Battery cages for poultry should be large enough for a bird to be able to stretch one wing at a time." Under current British practice, a cage for four or five laying hens has a floor area of twenty inches by eighteen inches, scarcely larger than a double page of the *New York Review of Books*. In this space, on a sloping wire floor (sloping so the eggs roll down, wire so the dung drops through) the birds live for a year or eighteen months while artificial lighting and temperature conditions combine with drugs in their food to squeeze the maximum number of eggs out of them. Table birds are also sometimes kept in cages. More often they are reared in sheds, no less crowded. Under these conditions all the birds' natural activities are frustrated, and they develop "vices" such as pecking each other to death. To prevent this, beaks are often cut off, and the sheds kept dark.

How many of those who support factory farming by buying its produce know anything about the way it is produced? How many have heard something about it, but are reluctant to check up for fear that it will make them uncomfortable? To non-speciesists, the typical consumer's mixture of ignorance, reluctance to find out the truth, and vague belief that nothing really bad could be allowed seems analogous to the attitudes of "decent Germans" to the death camps.

There are, of course, some defenders of factory farming. Their arguments are considered, though again rather sketchily, by John Harris. Among the most common: "Since they have never known anything else, they don't suffer." This argument will not be put by anyone who knows anything about animal behavior, since he will know that not all behavior has to be learned. Chickens attempt to stretch wings, walk around, scratch, and even dustbathe or build a nest, even though they have never lived under conditions that allowed these activities. Calves can suffer from maternal deprivation no matter at what age they were taken from their mothers. "We need these intensive methods to provide protein for a growing population." As ecologists and famine relief organizations know, we can produce far more protein per acre if we grow the right vegetable crop, soy beans for instance, than if we use the land to grow crops to be converted into protein by animals who use nearly 90 percent of the protein themselves, even when unable to exercise.

There will be many readers of this book who will agree that factory farming involves an unjustifiable degree of exploitation of sentient creatures, and yet will want to say that there is nothing wrong with rearing animals for food, provided it is done "humanely." These people are saying, in effect, that although we should not cause animals to suffer, there is nothing wrong with killing them.

There are two possible replies to this view. One is to attempt to show that this combination of attitudes is absurd. Roslind Godlovitch takes this course in her essay, which is an examination of some common attitudes to animals. She argues that from the combination of "animal suffering is to be avoided" and "there is nothing wrong with killing animals" it follows that all animal life ought to be exterminated (since all sentient creatures will suffer to some degree at some point in their lives). Euthanasia is a contentious issue only because we place some value on living. If we did not, the least amount of suffering would justify it. Accordingly, if we deny that we have a duty to exterminate all animal life, we must concede that we are placing some value on animal life.

This argument seems to me valid, although one could still reply that the value of animal life is to be derived from the pleasures that life can have for them, so that, provided their lives have a balance of pleasure over pain, we are justified in rearing them. But this would imply that we ought to produce animals and let them live as pleasantly as possible, without suffering.

At this point, one can make the second of the two possible replies to the view that rearing and killing animals for food is all right so long as it is done humanely. This second reply is that so long as we think that a nonhuman may be killed simply so that a human can satisfy his taste for meat, we are still thinking of nonhumans as means rather than as ends in themselves. The factory farm is nothing more than the application of technology to this concept. Even traditional methods involve castration, the separation of mothers and their young, the breaking up of herds, branding or ear-punching, and of course transportation to the abattoirs and the final moments of terror when the animal smells blood and senses danger. If we were to try rearing animals so that they lived and died without suffering, we should find that to do so on anything like the scale of today's meat industry would be a sheer impossibility. Meat would become the prerogative of the rich.

I have been able to discuss only some of the contributions to this book, saying nothing about, for instance, the essays on killing for furs and for sport. Nor have I considered all the detailed questions that need to be asked once we start thinking about other species in the radically different way presented by this book. What, for instance, are we to do about genuine conflicts of interest like rats biting slum children? I am not sure of the answer, but the essential point is just that we *do* see this as a conflict of interests, that we recognize that rats have interests too. Then we may begin to think about other ways of resolving the conflict—perhaps by leaving out rat baits that sterilize the rats instead of killing them.

I have not discussed such problems because they are side issues compared with the exploitation of other species for food and for experimental purposes. On these central matters, I hope that I have said enough to show that this book, despite its flaws, is a challenge to every human to recognize his attitudes to nonhumans as a form of prejudice no less objectionable than racism or sexism. It is a challenge that demands not just a change of attitudes, but a change in our way of life, for it requires us to become vegetarians.

Can a purely moral demand of this kind succeed? The odds are certainly against it. The book holds out no inducements. It does not tell us that we will become healthier, or enjoy life more, if we cease exploiting animals. Animal Liberation will require greater altruism on the part of mankind than any other liberation movement, since animals are incapable of demanding it for themselves, or of protesting against their exploitation by votes, demonstrations, or bombs. Is man capable of such genuine altruism? Who knows? If this book does have a significant effect, however, it will be a vindication of all those who have believed that man has within himself the potential for more than cruelty and selfishness.

Interest Criterion of Standing

Death, Misfortune and Species Inequality

Ruth Cigman

It has been argued that "speciesism—"unjust and discriminatory attitudes towards species other than our own—is a vice analogous to sexism and racism. Opposition to this phenomenon embraces two kinds of claims, one of them reasonable, the other by no means so. The weak claim, which I accept, is that we should treat many animals better than we do, and take whatever steps are necessary to oppose certain cruel practices toward them. The stronger claim is that, as women and blacks should have rights equal to those of men and whites, animals should have rights equal to those of persons, because difference of species does not constitute a morally relevant difference.

My view is that the stronger claim is sentimental and confused. Most important, it seriously misrepresents features of human experience such as attitudes to life and the misfortune of death. I shall attack it by exploring the relationship between (a) the kinds of obligations we have towards a creature (person, animal), and the correlative rights to which he or she is entitled; and (b) the kinds of misfortunes of which that creature may be a subject (or victim). . . .

I. Species Inequality

The phenomenon of speciesism must be described with care. One anti-speciesist has described it as the belief that it is justifiable "to treat a member of another species in a way in which it would be wrong to treat our own."[1] This definition isn't quite right; nor does it parallel the definitions of racism and sexism. A school which received an application from a parent for admission of her child and pet monkey would be quite justified in accepting the child and rejecting the monkey, however dull the child and bright the monkey; just as a dramatic director would be justified in turning down the most talented actress in the world in favor of an inferior actor, to fill the role of King Lear. Neither school nor director would be guilty of the "ism" in question. The vice abhorred by anti-speciesists is not the denial that animals and persons are in all respects identical (whatever this would mean), and therefore entitled to identical treatment; it is rather a much more plausible claim about the possession across species (many, not all) of certain morally relevent *capacties*. Specifically, speciesism may be seen as a failure to acknowledge the equal capacities of persons and animals to *suffer*, and (it is claimed) the moral equality which is a corollary of this fact.

As such, speciesism bears at least a superficial resemblance to sexism and racism, the error of which consists in part in a

---

[1] Peter Singer, "Animal Liberation," in *Moral Problems*, ed. James Rachels (New York: Harper and Row, 1975).

failure to understand what Bernard Williams has called the "useful tautology" that all human beings are human beings.[2] This phrase serves to remind anyone who believes that blacks or women are inherently inferior that these are not merely members of a certain species, but are also *human* or *persons*. The emphasis on these terms suggests certain capacities and related vulnerabilities which are more or less universally possessed by persons, and one is made to think of such truths as: all persons are able to suffer physical and mental pain, and to experience, and be frustrated in, affection for others. These truths give rise to certain moral claims which may be irrationally obscured by incidental characteristics such as skin color and sex.

Some anti-speciesists (notably Jeremy Bentham and, more recently, Peter Singer) have attacked speciesism along similar lines.[3] Species equality, they argue, is typically overlooked by virtue of morally insignificant features such as the number of legs a creature possesses, or the inability to talk. Equal capacity to suffer is the only reasonable ground for moral equality; it has been shown, moreover, that many species are in possession of nervous systems of comparable complexity to those of humans, and that they therefore suffer pain of comparable intensity.

However the equal capacity to suffer physical pain is only part of what the anti-sexist or anti-racist is getting at by emphasizing the humanity or personhood of all human beings. Implicit in this claim (the tautological status of which is, of course, more apparent than real) is an allusion to a *range* of vulnerabilities, or misfortunes, of which persons are able to be subjects, and by virtue of which they possess equal rights. Among these is the misfortune of death. Nothing that is said by the anti-speciesist about the suffering of physical pain suggests that animals are subject to the same range of misfortunes as persons, still less that death is a misfortune for an animal. Even if we grant that the equal capacity of persons and animals to suffer physical pain somehow yields equal rights not to be recipients of physical cruelty, it is far from clear why this should entail moral equality, that is, equality over a range of fundamental rights.

I want to suggest that a right to X entails the right to be protected from certain actions which will result in the misfortune, or possible misfortune, of not-X. A condition for being the subject of a right is therefore the *capacity* to be a subject of the corresponding misfortune. The relationship between capacity and desire in this context must be examined: for example, a creature may be a subject of the misfortune of death even if he or she doesn't *desire* not to die, so long as it is the case that he or she has the *capacity* to desire not to die. My suggestion is that, when we fill in the concept of desiring not to die in a way which is relevant to the misfortune of death and the right to life, we shall have to withhold this from animals.

II. Animal Misfortune and Human Misfortune

Of what kinds of misfortunes are animals subjects? A claim which may be rejected at the start is this: it is impossible to know exactly how much animals suffer, or what counts as a misfortune *for them;* it is therefore a form of speciesist arrogance to assume that their misfortunes are worthy of less concern than our own. Against this it must be said that the evidence we have that

---

[2]Bernard Williams. "The Idea of Equality," in *Problems of the Self* (Cambridge: Cambridge University Press, 1973).

[3]See Peter Singer, "Animal Liberation," where Bentham is quoted approvingly.

animals suffer *at all* is the same as the evidence which enables us to judge the nature and extent of this suffering. No philosopher has suggested this more powerfully than Wittgenstein, in his remarks about the deeply misunderstood relationship between behavior and the "inner life." It is worth quoting some of these:

> . . . only of a living human being and what resembles (behaves like) a living human being can one say: it has sensations; it sees; is blind; hears; is deaf; is conscious or unconscious.
>
> Look at a stone and imagine it having sensations. One says to oneself: How could one so much as get the idea of ascribing a *sensation* to a *thing?* One might as well ascribe it to a number!—And now look at a wriggling fly and at once these difficulties vanish and pain seems to get a foothold here, where before everything was, so to speak, too smooth for it.
>
> One can imagine an animal, angry, frightened, unhappy, happy, startled. But hopeful? And why not?
>
> A dog believes his master is at the door. But can he also believe his master will come the day after tomorrow?—And *what* can he not do here?[4]

Wittgenstein is not merely concerned in these passages with the difficulty of *imagining* the truth of certain mental descriptions (for example, "This dog is hopeful"; "This stone has sensations"). Maybe one *can* (or thinks one can—it may be hard to distinguish these) imagine these being true; what one cannot do is sensibly *consider* the possibility that they may be true, for to do this (Wittgenstein suggests) would be to remove the concept of hope from the context in which it has sense—where human beings talk and behave in ways which reveal their sense of the future, of alternative prospects, of concern for themselves and others, and so on. These form part of the structure, so to speak, of hope; it does not make sense to ascribe hope to a creature which manifests no awareness of future possibilities. Wittgenstein's choice of example may be questioned here; I think there do exist a small number of animals which may express hope in their behavior. But the point is sound: the mental experience which is sensibly attributed to a creature is commensurate with the complexity and nature of its behavioral expression. A wriggling fly may be supposed to feel pain; here, though, hope definitely fails to find a foothold.

If this is correct, two further conclusions must be drawn: (1) The "useful tautology" discussed earlier does not merely suggest certain vulnerabilities to which more or less everyone is subject; it also suggests, I think, certain complexities of experience surrounding these vulnerabilities, which are not attributable to animals. I have in mind, for example, the fear of death, or of contracting a fatal disease; the desire for respect or esteem from others; the desire to lead a fulfilling life (for one's life to have a "point," or "meaning"); the desire to achieve certain goals and resolve certain problems; and, finally, corresponding fears and desires on behalf of others. (2) These thoughts or experiences suggest a reason why persons deserve greater moral concern than animals. The capacity to talk does not *itself* provide such a reason; rather this capacity is related to, and is a condition for, the capacity to suffer complex and severe misfortunes, which animals are logically unable to suffer. Among these are the kinds of misfortunes which we call "tragic." It is with great strain that we say of an animal that he suffers a tragedy, even, I think, when he is destined for a premature death. The failure of Bentham and others to recognize this results from a crude conception

---

[4]Ludwig Wittgenstein, *Philosophical Investigations* (London: Basil Blackwell, 1953), pars. 281; 284; and p. 174.

of what it is to suffer a misfortune. Let us consider this briefly.

This conception is narrowly utilitarian. If one thinks, with Bentham, that all the good and bad things that can happen to one in life are quantities of pleasurable and painful experience, the comparison between animal and human misfortune will appear quite reasonable; for it is plausible, given this conception, to suggest that one can distinguish degrees of *intensity* of animal pain as well as one can do this with human pain. But notice that this view suggests (a) that all misfortune involves unpleasant experiences; (b) that all unpleasant experiences are measurable against one another—which is most implausible where tragedies and many other severe misfortunes are concerned; and (c) that death (as opposed to dying) is not a misfortune at all, for it involves no unpleasant experience, but rather an *absence* of experience. In fact, (c) is part of a famous argument by Lucretius, to the effect that the fear of death grows out of an irrational conception of death as a state which we *endure*, in which the loss of life is in some sense experienced. Lucretius argues that death is not experienced at all, for it is complete annihilation; therefore there is no subject *for whom* death can be a misfortune, and hence death is not a misfortune at all.

I do not want to suggest that Bentham is committed to this Lucretian view,[5] only that the identification of misfortune with unpleasant experience has this conception as a likely corollary. This identification seems to me *generally* adequate where animals are concerned; misfortunes for animals essentially consist in a rather limited range of unpleasant experiences (physical pain, emotional loss, and so on). To the extent that these are the kinds of misfortunes of which animals may be victims, I think it is correct to conclude that death is not a misfortune for an animal. For if the worst that can be said of the quick and painless death of an animal (of course suffering is another matter) is that it removes a quantity of pleasurable experience from the world, this does not justify calling that death a misfortune *for the animal who dies*. One may *prefer* that the death had not occurred, because one has a kind of utilitarian preference for a world containing as much pleasure as possible. This is very different from saying that it is the animal's misfortune. For this to make sense, it would have to be the case that the animal revealed a certain kind of *desire* to live, or was capable of having such a desire to live. . . .

Williams introduces the useful concept of a categorical desire. This is a desire which does not merely presuppose being alive (like the desire to eat when one is hungry), but rather answers the question whether one wants to remain alive. It may answer this question affirmatively or not. Williams discusses what he calls a rational forward-looking desire for suicide; this desire is categorical because it resolves (negatively), rather than assumes, the question of one's continued existence. Alternatively one may resolve this question affirmatively with a desire, for example, to raise children or write a book. Such desires give one reason to go on living, they give life a so-called point or meaning. Most persons have some such desires throughout substantial periods of their lives.

A person who possesses categorical desires of the second sort is, Williams suggests, vulnerable to the misfortune of death. . . . "To want something," says Williams, "is to that extent to have a reason for resisting what excludes having that thing: and death certainly does that, for a very large range of things that one wants." A subject of

---

[5] A Utilitarian like Bentham may argue that death is a misfortune because it prevents the satisfaction of certain desires. I find this unconvincing when applied to animals, however, for reasons which will be defended later on.

categorical desires, therefore, "has reason to regard possible death as a misfortune to be avoided, and we, looking at things from his point of view, would have reason to regard his actual death as a misfortune." The fear of death need not grow out of a confused conception of death as a state which is somehow suffered as Lucretius claims; it may be the entirely rational corollary of the desire to do certain things with one's life. . . .

It will be obvious from the earlier discussion that I reject the suggestion that a categorical desire, or anything of this nature, is attributable to animals. For consider what would have to be the case if this were so. First, animals would have to possess essentially the same conceptions of life and death as persons do. The subject of a categorical desire must either understand death as a condition which closes a possible future forever, and leaves behind one a world in which one has no part as an agent or conscious being of any sort; or he must grasp, and then reject, this conception of death, in favor of a belief in immortality. Either way, the radical and exclusive nature of the transition from life to death must be understood—it must at least be appreciated why people think in these terms—so that the full significance of the idea that "X is a reason for living" may be grasped.

One can only understand life and death in these ways if one possesses the related concepts of long-term future possibilities, of life itself as an object of value, of consciousness, agency, and their annihilation, and of tragedy and similar misfortunes. It is only by an imaginative leap that possession of these concepts seems attributable to animals as well as to persons; this leap is all the more tempting, and therefore all the more dangerous, because it is not *obviously* absurd. It is certainly the case, for example, that some animals experience emotions of a relatively sophisticated nature, and that these emotions involve a kind of recognition of such things as human misfortune, impending danger to another, potential loss, and so on. I see no reason to withhold the ascription of sympathy, anxiety, even grief, to some animals; I only want to deny (what may be suggested by an antispeciesist) that these emotions, and the range of awareness which they presuppose, give us a way into legitimately ascribing to animals an understanding of the finality, and potentially tragic significance, of death. Such understanding is necessary for a subject of categorical desires.

IV. Misfortunes and Rights

If my argument is correct, animals lack the very capacity which is necessary for the right to life: the capacity to have categorical desires. This capacity is necessary for a creature to be a possible subject of the misfortune of death, and *this* possibility is presupposed by the right to life; otherwise the right to life would be a right to be protected from something which could not conceivably be a misfortune, which does not make sense. I want to suggest, furthermore, that the capacity to be a subject of the misfortune of death is *sufficient* for possession of the right to life. I shall try to clarify this last point with reference to an article by Michael Tooley.[6]

Tooley points out that the concepts of a person and human being are usefully prized apart by employing the former as a purely moral concept, entailing the right to life, and the latter to denote membership of the species homo sapiens. The question may then be raised whether all human beings should be regarded as persons (how about fetuses and even newborn infants?), and whether some *non*-humans shouldn't be regarded as persons. The distinction is a valuable one, but its usefulness depends upon the discovery of criteria for personhood in

---

[6]Michael Tooley, "Abortion and Infanticide," in *Philosophy & Public Affairs* 2, no. I (Fall 1972).

this purely moral sense. Tooley suggests that possession of the concept of self as a continuing subject of experiences, and knowledge that one is such a self, are necessary and sufficient for personhood. His claim seems to be that the right to life is entailed by the *desire* for life as a continuing "self," which is present, or explicably absent (for example, through insanity or indoctrination) in most persons. He argues (rather as I have done) that such a desire presupposes a degree of conceptual sophistication which not all humans (for example, fetuses and newborn infants) possess.

Despite resemblances to my own position, there are important differences. For Tooley, a right to X is essentially an obligation on the part of others to respect the subject's *desire* for X; this is so, it seems, irrespective of whether or not the desire is reasonable or rational, good or evil. However it is most implausible to suggest that the right to life depends on the desire to live; one reason is that one does not forgo this right by *relinquishing* the desire to live. More generally, rights are independent of desires, for people may have desires without corresponding rights (for example, the desire to steal), and rights without corresponding desires (for example, the right to become an American citizen).

The connection between rights and misfortunes is a much more fruitful one. Not all possible misfortunes are matched by rights, though I believe the converse is true. Yet it seems reasonable to suggest that the reason why most human beings (biological concept) have the right to life is related to the fact that death is regarded as possibly a grave misfortune for a human being. The fact that most people desperately do not *want* to die is not what makes death a misfortune, or gives us the right to life; it is rather that this desire is an aspect of a rich understanding of what is not, so to speak, in our "interests" as human beings. Human beings have, we feel, the capacity clearly to recognize what is so appalling about death—its finality and inexorable quality for a self-conscious being—and this recognition is part of what makes death appalling. This, combined with the fact that death is something from which we can to some extent be protected, is part of the reason why we ascribe to human beings the right to life.

I suggest, therefore that the capacity to *see* death as a misfortune is sufficient for the truth of the claim that death *is* a misfortune for the person in question; also that this capacity is sufficient for the right to life. . . .

Life Criterion of Standing

On Being Morally Considerable

Kenneth E. Goodpaster

A thing is right when it tends to preserve the integrity, stability, and beauty of the biotic community.

It is wrong when it tends otherwise.

–Aldo Leopold

What follows is a preliminary inquiry into a question which needs more elaborate treatment than an essay can provide. The question can be and has been addressed in different rhetorical formats, but perhaps G. J. Warnock's formulation of it[1] is the best to start with:

> Let us consider the question to whom principles of morality apply from, so to speak, the other end—from the standpoint not of the agent, but of the "patient." What, we may ask here, is the condition of moral *relevance*? What is the condition of having a claim to be *considerred*, by rational agents to whom moral principles apply? (148) . . .

Neither rationality nor the capacity to experience pleasure and pain seem to me necessary (even though they may be sufficient) conditions on moral considerability. And only our hedonistic and concentric forms of ethical reflection keep us from acknowledging this fact. Nothing short of the condition of *being alive* seems to me to be a plausible and nonarbitrary criterion. . . .

Warnock . . . settles upon his own solution. The basis of moral claims, he says, may be put as follows:

> . . . just as liability to be judged as a moral agent follows from one's general capability of alleviating, by moral action, the ills of the predicament, and is for that reason confined to rational beings, so the condition of being a proper "beneficiary" of moral action is the capability of *suffering* the ills of the predicament—and for that reason is not confined to rational beings, nor even to potential members of that class (151).

The criterion of moral considerability then, is located in the *capacity to suffer:*

> For all A, X deserves moral consideration from A if and only if X is capable of suffering pain (or experiencing enjoyment).

And the defense involves appeal to what Warnock considers to be (analytically) the *object* of the moral enterprise: amelioration of "the predicament."

W. K. Frankena, in a recent paper,[2] joins forces:

> Like Warnock, I believe that there are right and wrong ways to treat infants, animals, imbeciles, and idiots even if or even though (as the case may be) they are not persons or human beings—just because they are capable of pleasure and suffering, and not just because their lives happen to have some value to or for those who clearly are persons or human beings.

And Peter Singer[3] writes:

> If a being is not capable of suffering, or of experiencing enjoyment or happiness, there is nothing to be taken into account. This is why the limit of sentience (using the term as a convenient, if not strictly accurate, shorthand for the capacity to suffer or experience enjoyment or happiness) is the only defensible boundary of concern for the interests of others (154).

. . . Although I acknowledge and even applaud the conviction expressed by these philosophers that the capacity to suffer (or perhaps better, *sentience*) is sufficient for moral considerability, I fail to understand their reasons for thinking such a criterion necessary. To be sure, there are hints at reasons in each case. Warnock implies that nonsentient beings could not be proper "beneficiaries" of moral action. Singer seems to think that beyond sentience "there is nothing to take into account." And Frankena suggests that nonsentient

---

[1] *The Object of Morality* (New York: Methuen, 1971); parenthetical page references to Warnock will be to this book.

[2] "Ethics and the Environment," in K. E. Goodpaster and K. M. Sayre, eds., *Ethics and Problems of the 21st Century* (Notre Dame, Ind.: University Press, 1978).

[3] "All Animals Are Equal," in Tom Regan and Peter Singer, *Animal Rights and Human Obligations* (Englewood Cliffs, N.J.: Prentice-Hall. 1976). See p. 316.

beings simply do not provide us with moral reasons for respecting them unless it be potentially for sentience.[4] Yet it is so clear that there *is* something to take into account, something that is not merely "potential sentience" and which surely does qualify beings as beneficiaries and capable of harm—namely, *life*—that the hints provided seem to me to fall short of good reasons.

Biologically, it appears that sentience is an adaptive characteristic of living organisms that provides them with a better capacity to anticipate, and so avoid, threats to life. This at least suggests, though of course it does not prove, that the capacities to suffer and to enjoy are ancillary to something more important rather than tickets to considerability in their own right. In the words of one perceptive scientific observer:

> If we view pleasure as rooted in our sensory physiology, it is not difficult to see that our neurophysiological equipment must have evolved via variation and selective retention in such a way as to record a positive signal to adaptationally satisfactory conditions and a negative signal to adaptationally unsatisfactory conditions. . . . The pleasure signal is only an evolutionarily derived indicator, not the goal itself. It is the applause which signals a job well done, but not the actual completion of the job.[5]

Nor is it absurd to imagine that evolution might have resulted (indeed might still result?) in beings whose capacities to maintain, protect, and advance their lives did not depend upon mechanisms of pain and pleasure at all. . . .

Joel Feinberg offers (51) what may be the clearest and most explicit case for a restrictive criterion on moral considerability (restrictive with respect to life). . . . The central thesis defended by Feinberg is that a being cannot intelligibly be said to possess moral rights (read: deserve moral consideration) unless that being satisfies the "interest principle," and that only the subclass of humans and higher animals among living beings satisfies this principle:

> . . . the sorts of beings who have rights are precisely those who have (or can have) interests. I have come to this tentative conclusion for two reasons: (1) because a right holder must be capable of being represented and it is impossible to represent a being that has no interests, and (2) because a right holder must be capable of being a beneficiary in his own person, and a being without interests is a being that is incapable of being harmed or benefited, having no good or "sake" of its own (51).

Implicit in this passage are the following two arguments, interpreted in terms of moral considerability:

(A1) Only beings who can be represented can deserve moral consideration. Only beings who have (or can have) interests can be represented. Therefore, only beings who have (or can have) interests can deserve moral consideration.

(A2) Only beings capable of being beneficiaries can deserve moral consideration. Only beings who have (or can have) interests are capable of being beneficiaries. Therefore, only beings

---

[4] "I can see no reason, from the moral point of view, why we should respect something that is alive but has no conscious sentiency and so can experience no pleasure or pain, joy or suffering, unless perhaps it is potentially a consciously sentient being, as in the case of a fetus. Why, if leaves and trees have no capacity to feel pleasure or to suffer, should I tear no leaf from a tree? Why should I respect its location any more than that of a stone in my driveway, if no benefit or harm comes to any person or sentient being by my moving it?" ("Ethics and the Environment.")

[5] Mark W. Lipsey, "Value Science and Developing Society," paper delivered to the Society for Religion in Higher Education, Institute on Society, Technology and Values (July 15–August 4, 1973), p. 11.

who have (or can have) interests can deserve moral consideration.

I suspect that these two arguments are at work between the lines in Warnock, Frankena, and Singer, though of course one can never be sure. In any case, I propose to consider them as the best defense of the sentience criterion in recent literature.

I am prepared to grant, with some reservations, the first premises in each of these obviously valid arguments. The second premises, though, are *both* importantly equivocal. To claim that only beings who have (or can have) interests can be represented might mean that "mere things" cannot be represented because they have nothing to represent, no "interests" as opposed to "usefulness" to defend or protect. Similarly, to claim that only beings who have (or can have) interests are capable of being beneficiaries might mean that "mere things" are incapable of being benefited or harmed—they have no "well-being" to be sought or acknowledged by rational moral agents. So construed, Feinberg seems to be right; but he also seems to be committed to allowing any *living* thing the status of moral considerability. For as he himself admits, even plants

> ... are not "mere things"; they are vital objects with inherited biological propensities determining their natural growth. Moreover we do say that certain conditions are "good" or "bad" for plants. thereby suggesting that plants, unlike rocks, are capable of having a "good" (51).

But Feinberg pretty clearly wants to draw the nets tighter than this—and he does so by intepreting the notion of "interests" in the two second premises more narrowly. The contrast term he favors is not "mere things" but "mindless creatures." And he makes this move by insisting that "interests" logically presuppose *desires* or *wants* or *aims*, the equipment for which is not possessed by plants (nor, we might add, by many animals or even some humans?).

But why should we accept this shift in strength of the criterion? In doing so, we clearly abandon one sense in which living organisms like plants do have interests that can be represented. There is no absurdity in imagining the representation of the needs of a tree for sun and water in the face of a proposal to cut it down or pave its immediate radius for a parking lot. We might of course, on reflection, decide to go ahead and cut it down or do the paving, but there is hardly an intelligibility problem about representing the tree's interest in our deciding not to. In the face of their obvious tendencies to maintain and heal themselves, it is very difficult to reject the idea of interests on the part of trees (and plants generally) in remaining alive.[6]

Nor will it do to suggest, as Feinberg does, that the needs (interests) of living things like trees are not really their own but implicitly *ours:* "Plants may need things in order to discharge their functions, but their functions are assigned by human interests, not their own" (54). As if it were human interests that assigned to trees the tasks of growth or maintenance! The interests at stake are clearly those of the living things themselves, not simply those of the owners or users or other human persons involved. Indeed, there is a suggestion in this passage that, to be capable of being represented, an organism must *matter* to human beings somehow—a suggestion whose implications for human rights (disenfranchisement) let alone the rights of animals (inconsistently for Feinberg, I think)—are grim.

The truth seems to be that the "interests" that nonsentient beings share with sentient beings (over and against "mere

---

[6]See Albert Szent-Gyorgyi, *The Living State* (New York: Academic Press, 1972), esp. chap. VI, "Vegetable Defense Systems."

things") are far more plausible as criteria of *considerability* than the "interests" that sentient beings share (over and against "mindless creatures"). This is not to say that interests construed in the latter way are morally irrelevant—for they may play a role as criteria of moral *significance*—but it is to say that psychological or hedonic capacities seem unnecessarily sophisticated when it comes to locating the minimal conditions for something's deserving to be valued for its own sake. Surprisingly, Feinberg's own reflections on "mere things" appear to support this very point:

> . . . mere things have no conative life: no conscious wishes, desires, and hopes; or urges and impulses; or unconscious drives, aims, and goals; or latent tendencies, direction of growth, and natural fulfillments. Interests must be compounded somehow out of conations; hence mere things have no interests (49).

Together with the acknowledgment, quoted earlier, that plants, for example, are not "mere things," such observations seem to undermine the interest principle in its more restrictive form. I conclude, with appropriate caution, that the interest principle either grows to fit what we might call a "life principle" or requires an arbitrary stipulation of psychological capacities (for desires, wants, etc.) which are neither warranted by (A1) and (A2) nor independently plausible.

Let us now turn to several objections that might be thought to render a "life principle" of moral considerability untenable quite independently of the adequacy or inadequacy of the sentience or interest principle. . . .

(O1) Consideration of life can serve as a criterion only to the degree that life itself can be given a precise definition; and it can't.

(R1) I fail to see why a criterion of moral considerability must be strictly decidable in order to be tenable. Surely rationality, potential rationality, sentience, and the capacity for or possession of interests fare no better here. Moreover, there do seem to be empirically respectable accounts of the nature of living beings available which are not intolerably vague or open-textured:

> The typifying mark of a living system . . . appears to be its persistent state of low entropy, sustained by metabolic processes for accumulating energy, and maintained in equilibrium with its environment by homeostatic feedback processes.[7]

Granting the need for certain further qualifications, a definition such as this strikes me as not only plausible in its own right, but ethically illuminating, since it suggests that the core of moral concern lies in respect for self-sustaining organization and integration in the face of pressures toward high entropy.

(O2) If life, as understood in the previous response, is really taken as the key to moral considerability, then it is possible that larger systems besides our ordinarily understood "linear" extrapolations from human beings (e.g., animals, plants, etc.) might satisfy the conditions, such as the biosystem as a whole. This surely would be a *reductio* of the life principle.

(R2) At best, it would be a *reductio* of the life principle in this form or without qualification. But it seems to me that such (perhaps surprising) implications, if true, should be taken seriously. There is some evidence that the biosystem as a whole exhibits behavior approximating to the definition sketched above,[8] and I see no reason

---

[7] K. M. Sayre, *Cybernetics and the Philosophy of Mind* (New York: Humanities, 1976), p. 91.

[8] See J. Lovelock and S. Epton, "The Quest for Gaia," *The New Scientist*, 65 935 (February 6, 1975): 304–09.

to deny it moral considerability on that account. Why should the universe of moral considerability map neatly onto our medium-sized framework of organisms?

(O3) There are severe epistemological problems about imputing interests, benefits, harms, etc. to nonsentient beings. What is it for a tree to have needs?

(R3) I am not convinced that the epistemological problems are more severe in this context than they would be in numerous others which the objector would probably not find problematic. Christopher Stone has put this point nicely:

> I am sure I can judge with more certainty and meaningfulness whether and when my lawn wants (needs) water than the Attorney General can judge whether and when the United States wants (needs) to take an appeal from an adverse judgment by a lower court. The lawn tells me that it wants water by a certain dryness of the blades and soil—immediately obvious to the touch—the appearance of bald spots, yellowing, and a lack of springiness after being walked on; how does "the United States" communicate to the Attorney General? (24).

We make decisions in the interest of others or on behalf of others every day—"others" whose wants are far less verifiable than those of most living creatures.

(O4) Whatever the force of the previous objections, the clearest and most decisive refutation of the principle of respect for life is that one cannot *live* according to it, nor is there any indication in nature that we were intended to. We must eat, experiment to gain knowledge, protect ourselves from predation (macroscopic and microscopic), and in general deal with the overwhelming complexities of the moral life while remaining psychologically intact. To take seriously the criterion of considerability being defended, all these things must be seen as somehow morally wrong.

(R4) This objection . . . can be met, I think, by recalling the distinction made earlier between regulative and operative moral consideration.[9] It seems to me that there clearly are limits to the operational character of respect for living things. We must eat, and usually this involves killing (though not always). We must have knowledge, and sometimes this involves experimentation with living things and killing (though not always). We must protect ourselves from predation and disease, and sometimes this involves killing (though not always). The regulative character of the moral consideration due to all living things asks, as far as I can see, for sensitivity and awareness, not for suicide (psychic or otherwise). But it is not vacuous, in that it does provide a *ceteris paribus* encouragement in the direction of nutritional, scientific, and medical practices of a genuinely life-respecting sort.

As for the implicit claim, in the objection, that since nature doesn't respect life, we needn't, there are two rejoinders. The first is that the premise is not so clearly true. Gratuitous killing in nature is rare indeed. The second, and more important, response is that the issue at hand has to do with the appropriate moral demands to be made on rational moral agents, not on beings who are not rational moral agents. Besides, this objection would tell equally against *any* criterion of moral considerability so far as I can see, if the suggestion is that nature is amoral.

---

[9]The distinction was described as follows: "Let us, then, say that the moral considerability of X is *operative* for an agent A if and only if the thorough acknowledgment of X by A is psychologically (and in general, causally) possible for A. If the moral considerability of X is defensible on all grounds independent of operativity, we shall say that it is *regulative*."—Eds.

THE NONSENTIENT ENVIRONMENT

Environmental Ethics and International Justice

Bernard E. Rollin

The past two decades have witnessed a major revolutionary thrust in social moral awareness, one virtually unknown in mainstream Western ethical thinking, although not unrecognized in other cultural traditions; for example, the Navajo, whose descriptive language for nature and animals is suffused with ethical nuances; the Australian Aboriginal people; and the ancient Persians. This thrust is the recognition that nonhuman entities enjoy some moral status as objects of moral concern and deliberation. Although the investigation of the moral status of nonhuman entities has sometimes been subsumed under the global rubric of environmental ethics, such a blanket term does not do adequate justice to the substantial conceptual differences of its components.

The Moral Status of Nonhuman Things

As a bare minimum, environmental ethics comprises two fundamentally divergent concerns—namely, concern with individual nonhuman animals as direct objects of moral concern and concern with species, ecosystems, environments, wilderness areas, forests, the biosphere, and other nonsentient natural or even abstract objects as direct objects of moral concern. Usually, although with a number of major exceptions,[1] those who give primacy to animals have tended to deny the moral significance of environments and species as direct objects of moral concern, whereas those who give moral primacy to enviro-ecological concerns tend to deny or at least downplay the moral significance of individual animals.[2] Significant though these differences are, they should not cloud the dramatic nature of this common attempt to break out of a moral tradition that finds loci of value only in human beings and, derivatively, in human institutions.

Because of the revolutionary nature of these attempts, they also remain somewhat undeveloped and embryonic. Writings in this area by and large have tended to focus more on making the case for the attribution of moral status to these entities than in working out detailed answers to particular issues.[3] Thus, in order to assess these thrusts in relation to international justice, one must first attempt to articulate a consensus concerning the basic issue of attributing moral status to nonhumans, an attribution that, prima facie, flies in the face of previous moral tradition. In attempting such an articulation, one cannot hope to capture all approaches to these issues, but rather to glean what appears most defensible when assessed against the tribunal of common moral practice, moral theory attempting to explain that practice, and common moral discourse.

The most plausible strategy in attempting to revise traditional moral theory and practice is to show that the seeds of the new moral notions or extensions of old moral notions are, in fact, already implicit in the old moral machinery developed to deal with other issues. Only when such avenues are exhausted will it make sense to recommend major rebuilding of the machinery, rather than putting it to new uses. The classic examples of such extensions are obviously found in the extension of the moral/legal machinery of Western democracies to cover traditionally disenfranchised groups such as women and minorities. The relatively smooth flow of such applications owes much of its smoothness to the plausibility of a simple argument of the form:

> Our extant moral principles ought to cover all humans.
> Women are humans.
> ∴ Our extant moral principles ought to cover women.

On the other hand, conceptually radical departures from tradition do not lend themselves to such simple rational reconstruction. Thus, for example, the principles of *favoring* members of traditionally disenfranchised groups at the expense of innocent members of nondisenfranchised groups for the sake of rectifying historically based injustice is viewed as much more morally problematic and ambivalent than simply according rights to these groups. Thus, it would be difficult to construct a simple syllogism in defense of this practice that would garner universal acquiescence with the case of the one indicated previously.

Thus, one needs to distinguish between moral revolutionary thrusts that are ostensibly paradoxical to common sense and practice because they have been ignored in a wholesale fashion, yet are in fact logical extensions of common morality, and those revolutionary thrusts that are genuinely paradoxical to previous moral thinking and practice because they are not implicit therein. Being genuinely paradoxical does not invalidate a new moral thrust—it does, however, place upon its proponents a substantially greater burden of proof. Those philosophers, like myself, who have argued for a recognition of the moral status of individual animals and the rights and legal status that derive therefrom, have attempted to place ourselves in the first category. We recognize that a society that kills and eats billions of animals, kills millions more in research, and disposes of millions more for relatively frivolous reasons and that relies economically on animal exploitation as a mainstay of social wealth, considers talk of elevating the moral status of animals as impossible and paradoxical. But this does not mean that such an elevation does not follow unrecognized from moral principles we all hold. Indeed, the abolition of slavery or the liberation of women appeared similarly paradoxical and economically impossible, yet gradually both were perceived as morally necessary, in part because both were implicit, albeit unrecognized, in previously acknowledged assumptions.[4]

My own argument for elevating the status of animals has been a relatively straightforward deduction of unnoticed implications of traditional morality. I have tried to show that no morally relevant grounds for excluding animals from the full application of our moral machinery will stand up to rational scrutiny. Traditional claims that rely on notions such as animals have no souls, are inferior to humans in power or intelligence or evolutionary status, are not moral agents, are not rational, are not possessed of free will, are not capable of language, are not bound by social contract to humans, and so forth, do not serve as justifiable reasons for excluding animals and their interests from the moral arena.

By the same token, morally relevant similarities exist between us and them in the case of the "higher" animals. Animals can suffer, as Jeremy Bentham said; they have interests; what we do to them matters to them; they can feel pain, fear, anxiety, loneliness, pleasure, boredom, and so on. Indeed, the simplicity and power of the argument calling attention to such morally relevant similarities has led Cartesians from Descartes to modern physiologists with a vested interest against attributing moral status to animals to declare that animals are machines with no morally relevant modes of awareness, a point often addressed today against moral claims such as mine. In fact, such claims have become a mainstay of what I have elsewhere called the "common sense of science." Thus, one who argues for an augmented moral status for animals finds it necessary to establish philosophically and scientifically what common sense takes for granted—namely, that animals *are* conscious.[5] Most people whose common sense is intact are not Cartesians and can see that moral talk cannot be withheld from animals and our treatment of them.

In my own work, appealing again to common moral practice, I have stressed our society's quasi-moral, quasi-legal notion of rights as a reflection of our commitment to the moral primacy of the individual, rather than the state. Rights protect what are hypothesized as the fundamental interests of human beings from cavalier encroachment by the common good—such interests as speech, assembly, belief, property, privacy, freedom from torture, and so forth. But those animals who are conscious also have fundamental interests arising out of *their* biologically given natures (or *teloi*), the infringement upon which matters greatly to them, and the fulfillment of which is central to their lives. Hence, I deduce the notion of animal rights from our common moral theory and practice and attempt to show that conceptually, at least, it is a deduction from the moral framework of the status quo rather than a major revision therein. Moral concern for individual animals follows from the hitherto ignored presence of morally relevant characteristics, primarily sentience, in animals. As a result, I am comfortable in attributing what Immanuel Kant called "intrinsic value," not merely use value, to animals if we attribute it to people.[6]

The task is far more formidable for those who attempt to make nonsentient natural objects, such as rivers and mountains, or, worse, quasi-abstract entities, such as species and ecosystems, into direct objects of moral concern. Interestingly enough, in direct opposition to the case of animals, such moves appear prima facie plausible to common morality, which has long expressed concern for the value and preservation of some natural objects, while condoning wholesale exploitation of others. In the same way, common practice often showed extreme concern for certain favored kinds of animals, while systematically exploiting others. Thus, many people in the United States strongly oppose scientific research on dogs and cats, but are totally unconcerned about such use of rodents or swine. What is superficially plausible, however, quite unlike the case of animals, turns out to be deeply paradoxical given the machinery of traditional morality.

Many leading environmental ethicists have attempted to do for nonsentient natural objects and abstract objects the same sort of thing I have tried to do for animals—namely, attempted to elevate their status to direct objects of intrinsic value, ends in themselves, which are morally valuable not only because of their relations and utility to sentient beings, but in and of themselves.[7] To my knowledge, none of these theorists has attempted to claim, as I do for animals, that the locus of such value lies in the fact that what we do to these entities matters to them. No one has argued that we can harm rivers, species, or ecosystems in ways that matter to them.

Wherein, then, do these theorists locate the intrinsic value of these entities? This is not at all clear in the writings, but seems to come down to one of the following doubtful moves:

1. Going from the fact that environmental factors are absolutely essential to the well-being or survival of beings that are loci of intrinsic value to the conclusion that environmental factors therefore enjoy a similar or even higher moral status. Such a move is clearly fallacious. Just because I cannot survive without insulin, and I am an object of intrinsic value, it does not follow that insulin is, too. In fact, the insulin is a paradigmatic example of instrumental value.
2. Going from the fact that the environment "creates" all sentient creatures to the fact that its welfare is more important than theirs. This is really a variation on (1) and succumbs to the same sort of criticism, namely, that this reasoning represents a genetic fallacy. The cause of something valuable need not itself be valuable and certainly not necessarily more valuable than its effect—its value must be established independently of its result. The Holocaust may have caused the state of Israel; that does not make the Holocaust more valuable than the state of Israel.
3. Confusing aesthetic or instrumental value for sentient creatures, notably humans, with intrinsic value and underestimating aesthetic value as a category. We shall return to this shortly, for I suspect it is the root confusion in those attempting to give nonsentient nature intrinsic value.
4. Substituting rhetoric for logic at crucial points in the discussions and using a poetic rhetoric (descriptions of natural objects in terms such as "grandeur," "majesty," "novelty," "variety") as an unexplained basis for according them "intrinsic value."
5. Going from the metaphor that infringement on natural objects "matters" to them in the sense that disturbance evokes an adjustment by their self-regulating properties, to the erroneous conclusion that such self-regulation, being analogous to conscious coping in animals, entitles them to direct moral status.

In short, traditional morality and its theory do not offer a viable way to raise the moral status of nonsentient natural objects and abstract objects so that they are direct objects of moral concern on a par with or even higher than sentient creatures. Ordinary morality and moral concern take as their focus the effects of actions on beings who can be helped and harmed, in ways that matter to them, either directly or by implication. If it is immoral to wreck someone's property, it is because it is someone's; if it is immoral to promote the extinction of species, it is because such extinction causes aesthetic or practical harm to humans or to animals or because a species is, in the final analysis, a group of harmable individuals.

There is nothing, of course, to stop environmental ethicists from making a recommendation for a substantial revision of common and traditional morality. But such recommendations are likely to be dismissed or whittled away by a moral version of Occam's razor: Why grant animals rights and acknowledge in animals intrinsic value? Because they are conscious and what we do to them matters to them? Why grant rocks, or trees, or species, or ecosystems rights? Because these objects have great aesthetic value, or are essential to us, or are basic for survival? But these are paradigmatic examples of *instrumental* value. A conceptual confusion for a noble purpose is still a conceptual confusion.

There is nothing to be gained by attempting to elevate the moral status of nonsentient natural objects to that of sentient ones. One can develop a rich environmental ethic by locating the value of nonsentient natural objects in their relation to sentient ones. One can argue for the preservation of habitats because their destruction harms animals; one can argue for preserving ecosystems on the grounds of unforeseen pernicious consequences resulting from their destruction, a claim for which much empirical evidence exists. One can argue for the preservation of animal species as the sum of a group of individuals who would be harmed by its extinction. One can argue for preserving mountains, snail darters, streams, and cockroaches on aesthetic grounds. Too many philosophers forget the moral power of aesthetic claims and tend to see aesthetic reasons as a weak basis for preserving natural objects. Yet the moral imperative not to destroy unique aesthetic objects and even nonunique ones is an onerous one that is well ingrained into common practice—witness the worldwide establishment of national parks, preserves, forests, and wildlife areas.

Rather than attempting to transcend all views of natural objects as instrumental by grafting onto nature a mystical intrinsic value that can be buttressed only by poetic rhetoric, it would be far better to nurture public appreciation of subtle instrumental value, especially aesthetic value. People can learn to appreciate the unique beauty of a desert, or of a fragile ecosystem, or even of a noxious creature like a tick, when they understand the complexity and history therein and can read the story each life form contains. I am reminded of a colleague in parasitology who is loath to destroy worms he has studied upon completing his research because he has aesthetically learned to value their complexity of structure, function, and evolutionary history and role.

It is important to note that the attribution of value to nonsentient natural objects as a relational property arising out of their significance (recognized or not) for sentient beings does not denigrate the value of natural objects. Indeed, this attribution does not even imply that the interests or desires of individual sentient beings always trump concern for nonsentient ones. Our legal system has, for example, valuable and irreplaceable property laws that forbid owners of aesthetic objects, say, a collection of Vincent van Gogh paintings, to destroy them at will, say, by adding them to one's funeral pyre. To be sure, this restriction on people's right to dispose of their own property arises out of a recognition of the value of these objects to other humans, but this is surely quite sensible. How else would one justify such a restriction? Nor, as we said earlier, need one limit the value of natural objects to their relationship to humans. Philosophically, one could, for example, sensibly (and commonsensically) argue for preservation of acreage from the golf-course developer because failure to do so would mean the destruction of thousands of sentient creatures' habitats—a major infringement of their interests—while building the golf course would fulfill the rarefied and inessential interests of a few.

Thus, in my view, one would accord moral concern to natural objects in a variety of ways, depending on the sort of object being considered. Moral status for individual animals would arise from their sentience. Moral status of species and their protection from humans would arise from the fact that a species is a collection of morally relevant individuals; moral status also would arise from the fact that humans have an aesthetic concern in not letting a unique and irreplaceable aesthetic object (or group of objects) disappear forever from our *Umwelt* (environment). Concern for wilderness areas, mountains, deserts, and so on would arise from their survival value for sentient animals as well as from their aesthetic value for humans. (Some writers have suggested that this aesthetic value is so great as to be essential to human mental/physical health, a point perfectly compatible with my position.[8])

Nothing in what I have said as yet tells us how to weigh conflicting interests, whether between humans and other sentient creatures or between human desires and environmental protection. How does one weigh the aesthetic concern of those who oppose blasting away part of a cliff against the pragmatic concern of those who wish to build on a cliffside? But the problem of weighing is equally thorny in traditional ethics—witness lifeboat questions or questions concerning the allocation of scarce medical resources. Nor does the intrinsic value approach help in adjudicating such issues. How does one weigh the alleged intrinsic value of a cliffside against the interests of the (intrinsic-value-bearing) homebuilders?

Furthermore, the intrinsic value view can lead to results that are repugnant to common sense and ordinary moral consciousness. Thus, for example, it follows from what has been suggested by one intrinsic value theorist that if a migratory herd of plentiful elk were passing through an area containing an endangered species of moss, it would be not only permissible but obligatory to kill the elk in order to protect the moss because in one case we would lose a species, in another "merely" individuals.[9] In my view, such a case has a less paradoxical resolution. Destruction of the moss does not matter to the moss, whereas elk presumably care about living or being injured. Therefore, one would give prima facie priority to the elk. This might presumably be trumped if, for example, the moss were a substratum from which was extracted an ingredient necessary to stop a raging, lethal epidemic in humans or animals. But such cases—and indeed most cases of conflicting interests—must be decided on the actual occasion. These cases are decided by a careful examination of the facts of the situation. Thus, our suggestion of a basis for environmental ethics does not qualitatively change the situation from that of current ethical deliberation, whereas granting intrinsic value to natural objects would leave us with a "whole new ball game"—and one where we do not know the rules.

In sum, then, the question of environmental ethics in relation to international justice must be analyzed into two discrete components. First are those questions that pertain to direct objects of moral concern—nonhuman animals whose sentience we have good reason to suspect—and that require the application of traditional moral notions to a hitherto ignored domain of moral objects. Second are those questions pertaining to natural objects or abstract natural objects. Although it is nonsensical to attribute intrinsic or direct moral value to these objects, they nonetheless must become (and are indeed becoming) central to our social moral deliberations. This centrality derives from our increasing recognition of the far-reaching and sometimes subtle instrumental value these objects have for humans and animals. Knowing that contamination of remote desert areas by pollutants can destroy unique panoplies of fragile beauty, or that dumping wastes into the ocean can destroy a potential source of antibiotics, or that building a pipeline can have undreamed-of harmful effects goes a long way toward making us think twice about these activities—a far longer way than endowing them with quasi-mystical rhetorical status subject to (and begging for) positivistic torpedoing.

The Environment and International Justice

How do both of these newly born areas of moral concern relate to issues of international justice? In the case of issues pertaining to moral awareness of the questions involved in the preservation and despoliation of nonsentient natural objects, processes, and abstract objects, the connection becomes increasingly clear as our knowledge increases. The interconnectedness of all things occupying the biosphere, the tenuousness and violability of certain natural objects and events whose permanence and invulnerability were long taken for granted have become dramatically clearer as environmental science has developed and the results of cavalier treatment of nature have become known.

Even those lacking any moral perspective on the instrumental values in nature now ought to have some prudential ones. Thus, even if one does not care about poisoning the air that other people and animals breathe, prudential reason would dictate that one realize that one is also poisoning oneself. Thus, the question of control of the actions of those who would or could harm another or everyone for the sake of selfish interests begins to loom large as our knowledge of environmental impact of individual actions begins to grow. These effects therefore enter into the dialectic of social justice. What constraints can legitimately be placed upon my freedoms in order to protect the environment? What social or individual benefits balance what costs to the environment or to natural objects? How much ought aesthetic values weigh against economic ones? Whole bureaucracies like the Environmental Protection Agency in the United States exist to ponder and regulate such questions in almost all civilized countries, and recent legal thinking has sought ways to codify the importance of natural objects in the law—for example, by granting them legal standing.[10] (Such a granting can and should be based on a realization of their instrumental value, not on intrinsic value; we already have such a precedent in legal standing for ships, cities, and corporations.)

Nevertheless, increased environmental knowledge has driven home a major but often ignored point: Environmental effects do not respect national boundaries. I recall traveling more than twenty years ago to the northernmost regions of eastern Canada that can be reached by road—areas inhabited almost exclusively by Native Americans to whom the benefits accruing from technological progress were manifestly limited. I was appalled to discover that in this land of few roads and fewer amenities, atmospheric pollutants such as sulfur dioxide and hydrogen sulfide reigned supreme—an unwelcome gift from factories hundreds of miles away across the U.S. border. I had no doubt that the respiratory systems of those native people were paying a heavy, and totally unjustified, price for another country's prosperity in which they did not share.

Similar examples abound. When propellant gases released by people in affluent societies (possibly) succeed in tearing a hole in the ozone layer, which hole then has cataclysmic effects on global weather, penetration of noxious rays, and so on, we again see that environmental damage does not respect national boundaries.

In a slightly different vein, one can consider underdeveloped countries struggling to raise the living standards of their populace. To do so, they must exploit and perhaps despoil resources and environments that, from the point of view of a detached observer, ought to be left alone or whose exploitation will or may in some measure ultimately threaten the whole biosphere. The detached observer may well be (and probably is) where he is in virtue of similar despoliation routinely engaged in by his country generations before environmental consciousness had dawned. Is the underdeveloped country to bear a burden of poverty just because its awakening is happening a hundred years late? Or is the new environmental knowledge to count for naught in the face of the need for development?

An excellent example of this point was recently given by an environmental scientist, Michael Mares, in an article in *Science*. Echoing the point we just made, Mares asserts that "broad-scale ecological problems have little to do with national boundaries. In our complex world, where multiple links of commerce, communications, and politics join all countries to a remarkable degree, the suggestion that ecological problems of large magnitude can or should be solved only at a local level is unrealistic. We are all involved in biospheric problems."[11]

Using the case of South America, for which massive extinction of species has been predicted and where wholesale destruction of rain forests has occurred, Mares points out that one cannot look at this situation strictly as South America's problem, but as one caused by global as well as local pressures with global and local consequences. With South American countries in economic difficulties, can one really expect governments there to take a long-run ecological perspective rather than acceding to short-term gain? If other countries in an immediate position to adopt a long-run perspective wish to do so, they must help South America with the requisite expertise as well as with significant financial assistance.

> South America's economies are in poor shape. Poverty is extensive, inflation rates in some countries are among the highest in the world, and the foreign debt is a crushing burden. Bare subsistence is often the only way of life. Impoverished farmers or unemployed workers engage in the illegal wildlife trade because they have nowhere else to turn. Their earnings, unlike the middle-level businessmen, are minimal, and they are frequently paid in goods, such as sugar or tobacco. Widespread poverty leads to desperation, and desperation causes people to eke out the barest of livings by using plant and animal resources, legally or illegally, with no thought to their renewability. The foreign debt, with its unending spiral fed by high interest rates, and the strict economic standards imposed by the International Monetary Fund on debtor nations lead to societal unrest and political instability, hopelessness, and increased poverty. When the United States demands repayment of loans, while telling the countries to increase their efforts at conservation, the reluctance or inability of South American countries to do more is understandable, as is the undercurrent of anti-American feeling that has increased over the last decade. Poor people and bankrupt countries have very little interest in conserving resources for themselves or for the richest nation on Earth. The poor economic panorama on the continent affects all areas of life. For example, educational opportunities decline as university budgets are cut back. Fewer students are trained in fields related to conservation needs. In addition, the continent is experiencing the most rapid human population growth in the world. This fact impacts negatively on all aspects of conservation biology.[12]

Mares points out that international cooperation is necessary in at least seven problem areas to solve the environmental problems of South America:

1. Lack of data
2. Lack of people trained in areas related to conservation
3. Lack of money
4. Lack of coordinated plans for the long term
5. Weak economics

6. The precedence of short-term planning strategies
7. An air of panic (suggesting that crisis is imminent and nothing can be done)[13]

Unlike many doomsayers, Mares argues that international cooperation can forestall the crisis: "We are all a part of this problem and must work together to find its solution. There is still time to act."[14]

The ultimate example is, of course, the ecological catastrophe of the nuclear winter that is projected to follow nuclear war. Those who would suffer from the effects of such a winter far outnumber the belligerents. Thus, nuclear war becomes a pressing matter not only to those nations with a penchant for annihilating one another, but even to those simple innocents thousands of miles and cultural light years away from the principals who have no notion of the ideological and economic disputes leading to the conflagration and no allegiance to either side.

Yet another striking example of the need for international cooperation and justice in environmental matters comes from the burgeoning area of biotechnology and genetic engineering. For some time, the United States has led in genetic engineering and also in attempts to create rules and guidelines for its regulation. Interest groups have brought suit against projects that might have untoward and unpredictable environmental consequences—for example, the ice nucleation experiments in California that use genetically engineered bacteria to protect crops from frost.[15] Demands for stringent federal regulation of such work have persisted, primarily on the grounds that such activities could wreak havoc with the environment in undreamed-of ways. What is all too often forgotten is that genetic engineering is a problem for international regulation, not merely for national rules. By and large, the technology for doing pioneering work in genetic engineering is relatively inexpensive, compared, for example, to the need for enormous amounts of capital to build particle accelerators. Thus, stringent regulation or even abolition of genetic engineering in a country such as the United States would not alone solve the problem; regulation would merely move genetic engineering into countries less concerned with potential national and global catastrophe. The net effect is that probably riskier, less supervised work would be done under less stringent conditions. Thus, by its very nature, genetic engineering must be controlled internationally if national control is to be effective.

The point about genetic engineering can be made even more strongly when one contemplates its use for military purposes. If there is a real possibility of environmental disaster arising adventitiously out of benign applications of biotechnology, this is a fortiori the case regarding those uses whose avowed purpose is destructive and whose sphere of effect is unpredictable. So much is manifest in the ratification of the Biological Weapons Convention of 1975, widely cited as the world's first disarmament treaty, "since it is the only one that outlaws the production and use of an entire class of weapons of mass destruction."[16] In October 1986, steps were taken to strengthen the verificational procedures of the treaty, but these essentially boil down to merely voluntary compliance, with no system of sanctions or enforcement.

The final example of environmental problems depending for their solution on some system of international justice concerns the extinction of species. Such problems fall into two distinct categories given the argument we have developed, although this distinction has traditionally been ignored. In my view, we must distinguish between threats of extinction involving sentient and nonsentient species. In the case of sentient species, the fact that a species is threatened is trumped by the fact that its members are sentient. First and foremost, the issue involves harming individual, direct objects of moral concern, just as genocide amounts to mass murder, not the elimination of an abstract entity.

Thus, from the point of view of primary loci of moral concern, killing *any* ten Siberian tigers is no different than killing the *last* ten. Our greater horror at the latter stems from invoking the relational value dimension to humans—no human will ever again be able to witness the beauty of these creatures; our world is poorer in the same way that it would be if one destroyed the last ten van Goghs, not just any ten; the loss of the last ten tigers may lead to other losses of which we are not aware. But we should not lose sight of the fact that the greater harm is to the animals, not to us. For this reason, I will discuss the destruction of sentient species separately, along with cases where individual animals are destroyed and hurt without endangering the species.

This still leaves us with the case of species extinction involving nonsentient species—plants or animals in whom we have no reason to suspect the presence of consciousness. Such extinction is not necessarily an evil. Few (albeit some) bemoaned the eradication of the smallpox virus, and David Baltimore recently remarked that, in his view, all viruses could be eradicated with no loss (save perhaps to intrinsic value theorists).[17] On the other hand, most cases of extinction presumably would be cases of (relational) evil because nonsentient species that do not harm us or other sentient creatures directly or indirectly are at worst neutral, and their loss is both an aesthetic loss for their uniqueness and beauty (the humblest organisms often contain great beauty—in symmetry, adaptation, complexity, or whatever, as my friend the parasitologist discovered), or a loss of a potential tool whose value is not yet detected (as a source of medicine, dye, and so on), or as crucial to the ecosystem in some unrecognized way.

The destruction of myriad species is a major problem. The greatest threat lies in the tropics, where species diversity is both the richest and under the greatest threat. It has been estimated that only one in ten to one in twenty species in the tropics are known to science.[18] A hectare of land in the Peruvian Amazon rain forest contains 41,000 species of insect alone, according to a recent count.[19] A *single tree* contained 43 species of ant. In ten separate hectare plots in Borneo, 700 species of tree were identified, matching the count for all of North America!ial[20] According to a report in *Science,* "The continued erosion of tropical rain forests—through small-scale slash and burn agriculture at one extreme to massive timber operations at the other—is . . . closing in on perhaps half the world's natural inventory of species. Most biologists agree that the world's rain forests will be all but obliterated at some point in the next century."[21] Furthermore, small parks and preserves could not harbor numbers and varieties of species proportional to their size. Thus, standard conservation compromises do not represent a viable solution to the problem.

Other habitats holding a large diversity of species also are threatened. These include coral reefs, coastal wetlands, such as those in California, and large African lakes. The last have been especially threatened by the attempt to cultivate within them varieties of fish not indigenous to the area. A mere documentation of species unknown to science and possibly threatened would require the life work of twenty-five thousand taxonomists; currently there are a mere fifteen hundred such individuals at work.[22] Standard techniques of conserving representative members of such species in zoos and herbaria or preserving germ plasm in essence represent the proverbial drop in the bucket, although they are of course better than nothing.

Scientists who have devoted a great deal of study to these issues again echo the point cited earlier from Mares: These concerns are not local, but international. Michael Robinson puts the point dramatically: "We are facing 'the enlightenment fallacy.' The fallacy is that if you educate the people of the Third World, the problem will disappear. It won't. The problems are not due to ignorance and stupidity. The problems . . . derive from the poverty of the poor and the greed of the rich."[23] *Science*, in concluding its analysis, asserted that "the problems are those of economics and politics. Inescapably, therefore, the solutions are to be found in those same areas."[24]

Some recognition of this politico-economic dimension of environmental problems has been slowly forthcoming politically. There are, for example, indications that policies of the World Bank, which lends development money to countries, are being restructured to take more cognizance of environmental concerns. The bank has been criticized for funding the Polonoroeste project in Brazil, which would have destroyed large forest areas in Brazil in order to allow mass migration of farmers from impoverished areas, and for funding cattle ranching projects in Africa that promote desertification.[25]

Thus, even a cursory examination of some major environmental issues affecting the nonsentient environment indicates that those problems are insoluble outside of the context of international justice. The question then becomes: What, if any, philosophical basis exists for a system of international justice in this area? History has shown, after all, that attempts to create viable machinery of international justice in any area, ranging from an end to genocide to the prevention of war, have run the gamut from laughable to ineffectual. Self-interest has always trumped justice; the situation among nations, it is often remarked, is essentially the Hobbesian "war of each against all." This historical point again blunts even the pragmatic justification for attributing intrinsic value to the nonsentient environment. After all, widespread recognition in the Western tradition of the intrinsic value of humans has not at all assisted in the development of effective mechanisms to ensure that such value is respected.

Ironically, if we begin with the Hobbesian insight, it actually may be easier to provide a rational (and pragmatically effective) basis for a system of international justice regarding environmental concerns rather than human rights. After all, there is no pragmatic reason for a nation to sacrifice its sovereignty in the international arena regarding matters of human rights. If a given country benefits significantly from oppressing all or some of its citizenry, what positive incentive is there for that nation to respond to other nations' protests, and what incentive is there for other nations to protest? In the latter case, of course, there may be moral or ideological reasons for a nation to protest another's human rights policies, but such concerns usually give way to more pragmatic pressures—for example, if the oppressive country stands in a mutually beneficial trade or defensive relationship with the concerned nation.

In the case of global environmental concerns—destruction of the ozone, pollution of air and water, nuclear winter, dangers arising out of genetic engineering, loss of species—*everyone* loses (or might lose) if these concerns are not addressed. A leitmotif of our discussion has been precisely the global nature of such concerns. We have, in the case of all of the examples cited previously, something closer to what game theorists call a game of cooperation rather than a game of competition. That is, if one nation loses its fight with an environmental problem, or simply does not address it, any other nation could, and in many cases would, be likely to suffer as well. Thus, if the United States, through excessive use of fluorocarbons, weakens the ozone barrier, the results will not be restricted to the United States, but will have global impact.

By the same token, even if a given nation X stands to gain by ignoring environmental despoliation, others may lose and, without a system of regulation, may in turn bear the brunt of Y's or Z's cavalier disregard of other aspects of the environment. Furthermore, there is good reason to believe that the short-run gains accruing to a nation by a disregard of environmental concerns may well be significantly outweighed in the long run by unforeseen or ignored consequences. Thus, the wholesale conversion of African grasslands into grazing lands for domestic animals not ecologically adapted to such an environment may yield short-term profits, but in the long run lead to desertification, which leaves the land of no use at all. By the same token, cavalier disregard of species loss in the deforestation of the tropics may certainly provide short-term windfall profits, but at the expense of far richer resources. *Time* magazine recounted a number of examples of these riches.

> These threatened ecosystems have already proved a valuable source of medicines, foods and new seed stock for crops. Nine years ago, for example, a strain of perennial, disease-resistant wild maize named *Zea diploperennis* was found in a Mexican mountain forest, growing in three small plots. Crossing domestic corn varieties with this maize produces hardy hybrids that should ultimately be worth billions of dollars to farmers. A great many of the prescription drugs sold in the U.S. are based on unique chemical compounds found in tropical plants. For example, vincristine, originally isolated from the Madagascan periwinkle, is used to treat some human cancers. Scientists are convinced that still undiscovered forest plants could be the source of countless new natural drugs.[26]

The fundamental argument, however, is still the Hobbesian one of rational self-interest. Any country, if utterly unbridled in its pursuit of short-term economic gains, or in its cavalier disregard for the impact of its activities on other nations, can permanently harm the interests of other nations. An irresponsibly genetically engineered microorganism does not respect national boundaries or military power, nor does oceanic or atmospheric pollution. The consequences of lack of control of environmental damage can range from loss of potential benefits—such as loss of new medication derived from plants, or loss of the delight and wonder in seeing a fragile tundra aglow in wildflowers—to positive and serious harm—the dramatic rise in cancers or other diseases produced by environmental despoliation of air, water, or the food chain, or even to a new ice age or tidal waves resulting from destruction of the ozone. Given modern technology, virtually any nation can damage any or all nations in any number of these ways; hence, a situation ripe for Hobbesian contractualism is reached.

In Hobbesian terms, of course, individuals engaged in a war of each against all are rendered equal by their ultimate vulnerability to harm and death by action on the part of others or combinations of others. Thus, we rationally relinquish our natural tendency toward rapaciousness in recognition of others' similar tendency, and our vulnerability thereto. Unrestricted greed is sacrificed for security and protection from the unrestricted greed of others, and a sovereign who, as it were, builds fences protecting each from all is constituted by each individual surrendering a portion of his or her unbridled autonomy. As we have seen, a precisely analogous situation exists regarding environmental vulnerability, and thus rationality would dictate that each nation surrender some of its autonomy to an international authority in order to protect itself, or the whole world including itself, from major disaster. This is of course especially clear, as we have seen earlier, in matters pertaining to biological warfare, where any nation can effectively annihilate any or all others.

In summary, then, the relevance of a viable mechanism of international justice to environmental ethical concerns is manifest. Indeed, many if not most environmental issues, and certainly the most vexing and important ones, entail major global consequences and thus cannot be restricted to local issues of sovereignty. An environmental ethics is inseparable from a system of international justice, not only in terms of policing global dangers and verifying and monitoring compliance with international agreements, but also in terms of implementing the distributive justice necessary to prevent poor countries from looking only at short-term gains. The rain forests are not only a problem for the countries in which they are found; if other developed nations are to benefit from the continued existence of the rain forests, we must be prepared to pay for that benefit. No country should be expected to bear the full brunt of environmental concerns. Classical economics does not work for ecological and environmental concerns; each unit pursuing its own interest will not enrich the biosphere, but deplete and devastate it. As E. O. Wilson put it in a recent conference on biodiversity, "The time has come to link ecology to economic and human development. . . . What is happening to the rain forests of Madagascar and Brazil will affect us all."[27] In other words, if a tree is felled in a primeval forest and there is no one else around, one should care about it anyway.

Animals and International Justice

But what of the other class of environmental moral issues—namely, those affecting nonhuman sentient beings? Does the solution of these issues require a system of international justice as well? Clearly, in many cases, the answer is an obvious yes. In the first place, animal populations do not always respect or adhere to geopolitical boundaries, the classic case being, of course, the numerous species of whales. Thus, any given country's commitment to protect the whales is meaningless in the face of other nations' commitment to "harvest" them, to use a common if odious locution. Thus, in such a case, some international guarantees are required to protect the animals. Such treaties, of course, currently exist, but, like the convention regulating biological weaponry, are readily and frequently abrogated in the face of national interest.

The whaling treaties, for example, are regularly ignored by various nations in the face of self-interest, and other nations look the other way because they are tied to the offending nation by ties of commerce and defense; which unequivocally trump the interests of the animals.[28] Only if some neutral, disinterested mechanism existed for enforcing such treaties could one assure that the interests of the animals were protected in the face of self-interest or even tradition—witness the recent case of the Faroe Islands whale slaughters, which are undertaken for fun, not meat or income.[29] Unfortunately, the surrender of the autonomy that makes such mechanisms possible does not, unlike the environmental areas of our previous discussion, follow plausibly from rational self-interest. The Japanese, for example, lose nothing by violating a treaty and killing whales; there is no parallel meaningful threat from other nations. The problem here is that concern for the animals does not rest upon rational self-interest, but on extended moral concern, similar to concern for human rights and their abridgment in other nations. Thus, we cannot even appeal to self-interest as a basis for moral concern; indeed, in such cases, moral concern may exact a cost in self-interest.

Nonetheless, the situation is not hopeless. The case of the Canadian harp seal hunt dramatically illustrates that nations can be motivated by a moral concern that is actually inimical to self-interest. The European Economic Community recently banned the importation of seal products derived from the barbaric Newfoundland hunt. This was done despite the fact that at least some European nations derived economic benefit from the seal hunt and despite the fact that the European public was a major traditional consumer of seal products. This case dramatically illustrates that human consciousness is being increasingly sensitized to the suffering and interests of animals.

Cynics might argue that the seal case derives from the sentiment attached to the furry cuteness of baby seals and the jarring image of their slaughter by clubbing—big eyes and blood on the white snow. Although there is some truth in this claim, it is by no means all. Until recently, moral concern as embodied in the "humane ethic" was highly selective and favored the cute, cuddly, and familiar. Thus, for example, the Animal Welfare Act of 1966 and 1970, the only legal constraint on animal research in the United States, exempted from its very limited purview (it concerned itself only with food, caging, transport, and so on and disavowed concern with the actual content and conduct of research) rats, mice, and farm animals, in fact, 90 percent of the animals used in research. For purposes of the act, a dead dog was defined as an animal, a live mouse was not. Recently, however, things have changed. With the rise of an articulated moral concern for sentient beings by philosophers such as Peter Singer, Tom Regan, Steven Sapontzis,[30] and myself, that concern has captured the social imagination nationally and internationally. New guidelines and laws extend concern even to the more prosaic and unlovely animals, and a new amendment to the Animal Welfare Act in the United States, which I helped to draft, now mandates control of pain, suffering, and distress, which is a direct insult to the ideology of science that treated these as unknowable. Similar thrusts have occurred in other countries; in Germany, a new law bans animal research for military and cosmetic purposes, as does a new Dutch law. By the same token, many countries, such as Britain, Switzerland, and Denmark, have put constraints on confinement agriculture—"factory farming"—even though a price is paid in "efficiency" and cost to the consumer.

We sometimes forget that there is an international dimension even to animal research and factory farming. Unilateral and major constraints on such practices by one country for the sake of moral concern for animals, with other countries not making similar moves, can lead, for example, to an erosion of the legislating country's agricultural economy if the constraints make its products prohibitively more expensive and drastically reduce a market for them. But a universal constraint applicable to all countries would merely put all competitors back at the same starting gate. Public education also can convince consumers to "put their money where their morality is."

In the case of animals in science, a parallel problem arises. Multinational corporations, and even individual researchers, when unable to do a particular kind of experiment in one country will simply go to another. Given that experimenters then are shifting the suffering from one animal to another who is not different morally, this is not a just solution. Here we cannot even use the rationalization we do with humans—"Their culture makes things tolerable to them that are not tolerable to us"—because, as a Dutch colleague of mine said, "All dogs bark in the same language." Thus, scientific research must also be regulated by internationally accepted rules, else the burden of injustice is merely shifted from one innocent animal to another who happens to be living in a different place. For this reason, the European Economic Community member nations are drafting rules designed to govern all member nations, which is a step in the right direction because it would probably be impractical for companies smarting under such rules to move out of Europe altogether to less enlightened countries.

There are many areas of animal abuse where the network of interests and thus the need for rules are obviously international. There are other cases—for example, a horrendous blood sport practiced in a small country—where there are fewer international connections and implications. Nonetheless, the key to stopping all such evils is, in the final analysis, the same. It lies in a widespread philosophical extension of widespread moral notions. Thus, the philosophical basis for a system of international justice that can stop, for example, the slaughter of rhinoceroses for frivolous consumer goods such as ornamental knives and aphrodisiacs (which reduced the black rhino population from 65,000 in 1970 to 4,500 today),[31] or the killing of the snow leopard for fur, lies in the expanded moral vision of many people in diverse nations. Such expanded awareness is contagious and creates a new gestalt on animals that finds expression in legislation, boycotts, embargos, and the like. Such concern is likely to manifest first on a national level, with demands for regulation of research and mandated protection of research animals (including recent demands for housing that respects their telos); legal constraints on agricultural practices that yield efficiency at the expense of animals' suffering; restriction of frivolous and painful testing on animals, such as the LD 50 and Draize tests used in developing cosmetics and the like; tighter controls imposed over zoos, circuses, and rodeos; and so on.

But as I said, animal exploitation does not stop at national boundaries, nor does moral concern for animals. Thus, such abuses as traffic in rare birds where vast shipments of them arrive dead and dying; unregulated transport of all varieties of animals; the murder of porpoises in pursuit of tuna; the slaughter of migrating whales in the Faroe Islands as a sport and "cultural tradition," will—whether happening in any or all countries—be subjected to international pressures for regulation. These inevitably will result in tighter monitoring and restriction of such activities, which in turn will require international cooperation of the sort that is starting to develop in order to control the drug traffic.

It is perhaps not totally utopian to suggest that expanded concern for animals, a concern crossing geopolitical barriers, may lead to expanded concern for other human beings in countries not one's own, in a lovely dialectical reversal of the traditional wisdom preached by St. Thomas Aquinas and Immanuel Kant, suggesting that concern for animals is merely disguised concern for human beings.

NOTES

1. See the chapters in Tom Regan, *All That Dwell Therein* (Berkeley: University of California Press, 1982).

2. See Aldo Leopold, *A Sand County Almanac* (Oxford: Oxford University Press, 1949); J. Baird Callicott, "Animal Liberation: A Triangular Affair," *Environmental Ethics* 2 (1980):311–338; Holmes Rolston III, *Philosophy Gone Wild* (Buffalo, N.Y.: Prometheus Books, 1986).
3. There are exceptions to this generalization—for example, my own work in abolishing multiple use of animals as a standard teaching practice in medical and veterinary schools and my efforts in writing and promoting new legislation on proper care of laboratory animals.
4. See the discussions of this point in Peter Singer, *Animal Liberation* (New York: New York Review of Books, 1975); and B. Rollin, *Animal Rights and Human Morality* (Buffalo, N.Y.: Prometheus Books, 1981).
5. See my "Animal Pain," in M. Fox and L. Mickley (eds.), *Advances in Animal Welfare Science 1985* (The Hague: Martinus Nijhoff, 1985); and my "Animal Consciousness and Scientific Change," *New Ideas in Psychology* 4, no. 2 (1986):141–152, as well as the replies to the latter by P. K. Feyeraend, H. Rachlin, and T. Leahey in the same issue, p. 153. See also my *Animal Consciousness, Animal Pain, and Scientific Change* (tentative title) (Oxford: Oxford University Press, forthcoming).
6. See my *Animal Rights*, Part I.
7. See the works mentioned in footnotes 1 and 2.
8. This point is made with great rhetorical force in Edward Abbey, *Desert Solitaire* (New York: Ballantine Books, 1971).
9. See Holmes Rolston, "Duties to Endangered Species," *Philosophy Gone Wild*.
10. See the seminal discussion in Christopher Stone, *Should Trees Have Standing? Toward Legal Rights for Natural Objects.* (Los Altos, Calif.: William Kaufmann, 1974).
11. Michael Mares, "Conservation in South America: Problems, Consequences, and Solutions," *Science* 233 (1986):734.
12. Ibid., p. 738.
13. Ibid., p. 736.
14. Ibid., p. 739.
15. For a discussion of various ethical issues surrounding genetic engineering, see my "The Frankenstein Thing," in J. W. Evans and A. Hollaender (eds.), *Genetic Engineering of Agricultural Animals* (New York: Plenum, 1986).
16. *Science* 234 (1986):143.
17. *Time*, November 3, 1986, p. 74.
18. *Science* 234 (1986):149.
19. Ibid.
20. Ibid.
21. Ibid.
22. Ibid., p. 150
23. Ibid.
24. Ibid.
25. *Science* 234 (1986):813.
26. *Time*, October 13, 1986, p. 80.
27. Ibid.
28. Maxine McCloskey, "Wildlife on a Geopolitical Planet" (Presentation by U.S. delegate to the International Whaling Commission, at the Animal Protection Institute annual meeting, Sacramento, California, October 18, 1986). See also N. Carter and A. Thornton, *Pirate Whaling 1985, and a History of the Subversion of International Whaling Regulations* (Glasgow: SAVE International, 1985).
29. See A. Thornton and J. Gibson, *Pilot Whaling in the Faroe Islands* (London: CACE, 1986).
30. Steven Sapontzis, *Morals, Reason, and Animals* (Philadelphia: Temple University Press, 1987).
31. *Science* 234 (1986):147.

Questions for Further Reflection

1. Should the religiously inspired anthropocentrist say that God gave the universe beyond earth to human beings? If not, how can we work out how we may deal with the creatures we may come to discover there?
2. As noted in the discussion of whether death is a bad thing, hedonists could select among the following versions of their view:
    a. The good consists in the absence of pain, and the bad consists in the presence of pain.

b. The good consists in the presence of pleasure and the absence of pain, and the bad consists in the presence of pain.
c. The good consists in the presence of pleasure and the absence of pain, and the bad consists in the absence of pleasure or the presence of pain.

To which version of hedonism should hedonists such as Peter Singer, who wish to defend animal rights, subscribe? Consider that in the first two versions of hedonism, nothing is wrong with painlessly killing a creature (whether human or nonhuman), because depriving a creature of pleasure is a matter of moral indifference as long as we also deprive it of pain. Only in the third position is there an objection to painlessly killing animals.

3. Cigman would say that cats do not have the right to life in part because they cannot desire to live, for to say that a creature desires a state of affairs presupposes that the creature is capable of representing that state of affairs to itself. However, cats are not sophisticated enough mentally to think of themselves as temporally extended beings.

Even if cats cannot think of themselves as temporally extended creatures, though, it is by no means clear that this inability precludes their thinking about the future. Does it? Is it plausible to say that cats can have desires about the future, including the desire to experience pleasure in the future? How does your answer affect the dispute between Cigman and Singer?

4. Readers inclined to agree with Epicurus's view that dying is not a bad thing because evil consists in the presence of pain (so that the absence of pleasure is not in and of itself a bad thing) will be hard-pressed to resist Cigman's (and Michael Tooley's) view that killing animals and unwanted infants (or adults, for that matter) is acceptable. On the other hand, readers who object to death on the grounds that it prevents people from satisfying desires they would otherwise find fulfilling might also object to killing animals and unwanted infants if those readers believe that such creatures are capable of wanting future pleasure. Construct a criterion of goodness that allows you to defend a plausible position about the importance of your own death, on one hand, and the importance of killing animals, infants, and adults on the other.

5. Suppose you grant Singer's claim that all creatures that can suffer have standing. How should you decide what to do when the interests of creatures from one species clash with the interests of creatures from another?

Further Readings

Cooper, David, and Joy Palmer, eds. *Just Environments: Intergenerational, International and Interspecies Issues.* London: Routledge, 1995. Examines environmental issues from a variety of viewpoints.

Frey, R. G. *Interests and Rights: The Case Against Animals.* Oxford, England: The Clarendon Press, 1980. Frey argues that animals have no rights because they lack interests.

Leopold, Aldo. *A Sand County Almanac.* London: Oxford University Press, 1949. One of the earliest defenses of the claim that the nonhuman realm has moral standing, but weak on argument.

Reagan, Thomas, and Peter Singer, eds. *Animal Rights and Human Obligations.* Englewood Cliffs, NJ: Prentice-Hall, 1976. Contains several good essays.

Regan, Tom. *The Case for Animal Rights.* Berkeley: University of California Press, 1983. Detailed defense of the animal rights view.

Rollin, Bernard. *Animal Rights and Human Morality.* Buffalo: Prometheus Books, 1981. An able defense of the interest criterion.

Singer, Peter. *Animal Liberation: A New Ethics for Our Treatment of Animals*. New York: New York Review of Books, 1975. Develops the theses Singer lays out in his essay "Animal Liberation."

Singer, Peter, ed. *In Defence of Animals*. Oxford, England: Basil Blackwell, 1985. Contains many helpful essays.

Sperlinger, David, ed. *Animals in Research: New Perspectives in Animal Experimentation*. New York: John Wiley & Sons, 1981. As the title suggests, this volume focuses on the use of animals in experiments.

Stone, Christopher. *Can Trees Have Standing? Towards Legal Rights for Natural Objects*. New York: Avon Books, 1975. *Earth and Other Ethics: The Case for Moral Pluralism*. New York: Harper & Row, 1987. Discussion of both the legal and ethical rights of nonhumans by the principal defender of the view that nonhuman entities (such as forests) should have legal standing.

CONTRIBUTING AUTHORS

Aristotle: Greek philosopher, student of Plato, and teacher of Alexander the Great.

Arkes, Hadly: Professor of Political Science at Amherst College.

Battin, Margaret P.: Professor of Philosophy at the University of Utah.

Black, Walter: Professor of Economics, College of the Holy Cross.

Cigman, Ruth: Professor of Philosophy at Iona College.

Confucius: 557–479 BCE. Chinese philosopher.

Engels, Friedrich: 1820–1895. German socialist and collaborator with Karl Marx on such works as the *Communist Manifesto*.

Epicurus: 342?–270 B.C. Greek philosopher who advocated hedonism. The term *Epicure* derives from Epicurus's name, but Epicurus himself rejected the life of the libertine.

Ericsson, Lars O.: Filosofiska Institutionen, Stockholms Universitet, Stockholm.

Friedman, Marilyn: Professor of Philosophy at Bowling Green State University.

Fullinwider, Robert K.: Professor of Philosophy at the University of Maryland.

Gauthier, David: Professor of Philosophy at the University of Pittsburgh.

Gilligan, Carol: Professor of Education at Harvard University.

Glover, Jonathan C.B.: Fellow, New College, Oxford University.

Goldman, Alan: Professor of Philosophy at the University of Miami.

Goodpaster, Kenneth E.: Professor, Department of General Management at the Harvard University Business School.

Graham, Daniel O. (General, USAF, Ret.): Views were influential during the Reagan administration.

Hardin, Garrett: Professor of Biology at the University of California at Santa Barbara.

Hare, R.M.: Formerly White's Professor of Moral Philosophy, University of Oxford.

Hospers, John: Retired Professor of Philosophy Emeritus at the University of Southern California; former presidential candidate of the libertarian party.

Hume, David: 1711–1776. Scottish empiricist philosopher.

Kant, Immanuel: 1724–1804. German philosopher.

Lackey, Douglas P.: Professor of Philosophy at Bernard Baruch College, New York.

LaFollette, Hugh: Professor of Philosophy and Humanities, East Tennessee State University.

Lao Tzu: Chinese philosopher who may have written the *Tao te Ching*.

Lee, Steven: Professor of Philosophy at Hobart and William Smith College.

Levin, Michael: Professor of Philosophy at the City University of New York.

Locke, John: 1632–1704. British empiricist philosopher.

Lucretius: 97?–54 B.C. Roman philosopher and poet; follower of Epicurus.

Luper, Steven: Professor of Philosophy at Trinity University, San Antonio, Texas.

Marighella, Carlos: 1912–1969. Brazilian Marxist and theorist of terrorism.

Marx, Karl: 1818–1883. German philosopher.

Mill, John Stuart: 1806–1873. British utilitarian.

Murphy, Timothy F.: Professor of Philosophy at Boston University.

Nathanson, Stephen: Professor of Philosophy at Northeastern University in Massachusetts.

Nietzsche, Friedrich: 1844–1900. German existentialist philosopher; precursor of existentialism.

Okin, Susan Moller: teaches political theory at Brandeis University.

O'Neill, Onora: Professor of Philosophy at the University of Essex in Colchester, England.

Parfit, Derek: Fellow, University of Oxford, Sub-Faculty of Philosophy.

Rachels, James: Professor of Philosophy at the University of Alabama.

Rawls, John: Professor of Philosophy at Harvard University.

Reagan, Ronald: Former President of the United States (1980–1988).

Reiman, Jeffrey: Professor of Philosophy and Religion at the American University in Washington, D.C.

Rifkin, Jeremy: Washington, D.C.-based opponent of genetic engineering and nuclear technology.

Ringer, Robert J.: Author of popular self-help books.

Rollin, Bernard: Professor of Philosophy, Colorado State University.

Ruse, Michael: Professor of Philosophy, University of Guelph, Ontario, Canada.

Sade, Donatien-Alphonse-François, Comte de: 1740–1814, French novelist. The term *sadism* derives from Sade's name.

Sartre, Jean-Paul: 1905–1980. French existentialist philosopher.

Schopenhauer, Arthur: 1788–1860. German philosopher.

Scruton, Roger: Editor, The Salisbury Review; formerly Professor of Philosophy at Boston University.

Singer, Peter: Professor of Philosophy at La Trobe University in Victoria, Australia.

Slote, Michael: Professor of Philosophy at the University of Maryland.

Smart, J.J.C.: Professor of Philosophy at the Research School of Social Sciences, Australian National University.

Steinbock, Bonnie: Professor of Philosophy at the State University of New York at Albany.

Storr, Anthony: Clinical Lecturer in Psychiatry at Oxford University.

Sullivan, Joseph V.: Was Ordinary of the Baton Rouge Diocese.

Szasz, Thomas, M.D.: Professor of Psychiatry, State University of New York, Upstate Medical Center.

Thomson, Judith Jarvis: Professor of Philosophy at the Massachusetts Institute of Technology.

Tolstoy, Leo: 1828–1910. Russian novelist.

van den Haag, Ernest: Professor of Jurisprudence and Public Policy at Fordham University.

Walzer, Michael: Professor of Social Science, Institute of Advanced Study, Princeton, New Jersey.

Wilson, James Q.: Collins Professor of Management and Public Policy at UCLA.

SOURCES

Aristotle — "Nicomachean Ethics"
Jonathan Barnes, ed., COMPLETE WORKS OF ARISTOTLE: THE REVISED OXFORD TRANSLATIONS. Bollingen Series 71, Copyright © 1984 Jowett Copyright Trustees. Excerpt, "Nichomachean Ethics" reprinted with permission of Princeton University Press.

Aristotle — "Happiness as Contemplation"
Jonathan Barnes, ed., COMPLETE WORKS OF ARISTOTLE: THE REVISED OXFORD TRANSLATIONS. Bollingen Series 71, Copyright © 1984 Jowett Copyright Trustees. Excerpts from Book Ten reprinted with permission of Princeton University Press.

Aristotle — "Friendship"
Jonathan Barnes, ed., COMPLETE WORKS OF ARISTOTLE: THE REVISED OXFORD TRANSLATIONS. Bollingen Series 71, Copyright © 1984 Jowett Copyright Trustees. Excerpts from Books Eight and Nine reprinted with permission of Princeton University Press.

Arkes, Hadley — "Prostitution"
Arkes, H., PHILOSOPHER IN THE CITY: MORAL DIMENSIONS OF URBAN POLITICS. Copyright (©) 1981 by Princeton University Press. Excerpt pp. 401–413 reprinted with permission of Princeton University Press.

Battin, Margaret — "Is There a Duty to Die?"
Margaret Battin, "Is There a Duty to Die?", Ethics 97 (1987). Reprinted by permission of The University of Chicago Press.

Block, Walter — "Drug Prohibition: A Legal and Economic Analysis"
Walter Block, "Drug Prohibition: A Legal and Economic Analysis," from DRUGS, MORALITY, AND THE LAW edited by Steven Luper and Curtis Brown. Published by Garland Publishing, Inc., 1994, Hamden, Connecticut.

Cigman, Ruth — "Death, Misfortune and Species Inequality"
Ruth Cigman, "Death, Misfortune and Species Inequality." *Philosophy & Public Affairs*, 10, no. 1 (Winter 1981). Copyright © 1981 Princeton University Press.

Confucius — "The Analects"
© Raymond Dawson 1993. Reprinted from *Confucius: The Analects* translated by Raymond Dawson (World's Classics, 1993) by permission of Oxford University Press.

657

de Sade, Marquis — "Philosophy in the Bedroom"
Reprinted by permission of Grove Weidenfeld. English translation copyright © 1965 by Richard Seaver and Austryn Wainhouse.

Engels, Frederick — "Marriage"
Engels, Frederick and Marx, Karl, "Marriage" from THE ORIGIN OF THE FAMILY, PRIVATE PROPERTY, AND THE STATE: SELECTED WORKS, V. 3, 1970.

Ericsson, Lars — "Charges Against Prostitution: An Attempt at a Philosophical Assessment"
Ericsson, Lars, "Charges Against Prostitution: An Attempt at a Philosophical Assessment"; *Ethics* Vol. 90 (1980), p. 335–366. Reprinted by permission of The University of Chicago Press and the author.

Friedman, Marilyn — "Friendship and Moral Growth"
Friedman, Marilyn, "Friendship and Moral Growth," *Journal of Value Inquiry* Vol. 23 (1989) pp. 3–13. Reprinted by permission of the publisher.

Fullinwider, Robert — "Reverse Discrimination and Equal Opportunity"
Robert Fullinwider, "Reverse Discrimination and Equal Opportunity," from NEW DIRECTIONS IN ETHICS by Robert Fullinwider, Joseph DeMarco and Richard Fox. Reprinted by permission of Routledge.

Fullinwider, Robert — "Understanding Terrorism"
Robert Fullinwider, "Understanding Terrorism," from PROBLEMS OF INTERNATIONAL JUSTICE edited by Steven Luper-Foy. Published by Westview Press, 1988, Boulder, Colorado.

Gauthier, David — "War and Nuclear Deterrence"
David Gauthier, "War and Nuclear Deterrence." Reprinted by permission of Westview Press from PROBLEMS OF INTERNATIONAL JUSTICE edited by Steven Luper-Foy. Published by Westview Press, 1988, Boulder, Colorado.

Gilligan, Carol — "Woman's Place in Man's Life Cycle"
Reprinted by permission of the publishers from IN A DIFFERENT VOICE by Carol Gilligan, Cambridge, Mass.: Harvard University Press, copyright © 1982 by Carol Gilligan. All rights reserved.

Glover, Jonathan — "Suicide and Gambling with Life"
Chapter 13 "Suicide and Gambling with Life" from CAUSING DEATH AND SAVING LIVES by Jonathan Glover (Penguin Books, 1977), copyright © Jonathan Glover, 1977.

Glover, Jonathan — "Decisions"
Chapter 3 "Decisions," from WHAT SORT OF PEOPLE SHOULD THERE BE? by Jonathan Glover (Penguin Books, 1984), copyright © Jonathan Glover, 1984.

Goldman, Alan — "Plain Sex"
Alan Goldman, "Plain Sex," *Philosophy and Public Affairs* 6 (Spring 1977). Copyright © 1977 by Princeton University Press. Reprinted by permission of Princeton University Press.

Goodpaster, Kenneth — "On Being Morally Considerable"
Kenneth E. Goodpaster, "On Being Morally Considerable." *Journal of Philosophy*, LXXV, 6 (June 1978), p. 308–325.

Graham, Daniel — "The Non-Nuclear Defense of Cities"
From THE NON-NUCLEAR DEFENSE OF CITIES. Daniel O. Graham. Cambridge, MA: Abt Books, 1983

Haag, Ernest van den — "Refuting Reiman and Nathanson"
Ernest van den Haag, "Refuting Reiman and Nathanson." *Philosophy & Public Affairs*, 14, no. 2 (Spring 1985). Copyright © 1985 Princeton University Press. Reprinted with permission of Princeton University Press.

Hardin, Garrett — "Living on a Lifeboat"
Garrett Hardin, 1974. "Living on a Lifeboat." *BioScience* 24(10), pp. 561–568. Reprinted by permission of the author.

Hare, R.M. — "A Kantian Approach to Abortion"
R.M. Hare, "A Kantian Approach to Abortion." Reprinted by permission of the author.

Hinayana and Mahayana Scriptures
From A SOURCEBOOK IN INDIAN PHILOSOPHY, edited by S. Radhakrishnan and C. Moore. Reprinted by permission of Princeton University Press.

Hospers, John — "What Libertarianism Is"
Hospers, John, "What Libertarianism Is," *The Libertarian Alternative* (1974). Ed. Tibor Machan. Reprinted by permission of Nelson-Hall Company.

Hume, David — "Of Suicide"
Hume, David, "Of Suicide" from ESSAYS MORAL, POLITICAL, AND LITERARY. Reprinted by permission of Liberty Fund, Inc., Liberty Classics, 1985.

Kant, Immanuel — "Duties Towards Animals"
Immanuel Kant, "Duties Towards Animals" in LECTURES ON ETHICS, 1979. Reprinted by permission of Methuen & Co.

Kant, Immanuel — "Suicide"
Kant, Immanuel, "Suicide" from LECTURES ON ETHICS, 1930. Reprinted by permission of Methuen & Co.

Kant, Immanuel — "Friendship"
Kant, Immanuel, "Friendship" from LECTURES ON ETHICS, 1930. Reprinted by permission of Methuen & Co.

Lackey, Douglas — "Prisoners and Chickens"
Douglas Lackey, "Prisoners and Chickens." Reprinted by permission of Westview Press from PROBLEMS OF INTERNATIONAL JUSTICE, edited by Steven Luper-Foy. Published by Westview Press, 1988, Boulder, Colorado.

LaFollette, Hugh — "Morality and Personal Relationships"
From PERSONAL RELATIONSHIPS: LOVE, IDENTITY, AND MORALITY by Hugh LaFollette. Reprinted with permission of Blackwell Publishers Ltd.

LaFollette, Hugh — "Licensing Parents"
Hugh LaFollette, "Licensing Parents." *Philosophy & Public Affairs*, 9, no. 2 (Winter 1980). Copyright © 1980 Princeton University Press. Reprinted with permission of Princeton University Press.

Lao Tzu — "Tao Te Ching"
From LAO TZU: TAO TE CHING, translated by D. C. Lao. Reprinted by permission of Penguin Books Ltd.

Lee, Steven — "The Moral Vision of Strategic Defense"
Steven Lee, "The Moral Vision of Strategic Defense." First published in *The Philosophical Forum*, Vol. XVIII, Number 1, Fall 1986.

Levin, Michael — "Why Homosexuality Is Abnormal"
Levin, Michael, "Why Homosexuality Is Abnormal." Copyright © 1984, *The Monist*, La Salle, Illinois 61301. Reprinted by permission.

Levin, Michael — "Affirmative Action"
Michael Levin, "Affirmative Action" from FEMINISM AND FREEDOM (1987). Reprinted by permission of Transaction Books.

Lucretius — "Death"
LUCRETIUS: ON THE NATURE OF THE UNIVERSE, translated by R.E. Latham (Penguin Classics, 1951), translation © R.E. Latham, 1951. Reproduced by permission of Penguin Books Ltd.

Luper, Steven — "Annihilation"
Steven Luper, "Annihilation." *Philosophical Quarterly*, vol. 27, no. 148 (July 1987), reprinted with permission of Blackwell Publishers Ltd.

Murphy, Timothy — "Homosexuality and Nature: Happiness and the Law at Stake"
Murphy, Timothy, "Homosexuality and Nature: Happiness and the Law at Stake," *Journal of Applied Philosophy*. Reprinted by permission of the author and the publisher.

Nathanson, Stephen — "Do Murderers Deserve to Die?"
Stephen Nathanson, "Do Murderers Deserve to Die?" from AN EYE FOR AN EYE? THE

MORALITY OF PUNISHING BY DEATH (1987). Reprinted with permission of Rowan-Littlefield Publishers.

Nietzsche — "What Is Noble?"
From BEYOND GOOD AND EVIL by Friedrich Nietzsche, translated by Walter Kaufmann. Copyright © 1966 by Random House, Inc. Reprinted by permission of the publisher.

Okin, Susan Moller — "Justice, Gender and the Family"
From JUSTICE, GENDER AND THE FAMILY, by Susan Moller Okin. Copyright © 1989 by Basic Books, Inc., Publishers, New York. Reprinted by permission of Basic Books, Inc., Publishers, New York.

O'Neill, Onora — "Kantianism and World Hunger"
From MATTERS OF LIFE AND DEATH 2/E by Regan, 1986. Reprinted by permission of McGraw-Hill Publishing Company.

Parfit, Derek — "Why We Should Not Be Biased Towards the Future"
Copyright © Derek Parfit 1984. Reprinted from REASONS AND PERSONS by Derek Parfit (1984) by permission of Oxford University Press.

Rachels, James — "Active and Passive Euthanasia" & "Euthanasia"
James Rachels, "Active and Passive Euthanasia," New England Journal of Medicine, Vol. 292, pp. 78–80, 1975. Copyright 1975 Massachusetts Medical Society.

Rawls, John — "Justice as Fairness"
Rawls, John, "Reply to Alexander and Musgrave," The Quarterly Journal of Economics, LXXXVIII (1974). Reprinted by permission of MIT Press.

Reiman, Jeffrey — "The Justice of the Death Penalty in an Unjust World"
Jeffrey Reiman, "The Justice of the Death Penalty in an Unjust World" from CHALLENGING CAPITAL PUNISHMENT by Haas and Inciardi. Reprinted by permission of Sage Publications, Inc.

Richards, David A.J. — "Drug Use and the Rights of the Person"
David A.J. Richards, "Drug Use and the Rights of the Person" from Sex, Drugs, Death and the Law: An Essay on Human Rights and Overcriminalization (1982). Reprinted by permission of the author.

Ringer, Robert — "The Friendship Hurdle"
Ringer, Robert, "The Friendship Hurdle" from LOOKING OUT FOR #1. Reprinted by permission of the author.

Rollin, Bernard E. — "Environmental Ethics and International Justice"
From PROBLEMS OF INTERNATIONAL JUSTICE edited by Steven Luper-Foy. Published by Westview Press, 1988, Boulder, Colorado.

Ruse, Michael — "Genesis Revisited: Can We Do Better than God?"
Michael Ruse, "Genesis Revisited: Can We do Better than God?"; Zygon, 19, 1984.

Sartre, Jean-Paul — "Existentialism and Humanism"
From EXISTENTIALISM AND HUMANISM by Jean-Paul Sartre, translated by P. Mairet. Reprinted by permission of Methuen & Co.

Schopenhauer, Arthur — "The World as Will and Representation" (2 excerpts)
From THE WORLD AS WILL AND REPRESENTATION by Arthur Schopenhauer, translated by R.B. Haldane and J. Kemp. Reprinted by courtesy of AMS Press Inc.

Scruton, Roger — "Sexual Morality" & "The Politics of Sex"
Reprinted with permission of the Free Press, a Division of Macmillan, Inc. from SEXUAL DESIRE: A MORAL PHILOSOPHY OF THE EROTIC by Roger Scruton. Copyright © 1986 by Roger Scruton.

Singer, Peter — "Famine, Affluence, and Morality"
Peter Singer, "Famine, Affluence, and Morality." Philosophy & Public Affairs 1, no. 3

(Spring 1972). Copyright © 1972 Princeton University Press. Reprinted with permission of Princeton University Press.

Singer, Peter — "Animal Liberation"
Reprinted from *The New York Review of Books*, April 5, 1973, by permission of the author. Copyright Peter Singer, 1973.

Slote, Michael — "Obedience and Illusions"
Slote, Michael, "Obedience and Illusions," from HAVING CHILDREN: PHILOSOPHICAL AND LEGAL REFLECTIONS ON PARENTHOOD, Onora O'Neill and William Ruddick, ed. (1979).

Smart, J.J.C. & Bernard Williams — "Hedonism"
Smart, J.J.C. and Williams, Bernard, UTILITARIANISM FOR AND AGAINST. Reprinted with the permission of Cambridge University Press.

Steinbock, Bonnie — "Drug Prohibition: A Public Health Perspective"
Bonnie Steinbock, "Drug Prohibition: A Public Health Perspective," from DRUGS, MORALITY, AND THE LAW edited by Steven Luper and Curtis Brown. Published by Garland Publishing, Inc., 1994, Hamden, Connecticut.

Storr, Anthony — "The Significance of Human Relationships"
Reprinted with permission of the Free Press, a Division of Macmillan, Inc. from SOLITUDE: A RETURN TO THE SELF by Anthony Storr. Copyright © 1988 by Anthony Storr.

Sullivan, Joseph — "The Immorality of Euthanasia"
Joseph Sullivan, "The Immorality of Euthanasia" from BENEFICIENT EUTHANASIA. Reprinted by permission of Prometheus Books.

Szasz, Thomas — "The Ethics of Suicide"
Szasz, Thomas, "The Ethics of Suicide" from The Antioch Review, 1971. Reprinted by permission of the author.

Thomson, Judith Jarvis — "A Defense of Abortion"
Judith J. Thomson, "A Defense of Abortion." *Philosophy & Public Affairs* 1, no. 1 (Fall 1971). Copyright © 1971 by Princeton University Press. Reprinted with permission of Princeton University Press.

Tolstoy, Leo — "Confessions"
A CONFESSION AND OTHER RELIGIOUS WRITINGS, Leo Tolstoy; translated by Jane Kentish (Penguin Classics, 1987) translation © Jane Kentish, 1987. Reproduced by permission of Penguin Books Ltd.

Wilson, James — "Against the Legalization of Drugs"
James Q. Wilson, "Against the Legalization of Drugs." Reprinted from *Commentary*, February 1990, by permission; all rights reserved.

CPSIA information can be obtained
at www.ICGtesting.com
Printed in the USA
BVHW042245260620
582458BV00002B/39